GLEN ARNOLD BSc(Econ), PhD
University of Salford

CORPORATE FINANCIAL MANAGEMENT

FOURTH EDITION

FT Prentice Hall
FINANCIAL TIMES

An imprint of Pearson Education
Harlow, England • London • New York • Boston • San Francisco • Toronto • Sydney • Singapore • Hong Kong
Tokyo • Seoul • Taipei • New Delhi • Cape Town • Madrid • Mexico City • Amsterdam • Munich • Paris • Milan

Pearson Education Limited
Edinburgh Gate
Harlow
Essex CM20 2JE
England

and Associated Companies throughout the world

Visit us on the World Wide Web at:
www.pearsoned.co.uk

First published in Great Britain under the
Financial Times Pitman Publishing imprint in 1998
Second edition published 2002
Third edition published 2005
Fourth edition published 2008

ISBN: 978-0-273-71041-7

British Library Cataloguing-in-Publication Data
A catalogue record for this book is available from the British Library

Library of Congress Cataloging-in-Publication Data

10 9 8 7 6 5 4 3
12 11 10 09

Typeset in Minion 10/11.5pt by 30
Printed and bound by Rotolito Lombarda, Italy

The publisher's policy is to use paper manufactured from sustainable forests

CORPORATE FINANCIAL MANAGEMENT

MyFinanceLab
The Power of Practice

With your purchase of a new copy of this textbook, you received a Student Access Kit for MyFinanceLab for *Corporate Financial Management fourth edition.* Follow the instructions on the card to register successfully and start making the most of the resources.

Don't throw it away!

The Power of Practice:

MyFinanceLab is an online study and testing resource that puts you in control of your study, providing extensive practice exactly where and when you need it.

MyFinanceLab gives you unrivalled resources:

- Sample tests for each chapter to see how much you have learned and where you still need practice
- A personalised study plan, which constantly adapts to your strengths and weaknesses, taking you to exercises you can practise over and again with different variables every time
- Guided solutions which break the problem into its component steps and guide you through with hints
- Audio animations to guide you step by step through the key concepts in corporate finance.
- Pod casts analysing topical issues and recent news items in finance.
- Video clips for each part of the book of CEOs and Financial Directors from large companies explaining how they make financial decisions.
- E text
- Online glossary which defines key terms and provides examples

See Using MyFinanceLab on page xxxi for more details.

To activate your registration go to **www.myfinancelab.com/register** and follow the instructions on screen to register as a new user.

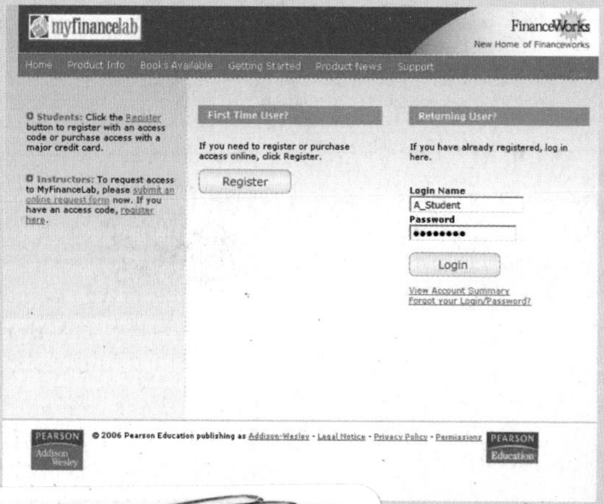

Brief contents

Contents

APPENDICES A:1

Topics covered in the book

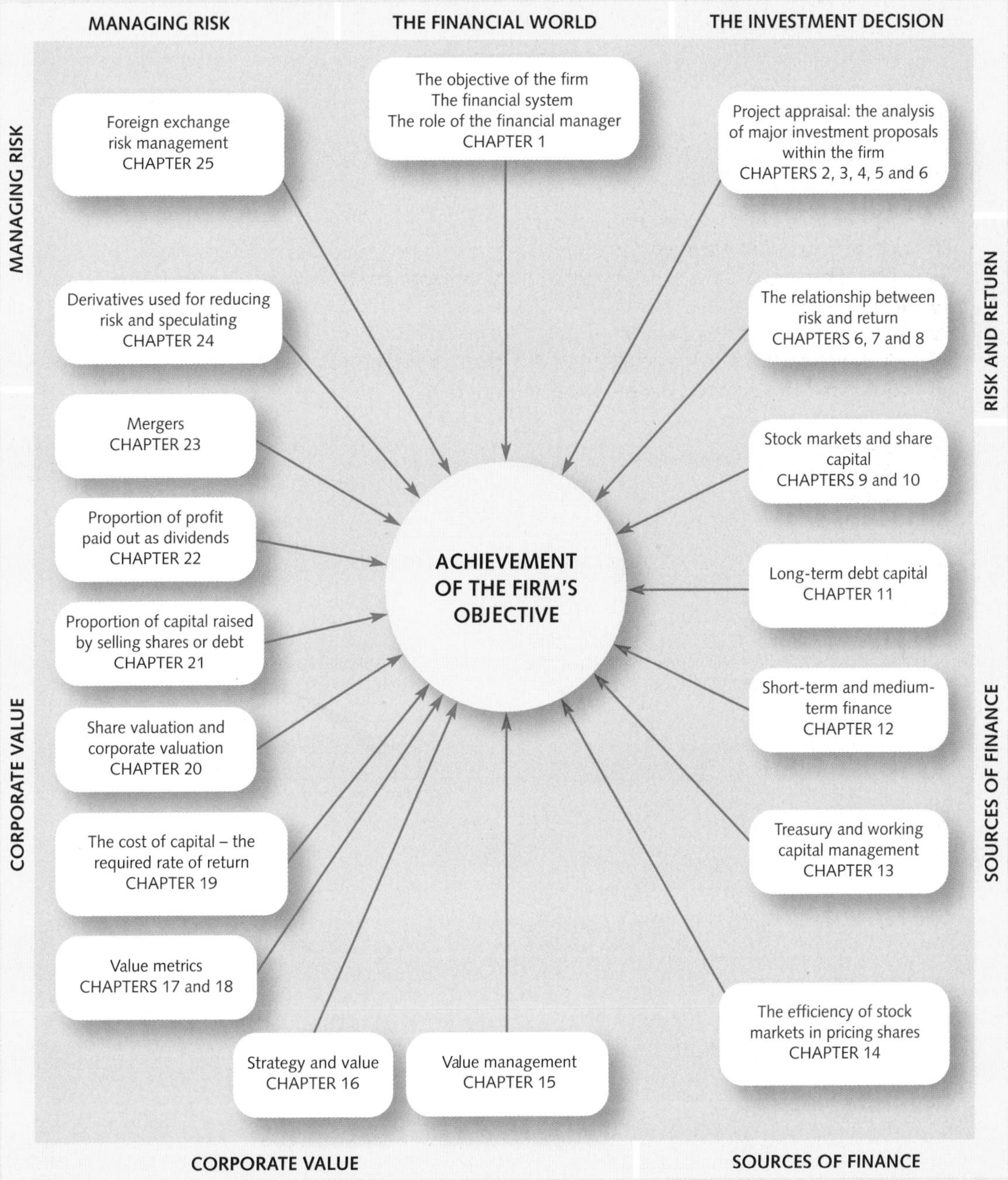

Introduction to the book

Aims of the book

This book is an introduction to the theory and practice of finance. It builds from the assumption of no knowledge of finance. It is comprehensive and aims to provide the key elements needed by business management, accounting and other groups of undergraduates, postgraduates and practising managers. Finance theory and practice are integrated throughout the text, reflecting the extent to which real-world practice has been profoundly shaped by theoretical developments.

Some of the features in this fourth edition are listed below.

- New sections on corporate governance, private equity and hedge funds in Chapter 1.
- Recent evidence on stock market inefficiency is presented in Chapter 14.
- Takeover panel rules are updated in Chapter 23.
- Excel spreadsheet solutions for many worked examples and test questions are now provided on the supporting website.
- Many recent *Financial Times* articles illustrate the practical application of theoretical material.
- Recent statistics – ranging from the number of corporate mergers, to the default rates on corporate bonds – are presented.
- Recent European stock exchange alliances, mergers, etc. are discussed in Chapter 9.
- Recommended case studies, drawn from the Harvard Business School website, are listed in each chapter.
- Key technical terms are now highlighted when first presented to the reader.
- The bank of multiple choice questions has been greatly increased.
- Flash cards on the companion website can be used to test learning by asking for definitions of key financial terms.
- **MyFinanceLab**, a new online study and testing resource, provides extra practice for students and an extensive range of assessment questions for lecturers. See page i and page xxxi for more details.

Themes in the book

Practical orientation

Every chapter describes and illustrates how financial techniques are used in the practical world of business. Throughout the text insight is offered into how and why practice may sometimes differ from sound theory. For example, in making major investment decisions, managers still use techniques with little theoretical backing (e.g. payback) alongside the more theoretically acceptable approaches. The extent of the use of traditional appraisal methods was revealed in a survey to which 96 finance directors from the largest UK-based firms responded. Their choice of analytical technique is not dismissed or regarded as 'bad practice', but there is an exploration of the reasons for the retention of these simple rule-of-thumb methods. This book uses theory, algebra and economic models where these are considered essential to assist learning about better decision making. Where these are introduced, however, they must always have passed the practicality test: 'Is this knowledge sufficiently useful out there, in the real world, to make it worth while for the reader to study it?' If it is not, then it is not included.

Clear, accessible style

Great care has been taken to explain sometimes difficult topics in an interesting and comprehensible way. An informal language style, and an incremental approach, which builds knowledge in a series of easily achieved steps, leads the reader to a high level of knowledge with as little pain as possible. The large panel of reviewers of the book assisted in the process of developing a text that is, we hope, comprehensive and easy to read.

Integration with other disciplines

Finance should never be regarded as a subject in isolation, separated from the workings of the rest of the organisation. This text, when considering the link between theoretical methods and practical financial decision making, recognises a wide range of other influences, from strategy to psychology. For example, important new developments in business thinking over the past twenty years have led to the adoption of shareholder value management, which integrates finance, strategy and organisational resource. Value-based management principles are sweeping across boardrooms the world over. This is the first major corporate finance textbook to recognise fully the importance of value-based approaches to managing companies today. The origins of the principles in the finance literature are described, and the significance and pervasiveness of the managerial challenge are explored.

Real-world relevance

Experience of teaching finance to undergraduates, postgraduates and managers on short courses has led to the conclusion that, in order to generate enthusiasm and commitment to the subject, it is vital continually to show the relevance of the material to what is going on in the world beyond the textbook. Therefore, this book incorporates vignettes/short case studies as well as a very large number of examples of real companies making decisions which draw on the models, concepts and ideas of financial management.

A UK/international perspective

There is a primary focus on the UK, but also regular reference to international financial markets and institutions. Care has been taken to avoid giving a parochial perspective and the international character of the book has been enhanced by the detailed evaluation of each chapter by a number of respected academics teaching at universities in Europe, Asia, Australasia and Africa. The richly integrated world of modern finance requires that a text of this nature reflects the globalised character of much financial activity. The financial world has moved on in the last few years with the development of new financial markets and methods of trading, and this is fully reflected in the text.

A re-evaluation of classical finance theory

There is considerable debate about the validity of the theories of the 1950s and 1960s which underpin much of modern finance, stimulated by fresh evidence generated over the last decade. For example, the theories concerning the relationship between the risk of a financial security and its expected return is under dispute, with some saying the old measure of risk, beta, is dead or dying. This issue and other financial economics theories are presented along with their assumptions and a consideration of recent revisions.

Real-world case examples

The publishers are part of the Pearson Group, which also includes the *Financial Times* and the *Investors Chronicle* (and part ownership of *The Economist*). It has been possible to include much more than the usual quantity of real-world case examples in this book by drawing on material from the *Financial Times*, *Investors Chronicle* and *The Economist*. The aim of these extracts is to bring the subject of finance to life for readers. A typical example is shown in Exhibit 1, which is used to illustrate some of the financial issues explored in the book.

Exhibit 1

Silverjet seeking fresh funding

FT

by Kevin Done,
Aerospace Correspondent

The first UK all-business class airline said it was seeking £22m of fresh funding to finance expansion and to meet higher-than-expected losses in its first year of operations.

Silverjet said it was raising £10m in a convertible loan from TFB (Mortgages), a Reuben brothers company, and was raising additional gross proceeds of £12m through an issue of new shares.

The airline, which is listed on Aim, raised net proceeds of £25.3m in an initial public offering in May last year and £24.6m in a further share offering last April.

Its share price, which reached a peak of 290p in March after the company was floated at 112p a share, has fallen steeply. It closed last night down $4^1/_2$p, at $71^1/_2$p.

Silverjet said it was planning to issue 20m new shares in the placement at 60p a share.

The £10m loan is convertible by TFB, by no later than February 11, into 18.3m shares. If the loan is converted the Reuben brothers will hold about 22 per cent of the Silverjet equity and will gain two seats on the seven-member board.

David Reuben said: 'We are long-term investors in the sector and look forward to helping Silverjet accelerate its development and growth.'

Source: Financial Times, 23 November 2007, p. 22. Reprinted with permission.

This article touches on many of the financial decisions which are explored in greater detail later in the book. Starting a new airline requires a lot of money. In November 2007 Silverjet, which flies business passengers across the Atlantic, raised more money to invest in the next stage of its development. There are two main pillars of finance:

1 *Raising finance and knowledge of financial markets* In the case of Silverjet it raised £25.3m by selling shares to investors when its shares first started trading on the London Stock Exchange's market for smaller companies, called the Alternative Investment Market (Aim) in May 2006. Share investors then pumped in another £24.6m in April 2007. Now, in November 2007, shareholders are buying another £12m shares. Also, TFB lent £10m but held a right to convert the loan into 18.3m shares. (Sources of finance are considered in the book in Chapters 9–14).

2 *Investment in real assets, tangible or intangible* There are techniques which help the process of deciding whether to make a major investment – these are discussed early in the book (Chapters 2–6). Silverjet will be investing in new aircraft and support facilities. It will need rigorous techniques to assist with the selection of projects. Amongst other things it will have to consider the risk relative to the reward on investments (risk and return are considered in Chapters 6, 7 and 8).

Another area of decision making for investors and management alike is the question of the most appropriate mixture of sources of finance: should the company borrow most of the money it needs, or should it obtain a larger proportion from shareholders? This is the 'gearing' question (*see* Chapter 21). Other financial decisions likely to affect Silverjet which are not mentioned in the article, but which may well be of importance for the company in the future, include:

- What proportion of profits should be distributed as dividends each year? (*See* Chapter 22.)
- What factors are to be considered when contemplating a merger with another company? (*See* Chapter 23.)
- What type of debt finance to use? Is bank borrowing better than selling a corporate bond? Should the Eurobond or the syndicated loan market be tapped? What are the advantages and disadvantages of financing equipment with a lease or hire purchase? (*See* Chapters 11 and 12.)
- How will the company's shares be valued on the stock market once the company has been floated? (*See* Chapter 20.) Does the market do a good job of pricing shares, taking into account the future potential of the company, or does it act in perverse and unpredictable ways? (*See* Chapter 14.)

- Should the company use derivative financial instruments, such as futures, options and swaps, to reduce its risk exposure to changes in interest rates, commodities (e.g. aviation fuel) and exchange rates? (*See* Chapters 24 and 25.)

These are just a few of the financial issues that have to be tackled by the modern corporation and trying to answer these questions forms the basis for this book.

Student learning features

Each chapter has the following elements to help the learning process:

- ***Learning objectives*** This section sets out the expected competencies to be gained by reading the chapter.
- ***Introduction*** The intention here is to engage the attention of the reader by discussing the importance and relevance of the topic to real business decisions.
- ***Worked examples*** New techniques are illustrated in the text, with sections which present problems, followed by detailed answers.
- ***Mathematical explanations*** Students with a limited mathematical ability should not be put off by this text. The basics are covered early and in a simple style. New skills are fully explained and illustrated, as and when required.
- ***Case studies and articles*** Extracts from recent articles from the *Financial Times*, *The Economist* and other sources are used to demonstrate the arguments in the chapter, to add a different dimension to an issue, or merely to show that it is worth taking time to understand the material because this sort of decision is being made in day-to-day business.
- ***Key points and concepts*** At the end of each chapter an outline is given of the essentials of what has been covered. New concepts, jargon and equations are summarised for easy referral.
- ***References and further reading*** One of the features of this text is the short commentaries in the list of articles and books referred to in the body of the chapter, or which are suggested for the interested student who wishes to pursue a topic in greater depth. These allow students to be selective in their follow-up reading. So, for example, if on the one hand a particular article takes a high-level, algebraic and theoretical approach or, on the other hand, is an easy-to-read introduction to the subject, this is highlighted, permitting the student to decide whether to obtain the article. A list of useful websites is also included.
- ***Self-review questions*** These short questions are designed to prompt the reader to recall the main elements of the topic. They can act as a revision aid and highlight areas requiring more attention.
- ***Questions and problems*** These vary in the amount of time required, from 5 minutes to 45 minutes or more. Many are taken from university second year and final year undergraduate examinations, and MBA module examinations. They allow the student to demonstrate a thorough understanding of the material presented in the chapter. Some of these questions necessitate the integration of knowledge from previous chapters with the present chapter. The answers to many of the questions can be found in Appendix VII at the end of the book.
- ***Assignments*** These are projects which require the reader to investigate real-world practice in a firm and relate this to the concepts and techniques learned in the chapter. These assignments can be used both as learning aids and as a way of helping firms to examine the relationship between current practice and finance theory and frameworks.
- ***Recommended case studies*** A list of case studies relevant to the chapter material is provided. These are drawn from the Harvard Business School website.

At the end of the book there are also the following elements:

- ***Appendices*** Appendices give a future value table (Appendix I), present value table (Appendix II), present value of annuity table (Appendix III), future value of an annuity (Appendix IV), areas under the standardised normal distribution (Appendix V), answers to questions in the Chapter 2, Appendix 2.1 reviewing mathematical tools for finance (Appendix VI), and answers to the numerical questions and problems (Appendix VII) – with the exception of those question numbers followed by an asterisk (*), which are answered in the *Lecturer's Guide.* Answers to discussion questions, essay and report questions can be found by reading the text.

- ***Glossary*** There is an extensive Glossary of terms, allowing the student quickly to find the meaning of new technical terms or jargon.
- ***Bibliography*** There is also a Bibliography of references for further reading.

Also:

- When you see the **MyFinanceLab** logo at the start and end of every chapter you can go online to complete your diagnostic test for the chapter and see where you need most help. You can practice further by completing the corresponding questions with additional supporting resources including videos, podcasts and audio animations. See page xxxi for more details.
- Recommended case study synopses.
- Flash cards tests

Support for lecturers

The website dedicated to this book contains a section designed to add value to the student learning process (for example by providing updated newspaper articles illustrating the concepts discussed in the chapters) and also includes a section for lecturers who adopt the book. Go to www.pearsoned.co.uk/arnold to access:

- Over 800 PowerPoint slides, which can also be downloaded as OHP masters.
- Extra questions and answers.
- Multiple-choice questions bank.
- Links to other websites, for example major stock exchanges around the world, banks, derivatives markets, the international financial press and professional bodies.
- Excel spreadsheets.
- A link to **MyFinanceLab**.

Lecturers Guide

This contains:

- Supplementary material for chapters, including learning objectives and key points and concepts listings.
- A multiple-choice question bank (also available on the website).
- Answers to the questions and problems marked with an asterisk * in the book.

Target readership

The book is aimed at second/final year undergraduates of accounting and finance, business/management studies, banking and economics, as well as postgraduate students on MBA/MSc courses in the UK, Europe and the rest of the world. It would be helpful if the student has an elementary knowledge of statistics, algebra, accounting and microeconomics, but this is not essential.

The practising manager, whether or not a specialist in financial decision making, should find the book useful – not least to understand the language and concepts of business and financial markets.

Students studying for examinations for the professional bodies will benefit from this text. The material is valuable for those working towards a qualification of one of the following organisations:

- Association of Corporate Treasurers
- Institute of Chartered Accountants in England and Wales

- Institute of Chartered Accountants of Scotland
- Chartered Institute of Public Finance and Accountancy
- Association of Chartered Certified Accountants
- Chartered Institute of Management Accountants
- Institute of Chartered Secretaries and Administrators
- Chartered Institute of Bankers

The applicability of finance knowledge for all organisations

Most of the theories and practical examples in the book are directed at the business operating in a competitive market environment. However, the fundamental principles and truths revealed by the logic and frameworks of finance are applicable to organisations other than commercial firms. Sound financial decision making is necessary in non-profit organisations and public sector bodies, ranging from schools and hospitals to charities and churches, and so the principles contained within the book have validity and applicability to any organisation needing to make decisions involving money.

Custom Publishing

Custom publishing allows academics to pick and choose content from one or more textbooks for their course and combine it into a definitive course text.

Here are some common examples of custom solutions which have helped over 500 courses across Europe:

- different chapters from across our publishing imprints combined into one book;
- lecturer's own material combined together with textbook chapters or published in a separate booklet;
- third-party cases and articles that you are keen for your students to read as part of the course;
- any combination of the above.

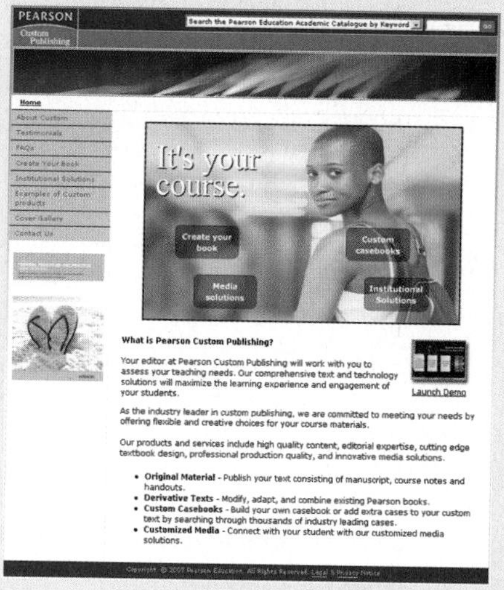

The Pearson Education custom text published for your course is professionally produced and bound – just as you would expect from a normal Pearson Education text. Since many of our titles have online resources accompanying them we can even build a Custom website that matches your course text.

If you are teaching a shorter course in Corporate Finance, you may find the shorter version of this text book, *Essentials of Corporate Financial Management*, more appropriate for your needs. Some adopters have found, however, that they require just one or two extra chapters from this larger volume or would like to select a range of chapters from both texts.

Custom publishing has allowed these adopters to provide access to additional chapters for their students both online and in print.

If, once you have had time to review this title, you feel Custom publishing might benefit you and your course, please do get in contact. However minor, or major the change, we can help you out.

You can contact us at: **www.pearsoncustom.co.uk** or via your local representative at: **www.pearsoned.co.uk/replocator**

Guided Tour

Aiding your understanding

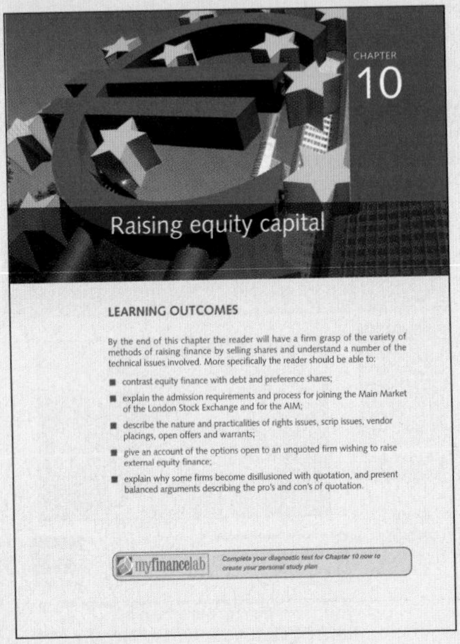

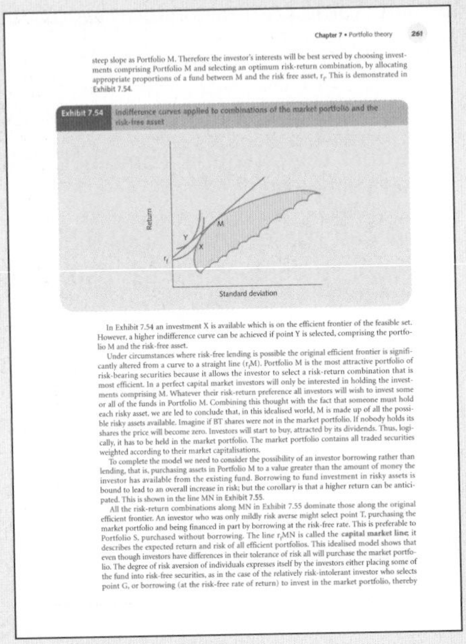

Learning outcomes introduce topics covered and summarise what you should have learnt by the end of the chapter.

Exhibits highlight important material covered in the text. Coloured figures provide visual representations of mathematical concepts and techniques, aiding intuitive understanding.

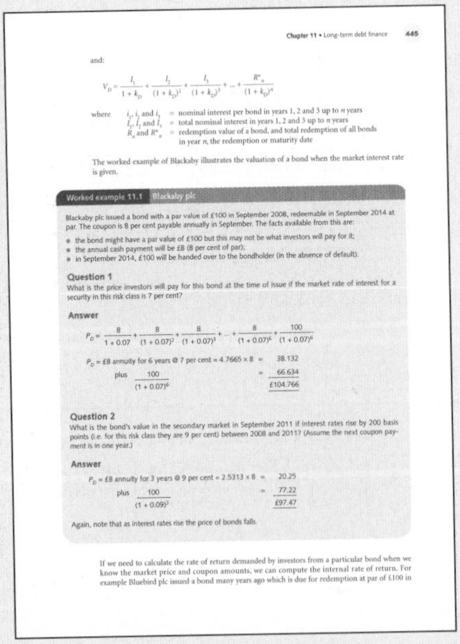

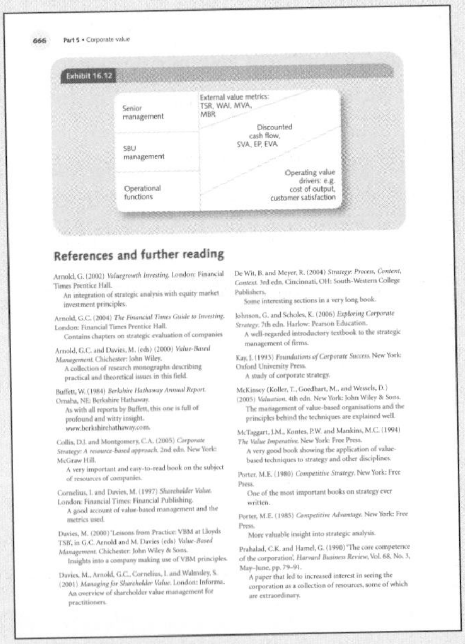

Worked examples illustrate new techniques and provide step by step answers guiding you through the workings out.

Use the extensive annotated sets of **References** and **Further Reading** as starting points for your independent reading to pursue individual topics in more depth.

Testing your learning

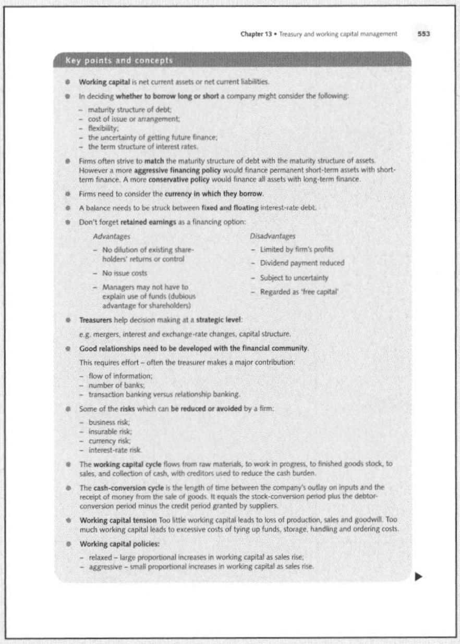

Chapter 13 • Treasury and working capital management 553

Key points and concepts

- **Working capital** is net current assets or net current liabilities.
- In deciding **whether to borrow long or short** a company might consider the following:
  - maturity structure of debt;
  - cost of issue or arrangement;
  - flexibility;
  - the uncertainty of getting future finance;
  - the term structure of interest rates.
- Firms often strive to **match** the maturity structure of debt with the maturity structure of assets. However a more **aggressive financing policy** would finance permanent short-term assets with short-term finance. A more **conservative policy** would finance all assets with long-term finance.
- Firms need to consider the **currency in which they borrow**.
- A balance needs to be struck between **fixed and floating** interest-rate debt.
- Don't forget **retained earnings** as a financing option:

Advantages	*Disadvantages*
– No dilution of existing shareholders' returns or control	– Limited by firm's profits
– No issue costs	– Dividend payment reduced
– Managers may not have to explain use of funds (dubious advantage for shareholders)	– Subject to uncertainty
	– Regarded as 'free capital'

- **Treasurers** help decision making at a **strategic level**:

  e.g. mergers, interest and exchange-rate changes, capital structure.
- **Good relationships need to be developed with the financial community.**

  This requires effort – often the treasurer makes a major contribution:
  - flow of information;
  - number of banks;
  - transaction banking versus relationship banking.
- Some of the **risks** which can **be reduced or avoided** by a firm:
  - business risk;
  - insurable risk;
  - currency risk;
  - interest-rate risk.
- The **working capital cycle** flows from raw materials, to work in progress, to finished goods stock, to sales, and collection of cash, with creditors used to reduce the cash burden.
- The **cash-conversion cycle** is the length of time between the company's outlay on inputs and the receipt of money from the sale of goods. It equals the stock-conversion period plus the debtor-conversion period minus the credit period granted by suppliers.
- **Working capital tension** Too little working capital leads to loss of production, sales and goodwill. Too much working capital leads to excessive costs of tying up funds, storage, handling and ordering costs.
- **Working capital policies:**
  - relaxed – large proportional increases in working capital as sales rise;
  - aggressive – small proportional increases in working capital as sales rise.

Revise using the summaries of **Key points and concepts** at the end of each chapter.

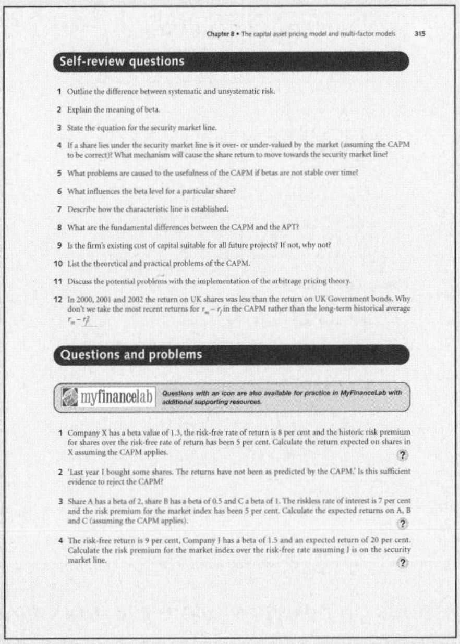

Chapter 8 • The capital asset pricing model and multi-factor models 315

Self-review questions

1 Outline the difference between systematic and unsystematic risk.

2 Explain the meaning of beta.

3 State the equation for the security market line.

4 If a share lies under the security market line is it over- or under-valued by the market (assuming the CAPM to be correct)? What mechanism will cause the share return to move towards the security market line?

5 What problems are caused to the usefulness of the CAPM if betas are not stable over time?

6 What influences the beta level for a particular share?

7 Describe how the characteristic line is established.

8 What are the fundamental differences between the CAPM and the APT?

9 Is the firm's existing cost of capital suitable for all future projects? If not, why not?

10 List the theoretical and practical problems of the CAPM.

11 Discuss the potential problems with the implementation of the arbitrage pricing theory.

12 In 2000, 2001 and 2002 the return on UK shares was less than the return on UK Government bonds. Why don't we take the most recent returns for $r_m - r_f$ in the CAPM rather than the long-term historical average $\overline{r_m - r_f}$?

Questions and problems

myfinancelab *Questions with an icon are also available for practice in MyFinanceLab with additional supporting resources.*

1 Company X has a beta value of 1.3, the risk-free rate of return is 8 per cent and the historic risk premium for shares over the risk-free rate of return has been 5 per cent. Calculate the return expected on shares in X assuming the CAPM applies. ?

2 'Last year I bought some shares. The returns have not been as predicted by the CAPM.' Is this sufficient evidence to reject the CAPM?

3 Share A has a beta of 2, share B has a beta of 0.5 and C a beta of 1. The riskless rate of interest is 7 per cent and the risk premium for the market index has been 5 per cent. Calculate the expected returns on A, B and C (assuming the CAPM applies). ?

4 The risk-free return is 9 per cent, Company J has a beta of 1.5 and an expected return of 20 per cent. Calculate the risk premium for the market index over the risk-free rate assuming J is on the security market line. ?

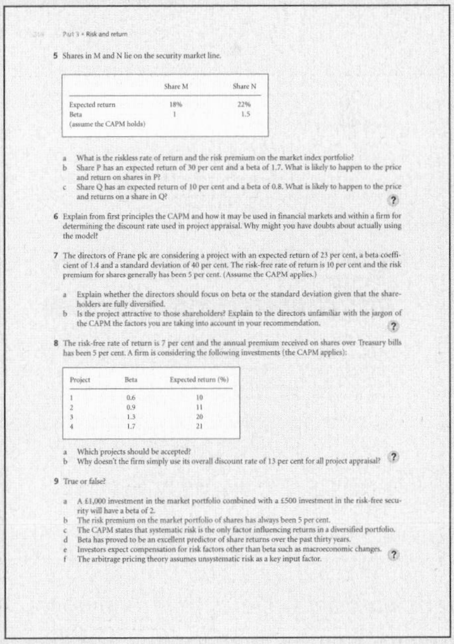

Part 3 • Risk and return

5 Shares in M and N lie on the security market line.

	Share M	Share N
Expected return	18%	22%
Beta	1	1.5
(assume the CAPM holds)		

a What is the riskless rate of return and the risk premium on the market index portfolio?
b Share P has an expected return of 30 per cent and a beta of 1.7. What is likely to happen to the price and return on shares in P?
c Share Q has an expected return of 10 per cent and a beta of 0.8. What is likely to happen to the price and returns on a share in Q? ?

6 Explain from first principles the CAPM and how it may be used in financial markets and within a firm for determining the discount rate used in project appraisal. Why might you have doubts about actually using the model?

7 The directors of Frane plc are considering a project with an expected return of 23 per cent, a beta coefficient of 1.4 and a standard deviation of 40 per cent. The risk-free rate of return is 10 per cent and the risk premium for shares generally has been 5 per cent. (Assume the CAPM applies.)

a Explain whether the directors should focus on beta or the standard deviation given that the shareholders are fully diversified.
b Is the project attractive to those shareholders? Explain to the directors unfamiliar with the jargon of the CAPM the factors you are taking into account in your recommendation. ?

8 The risk-free rate of return is 7 per cent and the annual premium received on shares over Treasury bills has been 5 per cent. A firm is considering the following investments (the CAPM applies):

Project	Beta	Expected return (%)
1	0.6	10
2	0.9	11
3	1.3	20
4	1.7	21

a Which projects should be accepted?
b Why doesn't the firm simply use its overall discount rate of 13 per cent for all project appraisal? ?

9 True or false?

a A £1,000 investment in the market portfolio combined with a £500 investment in the risk-free security will have a beta of 2.
b The risk premium on the market portfolio of shares has always been 5 per cent.
c The CAPM states that systematic risk is the only factor influencing returns in a diversified portfolio.
d Beta has proved to be an excellent predictor of share returns over the past thirty years.
e Investors expect compensation for risk factors other than beta such as macroeconomic changes.
f The arbitrage pricing theory assumes unsystematic risk as a key input factor. ?

Questions at the end of the chapter range from short **Self-review questions** to more extended **Questions and problems** taken from undergraduate and MBA examinations. Answers to many of the questions are provided in Appendix VII. Questions with the **question mark icon** ? have a corresponding question for you to practice in your online learning resource **MyFinanceLab**.

Corporate finance in the real world

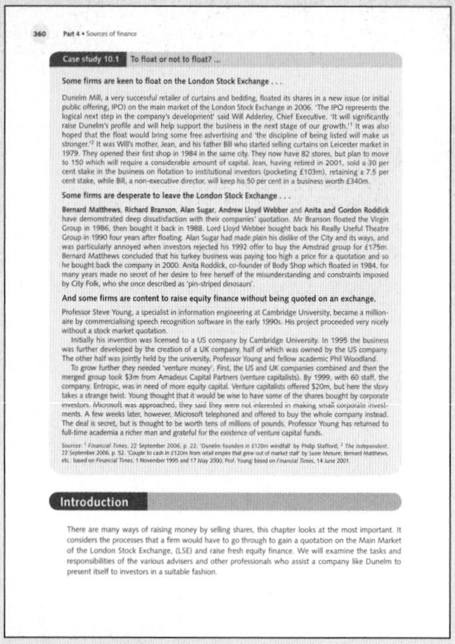

Short **case studies** in each chapter show real companies making decisions that draw on the models and concepts of financial management.

Bringing the theory to life, recent extracts from the *Financial Times* show financial management in action.

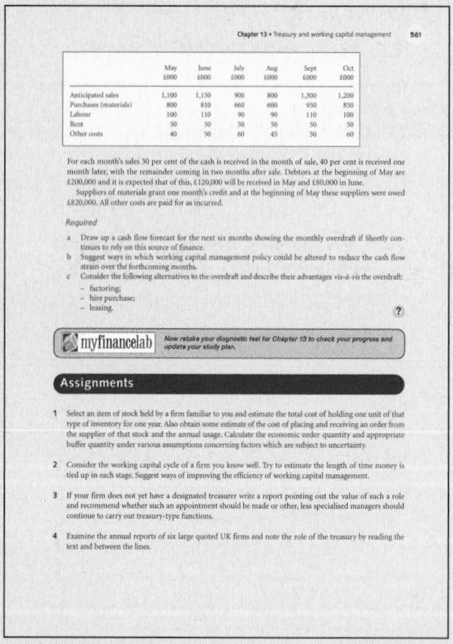

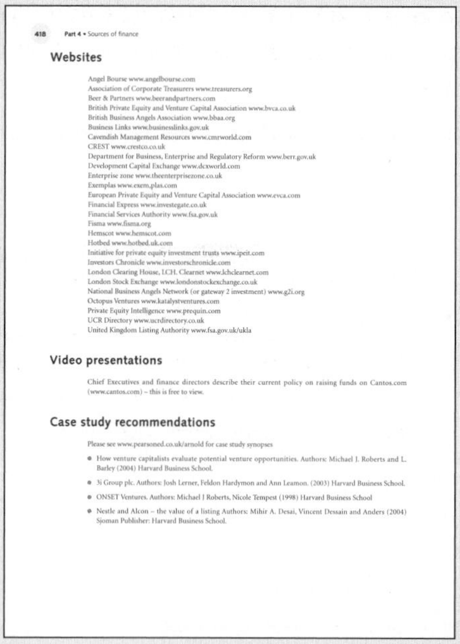

Assignments are projects that require you to investigate financial practice in a real firm, applying the financial techniques and concepts that you have learned in the chapter.

Suggestions on how to explore the workings of corporate finance in the real world, with lists of **recommended websites** and useful **case studies**. Some chapters include recommendations on **video presentations**, where you can view chief executives and finance directors discussing issues faced by their firms.

Using MyFinanceLab

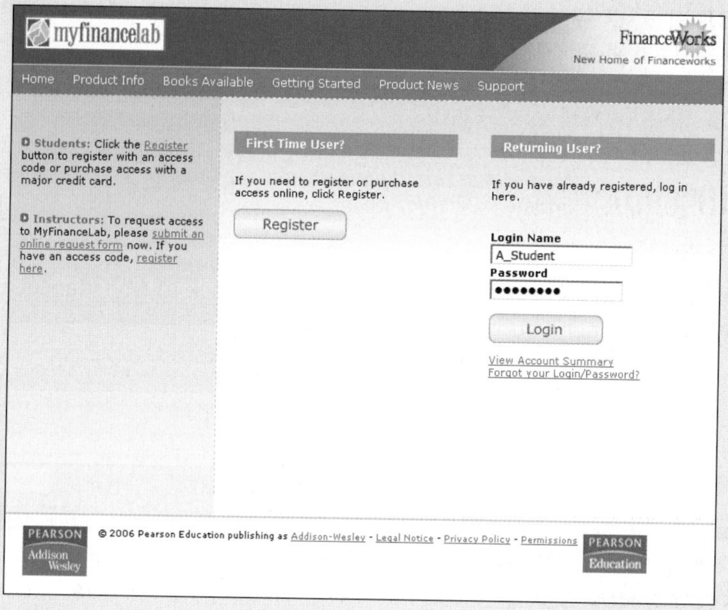

Packaged with every new copy of the fourth edition of *Corporate Financial Management*, **MyFinanceLab** puts you in control of your study. To register as a new user go to **www.myfinancelab.com/register** and follow the instructions on-screen using the code in your student access kit.

By using MyFinanceLab you test your understanding and practise what you have learned.

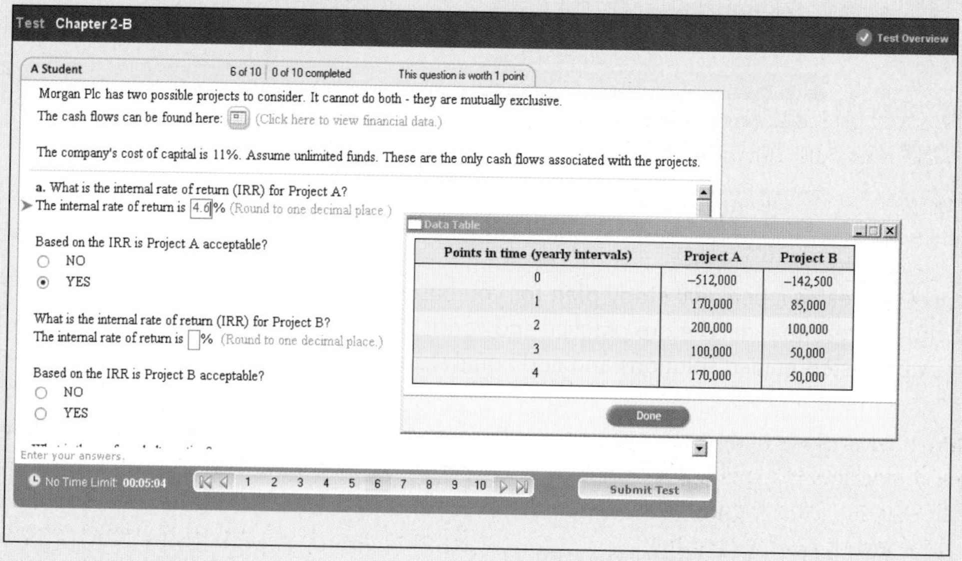

Sample tests (two for each chapter) enable you to test your understanding and identify the areas in which you need to do further work.

myfinancelab *Complete your diagnostic test for Chapter X now to create your personal study plan.*

When you see this icon in the text at the beginning of a chapter complete your **sample test (a)** in MyFinanceLab to create your personal study plan for the chapter.

myfinancelab *Now retake your diagnostic test for Chapter X to check your progress and update your study plan.*

When you see this icon in the text at the end of a chapter, go back to MyFinanceLab and take your **sample test (b)** to see how much you have improved.

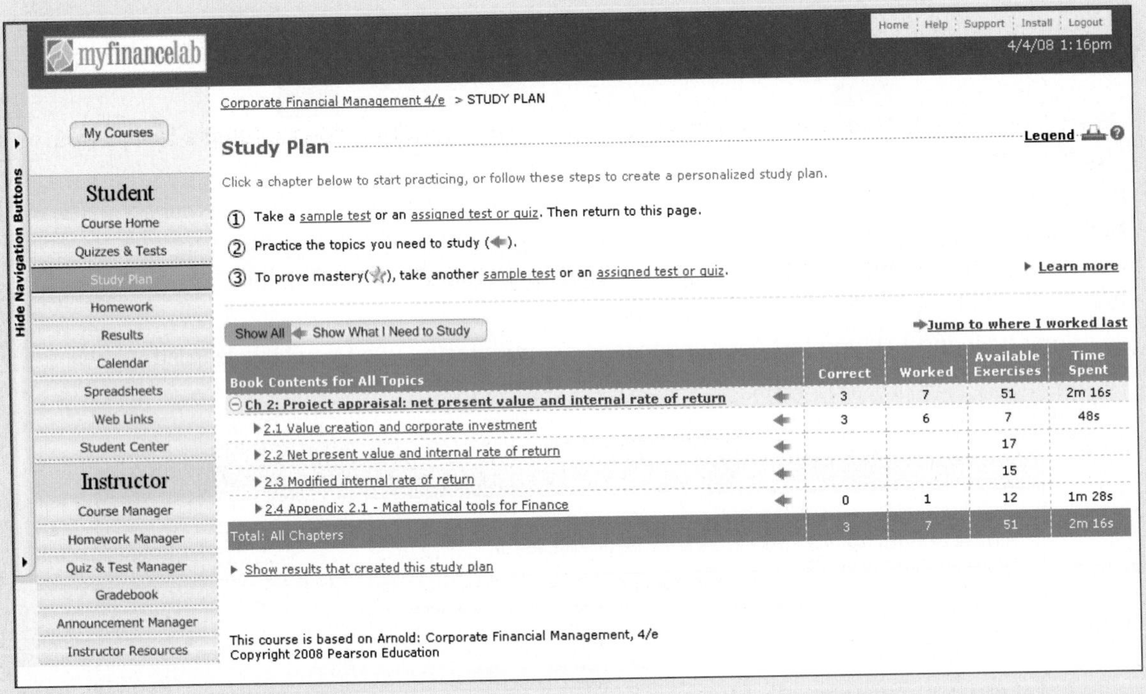

MyFinanceLab creates a personal **study plan** for you based on your performances in tests. The study plan diagnoses areas that need more practice and consists of a series of additional exercises with detailed step-by-step guided solutions and additional study tools to help you complete the exercises.

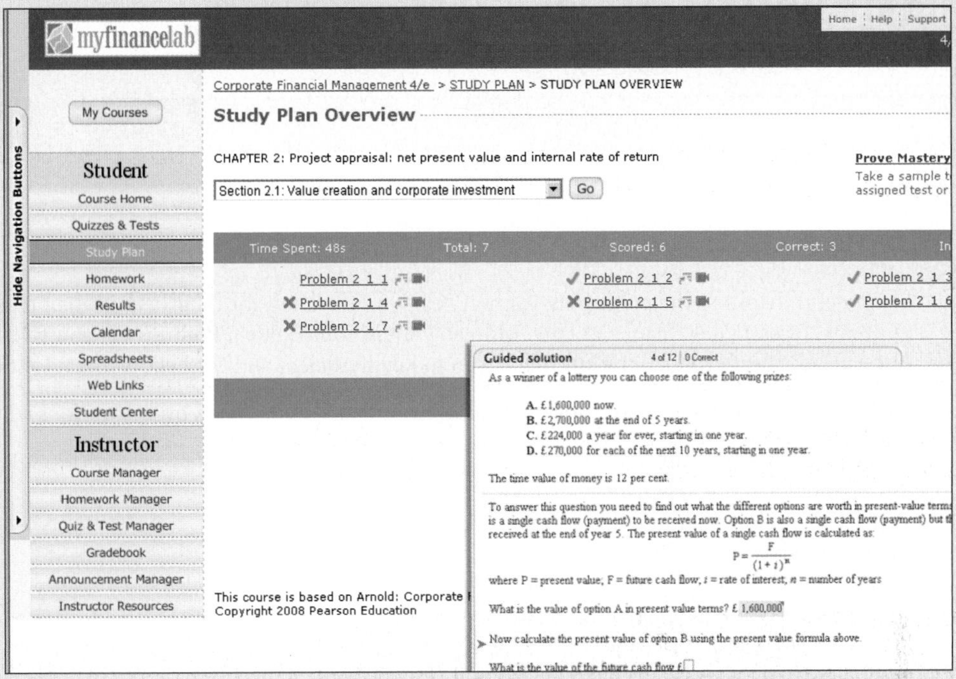

From the study plan exercises, you can link out to the **step-by-step guided solutions** to help you complete the exercise.

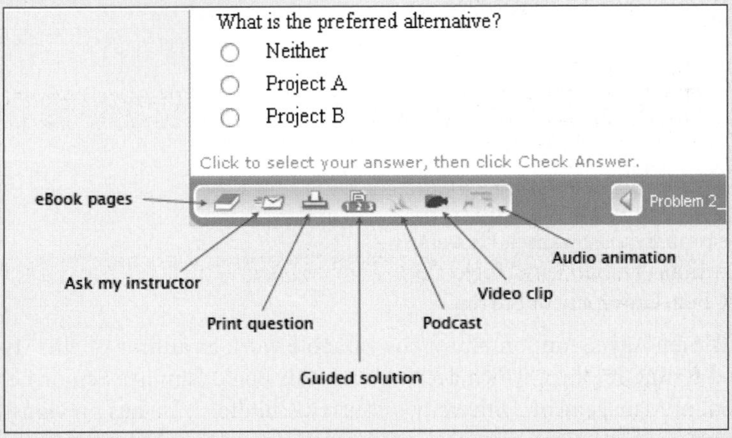

Additional resources such as **podcasts, videos, audio animations** of key concepts in corporate finance and an **electronic version of your text book** are also on hand to help you.

Acknowledgements

My grateful thanks to the publishing team at Pearson Education for their help in the preparation of this book. In particular, thanks to Ellen Morgan (Aquisitions Editor), Philippa Fiszzon (Desk Editor), Angela Hawksbee (Production Controller) and to Kevin Ancient and Michelle Morgan for design.

We thank the following reviewers for their valuable feedback on this book over its various editions:

Ian Jackson, Staffordshire University
Ruth Bender, Cranfield University
Vijay Lee, London South Bank University
Jean Bellemans, United Business Institutes, Belgium
Lars Vangaard, University of Southern Denmark
Dr Jan Jakobsen, Copenhagen Business School
Rob Jones, Newcastle University
Dr Stuart Hyde, Manchester Business School, University of Manchester
Heather Tarbert, Glasgow Caledonian University
Tony Boczko, University of Hull
Roger Henderson, Leeds Metropolitan University
David Bence, University of West England
Kay Pollock, Kingston University
Alex Stremme, Warwick University
Victor Murinde, University of Birmingham
Edel Barnes, National University of Cork
Edwards Jones, Heriot Watt University
Per Hiller, Stockholm School of Economics
Roger Lister, University of Salford
Robert Major, University of Portsmouth
Dr Liang Han, University of Hull
Dr Pornsawan Evans, Swansea University
Ruth Mattimoe, Dublin City University
Dr Jean Chen, University of Surrey

We thank Sam Agyei-Ampomah for his valuable work as author of the MyFinanceLab online study and testing resource which accompanies this book. Sam is a Senior Lecturer in Finance at the School of Management, University of Surrey, Guildford. He has previously taught on various finance courses at the Aston Business School and the University of Strathclyde. Sam also co-authors the *Chartered Institute of Management Accountants (CIMA) Study System on Risk and Control Strategy* – the official study text for CIMA's Strategic Level Paper 3.

We are grateful to the following for permission to reproduce copyright material:

Cadbury Schweppes plc for exhibits 21.3, 22.6 and details from *Cadbury Schweppes Annual Report and Accounts* 2003, 2005, 2006 and exhibit 17.12 reproduced with permission of Cadbury Schweppes plc; The Economist Newspaper Limited for extracts from "The use of economic profit is becoming more widespread" published in *The Economist* 18th November 2000, "The good company" published in *The Economist* 22nd January 2005, "Carry on speculating" published in *The Economist* 24th February 2007 and "Sizzling" published in *The Economist* 7th July 2007 copyright © The Economist Newspaper Limited, London 2000, 2005, 2007; Diageo Plc for company objectives from *Diageo Annual Report 2006* reproduced with permission of Diageo Plc; Marks and Spencer plc for their company objective from *Marks & Spencer Annual Review 2006* reproduced with permission of Marks and Spencer plc; Tate & Lyle plc for their company objective from *Tate & Lyle Annual Report 2006* reproduced with permission of Tate & Lyle plc; Elsevier Ltd for exhibit 4.2 from *The British Accounting Review*, Volume 38, Issue 2, June 2006, Pages 149–173 by Fadi Alkaraan and Deryl Northcott reproduced with permission of Elsevier Ltd, 2006. All rights reserved; Blackwell Publishing for exhibit 4.2 from *Accounting and Business Research 18(72)* autumn pg 341–51, 1988 "An empirical study of the adoption of sophisticated capital budgeting practices and decision-making effectiveness" by Pike; *Journal of Business Finance and Accounting 23(1)* Jan 1996 "A longitudinal survey of capital budgeting practices" by Pike and *Journal of Business Finance and Accounting 27(5)* and *(6)* June/July pg 603–26 "The theory practice gap in capital budgeting: evidence from the United Kingdom" by G Arnold and P Hatzopoulos 2000; exhibits 4.11, 4.12, 6.31, 19.7–19.9 from *Journal of Business Finance and Accounting 27(5)* and *(6)* June/July pg 603–26 "The theory practice gap in capital budgeting: evidence from the United Kingdom" by G Arnold and P Hatzopoulos 2000; and exhibit 14.15 from *Journal of Accounting Research 27*, 1989 Supplement, pg 1–36, "Post-earnings-announcement drift: delayed price response or risk premium?" by Bernard V & Thomas J reproduced with permission of Blackwell Publishers; CFA Institute for exhibits 7.49–7.51 'USA', 'UK', 'France', 'Germany' and 'International Diversification' from "Why Not Diversify Internationally Rather Than Domestically?" by Bruno H. Solnik from the *Financial Analysts Journal*, July-August 1974: 51 and exhibit 8.30 'A: Return and Three Risk Measures' from "Traditional versus Theoretical Risk Measure" by Russell J. Fuller and G. Wenchi Wong from the *Financial Analysts Journal*, March/April 1988: 55 copyright © 1974, 1988 CFA Institute. Reproduced and republished from Financial Analysts Journal with permission from CFA Institute. All rights reserved; Princeton University Press for exhibits 7.52, 8.10, 8.11 and 14.14 from *Triumph of the Optimists* copyright © 2002 Elroy Dimson, Paul Marks and Mike Staunton published by Princeton University Press, reproduced with permission of Princeton University Press and Mike Staunton; Barclays Capital for exhibits 7.56, 7.57, 8.4–8.9 from *Equity Gilt study* reproduced with permission of Barclays Capital (M. Capleton and F. Cleary 2003 and 2004); Elroy Dimson and Paul Marsh for exhibits 8.1–8.3 from *Global Investment Returns Yearbook 2008* by Dimson, Marsh & Staunton & reproduced with permission of the authors; Simon & Schuster Adult Publishing Group for an extract from *Contrarian Investment Strategies: The Next Generation* by David Dreman copyright © 1998 by Dreman Contrarian Group, Inc; Warren E Buffett and Berkshire Hathaway Inc for exhibits 22.2, 23.13, 23.23 and extracts from Warren E Buffett's 'letter to shareholders attached to the Annual Report of Berkshire Hathaway Inc' 1982, 1984, 1993, 1995 and 2000; exhibit 14.17 an edited transcript of a talk given at Columbia University 1984 and exhibits 14.16 and 23.7 and extracts from Berkshire Hathaway Annual Report 1981, 1984 and 2006 copyright © Warren E. Buffett and Berkshire Hathaway Inc, reproduced with permission; HarperCollins Publishers for an extract from *The Intelligent Investor: The Classic Text on Value Investing* by Benjamin Graham copyright © Benjamin Graham 1949, foreward copyright © John C Bogle, reproduced by permission of HarperCollins Publishers; World Federation of Exchanges for exhibits 9.1 and 9.4 from *World Federation of Exchanges December 2006* statistics www.world-exchanges.org copyright © World Federation of Exchanges; London Stock Exchange for exhibits 9.16, 9.17, 9.19, 19.21 and 10.5 from www.londonstockexchange.com, reproduced with permission; Office for National Statistics for exhibit 9.22 from *Share Ownership 2004* and exhibit 23.1 from *Financial Statistics.* Crown copyright material is reproduced with permission of the Controller of Her Majesty's Stationery Office and the Queen's Printer for Scotland; GlaxoSmithKline plc for exhibit 11.1 from the *GlaxoSmithKline Annual Report 2005/6* copyright © GlaxoSmithKline plc, reproduced with permission; Fitchratings for exhibit 11.9 from *Fitchratings Global Corporate Finance 2006 Transition and Default Study* www.fitchratings.com copyright © Fitchratings, reproduced with permission of Fitchratings; Bank for International Settlements for exhibit 11.8 from *BIS Quarterly Review Sept 2007* the full publication for which is available for free on the BIS website www.bis.org; Leeds University Business School for exhibit 12.8 "F Credit policy in the UK Economy" by Credit Management Research Centre, 2005 copyright © Leeds University Business School; The Association of Corporate Treasurers for exhibit 13.2 www.treasurers.org, reproduced with permission; Martin O'Donovan of the Association of Corporate Treasurers for his valuable comments and suggestions for improvement to Chapter 13; Salford Business School for exhibits 14.8 and 14.9 from 'Return reversal in UK shares' by Arnold & Baker published in

Salford Business School working paper 107/07, 2005, reproduced by permission; Thomson Financial Datastream for exhibits 15.3, 20.7, 25.1, 25.2, 25.3 reproduced with permission of Thomson Financial Datastream; Pearson Education for exhibit 20.1 from *Pearson plc Annual Review 2006*, reproduced with permission of Pearson Education; and ADVFN plc for exhbit 20.2 from the *ADVFN Annual Reports and Accounts 2007* reproduced with permission of ADVFN plc www.advfn.com.

We are grateful to the Financial Times Limited for permission to reprint the following material:

Text

Exhibit 1 Silverjet seeking fresh funding, © *Financial Times*, 23 November 2007; Exhibit 1.2 Profits fall 39% on scheduled flights, © *Financial Times*, 5 April 2000; Exhibit 1.3 United Airlines: the experiment that fell to earth, © *Financial Times*, 18 March 2003; Exhibit 1.4 Business put under pressure to disclose ethical risks, © *Financial Times*, 26 February 2004; Exhibit 1.5 Forget how the crow flies, © *Financial Times*, 17 January 2004; Chapter 1 quote from Lunch with the FT, Milton Friedman – the long view, © *Financial Times*, 7 June 2003; Exhibit 1.7 It is time to knock shareholder value off its pedestal, © *Financial Times*, 23 February 2005; Exhibit 1.9 Under-fire companies might find it's good to talk, © *Financial Times*, 17–18 January 2004; Exhibit 1.11 Severstal pledges high standards, © *Financial Times*, 7/8 October 2006; Exhibit 1.20 Indian premier to push for financial reform, © *Financial Times*, 9 October 2006; Exhibit 1.21 Capital gain: how London is thriving and taking on the global competition, © *Financial Times*, 27 March 2006; Exhibit 2.1 Panama Plan – a bigger canal can bring east and west closer, © *Financial Times*, 20 October 2006; Exhibit 2.10 Egdon Egged on by positive gas storage tests, © *Financial Times*, 29 June 2006; Exhibit 2.21 Storm over 'unacceptable gains' from PFI spreads to the secondary market, © *Financial Times*, 3 May 2006; Exhibit 3.5 Investor equity brings uneven outcomes, © *Financial Times*, 8 February 2006; Exhibit 3.18 JCB to buck trend and build engines, © *Financial Times*, 29 August 2003; Exhibit 4.1 BskyB to invest £400m building broadband arm, © *Financial Times*, 19 July 2006; Exhibit 4.6 More EU Lunacy, © *Financial Times*, 8 November 2004; Exhibit 4.7 Entrepreneur fires broad attack on manufacturers, © *Financial Times*, 17 January 2006; Exhibit 4.9 Tyranny of time, © *Financial Times*, 1 June 1999; Exhibit 6.33 Dear Economist resolving readers dilemmas with the tools of Adam Smith, © *Financial Times*, 12 February 2005; Exhibit 8.12 Big Bequest, © *Financial Times*, 1 August 1997; Exhibit 8.23 Equity beta the Lex column, © *Financial Times*, 4 September 2006; Exhibit 8.27 The time has come for the CAPM to RIP © *Financial Times*, 10/11 February 2007; Exhibit 9.2 France joins the stakeholder revolution, © *Financial Times*, 21 May 1999; Exhibit 9.3 A market appeals to the sceptical masses, © *Financial Times*, 21 May 2001; Chapter 9 quote from It's the liquidity that matters, © *Financial Times*, 28 March 2001; Exhibit 9.7 Peruvian miner lists in London in an attempt to regain global glories, © *Financial Times*, 9 November 2006; Exhibit 9.8 Indian groups check out Aim, © *Financial Times*, 1 September 2006; Exhibit 9.9 KarstadtQuelle eyes London, © *Financial Times*, 19 June 2007; Exhibit 9.10 Picsel proposes listing in London & Tokyo, © *Financial Times*, 1 November 2006; Exhibit 9.11 H K is China's preferred stock market, © *Financial Times*, 23 December 2005; Exhibit 9.12 Toyota to list in New York and London, © *Financial Times*, 8 September 1999; Exhibit 9.15 A Capital idea for emerging economies, © *Financial Times*, 30 May 2007; Exhibit 9.18 A mixed message for wondering naughty nomads, © *Financial Times*, 9 August 2005; Case Study 10.1 Talking his way to a fortune, © *Financial Times*, 14 June 2001 and In pursuit of a private life, © *Financial Times*, 1 November 1995; Exhibit 10.2 Golden share will corner Nottingham Forest buyer, © *Financial Times*, 25 November 1996; Exhibit 10.3 Flotation price of 275P Set for RHM, © *Financial Times*, 20 July 2005; Exhibit 10.6 Eddie Stobart drives on to LSE, © *Financial Times*, 16 August 2007; Exhibit 10.7 Booking the bids in the power sale, © *Financial Times*, 21 February 1995; Exhibit 10.8 Back to the start, © *Financial Times*, 21 February 1995; Exhibit 10.10 Cost of Aim flotation rises, especially for the minnows, © *Financial Times*, 27 April 2007; Exhibit 10.13 Aim augments the arduous process of listing, © *Financial Times*, 2 February 2007; Exhibit 10.14 Professional expenses prove a deterrent to maintaining stock market exposure, © *Financial Times*, 31 August 1999; Exhibit 10.16 Call to tighten Asian rules on dilution, © *Financial Times*, 2 April 2007; Exhibit 10.17 Corus raises £300m for revival, © *Financial Times*, 13 November 2003; Exhibit 10.18 Stock splits: time to query decades of dogma, © *Financial Times*, 7 April 2007; Case Study 10.3 The value of honesty and patience, © *Financial Times*, 1 February 2006; Exhibit 10.20 Haunted by the cost of dotcom crashing, © *Financial Times*, 22 May 2007; Exhibit 10.21 Limits are put to the test, © *Financial Times*, 24 April 2007; Exhibit 10.22 Baker set to pocket £6.5m if Boots sold, © *Financial Times*, 10 May 2007; Exhibit 10.23 Founding father and mentor of digital age Obituary of Eugene Kleiner, © *Financial Times*, 4 December 2003; Exhibit 10.25 Ingenious set to fund new bands to tune of £30m, © *Financial Times*, 17 January 2006; Exhibit 10.26 GSKs venture capital funds steps up European focus, © *Financial Times*, 24 April 2006; Exhibit 10.28 Your move bosses make small fortune, © *Financial Times*, 17 November 2006; Exhibit 10.29 Virgin accepts defeat with Victory delist, , © *Financial Times*, 24 November 2006; Exhibit 10.30 Praise the company that stays public, for it does good work, © *Financial Times*, 23 January 2007; Exhibit 10.31 JCB's reasons to be private, © *Financial Times*, 4 February 2003; Exhibit 10.32 Ferrari chief keen for IPO to drive growth, © *Financial Times*, 18 March 2002; Exhibit 10.33 The Lord is not for turning Haymarket over, © *Financial Times*, 18 June 2006; Exhibit 10.34 Monsoon chief to try to take group private, © *Financial Times*, 23/24 July 2005; Exhibit 10.35 Private equity demands only the best. © *Financial Times*, 28 September 2005; Exhibit 10.36 Chairman complains of City's short-termism, © *Financial Times*, 9 November 2005; 9 November 2005; Exhibit 10.37 The Dalek invasion stumbles on the corporate ladder, © *Financial Times*, 15 June 2004; Exhibit 10.38 Climbing aboard the flight from Flotation, © *Financial Times*, 6/7 September 2003; Exhibit 10.39 Enjoying life out of the spotlight, © *Financial Times*, 23 January 2003; Exhibit 10.40 AM Paper to examine options for a sale, © *Financial Times*, 21 May 1999; Exhibit 11.2 Photobition cautions on covenants, © *Financial Times*, 28 February 2001; Exhibit 11.4 Deutsche's exclusive deal with Invensys shatters cosy world of syndicated loans, © *Financial Times*, 10/11 April 2004; Exhibit 11.8 Weighing up the debt balancing act, © *Financial Times*, 12 March 2007; Exhibit 11.10 Mezzanine is starting to stake its claim, © *Financial Times*, 16 November 2006; Exhibit 11.12 Deferred return: risky investment?, © *Financial Times*, 27 September 2006; Exhibit 11.15 Brakes applied to convertible bond market, 6 April 2001; Exhibit 11.16 New bond raises $1bn for child jabs, © *Financial Times*, 8 November 2006; Exhibit 11.20 Autostrade returns to bond market after 40 year gap, © *Financial Times*, 13 May 2004; Exhibit 11.24 Property leasing link with market return discovered, © *Financial Times*, 3 November 2003; Exhibit 11.25 It's all a question of the right packaging, © *Financial Times*, 25 July 2007; Exhibit 11.26 A brief moment upside down, © *Financial Times*, 10 November 2006; Exhibit 12.2 NatWest deletes overdraft clause, © *Financial Times*, 21 November 2000; Exhibit 12.3 Branson wins £17, loan facility increase, © *Financial Times*, 12 June 2001; Exhibit 12.10 Sainsburys changes payment system in bank deal, © *Financial Times*, 24 November 2006; Exhibit 12.13 Cheque in the post' takes up 11.5m hours a week, © *Financial Times*, 24 May 2005; Exhibit 12.14 Late payments cost business £20bn a year, © *Financial Times*, 29 June 2004; Exhibit 12.17 Vital factor in surviving slump from SMEs, © *Financial Times*, 24 January 2002; Exhibit 12.20 EOS to launch transatlantic flights, © *Financial Times*, 4 October 2005; Exhibit 12.22 Companies balance sheets to set to get a new lease of life, © *Financial Times*, 21 February 2007; Exhibit 12.24 IFC makes move into Vietnam, © *Financial Times*, 1 November 1996; Exhibit 13.5 Pay now, live later is the new mantra of borrowing, © *Financial Times*, 9 April 2002; Exhibit 13.9 Relationship banking: Why Barcap's loyalty paid off, © *Financial Times*, 28 June 2006; Exhibit 13.15 Cash benefit: how big supermarkets fund expansion by using suppliers as bankers, 7 December 2005; Exhibit 14.11 Popularity of algorithmic trading assists wild change, © *Financial Times*, 23 April 2007; Exhibit 14.12 It does not always pay to follow the stars, © *Financial Times*, 15/16 May 2004; Exhibit 14.13 Measuring the impact of IFRS, © *Financial Times*, 21 April 2005; Exhibit 14.18 Forty years on, Fama holds to his big idea, © *Financial Times*, 3 June 2002; Exhibit 14.19 FSA boss admits defeat, © *Financial Times*, 3 July 2007; Exhibit 14.20 Life at the Sharpe end of economic modeling, © *Financial Times*, © *Financial Times*, 29 July 2002; Exhibit 15.2 The monoliths stir, © *Financial Times*, 28 September 1999; Chapter 15 quote from Problems kept coming out of the woodwork, © *Financial Times*, 19 January 2007; Exhibit 15.6 Motorola falls victim to its own success, © *Financial Times*, 19 March 2007; Exhibit 15.7 Non-financial measures just don't add up, © *Financial Times*, 29 March 2004; Chapter 15 quote from Return on investments, © *Financial Times*, 7 May 1996; Exhibit 15.12 Silicon Valley is starting to return cash to investors, © *Financial Times*, 14 March 2005; Exhibit 15.13 Gent's latest package raises acquisition fear, © *Financial Times*, 24 June 2002; Exhibit 15.15 Big feet, shrinking values, surred numbers, © *Financial Times*, 2 June 2003; Chapter 15 quote from Return on investments, © *Financial Times*, 7 May 1996; Exhibit 15.16 Stategy – the key issue suffering from neglect, © *Financial Times*, 8 March 2004; Exhibit 15.21 MMC reels as Daimler walks away, © *Financial Times*, 24/25 April 2004; Exhibit 16.9 Shell all but withdraws from Angola, © *Financial Times*, 10 April 2004; Exhibit 16.11 The Japanese art of performance, © *Financial Times*, 18 May 2004; Exhibit 17.14 VW to alter management focus, © *Financial Times*, 1 September 2003; Exhibit 17.15 Vodafone, © *Financial Times*, 4 June 2002; Exhibit 18.3 Investor warns companies on measures for executive pay, © *Financial Times*, 2 December 2003; Exhibit 19.4 LEX column – returns, © *Financial Times*, 11 February 2006; Exhibit 19.6 BSKYB/triple play, © *Financial Times*, 19 July 2006; Exhibit 19.10 The past is a poor guide to future share earnings, © *Financial Times*, 31 January 2006; Exhibit 19.11 Lex Column infrastructure returns, © *Financial Times*, 5 December 2006 and UK Airports, © *Financial Times*, 6 December 2006 and Lex column: Energy groups protest at Ofgems' price control plans, © *Financial Times*, 25 September 2007; Exhibit 20.4 £300bn binge ends in severe hangover write-downs, © *Financial Times*, 31 May 2006; Exhibit 20.5 Canary Wharf reflects change of sentiment to unloved sector, © *Financial Times*, 26 March 2004; Exhibit 20.10 Jefferson Smurfit, © *Financial Times*, 24 August 1995; Exhibit 20.11 Paper groups see few signs of upturn, © *Financial Times*, 24 October 2003; Exhibit 20.12 Why policymakers should take note, © *Financial Times*, 5 February 1996; Exhibit 20.15 Value model that ignores share price, © *Financial Times*, 25 October 2006; Exhibit 20.17 Private companies catching up, © *Financial Times*, 18 September 2006; Exhibit 20.18 The internet revolution, © *Financial Times*, 13 October 2000; Case Study 21.1 Whitbread looks to extend debt, © *Financial Times*, 15 June 2005 and O2 review could return more cash to investors, © *Financial Times*, 21 July 2005 and Resurgent BT planning £2bn share buy-back, © *Financial Times*, 5 May 2007; Exhibit 21.4 Goodbye gearing, © *Financial Times*, 9 October 1995; Exhibit 21.15 Glas Cymru launches bond campaign, © *Financial Times*, 9 April 2001; Exhibit 21.16 Demand to cut corporate relief cause alarm, © *Financial Times*, 12 February 2007; Exhibit 21.17 Rovers suppliers tighten terms, © *Financial Times*, 21 March 2005; Exhibit 21.18 NTL lost 73,400 customers during rescue talks, © *Financial Times*, 12 June 2002; Exhibit 21.21 Pressure building for public companies to utilise private equity tactics, © *Financial Times*, 12 August 2006; Exhibit 21.23 Bank puts assessment of risks into sharp focus, © *Financial Times*, 12 July 2006; Exhibit 21.24 Companies go back to basics in search for cash, © *Financial Times*, 1 October 2002; Exhibit 21.25 Matriarch in a waxed jacket, © *Financial Times*, 23 June 1997; Exhibit 21.26 A surplus of cash invariably leads to a shortage of sense, © *Financial Times*, 30 November 2005; Exhibit 21.27 Highest scores may not be most efficient, © *Financial Times*, 12 August 2003; Exhibit 22.1 Dividend payouts surge to new record, © *Financial Times*, © *Financial Times*, 2 April 2005; Exhibit 22.3 Double boost for HMV shareholders, © *Financial Times*, 19 January 2005; Exhibit 22.4 Arc agrees to hand back £50m, © *Financial Times*, 23/24 November 2002; Exhibit 22.7 Lurid acquisitions lose their edge as the retro dividend makes a comeback, © *Financial Times*, 15 September 2004; Exhibit 22.8 The dilemma of how best to share the wealth, © *Financial Times*, 17/18 July 2004; Exhibit 22.9 William Hill hands back £453m to investors, © *Financial Times*, 3 March 2005; Exhibit 22.10 Shareholders taking a stand on hand-outs, © *Financial Times*, 19 May 2007; Exhibit 23.3 Electric shock as ScotPower pulls US plug, © *Financial Times*, 22 May 2005; Exhibit 23.4 GE to face call for Gecas separation, © *Financial Times*, 6 June 2001; Exhibit 23.5 Valuing pharmas is not an exact science big acquisition premiums may be perfectly justified, © *Financial Times*, 8 June 2006; Exhibit 23.6 Chinese companies acquire a taste for western targets, © *Financial Times*, 19 October 2004; Exhibit 23.10 Vodafone's winning formula is now seen as a recipe for producing wrong numbers, © *Financial Times*, 28 June 2001; Exhibit 23.16 Bid tactics, © *Financial Times*, 14 February 2004; Exhibit 23.17 GEC given go-ahead to bid for VSEL, © *Financial Times*, 24 May 1995; Exhibit 23.19 KPMG withdraws merger study, © *Financial Times*, 29 November 1999; Exhibit 23.20 Funds furious over RBS bonuses, © *Financial Times*, 27 March 2001; Exhibit 23.22 How to make a corporate marriage work, © *Financial Times*, 7 February 2005; Exhibit 23.26 A sometimes fatal attraction, © *Financial Times*, 11 September 1995; Exhibit 23.27 Hearts and minds: Cadbury's recipe for merger success, © *Financial Times*, 27 April 2005; Exhibit 24.11 GM pays Fiat £1.55bn to end joint ventures, © *Financial Times*, 14 February 2005; Exhibit 24.16 Groups share shelter from the elements, © *Financial Times*, 18 October 2005; Exhibit 24.17 Leeson hid trading from the outset, © *Financial Times*, 18 October 1995; Exhibit 24.20 Betting on interest rates, © *Financial Times*, 1 November 1995; Exhibit 24.23 Rate rise is music to the ears of 'swappers', © *Financial Times*, 30 June 2007; Exhibit 24.24 TVA, EIB find winning formula, © *Financial Times*, 12 September 1996; Exhibit 24.26 Options mispricing caused loss, © *Financial Times*, 14 March 1997; Exhibit 25.4 London's dominance of global forex grows, © *Financial Times*, 26 September 2007; Exhibit 25.5 The mouse takes over the floor, © *Financial Times*, 27 May 2004; Exhibit 25.8 Balance sheets left reeling by Real, © *Financial Times*, 26 November 2002; Exhibit 25.9 Exchange rate woes hit GSK, © *Financial Times*, 26 April 2007; Exhibit 25.10 Small fry flounder in wake of surge, © *Financial Times*, 10 October 2007; Exhibit 25.15 Choose the correct path for a viable deal, © *Financial Times*, 25 January 2007; Exhibit 25.16 When a hedge is not a gardener's problem, © *Financial Times*, 18 August 1997; Exhibit 25.17 Sterling starts to stir, © *Financial Times*, 10 January 2004;

Graphics

Graphic from Case Study 3.1: Will it fly. Airbus's superjumbo, Building the superjumbo, © *Financial Times*, 2 November 2000; Exhibit 9.24 London Share Service extracts: Aerospace & Defence, © *Financial Times*, 10 September 2007; Exhibit 9.25 FTSE actuaries Share indices, © *Financial Times*, 11 September 2007; Exhibit 11.7 Examples of ratings on bonds in Sept 2007, © *Financial Times*, 12 September 2007; Exhibit 11.21 Global Investment Grade, © *Financial Times*, 21 September 2007; Chapter 11, © *Financial Times*, 20 October 2000; Exhibit 13.35 UK interest rates, © *Financial Times*, 8 March 2007; Exhibit 24.1 Call options on BSkyB shares, © *Financial Times*, 30 October 2007; Exhibit 24.6 Equity options shown in the Financial Times, 31 October 2007; Exhibit 24.14 Commodity prices, © *Financial Times*, 3–4 November 2007; Exhibit 24.18 Equity Index Futures, © *Financial Times*, 2 November 2007; Exhibit 24.19 Interest rate futures, © *Financial Times*, 2 November 2007; Exhibit 25.6 Currency rates, © *Financial Times*, 16 November 2007; Exhibit 25.13 Currency futures on the Chicago Mercantile Exchange and the NYBOT, © *Financial Times*, 16 November 2007;

We are grateful to the following for permission to use copyright material:

Exhibit 1.16 from Follow the money, *The Financial Times Limited*, 7/8 October 2006, © Mrs Moneypenny; Exhibit 10.19 from A wing and a prayer, *The Financial Times Limited*, 29/30 April 2006, © Monica Porter www.monicaporter.co.uk; Exhibit 14.1 from Inventors are taking the lead to help save the planet, *The Financial Times Limited*, 4 October 2006, © Douglas Ferrans & Peter Scales; Exhibit 15.17 from Investment community piles on pressure for better returns, *The Financial Times Limited*, 10 December 1999, © Nigel Page; Exhibit 22.5 from Dividends can be the best reward, *The Financial Times Limited*, 2/3 December 2006, © John Lee.

In some instances we have been unable to trace the owners of copyright material and we would appreciate any information that would enable us to do so.

PART 1

Introduction

CHAPTER 1

The financial world

LEARNING OUTCOMES

At the end of this chapter the reader will have a balanced perspective on the purpose and value of the finance function, at both the corporate and the national level. More specifically, the reader should be able to:

- describe alternative views on the purpose of the business and show the importance to any organisation of clarity on this point;
- describe the impact of the divorce of corporate ownership from day-to-day managerial control;
- explain the role of the financial manager;
- detail the value of financial intermediaries;
- show an appreciation of the function of the major financial institutions and markets

myfinancelab *Complete your diagnostic test for Chapter 1 now to create your personal study plan.*

Introduction

Before getting carried away with specific financial issues and technical detail, it is important to gain a broad perspective by looking at the fundamental questions and the place of finance in the overall scheme of things. The finance function is a vital one, both within an individual organisation and for society as a whole. In the UK, for example, the financial services industry accounts for a larger proportion of national output than the whole of manufacturing industry. There are now over 6 million UK employees in banking, finance and insurance. By contrast there are only 3.5 million in manufacturing. As recently as 1993 both sectors employed 4.4 million, so you can see that there has been an enormous shift in demand and resources in recent times. To some this is a cause of great alarm and regret but, given that this trend has occurred at a time when free choice in the marketplace largely dictates what is produced, presumably there must be something useful that financial firms are providing. We will examine the key role played by financial intermediaries and markets in a modern economy, and how an efficient and innovative financial sector contributes greatly to the ability of other sectors to produce efficiently. One of the vital roles of the financial sector is to encourage the mobilisation of savings to put them to productive use through investment. Without a vibrant and adaptable finance sector all parts of the economy would be starved of investment and society would be poorer.

This chapter also considers the most fundamental question facing anyone trying to make decisions within an organisation – what is the objective of the business? Without clarity on this point it is very difficult to run a business in a purposeful and effective manner. The resolution of this question is somewhat clouded in the large, modern corporation by the tendency for the owners to be distant from the running of the enterprise. Professional managers are usually left in control and they have objectives which may or may not match those of the owners.

Finally, to help the reader become orientated, a brief rundown is given of the roles, size and activities of the major types of financial institutions and markets. A little bit of jargon busting early on will no doubt be welcomed.

The objective of the firm

Cadbury Schweppes, widely regarded as one of the best-managed companies in the world, has a clear statement of its objective in the 2006 Annual Report and Accounts – *see* **Case study 1.1.**

Case study 1.1 Cadbury Schweppes

'Our aim is to deliver superior shareowner returns using all the levers of value creation: revenue growth, margin enhancement and increased capital efficiency. We will exploit and expand our business platforms through innovation, execution in the marketplace, investment and by ... extend[ing] our broad portfolio into new markets.'

Cadbury first establishes the ultimate aim of the company and then lists some goals and priorities in achieving this:

- 'Driving innovation through global categories (introducing new products or variations on products worldwide)
- Focusing on areas with the most potential
- Expanding our reach in confectionery
- Exploiting our beverage strength
- Increased efficiency and reducing costs
- Reinforcing our reputation (having engaged and committed workforce, and taking care of our environment and the communities where we live, work and operate)'

Source: Cadbury Schweppes Annual Report and Accounts 2006.

Notice that there is not a confusion of objectives (as there is in many companies) with no one knowing which of a long list of desirable outcomes is the dominant purpose of the firm. Cadbury Schweppes does not confuse the objective with the strategy to be employed to achieve the objective. Many managerial teams believe that it is their objective to operate within a particular market or take particular actions. They seem unable to distinguish market positions or actions from the ultimate purpose for the existence of the organisation. This will not only lead to poor strategic decisions but frequently makes intelligent financial decisions impossible.

This book is all about practical decision making in the real world. When people have to make choices in the harsh environment in which modern businesses have to operate, it is necessary to be clear about the purpose of the organisation; to be clear about what objective is set for management to achieve. A multitude of small decisions are made every day; more importantly, every now and then major strategic commitments of resources are made. It is imperative that the management teams are aware of, respect and contribute to the fundamental objective of the firm in all these large and small decisions. Imagine the chaos and confusion that could result from the opposite situation where there is no clear, accepted objective. The outcome of each decision, and the direction of the firm, will become random and rudderless. One manager on one occasion will decide to grant long holidays and a shorter working week, believing that the purpose of the institution's existence is to benefit employees; while on another occasion a different manager sacks 'surplus' staff and imposes lower wages, seeing the need to look after the owner's interests as a first priority. So, before we can make decisions in the field of finance we need to establish what it is we are trying to achieve.

You have probably encountered elsewhere the question, 'In whose interests is the firm run?' This is a political and philosophical as well as an economic question and many books have been written on the subject. Here we will provide a brief overview of the debate because of its central importance to making choices in finance. The list of interested parties in **Exhibit 1.1** could be extended, but no doubt you can accept the point from this shortened version that there are a number of claimants on a firm.

Sound financial management is necessary for the survival of the firm and for its growth. Therefore all of these stakeholders, to some extent, have an interest in seeing sensible financial decisions being taken. Many business decisions do not involve a conflict between the objectives of each of the stakeholders. However, there are occasions when someone has to decide which claimants are to have their **objectives maximised**, and which are merely to be **satisficed** – that is, given just enough of a return to make their contributions.

There are some strong views held on this subject. The pro-capitalist economists, such as Friedrich Hayek and Milton Friedman, believe that making shareholders' interests the paramount objective will benefit both the firm and society at large. This approach is not quite as extreme as it sounds because these thinkers generally accept that unbridled pursuit of shareholder returns, to the point of widespread pollution, murder and extortion, will not be in society's best interest and

Exhibit 1.1 A company has responsibilities to a number of interested parties

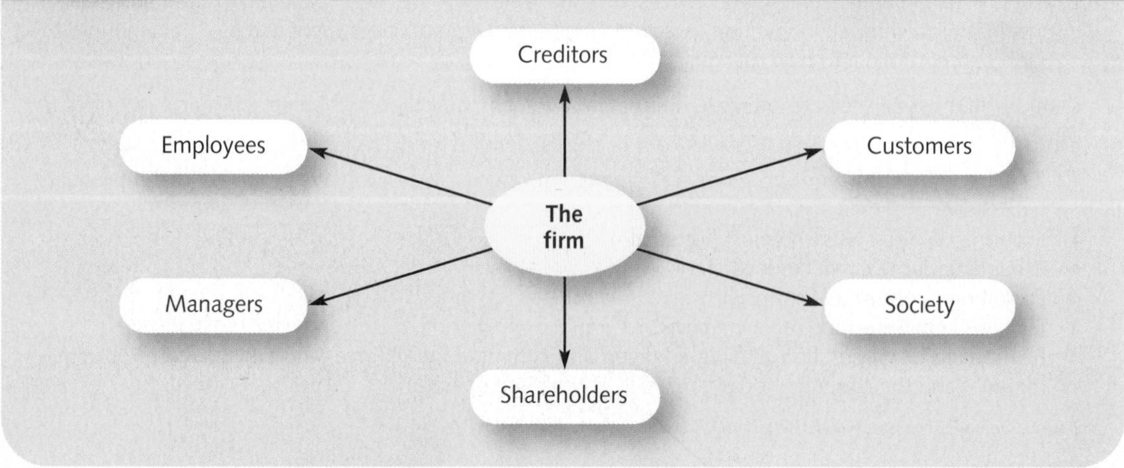

so add the proviso that maximising shareholder wealth is the desired objective provided that firms remain within 'the rules of the game'. This includes obeying the laws and conventions of society, behaving ethically and honestly.

At the opposite end of the political or philosophical spectrum are the left-wing advocates of the primacy of workers' rights and rewards. The belief here is that labour should have its rewards maximised. The employees should have all that is left over, after the other parties have been satisfied. Shareholders are given just enough of a return to provide capital, suppliers are given just enough to supply raw materials and so on.

Standing somewhere in the middle are those keen on a balanced stakeholder approach. Here the (often conflicting) interests of each of the claimants are somehow maximised but within the constraints set by the necessity to compromise in order to provide a fair return to the other stakeholders.

Some possible objectives

A firm can choose from an infinitely long list of possible objectives. Some of these will appear noble and easily justified, others remain hidden, implicit, embarrassing, even subconscious. The following represent some of the most frequently encountered.

- ***Achieving a target market share*** In some industrial sectors to achieve a high share of the market gives high rewards. These may be in the form of improved profitability, survival chances or status. Quite often the winning of a particular market share is set as an objective because it acts as a proxy for other, more profound objectives, such as generating the maximum returns to shareholders. On other occasions matters can get out of hand and there is an obsessive pursuit of market share with only a thin veneer of shareholder wealth espousement – *see* **Exhibit 1.2**.
- ***Keeping employee agitation to a minimum*** Here, return to the organisation's owners is kept to a minimum necessary level. All surplus resources are directed to mollifying employees. Managers would be very reluctant to admit publicly that they place a high priority on reducing workplace tension, encouraging peace by appeasement and thereby, it is hoped, reducing their own stress levels, but actions tend to speak louder than words. An example of this kind of prioritisation was evident in a number of state-owned UK industries in the 1960s and 1970s. Unemployment levels were low, workers were in a strong bargaining position and there were, generally, state funds available to bail out a loss-making firm. In these circumstances it was easier to buy peace by acquiescing to union demands than to fight on the picket lines.

  Some companies have tried to reduce workplace tension by giving workers a large proportion of the shares, i.e. making them part-owners. But, as the example of United Airlines shows, 'differences in expectations' can destroy the business. UA ended up with ever more extreme demands from the unions, followed by bankruptcy – *see* **Exhibit 1.3**.

Exhibit 1.2

Profits fall 39% on scheduled flights

FT

By Kevin Done, Aerospace Correspondent

International airlines last year suffered a 39 per cent fall in the net profits of their scheduled services to $1.9bn, the lowest level for five years, according to the International Air Transport Association (Iata).

Pierre Jeanniot, Iata director-general, warned that airlines should 'stop chasing the chimera of endless traffic growth at any price'.

'If governments are no longer going to subsidise such folly,' he said, 'why should we?'

Mr Jeanniot warned that most airline strategies continued to be based on market growth and on increasing market share instead of being driven by profits. Airline shareholders should be moved 'to the top of the priority list for rewards'.

Source: Financial Times, 5 April 2000, p. 13. Reprinted with permission.

Exhibit 1.3

United Airlines: the experiment that fell to earth

FT

The carrier's bankruptcy has raised serious doubts about the viability of workers controlling the companies they work for

write Caroline Daniel and Simon London

. . . Three months ago the world's second largest airline filed for bankruptcy amid spiralling losses. Last week, after nine years of 55 per cent employee ownership, workers at last dumped enough stock to push their stake below 20 per cent, triggering so-called 'sunset clauses'. The experiment was finally declared dead. . . .

Differences in expectations emerged quickly, says one former employee. 'The silliest of all was when John Edwardson, [then number two] had a meeting with the pilots' union early on and the union said: "Now we are owners, we have the right to fire one officer every year" and John just looked at him and understood it wasn't a joke. It was a tense moment. And he replied: "I suppose then that officers can fire one pilots' union leader every year." Then the light went on.'

Moreover, it was hard to get employees to think like owners. Middle managers in particular were uneasy about giving up precious power. 'We started to say: "We are all owners now, instead of just bosses and employees, so bosses needed to learn quickly how to supervise as coaches, cajolers, advisers – but not with a whip." But some supervisors didn't get it and said: "If I criticise one of my people, and they write to the chief executive, I'll be in trouble."' . . .

Along with restrictions over which aircraft would fly certain routes, the absurdity of some of the arcane work rules was underscored by the fact that the pilots' contract included a promise that the company would pick up the tab if a pilot moved city and his piano needed re-tuning, according to one employee. . . .

Employees were given just three out of 12 board seats. But they were also granted the ability to veto chief executives and strategic decisions, such as acquisitions.

Wielding that power required enlightened union leaders. Instead, unions exploited it, denying Mr Edwardson the chief executive's post and later ousting Jim Goodwin, their own appointee, when he warned United would perish without wage cuts. . . .

In 2000 pilots' wages soared an immediate 29 per cent, with 4.5 per cent rises scheduled to follow.

Mr Dubinsky, then head of United's pilots' union, gloated that he intended to choke the golden goose 'by its neck until it gives us every last egg'. . . .

A senior pilot recalls: 'From 2000 to 2002, labour costs rose $1.4bn (£886m) but at the same time revenues fell $5.5bn.'

The pilot continues: 'The problem was that United was employee-owned but union-controlled. Union leaders needed to satisfy their members who were concerned about work rules and wages, rather than valuation issues. There was a corrupting influence of politics on decision-making . . . the equity culture never caught on.' . . .

The implications of union control over time led to the bleeding of management talent. . . .

Source: Financial Times, 18 March 2003, p. 15. Reprinted with permission.

- ***Survival*** There are circumstances where the overriding objective becomes the survival of the firm. Severe economic or market shock may force managers to focus purely on short-term issues to ensure the continuance of the business. In firefighting they end up paying little attention to long-term growth and return to owners. However, this focus is clearly inadequate in the long run – there must be other goals. If survival were the only objective then putting all the firm's cash reserves into a bank savings account might be the best option. When managers say that their objective is survival what they generally mean is the avoidance of large risks which endanger the firm's future. This may lead to a greater aversion to risk, and a rejection of activities that shareholders might wish the firm to undertake. Shareholders are in a position to diversify their investments: if one firm goes bankrupt they may be disappointed but they have other companies' shares to fall back on. However, the managers of that one firm may have the majority of their income, prestige and security linked to the continuing existence of that firm. These managers may deliberately avoid high-risk/high-return investments and therefore deprive the owners of the possibility of large gains.
- ***Creating an ever-expanding empire*** This is an objective which is rarely openly discussed, but it seems reasonable to propose that some managers drive a firm forward, via organic growth or

mergers, because of a desire to run an ever-larger enterprise. Often these motives become clearer with hindsight; when, for instance, a firm meets a calamitous end the post-mortem often reveals that profit and efficiency were given second place to growth. The volume of sales, number of employees or overall stock market value of the firm has a much closer correlation with senior executive salaries, perks and status than do returns to shareholder funds. This may motivate some individuals to promote growth.

- ***Maximisation of profit*** This is a much more acceptable objective, although not everyone would agree that maximisation of profit should be the firm's purpose.
- ***Maximisation of long-term shareholder wealth*** While many commentators concentrate on profit maximisation, finance experts are aware of a number of drawbacks of profit. The maximisation of the returns to shareholders in the long term is considered to be a superior goal. We look at the differences between profit maximisation and wealth maximisation later.

This list of possible objectives can easily be extended but it is not possible within the scope of this book to examine each of them. Suffice it to say, there can be an enormous variety of objectives and a large potential for conflict and confusion. We have to introduce some sort of order.

The assumed objective for finance

The company should make investment and financing decisions with the aim of maximising long-term shareholder wealth. Throughout the remainder of this book we will assume that the firm gives primacy of purpose to the wealth of shareholders. This assumption is made mainly on practical grounds, but there are respectable theoretical justifications too.

The practical reason

If one may assume that the decision-making agents of the firm (managers) are acting in the best interests of shareholders then decisions on such matters as which investment projects to undertake, or which method of financing to use, can be made much more simply. If the firm has a multiplicity of objectives, imagine the difficulty in deciding whether to introduce a new, more efficient machine to produce the firm's widgets, where the new machine will both be more labour efficient (thereby creating redundancies), and will eliminate the need to buy from one half of the firm's suppliers. If one focuses solely on the benefits to shareholders a clear decision can be made. This entire book is about decision-making tools to aid those choices. These range from whether to produce a component in-house, to whether to buy another company. If for each decision scenario we have to contemplate a number of different objectives or some vague balance of stakeholder interests, the task is going to be much more complex. Once the basic decision-making frameworks are understood within the tight confines of shareholder wealth maximisation, we can allow for complications caused by the modification of this assumption. For instance, shareholder wealth maximisation is clearly not the only consideration motivating actions of organisations such as Body Shop or the Co-operative Bank, each with publicly stated ethical principles.

The theoretical reasons

The '**contractual theory**' views the firm as a network of contracts, actual and implicit, which specify the roles to be played by various participants in the organisation. For instance, the workers make both an explicit (employment contract) and an implicit (show initiative, reliability, etc.) deal with the firm to provide their services in return for salary and other benefits, and suppliers deliver necessary inputs in return for a known payment. Each party has well-defined rights and pay-offs. Most of the participants bargain for a limited risk and a fixed pay-off. Banks, for example, when they lend to a firm, often strenuously try to reduce risk by making sure that the firm is generating sufficient cash flow to repay, that there are assets that can be seized if the loan is not repaid and so on. The bankers' bargain, like that of many of the parties, is a low-risk one and so, the argument goes, they should be rewarded with just the bare minimum for them to provide their service to the firm. Shareholders, on the other hand, are asked to put money into the business at high risk. The deal here is, 'You give us your £10,000 nest egg that you need for your retirement and we, the directors of the firm, do not promise that you will receive a dividend or even see your capital again. We will try our hardest to produce a return on your money but we cannot give any guarantees. Sorry.' Thus the firm's owners are exposed to the possibilities that the firm may go bankrupt and all will be lost. Because of this unfair balance of risk between the different potential claimants on a firm's resources it seems reasonable that the owners should be entitled to any surplus returns which result after all the other parties have been satisfied.

Another theoretical reason hinges on the practicalities of operating in a free market system. In such a capitalist system, it is argued, if a firm chooses to reduce returns to shareholders because, say, it wishes to direct more of the firm's surplus to the workers, then this firm will find it difficult to survive. Some shareholders will sell their shares and invest in other firms more orientated towards their benefit. (United Airlines perhaps, where even the workers sold their shares?) In the long run those individuals who do retain their shares may be amenable to a takeover bid from a firm which does concentrate on shareholder wealth creation. The acquirer will anticipate being able to cut costs, not least by lowering the returns to labour. In the absence of a takeover the company would be unable to raise more finance from shareholders and this might result in slow growth and liquidity problems and possibly corporate death, throwing all employees out of work.

For over 200 years it has been argued that society is best served by businesses focusing on returns to the owner. Adam Smith (1776) expressed the argument very effectively:

> The businessman by directing . . . industry in such a manner as its produce may be of the greatest value, intends only his own gain, and he is in this, as in many other cases, led by an invisible hand to promote an end which was no part of his intention. Nor is it always the worse for society that it was no part of it. By pursuing his own interest he frequently promotes that of the society more effectually than when he really intends to promote it. I have never known much good done by those who affected to trade for the public good. It is an affectation, indeed, not very common among merchants.
>
> *Source*: Adam Smith, *The Wealth of Nations*, 1776, p. 400.

Adam Smith's objection to businessmen affecting to trade for the public good is echoed in Michael Jensen's writings in which he attacks the stakeholder approach (and its derivative, the Balanced Scorecard of Kaplan and Norton (1996)). His main worry is the confusion that results from having a multiplicity of targets to aim for, but he also takes a sideswipe at managers who are able to use the smokescreen of the stakeholder approach to cloak their actions in pursuit of benefits for themselves, or their pet 'socially beneficial' goals:

> Stakeholder theory effectively leaves managers and directors unaccountable for their stewardship of the firm's resources . . . [it] plays into the hands of managers by allowing them to pursue their own interests at the expense of the firm's financial claimants and society at large. It allows managers and directors to devote the firm's resources to their own favorite causes – the environment, arts, cities, medical research – without being held accountable . . . it is not surprising that stakeholder theory receives substantial support from them.
>
> (Jensen 2001).

However, Jensen goes on to say that companies cannot create shareholder value if they ignore important constituencies. They must have good relationships with customers, employees, suppliers, government and so on. This is a form of **corporate social responsibility, CSR**, within an overall framework of shareholder wealth maximisation. (Some of the CSR officers, consultants and departments take this a stage further to a belief that the firm must balance all the stakeholder interests to fulfil its social role – something Jensen disagrees with.) **Exhibit 1.4** shows that UK financial institutions, (large holders of shares) despite being keenly interested in the returns generated from the shares they hold, nevertheless want companies to act responsibly with regard to climate change, obesity, access by African AIDS patients to medicines, etc.

Also, simply to tell people to maximise shareholder value may not be enough to motivate them to deliver value. They must be turned on by a vision or a strategy, e.g. to put a PC on every desk, to produce a drug to cure AIDs or to build a state of the art aeroplane. Shareholder value can measure how successful you are, but it does not create superior vision or strategy – you need additional (but subsidiary) goals and measures, which may be identified and supported through a Balanced Scorecard approach, because it allows a greater understanding of what creates value.

John Kay also points out that firms going directly for 'shareholder value' may actually do less well for shareholders than those that focus on vision and excellence first and find themselves

Exhibit 1.4

Business put under pressure to disclose ethical risks

FT

By Sundeep Tucker and Alison Maitland

Shareholders may deploy a powerful new weapon against companies that fail to disclose the social, ethical and environmental risks to their business by refusing to endorse the company report and accounts, a leading investor lobby group warned yesterday.

The Association of British Insurers, whose members own a fifth of the London stock market, welcomed an explicit threat by Henderson Global Investors, the fund manager, to consider companies 'non-financial risk management' when deciding how to vote on a company's report and accounts.

The decision indicates that shareholder activists are beginning to pay as much attention to issues of corporate social responsibility as they do to executive pay – and piles even more pressure on business.

Controversies over climate change, obesity, access to medicines and labour standards in the clothing and computer supply chains are raising concerns among investors who fear their shareholdings could be damaged by factors such as negative publicity or litigation.

Nick Robins, head of socially responsible investment research at Henderson, said: 'Companies with inadequate disclosure on social, ethical and environmental factors are denying their investors the right to make informed investment decisions.'

'Corporate responsibility is not about creating a feel-good factor,' said Peter Montagnon, ABI head of investment affairs. 'We're talking about fundamental risk management. We want companies to have high-quality, sustainable earnings.'

Source: *Financial Times*, 26 February 2004, p. 3.

shareholder wealth maximisers in an **oblique way**. He argues that Boeing, in the 1990s, sacrificed its vision of being a company always on the cutting edge of commercial plane design, breaking through technological and marketplace barriers. This reduced the vibrancy of the pioneering spirit of the organisation, as it refocused on short-term financial performance measures – *see* **Exhibit 1.5**. However, it is possible to argue that Boeing's managers in the 1990s were not, in fact, shareholder wealth maximisers because they forgot the crucial 'long-term' focus. Being daring and at the cutting edge may be risky, but it often leads to the highest long-term shareholder wealth. Concentrating on short-term financial goals and presenting these as shareholder wealth-maximising actions can lead to slow pace and market irrelevance. So, being too fastidious in requiring immediately visible and quantifiable returns in an uncertain world can result in the rejection of extremely valuable projects that require a leap into the unknown by a team of enthusiasts. Where would Microsoft be today if in the 1970s it had required a positive number popping out of a rigorous financial analysis of the prospects for its operating systems, when sales of PCs numbered in hundreds?

In an interview in 2003 Milton Friedman focused on the main benefit of encouraging businesses to pursue high returns for owners. He said that this results in the best allocation of investment capital among competing industries and product lines. This is good for society because consumers end up with more of what they want because scarce investment money is directed to the best uses, producing the optimum mix of goods and services. 'The self-interest of employees in retaining their jobs will often conflict with this overriding objective.' He went on:

> the best system of corporate governance is one that provides the best incentives to use capital efficiently. . . . You want control . . . in the hands of those who are residual recipients [i.e. shareholders bear the residual risk when a company fails] because they are the ones with the direct interest in using the capital of the firm efficiently.
>
> *Source*: Simon London, *Financial Times Magazine*, 7 June 2003, p. 13.

One final and powerful reason for advancing shareholders' interests above all others (subject to the rules of the game) is very simple: they own the firm and therefore deserve any surplus it produces. The Companies Act 2006 reinforces this by stating that directors' primary duty is to promote the success of the company for the benefit of its members, that is, the shareholders. Yet in the fulfilment of that duty directors should have regard to the interests of employees, suppliers, cus-

Exhibit 1.5

Forget how the crow flies

FT

If you want to go in one direction, the best route may involve going in the other. Paradoxical as it sounds, goals are more likely to be achieved when pursued indirectly. So the most profitable companies are not the most profit-oriented, and the happiest people are not those who make happiness their main aim. The name of this idea? Obliquity

By John Kay

. . . I once said that Boeing's grip on the world civil aviation market made it the most powerful market leader in world business. Bill Allen was chief executive from 1945 to 1968, as the company created its dominant position. He said that his spirit and that of his colleagues was to eat, breathe, and sleep the world of aeronautics. 'The greatest pleasure life has to offer is the satisfaction that flows from participating in a difficult and constructive undertaking', he explained. . . .

The company's largest and riskiest project was the development of the 747 jumbo jet. When a non-executive director asked about the expected return on investment, he was brushed off: there had been some studies, he was told, but the manager concerned couldn't remember the results.

It took only 10 years for Boeing to prove me wrong in asserting that its market position in civil aviation was impregnable. The decisive shift in corporate culture followed the acquisition of its principal US rival, McDonnell Douglas, in 1997. The transformation was exemplified by the CEO, Phil Condit. The company's previous preoccupation with meeting 'technological challenges of supreme magnitude' would, he told Business Week, now have to change. 'We are going into a value-based environment where unit cost, return on investment and shareholder return are the measures by which you'll be judged. That's a big shift.'

The company's senior executives agreed to move from Seattle, where the main production facilities were located, to Chicago. More importantly, the more focused business reviewed risky investments in new civil projects with much greater scepticism. The strategic decision was to redirect resources towards projects for the US military that involved low financial risk. Chicago had the advantage of being nearer to Washington, where government funds were dispensed.

So Boeing's civil orderbook today lags behind that of Airbus, the European consortium whose aims were not initially commercial but which has, almost by chance, become a profitable business. . . . And what was the market's verdict on the company's performance in terms of unit cost, return on investment and shareholder return? Boeing stock, $48 when Condit took over, rose to $70 as he affirmed the commitment to shareholder value; by the time of his enforced resignation in December 2003 it had fallen to $38. . . .

At Boeing, the attempt to focus on simple, well defined objectives proved less successful than management with a broader, more comprehensive conception of objectives. . . .

Obliquity gives rise to the profit-seeking paradox: the most profitable companies are not the most profit-oriented. Boeing illustrates how a greater focus on shareholder returns was self-defeating in its own narrow terms. . . .

Collins and Porras compared the philosophy of George Merck ('We try never to forget that medicine is for the people. It is not for the profits. The profits follow, and if we have remembered that, they have never failed to appear. The better we have remembered it, the larger they have been') with that of John McKeen of Pfizer ('So far as humanly possible, we aim to get profit out of everything we do').

The individuals who are most successful at making money are not those who are most interested in making money. This is not surprising. The principal route to great wealth is the creation of a successful business, and building a successful business demands exceptional talents and hard work. There is no reason to think these characteristics are associated with greed and materialism: rather the opposite. People who are obsessively interested in money are drawn to get-rich-quick schemes rather than to business opportunities, and when these schemes come off, as occasionally they do, they retire to their villas in the sun. . . .

Although we crave time for passive leisure, people engaged in watching television reported low levels of contentment. Csikszentmihalyi's systematic finding is that the activities that yield the highest for satisfaction with life require the successful performance of challenging tasks.

John Kay is the author of *The Truth About Markets* (Allen Lane).

Source: John Kay, *Financial Times Magazine*, 17 January 2004, pp. 17–21. Reproduced with kind permission of the *Financial Times*.

tomers, the environment and corporate reputation. Thus in closing a factory, say, the interests of shareholders trump those of employees, but the latter concerns should not be completely ignored. *The Economist* presents a series of arguments in favour of shareholder supremacy in **Exhibit 1.6**.

Exhibit 1.6

The good company

FT

Companies today are exhorted to be 'socially responsible'. What, exactly, does this mean?

It will no longer do for a company to go quietly about its business, telling no lies and breaking no laws, selling things that people want, and making money. That is so passé. Today, all companies, but especially big ones, are enjoined from every side to worry less about profits and be socially responsible instead. Surprisingly, perhaps, these demands have elicited a willing, not to say avid, response in enlightened boardrooms everywhere. Companies at every opportunity now pay elaborate obeisance to the principles of corporate social responsibility. They have CSR officers, CSR consultants, CSR departments, and CSR initiatives coming out of their ears. A good thing, too, you might think. About time. What kind of idiot or curmudgeon would challenge the case for businesses to behave more responsibly? Thank you for asking.

Cynics and believers

The practices that caring, progressive CEOs mention when speaking at conferences on CSR come in all shapes and sizes. Treat your employees well; encourage loyalty among your customers and suppliers; avoid investing in 'unethical' industries, or in countries where workers are paid low wages or denied decent benefits; take care to save energy and recycle used envelopes; and so on. The range of such policies makes it hazardous to generalise. Some of them advance the interests of shareholders and of the wider world as well; others make everyone, except the office bureaucrats paid to dream them up, worse off. Motives vary too. Some CSR advocates are cynics: they pay lip service to the idea but are chuckling quietly. Others are true believers, born-again champions of a kinder, gentler capitalism.

The one thing that all the nostrums of CSR have in common is that they are based on a faulty – and dangerously faulty – analysis of the capitalist system they are intended to redeem. Admittedly, CSR is now so well entrenched and amply funded that to complain about it may be pointless. We are concerned that it may even be a socially irresponsible use of scarce newsprint. Nonetheless, if businessmen had a clearer understanding of the CSR mindset and its defects, they would be better at their jobs and everybody else would be more prosperous.

Simply put, advocates of CSR work from the premise that unadorned capitalism fails to serve the public interest. The search for profit, they argue, may be a regrettable necessity in the modern world, a sad fact of life if there is to be any private enterprise. But the problem is that the profits of private enterprise go exclusively to shareholders. What about the public good? Only if corporations recognise their obligations to society – to 'stakeholders' other than the owners of the business – will that broader social interest be advanced. Often, governments can force such obligations on companies, through taxes and regulation. But that does not fully discharge the enlightened company's debt to society. For that, one requires CSR.

This is wrong. The goal of a well-run company may be to make profits for its shareholders, but merely in doing that – provided it faces competition in its markets, behaves honestly and obeys the law – the company, without even trying, is doing good works. Its employees willingly work for the company in exchange for wages; the transaction makes them better off. Its customers willingly pay for the company's products; the transaction makes them better off also. All the while, for strictly selfish reasons, well-run companies will strive for friendly long-term relations with employees, suppliers and customers. There is no need for selfless sacrifice when it comes to stakeholders. It goes with the territory.

Thus, the selfish pursuit of profit serves a social purpose. And this is putting it mildly. The standard of living people in the West enjoy today is due to little else but the selfish pursuit of profit. It is a point that Adam Smith emphasised in 'The Wealth of Nations': 'It is not from the benevolence of the butcher, the brewer, or the baker, that we expect our dinner, but from their regard to their own interest.' This is not the fatal defect of capitalism, as CSR-advocates appear to believe; it is the very reason capitalism works.

Maybe so, those advocates might reply, but perhaps the system would work even better if there were a bit more benevolence in the boardroom and a bit less self-interest. In some cases, that might be so, but in general (as Smith also noted) one should be wary of businessmen proclaiming their benevolence. A question to ask of all outbreaks of corporate goodness is, who is paying? Following the Indian Ocean tsunami, many companies made generous donations to charities helping the victims. There could be no worthier cause – but keep in mind that, in the case of public companies, the managers authorising those donations were giving other people's money, not their own. Philanthropy at others' expense, even in a cause as good as that one, is not quite the real thing.

All things considered, there is much to be said for leaving social and economic policy to governments. They, at least, are accountable to voters. Managers lack the time for such endeavours, or should do. Lately they have found it a struggle even to discharge their obligations to shareholders, the people who are paying their wages. If they want to make the world a better place – a commendable aim, to be sure – let them concentrate for the time being on that.

Source: The Economist, 22 January 2005.

This is not the place to advocate one philosophical approach or another which is applicable to all organisations at all times. Many organisations are clearly not shareholder wealth maximisers and are quite comfortable with that. Charities, government departments and other non-profit organisations are fully justified in emphasising a different set of values to those espoused by the commercial firm. The reader is asked to be prepared for two levels of thought when using this book. While it focuses on corporate shareholder wealth decision making, it may be necessary to make small or large modifications to be able to apply the same frameworks and theories to organisations with different goals.

However, beware of organisations that try to balance a number of objectives. Take, for example, football clubs that have floated on the stock market. They have at least two parties to satisfy: (i) shareholders looking for good return on their savings: (ii) fans looking for more spending on players and lower ticket prices. It is very difficult to satisfy both – hence the dramatic tensions and suspicions at so many clubs.

The views of an opponent of shareholder wealth maximisation are presented in **Exhibit 1.7**.

Exhibit 1.7

It's time to knock shareholder value off its pedestal

FT

Michael Skapinker on managing

Are business schools destroying business? A growing number of business school professors believe they are. Now one of their best-liked colleagues has added his voice, posthumously. Sumantra Ghoshal of London Business School died last year aged 55, while he was still developing his critique of management educators and the damage they had wrought.

In his paper, 'Bad management Theories are Destroying Good Management Practices', published next month in the Academy of Management Learning and Education journal, is among many pieces of Ghoshal's work that will resonate after his premature death.

'Much of the worst excesses of recent management practices have their roots in a set of ideas that have emerged from the business school academics over the past 30 years,' Ghoshal wrote. Many of those bad ideas, he said, had their origins in the dismal influence of economists, and one economist in particular – Milton Friedman, who declared that managers' sole responsibility was to make money for shareholders.

The attraction of shareholder value, in its supporters' view, was that it set a standard against which managers could be judged. Asking managers to aim at anything else – the good of the wider community, for example – was a distraction from the central task. Other goals were too imprecise: how would you measure whether managers had succeeded or failed?

Having decided that managers' sole task was to make money for shareholders, the economists promptly declared they could not be trusted to do so. What was to stop managers pursuing their own interests, rather than those of shareholders? There were several attempts to solve this 'agency problem'. Giving managers share options to align their interests with shareholders' was the first. When that failed, amid the managerial excesses and fraud of the past few years, governments and regulators turned to controlling managers through independent directors. But, Ghoshal said, there was no evidence that corporate governance reform improved corporate performance.

Managerial malpractice, Ghoshal argued, was not the result of insufficient independent directors. It was the consequence of believing that shareholder return was all that mattered and that managers should battle their way through any obstacle to achieve it, free 'from any sense of moral or ethical responsibility for their actions'. It was also the result of assuming managers could not be trusted. Treated as untrustworthy, that is what they became.

> One problem with Ghoshal is that while he demolished shareholder value, he proposed nothing in its place

Business schools, he wrote, had been at the forefront of propagating shareholder value, agency theory and the rest, with all the baleful consequences of recent years.

What should we make of this? First, like Jeffrey Pfeffer of Stanford who endorses his views in the same journal, Ghoshal overstated business schools' importance. As Rosabeth Moss Kanter of Harvard Business School says in her response to Ghoshal, the business schools' ideas 'have hardly been foisted on innocent capitalists'.

It was not just that business schools propounded shareholder value: managers were all too ready to practise it. 'Why has there been such a receptive audience?' Prof Kanter asks. First, because what preceded it was so unattractive, a 'cosy managerialism' in which US business leaders ignored the threat, for example, from Japanese manufacturing. Nor, as Donald Hanibrick, another contributor, points out, were old-fashioned managers caring paternalists. They feathered their nests too, building company golf courses, among other things.

Prof Kanter adds that the rise of shareholder value coincided with capitalism's victory over communism. 'American theories and theorists had disproportionate influence. One-sided

Exhibit 1.7 continued

shareholder capitalism was in vogue,' Prof Kanter says. 'Valuing all stakeholders, being socially responsible and caring about people sounded a little "pinko" to business managers when the world had so roundly rejected socialism in any form. Greed was legitimated as producing a better society, not just better companies.'

The second objection to Ghoshal's argument was that Enron, Tyco, WorldCom and the others did not happen because managers put shareholders first. They happened because managers put themselves first. Shareholders suffered from their behaviour, along with employees. Share options and independent directors might not be the answer to the agency problem, but the corporate scandals demonstrated that there undoubtedly was an agency problem.

Third, while the shareholder value philosophy had its unattractive side, it had its successes too. For all the scandals, US companies remained the world's most innovative.

The final problem with Ghoshal's argument: having set out to demolish shareholder value, he proposed nothing in its place.

Source: *Financial Times*, 23 February 2005, p. 16.

What is shareholder wealth?

Maximising wealth can be defined as maximising purchasing power. The way in which an enterprise enables its owners to indulge in the pleasures of purchasing and consumption is by paying them dividends. The promise of a flow of cash in the form of dividends is what prompts investors to sacrifice immediate consumption and hand over their savings to a management team through the purchase of shares. Shareholders are interested in a flow of dividends over a long time horizon and not necessarily in a quick payback. Take the electronics giant Philips: it could raise vast sums for short-term dividend payouts by ceasing all research and development (R&D) and selling off surplus sites. But this would not maximise shareholder wealth because, by retaining funds within the business, it is believed that new products and ideas, springing from the R&D programme, will produce much higher dividends in the future. **Maximising shareholder wealth** means maximising the flow of dividends to shareholders *through time* – there is a long-term perspective.

Profit maximisation is not the same as shareholder wealth maximisation

Profit is a concept developed by accountants to aid decision making, one decision being to judge the quality of stewardship shown over the owner's funds. The accountant has to take what is a continuous process, a business activity stretching over many years, and split this into accounting periods of, say, a year, or six months. To some extent this exercise is bound to be artificial and fraught with problems. There are many reasons why accounting profit may not be a good proxy for shareholder wealth. Here are five of them:

- ***Prospects*** Imagine that there are two firms that have reported identical profits but one firm is more highly valued by its shareholders than the other. One possible reason for this is that recent profit figures fail to reflect the relative potential of the two firms. The stock market will give a higher share value to the company which shows the greater future growth outlook. Perhaps one set of managers have chosen a short-term approach and raised their profits in the near term but have sacrificed long-term prospects. One way of achieving this is to raise prices and slash marketing spend – over the subsequent year profits might be boosted as customers are unable to switch suppliers immediately. Over the long term, however, competitors will respond and profits will fall.
- ***Risk*** Again two firms could report identical historic profit figures and have future prospects which indicate that they will produce the same average annual returns. However, one firm's returns are subject to much greater variability and so there will be years of losses and, in a particularly bad year, the possibility of bankruptcy. **Exhibit 1.8** shows two firms which have identical average profit but Volatile Joe's profit is subject to much greater risk than that of Steady Eddie. Shareholders are likely to value the firm with stable income flows more highly than one with high risk.
- ***Accounting problems*** Drawing up a set of accounts is not as scientific and objective as some people try to make out. There is plenty of scope for judgement, guesswork or even cynical manipulation. Imagine the difficulty facing the company accountant and auditors of a clothes

Exhibit 1.8 Two firms with identical average profits but different risk levels

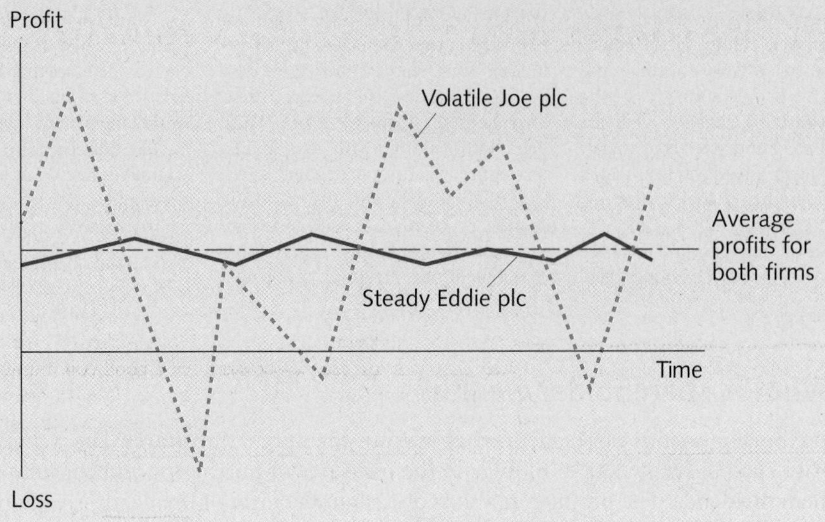

retailer when trying to value a dress which has been on sale for six months. Let us suppose the dress cost the firm £50. Perhaps this should go into the balance sheet and then the profit and loss account will not be affected. But what if the store manager says that he can only sell that dress if it is reduced to £30, and contradicting him the managing director says that if a little more effort was made £40 could be achieved? Which figure is the person who drafts the financial accounts going to take? Profits can vary significantly depending on a multitude of small judgements like this.

- ***Communication*** Investors realise and accept that buying a share is risky. However they like to reduce their uncertainty and nervousness by finding out as much as they can about the firm. If the firm is reluctant to tell shareholders about such matters as the origin of reported profits, then investors generally will tend to avoid those shares. Fears are likely to arise in the minds of poorly informed investors: did the profits come from the most risky activities and might they therefore disappear next year? Is the company being used to run guns to unsavoury regimes abroad? The senior executives of large quoted firms spend a great deal of time explaining their strategies, sources of income and future investment plans to the large institutional shareholders to make sure that these investors are aware of the quality of the firm and its prospects. Firms that ignore the importance of communication and image in the investment community may be doing their shareholders a disservice as the share price might fall.

The London Stock Exchange encourages companies to improve their communication with shareholders – *see* **Exhibit 1.9**.

- ***Additional capital*** Profits can be increased simply by making use of more shareholders' money. If shareholders inject more money into the company or the firm merely retains profits (which belong to shareholders) their future profits can rise, but the *return* on shareholders' money may fall to less than what is available elsewhere for the same level of risk. This is shareholder wealth destructive. For more on this see Chapter 15.

Exhibit 1.9

Under-fire companies might find it's good to talk

FT

Deborah Hargreaves

Communication matters to markets. Anyone who doubts this should look no further than the 7 per cent drop in Shell's shares last Friday after the disastrous announcement of a 20 per cent reduction in its estimate of proven crude reserves.

The change in classification of oilfields to represent fewer reserves than expected was enough of a shock on its own. But what really sent shareholders into a lather was the fact that no executive board members were available to explain the move. They wanted Sir Philip Watts, chief executive, who had been running the exploration business when these fields were first booked as reserves, to answer their queries.

The communications gaffe was the latest in a number by Sir Philip and has led some fuming fund managers to call for his head.

The absence of top directors from Friday's conference call has also fuelled traders' much-loved conspiracy theories. Maybe Sir Philip and Judy Boynton, finance director, know something even more damaging and did not want to be subjected to public scrutiny, the tattle runs.

This is why companies should try to offer credible explanations of material factors affecting them, if they want to avoid the market filling the void with rumours and gossip. . . .

It is hard to quantify the benefits of a good communications strategy, but so often an open chief executive reflects a wider company culture. One of the most important things that companies can lose is their reputation.

Source: Financial Times, 17–18 January 2004, p. M21. Reprinted with permission.

Exhibit 1.10 shows what some leading European companies say about their objectives.

Exhibit 1.10

What companies state as their objective

'Our main task – to create value for shareholders by developing a trusted brand and delighting customers'

Marks & Spencer Annual Review 2006

'Four strategic guidelines describe our path to the future: (1) We earn a premium on our cost of capital; (2) We help customers to be more successful; (3) We form the best team in industry; (4) We ensure sustainable development. We align our activities with these four guidelines. They are inextricably linked with one another, there combination makes us successful'

BASF, Corporate website

'Our purpose: To create the world's leading renewable ingredients business'

Tate and Lyle Annual Report 2006

'Diageo's success will be judged by our ability to deliver sustained business performance. But for today's global business, success is measured by more than sales or profits. Diageo continues its course as a strong and sustainable business and one that is trusted and respected by stakeholders around the world'

Diageo Annual Report 2006

Author's note: This section took longer to complete than expected because most annual reports examined failed to state any objective for the organisation so the search for something to quote was extended. Perhaps this is the most telling fact to emerge!

Corporate governance

In theory the shareholders, being the owners of the firm, control its activities. In practice, the large modern corporation has a very diffuse and fragmented set of shareholders and control often lies in the hands of directors. It is extremely difficult to marshall thousands of shareholders, each with a small stake in the business, to push for change. Thus in many firms we have what is called a separation, or **a divorce, of ownership and control**. In times past the directors would usually be the same individuals as the owners. Today, however, less than 1 per cent of the shares of most of the largest quoted firms are owned by the directors.

The separation of ownership and control raises worries that the management team may pursue objectives attractive to them, but which are not necessarily beneficial to the shareholders – this is termed '**managerialism**' or '**managementism**'. For example, raising their own pay perks, expanding their empire, avoiding risky projects, boosting short-term results at the expense of long-term performance. This conflict is an example of the **principal–agent problem**. The principals (the shareholders) have to find ways of ensuring that their agents (the managers) act in their interests. This means incurring costs, '**agency costs**', to (a) monitor managers' behaviour, and (b) create incentive schemes and controls for managers to encourage the pursuit of shareholders' wealth maximisation. These costs arise in addition to the agency cost of the loss of wealth caused by the extent to which prevention measures do not work and managers continue to pursue non-shareholder wealth goals.

Corporate governance means the system by which companies are managed and controlled. Its main focus is on the responsibilities and obligations placed on the executive directors and the non-executive directors, and on the relationships between the firm's owners, the board of directors and the top tier of managers. The interaction between these groups leads to the defining of the corporate objective, the placing of constraints on managerial behaviour and the setting of targets and incentive payments based on achievement.

The board of directors has the responsibility of overseeing the company, acting as a check on managerialism, so that shareholders' best interests are appropriately prioritised. The board sets company-wide policy and strategic direction, leaving the **executive directors** to manage day-to-day activities. It also decides who will be an executive director (subject to shareholder vote) and sets their pay. In addition the board oversees the reporting of accounting results to shareholders. The board should also take a keen interest in the ethical behaviour of senior managers.

Corporate governance regulations

There is a considerable range of legislation and other regulatory pressures designed to encourage directors to act in shareholders' interests. In the UK the Companies Acts require certain minimum standards of behaviour, as does the London Stock Exchange, LSE. For example, directors are forbidden to use their position to profit at the expense of shareholders, e.g. they cannot buy shares in their own company just before announcing unexpectedly high profits. There is the back-up of the financial industry regulator, the Financial Services Authority, FSA and the Financial Reporting Council, FRC.

Following a number of financial scandals, guidelines of best practice in corporate governance were issued by the Cadbury, Greenbury, Hampel, Higgs and Smith committees, now consolidated in the **Combined Code of Corporate Governance**, which is backed by the FSA, LSE and the FRC.

Under the code directors of companies listed on the London Stock Exchange are required to state in the accounts how the principles of the code have been applied. If the principles have not been followed they have to state why. The principles include:

- At least half the members of the board, excluding the chairman, should be independent[1] **non-executive directors** so that they can act as a powerful counterweight to the executive directors. These directors are not full-time and not concerned with day-to-day management. They may be able to take a broader view than executive directors, who may become excessively focused on detail. The experienced individuals who become non-executive directors are not expected to be dependent on the director's fee for income and can therefore afford to be independently minded. They are expected to 'constructively challenge and help develop proposals on strategy ... scrutinize the performance of management in meeting agreed goals and objectives and monitor the reporting of performance' (*Financial Services Authority, FSA*, 2003, p. 4).
- There should be a balance of power on the board such that no one individual can dominate and impose their will. The running of the board of directors (by a **chairman**) should be a separate responsibility which should be held by a separate person from that responsible for running the

[1] To be independent the non-executive directors should not, for example, be a customer, ex-employee, supplier, or a friend of the founding family or the chief executive.

business, i.e. the **chief executive officer (CEO)** or managing director (MD) (this is frequently ignored in practice, which is permitted, if a written justification is presented to shareholders).

- There should be transparency on directors' remuneration requiring a **remuneration committee** consisting exclusively of non-executive directors, independent of management. No director should be involved in deciding his or her remuneration. A significant proportion of remuneration should be linked to corporate and individual performance.
- The procedure for the appointment of board directors should be formal (nomination committee), objective (based on merit) and transparent (information on the terms and conditions made available). Directors are to retire by rotation at least every three years – they may be re-elected.
- The **audit committee** (responsible for validating financial figures, e.g. by appointing effective external auditors) should consist exclusively of independent non-executive directors, otherwise the committee would not be able to act as a check and balance to the executive directors.
- Directors are required to communicate with shareholders, e.g. to use the **annual general meeting** to explain the company's performance and encourage discussion.

The 'comply or explain' approach is in contrast to many other systems of regulation of corporate governance around the world – these are often strict rule-based systems with lawyers to the fore (e.g. Sarbanes–Oxley regulations in the US, which have frightened companies away from listing on a US stock market). 'The flexibility it offers [the "comply or explain" approach] has been widely welcomed both by company boards and by investors. It is for shareholders and others to evaluate the company's statement. While it is expected that companies will comply with the Code's provisions most of the time, it is recognized that departure from the provisions of the Code may be justified in particular circumstances' (FSA, 2003, pp. 1–2). Furthermore, some of the provisions do not apply to companies smaller than the largest 350 listed on the London Stock Exchange. However, failure to comply or explain properly will result in suspension from the stock exchange.

www.ecgi.org displays corporate governance codes in a range of countries.

There are various other (complementary) methods used to try to align the actions of senior management with the interests of shareholders, that is, to achieve 'goal congruence'.

- ***Linking rewards to shareholder wealth improvements*** A technique widely employed in industry is to grant directors and other senior managers **share options**. These permit managers to purchase shares at some date in the future at a price which is fixed now. If the share price rises significantly between the date when the option was granted and the date when the shares can be bought the manager can make a fortune by buying at the pre-arranged price and then selling in the marketplace. For example in 2008 managers might be granted the right to buy shares in 2013 at a price of £1.50. If the market price moves to say £2.30 in 2013 the managers can buy and then sell the shares, making a gain of 80p. The managers under such a scheme have a clear interest in achieving a rise in share price and thus congruence comes about to some extent. An alternative method is to allot shares to managers if they achieve certain performance targets, for example, growth in earnings per share or return on assets. Many companies have **long-term incentive plans (LTIPs)** for senior executives which at the end of three years or more pay bonuses if certain targets are surpassed, e.g. share price rise or high profit achieved.
- ***Sackings*** The threat of being sacked with the accompanying humiliation and financial loss may encourage managers not to diverge too far from the shareholders' wealth path. However, this method is employed in extreme circumstances only. It is sometimes difficult to implement because of difficulties of making a co-ordinated shareholder effort. It is made easier if the majority of directors are independent of the executives.
- ***Selling shares and the takeover threat*** Over 70 per cent of the shares of the typical company quoted on the London stock market are owned by financial institutions such as pension and insurance funds. These organisations generally are not prepared to put large resources into monitoring and controlling all the hundreds of firms of which they own a part. Quite often their first response, if they observe that management is not acting in what they regard as their best interest, is to sell the share rather than intervene. This will result in a lower share price, making the raising of funds more difficult. It may also lower rewards to managers whose renumeration partly depends on the share price level. If this process continues the firm may become vulnerable to a merger bid by another group of managers, resulting in a loss of top

management posts. Fear of being taken over can establish some sort of backstop position to prevent shareholder wealth considerations being totally ignored.

- ***Information flow*** The accounting profession, the stock exchange and the investing institutions have conducted a continuous battle to encourage or force firms to release more accurate, timely and detailed information concerning their operations. The quality of corporate accounts and annual reports has generally improved, as has the availability of other forms of information flowing to investors and analysts, such as company briefings and company announcements (which are available from financial websites e.g. www.advfn.com). All this helps to monitor firms, and identify any wealth-destroying actions by wayward managers early, but as a number of recent scandals have shown, matters are still far from perfect.

In some countries the interests of shareholders are often placed far below those of the controlling managers. In the absence of good corporate governance it is difficult for a firm to obtain funds for expansion. Many Russian companies have chosen to take on the high standards of corporate governance in London to make them acceptable to investors – see the case of Severstal in **Exhibit 1.11**.

Exhibit 1.11

Severstal pledges high standards

FT

Russian steelmaker plans for London listing
Half the board to be independent non-execs

By Peter Marsh

Severstal, the largest Russian steelmaker, yesterday said it would adopt high standards of corporate governance in pursuing a London listing as a prelude to becoming 'one of the top six steelmakers in the world' in the next five years.

As a way to win the confidence of investors, Mr Mordashov said Severstal intended to go beyond what had been done by most other Russian companies in adopting foreign listings and appoint an independent chairman 'who is a person known internationally and is of high reliability'.

The company would also make sure half the board consisted of independent non-executive directors, he added.

Before any acquisition of above $500m (267m) goes ahead, two-thirds of the board would have to agree to the project, giving the non-executives an effective veto.

'It's very important for us to be as public a company as possible with a lot of transparency,' said Mr Mordashov, who will remain the main shareholder after the group floats on the London stock market by the end of the year.

It is expected that Severstal will list about 15 per cent of its stock in London, raising roughly $1.7bn, leaving Mr Mordashov with 75 per cent. The remaining 10 per cent will continue to trade on the Moscow stock exchange where Severstal already has a listing.

Source: *Financial Times*, 7/8 October 2006, p. 17. Reprinted with permission.

Primitive and modern economies

A simple economy

Before we proceed to discuss the role of the financial manager and the part played by various financial institutions it is useful to gain an overview of the economy and the place of the financial system within society. To see the role of the financial sector in perspective it is, perhaps, of value to try to imagine a society without any financial services. Imagine how people would go about their daily business in the absence of either money or financial institutions. This sort of economy is represented in **Exhibit 1.12**. Here there are only two sectors in society. The **business sector** produces goods and services, making use of the resources of labour, land and commodities which are owned by the **household sector**. The household sector is paid with the goods and services produced by the business sector.

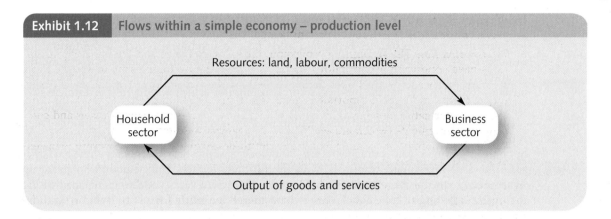

Exhibit 1.12 Flows within a simple economy – production level

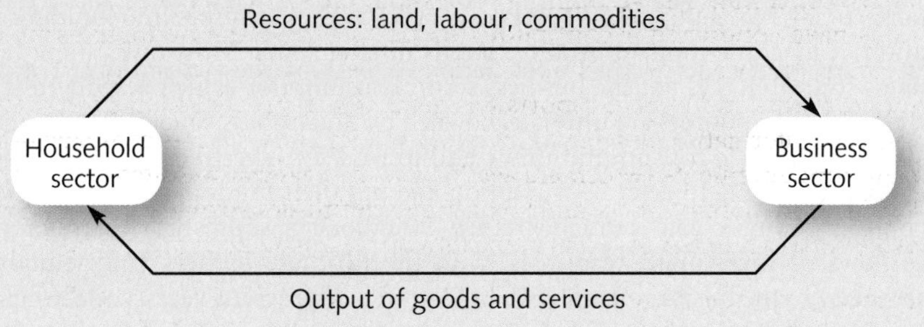

In this economy there is no money and therefore there are two choices open to the household sector upon receipt of the goods and services:

1. ***Consumption*** Commodities can be consumed now either by taking those specific items provided from the place of work and enjoying their consumption directly, or, under a barter system, by exchanging them with other households to widen the variety of consumption.
2. ***Investment*** Some immediate consumption could be forgone so that resources can be put into building assets which will produce a higher level of consumption in the future. For instance, a worker takes payment in the form of a plough so that in future years when he enters the productive (business) sector he can produce more food per acre.

The introduction of money

Under a barter system much time and effort is expended in searching out other households interested in trade. It quickly becomes apparent that a tool is needed to help make transactions more efficient. People will need something into which all goods and services received can be converted. That something would have to be small and portable, it would have to hold its value over a long period of time and have general acceptability. This will enable people to take the commodities given in exchange for, say, labour and then avoid the necessity of, say, carrying the bushels of wheat to market to exchange them for bricks. Instead **money** could be paid in exchange for labour, and money taken to the market to buy bricks. Various things have been used as a means of exchange ranging from cowry shells to cigarettes (in prisons particularly) but the most popular used to be a metal, usually gold or silver. (Now it is less tangible such as credit and debit card transactions.) The introduction of money into the system creates monetary as well as real flows of goods and services – *see* **Exhibit 1.13**.

Exhibit 1.13 Flows within a simple economy – production level plus money

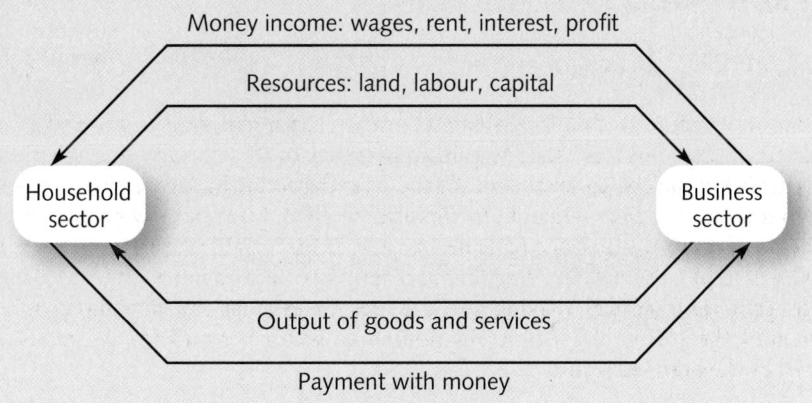

Investment in a money economy

Investment involves resources being laid aside now to produce a return in the future, for instance, today's consumption is reduced in order to put resources into building a factory and the creation of machine tools to produce goods in later years. Most investment takes place in the business sector but it is not the business sector consumption which is reduced if investment is to take place, as all resources are ultimately owned by households. Society needs individuals who are prepared to sacrifice consumption now and to wait for investments to come to fruition. These capitalists are willing to defer consumption and put their funds at risk within the business sector but only if they anticipate a suitable return. In a modern, sophisticated economy there are large-scale flows of investment resources from the ultimate owners (individuals who make up households) to the business sector. Even the profits of previous years' endeavours retained within the business belong to households – they have merely permitted firms to hold on to those resources for further investments on their behalf.

Investment in the twenty-first century is on a grand scale and the time gap between sacrifice and return has in many cases grown very large. This has increased the risks to any one individual investor and so investments tend to be made via pooled funds drawing on the savings of many thousands of households. A capital market has developed to assist the flow of funds between the business and household sectors. Amongst their other functions the financial markets reduce risk through their regulatory regimes and insistence on a high level of disclosure of information. In these more advanced financial structures businesses issue securities which give the holder the right to receive income in specified circumstances. Those that hold debt securities have a relatively high certainty of receiving a flow of interest. Those that buy a security called a share have less certainty about what they will receive but, because the return is based on a share of profit, they expect to gain a higher return than if they had merely lent money to the firm.

In **Exhibit 1.14** we can see household savings going into business investment. In exchange for this investment the business sector issues securities which show the claims that households have over firms. This exhibit shows three interconnected systems. The first is the flow of real goods and services. The second is a flow of money. The third is the investment system which enables production and consumption to be increased in the future. It is mainly in facilitating the flow of investment finance that the financial sector has a role in our society. The financial system increases the efficiency of the real economy by encouraging the flow of funds to productive uses.

Exhibit 1.14 Flows within a modern economy

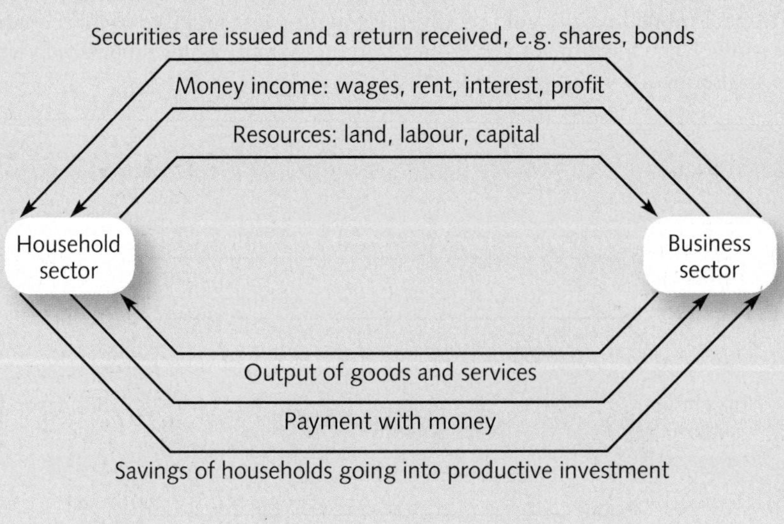

The role of the financial manager

To be able to carry on a business a company needs **real assets**. These real assets may be tangible, such as buildings, plant, machinery, vehicles and so on. Alternatively a firm may invest in intangible real assets, for example patents, expertise, licensing rights, etc. To obtain these real assets corporations sell financial claims to raise money; to lenders a bundle of rights are sold within a loan contract, to shareholders rights over the ownership of a company are sold as well as the right to receive a proportion of profits produced. The financial manager has the task of both raising finance by selling financial claims and advising on the use of those funds within the business. This is illustrated in **Exhibit 1.15**.

The financial manager plays a pivotal role in the following:

Interaction with the financial markets

In order to raise finance a knowledge is needed of the financial markets and the way in which they operate. To raise share (equity) capital awareness of the rigours and processes involved in 'taking a new company to market' might be useful. For instance, what is the role of an issuing house? What services do brokers, accountants, solicitors, etc. provide to a company wishing to float? Once a company is quoted on a stock market it is going to be useful to know about ways of raising additional equity capital – what about rights issues and open offers?

Knowledge of exchanges such as the Alternative Investment Market (UK) or the European market Euronext might be valuable. If the firm does not wish to have its shares quoted on an exchange perhaps an investigation needs to be made into the possibility of raising money through the venture capital industry.

Understanding how shares are priced and what it is that shareholders are looking for when sacrificing present consumption to make an investment could help the firm to tailor its strategy,

Exhibit 1.15 The flow of cash between capital markets and the firm's operations

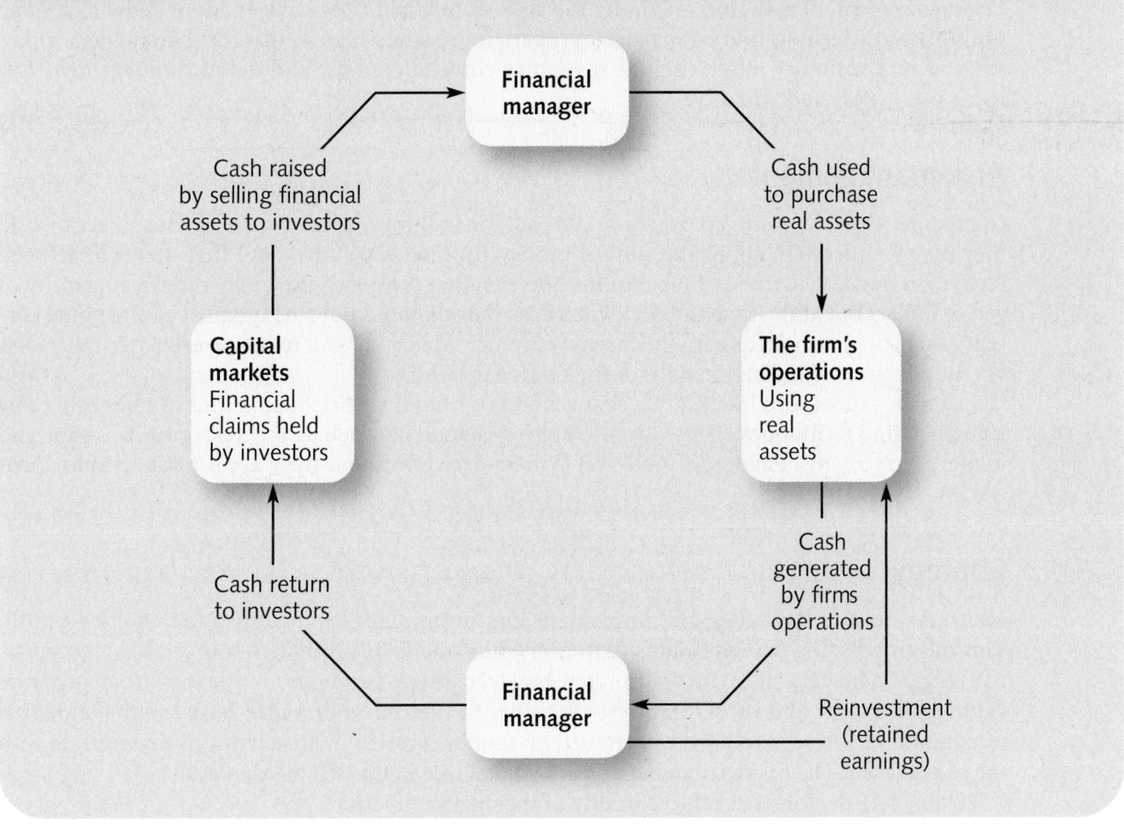

operations and financing decisions to suit their owners. These, and dozens of other equity finance questions, are part of the remit of the finance expert within the firm.

Another major source of finance comes from banks. Understanding the operation of banks and what concerns them when lending to a firm may enable you to present your case better, to negotiate improved terms and obtain finance which fits the cash-flow patterns of the firm. Then there are ways of borrowing which by-pass banks. Bonds could be issued either domestically or internationally. Medium-term notes, commercial paper, leasing, hire purchase and factoring are other possibilities.

Once a knowledge has been gained of each of these alternative financial instruments and of the operation of their respective financial markets, then the financial manager has to consider the issue of the correct balance between the different types. What proportion of debt to equity? What proportion of short-term finance to long-term finance and so on?

Perhaps you can already appreciate that the finance function is far from a boring 'bean-counting' role. It is a dynamic function with a constant need for up-to-date and relevant knowledge. The success or failure of the entire business may rest on the quality of the interaction between the firm and the financial markets. The financial manager stands at the interface between the two.

Investment

Decisions have to be made concerning how much to invest in real assets and which specific projects to undertake (**capital budgeting decisions**). In addition to providing analytical techniques to aid these sorts of decisions the financial expert has to be aware of a wide variety of factors which might have some influence on the wisdom of proceeding with a particular investment. These range from corporate strategy and budgeting restrictions to culture and the commitment of individuals likely to be called upon to support an activity.

There is also the opposite of investment – **divestment** or **disinvestment**. Assets, such as a factory or subsidiary, that are no longer contributing to shareholder wealth need to be disposed of to release capital.

Treasury management

The management of cash may fall under the aegis of the financial manager. Many firms have large sums of cash which need to be managed properly to obtain a high return for shareholders. Other areas of responsibility might include inventory control, creditor and debtor management and issues of solvency and liquidity.

Risk management

Companies that enter into transactions abroad, for example exporters, are often subject to risk: they may be uncertain about the sum of money (in their own currency) that they will actually receive on the deal. Three or four months after sending the goods they may receive a quantity of yen or dollars but at the time the deal was struck they did not know the quantity of the home currency that could be bought with the foreign currency. Managing and reducing exchange rate risk is yet another area calling on the skills of the finance director.

Likewise, exposure to interest rate changes and commodity price fluctuations can be reduced by using hedging techniques. These often employ instruments such as futures, options, swaps and forward agreements. Failure to understand these derivatives and their appropriate employment can lead to disaster.

Strategy

Managers need to formulate and implement long-term plans to maximise shareholder wealth. This means selecting markets and activities in which the firm, given its resources, has a competitive edge. Managers need to distinguish between those products or markets that generate value for the firm and those that destroy value. At the centre of **value-based management** is recognition of the need to produce a return on money invested in an activity commensurate with the risk is taken. The financial manager has a pivotal role in this strategic analysis.

Exhibit 1.16 demonstrates the centrality of the finance function.

Exhibit 1.16

Follow the money

FT

Take a look at the CVs of the most successful businesswomen, and one thing is clear – the path to the top starts with a good grounding in finance

By Heather McGregor

When PepsiCo named Indra Nooyi – a woman, born in India, who still routinely wears a sari and who used to front an all-female rock band – as its chief executive-designate in August, it was always going to draw comment. 'Ms Nooyi will become the world's most important female chief executive,' said *The Economist.*

Not much was written, though, about her chosen route to the top. Before she became chief executive, Nooyi was the president and chief financial officer of the soft drinks and food company – and this despite the fact that she is not a professional accountant. Her undergraduate degree, from Madras Christian College in India, was in chemistry, physics and maths; she earned a master's in finance and marketing from the Indian Institute of Management in Calcutta; and she also holds a master's in public and private management from the Yale School of Management. Her progress to the boardroom of PepsiCo was via several other positions (including at Asea Brown Boveri and Motorola, on whose board she still sits), and a stint in management consultancy.

It would be a strong bet to say that, when making their decision about Nooyi, the directors of PepsiCo would have been favourably impressed by her knowledge of the company and her ability to understand its every facet: her job as president and chief financial officer was described as being responsible for 'all of PepsiCo's corporate functions, including finance, strategy, business process optimisation, corporate platforms and innovation, procurement, investor relations and information technology'.

Kathleen O'Donovan, a former FTSE 100 finance director who used to hold a non-executive position at the Bank of England and now performs the same role at several of the UK's largest companies, believes that finance can help women reach the top, particularly because of the overall business view that it delivers. 'Finance as a career route has two big advantages,' she says. 'It's technical, so if you know your stuff you can establish credibility quickly; more importantly, it pervades all aspects of an organisation's activities, so it really is "access all areas".'

Jeremy Rickman of Russell Reynolds is a respected head-hunter who specialises in finding talented chief financial officers for some of Europe's most successful companies.

'If you look at some of Britain's most successful chief executives, male or female, many of them have held finance posts along the way.'

Liz Airey, the former finance director of Monument Oil & Gas and now, like O'Donovan, a multiple operator with positions that include senior independent non-executive director at Amec says finance can be a stepping stone for a variety of careers, including that of chief executive. 'The right individuals will be easily able to make the transition from the chief financial to the chief executive role, but even if you don't want to do that it opens such a wide range of career options in either the public or private sector. In my case it has enabled me to develop the plural career that I now have.'

Helen Weir endorses the view that a professional qualification will aid ambitious women: 'Every senior manager I know is very comfortable with numbers – they can look at a profit and loss account or balance sheet and understand what it's saying. Having that capability is a very important prerequisite for making it to the top of a business. Not all executives have a professional finance qualification, but I think it's a great place to start.'

Of course, not every woman who ends up as the chief executive of a public company has started life as an accountant or a lawyer, and some of them have deliberately chosen not to take that route. Belinda Earl, who was appointed chief executive of Debenhams at the age of 38 and is now the chief executive of Jaeger, studied economics at university. But even she stresses the importance of a good grounding in finance. 'I would encourage individuals who are keen to climb the corporate ladder to gain not only an appreciation of, but really a full grounding in finance, not just the standard balance sheet, or profit and loss, but a complete awareness of business levers. Retailing, from running a store through to buying and merchandising a product area, requires all of these skills.'

The overall lesson seems to be that if you are a woman and you want to make it in the corporate world, go out and get yourself a career in finance.

Source: FT magazine, 7/8 October, 2006, p. 26.

The flow of funds and financial intermediation

Exhibit 1.15 looked at the simple relationship between a firm and investors. Unfortunately the real world is somewhat more complicated and the flow of funds within the financial system involves a number of other institutions and agencies. **Exhibit 1.17** is a more realistic representation of the financial interactions between different groups in society.

Households generally place the largest proportion of their savings with **financial institutions**. These organisations then put that money to work. Some of it is lent back to members of the household sector in the form of, say, a mortgage to purchase a house, or as a personal loan. Some of the money is used to buy securities issued by the business sector. The institutions will expect a return on these loans and shares, which flows back in the form of interest and dividends. However, they are often prepared for businesses to retain profit within the firm for further investment in the hope of greater returns in the future. The government sector enters into the financial system in a number of ways, two of which are shown in Exhibit 1.17. Taxes are taken from businesses and this adds a further dimension to the financial manager's job – for example, taking taxation into account when selecting sources of finance and when analysing investment proposals. Second, governments usually fail to match their revenues with their expenditure and therefore borrow significant sums from the financial institutions. The diagram in Exhibit 1.17 remains a gross simplification; it has not allowed for overseas financial transactions, for example, but it does demonstrate a crucial role for financial institutions in an advanced market economy.

Primary investors

Typically the household sector is in financial surplus. This sector contains the savers of society. It is these individuals who become the main providers of funds used for investment in the business

Exhibit 1.17 The flow of funds and financial intermediation

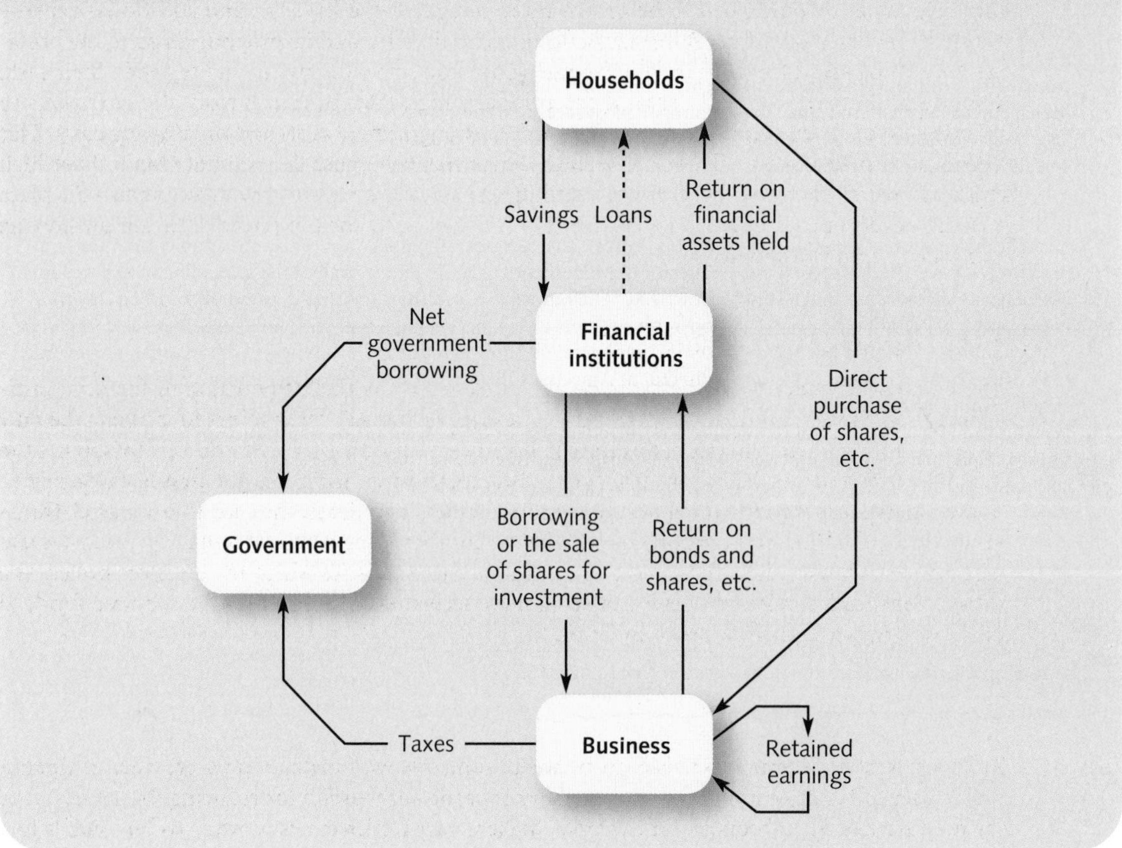

sector. **Primary investors** tend to prefer to exchange their cash for financial assets which (a) allow them to get their money back quickly should they need to (with low transaction cost of doing so) and (b) have a high degree of certainty over the amount they will receive back. That is, primary investors like high **liquidity** and low risk. Lending directly to a firm with a project proposal to build a North Sea oil platform which will not be sold until five years have passed is not a high-liquidity and low-risk investment. However, putting money into a sock under the bed is (if we exclude the possibility of the risk of sock theft).

Ultimate borrowers

In our simplified model the **ultimate borrowers** are in the business sector. These firms are trying to maximise the wealth generated by their activities. To do this companies need to invest in real plant, equipment and other assets, often for long periods of time. The firms, in order to serve their social function, need to attract funds for use over many years. Also these funds are to be put at risk, sometimes very high risk. (Here we are using the term 'borrower' broadly to include all forms of finance, even 'borrowing' by selling shares.)

Conflict of preferences

We have a **conflict of preference** between the primary investors wanting low-cost liquidity and certainty, and the ultimate borrowers wanting long-term risk-bearing capital. A further complicating factor is that savers usually save on a small scale, £100 here or £200 there, whereas businesses are likely to need large sums of money. Imagine some of the problems that would occur in a society which did not have any financial intermediaries. Here lending and share buying will occur only as a result of direct contact and negotiation between two parties. If there were no organised market where financial securities could be sold on to other investors the fund provider, once committed, would be trapped in an illiquid investment. Also the costs that the two parties might incur in searching to find each other in the first place might be considerable. Following contact a thorough agreement would need to be drawn up to safeguard the investor, and additional expense would be incurred obtaining information to monitor the firm and its progress. In sum, the obstacles to putting saved funds to productive use would lead many to give up and to retain their cash. Those that do persevere will demand exceptionally high rates of return from the borrowers to compensate them for poor liquidity, risk, search costs, agreement costs and monitoring costs. This will mean that few firms will be able to justify investments because they cannot obtain those high levels of return when the funds are invested in real assets. As a result few investments take place and the wealth of society fails to grow. **Exhibit 1.18** shows (by the top arrow) little money flowing from saving into investment.

The introduction of financial intermediaries

The problem of under-investment can be alleviated greatly by the introduction of financial institutions (e.g. banks) and financial markets (e.g. a stock exchange). Their role is to facilitate the flow of funds from primary investors to ultimate borrowers at a low cost. They do this by solving the conflict of preferences. There are two types of financial intermediation; the first is an agency or brokerage type operation which brings together lenders and firms, the second is an asset-transforming type of intermediation, in which the conflict is resolved by creating intermediate securities which have the risk, liquidity and volume characteristics which the investors prefer. The financial institution raises money by offering these securities, and then uses the acquired funds to purchase primary securities issued by firms.

Brokers

At its simplest an intermediary is a 'go-between', someone who matches up a provider of finance with a user of funds. This type of intermediary is particularly useful for reducing the **search costs** for both parties. Stockbrokers, for example, make it easy for investors wanting to buy shares in a

Exhibit 1.18 Savings into investment in an economy without financial intermediaries

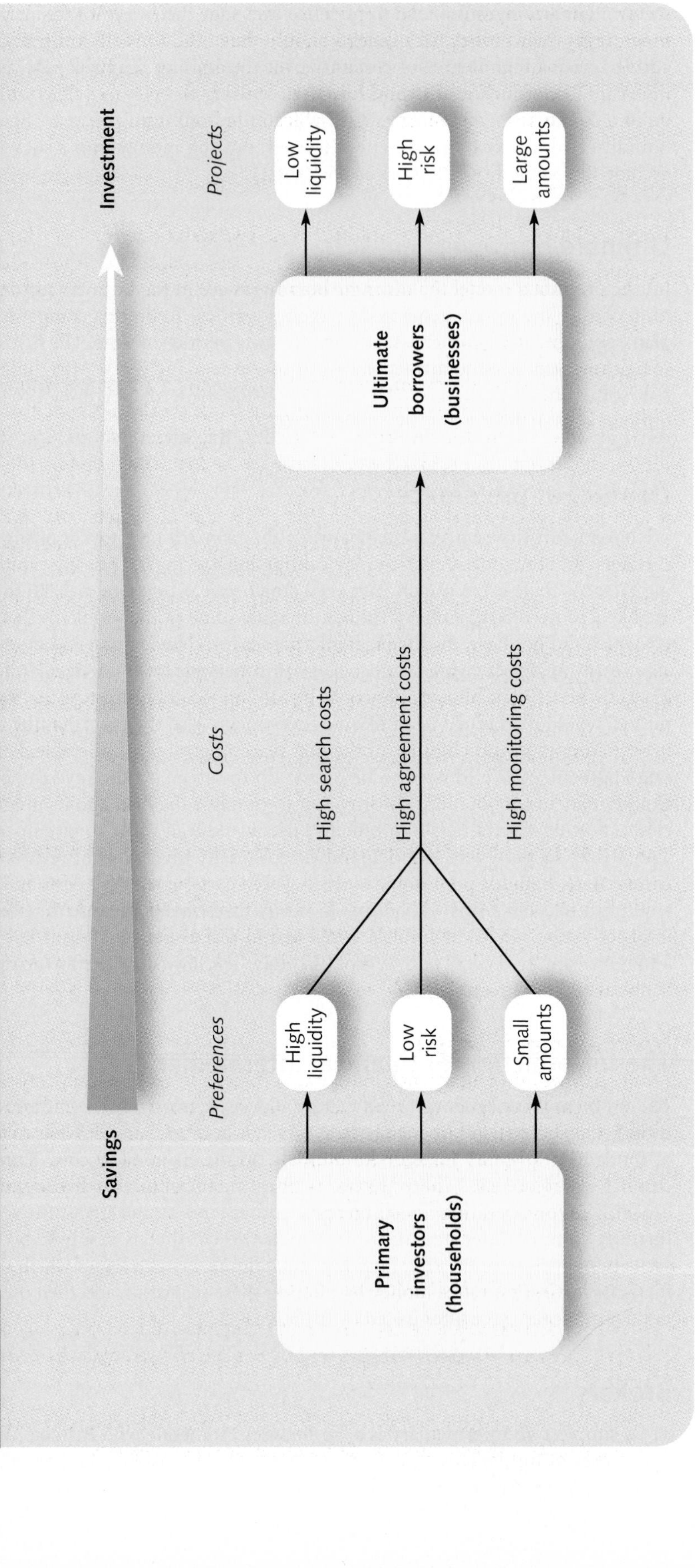

newly floated company. **Brokers** may also have some skill at collecting information on a firm and monitoring its activities, saving the investor time. They also act as middlemen when an investor wishes to sell to another, thus enhancing the liquidity of the fund providers. Another example is the Post Office which enables individuals to lend to the UK government in a convenient and cheap manner by buying National Savings certificates or Premium Bonds.

Asset transformers

Intermediaries, by creating a completely new security, the **intermediate security**, increase the opportunities available to savers, encouraging them to invest and thus reducing the cost of finance for the productive sector. The transformation function can act in a number of different ways.

Risk transformation

For example, instead of an individual lending directly to a business with a great idea, such as digging a tunnel under the English Channel, a bank creates a deposit or current account with relatively low risk for the investor's savings. Lending directly to the firm the saver would demand compensation for the probability of default on the loan and therefore the business would have to pay a very high rate of interest which would inhibit investment. The bank acting as an intermediary creates a special kind of security called a bank account agreement. The intermediary then uses the funds attracted by the new financial asset to buy a security issued by the tunnel owner (the **primary security**) when it obtains long-term debt capital. Because of the extra security that a lender has by holding a bank account as a financial asset rather than by making a loan direct to a firm, the lender is prepared to accept a lower rate of interest and the ultimate borrower obtains funds at a relatively low cost. The bank is able to reduce its risk exposure to any one project by diversifying its loan portfolio amongst a number of firms. It can also reduce risk by building up expertise in assessing and monitoring firms and their associated risk. Another example of **risk transformation** is when unit or investment companies (*see* later in this chapter) take savers' funds and spread these over a wide range of company shares.

Maturity (liquidity) transformation

The fact that a bank lends long term for a risky venture does not mean that the primary lender is subjected to illiquidity. Liquidity is not a problem because banks maintain sufficient liquid funds to meet their liabilities when they arise. You can walk into a bank and take the money from your account at short notice because the bank, given its size, exploits economies of scale and anticipates that only a small fraction of its customers will withdraw their money on any one day. Banks and building societies play an important role in borrowing 'short' and lending 'long'.

Volume transformation

Many institutions gather small amounts of money from numerous savers and re-package these sums into larger bundles for investment in the business sector. Apart from the banks and building societies, unit trusts are important here. It is uneconomic for an investor with, say, £50 per month, who wants to invest in shares, to buy small quantities periodically. Unit trusts gather together hundreds of individuals' monthly savings and invest them in a broad range of shares, thereby exploiting economies in transaction costs.

Intermediaries' economies of scale

The intermediary is able to accept lending to (and investing in shares of) companies at a relatively low rate of return because of the economies of scale enjoyed compared with the primary investor. These **economies of scale** include:

(a) *Efficiencies in gathering information* on the riskiness of lending to a particular firm. Individuals do not have access to the same data sources or expert analysis.

(b) *Risk spreading* Intermediaries are able to spread funds across a large number of borrowers and thereby reduce overall risk. Individual investors may be unable to do this.

(c) *Transaction costs* They are able to reduce the search, agreement and monitoring costs that would be incurred by savers and borrowers in a direct transaction. Banks, for example, are convenient, safe locations with standardised types of securities. Savers do not have to spend time examining the contract they are entering upon when, say, they open a bank account. How many of us read the small print when we opened a bank account?

The reduced **information costs**, convenience and passed-on benefits from the economies of operating on a large scale mean that primary investors are motivated to place their savings with intermediaries.

Apart from linking savers with ultimate borrowers there are financial services within the household sector and within the business sector. For example, transferring money between bank accounts or providing financial advice.

Financial markets

A financial market, such as a stock exchange, has two aspects; there is the **primary market** where funds are raised from investors by the firm, and there is the **secondary market** in which investors buy and sell securities, such as shares and bonds, between each other. The securities sold into the primary market are generally done so on the understanding that repayment will not be made for many years, if ever, and so it is beneficial for the original buyer to be able to sell on to other investors in the secondary market. In this way the firm achieves its objective of raising finance that will stay in the firm for a lengthy period and the investor has retained the ability to liquidate (turn into cash) a holding by selling to another investor. In addition a well-regulated exchange encourages investment by reducing search, agreement and monitoring costs – *see* **Exhibit 1.20**.

Exhibit 1.19 reports that the Prime Minister of India regards a reformed financial sector as crucial to 'mobilise long-term capital' and in sustaining economic growth.

Exhibit 1.19

Indian premier to push for financial reform

FT

By Lionel Barber, Jo Johnson and Victor Mallet in New Delhi

Manmohan Singh, prime minister of India, has pledged to push hard for reform of the insurance and banking sectors and to step up investment in infrastructure in the latter half of his term in office.

Sustaining a growth rate of 8–10 per cent would hinge on 'massive investments' in infrastructure that would require India to mobilise long-term capital more effectively than was currently possible in a short-termist debt market, he said.

'These are our two biggest priorities,' Mr Singh said.

Both he and P. Chidambaram, finance minister, are showing a new determination to try to move ahead with reforms that would in theory improve the efficiency with which capital is allocated in Asia's fourth-largest economy. 'Financial sector reforms must be completed by this fiscal,' Mr Chidambaram said in a speech in Munibal on Friday. 'The PM has put his weight behind the need for reforms in pension, insurance and banking. Look at the opportunities we are missing.'

Mr Singh said: 'We cannot achieve our social and economic objectives unless there is a reform of the insurance and banking system. Infrastructure requires long-term investment and our banking system is essentially short-term oriented.'

Source: Financial Times, 9 October 2006, p. 5. Reprinted with permission.

Exhibit 1.20 Savings into investment in an economy with financial intermediaries and financial markets

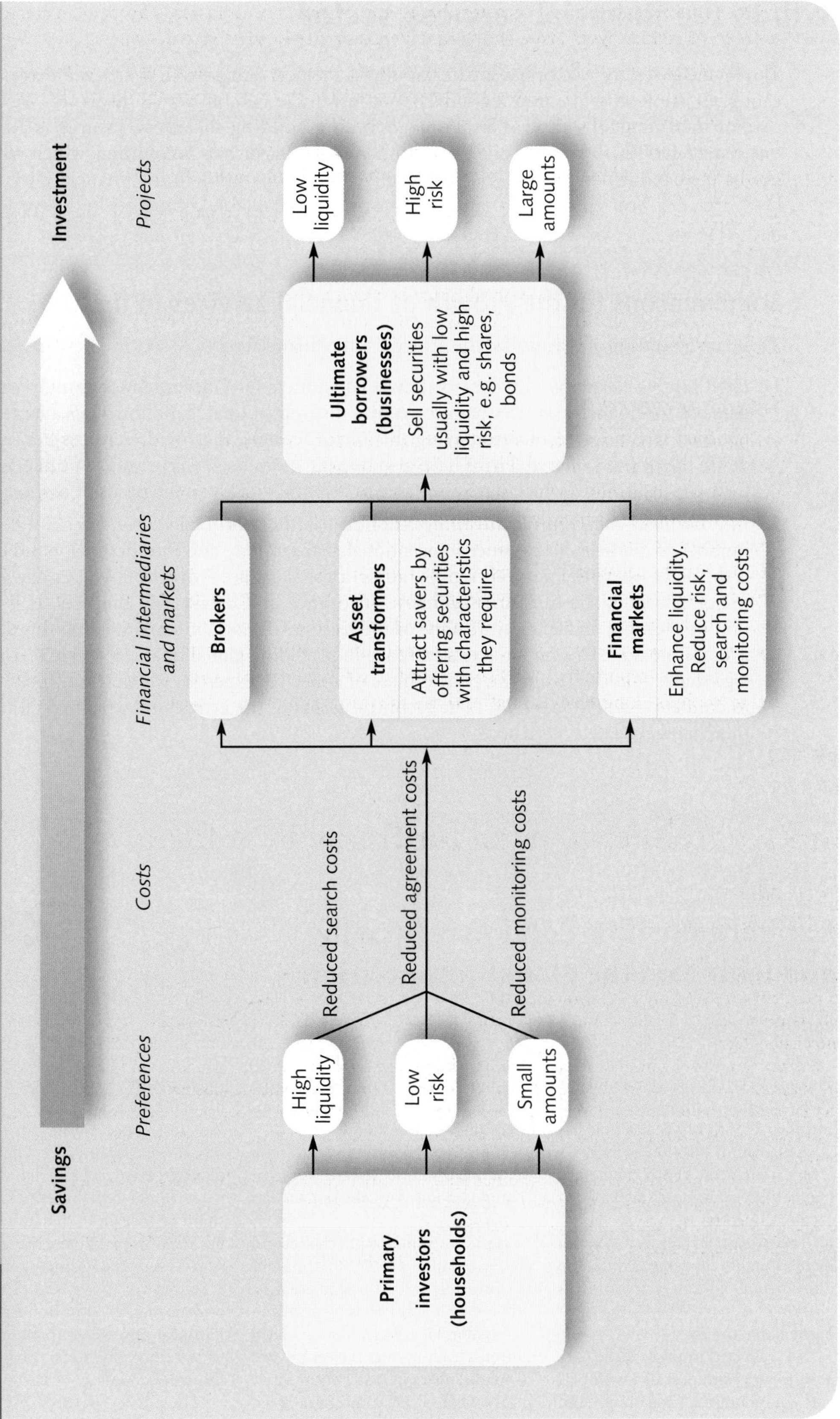

Growth in the financial services sector

The financial services sector has grown rapidly in the post-war period. It now represents a significant proportion of total economic activity, not just in the UK, but across the world. We define the core of the **financial sector** as banking (including building societies), insurance and various investment services. There are one or two other activities, such as accounting, which may or may not be included depending on your perspective. Firms operating in the financial services sector have, arguably, been the most dynamic, innovative and adaptable companies in the world over the past 30 years.

Some reasons for the growth of financial services in the UK

There are a number of reasons for the growth of the financial services sector. These include:

1 *High income elasticity.* This means that as consumers have become increasingly wealthy the demand for financial services has grown by a disproportionate amount. Thus a larger share of national income is devoted to paying this sector fees etc. to provide services because people desire the benefits offered. Firms have also bought an ever-widening range of financial services from the institutions which have been able to respond quickly to the needs of corporations.

2 *International comparative advantage.* London is the world's leading financial centre in a number of markets, for instance international share trading and international bond dealing. It is the place where the most currency transactions take place – over £500bn per day. It is also a major player in the fund management, insurance and derivatives markets. It is certainly Europe's leading financial centre. One of the reasons for London's maintaining this dominance is that it possesses a comparative advantage in providing global financial services. This advantage stems, not least, from the critical mass of collective expertise which it is difficult for rivals to emulate – *see* **Exhibit 1.21**. (The technical terms in the article are explained either later in this chapter or later in the book.)

Exhibit 1.21

The New City

FT

Capital gain: how London is thriving and taking on the global competition

Martin Dickson

There is a certain swagger about the City of London these days – a self-confidence born of success as it has strengthened its position as Europe's leading financial centre and as a magnet for capital and talent from around the world.

The swagger of this 'New City' is manifest in the changing skyline – be it the bulbous effrontery of Swiss Re's gherkin or Canary Wharf's cluster of big banking towers.

It is reflected in the way the City has grown geographically, with private equity houses, hedge funds and advisory boutiques gravitating to London's West End, and large investment and integrated banks to Dockland's new East End.

'The City today is more a state of mind than a square mile of central London,' says one senior fund manager.

'London is no longer the second city,' says James Cayne, chairman of US investment bank Bear Stearns. 'Right now it is as fast as New York.'

London, of course, has long been Europe's leading financial centre. But its market share in many of the disciplines where it has traditionally led the region has been on the rise or stable over the past five years, while it has captured a large share of some of the most important new opportunities. It now accounts for 20 per cent of cross-border bank lending, up from 16 per cent in 1992, while its share of foreign exchange turnover has risen from 27 per cent to 31 per cent over the same period. It accounts for 70 per cent of the secondary market in in bonds. Half of European investment banking activity is thought to be conducted through London.

The City's share of derivatives traded on exchanges may have fallen

Exhibit 1.21 Continued

Battle of the financial centres

How they line up (★ Ranking, based on survey of financial professionals, where four stars rate highest)

	Availability of skilled personnel	Regulatory environment	Availability of business infrastructure	Government responsiveness	Quality of life
London	★★★★	★★★★	★★★	★★★	★★
New York	★★★	★★★	★★★★	★★★★	★★★
Frankfurt	★	★★	★★	★★	★
Paris	★★	★	★	★	★★★★

	Culture and language	Quality/availability of commercial property
London	★★★★	★★★
New York	★★★	★★★★
Frankfurt	★	★★
Paris	★★	★

Overall rating

The sum of scores for each centre on 13 competitiveness factors

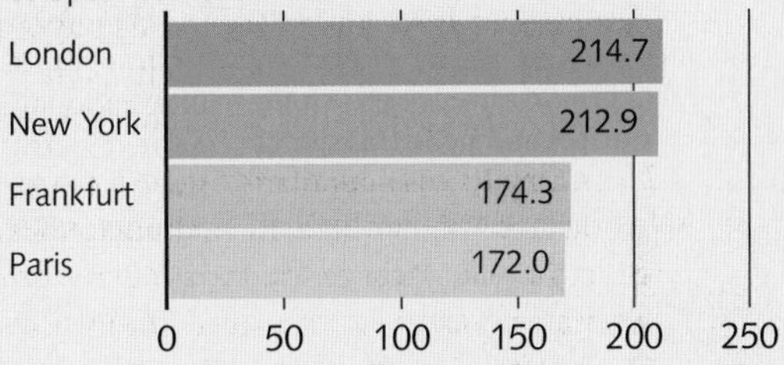

Sources: Z/year and Corporation of London report: www.ifsi.org.uk

over the past decade but it has reinforced its position as the leading centre for bespoke, over-the-counter products. It is thought to account for roughly 45 per cent of the fast-growing market in credit derivatives.

London has long been the leading centre for international fund management: over three-quarters of the region's [Europe] hedge fund assets are managed out of London, and nearly 50 per cent of private equity assets.

In quoted equities, the LSE has become Europe's leading exchange for emerging market listings, while its junior Aim market has become the region's most successful source of capital for small companies.

More generally, London's pull means that an increasing number of continental financial services operations are choosing to base themselves in the City. They range in size from Deutsche Bank, Germany's largest private-sector bank, which is now being run largely from London, to the likes of a private wealth management company with predominantly German clients who enjoy the opportunity to visit London.

So what factors are behind London's growing competitive advantage?

The UK's long tradition of laissez-faire capitalism and openness to competition have created an environment in which financial creativity can flourish. For example, in the 20 years since London's Big Bang deregulated financial markets, the make-up and ownership of the City's investment banks and broking houses has changed out of all recognition.

The first decade was characterised by the growing dominance of large, integrated American houses. The past few years have seen the emergence of a more mixed ecology. UK-owned broking houses have sprung up to serve small and mid-sized companies that are off the radar of the biggest banks. Banking advisory boutiques are being set up to meet clients' demands for a more personal service, free of potential conflicts of interest.

One of the biggest changes has been the international broadening of the talent pool

Decent regulation has also been crucial to London's success, be it self-regulation – as with the Takeover Panel, probably the world's best referee of bids – or state-imposed rules. Over the past few years the City has undergone a fundamental change of regulatory framework with the creation of the Financial Services Authority – a single, statutory institution replacing 10 self-regulatory bodies. London is the only major financial centre to have a single regulator with such concentrated powers, and a heavy-handed FSA could have done serious damage to London's creativity and competitiveness.

Instead, despite grumbling about its bureaucracy (some of it justified), the FSA is regarded as having struck a reasonable balance, and to be growing better at doing so. This matters in a world where strong but measured regulation, offering investor protection, is a source of competitive strength rather than weakness.

These fundamental factors – good regulation and a pro-competition orientation – have created the basis for a concentration of market liquidity and financial expertise. And once a centre captures these attributes, they tend to be self-reinforcing – in the absence of crass political interference – and create a strong client base for the sophisticated international

Exhibit 2.1 Continued

financial consultancy sector that is also one of the City's strengths.

London has certainly benefited from others' mistakes. For example, America's post-Enron Sarbanes-Oxley legislation has created a governance framework that discourages foreign companies from raising capital in the US. America's heavy-handed response to the 9/11 terrorist attacks may have made the US less attractive for Middle Eastern funds. And the collapse of Germany's poorly regulated Neuer Markt eliminated a potential competitor to London's Aim.

London also has softer attractions for international financiers. It is an agreeable place to live (despite high property prices and poor transport) and its increasingly cosmopolitan atmosphere is matched only by New York. Its tax regime has also been benign to foreign nationals.

Employment regulations have also been helpful to the financial services industry, allowing employers to bring in talent from all over the world. Indeed, one of the most remarkable changes in the City has been the broadening of the talent pool. Two decades ago investment bankers and fund managers would work surrounded by people like themselves – notably Oxbridge arts graduates – but now they are just as likely to be seated next to a mathematics wizard from Azerbaijan or Ukraine.

This creates another virtuous circle – the more outstanding the international talent in the City, the more it increases London's competitive advantage, and the greater the advantage, the more it attracts fresh talent from around the world.

Technology has also played a vital role in strengthening the City. Most obviously, new computer systems have allowed London's equity and derivatives exchanges to remain competitive with international rivals. Technology allows executives to be based in London while keeping a close eye on operations around the world. It has also democratised markets. Relatively cheap access to data means you no longer have to work for a large institution to make your mark. Set up your own hedge fund and the large, integrated investment banks will service you with leverage, stock lending, trade processing and investment ideas.

Source: Financial Times, 27 March 2006. Reprinted with permission.

Dynamism, innovation and adaptation – three decades of change

Since the 1970s there has been a remarkably proactive response by the financial sector to changes in the market environment. New financial instruments, techniques of intermediation and markets have been developed with impressive speed. Instruments which even in the 1980s did not exist have sprung to prominence to create multi-billion pound markets, with thousands of employees serving that market.

Until the mid-1970s there were clearly delineated roles for different types of financial institutions. Banks did banking, insurance firms provided insurance, building societies granted mortgages and so on. There was little competition between the different sectors, and cartel-like arrangements meant that there was only limited competition within each sector. Some effort was made in the 1970s to increase the competitive pressures, particularly for banks. The arrival of large numbers of foreign banks in London helped the process of reform in the UK but the system remained firmly bound by restrictions, particularly in defining the activities firms could undertake.

The real breakthrough came in the 1980s. The guiding philosophy of achieving efficiency through competition led to large-scale deregulation of activities and pricing. There was widespread competitive invasion of market segments. Banks became much more active in the mortgage market and set up insurance operations, stockbroking arms, unit trusts and many other services. Building societies, on the other hand, started to invade the territory of the banks and offered personal loans, credit cards, cheque accounts. They even went into estate agency, stockbroking and insurance underwriting. The Stock Exchange was deregulated in 1986 (in what is known as 'Big bang') and this move enabled it to compete more effectively on a global scale and reduce the costs of dealing in shares, particularly for the large institutional investors.

The 1970s and early 1980s were periods of volatile interest rates and exchange rates. This resulted in greater uncertainty for businesses. New financial instruments were developed to help manage risk. The volume of trading in LIFFE (the London International Financial Futures and Options Exchange) has rocketed since it was opened in 1982 – it now handles around £500bn worth of business every day.[2] (Euronext bought LIFFE in 2002 and it is now called 'Liffe, NYSE Euronext' following the merger of the New York Stock Exchange with Euronext.) Likewise the volume of swaps, options, futures, etc. traded in the informal 'over-the-counter' market (i.e. not on a regulated exchange) has grown exponentially.

[2] Source: www.euronext.com

Through the 1980s the trend towards globalisation in financial product trading and services continued apace. Increasingly a worldwide market was established. It became unexceptional for a company to have its shares quoted in New York, London, Frankfurt and Tokyo as well as its home exchange in Africa. Bond selling and trading became global and currencies were traded 24 hours a day. International banking took on an increasingly high profile, not least because the multinational corporations demanded that their banks provide multifaceted services ranging from borrowing in a foreign currency to helping manage cash.

Vast investments have been made in computing and telecommunications systems to cut costs and provide improved services. Automated teller machines (ATMs), banking by telephone and Internet, and payment by EFTPOS (electronic funds transfer at point of sale) are now commonplace. A more advanced use of technological innovation is in the global trading of the ever-expanding range of financial instruments. It became possible to sit on a beach in the Caribbean and trade pork belly futures in Chicago, interest rate options in London and shares in Singapore. In the 1990s there was a continuation of the blurring of the boundaries between different types of financial institutions to the point where organisations such as JPMorgan Chase and Barclays are referred to as 'financial supermarkets' (or 'universal banks' or '**financial services companies**') offering a wide range of services. The irony is that just as this title was being bandied about, the food supermarket giants such as Sainsbury's and Tesco set up comprehensive banking services, following a path trodden by a number of other non-banking corporations. Marks and Spencer provides credit cards, personal loans and even pensions. Virgin Money sells life insurance, pensions and Individual Savings Accounts (ISAs) over the telephone. The Internet has provided a new means of supplying financial services and lowered the barrier to entry into the industry. New banking, stockbroking and insurance services have sprung up. The Internet allows people to trade millions of shares at the touch of a button from the comfort of their home, to transfer the proceeds between bank accounts and to search websites for data, company reports, newspaper reports, insurance quotations and so on – all much more cheaply than ever before.

The globalisation of business and investment decisions has continued making national economies increasingly interdependent. Borrowers use the international financial markets to seek the cheapest funds, and investors look in all parts of the globe for the highest returns. Some idea of the extent of global financial flows can be gained by contrasting the *daily* turnover of foreign exchange (approximately £1,600bn)[3] with the *annual* output of all the goods and services produced by the people in the UK of less than this. Another effect of technological change is the increased mobility of activities within firms. For example, banks have transferred a high proportion of their operations to India, as have insurance companies and other financial firms.

Exhibit 1.22 Main features of change in financial services

1970s	• Roles strictly demarcated
1980s	• Deregulation • Competitive invasions of market segments • Globalisation
1990s and 2000s	• Continuation of boundary blurring • Increasing internationalisation • Disintermediation • New products (e.g. ever more exotic derivatives) • Internet services/trading • Growth of hedge funds and private equity funds

[3] Bank for International Settlement: www.BIS.org

Another feature of recent years has been the development of disintermediation. This means borrowing firms by-passing the banks and obtaining debt finance by selling debt securities, such as bonds, in the market. The purchasers can be individuals but are more usually the large savings institutions such as pension funds, insurance funds and hedge funds. Banks, having lost some interest income from lending to these large firms, have concentrated instead on fee income gained by arranging the sale and distribution of these securities as well as underwriting their issue. Hedge funds (free from most regulatory control) now account for a high proportion of financial market trading whereas they were barely heard of 15 years ago. Private equity funds, which invest in shares and other securities of companies outside a stock exchange, have grown tremendously over the last 10 years, owning stakes in companies which employ millions of workers.

The financial system

To assist with orientating the reader within the financial system and to carry out more jargon busting, a brief outline of the main financial services sectors and markets is given here.

The institutions

The banking sector

Retail banks

Put at its simplest, the **retail banks** take (small) deposits from the public which are re-packaged and lent to businesses and households. This is generally high-volume and low-value business which contrasts with wholesale (investment) banking which is low volume but each transaction is for high value. The distinction between retail and investment banks has become blurred over recent years as the large institutions have diversified their operations. The retail banks operate nationwide branch networks and a subset of banks provide a cheque clearance system (transferring money from one account to another) – these are the **clearing banks**. The five largest UK clearing banks are Barclays, Lloyds TSB, Royal Bank of Scotland (including NatWest), HSBC and HBOS group (including Bank of Scotland and Halifax). Loans, overdrafts and mortgages are the main forms of retail bank lending. The trend has been for retail banks to reduce their reliance on retail deposits and raise more wholesale funds from the financial markets. They also get together with other banks if a large loan is required by a borrower (say £150m) rather than provide the full amount themselves as this would create an excessive exposure to one customer – this is called syndicate lending, discussed in Chapter 11.

Investment banks

The terms **wholesale bank**, **merchant bank** and **investment bank** are often used interchangeably. There are subtle differences but for most practical purposes they can be regarded as the same. These institutions tend to deal in large sums of money – at least £250,000 – although some have set up retail arms. They concentrate on dealing with other large organisations, corporations, institutional investors and governments. While they undertake some lending their main focus is on generating commission income by providing advice and facilitating deals. There are five main areas of activity:

- ***Raising external finance for companies*** These banks provide advice and arrange finance for corporate clients. Sometimes they provide loans themselves, but often they assist the setting up of a bank syndicate or make arrangements with other institutions. They will advise and assist a firm issuing a bond, they have expertise in helping firms float on the Stock Exchange and make rights issues. They may 'underwrite' a bond or share issue. (This means that they will buy any part of the issue not taken up by other investors – see Chapter 10.) This assures the corporation that it will receive the funds it needs for its investment programme.
- ***Broking and dealing*** They act as agents for the buying and selling of securities on the financial markets, including shares and bonds. Some also have market-making arms which quote prices

they are willing buy or sell from or to, say, a shareholder or a bond holder, thus assisting the operation of secondary markets (see Chapter 9). They also trade in the markets on their own account and assist companies with export finance.

- ***Fund management (asset management)*** The investment banks offer services to rich individuals who lack the time or expertise to deal with their own investment strategies. They also manage unit and investment trusts as well as the portfolios of some pension funds and insurance companies. In addition corporations often have short-term cash flows which need managing efficiently (treasury management).
- ***Assistance in corporate restructuring*** Investment banks earn large fees from advising acquirers on mergers and assisting with the merger process. They also gain by helping target firms avoid being taken over too cheaply. Corporate disposal programmes, such as selling off a division, may also need the services of an investment bank.
- ***Assisting risk management using derivatives*** Risk can be reduced through hedging strategies using futures, options, swaps and the like. However this is a complex area with large room for error and terrible penalties if a mistake is made (*see* Chapters 24 and 25). The banks may have specialist knowledge to offer in this area.

International banks

There are two types of **international banking** in the UK:

- **Foreign banking** transactions in sterling with non-UK residents (lending/borrowing, etc.) by UK banks.
- **Eurocurrency banking** for transactions in a currency other than that of the host country, e.g. yen transactions in Canada. Thus for UK banks this involves transactions in currencies other than sterling with both residents and non-residents (Chapter 11 considers this further).

The major part of international banking these days is borrowing and lending in foreign currencies. There are over 300 non-UK banks operating in London, the most prominent of which are American, German and Japanese. Their initial function was mainly to provide services for their own nationals, for example for export and import transactions, but nowadays their main emphasis is in the Eurocurrency market and international securities (shares, bonds, etc.) trading. Often funds are held in the UK for the purpose of trading and speculation on the foreign exchange market.

Building societies

Building societies collect funds from millions of savers by enticing them to put their money in interest-bearing accounts. The vast majority of that deposited money is then lent to people wishing to buy a home – in the form of a mortgage. Thus, they take in short-term deposits (although they also borrow on the wholesale financial markets) and they lend money for long periods, usually for 25 years. The moves by the biggest societies to convert to banks has diminished building societies' significance in the mortgage market.

Finance houses[4]

Finance houses are responsible for the financing of hire purchase agreements and other instalment credit, for example, leasing. If you buy a large durable good such as a car or a washing machine you often find that the sales assistant also tries to get you interested in taking the item on credit, so you pay for it over a period of, say, three years. It is usually not the retailer that provides the finance for the credit. The retailer usually works with a finance house which pays the retailer the full purchase price of the good and therefore becomes the owner. You, the customer, get to use the good, but in return you have to make regular payments to the finance house, including

[4] The term 'finance house' is also used for broadly based financial-service companies carrying out a wide variety of financial activities from share brokerage to corporate lending. However we will confine the term to instalment credit and related services.

interest. Under a **hire purchase** agreement, when you have made enough payments you will become the owner. Under **leasing** the finance house retains ownership (for more detail *see* Chapter 12). Finance houses also provide **factoring** services – providing cash to firms in return for receiving income from the firms' debtors when they pay up. Most of the large finance houses are subsidiaries of the major conglomerate banks.

Long-term savings institutions

Pension funds

Pension funds are set up to provide pensions for members. For example, the University Superannuation Scheme (USS), to which university lecturers belong, takes 6.35 per cent of working members' salaries each month and puts it into the fund. In addition the employing organisation pays money into the scheme. When a member retires the USS will pay a pension. Between the time of making a contribution and payment in retirement, which may be decades, the pension trustees oversee the management of the fund. They may place some or all of the fund with specialist investment managers. This is a particularly attractive form of saving because of the generous tax relief provided. The long time horizon of the pension business means that large sums are built up and available for investment – currently around £800bn in the UK funds. A typical allocation of a fund is:

- 30–40 per cent in UK shares;
- 10–15 per cent lending to the UK government by buying bonds and bills;
- 20–30 per cent overseas securities;
- 5–15 per cent other (e.g. property, cash and overseas bonds).

Insurance funds

Insurance companies engage in two types of activities:

- **General insurance** This is insurance against specific contingencies such as fire, theft, accident, generally for a one-year period. The money collected in premiums is mostly held in financial assets which are relatively short term and liquid so that short-term commitments can be met.
- **Life assurance** With **term assurance**, your life is assured for a specified period. If you die your beneficiaries get a payout. If you live you get nothing at the end of the period. With **whole-of-life policies**, the insurance company pays a capital sum upon death whenever this occurs. **Endowment policies** are more interesting from a financial systems perspective because they act as a savings vehicle as well as cover against death. The premium will be larger but after a number of years have passed the insurance company pays a substantial sum of money even if you are still alive. The life company has to take the premiums paid over, say, 10 or 25 years, and invest them wisely to satisfy its commitment to the policy holder. Millions of UK house buyers purchase with an endowment mortgage. They simply pay interest to the lender (e.g. a building society) while also placing premiums into an endowment fund. The hope is that after 25 years or so the value of the accumulated fund will equal or be greater than the capital value of the loan.

Life assurance companies also provide **annuities**. Here a policy holder pays an initial lump sum and in return receives regular payments in subsequent years. They have also moved into personal pensions.

Life assurance companies have over £900bn under management. A typical fund allocation is:

- 30–50 per cent UK shares;
- 20 per cent lending to the UK government;
- 10 per cent property;
- 10–15 per cent overseas securities;
- 5–10 per cent other.

The risk spreaders

These institutions allow small savers a stake in a large diversified portfolio.

Unit trusts

Unit trusts are 'open-ended' funds, so the size of the fund and the number of units depends on the amount of money investors wish to put into the fund. If a fund of one million units suddenly doubled in size because of an inflow of investor funds it would become a fund of two million units through the creation and selling of more units. The buying and selling prices of the units are determined by the value of the fund. So if a two-million unit fund is invested in £2m worth of shares in the UK stock market the value of each unit will be £1. If over a period the value of the shares rises to £3m, the units will be worth £1.50 each. Unit holders sell units back to the managers of the unit trust if they want to liquidate their holding. The manager would then either sell the units to another investor or sell some of the underlying investments to raise cash to pay the unit holder. The units are usually quoted at two prices depending on whether you are buying (higher) or selling. There is also an ongoing management charge for running the fund. Trustees supervise the funds to safeguard the interests of unit holders but employ managers to make the investment decisions.

There is a wide choice of unit trust (over 2,000) specialising in different types of investments ranging from Japanese equities to privatised European companies. Of the £350bn invested in unit trusts and their cousins, OEICs, 50–60 per cent is devoted to UK company securities, with the remainder mostly devoted to overseas company securities. Instruments similar to unit trusts are called mutual funds in other countries.

Investment companies (investment trusts)

Investment companies differ from unit trusts because they are companies able to issue shares and other securities. Investors can purchase these securities when the investment company is first launched or purchase shares in the secondary market from other investors. These are known as closed-end funds because the company itself is closed to new investors – if you wished to invest your money you would go to an existing investor and not buy from the company. Investment companies usually spread the investors' funds across a range of other companies' shares. They are also more inclined to invest in a broader range of assets than unit trusts – even property and shares not listed on a stock market. Approximately one-half of the money devoted to the 400 or so UK investment companies (£80bn) is put into UK securities, with the remainder placed in overseas securities. The managers of these funds are able to borrow in order to invest. This has the effect of increasing returns to shareholders when things go well. Correspondingly if the value of the underlying investments falls the return to shareholders falls even more, because of the obligation to meet interest charges.

Open-ended investment companies (OEICs)

Open-ended investment companies are hybrid risk-spreading instruments which allow an investment in an open-ended fund. Designed to be more flexible and transparent than either investment companies or unit trusts, OEICs have just one price. However, as with unit trusts, OEICs can issue more shares, in line with demand from investors, and they can borrow.[5]

The risk takers

Private equity funds

These are funds that invest in companies that do not have a stock market trading quote for their shares. The firms are often young and on a rapid growth trajectory, but **private equity companies** also supply finance to well-established companies. The funds usually buy shares in these companies and occasionally supply debt finance. Frequently the private equity funds are themselves funded by other financial institutions, such as a group of pension funds. Private equity has grown tremen-

[5] There is much more on unit trusts, investment companies and OEICs in G.C. Arnold (2004), *The Financial Times Guide to Investing* (Harlow: FT Prentice Hall).

dously over the last 15 years to the point where now over one-fifth of non-government UK workers are employed by a firm financed by private equity. Private equity is discussed in Chapter 10.

Hedge funds

Hedge funds gather together investors' money and invest it in a wide variety of financial strategies largely outside of the control of the regulators, being created either outside of the major financial centres or as private investment partnerships. The investors include wealthy individuals as well as institutions, such as pension funds, insurance funds and banks. By being outside of normal regulatory control hedge funds are not confined to investing in particular types of security, or to using particular investment methods. For example, they have far more freedom than unit trusts in '**going short**', i.e. selling a security first and then buying it later, hopefully at a lower price. They can also borrow many times the size of the fund to punt on a small movement of currency rates, or share movements, orange juice futures, or whatever they judge will go up (or go down). If the punt goes well (or rather, a series of punts over the year) the fund managers earn million-pound bonuses (often on the basis of 2 per cent of funds under management fee plus 20 per cent of the profit made for client investors).

Originally, the term 'hedge' made some sense when applied to these funds. They would, through a combination of investments, including derivatives, try to **hedge** (lower or eliminate) risk while seeking a high absolute return (rather than a return relative to an index). Today the word 'hedge' is misapplied to most of these funds because they generally take aggressive bets on the movements of currencies, equities, interest rates, bonds, etc. around the world. For example one fund, Amaranth, bet on the movement of the price of natural gas, and lost US$6bn in a matter of days in 2006. Their activities would not be a concern if they had remained a relatively small part of the investment scene. However, today they command enormous power and billions more are being placed in these funds every week. Already over £1,000 billion is invested in these funds. Add to that the borrowed money – sometimes ten times the fund's base capital – and you can see why they are to be taken very seriously. Up to 50 per cent of the share trades on a typical day in London is said to be due to hedge funds, for example.

The markets

The money markets

The **money markets** are wholesale markets (usually involving transactions of £500,000 or more) which enable borrowing on a short-term basis (less than one year). The banks are particularly active in this market – both as lenders and as borrowers. Large corporations, local government bodies and non-banking financial institutions also lend when they have surplus cash and borrow when short of money.

The bond markets

While the money markets are concerned with short-term lending the capital markets deal with longer-term (> 1 year) debt (e.g. bond) and equity instruments. A **bond** is merely a document which sets out the borrower's promise to pay sums of money in the future – usually regular interest plus a capital amount upon the maturity of the bond. These are securities issued by a variety of organisations including governments and corporations. The UK bond markets are over three centuries old and during that time they have developed very large and sophisticated primary and secondary sub-markets encompassing gilts (UK government bonds), corporate bonds, local authority bonds and international bonds, amongst others. Bonds as a source of finance for firms will be examined in Chapter 11.

The foreign exchange markets (Forex or FX)

The **foreign exchange markets** are the markets in which one currency is exchanged for another. They include the ***spot* market** where currencies are bought and sold for 'immediate' delivery (in reality, one or two days later) and the ***forward* markets**, where the deal is agreed now to exchange currencies at some fixed point in the future. Also currency *futures* and *options* and other forex derivatives are employed to hedge risk and to speculate. The forex markets are dominated by the major banks, with dealing taking place 24 hours a day around the globe. Chapter 25 looks at how a company could use the forex market to facilitate international trade and reduce the risk attached to business transactions abroad.

The share markets

All major economies now have **share markets**. The London Stock Exchange is an important potential source of long-term equity (ownership) capital for UK companies and for hundreds of overseas companies. Firms can raise finance in the primary market by a new issue, a rights issue, open offer, etc., either in the main listed London Market, or on the Alternative Investment Market. Subsequently investors are able to buy and sell to each other on the very active secondary market. Chapters 9 and 10 examine stock markets and the raising of equity capital.

The derivative markets

A **derivative** is a financial instrument derived from other financial securities or some other underlying asset. For example, a **future** is the right to buy something (e.g. currency, shares, bonds) at some date in the future at an agreed price. This *right* becomes a saleable derived financial instrument. The performance of the derivative depends on the behaviour of the underlying asset. Companies can use these markets for the management and transfer of risk. They can be used to reduce risk (hedging) or to **speculate. Liffe** trades options and futures in shares, bonds and interest rates. This used to be the only one of the markets listed here to have a trading floor where face-to-face dealing took place on an **open outcry system** (traders shouting and signalling to each other, face to face in a trading pit, the price at which they are willing to buy and sell). Now all the financial markets (money, bond, forex, derivatives and share markets) are conducted using computers (and telephones) from isolated trading rooms located in the major financial institutions. In the derivative markets a high proportion of trade takes place on what is called the **over-the-counter (OTC)** market rather than on a regulated exchange. The OTC market flexibility allows the creation of tailor-made derivatives to suit a client's risk situation. The practical use of derivatives is examined in Chapters 24 and 25.

Concluding comments

We now have a clear guiding principle set as our objective for the myriad financial decisions discussed later in this book: maximise shareholder wealth. Whether we are considering a major investment programme, or trying to decide on the best kind of finance to use, the criterion of creating value for shareholders over the long run will be paramount. A single objective is set primarily for practical reasons to aid exposition in this text; however, many of the techniques described in later chapters will be applicable to organisations with other purposes as they stand; others will need slight modification.

There is an old joke about financial service firms: they just shovel money from one place to another making sure that some of it sticks to the shovel. The implication is that they contribute little to the well-being of society. Extremists even go so far as to regard these firms as parasites on the 'really productive' parts of the economies. And yet very few people avoid extensive use of financial services. Most have bank and building society accounts, pay insurance premiums and contribute to pension schemes. People do not put their money into a bank account unless they get something in return. Likewise building societies, insurance companies, pension funds, unit trusts, investment banks and so on can only survive if they offer a service people find beneficial and are willing to pay for. Describing the mobilisation and employment of money in the service of productive investment as pointless or merely 'shovelling it around the system' is as logical as saying that the transport firms which bring goods to the high street do not provide a valuable service because of the absence of a tangible 'thing' created by their activities.

Key points and concepts

- Firms should clearly define the **objective** of the enterprise to provide a focus for decision making.
- **Sound financial management** is necessary for the achievement of all **stakeholder** goals.
- Some stakeholders will have their returns **satisficed** – given just enough to make their contribution. One (or more) group(s) will have their returns **maximised** – given any surplus after all others have been satisfied.
- The assumed objective of the firm for finance is to **maximise shareholder wealth**. Reasons:
  - **practical**, a single objective leads to clearer decisions;
  - the **contractual theory**;
  - **survival** in a competitive world;
  - it is better for **society**;
  - counters the tendency of managers to pursue goals for their own benefit;
  - they **own** the firm.
- **Maximising shareholder wealth** is **maximising purchasing power** or **maximising the flow of discounted cash flow** to shareholders over a long time horizon.
- **Profit maximisation** is not the same as shareholder wealth maximisation. Some factors a profit comparison does not allow for:
  - future prospects;
  - risk;
  - accounting problems;
  - communication;
  - additional capital.
- **Corporate governance**. Large corporations usually have a **separation of ownership and control**. This may lead to **managerialism** where the agent (the managers) take decisions primarily with their interests in mind rather than those of the principals (the shareholders). This is a **principal–agent problem**. Some solutions:
  - corporate governance regulation;
  - link managerial rewards to shareholder wealth improvement;
  - sackings;
  - selling shares and the takeover threat;
  - improve information flow.
- **Financial institutions and markets** encourage growth and progress by **mobilising savings** and encouraging investment.
- Financial managers contribute to firms' success primarily through **investment and finance decisions**. Their knowledge of financial markets, investment appraisal methods, treasury, risk management and value analysis techniques are vital for company growth and stability.
- Financial institutions encourage the flow of saving into investment by acting as **brokers** and **asset transformers**, thus alleviating the **conflict of preferences** between the **primary investors** (households) and the **ultimate borrowers** (firms).
- **Asset transformation** is the creation of an intermediate security with characteristics appealing to the primary investor to attract funds, which are then made available to the ultimate borrower in a form appropriate to them. Types of asset transformation:
  - risk transformation;
  - maturity transformation;
  - volume transformation.
- Intermediaries are able to transform assets and encourage the flow of funds because of their **economies of scale** *vis-à-vis* the individual investor:
  - efficiencies in gathering information;
  - risk spreading;
  - transaction costs.

- The **secondary markets** in financial securities encourage investment by enabling investor liquidity (being able to sell quickly and cheaply to another investor) while providing the firm with long-term funds.
- The **financial services sector** has grown to be of great economic significance in the UK. Reasons:
  - high income elasticity;
  - international comparative advantage.
- The financial sector has shown remarkable **dynamism, innovation and adaptability** over the last three decades. Deregulation, new technology, globalisation and the rapid development of new financial products have characterised this sector.
- **Banking sector:**
  - **Retail banks** – high-volume and low-value business.
  - **Wholesale banks** – low-volume and high-value business. Mostly fee based.
  - **International banks** – mostly Eurocurrency transactions.
  - **Building societies** – still primarily small deposits aggregated for mortgage lending.
  - **Finance houses** – hire purchase, leasing, factoring.
- **Long-term savings institutions:**
  - **Pension funds** – major investors in financial assets.
  - **Insurance funds** – life assurance and endowment policies provide large investment funds.
- **The risk spreaders:**
  - **Unit trusts** – companies trusts which are open-ended investment vehicles.
  - **Investment companies** – companies which invest in other companies' financial securities, particularly shares.
  - **Open-ended investment companies** (OEICs) – a hybrid between unit and investment trusts.
- **The risk takers:**
  - **Private equity funds** – invest in companies not quoted on a stock exchange.
  - **Hedge funds** – wide variety of investment or speculative strategies outside regulators' control.
- **The markets:**
  - **The money markets** are short-term wholesale lending and/or borrowing markets.
  - **The bond markets** deal in long-term bond debt issued by corporations, governments, local authorities and so on, and usually have a secondary market.
  - **The foreign exchange market** – one currency is exchanged for another.
  - **The share market** – primary and secondary trading in companies' shares takes place.
  - **The derivatives market** – Liffe dominates the 'exchange-traded' derivatives market in options and futures. However there is a flourishing over-the-counter (OTC) market.

References and further reading

Students of finance, or any managerial discipline, should get into the habit of reading the *Financial Times* and *The Economist* to (a) reinforce knowledge gained from a course, and (b) appreciate the wider business environment.

Anthony, R.N. (1960) 'The trouble with profit maximisation', *Harvard Business Review*, Nov.–Dec., pp. 126–34.

Challenges the conventional economic view of profit maximisation on grounds of realism and morality.

Arnold, G.C. (2000) 'Tracing the development of value-based management'. In Glen Arnold and Matt Davies (eds), *Value-based Management: Context and Application*. London: Wiley.

A more detailed discussion of the objective of the firm is presented.

Arnold, G.C. (2004) *The Financial Times Guide to Investing*. Harlow: FT Prentice Hall.

This provides much more on the financial system and instruments.

Berle, A.A. and Means, G.C. (1932) *The Modern Corporation and Private Property*. New York: Macmillan.

An early discussion of the principal–agent problem and corporate governance.

Blake, D. (2000) *Financial Market Analysis*. 2nd edn. London: Wiley.

A more detailed introduction to the financial markets.

Brett, M. (2000) *How to Read the Financial Pages*. 5th edn. London: Random House.

A well-written simple guide to the financial markets.

Buckle, M. and Thompson, J. (2004) *The UK Financial System*. 4th edn. Manchester: Manchester University Press.
Clear, elegant and concise description.

'The Cadbury Report' (1992) *Report of the Committee on the Financial Aspects of Corporate Governance*. London: Gee.
The first and most thorough of the three reports on corporate governance – easy to read.

Donaldson, G. (1963) 'Financial goals: management vs. stockholders', *Harvard Business Review*, May–June, pp. 116–29.
Clear and concise discussion of the conflict of interest between managers and shareholders.

Doyle, P. (1994) 'Setting business objectives and measuring performance', *Journal of General Management*, Winter, pp. 1–19.
Western firms are over-focused on short-term financial goals (profit, ROI). Reconciling the interests of stakeholders should not be difficult as they are 'satisficers' rather than maximisers.

Fama, E.F. (1980) 'Agency problems and the theory of the firm', *Journal of Political Economy*, Spring, pp. 288–307.
Explains how the separation of ownership and control can lead to an efficient form of economic organisation.

Financial Services Authority (2003) *The Combined Code on corporate governance*, London. www.fsa.gov.uk/pubs/ukla
The current Combined Code is shown. There are likely to be minor changes in the code over time.

Financial Reporting Council. Various publications on corporate governance are display on the FRC website, including the updated Combined Code.

Friedman, M. (1970) 'The social responsibility of business is to increase its profits', *New York Times Magazine*, 30 Sept.
A viewpoint on the objective of the firm.

Galbraith, J. (1967) 'The goals of an industrial system' (excerpt from *The New Industrial State*). Reproduced in H.I. Ansoff, *Business Strategy*. London: Penguin, 1969.
Survival, sales and expansion of the 'technostructure' are emphasised as the goals in real-world corporations.

Ghoshal, S. (2005) 'Bad management theories are destroying good management practices', *Academy of Management's Learning and Education*, Vol. 4, No. 1, pp. 75–91.
Argues that the encouragement of shareholder wealth maximisation is wrong.

'The Greenbury Report' (1995) *Directors' remuneration: report of a Study Group chaired by Sir Richard Greenbury*. London: Gee.
One of the three reports designed to improve corporate governance.

Grinyer, J.R. (1986) 'An alternative to maximisation of shareholder wealth in capital budgeting decisions', *Accounting and Business Research*, Autumn, pp. 319–26.
Discusses the maximisation of monetary surplus as an alternative to shareholder wealth.

'The Hampel Report' (1998) *The Committee on Corporate Governance, Final report*. London: Gee.
The final report attempting to improve corporate behaviour.

Hart, O.D. (1995a) *Firms, Contracts and Financial Structure*. Oxford: Clarendon Press.
A clear articulation of the principal–agent problem.

Hart, O.D. (1995b) 'Corporate governance: some theory and implications'. *Economic Journal*, 105, pp. 678–9.
Principal–agent problem discussed.

Hayek, F.A. (1969) 'The corporation in a democratic society: in whose interests ought it and will it be run?'. Reprinted in H.I. Ansoff, *Business Strategy*. London: Penguin, 1969.
Objective should be long-run return on owners' capital subject to restraint by general legal and moral rules.

Jensen, M.C. (1986) 'Agency costs of free cash flow, corporate finance and takeovers', *American Economic Review*, Vol. 76, pp. 323–9.
Agency cost theory applied to the issue of the use to which managers put business cash inflows.

Jensen, M.C. (2001) 'Value maximisation, stakeholder theory, and the corporate objective function', *Journal of Applied Corporate Finance*, Vol. 14, No. 3, Fall.
Cogently argues against simple stakeholder balancing or a Balance Scorecard approach to directing a company because of the violation of the proposition that a single-valued objective is a prerequisite for purposeful or rational behaviour by any organisation, thus politicising the corporation and leaving managers empowered to exercise their own preferences.

Jensen, M.C. and Meckling, W.H. (1976) 'Theory of the firm: managerial behavior, agency costs and ownership structure', *Journal of Financial Economics*, Oct., Vol. 3, pp. 305–60.
Seminal work on agency theory.

Jones, G. and Gallagher-Kernstine, M. (2004) '"Walking on a tightrope": maintaining London as a financial centre', *Harvard Business Review*, May 27.
An easy-to-read discussion of the recent listing of the City and the role today.

Kaplan, R. and Norton, D.P. (1996) *The Balanced Scorecard*. Boston, MA: Harvard Business School Press.
The managerial equivalent of stakeholder theory in which multiple measures are used to evaluate performance.

Kay, J. (2004) 'Forget how the crow flies', *Financial Times Magazine*, 17–18 January, pp. 17–21.
An imporant argument on obliquity is presented.

Keasey, K., Thompson, S. and Wright, M. (1997) *Corporate Governance*. Oxford: Oxford University Press.
A collection of easy-to-read monographs on various aspects of corporate governance.

Levinson, M. (2006) *Guide to Financial Markets*. 5th edn. London: The Economist Books.
A clear, brief account of modern financial markets.

London, S. (2003) 'The long view: lunch with the FT, Milton Friedman', *Financial Times Magazine*, 7–8 June, pp. 12–13.

McKinsey and Company: Koller, T., Goedhart, M. and Wessels, D. (2005) *Valuation*. 4th edn. New York: John Wiley & Sons Ltd.
Contends that shareholder wealth should be the focus of managerial actions.

Simon, H.A. (1959) 'Theories of decision making in economics and behavioural science', *American Economic Review*, June.
Traditional economic theories are challenged, drawing on psychology. Discusses the goals of the firm: satisficing vs. maximising.

Simon, H.A. (1964) 'On the concept of organisational goals', *Administrative Science Quarterly*, 9(1), June, pp. 1–22.
Discusses the complexity of goal setting.

Smith, A. (1776) *The Wealth of Nations*. Reproduced in 1910 in two volumes by J.M. Dent, London.
An early viewpoint on the objective of the firm.

Smith, R. (chair) (2003) *Audit committees combined code guidance*. Published by the Financial Reporting Council. www.frc.org.uk
One of the contributions to the Combined Code on Corporate Governance.

The Economist (2005) 'A survey of corporate social responsibility', 22 January.
A forcefully argued piece on the dangers of advocating corporate social responsibility if that means less attention to shareholder wealth.

Higgs Report (2003) *Review of the role and effectiveness of non-executive directors*. The Department of Trade and Industry. www.dti.pdf file available
A key UK corporate governance report.

Tirole, J. (2005) *The Theory of Corporate Finance*. Princeton: Princeton University Press.
Provides a thorough overview of the principal–agent problem and corporate governance.

Vaitilingam, R. (2006) *The Financial Times Guide to using the Financial Pages*. 5th edn. London: Financial Times Prentice Hall.
Good introductory source of information. Clear and concise.

Valdez, S. (2007) *An Introduction to Global Financial Markets*, 5th edn. Basingstoke: Palgrave Macmillan.
An easy-to-follow overview of the financial markets.

Williamson, O. (1963) 'Managerial discretion and business behaviour', *American Economic Review*, 53, pp. 1033–57.
Managerial security, power, prestige, etc. are powerful motivating forces. These goals may lead to less than profit-maximising behaviour.

Websites

Association of British Insurers www.abi.org.uk
Association of Investment Companies www.theaic.co.uk or www.aitc.co.uk
Bank for International Settlement www.bis.org
Bank of England www.bankofengland.co.uk
British Bankers Association www.bba.org.uk
British Venture Capital Association www.bvca.co.uk
Building Societies Association www.bsa.org.uk
Combined Code of Corporate Governance www.fsa.gov.uk/pub/ukla
Companies House www.companieshouse.gov.uk
European Corporate Governance Institute www.ecgi.org
Euronext.liffe Euronext.com/home_derivatives
Finance and Leasing Association www.fla.org.uk
Financial Times www.FT.com
Financial Reporting Council www.frc.org
Institute of Financial Services www.ifslearning.com
Investment Management Association www.investmentuk.org
National Association of Pension Funds www.napf.co.uk
London Stock Exchange www.londonstockexchange.com

Self-review questions

1 Why is it important to specify a goal for the corporation?

2 How can 'goal congruence' for managers and shareholders be achieved?

3 How does money assist the well-being of society?

4 What are the economies of scale of intermediaries?

5 Distinguish between a primary market and a secondary market. How does the secondary market aid the effectiveness of the primary market?

6 Illustrate the flow of funds between primary investors and ultimate borrowers in a modern economy. Give examples of intermediary activity.

7 List as many financial intermediaries as you can. Describe the nature of their intermediation and explain the intermediate securities they create.

8 What is the principal–agent problem?

9 What is the 'contractual theory'? Do you regard it as a strong argument?

10 What difficulties might arise in state-owned industries in making financial decisions?

11 Briefly describe the following types of decisions (give examples):

a Financing
b Investment
c Treasury
d Risk management
e Strategic.

12 Briefly explain the role of the following:

a The money markets
b The bond markets
c The foreign exchange markets
d The share markets
e The derivatives market.

Questions and problems

myfinancelab ***Questions with an icon are also available for practice in MyFinanceLab with additional supporting resources.***

1 Explain the rationale for selecting shareholder wealth maximisation as the objective of the firm. Include a consideration of profit maximisation as an alternative goal.

2 What benefits are derived from the financial services sector which have led to its growth over recent years in terms of employment and share of GDP?

3 What is managerialism and how might it be incompatible with shareholder interests?

4 Why has an increasing share of household savings been channelled through financial intermediaries?

5 Discuss the relationship between economic growth and the development of a financial services sector.

6 Firm A has a stock market value of £20m (number of shares in issue x share price), while firm B is valued at £15m. The firms have similar profit histories:

	Firm A	Firm B
2004	1.5	1.8
2005	1.6	1.0
2006	1.7	2.3
2007	1.8	1.5
2008	2.0	2.0

Provide reasons why, despite the same total profit over the last five years, shareholders regard firm A as being worth £5m more (extend your thoughts beyond the numbers in the table).

7 The chief executive of Geight plc receives a salary of £80,000 plus 4 per cent of sales. Will this encourage the adoption of decisions which are shareholder wealth enhancing? How might you change matters to persuade the chief executive to focus on shareholder wealth in all decision making?

myfinancelab *Now retake your diagnostic test for Chapter 1 to check your progress and update your study plan.*

Assignments

1 Consider the organisations where you have worked in the past and the people you have come into contact with. List as many objectives as you can, explicit or implicit, that have been revealed to, or suspected by, you. To what extent was goal congruence between different stakeholders achieved? How might the efforts of all individuals be channelled more effectively?

2 Review all the financial services you or your firm purchase. Try to establish a rough estimate of the cost of using each financial intermediary and write a balanced report considering whether you or your firm should continue to pay for that service.

PART 2

The investment decision

CHAPTER

2

Project appraisal:

net present value and internal rate of return

LEARNING OUTCOMES

By the end of the chapter the student should be able to demonstrate an understanding of the fundamental theoretical justifications for using discounted cash flow techniques in analysing major investment decisions, based on the concepts of the time value of money and the opportunity cost of capital. More specifically the student should be able to:

- calculate net present value and internal rate of return;
- show an appreciation of the relationship between net present value and internal rate of return;
- describe and explain at least three potential problems that can arise with internal rate of return in specific circumstances;
- demonstrates awareness of the propensity for management to favour a percentage measure of investment performance and be able to use the modified internal rate of return.

Introduction

Shareholders supply funds to a firm for a reason. That reason, generally, is to receive a return on their precious resources. The return is generated by management using the finance provided to invest in real assets. It is vital for the health of the firm and the economic welfare of the finance providers that management employ the best techniques available when analysing which of all the possible investment opportunities will give the best return.

Someone (or a group) within the organisation may have to take the bold decision on whether it is better to build a new factory or extend the old; whether it is wiser to use an empty piece of land for a multi-storey car park or to invest a larger sum and build a shopping centre; whether shareholders would be better off if the firm returned their money in the form of dividends because shareholders can obtain a better return elsewhere, or whether the firm should pursue its expansion plan and invest in that new chain of hotels, or that large car showroom, or the new football stand.

These sorts of decisions require not only brave people, but informed people; individuals of the required calibre need to be informed about a range of issues: for example, the market environment and level of demand for the proposed activity, the internal environment, culture and capabilities of the firm, the types and levels of cost elements in the proposed area of activity, and, of course, an understanding of the risk appertaining to the project.

The Panama Canal Authority presumably considered all these factors before making its £2.81bn investment – *see* **Exhibit 2.1**.

Exhibit 2.1

Panama plan – a bigger canal can bring east and west closer

FT

The gigantic ships that ply trade routes have outgrown the central American waterway.

Robert Wright examines plans to upgrade it for the 21st century

While all the container ships in service before 1990 could fit through the canal's locks, nearly half those on order now are too large. And the canal is clogged with vessels: those that have not booked long in advance must often wait four days to get through.

But in 2014, a century after the opening, Panama should have a chance to celebrate properly. If a referendum on Sunday passes, which looks likely, an expansion to the canal should be completed around that year.

For the first time, it would accommodate a vessel more than 295 metres long and 33 metres wide – its current maximum.

Panamax container carriers, as the largest ships that can use the present canal are known, carry at most 5,000 twenty-foot equivalent units (TEUs) of containers. On other routes some container ships now have more than twice that capacity.

The canal authority wants to build a lane of locks, each 427m long by 55m wide. Three would lift ships up to the summit level while another three would lower them again at the, other side. Some approach channels would be dredged deeper, while the water level in the summit would be raised, to increase the depth of the Culebra Cut. It says the programme will cost $5.25bn (£2.81bn, €4.18bn), to be funded by higher tolls for canal users.

Source: Financial Times, 20 October 2006, p. 15. Reprinted with permission.

Bravery, information, knowledge and a sense of proportion are all essential ingredients when undertaking the onerous task of investing other people's money, but there is another element which is also of crucial importance, that is, the employment of an investment appraisal technique which leads to the 'correct' decision; a technique which takes into account the fundamental considerations.

In this chapter we examine two approaches to evaluating investments within the firm.[1] Both emphasise the central importance of the concept of the time value of money and are thus described as Discounted Cash Flow (DCF) techniques. Net present value (NPV) and internal rate of return (IRR) are in common usage in most large commercial organisations and are regarded as more complete than the traditional techniques of payback and accounting rate of return (e.g. Return on Capital Employed – ROCE). The relative merits and demerits of these alternative methods are discussed in Chapter 4 in conjunction with a consideration of some of the practical issues of project implementation. In this chapter we concentrate on gaining an understanding of how net present value and internal rate of return are calculated, as well as their theoretical underpinnings.

Value creation and corporate investment

If we accept that the objective of investment within the firm is to create value for its owners then the purpose of allocating money to a particular division or project is to generate cash inflows in the future, significantly greater than the amount invested. Thus, put most simply, the project appraisal decision is one involving the comparison of the amount of cash put into an investment with the amount of cash returned. The key phrase and the tricky issue is 'significantly greater than'. For instance, would you, as part-owner of a firm, be content if that firm asked you to swap £10,000 of your hard-earned money for some new shares so that the management team could invest it in order to hand back to you, in five years, the £10,000 plus £1,000? Is this a significant return? Would you feel that your wealth had been enhanced if you were aware that by investing the £10,000 yourself, by, for instance, lending to the government, you could have received a 5 per cent return per year? Or that you could obtain a return of 10 per cent per annum by investing in other shares on the stock market? Naturally, you would feel let down by a management team that offered a return of less than 2 per cent per year when you had alternative courses of action which would have produced much more.

This line of thought is leading us to a central concept in finance and, indeed, in business generally – the **time value of money**. Investors have alternative uses for their funds and they therefore have an opportunity cost if money is invested in a corporate project. The *investor's* **opportunity cost** is the sacrifice of the return available on the best forgone alternative.

Investments must generate at least enough cash for all investors to obtain their required returns. If they produce less than the investor's opportunity cost then the wealth of shareholders will decline.

Exhibit 2.2 summarises the process of good investment appraisal. The achievement of value or wealth creation is determined not only by the future cash flows to be derived from a project but also by the timing of those cash flows and by making an allowance for the fact that time has value.

The time value of money

When people undertake to set aside money for investment something has to be given up now. For instance, if someone buys shares in a firm or lends to a business there is a sacrifice of consumption. One of the incentives to save is the possibility of gaining a higher level of future consumption by sacrificing some present consumption. Therefore, it is apparent that compensation is required to induce people to make a consumption sacrifice. Compensation will be required for at least three things:

- ***Impatience to consume*** That is, individuals generally prefer to have £1.00 today than £1.00 in five years' time. To put this formally: the utility of £1.00 now is greater than £1.00 received five years hence. Individuals are predisposed towards **impatience to consume**, thus they need an appropriate reward to begin the saving process. The rate of exchange between certain future consumption and certain current consumption is the **pure rate of interest** – this occurs even

[1] The selection of investment projects is called capital expenditure – 'capex' – or capital budgeting.

Exhibit 2.2 Investment appraisal: objective, inputs and process

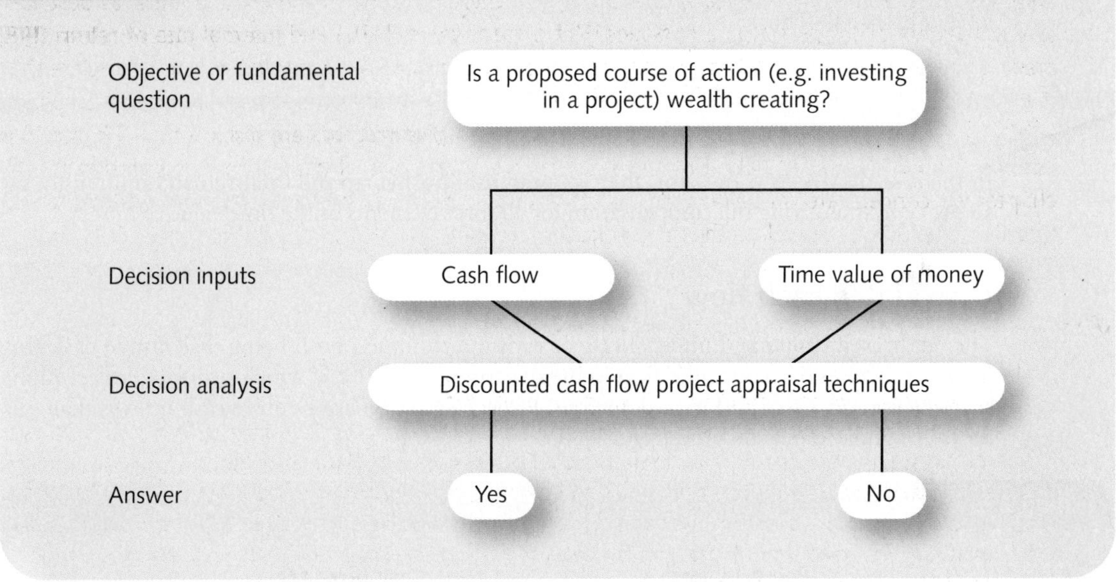

in a world of no inflation and no risk. If you lived in such a world you might be willing to sacrifice £100 of consumption now if you were compensated with £102 to be received in one year. This would mean that your pure rate of interest is 2 per cent.

- ***Inflation*** The price of time (or the interest rate needed to compensate for impatience to consume) exists even when there is no inflation, simply because people generally prefer consumption now to consumption later. If there is inflation then the providers of finance will have to be compensated for that loss in purchasing power as well as for time.
- ***Risk*** The promise of the receipt of a sum of money some years hence generally carries with it an element of risk; the payout may not take place or the amount may be less than expected. **Risk** simply means that the future return has a variety of possible values. Thus, the issuer of a security, whether it be a share, a bond or a bank account, must be prepared to compensate the investor for impatience to consume, inflation and risk involved, otherwise no one will be willing to buy the security.

Take the case of Mrs Ann Investor who is considering a £1,000 one-year investment and requires compensation for three elements of time value. First, a return of 2 per cent is required for the pure time value of money. Second, inflation is anticipated to be 3 per cent over the year. At time zero (t_0) £1,000 buys one basket of goods and services. To buy the same basket of goods and services at time t_1 (one year later) £1,030 is needed. To compensate the investor for impatience to consume and inflation the investment needs to generate a return of 5.06 per cent, that is:

$$(1 + 0.02)(1 + 0.03) - 1 = 0.0506$$

The figure of 5.06 per cent may be regarded here as the **risk-free return (RFR)**, the interest rate which is sufficient to induce investment assuming no uncertainty about cash flows.

Investors tend to view lending to reputable governments through the purchase of bonds or bills as the nearest they are going to get to risk-free investing, because these institutions have an almost unlimited ability to raise income from taxes or to create money. The RFR forms the bedrock for time value of money calculations as the pure time value and the expected inflation rate affect all investments equally. Whether the investment is in property, bonds, shares or a factory, if expected inflation rises from 3 per cent to 5 per cent then the investor's required return on all investments will increase by 2 per cent.

However, different investment categories carry different degrees of uncertainty about the outcome of the investment. For instance, an investment on the Russian stock market, with its high volatility, may be regarded as more risky than the purchase of a share in BP with its steady growth prospects. Investors require different **risk premiums** on top of the RFR to reflect the perceived level of extra risk. Thus:

Required return = RFR + Risk premium
(Time value of money)

In the case of Mrs Ann Investor, the risk premium pushes up the total return required to, say, 10 per cent, thus giving full compensation for all three elements of the time value of money.

Discounted cash flow

The net present value and internal rate of return techniques, both being **discounted cash flow** methods, take into account the time value of money. **Exhibit 2.3**, which presents Project Alpha, suggests that on a straightforward analysis, Project Alpha generates more cash inflows than outflows. An outlay of £2,000 produces £2,400.

Exhibit 2.3 Project Alpha, simple cash flow

Points in time (yearly intervals)	Cash flows (£)
0 Now	−2,000
1 (1 year from now)	+600
2	+600
3	+600
4	+600

However, we may be foolish to accept Project Alpha on the basis of this crude methodology. The £600 cash flows occur at different times and are therefore worth different amounts to a person standing at time zero. Quite naturally, such an individual would value the £600 received in one year more highly than the £600 received after four years. In other words, the present value of the pounds (at time zero) depends on when they are received.

It would be useful to convert all these different 'qualities' of pounds to a common currency, to some sort of common denominator. The conversion process is achieved by **discounting** all future cash flows by the time value of money, thereby expressing them as an equivalent amount received at time zero. The process of discounting relies on a variant of the **compounding** formula:

$$F = P(1 + i)^n$$

where F = future value
P = present value
i = interest rate
n = number of years over which compounding takes place

Note It will be most important for many readers to turn to Appendix 2.1 at the end of this chapter at this point to get to grips with the key mathematical tools which will be used in this chapter and throughout the rest of the book. Readers are also strongly advised to attempt the Appendix 2.1 exercises (answers for which are provided in Appendix VI at the end of the book).

If a saver deposited £100 in a bank account paying interest at 8 per cent per annum, after three years the account will contain £125.97:

$$F = 100\,(1 + 0.08)^3 = £125.97$$

This formula can be changed so that we can answer the following question: 'How much must I deposit in the bank now to receive £125.97 in three years?' We need to rearrange the formula so that we are calculating for present value, *P*.

$$P = \frac{F}{(1+i)^n} \text{ or } F \times \frac{1}{(1+i)^n}$$

$$P = \frac{125.97}{(1+0.08)^3} = 100$$

In this second case we have discounted the £125.97 back to a present value of £100. If this technique is now applied to Project Alpha to convert all the money cash flows of future years into their present value equivalents the result is as follows (assuming that the time value of money is 10 per cent) – *see* **Exhibit 2.4**.

Exhibit 2.4 Project Alpha, discounted cash flow

Points in time (yearly intervals)	Cash flows (£)	Discounted cash flows (£)	
0	−2,000		−2,000.00
1	+600	$\frac{600}{1+0.10}$	= +545.45
2	+600	$\frac{600}{(1+0.10)^2}$	= +495.87
3	+600	$\frac{600}{(1+0.10)^3}$	= +450.79
4	+600	$\frac{600}{(1+0.10)^4}$	= +409.81

We can see that, when these future pounds are converted to a common denominator, this investment involves a larger outflow (£2,000) than inflow (£1,901.92). In other words the return on the £2,000 is less than 10 per cent.

Technical aside

If your calculator has a 'powers' function (usually represented by x^y or y^x) then compounding and discounting can be accomplished relatively quickly. Alternatively, you may obtain discount factors from the table in Appendix II at the end of the book. If we take the discounting of the fourth year's cash flow for Alpha as an illustration:

$$\frac{1}{(1+0.10)^4} \times 600$$

Calculator: Input 1.10
Press y^x (or x^y)
Input 4
Press =
Display 1.4641
Press $^1/_x$
Display 0.6830
Multiply by 600
Answer 409.81

Using Appendix II, look down the column 10% and along the row 4 years to find discount factor of 0.683:

0.683 × £600 = £409.81

Net present value and internal rate of return

Net present value: examples and definitions

The conceptual justification for, and the mathematics of, the net present value and internal rate of return methods of project appraisal will be illustrated through an imaginary but realistic decision-making process at the firm of Hard Decisions plc. This example, in addition to describing techniques, demonstrates the centrality of some key concepts such as opportunity cost and time value of money and shows the wealth-destroying effect of ignoring these issues.

Imagine you are the finance director of a large publicly quoted company called Hard Decisions plc. The board of directors have agreed that the objective of the firm should be shareholder wealth maximisation. Recently, the board appointed a new director, Mr Brightspark, as an 'ideas' man. He has a reputation as someone who can see opportunities where others see only problems. He has been hired especially to seek out new avenues for expansion and make better use of existing assets. In the past few weeks Mr Brightspark has been looking at some land that the company owns near the centre of Birmingham. This is a ten-acre site on which the flagship factory of the firm once stood; but that was 30 years ago and the site is now derelict. Mr Brightspark announces to a board meeting that he has three alternative proposals concerning the ten-acre site.

Mr Brightspark stands up to speak: Proposal 1 is to spend £5m clearing the site, cleaning it up, and decontaminating it. [The factory that stood on the site was used for chemical production.] It would then be possible to sell the ten acres to property developers for a sum of £12m in one year's time. Thus, we will make a profit of £7m over a one-year period.

Proposal 1: Clean up and sell – Mr Brightspark's figures

Clearing the site plus decontamination, payable t_0	–£5m
Sell the site in one year, t_1	£12m
Profit	£7m

The chairman of the board stops Mr Brightspark at that point and turns to you, in your capacity as the financial expert on the board, to ask what you think of the first proposal. Because you have studied assiduously on your financial management course you are able to make the following observations:

Point 1 This company is valued by the stock market at £100m because our investors are content that the rate of return they receive from us is consistent with the going rate for our risk class of shares; that is, 15 per cent per annum. In other words, the opportunity cost for our shareholders of buying shares in this firm is 15 per cent. (Hard Decisions is an all-equity firm, no debt capital has been raised.) The alternative to investing their money with us is to invest it in another firm with similar risk characteristics yielding 15 per cent per annum. Thus, we may take this **opportunity cost of capital** as our minimum required return from any project we undertake. This idea of opportunity cost can perhaps be better explained by the use of a diagram (*see* **Exhibit 2.5**).

If we give a return of less than 15 per cent then shareholders will lose out because they can obtain 15 per cent elsewhere and will, thus, suffer an opportunity cost.

We, as managers of shareholders' money, need to use a discount rate of 15 per cent for any project of the same risk class that we analyse. The discount rate is the opportunity cost of investing in the project rather than the capital markets, for example, buying shares in other firms giving a 15 per cent return. Instead of accepting this project the firm can always give the cash to the shareholders and let them invest it in financial assets.

Point 2 I believe I am right in saying that we have received numerous offers for the ten-acre site over the past year. A reasonable estimate of its immediate sale value would be £6m. That is, I could call up one of the firms keen to get its hands on the site and squeeze out a price of about £6m. This

Exhibit 2.5 The investment decision: alternative uses of firm's funds

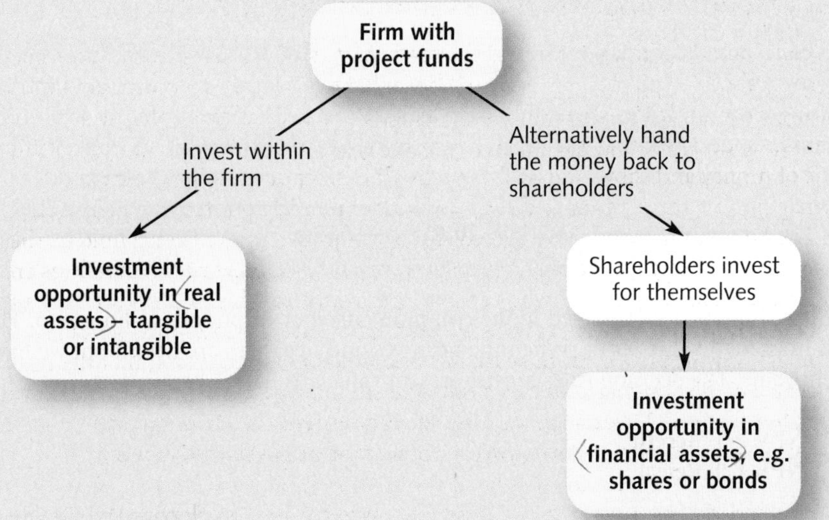

£6m is an opportunity cost of the project, in that it is the value of the best alternative course of action. Thus, we should add to Mr Brightspark's £5m of clean-up costs the £6m of opportunity cost because we are truly sacrificing £11m to put this proposal into operation. If we did not go ahead with Mr Brightspark's proposal, but sold the site as it is, we could raise our bank balance by £6m, plus the £5m saved by not paying clean-up costs.

Proposal 1: Clean up and sell – Year t_0 cash flows

Immediate sale value (opportunity cost)	£6m
Clean-up, etc.	£5m
Total sacrifice at t_0	£11m

Point 3 I can accept Mr Brightspark's final sale price of £12m as being valid in the sense that he has, I know, employed some high-quality experts to derive the figure, but I do have a problem with comparing the initial outlay *directly* with the final cash flow on a simple *nominal* sum basis. The £12m is to be received in one year's time, whereas the £5m is to be handed over to the clean-up firm immediately, and the £6m opportunity cost sacrifice, by not selling the site, is being made immediately.

If we were to take the £11m initial cost of the project and invest it in financial assets of the same risk class as this firm, giving a return of 15 per cent, then the value of that investment at the end of one year would be £12.65m. The calculation for this:

$$F = P(1 + k)$$

where k = the opportunity cost of capital:

$$11\,(1 + 0.15) = £12.65\text{m}$$

This is more than the return promised by Mr Brightspark.

Another way of looking at this problem is to calculate the **net present value** of the project. We start with the classic formula for net present value:

$$NPV = CF_0 + \frac{CF_1}{(1+k)^n}$$

where CF_0 = cash flow at time zero (t_0), and
CF_1 = cash flow at time one (t_1), one year after time zero:

$$NPV = -11 + \frac{12}{1+0.15} = -11 + 10.435 = -0.565\text{m}$$

All cash flows are expressed in the common currency of pounds at time zero. Thus, everything is in present value terms. When the positives and negatives are netted out we have the *net* present value. The decision rules for net present value are:

NPV ≥ 0 Accept
NPV < 0 Reject

Project proposal 1's negative NPV indicates that a return of less than 15 per cent per annum will be achieved.

An investment proposal's net present value is derived by discounting the future net cash receipts at a rate which reflects the value of the alternative use of the funds, summing them over the life of the proposal and deducting the initial outlay.

In conclusion, Ladies and Gentlemen, given the choice between:

(a) selling the site immediately raising £6m and saving £5m of expenditure – a total of £11m, or
(b) developing the site along the lines of Mr Brightspark's proposal,

I would choose to sell it immediately because £11m would get a better return elsewhere.

The chairman thanks you and asks Mr Brightspark to explain Project proposal 2.

Proposal 2: Office complex – Mr Brightspark's figures

Mr Brightspark: Proposal 2 consists of paying £5m immediately for a clean-up. Then, over the next two years, spending another £14m building an office complex. Tenants would not be found immediately on completion of the building. The office units would be let gradually over the following three years. Finally, when the office complex is fully let, in six years' time, it would be sold to an institution, such as a pension fund, for the sum of £40m (*see* **Exhibit 2.6**).

Mr Brightspark claims an almost doubling of the money invested (£25m invested over the first two years leads to an inflow of £47m).

The chairman turns to you and asks: Is this project really so beneficial to our shareholders?

You reply: The message rammed home to me by my finance textbook was that the best method of assessing whether a project is shareholder wealth enhancing is to discount all its cash flows at the opportunity cost of capital. This will enable a calculation of the net present value of those cash flows.

$$NPV = CF_0 + \frac{CF_1}{1+k} + \frac{CF_2}{(1+k)^2} + \frac{CF_3}{(1+k)^3} \dots + \frac{CF_n}{(1+k)^n}$$

So, given that Mr Brightspark's figures are true cash flows, I can calculate the NPV of Proposal 2 – *see* **Exhibit 2.7**. Note that we again use a 15 per cent discount rate, which implies that this

Exhibit 2.6 Project 2: Mr Brightspark's figures

Points in time (yearly intervals)	Cash flows (£m)	Event	
0 (now)	−5	Clean-up costs	
0 (now)	−6	Opportunity cost	
1	−4	Building cost	
2	−10	Building cost	
3	+1	Net rental income $\frac{1}{4}$ of offices let	
4	+2	Net rental income $\frac{1}{2}$ of offices let	
5	+4	Net rental income All offices let	
6	+40	Office complex sold	
Total	+22	Inflow	£47m
		Outflow	£25m
Profit	£22m		

Note: Mr Brightspark has accepted the validity of your argument about the opportunity cost of the alternative 'project' of selling the land immediately and has quickly added this –£6m to the figures

Exhibit 2.7 Proposal 2: Net present value

Points in time (yearly intervals)	Cash flows (£m)		Discounted cash flows (£m)
0	−5		−5
0	−6		−6
1	−4	$\frac{-4}{(1+0.15)}$	−3.48
2	−10	$\frac{-10}{(1+0.15)^2}$	−7.56
3	1	$\frac{1}{(1+0.15)^3}$	0.66
4	2	$\frac{2}{(1+0.15)^4}$	1.14
5	4	$\frac{4}{(1+0.15)^5}$	1.99
6	40	$\frac{40}{(1+0.15)^6}$	17.29
Net present value			−0.96

(An Excel spreadsheet version of this calculation is shown at www.pearsoned.co.uk/arnold)

project is at the same level of risk as project 1 and the same as the average of the existing set of risk projects carried out by the firm. If it is subject to higher risk an increased rate of return would be demanded (the calculation of the required rate of return is discussed in Chapter 19).

Proposal 2: Net present value

Because the NPV is less than 0, we would serve our shareholders better by selling the site and saving the money spent on clearing and building and putting that money into financial assets yielding 15 per cent per annum. Shareholders would end up with more in Year 6.

The chairman thanks you and asks Mr Brightspark for his third proposal.

Proposal 3: Worldbeater manufacturing plant

Mr Brightspark: Proposal 3 involves the use of the site for a factory to manufacture the product 'Worldbeater'. We have been producing 'Worldbeater' from our Liverpool factory for the past ten years. Despite its name, we have confined the selling of it to the UK market. I propose the setting up of a second 'Worldbeater' factory which will serve the European market. The figures are as follows (*see* **Exhibit 2.8**).

Exhibit 2.8 Proposal 3: Mr Brightspark's figures

Points in time (yearly intervals)	Cash flows (£m)	Event
0	-5	Clean-up
0	-6	Opportunity cost
1	-10	Factory building
2	0	
3 to infinity	+5	Net income from additional sales of 'Worldbeater'

Note: Revenue is gained in Year 2 from sales but this is exactly offset by the cash flows created by the costs of production and distribution. The figures for Year 3 and all subsequent years are net cash flows, that is, cash outflows are subtracted from cash inflows generated by sales.

The chairman turns to you and asks your advice.

You reply: Worldbeater is a well-established product and has been very successful. I am happy to take the cash flow figures given by Mr Brightspark as the basis for my calculations, which are set out in **Exhibit 2.9**.

This project gives an NPV that is positive, and therefore is shareholder wealth enhancing. The third project gives a rate of return which is greater than 15 per cent per annum. It provides a return of 15 per cent plus a present value of £5.5m. Based on these figures I would recommend that the board looks into Proposal 3 in more detail.

The chairman thanks you and suggests that this proposal be put to the vote.

Mr Brightspark (interrupts): Just a minute, are we not taking a lot on trust here? Our finance expert has stated that the way to evaluate these proposals is by using the NPV method, but in the firms where I have worked in the past, the internal rate of return (IRR) method of investment appraisal was used. I would like to see how these three proposals shape up when the IRR calculations are done.

The chairman turns to you and asks you to explain the IRR method, and to apply it to the figures provided by Mr Brightspark.

Exhibit 2.9 **Proposal 3: Net present value**

Points in time (yearly intervals)	Cash flows (£m)		Discounted cash flows (£m)
0	−11		−11
1	−10	$\frac{-10}{(1+0.15)}$	−8.7
2	0		
3 to infinity	5	Value of perpetuity at time t_2: $P = \frac{F}{k} = \frac{5}{0.15} = 33.33.$ This has to be discounted back two years: $\frac{33.33}{(1+0.15)^2}$	= 25.20
Net present value			+5.5

(An Excel spreadsheet version of this calculation is shown at www.pearsoned.co.uk/arnold)
Note: If these calculations are confusing you are advised to read the mathematical Appendix 2.1 at the end of this chapter.

Note

The perpetuity formula $\left(\frac{F}{k}\right)$ can be used on the assumption that the first payment arises one year from the time at which we are valuing. So, if the first inflow arises at time 3 we are valuing the perpetuity as though we are standing at time 2. The objective of this exercise is not to convert all cash flows to time 2 values, but rather to time 0 value. Therefore, it is necessary to discount the perpetuity value by two years.

Before continuing this boardroom drama it might be useful at this point to broaden the understanding of NPV by considering two worked examples.

Worked example 2.1 **Camarat plc**

Camrat plc requires a return on investment of at least 10 per cent per annum over the life of any proposed project with the same risk as its existing projects in order to meet the opportunity cost of its shareholders (Camrat is financed entirely by equity). The dynamic and thrusting strategic development team have been examining the possibility of entering the new market area of mosaic floor tiles. This will require an immediate outlay of £1m for factory purchase and tooling-up which will be followed by *net* (i.e. after all cash outflows, e.g. wages, variable costs, etc.) cash inflows of £0.2m in one year, and £0.3m in two years' time. Thereafter, annual net cash inflows will be £180,000.

Required

Given these cash flows, will this investment provide a 10 per cent return (per annum) over the life of the project? Assume for simplicity that all cash flows arise on anniversary dates.

Answer

First, lay out the cash flows with precise timing. (Note: the assumption that all cash flows arise on anniversary dates allows us to do this very simply.)

Points in time (yearly intervals)	0	1	2	3 to infinity
Cash flows (£)	−1m	0.2m	0.3m	0.18m

Second, discount these cash flows to their present value equivalents.

Points in time	0	1	2	3 to infinity
	CF_0	$\frac{CF_1}{1+k}$	$\frac{CF_2}{(1+k)^2}$	$\frac{CF_3}{k} \times \frac{1}{(1+k)^2}$
	−1m	$\frac{0.2}{1+0.1}$	$\frac{0.3}{(1+0.1)^2}$	$\frac{0.18}{0.1}$
				This discounts back two years: $\frac{0.18/0.1}{(1+0.1)^2}$
	−1m	0.1818	0.2479	$\frac{1.8}{(1.1)^2} = 1.4876$

Third, net out the discounted cash flows to give the net present value.

	−1.0000
	+0.1818
	+0.2479
	+1.4876
Net present value	+0.9173

Conclusion

The positive NPV result demonstrates that this project gives not only a return of 10 per cent per annum but a large surplus above and beyond a 10 per cent per annum return. This is an extremely attractive project: on a £1m investment the surplus generated beyond the opportunity cost of the shareholders (their time value of money) is £917,300; thus by accepting this project we would increase shareholder wealth by this amount.

Worked example 2.2 Actarm plc

Actarm plc is examining two projects, A and B. The cash flows are as follows:

	A £	B £
Initial outflow, t_0	240,000	240,000
Cash inflows:		
Time 1 (one year after t_0)	200,000	20,000
Time 2	100,000	120,000
Time 3	20,000	220,000

Using discount rates of 8 per cent, and then 16 per cent, calculate the NPVs and state which project is superior. Why do you get a different preference depending on the discount rate used?

Answer

Using 8 per cent as the discount rate

$$NPV = CF_0 + \frac{CF_1}{1+k} + \frac{CF_2}{(1+k)^2} + \frac{CF_3}{(1+k)^3}$$

Project A

$$-240{,}000 + \frac{200{,}000}{1 + 0.08} + \frac{100{,}000}{(1 + 0.08)^2} + \frac{20{,}000}{(1 + 0.08)^3}$$

$$-240{,}000 + 185{,}185 + 85{,}734 + 15{,}877 = +£46{,}796$$

Project B

$$-240{,}000 + \frac{20{,}000}{1 + 0.08} + \frac{120{,}000}{(1 + 0.08)^2} + \frac{220{,}000}{(1 + 0.08)^3}$$

$$-240{,}000 + 18{,}519 + 102{,}881 + 174{,}643 = +£56{,}043$$

Using an 8 per cent discount rate both projects produce positive NPVs and therefore would enhance shareholder wealth. However, Project B is superior because it creates more value than Project A. Thus, if the accepting of one project excludes the possibility of accepting the other then B is preferred.

Using 16 per cent as the discount rate

Project A

$$-240{,}000 + \frac{200{,}000}{1.16} + \frac{100{,}000}{(1.16)^2} + \frac{20{,}000}{(1.16)^3}$$

$$-240{,}000 + 172{,}414 + 74{,}316 + 12{,}813 = +£19{,}543$$

Project B

$$-240{,}000 + \frac{20{,}000}{1.16} + \frac{120{,}000}{(1.16)^2} + \frac{220{,}000}{(1.16)^3}$$

$$-240{,}000 + 17{,}241 + 89{,}180 + 140{,}945 = +£7{,}366$$

With a 16 per cent discount rate Project A generates more shareholder value and so would be preferred to Project B. This is despite the fact that Project B, in pure undiscounted cash flow terms, produces an additional £40,000.

The different ranking (order of superiority) occurs because Project B has the bulk of its cash flows occurring towards the end of the project's life. These large distant cash flows, when discounted at a high discount rate, become relatively small compared with those of Project A, which has its high cash flows discounted by only one year.

(An Excel spreadsheet showing these calculations is available at www.pearsoned.co.uk/arnold)

NPV is used by many people besides corporate finance teams. For example, as **Exhibit 2.10** shows, stockbrokers sometimes calculate NPV to help estimate share values.

Internal rate of return

We now return to Hard Decisions plc. The chairman has asked you to explain internal rate of return (IRR).

You respond: The **internal rate of return** is a very popular method of project appraisal and it has much to commend it. In particular it takes into account the time value of money. I am not surprised to find that Mr Brightspark has encountered this appraisal technique in his previous employment. Basically, what the IRR tells you is the rate of return you will receive by putting your money into a project. It describes by how much the cash inflows exceed the cash outflows on an annualised percentage basis, taking account of the timing of those cash flows.

The internal rate of return is the rate of return which equates the present value of future cash flows with the outlay (or, for some projects, it equates discounted future cash outflows with initial inflow):

Outlay = Future cash flows discounted at rate *r*

Exhibit 2.10

Egdon egged on by positive gas storage tests

FT

By Neil Hume and Robert Orr

Egdon Resources jumped 36 per cent to 134½p as tests showed its site on the Isle of Portland in Dorset could be used as a giant underground gas storage facility. There is a shortage of such facilities in the UK, which stores only enough gas to last 12 days compared with 91 days in France or 77 days in Germany. Although Egdon needs to apply for planning permission, house broker Seymour Pierce said the facility had a **net present value** equivalent to 341p a share and said it had 'no hesitation' in reiterating a 'buy' rating.

Source: Financial Times, 29 June 2006, p. 42. Reprinted with permission.

Thus:

$$CF_0 = \frac{CF_1}{1+r} + \frac{CF_2}{(1+r)^2} + \frac{CF_3}{(1+r)^3} \cdots \frac{CF_n}{(1+r)^n}$$

IRR is also referred to as the 'yield' of a project. NPV = 0

Alternatively, the internal rate of return, r, is the discount rate at which the net present value is zero. It is the value for r which makes the following equation hold:

$$CF_0 + \frac{CF_1}{1+r} + \frac{CF_2}{(1+r)^2} + \frac{CF_3}{(1+r)^3} \cdots \frac{CF_n}{(1+r)^n} = 0$$

(*Note*: in the first formula CF_0 is expressed as a positive number, whereas in the second it is usually a negative.)

These two equations amount to the same thing. They both require knowledge of the cash flows and their precise timing. The element which is unknown is the rate of return which will make the time-adjusted outflows and inflows equal to each other.

I apologise, Ladies and Gentlemen, if this all sounds like too much jargon. Perhaps it would be helpful if you could see the IRR calculation in action. Let's apply the formula to Mr Brightspark's Proposal 1.

Proposal 1: Internal rate of return

Using the second version of the formula, our objective is to find an r which makes the discounted inflow at time 1 of £12m plus the initial £11m outflow equal to zero:

$$CF_0 + \frac{CF_1}{1+r} = 0$$

$$-11 + \frac{12}{1+r} = 0$$

The method I would recommend for establishing r is trial and error (assuming we do not have the relevant computer program available). So, to start with, simply pick a discount rate and plug it into the formula. (You can pick any (reasonable) discount rate to begin with in the trial and error approach.)

Let us try 5 per cent:

$$-11 + \frac{12}{1+0.05} = £0.42857\text{m or } £428,571$$

A 5 per cent rate is not correct because the discounted cash flows do not total to zero. The surplus of approximately £0.43m suggests that a higher interest rate will be more suitable. This will reduce the present value of the future cash inflow.

Try 10 per cent:

$$-11 + \frac{12}{1 + 0.1} = -0.0909 \text{ or } -£90{,}909$$

Again, we have not hit on the correct discount rate.

Try 9 per cent:

$$-11 + \frac{12}{1 + 0.09} = +0.009174 \text{ or } +£9{,}174$$

The last two calculations tell us that the discount rate which causes the discounted future cash flow to equal the inital outflow lies somewhere between 9 per cent and 10 per cent. The precise rate can be found through interpolation.

Interpolation for Proposal 1

First, display all the facts so far established (*see* **Exhibit 2.11**).

Exhibit 2.11 Interpolation

Discount rate	9%	?	10%
Net present value	+£9,174	0	–£90,909
Point	A	B	C

Exhibit 2.11 illustrates that there is a yield rate (r) which lies between 9 per cent and 10 per cent which will produce an NPV of zero. The way to find that discount rate is to first find the distance between points A and B as a proportion of the entire distance between points A and C.

$$\frac{A \rightarrow B}{A \rightarrow C} = \frac{9{,}174 - 0}{9{,}174 + 90{,}909} = 0.0917$$

Thus the ? lies at a distance of 0.0917 away from the 9 per cent point.

Thus, IRR:

$$= 9 + \left(\frac{9{,}174}{100{,}083}\right) \times (10 - 9) = 9.0917 \text{ per cent}$$

To double-check our result:

$$-11 + \frac{12}{1 + 0.090917}$$

$$-11 + 11 = 0$$

Internal rate of return: examples and definitions

The rule for internal rate of return decisions is:

If $k > r$ reject

If the opportunity cost of capital (k) is greater than the internal rate of return (r) on a project then the investor is better served by not going ahead with the project and applying the money to the best alternative use.

If $k \leq r$ accept

Here, the project under consideration produces the same or a higher yield than investment elsewhere for a similar risk level.

The IRR of Proposal 1 is 9.091 per cent, which is below the 15 per cent opportunity cost of capital used by Hard Decisions plc for projects of this risk class. Therefore, using the IRR method as well as the NPV method, this project should be rejected.

It might be enlightening to consider the relationship between NPV and IRR. **Exhibits 2.12** and **2.13** show what happens to NPV as the discount rate is varied between zero and 10 per cent for

Exhibit 2.12 The relationship between NPV and the discount rate (using Proposal 1's figures)

Discount rate (%)	NPV
10	–90,909
9.0917	0
9	9,174
8	111,111
7	214,953
6	320,755
5	428,571
4	538,461
3	650,485
2	764,706
1	881,188
0	1,000,000

Exhibit 2.13 The relationship between NPV and the discount rate for Project proposal 1

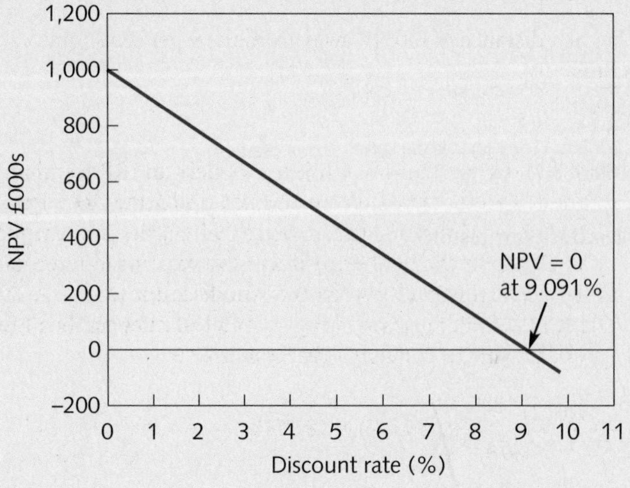

Proposal 1. At a zero discount rate the £12m received in one year is not discounted at all, so the NPV of £1m is simply the difference between the two cash flows. When the discount rate is raised to 10 per cent the present value of the year 1 cash flow becomes less than the current outlay. Where the line crosses the *x* axis, i.e. when NPV is zero, we can read off the internal rate of return.

It should be noted that in the case of Project proposal 1 the NPV/discount rate relationship is nearly a straight line. This is an unusual case. When cash flows occur over a number of years the line is likely to be more curved and concave to the origin.

If the board will bear with me I can quickly run through the IRR calculations for Project proposals 2 and 3.

Proposal 2: IRR

To calculate the IRR for Proposal 2 we first lay out the cash flows in the discount formula:

$$-11 + \frac{-4}{(1+r)} + \frac{-10}{(1+r)^2} + \frac{1}{(1+r)^3}$$

$$+ \frac{2}{(1+r)^4} + \frac{4}{(1+r)^5} + \frac{40}{(1+r)^6} = 0$$

Then we try alternative discount rates to find a rate, *r*, that gives a zero NPV:

Try 14 per cent:

NPV (approx.) = –£0.043 or –£43,000

At 13 per cent:

NPV = £932,000

Interpolation is required to find an internal rate of return accurate to at least one decimal place (*see* **Exhibit 2.14**).

Exhibit 2.14 Interpolation

Discount rate	13%	?	14%
NPV	+932,000	0	–43,000

$$13 + \frac{932{,}000}{975{,}000} \times (14 - 13) = 13.96\%$$

From **Exhibit 2.15**, we see that this project produces an IRR less than the opportunity cost of shareholders' funds; therefore it should be rejected under the IRR method. The curvature of the line is exaggerated to demonstrate the absence of linearity and emphasise the importance of having a fairly small gap in trial and error interest rates prior to interpolation. The interpolation formula assumes a straight line between the two discount rates chosen and this may lead to a false result. The effect of taking a wide range of interest rates can be illustrated if we calculate on the basis of 5 per cent and 30 per cent – *see* **Exhibit 2.16**.

$$5 + \left(\frac{11.6121}{11.6121 + 9.4743}\right)(30 - 5) = 18.77\%$$

Exhibit 2.15 Graph of NPV for Proposal 2

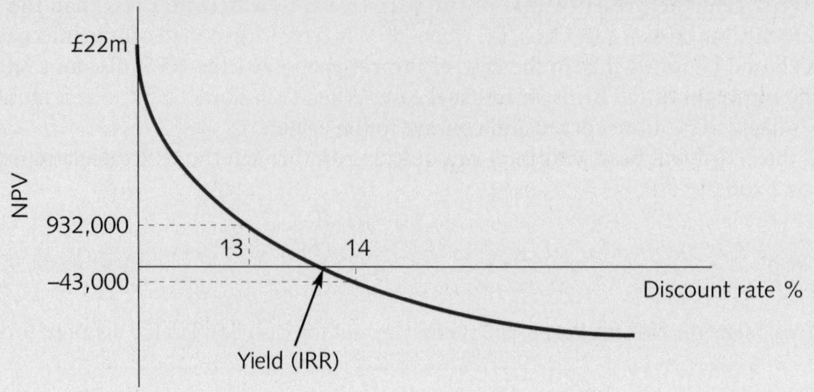

(An Excel spreadsheet showing the IRR calculation for proposal 2 is available at www.pearsoned.co.uk/Arnold)

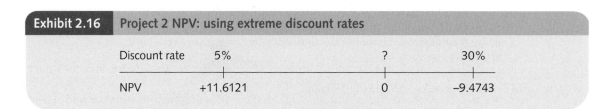

Exhibit 2.16 Project 2 NPV: using extreme discount rates

Discount rate	5%	?	30%
NPV	+11.6121	0	–9.4743

From **Exhibit 2.17** we see that the non-linearity of the relationship between NPV and the discount rate has created an IRR almost 5 per cent removed from the true IRR. This could lead to an erroneous acceptance of this project given the company's hurdle rate of 15 per cent. In reality this project yields less than the company could earn by placing its money elsewhere for the same risk level.

Exhibit 2.17 The accuracy of the IRR calculated may depend on the size of the gap between the discount rates used in the interpolation calculation

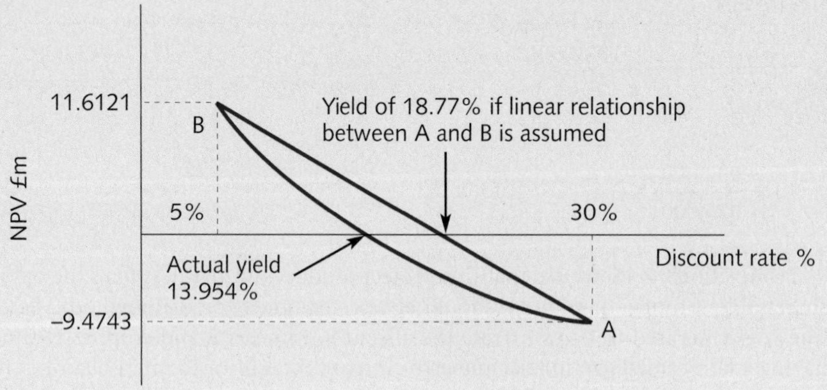

Proposal 3: IRR

$$CF_0 + \frac{CF_1}{1+r} + \frac{CF_3/r}{(1+r)^2} = 0$$

Try 19 per cent:

$$-11 + \frac{-10}{1 + 0.19} + \frac{5/0.19}{(1 + 0.19)^2} = -£0.82\text{m}$$

Try 18 per cent:

$$-11 + \frac{-10}{1 + 0.18} + \frac{5/0.18}{(1 + 0.18)^2} = £0.475\text{m}$$

Exhibit 2.18 Linear interpolation

Discount rate	18%	?	19%
NPV	+475,000	0	–820,000

(An Excel spreadsheet showing the IRR calculation for proposed project 3 is available at www.pearsoned.co.uk/arnold)

$$18 + \frac{475{,}000}{1{,}295{,}000} \times (19 - 18) = 18.37\%$$

Project 3 produces an internal rate of return of 18.37 per cent which is higher than the opportunity cost of capital and therefore is to be commended.

We temporarily leave the saga of Mr Brightspark and his proposals to reinforce understanding of NPV and IRR through the worked example of Martac plc.

Worked example 2.3 Martac plc

Martac plc is a manufacturer of *Martac-aphro*. Two new automated process machines used in the production of *Martac-aphro* have been introduced to the market, the CAM and the ATR. Both will give cost savings over existing processes:

£000s	CAM	ATR
Initial cost (machine purchase and installation, etc.)	120	250
Cash flow savings:		
At Time 1 (one year after the initial cash outflow)	48	90
At Time 2	48	90
At Time 3	48	90
At Time 4	48	90

All other factors remain constant and the firm has access to large amounts of capital. The required return on projects is 8 per cent. Production ceases after four years and the machines will then have a zero scrap value.

Required

(a) Calculate the IRR for CAM.
(b) Calculate the IRR for ATR.
(c) Based on IRR which machine would you purchase?
(d) Calculate the NPV for each machine.
(e) Based on NPV which machine would you buy?
(f) Is IRR or NPV the better decision tool?

Answers

In this problem the total cash flows associated with the alternative projects are not given. Instead the incremental cash flows are provided, for example, the additional savings available over the existing costs of production. This, however, is sufficient for a decision to be made about which machine to purchase.

(a) IRR for CAM

$$CF_0 + \frac{CF_1}{1+r} + \frac{CF_2}{(1+r)^2} + \frac{CF_3}{(1+r)^3} + \frac{CF_4}{(1+r)^4} = 0$$

Try 22 per cent:

$$-120{,}000 + 48{,}000 \times \text{annuity factor (af) for 4 years @ } 22\%$$

(*See* Appendix 2.1 to this chapter for annuity calculations and Appendix III at the end of the book for an annuity table.)

The annuity factor tells us the present value of four lots of £1 received at four annual intervals. This is 2.4936, meaning that the £4 in present value terms is worth just over £2.49.

$$-120{,}000 + 48{,}000 \times 2.4936 = -£307.20$$

Try 21 per cent:

$$-120{,}000 + 48{,}000 \times \text{annuity factor (af) for 4 years @ } 21\%$$

$$-120{,}000 + 48{,}000 \times 2.5404 = +£1{,}939.20$$

See **Exhibit 2.19**.

Exhibit 2.19 Interpolation

Discount rate	21%	?	22%
NPV	1,939.2	0	−307

$$21 + \left(\frac{1939.2}{1939.2 + 307}\right) \times (22 - 21) = 21.86\%$$

(b) IRR for ATR

Try 16 per cent:

$$-250{,}000 + 90{,}000 \times 2.7982 = +£1{,}838$$

Try 17 per cent:

$$-250{,}000 + 90{,}000 \times 2.7432 = -£3{,}112$$

See **Exhibit 2.20**.

Exhibit 2.20 Interpolation

Discount rate	16%	?	17%
NPV	+1,838	0	−3,112

$$16 + \left(\frac{1{,}838}{1{,}838 + 3{,}112}\right) \times (17 - 16) = 16.37\%$$

(c) Choice of machine on basis of IRR

If IRR is the only decision tool available then as long as the IRRs exceed the discount rate (or cost of capital) the project with the higher IRR might appear to be the preferred choice. In this case CAM ranks higher than ATR.

(d) NPV for machines: CAM

$$-120{,}000 + 48{,}000 \times 3.3121 = +\pounds 38{,}981$$

NPV for ATR

$$-250{,}000 + 90{,}000 \times 3.3121 = +\pounds 48{,}089$$

(e) Choice of machine on basis of NPV

ATR generates a return which has a present value of £48,089 in addition to the minimum return on capital required. This is larger than for CAM and therefore ATR ranks higher than CAM if NPV is used as the decision tool.

(f) Choice of decision tool

This problem has produced conflicting decision outcomes, which depend on the project appraisal method employed. NPV is the better decision-making technique because it measures in absolute amounts of money. That is, it gives the increase in shareholder wealth available by accepting a project. In contrast IRR expresses its return as a percentage which may result in an inferior low-scale project being preferred to a higher-scale project.

(An Excel spreadsheet showing this calculation is shown at www.pearsoned.co.uk/arnold)

Exhibit 2.21 illustrates a practical use of IRR ('private finance initiative' is a scheme whereby private companies design, build, maintain and operate hospitals etc. for the government. 'Refinancing' is where, once the project is producing a stable cashflow, the loans used to start the project can be replaced with cheaper (lower interest) debt and more of it, allowing the shareholder to take money out, e.g. by paying dividends.)

Exhibit 2.21

Storm over 'unacceptable gains' from PFI spreads to the secondary market

FT

Nicholas Timmins

Some of the biggest operators in the private finance initiative were condemned yesterday, for making gains that are 'unacceptable, even for an early PFI deal' from the refinancing of Norfolk and Norwich hospital.

David Metter, the chief executive of Innisfree, which has a 25 per cent stake in the Norfolk and Norwich hospital project, defended the refinancing. It was an early deal, said Mr Metter, struck in 1998 when interest rates were much higher and banks saw the PFI as much riskier than they do now.

That combination of circumstances, he said, had indeed 'given rise to some very large refinancing gains of which Norfolk and Norwich was one'.

But those big gains – £95m for the Octagon consortium, which built and runs the hospital, after it had given the hospital a £34m share under the Treasury's voluntary code of conduct had to be offset against losses elsewhere, he said.

He noted that John Laing, a member of the Octagon consortium, had lost £80m on the PFI contract for the National Physical Laboratory, a loss that contributed to the destruction of its construction arm.

Forty-seven refinancings have resulted in internal rates of return for the private investors ranging from a mere 10 per cent to more than 70 per cent on Debden Park school and the Bromley PFI hospital and to returns of 56 and 60 per cent on the Darent Valley and Norfolk and Norwich hospitals respectively.

Source: Financial Times 3 May 2006. Reprinted with permission.

Exhibit 2.21 Continued

Return to investors

Project	Projected internal rate of return to investors: At contract letting (%)	Projected internal rate of return to investors: Just after the refinancing (%)	Substantial increase on borrowings at time of refinancing
Norfolk & Norwich Hospital	**19**	**60**	Yes
Darent Valley Hospital	**21**	**56**	Yes
Fazakerley Prison	**13**	**39**	No
Ministry of Defence: Joint Services Command and Staff College	**18**	**31**	Yes

Shareholders in octagon
(Norfolk and Norwich)
Percent

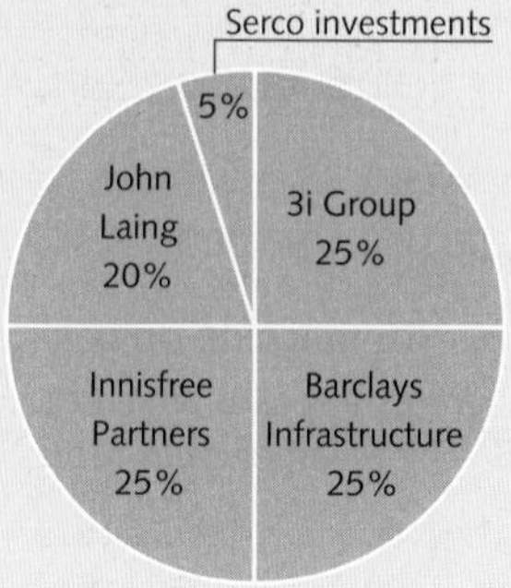

Source: Committee of Public Accounts

Problems with internal rate of return

We now return to Hard Decisions plc.

Mr Brightspark: I have noticed your tendency to prefer NPV to any other method. Yet, in the three projects we have been discussing, NPV and IRR give the same decision recommendation. That is, reject Projects 1 and 2 and accept Project 3. So, why not use IRR more often?

You reply: It is true that the NPV and IRR methods of capital investment appraisal are closely related. Both are **'time-adjusted' measures of profitability**. The NPV and IRR methods gave the same result in the cases we have considered today because the problems associated with the IRR method are not present in the figures we have been working with. In the appraisal of other projects we may encounter the severe limitations of the IRR method and therefore I prefer to stick to the theoretically superior NPV technique. IRR方法的局限性

I will illustrate three of the most important problems, **multiple solutions**, **ranking** and confusion between **investing-type decisions** and **financing-type decisions**.

Multiple solutions

There may be a number of possible IRRs. This can be explained by examining the problems Mr Flummoxed is having (*see* Worked example 2.4).

Worked example 2.4 Mr Flummoxed

Mr Flummoxed of Deadhead plc has always used the IRR method of project appraisal. He has started to have doubts about its usefulness after examining the proposal, 'Project Oscillation'.

Project Oscillation

Points in time (yearly intervals)	0	1	2
Cash flow	−3,000	+15,000	−13,000

Internal rates of return are found at 11.56 per cent *and* 288.4 per cent.

Given that Deadhead plc has a required rate of return of 20 per cent, it is impossible to decide whether to implement Project Oscillation using an unadjusted IRR methodology. If there are a number of possible IRRs this means they are all meaningless.

The cause of multiple solutions is **unconventional cash flows**. Conventional cash flows occur when an outflow is followed by a series of inflows or a cash inflow is followed by a series of cash outflows. Unconventional cash flows are a series of cash flows with more than one change in sign. In the case of Project Oscillation the sign changes from negative to positive once, and from positive to negative once. Multiple yields can be adjusted for whilst still using the IRR method, but the simplest approach is to use the NPV method.

Ranking

The IRR decision rule does not always rank projects in the same way as the NPV method. Sometimes it is important to find out, not only which project gives a positive return, but which one gives the greater positive return. For instance, projects may be mutually exclusive, that is, only one may be undertaken and a choice has to be made. The use of IRR alone sometimes leads to a poor choice (*see* **Exhibit 2.22**).

Exhibit 2.22 Illustration of the IRR ranking problem

Project	Cash flows £m Time 0	Cash flows £m One year later	IRR%	NPV (at 15%) £
A	–20	+40	100%	+14.78m
B	–40	+70	75%	+20.87m

NPV at different discount rates

Discount rate (%)	Project A	Project B
0	20	30
20	13.33	18.33
50	6.67	6.67
75	2.86	0
100	0	–5
125	–2.22	–8.89

From **Exhibit 2.23**, it is clear that the ranking of the projects by their IRRs is constant at 75 per cent and 100 per cent, regardless of the opportunity cost of capital (discount rate). Project A is always better. On the other hand, ranking the projects by the NPV method is not fixed. The NPV ranking depends on the discount rate assumed. Thus, if the discount rate used in the NPV calculation is higher than 50 per cent, the ranking under both IRR and NPV would be the same, i.e. Project A is superior. If the discount rate falls below 50 per cent, Project B is the better choice. One of the major elements leading to the theoretical dominance of NPV is that it takes into account the scale of investment; thus the shareholders are made better off by undertaking Project B by £20.87m because the initial size of the project was larger. NPVs are measured in absolute amounts.

Exhibit 2.23 NPV at different discount rates

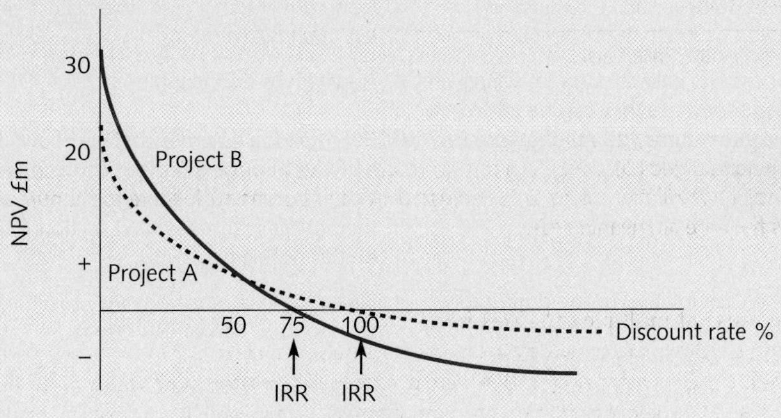

Confusion over investing-type decisions versus financing-type decisions

Hard Decisions plc's Proposal 1 required a cash outflow of £11m at time zero followed by a cash inflow of £12m one year later. This resulted in an IRR of 9.0917 per cent and negative NPV of –£0.565m, thus the project is rejected under both methods given the required rate of return of 15 per cent. This is an investing-type decision, because the initial cash flow is an outflow. Now consider a project that resulted in £11m being *received* at time zero and £12m *flowing out* at time 1 (one year later). Here we have a financing-type decision. You need to be careful in interpreting the results of a financing-type decision IRR. The IRR is again 9.0917 and given the opportunity cost of capital there is a danger of automatically rejecting the project if you have it stuck in your mind that the IRR must exceed 15 per cent for the project to be accepted. This would be wrong because you are being offered the chance to receive £11m, which can then be invested at 15 per cent per year at that risk level. This will outweigh the outflow that occurs at time one of £12m. In other words, this project gives a positive NPV and should be accepted.

$$\text{NPV} = £11\text{m} - £12\text{m}/(1.15) = +£0.565\text{m}$$

This leads us to reverse the IRR rules for a financing-type situation. To avoid confusion use NPV.

Exhibit 2.24 Characteristics of NPV and IRR

NPV	IRR
• It recognises that £1 today is worth more than £1 tomorrow.	• Also takes into account the time value of money.
• In conditions where all worthwhile projects can be accepted (i.e. no mutual exclusivity) it maximises shareholder utility. Projects with a positive NPV should be accepted since they increase shareholder wealth, while those with negative NPVs decrease shareholder wealth.	• In situations of non-mutual exclusivity, shareholder wealth is maximised if all projects with a yield higher than the opportunity cost of capital are accepted, while those with a return less than the time value of money are rejected.
• It takes into account investment size – absolute amounts of wealth change.	• Fails to measure in terms of absolute amounts of wealth changes. It measures percentage returns and this may cause ranking problems in conditions of mutual exclusivity, i.e. the wrong project may be rejected.
• It is not as intuitively understandable as a percentage measure.	• It is easier to communicate a percentage return than NPV to other managers and employees, who may not be familiar with the details of project appraisal techniques. The appeal of quick recognition and conveyance of understanding should not be belittled or underestimated.
• It can handle non-conventional cash flows.	• Non-conventional cash flows cause problems, e.g. multiple solutions.
• **Additivity** is possible: because present values are all measured in today's £s they can be added together. Thus the returns (NPVs) of a group of projects can be calculated.	• Additivity is not possible.
	• IRR implicitly assumes that cashflows received, say halfway through a project, can be invested elsewhere at a rate equal to the IRR until the end of the project's life – see next section for more detail on this problem.
• It assumes that cash inflows arising during the life of a project are reinvested at the opportunity cost of capital – a reasonable assumption.	• Financing-type decisions may result in misinterpretation of IRR results.

The board of directors of Hard Decisions are now ready for a coffee break and time to digest these concepts and techniques. The chairman thanks you for your clarity and rigorous analysis. He also thanks Mr Brightspark for originating three imaginative and thought-provoking proposals to take the business forward towards its goal of shareholder wealth enhancement.

Modified internal rate of return

The fourth characteristic listed for IRR in Exhibit 2.24 is a powerful force driving its adoption in the practical world of business where few individuals have exposed themselves to the rigours of financial decision-making models, and therefore may not comprehend NPV. These issues are examined in more detail in Chapter 4, but it is perhaps worth explaining now the consequences of sticking rigidly to IRR.

One problem centres on the reinvestment assumption. With NPV it is assumed that cash inflows arising during the life of the project are reinvested at the opportunity cost of capital. In contrast the IRR implicitly assumes that the cash inflows that are received, say, half-way through a project, can be reinvested elsewhere at a rate equal to the IRR until the end of the project's life. This is intuitively unacceptable. In the real world, if a firm invested in a very high-yielding project and some cash was returned after a short period, this firm would be unlikely to be able to deposit this cash elsewhere until the end of the project and reach the same extraordinary high yield, and yet this is what the IRR implicitly assumes. The more likely eventuality is that the intra-project cash inflows will be invested at the 'going rate' or the opportunity cost of capital. In other words, the firm's normal discount rate is the better estimate of the reinvestment rate. The effect of this erroneous reinvestment assumption is to inflate the IRR of the project under examination.

For example, Project K below has a very high IRR, at 61.8 per cent; thus the £1,000 received after one year is assumed to be taken back into the firm and then placed in another investment, again yielding 61.8 per cent until time 2. This is obviously absurd: if such an investment existed why has the firm not already invested in it – given its cost of capital of only 15 per cent?

Project K (required rate of return 15 per cent)

Points in time (yearly intervals)	0	1	2
Cash flows (£)	–1,000	+1,000	+1,000

IRR

Try 60 per cent: NPV = 15.63.
Try 62 per cent: NPV = –1.68.

Interpolation

Exhibit 2.25 Project K

Discount rate	60%	?	62%
NPV	15.63	0	–1.68

$$60 + \left(\frac{15.63}{15.63 + 1.68}\right) \times (62 - 60) = 61.8\%$$

The reinvestment assumption of 61.8 per cent, for the £1,000 receivable at time 1, is clearly unrealistic, especially in the light of the fact that most investors can only obtain a return of 15 per cent for taking this level of risk.

The IRR of Project K assumes the following:

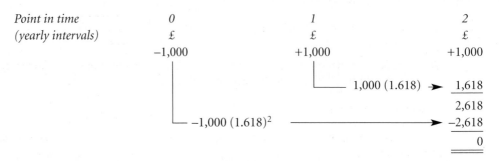

Point in time	*0*	*1*	*2*
(yearly intervals)	£	£	£
	−1,000	+1,000	+1,000
		1,000 (1.618) →	1,618
			2,618
	−1,000 $(1.618)^2$ →		−2,618
			0

The £2,618 compounded cash flows at the terminal date of the project are equivalent to taking the original investment of £1,000 and compounding it for two years at 61.8 per cent. However, an NPV calculation assumes that the intra-project cash inflow is invested at 15 per cent:

Points in time	*0*	*1*	*2*
(yearly intervals)	£	£	£
	−1,000	+1,000.00	+1,000.00
		1,000 (1.15) →	1,150.00
			2,150.00
	−1,000 $(1.15)^2$ →		−1,322.50
			827.50

Discounting £827.50 back two years gives the NPV of £625.71.

If, for reasons of pragmatism or communication within the firm, it is necessary to describe a project appraisal in terms of a percentage, then it is recommended that the **modified internal rate of return (MIRR)** is used. This takes as its starting point the notion that, for the sake of consistency with NPV, any cash inflows arising during the project are reinvested at the opportunity cost of funds. That is, at the rate of return available on the next best alternative use of the funds in either financial or real assets. The MIRR is the rate of return, *m*, which, if used to compound the initial investment amount (the original cash outlay) produces the same terminal value as the project's cash inflows. The value of the project's cash inflows at the end of the project's life after they have been expressed in the terminal date's £s is achieved through compounding at the opportunity cost of funds. In other words, the common currency this time is not time 0 £s, but time 4, or time 6, or time '*n*' £s.

What we are attempting to do is find that rate of compounding which will equate the terminal value of the intra-project cash flows with the terminal value of the initial investment.

Modified internal rate of return for Project K

First, calculate the terminal value of the cash flows excluding the t_0 investment using the opportunity cost of capital.

		Terminal value (£)
t_1 1,000 (1.15)		1,150.00
t_2 1,000	already expressed as a terminal value because it occurs on the date of termination	1,000.00
	Total terminal value	2,150.00

The modified internal rate of return is the rate of compounding applied to the original investment necessary to produce a future (terminal) value of £2,150.00 two years later.

$$1{,}000\,(1 + m)^2 = 2{,}150$$

Solve for *m*. (The mathematical tools – *see* Appendix 2.1 – may be useful here.) Divide both sides of the equation by 1,000:

$$(1 + m)^2 = \frac{2{,}150}{1{,}000}$$

Then, take roots to the power of 2 of both sides of the equation:

$$\sqrt[2]{(1 + m)^2} = \sqrt[2]{\frac{2{,}150}{1{,}000}}$$

$$m = \sqrt[2]{\frac{2{,}150}{1{,}000}} - 1 = 0.466 \text{ or } 46.6\%$$

or more generally:

$$m = \sqrt[n]{\frac{F}{P}} - 1$$

Thus, the MIRR is 46.6 per cent compared with the IRR of 61.8 per cent. In the case of Project K this reduced rate is still very high and the project is accepted under either rule. However, in a number of situations, the calculation of the MIRR may alter the decision given under the IRR method. This is true in the worked example of Switcharound plc for projects Tic and Cit, which are mutually exclusive projects and thus ranking is important.

Worked example 2.5 Switcharound plc

The business development team of Switcharound plc has been working to find uses for a vacated factory. The two projects it has selected for further consideration by senior management both have a life of only three years, because the site will be flattened in three years when a new motorway is constructed. On the basis of IRR the business development team is leaning towards acceptance of Cit but it knows that the key Senior Manager is aware of MIRR and therefore feels it is necessary to present the data calculated through both techniques. The opportunity cost of capital is 10 per cent.

Cash flows

Points in time (yearly intervals)	*0*	*1*	*2*	*3*	*IRR*
Tic (£m)	–1	0.5	0.5	0.5	23.4%
Cit (£m)	–1	1.1	0.1	0.16	27.7%

However, on the basis of MIRR, a different preference emerges.

Tic: MIRR

		Terminal value £m
t_1	$0.5 \times (1.1)^2$	0.605
t_2	0.5×1.1	0.550
t_3	0.5	0.500
Total terminal value		1.655

$$1{,}000{,}000\,(1 + m)^3 = 1{,}655{,}000$$

$$m = \sqrt[n]{\frac{F}{P}} - 1$$

$$m = \sqrt[3]{\frac{1{,}655{,}000}{1{,}000{,}000}} - 1 = 0.183 \text{ or } 18.3\%$$

Cit: MIRR

		Terminal value £m
t_1	$1.1 \times (1.1)^2$	1.331
t_2	0.1×1.1	0.110
t_3	0.16	0.16
Total terminal value		1.601

$$1{,}000{,}000\,(1 + m)^3 = 1{,}601{,}000$$

$$m = \sqrt[n]{\frac{F}{P}} - 1$$

$$m = \sqrt[3]{\frac{1{,}601{,}000}{1{,}000{,}000}} - 1 = 0.17 \text{ or } 17\%$$

Of course, a more satisfactory answer can be obtained by calculating NPVs, but the result may not be persuasive if the senior management team do not understand NPVs.

NPVs for Tic and Cit

Tic $-1 + 0.5 \times$ annuity factor, 3 years @ 10%

$-1 + 0.5 \times 2.4869 = 0.24345$ or £243,450

Cit
$$-1 + \frac{1.1}{1 + 0.1} + \frac{0.1}{(1 + 0.1)^2} + \frac{0.16}{(1 + 0.1)^3} = 0.202855 \text{ or } £202{,}855$$

Therefore, Tic contributes more towards shareholder wealth.

Summary table

Ranking

	NPV	**IRR**	**MIRR**
Tic	£243,450 (1)	23.4% (2)	18.3% (1)
Cit	£202,855 (2)	27.7% (1)	17.0% (2)

Concluding comments

This chapter has provided insight into the key factors for consideration when an organisation is contemplating using financial (or other) resources for investment. The analysis has been based on the assumption that the objective of any such investment is to maximise economic benefits to the owners of the enterprise. To achieve such an objective requires allowance for the opportunity cost of capital or time value of money as well as robust analysis of relevant cash flows. Given that time has a value, the precise timing of cash flows is important for project analysis. The net present value (NPV) and internal rate of return (IRR) methods of project appraisal are both discounted cash flow techniques and therefore allow for the time value of money. However, the IRR method does present problems in a few special circumstances and so the theoretically preferred method is NPV. On the other hand, NPV requires diligent studying and thought in order to be fully understood, and therefore it is not surprising to find in the workplace a bias in favour of communicating a project's viability in terms of percentages. Most large organisations, in fact, use three or four methods of project appraisal, rather than rely on only one for both rigorous analysis and communication – *see* Chapter 4 for more detail. If a percentage approach is regarded as essential in a particular organisational setting then the MIRR is to be preferred to the IRR. Not only does the MIRR rank projects more appropriately and so is useful in mutual exclusivity situations; it also avoids biasing upward expectations of returns from an investment. The fundamental conclusion of this chapter is that the best method for maximising shareholder wealth in assessing investment projects is net present value.

Key points and concepts

- ***Time value of money*** has three component parts each requiring compensation for a delay in the receipt of cash:
  - the pure time value, or impatience to consume,
  - inflation,
  - risk.
- ***Opportunity cost of capital*** is the yield forgone on the best available investment alternative – the risk level of the alternative being the same as for the project under consideration.
- Taking account of the time value of money and opportunity cost of capital in project appraisal leads to **discounted cash flow analysis** (DCF).
- **Net present value** (NPV) is the present value of the future cash flows after netting out the initial cash flow. Present values are achieved by discounting at the opportunity cost of capital.

$$\text{NPV} = CF_0 + \frac{CF_1}{1+k} + \frac{CF_2}{(1+k)^2} + \dots \frac{CF_n}{(1+k)^n}$$

- **The net present value decision rules** are:

  NPV ≥ 0 accept
  NPV < 0 reject

- **Internal rate of return** (IRR) is the discount rate which, when applied to the cash flows of a project, results in a zero net present value. It is an '*r*' which results in the following formula being true:

$$CF_0 + \frac{CF_1}{1+r} + \frac{CF_2}{(1+r)^2} + \dots \frac{CF_n}{(1+r)^n} = 0$$

- **The internal rate of return decision rule** is:

  IRR ≥ opportunity cost of capital – accept
  IRR < opportunity cost of capital – reject

- IRR is poor at handling situations of unconventional cash flows. **Multiple solutions** can be the result.
- There are circumstances when IRR ranks one project higher than another, whereas NPV ranks the projects in the opposite order. This **ranking problem** becomes an important issue in situations of mutual exclusivity.
- The IRR decision rule is reversed for financing-type decisions
- NPV measures in **absolute amounts of money**. IRR is a percentage measure.

- IRR assumes that intra-project cash flows can be invested at a rate of return equal to the IRR. This biases the IRR calculation.
- If a percentage measure is required, perhaps for communication within an organisation, then the **modified internal rate of return** (MIRR) is to be preferred to the IRR.

Appendix 2.1 Mathematical tools for finance

The purpose of this appendix is to explain essential mathematical skills that will be needed for this book. The author has no love of mathematics for its own sake and so only those techniques of direct relevance to the subject matter of this textbook will be covered in this section.

Simple and compound interest

When there are time delays between receipts and payments of financial sums we need to make use of the concepts of simple and compound interest.

Simple interest

Interest is paid only on the original principal. No interest is paid on the accumulated interest payments.

Example 1

Suppose that a sum of £10 is deposited in a bank account that pays 12 per cent per annum. At the end of year 1 the investor has £11.20 in the account. That is:

$$F = P(1 + i)$$
$$11.20 = 10(1 + 0.12)$$

where F = Future value, P = Present value, i = Interest rate.

The initial sum, called the principal, is multiplied by the interest rate to give the annual return. At the end of five years:

$$F = P(1 + in)$$

where n = number of years. Thus,

$$16 = 10(1 + 0.12 \times 5)$$

Note from the example that the 12 per cent return is a constant amount each year. Interest is not earned on the interest already accumulated from previous years.

Compound interest

The more usual situation in the real world is for interest to be paid on the sum which accumulates – whether or not that sum comes from the principal or from the interest received in previous periods.

Example 2

An investment of £10 is made at an interest rate of 12 per cent with the interest being compounded. In one year the capital will grow by 12 per cent to £11.20. In the second year the capital will grow by 12 per cent, but this time the growth will be on the accumulated value of £11.20 and thus will amount to an extra £1.34. At the end of two years:

$F = P(1 + i)(1 + i)$
$F = 11.20(1 + i)$
$F = 12.54$

Alternatively,

$$F = P(1 + i)^2$$

Exhibit 2.26 displays the future value of £1 invested at a number of different interest rates and for alternative numbers of years. This is extracted from Appendix I at the end of the book.

Exhibit 2.26 The future value of £1

Year	Interest rate (per cent per annum) 1	2	5	12	15
1	1.0100	1.0200	1.0500	1.1200	1.1500
2	1.0201	1.0404	1.1025	1.2544	1.3225
3	1.0303	1.0612	1.1576	1.4049	1.5209
4	1.0406	1.0824	1.2155	1.5735	1.7490
5	1.0510	1.1041	1.2763	1.7623	2.0114

From the second row of the table in Exhibit 2.26 we can read that £1 invested for two years at 12 per cent amounts to £1.2544. Thus, the investment of £10 provides a future capital sum 1.2544 times the original amount:

$$£10 \times 1.2544 = £12.544$$

Over five years the result is:

$F = P(1 + i)^n$
$17.62 = 10(1 + 0.12)^5$

The interest on the accumulated interest is therefore the difference between the total arising from simple interest and that from compound interest:

$$£17.62 - £16.00 = £1.62$$

Almost all investments pay compound interest and so we will be using compounding throughout the book.

Present values

There are many occasions in financial management when you are given the future sums and need to find out what those future sums are worth in present-value terms today. For example, you wish to know how much you would have to put aside today which will accumulate, with compounded interest, to a defined sum in the future; or you are given the choice between receiving £200 in five years or £100 now and wish to know which is the better option, given anticipated interest rates; or a project gives a return of £1m in three years for an outlay of £800,000 now and you need to establish if this is the best use of the £800,000. By the process of discounting a sum of money to be received in the future is given a monetary value today.

Example 3

If we anticipate the receipt of £17.62 in five years' time we can determine its present value. Rearrangement of the compound formula, and assuming a discount rate of 12 per cent, gives:

$$P = \frac{F}{(1+i)^n} \text{ or } P = F \times \frac{1}{(1+i)^n}$$

$$10 = \frac{17.62}{(1+0.12)^5}$$

Alternatively, discount factors may be used, as shown in **Exhibit 2.27** (this is an extract from Appendix II at the end of the book). The factor needed to discount £1 receivable in five years when the discount rate is 12 per cent is 0.5674.

Therefore the present value of £17.62 is:

$$0.5674 \times £17.62 = £10$$

Exhibit 2.27 The present value of £1

	Interest rate (per cent per annum)				
Year	**1**	**5**	**10**	**12**	**15**
1	0.9901	0.9524	0.9091	0.8929	0.8696
2	0.9803	0.9070	0.8264	0.7972	0.7561
3	0.9706	0.8638	0.7513	0.7118	0.6575
4	0.9610	0.8227	0.6830	0.6355	0.5718
5	0.9515	0.7835	0.6209	0.5674	0.4972

Examining the present value table in Exhibit 2.27 you can see that as the discount rate increases the present value goes down. Also the further into the future the money is to be received, the less valuable it is in today's terms. Distant cash flows discounted at a high rate have a small present value; for instance, £1,000 receivable in 20 years when the discount rate is 17 per cent has a present value of £43.30. Viewed from another angle, if you invested £43.30 for 20 years it would accumulate to £1,000 if interest compounds at 17 per cent.

Determining the rate of interest

Sometimes you wish to calculate the rate of return that a project is earning. For instance, a savings company may offer to pay you £10,000 in five years if you deposit £8,000 now, when interest rates on accounts elsewhere are offering 6 per cent per annum. In order to make a comparison you need to know the annual rate being offered by the savings company. Thus, we need to find i in the discounting equation.

To be able to calculate i it is necessary to rearrange the compounding formula. Since:

$$F = P(1+i)^n$$

first, divide both sides by P:

$$F/P = (1+i)^n$$

(The Ps on the right side cancel out.)

Second, take the root to the power n of both sides and subtract 1 from each side:

$$i = \sqrt[n]{[F/P]} - 1 \text{ or } i = [F/P]^{1/n} - 1$$

Example 4

In the case of a five-year investment requiring an outlay of £10 and having a future value of £17.62 the rate of return is:

$$i = \sqrt[5]{\frac{17.62}{10}} - 1 \quad i = 12\%$$

$$i = [17.62/10]^{1/5} - 1 \quad i = 12\%$$

Technical aside

You can use the $\sqrt[x]{y}$, the $\sqrt[y]{x}$ button or a combination of the y^x and $\frac{1}{x}$ buttons depending on the calculator.

Alternatively, use the future value table, an extract of which is shown in Exhibit 2.26. In our example, the return on £1 worth of investment over five years is:

$$\frac{17.62}{10} = 1.762$$

In the body of the future value table look at the year 5 row for a future value of 1.762. Read off the interest rate of 12 per cent.

An interesting application of this technique outside finance is to use it to put into perspective the pronouncements of politicians. For example, in 1994 John Major made a speech to the Conservative Party conference promising to double national income (the total quantity of goods and services produced) within 25 years. This sounds impressive, but let us see how ambitious this is in terms of an annual percentage increase.

$$i = \sqrt[25]{\frac{F}{P}} - 1$$

F, future income, is double *P*, the present income.

$$i = \sqrt[25]{\frac{2}{1}} - 1 = 0.0281 \text{ or } 2.81\%$$

The result is not too bad compared with the previous 20 years. However, performance in the 1950s and 1960s was better and countries in the Far East have annual rates of growth of between 5 per cent and 10 per cent.

The investment period

Rearranging the standard equation so that we can find n (the number of years of the investment), we create the following equation:

$$F = P(1 + i)^n$$
$$F/P = (1 + i)^n$$
$$\log(F/P) = \log(1 + i)n$$

$$n = \frac{\log(F/P)}{\log(1 + i)}$$

Example 5

How many years does it take for £10 to grow to £17.62 when the interest rate is 12 per cent?

$$n = \frac{\log(17.62/10)}{\log(1 + 0.12)} \text{ Therefore } n = 5 \text{ years}$$

An application outside finance How many years will it take for China to double its real national income if growth rates continue at 10 per cent per annum?
Answer:

$$n = \frac{\log(2/1)}{\log(1 + 0.1)} = 7.3 \text{ years}$$ (quadrupling in less than 15 years. At this rate it won't be long before China overtakes the USA as the world's biggest economy)

Annuities

Quite often there is not just one payment at the end of a certain number of years. There can be a series of identical payments made over a period of years. For instance:

- bonds usually pay a regular rate of interest;
- individuals can buy, from saving plan companies, the right to receive a number of identical payments over a number of years;
- a business might invest in a project which, it is estimated, will give regular cash inflows over a period of years;
- a typical house mortgage is an annuity.

An annuity is a series of payments or receipts of equal amounts. We are able to calculate the present value of this set of payments.

Example 6

For a regular payment of £10 per year for five years, when the interest rate is 12 per cent, we can calculate the present value of the annuity by three methods.

Method 1

$$P_{an} = \frac{A}{(1+i)} + \frac{A}{(1+i)^2} + \frac{A}{(1+i)^3} + \frac{A}{(1+i)^4} + \frac{A}{(1+i)^5}$$

where A = the periodic receipt.

$$P_{10,5} = \frac{10}{(1.12)} + \frac{10}{(1.12)^2} + \frac{10}{(1.12)^3} + \frac{10}{(1.12)^4} + \frac{10}{(1.12)^5} = £36.05$$

Method 2

Using the derived formula:

$$P_{an} = \frac{1 - 1/(1+i)^n}{i} \times A$$

$$P_{10,5} = \frac{1 - 1/(1+0.12)^5}{0.12} \times 10 = £36.05$$

Method 3

Use the 'present value of an annuity' table. (*See* **Exhibit 2.28**, an extract from the more complete annuity table at the end of the book in Appendix III.) Here we simply look along the year 5 row and 12 per cent column to find the figure of 3.605. This refers to the present value of five annual receipts of £1. Therefore we multiply by £10:

$$3.605 \times £10 = £36.05$$

Exhibit 2.28 The present value of an annuity of £1 per annum

	Interest rate (per cent per annum)				
Year	1	5	10	12	15
1	0.9901	0.9524	0.9091	0.8929	0.8696
2	1.9704	1.8594	1.7355	1.6901	1.6257
3	2.9410	2.7232	2.4869	2.4018	2.2832
4	3.9020	3.5459	3.1699	3.0373	2.8550
5	4.8535	4.3295	3.7908	3.6048	3.3522

The student is strongly advised against using Method 1. This was presented for conceptual understanding only. For any but the simplest cases, this method can be very time consuming.

Perpetuities

Some contracts run indefinitely and there is no end to a series of identical payments. Perpetuities are rare in the private sector, but certain government securities do not have an end date; that is, the amount paid when the bond was purchased by the lender will never be repaid, only interest payments are made. For example, the UK government has issued Consolidated Stocks or War Loans which will never be redeemed. Also, in a number of project appraisals or share valuations it is useful to assume that regular annual payments go on forever. Perpetuities are annuities which continue indefinitely. The value of a perpetuity is simply the annual amount received divided by the interest rate when the latter is expressed as a decimal.

$$P = \frac{A}{i}$$

If £10 is to be received as an indefinite annual payment then the present value, at a discount rate of 12 per cent, is:

$$P = \frac{10}{0.12} = £83.33$$

It is very important to note that in order to use this formula we are assuming that the first payment arises 365 days after the time at which we are standing (the present time or time zero).

Discounting semi-annually, monthly and daily

Sometimes financial transactions take place on the basis that interest will be calculated more frequently than once a year. For instance, if a bank account paid 12 per cent nominal return per year, but credited 6 per cent after half a year, in the second half of the year interest could be earned on the interest credited after the first six months. This will mean that the true annual rate of interest will be greater than 12 per cent.

The greater the frequency with which interest is earned, the higher the future value of the deposit.

Example 7

If you put £10 in a bank account earning 12 per cent per annum then your return after one year is:

$$10(1 + 0.12) = £11.20$$

If the interest is compounded semi-annually (at a nominal annual rate of 12 per cent):

$$10(1 + [0.12/2])(1 + [0.12/2]) = 10(1 + [0.12/2])^2 = £11.236$$

In Example 7 the difference between annual compounding and semi-annual compounding is an extra 3.6p. After six months the bank credits the account with 60p in interest so that in the following six months the investor earns 6 per cent on the £10.60.

If the interest is compounded quarterly:

$$10(1 + [0.12/4])^4 = £11.255$$

Daily compounding:

$$10(1 + [0.12/365])^{365} = £11.2747$$

Example 8

If £10 is deposited in a bank account that compounds interest quarterly and the nominal return per year is 12 per cent, how much will be in the account after eight years?

$$10(1 + [0.12/4])^{4\times8} = £25.75$$

Continuous compounding

If the compounding frequency is taken to the limit we say that there is continuous compounding. When the number of compounding periods approaches infinity the future value is found by $F = Pe^{in}$ where e is the value of the exponential function. This is set as 2.71828 (to five decimal places, as shown on a scientific calculator).

So, the future value of £10 deposited in a bank paying 12 per cent nominal compounded continuously after eight years is:

$$10 \times 2.71828^{0.12\times8} = £26.12$$

Converting monthly and daily rates to annual rates

Sometimes you are presented with a monthly or daily rate of interest and wish to know what that is equivalent to in terms of Annual Percentage Rate (APR) (or Effective Annual Rate (EAR)).

If m is the monthly interest or discount rate, then over 12 months:

$$(1 + m)^{12} = 1 + i$$

where i is the annual compound rate.

$$i = (1 + m)^{12} - 1$$

Thus, if a credit card company charges 1.5 per cent per month, the annual percentage rate (APR) is:

$$i = (1 + 0.015)^{12} - 1 = 19.56\%$$

If you want to find the monthly rate when you are given the APR:

$$m = (1 + i)^{1/12} - 1 \text{ or } m = \sqrt[12]{(1 + i)} - 1$$
$$m = (1 + 0.1956)^{1/12} - 1 = 0.015 = 1.5\%$$

Daily rate:

$$(1 + d)^{365} = 1 + i$$

where d is the daily discount rate.

The following exercises will consolidate the knowledge gained by reading through this appendix (answers are provided at the end of the book in Appendix VI).

Exercise Mathematical tools exercise

1 What will a £100 investment be worth in three years' time if the rate of interest is 8 per cent, using: (a) simple interest? (b) annual compound interest? ?

2 You plan to invest £10,000 in the shares of a company.

  a If the value of the shares increases by 5 per cent a year, what will be the value of the shares in 20 years?

  b If the value of the shares increases by 15 per cent a year, what will be the value of the shares in 20 years? ?

3 How long will it take you to double your money if you invest it at: (a) 5 per cent? (b) 15 per cent? ?

4 As a winner of a lottery you can choose one of the following prizes:

  a £1,000,000 now.

  b £1,700,000 at the end of five years.

  c £135,000 a year for ever, starting in one year.

  d £200,000 for each of the next 10 years, starting in one year.

  If the time value of money is 9 per cent, which is the most valuable prize? ?

5 A bank lends a customer £5,000. At the end of 10 years he repays this amount plus interest. The amount he repays is £8,950. What is the rate of interest charged by the bank? ?

6 The Morbid Memorial Garden company will maintain a garden plot around your grave for a payment of £50 now, followed by annual payments, in perpetuity, of £50. How much would you have to put into an account which was to make these payments if the account guaranteed an interest rate of 8 per cent? ?

7 If the flat (nominal annual) rate of interest is 14 per cent and compounding takes place monthly, what is the effective annual rate of interest (the Annual Percentage Rate)? ?

8 What is the present value of £100 to be received in 10 years' time when the interest rate (nominal annual) is 12 per cent and (a) annual discounting is used? (b) semi-annual discounting is used? ?

9 What sum must be invested now to provide an amount of £18,000 at the end of 15 years if interest is to accumulate at 8 per cent for the first 10 years and 12 per cent thereafter? ?

10 How much must be invested now to provide an amount of £10,000 in six years' time assuming interest is compounded quarterly at a nominal annual rate of 8 per cent? What is the effective annual rate? ?

11 Supersalesman offers you an annuity of £800 per annum for 10 years. The price he asks is £4,800. Assuming you could earn 11 per cent on alternative investments would you buy the annuity? ?

12 Punter buys a car on hire purchase paying five annual instalments of £1,500, the first being an immediate cash deposit. Assuming an interest rate of 8 per cent is being charged by the hire purchase company, how much is the current cash price of the car? ?

References and further reading

Bierman, H. and Smidt, S. (2006) *The Capital Budgeting Decision*, 9th edn. London: Routledge.
A clear introductory exposition of the concepts discussed in this chapter.

Bierman, H. and Smidt, S. (2006) *Advanced Capital Budgeting*. London: Routledge.
A book for those interested in pursuing the technical issue in depth.

Dean, J. (1951) *Capital Budgeting*. New York: Columbia University Press.
Dean introduced an analytical framework for a systemised approach to investment within the firm based on discounted cash flow. Easy to read.

Fama, E.F. and Miller, M.H. (1972) *The Theory of Finance*. New York: Holt, Rinehart & Winston.
A more detailed consideration of IRR and NPV.

Fisher, I. (1930) *The Theory of Interest*. Reprinted in 1977 by Porcupine Press.
Originator of the present value rule.

Hirshleifer, J. (1958) 'On the theory of optimal investment decision', *Journal of Political Economy*, 66 (August), pp. 329–52.
Early theory.

Hirshleifer, J. (1961) 'Risk, the discount rate and investment decisions', *American Economic Review*, May, pp. 112–20.
Theoretical justification for the use of net present value.

McDaniel, W.R., McCarty, D.E. and Jessell, K.A. (1988) 'Discounted cash flow with explicit reinvestment rates: Tutorial and extension', *The Financial Review*, August.
Modified internal rate of return discussed in more detail as well as other theoretical developments.

Solomon, E. (1963) *The Theory of Financial Management*. New York: Columbia University Press.
An early advocate of net present value.

Wilkes, F.M. (1980) 'On multiple rates of return', *Journal of Business Finance and Accounting*, 7(4).
Theoretical treatment of a specific issue.

Websites

Investopedia www. investopedia.com
As well as tutorials on finance this website has quick definitions and quick calculators, e.g. for NPV.

Case study recommendations

Please see www.pearsoned.co.uk/arnold for case study synopses.

- Ginny' Restaurant: An introduction to capital investment valuation. Author: Mark Mitchell (2001) Harvard Business School.
- Tree Values: Authors: R.S. Ruback and K. S. Luchs (2000) Harvard Business School.

Self-review questions

1 What are the theoretical justifications for the NPV decision rules?

2 Explain what is meant by conventional and unconventional cash flows and what problems they might cause in investment appraisal.

3 Define the time value of money.

4 What is the reinvestment assumption for project cash flows under IRR? Why is this problematical? How can it be corrected?

5 Rearrange the compounding equation to solve for: (a) the annual interest rate, and (b) the number of years over which compounding takes place.

6 What is the 'yield' of a project?

7 Explain why it is possible to obtain an inaccurate result using the trial and error method of IRR when a wide difference of two discount rates is used for interpolation.

Questions and problems

myfinancelab ***Questions with an icon are also available for practice in MyFinanceLab with additional supporting resources.***

1 Proast plc is considering two investment projects whose cash flows are:

Points in time (yearly intervals)	Project A	Project B
0	–120,000	–120,000
1	60,000	15,000
2	45,000	45,000
3	42,000	55,000
4	18,000	60,000

The company's required rate of return is 15 per cent.

a Advise the company whether to undertake the two projects.
b Indicate the maximum outlay in year 0 for each project before it ceases to be viable.

(An Excel spreadsheet solution to the question is at www.pearsoned.co.uk/arnold)

?

2 Highflyer plc has two possible projects to consider. It cannot do both – they are mutually exclusive. The cash flows are:

Points in time (yearly intervals)	Project A	Project B
0	–420,000	–100,000
1	150,000	75,000
2	150,000	75,000
3	150,000	0
4	150,000	0

Highflyer's cost of capital is 12 per cent. Assume unlimited funds. These are the only cash flows associated with the projects.

a Calculate the internal rate of return (IRR) for each project.
b Calculate the net present value (NPV) for each project.
c Compare and explain the results in (a) and (b) and indicate which project the company should undertake and why.

(An Excel spreadsheet solution to the question is at www.pearsoned.co.uk/arnold)

?

3* Mr Baffled, the managing director of Confused plc, has heard that the internal rate of return (IRR) method of investment appraisal is the best modern approach. He is trying to apply the IRR method to two new projects.

	Cash flows		
Year	0	1	2
Project C	–3,000	+14,950	–12,990
Project D	–3,000	+7,500	–5,000

a Calculate the IRRs of the two projects.
b Explain why Mr Baffled is having difficulties with the IRR method.
c Advise Confused whether to accept either or both projects. (Assume a discount rate of 25 per cent.)

?

4 Using a 13 per cent discount rate find the NPV of a project with the following cash flows:

Points in time (yearly intervals)	t_0	t_1	t_2	t_3
Cash flow (£)	–300	+260	–200	+600

Explain the difficulties you might have analysing this project using the IRR method.

?

5 a Find the total terminal value of the following cash flows when compounded at 15 per cent. Cash flows occur at annual intervals and the fourth year's cash flow is the last.

Points in time (yearly intervals)	t_1	t_2	t_3	t_4
Cash flow (£)	+200	+300	+250	+400

b If £900 is the initial cash outflow at time 0 calculate the compounding rate that will equate the initial cash outflow with the terminal value as calculated in (a) above.

c You have calculated the modified internal rate of return (MIRR), now calculate the IRR for comparison.

?

6 a If the cost of capital is 14 per cent find the modified internal rate of return for the following investment and state if you would implement it.

Points in time (yearly intervals)	t_0	t_1	t_2	t_3	t_4
Cash flow	–9,300	5,400	3,100	2,800	600

b Is this project to be accepted under the internal rate of return method?

?

7* Seddet International is considering four major projects which have either two- or three-year lives. The firm has raised all of its capital in the form of equity and has never borrowed money. This is partly due to the success of the business in generating income and partly due to an insistence by the dominant managing director that borrowing is to be avoided if at all possible. Shareholders in Seddet International regard the firm as relatively risky, given its existing portfolio of projects. Other firms' shares in this risk class have generally given a return of 16 per cent per annum and this is taken as the opportunity cost of capital for the investment projects. The risk level for the proposed projects is the same as that of the existing range of activities.

Project		Net cash flows		
Points in time (yearly intervals)	t_0	t_1	t_2	t_3
A	–5,266	2,500	2,500	2,500
B	–8,000	0	0	10,000
C	–2,100	200	2,900	0
D	–1,975	1,600	800	0

Ignore taxation and inflation.

a The managing director has been on a one-day intensive course to learn about project appraisal techniques. Unfortunately, during the one slot given over to NPV he had to leave the room to deal with a business crisis, and therefore does not understand it. He vaguely understands IRR and insists that you use this to calculate which of the four projects should be proceeded with, if there are no limitations on the number which can be undertaken.

b State which is the best project if they are mutually exclusive (i.e. accepting one excludes the possibility of accepting another), using IRR.

c Use the NPV decision rule to rank the projects and explain why, under conditions of mutual exclusivity, the selected project differs from that under (b).

d Write a report for the managing director, detailing the value of the net present value method for shareholder wealth enhancement and explaining why it may be considered of greater use than IRR.

?

Assignments

1 Try to discover the extent to which NPV, IRR and MIRR are used in your organisation. Also try to gauge the degree of appreciation of the problems of using IRR.

2 If possible, obtain data on a real project, historical or proposed, and analyse it using the techniques learned in this chapter.

CHAPTER 3

Project appraisal:

cash flow and applications

LEARNING OUTCOMES

By the end of this chapter the reader will be able to identify and apply relevant and incremental cash flows in net present value calculations. The reader will also be able to recognise and deal with sunk costs, incidental costs and allocated overheads and be able to employ this knowledge to the following:

- the replacement decision/the replacement cycle;
- the calculation of annual equivalent annuities;
- the make or buy decision;
- optimal timing of investment;
- fluctuating output situations.

myfinancelab — *Complete your diagnostic test for Chapter 3 now to create your personal study plan*

Introduction

The last chapter outlined the process of project evaluation. This required consideration of the fundamental elements; first, recognition of the fact that time has a value and that money received in the future has to be discounted at the opportunity cost of capital; second, the identification of relevant cash flows that are to be subject to the discounting procedure. It is to this second issue that we now turn.

This chapter examines the estimation of the cash flows appropriate for good decision making. The relevant cash flows are not always obvious and easy to obtain and therefore diligent data collection and rigorous analysis are required. Defining and measuring future receipts and outlays accurately is central to successful project appraisal.

In **Case study 3.1** Airbus would have had to consider carefully which projected cash flows are, and are not, relevant to the decision whether to go ahead with producing an aircraft capable of carrying 555 passengers.

Having completed the essential groundwork the chapter moves on to demonstrate the practical application of the net present value (NPV) method. This deals with important business decisions, such as whether to replace a machine with a new more efficient (but expensive) version or whether it is better to persevere with the old machine for a few more years despite its rising maintenance costs and higher raw material inputs. Another area examined is replacement cycles, that is, if you have machinery which costs more to run as it gets older and you know that you will continue to need this type of machine and therefore have to replace it at some stage should you regularly replace after one year or two, three or four years? An example is a car hire company that replaces its fleet of cars on a regular cycle. Other topics include the make or buy decision and optimal timing for the implementation of a project.

Case study 3.1 Will it fly?

Airbus's superjumbo

(This case study describes the difficult decision to go ahead and produce the A380. Chapter 6 describes what happened afterwards – it was not all plain sailing!)

Surely one of the biggest investment appraisal decisions ever made was when Airbus decided to go ahead and produce the A380 superjumbo. This is one of those 'bet the company' type investments. A massive £6,500 million will be needed to create this monster aircraft.

It was touch and go all through 2000 as to whether Airbus would dare to invest so much money. Before they said 'yes let's do it' they had to have firm orders for at least 50 aircraft. Finally, just before Christmas the sixth major buyer signed up, to take the order book to 50 'definites' and 42 on option (the airlines have the right to buy, but not the obligation).

The A380 will be significantly larger than Boeing's highly successful 747. It will carry 555 passengers (compared with 416). It will also cut direct operating costs for the airlines by 15–20 per cent compared with Boeing's B747–400 and will be able to fly 10 per cent further (8,150 nautical miles).

So, where is all the money on development and build going? This is a project at the cutting edge of technology. The remarkable innovations cost a tremendous amount in terms of up-front cost but the benefit will be spread out over many decades.

Some of the innovations include improved aerodynamics, weight-saving materials such as carbon-fibre, aluminium and glass-fibre.

Rivalry in the skies: contrasting views

Traffic volume in 2019

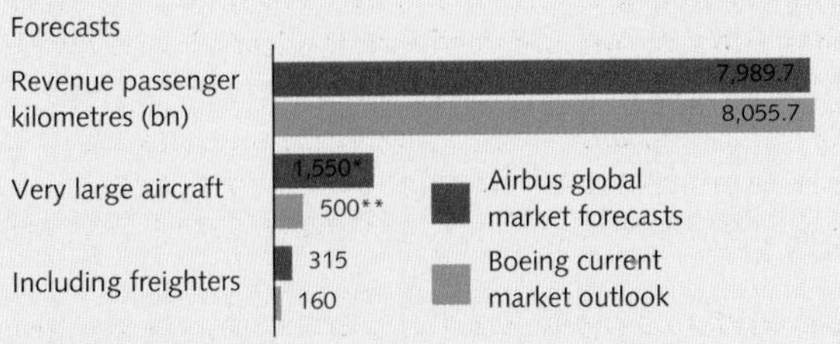

Profit potential

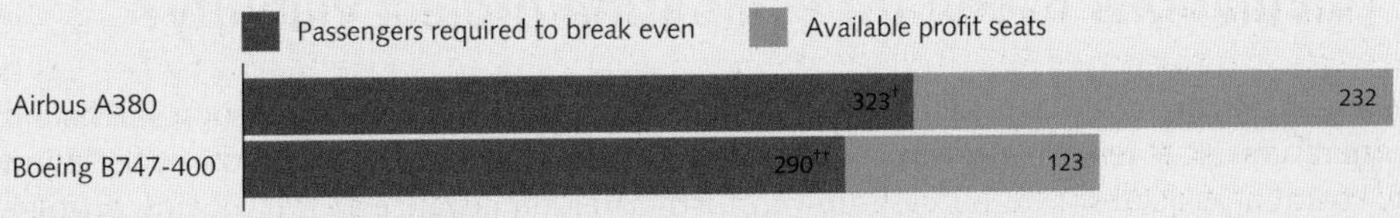

* 500 seats and above ** Larger than 747
† Assuming same revenue per passenger as B747–400 †† Break-even load factor assumed for B747–400; 70%

Source: Financial Times, 2 November 2000, p. 28, Kevin Done. Reprinted with permission. Data from Airbus.

Airbus reckon that they need to sell at least 250 aircraft to break even in cash-flow terms (presumably meaning that nominal cumulative cash inflows equal nominal cumulative cash outflows). To achieve a positive net present value would require the sale of hundreds more aircraft. Each aircraft has a list price of around \$216m–\$230m – but don't pay too much attention to that, as airlines receive substantial discounts. At full capacity something like 96,000 people will be working on this aircraft.

And yet it could so easily have been abandoned. Boeing had decided not to develop a superjumbo because it estimated the maximum market at 500 aircraft – they believe that airlines are generally content to continue using the 747. Airbus estimated the market for jumbos and superjumbos at 1,550. It expects to take two-thirds of that business, worth \$400bn in today's prices.

This is a high-impact project appraisal if ever there was one. Many of the techniques you have learned in Chapter 2 and will learn in this chapter will have been employed by the management of Airbus to help them decide whether or not to press the button to 'go' or the button to 'stop'.

Quality of information

Good decisions are born of good information. This principle applies to all types of business decisions but is especially appropriate in the case of capital investment decisions in which a substantial proportion of the firm's assets can be put at risk. Obtaining relevant and high-quality information reduces the extent of the risk for the enterprise. Information varies greatly in its reliability, which often depends upon its source. The financial manager or analyst is often dependent on the knowledge and experience of other specialists within the organisation to supply data. For example the marketing team may be able to provide an estimate of likely demand while the production team could help establish the costs per unit. Allowance will have to be made for any bias that may creep into the information passed on; for instance, a manager who is particularly keen on encouraging the firm to expand in a particular geographical area might tend to be over-optimistic concerning market demand. For some elements of a project there might be high-quality information, whereas other aspects have a lower quality. Take the case of the investment in a new lorry for a courier firm; the cost of purchase can be estimated with high precision, whereas the reaction of competitor firms is subject to much more uncertainty.

The sources of information which are useful as inputs for decision making vary widely; from accounting systems and special investigations, to those of the informal, 'just-between-you-and-me-and-the-gatepost' type. Whatever its source all information should, as far as possible, have the following characteristics:

- relevance;
- completeness;
- consistency;
- accuracy;
- reliability;
- timeliness;
- low cost of collection compared with benefit to be gained by gathering more detail.

Are profit calculations useful for estimating project viability?

Accountants often produce a wealth of numerical information about an organisation and its individual operations. It is tempting to simply take the profit figures for a project and put these into the NPV formula as a substitute for cash flow. A further reason advanced for favouring profit-based evaluations is that managers are often familiar with the notion of 'the bottom line' and frequently their performance is judged using profit. However, as was noted in Chapter 1, determining whether a project is 'profitable' is not the same as achieving shareholder wealth maximisation.

Profit is a concept developed by accountants in order to assist them with auditing and reporting. Profit figures are derived by taking what is a continuous process, a change in a company's worth over time, and allocating these changes to discrete periods of time, say a year (*see* **Exhibit 3.1**). This is a difficult task. It is a complex task with rules, principles and conventions in abundance.

Profit uses two carefully defined concepts: income and expenses. Income is not cash inflow, it is the amount earned from business activity whether or not the cash has actually been handed over. So, if a £1,000 sofa has been sold on two years' credit the accountant's income arises in the year of sale despite the fact that cash actually flows in two years later. Expense relates the use of an asset to a particular time period whether or not any cash outflow relating to that item occurs in that period. If a firm pays immediately for a machine which will have a ten-year useful life it does not write off the full cost of the machine against the first year's profit, but allocates a proportion of the cost to each of the ten years. The cash outflow occurs in the first year but the expense (use) of the asset occurs over ten years.

Shareholders make current consumption sacrifices, or they give up the return available elsewhere when they choose to invest their money in a firm. They do this in anticipation of receiving more £s in the future than they laid out. Hence what is of interest to them are the future cash flows and the precise timing of these cash flows. The accountant does a difficult and important job but the profit figures produced are not suitable for project appraisal. Profit is a poor approach for two main reasons, first, depreciation and second, working capital.

Exhibit 3.1 **Business activity is a continuous process; this is difficult to capture in periodic accounts**

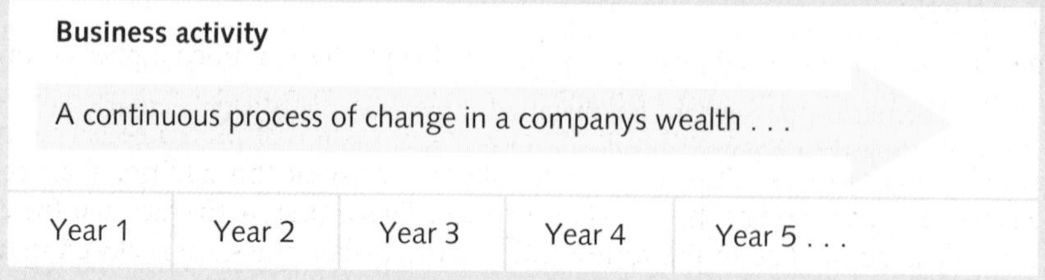

Depreciation

Accounting profit is calculated after deducting depreciation, whereas what we are interested in is net cash inflows for a year. Depreciation should not be deducted to calculate net cash inflows. For example, if a firm buys a machine for £20,000 which is expected to be productive for four years and have a zero scrap value, the firm's accountant may allocate the depreciation on the machine over the four years to give the profit figures of say, a stable £7,000 per year (*see* **Exhibit 3.2**). The reason for doing this may be so that the full impact of the £20,000 payout in the first year is not allocated solely to that year's profit and loss account, but is spread over the economic life of the asset. This makes good sense for calculating accounting profit. However, this is not appropriate for project appraisal based on NPV because these figures are not true cash flows. We need to focus on the cash flows at the precise time they occur and should not discount back to time zero the figure of £7,000, but cash flows at the time they occur.

Exhibit 3.2 ABC plc: An example of adjustment to a profit and loss projection

Machine cost £20,000, at time 0. **Productive life of four years.**

Accountant's figures

Year	1 £	2 £	3 £	4 £
Profit before depreciation	12,000	12,000	12,000	12,000
Depreciation	5,000	5,000	5,000	5,000
Profit after depreciation	7,000	7,000	7,000	7,000

Cash flow

Point in time (yearly intervals)	0 £	1 £	2 £	3 £	4 £
Cash outflow	-20,000				
Cash inflow		12,000	12,000	12,000	12,000

Working capital

When a project is accepted and implemented the firm may have to invest in more than the large and obvious depreciable assets such as machines, buildings, vehicles and so forth. Investment in a new project often requires an additional investment in **working capital**, that is, the difference between short-term assets and liabilities. The main short-term assets are cash, stock (inventories) and debtors. The principal short-term liabilities are creditors.

So, a firm might take on a project which involves an increase in the requirements for one of these types of working capital. Each of these will be taken in turn.

Cash floats

It may be that the proposed project requires the firm to have a much higher amount of cash float. For instance, a firm setting up a betting shop may have to consider not only the cash outflow for building or refurbishment, but also the amount of extra cash float needed to meet minute-by-minute betting payouts. Thus, we have to take into account this additional aspect of cash inputs when evaluating the size of the initial investment. This is despite the fact that the cash float will be recoverable at some date in the future (for instance, when the shop is closed in, e.g., three years' time). The fact that this cash is being used to lubricate day-to-day business and is therefore not available to shareholders means that a sacrifice has been made at a particular point. The owners of that money rightfully expect to receive a suitable return while that money is tied up and unavailable for them to use as they wish.

Stock (inventories)

Examples of stock are raw materials and finished goods. If a project is undertaken which raises the level of inventories then this additional cash outflow has to be allowed for. So, for a retail business opening a number of new shops the additional expenditure on stock is a form of investment. This extra cash being tied up will not be recognised by the profit and loss accounts because all that has happened is that one asset, cash, has been swapped for another, inventory. However, the cash use has to be recognised in any NPV calculation. With some projects there may be a reduction in inventory levels. This may happen in the case of the replacement of an inefficient machine with a new piece of equipment. In this case the stock reduction releases cash and so results in a positive cash flow.

Debtors

Accounting convention dictates that if a sale is made during a year it is brought into the profit and loss account for that year. But in many cases a sale might be made on credit and all the firm has is a promise that cash will be paid in the future, the cash inflow has not materialised in the year the sale was recorded. Also, at the start of the financial year this firm may have had some outstanding debtors, that is, other firms or individuals owing this firm money, and in the early months of the year cash inflow is boosted by those other firms paying off their debt.

If we want to calculate the cash flow for the year then the annual profit figure has to be adjusted to exclude the closing balance of debtors (cash owed by customers at the end of the year but not yet paid over), and include the opening balance of debtors (cash owed by the customers at the beginning of the year which is actually received in this year for sales that took place the previous year).

Creditors

Whether suppliers send input goods and services to this firm for payment on 'cash on delivery terms' or 'credit terms' the accountant, rightly, records the value of these as an expense (if they are used up this year), and deducts this from the profit and loss account, in the year of delivery. The cash flow analyst needs to make an adjustment here because the full amount of the expense may not yet have flowed out in cash. So, if creditor balances increase we need to recognise that the profit and loss account has overstated the outflow of cash. We need then to add back the extent to which the creditor amount outstanding has increased from the beginning of the year to the end to arrive at the cash flow figure.

Thus we may have four working capital adjustments to make to the profit and loss account figures to arrive at cash flow figures. The value of the firm's investment in net working capital, associated with a project, is found by the:

increase in cash floats

increase in stocks

increase in debtors

less the increase in creditors

Net operating cash flow

The **net operating cash flow** associated with a new investment is equal to the profit, with depreciation[1] added back plus or minus any change in working capital. If the project results in an increase in working capital then:

Net operating cash flow = Profit before depreciation – Periodic investment in net working capital

An example of the differences between profit and cash flow

We now turn to an example of the firm, ABC plc, carrying out a project appraisal. The finance manager has been provided with forecast profit and loss accounts and has to adjust these figures to arrive at cash flow (*see* **Exhibit 3.3**). This project will require investment in machinery of £20,000 at the outset. The machinery will have a useful life of four years and a zero scrap value when production ceases at the end of the fourth year.

ABC's business involves dealing with numerous customers and the cash flows within any particular week are unpredictable. It therefore needs to maintain a cash float of £5,000 to be able to pay for day-to-day expenses. (Note: this cash float is not used up, and cannot therefore be regarded as a cost – in some weeks cash outflows are simply greater than cash inflows and to provide adequate liquidity £5,000 is needed for the firm to operate efficiently. The £5,000 will not be needed when output ceases.)

To produce the product it will be necessary to have a stock of raw materials close to hand. The investment in this form of inventory together with the cash committed to work in progress and finished goods amounts to £2,000 at the beginning of production. However, more cash (an extra £1,000) is expected to be required for this purpose at the end of the second year. When the new business is begun a large proportion of raw materials will come from suppliers who will grant additional credit. Therefore the level of creditors will rise by £1,000 over the period of the project.

To illustrate some of the differences between profit and cash flow there follows a conversion from projected accounting figures to cash flow. First it is necessary to add back the depreciation and instead account for the cost of the machine at time 0, the start date for the project when the cash actually left the firm. To capture the cash flow effect of the investment in inventories (stock) we need to see if any additional cash has been required between the beginning of the year and its end. If cash has been invested in inventory then the net stock adjustment to the cash flow calculation is negative. If cash has been released by the running down of inventory the cash flow effect is positive.

Now we turn to creditors. The accounting profit is derived after subtracting the expense of all inputs in a period, whether or not the payment for those inputs has been made in that period. If at the start ABC's suppliers provide goods and services to the value of £1,000 without requiring immediate payment then £1,000 needs to be added to the accountant's figures for true cash flow at that point. If the creditor's adjustment is not made then we are denying that of the £2,000 of stock delivered on the first day of trading half is bought on credit. It is not necessary for ABC to pay £2,000 at the start to suppliers; they pay only £1,000 and thus the creditor adjustment shows a positive cash flow at time 0, offsetting the outflow on stock. (In other examples, later in the book, it may be assumed that all stock is bought on trade credit and therefore there would not be a cash outflow for stock payments at time 0. In these examples all creditor and debtor adjustments are made at the year ends and not at time 0.) In subsequent years the prior year's creditor debts actually paid match the amount outstanding at the year end, thus no net cash flow effect adjustment is necessary.

In this simplified example it is assumed that after exactly four years all production ceases and outstanding creditors and debtors are settled on the last day of the fourth year. Also on the last day

[1] Other non-cash deductions such as for amortisation of intangible assets may also be added back.

Exhibit 3.3 ABC plc: an example of profit to cash flow conversion

- Machinery cost £20,000 at time 0, life of four years, zero scrap value.
- Extra cash floats required: £5,000, at time 0.
- Additional stock: £2,000 at time 0, £3,000 at time 2.
- Increase in creditors: £1,000.

ABC plc	Accounting year				
Point in time (yearly intervals)	0 £	1 £	2 £	3 £	4 £
Accounting profit		7,000	7,000	7,000	7,000
Add back depreciation		5,000	5,000	5,000	5,000
		12,000	**12,000**	**12,000**	**12,000**
Initial machine cost	**–20,000**				
Cash float	**–5,000**				**5,000**
Stock					
Closing stock	2,000	2,000	3,000	3,000	0
Opening stock		2,000	2,000	3,000	3,000
Net stock adjustment (Outflow –tive, Inflow +tive)	**–2,000**	**0**	**–1,000**	**0**	**+3,000**
Creditors					
End of year	1,000	1,000	1,000	1,000	0
Start of year		1,000	1,000	1,000	–1,000
Cash flow effect of creditors (Outflow –tive, Inflow +tive)	**+1,000**	**0**	**0**	**0**	**–1,000**
Net operating cash flow	**–26,000**	**12,000**	**11,000**	**12,000**	**19,000**

Point in time (yearly intervals)	**0**	**1**	**2**	**3**	**4**
Cash flow	–26,000	12,000	11,000	12,000	19,000

Cost of capital 12%

$$\text{NPV} = -26{,}000 + \frac{12{,}000}{(1+0.12)} + \frac{11{,}000}{(1+0.12)^2} + \frac{12{,}000}{(1+0.12)^3} + \frac{19{,}000}{(1+0.12)^4} = +£14{,}099$$

This project produces a positive NPV, i.e. it generates a return which is more than the required rate of 12%, and therefore should be accepted.
(An Excel spreadsheet version of this calculation is available at www.pearsoned.co.uk/arnold)

of the fourth year the money tied up in cash float and stock is released. Furthermore, the net cash flows from each year's trading all arrive on the last day of the respective year. These assumptions are obviously unrealistic, but to make the example more realistic would add to its complexity.

Strictly speaking we should allow for the fact that a business generally receives and pays cash flows fairly evenly through the year rather than assume that all cash flows occur at the end of the year. So, in theory, we should discount cash flows weekly or even daily (365 discount calculations per year!).

The practice of simplifying to one net cash flow per year, followed by most managers, is justified on the grounds of practical necessity to avoiding over-complicated calculations. Furthermore, by assuming cash comes in at the end of the year, and not any earlier, managers are, if anything, underestimating NPV. This more conservative estimate of project viability encourages greater confidence in the likelihood of project acceptance boosting shareholder wealth. An alternative is to assume cash inflows half-way through the year, in which case the discount factor becomes $\frac{1}{(1+r)^{0.5}}$, $\frac{1}{(1+r)^{1.5}}$, etc.

Incremental cash flows

A fundamental principle in project appraisal is to include only **incremental cash flows**. These are defined as the cash flows dependent on the project's implementation. Only those cash flows that are induced by the investment at time 0 and in subsequent years are regarded as incremental. Some of these cash flows are easy to establish but others are much more difficult to pin down.

Incremental cash flow = Cash flow for firm with the project − Cash flow for firm without project

Here are some guideposts for finding relevant/incremental cash flows.

Include all opportunity costs

The direct inputs into a project are generally easy to understand and measure. However, quite often a project uses resources which already exist within the firm but which are in short supply and which cannot be replaced in the immediate future. That is, the project under consideration may be taking resources away from other projects. The loss of net cash flows from these other projects is termed an opportunity cost. For example, a firm may be considering a project that makes use of a factory which at present is empty. Because it is empty we should not automatically assume that the opportunity cost is zero. Perhaps the firm could engage in the alternative project of renting out the factory to another firm. The forgone rental income is a cost of the project under consideration.

Likewise if a project uses the services of specialist personnel this may be regarded as having an opportunity cost. The loss of these people to other parts of the organisation may reduce cash flows on other projects. If they cannot be replaced with equally able individuals then the opportunity cost will be the lost net cash flows. If equally able hired replacements are found then the extra cost imposed, by the additional salaries etc., on other projects should be regarded as an opportunity cost of the new project under consideration.

For a third example of opportunity cost, imagine your firm bought, when the price was low, a stock of platinum to use as a raw material. The total cost was £1m. It would be illogical to sell the final manufactured product at a price based on the old platinum value if the same quantity would now cost £3m. An alternative course of action would be to sell the platinum in its existing state, rather than to produce the manufactured product. The current market value of the raw platinum (£3m) then is the opportunity cost.

Include all incidental effects

It is possible for a new project to either increase or reduce sales of other products of the company. Take the case of an airline company trying to decide whether to go ahead with a project to fly between the USA and Japan. The direct cash flows of selling tickets, etc. on these flights may not give a positive NPV. However, it could be that the new service generates additional net revenue not only for USA–Japan flights but also on existing routes as customers switch to this airline because it now offers a more complete worldwide service. If this additional net cash flow is included the project may be viable.

On the other hand if a clothes retailer opens a second or a third outlet in the same town, it is likely to find custom is reduced at the original store. This loss elsewhere in the organisation becomes a relevant cash flow in the appraisal of the *new* project, that is, the new shop.

In the soft drink business the introduction of a new brand can reduce the sales of the older brands. This is not to say that a company should never risk any cannibalisation, only that if a new product is to be launched it should not be viewed in isolation. All **incidental effects** have to be allowed for, including those effects not directly associated with the new product or service.

Royal Dutch/Shell are to include the incidental effect of carbon emissions in all future projects (*see* **Exhibit 3.4**).

Exhibit 3.4

Environmental cost included in project appraisals

Royal Dutch/Shell, the Anglo-Dutch energy company, has decided to include a cost for carbon emissions in all big projects. Each project is now required to achieve a satisfactory internal rate of return after the deduction of \$5 per tonne of carbon dioxide in the years 2005–2009, rising to \$20 per tonne in 2010.

Ignore sunk costs

Do not include **sunk costs**. For example, the project to build Concorde involved an enormous expenditure in design and manufacture. At the point where it had to be decided whether to put the aeroplane into service, the costs of development became irrelevant to the decision. Only incremental costs and inflows should be considered. The development costs are in the past and are bygones; they should be ignored. The money spent on development is irrecoverable, whatever the decision on whether to fly the plane. Similarly with Eurotunnel, the fact that the overspend runs into billions of pounds and the tunnel service is unlikely to make a profit does not mean that the incremental cost of using some electricity to power the trains and the cost of employing some train drivers should not be incurred. The £9bn+ already spent is irrelevant to the decision on whether to transport passengers and freight between France and the UK. So long as incremental costs are less than incremental benefits (cash flows when discounted) then the service should operate.

A common mistake in this area is to regard pre-project survey work already carried out or committed to (market demand screening, scientific study, geological survey, etc.) as a relevant cost. After all, the cost would not have been incurred but for the *possibility* of going ahead with the project. However, at the point of decision on whether to proceed, the survey cost is sunk – it will be incurred whether or not implementation takes place, and it therefore is not incremental. Sunk costs can be either costs for intangibles (such as research and development expenses), or costs for tangibles that may not be used for other purposes (such as the cost of the Eurotunnel). When dealing with sunk costs it is sometimes necessary to be resolute in the face of comments such as 'good money is being thrown after bad' but always remember the 'bad' money outflow happened in the past and is no longer an input factor into a rigorous decision-making process.

Be careful with overheads

Overheads consist of such items as managerial salaries, rent, light, heat, etc. These are costs that are not directly associated with any one part of the firm or one item produced. An accountant often allocates these overhead costs amongst the various projects a firm is involved in. When trying to assess the viability of a project we should only include the incremental or extra expenses that would be incurred by going ahead with a project. Many of the general overhead expenses may be incurred regardless of whether the project takes place.

There are two types of overhead. The first type is truly incremental costs resulting from a project. For example, extra electricity, rental and administrative staff costs may be incurred by going ahead rather than abstaining. The second type of overhead consists of such items as head office managerial salaries, legal expertise, public relations, research and development and even the corporate jet. These costs are not directly associated with any one part of the firm or one project and will be incurred regardless of whether the project under consideration is embarked upon. The accountant generally charges a proportion of this overhead to particular divisions and projects. When trying to assess the viability of a project only the incremental costs incurred by going ahead are relevant. Those costs which are unaffected are irrelevant.

Dealing with interest

Interest on funds borrowed to invest does represent a cash outflow. However, it is wrong to include this element in the cash flow calculations. **To repeat, interest should not be deducted from the net cash flows.** This is because if it were subtracted this would amount to double counting because the opportunity cost of capital used to discount the cash flows already incorporates a cost of these funds. The net cash flows are reduced to a present value by allowing for the weighted average cost of finance to give a return to shareholders and lenders. If the un-discounted cash flows also had interest deducted there would be a serious understatement of NPV. For more details see Chapter 19 on the calculation of the firm's discount rate (cost of capital).

Worked example 3.1 Tamcar plc

The accountants at Tamcar plc, manufacturers of hairpieces, are trying to analyse the viability of a proposed new division, 'Baldies heaven'. They estimate that this project will have a life of four years before the market is swamped by the lifting of the present EU import ban on hairpieces. The estimated sales, made on three months' credit, are as follows:

Year	*Sales (£)*
20X1	1.5m
20X2	2.0m
20X3	2.5m
20X4	3.0m

There are no bad debts.

Costs of production can be assumed to be paid for on the last day of the year. There are no creditors.

Year	*Cost of production (£)*
20X1	0.75m
20X2	1.00m
20X3	1.25m
20X4	1.50m

At the start of the project an investment of £1m will be required in buildings, plant and machinery. These items will have a net worth of zero at the end of this project. The accountants depreciate the buildings and machinery at 25 per cent per annum on a straight line basis.

A cash float of £0.5m will be required at the start. Also stocks will increase by £0.3m. These are both recoverable at the end of the project's life.

A £1m invoice for last year's scientific study of 'Baldies heaven' hairpiece technology (e.g. wind resistance and combability) has yet to be paid.

The head office always allocates a proportion of central expenses to all divisions and projects. The share to be borne by 'Baldies heaven' is £500,000 per annum. The head office costs are unaffected by the new project.

The accountants have produced the following projected profit and loss accounts:

Year	**20X1 £m**	**20X2 £m**	**20X3 £m**	**20X4 £m**
Sales	1.50	2.00	2.50	3.00
Costs of production	0.75	1.00	1.25	1.50
Depreciation	0.25	0.25	0.25	0.25
Scientific survey	0.25	0.25	0.25	0.25
Head office	0.50	0.50	0.50	0.50
Profit/loss	–0.25	0	0.25	0.50

Accountants' summary

Investment: £2m Return: £0.5m over 4 years

$$\text{Average Return on Investment (ROI)} = \frac{\text{Average profit}}{\text{Investment}} = \frac{0.5 \div 4}{2} = 0.0625 \text{ or } 6.25\%$$

Recommendation: do not proceed with this project as 6.25% is a poor return.

Required

Calculate the Net Present Value and recommend whether to accept this project or invest elsewhere.

Assume

- No tax.
- The return required on projects of this risk class is 11%.
- Start date of the project is 1.1.20X1.

Answer

- Depreciation is not a cash flow and should be excluded.
- The scientific survey is a sunk cost. This will not alter whether Tamcar chooses to go ahead or refuses to invest – it is irrelevant to the NPV calculation.
- Head office costs will be constant regardless of the decision to accept or reject the project, they are not incremental.

The sales figures shown in the first line of the table below are not the true cash receipts for each of those years because three months' credit is granted. Thus, in year 1 only three-quarters of £1.5m is actually received. An adjustment for debtors shows that one-quarter of the first year's sales are deducted. Thus £375,000 is received in the second year and therefore this is added to time 2's cash flow. However, one-quarter of the £2m of time 2's sales is subtracted because this is not received until the following year.

An assumption has been made concerning the receipt of debtor payments after production and distribution has ceased. In 20X4 sales are on the last day and given the three months' credit, cash is received after three months at time 4.25.

Tamcar cash flows

Time (annual intervals)	**0**	**1**	**2**	**3**	**4**	**4.25**
	start	**end**	**end**	**end**	**end**	
Year	**20X1**	**20X1**	**20X2**	**20X3**	**20X4**	**20X5**
Sales		+1.5	+2.0	+2.5	+3.0	
Buildings, plant, machinery	–1.0					
Cash float	–0.5				+0.5	
Stocks	–0.3				+0.3	
Costs of production		–0.75	–1.0	–1.25	–1.50	
Adjustment for debtors:						
Opening debtors	*0*	*0*	*0.375*	*0.500*	*0.625*	*0.75*
Closing debtors	*0*	*0.375*	*0.500*	*0.625*	*0.750*	*0*
Cash flow adjustment for debtors		–0.375	–0.125	–0.125	–0.125	+0.75
Cash flow	–1.8	+0.375	+0.875	+1.125	+2.175	+0.75
Net present value	$-1.8 +$	$\frac{0.375}{(1.11)} +$	$\frac{0.875}{(1.11)^2} +$	$\frac{1.125}{(1.11)^3} +$	$\frac{2.175}{(1.11)^4} +$	$\frac{0.75}{(1.11)^{4.25}}$
	–1.8	+0.338	+0.710	+0.823	+1.433	+0.481

NPV = + £1.985m

This is a project that adds significantly to shareholder wealth, producing £1.985m more than the minimum rate of return of 11 per cent required by the firm's finance providers.

(An Excel spreadsheet version of the calculation is available at www.pearsoned.co.uk/arnold)

Worked example 3.2 The International Seed Company (TISC)

As the newly appointed financial manager of TISC you are about to analyse a proposal for the marketing and distribution of a range of genetically engineered vegetable seeds which have been developed by a bio-technology firm. This firm will supply the seeds and permit TISC to market and distribute them under a licence.

Market research, costing £100,000, has already been carried out to establish the likely demand. After three years TISC will withdraw from the market because it anticipates that these products will be superseded by further bio-technological developments.

The annual payment to the bio-technology firm will be £1m for the licence; this will be payable at the end of each accounting year.

Also £500,000 will be needed initially to buy a fleet of vehicles for distribution. These vehicles will be sold at the end of the third year for £200,000.

There will be a need for a packaging and administrative facility. TISC is large and has a suitable factory with offices, which at present are empty. Head office has stated that they will let this space to your project at a reduced rent of £200,000 per annum payable at the end of the accounting year (the open market rental value is £1m p.a.).

The project would start on 1.1.20X1 and would not be subject to any taxation because of its special status as a growth industry. A relatively junior and inexperienced accountant has prepared forecast profit and loss accounts for the project as shown in the following table.

Year	**20X1**	**20X2**	**20X3**
	£m	**£m**	**£m**
Sales	5	6	6
Costs			
Market research	0.1		
Raw material (seeds)	2.0	2.4	2.4
Licence	1.0	1.0	1.0
Vehicle fleet depreciation	0.1	0.1	0.1
Direct wages	0.5	0.5	0.5
Rent	0.2	0.2	0.2
Overhead	0.5	0.5	0.5
Variable transport costs	0.5	0.5	0.5
Profit	0.1	0.8	0.8

By expanding its product range with these new seeds the firm expects to attract a great deal of publicity which will improve the market position, and thus the profitability, of its other products. The benefit is estimated at £100,000 for each of the three years.

Head office normally allocates a proportion of its costs to any new project as part of its budgeting/costing process. This will be £100,000 for this project and has been included in the figures calculated for overhead by the accountant. The remainder of the overhead is directly related to the project.

The direct wages, seed purchases, overhead and variable transport costs can be assumed to be paid at the end of each year. Most of the sales revenue may be assumed to be received at the end of each year. However, the firm will grant two months' credit to its customers which means that for some of the sales recorded by the accountant for a year the actual cash is received in the following year. An initial cash float of £1m will be needed. This will be returned at the end of the third year.

Assume no inflation. An appropriate discount rate is 15 per cent.

Required

Assess the viability of the proposed project using the discounted cash flow technique you feel to be most appropriate.

Suggestion

Try to answer this question before reading the model answer.

Answer

Notes

- Market research cost is non-incremental.
- Opportunity cost of factory is £1m per annum.
- Vehicle depreciation does not belong in a cash flow calculation.
- The effect on TISC's other products is an incidental benefit.
- Head office cost apportionment should be excluded.

Cash flows

£m	20X1 start	20X1 end	20X2 end	20X3 end	20X3 end	20X4 2 months
Inflows						
Sales		5.0	6.0	6.0		
Benefit to divisions		0.1	0.1	0.1		
Cash at end					1.0	
Vehicles					0.2	
Total inflows	0	5.1	6.1	6.1	1.2	0
Outflows						
Licence		1.0	1.0	1.0		
Vehicles	0.5					
Property rent (opportunity cost)		1.0	1.0	1.0		
Raw materials		2.0	2.4	2.4		
Direct wages		0.5	0.5	0.5		
Overheads		0.4	0.4	0.4		
Variable transport		0.5	0.5	0.5		
Initial cash	1.0					
Cash flows after outflows	−1.5	−0.3	0.3	0.3	1.2	0
Adjustment for debtors						
Debtor: start		0	0.833	1.00		1.0
end		0.833	1.000	1.00		0
Cash flow effect of debtors		−0.833	−0.167	0	0	+1.0
Cash flows	**−1.5**	**−1.133**	**+0.133**	**+0.3**	**+1.2**	**+1.0**

Net present value

$$NPV = -1.5 + \frac{-1.133}{(1.15)} + \frac{0.133}{(1.15)^2} + \frac{0.3}{(1.15)^3}$$

$$+ \frac{1.2}{(1.15)^3} + \frac{1.00}{(1.15)^{3.167}}$$

NPV = −1.5 − 0.985 + 0.101 + 0.197 + 0.789 + 0.642 = −£0.756

Conclusion

Do not proceed with the project as it returns less than 15 per cent.

(An Excel spreadsheet version of the calculation is available at www.pearsoned.co.uk/arnold)

Carillion, Mowlem and Amey had to pay a great deal of attention to the estimated relevant cash flows associated when building and operating key national assets such as the M6 toll road, GCHQ and the London Underground. In many cases they overestimated the likely revenue and therefore destroyed shareholder wealth (*see* **Exhibit 3.5**).

Exhibit 3.5

Investor equity brings uneven outcomes

FT

For some investors the private finance initiative has been a blessing but for others it has been a curse.

In the early 1990s, companies rushed to grab a share of the equity in UK public sector projects that – so long as they performed – offered long-term earnings, cash flows in effect guaranteed by the government and high returns: criteria that investors value highly. Many have since seen the value of their investments rocket but political sensitivities have made them reluctant to gloat.

Carillion, a leading PFI contractor, holds equity investments in 19 public sector projects, including the M6 toll road and the GCHQ communications centre in Cheltenham – and has seen its stakes almost triple in value over the past two years. An original investment of £29m has a **net present value** of £84m.

Mowlem, the construction company, generated £27m in cash from the sale of its 40 per cent stake in the company that runs part of the Docklands Light Railway in London. This was a return of 4.8 times its original investment.

But the market does contain risks and some companies' balance sheets and cash flows have suffered. Jarvis, one of the PFI losers, bid for more contracts than it could afford and underpriced them. These miscalculations led to a working capital crisis and a pile of debt.

Worked stopped abruptly on all its 14 construction projects as the company was unable to pay its subcontractors. Jarvis only narrowly avoided administration after it secured a refinancing including a £378m debt-for-equity swap.

Amey, another entrant, was hurt by high bidding costs, in particular for a contract to run part of the London Underground. The company also had to take a £40m charge in 2003 for its investment in the Croydon Tram Link project, which drew many fewer passengers than expected.

Even Carillion, considered a PFI success story, underestimated the cost of its Nottingham tram project, which led to a £10m dent in 2003 profits.

Source: Financial Times, 8 February 2006, p. 15. Reprinted with permission.

The replacement decision

In the dynamic and competitive world of business it is important to review operations continually to ensure efficient production. Technological change brings with it the danger that a competitor has reduced costs and has leaped ahead. Thus, it is often wise to examine, say, the machinery used in the production process to see if it should be replaced with a new improved version. This is a continual process in many industries, and the frustrating aspect is that the existing machine may have years of useful life left in it. Despite this the right decision is sometimes to dispose of the old and bring in the new. If your firm does not produce at lowest cost, another one will.

In making a **replacement decision** the increased costs associated with the purchase and installation of the new machine have to be weighed against the savings from switching to the new method of production. In other words the incremental cash flows are the focus of attention. The worked example of Amtarc plc demonstrates the incremental approach.

Worked example 3.3 Amtarc plc

Amtarc plc produces Tarcs with a machine which is now four years old. The management team estimates that this machine has a useful life of four more years before it will be sold for scrap, raising £10,000.

Q-leap, a manufacturer of machines suitable for Tarc production, has offered its new computer-controlled Q-2000 to Amtarc for a cost of £800,000 payable immediately.

If Amtarc sold its existing machine now, on the secondhand market, it would receive £70,000. (Its book value, after depreciation, is £150,000.) The Q-2000 will have a life of four years before being sold for scrap for £20,000.

The attractive features of the Q-2000 are its lower raw material wastage and its reduced labour requirements. Selling price and variable overhead will be the same as for the old machine.

The accountants have prepared the figures shown below on the assumption that output will remain constant at last year's level of 100,000 Tarcs per annum.

	Profit per unit of Tarc	
	Old machine	**Q-2000**
	£	**£**
Sale price	45	45
Costs		
Labour	10	9
Materials	15	14
Variable overhead	7	7
Fixed overhead		
Factory admin., etc.	5	5
Depreciation	0.35	1.95
Profit per Tarc	7.65	8.05

The depreciation per unit has been calculated as follows:

$$\frac{\text{Total depreciation for a year}}{\text{Output for a year}}$$

Old machine: $$\frac{(150{,}000 - 10{,}000)/4}{100{,}000} = £0.35$$

Q-2000: $$\frac{(800{,}000 - 20{,}000)/4}{100{,}000} = £1.95$$

An additional benefit of the Q-2000 will be the reduction in required raw material buffer stocks – releasing £120,000 at the outset. However, because of the lower labour needs, redundancy payments of £50,000 will be necessary after one year.

Assume

- No inflation or tax.
- The required rate of return is 10 per cent.
- To simplify the analysis sales, labour costs, raw material costs and variable overhead costs all occur on the last day of each year.

Required

Using the NPV method decide whether to continue using the old machine or to purchase the Q-2000.

Hints

Remember to undertake incremental analysis. That is, analyse only the difference in cash flow which will result from the decision to go ahead with the purchase. Remember to include the £10,000 opportunity cost of scrapping the old machine in four years if the Q-2000 is purchased.

Answers

Stage 1

Note the irrelevant information:

1 Depreciation is not a cash flow and should not be included.
2 The book value of the machine is merely an accounting entry and has little relationship with the market value. Theoretically book value has no influence on the decision. (In practice, however, senior management may be reluctant to write off the surplus book value through the profit and loss account as this may prejudice an observer's view of their performance – despite there being no change in the underlying economic position.)

Stage 2

Work out the annual incremental cost savings.

	Savings per Tarc		
	Old machine £	Q-2000 £	Saving £
Labour	10	9	1
Materials	15	14	1
Total saving			2

Total annual saving £2 × 100,000 = £200,000.

Stage 3 Incremental cash flow table

Time £000s	0	1	2	3	4
Purchase of Q-2000	−800				
Scrap of old machine	+70				
Raw material stocks	+120				
Opportunity cost (old machine)					−10
Redundancy payments		−50			
Sale of Q-2000					+20
Annual cost savings		+200	+200	+200	+200
	−610	+150	+200	+200	+210

Stage 4 Calculate NPV

$$\text{Discounted cash flows} \quad -610 + \frac{150}{1.1} + \frac{200}{(1.1)^2} + \frac{200}{(1.1)^3} + \frac{210}{(1.1)^4}$$

NPV = −£14,660.

The negative NPV indicates that shareholder wealth will be higher if the existing machine is retained.

Replacement cycles

Many business assets, machinery and vehicles especially, become increasingly expensive to operate and maintain as they become older. This rising cost burden prompts the thought that there must be a point when it is better to buy a replacement than to face rising repair bills. Assets such as vehicles are often replaced on a regular cycle, say every two or three years, depending on the comparison between the benefit to be derived by delaying the replacement decision (that is, the postponed cash outflow associated with the purchase of new assets) and the cost in terms of higher maintenance costs (and lower secondhand value achieved with the sale of the used asset).

Consider the case of a car rental firm which is considering a switch to a new type of car. The cars cost £10,000 and a choice has to be made between four alternative (mutually exclusive) projects (four alternative regular replacement cycles). Project 1 is to sell the cars on the secondhand market after one year for £7,000. Project 2 is to sell after two years for £5,000. Projects 3 and 4 are three-year and four-year cycles and will produce £3,000 and £1,000 respectively on the secondhand market. The cost of maintenance rises from £500 in the first year to £900 in the second, £1,200 in the third and £2,500 in the fourth. The cars are not worth keeping for more than four years because of the bad publicity associated with breakdowns. The revenue streams and other costs are unaffected by which cycle is selected. We will focus on achieving the lowest present value of the costs.

If we make the simplifying assumption that all the cash flows occur at annual intervals then the relevant cash flows are as set out in **Exhibit 3.6**.

Exhibit 3.6 Relevant cash flows

	Point in time (yearly intervals)	0	1	2	3	4
		£	£	£	£	£
Project 1 *Replace after one year*	Purchase cost	−10,000				
	Maintenance		−500			
	Sale proceeds		+7,000			
	Net cash flow	−10,000	+6,500			
Project 2 *Replace after two years*	Purchase cost	−10,000				
	Maintenance		−500	−900		
	Sale proceeds			+5,000		
	Net cash flow	−10,000	−500	+4,100		
Project 3 *Replace after three years*	Purchase cost	−10,000				
	Maintenance		−500	−900	−1,200	
	Sale proceeds				+3,000	
	Net cash flow	−10,000	−500	−900	+1,800	
Project 4 *Replace after four years*	Purchase cost	−10,000				
	Maintenance		−500	−900	−1,200	−2,500
	Sale proceeds					+1,000
	Net cash flow	−10,000	−500	−900	−1,200	−1,500

Assuming a discount rate of 10 per cent the Present Values (PVs) of costs of one cycle of the projects are:

$$PV_1 \quad -10{,}000 + \frac{6{,}500}{1.1} = -4{,}090.90$$

$$PV_2 \quad -10{,}000 - \frac{500}{1.1} + \frac{4{,}100}{(1.1)^2} = -7{,}066.12$$

$$PV_3 \quad -10{,}000 - \frac{500}{1.1} - \frac{900}{(1.1)^2} + \frac{1{,}800}{(1.1)^3} = -9{,}845.98$$

$$PV_4 \quad -10{,}000 - \frac{500}{1.1} - \frac{900}{(1.1)^2} - \frac{1{,}200}{(1.1)^3} - \frac{1{,}500}{(1.1)^4} = -13{,}124.44$$

At first sight the figures in Exhibit 3.6 might suggest that the first project is the best. Such a conclusion would be based on the normal rule with mutually exclusive projects of selecting the one with the lowest present value of costs. However, this is not a standard situation because purchases and sales of vehicles have to be allowed for far beyond the first round in the replacement cycle. If we can make the assumption that there are no increases in costs and the cars can be replaced with identical models on regular cycles in the future[2] then the pattern of cash flows for the third project, for example, are as shown in **Exhibit 3.7**.

Exhibit 3.7 Cash flows for Project 3

Time (years)	0	1	2	3	4	5	6	7 ...
Cash flows (£)								
1st generation	–10,000	–500	–900	+1,800				
2nd generation				–10,000	–500	–900	+1,800	
3rd generation							–10,000	–500 ...

One way of dealing with a long-lived project of this kind is to calculate the present values of numerous cycles stretching into the future. This can then be compared with other projects' present values calculated in a similarly time-consuming fashion. Fortunately there is a much quicker technique available called the annual equivalent annuity method (AEA). This third project involves three cash outflows followed by a cash inflow within one cycle as shown in **Exhibit 3.8**.

Exhibit 3.8 Cash outflows and cash inflow in one cycle

Time (years)	0	1	2	3
Cash flows (£)	–10,000	–500	–900	+1,800

This produces a one-cycle present value of –£9,845.98. The **annual equivalent annuity** (AEA) method finds the amount that would be paid in each of the next three years if each annual payment were identical and the three payments gave the same (equivalent) present value of –£9,845.98, that is, the constant amount which would replace the ? in **Exhibit 3.9**.

Exhibit 3.9 Using the AEA

Time (years)	0	1	2	3	Present value
Actual cash flows (£)	–10,000	–500	–900	+1,800	-9,845.98
Annual equivalent annuity (£)		?	?	?	-9,845.98

(Recall that the first cash flow under an 'immediate' annuity arises after one year.)

To find the AEA we need to employ the annuity table in Appendix III. This table gives the value of a series of £1 cash flows occurring at annual intervals in terms of present money. Normally these 'annuity factors' (af) are multiplied by the amount of the cash flow that is received regularly, the annuity (A), to obtain the present value, PV. In this case we already know the PV and we can obtain the af by looking at the three-year row and the 10 per cent column. The missing element is the annual annuity.

$$PV = A \times af$$

$$\text{or } A = \frac{PV}{af}$$

[2] This is a bold assumption. More realistic assumptions could be made, e.g. allowing for inflation, but the complexity that this produces is beyond the scope of this book.

In the case of the three-year replacement:

$$A = \frac{-£9,845.98}{2.4869} = -£3,959.14$$

Thus, two alternative sets of cash flows give the same present value (*see* **Exhibit 3.10**).

Exhibit 3.10 Cash flow 1 and Cash flow 2

Time (years)	0 £	1 £	2 £	3 £
Cash flow 1	-10,000	-500	-900	+1,800
Cash flow 2		-3,959.14	-3,959.14	-3,959.14

The second generation of cars bought at the end of the third year will have a cost of –£9,845.98 when discounted to the end of the third year (assuming both zero inflation and that the discount rate remains at 10 per cent). The present value of the costs of this second generation of vehicle is equivalent to the present value of an annuity of –£3,959.14. Thus replacing the car every three years is equivalent to a cash flow of –£3,959.14 every year to infinity (*see* **Exhibit 3.11**).

Exhibit 3.11 Replacing the car every three years

Time (years)	0	1	2	3	4	5	6	7 ...
Cash flows (£)								
First generation	-10,000	-500	-900	+1,800				
Second generation				-10,000	-500	-900	+1,800	
Third generation							-10,000	-500 ...
Annual equivalent annuity	0	-3,959.14	-3,959.14	-3,959.14	-3,959.14	-3,959.14	-3,959.14	-3,959.14

If all the other projects are converted to their annual equivalent annuities a comparison can be made (*see* **Exhibit 3.12**).

Exhibit 3.12 Using AEAs for all projects

Cycle	Present value of one cycle (PV)	Annuity factor (af)	Annual equivalent annuity (PV/af)
1 year	-4,090.90	0.9091	-4,500.00
2 years	-7,066.12	1.7355	-4,071.52
3 years	-9,845.98	2.4869	-3,959.14
4 years	-13,124.44	3.1699	-4,140.33

Thus Project 3 requires the lowest equivalent annual cash flow and is the optimal replacement cycle. This is over £540 per year cheaper than replacing the car every year.

A valid alternative to the annual equivalent annuity is the **lowest common multiple (LCM) method**. Here the alternatives are compared using the present value of the costs over a timespan equal to the lowest common multiple of the cycle lengths. So the cash flow for 12 cycles of Project

1 would be discounted and compared with six cycles of Project 2, four cycles of Project 3 and three cycles of Project 4. The AEA method is the simplest and quickest method in cases where the lowest common multiple is high. For instance the LCM of five-, six- and seven-year cycles is 210 years, and involves a great many calculations.

Worked example 3.4 Brrum plc

Suppose the firm Brrum has to decide between two machines, A and B, to replace an old worn-out one. Whichever new machine is chosen it will be replaced on a regular cycle. Both machines produce the same level of output. Because they produce exactly the same output we do not need to examine the cash inflows at all to choose between the machines; we can concentrate solely on establishing the lower-cost machine.

Brrum plc

- Machine A costs £30m, lasts three years and costs £8m a year to run.
- Machine B costs £20m, lasts two years and costs £12m a year to run.

Cash flows

Point in time (yearly intervals)	**0**	**1**	**2**	**3**	**PV (6%)**
Machine A (£m)	−30	−8	−8	−8	−51.38
Machine B (£m)	−20	−12	−12	–	−42.00

Because Machine B has a lower PV of cost, should we jump to the conclusion that this is the better option? Well, Machine B will have to be replaced one year before Machine A and therefore, there are further cash flows to consider and discount.

If we were to assume a constant discount rate of 6 per cent and no change in costs over a number of future years, then we can make a comparison between the two machines. To do this we need to convert the total PV of the costs to a cost per year. We convert the PV of the costs associated with each machine to the equivalent annuity.

Machine A

Machine A has a PV of −£51.38m. We need to find an annuity with a PV of −£51.38m which has regular equal costs occurring at years 1, 2 and 3.

Look in the annuity table along the row of 3 years and down the column of 6% to get the three-year annuity factor.

PV = Annual annuity payment (A) × 3-year annuity factor (af)

$$-51.38 = A \times 2.673$$
$$A = -51.38/2.673 = -£19.22\text{m per year}$$

Point in time (yearly intervals)	**0**	**1**	**2**	**3**	**PV (6%)**
Cash flows (£m)	−30	−8	−8	−8	−51.38
Equivalent 3-year annuity (£m)		−19.22	−19.22	−19.22	−51.38

When Machine A needs to be replaced at the end of the third year, if we can assume it is replaced by a machine of equal cost we again have a PV of costs for the end of year 3 of £51.38m. This too has an equivalent annuity of −£19.22m. Thus, the −£19.22m annual costs is an annual cost for many years beyond year 3.

Machine B

$$PV = A \times af$$
$$-42 = A \times 1.8334$$
$$A = -42/1.8334 = -£22.908\text{m}$$

Point in time (yearly intervals)	0	1	2	PV (6%)
Cash flows (£m)	−20	−12	−12	−42
Equivalent 2-year annuity (£m)		−22.91	−22.91	−42

Again, if we assume that at the end of two years the machine is replaced with an identical one, with identical costs, then the annuity of −£22.91m can be assumed to be continuing into the future.

Comparing the annual annuities

Machine A: (£m) −19.22.
Machine B: (£m) −22.91.

When we compare the annual annuities we see that Machine A, in fact, has the lower annual cost and is therefore the better buy.

When to introduce a new machine

Businesses, when switching from one kind of a machine to another, have to decide on the timing of that switch. The best option may not be to dispose of the old machine immediately. It may be better to wait for a year or two because the costs of running the old machine may amount to less than the equivalent annual cost of starting a regular cycle with replacements. However, eventually the old machine is going to become more costly due to its lower efficiency, increased repair bills or declining secondhand value. Let us return to the case of the car rental firm. It has been established that when a replacement cycle is begun for the new type of car, it should be a three-year cycle. The existing type of car used by the firm has a potential further life of two years. The firm is considering three alternative courses of action. The first is to sell the old vehicles immediately, raising £7,000 per car, and then begin a three-year replacement cycle with the new type of car. The second possibility is to spend £500 now to service the vehicles ready for another year's use. At the end of the year the cars could be sold for £5,200 each. The third option is to pay £500 for servicing now, followed by a further £2,000 in one year to maintain the vehicles on the road for a second year, after which they would be sold for £1,800. The easiest approach for dealing with a problem of this

Exhibit 3.13 Cash flow per car (excluding operating revenues, etc.)

Point in time (yearly intervals)		0 £	1 £	2 £	$3 \rightarrow \infty$ £
Option 1 – sell old car at time 0	Secondhand value	+7,000			
	New car		−3,959.14	−3,959.14	−3,959.14
	Net cash flow	+7,000	−3,959.14	−3,959.14	−3,959.14
Option 2 – sell old car after one year	Secondhand value		+5,200		
	Maintenance	−500			
	New car			−3,959.14	−3,959.14
	Net cash flow	−500	+5,200	−3,959.14	−3,959.14
Option 3 – sell old car after two years	Secondhand value			+1,800	
	Maintenance	−500	−2,000		
	New car				−3,959.14
	Net cash flow	−500	−2,000	+1,800	−3,959.14

nature is to calculate NPVs for all the possible alternatives. We will assume that the revenue aspect of this car rental business can be ignored as this will not change regardless of which option is selected. The relevant cash flows are shown in **Exhibit 3.13**. Note that the annual equivalent annuity cash flow, rather than the actual cash flows for the three-year cycle of new cars, is incorporated and is assumed to continue to infinity. It is therefore a perpetuity.

(Note that the sums of £3,959.14 are perpetuities starting at times 1, 2 and 3, and so are valued at times 0, 1 and 2. The latter two therefore have to be discounted back one and two years respectively.) The net present value calculations are as set out in **Exhibit 3.14**. The switch to the new cars should take place after one year. Thereafter the new cars should be replaced every three years. This policy is over £800 cheaper than selling off the old cars immediately.

Exhibit 3.14 **Present value calculations**

Option 1: $$+7{,}000 - \frac{3{,}959.14}{0.1} = -£32{,}591.4$$

Option 2: $$-500 + \frac{5{,}200}{1.1} - \frac{3{,}959.14}{0.1} \times \frac{1}{1.1} = -£31{,}764.91$$

Option 3: $$-500 - \frac{2{,}000}{1.1} + \frac{1{,}800}{(1.1)^2} - \frac{3{,}959.14}{0.1} \times \frac{1}{(1.1)^2} = -£33{,}550.74$$

Drawbacks of the annual equivalent annuity method

It is important to note that annual equivalent annuity analysis relies on there being a high degree of predictability of cash flows stretching into the future. While the technique can be modified reasonably satisfactorily for the problems caused by inflation we may encounter severe problems if the assets in question are susceptible to a high degree of technical change and associated cash flows. An example here would be computer hardware where simultaneously, over short time periods both technical capability increases and cost of purchase decreases. The absence of predictability means that the AEA approach is not suitable in a number of situations. The requirement that identical replacement takes place can be a severe limitation but the AEA approach can be used for approximate analysis, which is sufficient for practical decisions in many situations – provided the analyst does not become too preoccupied with mathematical preciseness and remembers that good judgement is also required.

Timing of projects

In some industries the mutually exclusive projects facing the firm may simply be whether to take a particular course of action now or to make shareholders better off by considering another possibility, for instance, to implement the action in a future year. It may be that taking action now would produce a positive NPV and is therefore attractive. However, by delaying action an even higher NPV can be obtained. Take the case of Lochglen distillery. Ten years ago it laid down a number of vats of whisky. These have a higher market value the older the whisky becomes. The issue facing the management team is to decide in which of the next seven years to bottle and sell it. The table in **Exhibit 3.15** gives the net cash flows available for each of the seven alternative projects.

The longer the firm refrains from harvesting, the greater the size of the money inflow. However, this does not necessarily imply that shareholders will be best served by delaying as long as possible. They have an opportunity cost for their funds and therefore the firm must produce an adequate return over a period of time. In the case of Lochglen the assumption is that the firm requires a 9 per cent return on projects. The calculation of the NPVs for each project is easy (*see* **Exhibit 3.16**).

Exhibit 3.15 Lochglen distillery's choices

	Year of bottling						
Point in time (yearly intervals)	**0**	**1**	**2**	**3**	**4**	**5**	**6**
Net cash flow £000s per vat	60	75	90	103	116	129	139
Percentage change on previous year		25%	20%	14.4%	12.6%	11.2%	7.8%

Exhibit 3.16 NPVs for Lochglen distillery's choices

	Year of bottling						
Point in time (yearly intervals)	**0**	**1**	**2**	**3**	**4**	**5**	**6**
£000s per vat		$\frac{75}{1.09}$	$\frac{90}{(1.09)^2}$	$\frac{103}{(1.09)^3}$	$\frac{116}{(1.09)^4}$	$\frac{129}{(1.09)^5}$	$\frac{139}{(1.09)^6}$
Net present value	60	68.8	75.8	79.5	82.2	83.8	82.9

As shown in Exhibit 3.16, the optimal point is at Year 5 when the whisky has reached the ripe old age of 15. Note also that prior to the fifth year the value increased at an annual rate greater than 9 per cent. After Year 5 (or 15 years old) the rate of increase is less than the cost of capital. Another way of viewing this is to say that if the whisky was sold when at 15 years old, the cash received could be invested elsewhere (for the same level of risk) and receive a return of 9 per cent, which is more than the 7.8 per cent available by holding the whisky one more year.

The make or buy decision

A perennial issue that many organisations need to address is whether it is better to buy a particular item, such as a component, from a supplier or to produce the item in-house. If the firm produces for itself it will incur the costs of set-up as well as the ongoing annual costs. These costs can be avoided by buying in but this has the potential drawback that the firm may be forced to pay a high market price.

Exhibit 3.17 Cash flows for producing 'eyes' in-house

Points in time (yearly intervals) £000s	**0**	**1**	**2**	**3**	**4**
1 Cash flows of self-production	40	80	85	92	100
2 Plus opportunity costs		20	20	20	20
3 Relevant cash flows of making	40	100	105	112	120
4 Costs of purchasing component		105	120	128	132
Incremented cash flow due to making (line 4 – line 3)	–40	5	15	16	12

Net present value of incremental cash flows

$$-40 + \frac{5}{1.11} + \frac{15}{(1.11)^2} + \frac{16}{(1.11)^3} + \frac{12}{(1.11)^4}$$

NPV = –£3,717

This is essentially an incremented cash flow problem. We need to establish the difference between the costs of set-up and production in-house and the costs of purchase. Take the case of Davis and Davies plc who manufacture fishing rods. At the moment they buy in the 'eyes' for the rods from I'spies plc at £1 per set. They expect to make use of 100,000 sets per annum for the next few years. If Davis and Davies were to produce their own 'eyes' they would have to spend £40,000 immediately on machinery, setting up and training. The machinery will have a life of four years and the annual cost of production of 100,000 sets will be £80,000, £85,000, £92,000 and £100,000 respectively. The cost of bought-in components is not expected to remain at £1 per set. The more realistic estimates are £105,000 for year 1, followed by £120,000, £128,000 and £132,000 for years 2 to 4 respectively, for 100,000 sets per year. The new machinery will be installed in an empty factory the open market rental value of which is £20,000 per annum and the firm's cost of capital is 11 per cent. The extra cash flows associated with in-house production compared with buying in are as set out in **Exhibit 3.17**.

As the incremental NPV is negative Davis and Davies should continue to purchase 'eyes'. The present values of the future annual savings are worth less than the initial investment for self-production.

An example of this sort of buy-in or build decision is shown for JCB in **Exhibit 3.18**.

Exhibit 3.18

JCB to buck trend and build engines

FT

By Dan Roberts, Industrial Editor

JCB is due to buck the trend in British engineering decline by launching one of the first new engines designed and built entirely in the UK for over a decade.

The Staffordshire manufacturer of construction equipment says signs of recovery in several of its main export markets have encouraged it to commit £50m to replace existing diesel engines bought from foreign-owned suppliers.

Although the capital expenditure is small by global standards, it reflects growing confidence in one of the UK's biggest privately-owned companies and contradicts warnings that the specialist expertise required has been lost. . . .

'Until recently we have never had the volume of sales to support the development of a new engine but we have been developing the project in secret for the last four years', said Mr Patterson. . . .

JCB says annual vehicle sales are more than 30,000, up from 11,000 in 1993. . . .

Source: Financial Times, 29 August 2003, p. 4. Reprinted with permission.

Fluctuating output

Many businesses and individual machines operate at less than full capacity for long periods of time. Sometimes this is due to the nature of the firm's business. For instance, electricity demand fluctuates through the day and over the year. Fluctuating output can produce some interesting problems for project appraisal analysis. Take the case of the Potato Sorting Company, which grades and bags potatoes in terms of size and quality. During the summer and autumn its two machines work at full capacity, which is the equivalent of 20,000 bags per machine per year. However, in the six months of the winter and spring the machines work at half capacity because fewer home grown potatoes need to be sorted. The operating cost of the machine per bag is 20 pence. The machines were installed over 50 years ago and can be regarded as still having a very long productive life. Despite this they have no secondhand value because modern machines called Fastsort now dominate the market. Fastsort has an identical capacity to the old machine but its running cost is only 10 pence per bag. These machines are also expected to be productive indefinitely, but they cost £12,000 each to purchase and install. The new production manager is keen on getting rid of the two old machines and replacing them with two Fastsort machines. She has presented the figures given in **Exhibit 3.19** to a board meeting on the assumption of a cost of capital of 10 per cent.

The production manager has identified a way to save the firm £6,000 and is duly proud of her presentation. The newly appointed finance director thanks her for bringing this issue to the attention of the board but thinks that they should consider a third possibility. This is to replace only one of the machines. The virtue of this approach is that during the slack six months only the Fastsort will be used and can be supplemented with the old machine during the busy period, thus avoiding £12,000 of initial investment. The figures work out as set out in **Exhibit 3.20**.

Exhibit 3.19 Comparison of old machines with Fastsort

Cost of two old machines

Output per machine per year	=	rate of 20,000 p.a. for six months $20{,}000 \times 0.5$	=	10,000
	+	rate of 10,000 p.a. for six months $10{,}000 \times 0.5$	=	5,000
				15,000

15,000 bags @ 20p × 2 = £6,000.

Present value of a perpetuity of £6,000: $\frac{6{,}000}{0.1}$ = £60,000

Cost of the Fastsorts

Annual output – same as under old machines, 30,000 bags p.a.

Annual operating cost 30,000 × 10p = £3,000

Present value of operating costs $\frac{3{,}000}{0.1}$ = £30,000

Plus initial investment	£24,000
Overall cost in present value terms	£54,000

Exhibit 3.20 Replacing only one old machine

	Fastsort		Old machine	
Output	20,000 bags		10,000 bags	
Initial investment	£12,000			
Operating costs	10p × 20,000	= £2,000	20p × 10,000	= £2,000
Present value of operating costs	$\frac{2{,}000}{0.1}$	= £20,000	$\frac{2{,}000}{0.1}$	= £20,000
Total present value of costs	£12,000	+ £20,000	+ £20,000	= £52,000

The board decides to replace only one of the machines as this saves £8,000 compared with £6,000 under the production manager's proposal.

Concluding comments

Finding appropriate cash flows to include in a project appraisal often involves some difficulty in data collection and requires some thoughtfulness in applying the concepts of incremental cash flow. The reader who has diligently worked through this chapter and has overcome the barriers to understanding may be more than a little annoyed at being told that the understanding of these issues is merely one of the stages leading to successful application of net present value to practical business problems. The logical, mathematical and conceptual knowledge presented above has to be married to an appreciation of real-world limitations imposed by the awkward fact that it is people who have to be persuaded to act to implement a plan. This is an issue examined in the next chapter. Further real-world complications such as the existence of risk, of inflation and taxation and of limits placed on availability of capital are covered in subsequent chapters.

Key points and concepts

- **Raw data** have to be checked for accuracy, reliability, timeliness, expense of collection, etc.
- **Depreciation** is not a cash flow and should be excluded.
- **Profit** is a poor substitute for cash flow. For example, working capital adjustments may be needed to modify the profit figures for NPV analysis.
- Analyse on the basis of **incremental cash flows**. That is the difference between the cash flows arising if the project is implemented and the cash flows if the project is not implemented:
  - **opportunity costs** associated with, say, using an asset which has an alternative employment are relevant;
  - **incidental effects**, that is, cash flow effects throughout the organisation, should be considered along with the obvious direct effects;
  - **sunk costs** – costs which will not change regardless of the decision to proceed are clearly irrelevant;
  - **allocated overhead** is a non-incremental cost and is irrelevant;
  - **interest** should not be double counted by both including interest as a cash flow and including it as an element in the discount rate.
- **The replacement decision** is an example of the application of incremental cash flow analysis.
- **Annual equivalent annuities (AEA)** can be employed to estimate the **optimal replacement cycle** for an asset under certain restrictive assumptions. The **lowest common multiple (LCM)** method is sometimes employed for short-lived assets.
- Whether to repair the old machine or sell it and buy a new machine is a very common business dilemma. Incremental cash flow analysis helps us to solve these types of problems. Other applications include **the timing of projects**, the issue of **fluctuating output** and the **make** or **buy decision**.

References and further reading

Bierman, H. and Smidt, S. (2006) *The Capital Budgeting Decision*, 9th edn. London: Routledge.
Contains some good chapters for the beginner.

Bierman, H. and Smidt, S. (2006) *Advanced Capital Budgeting*. London: Routledge.
Good for those wanting to pursue these topics in more depth.

Carsberg, B.V. (1975) *Economics of Business Decisions*. Harmondsworth: Penguin.
An economist's perspective on relevant cash flows.

Coulthurst, N.J. (1986) 'The application of the incremental principle in capital investment project evaluation', *Accounting and Business Research*, Autumn.
A discussion of the theoretical and practical application of the incremental cash flow principle.

Damodaran, A. (1999) *Applied Corporate Finance*. New York: Wiley.
A clear account of some of the issues discussed in this chapter.

Gordon, L.A. and Stark, A.W. (1989) 'Accounting and economic rates of return: a note on depreciation and other accruals', *Journal of Business Finance and Accounting*, 16(3), pp. 425–32.
Considers the problem of depreciation – an algebraic approach.

Pohlman, R.A., Santiago, E.S. and Markel, F.L. (1988) 'Cash flow estimation practices of larger firms', *Financial Management*, Summer.
Evidence on large US corporation cash flow estimation practices.

Reinhardt, U.E. (1973) 'Break-even analysis for Lockheed's Tristar: an application of financial theory', *Journal of Finance*, 28, pp. 821–38, September.
An interesting application of the principle of the opportunity cost of funds.

Wilkes, F.M. (1983) *Capital Budgeting Techniques*, 2nd edn. Chichester: Wiley.
Useful if your maths is up to scratch.

Case study recommendations

Please see www.pearsoned.co.uk/arnold for case study synopses.

- TechnoServe and the Tanzanian Specialty Coffee Industry. Authors: P.A. Hecht and S. Haji (2004) Harvard Business School.
- Wabash Music, Inc. Author: T. Luehrman (2005) Harvard Business School.

Self-review questions

1 Imagine the Ministry of Defence have spent £50m researching and developing a new guided weapon system. Explain why this fact may be irrelevant to the decision on whether to go ahead with production.

2 'Those business school graduates don't know what they are talking about. We have to allocate overheads to every department and activity. If we simply excluded this cost there would be a big lump of costs not written off. All projects must bear some central overhead.' Discuss this statement.

3 What is an annual equivalent annuity?

4 What are the two main techniques available for evaluating mutually exclusive repeated projects with different lengths of life? Why is it not valid simply to use NPVs?

5 Arcmat plc owns a factory which at present is empty. Mrs Hambicious, a business strategist, has been working on a proposal for using the factory for doll manufacture. This will require complete modernisation. Mrs Hambicious is a little confused about project appraisal and has asked your advice about which of the following are relevant and incremental cash flows.

a The future cost of modernising the factory.
b The £100,000 spent two months ago on a market survey investigating the demand for these plastic dolls.
c Machines to produce the dolls – cost £10m payable on delivery.
d Depreciation on the machines.
e Arcmat's other product lines are expected to be more popular due to the complementary nature of the new doll range with these existing products – the net cash flow effect is anticipated at £1m.
f Three senior managers will be drafted in from other divisions for a period of a year.
g A proportion of the US head office costs.
h The tax saving due to the plant investment being offset against taxable income.
i The £1m of additional raw material stock required at the start of production.
j The interest that will be charged on the £20m bank loan needed to initiate this project.
k The cost of the utility services installed last year.

6 In a 'make or buy' type of decision should we also consider factors not easily quantified such as security of supply, convenience and the morale of the workforce? (This question is meant to start you thinking about the issues discussed in Chapter 4. You are not expected to give a detailed answer yet.)

7 'Depreciation is a cost recognised by tax authorities so why don't you use it in project appraisal?' Help the person who asked this question.

8 A firm is considering the implementation of a new project to produce slippers. The already owned equipment to be used has sufficient spare capacity to allow this new production without affecting existing product ranges. The production manager suggests that because the equipment has been paid for it is a sunk cost and should not be included in the project appraisal calculations. Do you accept his argument?

Questions and problems

myfinancelab **Questions with an icon are also available for practice in MyFinanceLab with additional supporting resources.**

An asterisk* indictates that the answers are provided in the lecturer's guide only.

1 The Tenby-Saundersfoot Dock company is considering the reopening of one of its mothballed loading docks. Repairs and new equipment will cost £250,000 payable immediately. To operate the new dock will require additional dockside employees costing £70,000 per year. There will also be a need for additional administrative staff and other overheads such as extra stationery, insurance and telephone costs amounting to £85,000 per year. Electricity and other energy used on the dock is anticipated to cost £40,000 per year. The London head office will allocate £50,000 of its (unchanged) costs to this project. Other docks will experience a reduction in receipts of about £20,000 per year due to some degree of cannibalisation. Annual fees expected from the new dock are £255,000 per year.

Assume

- all cash flows arise at the year ends except the initial repair and equipment costs which are incurred at the outset;
- no tax or inflation;
- no sales are made on credit.

a Lay out the net annual cash flow calculations. Explain your reasoning.
b Assume an infinite life for the project and a cost of capital of 17 per cent. What is the net present value?

?

2 A senior management team at Railcam, a supplier to the railway industry, is trying to prepare a cash flow forecast for the years 20X2–20X4. The estimated sales are:

Year	20X1	20X2	20X3	20X4	20X5
Sales (£)	20m	22m	24m	21m	25m

These sales will be made on three months' credit and there will be no bad debts.

There are only three cost elements. First, wages amounting to £6m per year. Second, raw materials costing one-half of sales for the year. Raw material suppliers grant three months of credit. Third, direct overhead (only incurred if the project is undertaken) at £5m per year. Start date: 1.1.20X1.

Calculate the net operating cash flow for the years 20X2–20X4.

?

3 (*Examination level*) Pine Ltd have spent £20,000 researching the prospects for a new range of products. If it were decided that production is to go ahead an investment of £240,000 in capital equipment on 1 January 20X1 would be required.

The accounts department has produced budgeted profit and loss statements for each of the next five years for the project. At the end of the fifth year the capital equipment will be sold and production will cease.

The capital equipment is expected to be sold for scrap on 31.12.20X5 for £40,000.

	Year end 31.12.20X1	Year end 31.12.20X2	Year end 31.12.20X3	Year end 31.12.20X4	Year end 31.12.20X5
Sales	400	400	400	320	200
Materials	240	240	240	192	120
Other variable costs	40	40	40	32	20
Overheads	20	20	24	24	24
Depreciation	40	40	40	40	40
Net profit/(loss)	60	60	56	32	(4)

(All figures in £000s)

When production is started it will be necessary to raise material stock levels by £30,000 and other working capital by £20,000.

Both the additional stock and other working capital increases will be released at the end of the project.

Customers receive one year's credit from the firm.

The overhead figures in the budgeted accounts have two elements – 60 per cent is due to a reallocation of existing overheads, 40 per cent is directly incurred because of the take-up of the project.

For the purposes of this appraisal you may regard all receipts and payments as occurring at the year end to which they relate, unless otherwise stated. The company's cost of capital is 12 per cent.

Assume no inflation or tax.

Required

a Use the net present value method of project appraisal to advise the company on whether to go ahead with the proposed project.

b Explain to a management team unfamiliar with discounted cash flow appraisal techniques the significance and value of the NPV method.

(In addition to the solution given in Appendix VII there is an Excel spreadsheet solution available at www.pearsoned.co.uk/arnold)

?

4* (*Examination level*) Mercia plc owns two acres of derelict land near to the centre of a major UK city. The firm has received an invoice for £50,000 from consultants who were given the task of analysis, investigation and design of some project proposals for using the land. The consultants outline the two best proposals to a meeting of the board of Mercia.

Proposal 1 is to spend £150,000 levelling the site and then constructing a six-level car park at an additional cost of £1,600,000. The earthmoving firm will be paid £150,000 on the start date and the construction firm will be paid £1.4m on the start date, with the balance payable 24 months later.

It is expected that the car park will be fully operational as from the completion date (365 days after the earthmovers first begin).

The annual income from ticket sales will be £600,000 to an infinite horizon. Operational costs (attendants, security, power, etc.) will be £100,000 per annum. The consultants have also apportioned £60,000 of Mercia's central overhead costs (created by the London-based head office and the executive jet) to this project.

The consultants present their analysis in terms of a commonly used measure of project viability, that of payback.

This investment idea is not original; Mercia investigated a similar project two years ago and discovered that there are some costs which have been ignored by the consultants. First, the local council will require a payment of £100,000 one year after the completion of the construction for its inspection services and a trading and environmental impact licence. Second, senior management will have to leave aside work on other projects, resulting in delays and reduced income from these projects amounting to £50,000 per year once the car park is operational. Also, the proposal is subject to depreciation of one-fiftieth (1/50) of the earthmoving and construction costs each year.

Proposal 2 is for a health club. An experienced company will, for a total cost of £9m payable at the start of the project, design and construct the buildings and supply all the equipment. It will be ready for Mercia's use one year after construction begins. Revenue from customers will be £5m per annum and operating costs will be £4m per annum. The consultants allocate £70,000 of central general head office overhead costs for each year from the start. After two years of operating the health club Mercia will sell it for a total of £11m.

Information not considered by the consultants for Proposal 2

The £9m investment includes £5m in buildings not subject to depreciation. It also includes £4m in equipment, 10 per cent of which has to be replaced each year. This has not been included in the operating costs.

A new executive will be needed to oversee the project from the start of the project – costing £100,000 per annum.

The consultants recommend that the board of Mercia accept the second proposal and reject the first.

Assume

- If the site was sold with no further work carried out it would fetch £100,000.
- No inflation or tax.
- The cost of capital for Mercia is 10 per cent (this is the relevant rate for this project).
- It can be assumed, for simplicity of analysis, that all cash flows occur at year ends except those occurring at the start of the project.

Required

a Calculate the net present value of each proposal.
State whether you would recommend Proposal 1 or 2.

b Calculate the internal rate of return for each proposed project.

(In addition to the solution given in the Lecturer's Guide there is an Excel spreadsheet solution available at www.pearsoned.co.uk/arnold (Lecturer's Guide))

?

5* (*Examination level*) Mines International plc

The Albanian government is auctioning the rights to mine copper in the east of the country. Mines International plc (MI) is considering the amount they would be prepared to pay as a lump sum for the five-year licence. The auction is to take place very soon and the cash will have to be paid immediately following the auction.

In addition to the lump sum the Albanian government will expect annual payments of £500,000 to cover 'administration'. If MI wins the licence, production would not start until one year later because it will take a year to prepare the site and buy in equipment. To begin production MI would have to commission the manufacture of specialist engineering equipment costing £9.5m, half of which is payable immediately, with the remainder due in one year.

MI has already conducted a survey of the site which showed a potential productive life of four years with its new machine. The survey cost £300,000 and is payable immediately.

The accounts department have produced the following projected profit and loss accounts.

	Year				
Projected profit and loss (£m)	1	2	3	4	5
Sales	0	8	9	9	7
Less expenses					
Materials and consumables	0.6	0.4	0.5	0.5	0.4
Wages	0.3	0.7	0.7	0.7	0.7
Overheads	0.4	0.5	0.6	0.6	0.5
Depreciation of equipment	0	2.0	2.0	2.0	2.0
Albanian govt. payments	0.5	0.5	0.5	0.5	0.5
Survey costs written off	0.3				
Profit (loss) excluding licence fee	(2.1)	3.9	4.7	4.7	2.9

The following additional information is available:

a Payments and receipts arise at the year ends unless otherwise stated.
b The initial lump sum payment has been excluded from the projected accounts as this is unknown at the outset.
c The customers of MI demand and receive a credit period of three months.
d The suppliers of materials and consumables grant a credit period of three months.
e The overheads contain an annual charge of £200,000 which represents an apportionment of head office costs. This is an expense which would be incurred whether or not the project proceeds. The remainder of the overheads relate directly to the project.
f The new equipment will have a resale value at the end of the fifth year of £1.5m.
g During the whole of Year 3 a specialised item of machinery will be needed, which is currently being used by another division of MI. This division will therefore incur hire costs of £100,000 for the period the machinery is on loan.
h The project will require additional cash reserves of £1m to be held in Albania throughout the project for operational purposes. These are recoverable at the end of the project.
i The Albanian government will make a one-off refund of 'administration' charges one and a half months after the end of the fifth year of £200,000.

The company's cost of capital is 12 per cent.

Ignore taxation, inflation and exchange rate movements and controls.

Required

a Calculate the maximum amount MI should bid in the auction.
b What would be the Internal Rate of Return on the project if MI did not have to pay for the licence?
c The board of directors have never been on a finance course and do not understand any of the finance jargon. However, they have asked you to persuade them that the appraisal method you have used in (a) above can be relied on. Prepare a presentation for the board of directors explaining the reasoning and justification for using your chosen project appraisal technique and your treatment of specific items in the accounts. You will need to explain concepts such as the time value of money, opportunity cost and sunk cost in plain English.

?

6 Find the annual equivalent annuity at 13 per cent for the following cash flow:

Point in time (yearly intervals)	0	1	2	3
Cash flow (£)	–5,000	+2,000	+2,200	+3,500

?

7* (*Examination question if combined with Question 8*) Reds plc is attempting to decide a replacement cycle for new machinery. This machinery costs £10,000 to purchase. Operating and maintenance costs for the future years are:

Point in time (yearly intervals)	0	1	2	3
Operating and maintenance costs (£)	0	12,000	13,000	14,000

The values available from the sale of the machinery on the secondhand market are:

Point in time (yearly intervals)	0	1	2	3
Secondhand value (£)	0	8,000	6,500	3,500

Assume

– replacement by an identical machine to an infinite horizon;
– no inflation, tax or risk;
– the cost of capital is 11 per cent.

Should Reds replace this new machine on a one-, two- or three-year cycle?

?

8* The firm Reds plc in Question 7 has not yet purchased the new machinery and is considering postponing such a cash outflow for a year or two. If it were to replace the existing machine now it could be sold immediately for £4,000. If the firm persevered with the old machine for a further year then £2,000 would have to be spent immediately to recondition it. The machine could then be sold for £3,000 in 12 months' time. The third possibility is to spend £2,000 now, on reconditioning, and £1,000 on maintenance in one year, and finally sell the machine for £1,500, 24 months from now. Assuming all other factors remain constant regardless of which option is chosen, which date would you recommend for the commencement of the replacement cycle?

?

9 Quite plc has an ageing piece of equipment which is less efficient than more modern equivalents. This equipment will continue to operate for another 15 years but operating and maintenance costs will be £3,500 per year. Alternatively it could be sold, raising £2,000 now, and replaced with its modern equivalent which costs £7,000 but has reduced operating and maintenance costs at £3,000 per year. This machine could be sold at the end of its 15-year life for scrap for £500. The third possibility is to spend £2,500 for an immediate overhaul of the old machine which will improve its efficiency for the rest of its life, so that operating and maintenance costs become £3,200 per annum. The old machine will have a zero scrap value in 15 years, whether or not it is overhauled. Quite plc requires a return of 9 per cent on projects in this risk class. Select the best course of action. (Assume that cash flows arise at the year ends.)

?

10* The managing director of Curt plc is irritated that the supplier for the component widgets has recently increased prices by another 10 per cent following similar rises for each of the last five years. Based on the assumption that this pattern will continue, the cost of these widgets will be:

Points in time (yearly intervals)	1	2	3	4	5
Payments for widgets (£)	100,000	110,000	121,000	133,100	146,410

The managing director is convinced that the expertise for the manufacture of widgets exists within Curt. He therefore proposes the purchase of the necessary machine tools and other items of equipment to produce widgets in-house, at a cost of £70,000. The net cash outflows associated with this course of action are:

Points in time (yearly intervals)	0	1	2	3	4	5
Cash outflows	70,000	80,000	82,000	84,000	86,000	88,000

Note: The figures include the £70,000 for equipment and operating costs, etc.

The machinery has a life of five years and can be sold for scrap at the end of its life for £10,000. This is not included in the £88,000 for year 5. The installation of the new machine will require the attention of the technical services manager during the first year. She will have to abandon other projects as a result, causing a loss of net income of £48,000 from those projects. This cost has not been included in the above figures.

The relevant discount rate is 16 per cent, and all cash flows occur at year ends except the initial investment.

Help Curt plc to decide whether to produce widgets for itself. What other factors might influence this decision?

?

11 The Borough Company is to replace its existing machinery. It has a choice between two new types of machine having different lives. The machines have the following costs:

Points in time (yearly intervals)		Machine X	Machine Y
0	Initial investment	£20,000	£25,000
1	Operating costs	£5,000	£4,000
2	Operating costs	£5,000	£4,000
3	Operating costs	£5,000	£4,000
4	Operating costs		£4,000

Machine X ceases to operate and is worth nothing after three years. Machine Y ceases to operate and is worth nothing after four years.

Each machine will be replaced at the end of its life by identical machines with identical costs. This cycle will continue indefinitely. The cost of capital is 13 per cent.

Which machine should Borough buy?

?

12* Netq plc manufactures Qtrans, for which demand fluctuates seasonally. Netq has two machines, each with a productive capacity of 1,000 Qtrans per year. For four months of the year each machine operates at full capacity. For a further four months the machines operate at three-quarters of their full capacity and for the remaining months they produce at half capacity. The operating cost of producing a Qtran is £4 and the machines are expected to be productive to an indefinite horizon. Netq is considering scrapping the old machines (for which the firm will receive nothing) and replacing them with new improved versions. These machines are also expected to last forever if properly maintained but they cost £7,000 each. Each has an annual capacity of 1,000 Qtrans. Operating costs (including maintenance) will, however, fall to £1.80 per Qtran. The appropriate cost of capital is 13 per cent. Should Netq replace both of its machines, one of them, or neither? Assume output is the same under each option and that the new machines have the same productive capacity as the old.

?

13 Clipper owns 100 acres of mature woodland and is trying to decide when to harvest the trees. If it harvests immediately the net cash flow, after paying the professional loggers, will be £10,000. If it waits a year the trees will grow, so that the net cash flow will be £12,000. In two years, £14,000 can be obtained. After three years have elapsed, the cash flow will be £15,500, and thereafter will increase in value by £1,000 per annum.

Calculate the best time to cut the trees given a cost of capital of 10 per cent. ?

14* (*Examination level*) Opti plc operates a single machine to produce its output. The senior management are trying to choose between four possibilities. First, sell the machine on the secondhand market and buy a new one at the end of one year. Second, sell in the secondhand market and replace at the end of two years. The third is to replace after three years. Finally, the machine could be scrapped at the end of its useful life after four years. These replacement cycles are expected to continue indefinitely. The management team believe that all such replacements will be for financially identical equipment, i.e. the cash inflows produced by the new and old equipment are the same. However, the cost of maintenance and operations increases with the age of the machine. These costs are shown in the table, along with the secondhand and scrap values.

Points in time (yearly intervals)	0	1	2	3	4
Initial outlay (£)	20,000				
Operating and maintenance costs (£)		6,000	8,000	10,000	12,000
Secondhand/scrap value (£)		12,000	9,000	6,000	2,000

Assume

- The cost of capital is 10 per cent.
- No inflation.
- No technological advances.
- No tax.
- All cash flows occur on anniversary dates.

Required

Choose the length of the replacement cycle which minimises the present values of the costs of an infinite number of cycles. ?

15 (*Examination level*) Hazel plc produces one of the components used in the manufacture of car bumpers. The production manager is keen on obtaining modern equipment and he has come to you, the finance director, with details concerning two alternative machines, A and B.

The cash flows and other assumptions are as follows.

		£000s	£000s	£000s
Points in time (yearly intervals)	0	1	2	3
Machine A	–200	+220	+242	0
Machine B	–240	+220	+242	+266

Machine A would have to be replaced by an identical machine on a two-year cycle.
Machine B would be replaced by an identical machine every three years.
It is considered reasonable to assume that the cash flows for the future replacements of A and B are the same as in the above table.
The opportunity cost of capital for Hazel is 15 per cent.
Ignore taxation.
The acceptance of either project would leave the company's risk unchanged.
The cash flows occur on anniversary dates.

Required

a Calculate the net present value of Machine A for its two-year life.

b Calculate the net present value of Machine B for its three-year life.

c Calculate the annual equivalent annuities for Machines A and B and recommend which machine should be selected.

d You are aware that the production manager gets very enthusiastic about new machinery and this may cloud his judgement. You suggest the third possibility, which is to continue production with Machine C which was purchased five years ago for £400,000. This is expected to produce +£160,000 per year. It has a scrap value now of £87,000 and is expected to last another five years. At the end of its useful life it will have a scrap value of £20,000.
Should C be kept for another five years?

e The production manager asks why you are discounting the cash flows. Briefly explain the time value of money and its components.

?

myfinancelab ***Now retake your diagnostic test for Chapter 3 to check your progress and update your study plan.***

Assignments

1 Try to obtain budgeted profit and loss accounts for a proposed project and by combining these with other data produce cash flow estimates for the project. Calculate the NPV and contrast your conclusions on the viability of the project with that suggested by the profit and loss projections.

2 Examine some items of machinery (e.g. shopfloor machine tools, vehicles, computers). Consider whether to replace these items with the modern equivalent, taking into account increased maintenance costs, loss or gain of customer sales, secondhand values, higher productivity, etc.

3 Apply the technique of annual equivalent annuities to an asset which is replaced on a regular cycle. Consider alternative cycle lengths.

CHAPTER 4

The decision-making process for investment appraisal

LEARNING OUTCOMES

The main outcome expected from this chapter is that the reader is aware of both traditional and discounted cash flow investment appraisal techniques and the extent of their use. The reader should also be aware that these techniques are a small part of the overall capital-allocation planning process. The student is expected to gain knowledge of:

- the empirical evidence on techniques used;
- the calculation of payback, discounted payback and accounting rate of return (ARR);
- the drawbacks and attractions of payback and ARR;
- the balance to be struck between mathematical precision and imprecise reality;
- the capital-allocation planning process.

myfinancelab *Complete your diagnostic test for Chapter 4 now to create your personal study plan*

Introduction

An organisation may be viewed simply as a collection of projects, some of which were started a long time ago, some only recently begun, many being major 'strategic' projects and others minor operating-unit-level schemes. It is in the nature of business for change to occur, and through change old activities, profit centres and methods die, to be replaced by the new. Without a continuous process of regeneration firms will cease to progress and be unable to compete in a dynamic environment. It is vital that the processes and systems that lead to the development of new production methods, new markets and products, and so on are efficient. That is, both the project appraisal techniques and the entire process of proposal creation and selection lead to the achievement of the objective of the organisation. Poor appraisal technique, set within the framework of an investment process that does not ask the right questions and which provides erroneous conclusions, will destroy the wealth of shareholders.

The payback and accounting rate of return (ARR) methods of evaluating capital investment proposals have historically been, and continue to be, very popular approaches. This is despite the best efforts of a number of writers to denigrate them. It is important to understand the disadvantages of these methods, but it is also useful to be aware of why practical business people still see a great deal of merit in observing the outcome of these calculations.

The employment of project appraisal techniques must be seen as merely one of the stages in the process of the allocation of resources within a firm. The appraisal stage can be reached only after ideas for the use of capital resources have been generated and those ideas have been filtered through a consideration of the strategic, budgetary and business resource capabilities of the firm. Following the appraisal stage are the approval, implementation and post-completion auditing stages.

Any capital allocation system has to be viewed in the light of the complexity of organisational life. This aspect has been ignored in Chapters 2 and 3, where mechanical analysis is applied. The balance is corrected in this chapter. Investment, as in the case of BSkyB's broadband business (*see* **Exhibit 4.1**), needs to be thoroughly evaluated. This chapter considers the process of project development, appraisal and post-investment monitoring.

Exhibit 4.1

BSkyB to invest £400m building broadband arm

FT

Satellite broadcaster to target 3m customers by 2010

By Andrew Edgecliffe-Johnson, Emiko Terazono and Andrew Parker

British Sky Broadcasting will pour £400m into building a broadband access business over the next three years in the hope of expanding from its £4bn pay television market to take a piece of the £25bn internet, telecommunications and entertainment market by 2010.

Its aggressive challenge to rivals such as BT Group, NTL and Carphone Warehouse will entail unexpectedly high upfront investment. Shares in BSkyB fell by $23\frac{1}{2}$p to $517\frac{1}{2}$p as analysts cut 2007 forecasts by as much as 10 per cent.

Expectations of an intensifying war for broadband customers also hit shares in BT Group by $3\frac{1}{2}$p to $226\frac{3}{4}$p and knocked Carphone Warehouse by 12p to $263\frac{1}{2}$p.

Mr Murdoch defended the upfront investment, saying: 'It's a couple of quarters of operating profit to build a franchise that is going to have the durability of decades and open up millions of customers. I'll make that trade any day.'

The group is building on the Easynet broadband network it bought last year for £211m.

The bulk of the initial investment will include subscriber acquisition costs of about £80, on average, for a customer. BSkyB said the broadband product was expected to begin reaping profits in the year to June 30, 2010.

Source: Financial Times, 19 July 2006, p. 21. Reprinted with permission.

Evidence on the employment of appraisal techniques

A number of surveys enquiring into the appraisal methods used in practice have been conducted. The results from surveys conducted by Pike, by the author jointly with Panos Hatzopoulos and by Alkaraan and Northcott are displayed in **Exhibit 4.2**. Some striking features emerge from these and other studies. Payback remains in wide use, despite the increasing application of discounted cash flow techniques. Internal rate of return is popular, but net present value is the preferred method in large companies. Accounting rate of return continues to be the laggard, but is still used in over 50 per cent of large firms. One observation that is emphasised in many studies is the tendency for decision makers to use more than one method. In the Arnold and Hatzopoulos study 67 per cent of firms use three or four of these techniques. These methods are regarded as being complementary rather than competitors.

Exhibit 4.2 Appraisal techniques used

Proportion of companies using technique

	Pike surveys[a]				Arnold and Hatzopoulos survey[b]				Alkaraan & Northcott[c]
	1975 %	1980 %	1986 %	1992 %	1997 Small %	Medium %	Large %	Total %	2002 Large%
Payback	73	81	92	94	71	75	66	70	96
Accounting rate of return	51	49	56	50	62	50	55	56	60
Internal rate of return	44	57	75	81	76	83	84	81	89
Net present value	32	39	68	74	62	79	97	80	99

Capital budget (per year) for companies in Arnold and Hatzopoulos study approx.
Small: £1–50m. Medium: £51–100m. Large: £100m+

Notes

(a) *Pike's studies focus on 100 large UK firms.*

(b) *In the Arnold and Hatzopoulos study (2000), 300 finance directors of UK companies taken from* The Times 1000 *(London: Times Books), ranked according to capital employed (excluding investment trusts), were asked dozens of questions about project appraisal techniques, sources of finance and performance measurement. The first 100 (Large size) of the sample are the top 100; another 100 are in the rankings at 250–400 (Medium size); the final 100 are ranked 820–1,000 (Small size). The capital employed ranges between £1.3bn and £24bn for the large firms, £207m and £400m for the medium-sized firms, and £40m and £60m for the small companies. Ninety-six usable replies were received: 38 large, 24 medium and 34 small.*

(c) *Alkaraan and Northcott focus on UK manufacturing companies each with at least a turnover of £100m, 1000 employees and assets of £50m. 83 companies returned questionaires.*

Sources: Pike (1988 and 1996), Arnold and Hatzopoulos (2000) and Alkaraan and Northcott (2006)

There is an indication in the literature that while some methods have superior theoretical justification, other, simpler methods are used for purposes such as communicating project viability and gaining commitment throughout an organisation. It is also suggested that those who sponsor and advance projects within organisations like to have the option of presenting their case in an alternative form which shows the proposal in the best light.

Another clear observation from the literature is that small and medium-sized firms use the sophisticated formal procedures less than their larger brethren.

Payback

The **payback** period for a capital investment is the length of time before the cumulated stream of forecasted cash flows equals the initial investment.

The decision rule is that if a project's payback period is less than or equal to a predetermined threshold figure it is acceptable.

Consider the case of Tradfirm's three mutually exclusive proposed investments (*see* **Exhibit 4.3**).

Exhibit 4.3 Tradfirm

	Cash flows (£m)						
Points in time (yearly intervals)	**0**	**1**	**2**	**3**	**4**	**5**	**6**
Project A	–10	6	2	1	1	2	2
Project B	–10	1	1	2	6	2	2
Project C	–10	3	2	2	2	15	10

Note: Production ceases after six years, and all cash flows occur on anniversary dates.

There is a boardroom battle in Tradfirm, with older members preferring the payback rule. They set four years as the decision benchmark. For both A and B the £10m initial outflow is recouped after four years. In the case of C it takes five years for the cash inflows to cumulate to £10m. Thus payback for the three projects is as follows:

Project A: 4 years
Project B: 4 years
Project C: 5 years

If the payback rule is rigidly applied, the older members of the board will reject the third project, and they are left with a degree of indecisiveness over whether to accept A or B. The younger members prefer the NPV rule and are thus able to offer a clear decision.

As **Exhibit 4.4** shows, Project A has a positive NPV and is therefore shareholder wealth enhancing. Project B has a negative NPV; the firm would be better served by investing the £10m in the alternative that offers a 10 per cent return. Project C has the largest positive NPV and is therefore the one that creates most shareholder wealth.

Exhibit 4.4 Tradfirm: Net Present Values (£m)

Project A $$-10 + \frac{6}{1.1} + \frac{2}{(1.1)^2} + \frac{1}{(1.1)^3} + \frac{1}{(1.1)^4} + \frac{2}{(1.1)^5} + \frac{2}{(1.1)^6} = £0.913\text{m}$$

Project B $$-10 + \frac{1}{1.1} + \frac{1}{(1.1)^2} + \frac{2}{(1.1)^3} + \frac{6}{(1.1)^4} + \frac{2}{(1.1)^5} + \frac{2}{(1.1)^6} = -£0.293\text{m}$$

Project C $$-10 + \frac{3}{1.1} + \frac{2}{(1.1)^2} + \frac{2}{(1.1)^3} + \frac{2}{(1.1)^4} + \frac{15}{(1.1)^5} + \frac{10}{(1.1)^6} = £12.208\text{m}$$

Note: The discount rate is 10 per cent.

Drawbacks of payback

The first drawback of payback is that it makes no allowance for the time value of money. It ignores the need to compare future cash flows with the initial investment after they have been discounted to their present values. The second drawback is that receipts beyond the payback period are ignored. This problem is particularly obvious in the case of Project C. A third disadvantage is the arbitrary selection of the cut-off point. There is no theoretical basis for setting the appropriate time period and so guesswork, whim and manipulation take over.

Discounted payback

With **discounted payback** the future cash flows are discounted prior to calculating the payback period. This is an improvement on the simple payback method in that it takes into account the time value of money. In **Exhibit 4.5** the *discounted* cash inflows are added together to calculate payback. In the case of Project B the discounted cash inflows never reach the level of the cash outflow.

Exhibit 4.5 Discounted payback: Tradfirm plc (£m)

Points in time (yearly intervals)	0	1	2	3	4	5	6	Discounted payback
Project A								
Undiscounted cash flow	−10	6	2	1	1	2	2	
Discounted cash flow	−10	5.45	1.65	0.75	0.68	1.24	1.13	Year 6
Project B								
Undiscounted cash flow	−10	1	1	2	6	2	2	Outflow −10m
Discounted cash flow	−10	0.909	0.826	1.5	4.1	1.24	1.13	Inflow +£9.7m
Project C								
Undiscounted cash flow	−10	3	2	2	2	15	10	
Discounted cash flow	−10	2.72	1.65	1.5	1.37	9.3	5.64	Year 5

Note: The discount rate is 10 per cent.

This modification tackles the first drawback of the simple payback method but it is still necessary to make an arbitrary decision about the cut-off date and it ignores cash flows beyond that date.

Reasons for the continuing popularity of payback

Payback remains a widely used project appraisal method despite its drawbacks. This requires some explanation. The first fact to note is that payback is rarely used as the primary investment technique, but rather as a secondary method which supplements the more sophisticated methods. Although it appears irrational to employ payback when the issue is examined in isolation, we may begin to see the logic behind its use if we take into account the organisational context and the complementary nature of alternative techniques. For example, payback may be used at an early stage to filter out projects which have clearly unacceptable risk and return characteristics. Identifying those projects at a preliminary stage avoids the need for more detailed evaluation through a discounted cash flow method, thus increasing the efficiency of the appraisal process. This early sifting has to be carefully implemented so as to avoid premature rejection.

Payback also has one extraordinarily endearing quality to busy managers and hard-pressed students alike – it is simple and easy to use. Executives often admit that the payback rule, used indiscriminately, does not always give the best decisions, but it is the simplest way to communicate an idea of project profitability. NPV is difficult to understand and so it is useful to have an alternative measure which all managers can follow. In the workplace a project's success often relies on the gaining of widespread employee commitment. Discussion, negotiation and communication of ideas often need to be carried out in a simple form so that non-quantitative managers can make their contribution and, eventually, their commitment. Communication in terms of the sophisticated models may lead to alienation and exclusion and, ultimately, project failure.

Another argument advanced by practitioners is that projects which return their outlay quickly reduce the exposure of the firm to risk. In the world beyond the simplifications needed in academic exercises, as described in Chapters 2 and 3, there is a great deal of uncertainty about future cash flows. Managers often distrust forecasts for more distant years. Payback has an implicit assumption that the risk of cash flows is directly related to the time distance from project implementation date. By focusing on near-term returns this approach uses only those data in which management have greatest faith. Take the case of the web-based music provider industry. Here, competitive forces and technology are changing so rapidly that it is difficult to forecast for eight months ahead, let alone for eight years. Thus, managers may choose to ignore cash flow projections beyond a certain number of years. They accept only those projects immune to the risk of total market collapse a few years down the line or the risk of company failure due to an inability to meet debts as they become due. Those who advocate NPV counter this approach by saying that risk is accounted for in a better way in the NPV model than is done by simply excluding data – it certainly does not completely ignore cash flows beyond the payback period. Risk analysis applied to NPV is examined in Chapter 6.

A further advantage of payback, as perceived by many managers, is its use in situations of capital shortage. If funds are limited, there is an advantage in receiving a return on projects earlier rather than later, as this permits investment in other profitable opportunities. Theoretically this factor can be allowed for in a more satisfactory way with the NPV method; capital rationing is discussed in Chapter 5.

This section is not meant to promote the use of payback. It remains a theoretically inferior method to the discounted cash flow approaches. Payback has a number of valuable attributes, but the primary method of project appraisal in most organisations should take into account all of the relevant cash flows and then discount them.

Accounting rate of return

The **accounting rate of return (ARR)** method may be known to readers by other names such as the **return on capital employed (ROCE)** or **return on investment (ROI)**. The ARR is a ratio of the accounting profit to the investment in the project, expressed as a percentage.

The *decision rule* is that if the ARR is greater than, or equal to, a hurdle rate then accept the project.

This ratio can be calculated in a number of ways but the most popular approach is to take profit after the deduction of depreciation. For the investment figure we regard any increases in working capital as adding to the investment required. Three alternative versions of ARR are calculated for Timewarp plc which give markedly different results (*see* Worked example 4.1). Note: these are just three of all the possible ways of calculating ARR – there are many more.

Worked example 4.1 Timewarp plc

Timewarp is to invest £30,000 in machinery for a project which has a life of three years. The machinery will have a zero scrap value and will be depreciated on a straight-line basis.

Accounting rate of return, version 1 (annual basis)

$$\text{ARR} = \frac{\text{Profit for the year}}{\text{Asset book value at start of year}} \times 100$$

Time (year)	1 £	2 £	3 £
Profit before depreciation	15,000	15,000	15,000
Less depreciation	10,000	10,000	10,000
Profit after depreciation	5,000	5,000	5,000
Value of asset (book value)			
Start of year	30,000	20,000	10,000
End of year	20,000	10,000	0
Accounting rate of return	$\frac{5,000}{30,000} = 16.67\%$	$\frac{5,000}{20,000} = 25\%$	$\frac{5,000}{10,000} = 50\%$

On average the ARR is: 1/3 × (16.67 + 25 + 50)% = 30.55%.
Note the illusion of an annual rise in profitability despite profits remaining constant year on year.

Accounting rate of return, version 2 (total investment basis)

$$\text{ARR} = \frac{\text{Average annual profit}}{\text{Initial capital invested}} \times 100$$

$$\text{ARR} = \frac{(5{,}000 + 5{,}000 + 5{,}000)/3}{30{,}000} \times 100 = 16.67\%$$

Accounting rate of return, version 3 (average investment basis)

$$\text{ARR} = \frac{\text{Average annual profit}}{\text{Average capital invested}} \times 100$$

$$\text{Average capital invested: } \frac{30{,}000}{2} = 15{,}000$$

(At time 0 the machinery has a value of £30,000, three years later it has a value of zero. If we assume constant devaluation then the average value of the machinery is £15,000.)

$$\text{ARR} = \frac{(5{,}000 + 5{,}000 + 5{,}000)/3}{15{,}000} \times 100 = 33.33\%$$

If we now make the example slightly more sophisticated by assuming that the machinery has a scrap value of £8,000 at the end of year 3, then the average capital invested figure becomes:

0.5 (initial outlay + scrap value)
0.5 (30,000 + 8,000) = 19,000

The profit figures also change.

	Year 1 £	Year 2 £	Year 3 £
Profit before depreciation	15,000	15,000	15,000
Depreciation	7,333	7,333	7,333
Profit after depreciation	7,667	7,667	7,667

$$\text{The ARR (version 3) is: } \frac{7{,}667}{19{,}000} \times 100 = 40.35\%$$

Drawbacks of accounting rate of return

The number of alternative ARR calculations can be continued beyond the three possibilities described in Worked example 4.1. Each alternative would be a legitimate variant and would find favour with some managers and accountants. The almost wide-open field for selecting profit and asset definitions is a major weakness of ARR. This flexibility may tempt decision makers to abuse the technique to suit their purposes. Secondly, as explained in Chapter 3, the inflow and outflow of cash should be the focus of investment analysis appraisals. Profit figures are very poor substitutes for cash flow. The most important criticism of accounting rate of return is that it fails to take account of the time value of money. There is no allowance for the fact that cash received in year 1 is more valuable than an identical sum received in year 3. Also there is a high degree of arbitrariness in defining the cut-off or hurdle rate. There is no reason for selecting 10, 15 or 20 per cent as an acceptable ARR. This arbitrariness contrasts with NPV, which has a sound theoretical base to its decision rule: accept if the project's cash flows deliver more than the finance provider's opportunity cost of capital.

Accounting rate of return can lead to some perverse decisions. For example, suppose that Timewarp use the second version, the total investment ARR, with a hurdle rate of 15 per cent, and the appraisal team discover that the machinery will in fact generate an additional profit of £1,000 in a fourth year. Common sense suggests that if all other factors remain constant this new situation is better than the old one, and yet the ARR declines to below the threshold level because the profits are averaged over four years rather than three and the project is therefore rejected.

The original situation is:

$$\text{ARR} = \frac{(5{,}000 + 5{,}000 + 5{,}000)/3}{30{,}000} = 16.67\%. \text{ Accepted}$$

The new situation is:

$$\text{ARR} = \frac{(5{,}000 + 5{,}000 + 5{,}000 + 1{,}000)/4}{30{,}000} = 13.33\%. \text{ Rejected}$$

An alternative way of viewing this problem is to think of two projects that are identical except that one offers the additional £1,000. If only one project can be accepted which will the managers go for? If they are motivated by ARR (e.g. by bonuses related to ARR achieved) they may be inclined to accept the project that offers the higher ARR even if this means sacrificing £1,000 of shareholders' money.

Reasons for the continued use of accounting rate of returns

Exhibit 4.2 shows that over one-half of large firms calculate ARR when appraising projects and so the conclusion must be that, in the practical world of business, some merit is seen in this technique. One possible explanation is that managers are familiar with this ancient and extensively used profitability measure. The financial press regularly report accounting rates of return. Divisional performance is often judged on a profit-to-assets-employed ratio. Indeed, the entire firm is often analysed and management evaluated on this ratio. Because performance is measured in this way, managers have a natural bias towards using it in appraising future projects. Conflicting signals are sometimes sent to managers controlling a division. They are expected to use a discounted cash flow approach for investment decisions, but find that their performance is being monitored on a profit-to-investment ratio basis. This dichotomy may produce a resistance to proposed projects which produce low returns in the early years and thus report a low ARR to head office. This may result in excellent long-term opportunities being missed. (Some additional reasons for the continued use of ARR and payback are given in the Arnold and Hatzopoulos (2000) paper.)

Exhbit 4.6 illustrates what can happen if too much emphasis is placed on accounting numbers.

Exhibit 4.6

More EU lunacy

FT

By John Plender

Mrs Loyola de Palacio, the European Union's transport commissioner, complains bitterly that the International Accounting Standards Board and the European Financial Reporting Advisory Group pose a threat to the development of Europe's infrastructure. They are, she believes, too academic in dealing with the time gap between the vast negative cash flow incurred during construction and the subsequent revenue build-up.

The fear is that enormous accounting losses will have to be recognised in the early years of projects, while in the later years 'exaggerated' profits will appear.

The laughable assumption underlying this latest attempt by the European Commission to subvert standard setting in accountancy is that entrepreneurs and financial institutions are incapable of doing **net present value** calculations. So to recognise what she calls the reality of 'the construction sector' Mrs de Palacio wants the accountants to distort economic reality and cook the books.

Source: *Financial Times*, 8 November 2004, p. 22. Reprinted with permission.

Internal rate of return: reasons for continued popularity

Exhibit 4.2 shows that firms use IRR as much as the theoretically superior NPV. Given the problems associated with IRR described in Chapter 2, this may seem strange. It is all the more perplexing if one considers that IRR is often more difficult to calculate manually than NPV (although, with modern computer programs, the computational difficulties virtually disappear). Some possible explanations follow.

- ***Psychological*** Managers are familiar with expressing financial data in the form of a percentage. It is intuitively easier to grasp what is meant by an IRR of 15 per cent than, say, an NPV of £2,000.
- ***IRR can be calculated without knowledge of the required rate of return*** Making a decision using the IRR involves two separate stages. Stage 1 involves gathering data and then computing the IRR. Stage 2 requires comparing this with the cut-off rate. By contrast, it is not possible to calculate NPV without knowing the required rate of return. The proposal has to be analysed in one stage only. In a large company it is possible for senior managers to request that profit centres and divisions appraise projects on the basis of their IRRs, while refusing to communicate in advance the rate of return required. This has at least two potential advantages. First, the required rate may change over time and it becomes a simple matter of changing the cut-off comparison rate at head office once the IRR computations are received from lower down the organisation. With NPV, each project's cash flows would need to be calculated again at the new discount rate. Secondly, managers are only human and there is a tendency to bias information passed upwards so as to achieve their personal goals. For instance, it has been known for ambitious managers to be excessively optimistic concerning the prospects for projects that would lead to an expansion of their domain. If they are provided with a cut-off rate prior to evaluating projects you can be sure that all projects they sponsor will have cash flows 'forecasted' to produce a return greater than the target. If the head office team choose not to communicate a cut-off rate, this leaves them free to adjust the required return to allow for factors such as over-optimism. They may also adjust the minimum rate of return for perceived risk associated with particular projects or divisions.
- ***Ranking*** Some managers are not familiar with the drawbacks of IRR and believe that ranking projects to select between them is most accurately and most easily carried out using the percentage-based IRR method. This was, in Chapter 2, shown not to be the case.

The managerial 'art' of investment appraisal

This book places strong emphasis on the formal methods of project appraisal, so a word of warning is necessary at this point. Mathematical technique is merely one element needed for successful project appraisal. The quantitative analysis is only the starting point for decision making. In most real-world situations there are many qualitative factors which need to be taken into account. The techniques described in Chapters 2 and 3 cannot be used in a mechanical fashion. Management is largely an art form with a few useful quantitative techniques to improve the quality of the art. For instance, in generating and evaluating major investments the firm has to take into account:

- ***Strategy*** The relationship between the proposed project and the strategic direction of the firm is very important. A business-unit investment isolated from the main thrust of the firm may be a distraction in terms of managerial attention and financial resources. A project that looks good at divisional level may not be appropriate when examined from the whole-firm perspective. It may even be contradictory to the firm's goals. For example, luxury goods companies are sometimes enticed to produce lower-priced items for the mass market or to stretch the brand into unrelated areas. The project, when judged on its own, appears to have a very high NPV. But there is the danger of losing the premium brand (expensive and exclusive) strategic position in the existing product ranges by association with something that does not quite fit the image the firm has nurtured.
- ***Social context*** The effect on individuals is a crucial consideration. Projects require people to implement them. Their enthusiasm and commitment will be of central importance. Neglecting

this factor may lead to resentment and even sabotage. Discussion and consensus on major project proposals may matter more than selecting the mathematically correct option. In many cases, quantitative techniques are avoided because they are precise. It is safer to sponsor a project in a non-quantified or judgemental way at an early stage in its development. If, as a result of discussion with colleagues and superiors, the idea becomes more generally accepted and it fits into the pervading view on the firm's policy and strategy, the figures are presented in a report. Note here the order of actions. First, general acceptance. Second, quantification. A proposal is usually discussed at progressively higher levels of management before it is 'firmed up' into a project report. One reason for this is that continuing commitment and support from many people will be needed if the project is to succeed. In order to engender support and to improve the final report it is necessary to start the process in a rather vague way, making room for modifications in the light of suggestions. Some of these suggestions will be motivated by shareholder wealth considerations, others will be motivated by goals closer to the hearts of key individuals. Allowing adaptability in project development also means that if circumstances change, say, in the competitive environment, the final formal appraisal takes account of this. The sponsor or promoter of a capital investment has to be aware of, and to adjust for, social sub-systems within the organisation (see Ekanem (2005) for eight case studies showing the importance of social context).

- ***Expense*** Sophisticated project evaluation can cost a considerable amount of money. The financial experts' input is costly enough, but the firm also has to consider the time and trouble managers throughout the organisation might have to devote to provide good-quality data and make their contribution to the debate. In a firm of limited resources it may be more efficient to search for projects at an informal or judgement level, thus generating a multitude of alternative avenues for growth, rather than to analyse a few in greater quantitative depth.
- ***Stifling the entrepreneurial spirit*** Excessive emphasis on formal evaluatory systems may be demotivating to individuals who thrive on free thinking, fast decision making and action. The relative weights given to formal approaches and entrepreneurialism will depend on the context, such as the pace of change in the marketplace.

A leading businessman describes the problems arising from overemphasis on accounting [finance?] numbers – *see* **Exhibit 4.7**.

Exhibit 4.7

Entrepreneur fires broad attack

FT

By Peter Marsh

British manufacturers have failed to invest enough in marketing and given too much management control to accountants, according to Edward Atkin, one of the country's most successful engineering entrepreneurs of the past decade.

Until recently Mr Atkin was the managing director and majority owner of Avent, one of the world's biggest makers of babies' bottles.

He sold Avent to a venture capital company for £300m, of which £225m (minus advisers' fees) came to Mr Atkin and his family. The entrepreneur is now weighing up several ideas about ways in which to invest some of the cash in innovative businesses.

In a speech to the Institution of Electrical Engineers Mr Atkin will say that most successful manufacturers require a stable investment climate and an interest in making world beating products.

These factors are more likely to be in place if the businesses are owned privately, and also have people with an interest in engineering at the helm, rather than accountants.

'As soon as financial criteria become the main method used for evaluating investment opportunities, the company is almost certainly doomed,' Mr Atkin will say.

'It is impossible to forecast variables like volumes, competitive pricing, raw material costs, interest rates or currencies three or five years out,' Mr Atkin will say. 'What is very easy, however, is to appreciate that speeding up a process, reducing waste, eliminating direct labour and improving tolerances and reliability will enhance both the products and their manufacturer, as well as the experience of the end-user. These benefits will be long-term and valid, irrespective of the output, exchange rate, raw material costs and all the other variables.'

Successful manufacturers such as US semiconductor maker Intel, and BMW and Toyota, two of the world's biggest car producers, have made as a centre of their businesses 'an unbroken trend of consistent [product] development, decade after decade.'

This is a culture, Mr Atkin will say, that makes it relatively easy to build up strong teams of engineering and marketing experts within the company that will stay for long periods. It also makes it easier to establish long-term brand loyalty.

Source: Financial Times, 17 January 2006, p. 5. Reprinted with permission.

- ***Intangible benefits*** Frequently, many of the most important benefits that flow from an investment are difficult to measure in money terms. Improving customer satisfaction through better service, quality or image may lead to enhanced revenues, but it is often difficult to state precisely the quantity of the increased revenue flow. For example, new technology often provides a number of intangible benefits, such as reduced time needed to switch machine tools to the production of other products, thereby reducing risk in fluctuating markets, or a quicker response to customer choice. These non-quantifiable benefits can amount to a higher value than the more obvious tangible benefits (see Alkaraan and Northcott (2006) for a survey of just how important these factors are for UK firms). An example of how intangible benefits could be allowed for in project appraisal is shown through the example of Crowther Precision plc.

Worked example 4.2 Crowther Precision plc

Crowther Precision plc produces metal parts for the car industry, with machinery that is now more than 20 years old. With appropriate maintenance these machines could continue producing indefinitely. However, developments in the machine tool industry have led to the creation of computer-controlled multi-use machines. Crowther is considering the purchase of the Z200 which would provide both quantifiable and non-quantifiable benefits over the old machine. The Z200 costs £1.2m but would be expected to last indefinitely if maintenance expenditure were increased by £20,000 every year forever.

The quantifiable benefits are:

(a) reduced raw material requirements, due to lower wastage, amounting to £35,000 in each future year;
(b) labour cost savings of £80,000 in each future year.

These quantifiable benefits are analysed using the NPV method (*see* **Exhibit 4.8**).

Exhibit 4.8 Incremental net present value analysis of Z200

		Present value £
Purchase of machine		−1,200,000
Present value of raw material saving	$\frac{35,000}{0.1}$	+350,000
Present value of labour saving	$\frac{80,000}{0.1}$	+800,000
Less present value of increased maintenance costs	$\frac{20,000}{0.1}$	−200,000
Net present value		−250,000

Note: Assume discount rate of 10 per cent, all cash flows arise at the year ends, zero scrap value of old machine.

Examining the quantifiable elements in isolation will lead to a rejection of the project to buy the Z200. However, the non-quantifiable benefits are:

- reduced time required to switch the machine from producing one version of the car component to one of the other three versions Crowther presently produces;
- the ability to switch the machine over to completely new products in response to changed industry demands, or to take up, as yet unseen, market opportunities in the future;
- improved quality of output leading to greater customer satisfaction.

It is true that the discounted cash flow analysis has failed to take into account all the relevant factors, but this should not lead to its complete rejection. In cases where non-quantifiable elements are present, the problem needs to be separated into two stages.

1 Analyse those elements that are quantifiable using NPV.
2 If the NPV from Stage 1 is negative, then managerial judgement will be needed to subjectively assess the non-quantifiable benefits. If these are judged to be greater than the 'loss' signalled in Stage 1 then the project is viable. For Crowther, if the management team consider that the intangible benefits are worth more than £250,000 they should proceed with the purchase of the Z200.

This line of thought is continued in Chapter 6 (pp. 203–12), where operational and strategic decisions with options (real options) are considered. As the article in **Exhibit 4.9** shows, the decision to commit to an investment means the loss of options.

Exhibit 4.9 Sacrificing options

Tyranny of time

FT

By their very nature capital investment decisions threaten to place a straitjacket on companies. There is no easy way out.

By Peter Martin

When you make a capital investment decision, you freeze time. In fast-moving industries, this may be the most important aspect of the decision – more important than its actual content. But it is rarely assessed in this light.

There is any amount of theory about how to take capital investment decisions.

All such approaches assume that there are financial and easily quantifiable costs of taking the decision; and less measurable benefits to set against it. The techniques all revolve around ways of making imponderable future benefits more tangible. There is a reason for this: managers usually want to take investment decisions while their superiors usually do not. So the techniques are ever more elaborate ways of capturing the discounted value of blue sky.

But there are also intangible costs of taking the decision, and they are not given the attention they deserve. The cost of freezing time is one of the most important.

Here is how it works. When you make a big capital investment decision, it will usually take between 18 months and five years to bring the plant fully into operation. The cost of tying up capital for that time is reflected in the investment appraisal. But the broader implications of tying up the company are not.

When you have committed yourself to a big new plant, you have not just signed a cheque for the money. You have also sold your soul to this technology, on this scale, in this site. That is what freezing time means. Until the plant is complete, and it is clear whether it works and whether there is a market for its products, time stands still. For you, but not for your rivals.

They are free to react, to adjust technology, to play around with the pricing and volume. You are not. Unless you have built an implausibly flexible new plant, you are on a convergence course with a straitjacket.

Once your new plant is up and running, you can start to adjust the pattern of its output, and strive to reduce its costs. But until then, your options are more limited: press on, or give up.

The semiconductor industry illustrates this dilemma in a big way. In the mid-1990s, the UK looked like a good home for a bunch of new chip plants. Siemens, LG Group and Hyundai all targeted the British regions for big state-of-the-art factories. One of them – Siemens' factory on Tyneside – opened and promptly shut down again. The other two have never made it into production, and look more questionable by the moment: the Asian crisis undermined their parents and their markets simultaneously.

The decisions all three companies had to make were unenviable, because they were all or nothing. Technology had moved on while the plants were being prepared. Once the Siemens plant came into production, it was clear that it was the wrong plant, making the wrong sort of chip, in the wrong place.

So the company shut it down, at vast cost – only to invest another huge sum in a different plant to make different chips in France. For LG and Hyundai the moment of decision comes even before they have had the satisfaction of seeing their plants up and running.

The problem is not so much the risk that a plant's technology may

Exhibit 4.9 continued

prove inappropriate, or that its markets may not meet expectations: these are the normal risks of doing business in a capital intensive industry. It is more that the process of building the factory shuts out other alternatives, freezing the company's options and its internal clock.

What can companies do to avoid this risk? First, look for investment decisions that can be made piece by piece, and implemented quickly, minimising the freezing effect. Engineers usually hate this approach, because it means they are never designing plants at the cutting edge of the technology, or at maximum efficient scale. That's tough.

Second, once an investment has been approved, managers must resist the temptation to make the decision sacrosanct. It needs revisiting, in the light of changing technology and markets, just as much as plants that are already operating. This is a difficult balance to strike, because every big investment decision usually had to be made in the teeth of the opposition of a faction that wanted something bigger, smaller, older, newer, or somewhere else. This group of dissidents will never be happy with the decision, and they may even be right.

Third, keep a close eye on the relationship between the product cycle time in your industry and the time it takes to get a new plant commissioned.

If the former is shrinking while the latter is lengthening – a common feature of any high-technology industry that has to cater to retail consumers – there will come a point at which the price of freezing time will outstrip the benefits of new plant.

If you cannot keep going by patching the old factory, it is time to think of some revolutionary new process that will replace one big capital investment decision with a lot of small ones. Or give up.

Source: Financial Times, 1 June 1999, p. 18. Reprinted with permission.

The investment process

There is a great deal more to a successful investment programme than simply project appraisal. As Exhibit 4.10 demonstrates, project appraisal is one of a number of stages in the investment process. The emphasis in the academic world on ever more sophistication in appraisal could be seriously misplaced. Attention paid to the evolution of investment ideas, their development and sifting may produce more practical returns. Marrying the evaluation of projects once screened with strategic, resource and human considerations may lead to avoidance of erroneous decisions. Following through the implementation with a review of what went right, what went wrong, and why, may enable better decision making in the future.

Investment by a firm is a process often involving large numbers of individuals up and down an organisational hierarchy. It is a complex and infinitely adaptable process which is likely to differ from one organisation to another. However, we can identify some common threads.

Generation of ideas

A firm is more likely to founder because of a shortage of good investment ideas than because of poor methods of appraisal. A good investment planning process requires a continuous flow of ideas to regenerate the organisation through the exploitation of new opportunities. Thought needs to be given to the development of a system for the encouragement of idea generation and subsequent communication through the firm. Indeed, one of the central tasks of senior management is to nurture a culture of search for and sponsorship of ideas. In the absence of a well-functioning system, the danger remains that investment proposals only arise in a reactive manner. For example, a firm examines new product possibilities only when it is realised that the old product is becoming, or has become, obsolete. Or else the latest technology is installed in reaction to its adoption by a competitor. A system and culture is needed to help the firm 'get ahead of the game' and be proactive rather than reactive.

One of the main inputs into a more systematic search for ideas is likely to be an environment-scanning process. It is also helpful if all potential idea-generators are made aware of the general strategic direction of the firm and the constraints under which it operates. Idea-generators often become sponsors of their proposals within the organisation. These individuals, in a poorly operating system, can see themselves taking a high risk for very little reward. Their reputation and career prospects can be intimately associated with a project. If it goes badly then they may find themselves blamed for that failure. In a system with such poor incentives the natural response of most

Exhibit 4.10 The investment process

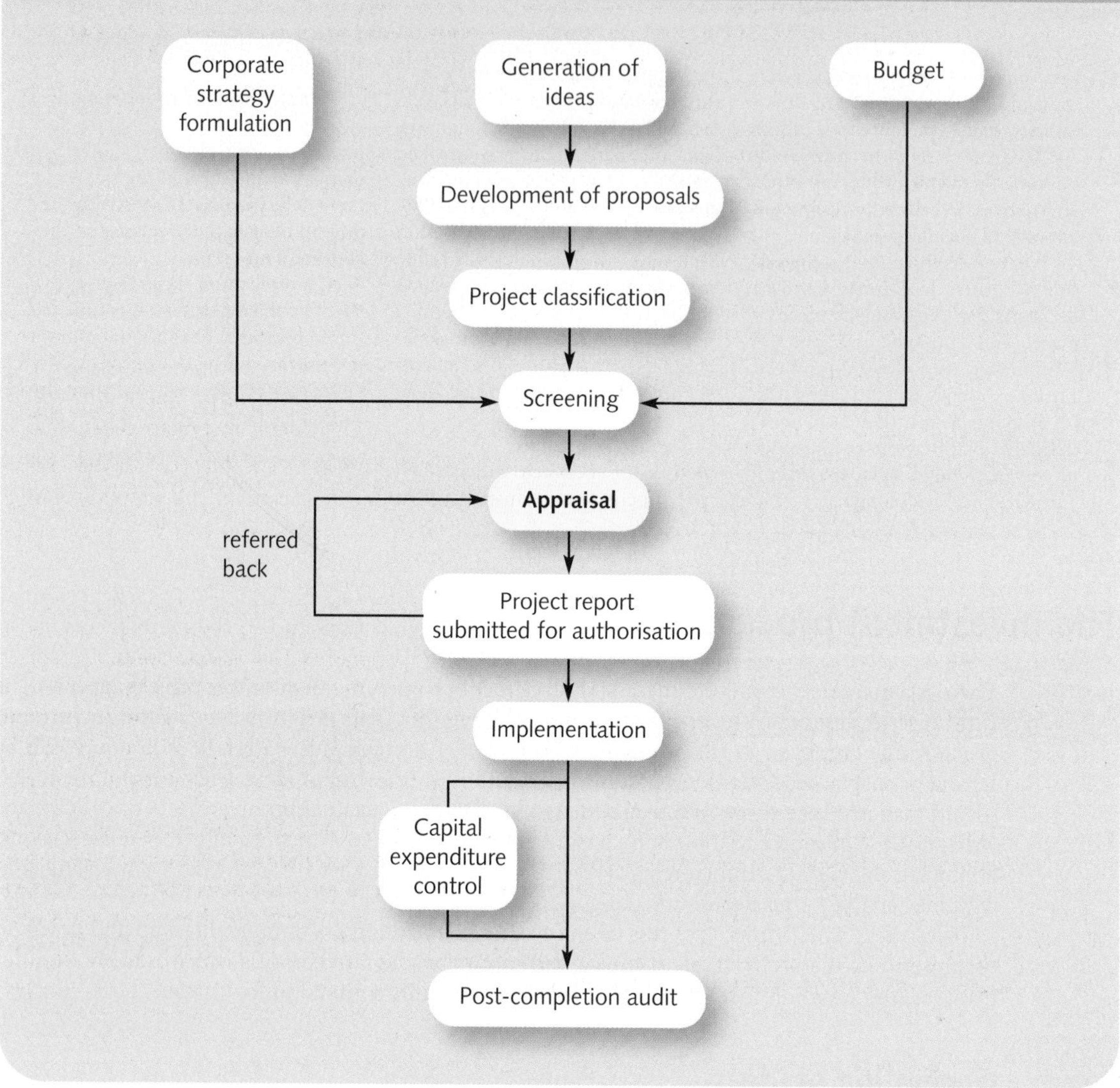

people would be to hold back from suggesting ideas and pushing them through, and concentrate on day-to-day management. This defensive attitude could be bad for the organisation and it is therefore incumbent on senior management to develop reward systems that do not penalise project idea-generators and sponsors.

Development and classification

As the sponsor or the division-level team gather more data and refine estimates, some degree of early filtering takes place. Ideas that may have looked good in theory do not necessarily look so good when examined more closely. In a well-functioning system, idea generation should be propagated in an unstructured, almost random manner, but the development phase starts to impose some degree of order and structure. Many firms like to have a bottom-up approach, with ideas coming from plant level and being reviewed by divisional management before being presented to senior management. At the development stage the sponsor elaborates and hones ideas in consultation with colleagues. The divisional managers may add ideas, ask for information and suggest alternative scenarios. There may also be division-level projects which need further consideration. As the discussions and data gathering progress the proposal generally starts to gain commitment from a number of people who become drawn in and involved.

The classification stage involves matching projects to identified needs. Initially, there may be a long list of imaginative project ideas or solutions to a specific problem, but this may be narrowed down in these early stages to two or three. Detailed evaluation of all projects is expensive. Some types of project do not require the extensive search for data and complex evaluation that others do. The following classification may allow more attention to be directed at the type of project where the need is greatest:

1 ***Equipment replacement*** Equipment obsolescence can occur because of technological developments which create more efficient alternatives, because the old equipment becomes expensive to maintain or because of a change in the cost of inputs, making an alternative method cheaper (for example, if the oil price quadruples, taxi firms may shift to smaller cars).
2 ***Expansion or improvement of existing products*** These investments relate to increasing the volume of output and/or improving product quality and market position.
3 ***Cost reduction*** A continuous process of search and analysis may be necessary to ensure that the firm is producing at lowest cost. Small modifications to methods of production or equipment, as well as the introduction of new machines, may bring valuable incremental benefits.
4 ***New products*** Many firms depend on a regular flow of innovatory products to permit continued expansion. Examples are Intel, GlaxoSmithKline and 3M. These firms have to make huge commitments to research and development, market research and promotion. Vast investments are needed in new production facilities around the world.
5 ***Statutory and welfare*** Investments may be required by law for such matters as safety, or pollution control. These do not, generally, give a financial return and so the focus is usually to satisfy the requirement at minimum cost. Welfare investments may lead to some intangible benefits which are difficult to quantify, such as a more contented workforce. The Arnold and Hatzopoulos (2000) survey showed that 78 per cent of the firms undertook non-economic projects directed at health and safety issues; 74 per cent accepted projects motivated by legislation; and 54 per cent had paid for uneconomic projects for social and environmental reasons.

The management team need to weigh up the value of a more comprehensive analysis against the cost of evaluation. Regular equipment replacement, cost reduction and existing product expansion decisions are likely to require less documentation than a major strategic investment in a new product area. Also, the information needs are likely to rise in proportion to the size of the investment. A £100m investment in a new pharmaceutical plant is likely to be treated differently to a £10,000 investment in a new delivery vehicle.

Screening

At this stage, each proposal will be assessed to establish whether it is sufficiently attractive to receive further attention through the application of sophisticated analysis. Screening decisions should be made with an awareness of the strategic direction of the firm and the limitations imposed by the financial, human and other resources available. There should also be a check on the technical feasibility of the proposal and some preliminary assessment of risk.

Strategy

Capital allocation is a pivotal part of the overall strategic process. A good investment appraisal system must mesh with the firm's long-term plan. The managers at plant or division level may not be able to see opportunities at a strategic level, such as the benefits of combining two divisions, or the necessity for business-unit divestment. Thus, the bottom-up flow of ideas for investment at plant level should complement the top-down strategic planning from the centre. Each vantage point has a valuable contribution to make.

Budget

Most large firms prepare capital budgets stretching over many years. Often a detailed budget for capital expenditure in the forthcoming year is set within the framework of an outline plan for the next five years. Individual projects are required to conform to the corporate budget. However, the budget itself, at least in the long run, is heavily influenced by the availability of project proposals. The Arnold and Hatzopoulos (2000) survey shows the use of budgets by UK firms (*see* **Exhibit 4.11**).

Exhibit 4.11 Capital expenditure budgets for UK firms

	Small firms %	Medium-sized firms %	Large firms %
Outline capital expenditure budgets are prepared for:			
1 year ahead	18	8	–
2 years ahead	18	25	13
3 years ahead	35	50	18
4 years ahead	9	–	5
More than 4 years ahead	21	13	61
Blank	–	4	3
Detailed capital expenditure budgets are prepared for:			
1 year ahead	70	79	55
2 years ahead	21	13	21
3 years ahead	9	4	8
4 years ahead	–	–	5
More than 4 years ahead	–	4	11

Note: 96 firms completed the survey questionnaire.

Source: Arnold and Hatzopoulos (2000).

Appraisal

It is at the appraisal stage that detailed cash flow forecasts are required as inputs to the more sophisticated evaluation methods, such as net present value. Manuals provide detailed checklists which help the project sponsor to ensure that all relevant costs and other factors have been considered. These manuals may explain how to calculate NPV and IRR and may also supply the firm's opportunity cost of capital. (If risk adjustment is made through the discount rate there may be more than one cost of capital and the sponsor then has to classify the project into, say, high-, medium- or low-risk categories – *see* Chapter 6.) The project promoter may seek the aid of specialists, such as engineers, accountants and economists, in the preparation of the formal analysis.

Report and authorisation

Many firms require that project proposals are presented in a specific manner through the use of **capital appropriation request forms**. Such forms will detail the nature of the project and the amount of finance needed, together with the forecasted cash inflows and the NPV, IRR, ARR and/or payback. Some analysis of risk and a consideration of alternatives to the proposed course of action may also be required.

Expenditure below a threshold, say £100,000, will gain authorisation at division level, while that above the threshold will need approval at corporate level. At head office a committee consisting of the most senior officers (chairman, chief executive, finance director, etc.) will meet on a regular basis to consider major capital projects. Very few investment proposals are turned down by this committee, mainly because these project ideas will have already been through a number of stages of review and informal discussion up and down the organisation, and the obviously non-viable will have been eliminated. Also, even marginally profitable projects may get approval to give a vote of confidence to the sponsoring management team. The alternative of refusal may damage motivation and may cause loss of commitment to developing other projects. If the senior management had had doubts about a proposal they would have influenced the sponsoring division(s) long before the proposal reached the final report stage. In most cases there is a long period of consultation between head office and division managers, and informal pressures to modify or drop proposals can be both more efficient and politically astute ways of proceeding than refusal at the last hurdle.

Implementation

Capital expenditure controls

Firms must keep track of investment projects so as to be quickly aware of delays and cost differences compared with the plan. When a project is authorised there is usually a specified schedule of expenditure, and the accountants and senior management will keep a watchful eye on cash outflows. During the installation, purchasing and construction phases, comparisons with original estimates will be made on a periodic basis. Divisions may be permitted to overspend by, say, 10 per cent before a formal request for more funds is required. A careful watch is also kept on any changes to the projected start and completion dates. Deviations from projected cash flows are often caused by the following two factors:

a inaccuracy in the original estimate, that is, the proposal report did not reflect reality perfectly;

b poor control of costs.

It is often difficult to isolate each of these elements. However, deviations need to be identified and explained as the project progresses. This may permit corrective action to be taken to avoid further overspending and may, in extreme circumstances, lead to the cancellation of the project.

Post-completion audit

Post-completion auditing is the monitoring and evaluation of the progress of a capital investment project through a comparison of the actual cash flows and other costs and benefits with those forecasted at the time of authorisation. Companies need a follow-up procedure which examines the performance of projects over a long timespan, stretching over many years. It is necessary to isolate and explain deviations from estimated values.

Exhibit 4.12 shows the extent of the use of post-competition audits by UK companies.

Exhibit 4.12 Replies to the question: 'Does your company conduct post-audits of major capital expenditure?'

	Small %	Medium-sized %	Large %	Composite %
Always	41	17	24	28
Sometimes/on major projects	41	67	71	59
Rarely	12	17	5	10
Never	6	–	–	2

Note: 96 companies responded to the survey.

Source: Arnold and Hatzopoulos (2000).

There are three main reasons for carrying out a post-completion audit:

1 ***Financial control mechanism*** This monitoring process helps to identify problems and errors evident in a particular project. A comparison with the original projections establishes whether the benefits claimed prior to approval actually materialise. If a problem is encountered then modifications or abandonment may be possible before it is too late.

2 ***Insight gained may be useful for future capital investment decisions*** One benefit of auditing existing projects is that it might lead to the identification of failings in the capital investment

process generally. It may be discovered that data collection systems are inadequate or that appraisal methods are poor. Regular post-completion auditing helps to develop better decision making. For instance, past appraisals may have paid scant regard to likely competitor reaction; once recognised this omission will be corrected for in all future evaluations.

3 ***The psychological effect*** If potential project sponsors are aware that implemented proposals are monitored and reviewed they may be encouraged to increase their forecasting accuracy. They may also be dissuaded from playing 'numbers games' with their project submission, designed to draw more resources to their divisions or pet schemes unjustifiably. In addition, they may take a keener interest in the implementation phase.

Senior management must conduct a careful balancing act because the post-completion audit may encourage another sort of non-optimal behaviour. For instance, if managers are judged on the extent to which project outcomes exceed original estimates, there will be a tendency to deliberately understate the forecast. Also, if the audit is too inquisitorial, or if it too forcefully apportions blame for results which are only partially under the control of managers, then they may be inclined to suggest only relatively safe projects with predictable outcomes. This may result in a loss of opportunities. Ideally, regular post-completion reviews are needed, but many firms settle for an audit one year after the asset has been put in place. This may be inadequate for projects producing returns over many years. Some firms do manage an annual review of progress, and some even go as far as monthly monitoring during the first year followed by annual reviews thereafter. On the other hand, many projects involve only minor commitment of resources and are routine in nature. The need for post-completion auditing is not as pressing for these as it would be for strategic projects requiring major organisational resource commitment. Given the costs involved in the auditing process, many firms feel justified in being highly selective and auditing only a small proportion. Another reason for not carrying out a post-completion audit in all cases is the difficulty of disentangling the costs and benefits of a specific project in a context of widespread interaction and interdependence.

Concluding comments

The typical student of finance will spend a great deal of time trying to cope with problems presented in a mathematical form. This is necessary because these are often the most difficult aspects of the subject to absorb. However, readers should not be misled into thinking that complex computations are at the centre of project investment in the practical world of business. Managers are often either ignorant of the principles behind discounted cash flow techniques or choose to stress more traditional rule-of-thumb techniques, such as payback and accounting rate of return, because of their communicatory or other perceived advantages. These managers recognise that good investment decision making and implementation require attention to be paid to the social and psychological factors at work within an organisation. They also know that formal technical appraisal takes place only after a long process of idea creation and development in a suitably nurturing environment. There is also a long period of discussion and commitment forming, and continuous re-examination and refinement. The real art of management is in the process of project creation and selection and not in the technical appraisal stage.

Key points and concepts

- **Payback and ARR** are widely used methods of project appraisal, but discounted cash flow methods are the most popular.
- Most large firms use **more than one appraisal method**.
- **Payback** is the length of time for cumulated future cash inflows to equal an initial outflow. Projects are accepted if this time is below an agreed cut-off point.

- **Payback has a few drawbacks:**
  - no allowance for the time value of money;
  - cash flows after the cut-off are ignored;
  - arbitrary selection of cut-off date.
- **Discounted payback** takes account of the time value of money.
- **Payback's attractions:**
  - it complements more sophisticated methods;
  - simple, and easy to use;
  - good for communication with non-specialists;
  - makes allowance for increased risk of more distant cash flows;
  - projects returning cash sooner are ranked higher. Thought to be useful when capital is in short supply.
- **Accounting rate of return** is the ratio of accounting profit to investment, expressed as a percentage.
- **Accounting rate of return has a few drawbacks:**
  - it can be calculated in a wide variety of ways;
  - profit is a poor substitute for cash flow;
  - no allowance for the time value of money;
  - arbitrary cut-off rate;
  - some perverse decisions can be made.
- **Accounting rate of return attractions:**
  - familiarity, ease of understanding and communication;
  - managers' performances are often judged using ARR and therefore they wish to select projects on the same basis.
- **Internal rate of return** is used more than NPV:
  - psychological preference for a percentage;
  - can be calculated without cost of capital;
  - thought (wrongly) to give a better ranking.
- **Mathematical technique is only one element** needed for successful project appraisal. Other factors to be taken into account are:
  - strategy;
  - social context;
  - expense;
  - entrepreneurial spirit;
  - intangible benefits.
- **The investment process** is more than appraisal. **It has many stages:**
  - generation of ideas;
  - development and classification;
  - screening;
  - appraisal;
  - report and authorisation;
  - implementation;
  - post-completion auditing.

References and further reading

Alkaraan, F. and Northcott, D. (2006) 'Strategic capital investment decision-making: a role for emergent analysis tools? A study of practice in large UK manufacturing companies', *British Accounting Review*, 38, pp. 149–73.
As well as providing survey evidence on appraisal techniques used this paper considers the issue of using alternative techniques for strategies investments.

Arnold, G.C. and Hatzopoulos, P.D. (2000) 'The theory–practice gap in capital budgeting: evidence from the United Kingdom', *Journal of Business Finance and Accounting*, 27(5) and (6), June/July, pp. 603–26.
Evidence of techniques used by UK firms, discussion of reasons for continued use of rule-of-thumb methods.

Arya, A., Fellingham, J.C. and Glover, J.C. (1998) 'Capital budgeting: some exceptions to the net present value rule', *Issues in Accounting Education*, 13(3), August, pp. 499–508.
Discussion on the use of NPV.

Bhasker, K. (1979) 'A multiple objective approach to capital budgeting', *Accounting and Business Research*, Winter.
Discussion of investment appraisal.

Bierman, H. (1988) *Implementing Capital Budgeting Techniques*, revised edn. Cambridge, MA: Ballinger Publishing.
Practical issues.

Bierman, H. and Smidt, S. (2006) *The Capital Budgeting Decision*, 9th edn. London: Routledge.
Beginner's guide.

Bierman, H. and Smidt, S. (2006) *Advanced Capital Budgeting*. London: Routledge.
For those who need more depth.

Boardman, C.M., Reinhard, W.J. and Celec, S.G. (1982) 'The role of the payback period in the theory and application of duration to capital budgeting', *Journal of Business Finance and Accounting*, 9(4), Winter, pp. 511–22.
Payback critically assessed.

Bower, J.L. (1972) *Managing the Resource Allocation Process*. Illinois: Irwin.
Provides insight into the managerial processes involved in investment decision taking.

Bromwich, M. and Bhimani, A. (1991) 'Strategic investment appraisal', *Management Accounting*, March.
Short article describing appraisal of non-quantifiable benefits of a project.

Chartered Institute of Public Finance and Accountancy (1983) 'Management of capital programmes', *Financial System Review* 8.
Advice on project processes in the public sector.

Christy, G.A. (1966) *Capital Budgeting – Current Practices and their Efficiency*. Bureau of Business and Economic Research, University of Oregon.
More evidence of use.

Cooper, D.J. (1975) 'Rationality and investment appraisal', *Accounting and Business Research*, Summer, pp. 198–202.
Capital budgeting set in context.

Dean, J. (1951) *Capital Budgeting*. New York: Columbia University Press.
The first comprehensive capital budgeting book. An early rejection of payback.

Demski, J.S. (1994) *Managerial Uses of Accounting Information*. Boston: Kluwer Academic Pub.
Includes a discussion of the practical employment of NPV.

Dixit, A.K. and Pindyck, R.S. (1994) *Investment Under Uncertainty*. Princeton, NJ: Princeton University Press.
Higher-level discussion.

Ekanem, I. (2005) '"Bootstrapping": the investment decision-making process in small firms', *British Accounting Review*, 37, pp. 299–318.
Describes how investment decisions are made in eight small firms – somewhat differently to textbook theory.

Emmanuel, C., Otley, D. and Merchant, K. (1990) *Accounting for Management Control*, 2nd edn. London: Chapman and Hall.
An advanced accounting text that deals with investment appraisal.

Finnie, J. (1988) 'The role of financial appraisal in decisions to acquire advanced manufacturing technology', *Accounting and Business Research*, 18(70), pp. 133–9.
Argues that better management of the appraisal process is required for projects using advanced manufacturing technology.

Fisher, F.M. and McGowan, J.I. (1983) 'On the misuse of accounting rates of return to infer monopoly profits', *American Economic Review*, 73, March, pp. 82–97.
Highlights a number of problems with ARR.

Gadella, J.W. (1992), 'Post-project appraisal', *Management Accounting*. March, pp. 52 and 58.
Yet more on post-completion auditing.

Gitman, L.J. and Forrester, J.R. (1977) 'A survey of capital budgeting techniques used by major US firms', *Financial Management*, Fall, pp. 66–76.
Empirical evidence from the USA.

Gitman, L.J. and Maxwell, C.E. (1987) 'A longitudinal comparison of capital budgeting techniques used by major US firms: 1986 versus 1976', *Journal of Applied Business Research*, Fall, pp. 41–50.
Empirical evidence from the USA.

Gitman, L.J. and Mercurio, V.A. (1982) 'Cost of capital techniques used in major US firms', *Financial Management*, Winter, pp. 21–9.
Empirical evidence from the USA.

Goffin, K. and Mitchell, R. (2006) 'Learning to avoid the net present value trap', *Financial Times*, Mastering Financial Management (part 1), 26 May, p. 2.
Deals with the difficulties of evaluating highly innovative projects – easy to read.

Gordon, L.A. and Myers, M.D. (1991) 'Postauditing capital projects', *Management Accounting* (US), January, pp. 39–42.

Graham, J.R. and Harvey, C.R. (2001) 'The theory and practice of corporate finance: evidence from the field', *Journal of Financial Economics*, 60(2–3), May, pp. 187–243.
Provides evidence of US corporate use of project appraisal techniques together with an easy-to-follow discussion.

Grayson, C.J. (1966) 'The use of statistical techniques in capital budgeting', in A.A. Robichek, (ed.) *Financial Research and Management Decisions*. New York: Wiley, pp. 90–132.
Early discussion.

Gurnani, C. (1984) 'Capital budgeting: theory and practice', *Engineering Economist*, Fall, pp. 19–46.
Discussion of the theory–practice gap.

Hajdasinski, M.M. (1993) 'The payback period as a measure of profitability and liquidity', *Engineering Economist*, 38(3), Spring, pp. 177–91.
Payback's usefulness.

Haka, S.F., Gordon, L.A. and Pinches, G.E. (1985) 'Sophisticated capital budgeting selection techniques and firm performance', *Accounting Review*, October, pp. 651–69.
Do firms that adopt textbook best practice perform the best?

Harris, M., Kriebel, C.H. and Raviv, A. (1982) 'Asymmetric information, incentives and intrafirm resource allocation', *Management Science*, 28(6), June, pp. 604–20.
Explanations for the theory–practice gap.

Ho, S.M. and Pike, R.H. (1991) 'Risk analysis techniques in capital budgeting contexts', *Accounting and Business Research*, 21(83).
Survey of 146 UK firms' project risk analysis practices.

Hodgkinson, L. (1987) 'The capital budgeting decision of corporate groups', Plymouth Business School Paper.
An interesting survey of the capital investment process in medium-sized UK companies.

Jones, T.C. and Dugdale, D. (1994) 'Academic and practitioner rationality: the case of investment appraisal', *British Accounting Review*, 26, pp. 3–25.
Theory–practice gap explored.

Kaplan, R.S. (1986) 'Must CIM be justified by faith alone?', *Harvard Business Review*, March/April, pp. 87–95.
DCF analysis applied to computer-integrated manufacturing projects – interesting application of principles.

Kaplan, R.S. and Atkinson, A.A. (1998) *Advanced Management Accounting*, International Edition. Englewood Cliffs, NJ: Prentice-Hall.
Theory–practice gap explored.

Kay, J.A. (1976) 'Accountants, too, could be happy in a golden age: the accountant's rate of profit and the internal rate of return', *Oxford Economic Papers*, 28, pp. 447–60.
A technical/mathematical consideration of the link between ARR and IRR.

Kee, R. and Bublitz, B. (1988) 'The role of payback in the investment process', *Accounting and Business Research*, 18(70), pp. 149–55.
Value of payback discussed.

Kennedy, A. and Mills, R. (1990) *Post Completion Audit of Capital Expenditure Projects*. London: CIMA. Management Accounting Guide 9.
Post-completion auditing evidence.

Kennedy, A. and Mills, R. (1992) 'Post completion auditing: a source of strategic direction?', *Management Accounting* (UK), May, pp. 26–8.
Post-completion auditing evidence.

Kennedy, A. and Mills, R. (1993a) 'Post completion auditing in practice', *Management Accounting*, October, pp. 22–5.
Post-completion auditing evidence.

Kennedy, A. and Mills, R. (1993b) 'Experiences in operating a post-audit system', *Management Accounting*, November.
Post-completion auditing evidence.

Kim, S.H. (1982) 'An empirical study of the relationship between capital budgeting practices and earning performance', *Engineering Economics*, 27(3), Spring, pp. 185–96.
Does the adoption of theoretical best practice result in outperformance?

Kim, S.H. and Farragher, E.J. (1981) 'Current capital budgeting practices', *Management Accounting* (US), June, pp. 26–33.
Empirical evidence.

Kim, S.H., Crick, T. and Kim, S.H. (1986) 'Do executives practice what academics preach?', *Management Accounting* (US), November, pp. 49–52.
Theory–practice gap.

King, P. (1975) 'Is the emphasis of capital budgeting theory misplaced?', *Journal of Business Finance and Accounting*, 2(1), p. 69.
Theory–practice gap.

Klammer, T., Koch, B. and Wilner, N. (1991) 'Capital budgeting practices – a survey of corporate use', *Journal of Management Accounting Research*, Fall, pp. 447–64.
Empirical evidence.

Lawrence, A.G. and Myers, M.D. (1991) 'Post-auditing capital projects', *Management Accounting*, January, pp. 39–42.
Survey of 282 large US firms' post-auditing objectives, method and thoroughness.

Lefley, F. (1996) 'Strategic methodologies of investment appraisal of AMT projects: a review and synthesis', *Engineering Economist*, 41(4), Summer, pp. 345–61.
Quantitative analysis and judgement are both needed in order to assess advanced manufacturing technology projects.

Lefley, F. (1997) 'The sometimes overlooked discounted payback method', *Management Accounting* (UK), November, p. 36.
Payback's virtues.

Litzenberger, R.M. and Joy, O.M. (1975) 'Decentralized capital budgeting decisions and shareholder wealth maximisation', *Journal of Finance*, 30(4), pp. 993–1002.
Practical DCF.

Longmore, D.R. (1989) 'The persistence of the payback method: a time-adjusted decision rule perspective', *Engineering Economist*, 43(3), Spring, pp. 185–94.
Payback's use.

Lowenstein, L. (1991) *Sense and Nonsense in Corporate Finance*. Reading, MA: Addison Wesley.
Criticism of over-preciseness in project appraisal and the underplaying of unquantifiable elements.

Lumijärvi, O.P. (1991) 'Selling of capital investments to top management', *Management Accounting Research*, 2, pp. 171–88.
Describes a real-world case of a lower-level manager influencing superiors so that desired investment funds are received.

McIntyre, A.D. and Coulthurst, N.J. (1986) *Capital Budgeting Practices in Medium-Sized Businesses – A Survey*. London: Institute of Cost and Management Accountants.
Interesting survey of investment appraisal practices in UK medium-sized firms. More detailed than the later (1987) article.

McIntyre, A.D. and Coulthurst, N.J. (1987) 'Planning and control of capital investment in medium-sized UK companies', *Management Accounting*, March, pp. 39–40.
Interesting summary of empirical work explaining the capital budgeting processes in 141 medium-sized firms with turnovers in the range £1.4m–£5.75m.

Mills, R.W. (1988) 'Capital budgeting techniques used in the UK and the USA', *Management Accounting*, January, pp. 26–7.
Empirical evidence on investment appraisal methods used in practice.

Mills, R.W. and Herbert, P.J.A. (1987) 'Corporate and divisional influence in capital budgeting', Chartered Institute of Management Accountants, Occasional Paper Series.
Internal issues associated with capital budgeting.

Mills, R., Robertson, J. and Ward, T. (1992) 'Why financial economics is vital in measuring business value', *Management Accounting* (UK), January, pp. 39–42.
Theoretical discussion.

Neale, B. and Holmes, D. (1988) 'Post-completion audits: the costs and benefits', *Management Accounting*, March, pp. 27–30.
Post-completion audits discussion.

Neale, C.W. and Holmes, D.E.A. (1988) 'Post-completion audits: the costs and benefits', *Management Accounting*, 66(3).
Benefits of post-completion auditing. Evidence from a survey of 384 UK and USA large firms.

Northcott, D. (1991) 'Rationality and decision making in capital budgeting', *British Accounting Review*, Sept., pp. 219–34.
Theory–practice gap explored.

Patterson, C.S. (1989) 'Investment decision criteria used by listed New Zealand companies', *Accounting and Finance*, 29(2), November, pp. 73–89.
Evidence from the Pacific.

Pike, R.H. (1982) *Capital Budgeting in the 1980s*. London: Chartered Institute of Management Accountants.
Clearly describes evidence on the capital investment practices of major British companies.

Pike, R.H. (1983) 'A review of recent trends in formal capital budgeting processes', *Accounting and Business Research*, Summer, pp. 201–8.
More evidence.

Pike, R.H. (1985) 'Owner–manager conflict and the role of payback', *Accounting and Business Research*, Winter, pp. 47–51.
Comparison of methods.

Pike, R.H. (1988) 'An empirical study of the adoption of sophisticated capital budgeting practices and decision-making effectiveness', *Accounting and Business Research*, 18(72), Autumn, pp. 341–51.
Observes the trend within 100 large UK firms over 11 years towards sophisticated methods – NPV, post-completion audits, probability analysis.

Pike, R.H. (1996) 'A longitudinal survey of capital budgeting practices', *Journal of Business Finance and Accounting*, 23(1), January.
Excellent, short and clear article surveying appraisal methods in UK large firms.

Pike, R.H. and Wolfe, M. (1988) *Capital Budgeting in the 1990s*. London: Chartered Institute of Management Accountants.
Some interesting evidence on appraisal methods used in practice. Clearly expressed.

Pinches, G.E. (1982) 'Myopia, capital budgeting and decision-making', *Financial Management*, Autumn, pp. 6–19.

Ross, S.A. (1995) 'Uses, abuses, and alternatives to the net-present-value rule', *Financial Management*, 24(3), Autumn, pp. 96–102.
Discussion of the value of NPV.

Sangster, A. (1993) 'Capital investment appraisal techniques: a survey of current usage', *Journal of Business Finance and Accounting*, 20(3), April, pp. 307–33.
Evidence of use.

Scapens, R.W. and Sale, J.T. (1981) 'Performance measurement and formal capital expenditure controls in divisionalised companies', *Journal of Business Finance and Accounting*, 8, pp. 389–420.
The capital investment process in large UK and US firms.

Scapens, R.W., Sale, J.T. and Tikkas, P.A. (1982) *Financial Control of Divisional Capital Investment*. London: Institute of Cost and Management Accountants, Occasional Papers Series.
Good insight into the capital investment process in large UK and US companies.

Statman, M. (1982) 'The persistence of the payback method: a principal–agent perspective', *Engineering Economist*, Summer, pp. 95–100.
Payback's usefulness.

Statman, M. and Sepe, J.F. (1984) 'Managerial incentive plans and the use of the payback method', *Journal of Business Finance and Accounting*, 11(1), Spring, pp. 61–5.
Payback's usefulness.

Steele, R. and Albright, C. (2004) 'Games managers play at budget time', *MIT Sloan Management Review*, Spring, pp. 81–4.
Executive game-play tactics revealed.

Tyrrall, D.E. (1998) 'Discounted cash flow: rational calculation or psychological crutch?', *Management Accounting* (UK), February, pp 46–8.
Discussion of theory–practice relationship.

Wardlow, A. (1994), 'Investment appraisal criteria and the impact of low inflation', *Bank of England Quarterly Bulletin*, 34(3), August, pp. 250–4.
Discussion of the failure to adjust to a low and stable inflation environment. Easy to read.

Weingartner, H.M. (1969) 'Some new views on the payback period and capital budgeting', *Management Science*, 15, pp. 594–607.
Why payback is frequently employed.

Weingartner, H.M. (1977) 'Capital rationing: *n* authors in search of a plot', *Journal of Finance*, December, pp. 1403–31.
Critical discussion.

Zimmerman, J.L. (1997) *Accounting for Decision Making and Control*, 2nd edn. Boston: Irwin/McGraw-Hill.
Contains a useful discussion on discounted cash flow methods.

Case study recommendations

Please see www.pearsoned.co.uk/arnold for case study synopses.

- Innocent Drinks. Authors: W. A. Sahlman and D. Heath, (November 2004) Harvard Business School.
- The Super Project. Author: H.E. Wyman, (May 2004) Harvard Business School.

Self-review questions

1 Payback is dismissed as unsound. Discuss.

2 Define accounting rate of return and compare it with net present value.

3 Describe discounted payback.

4 Do you believe the arguments for using IRR are strong enough to justify relying on this technique alone?

5 Why is investment project generation, selection and implementation closer to an art form than a science?

6 How would you appraise a project with a high proportion of non-quantifiable benefits?

7 If you were chief executive of a large corporation, how would you encourage project idea generation, communication and sponsorship?

8 Why is project screening necessary?

9 Invent five projects, each of which falls into a different project category.

10 Why are few projects rejected at the report stage?

11 When do capital expenditure controls and post-completion audits become an excessive burden, and when are they very important?

12 Comment on the following statement:

'The firm should choose the investment with a short payback rather than one with a larger net present value.'

Questions and problems

myfinancelab **_Questions with an icon are also available for practice in MyFinanceLab with additional supporting resources._**

1 For the following projects, calculate the payback and the discounted payback.

Point in time (yearly intervals)	0 £	1 £	2 £	3 £	4 £	5 £	6 £	7 £
A	−3,000	500	500	500	500	500	500	500
B	−10,000	2,000	5,000	3,000	2,000	–	–	–
C	−15,000	5,000	4,000	4,000	5,000	10,000	–	–
D	−4,000	1,000	1,000	1,000	1,000	7,000	7,000	7,000
E	−8,000	500	500	500	2,000	5,000	10,000	–

The cost of capital is 12 per cent.

2 A project has a £10,000 initial investment and cash inflows of £3,334 per year over six years. What is the payback period? What will be the payback period if the receipts of £3,334 per year occur for only three years? Explain the significance of your answer.

3* (*Examination level*) Oakland plc is considering a major investment project. The initial outlay of £900,000 will, in subsequent years, be followed by positive cash flows, as shown below. (These occur on the anniversary dates.)

Year	1	2	3	4	5
Cash flow (£)	+50,000	+120,000	+350,000	+80,000	+800,000

After the end of the fifth year this business activity will cease and no more cash flows will be produced.

The initial £900,000 investment in plant and machinery is to be depreciated over the five-year life of the project using the straight-line method. These assets will have no value after Year 5.

The management judge that the cash inflows shown above are also an accurate estimation of the profit before depreciation for each of the years. They also believe that the appropriate discount rate to use for the firm's projects is 10 per cent per annum.

The board of directors are used to evaluating project proposals on the basis of a payback rule which requires that all investments achieve payback in four years.

As the newly appointed executive responsible for project appraisal you have been asked to assess this project using a number of different methods and to advise the board on the advantages and disadvantages of each. Do this in the following sequence.

(1) a Calculate the payback period.
b Calculate the discounted payback period.
c Calculate an accounting rate of return.
d Calculate the internal rate of return.
e Calculate the net present value.

(2) Compare the relative theoretical and practical merits and demerits of each of the methods used.

Assume: No tax or inflation.

?

4 A firm is considering investing in a project with the following cash flows:

Year	1	2	3	4	5	6	7	8
Net cash flow (£)	1,000	1,500	2,000	1,750	1,500	1,000	500	500

The initial investment is £6,250. The firm has a required rate of return of 10 per cent. Calculate:

a the payback period;
b the discounted payback;
c the net present value.

What are the main objections to the use of payback? Why does it remain a very popular method?

?

5 Maple plc is considering which of two mutually exclusive projects to accept, each with a five-year life. Project A requires an initial expenditure of £2,300,000 and is forecast to generate annual cash flows before depreciation of £800,000. The equipment purchased at time zero has an estimated residual value after five years of £300,000. Project B costs £660,000 for equipment at the start. This has a residual value of £60,000 after five years. Cash inflows before depreciation of £250,000 per annum are anticipated. The company has a straight-line depreciation policy and a cost of capital of 15 per cent (relevant for projects of this risk class). You can assume that the cash flows are also equal to the profits before depreciation. Calculate:

a an accounting rate of return;
b the net present value.

What are the disadvantages of using ARR?

6 Explain why empirical studies show that, in practice, firms often prefer to evaluate projects using traditional methods.

7 Camelia plc has been run in an autocratic style by the chief executive and main shareholder, Mr Linedraw, during its 40-year history. The company is now too large for Mr Linedraw to continue being involved in all decisions. As part of its reforms the firm intends to set up a structured programme of capital investment. You have been asked to compile a report which will guide management. This will detail the investment process and will not be confined to appraisal techniques.

8 'The making of good investment decisions is as much about understanding human psychology as it is about mathematics.' Explain this statement.

9 Explain how each of the following can lead to a sub-optimal investment process:

a relying on top-down idea generation;
b managers being judged solely on accounting rate of return;
c a requirement that projects have a quick payback;
d post-auditing once only, one year after completion;
e post-auditing conducted by managers from 'rival' divisions;
f over-optimism of project sponsors.

myfinancelab *Now retake your diagnostic test for Chapter 4 to check your progress and update your study plan.*

Assignment

Investigate the capital investment process in a firm you know well. Relate the stages and methods used to the process outlined in this chapter. Consider areas for improvement.

CHAPTER

5

Project appraisal:

Capital rationing, taxation and inflation

LEARNING OUTCOMES

By the end of this chapter the reader should be able to cope with investment appraisal in an environment of capital rationing, taxation and inflation. More specifically, he/she should be able to:

- explain why capital rationing exists and use the profitability ratio in one-period rationing situations;
- show awareness of the influence of taxation on cash flows;
- discount money cash flows with a money discount rate, and real cash flows with a real discount rate.

myfinancelab *Complete your diagnostic test for Chapter 5 now to create your personal study plan*

Introduction

In all the analysis conducted so far in this book, bold simplifying assumptions have been made in order to convey the essential concepts and techniques of project appraisal. First, it was assumed that there are no limits placed on finance available to fund any project the firm thinks viable, that is, there is no capital rationing. Secondly, it was assumed that individuals and firms do not have to concern themselves with taxation – oh, if only it were so! Thirdly, it was assumed that there is no such thing as inflation to distort cash flow projections and cost of capital calculations. The analysis is made more sophisticated in this chapter by dropping these assumptions and allowing for greater realism.

Capital rationing

Our discussion, until now, has rested on the assumption that if a project had a positive net present value then it both *should* be undertaken, and *could* be undertaken. The wealth of shareholders is highest if the firm accepts every project that has a positive NPV. But to undertake every possible project assumes that the firm has sufficient funds available. Quite often, in the practical world of business, there are limits placed on the availability of project finance and a choice has to be made between a number of positive NPV projects. This is the capital rationing problem.

Capital rationing occurs when funds are not available to finance all wealth-enhancing projects. There are two types of capital rationing: soft rationing and hard rationing.

Soft rationing

Soft capital rationing is internal management-imposed limits on investment expenditure. Such limits may be linked to the firm's financial control policy. Senior management may try to retain financial control over divisions by placing limits on the amount any particular division can spend on a set of projects. Some ambitious managers may be tempted to overstate the extent of investment opportunities within their sector of responsibility. To sort out the good projects from the bad, head office could examine each individually, but this would be bureaucratic and time consuming. The alternative is to impose a limit on the amount a division may invest in projects within a particular time frame. It is then the division's responsibility to decide which projects rank higher than others.

Some firms operate in very dynamic sectors and have a large number of potentially profitable expansion opportunities. To undertake all of them would put intolerable strains on the management and the organisation because of the excessive growth this might imply. For example, Microsoft's thousands of technically able employees might generate dozens or even hundreds of ideas for significant new businesses, ranging from new software and multimedia to links with television broadcasters and book publishers. Over-rapid expansion may lead to difficulties in planning and control. Intangible stresses and strains are difficult to quantify and therefore the rationing of capital is used to place some limits to growth. Capital rationing acts as a proxy for other types of resources in short supply, such as managerial talent or time, technical expertise or even equipment.

Firms may aim to avoid exceeding certain values for key financial ratios. One of the most important ratios examined is the relationship between borrowing and asset levels. Management may be fearful of the increasing risk associated with extensive borrowing and become reluctant to enter into the capital markets to borrow. Unwillingness to borrow more money has elements of soft and hard capital rationing. It is a form of self-imposed rationing, but it may have been prompted by signals from the capital markets that borrowing would be difficult or would be available only with onerous strings attached.

Another limit on the availability of finance can be created because the existing owner-manager or family shareholders do not wish to lose control by permitting the firm to raise equity finance by selling new shares to outsiders.

Hard rationing

Hard capital rationing relates to capital from external sources. Agencies (e.g. shareholders) external to the firm will not supply unlimited amounts of investment capital, even though positive NPV projects are identified. In a perfect capital market hard rationing should never occur, because if a firm has positive NPV projects it will be able to raise any finance it needs. Hard rationing, therefore, implies market imperfections (two elements of which might be the principal–agent problem and information asymmetry leading to a lack of trust in managers' claims). This is a problem that has been evident since business activity first started. It is a particular problem for smaller, less profitable and more high-risk firms. Numerous governments have tried to improve the availability of funds to firms. Also, stock exchanges, over recent years, have encouraged the development of equity markets specifically targeted at small firms trying to raise finance. In addition, a venture capital market has been developed by institutions to provide for start-up and early stage development. (Sources of equity capital are examined in Chapters 9 and 10.) Despite all these advances companies still complain regularly in the press about the gap between the amount of capital firms would like to use and that which is made available.

One-period capital rationing

The simplest and most straightforward form of rationing occurs when limits are placed on finance availability for only one year; for all the other years funds are unlimited. There are two possibilities within this one-period rationing situation.

1 ***Divisible projects*** The nature of the proposed projects is such that it is possible to undertake a fraction of a total project. For instance, if a project is established to expand a retail group by opening a further 100 shops, it would be possible to take only 30 per cent (that is 30 shops) or any other fraction of the overall project. To make the mathematical calculations less complicated, and to make conceptual understanding easier, it is often assumed that all cash flows change in proportion to the fraction of the project implemented.

2 ***Indivisible projects*** With some projects it is impossible to take a fraction. The choice is between undertaking the whole of the investment or none of it (for instance, a project to build a ship, or a bridge or an oil platform).

Divisible projects

A stylised example of a one-period constraint problem with divisible projects is Bigtasks plc, a subsidiary of a major manufacturing group.

Worked example 5.1 Bigtasks plc

Bigtasks has four positive NPV projects to consider. Capital at time zero has been rationed to £4.5m because of head office planning and control policies, and because the holding company has been subtly warned that another major round of fresh borrowing this year would not be welcomed by the financial institutions in the City of London. However, funds are likely to be effectively unlimited in future years. The four projects under consideration can each be undertaken once only and the acceptance of one of the projects does not exclude the possibility of accepting another one. The cash flows are as follows:

Point in time (yearly intervals)	0 £m	1 £m	2 £m	NPV at 10% £m
Project A	−2	6	1	4.281
Project B	−1	1	4	3.215
Project C	−1	1	3	2.388
Project D	−3	10	10	14.355

All these projects have positive net present values and would therefore all be accepted in the absence of capital rationing. We need to determine the optimal combination of projects which will require a total investment the same as, or less than, the capital constraint. Ranking projects by the absolute NPV will usually give an incorrect result. Such an approach will be biased towards the selection of large projects. It may be better to invest in a number of smaller projects with lower individual NPVs. If we do select according to the highest absolute NPV, the total NPV produced is £17.566m, because we would allocate £3m first to Project D, and then the remaining £1.5m would be invested in three-quarters of Project A because this has the next highest absolute NPV.

Ranking according to absolute NPV

	Initial outlay	NPV (£m)
All of Project D	3	14.355
3/4 of Project A	1.5	3.211
	4.5	Total NPV 17.566

To achieve an optimum allocation of the £4.5m we need to make use of either the **profitability index (PI)** or the **benefit–cost ratio**.[1]

$$\text{Profitability index} = \frac{\text{Gross present value}}{\text{Initial outlay}}$$

$$\text{Benefit–cost ratio} = \frac{\text{Net present value}}{\text{Initial outlay}}$$

The **gross present value** is the total present value of all the cash flows excluding the initial investment. Both ratios provide a measure of profitability per £ invested. For example, in **Exhibit 5.1**, for every £1 invested in Project A, £3.14 is returned in future cash flows when discounted. The benefit–cost ratio is, of course, closely related to the profitability index and for Project A shows that £1 committed at time zero will produce a *net* present value of £2.14.

Exhibit 5.1 Bigtasks plc: Profitability indices and benefit-cost ratios

Project	NPV (@ 10%)	GPV (@ 10%)	Profitability index	Benefit–cost ratio
A	4.281	6.281	$\frac{6.281}{2} = 3.14$	$\frac{4.281}{2} = 2.14$
B	3.215	4.215	$\frac{4.215}{1} = 4.215$	$\frac{3.215}{1} = 3.215$
C	2.388	3.388	$\frac{3.388}{1} = 3.388$	$\frac{2.388}{1} = 2.388$
D	14.355	17.355	$\frac{17.355}{3} = 5.785$	$\frac{14.355}{3} = 4.785$

The use of profitability indices or benefit–cost ratios is a matter of personal choice. Whichever is used, the next stage is to arrange the projects in order of the highest profitability index or benefit–cost ratio. Then work down the list until the capital limit is reached. Here, the profitability index (PI) will be used (*see* **Exhibit 5.2**).

[1] The use of these terms is often muddled and they may be used interchangeably in the literature and in practice, so you should ensure that it is clearly understood how the ratio used in a particular situation is calculated.

Exhibit 5.2 Bigtasks plc: Ranking according to the highest profitability index

Profit	Profitability index	Initial outlay £m	NPV £m
D	5.785	3	14.355
B	4.215	1	3.215
1/2 of C	3.388	0.5	1.194
Nothing of A	3.14	0	0
Total investment		4.5	18.764

With the profitability index, Project D gives the highest return and so is the best project in terms of return per £ of outlay. However, Project A no longer ranks second because this provides the lowest return per unit of initial investment. The smaller projects, B and C, give a higher PI.

The overall result for Bigtasks is that an extra £1.198m (£18.764–£17.566m) is created for shareholders by selecting projects through one of the ratios rather than sticking rigidly to NPV.

Indivisible projects

In practice, few projects are divisible and so the profitability index is inappropriate. Now, assume that it is not possible to take a fraction of Bigtask's projects and that the capital limit at time zero is £3m. In these circumstances the easiest approach is to examine the total NPV values of all the feasible alternative combinations of whole projects, in other words, trial and error. (*See* **Exhibit 5.3**.)

Exhibit 5.3 Individual project with capital constraint of £3m

Feasible combination 1		NPV (£m)
£2m invested in Project A		4.281
£1m invested in Project B		3.215
	Total NPV	7.496

Feasible combination 2		NPV (£m)
£2m invested in Project A		4.281
£1m invested in Project C		2.388
	Total NPV	6.669

Feasible combination 3		NPV (£m)
£1m invested in Project B		3.215
£1m invested in Project C		2.388
	Total NPV	5.603

Feasible combination 4		NPV (£m)
£3m invested in Project D	Total NPV	14.355

Multi-period capital rationing

If capital constraints are likely in more than one time period, then the calculations to derive an optimal solution become significantly more complicated. For example, Small Decisions Ltd (*see* **Exhibit 5.4**) is trying to decide how to allocate its resources between six projects. All the projects

Exhibit 5.4 Small Decisions Ltd: Cash flows

Point in time (yearly intervals)	0 £000s	1 £000s	2 £000s	3 £000s
Project A	-200	-100	-20	500
Project B	0	-120	70	200
Project C	-10	0	-80	200
Project D	-80	-120	70	200
Project E	-30	-240	200	150
Project F	-60	-110	50	320

are independent (that is, not mutually exclusive) and no one project can be repeated. The firm is aware of a capital limit of £240,000 at time zero and a further constraint of £400,000 at time one.

To find a solution to a problem like this, with fund constraints in more than one period, we cannot use a method based on the profitability index. A mathematical programme will be required and a computer would normally be employed. If the projects are divisible then linear programming is used. If the projects are indivisible the solution is found through integer programming. However, these techniques are beyond the scope of this book. The reader wishing to examine this issue in more detail is referred to the references and further reading list at the end of this chapter.

Taxation and investment appraisal

Taxation can have an important impact on project viability. If management are implementing decisions that are shareholder wealth enhancing, they will focus on the cash flows generated which are available for shareholders. Therefore, they will evaluate the after-tax cash flows of a project. There are two rules to follow in investment appraisal in a world with taxation:

- ***Rule 1*** If acceptance of a project changes the tax liabilities of the firm then incremental tax effects need to be accommodated in the analysis.
- ***Rule 2*** Get the timing right. Incorporate the cash outflow of tax into the analysis at the correct time. For example, it is often the case (for small firms) that tax is paid one year or more after the receipt of the related cash flows.

Tax rates and systems can change rapidly and any example presented using rates applicable at the time of writing is likely to be soon out of date. We will not get too involved in the details of the UK taxation system, but will concentrate on the general principles of how tax is taken into account in project appraisal.

In the UK HM Revenue and Customs collect corporation tax based on the taxable income of companies. Specific projects are not taxed separately, but if a project produces additional profits in a year, then this will generally increase the tax bill. If losses are made on a project, then the overall tax bill will generally be reduced. Taxable income is rarely the same as the profit reported in the annual reports and accounts because some of the expenses deducted to produce the reported profit are not permitted by HMRC when calculating taxable income. For example, depreciation is not an allowable cost. HMRC permit a 'writing-down' allowance rather than depreciation. So for most plant and machinery in the UK, a writing-down allowance of 25 per cent on a declining balance is permitted. In a firm's accounts, such equipment may be depreciated by only, say, 10 per cent a year, whereas the tax authorities permit the taxable income to be reduced by 25 per cent of the equipment value. Thus, reported profit will often be higher than taxable income. Other types of long-lived assets, such as industrial buildings, have different percentage writing-down allowances – some assets carry a 100 per cent writing-down allowance in the year of purchase.

Worked example 5.2 Snaffle plc

Snaffle plc is considering a project which will require the purchase of a machine for £1,000,000 at time zero. This machine will have a scrap value at the end of its four-year life: this will be equal to its written-down value (this simplifying assumption will be dropped later). HMRC permit a 25 per cent declining balance writing-down allowance on the machine each year. Corporation tax, at a rate of 30 per cent of taxable income, is payable. Snaffle's required rate of return is 12 per cent.[2] Operating cash flows, excluding depreciation, and before taxation, are forecast to be:

Time (year)	1 £	2 £	3 £	4 £
Cash flows before tax	400,000	400,000	220,000	240,000

Note: All cash flows occur at year ends.

In order to calculate the net present value, first calculate the annual writing-down allowances (WDA). Note that each year the WDA is equal to 25 per cent of the asset value at the start of the year. (*See* **Exhibit 5.5**).

Exhibit 5.5 Calculation of written-down allowances

Point in time (yearly intervals)	Annual writing-down allowance £	Written-down value £
0	0	1,000,000
1	1,000,000 × 0.25 = 250,000	750,000
2	750,000 × 0.25 = 187,500	562,500
3	562,500 × 0.25 = 140,625	421,875
4	421,875 × 0.25 = 105,469	316,406

The next step is to derive the project's incremental taxable income and to calculate the tax payments (**Exhibit 5.6**).

Exhibit 5.6 Calculation of corporation tax

Year	1 £	2 £	3 £	4 £
Net income before writing-down allowance and tax	400,000	400,000	220,000	240,000
Less writing-down allowance	250,000	187,500	140,625	105,469
Incremental taxable income	150,000	212,500	79,375	134,531
Tax at 30% of incremental taxable income	45,000	63,750	23,813	40,359

Finally, the total cash flows and NPV are calculated (*see* **Exhibit 5.7**).

The assumption that the machine can be sold at the end of the fourth year, for an amount equal to the written-down value, may be unrealistic. It may turn out that the machine is sold for the larger sum of

[2] If we are dealing with after-tax cash flows the discount rate will be the after-tax discount rate.

Exhibit 5.7 Calculation of cash flows

Year	0 £	1 £	2 £	3 £	4 £
Incremental cash flow before tax	–1,000,000	400,000	400,000	220,000	240,000
Sale of machine					316,406
Tax	0	–45,000	–63,750	–23,813	–40,359
Net cash flow	–1,000,000	355,000	336,250	196,187	516,047

$$\text{Discounted cash flow} \quad -1{,}000{,}000 + \frac{355{,}000}{1.12} + \frac{336{,}250}{(1.12)^2} + \frac{196{,}187}{(1.12)^3} + \frac{516{,}047}{(1.12)^4}$$

$$-1{,}000{,}000 \quad +316{,}964 \quad +268{,}056 \quad +139{,}642 \quad +327{,}957$$

Net present value = + £52,619

Note: tax is payable in the same year that the income was earned in this case, this is generally the position for larger UK firms.

£440,000. If this is the case, a *balancing charge* will need to be made, because by the end of the third year HMRC have already permitted write-offs against taxable profit such that the machine is shown as having a written-down value of £421,875. A year later its market value is found to be £440,000. The balancing charge is equal to the sale value at Time 4 minus the written-down book value at Time 3, viz:

£440,000 – £421,875 = £18,125

Taxable profits for Year 4 are now:

	£
Pre-tax cash flows	240,000
Plus balancing charge	18,125
	258,125

This results in a tax payment of £258,125 × 0.30 = £77,438 rather than £40,359.

Of course, the analyst does not have to wait until the actual sale of the asset to make these modifications to a proposed project's projected cash flows. It may be possible to estimate a realistic scrap value at the outset.

An alternative scenario, where the scrap value is less than the Year 4 written-down value, will require a balancing allowance. If the disposal value is £300,000 then the machine cost the firm £700,000 (£1,000,000 – £300,000) but the tax writing-down allowances amount to only £683,594 (£1,000,000 – £316,406). The firm will effectively be overcharged by HMRC. In this case a balancing adjustment, amounting to £16,406 (£700,000 – £683,594), is made to reduce the tax payable (*see* **Exhibit 5.8**).

Exhibit 5.8 Year 4 taxable profits

	£
Pre-tax cash flows	240,000
Less annual writing-down allowance	105,469
Less balancing allowance	16,406
Taxable profits	118,125
Tax payable @ 30%	35,438

Inflation

Annual inflation in the UK has varied from 1 per cent to 26 per cent since 1945. It is important to adapt investment appraisal methods to cope with the phenomenon of price movements. Future rates of inflation are unlikely to be precisely forecasted; nevertheless, we will assume in the analysis that follows that we can anticipate inflation with reasonable accuracy. Unanticipated inflation is an additional source of risk and methods of dealing with this are described in the next chapter. **Case study 5.1** shows the importance of allowing for inflation.

Case study 5.1 **Eurotunnel's inflation allowance**

Peter Puplett, writing in the *Investors Chronicle*, pointed out some of the forecasting errors made in Eurotunnel's pathfinder prospectus issued in November 1987, one of which was to do with inflation:

> The total cost of the project was stated as £4,874m in the prospectus, as shown in the table. The uplift directors made for inflation was less than 14%, even though they knew the project would take at least six years to complete.

General inflation in the UK was far higher than 14 per cent over this period. The projected costs, therefore, were too low.

1987 Eurotunnel costs

	£m
Construction @ 1987 prices	2,788
Corporate costs @ 1987 prices	642
	3,430
Plus:	
Provision for inflation	469
Building cost	3,899
Net financing costs	975
Total project cost	4,874

Source: Based on *Investors Chronicle*, 19 April 1996, p. 20.

Two types of inflation can be distinguished. **Specific inflation** refers to the price changes of an individual good or service. **General inflation** is the reduced purchasing power of money and is measured by an overall price index which follows the price changes of a 'basket' of goods and services through time. Even if there was no general inflation, specific items and sectors might experience price rises.

Inflation creates two problems for project appraisal. First, the estimation of future cash flows is made more troublesome. The project appraiser will have to estimate the degree to which future cash flows will be inflated. Second, the rate of return required by the firm's security holders, such as shareholders, will rise if inflation rises. Thus, inflation has an impact on the discount rate used in investment evaluation. We will look at the second problem in more detail first.

'Real' and 'money' rates of return

A point was made in Chapter 2 of demonstrating that the rate of return represented by the discount rate usually takes account of three types of compensation:

- the pure time value of money, or impatience to consume;
- risk;
- inflation.

Thus, the interest rates quoted in the financial markets are sufficiently high to compensate for all three elements. A 10-year loan to a reputable government (such as the purchase of a bond) may pay an interest rate of 9 per cent per annum. Some of this is compensation for time preference and a little for risk, but the majority of that interest is likely to be compensation for future inflation. It is the same for the cost of capital for a business. When it issues financial securities, the returns offered include a large element of inflation compensation.

To illustrate: even in a situation of no inflation, given the choice between receiving goods and services now or receiving them some time in the future, shareholders would rather receive them now. If these pure time and risk preferences were valued, the value might turn out to be 8 per cent per annum. That is, in a world without inflation, investors are indifferent as to whether they receive a given basket of commodities today or receive a basket of commodities which is 8 per cent larger in one year's time.

The **real rate of return** is defined as the rate of return that would be required in the absence of inflation. In the example in **Exhibit 5.9**, the real rate of return is 8 per cent.

Exhibit 5.9 Rate of return without inflation

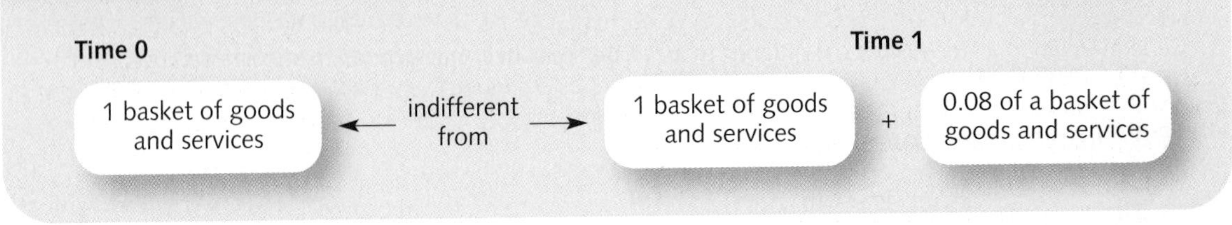

If we change the assumption so that prices do rise then investors will demand compensation for general inflation. They will require a larger monetary amount at Time 1 to buy 1.08 baskets. If inflation is 4 per cent then the money value of the commodities at Time 1, which would leave the investor indifferent when comparing it with one basket at Time 0, is:

$$1.08 \times 1.04 = 1.1232$$

That is, investors will be indifferent as to whether they hold £1,000 now or receive £1,123.20 one year hence. Since the money cash flow of £1,123.20 at Time 1 is financially equivalent to £1,000 now, the **money rate of return** is 12.32 per cent. The money rate of return includes a return to compensate for inflation.

The generalised relationship between real rates of return and money (or market, or nominal) rates of return and inflation is expressed in Fisher's (1930) equation:

$$(1 + \text{money rate of return}) = (1 + \text{real rate of return}) \times (1 + \text{anticipated rate of inflation})$$
$$(1 + m) = (1 + h) \times (1 + i)$$
$$(1 + 0.1232) = (1 + 0.08) \times (1 + 0.04)$$

'Money' cash flows and 'real' cash flows

We have now established two possible discount rates, the money discount rate and the real discount rate. There are two alternative ways of adjusting for the effect of future inflation on cash flows. The first is to estimate the likely specific inflation rates for each of the inflows and outflows of cash and calculate the actual monetary amount paid or received in the year that the flow occurs. This is the **money cash flow** or the **nominal cash flow**.

With a money cash flow, all future cash flows are expressed in the prices expected to rule when the cash flow occurs.

The other possibility is to measure the cash flows in terms of real prices. That is, all future cash flows are expressed in terms of, say, Time 0's prices.

With **real cash flows**, future cash flows are expressed in terms of constant purchasing power.

Adjusting for inflation

There are two correct methods of adjusting for inflation when calculating net present value. They will lead to the same answer:

- *Approach 1* Estimate the cash flows in money terms and use a money discount rate.
- *Approach 2* Estimate the cash flows in real terms and use a real discount rate.

For now we will leave discussion of conversion to real prices and focus on the calculations using money cash flow. This will be done through the examination of an appraisal for Amplify plc.

Worked example 5.3 Amplify plc

Cash flow in money terms and money discount rate

Amplify plc is considering a project which would require an outlay of £2.4m at the outset. The money cash flows receivable from sales will depend on the specific inflation rate for Amplify's product. This is anticipated to be 6 per cent per annum. Cash outflows consist of three elements: labour, materials and overheads. Labour costs are expected to increase at 9 per cent per year, materials by 12 per cent and overheads by 8 per cent. The discount rate of 12.32 per cent that Amplify uses is a money discount rate, including an allowance for inflation. One of the key rules of project appraisal is now followed: if the discount rate is stated in money terms, then consistency requires that the cash flows be estimated in money terms. (It is surprising how often this rule is broken.)

$$NPV = M_0 + \frac{M_1}{1+m} + \frac{M_2}{(1+m)^2} \dots \frac{M_n}{(1+m)^n}$$

where M = actual or money cash flow
m = actual or money rate of return

Annual cash flows in present (Time 0) prices are as follows:

	£m	Inflation
Sales	2	6%
Labour costs	0.3	9%
Material costs	0.6	12%
Overhead	0.06	8%

All cash flows occur at year ends except for the initial outflow.

The first stage is to calculate the money cash flows. We need to restate the inflows and outflows for each of the years at the amount actually changing hands in nominal terms. (*See* **Exhibit 5.10**.)

Exhibit 5.10 Amplify plc: Money cash flow

Point in time (yearly intervals)	Cash flow before allowing for price rises £m	Inflation adjustment	Money cash flow £m
0 Initial outflow	–2.4	1	–2.4
1 Sales	2	1.06	2.12
Labour	–0.3	1.09	–0.327
Materials	–0.6	1.12	–0.672
Overheads	–0.06	1.08	–0.065
Net money cash flow for Year 1			+1.056

2 Sales	2	$(1.06)^2$	2.247
Labour	–0.3	$(1.09)^2$	–0.356
Materials	–0.6	$(1.12)^2$	–0.753
Overheads	–0.06	$(1.08)^2$	–0.070
Net money cash flow for Year 2			+1.068
3 Sales	2	$(1.06)^3$	2.382
Labour	–0.3	$(1.09)^3$	–0.389
Materials	–0.6	$(1.12)^3$	–0.843
Overheads	–0.06	$(1.08)^3$	–0.076
Net money cash flow for Year 3			+1.074

Then we discount at the money rate of return (*see* **Exhibit 5.11**).

Exhibit 5.11 **Amplify plc: Money cash flows discounted at the money discount rate**

Point in time (yearly intervals)	**0 £m**	**1 £m**	**2 £m**	**3 £m**
Undiscounted cash flows	–2.4	1.056	1.068	1.074
Discounting calculation	–2.4	$\frac{1.056}{1 + 0.1232}$	$\frac{1.068}{(1 + 0.1232)^2}$	$\frac{1.074}{(1 + 0.1232)^3}$
Discounted cash flows	–2.4	0.9402	0.8466	0.7579

Net present value = +£0.1447 million.

(An Excel spreadsheet version of the calculation is available at www.pearsoned.co.uk/arnold)

This project produces a positive NPV and is therefore to be recommended.

Cash flow in real terms and real discount rate

The second approach is to calculate the net present value by discounting real cash flow by the real discount rate. A real cash flow is obtainable by discounting the money cash flow by the general rate of inflation, thereby converting it to its current purchasing power equivalent.

The general inflation rate is derived from Fisher's equation:

$$(1 + m) = (1 + h) \times (1 + i),$$

where m = money rate of return;
h = real rate of return;
i = inflation rate.

m is given as 0.1232, h as 0.08, i as 0.04.

$$i = \frac{(1 + m)}{(1 + h)} - 1 = \frac{1 + 0.1232}{1 + 0.08} - 1 = 0.04$$

Under this method net present value becomes:

$$NPV = R_0 + \frac{R_1}{1 + h} + \frac{R_2}{(1 + h)^2} + \frac{R_3}{(1 + h)^3} + \dots$$

The net present value is equal to the sum of the real cash flows R_t discounted at a real required rate of return, *h*.

The first stage is to discount money cash flows by the general inflation rate to establish real cash flows (**Exhibit 5.12**).

Exhibit 5.12 Amplify plc: Discounting money cash flows by the genera inflation rate

Points in time (yearly intervals)	Cash flow £m	Calculation	Real cash flow £m
0	−2.4	–	−2.4
1	1.056	$\frac{1.056}{1 + 0.04}$	1.0154
2	1.068	$\frac{1.068}{(1 + 0.04)^2}$	0.9874
3	1.074	$\frac{1.074}{(1 + 0.04)^3}$	0.9548

The second task is to discount real cash flows at the real discount rate (**Exhibit 5.13**).

Exhibit 5.13 Amplify plc: Real cash flows discounted at the real discount rate

Point in time (yearly intervals)	0 £m	1 £m	2 £m	3 £m
Real cash flow	−2.4	1.0154	0.9874	0.9548
Discounting calculation	−2.4	$\frac{1.0154}{1 + 0.08}$	$\frac{0.9874}{(1 + 0.08)^2}$	$\frac{0.9548}{(1 + 0.08)^3}$
Discounted cash flow	−2.4	0.9402	0.8465	0.7580

Net present value = +£0.1447 million.

Note that the net present value is the same as before. To discount at the general inflation rate, *i*, followed by discounting at the real rate of return, *h*, is arithmetically the same as discounting money cash flows at the money rate, *m*. Often, in practice, to calculate future cash flows the analyst, instead of allowing for specific inflation rates, will make the simplifying assumption that all prices will stay the same, at Time 0's prices and then apply a real discount rate. This could lead to errors if a cost item (e.g. oil) is a major component and is subject to a very high specific inflation. However, in most cases reasonably accurate results can be obtained.

Note in the example of Amplify that the money cash flows are deflated by the general rate of inflation, not by the specific rates. This is because the ultimate beneficiaries of this project are interested in their ability to purchase a basket of goods generally and not their ability to buy any one good, and therefore the link between the real cost of capital and the money cost of capital is the general inflation rate.

The two methods for adjusting for inflation produce the same result and therefore it does not matter which method is used. The first method, using money discount rates, has the virtue of requiring only one stage of discounting.

Internal rate of return and inflation

The logic applied to the NPV analysis can be transferred to an internal rate of return approach. That is, two acceptable methods are possible, either:

(**a**) compare the IRR of the money cash flows with the opportunity cost of capital expressed in money terms; or

(**b**) compare the IRR of the real cash flows with the opportunity cost of capital expressed in real terms.

A warning

Never do either of the following:

1 Discount money cash flows with the real discount rate. This gives an apparent NPV much larger than the true NPV and so will result in erroneous decisions to accept projects which are not shareholder wealth enhancing.

2 Discount real cash flows with the money discount rate. This will reduce the NPV from its true value which causes the rejection of projects which will be shareholder wealth enhancing.

The treatment of inflation in practice

Exhibit 5.14 shows that UK companies generally either specify cash flow in constant prices and apply a real rate of return or express cash flows in inflated price terms and discount at the market rate of return.

Exhibit 5.14 Inflation adjustment methods used for investment appraisal by UK firms

	Small %	Medium-sized %	Large %	Composite %
Specify cash flow in constant prices and apply a real rate of return	47	29	45	42
All cash flows expressed in inflated price terms and discounted at the market rate of return	18	42	55	39
Considered at risk analysis or sensitivity stage	21	13	16	17
No adjustment	18	21	3	13
Other	0	0	3	1

Source: Arnold and Hatzopoulos (2000).

Concluding comments

This chapter deals with some of the more technical aspects of project appraisal. These are issues that are of great concern to managers and should never be neglected in an investment evaluation. Serious misunderstanding and poor decision making can result from a failure to consider all relevant information.

Key points and concepts

- **Soft capital rationing** – internal management-imposed limits on investment expenditure despite the availability of positive NPV projects.
- **Hard capital rationing** – externally imposed limits on investment expenditure in the presence of positive NPV projects.
- For **divisible one-period capital rationing problems**, focus on the returns per £ of outlay:

$$\text{Profitability index} = \frac{\text{Gross present value}}{\text{Initial outlay}}$$

$$\text{Benefit–cost ratio} = \frac{\text{Net present value}}{\text{Initial outlay}}$$

- For **indivisible one-period capital rationing problems**, examine all the feasible alternative combinations.
- Two rules for **allowing for taxation** in project appraisal:
  - include incremental tax effects of a project as a cash outflow;
  - get the timing right.
- **Taxable profits are not the same as accounting profits**. For example, depreciation is not allowed for in the taxable profit calculation, but writing-down allowances are permitted.
- **Specific inflation** – price changes of an individual good or service over a period of time.
- **General inflation** – the reduced purchasing power of money.
- General inflation affects the rate of return required on projects:
  - **real rate of return** – the return required in the absence of inflation;
  - **money rate of return** – includes a return to compensate for inflation.
- **Fisher's equation**

  (1 + money rate of return) = (1 + real rate of return) × (1 + anticipated rate of inflation)

  $(1 + m) = (1 + h) \times (1 + i)$
- Inflation affects future cash flows:
  - **money cash flows** – all future cash flows are expressed in the prices expected to rule when the cash flow occurs;
  - **real cash flows** – future cash flows are expressed in constant purchasing power.
- **Adjusting for inflation in project appraisal:**
  - Approach 1 – Estimate the cash flows in money terms and use a money discount rate.
  - Approach 2 – Estimate the cash flows in real terms and use a real discount rate.

References and further reading

Arnold, G.C. and Hatzopoulos, P.D. (2000) 'The theory-practice gap in capital budgeting: evidence from the United Kingdom', *Journal of Business Finance and Accounting*, 27(5) and (6), June/July, pp. 603–26.

Empirical evidence on the treatment of inflation.

Bierman, H. and Smidt, S. (2006) *The Capital Budgeting Decision*, 9th edn. London: Routledge.

Some good chapters for the beginner.

Bierman, H. and Smidt, S. (2006) *Advanced Capital Budgeting*. London: Routledge.

Good for the student who wishes to pursue these topics in more depth.

Carsberg, B.V. and Hope, A. (1976) *Business Investment Decisions Under Inflation: Theory and Practice*. London: Institute of Chartered Accountants in England and Wales.

A study of investment appraisal practices adopted by large British firms with particular reference to the treatment of inflation. Clear description of NPV theory, suitable for the beginner.

Coulthurst, N.J. (1986) 'Accounting for inflation in capital investment: state of the art and science', *Accounting and Business Research*, Winter, pp. 33–42.

A clear account of the impact of inflation on project appraisal. Also considers empirical evidence on the adjustments made in practice. Good for the beginner.

Fama, E.F. (1981) 'Stock returns, real activity, inflation and money', *American Economic Review*, 71 (Sept.), pp. 545–64.

On the complex relationship between returns on shares and inflation – high level economics.

Fisher, I. (1930) *The Theory of Interest*. New York: Macmillan.

Early theory – interest rates and inflation.

Pike, R.H. (1983) 'The capital budgeting behaviour and corporate characteristics of capital-constrained firms', *Journal of Business Finance and Accounting*, 10(4), Winter, pp. 663–71.

Examines real-world evidence on capital rationing and its effects – easy to read.

Case study recommendations

Please see www.pearsoned.co.uk/arnold for case study synopses.

- Electrosteel Castings Limited. Authors: R. Klassen and N. Bahl (2002) Richard Ivory School of Business (available from Harvard Business School case study website).
- Whirlpool Europe. Authors: S. Balachandran and R. Ruback (2003) Harvard Business School.

Self-review questions

1 Explain why hard and soft rationing occur.

2 If the general rate of inflation is 5 per cent and the market rate of interest is 9 per cent, what is the real interest rate?

3 Explain the alternative methods of dealing with inflation in project appraisal.

4 Why not simply rank projects on the basis of the highest NPV in conditions of capital rationing?

5 Distinguish between a money cash flow and a real cash flow.

6 How should tax be allowed for in project appraisal?

7 Why is capital rationing impossible in perfect capital markets?

8 What are a balancing charge and a balancing allowance for capital items subject to a writing-down allowance?

9 Describe the two major effects inflation has on the evaluation of investments.

10 Name two great 'don'ts' in inflation adjustment for projects and explain the consequences of ignoring these.

11 What will be the effect of under-allowance for future inflation when using a money discount rate?

Questions and problems

myfinancelab *Questions with an icon are also available for practice in MyFinanceLab with additional supporting resources.*

Answers for those questions marked with an asterisk* are reserved for the Lecturer's guide.

1 The washer division of Plumber plc is permitted to spend £5m on investment projects at Time 0. The cash flows for five proposed projects are:

	Points in time (yearly intervals)				
	0	*1*	*2*	*3*	*4*
Project	*£m*	*£m*	*£m*	*£m*	*£m*
A	–1.5	0.5	0.5	1.0	1.0
B	–2.0	0	0	0	4.0
C	–1.8	0	0	1.2	1.2
D	–3.0	1.2	1.2	1.2	1.2
E	–0.5	0.3	0.3	0.3	0.3

The cost of capital is 12 per cent, all projects are divisible and none may be repeated. The projects are not mutually exclusive.

a Which projects should be undertaken to maximise NPV in the presence of the capital constraint?
b If the division was able to undertake all positive NPV projects, what level of NPV could be achieved?
c If you now assume that these projects are indivisible, how would you allocate the available £5m?

2 The Telescope Company plc is considering five projects: **?**

Project	*Initial outlay*	*Profitability index*
A	6,000	1.2
B	4,000	1.05
C	10,000	1.6
D	8,000	1.4
E	7,000	1.3

Projects C and D are mutually exclusive and the firm has £20,000 available for investment. All projects can only be undertaken once and are divisible. What is the maximum possible NPV? **?**

3 The business insurance premiums of £20,000 for the next year have just been paid. What will these premiums be in three years' time, if the specific rate of inflation for insurance premiums is 8 per cent per annum?
If the money rate of return is 17 per cent and the general inflation rate is anticipated to average 9 per cent over three years, what is the present value of the insurance premiums payable at Time 3? **?**

4* (*Examination level*) Wishbone plc is considering two mutually exclusive projects. Project X requires an immediate cash outflow of £2.5m and Project Y requires £2m. If there was no inflation then the cash flows for the three-year life of each of the projects would be:

Annual cash flows	*Project X*		*Project Y*	
	£	£	£	£
Inflow from sales		2,100,000		1,900,000
Cash outflows:				
Materials	800,000		200,000	
Labour	300,000		700,000	
Overheads	100,000		50,000	
		(1,200,000)		(950,000)
Net cash flow		900,000		950,000

These cash flows can be assumed to arise at the year ends of each of the three years.
Specific annual inflation rates have been estimated for each of the cash flow elements.

Sales	5%
Materials	4%
Labour	10%
Overheads	7%

The money cost of capital is 17 per cent per annum.

a Use the money cash flows and money cost of capital to calculate the NPV of the two projects and recommend the most appropriate course of action.
b Now assume that the general inflation rate is anticipated to be 8 per cent per annum. Calculate the real cash flows and the real cost of capital and use these to calculate the NPVs.

(In addition to the solution given in the Lecturer's Guide there is an Excel spreadsheet solution available at www.pearsoned.co.uk/arnold)

?

5 Hose plc is trying to make a decision on whether to make a commitment of £800,000 now to a project with a life of seven years. At present prices the project will return net cash flows of £150,000 per annum at the year ends. Prices are not expected to remain constant and general inflation is anticipated at 6 per cent per annum. The annual net cash inflows of this project are expected to rise in accordance with general inflation. The money rate of return is 13 per cent. Advise Hose on the viability of this project.

?

6 A machine costs £10,000 and has a five-year life. By how much can taxable profit be reduced through the writing-down allowance (WDA) in the third year, if the annual WDA is 25 per cent on a declining balance? If the tax rate is 30 per cent, what is the present value of the WDA in Year 4 to the machine's owners?
If the machine has a scrap value of £1,000 after five years, what will be the fifth year's adjustment to the WDA?
The required rate of return is 10 per cent.

?

7* Bedford Onions plc is examining the possibility of purchasing a machine for a new venture. The machine will cost £50,000, have a four-year life and a scrap value of £10,000. An additional investment of £15,000 in working capital will be needed at the outset. This is recoverable at the end of the project. The accountant's figures for the annual trading accounts are as follows:

	£
Sales	100,000
Labour	(20,000)
Materials	(10,000)
Direct overhead	(20,000)
Allocated overhead	(15,000)
Depreciation	(10,000)
Annual profit	25,000

Allocated overhead consists of central administrative costs which are incurred with or without this project. The machine will be eligible for a 25 per cent writing-down allowance (on a declining balance). Tax is payable at 30 per cent in the year of profit creation.
For a project of this risk class a minimum return of 14 per cent is considered acceptable.
Assume no inflation.

Required

Calculate the net present value of this investment.

?

8* (*Examination level*) Clipper plc is considering five project proposals. They are summarised below:

Project	*Initial investment (£000)*	*Annual revenue (£000)*	*Annual fixed costs (cash outflows) (£000)*	*Life of project (years)*
A	10	20	5	3
B	30	30	10	5
C	15	18	6	4
D	12	17	8	10
E	18	8	2	15

Variable costs (cash outflows) are 40 per cent of annual revenue. Projects D and E are mutually exclusive. Each project can only be undertaken once and each is divisible.

Assume

- The cash flows are confined to within the lifetime of each project.
- The cost of capital is 10 per cent.
- No inflation.
- No tax.
- All cash flows occur on anniversary dates.

If the firm has a limit of £40,000 for investment in projects at Time 0, what is the optimal allocation of this sum among these projects, and what is the maximum net present value obtainable?

?

9 (*Examination level*)

a Oppton plc's managers are ambitious and wish to expand their range of activities. They have produced a report for the parent company's board of directors detailing five projects requiring large initial investments. After reading the report the main board directors say that they have a policy of permitting subsidiary managers to select investment projects without head office interference. However, they do set a limit on the amount spent in any one period. In the case of Oppton this limit is to be £110,000 at Time 0 for these projects, which if accepted will commence immediately. The five projects are not mutually exclusive (that is, taking on one does not exclude the possibility of taking on another), each one can only be undertaken once and they are all divisible.

The cash flow details are as follows:

	Point in time (yearly intervals)				
	0 (£000)	*1 (£000)*	*2 (£000)*	*3 (£000)*	*4 (£000)*
Project 1	–35	0	60	0	0
Project 2	–50	30	30	30	0
Project 3	–20	10	10	10	10
Project 4	–30	15	15	15	15
Project 5	–60	70	0	0	0

None of the projects lasts more than four years and cash flows are confined to within the four-year horizon.

Assume

- The cost of capital is 10 per cent.
- No inflation.
- No tax.
- All cash flows occur on anniversary dates.

What is the optimal allocation of the £110,000 and the resulting net present value?

b Distinguish between 'soft' and 'hard' capital rationing and explain why these forms of rationing occur.

?

10 Cartma plc's superb strategic planning group have identified five projects they judge to be shareholder wealth enhancing, and therefore feel that the firm should make these investment commitments.

The strategic planning group are keen on getting approval for the release of £42m to invest in all these projects. However, Cartma is a subsidiary of PQT and the holding company board have placed limits on the amount of funds available in any one year for major capital projects for each of its subsidiaries. They were prompted to do this by the poor response of debt holders to a recent capital raising exercise due to the already high borrowing levels. Also they feel a need to counteract the excessive enthusiasm in subsidiary strategic planning groups which could lead to over-rapid expansion if all positive NPV projects are accepted, placing a strain on management talent. The limit that has been imposed on Cartma for the forthcoming year is £38m.

The figures are:

Point in time (yearly intervals)	0 *£m*	1 *£m*	2 *£m*	3 *£m*	4 *£m*	5 *£m*	*NPV*
Project A							
Cash flow	–10	0	0	+20	0	0	
Discounted cash flows	–10	0	0	$20/(1.1)^3$	0	0	+5
Project B							
Cash flow	–15	5	5	5	5	5	
Discounted cash flow	–15	5 × Annuity factor for 5 years @ 10%					
	–15	+ 5 × 3.7908					+3.95
Project C							
Cash flow	–8	1	12	0	0	0	
Discounted cash flows	–8	1/1.1	$12/(1.1)^2$	0	0	0	+2.83
Project D							
Cash flow	–5	2	2	2	2	2	
Discounted cash flow	–5	2 × Annuity factor for 5 years @ 10%					
	–5	+ 2 × 3.7908					+2.58
Project E							
Cash flow	–4	0	0	3	3	3	
Discounted cash flow	–4	$(3 \times \text{Annuity factor for 3 years @ 10\%})/(1.1)^2$					
	–4	0	0	$\frac{3 \times 2.4868}{(1.1)^2}$			+2.17

Assume

- No inflation or tax.
- The rate of return required on projects of this risk class is 10 per cent.
- All project cash flows are confined within the five-year period.
- All projects are divisible (a fraction of the project can be undertaken), and none can be undertaken more than once.

What is the maximum NPV available if projects are selected on the basis of NPV alone?

Now calculate profitability indices (or benefit–cost ratios) for each project and calculate the maximum potential NPV if the £38m limit is adhered to.

?

Assignments

1 Investigate the capital rationing constraints placed on a firm you are familiar with. Are these primarily soft or hard forms of rationing? Are they justified? What are the economic costs of this rationing? What actions do you suggest to circumvent irrational constraints?

2 Write a report on how inflation and tax are allowed for in project appraisal within a firm you know well. To what extent are the rules advocated in this chapter obeyed?

PART 3
Risk and return

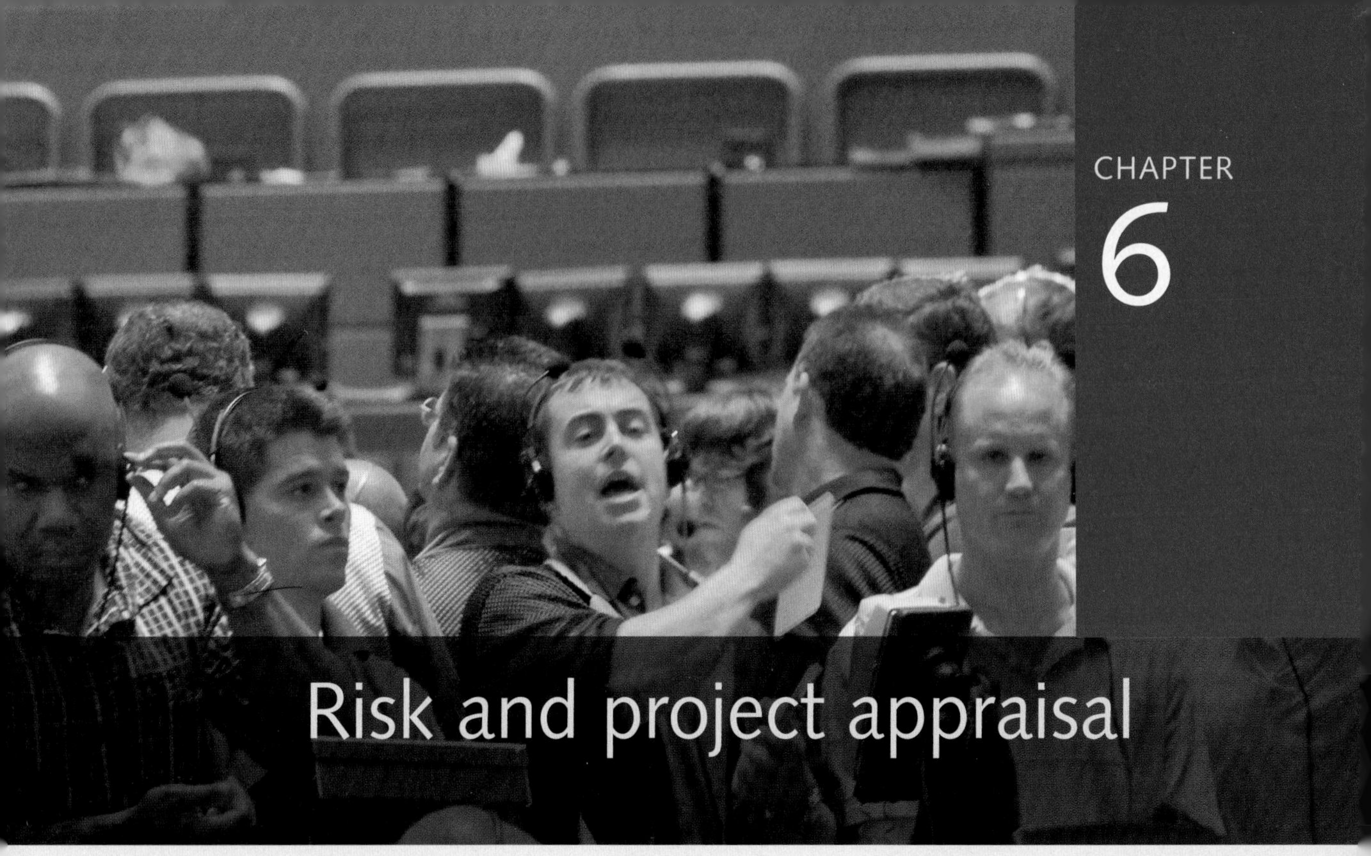

CHAPTER

6

Risk and project appraisal

LEARNING OUTCOMES

The reader is expected to be able to present a more realistic and rounded view of a project's prospects by incorporating risk in an appraisal. This enables more informed decision making. Specifically the reader should be able to:

- adjust for risk by varying the discount rate;
- present a sensitivity graph and discuss break-even NPV;
- undertake scenario analysis;
- make use of probability analysis to describe the extent of risk facing a project and thus make more enlightened choices;
- explain the nature of real options and the advantage in recognising their value;
- discuss the limitations, explain the appropriate use and make an accurate interpretation of the results of the four risk techniques described in this chapter.

myfinancelab

Complete your diagnostic test for Chapter 6 now to create your personal study plan

Case study 6.1 Two risky ventures . . .

One that will (probably) not pay off . . .

The £200 billion gamble – wireless telecommunications

In 2000 the telecommunication companies of Europe committed themselves to what may prove to be one of the biggest gambles ever. They agreed to pay £80–£100 billion to purchase 3G (third-generation) licences from various European governments. As a result they are now able to offer Internet access from mobile phones.

The 'winners' of the auctions for licences in addition to handing over thousands of millions of pounds to government, invested another £100 billion building the infrastructure needed to deliver the service to the customer supposedly hungry for video and Internet-enabled phones. As quickly as the middle of 2001 so great was the outflow of cash that major telecommunication companies had become burdened with extraordinary amounts of debt. For example, in 1998 BT had debts of roughly £1 billion. Over the next three years these rose to over £20 billion and serious concern was expressed in the City of London about the excessive debt. Shares tumbled as shareholders worried that too much was being paid for projects based on a high degree of optimism. 3G has been a disappointment. It took until 2005 to roll out 3G services actively, and even with the delay the engineers produced a poor customer experience, with low quality of content and few 3G tailored websites. Furthermore, the level of competition is likely to be so intense that the companies may lose money even with millions of customers.

Perhaps, as the new technology develops, an application will be discovered that is very attractive to consumers and the investment projects turn out to be very rewarding for shareholders. Perhaps the 3G projects will be superseded by new technology (WiMAX?) before they are properly up and running. The truth is that we will not know for many years. Such is the fun and excitement of real-world business decisions!

and one that did . . .

Camelot

Camelot bid for, and won, the right to create the UK's national lottery. They invested in a vast computer network linking 30,000 retail outlets and paid for three hundred man years to develop specialised software. Camelot also had to train 91,000 staff to operate the system, which can handle over 30,000 transactions a minute, and spend large amounts on marketing. The gamble seems to have paid off. It now regularly produces an annual profit of around £50m. The owners of Camelot – Cadbury Schweppes, De La Rue, Fujitsu, Thales Electronics and Royal Mail Enterprises – have a political battle on their hands trying to persuade the public and authorities that they took a risk and things happened to turn out well. It could have been so different; they could have made a multi-million pound investment followed by public indifference and enormous losses.

Introduction

Businesses operate in an environment of uncertainty. The 3G investment and Camelot examples in **Case study 6.1** show that managers can never by sure about what will happen in the future. There is the upside possibility of events turning out to be better than anticipated and the downside possibility of everything going wrong. Implementing an investment project requires acceptance of the distinct possibility that the managers have got it wrong; that the project or enterprise will result in failure. However, to avoid any chance of failure means the adoption of a 'play-safe' or 'do-nothing' strategy. This may itself constitute a worse business sin, that of inertia, and will result in greater failure. There has to be an acceptance of risk and of the potential for getting decisions wrong, but this does not mean that risk cannot by analysed and action taken to minimise its impact.

What is risk?

A key feature of project appraisal is its orientation to the future. Management rarely have precise forecasts regarding the future return to be earned from an investment. Usually the best that can be done is to make an estimate of the range of the possible future inflows and outflows. There are two types of expectations individuals may have about the future: certainty and uncertainty.

1 ***Certainty*** Under expectations of **certainty** future outcomes can be expected to have only one value. That is, there is not a variety of possible future eventualities – only one will occur. Such situations are rare, but there are some investments which are a reasonable approximation to certainty, for instance, lending to a reputable government by purchasing three-month treasury bills. Unless you are very pessimistic and expect catastrophic change over the next three months, such as revolution, war or major earthquake, then you can be certain of receiving your original capital plus interest. Thus a firm could undertake a project that had almost complete certainty by investing its funds in treasury bills, and receiving a return of, say, 5 per cent per year. Shareholders may not, however, be very pleased with such a low return.
2 ***Risk and uncertainty*** The terms *risk* and *uncertainty* are used interchangeably in the subsequent analysis. They both describe a situation where there is not just one possible outcome, but an array of potential returns. Strictly speaking, **risk** occurs when specific probabilities can be estimated for the possible outcomes. **Uncertainty** applies in cases when it is not possible to assign probabilities (or even identify all the possible outcomes). The range and distribution of these possible outcomes may be estimated on the basis of either objective probabilities or subjective probabilities (or a combination of the two).

Objective probabilities

An **objective probability** can be established mathematically or from historical data. The mathematical probability of a tossed coin showing a head is 0.5. The probability of taking the Ace of Hearts from a pack of 52 cards is 0.0192 (or 1/52). A probability of 0 indicates nil likelihood of outcome. A probability of 1 denotes that there is absolute certainty that this outcome will occur. A probability of 0.3 indicates that in three times out of ten this will occur. The probabilities for all possible outcomes must sum to 1. We will now examine an example of an objective probability assessment based on historical data for the supermarket retailer Safeburys. If the firm is considering a project which is similar to numerous projects undertaken in the past it may be able to obtain probabilities for future profitability. For instance, the Safeburys supermarket chain is examining the proposal to build and operate a new supermarket in Birmingham. Because the firm has opened and operated 100 other supermarkets in the past, and has been able to observe their profitability, it is able to assign probabilities to the performance of the supermarket it is proposing to build (*see* **Exhibits 6.1** and **6.2**).

The examination of this sort of historical record may be a useful first step in the process of making a decision. However, it must be borne in mind that the probabilities may have to be modi-

Exhibit 6.1 Safebury's profitability frequency distribution of existing 100 supermarkets

Profitability range (£m)	Frequency (Number of stores)	Probability
–30 to –20.01	1	0.01
–20 to –10.01	3	0.03
–10 to –0.01	11	0.11
0 to 9.99	19	0.19
10 to 19.99	30	0.30
20 to 29.99	20	0.20
30 to 39.99	10	0.10
40 to 49.99	6	0.06
TOTAL	100	1.00

Exhibit 6.2 Frequency distribution of supermarket profitability

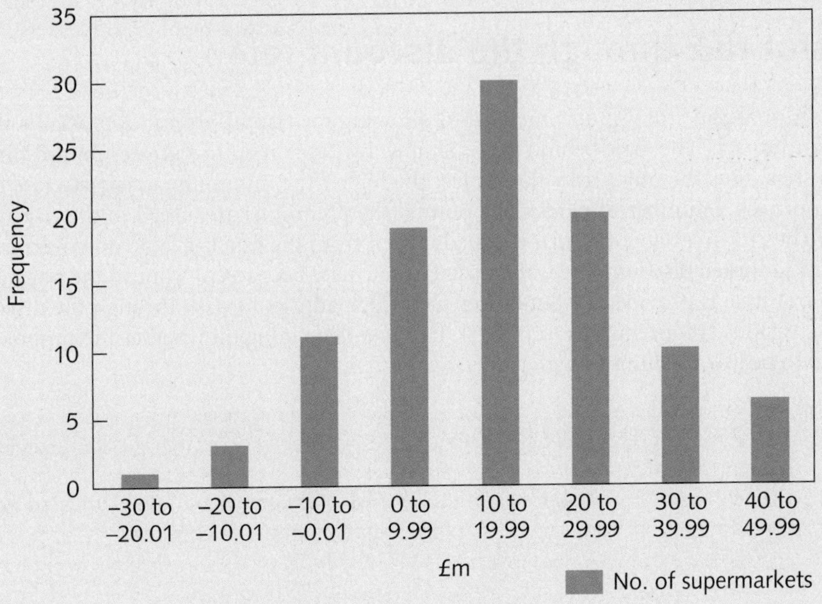

fied to take into account the particular circumstances surrounding the site in Birmingham. For instance demographic trends, road connections and competitor activity may influence the probabilities for profit or loss. Even with large quantities of historical data there is often still a lot of room for subjective assessment in judging the range of possible outcomes.

Subjective probabilities

In many project assessments there is a complete absence of any past record to help in the creation of the distribution of probabilities profile. For instance, the product may be completely new, or a foreign market is to be entered. In situations like these, **subjective probabilities** are likely to dominate, that is, personal judgement of the range of outcomes along with the likelihood of their occurrence. Managers, individually or collectively, must assign probability numbers to a range of outcomes.

It must be acknowledged that the probabilities assigned to particular eventualities are unlikely to be entirely accurate and thus the decision making that follows may be subject to some margin of error. But consider the alternative of merely stating the most likely outcomes. This can lead to less well-informed decisions and greater errors. For example, a firm might be considering two mutually exclusive projects, A and B (*see* **Exhibit 6.3**). Both projects are expected to be shareholder wealth enhancing, based on the estimate of the most likely outcome. The most likely outcome for A is for it to be shareholder wealth enhancing, with a 95 per cent chance of occurrence. Similarly the most likely outcome for B is a shareholder wealth enhancing return, with a 55 per cent chance of occurrence.

By using probabilities, a more informed decision is made. The project appraiser has been forced to consider the degree of confidence in the estimate of expected viability. It is clear that Project A is unlikely to fail, whereas Project B has a fairly high likelihood of failure. We will examine in detail

Exhibit 6.3 Probability outcome for two projects

Outcome	Project A probability	Project B probability
Shareholder wealth enhancing	0.95	0.55
Not shareholder wealth enhancing	0.05	0.45

the use of probability distribution for considering risk later in the chapter. We now turn to more pragmatic, rule-of-thumb and intuitively easier methods for dealing with project risk.

Adjusting for risk through the discount rate

A traditional and still popular method of allowing for risk in project appraisal is the risk premium approach. The logic behind this is simple: investors require a greater reward for accepting a higher risk, thus the more risky the project the higher the minimum acceptable rate of return. In this approach a number of percentage points (the premium) are added to the risk-free discount rate. (The risk-free rate of return is usually taken from the rate available on government bonds.) The risk-adjusted discount rate is then used to calculate net present value in the normal manner.

An example is provided by Sunflower plc, which adjusts for risk through the discount rate by adding various risk premiums to the risk-free rate depending on whether the proposed project is judged to be low, medium or high risk (*see* **Exhibit 6.4**).

Exhibit 6.4 Adjusting for risk – Sunflower plc

Level of risk	Risk-free rate (%)	Risk premium (%)	Risk-adjusted rate (%)
Low	9	+3	12
Medium	9	+6	15
High	9	+10	19

The project currently being considered has the following cash flows:

Point in time (yearly intervals)	0	1	2
Cash flow (£)	–100	55	70

If the project is judged to be low risk:

$$\text{NPV} = -100 + \frac{55}{1 + 0.12} + \frac{70}{(1 + 0.12)^2} = +£4.91$$

Accept.

If the project is judged to be medium risk:

$$\text{NPV} = -100 + \frac{55}{1 + 0.15} + \frac{70}{(1 + 0.15)^2} = +£0.76$$

Accept.

If the project is judged to be high risk:

$$\text{NPV} = -100 + \frac{55}{1 + 0.19} + \frac{70}{(1 + 0.19)^2} = -£4.35$$

Reject.

This is an easy approach to understand and adopt, which explains its continued popularity.

Drawbacks of the risk-adjusted discount rate method

The risk-adjusted discount rate method relies on an accurate assessment of the riskiness of a project. Risk perception and judgement are bound to be, to some extent, subjective and susceptible to personal bias. There may also be a high degree of arbitrariness in the selection of risk premiums. In reality it is extremely difficult to allocate projects to risk classes and identify appropriate risk premiums as personal analysis and casual observation can easily dominate.

Sensitivity analysis

The net present values calculated in previous chapters gave a static picture of the likely future outcome of an investment project. In many business situations it is desirable to generate a more complete and realistic impression of what may happen to NPV (or IRR) in conditions of uncertainty. Net present value calculations rely on the appraiser making assumptions about some crucial variables: for example the sale price of the product, the cost of labour and the amount of initial investment are all set at single values for input into the formula. It might be enlightening to examine the degree to which the viability of the project changes, as measured by NPV, as the assumed values of these key variables are altered. An interesting question to ask might be: if the sale price was raised by 10 per cent, by how much would NPV increase? In other words, it would be useful to know how sensitive NPV is to changes in component values. Sensitivity analysis is essentially a 'what-if' analysis, for example what if labour costs are 5 per cent lower? or what if the raw materials double in price? By carrying out a series of calculations it is possible to build up a picture of the nature of the risks facing the project and their impact on project profitability. Sensitivity analysis can identify the extent to which variables may change before a negative NPV is produced.

Sensitivity analysis examines the impact of a change in the value of one variable on the project NPV.

A series of 'what-if' questions are examined in the example of Acmart plc.

Worked example 6.1 Acmart plc

Acmart plc has developed a new product line called Marts. The marketing department in partnership with senior managers from other disciplines have estimated the likely demand for Marts at 1,000,000 per year, at a price of £1, for the four-year life of the project. (Marts are used in mobile telecommunications relay stations and the market is expected to cease to exist or be technologically superseded after four years.)

If we can assume perfect certainty about the future then the cash flows associated with Marts are as set out in Exhibit 6.5.

Exhibit 6.5 Cash flows of Marts

Initial investment	£800,000	
Cash flow per unit		£
Sale price		1.00
Costs		
Labour	0.20	
Materials	0.40	
Relevant overhead	0.10	
		0.70
Cash flow per unit		0.30

The finance department have estimated that the appropriate required rate of return on a project of this risk class is 15 per cent. They have also calculated the expected net present value.

Annual cash flow = 30p × 1,000,000 = £300,000.

Present value of annual cash flows = 300,000 × annuity factor for 4 years @ 15%

		£
	= 300,000 × 2.855	= 856,500
Less initial investment		−800,000
Net present value		+56,500

The finance department are aware that when the proposal is placed before the capital investment committee they will want to know how the project NPV changes if certain key assumptions are altered. As part of the report the finance team ask some 'what-if' questions and draw a sensitivity graph.

- What if the price achieved is only 95p (5 per cent below the expected £1) for sales of 1m units (all other factors remaining constant)?

  Annual cash flow = 25p × 1m = £250,000.

	£
250,000 × 2.855	713,750
Less initial investment	800,000
Net present value	−86,250

- What if the price rose by 1 per cent?

  Annual cash flow = 31p × 1m = £310,000.

	£
310,000 × 2.855	885,050
Less initial investment	800,000
Net present value	+85,050

- What if the quantity demanded is 5 per cent more than anticipated?

  Annual cash flow = 30p × 1.05m = £315,000.

	£
315,000 × 2.855	899,325
Less initial investment	800,000
Net present value	+99,325

- What if the quantity demanded is 10 per cent less than expected?

  Annual cash flow = 30p × 900,000 = £270,000.

	£
270,000 × 2.855	770,850
Less initial investment	800,000
Net present value	−29,150

- What if the appropriate discount rate is 20 per cent higher than originally assumed (that is, it is 18 per cent rather than 15 per cent)?

  300,000 × annuity factor for 4 years @ 18%.

	£
300,000 × 2.6901	807,030
Less initial investment	800,000
	+7,030

- What if the discount rate is 10 per cent lower than assumed (that is, it becomes 13.5 per cent)?

  300,000 × annuity factor for 4 years @ 13.5%.

	£
300,000 × 2.9438	883,140
Less initial investment	800,000
	+83,140

Exhibit 6.6 Sensitivity graph for Marts

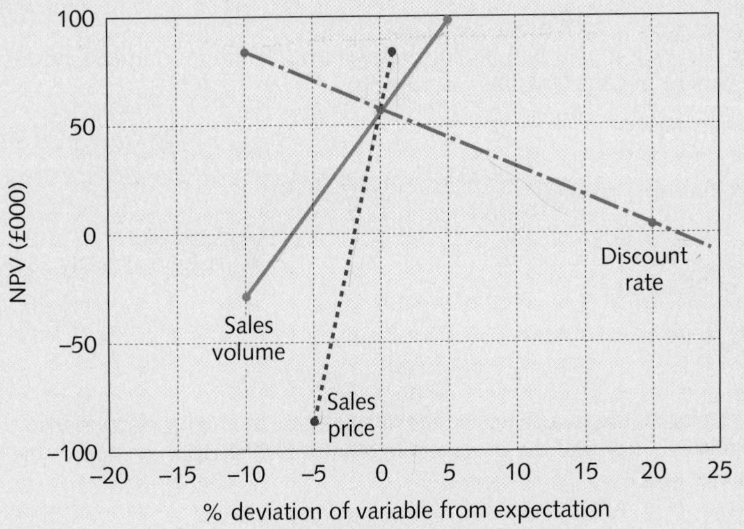

These findings can be summarised more clearly in a sensitivity graph (*see* **Exhibit 6.6**).

An examination of the sensitivity graph in Exhibit 6.6 gives a clear indication of those variables to which NPV is most responsive. This sort of technique can then be extended to consider the key factors that might cause a project to become unviable. This allows the management team to concentrate their analysis, by examining in detail the probability of actual events occurring which would alter the most critical variables. They may also look for ways of controlling the factors to which NPV is most sensitive in any future project implementation. For example, if a small change in material costs has a large impact, the managers may investigate ways of fixing the price of material inputs.

(An Excel spreadsheet version of the calculations is available at www.myfinancelab.com/arnold)

The break-even NPV

The break-even point, where NPV is zero, is a key concern of management. If the NPV is below zero the project is rejected; if it is above zero it is accepted.

The finance team at Acmart now calculate the extent to which some of the variables can change before the decision to accept switches to a decision to reject. (We will not go through all the possible variables.)

Initial investment

A rise of £56,500 will leave NPV at zero. A percentage increase of:

$$\frac{£56{,}500}{£800{,}000} \times 100 = 7.06\%$$

Sales price

The cash flow per unit (after costs), *c*, can fall to 28 pence before break-even is reached:

$$800{,}000 = c \times 1{,}000{,}000 \times 2.855$$

$$c = \frac{800{,}000}{2.855 \times 1{,}000{,}000} = 0.2802$$

Thus the price can decline by only 2 per cent from the original price of £1. An alternative approach is to look up the point at which the sales price line crosses the NPV axis in the sensitivity graph.

Material cost

If the cash flow per unit can fall to 28 pence before break-even is reached 2 pence can be added to the price of materials before the project produces a negative net present value (assuming all other factors remain constant). In percentage terms the material cost can rise by 5 per cent ((2 ÷ 40) × 100) before break-even is reached.

Discount rate

One approach is to calculate the annuity factor that will lead to the four annual inflows of £300,000 equalling the initial outflow of £800,000 after discounting.

$$300{,}000 \times \text{annuity factor} = 800{,}000$$

$$\text{Annuity factor (four-year annuity)} = \frac{800{,}000}{300{,}000} = 2.667$$

The interest rate corresponding to a four-year annuity factor of 2.667 is approximately 18.5 per cent. This is a percentage rise of 23.3 per cent.

$$\frac{18.5 - 15}{15} \times 100 = 23.3$$

This project is relatively insensitive to a change in the discount rate but highly responsive to a change in the sales price. This observation may lead the managers to request further work to improve the level of confidence in the sales projections.

Advantages of using sensitivity analysis

Sensitivity analysis has the following advantages:

- ***Information for decision making*** At the very least it allows the decision makers to be more informed about project sensitivities, to know the room they have for judgemental error and to decide whether they are prepared to accept the risks.
- ***To direct search*** It may lead to an indication of where further investigation might be worth while. The collection of data can be time consuming and expensive. If sensitivity analysis points to some variables being more crucial than others, then search time and money can be concentrated.
- ***To make contingency plans*** During the implementation phase of the investment process the original sensitivity analysis can be used to highlight those factors which have the greatest impact on NPV. Then these parameters can be monitored for deviation from projected values. The management team can draw on contingency plans if the key parameters differ significantly from the estimates. For example, a project may be highly sensitive to the price of a bought-in component. The management team after recognising this from the sensitivity analysis prepare contingency plans to: (a) buy the component from an alternative supplier, should the present one increase prices excessively, (b) produce the component in-house, or (c) modify the product so that a substitute component can be used. Which of the three is implemented, if any, will be decided as events unfold.

One can only hope that the Airbus contingency plans were thoroughly thought through prior to starting the project (see **Exhibit 6.7**).

Drawbacks of sensitivity analysis

The absence of any formal assignment of probabilities to the variations of the parameters is a potential limitation of sensitivity analysis. For Marts the discount rate can change by 23.3 per cent before break-even NPV is reached, whereas the price can only change by 2 per cent. Thus, at first glance, you would conclude that NPV is more vulnerable to the price changes than to variability in the discount rate. However, if you are now told that the market price for Marts is controlled by government regulations and therefore there is a very low probability of the price changing, whereas the probability of the discount rate rising by more than 23.3 per cent is high, you might change your assessment of the nature of the relative risks. This is another example where following the strict mathematical formula is a poor substitute for judgement. At the decision-making

Exhibit 6.7

Airbus A380 – A turbulent flight path

The first test flight of the superjumbo was in 2005. Everything looked to be progressing reasonably well until the summer of 2006 when Airbus announced that there would be another delay of seven months in the deliveries of the 555-seat airliner, following an earlier six-month delay. The shares of the parent company, EADS, fell by 26 per cent in one day, wiping €5.5bn off the value of the firm. By 2007 the estimated delay in delivery of the first aircraft was two years, which will knock €4.8bn off profits. The delay was blamed on a problem with installing the complicated electrical wiring system, but it goes much deeper than that.

Even before the summer 2006 announcement orders had flowed to a standstill – only 159 had been ordered. Also costs were £1.5bn greater than anticipated at €12bn (£8bn). Worse, the production problems meant that Airbus now had to tell customers that its factories were overloaded and any new orders would not be fulfilled for six years – very off-putting for customers.

In the months following the announcement airline companies lined up either to cancel orders or to rule out buying A380s. For example, FedEx scrapped its order for 10 freighter versions. 'The problem simply became that with two delays and the continued growth in the marketplace, we were in danger of not being able to continue to expand to meet customer demand,' said Fred Smith, CEO. Instead they ordered 15 Boeing B777s. Some customers pressed for compensation to pay for the leasing of smaller aircraft to plug the gap.

However, it still had some fans, for example, Quantas placed firm orders for eight more to take its total to 20, but the 'break-even point' moved up to 420 aircraft (from 250 when the project was first given the go ahead in 2000).

Critics had always maintained that the politically inspired approach to manufacturing in four European countries (e.g. the wings are made in the UK) and then assembling the plane in Toulouse was inefficient. The lack of coordination (and trust) between German and French factories was particularly acute. The in-fighting within the ranks of senior management was very embarrassing.

To try to contain cost the management are pushing for the adoption of a contingency plan, part of which would result in shifting Hamburg's A380 production to France and closing a number of production sites, in the teeth of fierce political opposition (Airbus cannot lose the support of the politicians as they rely on government refundable aid to finance initial production). Overheads are to be slashed by 30 per cent, with many job losses, to try to cut costs by €1bn per year. The management are even considering buying in more elements of the aircraft rather than making in-house. To speed up production better coordination of the two halves of the wiring is being planned (apparently the wiring in the back half of the plane did not mesh with the rest so it had to be pulled out and installed again!).

stage the formal sensitivity analysis must be read in the light of subjective or objective probabilities of the parameter changing.

The second major criticism of sensitivity analysis is that each variable is changed in isolation while all other factors remain constant. In the real world it is perfectly conceivable that a number of factors will change simultaneously. For example, if inflation is higher then both anticipated selling prices and input prices are likely to be raised. The next section presents a partial solution to this problem.

Scenario analysis

With sensitivity analysis we change one variable at a time and look at the result. Managers may be especially concerned about situations where a number of factors change. They are often interested in establishing a worst-case and a best-case **scenario**. That is, what NPV will result if all the assumptions made initially turned out to be too optimistic? And what would be the result if, in the event, matters went extremely well on all fronts?

Exhibit 6.8 describes only a worst-case and a best-case scenario for Marts but management may like to try alternative scenarios. Having carried out sensitivity, break-even NPV and scenario analysis the management team have a more complete picture of the project. They then need to apply the vital element of judgement to make a sound decision.

Exhibit 6.8 Acmart plc: Project proposal for the production of Marts – worst-case and best-case scenarios

Worst-case scenario

Sales	900,000 units
Price	90p
Initial investment	£850,000
Project life	3 years
Discount rate	17%
Labour costs	22p
Material costs	45p
Overhead	11p

Cash flow per unit		£
Sale price		0.90
Costs		
Labour	0.22	
Material	0.45	
Overhead	0.11	
		0.78
Cash flow per unit		0.12

Annual cash flow = 0.12 × 900,000 = £108,000

	£
Present value of cash flows 108,000 × 2.2096 =	238,637
Less initial investment	−850,000
Net present value	−611,363

Best-case scenario

Sales	1,200,000 units
Price	120p
Initial investment	£770,000
Project life	4 years
Discount rate	14%
Labour costs	19p
Material costs	38p
Overhead	9p

Cash flow per unit		£
Sale price		1.20
Costs		
Labour	0.19	
Material	0.38	
Overhead	0.09	
		0.66
Cash flow per unit		0.54

Annual cash flow = 0.54 × 1,200,000 = £648,000

	£
Present value of cash flows 648,000 × 2.9137 =	1,888,078
Less initial investment	−770,000
Net present value	1,118,078

Probability analysis

A further technique to assist the evaluation of the risk associated with a project is to use probability analysis. If management have obtained, through a mixture of objective and subjective methods, the probabilities of various outcomes this will help them to decide whether to go ahead with a project or to abandon the idea. We will look at this sort of decision making for the firm Pentagon plc, a firm trying to decide between five mutually exclusive one-year projects (*see* **Exhibit 6.9**).

Exhibit 6.9 Pentagon plc: Use of probability analysis

	Return	Probability of return occurring
Project 1	16	1.0
Project 2	20	1.0
Project 3	–16	0.25
	36	0.50
	48	0.25
Project 4	–8	0.25
	16	0.50
	24	0.25
Project 5	–40	0.10
	0	0.60
	100	0.30

Projects 1 and 2 represent perfectly certain outcomes. For both projects the chance of not receiving the returns is so small as to be regarded as zero. These securities carry no risk. However, Project 2 has a higher return and is therefore the obvious preferred choice. (These projects, with different returns for zero risk, only exist in an inefficient market environment because you should find increased return is only available for accepting increased risk; market efficiency is discussed in Chapter 14.)

In comparing Project 2 with Projects 3, 4 and 5 we have a problem: which of the possible outcomes should we compare with Project 2's outcome of 20? Take Project 3 as an example. If the outcome is –16 then clearly Project 2 is preferred. However, if the outcome is 36, or even better, 48, then Project 3 is preferred to Project 2.

Expected return

A tool that will help Pentagon choose between these projects is the expected return.

The **expected return** is the mean or average outcome calculated by weighting each of the possible outcomes by the probability of occurrence and then summing the result (*see* **Exhibit 6.10**).

Algebraically:

$$\overline{x} = x_1\,p_1 + x_2\,p_2 + \ldots\, x_n\,p_n$$

or

$$\overline{x} = \sum_{i=1}^{i=n} (x_i\,p_i)$$

Exhibit 6.10 Pentagon plc: Expected returns

Pentagon plc	Expected returns	
Project 1	16 × 1	16
Project 2	20 × 1	20
Project 3	−16 × 0.25 = −4	
	36 × 0.50 = 18	
	48 × 0.25 = 12	
		26
Project 4	−8 × 0.25 = −2	
	16 × 0.50 = 8	
	24 × 0.25 = 6	
		12
Project 5	−40 × 0.1 = −4	
	0 × 0.6 = 0	
	100 × 0.3 = 30	
		26

where $\bar{x}$ = the expected return
i = each of the possible outcomes (outcome 1 to outcome n)
p = probability of outcome i occurring
n = the number of possible outcomes
$\sum_{i=1}^{i=n}$ means add together the results for each of the possible outcomes i from the first to the nth outcome.

The preparation of probability distributions gives the management team some impression of likely outcomes. The additional calculation of expected returns adds a further dimension to the informed vision of the decision maker. Looking at expected returns is more enlightening than simply examining the single most likely outcome which is significantly different from the expected return of 26. For Project 5 the most likely outcome of 0 is not very informative and does not take into account the range of potential outcomes.

It is important to appreciate what these statistics are telling you. The expected return represents the outcome expected if the project is undertaken many times. If Project 4 was undertaken 1,000 times then on average the return would be 12. If the project was undertaken only once, as is the case in most business situations, there would be no guarantee that the actual outcome would equal the expected outcome.

The projects with the highest expected returns turn out to be Projects 3 and 5, each with an expected return of 26. However, we cannot get any further in our decision making by using just the expected return formula. This is because the formula fails to take account of risk. Risk is concerned with the likelihood that the actual performance might diverge from what is expected. Note that risk in this context has both positive and negative possibilities of diverging from the mean, whereas in everyday speech 'risk' usually has only negative connotations. If we plot the possible outcomes for Projects 3 and 5 against their probabilities of occurrence we get an impression that the outcome of Project 5 is more uncertain than the outcome of Project 3 (*see* **Exhibit 6.11**). The range of possible outcomes is relatively narrow for Project 3 and therefore presents an impression of lower risk. This is only a general indication. We need a more precise measurement of the dispersion of possible outcomes. This is provided by the standard deviation.

Exhibit 6.11 Pentagon plc: Probability distribution for Projects 3 and 5

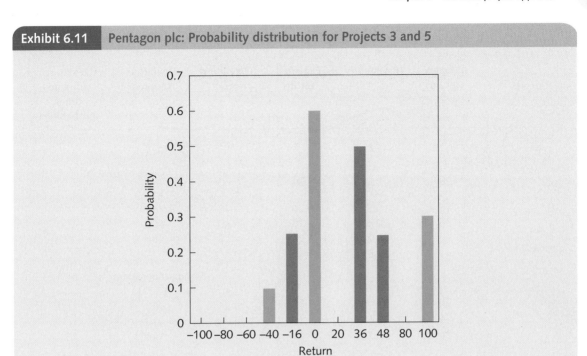

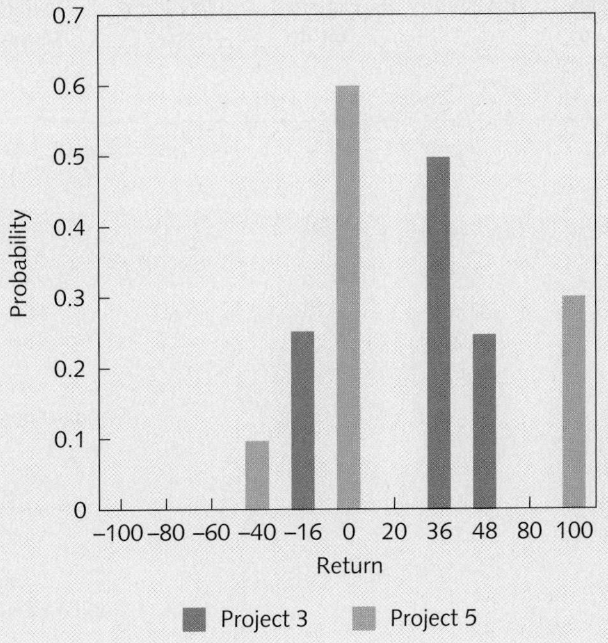

Standard deviation

The **standard deviation**, σ, is a statistical measure of the dispersion around the expected value. The standard deviation is the square root of the **variance**, σ^2.

$$\text{Variance of } x = \sigma_x^2 = (x_1 - \bar{x})^2 p_1 + (x_2 - \bar{x})^2 p^2 + \dots (x_n - \bar{x})^2 p_n$$

or $$\sigma_x^2 = \sum_{i=1}^{i=n} \{(x_i - \bar{x})^2 p_i\}$$

Standard deviation

$$\sigma_x = \sqrt{\sigma_x^2} \text{ or } \sqrt{\sum_{i=1}^{i=n} \{(x_i - \bar{x})^2 p_i\}}$$

Calculating the variance is straightforward if you take it in stages:

- **Stage 1**. First obtain the deviation of each potential outcome from the expected outcome $(x_i - \bar{x})$. So, in the case of Project 3 the first outcome is –16 (this is our x_i) and the expected outcome ($\bar{x}$) is 26. So, subtracting the second number from the first we have –42.
- **Stage 2**. Square the result from Stage 1 for each of the outcomes $(x_i - \bar{x})^2$. So, for the first outcome of Project 3 we take the –42 and multiply it by itself: –42 × –42 = 1,764.
- **Stage 3**. Multiply the number generated in Stage 2 by the probability of that outcome occurring. In the case of the first outcome of Project 3 we multiply 1,764 by 0.25 = 441. That is, $(x_i - \bar{x})^2 p_i$.
- **Stage 4**. Finally, add together the results of all these calculations for that particular project. So, for Project 3 we add 441 to 50 to 121, which gives a variance of 612 (see **Exhibit 6.12**).

Note that the variances are very large numbers compared with the original potential outcomes. For Project 3 these are –16, 36 and 48 whereas the variance is over 600. This is because the variance measures are in pounds squared or returns squared, etc. Thus, the next stage is to obtain the standard deviation σ, by taking the square root of the variance. This measures variability around the expected value in straightforward pound or return terms. The standard deviation provides a

Exhibit 6.12 Pentagon plc: Calculating the standard deviations for the five projects

Project	Outcome (return) x_i	Probability p_i	Expected return $\bar{x}$	Deviation $x_i - \bar{x}$	Deviation squared $(x_i - \bar{x})^2$	Deviation squared times probability $(x_i - \bar{x})^2 p_i$
1	16	1.0	16	0	0	0
2	20	1.0	20	0	0	0
3	−16	0.25	26	−42	1,764	441
	36	0.5	26	10	100	50
	48	0.25	26	22	484	121
					Variance =	612
					Standard deviation =	24.7
4	−8	0.25	12	−20	400	100
	16	0.5	12	4	16	8
	24	0.25	12	12	144	36
					Variance =	144
					Standard deviation =	12
5	−40	0.1	26	−66	4,356	436
	0	0.6	26	−26	676	406
	100	0.3	26	74	5,476	1,643
					Variance =	2,485
					Standard deviation =	49.8

(An Excel spreadsheet version of these calculations is available at www.myfinancelab.com/arnold)

common yardstick to use when comparing the dispersions of possible outcomes for a number of projects. So, for Project 3, the standard deviation is $\sqrt{612} = 24.7$.

If we now put together the two sets of measurements about the five projects, as shown in **Exhibit 6.13**, we might be able to make a decision on which one should be selected.

Exhibit 6.13 Pentagon plc: Expected return and standard deviation

	Expected return $\bar{x}$	Standard deviation σ_x
Project 1	16	0
Project 2	20	0
Project 3	26	24.7
Project 4	12	12
Project 5	26	49.8

Project 1 would not, presumably, be chosen by anyone. Also, Project 4 is obviously inferior to Project 2 because it has both a lower expected return and a higher standard deviation. That leaves us with Projects 2, 3 and 5. To choose between these we need to introduce a little utility theory in order to appreciate the significance of the standard deviation figures.

Risk and utility

Utility theory recognises that money in itself is unimportant to human beings. What is important is the well-being, satisfaction or utility to be derived from money. For most people a doubling of annual income will not double annual well-being. Money is used to buy goods and services. The first £8,000 of income will buy the most essential items – food, clothing, shelter, etc. Thus an individual going from an income of zero to one of £8,000 will experience a large increase in utility. If income is increased by a further £8,000 then utility will increase again, but the size of the increase will be less than for this first £8,000, because the goods and services bought with the second £8,000 provide less additional satisfaction. If the process of adding incremental amounts to annual income is continued then, when the individual has an income of, say, £150,000, the additional utility derived from a further £8,000 becomes very small. For most people the additional utility from consumption diminishes as consumption increases. This is the concept of **diminishing marginal utility**. Now consider the case of an individual who must choose between two alternative investments, A and B (*see* **Exhibit 6.14**).

Exhibit 6.14 Returns and utility

	Investment A		Investment B	
	Return	Probability	Return	Probability
Poor economic conditions	2,000	0.5	0	0.5
Good economic conditions	6,000	0.5	8,000	0.5
Expected return	4,000		4,000	

Both investments give an expected return of £4,000, but the outcomes of B are more widely dispersed. In other words, Investment B is more risky than Investment A. Suppose the individual has invested in A but is considering shifting all her money to B. As a result, in a poor year she will receive £2,000 less on Investment B than she would have received if she had stayed with A. In a good year Investment B will provide £2,000 more than if she had left her money in A. So the question is: is it worthwhile to shift from Investment A to Investment B? The answer hinges on the concept of diminishing marginal utility. While Investments A and B have the same expected returns they have different utilities. The extra utility associated with B in a good year is small compared with the loss of utility in a bad year when returns fall by an extra £2,000. Investment A is preferred because utility is higher for the first £2,000 of return than for the last £2,000 of return (increasing return from £6,000 to £8,000 by switching from A to B). Investors whose preferences are characterised by diminishing marginal utility are called risk averters.

A *risk averter* prefers a more certain return to an alternative with an equal but more risky expected outcome. The alternative to being a risk averter is to be a *risk lover* (risk seeker). These investors are highly optimistic and have a preference rather than an aversion for risk. For these people the marginal utility of each £ increases.

A risk lover prefers a more uncertain alternative to an alternative with an equal but less risky expected outcome. These are rare individuals and it is usually assumed that shareholders are risk averters (however, some are less risks averse than other. Don't confuse this lower aversion with risk loving.) When a risk averter is faced with two investments, each with the same expected return, he/she will select the one with the lower standard deviation or variance. This brings us to the mean-variance rule.

Mean-variance rule

Project X will be preferred to Project Y if at least one of the following conditions apply:

1 The expected return of X is at least equal to the expected return of Y, and the variance is less than that of Y.

2 The expected return of X exceeds that of Y and the variance is equal to or less than that of Y.

So, returning to Pentagon plc, we can see from **Exhibit 6.15** that Project 5 can be eliminated from any further consideration using the mean-variance rule because it has the same expected return as Project 3 but a wider dispersion of possible outcomes.

Exhibit 6.15 Pentagon plc: Expected returns and standard deviations

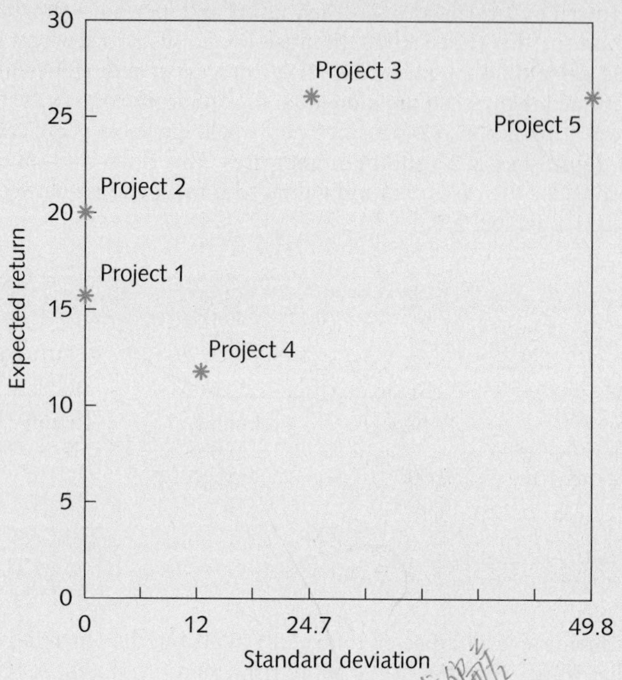

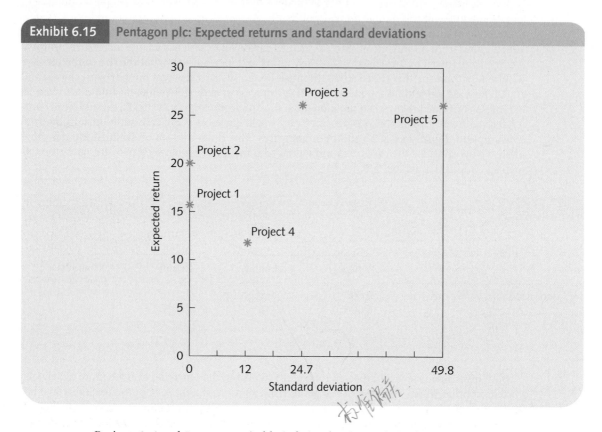

Projects 1, 4 and 5 are recognisably inferior, leaving a choice between Projects 2 and 3. From this point on there is no simple answer. The solution depends on the risk-return utility attitude of the decision maker. This is fundamentally a matter for subjective judgement and different management teams will make different choices. When the author has put the choice between Projects 2 and 3 to MBA classes of middle and senior managers approximately one-half take the safe option of Project 2. However, others in the class say that for the sake of a little more risk Project 3 gives a significantly higher return and so should be accepted. The board of directors of Pentagon need to weigh up the risk preferences of the owners of the company and choose one project or the other. In doing so they may like to consider how this new project fits with the rest of the company's projects. If the firm already has other projects (operations, strategic business units, product lines, etc.) and many of these projects tend to do well in circumstances when Project 3 does badly, and vice versa, they may consider the benefits of diversification incline them to accept this investment.

Another factor in the decision equation is that variability (standard deviation) may not be a worry if the project forms a small part of the firm's assets. If, however, choosing either Project 2 or Project 3 would entail the commitment of most of the company's assets the directors may take the safer option.

Expected net present values and standard deviation

In the example of Pentagon plc we have simply taken the potential returns of the projects as given. Now we will look at a project under circumstances of risk when you are not handed the *returns*, but have to calculate the NPV and the standard deviation of NPV using the cash flows associated with the investment. In addition, these cash flows will occur over a number of years and so the analysis becomes both more sophisticated and more challenging. First, the notation of the statistical formulae needs to be changed.

The expected net present value is:

$$\overline{NPV} = \sum_{i=1}^{i=n} (NPV_i p_i)$$

where $\overline{NPV}$ = expected net present value
NPV_i = the NPV if outcome i occurs
p_i = probability of outcome i occurring
n = number of possible outcomes
$\sum_{i=1}^{i=n}$ means add together the results of all the $NPV \times p$ calculations for each outcome i from the first to the nth outcome

The standard deviation of the net present value is:

$$\sigma_{NPV} = \sqrt{\sum_{i=1}^{i=n} \{(NPV_i - \overline{NPV})^2 p_i\}}$$

This more realistic application of probability analysis will be illustrated through the example of Horizon plc, which buys old pubs and invests a great deal of money on refurbishment and marketing. It then sells the pubs at the end of two years in what the firm hopes is a transformed and thriving state. The management are considering buying one of the pubs close to a university campus. The purchase of the freehold will cost, at Time 0, £500,000. The cost of refurbishment will be paid at the outset to the shopfitting firm which Horizon always uses (in order to obtain a discount). Thus an additional £200,000 will be spent at Time 0.

Purchase price, t_0	£500,000
Refurbishment, t_0	£200,000
	£700,000

Experience has taught the management team of Horizon that pub retailing is a very unpredictable game. Customers are fickle and the slightest change in fashion or trend and the level of customers drops dramatically. Through a mixture of objective historical data analysis and subjective 'expert' judgement the managers have concluded that there is a 60 per cent probability that the pub will become a trendy place to be seen in and meet people. There is a 40 per cent chance that potential customers will not switch to this revamped hostelry within the first year.

The Year 1 cash flows are as follows:

	Probability	Cash flow at end of Year 1
Good customer response	0.6	£100,000
Poor customer response	0.4	£10,000

Note: For simplicity it is assumed that all cash flows arise at the year ends.

If the response of customers is good in the first year there are three possibilities for the second year.

1. The customer flow will increase further and the pub can be sold at the end of the second year for a large sum. The total of the net operating cash flows for the second year and the sale proceeds will be £2m. This eventuality has a probability of 0.1 or 10 per cent.
2. Customer levels will be the same as in the first year and at the end of the second year the total cash flows will be £1.6m. The probability of this is 0.7 or 70 per cent.
3. Many customers will abandon the pub. This may happen because of competitor action, for example other pubs in the area are relaunched, or perhaps the fashion changes. The result will be that the pub will have a net cash outflow on trading, and will have a much lower selling price. The result will be a cash inflow for the year of only £800,000. This has a 20 per cent chance of occurring.

If, however, the response in the first year is poor then one of two eventualities may occur in the second year:

1 Matters continue to deteriorate and sales fall further. At the end of the second year the cash flows from trading and the sale of the pub total only £700,000. This has a probability of 0.5, or a 50:50 chance.
2 In the second year sales rise, resulting in a total t_2 cash flow of £1.2m. Probability: 0.5.

The conditional probabilities (conditional on what happens in the first year) for the second year are as follows:

If the first year elicits a *good response* then:

	Probability	Cash flow at end of Year 2
1 Sales increase in second year	0.1	£2m
or		
2 Sales are constant	0.7	£1.6m
or		
3 Sales decrease	0.2	£0.8m

If the first year elicits a *poor response* then:

	Probability	Cash flow at end of Year 2
1 Sales fall further	0.5	£0.7m
or		
2 Sales rise slightly	0.5	£1.2m

Note: All figures include net trading income plus sale of pub.

Exhibit 6.16 An event tree showing the probabilities of the possible returns for Horizon plc

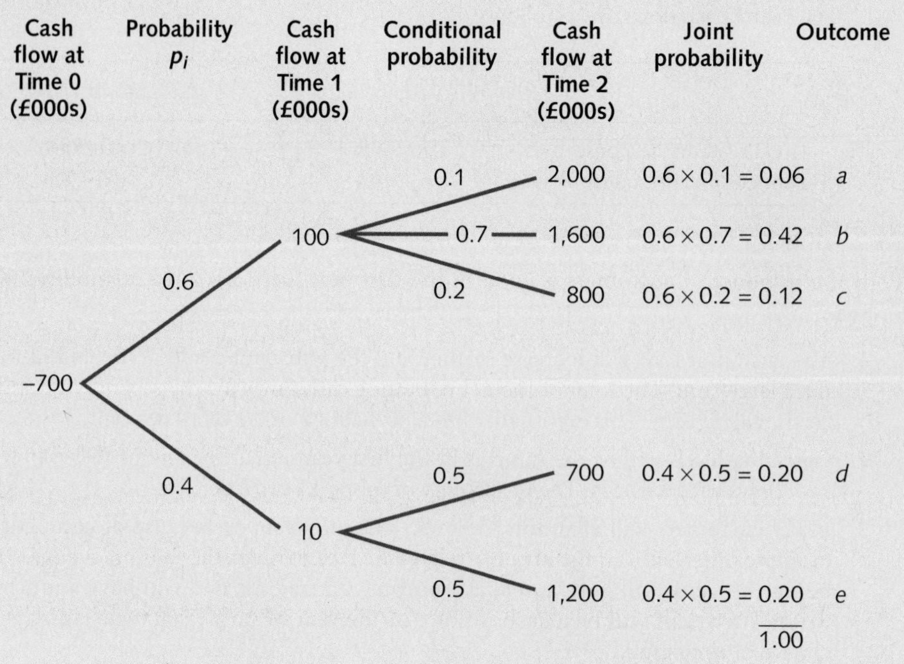

Exhibit 6.17 Expected net present value, Horizon plc

Outcome		Net present values (£000s)	NPV × Probability
a	$-700 + \frac{100}{1.1} + \frac{2,000}{(1.1)^2}$	= 1,044	1,044 × 0.06 = 63
b	$-700 + \frac{100}{1.1} + \frac{1,600}{(1.1)^2}$	= 713	713 × 0.42 = 300
c	$-700 + \frac{100}{1.1} + \frac{800}{(1.1)^2}$	= 52	52 × 0.12 = 6
d	$-700 + \frac{10}{1.1} + \frac{700}{(1.1)^2}$	= –112	–112 × 0.20 = –22
e	$-700 + \frac{10}{1.1} + \frac{1,200}{(1.1)^2}$	= 301	301 × 0.20 = 60
Expected net present value			407 or £407,000

Note: Assuming a 10% opportunity cost of capital.

To be able to calculate the expected return and standard deviation for a project of this nature, we first need to establish the probability of each of the possible outcomes. This is shown in **Exhibit 6.16**. This shows that there are five possible outcomes. The probability that the initial expenditure is followed by a cash inflow of £100,000 after one year, and £2m after two years (that is, outcome *a*) is very low. This is as we might expect given that this is an extreme, positive outcome. The overall probability of this path being followed is the first year's probability (0.6) multiplied by the second year's probability (0.1) to give 0.06 or a 6 per cent chance of occurrence. The most likely outcome is for the first year to be successful (£100,000) followed by a continuation of the same sales level resulting in Year 2 cash flow of £1.6m (outcome *b*) with a probability of 0.42.

The second stage is to calculate the expected return making use of the probabilities calculated in Exhibit 6.16 (*see* **Exhibit 6.17**).

Then the standard deviation for this pub project can be calculated (*see* **Exhibit 6.18**).

Exhibit 6.18 Standard deviation for Horizon plc

Outcome £000s NPV_i		Probability p_i	Expected NPV $\overline{NPV}$	Deviation $NPV_i - \overline{NPV}$	Deviation squared $(NPV_i - \overline{NPV})^2$	Deviation squared times probability $(NPV_i - \overline{NPV})^2 p_i$
a	1,044	0.06	407	637	405,769	24,346
b	713	0.42	407	306	93,636	39,327
c	52	0.12	407	–355	126,025	15,123
d	–112	0.20	407	–519	269,361	53,872
e	301	0.20	407	–106	11,236	2,247
					Variance =	134,915
				Standard deviation =	$\sqrt{134,915}$ =	367
					or	£367,000

(An Excel spreadsheet version of all the calculations for Horizon is available at www.myfinancelab.com/arnold)

Now that the management team have a calculated expected NPV of £407,000 and a standard deviation of £367,000 they are in a position to make a more informed decision. The probability analysis can be taken on to further stages; for example, an additional dimension that may affect their judgement of the worth of the project is the probability of certain extreme eventualities occurring, such as the project outcome being so bad as to lead to the insolvency of the company. This technique is described later. First we broaden the application of probability analysis.

Independent probabilities

In the case of Horizon the possible outcomes in the second year depend upon what happens in the first year. That is, they are conditional probabilities. We now turn to a case where the second year's outcomes are independent of what happens in the first year, and therefore there can be any combination of first and second year outcomes (*see* **Exhibit 6.19**).

Exhibit 6.19 Independent probabilities

Year 1		Year 2	
Cash flow (£000s)	Probability	Cash flow (£000s)	Probability
100	0.2	50	0.6
150	0.7	160	0.4
180	0.1		

The six possible overall outcomes are (£000s):

- 100 + 50
- 100 + 160
- 150 + 50
- 150 + 160
- 180 + 50
- 180 + 160

The initial cash outflow is £150,000. One method of calculating the expected NPV is to first calculate the expected cash flow in each year (*see* **Exhibit 6.20**).

Exhibit 6.20 Expected cash flow for each year

Year 1

Cash flow (£000s)	Probability	Cash flow × probability (£000s)
100	0.2	20
150	0.7	105
180	0.1	18
		143

Year 2

Cash flow (£000s)	Probability	Cash flow × probability (£000s)
50	0.6	30
160	0.4	64
		94

Note: The discount rate is 10%.

The expected NPV is given by:

$$-150 + \frac{143}{1.1} + \frac{94}{(1.1)^2} = +57.69 \text{ or } £57{,}690$$

Expected NPV and standard deviation can be computed in one table as shown in **Exhibit 6.21**.

Exhibit 6.21 Expected NPV and standard deviation

Cash flow Year 1	(£000s) Year 2	Probability p_i	*NPV*	$NPV \times p_i$	Expected *NPV*	$(NPV_i - \overline{NPV})^2 p_i$
100	50	0.2 × 0.6 = 0.12	−17.77	−2.13	57.69	683.31
100	160	0.2 × 0.4 = 0.08	73.14	5.85	57.69	19.10
150	50	0.7 × 0.6 = 0.42	27.69	11.63	57.69	378.00
150	160	0.7 × 0.4 = 0.28	118.59	33.21	57.69	1,038.47
180	50	0.1 × 0.6 = 0.06	54.96	3.30	57.69	0.45
180	160	0.1 × 0.4 = 0.04	145.87	5.83	57.69	311.03
		1.00	Expected NPV 57.69			

Variance σ^2 = 2,430.36
Standard deviation σ = 49.3

This project has an expected outcome of £57,690 but a fairly high standard deviation of £49,300. This means that there is a distinct possibility of the outcome being significantly under £57,690, at say £27,690, or £17,690, or even –£1,090. On the other hand, there are similar chances of obtaining £87,690, or £97,690, or even £116,470. To put more precise probability estimates on particular outcomes occurring we need to understand the Z statistic. It is to this that we now turn. The Z statistic will be explained by using it to tackle the problem of the probability of a project leading to insolvency.

The risk of insolvency

On occasions a project may be so large relative to the size of the firm that if the worst-case scenario occurred the firm would be made bankrupt. It is sometimes of interest to managers to know the probability that a project will have a sufficiently poor outcome as to threaten the survival of the company. We can estimate this probability if we know the shape of the probability distribution. We usually assume that the probability distribution of a project's potential return is 'normal, bell-shaped' (*see* **Exhibit 6.22**).

Exhibit 6.22 The normal curve

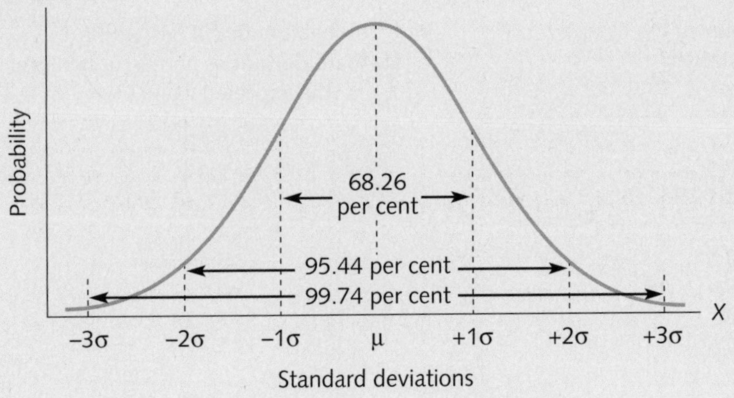

The distribution of possible outcomes is symmetrical about the expected return, μ. This means that the probability of an outcome, X, occurring between the expected return and one standard deviation away from the expected return is 34.13 per cent (one half of 68.26 per cent). That is, the chances of the outcome landing in the shaded area of **Exhibit 6.23** are 34.13 per cent.

Exhibit 6.23 **Probability of outcome being between expected return and one standard deviation from expected return**

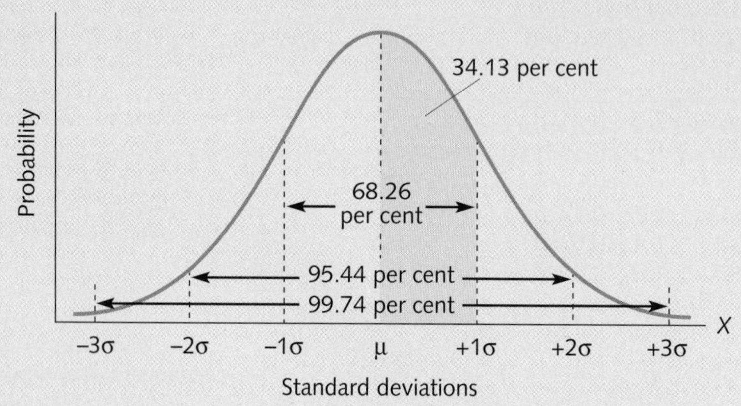

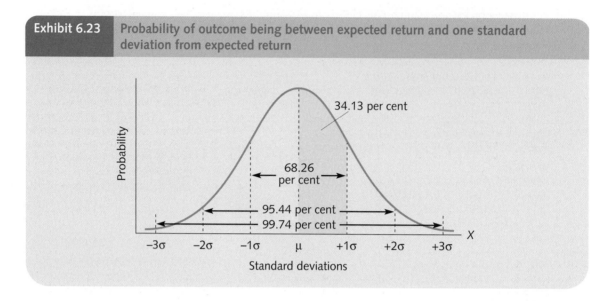

The probability of the outcome being between the expected value and two standard deviations from the expected value is 47.72 per cent (one-half of 95.44 per cent). To find the probability that the outcome will be between two particular values we first need to obtain the **Z statistic**. This simply shows the number of standard deviations from the mean to the value that interests you.

$$Z = \frac{X - \mu}{\sigma}$$

where
- Z is the number of standard deviations from the mean
- X is the outcome that you are concerned about
- μ is the mean of the possible outcomes
- σ is the standard deviation of the outcome distribution

We also need to use the standard normal distribution table. This is in Appendix V at the end of the book but an extract is presented in **Exhibit 6.24**.

Exhibit 6.24 **The standard normal distribution**

Value of the Z statistic	Probability that X lies within Z standard deviations above (or below) the expected value (%)
0.0	0.00
0.2	7.93
0.4	15.54
1.0	34.13
1.2	38.49
1.6	44.52
2.0	47.72
3.0	49.87

The use of the standard normal distribution table will be illustrated by the example of Roulette plc in Worked example 6.2.

Worked example 6.2 Roulette plc

Roulette plc is considering undertaking a very large project and if the economy fails to grow there is a risk that the losses on this project will cause the liquidation of the firm. It can take a maximum loss of £5m (NPV of £5m) and still keep the rest of the business afloat. But if the loss is more than £5m the firm will become bankrupt. The managers are keen to know the percentage probability that more than £5m will be lost.

The expected NPV has already been calculated at £8m but there is a wide variety of possible outcomes. If the economy booms the firm will make a fortune. If it is reasonably strong it will make a respectable return and if there is zero or negative growth large sums will be lost. These NPVs are judged to be normally distributed, that is, a bell-shaped distribution. The standard deviation is £6.5m.

To calculate the probability of insolvency we first calculate the Z statistic, when the X in which we are interested is at a value of –5.

$$Z = \frac{X - \mu}{\sigma}$$

$$Z = \frac{-5 - 8}{6.5} = -2$$

The value of –2 means that the distance between the expected outcome and the point of bankruptcy is two standard deviations. From the standardised normal distribution table (Appendix V) we can see that the probability that the return will lie between the mean and two standard deviations below the mean is 47.72 per cent (*see* **Exhibit 6.25**).

Exhibit 6.25 Probability of outcome between μ and 2σ from μ

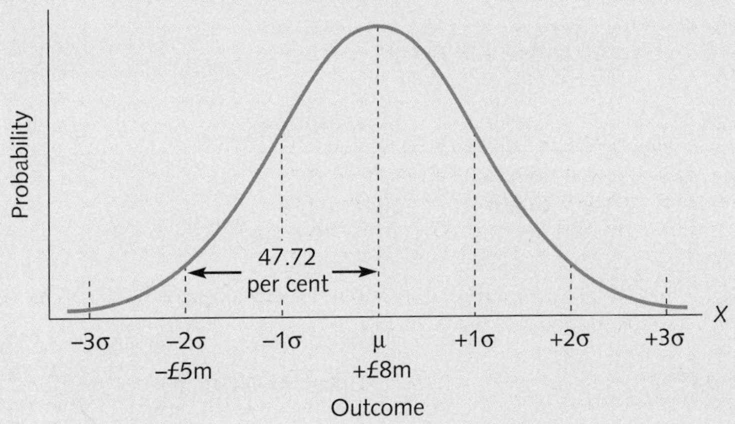

The probability distribution is symmetrical about the mean; therefore, the probability that the return will be above the mean (£8m) is 50 per cent. Thus, the probability of the firm achieving an NPV greater than a loss of £5m is 97.72 per cent (47.72 per cent plus 50 per cent). To make the final decision on whether to proceed with this project we need to consider the owners' and the managers' attitude to this particular level of risk of insolvency. This is likely to vary from one company to another. In some situations shareholders and managers will have well-diversified interests and so are reasonably sanguine about this risk. Other decision makers will not even take a 2.28 per cent (100 per cent – 97.72 per cent) chance of insolvency.

Interpreting probability distributions using different discount rates

In calculating NPVs and their standard deviations, two alternative discount rates may be used:

- the risk-free discount rate;
- a risk-adjusted discount rate (that is, with a risk premium added).

Regardless of which of these is used to calculate the probability of certain eventualities through the standard normal distribution, careful interpretation of the results is needed. This is illustrated through the example of Brightlight plc.

Brightlight plc is considering a project with the cash flows shown in **Exhibit 6.26**.

Exhibit 6.26 Brightlight plc: cash flows

Initial outlay 100

Economic conditions	**Time (year)** 1	2	**Probability of economic event** p_i
Economic boom	130	130	0.15
Good growth	110	110	0.20
Growth	90	90	0.30
Poor growth	70	70	0.20
Recession	50	50	0.15

The risk-free discount rate is 6 per cent. Applying this the project produces an expected NPV of 65 and a standard deviation of 46.4 (*see* **Exhibit 6.27**).

Exhibit 6.27 Applying the risk-free discount rate

Economic conditions	***NPV***	***NPV*** $\times p_i$	$(NPV - \overline{NPV})^2 p_i$
Economic boom	138.342	20.7513	806.725
Good growth	101.674	20.3348	268.908
Growth	65.006	19.5018	0.000
Poor growth	28.338	5.6676	268.908
Recession	−8.330	−1.2495	806.725
		Expected NPV = 65.0060	Variance = 2,151.266

Standard deviation = $\sqrt{2{,}151.27} = 46.4$

The management team are interested in discovering the probability of the project producing a negative NPV if the risk-free discount rate is used. Thus, in the Z statistic formula, X is set at a value of 0:

$$Z = \frac{X - \mu}{\sigma}$$

$$Z = \frac{0 - 65}{46.4} = -1.4$$

The probability of the outcome giving an NPV of between 0 and +65 is 41.92 per cent (1.4 standard deviations) according to Appendix V. Therefore, the probability of a negative NPV (the shaded area in **Exhibit 6.28**) is 8.08 per cent (50 per cent – 41.92 per cent). The interpretation of this result is that there is an 8.08 per cent probability of this project producing a return of *less than the risk-free rate*. The decision now has to be made as to whether this probability is acceptable, given that the rate set is merely the risk-free rate. If a number of mutually exclusive projects were being compared then to be consistent the risk-free rate must be used for all of them.

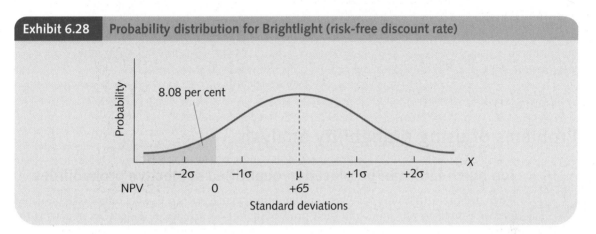

Exhibit 6.28 Probability distribution for Brightlight (risk-free discount rate)

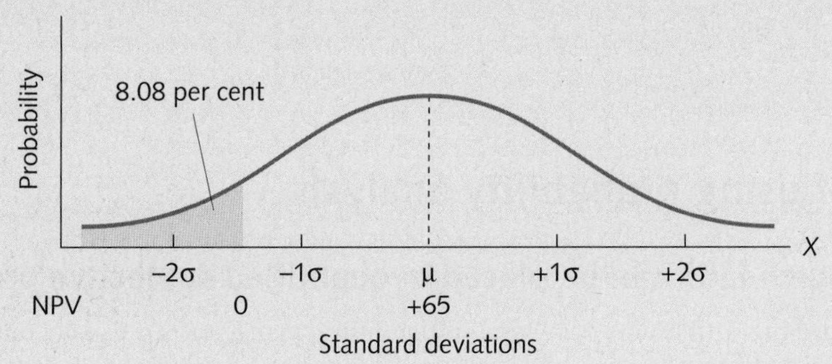

Brightlight also considers this project using a discount rate with a risk premium of 5 per cent added to the risk-free rate, that is, 6 + 5 = 11 per cent (*see* **Exhibit 6.29**).

Exhibit 6.29 Applying a discount rate including a risk premium of 5 per cent

Economic conditions	*NPV*	$NPV \times p_i$	$(NPV - \overline{NPV})^2 p_i$
Boom	122.625	18.394	703.8375
Good growth	88.375	17.675	234.6125
Growth	54.125	16.237	0
Poor growth	19.875	3.975	234.6125
Recession	−14.375	−2.156	703.8375
		Expected NPV = 54.125	Variance = 1,876.90
			Standard deviation = 43.3

The probability of a negative NPV is:

$$Z = \frac{X - \mu}{\sigma}$$

$$Z = \frac{0 - 54.125}{43.30} = -1.25$$

A standard deviation of 1.25 gives a probability of 39.44 per cent of the outcome being between X and μ. Thus the probability of the project producing less than the required return of 11 per cent is 10.56 per cent (50 per cent – 39.44 per cent). Using the risk-adjusted discount rate tells the appraiser that this project is expected to produce a positive NPV of 54.125 when using a discount rate which takes account of risk. Also, if it is decided to implement this project, there is a 10.56 per cent probability of the decision being incorrect, in the sense that the NPV will turn out to be negative and therefore will not be shareholder wealth enhancing (*see* **Exhibit 6.30**).

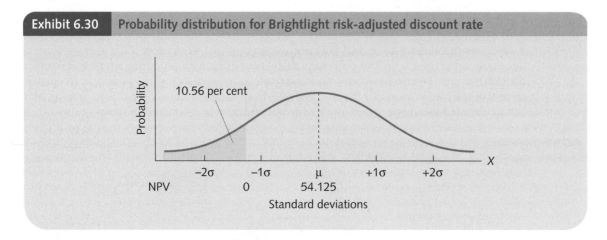

Exhibit 6.30 Probability distribution for Brightlight risk-adjusted discount rate

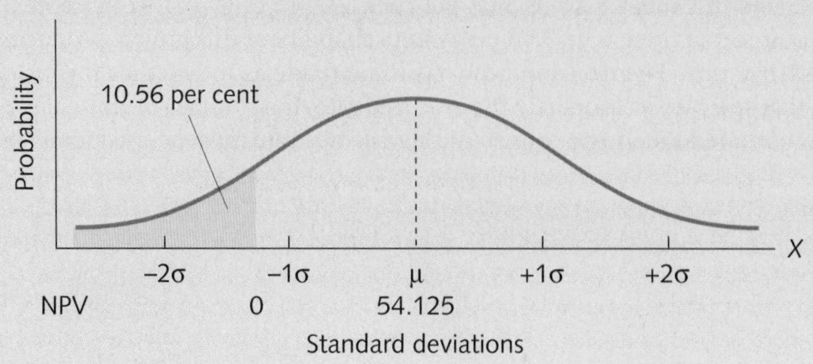

Problems of using probability analysis

Too much faith can be placed in quantified subjective probabilities

When dealing with events occurring in the future, managers can usually only make informed guesses as to likely outcomes and their probabilities of occurrence. A danger lies in placing too much emphasis on analysis of these subjective estimates once they are converted to numerical form. It is all too easy to carry out detailed computations with accuracy to the nth degree, forgetting that the fundamental data usually have a small objective base. Again, mathematical purity is no substitute for thoughtful judgement.

The alternative to the assignment of probabilities, that of using only the most likely outcome estimate in the decision-making process, is both more restricted in vision and equally subjective. At least probability analysis forces the decision maker to explicitly recognise a range of outcomes and the basis on which they are estimated, and to express the degree of confidence in the estimates.

Too complicated

Investment decision making and subsequent implementation often require the understanding and commitment of large numbers of individuals. Probability analysis can be a poor communicating tool if important employees do not understand what the numbers mean. Perhaps here there is a need for education combined with good presentation.

Projects may be viewed in isolation

The context of the firm may be an important variable, determining whether a single project is too risky to accept, and therefore a project should never be viewed in isolation. Take a firm with a large base of stable low-risk activities. It may be willing to accept a high-risk project because the overall profits might be very large and even if the worst happened the firm will survive. On the other hand a small firm that already has one risky activity may only accept further proposals if they are low risk.

The other aspect to bear in mind here is the extent to which a project increases or reduces the overall risk of the firm. This is based on the degree of negative covariance of project returns. (This is an aspect of portfolio theory which is discussed in the next chapter.)

Despite these drawbacks, probability analysis has an important advantage over scenario analysis. In scenario analysis the focus is on a few highly probable scenarios. In probability analysis consideration must be given to all possible outcomes (or at least an approximation of all outcomes) so that probabilities sum to one. This forces a more thorough consideration of the risk of the project.

Evidence of risk analysis in practice

Exhibit 6.31 summarises the risk analysis techniques used by UK firms.

Exhibit 6.31 Risk analysis techniques used in UK firms

	Arnold and Hatzopoulos				Alkaraan and Northcott
	Small %	Medium %	Large %	Total %	%
Sensitivity/Scenario analysis	82	83	89	85	89
Reduced payback period	15	42	11	20	75
Risk-adjusted discount rate	42	71	50	52	82
Probability analysis	27	21	42	31	77
Beta analysis	3	0	5	3	43
Subjective assessment	44	33	55	46	–

Sources: Arnold and Hatzopoulos (2000) sample of 96 firms: 34 small, 24 medium, 38 large. Survey date July 1997. Alkaraan and Northcott (2006): 83 large companies returned questionnaires in 2002.

UK firms have increased the extent of risk analysis in project appraisal over the past 20 years (evident from surveys conducted by Pike (1988, 1996) and Ho and Pike (1991)). This trend has been encouraged by a greater awareness of the techniques and aided by the availability of computing software. Sensitivity and scenario analysis remain the most widely adopted approaches. Probability analysis is now used more widely than in the past but few smaller firms use it on a regular basis. Beta analysis, based on the capital-asset pricing model (discussed in Chapter 8) is rarely used. Simple, rule-of-thumb approaches have not been replaced by the more complex methods. Firms tend to be pragmatic and to use a multiplicity of techniques in a complementary fashion.

Real options

Traditional project appraisal, based on the calculation of NPV, generally implicitly assumes that the investment being analysed is a straightforward go-now-or-don't-go-ever decision. That you either accept the project in its entirety at the outset or forget about the whole idea. So, if a company is considering a project with cash flow spread over, say, eight years it would estimate the expected cash flows and discount all eight of them (usually following a probability analysis to allow for uncertainty). Under this view of decision making there is only the initial decision to accept or reject; and if accepted the project is persisted with for the full term analysed (say, eight years).

Some business decisions are like this. For example, if the project is to build a bridge for a government, then once you have signed the contract, regardless of what happens in the future, you are obligated to deliver a bridge. You cannot delay the start date, nor can you abandon the project halfway through if new information is received indicating that the worst-case scenario is now likely to happen (say, building costs double).

However, with most projects the managers are not making all-or-nothing decisions at the outset. They are able to respond to changing circumstances as they unfold over the life of the project. For example, if events turn out badly they can react by abandoning the project. So a company that goes ahead with wind powered electricity machinery production on the basis of a positive NPV given the government's current support for subsidising renewable energy it may abandon the project if government policy changes two years later. The option to abandon rather than be forced to persist has value. This value is usually ignored in traditional NPV analysis.

Sometimes it is the option to expand if events turn out well that is extremely valuable. On other occasions the decision to go ahead or not to go ahead is not now-or-never but to consider a range of dates for going ahead; this year, next year or the year after. That is, the company has the option to defer the project, e.g. developing a copper mine only when the world market price of copper rises sufficiently. Going ahead now would destroy value at current low copper prices (a negative NPV) but the *option* to develop has value. The ability to abandon, expand or defer a project can add considerable value compared with a project without one of these flexibilities.

The real options perspective takes account of future managerial flexibility whereas the traditional NPV framework tends to assume away such flexibility.

Real options ('capital investment options') give the right, but not the obligation, to take an action in the future. They give value by presenting managers with the opportunity to exploit an uncertain future in which conditions change unpredictably, making one decision choice better than the other(s). By holding a real option we have the right to select whatever decision suits us best at the time. They differ from financial options traded in the market (*see* Chapter 24) in that their value does not depend on the movement of a financial security or instrument, such as a share, or currency rate, but on the cash flows of real investment projects within the firm.

Some simple examples of valuable real options

Firms sometimes undertake projects which apparently have negative NPVs. They do so because an option is thereby created to expand, should this be seen to be desirable. The value of the option outweighs the loss of value on the project. For example, many Western firms have set up offices, marketing and production operations in China which run up losses. This has not led to a pull-out because of the long-term attraction to expand within the world's largest market. If they withdrew they would find it very difficult to re-enter, and would therefore sacrifice the option to expand. This option is considered to be so valuable that some firms are prepared to pay the price of many years of losses.

Another example would be where a firm has to decide whether to enter a new technological area. If it does it may make losses but at least it has opened up the choices available to the firm. To have refused to enter at all on the basis of a crude NPV calculation could close off important future avenues for expansion. The pharmaceutical giants run dozens of research programmes showing apparent negative NPVs: they do so for what is often described as 'strategic reasons'. We might alternatively call this intuitive option analysis. Perhaps the drugs a company is currently developing in a field of medicine, say, for the treatment of Alzheimer's disease, show negative NPVs when taken in isolation. However, by undertaking this activity the firm builds capabilities within this specialism allowing the firm to stay in the game and participate in future generations of drugs which may have very high payoffs.

If a property developer purchases a prime site near a town centre there is, in the time it takes to draw up plans and gain planning permission, the alternative option of selling the land (abandonment option). Flexibility could also be incorporated in the construction process itself – for example, perhaps alternative materials can be used if the price of the first choice increases. Also, the buildings could be designed in such a way that they could be quickly and cheaply switched from one use to another (switching option), for example from offices to flats, or from hotel to shops. At each stage there is an option to abandon plan A and switch to plan B. Having plan B available has value. To have only plan A leaves the firm vulnerable to changing circumstances.

Perhaps in the example of the property developer it may be possible to create more options by creating conditions that do not compel the firm to undertake investment at particular points in time. If there was an option to wait a year, or two years, then the prospects for rapid rental growth for office space *vis-à-vis* hotels, flats and shops could be more accurately assessed (deferral option or timing option). Thus a more informed, and in the long run more value-creating, decision can be made.

True NPV

Thus we need to raise the sophistication of NPV analysis by allowing for the value of flexibility during the life of the project. A project in which there is the ability to take further action after uncertainty has been resolved or reduced significantly is more valuable than one that is rigid.

True NPV = Crude NPV + NPV of expansion option + NPV of the option to abandon + NPV of timing option + NPV of other option possibilities

Exhibit 6.32 uses option theory in an unusual way.

Exhibit 6.32

Dear Economist: Resolving readers' dilemmas with the tools of Adam Smith

FT

By Tim Harford

Dear Economist,

I've been seeing my girlfriend for the past three years, and we've been living together for the past 18 months. I just can't decide whether to propose to her this Valentine's Day, or wait until next year. What would you suggest?

Yours sincerely,

Mr C. Johnson, Bristol

Dear Mr Johnson,

Evidently you intend to marry this lucky girl, eventually, since your question implies that whether you propose now or later, the expected **net present value** created will be positive.

As the poet Andrew Marvell once explained, value creating moves usually should be made sooner, rather than later, since time's winged chariot hurries near. But Marvell failed to anticipate advances in real option theory which demonstrate that it can be worth delaying decisions to obtain more information. You need to weigh up the cost of delay against the value of waiting to gain new information.

The cost of delay is small if you are young and patient. The value of waiting is large if you have the kind of exciting relationship where every day you learn something new about your belle. This is why young people are often counselled against rash betrothals.

On the other hand, you've been living with the girl for a while. Perhaps another year is unlikely to bring important information. If so, what are you waiting for? This reasoning has served your correspondent very well.

There is another important consideration: the window of opportunity for exercising an option can slam shut, in which case the option value is zero. There is no point learning everything you need to know to propose, if on Valentine's Day 2006 your girlfriend is dating somebody else. Before you decide to wait another year, it might be wise to be sure that she will wait too.

Source: FT Weekend Magazine, 12 February 2005, p. 12. Reprinted with permission.

Option to abandon

Imagine you are the chief executive of a company that designs, creates and sells computer games. A film studio is about to start shooting a major action thriller film. It will reach the box office in one year from now. The film company have contacted you offering you the right to develop and market a game based on the film (with film clips and voice-overs from the principal actors). You would have to pay £10m now for this. From previous experience you estimate that there is a 50:50 chance of the film being a success or a box office flop. If it is a success the present value of all the future cash flows for the game will amount to £50m. If, however, it is a flop the high costs of development and promotion will mean a present value of all the future cash flows associated with the game will be negative £50m.

Should you pay £10m now for the game rights?

Conventional NPV analysis is likely to mislead you in this decision. You would set out the cash flows and their probabilities and calculate an expected NPV from them, which will be –£10m (*see* Exhibit 6.33). Hence you would reject the project.

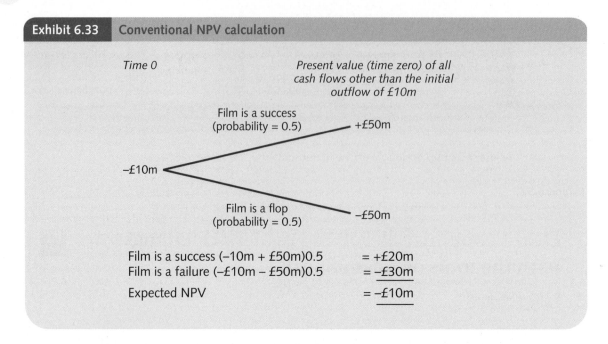

Exhibit 6.33 Conventional NPV calculation

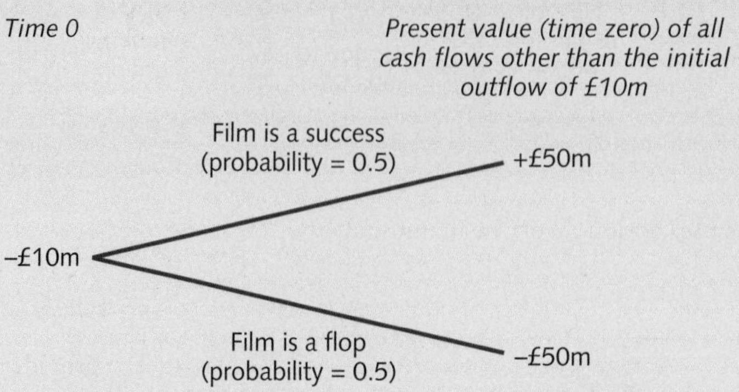

Film is a success (–10m + £50m)0.5	= +£20m
Film is a failure (–£10m – £50m)0.5	= –£30m
Expected NPV	= –£10m

The fact that you would be purchasing merely an option to develop the game, without the obligation to do so, is very significant in the valuation of this project. You can abandon the whole plan in one year's time when you have some vital information: how the film performs at the box office after release. If it is a success then continue. If it is a failure then do not invest any more than the original £10m and save yourself £50m.

With this flexibility built in, your cash flows in the future are +£50m if the film is well received, and zero if it is hammered by the critics and audiences stay away. Each of these has a 50 per cent chance of occurring (*see* **Exhibit 6.34**).

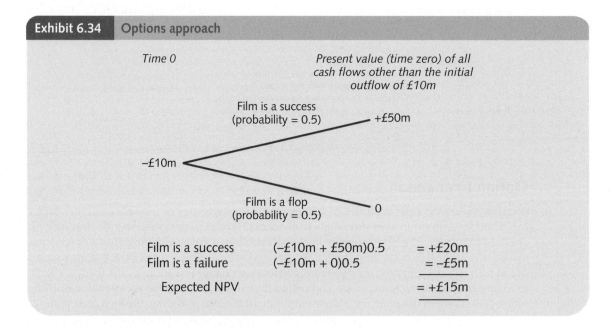

Exhibit 6.34 Options approach

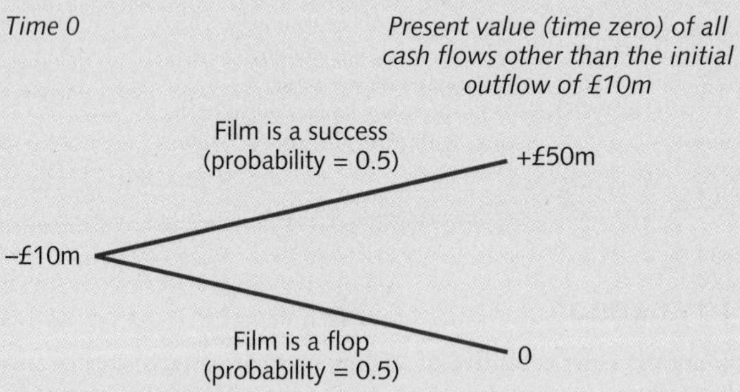

Film is a success	(–£10m + £50m)0.5	= +£20m
Film is a failure	(–£10m + 0)0.5	= –£5m
Expected NPV		= +£15m

The important point is that we don't view the project as a take-it-now-in-its-entirety-or-forget-it deal, but rather consider the possibility of future managerial choices. In other words managers are not passive, but active over the life of the project. There are contingent future decisions which can boost NPV. We need to allow for these possibilities now, when deciding whether to buy the game rights.

The payoff when the real option to abandon is considered is +£15m and it is correct to pay £10m for the game rights now.

The value of the option to abandon is calculated as the difference between the NPV if obligated to go ahead with the entire project and the NPV with the option to abandon.

NPV with option – NPV if there is no option

+£15 – (–£10m) = £25m

Welcoming risk

In traditional NPV analysis the greater the degree of uncertainty about the future cash flows the lower the value of the project. The higher standard deviation is offputting to a risk-averse shareholder, and their agents, the managers.

Real option analysis takes a different perspective. Uncertainty provides value because the opportunity to exercise the option to take action later becomes all the more precious. To illustrate, let us double the range of the present value of the cash flows after the initial payment. So there is now a 50 per cent chance of +£100m and a 50 per cent chance of –£100m. The expected NPV under traditional analysis of this remains at –£10m but the range of outcomes has increased, i.e. risk has risen.

Film is a success	(–£10m + £100m)0.5	= +£45m
Film is a failure	(–£10m – £100m)0.5	= –£55m
	Crude NPV	= –£10m

This project is even more unattractive under traditional NPV analysis than the original situation because of the higher risk for the same return.

The options perspective shows the more volatile cash flow project to be more valuable than the less volatile one because managers can avoid the downside risk by simply abandoning the project if the news turns out to be bad in one year's time. Risk is no longer symmetrical, that is, with equal probabilities of negative outcomes and positive outcomes around the expected return. It is asymmetrical: you benefit if things go well and do not lose if things go badly (at least you lose no more than you put down as a 'premium' to purchase the option in the first place).

Film is a success	(–£10m + £100m)0.5	= £45m
Film is a failure	(–£10m + 0)0.5	= –£5m
	Option perspective NPV	= £40m

Uncertainty can therefore be a good thing, if you hold an option to exploit the change in circumstances as time goes on. If you do not have flexibility to respond then uncertainty is a bad thing and reduces value. Traditional NPV analysis assumes away the possibility of response to contingencies, resulting in a symmetric risk profile. Thus traditional NPV can seriously underestimate the true NPV of many capital investments.

Don't sacrifice options lightly or cheaply

Most projects include an ability to abandon. If cash flows fall dramatically due to unforeseen events managers usually have a chance to 'cut their losses': exercise their option to abandon. If you are contemplating the initiation of a project that does not have the option to abandon then consider whether you should renegotiate the contract or adjust the method of implementation to see if you can build in an option to abandon. Such a clause or operational flexibility may one day save your bacon in a project with the potential for negative outcomes.

If your investment is in items with an active secondhand market then the abandonment option is easier to implement, e.g. purchase of a fleet of cars for car hire or a set of houses for rental. Building a specialist item with no secondhand market leaves you vulnerable, e.g. producing an information technology system for a government department. Think carefully in such situations about who bears the risk of future change in areas such as cost over-runs, delay and obsolescence if you are giving up the right to abandon.

In some cases the abandonment option may be better described as a switching option. For example you might be contemplating the purchase of machine tools to enable a project to go ahead. Even though machinery that is capable of producing many alternative products is more expensive than the dedicated version capable of producing only the products associated with this project, it may be worthwhile paying the extra because the option to switch from the manufacture of one item to another is so valuable. Thus car plants are often capable of producing more than one type of car on the assembly line. The assemblers can switch depending on the growth in demand of particular models. Electricity producers often build in the flexibility to switch from one type of fuel to another (e.g. oil or gas) in response to market prices.

Option to expand

A retail company has dreamed up a completely new retail concept. It has a plan to spend £200m now to open 50 branches across the country. There is a 50 per cent chance that the venture will be a success and the present value of all future cash flow will be £300m. There is also a 50 per cent chance that consumers will not flock to this new concept, in which case the present value of all future cash flows is £40m. Conducting a traditional NPV analysis leads the managers to reject the project (*see* **Exhibit 6.35**).

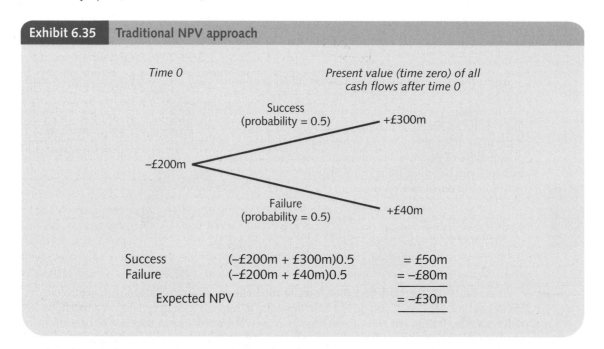

Exhibit 6.35 Traditional NPV approach

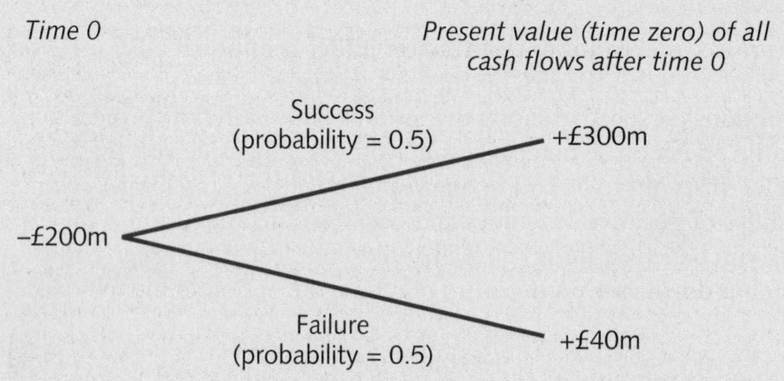

Success	(–£200m + £300m)0.5	= £50m
Failure	(–£200m + £40m)0.5	= –£80m
Expected NPV		= –£30m

An alternative is to create an option to expand rather than commit fully at the outset. The managers could set up a pilot by opening five shops to test the concept. This will resolve the uncertainty about the success of the concept. Full commitment only occurs after the information from the pilot is received. The cost of the pilot is £20m at time 0. There is a 50 per cent chance of the five shops succeeding, which means there is a 50 per cent chance of the entire 50 shops being successful (a suspect simplification for the sake of exposition). If the pilot is unsuccessful (50 per cent probability) the option to expand is abandoned (*see* **Exhibit 6.36**).

The *Lord of the Rings* trilogy was shot at the same time and then released as three separate films in three different years. In this case to produce the sequels at the same time as making the first film made sense. There were economies of scale and artistic quality would have been lowered by gathering actors, etc. together at a later date (and they might have exercised their option to ask for more pay for later films if the first film was a success). Also box office success was virtually assured and therefore risk of failure of the first or second film relatively low. However, in most cases

Exhibit 6.36 Option to expand approach

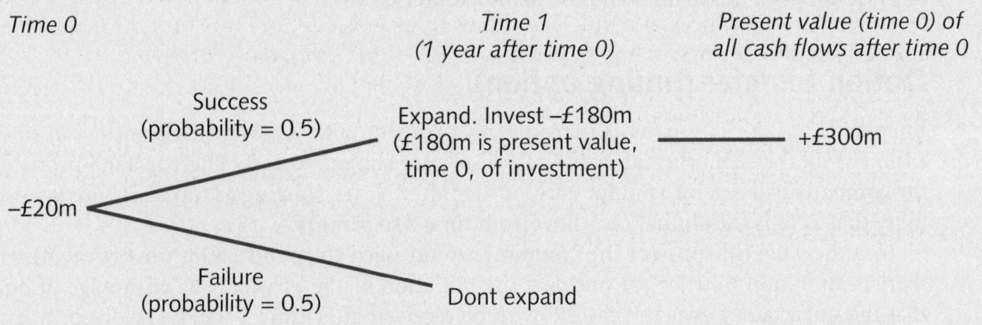

Success	(–£200m + £300m)0.5	= £50m
Failure	(–£20m + 0)0.5	= –£10m
Expected NPV		= +£40m

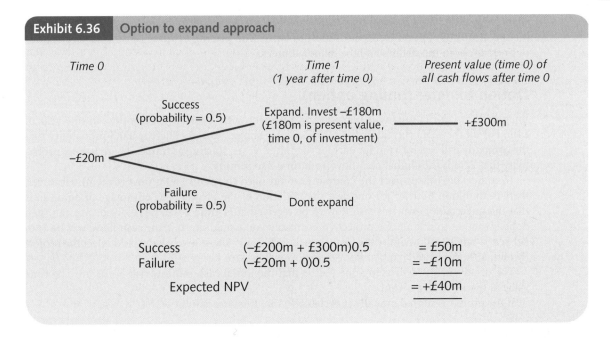

sequels are not made at the same time as the first film. The studio produces one film while being very careful to hold on to the right, but not the obligation, to produce more in the series. By making the first film the studio creates value in the option. However, if the first film flops at the box office the studio can let the option to expand lapse. Analysing the NPV of the first film in isolation may give an artificially low NPV as the present value of the option to expand by producing sequels can be very large. So even if the probability of making the sequel is low the expected NPV rises significantly if a hit series is possible because of the extraordinarily high cash flows these can generate, as in the case of *Toy Story* or *Shrek*. Note that the degree of uncertainty of success is crucial to the decision of whether to produce simultaneously or to buy an option to expand. If uncertainty is high the option is the best bet.

Many mobile phone operators make losses selling 3G services. So why do they persist? One explanation is a Darwinian view of business – businessmen carry on in the field of activity that they are familiar with until stopped by market forces (e.g. liquidation due to inability to compete) or by finance providers starving them of the cash to carry on. An alternative view is that they are rational and shareholder wealth maximising in their perseverance because of the option to expand in this field. Even though 3G may be value destructive, by engaging in this business companies gain knowledge, capabilities and reputation (e.g. brand recognition) which allow them the option to be leading players in the next generation of the technology (4G?) and the one after that. This option to expand can be very valuable. There is a danger in this argument: in some cases managers will use optimistic projections of cash flows from the next generation to justify continued losses. Take, for example, the biotechnology sector where company after company has promised lots of jam tomorrow and then after years of cash burn has nothing to show for it. Amazon.com could go either way. Its years of losses could yet be justified by its market position allowing expansion and extension.

Alliances can be used to create options to expand. For example Corning Glass started research on optical fibres in the 1970s in alliance with telecommunication firms and research companies. This led to more knowledge and a resolution of some uncertainties. It later allied itself with a number of manufacturers. When the success of the project looked assured it exercised its options to fully own and manage the key businesses.

When airlines are considering ordering aircraft from manufacturers they are often uncertain as to how many they will need over, say, the next 20 years. However, because of the long lead times between order and delivery they are compelled to order years in advance. This means they are vulnerable to making the mistake of ordering planes that they may not need. By waiting to see how high demand is before ordering they may suffer from being put to the back of the queue for delivery and the price may have risen. However, by purchasing an option on aircraft the airline gets a fixed price and delivery date. It is up to the airline to decide whether to exercise the option many years from now. Thus the company can wait to see if passenger demand is sufficient to justify buying; if not the option to expand is left to lapse. The pricing of these options is very serious business for both the airlines and the manufacturers.

Option to defer (timing option)

Imagine that your company is considering a project with a certain cash inflow in one year of £4m. For all the years thereafter the cash flows are subject to risk. There is a 0.5 probability that the company will receive £6m for each of the future years, starting at time 2. There is a 0.5 probability that £2m is the annual cash flow from time 2 to infinity.

To undertake this project the company would need to spend £30m now (time 0). However, there is an option to defer for one year the initiation of the project. The advantage of doing so is that the uncertainty over the cash flow to be received after time 1 will be resolved. You can then decide whether to initiate the project (presumably you would do so if the cash flows will be £6m per year – but we will wait for the formal analysis below). Alternatively you could reject the project (presumably this would happen if the cash flow will be £2m per year).

The disadvantage of delaying one year is that the initial cash outflow rises to £33m. The time value of money is 10 per cent.

If the project is started now the expected NPV is £10m (*see* **Exhibit 6.37**).

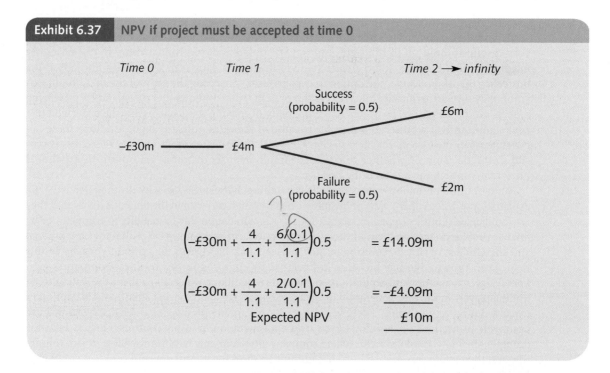

Exhibit 6.37 NPV if project must be accepted at time 0

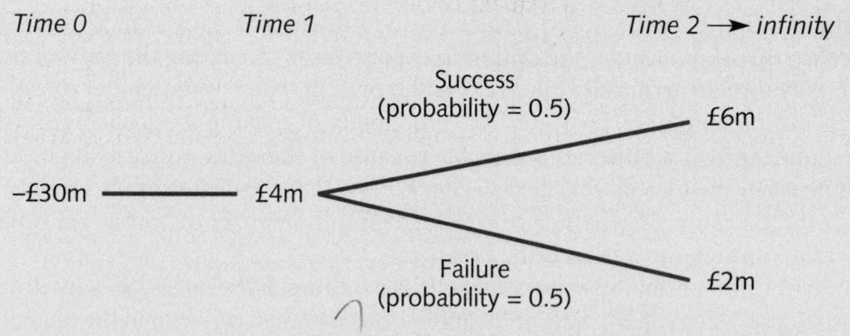

$$\left(-£30\text{m} + \frac{4}{1.1} + \frac{6/0.1}{1.1}\right)0.5 \qquad = £14.09\text{m}$$

$$\left(-£30\text{m} + \frac{4}{1.1} + \frac{2/0.1}{1.1}\right)0.5 \qquad = -£4.09\text{m}$$

Expected NPV £10m

This is a positive NPV and therefore, in the absence of a better mutually exclusive alternative, would be accepted. However, there is a more attractive alternative which is to defer the decision for one year until information on future demand has been received (*see* **Exhibit 6.38**).

Even though the delay of one year results in costs of implementing the project rising by £3m to £33m it is best to defer the project at time 0 so that if the information at time 1 suggests a poor level of sales the project idea can be rejected.

Naturally, if you were making the decision to invest at time 1 you would be faced with one of the future cash flows, either £6m or £2m per year, as the uncertainty is resolved. This would be an easy decision to make. However, this is not the decision you have to make at time 0. Right now you have to decide whether to go ahead or defer for one year. At time 0 you don't know what market demand will be so you still have to calculate expected NPV allowing for the equal probabilities of £6m or £2m being the outcome. What you do know at time 0 is that if the future cash flows are £2m p.a. then you would not go ahead. Thus there is a 50 per cent chance of 'no-go' on the project.

Exhibit 6.38 NPV if option to defer is included

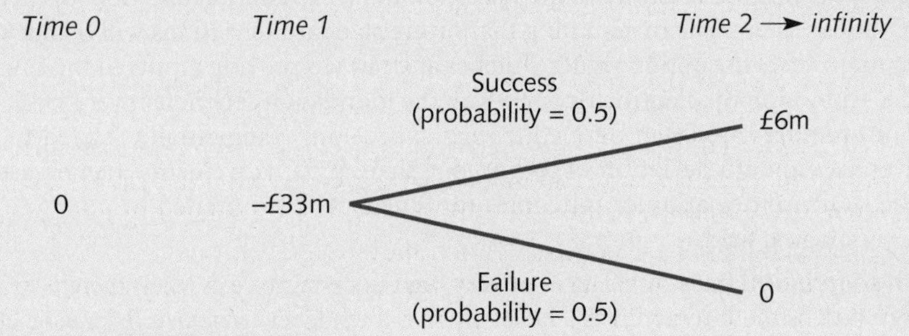

$$\left(\frac{-£33m}{1.1} + \frac{6/0.1}{1.1}\right)0.5 \quad = £12.27m$$

$$0 \times 0.5 \quad = \quad 0$$

$$£12.27m$$

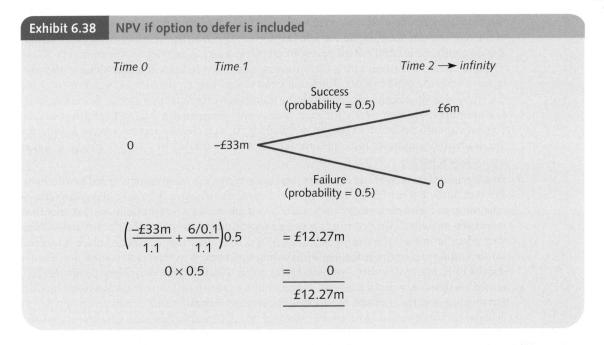

The value of the option to defer is the difference between the NPV if there was no possibility of delay and the NPV with the deferment flexibility, that is £12.27 – £10m = £2.27m.

Greater uncertainty increases the value of the deferral option. If the cash flow for year 2 to infinity changes to £7m (probability 0.5) or £1m (probability 0.5) the expected NPV calculated conventionally as a project to be undertaken at time 0 remains at £10m. The value of being able to wait until the resolution of the cash flow uncertainty increases the NPV to £16.82m.

$$\left(\frac{-£33m}{1.1} + \frac{7/0.1}{1.1}\right)0.5 \quad = £16.82m$$

$$0 \times 0.5 \quad = \quad 0$$

$$£16.82m$$

If a company owns the rights to extract oil (or some other commodity) the NPV of going ahead and doing so right now is often negative. This does not make the ownership of the land and extraction rights worthless. The company could pump the oil whenever it likes, and it is conceivable, given the volatility of the price of oil, that there will come a time when the oil field will become very valuable. Indeed, in order to retain their drilling or mining rights companies have been known to reject multi-million pound offers for unused land (from, say, property developers) because the real option to defer production is worth much more.

Difficulties with real option analysis

- ***Complexity of the valuation process*** This book has explained real options using very simple mathematical examples. Analysts in this field actually make use of complex models, e.g. the Black and Scholes option price model (*see* Appendix to Chapter 24). This complexity means that most managers are unable to participate in the valuation process in an informed manner without extensive training. The danger is that untrained managers treat the exercise as black box decision making: supplying some inputs, e.g. standard deviation of key cost or revenue components, then handing the numbers over to the financial wizards who put them into the model and out pops the answer. The managers are totally unable critically to assess the machinations within the black box. It may be necessary to question the assumptions behind the calculations but the key managers are not empowered to do so. This could lead to poor decision making because the quality of inputs is often poor (*see* next point) and to cynicism about the real options approach throughout the organisation.

- ***Measuring uncertainty*** There is a practical constraint of not being able to measure the degree of uncertainty, and therefore the value of an option. Historic data is usually used (where available), e.g. historic volatility of oil prices for an oil exploration and development project. A leap of faith is then made in assuming that future standard deviations will be like those in the past. In many cases the option valuer clutches at straws to provide inputs to the calculations – giving the impression of scientific rigour, when the foundations are in fact very weak. Standard deviation numbers are often derived from a source only tangentially related to the project, e.g. average standard deviation of technology share price movements may be used as a proxy for the standard deviation of outcomes for a new project initiated by a new company in a new technological field.
- ***Over optimism*** In circumstances of very high uncertainty, e.g. when there is brand new technology such as the Internet in the 1990s, there is a tendency to be overoptimistic about the value of expanding. In 1999 new 'dotcom' companies joined the stock market proclaiming that once their model was established the potential for scaling up was almost limitless. The market was so huge, they said, that even if the company had an 80 per cent chance of complete failure it was still worth backing as it might be the one left standing with options to expand to control the industry standard (the one most visited by travellers, pet owners, book buyers, etc.). These companies presented 'analysis' from 'independent' experts on the growth of Internet connections (usually exponential) and the revenues in this field (again exponentially rising). Sadly too many people believed the hype. Similar hype can be exhibited by junior and middle managers about a growth area they are particularly enthusiastic about. Senior managers need to view the high ranges of likely outcomes presented to them with scepticism. In particular they should ask whether the firm's competitors are really going to do nothing while they take all this market for themselves.
- ***What is the life of an option?*** It may not be clear how long the option value will be available to the firm. For example, a pharmaceutical company may have invested considerably in cardiovascular drug R & D, providing it with potential competitive advantages for many years to come through its options to expand to new generations of drugs. But it is impossible to be precise on how many years the option to develop more drugs in this field will be valuable: is it three years? five or 20 years? The life of the option depends on so many variables, e.g. developments in surgery or competitors' actions.

Perhaps it is because of these difficulties that only 3.6 per cent of large UK firms say that a real options approach to investment analysis is 'important' – none replied that it was 'very important' and 56.6 per cent said it was 'not important' (Alkaraan and Northcott, 2006).

Some risk analysis

For the purposes of analysing **Case study 6.2** we will make a number of bold simplifying assumptions in order to make the analysis manageable in the context of this textbook. The estimates that follow are based on one of many potential adjustments to the basic data. You may like to make your own assumptions and forecasts based on alternative perspectives. (The author is not privy to non-public data held only by RJB (now UK Coal) and therefore is unable to provide a true representation of the prospects for this project.)

Case study 6.2 RJB Mining: risky coalfields

Background

RJB Mining, led by Richard Budge, was a small company only recently quoted on the London Stock Exchange, when in November 1994 it tried to raise over £1bn of funds to buy the English mining regions of British Coal. In the accounts to 1994, RJB Mining made pre-tax profits of £12m on a turnover of £75m and was capitalised on the stock exchange at less than £160m.

The sale of the 17 deep mines and 16 open-cast sites was part of the UK government's privatisation programme and RJB was negotiating around a price of £914m, at least 50 per cent more than the nearest rival. If RJB's projections were correct and it could produce profits of over £200m per year, then £914m could be regarded as cheap. But it is a large 'if'. Richard Budge had a hard time trying to persuade City institutions that the project was viable. Together with advisers Barclays de Zoete Wedd, the company set about the task of trying to raise £425m in equity and £628m in debt to both finance the bid and provide working capital. In some parts of the financial world there was great scepticism concerning the projections put forward by RJB. The key features are these:

Financial projections

Year end Dec. 31

(£m)	95	96	97	98	99	Total
Turnover	1,244	1,276	1,258	1,218	1,238	6,234
Costs	1,073	1,052	1,029	1,033	1,031	
Profit before interest and taxation	171	224	229	185	207	1,016
Pro-forma net interest	(55)	(36)	(18)	1	13	
Profit before taxation	116	188	211	186	220	
Operating cash flow*	255	278	292	269	261	1,355
Cumulative cash flow*	255	533	825	1,094	1,355	

*Before interest, dividends and taxation. NB Projections exclude results for the existing RJB Group.

Key assumptions

	95	96	97	98	99
Volume sold (million tonnes)	35.3	35.7	34.7	34.1	33.8
Volume produced (million tonnes)	33.4	34.4	33.6	33.6	35.2
Ave. selling price/gigajoule (1994 prices) (£)	1.43	1.40	1.38	1.32	1.32
Ave. cost/tonne (£) (incl. overheads and inflation)	30.4	29.5	29.7	30.3	30.5

Inflation 3 per cent a year.

Market requirements for coal*

	Conservative case 31 Mar. 2000	Favourable case 31 Mar. 2000	RJB projection 31 Dec. 1999
ESI (Electricity)	27.1	43.0	
Industrial	6.4	8.5	
Domestic	2.0	3.0	
Total	**35.5**	**54.5**	**33.8**

* Million tonnes.

RJB was thought, by some analysts, to have overestimated the size of the post-1998 market by a large percentage and that even the 'conservative' estimates were at the high end of the likely outcome. Mr Charles Kernot, an analyst at Credit Lyonnais Laing, commented, 'He may be able to make £220m in 1998, but it looks tight.'

The bank lenders were being asked to provide £528m (the remaining £100m was to be derived from a corporate bond issue) on the expectation that RJB would have paid them back all their capital before 1998. The year 1998 is so important, because prior to that date the company would have firm contracts, inherited from British Coal, to sell 29m tonnes a year to the electricity generators at agreed prices. Thus, a total annual volume of around 35m tonnes for the first three years seemed credible. Raising the debt capital was likely to be less troublesome than the equity. Potential shareholders were concerned about the less predictable years after 1998. RJB were confident that volumes and prices would not fall dramatically, whereas others suggested that RJB would struggle to sell 25m tonnes a year and the price would fall to £1.15 a gigajoule or less, given the potential for intense competition.

Source of data: RJB annual reports and accounts www.rjb.co.uk. Reproduced by permission of COAL.

Background reading: *Financial Times*, 18 November 1994.

Note: RJB Mining changed its name to UK Coal in 2001.

The financial projections for turnover and operating cash flow are as set out in **Exhibit 6.39**.

Exhibit 6.39 Turnover and cash flow projections

Year £m	1995	1996	1997	1998	1999
Turnover	1,244	1,276	1,258	1,218	1,238
Operating cash flow	255	278	292	269	261

We will assume that the annual cash flows for the year 2000 and beyond are the same as for 1999.

Imagine you are an analyst advising a pension fund on whether to provide equity and debt finance for this enterprise and you believe the following outcomes are possible:

1 Turnover is the same as RJB's projections – probability 0.25.
2 Turnover is 10 per cent greater than RJB's projections – probability 0.10.
3 Turnover is 25 per cent less than the projections – probability 0.65.

To simplify the calculations, assume costs, interest and tax are unaffected by turnover changes, thus any lost or gained turnover feeds directly into cash flows. (This is an unforgivable oversimplification of the real world, but the calculation would be too complicated for the reader to focus on the risk analysis if more realistic assumptions were made.) Also assume that the 'operating cash flows' as calculated by RJB are truly reflective of the theoretically correct cash flows we would arrive at using our textbook knowledge.

The cost of capital is 9 per cent, time 0 is 1 January 1995 and the cash flows occur at year ends.

Expected net present value assuming £914m is the initial outflow

If turnover is as expected:

$$\text{NPV} = -914 + \frac{255}{1.09} + \frac{278}{(1.09)^2} + \frac{292}{(1.09)^3} + \frac{269}{(1.09)^4} + \frac{261}{(1.09)^5} + \frac{261}{0.09} \div (1.09)^5 = £2{,}024\text{m}$$

If turnover is 10 per cent greater than projections

Time (years)	0	1	2	3	4	5	6→∞
RJB's projected cash flows (£m)	–914	255	278	292	269	261	261
plus 10% of projected turnover		124.4	127.6	125.8	121.8	123.8	123.8
	–914	379.4	405.6	417.8	390.8	384.8	384.8

Discounted cash flows:

$$NPV = -914 + \frac{379.4}{1.09} + \frac{405.6}{(1.09)^2} + \frac{417.8}{(1.09)^3} + \frac{390.8}{(1.09)^4} + \frac{384.8}{(1.09)^5} + \frac{384.8}{0.09} \div (1.09)^5 = £3{,}403.84m$$

If turnover is 25 per cent less than projections

Time (years)	0	1	2	3	4	5	6→∞
RJB's projected cash flows (£m)	–914	255	278	292	269	261	261
less 25% of projected turnover		311	319	314.5	304.5	309.5	309.5
	–914	–56	–41	–22.5	–35.5	–48.5	–48.5

Discounted cash flows:

$$NPV = -914 - \frac{56}{1.09} - \frac{41}{(1.09)^2} - \frac{22.5}{(1.09)^3} - \frac{35.5}{(1.09)^4} - \frac{48.5}{(1.09)^5} - \frac{48.5}{0.09} \div (1.09)^5 = -£1{,}424.17m$$

Expected NPV

$$(2{,}024.42 \times 0.25) + (3{,}403.84 \times 0.1) + (-1{,}424.17 \times 0.65) = -£79.22m$$

Standard deviation of NPV

NPV	Probability, p_i	Expected NPV ($\overline{NPV}$)	$(NPV - \overline{NPV})^2 p_i$
2024.42	0.25	–79.22	1,106,304
3403.84	0.1	–79.22	1,213,157
–1424.17	0.65	–79.22	1,175,814
			Variance = 3,495,275
			Standard deviation = 1,869.56

If we assume that the distribution of returns is normal and bell shaped, we can answer some further questions.[1]

What is the probability of the rate of return being less than the required rate of return (9 per cent)?

This question relates to the probability of a negative NPV (*see* **Exhibit 6.40**).

$$Z = \frac{X - \mu}{\sigma}$$

$$Z = \frac{0 - (-79.22)}{1{,}869.56} = 0.0424$$

The probability of an outcome between –79.22 and 0 = 1.6 per cent.
Therefore the probability of an outcome less than 0 = 51.6 per cent.

[1] Strictly speaking, we are making a statistical gaffe here because the probability distribution is not symmetrical. But for the purpose of illustrating the usefulness of risk analysis we take the chance of upsetting statisticians.

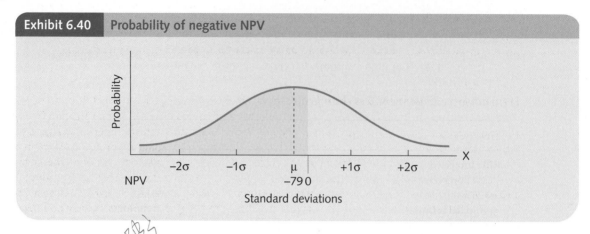

Exhibit 6.40 Probability of negative NPV

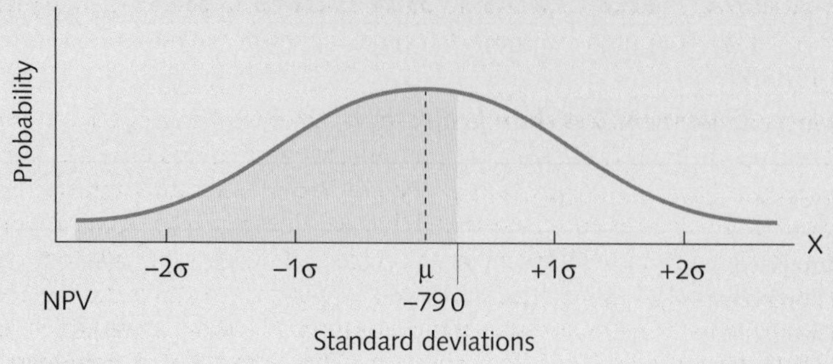

If insolvency occurs at an NPV of negative £200m, what is the probability of insolvency?

$$Z = \frac{X - \mu}{\sigma}$$

$$Z = \frac{-200 - (-79.22)}{1,869.56} = -0.065$$

The probability of an outcome between −200 and −79.22 = 2.6 per cent.
The probability of insolvency = 50 per cent − 2.6 per cent = 47.4 per cent.

If the champagne corks can start to fly at an NPV of £1,000m, what is the probability of this being achieved?

$$Z = \frac{X - \mu}{\sigma}$$

$$Z = \frac{1,000 - (-79.22)}{1,869.56} = 0.577$$

The probability of an outcome between −79.22 and 1,000 = 21.8 per cent.
The probability of an outcome greater than £1,000m = 50% − 21.8% = 28.2 per cent.

The data can be used to practise risk profiling by employing the other techniques shown in this chapter. Perhaps the reader would like to make a few assumptions and practise using the risk-adjusted discount rate method, sensitivity and scenario analysis.

Comment

In this analysis we have taken a much more pessimistic view of the prospects than did RJB. Perhaps it is far too pessimistic to assume that there is a 65 per cent chance that turnover will be only 75 per cent of the level forecast by the professionals at RJB and BZW. Having completed the statistical analysis we have a better picture of the nature of this project and can make far more informed choices. However, we cannot second-guess the risk appetite of the pension fund managers, given their particular context.

At the end of the negotiating period, RJB Mining paid £99m less than was first mooted, at £815m, and it raised a total of £894m mainly from the major institutions, although a few small shareholders did contribute. By mid-1995 the company had performed so well that it reduced its bank debt to around £150m. By mid-1996 RJB was regarded as having such a strong balance sheet, with gearing at 49 per cent, that the group felt confident enough to announce a £100m share buy-back programme. In addition, the company started an overseas expansion, spending £71.5m to acquire 43 per cent of CIM Resources of Australia. The share price almost doubled during the 18 months following the English coalfields purchase. However, it collapsed in late 1997 as reports on the negotiations over the electricity generator contracts starting in 1998 were pessimistic.

Events after 1998

Life got a lot tougher for RJB. As can be seen from **Exhibit 6.41** turnover was much less than projected at the time of the fund raising: for example, for 1999 it was expected to be £1,238m; it was actually £688m. With the deregulation of the electricity generating industry there was a rush to produce electricity using gas and the demand for coal slumped. The electricity producers were in a strong bargaining position when negotiating future coal prices, especially as the price on the international market for coal was depressed. RJB sells 85 per cent of its coal to the electricity producers and so was unable to resist the pressure to lower prices. The share price, which had peaked at 625p in 1996, slumped to 25p in 2000. The original £400m or more of shareholders' money had been reduced to about £30m.

Exhibit 6.41 RJB

		1997	1998	1999	2000	2001	2002	2003
Turnover	£m	1,125	823	688	705	663	597	564
Profit before interest and tax (and exceptional items)	£m	190	60	28	(26)	(21)	14	(1)
Costs	£m	942	764	675	736	687	662	556
Net interest	£m	19	20	17	8	5	6	7
Operating cash flow	£m	281	96	85	82	116	9	46
Volume sold (million tonnes)		31.2	25.9	22.5	22.2	20	19.5	17.9
Average selling price £/GJ (current price)	£	1.60	1.40	1.25	1.26	n/a	1.19	1.12
Average income/tonne	£	35	31	29.3	29.9	30.3	n/a	n/a
Average cost/tonne	£	30	29	28.8	32	31.4	n/a	n/a
Market requirements for coal		54	54	45	46	51	n/a	n/a

Sources: Financial Times (numerous articles), RJB annual reports and accounts, www.rjb.co.uk

In the years 2004, 2005 and 2006 the company made losses on its operations. However, despite everything going wrong with the coal business the share price rocketed to over £4 and equity market capitalisation to £700m in early 2008. The reason for this was that the firm owned hundreds of valuable real options. It owned 50,000 acres of land and much of it was well placed for property development. It applied for planning permission for 14,000 homes and 25m sq. feet of commercial and industrial property. The landbank was valued at around £600m–£800m.

Concluding comments

This chapter, and the previous one, have dealt with some of the more sophisticated aspects of project analysis. They have, it is hoped, encouraged the reader to consider a wider range of factors when embarking on investment appraisal. Taking into account more real-world influences such as inflation, rationing, tax and risk will enable the appraiser and the decision maker to obtain a clearer picture of the nature of the proposal being discussed. Greater realism and more information clears away some of the fog which envelops many capital investment decision-making processes.

However, this chapter has focused primarily on the technical/mathematical aspects of the appraisal stage of the investment process sequence. While these aspects should not be belittled, as we ought to improve the analysis wherever we can, it should be noted that a successful programme of investment usually rests far more on quality management of other stages in the process. Issues of human communication, enthusiasm and commitment are as vital to investment returns as, for example, assessing risk correctly.

Key points and concepts

- **Risk** – more than one possible outcome.
- **Objective probability** – likelihood of outcomes established mathematically or from historic data.
- **Subjective probability** – personal judgement of the likely range of outcomes along with the likelihood of their occurrence.
- **Risk can be allowed for by raising or lowering the discount rate:**

  Advantages:

  - easy to adopt and understand;
  - some theoretical support.

  Drawbacks: susceptible to subjectivity in risk premium and risk class allocation.
- **Sensitivity analysis** views a project's NPV under alternative assumed values of variables, changed one at a time. It permits a broader picture to be presented, enables search resources to be more efficiently directed and allows contingency plans to be made.

  Drawbacks of sensitivity analysis:

  - does not assign probabilities and these may need to be added for a fuller picture;
  - each variable is changed in isolation.
- **Scenario analysis** permits a number of factors to be changed simultaneously. Allows best- and worst-case scenarios.
- **Probability analysis** allows for more precision in judging project viability.
- **Expected return** – the mean or average outcome is calculated by weighting each of the possible outcomes by the probability of occurrence and then summing the result:

$$\bar{x} = \sum_{i=1}^{i=n} (x_i p_i)$$

- **Standard deviation** – a measure of dispersion around the expected value:

$$\sigma_x = \sqrt{\sigma_x^2} \text{ or } \sqrt{\sum_{i=1}^{i=n} \{(x_i - \bar{x})^2 p_i\}}$$

- It is assumed that most people are **risk averters** who demonstrate **diminishing marginal utility**, preferring less risk to more risk.
- **Mean-variance rule:**

  Project X will be preferred to Project Y if at least one of the following conditions applies:

  1. The expected return of X is at least equal to the expected return of Y, and the variance is less than that of Y.
  2. The expected return of X exceeds that of Y and the variance is equal to or less than that of Y.
- If a normal, bell-shaped distribution of possible outcomes can be assumed, the probabilities of various events, for example insolvency, can be calculated using the **Z statistic**.

$$Z = \frac{X - \mu}{\sigma}$$

- **Careful interpretation** is needed when using a risk-free discount rather than a risk-adjusted discount rate for probability analysis.
- **Problems with probability analysis:**
  - undue faith can be placed in quantified results;
  - can be too complicated for general understanding and communication;
  - projects may be viewed in isolation rather than as part of the firm's mixture of projects.
- Sensitivity analysis and scenario analysis are the most popular methods of allowing for project risk.
- The **real options** perspective takes account of future managerial flexibility whereas the traditional NPV famework tends to assume away such flexibility. Real options give the right, but not the obligation to take action in the future.

References and further reading

Alkaraan, F. and Northcott, D. (2006) 'Strategic capital investment decision-making: a role for emergent analysis tools? A study of practice in large UK manufacturing companies', *British Accounting Review*, 38, pp. 149–73.

Arnold, G.C. and Hartzopoulos, P.D. (2000) 'The theory-practice gap in capital budgeting: evidence from the United Kingdom', *Journal of Business Finance and Accounting*, 27(5) and (6), June/July, pp. 603–26.
Discussion on the use of alternative risk adjustment methods is provided.

Amran, M. and Kulatilaka, N. (1999) *Real Options: Managing Strategic Investment in an Uncertain World*. Boston, MA: Harvard Business School Press.

Bierman, H. and Smidt, S. (2006) *The Capital Budgeting Decision*, 9th edn. London: Routledge.
An introduction to risk in project appraisal.

Bierman, H. and Smidt, S. (2006) *Advanced Capital Budgeting*. London: Routledge.

Brealey, R.A., Myers, S.C. and Allan, F. (2008) *Principles of Corporate Finance*. 9th edn. New York: McGraw Hill.
Contains an intermediate-level discussion of real options including the application of option valuation models.

Brennan, M.J. and Schwartz, E.S. (1985) 'Evaluating natural resource investments', *Journal of Business*, Vol. 58, pp. 135–57.
A pioneering paper in the field of real options.

Brennan, M.J. and Trigeorgis, L. (eds) (2000) *Project Flexibility, Agency, and Competition: New Developments in the Theory and Application of Real Options*. Oxford, New York: Oxford University Press.
Contains a number of important papers on real options.

Childs, P.D., Ott, S.M. and Triantis, A.J. (1998) 'Capital budgeting for interrelated projects: a real options approach', *Journal of Financial and Quantitative Analysis*, Vol. 33(3), pp. 305–34.
Applications of the real options approach to the case of development-stage expenditure for mutually exclusive projects. Advanced level.

Chittenden, F. and Darregia, M. (2004) 'Capital Investment decision making: some results from studying entrepreneurial businesses', www.icaew.co.uk.
Many entrepreneurial firms rely more on qualitative assessments than formal capital budgeting. Also they build in options through leasing, hiring and renting because they are cheap to get out of.

Copeland, T. and Antikarov, V. (2001) *Real Options: A Practitioner's Guide*. New York: Texere.
A technical and mathematical approach to the subject.

Copeland, T. and Tufano, P. (2004) 'A real-world way to manage real options', *Harvard Business Review*, March, pp. 1–11.
A simplified use of option analysis.

Dixit, A. and Pindyck, R. (1994) *Investment Under Uncertainty*. Princeton, NJ: Princeton University Press.

Dixit, A.K. and Pindyck, R.S. (1995) 'The options approach to capital investment', *Harvard Business Review*, May–June. (Also reproduced in J. Rutterford (ed.) *Financial Strategy*. New York: John Wiley, 1998.)
An easy-to-follow discussion of inadequacy of the traditional simple NPV approach and an introduction to the real options perspective.

Graham, J.R. and Harvey, C.R. (2001) 'The theory and practice of corporate finance: evidence from the field', *Journal of Financial Economics*, Vol. 60, Nos 2–3, May, pp. 187–243.
It shows the use of risk techniques in US corporations.

Hertz, D.B. (1964) 'Risk analysis in capital investment', *Harvard Business Review*, January/ February, pp. 95–106.
Excellent discussion of risk and the use of probability analysis.

Hertz, D.B and Thomas, H. (1984) *Practical Risk Analysis: An Approach through Case Histories.* Chichester: Wiley.
Contains some interesting case studies of companies applying the principles and techniques discussed in this chapter.

Hillier, F.S. (1963) 'The derivation of probabilistic information for the evaluation of risky investments', *Management Science*, April, pp. 443–57.
The use of standard deviation in project appraisal.

Ho, S. and Pike, R.H. (1991) 'Risk analysis in capital budgeting contexts: simple or sophisticated', *Accounting and Business Research*, Summer, pp. 227–38.
Excellent survey of risk-handling techniques adopted in 146 large companies.

Howell, S., Stark, A., Newton, D., Paxson, D., Cavus, M. and Pereira, J. (2001) *Real Options: Evaluating Corporate Investment Opportunities in a Dynamic World.* Harlow: Financial Times Prentice Hall.
An intermediate-level book that tries to make mathematical real option analysis digestible.

Journal of Applied Corporate Finance (2001), Summer, contains many articles on real options.

Magee, J.F. (1964a) 'Decision trees for decision making', *Harvard Business Review*, July/August, pp. 126–38.
The use of decision trees is explained in clear terms.

Magee, J.F. (1964b) 'How to use decision trees in capital investment', *Harvard Business Review*, September/October, pp. 79–96.
Decision trees applied to project appraisal.

Markowitz, H. (1959) *Portfolio Selection.* New York: Wiley.
Utility foundations of mean-variance analysis.

Merton, R.C. (1998) 'Application of option-pricing theory: twenty-five years later', *American Economic Review*, June, No. 3, pp. 323–49.
Mostly focused on option price theory. Advanced level.

Moel, A. and Tufano, P. (2002) 'When are real options exercised? An empirical study of mine closings', *The Review of Financial Studies*, Spring, Vol. 15, No. 1, pp. 35–64.
The usefulness of real option analysis is demonstrated.

Pike, R.H. (1988) 'An empirical study of the adoption of sophisticated capital budgeting practices and decision-making effectiveness', *Accounting and Business Research*, 18(72), pp. 341–51.
Interesting evidence on the practical use of risk analysis techniques.

Pike, R.H. (1996) 'A longitudinal survey of capital budgeting practices', *Journal of Business Finance and Accounting*, 23(1), January.
Clearly described evidence on the capital investment appraisal practices of major UK companies.

Quigg, L. (1993) 'Empirical testing of real option pricing models', *Journal of Finance*, Vol. 48, No. 2, pp. 621–40.
An early application of real option theory. Advanced level.

Schwartz, E.S. and Trigeorgis, L. (eds) (2001) *Real Options and Investment Under Uncertainty: Classical Readings and Recent Contributions.* London, Cambridge, MA: MIT Press.
The major articles in the field are included – dozens of them.

Swalm, R.O. (1966) 'Utility theory – insights into risk taking', *Harvard Business Review*, November/December, pp. 123–36.
An accessible account of utility theory.

Triantis, A.J. and Hodder, J.E. (1990) 'Valuing flexibility as a complex option', *Journal of Finance*, Vol. 45, pp. 545–66.
An application to manufacturing systems. Advanced level.

Trigeorgis, L. (1996) *Real Options: Managerial Flexibility and Strategy in Resource Allocation.* Cambridge, MA: MIT Press.

Van Putten, A. B. and MacMillan I.C. (2004) 'Making real options really work', *Harvard Business Review*, December, pp. 1–8.
Easy-to-read article explaining the complementary use of real option analysis and DCF analysis.

Case study recommendations

Please see www.pearsoned.co.uk/arnold for case study synopses.

- Phuket Beach Hotel: Valuing mutually exclusive capital projects. Authors: S.H. Chan, K. Wang and M. Ho (2001). Centre for Asian Business Cases. (Also available via Harvard.)
- Airbus A3XX: Developing the world's largest commercial jet (A). Authors: B. Esty and M. Kane (2004) Harvard Business School.

Self-review questions

1 Explain, with reference to probability and sensitivity analysis, why the examination of the most likely outcome of an investment in isolation can both be limiting and give a false impression.

2 What do you understand by the following?

a Risk-lover.
b Diminishing marginal utility.
c Standard deviation.

3 Discuss the consequences of the quantification of personal judgements about future eventualities. Are we right to undertake precise analysis on this sort of basis?

4 Explain the attraction of using more than one method to examine risk in project appraisal.

5 Why has the development of powerful computers helped the more widespread adoption of scenario analysis?

6 Suggest reasons why probability analysis is used so infrequently by major international corporations.

7 'The flatter the line on the sensitivity graph, the less attention we have to pay to that variable.' Is the executive who made this statement correct in all cases?

8 If one project has a higher standard deviation and a higher expected return than another, can we use the mean-variance rule?

9 What does it mean if a project has a probability of a negative NPV of 20 per cent when (a) the risk-free discount rate is used, (b) the risk-adjusted discount rate is used?

10 What is the probability of an outcome being within 0.5 of a standard deviation from the expected outcome?

Questions and problems

myfinancelab ***Questions with an icon are also available for practice in MyFinanceLab with additional supporting resources.***

Answers for those questions marked with an asterisk are reserved for the Lecturer's guide.

1 Calculate the NPV of the following project with a discount rate of 9 per cent.

Point in time (yearly intervals)	0	1	2	3	4
Cash flow (£000s)	–800	300	250	400	500

Now examine the impact on NPV of raising the discount rate by the following risk premiums:

a 3 percentage points;
b 6 percentage points.

?

2* (*Examination level*) Cashion International are considering a project that is susceptible to risk. An initial investment of £90,000 will be followed by three years each with the following 'most likely' cash flows (there is no inflation or tax):

	£	£
Annual sales (volume of 100,000 units multiplied by estimated sales price of £2)		200,000
Annual costs		
Labour	100,000	
Materials	40,000	
Other	10,000	
	150,000	(150,000)
		50,000

The initial investment consists of £70,000 in machines, which have a zero scrap value at the end of the three-year life of the project and £20,000 in additional working capital which is recoverable at the end. The discount rate is 10 per cent.

Required

a Draw a sensitivity graph showing the sensitivity of NPV to changes in the following:
   - sales price;
   - labour costs;
   - material costs;
   - discount rate.

b For the four variables considered in (a) state the break-even point and the percentage deviation from 'most likely' levels before break-even NPV is reached (assuming all other variables remain constant).

(An Excel spreadsheet version of these calculations is available in the Lecturers-only section at www.pearsoned.co.uk/arnold)

?

3* Use the data in question 2 to calculate the NPV in two alternative scenarios:

Worst-case scenario		***Best-case scenario***	
Sales volume	90,000	Sales volume	110,000
Sales price	£1.90	Sales price	£2.15
Labour costs	£110,000	Labour costs	£95,000
Material costs	£44,000	Material costs	£39,000
Other costs	£13,000	Other costs	£9,000
Project life	3 years	Project life	3 years
Discount rate	13%	Discount rate	10%
Initial investment	£90,000	Initial investment	£90,000

?

4 (*Examination level*) A company is trying to decide whether to make a £400,000 investment in a new product area. The project will last 10 years and the £400,000 of machinery will have a zero scrap value. Other best estimate forecasts are:

- sales volume of 22,000 units per year;
- sales price £21 per unit;
- variable direct costs £16 per unit.

There are no other costs and inflation and tax are not relevant.

a The senior management team have asked you to calculate the internal rate of return (IRR) of this project based on these estimates.

b To gain a broader picture they also want you to recalculate IRR on the assumption that each of the following variables changes adversely by 5 per cent in turn:
   - sales volume;
   - sales price;
   - variable direct costs.

c Explain to the management team how this analysis can help to direct attention and further work to improve the likelihood of a successful project implementation.

(In addition to the solution in Appendix VII an Excel spreadsheet version of these calculations is available at www.pearsoned.co.uk/arnold)

?

5 Project W may yield a return of £2m with a probability of 0.3, or a return of £4m with a probability of 0.7. Project X may earn a negative return of £2m with a probability of 0.3 or a positive return of £8m with a probability of 0.7. Project Y yields a return of £2m which is certain. Compare the mean return and risk of the projects.

?

6 The returns from a project are normally distributed with a mean of £220,000 and a standard deviation of £160,000. If the project loses more than £80,000 the company will be made insolvent. What is the probability of insolvency?

?

7 (*Examination level*) Toughnut plc is considering a two-year project that has the following probability distribution of returns:

Year 1		*Year 2*	
Return	*Probability*	*Return*	*Probability*
8,000	0.1	4,000	0.3
10,000	0.6	8,000	0.7
12,000	0.3		

The events in each year are independent of other years (that is, there are no conditional probabilities). An outlay of £15,000 is payable at Time 0 and the other cash flows are receivable at the year ends. The risk-adjusted discount rate is 11 per cent.

Calculate

a The expected NPV.
b The standard deviation of NPV.
c The probability of the NPV being less than zero assuming a normal distribution of return – (bell shaped and symmetrical about the mean).
d Interpret the figure calculated in (c).

?

8 A project with an initial outlay of £1m has a 0.2 probability of producing a return of £800,000 in Year 1 and a 0.8 probability of delivering a return of £500,000 in Year 1. If the £800,000 result occurs then the second year could return either £700,000 (probability of 0.5) or £300,000 (probability of 0.5). If the £500,000 result for Year 1 occurs then either £600,000 (probability 0.7) or £400,000 (probability 0.3) could be received in the second year. All cash flows occur on anniversary dates. The discount rate is 12 per cent.

Calculate the expected return and standard deviation. ?

(An Excel spreadsheet version of the calculation is available at www.pearsoned.co.uk/arnold)

9 A project requires an immediate outflow of cash of £400,000 in return for the following probable cash flows:

State of economy	*Probability*	*End of Year 1 (£)*	*End of Year 2 (£)*
Recession	0.3	100,000	150,000
Growth	0.5	300,000	350,000
Boom	0.2	500,000	550,000

Assume that the state of the economy will be the same in the second year as in the first. The required rate of return is 8 per cent. There is no tax or inflation.

a Calculate the expected NPV.

b Calculate the standard deviation of NPV. ?

10 (*Examination level*) RJW plc is a quoted firm which operates ten lignite mines in Wales. It has total assets of £50m and the value of its shares is £90m. RJW plc's directors perceive a great opportunity in the UK government's privatisation drive. They have held preliminary discussions with the government about the purchase of the 25 lignite mines in England. The purchase price suggested by the Treasury is £900m.

For two months the directors have been engaged in a fund-raising campaign to persuade City financial institutions to provide £500m of new equity capital for RJW and £400m of fixed interest rate debt capital in the form of bank loans.

You are a senior analyst with the fund management arm of Klein-Ben Wensons and last week you listened attentively to RJW's presentation. You were impressed by their determination, acumen and track record but have some concerns about their figures for the new project.

RJW's projections are as follows, excluding the cost of purchasing the mines:

Table 1: Cash flows for the English lignite mines: RJW's estimate

Time t	*0*	*1*	*2*	*3*	*4*	*5 and all subsequent years*
Sales (£m) (cash inflows)		1,200	1,250	1,300	1,320	1,350
Less operating costs (£m) (cash outflows)		1,070	1,105	1,150	1,190	1,200
Net cash flows (£m)		130	145	150	130	150

You believe the probability of RJW's projections being correct to be 50 per cent (or 0.5). You also estimate that there is a chance that RJW's estimates are over-cautious. There is a 30 per cent probability of the cash flows being as shown in Table 2 (excluding the cost of purchasing the mines).

Table 2: A more optimistic forecast

Time t	*0*	*1*	*2*	*3*	*4*	*5 and all subsequent years*
Sales (£m) (cash inflows)		1,360	1,416.7	1,473.33	1,496	1,530
Less operating costs (£m) (cash outflows)		1,100	1,140	1,190	1,225	1,250
Net cash flows (£m)		260	276.7	283.33	271	280

On the other hand, events may not turn out as well as RJW's estimates. There is a 20 per cent probability that the cash flows will be as shown in Table 3.

Table 3: A more pessimistic scenario (excluding purchase cost of mines)

Time t	*0*	*1*	*2*	*3*	*4*	*5 and all subsequent years*
Sales (£m) (cash inflows)		1,166.67	1,216.7	1,266.67	1,144	1,170
Less operating costs (£m)(cash outflows)		1,070	1,105	1,150	1,165	1,150
Net cash flows (£m)		96.67	111.7	116.67	–21	20

Assume

1 The cost of capital can be taken to be 14 per cent.

2 Cash flows will arise at year ends except the initial payment to the government which occurs at Time 0.

Required

a Calculate the expected net present value (NPV) and the standard deviation of the NPV for the project to buy the English lignite mines if £900m is taken to be the initial cash outflow.

b There is a chance that events will turn out to be much worse than RJW would like. If the net present value of the English operation turns out to be worse than negative £550m, RJW will be liquidated. What is the probability of avoiding liquidation?

c If the NPV is greater than positive £100m then the share price of RJW will start to rise rapidly in two or three years after the purchase. What is the probability of this occurring?

?

11 (*Examination level*) Alder plc is considering four projects, for which the cash flows have been calculated as follows:

	Points in time (yearly intervals)					
Project	*0*	*1*	*2*	*3*	*4*	
A	–£500,000	+£600,000				Project ends after 1 year.
B	–£200,000	+£200,000	+£150,000			Project ends after 2 years.
C	–£700,000	0	£1million			Project ends after 2 years.
D	–£150,000	+£60,000	+£60,000	+£60,000	+£60,000	Project ends after 4 years.

The appropriate rate of discount is judged to be 10 per cent for risk-free projects.

Accepting one of the projects does not exclude the possibility of accepting another one, and each can only be undertaken once.

Assume that the annual cash flows arise on the anniversary dates of the initial outlay and that there is no inflation or tax.

Required

a Calculate the net present value for each of the projects on the assumption that the cash flows are not subject to any risk. Rank the projects on the basis of these calculations, assuming there is no capital rationing.

b Briefly explain two reasons why you might regard net present value as being superior to internal rate of return for project appraisal.

c Now assume that at Time 0 only £700,000 of capital is available for project investment. Calculate the wisest allocation of these funds to achieve the optimum return on the assumption that each of the projects is divisible (fractions may be undertaken). What is the highest net present value achievable using the risk-free discount rate?

d A change in the law now makes the outcome of Project D subject to risk because the cash flows depend upon the actions of central government. The project will still require an initial cash outflow of £150,000. If the government licensing agency decides at Time 0 to permit Alder a licence for a one-year trial production and sale of the product, then the net cash in flow at the end of the first year will be +£50,000. If the agency decides to allow the product to go on sale from time 0 under a four-year licence without a trial run the cash inflow in at the end of Year 1 will be +£70,000. The probability of the government insisting on a trial run is 50 per cent and the probability of full licensing is 50 per cent.

If the trial run takes place then there are two possibilities for future cash flows. The first, with a probability of 30 per cent, is that the product is subsequently given a full licence for the remaining three years, resulting in a net cash flow of +£60,000 per year. The second possibility, with a probability of 70 per cent, is that the government does not grant a licence and production and sales cease after the first year.

If a full licence is granted at time 0 then there are two possible sets of cash flows for the subsequent three years. First, the product sells very well, producing an annual net cash flow of +£80,000 – this has a probability of 60 per cent. Secondly, the product sells less well, producing annual cash flows of +£60,000 – this has a probability of 40 per cent.

The management wish you to calculate the probability of this product producing a negative net present value (assume a normal distribution). The appropriate discount rate for a project of this risk class is 13 per cent.

?

12* (Examination level) The UK manufacturer of footwear, Willow plc, is considering a major investment in a new product area, novelty umbrellas. It hopes that these products will become fashion icons.

The following information has been collected:

- The project will have a limited life of 11 years.
- The initial investment in plant and machinery will be £1m and a marketing budget of £200,000 will be allocated to the first year.
- The net cash flows before depreciation of plant and machinery and before marketing expenditure for each umbrella will be £1.
- The products will be introduced both in the UK and in France.
- The marketing costs in Years 2 to 11 will be £50,000 per annum.
- If the product catches the imagination of the consumer in both countries then sales in the first year are anticipated at 1m umbrellas.
- If the fashion press ignore the new products in one country but become enthusiastic in the other the sales will be 700,000 umbrellas in Year 1.
- If the marketing launch is unsuccessful in both countries, first year sales will be 200,000 umbrellas.

The probability of each of these events occurring is:

- 1m sales: 0.3
- 0.7m sales: 0.4
- 0.2m sales: 0.3

If the first year is a success in both countries then two possibilities are envisaged:

a. Sales levels are maintained at 1m units per annum for the next 10 years – probability 0.3.
b. The product is seen as a temporary fad and sales fall to 100,000 units for the remaining 10 years – probability 0.7.

If success is achieved in only one country in the first year then for the remaining 10 years there is:

a. a 0.4 probability of maintaining the annual sales at 700,000 units; and
b. a 0.6 probability of sales immediately falling to 50,000 units per year.

If the marketing launch is unsuccessful in both countries then production will cease after the first year.

The plant and machinery will have no alternative use once installed and will have no scrap value.

The annual cash flows and marketing costs will be payable at each year end.

Assume

- Cost of capital: 10 per cent.
- No inflation or taxation.
- No exchange rate changes.

Required

a. Calculate the expected net present value for the project.
b. Calculate the standard deviation for the project.
c. If the project produces a net present value less than minus £1m the directors fear that the company will be vulnerable to bankruptcy. Calculate the probability of the firm avoiding bankruptcy. Assume a normal distribution.

?

(An Excel spreadsheet version of these calculations is available in the Lecturers-only section at www.pearsoned.co.uk/arnold)

Assignments

1 Gather together sufficient data on a recent or forthcoming investment in a firm you know well to be able to carry out the following forms of risk analysis:

a Sensitivity analysis.
b Scenario analysis.
c Risk-adjusted return analysis.
d Probability analysis (expected return, standard deviation, probabilities of various eventualities).

Write a report giving as full a picture of the project as possible.

2 Comment on the quality of risk assessment for major investments within your firm. Provide implications and recommendations sections in your report.

CHAPTER 7

Portfolio theory

LEARNING OUTCOMES

This chapter should enable the student to understand, describe and explain in a formal way the interactions between investments and the risk-reducing properties of portfolios. This includes:

- calculating two-asset portfolio expected returns and standard deviations;
- estimating measures of the extent of interaction – covariance and correlation coefficients;
- being able to describe dominance, identify efficient portfolios and then apply utility theory to obtain optimum portfolios;
- recognise the properties of the multi-asset portfolio set and demonstrate the theory behind the capital market line.

myfinancelab *Complete your diagnostic test for Chapter 7 now to create your personal study plan*

Introduction

The principles discussed in this chapter are as old as the hills. If you are facing a future which is uncertain, as most of us do, you will be vulnerable to negative shocks if you rely on a single source of income. It is less risky to have diverse sources of income or, to put it another way, to hold a portfolio of assets or investments. You do not need to study high-level portfolio theory to be aware of the common sense behind the adage 'don't put all your eggs in one basket'.

Here we examine the extent of risk reduction when an investor switches from complete commitment to one asset, for example shares in one company or one project, to the position where resources are split between two or more assets. By doing so it is possible to maintain returns while reducing risk. In this chapter we will focus on the use of portfolio theory particularly in the context of investment in financial securities, for instance shares in companies. The reader needs to be aware, however, that the fundamental techniques have much wider application – for example, observing the risk-reducing effect of having a diversity of projects within the firm.

The basis of portfolio theory was first developed in 1952 by Harry Markowitz. The thinking behind the explanation of the risk-reducing effect of spreading investment across a range of assets is that in a portfolio unexpected bad news concerning one company will be compensated for to some extent by unexpected good news about another. Markowitz gave us the tools for identifying portfolios which give the highest return for a particular level of risk. Investors can then select the optimum risk-return trade-off for themselves, depending on the extent of personal risk aversion. For example, a retired person dependent on investments for income may prefer a low-risk and low-return portfolio, whereas a young person with alternative sources of income may prefer to choose a portfolio with a higher return and concomitant higher risk. The fundamental point is this: despite the different preferences, each investor will be able to invest in an efficient portfolio; that is, one that gives the highest return for a given level of risk.

Holding period returns

To invest in a share is to become part owner of a business. If the business performs well then high returns will be earned. If the business does less well the holders of other types of securities, for instance the lenders, have the right to demand their contractual return before the ordinary shareholders receive anything. This can result in the share investor receiving little or nothing. The return earned on a share is defined by the **holding period returns**: R. For one year this is:

$$\text{Return} = \frac{\text{Dividends received} + (\text{Share price at end of period} - \text{Purchase price})}{\text{Purchase price}}$$

$$R = \frac{D_1 + P_1 - P_0}{P_0}$$

The return is the money received less the cost, where P_0 is the purchase price, P_1 the securities value at the end of the holding period and D_1 the dividend paid during the period (usually assumed to occur at the end, for ease of calculations). Thus the return on a share consists of two parts: first, a dividend; and second, a capital gain (or loss), $P_1 - P_0$. For example if a share was bought for £2, and paid a dividend after one year of 10p and the share was sold for £2.20 after one year the return was:

$$\frac{0.10 + 2.20 - 2.00}{2} = 0.15 \text{ or } 15\%$$

If another share produced a holding period return of, say, 10 per cent over a six-month period we cannot make a direct comparison between the two investments. However, a one-year return and a six-month return are related through the formula:

$$(1 + s)^2 = 1 + R$$

where: s = semi-annual rate
R = annual rate[1]

Thus if the semi-annual return is converted to an annual rate we have a true comparison (*see* **Exhibit 7.1**).

Exhibit 7.1 Comparison of returns

First investment	Second investment
	$(1 + 0.1)^2 = 1 + R$
	$R = (1 + 0.1)^2 - 1$
Return = 0.15 or 15%	Return = 0.21 or 21%

For a three-year holding period, with dividends received at Time 1, 2 and 3 (yearly intervals) the annual rate of return is obtained by solving for R in the following formula:

$$P_0 = \frac{D_1}{1+R} + \frac{D_2}{(1+R)^2} + \frac{D_3}{(1+R)^3} + \frac{P_3}{(1+R)^3}$$

So, for example if the initial share price was £1 and the share price three years later (P_3) was £1.20 and a dividend of 6p was paid at the end of Year 1 (D_1), 7p was paid at the end of Year 2 (D_2) and 8p was paid at the end of Year 3 (D_3), the annual rate of return can be found by trial and error:[2]

Try 13%

	Pence	Discounted
D_1	6	5.31
D_2	7	5.48
D_3	8	5.54
P_3	120	83.17
		99.50

Try 12%

	Pence	Discounted
D_1	6	5.36
D_2	7	5.58
D_3	8	5.69
P_3	120	85.41
		102.04

[1] See Appendix 2.1 for mathematical tools.

[2] Normally a calculator or computer with an internal rate of return function would be used. We do this the long-winded way here to show the underlying logic. It can be found using the goal seek function in Excel – see www.pearsoned.co.uk/arnold

12	?	13
102.04	100	99.50

$$12 + \frac{2.04}{(102.04 - 99.50)}(13 - 12) = 12.8\%$$

If the annual rate of return was 12.8 per cent then the three-year holding period return was (assuming dividend income was reinvested at the internal rate of return):

$$(1 + 0.128)^3 - 1 = 43.5\%$$

or

$$P(1 + i)^n = F$$
$$£100(1 + 0.128)^3 = £143.52$$

(An Excel spreadsheet version of this calculation is available at www.pearsoned.co.uk/arnold)

The analysis so far has been backward looking, as it focused on the certain returns that have already been received. Given perfect hindsight it is easy to make a choice between investments. When making investment decisions we are concerned with the future. The only certain fact the investor has is the price P_0 to be paid. The uncertainty over the future dividend has to be taken into account and, in addition, the even more difficult task of estimating the market value of the share at the end of the period has to be undertaken. Pearson, the owner of the *Financial Times* and FT Prentice Hall, has steadily raised its dividend year on year and therefore the estimation of the dividend one year hence can be predicted with a reasonable amount of confidence. However, forecasting the future share price is more formidable. This is subject to a number of influences ranging from the talent of the editorial team to the general sentiment in the stock market about macroeconomic matters.

So when dealing with the future we have to talk about expected returns. An expected return is derived by considering a variety of possibilities and weighting the possible outcomes by the probability of occurrence. The list of possible outcomes along with their probability of occurrence is called the **frequency function**.

Expected return and standard deviation for shares

A frequency function or probability distribution for shares in Ace plc is described in **Exhibit 7.2**. If the economy booms over the next year then the return will be 20 per cent. If normal growth occurs the return will be 5 per cent. A recession will produce a negative return, losing an investor 10 per cent of the original investment.

Exhibit 7.2 Ace plc

A share costs 100p to purchase now and the estimates of returns for the next year are as follows.

Event	Estimated selling price, P_1	Estimated dividend, D_1	Return R_i	Probability
Economic boom	114p	6p	+20%	0.2
Normal growth	100p	5p	+5%	0.6
Recession	86p	4p	−10%	0.2
				1.0

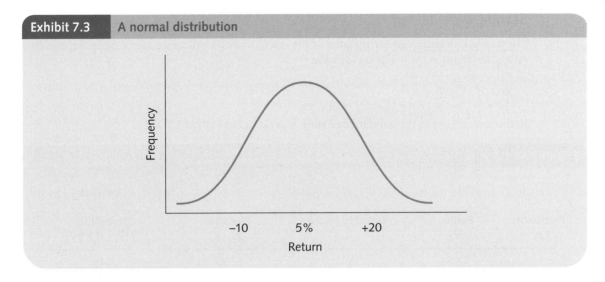

Exhibit 7.3 A normal distribution

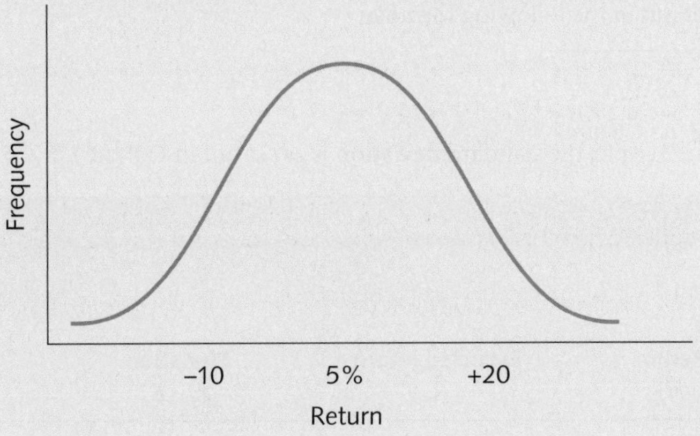

The example shown in Exhibit 7.2 lists only three possibilities. This small number was chosen in order to simplify the analysis, but it is possible to imagine that in reality there would be a number of intermediate outcomes, such as a return of 6 per cent or –2 per cent. Each potential outcome would have a defined probability of occurrence but the probability of all the outcomes would sum to 1.0. This more sophisticated approach to probability distribution is illustrated in **Exhibit 7.3** where the distribution is assumed to be normal, symmetrical and bell shaped.

We could add to the three possible events shown in Exhibit 7.2, for example slow growth, bad recession, moderate recession and so on, and thereby draw up a more complete representation of the distribution of the probabilities of eventualities. However, to represent all the possibilities would be an enormous task and the table would become unwieldy. Furthermore, the data we are dealing with, namely, future events, do not form a suitable base for such precision. We are better off representing the possible outcomes in terms of two summary statistics, the expected return and standard deviation.

The expected return

The expected return is represented by the following formula:

$$\overline{R} = \sum_{i=1}^{n} R_i p_i$$

where:

$\overline{R}$ = expected return
R_i = return if event i occurs
p_i = probability of event i occurring
n = number of events

In the case of Ace plc the expected return is as set out in **Exhibit 7.4**.

Exhibit 7.4 Expected return, Ace plc

Event	Probability of event p_i	Return R_i	$R_i \times p_i$	
Boom	0.2	+20	4	
Growth	0.6	+5	3	
Recession	0.2	–10	–2	
		Expected return	5	or 5%

Standard deviation

The standard deviation gives a measure of the extent to which outcomes vary around the expected return, as set out in the following formula:

$$\sigma = \sqrt{\sum_{i=1}^{n} (R_i - \bar{R}_i)^2 \, p_i}$$

In the case of Ace plc, the standard deviation is as set out in **Exhibit 7.5**.

Exhibit 7.5 Standard deviation, Ace plc

Probability p_i	Return R_i	Expected return $\bar{R}_i$	Deviation $R_i - \bar{R}_i$	Deviation squared × probability $(R_i - \bar{R}_i)^2 p_i$
0.2	20%	5%	15	45
0.6	5%	5%	0	0
0.2	–10%	5%	–15	45
			Variance σ^2	90
			Standard deviation σ	9.49%

Comparing shares

If we contrast the expected return and standard deviation of Ace with that for a share in a second company, Bravo, then using the mean-variance rule described in the previous chapter we would establish a preference for Ace (*see* **Exhibits 7.6** and **7.7**).

Exhibit 7.6 Returns for a share in Bravo plc

Event	Return R_i	Probability p_i
Boom	–15%	0.2
Growth	+5%	0.6
Recession	+25%	0.2
		1.0

The expected return is:
$(-15 \times 0.2) + (5 \times 0.6) + (25 \times 0.2) = 5$ per cent.

Exhibit 7.7 Standard deviation, Bravo plc

Probability p_i	Return R_i	Expected return $\bar{R}_i$	Deviation $R_i - \bar{R}_i$	Deviation squared × probability $(R_i - \bar{R}_i)^2 p_i$
0.2	–15%	5%	–20	80
0.6	+5%	5%	0	0
0.2	+25%	5%	+20	80
1.0			Variance σ^2	160
			Standard deviation σ	12.65%

The standard deviation for Bravo is as set out in Exhibit 7.7.

If we had to choose between these two shares then we would say that Ace is preferable to Bravo for a risk-averse investor because both shares have an expected return of 5 per cent but the standard deviation for Ace is lower at 9.49.

Combinations of investments

In the last section we confined our choice to two options – either invest all the money in Ace, or, alternatively, invest everything in Bravo. If the option were taken to invest in Ace then over a few years the returns might turn out to be as shown in **Exhibit 7.8**.

Note, in Exhibit 7.8, the large variability from one year to the next. The returns on Ace are high when the economy is doing well but fall dramatically when recession strikes. There are numerous industries which seem to follow this sort of pattern. For example, the luxury car market is vulnerable to the ups and downs of the economy, as are the hotel and consumer goods sectors.

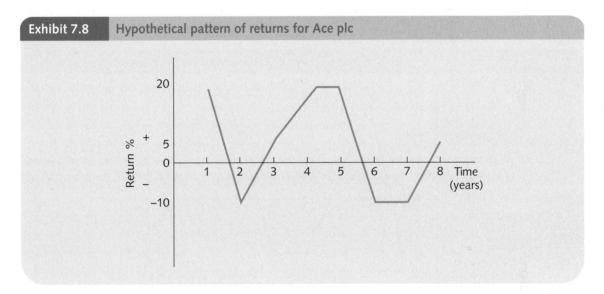

Exhibit 7.8 Hypothetical pattern of returns for Ace plc

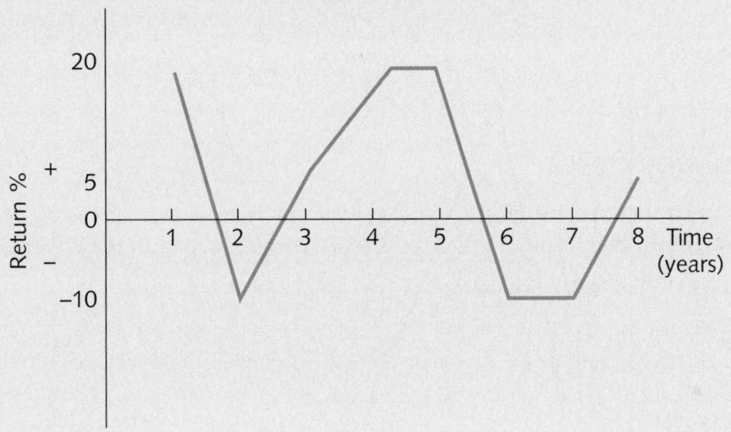

If all funds were invested in Bravo in isolation then the patterns of future returns might turn out as shown in **Exhibit 7.9**.

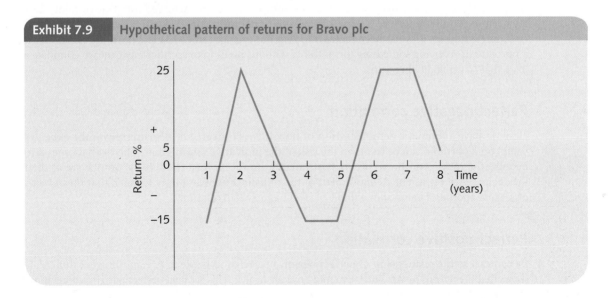

Exhibit 7.9 Hypothetical pattern of returns for Bravo plc

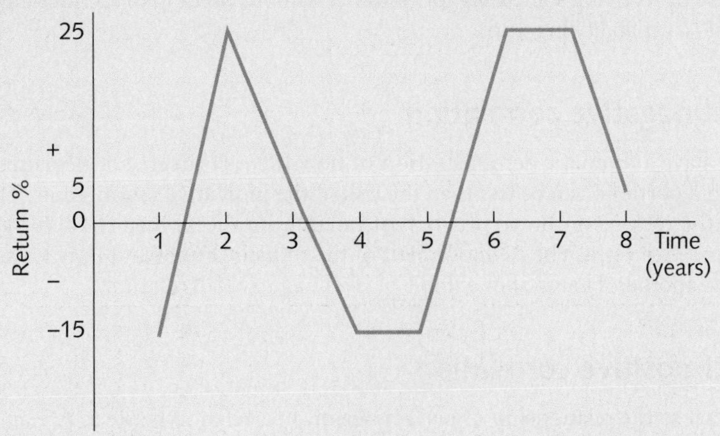

Bravo is in the sort of industry that performs best in recession years; for example, it could be an insolvency practice. Again, note the wild swings in returns from year to year.

Now assume that the investor is not confined to a pure investment in either Ace's shares or Bravo's shares. Another possibility is to buy a portfolio, in other words, to split the fund between the two companies. We will examine the effect on return and risk of placing £571 of a fund totalling £1,000 into Ace, and £429 into Bravo (*see* **Exhibits 7.10** and **7.11**).

Exhibit 7.10 Returns over one year from placing £571 in Ace and £429 in Bravo

Event	Returns Ace £	Returns Bravo £	Overall returns on £1,000	Percentage returns
Boom	571(1.2) = 685	429 – 429(0.15) = 365	1,050	5%
Growth	571(1.05) = 600	429(1.05) = 450	1,050	5%
Recession	571 – 571(0.1) = 514	429(1.25) = 536	1,050	5%

Exhibit 7.11 Hypothetical pattern of returns for Ace, Bravo and the two-asset portfolio

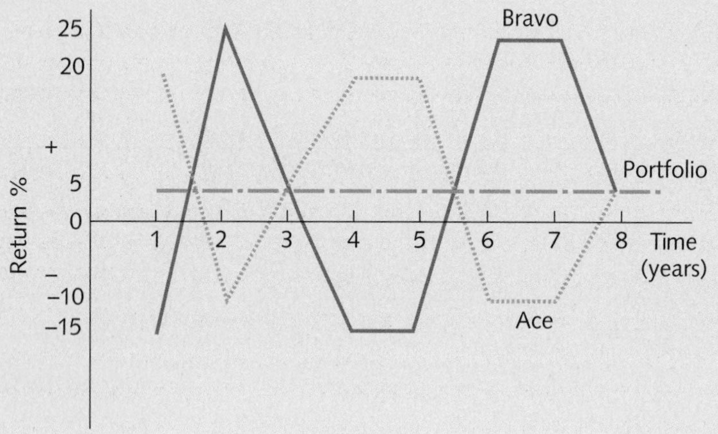

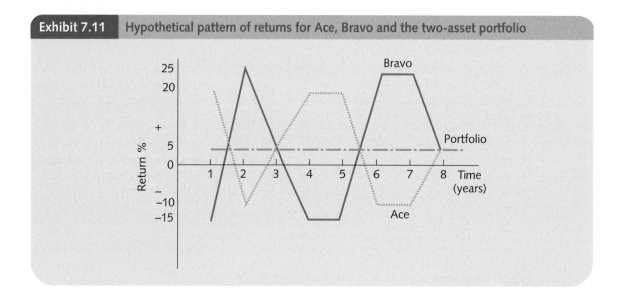

By spreading the investment between these two companies we have achieved complete certainty. Year after year a constant return of 5 per cent is assured rather than the fluctuations experienced if only one share is chosen. Risk has been reduced to zero but average return has remained the same. This is a rare case of receiving something for nothing: without needing to sacrifice any gain we eliminate a 'bad', that is, variability in return.

Perfect negative correlation

Here we have a dramatic demonstration of how the risk (degree of deviation from the expected value) on a portfolio can be less than the risk of the individual constituents. The risk becomes zero because the returns on Bravo are highest in circumstances when the returns on Ace are at their lowest, and vice versa. The co-movement of the returns on Ace and Bravo is such that they exactly offset one another. That is, they exhibit **perfect negative correlation.**

Perfect positive correlation

By contrast to the relationship of perfect negative correlation between Ace and Bravo **Exhibit 7.12** shows that the returns on Ace and Clara move exactly in step. This is called **perfect positive correlation.**

Exhibit 7.12 Annual returns on Ace and Clara

Event *i*	Probability p_i	Returns on Ace %	Returns on Clara %
Boom	0.2	+20	+50
Growth	0.6	+5	+15
Recession	0.2	–10	–20

If a portfolio were constructed from equal investments of Ace and Clara the result would be as shown in **Exhibit 7.13**.

Exhibit 7.13 Returns over a one-year period from placing £500 in Ace and £500 in Clara

Event *i*	Outcome for Ace £	Outcome for Clara £	Overall outcome on £1,000 investment	Percentage return
Boom	600	750	1,350	35%
Growth	525	575	1,100	10%
Recession	450	400	850	–15%

The situation portrayed in Exhibit 7.13 indicates that, compared with investing all the funds in Ace, the portfolio has a wider dispersion of possible percentage return outcomes. A higher percentage return is earned in a good year and a lower return in a recession year. However, the portfolio returns are less volatile than an investment in Clara alone. There is a general rule for a portfolio consisting of perfectly positively correlated returns: both the expected returns and the standard deviation of the portfolio are weighted averages of returns and standard deviations of the constituents respectively. Thus because half of the portfolio is from Ace and half from Clara the expected return is half-way between the two individual shares. Also the degree of oscillation is half-way between the small variability of Ace and the large variability of Clara. Perfectly positively correlated investments are at the opposite extreme to perfectly negatively correlated investments. In the former case risk is not reduced through diversification, it is merely averaged. In the latter case risk can be completely eliminated by selecting the appropriate proportions of each investment.

A typical pattern of returns over an eight-year period might be as shown in **Exhibit 7.14** for Ace and Clara and a 50 : 50 portfolio.

Exhibit 7.14 Hypothetical pattern of returns for Ace and Clara

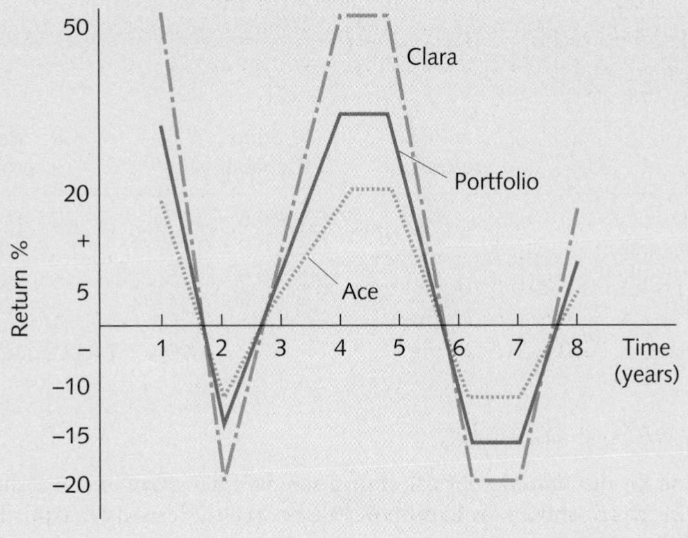

Independent investments

A third possibility is that the returns on shares in two firms are completely unrelated. Within a portfolio of two **statistically independent shares** we find that when one firm gives a high return the other one may give a high return *or* it may give a low return: that is, we are unable to state any correlation between the returns. The example of X and Y in **Exhibits 7.15–7.18** shows the effect on risk of this kind of zero correlation situation when two shares are brought together in a portfolio. Shares in X have a 0.5 probability of producing a return of 35 per cent and a 0.5 probability of producing a return of negative 25 per cent. Shares in Y have exactly the same returns and probabilities but which of the two outcomes will occur is totally independent of the outcome for X.

Exhibit 7.15 Expected returns for shares in X and shares in Y

Expected return for shares in X	Expected returns for shares in Y
Return × Probability	Return × Probability
−25 × 0.5 = −12.5	−25 × 0.5 = −12.5
35 × 0.5 = 17.5	35 × 0.5 = 17.5
5.0%	5.0%

Exhibit 7.16 Standard deviations for X or Y as single investments

Return R_i	Probability p_i	Expected return $\bar{R}_i$	Deviation $R_i - \bar{R}$	Deviation squared × probability $(R_i - \bar{R})^2 p_i$
−25%	0.5	5%	−30	450
35%	0.5	5%	30	450
			Variance σ^2	900
			Standard deviation σ	30%

If a 50:50 portfolio is created we see that the expected returns remain at 5 per cent, but the standard deviation is reduced (*see* Exhibits 7.17 and 7.18).

Exhibit 7.17 A mixed portfolio: 50 per cent of the fund invested in X and 50 per cent in Y, expected return

Possible outcome combinations	Joint returns	Joint probability	Return × probability	
Both firms do badly	−25	0.5 × 0.5 = 0.25	−25 × 0.25 =	−6.25
X does badly Y does well	5	0.5 × 0.5 = 0.25	5 × 0.25 =	1.25
X does well Y does badly	5	0.5 × 0.5 = 0.25	5 × 0.25 =	1.25
Both firms do well	35	0.5 × 0.5 = 0.25	35 × 0.25 =	8.75
		1.00	Expected return	5.00%

The reason for the reduction in risk from a standard deviation of 30 (as shown in Exhibit 7.16) to one of 21.21 (as shown in Exhibit 7.18), is that there is now a third possible outcome.

Exhibit 7.18 Standard deviation, mixed portfolio

Return R_i	Probability p_i	Expected return $\bar{R}$	Deviation $R_i - \bar{R}$	Deviation squared × probability $(R_i - \bar{R})^2 p_i$
–25	0.25	5	–30	225
5	0.50	5	0	0
35	0.25	5	30	225
			Variance σ^2	450
			Standard deviation σ	21.21%

Previously the only outcomes were –25 and +35. Now it is possible that one investment will give a positive result and one will give a negative result. The overall effect is that there is a 50 per cent chance of an outcome being +5. The diversified portfolio reduces the dispersion of the outcomes and the chance of suffering a major loss of 25 per cent is lowered from a probability of 0.5 to only 0.25 for the mixed portfolio.

A correlation scale

We have examined three extreme positions which will provide the foundation for more detailed consideration of portfolios. The case of Ace and Bravo demonstrated that when investments produce good or bad outcomes which vary in exact opposition to each other, risk can be eliminated. This relationship, described as perfect negative correlation, can be assigned the number –1 on a **correlation scale** which ranges from –1 to +1. The second example, of Ace and Clara, showed a situation where returns on both shares were affected by the same events and these returns moved in lock-step with one another. This sort of perfect positive correlation can be assigned a value of +1 on a correlation scale. The third case, of X and Y where returns are independent, showed that risk is not entirely eliminated but it can be reduced. (Extreme outcomes are still possible, but they are less likely.) Independent investments are assigned a value of zero on the correlation scale (*see* **Exhibit 7.19**).

Exhibit 7.19 Correlation scale

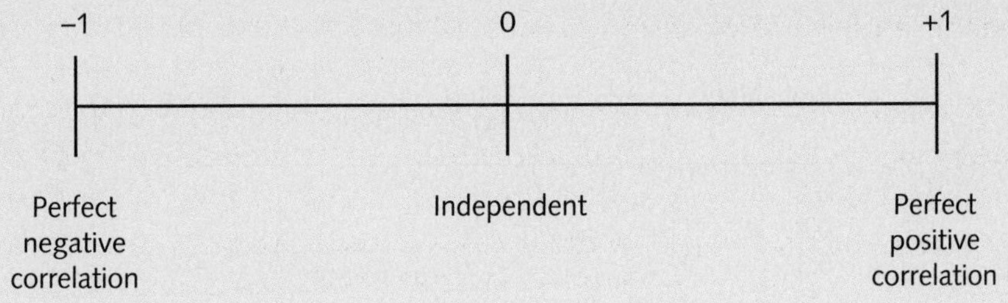

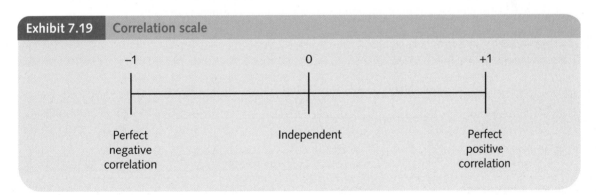

This leads to an important conclusion from portfolio theory:

So long as the returns of constituent assets of a portfolio are not perfectly positively correlated, diversification can reduce risk. The degree of risk reduction depends on:

(a) the extent of statistical interdependence between the returns of the different investments: the more negative the better; and

(b) the number of securities over which to spread the risk: the greater the number, the lower the risk.

This is an amazing conclusion because it is only in the very extreme and rare situation of perfect positive correlation that risk is not reduced.

It is all very well focusing on these three unusual types of relationships but what about the majority of investments in shares, projects or whatever? Real-world assets tend to have returns which have some degree of correlation with other assets but this is neither perfect nor zero. It is to this slightly more complex situation we now turn.

Initially the mathematics of portfolio theory may seem daunting but they do break down into manageable components. The algebra and theory are necessary to gain a true appreciation of the uses of portfolio theory, but the technical aspects are kept to a minimum.

The effects of diversification when security returns are not perfectly correlated

We will now look at the risk-reducing effects of diversification when two financial securities, two shares, have only a small degree of interrelatedness between their returns. Suppose that an investor has a chance of either investing all funds in one company, A or B, or investing a fraction in one with the remainder purchasing shares in the other. The returns on these companies respond differently to the general activity within the economy. Company A does particularly well when the economy is booming. Company B does best when there is normal growth in the economy. Both do badly in a recession. There is some degree of 'togetherness' or correlation of the movement of the returns, but not much (*see* **Exhibit 7.20**).

Exhibit 7.20 Returns on shares A and B for alternative economic states

Event i State of the economy	Probability p_i	Return on A R_A	Return on B R_B
Boom	0.3	20%	3%
Growth	0.4	10%	35%
Recession	0.3	0%	–5%

Before examining portfolio risk and returns we first calculate the expected return and standard deviation for each of the companies' shares as single investments (*see* **Exhibits 7.21–7.25**).

Exhibit 7.21 Company A: Expected return

Probability p_i	Return R_A	$R_A \times p_i$
0.3	20	6
0.4	10	4
0.3	0	0
		10%

Exhibit 7.22 Company A: Standard deviation

Probability p_i	Return R_A	Expected return $\bar{R}_A$	Deviation $(R_A - \bar{R}_A)$	Deviation squared × probability $(R_A - \bar{R}_A)^2 p_i$
0.3	20	10	10	30
0.4	10	10	0	0
0.3	0	10	–10	30
			Variance σ^2	60
			Standard deviation σ	7.75%

Exhibit 7.23 Company B: Expected return

Probability p_i	Return R_B	$R_B \times p_i$
0.3	3	0.9
0.4	35	14.0
0.3	–5	–1.5
		13.4%

Exhibit 7.24 Company B: Standard deviation

Probability p_i	Return R_B	Expected return $\bar{R}_B$	Deviation $(R_B - \bar{R}_B)$	Deviation squared × probability $(R_B - \bar{R}_B)^2 p_i$
0.3	3	13.4	10.4	32.45
0.4	35	13.4	21.6	186.62
0.3	–5	13.4	–18.4	101.57
			Variance σ^2	320.64
			Standard deviation σ	17.91%

Exhibit 7.25 Summary table: Expected returns and standard deviations for Companies A and B

	Expected return	Standard deviation
Company A	10%	7.75%
Company B	13.4%	17.91%

Compared with A, Company B is expected to give a higher return but also has a higher level of risk. If the results are plotted on a diagram we can give an impression of the relative risk-return profiles (*see* **Exhibit 7.26**).

Exhibit 7.26 Return and standard deviation for shares in companies A and B

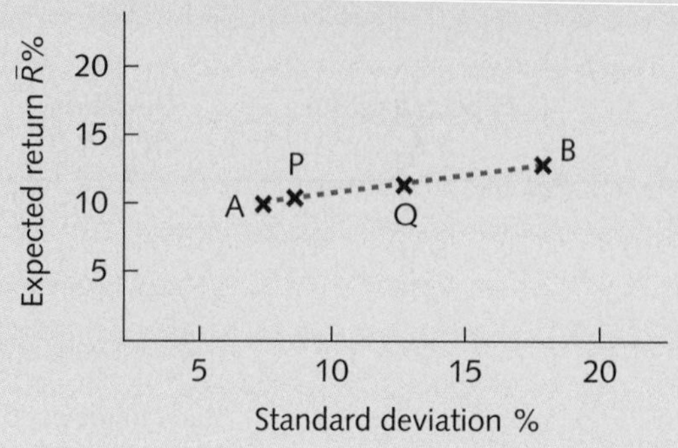

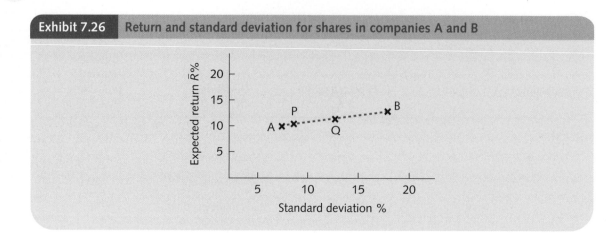

From a first glance at Exhibit 7.26 it might be thought that it is possible to invest in different proportions of A and B and obtain a risk-return combination somewhere along the dotted line. That is, a two-asset portfolio of A and B has an expected return which is a weighted average of the expected returns on the individual investments *and* the standard deviation is a weighted average of the risk of A and B depending on the proportions of the portfolio devoted to A and B. So if point Q represented a 50 : 50 split of capital between A and B the expected return, following this logic, would be:

$$(10 \times 0.5) + (13.4 \times 0.5) = 11.7\%$$

and the standard deviation would be:

$$(7.75 \times 0.5) + (17.91 \times 0.5) = 12.83\%$$

Point P represents 90 per cent of the fund in A and 10 per cent in B. If this portfolio was on the dotted line the expected return would be:

$$(10 \times 0.9) + (13.4 \times 0.1) = 10.34\%$$

and the standard deviation would be:

$$(7.75 \times 0.9) + (17.91 \times 0.1) = 8.766\%$$

However, this would be **wrong** because the risk of any portfolio of A and B is less than the weighted average of the two individual standard deviations. You can, in fact, reduce risk at each level of return by investing in a portfolio of A and B. This brings us to a general rule in portfolio theory:

Portfolio returns are a weighted average of the expected returns on the individual investments . . .

BUT . . .

Portfolio standard deviation is less than the weighted average risk of the individual investments, except for perfectly positively correlated investments.

Portfolio expected return and standard deviation

The rule stated above will now be illustrated by calculating the expected return and standard deviation when 90 per cent of the portfolio funds are placed in A and 10 per cent are placed in B.

Expected returns, two-asset portfolio

The expected returns from a two-asset portfolio are as follows.

Proportion of funds in A = a = 0.90
Proportion of funds in B = 1 – a = 0.10

The expected return of a portfolio R_p is solely related to the proportion of wealth invested in each constituent. Thus we simply multiply the expected return of each individual investment by their weights in the portfolio, 90 per cent for A and 10 per cent for B.

$$\bar{R}_p = a\bar{R}_A + (1-a)\bar{R}_B$$
$$\bar{R}_p = 0.90 \times 10 + 0.10 \times 13.4 = 10.34\%$$

Standard deviation, two-asset portfolio

Now comes the formula that for decades has made the hearts of students sink when first seen – the formula for the standard deviation of a two-asset portfolio. This is:

$$\sigma_p = \sqrt{a^2\,\sigma_A^2 + (1-a)^2\,\sigma_B^2 + 2a(1-a)\,\text{cov}\,(R_A, R_B)}$$

where:

σ_p = portfolio standard deviation
σ_A^2 = variance of investment A
σ_B^2 = variance of investment B
cov (R_A, R_B) = covariance of A and B

The formula for the standard deviation of a two-asset portfolio may seem daunting at first. However, the component parts are fairly straightforward. To make the formula easier to understand it is useful to break it down to three terms:

1 The first term, $a^2\sigma_A^2$, is the variance for A multiplied by the square of its weight – in the example $a^2 = 0.90^2$.
2 The second term $(1-a)^2\sigma_B^2$, is the variance for the second investment B multiplied by the square of its weight in the portfolio, 0.10^2.
3 The third term, $2a(1-a)$ cov (R_A, R_B), focuses on the covariance of the returns of A and B, which is examined below.

When the results of all three calculations are added together the square root is taken to give the standard deviation of the portfolio. The only piece of information not yet available is the covariance. This is considered next.

Covariance

The **covariance** measures the extent to which the returns on two investments 'co-vary' or 'co-move'. If the returns tend to go up together and go down together then the covariance will be a positive number. If, however, the returns on one investment move in the opposite direction to the returns on another when a particular event occurs then these securities will exhibit negative covariance. If there is no co-movement at all, that is, the returns are independent of each other, the covariance will be zero. This positive–zero–negative scale should sound familiar, as covariance and the correlation coefficient are closely related. However, the correlation coefficient scale has a strictly limited range from –1 to +1 whereas the covariance can be any positive or negative value. The covariance formula is:

$$\text{cov}\,(R_A, R_B) = \sum_{i=1}^{n} \{(R_A - \bar{R}_A)(R_B - \bar{R}_B)p_i\}$$

To calculate covariance take each of the possible events that could occur in turn and calculate the extent to which the returns on investment A differ from expected return ($R_A - \bar{R}_A$) – and note whether this is a positive or negative deviation. Follow this with a similar deviation calculation for an investment in B if those particular circumstances (that is, boom, recession, etc.) prevail ($R_B - \bar{R}_B$). Then multiply the deviation of A by the deviation of B and the probability of that event occurring, p_i. (Note that if the deviations are both in a positive direction away from the mean, that is, a higher return than average, or both negative, then the overall calculation will be positive. If one of the deviations is negative while the other is positive the overall result is negative.) Finally the results from all the potential events are added together to give the covariance.

Applying the formula to A and B will help to clarify matters (*see* **Exhibit 7.27**).

Exhibit 7.27 Covariance

Event and probability of event p_i		Returns R_A	Returns R_B	Expected returns $\bar{R}_A$	Expected returns $\bar{R}_B$	Deviations $R_A - \bar{R}_A$	Deviations $R_B - \bar{R}_B$	Deviation of A × deviation of B × probability $(R_A - \bar{R}_A)(R_B - \bar{R}_B)p_i$	
Boom	0.3	20	3	10	13.4	10	−10.4	10 × −10.4 × 0.3 =	−31.2
Growth	0.4	10	35	10	13.4	0	21.6	0 × 21.6 × 0.4 =	0
Recession	0.3	0	−5	10	13.4	−10	−18.4	−10 × −18.4 × 0.3 =	55.2
								Covariance of A and B, cov (R_A, R_B) =	+24

(An Excel spreadsheet showing these covariance calculations is available at www.pearsoned.co.uk/arnold)

It is worth spending a little time dwelling on the covariance and seeing how a positive or negative covariance comes about. In the calculation for A and B the 'Boom' eventuality contributed a negative 31.2 to the overall covariance. This is because A does particularly well in boom conditions and the returns are well above expected returns, but B does badly compared with its expected return of 13.4 and therefore the co-movement of returns is a negative one. In a recession both firms experience poor returns compared with their expected values, thus the contribution to the overall covariance is positive because they move together. This second element of co-movement outweighs that of the boom possibility and so the total covariance is positive 24.

Now that we have the final piece of information to plug into the standard deviation formula we can work out the risk resulting from splitting the fund, with 90 per cent invested in A and 10 per cent in B.

$$\sigma_p = \sqrt{a^2\sigma_A^2 + (1-a)^2\sigma_B^2 + 2a(1-a)\,\text{cov}(R_A, R_B)}$$

$$\sigma_p = \sqrt{0.90^2 \times 60 + 0.10^2 \times 320.64 + 2 \times 0.90 \times 0.10 \times 24}$$

$$\sigma_p = \sqrt{48.6 + 3.206 + 4.32}$$

$$\sigma_p = 7.49\%$$

A 90:10 portfolio gives both a higher return and a lower standard deviation than a simple investment in A alone (*see* **Exhibit 7.28**).

Exhibit 7.28 Summary table: expected return and standard deviation

	Expected return (%)	Standard deviation (%)
All invested in Company A	10	7.75
All invested in Company B	13.4	17.91
Invested in a portfolio (90% in A, 10% in B)	10.34	7.49

(An Excel spreadsheet showing all the calculations for A and B is available at www.pearsoned.co.uk/arnold)

In the example shown in Exhibit 7.29 the degree of risk reduction is so slight because the returns on A and B are positively correlated. Later we will consider the example of Augustus and Brown, two shares which exhibit negative correlation. Before that, it will be useful to examine the relationship between covariance and the correlation coefficient.

Exhibit 7.29 Expected returns and standard deviation for A and B and a 90:10 portfolio of A and B

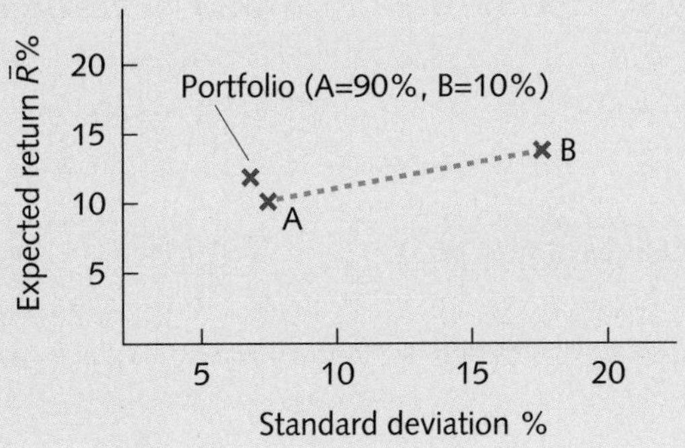

Correlation coefficient

Both the covariance and the correlation coefficient measure the degree to which returns move together. The covariance can take on any value and so it is difficult to use the covariance to compare relationships between pairs of investments. A 'standardised covariance' with a scale of interrelatedness is often more useful. This is what the correlation coefficient gives us. To calculate the correlation coefficient, R_{AB}, divide the covariance by the product (multiplied together) of the individual investment standard deviations.

So for investments A and B:

$$R_{AB} = \frac{\text{cov}\,(R_A, R_B)}{\sigma_A\,\sigma_B}$$

$$R_{AB} = \frac{24}{7.75 \times 17.91} = +0.1729$$

The correlation coefficient has the same properties as the covariance but it measures co-movement on a scale of –1 to +1 which makes comparisons easier. It also can be used as an alternative method of calculating portfolio standard deviation:

$$\text{If } R_{AB} = \frac{\text{cov}\,(R_A, R_B)}{\sigma_A\,\sigma_B} \text{ then cov}\,(R_A, R_B) = R_{AB}\sigma_A\sigma_B$$

This can then be used in the portfolio standard deviation formula:

$$\sigma_p = \sqrt{a^2\,\sigma_A^2 + (1-a)^2\sigma_B^2 + 2a\,(1-a)\,R_{AB}\sigma_A\sigma_B}$$

Exhibit 7.30 illustrates the case of perfect positively correlated returns ($R_{FG} = +1$) for the shares F and G. All the plot points lie on a straight upward-sloping line.

If the returns on G vary in an exactly opposite way to the returns on F we have perfect negative correlation, $R_{FG} = -1$ (*see* Exhibit 7.31).

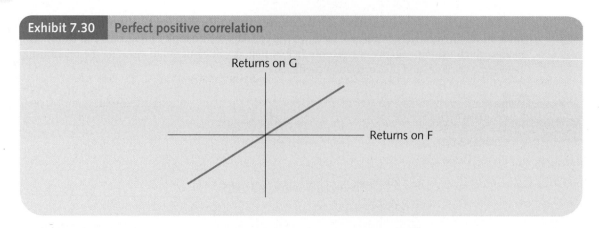

Exhibit 7.30 Perfect positive correlation

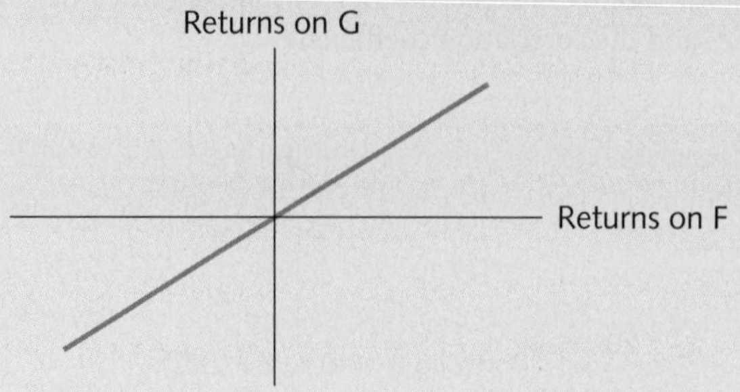

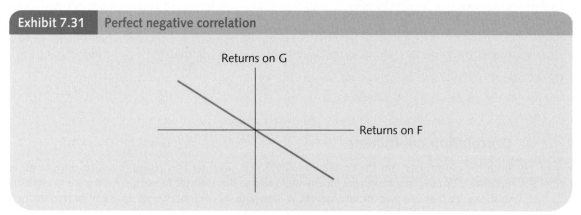

Exhibit 7.31 Perfect negative correlation

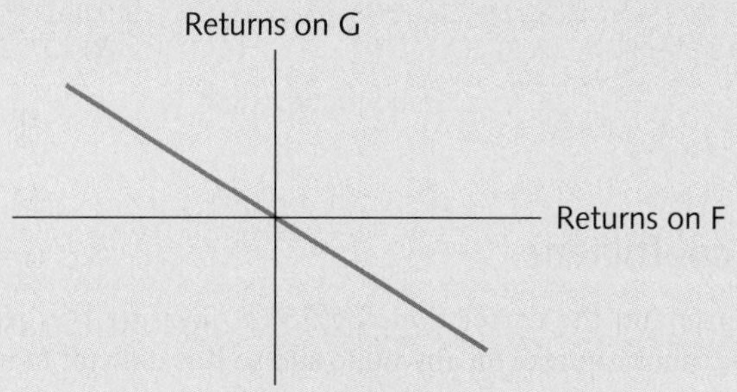

If the securities have a zero correlation coefficient ($R = 0$) we are unable to show a line representing the degree of co-movement (*see* **Exhibit 7.32**).

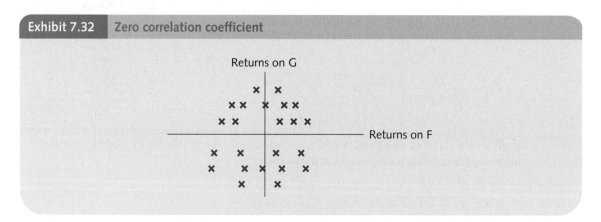

Exhibit 7.32 Zero correlation coefficient

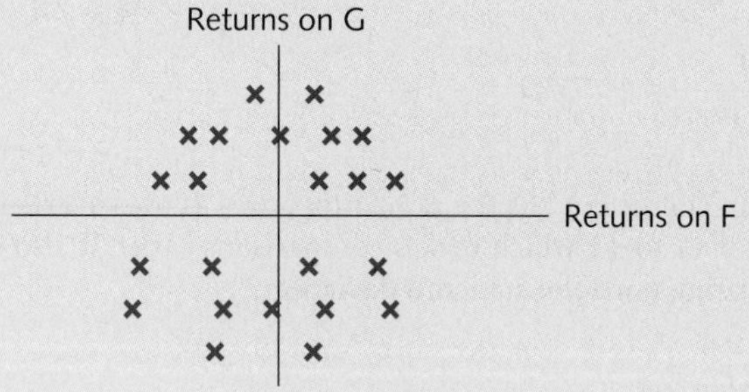

Dominance and the efficient frontier

Suppose an individual is able to invest in shares of Augustus, in shares of Brown or in a portfolio made up from Augustus and Brown shares. Augustus is an ice cream manufacturer and so does well if the weather is warm. Brown is an umbrella manufacturer and so does well if it rains. Because the weather is so changeable from year to year an investment in one of these firms alone is likely to be volatile, whereas a portfolio will probably reduce the variability of returns (*see* **Exhibits 7.33–7.35**).

Exhibit 7.33 Returns on shares in Augustus and Brown

Event (weather for season)	Probability of event	Returns on Augustus	Returns on Brown
	p_i	R_A	R_B
Warm	0.2	20%	–10%
Average	0.6	15%	22%
Wet	0.2	10%	44%
Expected return		15%	20%

Exhibit 7.34 Standard deviation for Augustus and Brown

Probability p_i	Returns on Augustus R_A	$(R_A - \bar{R}_A)^2 p_i$	Returns on Brown R_B	$(R_B - \bar{R}_B)^2 p_i$
0.2	20	5	–10	180.0
0.6	15	0	22	2.4
0.2	10	5	44	115.2
	Variance, σ^2_A	10	Variance, σ^2_B	297.6
	Standard deviation, σ_A	3.162	Standard deviation, σ_B	17.25

Exhibit 7.35 Covariance

Probability p_i	Returns R_A	Returns R_B	Expected returns $\bar{R}_A$	Expected returns $\bar{R}_B$	Deviations $R_A - \bar{R}_A$	Deviations $R_B - \bar{R}_B$	Deviation of A × deviation of B × probability $(R_A - \bar{R}_A)(R_B - \bar{R}_B)p_i$	
0.2	20	–10	15	20	5	–30	5 × –30 × 0.2 =	–30
0.6	15	22	15	20	0	2	0 × 2 × 0.6 =	0
0.2	10	44	15	20	–5	24	–5 × 24 × 0.2 =	–24
							Covariance (R_A, R_B) =	–54

The correlation coefficient is:

$$R_{AB} = \frac{\text{cov}\,(R_A, R_B)}{\sigma_A \sigma_B}$$

$$R_{AB} = \frac{-54}{3.162 \times 17.25} = -0.99$$

There are an infinite number of potential combinations of Augustus and Brown shares giving different levels of risk and return. To make the analysis easier we will examine only five portfolios. These are shown in **Exhibit 7.36**.

Exhibit 7.36 Risk-return correlations: two-asset portfolios for Augustus and Brown

Portfolio	Augustus weighting (%)	Brown weighting (%)	Expected return (%)	Standard deviation	
A	100	0	15		= 3.16
J	90	10	15.5	$\sqrt{0.9^2 \times 10 + 0.1^2 \times 297.6 + 2 \times 0.9 \times 0.1 \times -54}$	= 1.16
K	85	15	15.75	$\sqrt{0.85^2 \times 10 + 0.15^2 \times 297.6 + 2 \times 0.85 \times 0.15 \times -54}$	= 0.39
L	80	20	16.0	$\sqrt{0.8^2 \times 10 + 0.2^2 \times 297.6 + 2 \times 0.8 \times 0.2 \times -54}$	= 1.01
M	50	50	17.5	$\sqrt{0.5^2 \times 10 + 0.5^2 \times 297.6 + 2 \times 0.5 \times 0.5 \times -54}$	= 7.06
N	25	75	18.75	$\sqrt{0.25^2 \times 10 + 0.75^2 \times 297.6 + 2 \times 0.25 \times 0.75 \times -54}$	= 12.16
B	0	100	20		= 17.25

Exhibit 7.37 shows the risk-return profile for alternative portfolios. Portfolio K is very close to the minimum risk combination that actually occurs with a portfolio consisting of 84.6 per cent in Augustus and 15.4 per cent in Brown. The formula for calculating this minimum standard deviation point is shown in Worked example 7.1.

Exhibit 7.37 Risk-return profile for alternative portfolios of Augustus and Brown

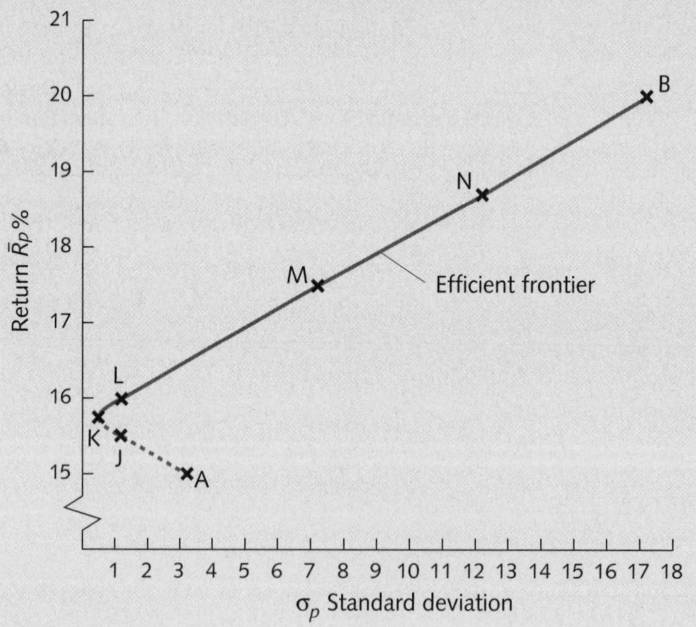

Worked example 7.1 Finding the minimum standard deviation for combinations of two securities

If a fund is to be split between two securities, A and B, and *a* is the fraction to be allocated to A, then the value for *a* which results in the lowest standard deviation is given by:

$$a = \frac{\sigma_B^2 - \text{cov}(R_A, R_B)}{\sigma_A^2 + \sigma_B^2 - 2\,\text{cov}(R_A, R_B)}$$

In the case of Augustus and Brown:

$$a = \frac{297.6 - (-54)}{10 + 297.6 - 2 \times -54} = 0.846 \text{ or } 84.6\%$$

To obtain the minimum standard deviation (or variance) place 84.6 per cent of the fund in Augustus and 15.4 per cent in Brown.

We can now calculate the minimum standard deviation:

$$\sigma_p = \sqrt{a^2\sigma_A^2 + (1-a)^2\sigma_B^2 + 2a(1-a)\,\text{cov}(R_A, R_B)}$$

$$\sigma_p = \sqrt{0.846^2 \times 10 + 0.154^2 \times 297.6 + 2 \times 0.846 \times 0.154 \times -54}$$

$$\sigma_p = 0.38\%$$

Thus, an extremely risk-averse individual who was choosing a combination of shares in Augustus and Brown can achieve a very low variation of income of a tiny standard deviation of 0.38 per cent by allocating 84.6 per cent of the investment fund to Augustus.

The risk-return line drawn, sometimes called the **opportunity set**, or **feasible set**, has two sections. The first, with a solid line, from point K to point B, represents all the **efficient portfolios**. This is called the **efficient frontier**. Portfolios between K and A are **dominated** by the efficient portfolios. Take L and J as examples: they have (almost) the same risk levels but portfolio L dominates portfolio J because it has a better return. All the portfolios between K and A are *inefficient* because for each possibility there is an alternative combination of Augustus and Brown on the solid line K to B which provides a higher return for the same risk.

An efficient portfolio is a combination of investments which maximises the expected return for a given standard deviation.

Identifying the efficient portfolios helps in the quest to find the optimal portfolio for an investor as it eliminates a number of inferior possibilities from further consideration. However, there remains a large range of risk-return combinations available in the efficient zone and we need a tool to enable us to find the best portfolio for an individual given that person's degree of risk aversion. For instance a highly risk-averse person will probably select a portfolio with a high proportion of Augustus (but not greater than 84.6 per cent), perhaps settling for the low-return and low-risk combination represented by portfolio L. A less risk-averse investor may be prepared to accept the high standard deviation of portfolio N if compensated by the expectation of greater reward. To be more accurate in choosing between efficient portfolios we need to be able to represent the decision makers' attitude towards risk. Indifference curve analysis is one tool which has been tried by economists.

Indifference curves

Indifference curve analysis draws on the concept of utility to present alternative trade-offs between risk and return each equally acceptable to the investor. Every individual will exhibit unique preferences for risk and return and so everyone has a unique set of indifference curves. Consider Mr Chisholm who is hypothetically allocated portfolio W represented in **Exhibit 7.38**. This portfolio has a return of 10 per cent and a standard deviation of 16 per cent. Now imagine you asked Mr Chisholm, 'If we were to change the constituents of the portfolio so that the risk

Exhibit 7.38 Indifference curve for Mr Chisholm

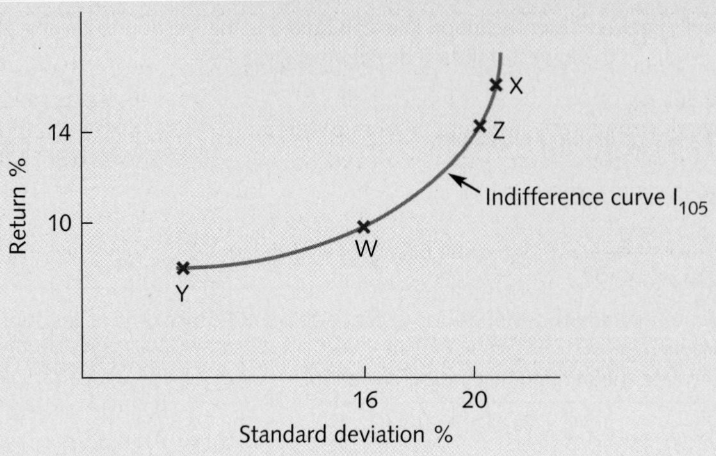

increased to a standard deviation of 20 per cent how much extra return would you require to compensate for the increased risk to leave your overall utility unchanged?' According to this simple model an extra return of 4 per cent is required. That is, Mr Chisholm is indifferent between W and the portfolio Z with a standard deviation of 20 per cent and return of 14 per cent. His utility (or well-being) is identical for each portfolio.

In fact all the risk-return combinations along the indifference curve I_{105} in Exhibit 7.38 have the same level of desirability to Mr Chisholm. (The 105 is just a label; it has no more significance than that.) Portfolio X has a higher risk than portfolio Y and is therefore less desirable on this factor. However, exactly offsetting this is the attraction of the increased return.

Now consider **Exhibit 7.39** where there are a number of indifference curves drawn for Mr Chisholm. Even though Mr Chisholm is indifferent between W and Z, he will not be indifferent between W and S. Portfolio S has the same level of risk as W but provides a higher level of return and is therefore preferable.

Exhibit 7.39 A map of indifference curves

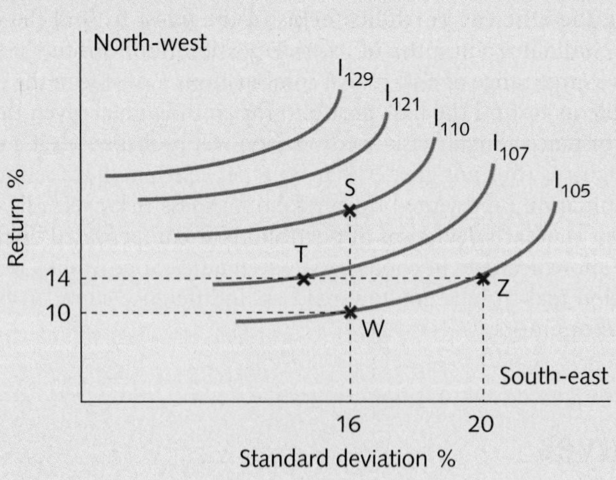

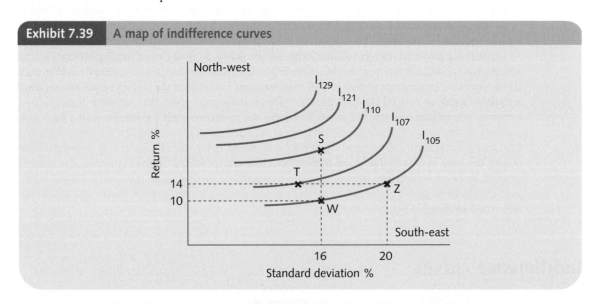

Likewise portfolio T is preferred to portfolio Z because for the same level of return a lower risk is obtainable. All portfolios along I_{110} provide a higher utility than any of the portfolios along I_{105}.

Similarly I_{121} portfolios are better than I_{110}. Indifference curve I_{129} gives the highest utility of all the curves represented in Exhibit 7.39, whereas I_{105} gives the lowest. The further 'north-west' the indifference curve, the higher the desirability, and therefore an investor will strive to obtain a portfolio which is furthest in this direction. Note that Exhibit 7.39 shows only five possible indifference curves whereas in reality there will be an infinite number, each representing alternative utility levels.

An important rule to bear in mind when drawing indifference curves is that they must never cross. To appreciate this rule consider point M in **Exhibit 7.40**. Remember that I_{105} represents alternative portfolios with the same level of utility for Mr Chisholm and he is therefore indifferent between the risk-return combinations offered along I_{105}. If M also lies on I_{101} this is saying that Mr Chisholm is indifferent between any of the I_{101} portfolios and point M. It is illogical to suppose that Mr Chisholm is indifferent between I_{105} and I_{101}. To the right of point M, I_{105} is clearly preferred. To the left of M, I_{101} gives the higher utility level. This logical contradiction is avoided by never allowing indifference curves to cross.

Exhibit 7.40 Intersecting indifference curves

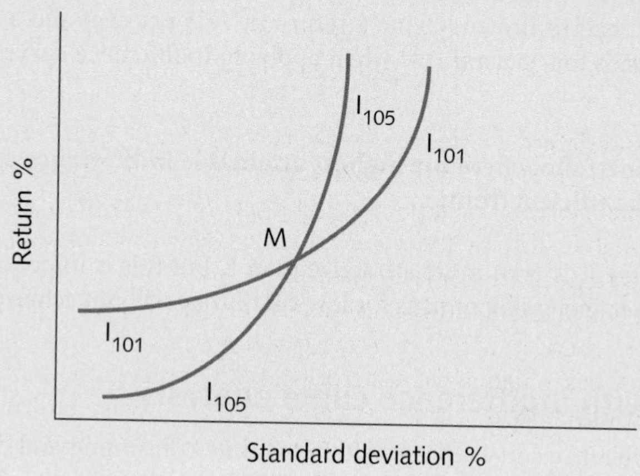

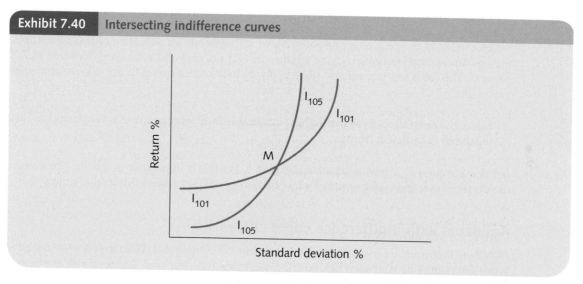

Mr Chisholm's personality and circumstances led to the drawing of his unique indifference curves with their particular slope. Other investors may be less risk averse than Mr Chisholm, in which case the increase in return required to compensate for each unit of increased risk will be less. That is, the indifference curves will have a lower slope. This is represented in **Exhibit 7.41(b)**. Alternatively, individuals may be less tolerant of risk and exhibit steeply sloped indifference curves, as demonstrated in **Exhibit 7.41(c)**. Here large increases in return are required for small increases in risk.

Exhibit 7.41 Varying degrees of risk aversion as represented by indifference curves

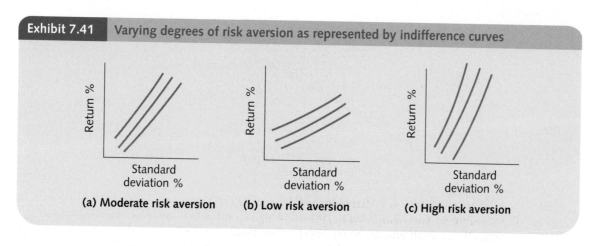

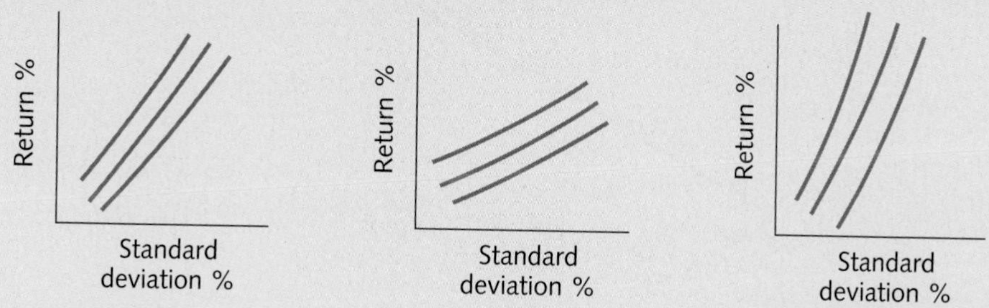

(a) Moderate risk aversion **(b) Low risk aversion** **(c) High risk aversion**

Choosing the optimal portfolio

We can now return to the investor considering investment in Augustus and Brown and apply indifference curve analysis to find the optimal portfolio. By assuming that this investor is moderately risk averse we can draw three of his indifference curves on to the risk-return profile diagram for two-asset portfolios of Augustus and Brown. This is shown in Exhibit 7.42. One option available is to select portfolio N, putting 25 per cent of the fund into Augustus and the remainder in Brown. This will give a respectable expected return of 18.75 per cent for a risk level of 12.2 per cent for the standard deviation. It is interesting to note that this investor would be just as content with the return of 15.5 per cent on portfolio J if risk were reduced to a standard deviation of 1.16 per cent. I_1 represents quite a high level of utility and the investor would achieve a high level of well-being selecting either N or J. However, this is not the highest level of utility available – which is what the investor is assumed to be trying to achieve. By moving on to the indifference curve I_2, further to the north-west, the investor will increase his satisfaction. This curve touches the risk-return combination line at only one point, M, which represents an allocation of half of the funds to Augustus and half to Brown, giving a return of 17.5 per cent and a standard deviation of 7.06 per cent. This leads to a general rule when applying indifference curves to the risk-return combination line:

Select the portfolio where the highest attainable indifference curve is tangential to (just touching) the efficient frontier.

Indifference curve I_3 is even more attractive than I_2 but this is impossible to obtain. The investor can dream of ever-increasing returns for low risk but he will not achieve this level of utility.

Problems with indifference curve analysis

Obtaining indifference curves for individuals is time consuming and difficult. It is also subject to error. Try estimating your own risk-return preferences and your own degree of risk aversion to gain an impression involved in drawing up curves from subjective material such as thoughts and

Exhibit 7.42 Optimal combination of Augustus and Brown

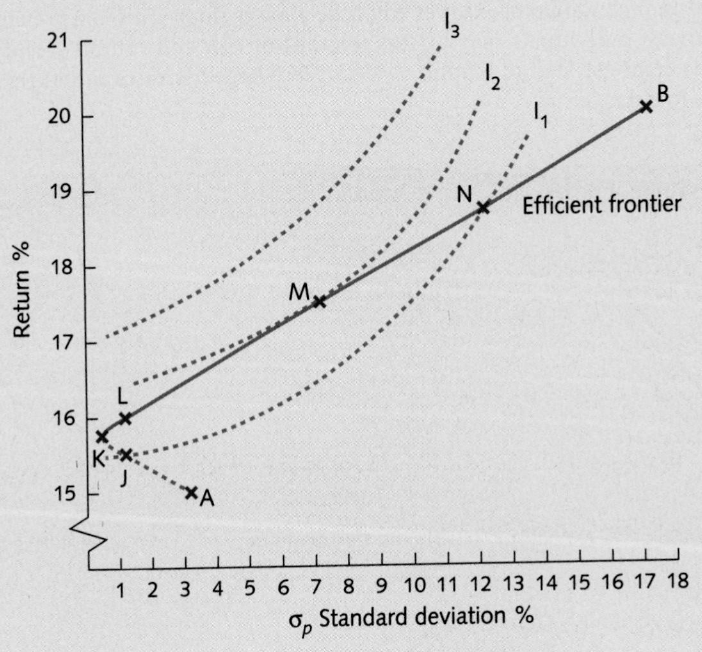

feelings. Even if you did arrive at firm conclusions at one specific time, are you confident that these will not change as your circumstances alter? It is plain that there are serious drawbacks to excessive reliance on mathematically precise curves when they are based on imprecise opinion. However it would be wrong to 'throw the baby out with the bathwater' and reject utility analysis completely. The model used does give us a representation of the different risk tolerances of individuals and permits us to come to approximate conclusions concerning likely optimal portfolios for particular individuals based on their risk-reward preferences. For instance a highly risk-averse person is unlikely to elect to place all funds in Brown but will tend to select portfolios close to L or K. The exact allocation is less important than the general principles of (a) identifying efficient portfolios and (b) selecting an efficient portfolio which roughly matches the degree of risk aversion of the decision maker.

The boundaries of diversification

We can now consider the extreme circumstances of perfect negative, perfect positive and zero correlation to demonstrate the outer boundaries of the risk-return relationships.

Consider the two securities C and D, the expected returns and standard deviations for which are presented in **Exhibit 7.43**.

Exhibit 7.43 Expected return and standard deviation, Companies C and D

	Company C	Company D
Expected return	$\bar{R}_C = 15\%$	$\bar{R}_D = 22\%$
Standard deviation	$\sigma_C = 3\%$	$\sigma_D = 9\%$

Perfect negative correlation

If we first assume that C and D are perfectly negatively correlated, $R_{CD} = -1$, then the point of minimum standard deviation is found as follows:

a = proportion of funds invested in C

$$a = \frac{\sigma_D^2 - \text{cov}\,(R_C, R_D)}{\sigma_C^2 + \sigma_D^2 - 2\,\text{cov}\,(R_C, R_D)}$$

or, given that $\text{cov}\,(R_C, R_D) = R_{CD}\sigma_C\sigma_D$:

$$a = \frac{\sigma_D^2 - R_{CD}\,\sigma_C\sigma_D}{\sigma_C^2 + \sigma_D^2 - 2R_{CD}\,\sigma_C\sigma_D}$$

$$a = \frac{9^2 - (-1 \times 3 \times 9)}{3^2 + 9^2 - (2 \times -1 \times 3 \times 9)} = 0.75$$

The portfolio which will reduce risk to zero is one which consists of 75 per cent of C and 25 per cent of D.

The return available on this portfolio is:

$$R_P = aR_C + (1 - a)\,R_D$$

$$= 0.75 \times 15 + 0.25 \times 22 = 16.75\%$$

Exhibit 7.44 The boundaries of diversification

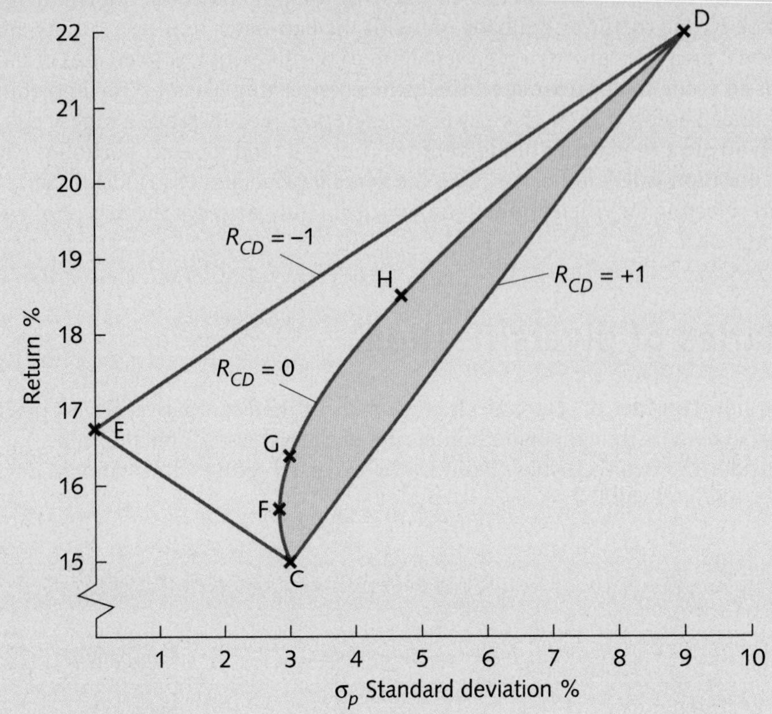

To confirm that this allocation will give the minimum risk the portfolio standard deviation could be calculated.

$$\sigma_p = \sqrt{a^2\sigma_C^2 + (1-a)^2\sigma_D^2 + 2a(1-a)\,R_{CD}\,\sigma_C\,\sigma_D}$$

$$\sigma_p = \sqrt{0.75^2 \times 3^2 + 0.25^2 \times 9^2 + 2 \times 0.75 \times 0.25 \times -1 \times 3 \times 9} = 0$$

This minimum variance portfolio has been labelled E in **Exhibit 7.44**. In the circumstances of a correlation coefficient of –1 all the other risk-return combinations are described by the dog-legged line CED. This describes the left boundary of the feasible set of portfolio risk-return lines.

Perfect positive correlation

The risk-return line for portfolios of C and D under the assumption of a correlation coefficient of +1 is a straight line joining C and D. This line forms the right boundary of possible portfolios. If the investment fund is evenly split between C and D both the expected return and the standard deviation will be weighted averages of those for single shares:

Expected return: $(15 \times 0.5) + (22 \times 0.5) = 18.5\%$
Standard deviation: $(3 \times 0.5) + (9 \times 0.5) = 6\%$

Zero correlation

The risk-return portfolio combinations for all correlation coefficients of less than +1 lie to the left of the line CD and exhibit non-linearity (that is, they are curved). The non-linearity becomes increasingly pronounced as the correlation coefficient approaches –1. The line CFGHD represents an intermediate level of the risk-reducing effect of diversification. For this line the correlation coefficient between C and D is set at 0. The plot points for the various portfolios are shown in **Exhibit 7.45**.

Exhibit 7.45 Risk-return combinations for C and D with a correlation coefficient of 0

Portfolio	C weighting (%)	D weighting (%)	Expected return (%)	Standard deviation
C	100	0	15	3.00
F	90	10	15.7	$\sqrt{0.9^2 \times 3^2 + 0.1^2 \times 9^2 + 0} = 2.85$
G	80	20	16.4	$\sqrt{0.8^2 \times 3^2 + 0.2^2 \times 9^2 + 0} = 3.00$
H	50	50	18.5	$\sqrt{0.5^2 \times 3^2 + 0.5^2 \times 9^2 + 0} = 4.74$
D	0	100	22	9.00

(All the calculations for C and D are shown in Excel spreadsheet form at www.pearsoned.co.uk/arnold)

For most investments in the real world, correlation coefficients tend to lie between 0 and +1. This is because general economic changes influence the returns on securities in similar ways, to a greater or lesser extent. This is particularly true for the returns on shares. This implies that risk reduction is possible through diversification but the total elimination of risk is unlikely. The shaded area in Exhibit 7.44 represents the risk-return region for two-asset portfolios for most ordinary shares.

Even private investors have adopted portfolio theory. The article in **Exhibit 7.46** is one of many discussing the qualities of shares in terms of covariances and standard deviations.

Exhibit 7.46

The dangers of risk

In this week's instalment of our monthly series on how to build more efficient portfolios of investments, we explain why even low-risk portfolios may not be as safe as they seem

How do you build a low-risk equity portfolio? If you think the answer is simply to stuff it with low-risk shares, go to the back of the class. If you want to reduce the riskiness of your portfolio, simply looking at the riskiness of individual shares isn't enough. You must also consider the covariances between shares – the degree to which they rise and fall together … two risky shares can make a safer portfolio, if one rises when the other falls.

A simple example shows how important covariances are. Imagine that since the start of 1998 your shareholdings had comprised equal weightings of just two stocks – Bass and Granada. Since 1988, this portfolio would have had a standard deviation of quarterly returns of 11.06 per cent. That's riskier than Bass alone. But had your portfolio comprised Bass and HSBC, its standard deviation would have been 9.35 per cent. Replacing Granada with HSBC would have cut your risk by 15 per cent, even though HSBC is a riskier stock than Granada.

This is possible because the covariance between Bass and HSBC is much lower than that between Bass and Granada. So falls in Bass have often been offset by rises in HSBC, and vice versa. Even high-risk stocks can have a place in a low-risk portfolio, if they have low covariances with other stocks. Not only is this a simple lesson, it's also a profitable one. Higher-risk stocks often have higher returns. So if you can get some of these in your portfolio, you may be able to achieve little risk without giving up decent returns.

In building a low-risk portfolio, your task, therefore, is to find stocks with low covariances. Sadly, this is harder than it sounds. Covariances, like share returns themselves, can vary over time. Just as past returns are no guide to future returns, so past covariances may be no guide to future covariances.

Take, for example, BP and J Sainsbury. Since the start of 1988, the covariance between the two – again using quarterly returns – has been minus five. That's very low indeed, suggesting the two stocks will often move in different directions. Often, but not always. Between December 1993 and March 1994, Sainsbury's price fell by over 15 per cent. But BP's price also fell, by 3 per cent. On that occasion, BP would have offered no protection against a fall in Sainsbury's price.

Source: Investors Chronicle, 7 August 1998, p. 11. Reprinted with permission.

Extension to a large number of securities

To ensure that the analysis is manageable we have so far confined ourselves to two-asset portfolios. Investors rarely construct portfolios from shares in just two firms. Most realise that if risk can be reduced by moving from a single investment to a portfolio of two shares it can be further reduced by adding a third and fourth security, and so on. Consider the three securities represented in **Exhibit 7.47**. If the investor were to limit the extent of diversification by dividing the fund between two shares, three possible portfolio risk-return combination lines are possible. Curve 1 represents portfolios made by varying allocations of a fund between A and B. Curve 2 shows the alternative risk and return profiles available by investing in B and C; and Curve 3 represents A and C portfolios. With three securities the additional option arises of creating three-asset portfolios. Curve 4 shows the further reduction in return fluctuations resulting from adding the third share.

For two-asset portfolios the alternative risk-return combinations are shown by a line or curve. For a three- (or more) asset portfolio the possible combinations are represented by an area. Thus

Exhibit 7.47 A three-asset portfolio

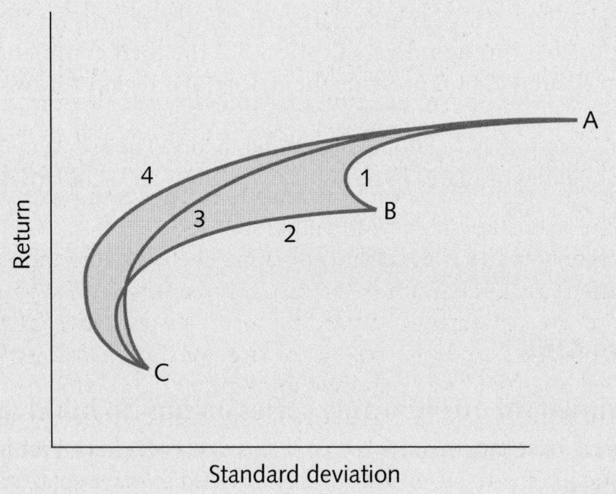

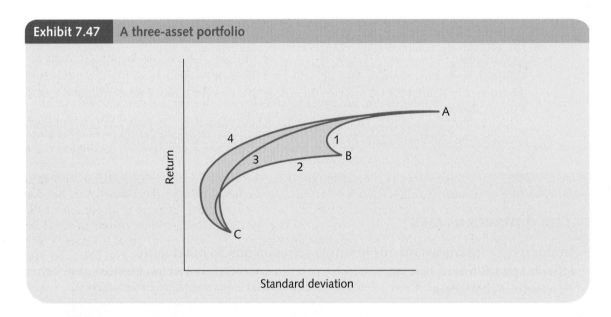

Exhibit 7.48 The opportunity set for multi-security portfolios and portfolio selection for a highly risk-averse person and for a slightly risk-averse person

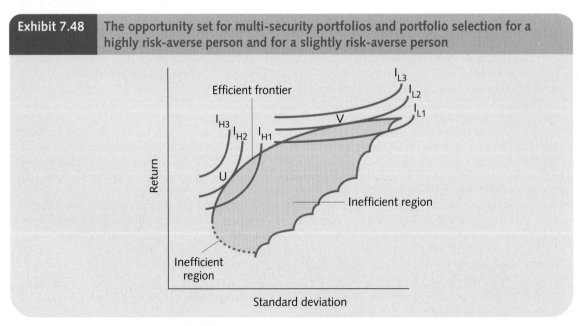

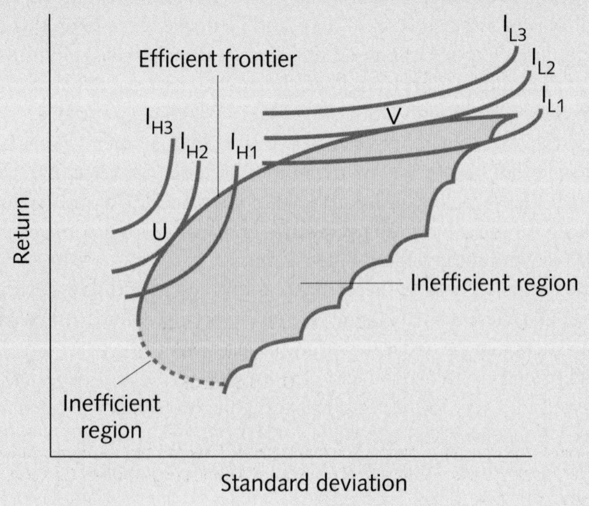

any risk-return combination within the shaded area of Exhibit 7.47 is potentially available to the investor. However, most of them will be unattractive because they are dominated by more efficient alternatives. In fact the rational investor will only be interested in portfolios lying on the upper part of Curve 4. This is the **efficient frontier** or **efficient boundary**. If the number of securities is raised the area representing the whole population of potential risk-return combinations comes to resemble an umbrella battling against a strong wind.

From Exhibit 7.47 it is not possible to establish which portfolio a rational investor would choose. This would depend on the individual's attitude to risk. Two types of investor attitudes are shown in **Exhibit 7.48** by drawing two sets of indifference curves. Indifference curves I_H are for a highly risk-averse person who would select the multi-asset portfolio U, which gives a relatively low return combined with a low risk. The less risk-averse person's attitude to risk is displayed in the indifference curves I_L. This person will buy portfolio V, accepting high risk but also anticipating high return. In this manner both investors achieve their optimum portfolios and the highest possible levels of utility.

Evidence on the benefits of diversification

A crucial question for a risk-averse investor is: 'How many securities should be included in a portfolio to achieve a reasonable degree of risk reduction?' Obviously the greater the number of securities the lower the risk. But many investors, particularly small ones, are not keen on dividing their resources into ever smaller amounts, particularly given the transaction cost of buying financial securities. So it would be useful to know the extent to which risk is reduced as additional securities are added to a portfolio. Solnik (1974) investigated this issue for shares in eight countries. The result for the UK is shown in **Exhibit 7.49**. The vertical axis measures portfolio risk as a percentage of the risk of holding an individual security.

Solnik randomly generated portfolios containing between one and 50 shares. Risk is reduced in a dramatic manner by the addition of the first four securities to the portfolio. Most of the benefits of diversification are generated by a portfolio of 10–15 securities. Thus up to 90 per cent of the benefit of diversification can be gained by holding a relatively small portfolio. Beyond this level the marginal risk reduction becomes relatively small. Also note that there is a level of risk below which the curve cannot fall even if larger numbers of securities are added to the portfolio. This is because there are certain risk factors common to all shares and these cannot be diversified away. This is called systematic (or market) risk and will be discussed in more detail in the next chapter.

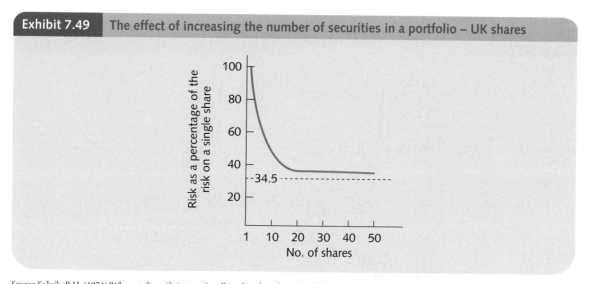

Exhibit 7.49 The effect of increasing the number of securities in a portfolio – UK shares

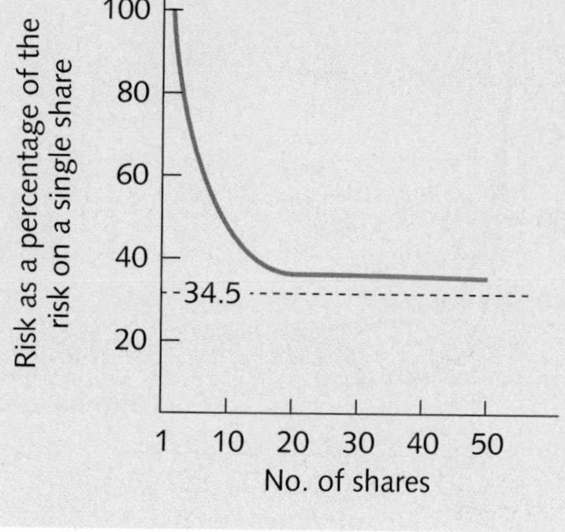

Source: Solnik, B.H. (1974) 'Why not diversify internationally rather than domestically?', *Financial Analysts Journal*, July–August, pp. 48–54. Copyright 1974, Association for Investment Management and Research. Reproduced and republished from *Financial Analysts Journal* with permission from the Association for Investment Management and Research. All rights reserved.

International diversification

We have seen that it is possible to reduce risk by diversifying within the boundaries of one country. It logically follows that further risk reduction is probably available by investing internationally. Exhibit 7.49 showed that there is a limit to the gains experienced by spreading investment across a range of shares in one country. This is because of the economy-wide risk factors such as interest rates and the level of economic activity, which influence all share returns simultaneously. Researchers have demonstrated that this limit can be side-stepped to some extent and that substantial further benefits can be attained through portfolio diversification into foreign shares. Solnik (1974) described a study for Germany in which 43.8 per cent of risk remains even after complete diversification through buying shares within the domestic stock market. While the figures for France and the USA were better, at 32.67 per cent and 27 per cent respectively, there was still a large amount of risk remaining, which could be reduced further by purchasing shares in other countries (*see* Exhibit 7.50).

The benefits of international diversification shown in Exhibit 7.51 are very significant. An internationally diversified portfolio reduced risk to less than half the level of a domestically focused portfolio. The international portfolio was around one-tenth as risky as holding a single company's shares.

Exhibit 7.50 The effect of increasing portfolio size with domestic shares

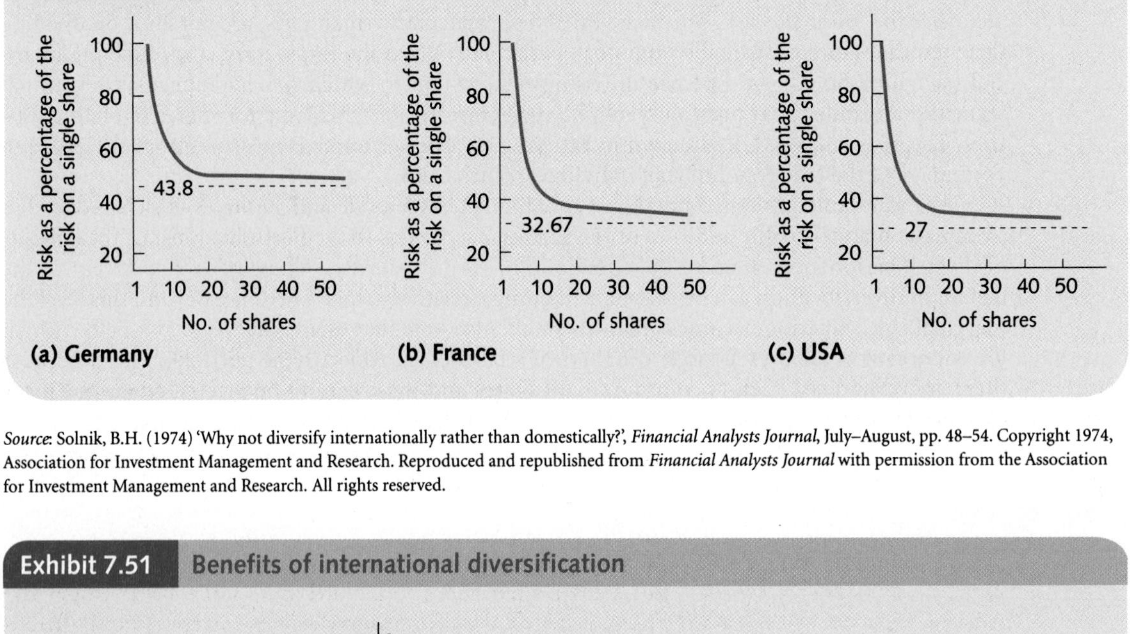

Source: Solnik, B.H. (1974) 'Why not diversify internationally rather than domestically?', *Financial Analysts Journal*, July–August, pp. 48–54.

Exhibit 7.51 Benefits of international diversification

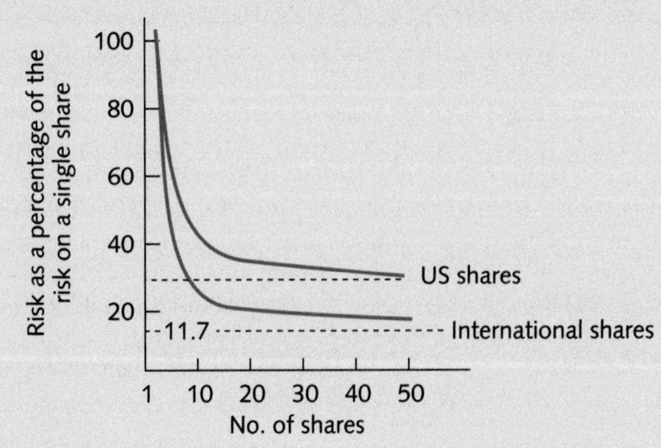

Source: Solnik, B.H. (1974) 'Why not diversify internationally rather than domestically?', *Financial Analysts Journal*, July–August, pp. 48–54.

If the world economy were so intimately linked that stock markets in different countries moved together, there would be little to gain from diversifying abroad. Fortunately, this sort of perfect positive correlation of markets does not occur. **Exhibit 7.52** shows that the correlation coefficients between national stock markets are significantly less than +1. The correlation between the USA and Canada (0.8 over 101 years or 0.78 over 1996–2000) is quite strong because their economies are closely linked whereas the correlation between Japan and European equity market returns has been relatively low.[3]

Exhibit 7.52 Correlation coefficients between world equity markets*

	Wld	US	UK	Swi	Swe	Spa	SAf	Neth	Jap	Ita	Ire	Ger	Fra	Den	Can	Bel	Aus
Wld		.93	.77	.59	.62	.67	.54	.73	.68	.52	.69	.69	.73	.57	.82	.54	.69
US	**.85**		.67	.44	.46	.53	.46	.57	.49	.40	.66	.56	.56	.46	.78	.45	.57
UK	**.70**	**.55**		.58	.44	.63	.31	.71	.42	.39	.73	.58	.59	.57	.57	.59	.56
Swi	**.68**	**.50**	**.62**		.39	.60	.19	.72	.36	.45	.57	.53	.64	.58	.35	.63	.37
Swe	**.62**	**.44**	**.42**	**.54**		.63	.38	.63	.34	.49	.27	.76	.76	.44	.61	.29	.44
Spa	**.41**	**.25**	**.25**	**.36**	**.37**		.35	.63	.32	.64	.50	.64	.75	.56	.51	.55	.54
SAf	**.55**	**.43**	**.49**	**.39**	**.34**	**.26**		.30	.44	.24	.31	.42	.37	.25	.62	.10	.66
Neth	**.57**	**.39**	**.42**	**.51**	**.43**	**.28**	**.29**		.39	.59	.63	.74	.77	.64	.55	.70	.46
Jap	**.45**	**.21**	**.33**	**.29**	**.39**	**.40**	**.31**	**.25**		.18	.33	.25	.36	.24	.50	.17	.59
Ita	**.54**	**.37**	**.43**	**.52**	**.39**	**.41**	**.41**	**.32**	**.34**		.33	.55	.71	.50	.40	.51	.38
Ire	**.58**	**.38**	**.73**	**.70**	**.42**	**.35**	**.42**	**.46**	**.29**	**.43**		.42	.45	.49	.54	.57	.50
Ger	**.30**	**.12**	**-.01**	**.22**	**.09**	**-.03**	**.05**	**.27**	**.06**	**.16**	**.03**		.83	.61	.57	.59	.46
Fra	**.62**	**.36**	**.45**	**.54**	**.44**	**.47**	**.38**	**.48**	**.25**	**.52**	**.53**	**.19**		.63	.60	.66	.48
Den	**.57**	**.38**	**.40**	**.51**	**.56**	**.34**	**.31**	**.50**	**.46**	**.38**	**.55**	**.22**	**.45**		.55	.54	.30
Can	**.80**	**.80**	**.55**	**.48**	**.53**	**.27**	**.54**	**.34**	**.30**	**.37**	**.41**	**.13**	**.35**	**.46**		.30	.65
Bel	**.58**	**.38**	**.40**	**.57**	**.43**	**.40**	**.29**	**.60**	**.25**	**.47**	**.49**	**.26**	**.68**	**.42**	**.35**		.30
Aus	**.66**	**.47**	**.66**	**.51**	**.50**	**.28**	**.56**	**.41**	**.28**	**.43**	**.62**	**.04**	**.47**	**.42**	**.62**	**.35**	

* *Correlations in bold (lower left-hand triangle) are based on 101 years of real dollar returns, 1900–2000. Correlations in roman (top right-hand triangle) are based on 60 months of real dollar returns, 1996–2000, from FTSE World (Ireland and South Africa) and MSCI (all others).*

Source: Dimson, E., Marsh, P. and Staunton, M. (2002) *Triumph of the Optimists: 101 Years of Global Investment Returns.* Princeton, NJ and Oxford: Princeton University Press.

Plainly, risk can be reduced by international diversification but some risk remains even for the broadest portfolio. There is an increasing degree of economic integration across the globe. The linkages mean that the economic independence of nations is gradually being eroded and there is some evidence that stock markets are becoming more correlated. A poor performance on Wall Street often ricochets across the Pacific to Tokyo and other Far East markets and causes a wave of depression on the European exchanges – or vice versa.

Despite the long-term trend to higher correlation there is still much to be gained from spreading investments internationally. Karen Lewis (1996) estimates that an American who invested globally between 1969 and 1993 would have been 10 per cent to 50 per cent better off than an individual who invested in the US domestic market. It is perhaps surprising to find that, typically, US investors assign only 15 per cent of their individual equity portfolios to foreign shares.[4] This contrasts with the fact that US shares now constitute about one-half of the total world equity capitalisation. For UK institutional investors (pension funds, insurance companies, etc.) the proportion of their portfolio in foreign equities rose substantially through the 1980s and 1990s as

[3] These correlation coefficients need to be treated with great caution as they tend to vary from one study to another. They also change a great deal over time; for example the correlation coefficient between the UK and the USA has varied from 0.67 to zero during the past century.

[4] Solnik and McLeavey (2003).

a number of restrictions were removed and now typically stands at over one-quarter of their equity funds.

However, around the world there is still a bias towards home investment. This disinclination to buy abroad is the result of many factors. These include: a lack of knowledge of companies and markets in faraway places; exchange rate problems; legal restrictions; cost; political risk. Many of these barriers can be, and are being, overcome and so the trend towards increasing internationalisation of security investment will probably continue.

The capital market line

Consider Portfolio A on the efficient frontier of a multi-asset portfolio feasibility set in **Exhibit 7.53**. An investor could elect to place all funds into such a portfolio and achieve a particular risk-return trade-off. Alternatively, point B could be selected. Here the investor places half the funds invested in an efficient portfolio, C, and half in a risk-free asset such as bonds or Treasury bills issued by a reputable government. These bonds are represented by point r_f which demonstrates a relatively low return but a corresponding zero standard deviation. By purchasing government bonds the investor is effectively lending to the government. Any combination containing a proportion of a share portfolio, such as C, and the risk-free asset will have an expected return which is a simple weighted average of the expected return of the share portfolio C and the risk-free asset r_f. More significantly, if the risk-free asset has a zero standard deviation, the standard deviation of a portfolio containing C and the risk-free asset will also be a simple weighted average. This results in the straight line between C and r_f representing all the possible allocations of a fund between these two types of investment.

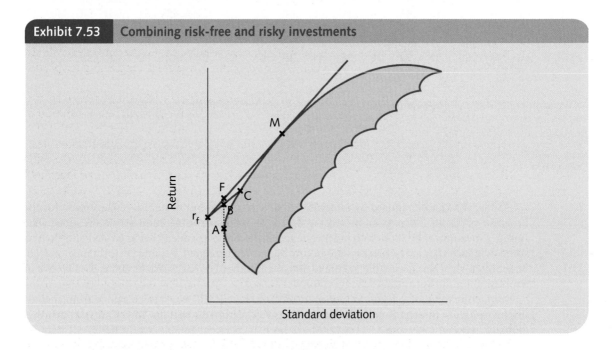

Exhibit 7.53 Combining risk-free and risky investments

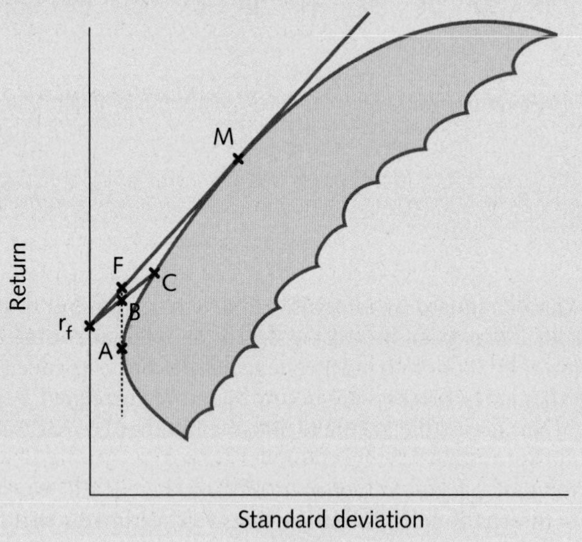

Point B in Exhibit 7.53 is obviously a more efficient combination of investments than point A because for the same level of risk a higher return is achievable. However, this is not the best result possible. If a fund were split between a portfolio of shares represented by M and the risk-free investment then all possible allocations between r_f and M would dominate those on the line r_fC. If the fund were divided so that risk-free lending absorbed most of the funds, with approximately one-quarter going into shares of portfolio M, then point F would be reached. This dominates points B and A and is therefore more efficient. The schedule r_fM describes the best possible risk-return combinations. No other share portfolio when combined with a riskless asset gives such a steep slope as Portfolio M. Therefore the investor's interests will be best served by choosing investments comprising Portfolio M and selecting an optimum risk-return combination, by allocating appropriate proportions of a fund between M and the risk free asset, r_f. This is demonstrated in **Exhibit 7.54**.

Exhibit 7.54 Indifference curves applied to combinations of the market portfolio and the risk-free asset

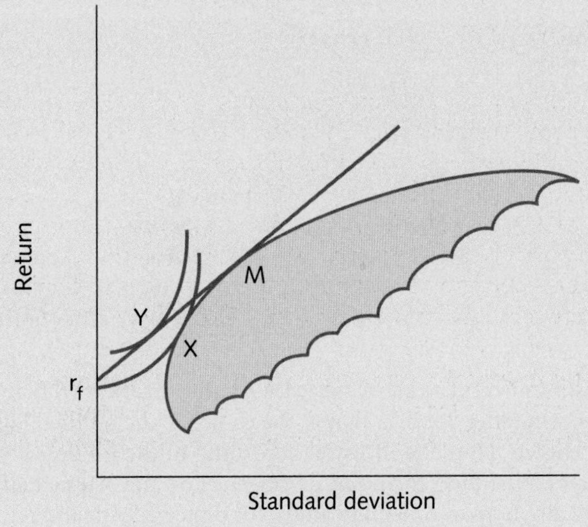

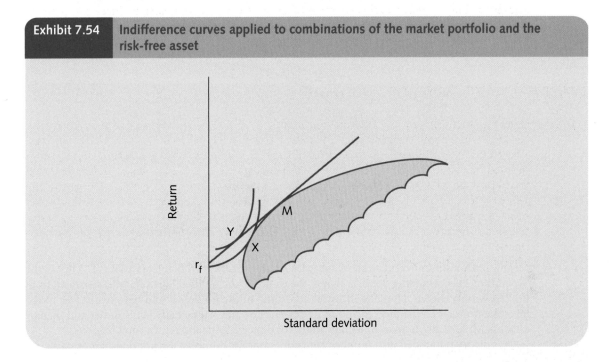

In Exhibit 7.54 an investment X is available which is on the efficient frontier of the feasible set. However, a higher indifference curve can be achieved if point Y is selected, comprising the portfolio M and the risk-free asset.

Under circumstances where risk-free lending is possible the original efficient frontier is significantly altered from a curve to a straight line (r_fM). Portfolio M is the most attractive portfolio of risk-bearing securities because it allows the investor to select a risk-return combination that is most efficient. In a perfect capital market investors will only be interested in holding the investments comprising M. Whatever their risk-return preference all investors will wish to invest some or all of the funds in Portfolio M. Combining this thought with the fact that someone must hold each risky asset, we are led to conclude that, in this idealised world, M is made up of all the possible risky assets available. Imagine if BT shares were not in the market portfolio. If nobody holds its shares the price will become zero. Investors will start to buy, attracted by its dividends. Thus, logically, it has to be held in the market portfolio. The market portfolio contains all traded securities weighted according to their market capitalisations.

To complete the model we need to consider the possibility of an investor borrowing rather than lending, that is, purchasing assets in Portfolio M to a value greater than the amount of money the investor has available from the existing fund. Borrowing to fund investment in risky assets is bound to lead to an overall increase in risk; but the corollary is that a higher return can be anticipated. This is shown in the line MN in **Exhibit 7.55**.

All the risk-return combinations along MN in Exhibit 7.55 dominate those along the original efficient frontier. An investor who was only mildly risk averse might select point T, purchasing the market portfolio and being financed in part by borrowing at the risk-free rate. This is preferable to Portfolio S, purchased without borrowing. The line r_fMN is called the **capital market line**; it describes the expected return and risk of all efficient portfolios. This idealised model shows that even though investors have differences in their tolerance of risk all will purchase the market portfolio. The degree of risk aversion of individuals expresses itself by the investors either placing some of the fund into risk-free securities, as in the case of the relatively risk-intolerant investor who selects point G, or borrowing (at the risk-free rate of return) to invest in the market portfolio, thereby

Exhibit 7.55 The capital market line

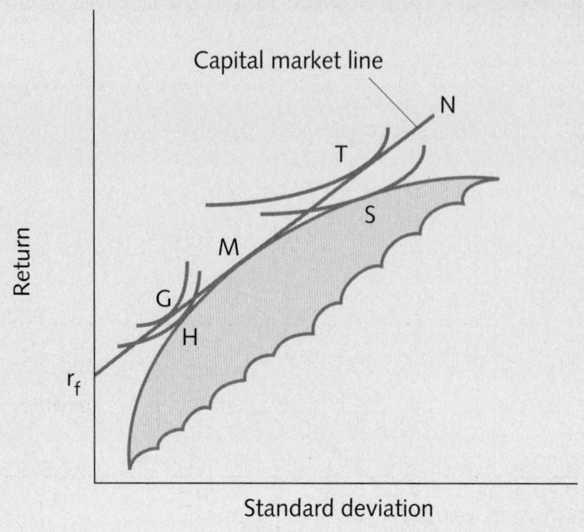

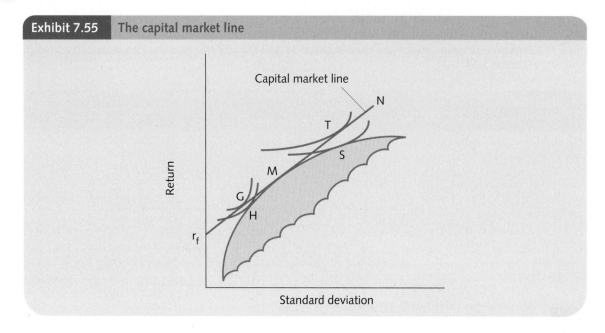

raising both risk and return, as in the case of the investor who selects point T. This is the **Separation Theorem** (after Tobin),[5] that is, the choice of the optimal Portfolio M is separated from the risk/return choice. Thus the investor, according to the model, would have two stages to the investment process. First, find the point of tangency on the original efficient frontier and thereby establish M; secondly, borrow or lend to adjust for preferred risk and return combinations.

This theory is founded on a number of major (some say dubious) assumptions, for example:

1 There are no transaction costs or taxes.
2 Investors can borrow or lend at the risk-free rate of return.
3 Investors have all relevant information regarding the range of investment opportunities. They make their choices on the basis of known expected returns and standard deviations.
4 Maximisation of utility is the objective of all investors.

A practical application of portfolio theory

Mark Capleton and Fred Cleary, writing in *Barclays Capital 2003 Equity Gilt Study*, provide an example of portfolio theory in use. They examine four possible investments. First, investing in equities (a broad range of shares). Secondly, investing by lending to the UK government by purchasing gilts (bonds in which the UK government promises to pay a capital sum after, say, 10 years, and in the meantime pays interest each year). Thirdly, buying gold. Fourthly, investing in **index-linked government bonds**. These are considered even lower risk than conventional gilts because whatever happens to inflation over the life of the bond you will receive a return of about 1–2 per cent above inflation.[6] Conventional gilts offer a nominal return without an inflation uplift. So if you buy a conventional bond yielding 5 per cent for £100 with a time to maturity of 10 years and after two years inflation rises to, say, 8 per cent, and stays at that level until the end of the bond's life, even though you receive £5 per year and £100 on maturity of the bond your purchasing power is reduced. By contrast the purchase of an index-linked bond would insulate you from inflation because the payout is always more than the inflation rate.

[5] Tobin's Separation Theorem was first discussed in his 1958 article.

[6] As you can see from Exhibit 7.56 the historic return above inflation has averaged 4 per cent. However, the current (2007) rate available over and above inflation is between 1 and 2 per cent.

Exhibit 7.56 Risk against return – UK equities, gilts, index-linked and gold, using annual data since end-1981

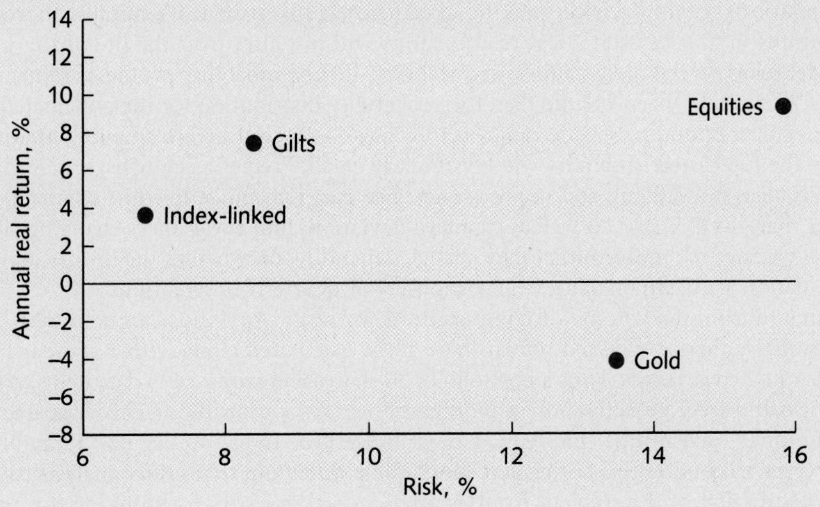

Source: Capleton, M. and Cleary, F.: Barclays Capital (2003) *Equity Gilt Study*. London: Barclays Capital. The authors also used Thompson Financial Data.

Exhibit 7.56 shows the returns and standard deviations of the four single investments over the period 1982 to 2002. Gold has performed very badly. However, because of its low correlation with the other assets it might still make sense to include it in portfolio comprised of the four investments. The researchers tested this by constructing an efficient frontier, shown in Exhibit 7.57. It is apparent that gold, if it shows the same risk and return characteristics over the next few years as it did over the previous 20, is best avoided in any portfolio – no portfolio on the efficient frontier contains gold. It is also apparent that a highly risk-averse person (e.g. some retired people) would select a portfolio containing large amounts of index-linked bonds and very few equities, whereas the less risk averse would select a high proportion of shares and reap the extra annual return.

Exhibit 7.57 Efficient frontier of four-asset portfolios, when equities, gilts, linkers and gold are available

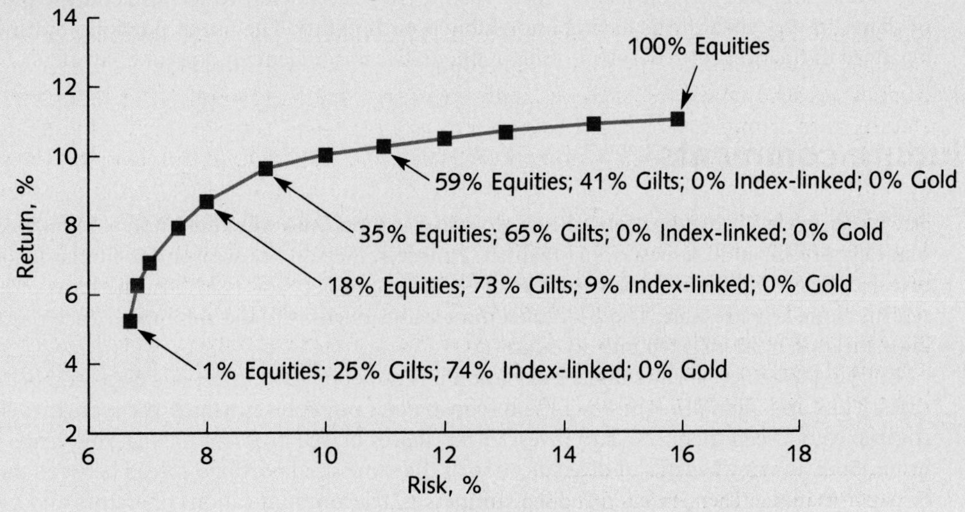

Source: Capleton, M. and Cleary, F.: Barclays Capital (2003) *Equity Gilt Study*. London: Barclays Capital. The authors also used Thompson Financial Data.

Problems with portfolio theory

The portfolio theory model is usually implemented using *historic* returns, standard deviations and correlations to aid decision making about *future* investment. Generally, there is the implicit assumption that key statistical relationships will not alter over the life of the investment. The model relies on the predictability and stability of the probability profile of returns. If the returns have, historically, been volatile then the probability distribution for the anticipated returns will be given a correspondingly wide range; if they have been confined to small fluctuations in the past, then the forecasted variability will be similarly small. Predicting returns, standard deviations and covariances is a difficult and imprecise art. The past may guide to some degree, but there remain large margins for error. As well as standard deviations and covariances changing significantly over time, we have the problem that they change depending on whether the historic data used for their calculation are based on daily, weekly, monthly or quarterly observations.

In addition, the volume of computations for large portfolios can be inhibiting. If there are n securities then n expected returns have to be calculated along with n standard deviations and $n(n-1)/2$ covariances. Thus a portfolio of 30 shares will require 495 data items to be calculated.

Also, the accurate estimation of indifference curves is probably an elusive goal and therefore the techniques used in this chapter can be criticised for trying to use unobtainable information. However, to counter this criticism it should be pointed out that utility analysis combined with an approximation of the efficient frontier provides a framework for thinking through the implications of portfolio selection. It is perhaps true that people cannot express their indifference curves exactly, but they will probably be able to state their risk preferences within broad categories, such as 'highly risk averse' or 'moderately risk averse' and so on. Through such approximate methods more appropriate portfolio selection can be made than would be the case without the framework. The model has been particularly useful in the fund management industry for constructing portfolios of different risk-return characteristics by weighting classes of investment assets differently, for example domestic shares, cash, bonds, foreign shares, property. Theorists have gone a stage further and developed 'portfolio optimisers'. These are mathematical computer programs designed to select an optimal portfolio. Relatively few investment managers have adopted these models, despite their familiarity with the principles and technical aspects of portfolio theory. It appears that traditional approaches to investment selection are valued more highly than the artificial precision of the optimisers. The problem seems to stem from the difficulty of finding high-quality data to put into the system on expected returns, standard deviations, covariances and so on – because of the necessity to rely on past returns. Extreme historical values such as an extraordinarily low standard deviation can lead the program to suggest counter-intuitive and uninvestable portfolios. They have a tendency to promote a high turnover of shares within the portfolio by failing to take into account transaction costs. Also there is a tendency to recommend the purchasing of shares in very small firms having impossibly poor liquidity. The use of portfolio optimisers fits a pattern in finance: entirely substituting mathematics for judgement does not pay off.

Concluding comments

The criticisms levelled at portfolio theory do strike at those who would use it in a dogmatic, mathematically precise and unquestioning manner. However, they do not weaken the fundamental truths revealed. Selecting shares (or other types of securities, projects or assets) on the basis of expected returns alone is inadequate. The additional dimensions of risk and the ability to reduce risk through diversification must be taken into account.

In trying to achieve a low standard deviation it is not enough to invest in a large number of securities. The fundamental requirement is to construct a portfolio in which the securities have low covariance between them. Thus to invest in the shares of 100 different engineering firms will not bring about as many benefits of diversification as the same sized portfolio spread between the sectors of paper manufacturers, retailers, media companies, telecommunications operators and computer software producers, etc. Returns on firms in the same industry are likely to respond in similar ways to economic and other events, to greater or lesser degrees, and so may all do badly at the same time. Firms in different industries are likely to have lower covariances than firms within an industry.

Key points and concepts

- The one-year holding period return:

  $$R = \frac{D_1 + P_1 - P_0}{P_0}$$

  Use IRR-type calculations for multi-period returns.

- With **perfect negative correlation** the risk on a portfolio can fall to zero if an appropriate allocation of funds is made.

- With **perfect positive correlations** between the returns on investments, both the expected returns and the standard deviations of portfolios are weighted averages of the expected returns and standard deviations, respectively, of the constituent investments.

- In cases of **zero correlation** between investments risk can be reduced through diversification, but it will not be eliminated.

- The **correlation coefficient** ranges from –1 to +1. Perfect negative correlation has a correlation coefficient of –1. Perfect positive correlation has a correlation coefficient of +1.

- **The degree of risk reduction** for a portfolio depends on:

  a the extent of statistical interdependency between the returns on different investments; and
  b the number of securities in the portfolio.

- **Portfolio expected returns** are a weighted average of the expected returns on the constituent investments:

  $$R_P = aR_A + (1 - a)R_B$$

- **Portfolio standard deviation** is less than the weighted average of the standard deviation of the constituent investments (except for perfectly positively correlated investments):

  $$\sigma_P = \sqrt{a^2\sigma_C^2 + (1 - a)^2\sigma_D^2 + 2a(1 - a) \operatorname{cov}(R_C, R_D)}$$

  $$\sigma_P = \sqrt{a^2\sigma_C^2 + (1 - a)^2\sigma_D^2 + 2a(1 - a) R_{CD}\sigma_C\sigma_D}$$

- **Covariance** means the extent to which the returns on two investments move together:

  $$\operatorname{cov}(R_A, R_B) = \sum_{i=1}^{n} \{(R_A - \bar{R}_A)(R_B - \bar{R}_B)p_i\}$$

- **Covariance and the correlation coefficient** are related. Covariance can take on any positive or negative value. The correlation coefficient is confined to the range –1 to +1:

  $$R_{AB} = \frac{\operatorname{cov}(R_A, R_B)}{\sigma_A\sigma_B}$$

  or $\operatorname{cov}(R_A, R_B) = R_{AB}\sigma_A\sigma_B$

- **Efficient portfolios** are on the **efficient frontier**. These are combinations of investments which maximise the expected returns for a given standard deviation. Such portfolios **dominate** all other possible portfolios in an **opportunity set** or **feasible set**.

- To find the proportion of the fund, *a*, to invest in investment C in a two-asset portfolio to achieve **minimum variance** or **standard deviation**:

  $$a = \frac{\sigma_D^2 - \operatorname{cov}(R_C, R_D)}{\sigma_C^2 + \sigma_D^2 - 2\operatorname{cov}(R_C, R_D)}$$

- **Indifference curves** for risk and return:
  - are upward sloping;
  - do not intersect;
  - are preferred if they are closer to the 'north-west';
  - are part of an infinite set of curves;
  - have a slope which depends on the risk aversion of the individual concerned.
- **Optimal portfolios** are available where the highest attainable indifference curve is tangential to the efficient frontier.
- **Most securities** have correlation coefficients in the range of 0 to +1.
- The feasible set for **multi-asset portfolios** is an area that resembles an umbrella.
- **Diversification within a home stock market** can reduce risk to less than one-third of the risk on a typical single share. Most of this benefit is achieved with a portfolio of 10 securities.
- **International diversification** can reduce risk even further than domestic diversification.
- **Problems with portfolio theory:**
  - relies on past data to predict future risk and return;
  - involves complicated calculations;
  - indifference curve generation is difficult;
  - few investment managers use computer programs because of the nonsense results they frequently produce.

References and further reading

Barclays Capital *Equity Gilt Studies*. London: Barclays Capital.

Annual reports packed with data on security returns and articles on current investment debates.

Barry, C.B., Peavy J.W. (III) and Rodriguez, M. (1998) 'Performance characteristics of emerging capital markets', *Financial Analysts Journal*, January/February, pp. 72–80.

Some useful evidence/data of relevance to international diversification.

Blake, D. (2000) *Financial Market Analysis*. Chichester: Wiley.

A more detailed and mathematical treatment.

Bodie, Z., Kane, A. and Marcus, A. J. (2005) *Investments*, 6th edn. New York: McGraw-Hill.

Contains a relatively easy-to-follow discussion of portfolio theory and CAPM.

Cochrane, J.H. (2001) *Asset Pricing*. Princeton, NJ, and Oxford: Princeton University Press.

An examination of asset pricing theory aimed at PhD students and academics.

Cooper, I. and Kaplanis, E. (1994) 'Home bias in equity portfolios, inflation hedging and international capital market equilibrium', *Review of Financial Studies*, 7(1), pp. 45–60.

Examines the general bias of investors toward investing in their domestic stock market.

Dimson, E., Marsh, P. and Staunton, M. (2002) *Triumph of the Optimists: 101 Years of Global Investment Returns*. Princeton, NJ, and Oxford: Princeton University Press.

An excellent source of data and thought-provoking discussion of equity risk premiums.

Divecha, A.B., Drach, J. and Stefek, D. (1992) 'Emerging markets: a quantitative perspective', *Journal of Portfolio Management*, Fall, pp. 41–50.

An investigation of the risk-reducing benefits of international diversification.

Economist, The (1991) 'School brief: risk and return', 2 February.

Concise and clear discussion of portfolio theory.

Economist, The (1996) 'Economic focus: stay-at-home shareholders', 17 February.

Discusses the attractions and problems of international diversification.

Elton, E.J., Gruber, M.J., Brown, S.J. and Goetzmann, W.N. (2007) *Modern Portfolio Theory and Investment Analysis*, 7th edn. Chichester: John Wiley & Sons.

From introductory to advanced portfolio theory. Well written and easy to follow. Suffers from inadequate updating.

Fama, E.F. and Miller, M.H. (1972) *The Theory of Finance*. Orlando, FL: Holt, Rinehart & Winston.

Utility analysis and indifference curve theory.

Frost, P.A. and Savarino, J.E. (1986) 'Portfolio size and estimation risk', *Journal of Portfolio Management*, 12, Summer, pp. 60–4.
Discussion of portfolio theory.

Goetzman, W.N., Lingfeng, L. and Rouwenhorst, K.G. (2005) 'Long-term global market correlations', *Journal of Business* 78(1), pp. 1–38.
Shows correlations of shares across countries over 150 years. Correlations shift overtime.

Haugen, R.A. (2001) *Modern Investment Theory*, 5th edn. Upper Saddle River, NJ: Prentice-Hall.
A more technical and advanced treatment of portfolio theory.

Jorion, P. (1992) 'Portfolio optimisation in practice', *Financial Analysts Journal*, 48, January/February, pp. 68–74.
The use of portfolio theory investigated.

Kaplanis, E. and Schaefer, S. (1991) 'Exchange risk and international diversification in bond and equity portfolios', *Journal of Economics and Business*, 43, pp. 287–307.
Considers the problem of exchange-rate risk on internationally diversified portfolios.

Lewis, K. (1996) 'Consumption, stock returns, and the gains from international risk-sharing', *NBER Working Paper*, No. 5410, January.
Advanced theoretical discussion of the gains from international diversification.

Lintner, J. (1965) 'The valuation of risky assets and the selection of risky investments in stock portfolios and capital budgets', *Review of Economics and Statistics*, 47, February, pp. 13–37.
Theoretical paper contributing to the development of portfolio theory.

Markowitz, H.M. (1952) 'Portfolio selection', *Journal of Finance*, 7, pp. 77–91.
Pioneering theory.

Markowitz, H.M. (1959) *Portfolio Selection: Efficient Diversification of Investments.* New York: John Wiley & Sons (1991); 2nd edn: Cambridge, MA: Basil Blackwell.
The Nobel Prize winner explains his ideas.

Markowitz, H.M. (1991) 'Foundations of portfolio theory', *Journal of Finance*, June.
Markowitz describes some of his thinking in the development of portfolio theory. Plus some advanced utility theory.

Michaud, R.O. (1989) 'The Markowitz optimization enigma: Is "optimized" optimal?', *Financial Analysts Journal*, 45, January–February, pp. 31–42.
Discusses reasons for the low rate of adoption of portfolio optimiser programmes by the investment community.

Michaud, R.O., Bergstorm, G.L., Frashure, R.D. and Wolahan, B.K. (1996) 'Twenty years of international equity investment', *Journal of Portfolio Management*, Fall, pp. 9–22.
Diversifying into well-developed markets did not reduce risk substantially.

Mossin, J. (1966) 'Equilibrium in a capital asset market', *Econometrica*, 34, October, pp. 768–83.
Theoretical paper taking forward portfolio theory and discussing the 'market line'.

Sharpe, W.F. (1963) 'A simplified model for portfolio analysis', *Management Science*, 9, pp. 277–93.
Builds on Markowitz's work, focusing on the determination of the efficient set.

Sharpe, W.F., Alexander, G.J. and Bailey, J.V. (1999) *Investments*, 6th edn. Upper Saddle River, NJ: Prentice-Hall.
Chapters 6, 7, 8 and 9 contain expositions of portfolio theory.

Solnik, B.H. (1974) 'Why not diversify internationally rather than domestically?', *Financial Analysts Journal*, July–August, pp. 48–54.
Empirical investigation on the effect of diversification for eight countries.

Solnik, B.H. and McLeavey, D. (2003) *International Investments*, 5th edn. Boston, MA: Pearson Education.
The benefits of international diversification are discussed in an accessible manner – some good data.

Spiedell, L.S. and Sappenfield, R. (1992) 'Global diversification in a shrinking world', *Journal of Portfolio Management*, Fall, pp. 57–67.
Diversifying into emerging markets enables significant risk reduction.

Tobin, J. (1958) 'Liquidity preference as behaviour toward risk', *Review of Economic Studies*, February, 26, pp. 65–86.
The first discussion of the separation of the selection of the efficient market portfolio and the individual's risk return choice.

Wagner, W.H. and Lau, S. (1971) 'The effects of diversification on risk', *Financial Analysts Journal*, November–December.
Empirical evidence of the effect on standard deviation of increasing portfolio size.

Case study recommendations

Please see www.pearsoned.co.uk/arnold for case study synopses.

- Pension policy at the Boots Co. plc. Authors: Viceira, L.M. and A.M. Mitsui (2003) Harvard Business School.
- Susan Griffin: Formulation of a long-term investment strategy. Authors: D.B. Crane and J.D. Stevens (2003). Harvard Business School.
- Harvard Management Company. Author: J.O. Light (2001) Harvard Business School.
- Portfolio and Partnership. Authors: F. Hardymon and A. Leamon (2003) Harvard Business School.

Self-review questions

1 How do you calculate the risk on a two-asset portfolio?

2 What is a dominant portfolio?

3 What are indifference curves and why can they never intersect?

4 How are holding-period returns calculated?

5 Show how the covariance and correlation coefficient are related.

6 Explain the necessary conditions for the standard deviation on a portfolio to be zero.

7 Illustrate the efficient frontier and explain why all portfolios on the frontier are not necessarily optimal.

8 A risk-averse investor currently holds low-risk shares in one company only. In what circumstances would it be wise to split the fund by purchasing shares in a high-risk and high-return share?

9 'The objective of portfolio investment is to minimise risk.' Do you agree?

10 Why is the standard deviation on a portfolio not a weighted average of the standard deviations of the constituent securities?

11 Describe why investors do not routinely calculate portfolio standard deviations and indifference curves.

12 How are the gains from diversification linked to correlation coefficients?

Questions and problems

myfinancelab ***Questions with an icon are also available for practice in MyFinanceLab with additional supporting resources.***

1 What is the holding-period return for a share which cost £2.50, was held for a year and then sold for £3.20, and which paid a dividend at the end of the holding period of 10p?

2 Calculate the percentage holding-period return for a share which is held for three months and sold for £5. The purchase price was £4.80 and no dividend is payable.

3 Shares in Whitchat plc can be purchased today for £1.20. The expected dividend in one year is 5p. This is expected to be followed by annual dividends of 6p and 7p respectively in the following two years. The shares are expected to be sold for £2 in three years. What is the average annual rate of return? What is the three-year holding-period return?

?

4* *(Examination level if combined with Questions 5 and 6)* The probability of a hot summer is 0.2. The probability of a moderately warm summer is 0.6, whereas the probability of a wet and cold summer is 0.2. If a hot summer occurs then the return on shares in the Ice Cream Manufacturing Company will be 30 per cent. If moderately warm the return will be 15 per cent, and if cold 2 per cent.

a What is the expected return?
b What is the standard deviation of that return?

?

5* Splash plc owns a swimming pool near to a major seaside resort town. Holidaymakers boost the turnover of this firm when they are unable to use the beach on cold and wet days. Thus Splash's returns are best when the weather is poor. The returns on the shares are shown in the table below, together with the probability of when a particular weather 'event' may occur.

Event	Probability	Returns on shares in Splash plc (%)
Hot weather	0.2	5
Modestly warm	0.6	15
Cold weather	0.2	20
	1.0	

Calculate

a The expected return for a share in Splash plc.
b The standard deviation of a share in Splash plc.

?

6* a Given the data on the Ice Cream Manufacturing Company (ICMC) in Question 4 and Splash plc in Question 5, now calculate the expected returns and standard deviation of the following portfolios.

Portfolio	Proportion of funds invested in ICMC	Proportion of funds invested in Splash
A	0.80	0.20
B	0.50	0.50
C	0.25	0.75

b Calculate the correct allocation of resources between ICMC and Splash which will give the minimum standard deviation. Draw a risk-return line on graph paper using the data you have generated from Questions 4, 5 and 6a.

(An Excel spreadsheet showing the calculations for Questions 4, 5 and 6 is available in the Lecturers-only section at www.pearsoned.co.uk/arnold)

?

7 Given the following expected returns and standard deviations for shares X and Y,

$\bar{R}_X = 25\%, \bar{R}_Y = 35\%, \sigma_X = 15\%, \sigma_Y = 20\%$

a What is the expected return and standard deviation for a portfolio composed of 50 per cent of X and 50 per cent of Y assuming X and Y have a correlation coefficient of –0.7?
b What is the expected return and standard deviation for a portfolio composed of 30 per cent of X and 70 per cent of Y, assuming X and Y have a correlation coefficient of +0.5?

?

8 The returns on shares S and T vary depending on the state of economic growth.

State of economy	Probability of economic state occurring	Returns on S if economic state occurs (%)	Returns on T if economic state occurs (%)
Boom	0.15	45	18
Growth	0.70	20	17
Recession	0.15	–10	16

Required

a Calculate the expected return and standard deviation for share S.
b Calculate the expected return and standard deviation for share T.
c What are the covariance and the correlation coefficient between returns on S and returns on T?
d Determine a portfolio expected return and standard deviation if two-thirds of a fund are devoted to S and one-third devoted to T.

?

(An Excel spreadsheet showing the calculations for Question 8 is available at www.pearsoned.co.uk/arnold)

9 Using the results generated in Question 8 and three or four additional calculations, display the efficient frontier for a two-asset portfolio consisting of S and T.

Show a set of indifference curves for a highly risk-averse investor and select an optimal portfolio on the assumption that the investor can only invest in these two shares.

?

10 An investor has £100,000 to invest in shares of Trent or Severn the expected returns and standard deviations of which are as follows.

The correlation coefficient between those two shares is –0.2.

	$\bar{R}$	σ
Trent	10	5
Severn	20	12

Required

a Calculate the portfolio expected returns and standard deviations for the following allocations.

Portfolio	Trent (%)	Severn (%)
A	100	0
B	75	25
C	50	50
D	25	75
E	0	100

b Calculate the minimum standard deviation available by varying the proportion of Trent and Severn shares in the portfolio.
c Create a diagram showing the feasible set and the efficient frontier.
d Select an optimal portfolio for a slightly risk-averse investor using indifference curves. ?

11 Big Trucks plc is considering two major projects. The first is to expand production at the Midlands factory. The second is to start production in the Far East. The returns in terms of internal rates of return depend on world economic growth. These are as follows.

World growth	Probability of growth occurring	IRR for Midlands project (%)	IRR for Far East project (%)
High	0.3	20	50
Medium	0.4	18	30
Low	0.3	16	0

Calculate

a The expected return and standard deviation of each project.
b An alternative to selecting one project or the other is to split the available investment funds between the two projects. Now calculate the expected return and standard deviation if half of the funds were devoted to the Midlands project and half to the Far East. Assume returns per pound invested remain constant regardless of the size of the investment.
c Calculate the expected return and standard deviation for a series of four other possible allocations of the funds and construct a risk-return line.
d Suggest an approach for choosing the optimal allocation of funds assuming a highly risk-averse management and shareholders own shares in this one firm only. ?

12 Shares in F and G are perfectly negatively correlated.

	$\bar{R}$	σ
F	17	6
G	25	10

a Calculate the expected return and standard deviation from a portfolio consisting of 50 per cent of F and 50 per cent of G.
b How would you allocate the fund to achieve a zero standard deviation? ?

13 Suppose that Mrs Qureshi can invest all her savings in shares of Ihser plc, or all her savings in Resque plc. Alternatively she could diversify her investment between these two. There are three possible states of the economy, boom, growth or recession, and the returns on Ihser and Resque depend on which state will occur.

State of the economy	Probability of state of the economy occurring	Ihser return (%)	Resque return (%)
Boom	0.3	40	10
Growth	0.4	30	15
Recession	0.3	–10	20

Required

a Calculate the expected return, variance and standard deviation for each share.

b Calculate the expected return, variance and standard deviation for the following diversifying allocations of Mrs Qureshi's savings:

(i) 50% in Ihser, 50% in Resque;

(ii) 10% in Ihser, 90% in Resque.

c Explain the relationship between risk reduction and the correlation between individual financial security returns.

?

14* *(Examination level)* **Horace Investments**

Your Uncle Horace is a wealthy man with investments in a variety of businesses. He is also a generous person, especially to his nieces and nephews. He has written explaining that he will be distributing some of his shareholdings amongst the next generation. To your surprise, he has offered you £100,000 of shares in two firms of great sentimental value to him: Ecaroh and Acehar. You may allocate the £100,000 in any one of four ways. The first two options are to put all of the money into one of the firms. An alternative is to allocate half to Ecaroh and half to Acehar. Finally you may have £90,000 of Ecaroh shares and £10,000 of Acehar shares. During the week you are given to make your decision you contact a friend who is a corporate analyst with access to extensive brokers' and other reports on firms. The information he provides could help you to allocate this generous gift. He tells you that the market consensus is that Ecaroh is a relatively unexciting but steady, reliable firm producing profits which do not vary in an erratic fashion. If the economy is growing strongly then the returns on Ecaroh are expected to be 10 per cent per year. If normal economic growth occurs then the returns will be 15 per cent and if poor growth is the outcome the returns will be 16 per cent.

Acehar, a consumer electronics firm, is a much more exciting and dynamic but risky firm. Profits vary in dramatic ways with the general level of activity in the economy. If growth is strong then Acehar will return 50 per cent; if normal, 25 per cent; and, if poor, there will be no return. You generate your own estimates of the probabilities of particular economic growth rates occurring by amalgamating numerous macroeconomic forecasts and applying a dose of scepticism to any one estimate. Your conclusions are that there is a 30 per cent chance of strong growth, a 40 per cent chance of normal growth and the probability of slow growth is put at 30 per cent.

Because of Horace's emotional attachment to these firms he insists that these are the only investment(s) you hold, as he puts it, to 'engender commitment and interest in the success of his corporate babies'.

Required

a For each of the alternatives on offer calculate returns and standard deviation.

b Draw a risk and return diagram on graph paper displaying the four options and then add a reasonable risk-return line for all possible allocations between Acehar and Ecaroh. (This is hypothetical to some extent because you do not know the minimum standard deviation point.)

State which of the four options are efficient portfolios and which are inefficient given your risk-return line.

c You are young and not as risk averse as most people, because you feel you will be able to bounce back from a financial disaster should one occur. Draw indifference curves on the diagram for a person who is only slightly risk averse. Demonstrate an optimal risk-return point on the risk-return line by labelling it point 'J'.

d Briefly discuss the benefits of greater diversification. Do these benefits continue to increase with ever greater diversification?

?

15 *(Examination level)* You have been bequeathed a legacy of £100,000 and you are considering placing the entire funds either in shares of company A or in shares in company B.

When you told your stock broker about this plan he suggested two alternative investment approaches.

a Invest some of the money in A and some in B to give you at least a small degree of diversification. The proportions suggested are given in Table 2 below.

b Invest the entire sum in a broad range of investments to reduce risk. This portfolio is expected to produce a return of 23 per cent per year with a standard deviation of 6 per cent.

To assist your final decision the broker provides you with forecasts by expert City analysts for shares in A and B given various states of the economy – *see* Table 1.

Table 1

State of the economy	Probability of that state of the economy	Returns on A (%)	Returns on B (%)
Recession	0.25	10	15
Growth	0.50	20	55
Boom	0.25	30	–10

Table 2

Portfolio	Proportion of portfolio invested in A (%)	Proportion of portfolio invested in B (%)
1	25	75
2	75	25
3	90	10

Required

a Compare the risk and return of the alternatives (including your original intention of putting all the money into either A or B).

b Display the results on graph paper and draw an estimated portfolio risk-return line based on the plot points for the two-share portfolio. (There is no requirement to calculate the minimum risk portfolio.)

c Describe the efficient and inefficient region.

d Use indifference curves to select the optimal portfolio to give the highest utility assuming that you are highly risk averse.

e Define the Market Portfolio in Modern Portfolio Theory.

?

Assignments

1 If you have access to information on financial security return probability profiles then draw up a report showing the efficient frontier for a two-asset portfolio. Draw indifference curves based on canvassed opinion and/or subjective judgement and select an optimal portfolio.

2 If you have access to the estimated probability distribution of returns for some projects within the firm, consider the impact of accepting these projects on the overall risk-return profile of the firm. For instance, are they positively or negatively correlated with the existing set of activities?

CHAPTER

8

The capital asset pricing model and multi-factor models

LEARNING OUTCOMES

The ideas, frameworks and theories surrounding the relationship between the returns on a security and its risk are pivotal to most of the issues discussed in this book. At times it may seem that this chapter is marching you up to the top of the hill only to push you down again. But remember, sometimes what you learn on a journey and what you see from new viewpoints are more important than the ultimate destination. By the end of this chapter the reader should be able to:

- describe the fundamental features of the Capital Asset Pricing Model (CAPM);
- show an awareness of the empirical evidence relating to the CAPM;
- explain the key characteristics of multi-factor models, including the Arbitrage Pricing Theory (APT) and the three-factor model;
- express a reasoned and balanced judgement of the risk-return relationship in financial markets.

Introduction

One financial theory has dominated the academic literature and influenced greatly the practical world of finance and business for over three decades since it was first expounded by the Nobel prizewinner William Sharpe and other theoreticians.[1] This is the Capital Asset Pricing Model (CAPM). At its heart the CAPM (pronounced cap-em) has an old and common observation – the returns on a financial asset increase with risk. The 'breakthrough' in the 1960s was to define risk in a very precise way. It was no longer enough to rely on standard deviation after the work of Markowitz and others (see Chapter 7) had shown the benefits of diversification. The argument goes that it is illogical to be less than fully diversified so investors tend to create large portfolios. When a portfolio is formed one type of risk factor is eliminated – that which is specifically associated with the fortunes and misfortunes of particular companies. This is called unsystematic risk or unique risk. Once this is taken from the scene the investor merely has to concentrate on risks which cannot be eliminated by holding ever larger portfolios. This is systematic risk, an element of risk common to all firms to a greater or lesser extent.

A central tenet of the CAPM is that systematic risk, as measured by beta, is the *only* factor affecting the level of return required on a share for a completely diversified investor. For practical use this risk factor is considered to be the extent to which a particular share's returns move when the stock market as a whole moves. Furthermore, the relationship between this beta factor and returns is described by a straight line (it is linear). This neat and, at first sight, apparently complete model changed the way people viewed the world of finance and influenced their actions.

Its far-reaching consequences changed the way in which portfolios were constructed for pension and insurance funds of millions of people. It contributed to the strengthening of the notion of stock market efficiency – the idea that the stock market 'correctly' prices shares (*see* Chapter 14). It has affected the investment philosophies of large numbers of investors. It has influenced the calculation of the cost of capital for a firm, or to express it another way, the required rate of return on projects. By providing a target figure of the return required by shareholders the CAPM has enabled management to vary the discount rate by which project cash flows were discounted, depending on the perceived level of systematic risk as defined by beta. Thus countless investment proposals have been accepted or rejected on the strength of what the CAPM has to say about the minimum return demanded by shareholders. In the view of many this is regrettable. Some see the CAPM as artificially restricting the investment opportunities undertaken by firms in national economies and this has led to charges of under-investment, economic backwardness and short-termism.

Far more damning criticism was to come for the CAPM in the 1980s and 1990s when researchers looked at the relationship between the the CAPM's systematic risk measure, beta, and the returns on shares over the period since the mid-1960s. They discovered either that there was absolutely no relationship at all or that beta had only a weak influence on the return shares produced. They commented that there were other factors determining the returns on shares. This opened up a raging debate within the academic community, with some saying beta was dead, some saying that it was only wounded, and some saying it was alive and well.

The irony is that just as the academic community is having serious doubts about the model, in the outside world the CAPM is reaching new heights of popularity. Hundreds of thousands, if not millions, have studied the CAPM in universities over the past three decades and are now placed in important positions around the world ready to make key decisions often under the subliminal influence of the CAPM. Indeed, a new industry has been built selling data and information which can be plugged into CAPM-based decision-making frameworks in the workplace.

Partly in response to the empirical evidence, and partly from theoretical doubts about the CAPM, academics began exploring models which were based on a number of explanatory factors influencing the returns on shares rather than the one solitary variable considered in the CAPM. The most prominent is the Arbitrage Pricing Theory (APT) which permits factors other than beta to explain share returns. But wait! We are running ahead of the story. First we have to understand the workings of the

[1] Sharpe (1964), Lintner (1965), Mossin (1966), Treynor (1965) and Black (1972).

CAPM, its theoretical underpinnings and the various items of jargon that have grown up within this area of finance. Only then will a full appreciation of its limitations be possible, along with a consideration of alternative risk-return approaches.

A short history of shares, bonds and bills

Returns

We begin with an examination of the rate of return earned on shares and other classes of financial securities over the period since the end of 1899. Elroy Dimson, Paul Marsh and Mike Staunton from the London Business School, in collaboration with the bank ABN Amro, regularly produce analyses of the returns earned on shares, **government bonds** (lending to the UK government by buying long-term financial investments, often called '**gilts**') and **Treasury bills** (short-term lending to the UK government – usually for three months) since the end of 1899. As can be seen from Exhibit 8.1 shares have produced a much better return than the other two classes of investment. Even if the effects of inflation are removed, an investor placing £100 in a portfolio of shares at the end of 1899 would, by the beginning of 2008, be able to purchase 328 times as many goods and services as could be purchased in 1899 with the initial amount invested.

Exhibit 8.1 What a £100 investment in January 1900 would be worth at the end of 2007 with all income reinvested

	If invested in equities (shares)	If invested in bonds (gilts)	If invested in Treasury bills
Money (nominal) return	£2.2m	£27,600	£20,400
Real return	£32,800	£410	£300

Source: Dimson, E., Marsh, P., Staunton, M. (2008) *Global investment returns yearbook 2008*. ABN AMRO.

The Dimson, Marsh and Staunton research shows that equities (shares) have produced average annual real returns (after reinvestment of dividends) much higher than that on gilts or Treasury bills (*see* Exhibit 8.2).

Exhibit 8.2 Real returns on UK financial securities (per cent per annum)

Geometric means

	108 years[a] (1900–1.1.2008)	50 years[b] (1957–1.1.2007)	20 years[b] (1987–1.1.2007)
Equities	5.5	7.1	6.9
Gilts	1.3	2.2	5.6
Treasury bills	1.0	2.0	3.7
Inflation	4.0		

Source: [a]Dimson, E., Marsh, P., Staunton, M. (2008) *Global investment returns yearbook 2008*. ABN AMRO.
[b]Barclays Capital (2007) Equity Gilt Study.

The study shows an extra return for equities compared with gilts of 4.2 per cent (5.5 per cent – 1.3 per cent) on the basis of **geometric means**. (For a discussion on geometric and **arithmetic means** consult Appendix 8.1.) Over 107 years (1900–2006), in a different study conducted by Barclays Capital, shares gave an annual average return of 4.2 per cent (5.3 per cent – 1.1 per cent) greater than gilts and 4.3 per cent greater than Treasury bills.

If a 50-year history of financial security returns is examined then the premium received by share investors rises. According to Barclays Capital the extra annual return over gilts is 4.9 per cent (7.1 per cent – 2.2 per cent). The premium over Treasury bills is larger at 5.1 per cent. Clearly the size of the additional return achieved by equity investors compared with government bond or Treasury bill investors has varied over time. Indeed during 2001 and 2002, the premium became negative as investors lost money on shares while the return on gilts remained positive.

To state definitively the return premium share investors generally receive over gilt and Treasury bill investors is obviously impossible as it depends on the period of time studied. What we can do is apply a principle when trying to establish a usable figure for the 'equity risk premium' (this is a vital number in finance). We would look at data for a long time period because the relationship between the returns on shares and bonds (or bills) is subject to a great deal of fluctuation in the short term (witness 2000–2003 when shares fell). If we used the two longest periods in Exhibit 8.2 we would say the extra return on shares is under 5 per cent. If we round up to 5 per cent for the remainder of this book we will, for practical purposes, assume an historic premium for shares over reputable government bond securities of 5 per cent.[2] However, this is a contentious area. Many informed thinkers (e.g. Dimson *et al.* (2006)) believe that an equity risk premium for US, UK and world equities today lies in the region of 3–3½ per cent. Fama and French (2002) suggest an equity premium of 2.5 per cent to 4.3 per cent for US shares, while other textbooks (e.g. Brealey, Myers and Allen 2006) stick to higher numbers (5 per cent to 8 per cent). Considering how crucial this number is to many areas of finance theory it may surprise you to find that there is so much room for choosing the equity risk premium.

Exhibit 8.3 shows that investors in other countries' shares have received higher returns than if they had opted to invest in government securities. Generally the extra return on shares over government bonds is in the region 4 per cent to 6 per cent. Chapter 19 contains a further consideration of the equity premium.

Exhibit 8.3 **Real returns on equities and government bonds: an international comparison, 1900–2007, 108 years (geometic means)**

	Annualised percentage returns	
	Equity	Bonds
Sweden	7.8	2.4
Australia	7.9	1.3
South Africa	7.5	1.7
USA	6.5	1.9
Canada	6.3	2.0
Netherlands	5.4	1.3
UK	5.5	1.3
Ireland	4.6	1.0
Denmark	5.3	3.0
Switzerland (equity from 1911)	4.5	2.6
Norway	4.5	1.6
Japan	4.3	–1.3
Spain	4.0	1.3
France	3.7	–0.3
Germany (bonds and bills: 99 years excl. 1922/3)	3.4	–1.8
Italy	2.5	–1.8
Belgium	2.5	–0.2

Sources: Dimson, E., Marsh, P., Staunton, M. (2008) *Global Investment Returns Yearbook, 2008*. ABN AMRO.

[2] Five per cent would be well within the confidence interval for the equity risk premium range shown in the most recent serious studies.

Risk

Treasury bills are regarded as the safest possible investment. It is highly unlikely that the UK government will default and the fact they mature in a matter of days means that their prices do not vary a great deal.

Long-term government bonds also have a low risk of default but they do suffer from uncertainty concerning the price that can be achieved in the market when selling to another investor

Exhibit 8.4 Annual real cash (Treasury bills) returns (%), 1900–2006

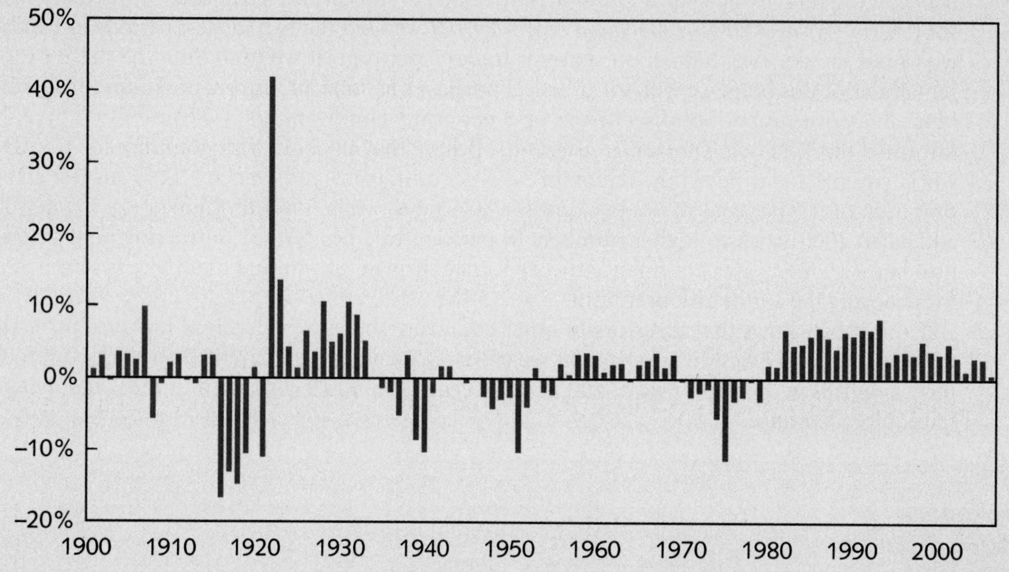

Source: Barclays Capital. Various Equity Gilt Studies. London: Barclays Capital.

Exhibit 8.5 Annual real gilt returns (%), 1900–2006

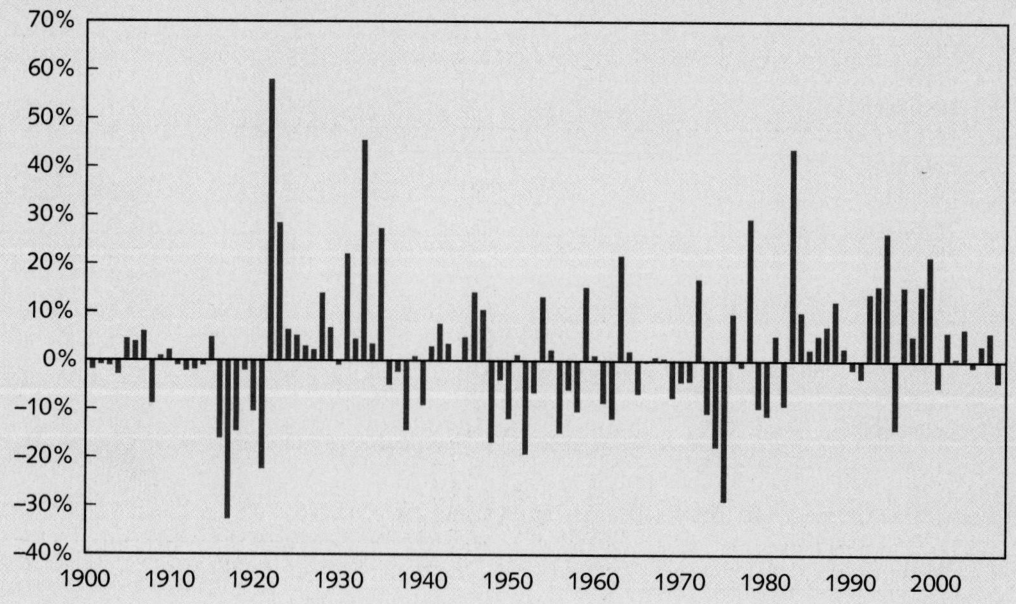

Source: Barclays Capital. Various Equity Gilt Studies. London: Barclays Capital.

prior to the maturity date. The prices fluctuate inversely to interest rates. If interest rates rise due to, say, a perceived increase in inflation, then the price of bonds will fall, producing a capital loss. Often these capital losses over a period of a year outweigh the gain from the interest paid, producing an overall negative annual return. (*See* Chapter 11 for a more detailed discussion of bonds.) Despite these yearly ups and downs, for practical purposes bonds issued by a reputable government may be viewed as being risk free if a long-term (to maturity) perspective is taken. This is because the promised payments by the government are highly unlikely to be missed, therefore the nominal return is guaranteed (unexpected inflation may be a problem for real returns, but

Exhibit 8.6 Annual real equity returns (%), 1900–2006

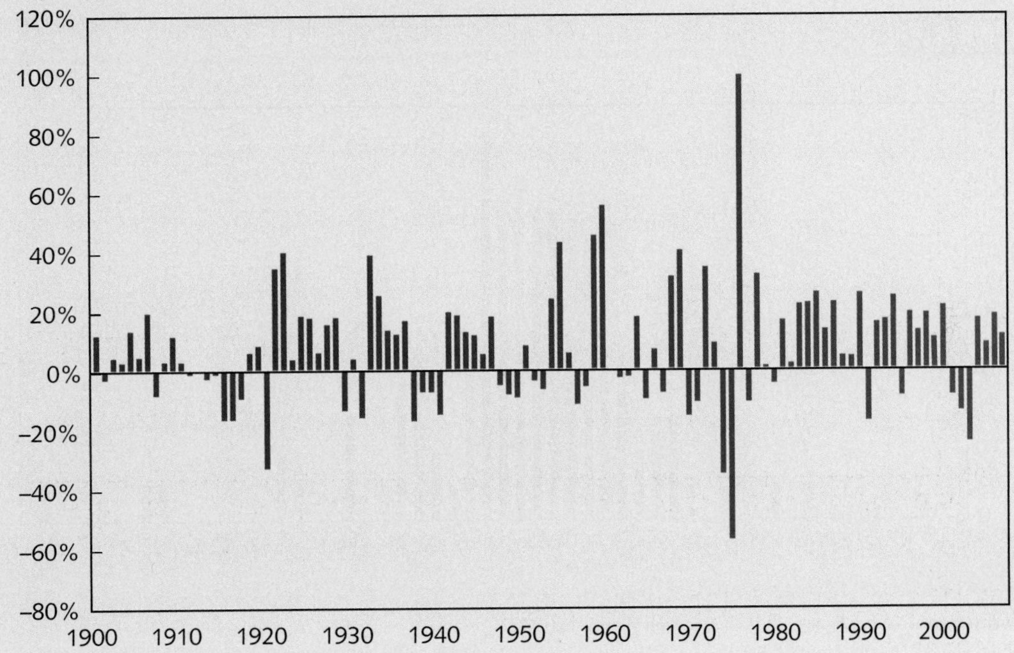

Source: Barclays Capital. Various Equity Gilt Studies. London: Barclays Capital.

Exhibit 8.7 Distribution of real annual cash (Treasury bill) returns, 1900–2006

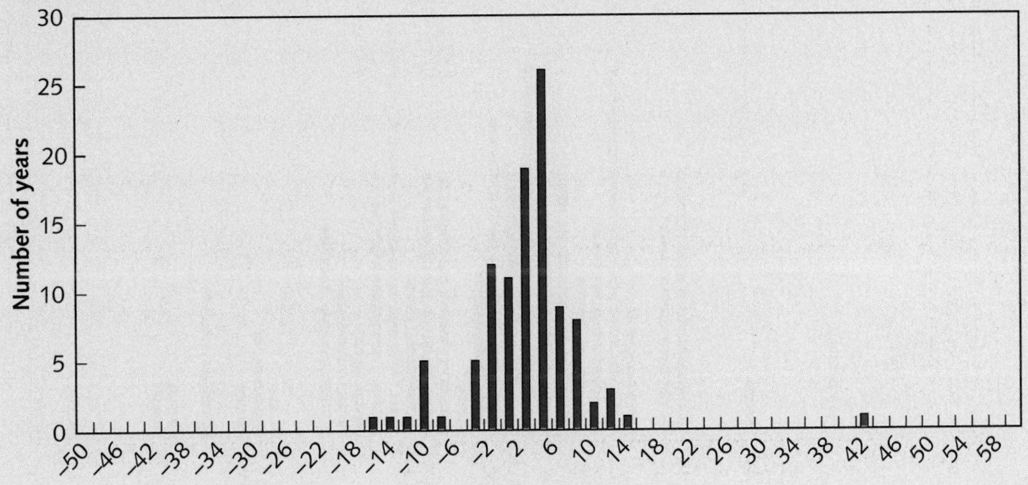

Source: Barclays Capital Various Equity Gilt Studies. London: Barclays Capital.

government bonds and bills are the nearest we are going to get to risk-free securities). Shares carry the highest risk because their payouts of dividends and capital gains and losses depend on the performance of the underlying businesses. We now examine the extent to which total returns (dividends or interest plus capital gain or loss) have varied over the years.

A general impression of the degree of volatility associated with each class of investment can be found by examining **Exhibits 8.4, 8.5** and **8.6**. An investor in Treasury bills in any year is unlikely to experience a real (after inflation) loss greater than 5 per cent. The investor in gilts, on the other hand, has a fairly high chance of making a significant negative return over the period of a year. There is also the possibility of large gains, many of which are over 10 per cent. Shares can show spectacular year-on-year gains and equally extraordinary losses. Take the years 1973 and 1974: a purchaser of shares at the start of 1973 lost 35 per cent in the first year followed by 58.1 per cent in 1974. The pain

Exhibit 8.8 Distribution of real annual gilt returns, 1900–2006

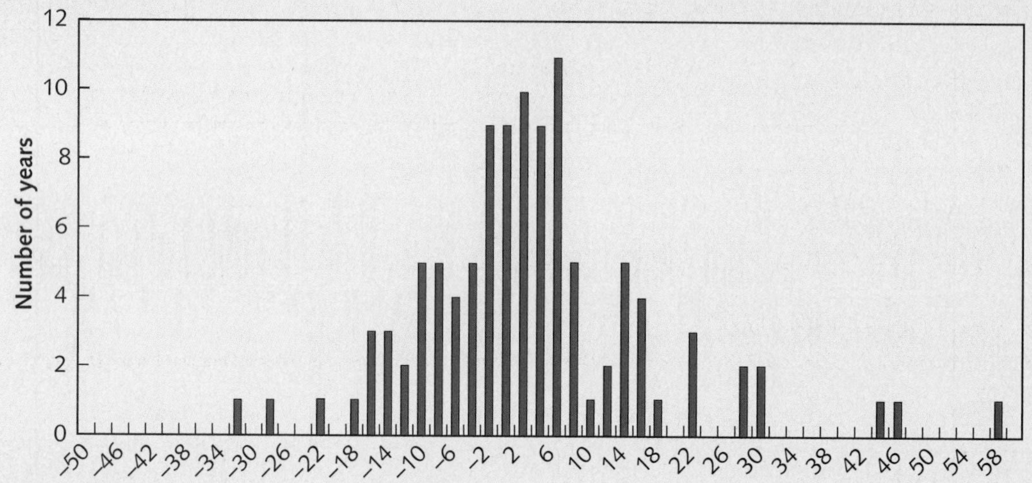

Source: Barclays Capital. Various Equity Gilt Studies. London: Barclays Capital.

Exhibit 8.9 Distribution of real annual equity return, 1900–2006

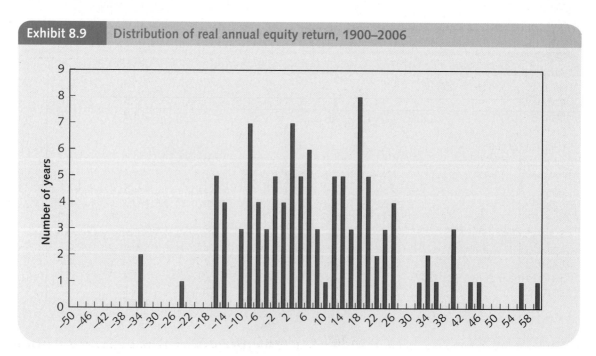

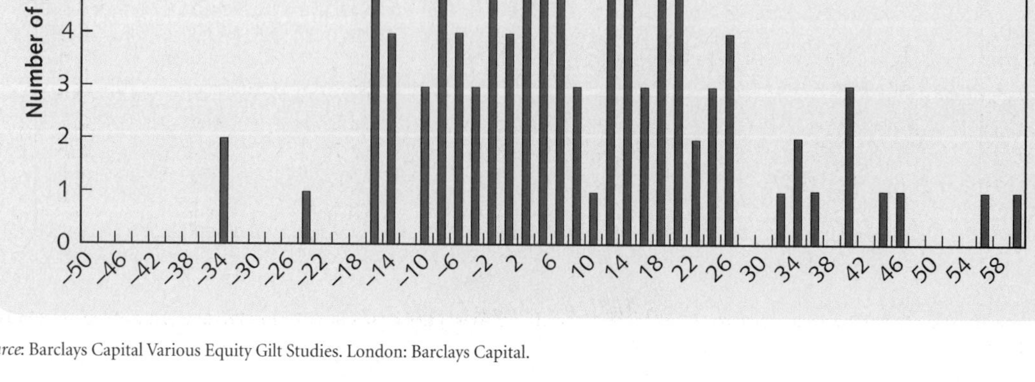

Source: Barclays Capital Various Equity Gilt Studies. London: Barclays Capital.

was offset by the bounce-back of 1975 but the fear and dislike of sharp stock market collapse is bound to haunt the experienced equity investor, given the history of stock market returns.

The frequency distribution of returns for the three asset classes is shown in **Exhibits 8.7, 8.8** and **8.9**. These show the number of years that each type of investment had a return within a particular range. For Treasury bills (cash) the returns vary from a negative 16 per cent to a positive 14 per cent (if we ignore the outlier at 41.5 per cent). The range for bonds is much wider, and for equities wider still. (The two most extreme returns for shares, –58.1 per cent in 1974 and +99.6 per cent in 1975, were excluded as outliers.)

We now have data for the average annual return on each class of asset, and some impression of the annual variability of those returns. These two characteristics are brought together in **Exhibit 8.10**, where standard deviation provides a measure of volatility. This confirms that equities are the most risky asset class of the three. The standard deviation of equities is much larger than that for

Exhibit 8.10 Return and risk on financial securities, 1900–2000[a]

	Arithmetic mean returns %	Standard deviation %
Equities	7.6	20.0
Gilts	2.3	14.5
Treasury bills	1.2	6.6
Inflation	4.3	6.9

Note a – Based on real returns after inflation.

Source: Dimson, E., Marsh, P. and Staunton, M. (2002) *Triumph of the Optimists: 101 Years of Global Investment Returns*. Princeton, NJ, and Oxford: Princeton University Press.

Exhibit 8.11 Means (arithmetic) and standard deviations of annual real returns for financial securities in 15 countries, 1900– January 2001

Country	Equities		Bonds		Bills	
	Arithmetic mean %	Standard deviation %	Arithmetic mean %	Standard deviation %	Arithmetic mean %	Standard deviation %
Australia	9.0	17.7	1.9	13.0	0.6	5.6
Belgium	4.8	22.8	0.3	12.1	0.0	8.2
Canada	7.7	16.8	2.4	10.6	1.8	5.1
Denmark	6.2	20.1	3.3	12.5	3.0	6.4
France	6.3	23.1	0.1	14.4	–2.6	11.4
Germany (equity 99 years excl. 1922/3)	8.8	32.3	0.3	15.9	0.1	10.6
Ireland	7.0	22.2	2.4	13.3	1.4	6.0
Italy	6.8	29.4	–0.8	14.4	–2.9	12.0
Japan	9.3	30.3	1.3	20.9	–0.3	14.5
Netherlands	7.7	21.0	1.5	9.4	0.8	5.2
South Africa	9.1	22.8	1.9	10.6	1.0	6.4
Spain	5.8	22.0	1.9	12.0	0.6	6.1
Sweden	9.9	22.8	3.1	12.7	2.2	6.8
Switzerland (equity from 1911)	6.9	20.4	3.1	8.0	1.2	6.2
USA	8.7	20.2	2.1	10.0	1.0	4.7

Source: Dimson, E., Marsh, P. and Staunton, M. (2002) *Triumph of the Optimists: 101 Years of Global Investment Returns*. Princeton, NJ, and Oxford: Princeton University Press.

bonds, and at least three times that for Treasury bills. The exhibits examined so far endorse the belief in a positive relationship between return and risk. This is confirmed to be the case for a number of other countries in Exhibit 8.11.

The article excerpted in Exhibit 8.12 describes the remarkable rewards for accepting additional risk by investing in shares (American, this time) rather than something safer.

Exhibit 8.12

Big bequest: Former Chicago secretary Gladys Holm, who never earned more than \$15,000 (£9,202) a year, left \$18m to a hospital in her will. She used to invest any spare earnings on the stock market.

FT

Source: *Financial Times*, 1 August 1997. Reprinted with permission.

The article from *Investors Chronicle* in Exhibit 8.13 gives some reasons why investors require a higher return on shares than on bonds. The author takes the line that the equity risk premium is too high.

Exhibit 8.13

The long-term charms of equities

History suggests the recent fall in equities could be a great buying opportunity. But is history a good guide? To see the answer, we must remember, says John Cochrane of the University of Chicago, that 'high average returns are only earned as a compensation for risk'. The equity premium has only existed because some people have shunned equities, believing them to be too risky. As a result, other investors have reaped high rewards.

Fortunately, there are reasons why some may continue to shy away from equities, allowing the rest of us to get good returns.

- *Misjudging risk* 'An investor who computed the value of her portfolio every day would find stocks very unattractive,' says Jeremy Siegel of the University of Pennsylvania. That's because, on any given day, even in good times, shares are almost as likely to fall as to rise. And if people suffer more pain from losses than they get pleasure from gains, they'll be keener to avoid equities.
- *Equities let you down when you need them* Financial assets are useful because they allow us to spend money even when our income has fallen. Equities, however, are a poor way of protecting our spending power, because they often fall in recessions – which is precisely when our salaries are falling. 'Consumers are afraid of holding stocks not because they fear the wealth volatility *per se*, but because bad stock returns tend to happen in recessions, and times of belt-tightening,' says Professor Cochrane.
- *Nervousness* In theory, high returns on equities could simply reflect the fact that people are so averse to short-term risk that they need huge returns to compensate for holding equities. Most economists believe people in general are not that risk-averse. But some might be.
- *Barriers to entry* Some people would like to own shares, but can't afford them. Even now, after recent building society flotations and the spread of private pensions, about 60 per cent of the adult population do not own shares.

Some people, therefore, will continue to perceive equities as inaccessible, or too risky. As a result, the rest of us should, over the long run, continue to enjoy an equity premium.

There is, as always, the small chance of a catastrophe that will hit long-run equity returns. Professor Siegel believes one reason for the equity premium in the past is precisely that investors have attached a small probability to such a calamity, and so avoided shares.

It's easy to imagine such disasters: deflation; the collapse of global capitalism; or entry into a Japanese-style stationary state, in which earning growth ceases for many years.

These, however, are remote possibilities – and the likeliest, deflation, isn't always bad for shares, as the experience of the 1920s teaches. So chances are the equity premium will continue.

Source: *Investors Chronicle*, 23 October 1998, p. 21. Reprinted with permission.

The capital asset pricing model

From the Capital Market Line (CML) to the Security Market Line (SML)

The Capital Market Line was described in Chapter 7 as an expression of the relationship between risk and return for a fully diversified investor. If an investor is able to first identify and invest in the *market portfolio*; and secondly, able to lend or borrow at the risk-free rate of return then the alternative risk–return combinations available to the investor lie on a straight line – there is a positive linear association. An example of this relationship is shown in **Exhibit 8.14**.

Exhibit 8.14 A hypothetical Capital Market Line

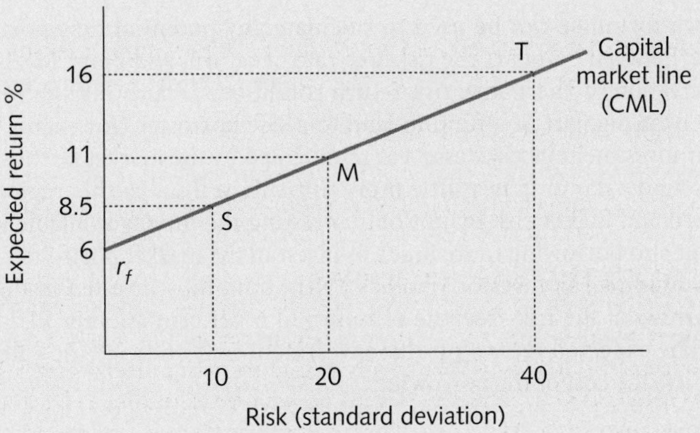

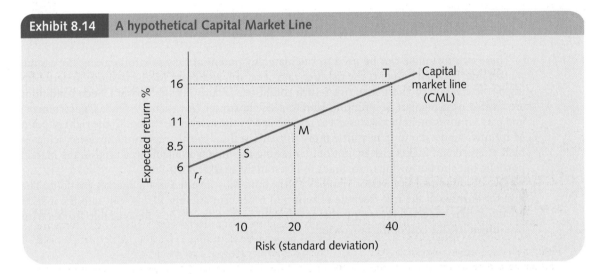

Ideally, when referring to the market portfolio, we should include all assets, ranging from gold through to bonds, property and shares. In practice, to make the CAPM workable, we use a proxy for the market portfolio, usually a broadly based index of shares such as the FTSE Actuaries All-Share Index which contains about 700 shares.

At least two possible options are open to a potential investor. The first is to place all funds into risk-free securities.[3] In the example given in Exhibit 8.14 this would result in a return of 6 per cent per year. (In reality the risk-free rate varies from day to day depending on supply and demand in the bond and bill markets.) The second option is to invest all the funds in the market portfolio. The share index proxies studied in empirical work such as the Barclays Capital and Dimson *et al.* studies generally show that over the past 50–107 years investors in shares have received a return of about 4 to 5 per cent more than if they had invested in risk-free securities.[4] We will use a figure of 5 per cent – thus, if anything, biasing the calculations upwards. Thus an investor in the market portfolio will expect, in this assumed model, a return of 6 per cent plus, say, 5 per cent. Having established the two benchmarks, of 11 per cent return for a risk level with a standard deviation of 20 per cent and a return of 6 per cent for zero risk in this hypothetical but representative model, we can now calculate alternative risk-return combinations constructed by varying the amount of a fund going into each of these two types of investment. For example, if half of the fund were placed in the market portfolio and half in the risk-free asset, the standard deviation on this new portfolio would be a weighted average of the two constituent standard deviations:

---

[3] Real returns on government Treasury bills have not had a zero standard deviation when measured on a year-to-year basis. However, over the three-month life of a Treasury bill the rate of return is fixed and the risk of default is virtually zero. Returns on government bonds may fluctuate from year to year, but the government is highly unlikely to default, and so they may be regarded as risk free for practical purposes (in nominal terms, at least) if they are held to maturity.

[4] For illustrative purposes we are using data supplied by Barclays Capital and Dimson *et al.* while also referring to the FTSE All-Share Index. These data, while being based on share returns, are not identical. Also they are mere proxies for the true market portfolio (*see* the discussion of the market portfolio later in this chapter).

0.5 × (standard deviation of risk-free asset) + 0.5 × (standard deviation of market portfolio)

$0.5 \times 0 + 0.5 \times 20 = 10$

For calculating the expected return a slightly more complicated formula is needed because the CML does not start at a zero expected return. This is as follows:

$$\text{expected return} = \text{risk-free return} + \begin{array}{c}\text{risk premium}\\ \text{for market}\\ \text{portfolio}\end{array} \times \left[\frac{\text{risk of new portfolio, S}}{\text{risk of market portfolio}}\right]$$

$r_j = 6 + 5 \times (10/20) = 8.5\%$

These two formulae can be used to calculate any potential new portfolio along the capital market line. Between points r_f, the risk-free rate of return, and point M, the intuitive understanding of the creation of alternative risk-return conditions is fairly straightforward. Such conditions are created by using part of a fund to lend to a safe borrower (for example the UK government) and part for investment in risky assets as represented by the market portfolio. To the right of point M intuitive understanding is a little more difficult at first. In this region the investor achieves higher return and higher risk by not only investing the money available in a fund in the market portfolio but also borrowing more funds to invest in the market portfolio.

Take, for example, an investor who has a £1m fund fully invested in the market portfolio. The investor borrows at the risk-free rate of return of 6 per cent another £1m to put into the market portfolio. The expected return on this investment will be twice the rate available from a £1m investment less the cost of the borrowing:

	£
11% return on shares (£110,000 × 2)	220,000
Less interest	60,000
	£160,000

This is a return of 16 per cent for a fund belonging to the investor of £1m. Before everyone rushes out to gear up their portfolios in this way, note that this is the expected return – the statistical mean. We saw in the last section how volatile share returns can be. It could be that the investor will receive no return from the market portfolio at all and yet will still have to pay the interest. Investors such as this one expose themselves to a greater variation in possible outcomes, that is, risk. The standard deviation for portfolio T is:

$$\frac{(2{,}000{,}000 \times 20\%) - (1{,}000{,}000 \times 0\%)}{1{,}000{,}000} = 40\%$$

With such a high standard deviation there is a high probability of negative returns for a year – roughly a one in three chance – Beta is discussed after some technical points on the market portfolio (*see* **Exhibit 8.15**).

From this section we can conclude that if the conditions leading to the establishment of the CML are fulfilled (such as a perfect capital market with no taxes, no transaction costs, full information about future return distributions disclosed to all investors and the ability to borrow and lend at the risk-free rate of interest) then an investor can achieve any point along the CML simply by varying the manner in which the portfolio is constructed from the two components of the market portfolio and the risk-free asset.

To get to a full understanding of the CAPM the reader is recommended to temporarily suspend disbelief. Of course the simplifying assumptions do not match reality, but such extraordinary artificiality is necessary to make a model intelligible and usable. What matters is whether the CAPM explains and predicts reality accurately and this is something examined much later in the chapter. For now we need to introduce the concept of beta to provide a bridge between the capital market line analysis and the capital asset pricing model.

Exhibit 8.15 The market portfolio

A linchpin of the CAPM is the market portfolio, because all investors are assumed to hold this in combination with risk-free lending and borrowing. In theory the market portfolio consists of a portion of all the potential assets in the world weighted in proportion to their respective market values. In practice, just identifying, let alone obtaining, the market portfolio is pretty well impossible. Consider what you would need to do. It would be necessary to identify all possible assets: that is, all the securities issued by firms in every country of the world, as well as all government debt, buildings and other property, cash and metals. Other possibilities for inclusion would be consumer durables and what is called human capital – the skills and knowledge of people. The value of these assets is clearly very difficult to assess. Because of these difficulties practitioners of the CAPM use market portfolio proxies such as broad share indices. Richard Roll (1977) has put forward the argument that the impossibility of obtaining or even identifying the market portfolio means that the CAPM is untestable. Using proxies can lead to conflicting results and the CAPM is not being properly employed.

Beta

In the previous chapter a number of graphs demonstrated the risk-reducing effect of adding securities to a portfolio. If there is only one company's shares in a 'portfolio' then risk is very high. Adding a second reduces risk (except in the rare cases of perfect positive correlation). The addition of a third and fourth continues to reduce risk but by smaller amounts. This sort of effect is demonstrated in **Exhibit 8.16**. The reason for the risk reduction is that security returns generally do not vary with perfect positive correlation. At any one time the good news about one share is offset to some extent by bad news about another.

Generally within a portfolio of shares if one is shooting up, others are stable, going down or rising. Each share movement depends mostly on the news emanating from the company. News is generally particular to companies and so we should not expect them each to report good (or bad) news on the same day. So, if on one day a share in the portfolio reports the resignation of a brilliant chief executive we might expect that share to fall. But, because the portfolio owner is diversified the return on the portfolio will not move dramatically downward. Other companies are reporting marketing coups, big new contracts, etc., pushing up their share prices. Others (the majority) are not reporting any news and their share prices do not move much at all. The point is by not having all your eggs in one basket you reduce the chance of the collective value of your investments falling off a cliff (how is that for a mixed metaphor!).

So, despite the fact that returns on individual shares can vary dramatically, a portfolio will be relatively stable. The type of risk that is being reduced through diversification is referred to as **unique** or **unsystematic risk** (or **idiosyncratic** or **specific risk** – you wouldn't expect financial economists to make things easy by having one word for it, would you?). This element of variability in a share's return is due to the particular circumstances of the individual firm. In a portfolio these individual ups and downs tend to cancel out. Another piece of jargon applied to this type of risk is that it is '**diversifiable**'. That is, it can be eliminated simply by holding a sufficiently large portfolio.

Exhibit 8.16 Systematic and unsystematic risk

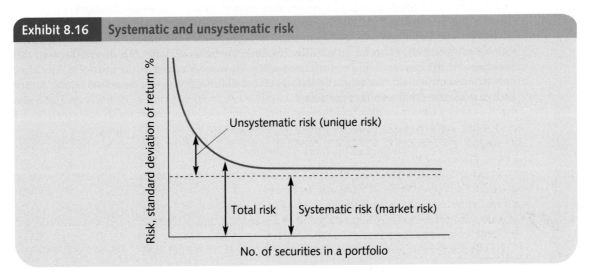

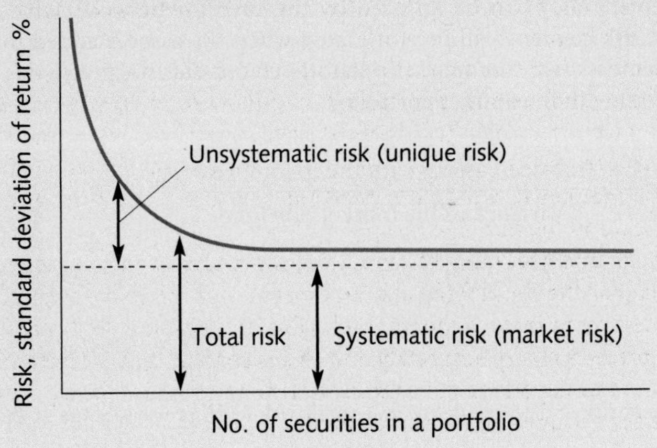

However, no matter how many shares are held, there will always be an element of risk that cannot be cancelled out by broadening the portfolio. This is called **systematic** or **market risk**. There are some risk factors that are common to all firms to a greater or lesser extent. These include macroeconomic movements such as economic growth, inflation and exchange rate changes. No firm is entirely immune from these factors. For example, a deceleration in gross domestic product (GDP) growth or a rise in tax rates is likely to impact on the returns of all firms within an economy. Note, however, that while all shares respond to these system-wide risk factors they do not all respond equally. Some shares will exhibit a greater sensitivity to these systematic risk elements than others. The revenues of the consumer and luxury goods sectors, for example, are particularly sensitive to the ups and downs of the economy. Spending on electrical goods and sports cars rises when the economy is in a strong growth phase but falls off significantly in recession. On the other hand, some sectors experience limited variations in demand as the economy booms and shrinks; the food-producing and retailing sector are prime examples here. People do not cut down significantly on food bought for home consumption even when their incomes fall.

It is assumed, quite reasonably, that investors do not like risk. If this is the case, then the logical course of action is going to be to eliminate as much unsystematic risk as possible by diversifying. Most of the shares in UK companies are held by highly diversified institutional investors such as pension funds, insurance funds, unit trusts and investment trusts. While it is true that many small investors are not fully diversified, it is equally true that the market, and more importantly market returns, are dominated by the actions of fully diversified investors. These investors ensure that the market does not reward investors for bearing some unsystematic risk. To understand this imagine that by some freak accident a share offered a return of, say, 50 per cent per annum which includes compensation for both unsystematic and systematic risk. There would be a mad scramble to buy these shares, especially by the major diversified funds which are not concerned about the unsystematic risk on this share – they have other share returns to offset the oscillations of this new one. The buying pressure would result in a rise in the share price. This process would continue until the share offered the same return as other shares offering that level of systematic risk. Let us assume that the price doubles and therefore the return falls to 25 per cent. Undiversified investors will be dismayed that they can no longer find any share which will compensate for what they perceive as the relevant risk for them, consisting of both unsystematic and systematic elements.

In the financial markets the risk that matters is the degree to which a particular share tends to move when the market as a whole moves. This is the only issue of concern to investors that are fully diversified, because ups and downs due to specific company events do not affect the return on the portfolio – only market-wide events affect the portfolio's return.

This is leading to a new way of measuring risk. For the diversified investor, the relevant measure of risk is no longer standard deviation, it is systematic risk.

The **capital asset pricing model (CAPM)** defined this systematic risk as beta.[5] **Beta (β)** measures the covariance between the returns on a particular share with the returns on the market as a whole (usually measured by a market index e.g. the FTSE All-Share index).

In the CAPM model, because all investors are assumed to hold the market portfolio, an individual asset (e.g. a share) owned by an investor will have a risk that is defined as the amount of risk that it adds to the market portfolio. Assets that tend to move a lot when the market portfolio moves will be more risky to the fully diversified investor than those assets that move a little when the market portfolio moves. To the extent that asset movements are unrelated to the market portfolio's movement they can be ignored by the investor because, with full diversification, this unsystematic risk element will be eliminated when the asset is added to the portfolio. Therefore only co-movements with the market portfolio count. Statistically, risk is measured by the covariance of the asset with the market portfolio:

$$\text{Beta of asset, } j = \frac{\text{Covariance of asset } j \text{ with the market portfolio}}{\text{Variance of the market portfolio}}$$

$$\beta_j = \frac{\text{Cov}\,(R_j, R_M)}{\sigma^2_M}$$

[5] Other models of risk and return define systematic risk in other ways. Some of these are discussed later in the chapter.

The beta value for a share indicates the sensitivity of that share to general market movements. A share with a beta of 1.0 tends to have returns which move broadly in line with the market index. A share with a beta greater than 1.0 tends to exhibit amplified return movements compared to the index. For example, Barclays in 2007 had a beta of 1.19 and, according to the CAPM, when the market index return rises by, say, 10 per cent, the returns on Barclays shares will tend to rise by 11.9 per cent. Conversely, if the market falls by 10 per cent, the returns on Barclays shares will tend to fall by 11.9 per cent.

Shares with a beta of less than 1.0, such as Marks and Spencer with a beta of 0.64, will vary less than the market as a whole. So, if the market is rising, shares in M&S will not enjoy the same level of upswing. However, should the market ever suffer a downward movement, for every 10 per cent decline in shares generally, M&S will, according to CAPM theory, give a return decline of only 6.4 per cent. Note that these co-movements are to be taken as statistical expectations rather than precise predictions. Thus, over a large sample of return movements M&S's returns will move by 6.4 per cent for a 10 per cent market movement if beta is a correct measure of company to market returns. On any single occasion the co-movements may not have this relationship. **Exhibit 8.17** displays the betas for some large UK companies.

Exhibit 8.17 Betas as measured in 2007

Share	Beta	Share	Beta
Barclays Bank	1.19	Sainsbury's (J)	1.19
Marks and Spencer	0.64	BT	1.28

Source: Thomson Financial Datastream.

The basic features of beta are:

When

$\beta = 1$	A 1 per cent change in the market index return generally leads to a 1 per cent change in the return on a specific share.
$0 < \beta < 1$	A 1 per cent change in the market index return generally leads to a less than 1 per cent change in the returns on a specific share.
$\beta > 1$	A 1 per cent change in the market index return generally leads to a greater return than 1 per cent on a specific company's share.

The Security Market Line (SML)

In Chapter 2 it was explained that investors require a risk premium (extra return) on top of what they can receive on a risk-free investment r_f to induce them to invest in something risky like a share. Thus the return expected on a share J is $r_j = r_f + \text{RP}$, where RP is the risk premium. To calculate the expected return on an average share (or share market as a whole return) we need two figures: (i) the current risk-free rate of return available to investors, and (ii) the RP for the average share. However, this is not enough information when we are examining shares that are not in the same risk category as the market as a whole. So, we must adjust (up or down) the RP for the averagely risky share to calculate the required return on a specific share.

Risk has been redefined for a fully diversified investor in an efficient market as systematic risk because this is the risk that cannot be diversified away and so a higher return is required if an investor is to bear it. In the CAPM the relationship between risk as measured by beta and expected return is shown by the **security market line** as in **Exhibit 8.18**. Shares perfectly correlated with the market return (M) will have a beta of 1.0 and are expected to produce an annual return of 11 per

Exhibit 8.18 A hypothetical Security Market Line (SML)

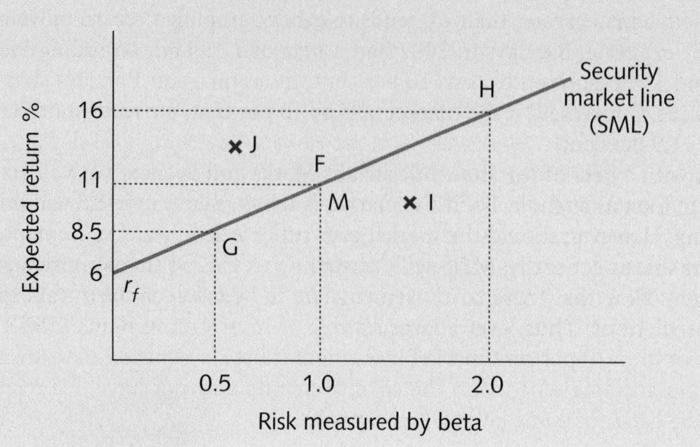

cent in the circumstances of a risk-free rate of return at 6 per cent and the risk premium on the market portfolio of shares over safe securities at 5 per cent (point M). Shares which are twice as risky, with a beta of 2.0, will have an expected return of 16 per cent; shares which vary half as much as the market index are expected to produce a return of 8.5 per cent in this particular hypothetical **risk-return line.**

To find the level of return expected for a given level of beta risk along the SML the following equation can be used:

Expected return = risk-free rate + beta × The average risk premium for shares (expected return on the market minus the risk-free rate)

or $r_j = r_f + \beta\,(r_m - r_f)$

Thus for a share with a beta of 1.31 the expected return will be:

$r_j = 6 + 1.31\,(11 - 6) = 12.55\%$

The better way of presenting this is to place the risk premium (RP) in the brackets rather than r_m and r_f separately because this reminds us that what is important is the required extra return over the risk-free rate as revealed by investors over many years – not the current risk-free rate. It is amazing how often financial journalists get this wrong and fixate on the current r_m and r_f rather than the long-term historical difference between the two. The market risk premium $(r_m - r_f)$ is fairly stable over time as it is taken from a long-term historical relationship. Indeed, taking a short period to estimate this would result in wild fluctuations from year to year). None of these fluctuations would reflect the premiums investors' demand for holding a risky portfolio of shares compared with a risk-free security. It is only over long periods that we can get a clearer view of returns required by shareholders as an acceptable premium.

At any one time the position of the SML depends primarily on the risk-free rate of return.[6] If the interest rate on government securities rises by, say, four percentage points, the SML lifts upwards by 4 per cent (*see* **Exhibit 8.19**). Note that the slope of the SML does not change even though the r_f in $(r_m - r_f)$ changes because $r_m - r_f$ is the *long-term* historical risk premium for shares over the risk-free rate.

According to the CAPM all securities lie on the security market line, their exact position being determined by their beta. But what about shares J and I in Exhibit 8.18? These are shares that are not in equilibrium. J offers a particularly high level of return for the risk its holders have to bear. This will not last for long in an efficient market because investors are constantly on the prowl for shares like this. As they start to buy in large quantities the price will rise and correspondingly the expected return will fall (assuming that future cash flows attached to the share remain constant). This will continue until the share return is brought on to the SML. Conversely, share I will be sold until the price falls sufficiently to bring about equilibrium, that is, I is placed on the SML.

Exhibit 8.19 Shifts in the SML: a 4 percentage point rise in the risk-free rate

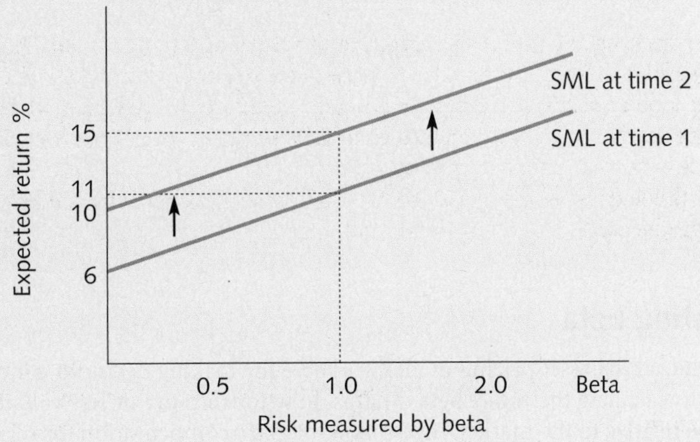

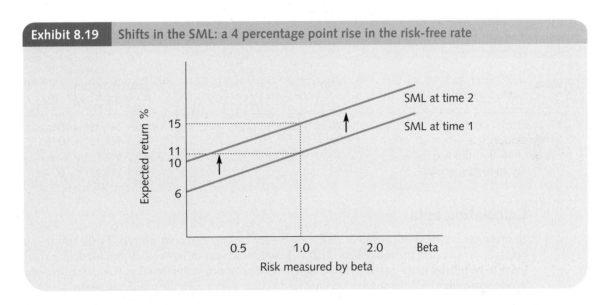

[6] We generally focus on a risk-free rate derived from long-term government bonds and a risk premium for shares above the government bond rate (rather than the Treasury bill rate) because in most applications we are concerned with rates of returns for projects with medium-term or long lives. The risk-free rate used should match the time horizon of the analysis. The risk-free rate is a completely certain return. For complete certainty two conditions are needed:

- The risk of default is zero.
- When intermediate cash flows are earned on a multi-year investment there is no uncertainty about reinvestment rates.

The return available on a zero-coupon reputable government bond which has a time horizon equal to the cash flow (of a project, share investment, etc.) being analysed is the closest we are going to get to the theoretically correct risk-free rate of return. Business projects usually involve cash flows arising at intervals, rather than all at the end of an investment. Theoretically, each of these separate cash flows should be discounted using different risk-free rates. So, for the cash flows arising after one year on a multi-year project, the rate on a one-year zero-coupon government bond should be used as part of the calculation of the cost of capital. The cash flows arising in Year 5 should be discounted on the basis of a cost of capital calculated using the five-year zero-coupon rate, and so on. However, this approach is cumbersome, and there is a practical alternative that gives a reasonable approximation to the theoretical optimum. It is considered acceptable to use a long-term government rate on all the cash flows of a project that has a long-term horizon. Furthermore, the return on a government bond with coupons, rather than a zero-coupon bond, is generally taken to be acceptable. The rule of thumb is to use the return available on a reputable government security having the same time horizon as the project under consideration – so a short-term project should use the discount rate that incorporates the short-term government security rate, for a 10-year project use the 10-year gilt rate.

Estimating some expected returns

To calculate the returns investors require from particular shares it is necessary to obtain three numbers using the CAPM: (a) the risk-free rate of return, r_f, (b) the risk premium for the market portfolio (or proxy index), $(r_m - r_f)$, and (c) the beta of the share. Betas are available from commercial information suppliers such as Datastream, the London Business School Risk Measurement Service or from many financial websites.

In 2007 the returns on UK government securities are about 4–5 per cent. For practical use we will take a risk premium of 5 per cent. We could plump for a much lower figure if we accept the argument that investors were surprised by the size of the premium they actually received; they weren't demanding it a priori, it was just that the optimists (share investors) were lucky and got it anyway – see Shiller (2000) and Dimson, Marsh and Staunton (2002, 2006) for this view – in future, it is argued, they will get a smaller return above the government bond rate. **Exhibit 8.20** calculates the returns required on shares of some leading UK firms using beta as the only risk variable influencing returns, a risk-free rate of 4.5 per cent and a risk premium of 5 per cent.

Exhibit 8.20 Returns expected by investors based on the capital asset pricing model

Share	Beta (β)	Expected returns $r_f + \beta(r_m - r_f)$
BT	1.28	4.5 + 5(1.28) = 10.9
Sainsbury's (J)	1.19	4.5 + 5(1.19) = 10.5
Barclays Bank	1.19	4.5 + 5(1.19) = 10.5
Marks and Spencer	0.64	4.5 + 5(0.64) = 7.7

Calculating beta

To make the capital asset pricing model workable for making decisions concerning the future it is necessary to calculate the *future* beta. That is, how much more or less voltaile is a particular share going to be relative to the market. Investors want extra compensation for relative volatility over the period when they hold the share – i.e. time yet to come. Obviously, the future cannot be foreseen, and so it is difficult to obtain an estimate of the likely co-movements of the returns on a share and the market portfolio. One approach is to substitute subjective probability beliefs, but this has obvious drawbacks. The most popular method is to observe the historic relationship between returns and to assume that this covariance will persist into the future. This is called *ex-post* analysis because it takes place after the event.

Exhibit 8.21 shows a simplified and idealised version of this sort of analysis. Here are shown 12 monthly observations for, say, 2007. (Commercially supplied beta calculations are usually based

Exhibit 8.21 The characteristic line; no unsystematic risk

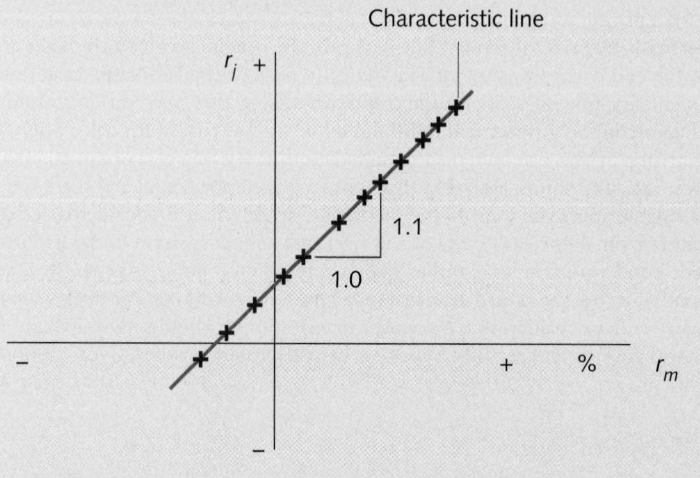

on at least 60 monthly observations stretching back over five years.) Each plot point expresses the return on the market index portfolio for a particular month and the return on the specific shares being examined in that same month.

In an analysis such as that presented in Exhibit 8.21 the market portfolio will be represented by some broad index containing many hundreds of shares. In this highly idealised example the relative returns plot along a straight line referred to as the **characteristic line**. Exhibit 8.21 shows a perfect statistical relationship, in that there is no statistical 'noise' causing the plot points to be placed off the line. The characteristic line has a form described by the following formula:

$$r_j = \alpha + \beta_j r_m + e$$

where: r_j = rate of return on the jth share
r_m = rate of return on the market index portfolio
α = regression line intercept
e = residual error about the regression line (in this simple case this has a value of zero because all the plot points are on a straight line)
β_j = the beta of security j

Thus the slope of the characteristic line is the beta for share j. That is:

$$\frac{\text{Change in } r_j}{\text{Change in } r_m} = \frac{\Delta r_j}{\Delta r_m} = \beta$$

In this case the slope is 1.1 and therefore $\beta = 1.1$.

A more realistic representation of the relationship between the monthly returns on the market and the returns on a specific share is shown in **Exhibit 8.22**. Here very few of the plot points fall on the fitted regression line (the line of best fit). The reason for this scatter of points is that the unsystematic risk effects in any one month may cause the returns on a specific share to rise or fall by a larger or smaller amount than they would if the returns on the market were the only influence.

To gain an appreciation of what the model presented in Exhibit 8.22 reveals, we will examine two of the plot points. Take point A: this represents the returns for the market and for share j in the month of, say, August 2007. Part of the movement of j is explained by the general market changes – this is the distance UV. However a large element of j's returns in that month is attributable to unsystematic risk factors – this is represented by the distance AU. Now consider point B for the month of November. If systematic risk was the only influence on the return of a single share then we would expect the change in j's return to be XW. However, unsystematic risk influences have reduced the extent of variation to only BX. The distance AU and WB make up part of the error term e in the market model formula.

Exhibit 8.22 The characteristic line: with unsystematic risk

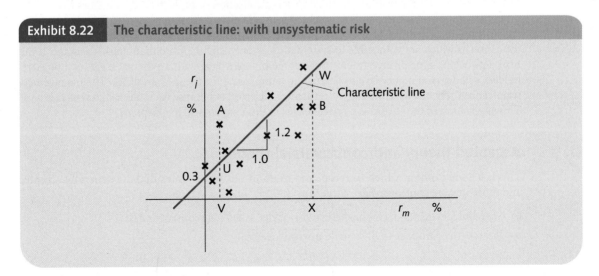

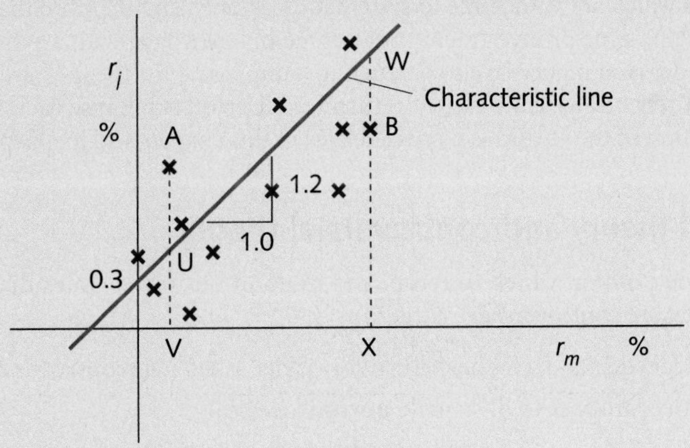

Applications of the CAPM

In this section we present a few examples of how the CAPM has been employed.

Investment in the financial markets

Portfolio selection

The beta metric has been used to construct different types of portfolio. For highly risk-averse investors a portfolio consisting of low beta securities may be chosen. If the average beta of the portfolio is 0.7 then for every 1 per cent change in the index the portfolio is expected to change by only 0.7 per cent. Similarly a high-risk portfolio could be created which consisted of high beta stocks and this will be expected to outperform the market in an upswing but underperform in a market correction.

Mispriced shares

Investors have used beta estimates to identify shares with anomalous risk-return characteristics. A share with an unusually attractive expected return for its beta level would be a 'buy' opportunity and one with an unusually low anticipated return a 'sell'. Getting this analysis correct is easier said than done, even if the CAPM worked perfectly.

Measuring portfolio performance

If a fund manager produces a high annual return of, say, 15 per cent how do you judge if this is due to good share selection? Well, one of the elements to consider is the systematic risk of the fund. If the 15 per cent return has been achieved because particularly risky shares were selected then perhaps you would hesitate to congratulate the manager. For example, if the beta risk is 1.7, the risk-free rate of return is 8 per cent and the historic risk premium for the market index over the risk-free investment $(r_m - r_f)$ has been 5 per cent then you would expect a return of 16.5 per cent:

$$r_j = r_f + \beta\,(r_m - r_f) = 8 + 1.7(5) = 16.5\%$$

On the other hand, if the beta of the portfolio is only 0.8 you might be willing to agree to that promotion the fund manager has been pushing for (expected return on the fund would be 8 + 0.8(5) = 12%).

Treynor's ratio measures return above the risk-free rate divided by beta. This allows you to observe return per unit of beta risk. **Sharpe's ratio** is return above the risk-free rate divided by standard deviation.

Calculating the required rate of return on a firm's investment projects

If it is true that shareholders price a company's shares on the basis of the perceived beta risk of the firm as a whole, and the firm may be regarded as a collection of projects, then investors will require different rates of return depending on the systematic risk of each new project that the company embarks upon. Consider a firm which at present has a beta of 1.1 because its existing projects produce returns which are vulnerable to systematic risk only slightly more than market average. If this firm now begins a major investment programme in a new area with a systematic risk of 1.8, shareholders will demand higher levels of return to compensate for the increased risk. The management team cannot rely on the same rate of return for all projects because each has a different risk level. This application of the CAPM is discussed later in this chapter and in Chapter 19.

Accepted theory and controversial theory

This is a good point at which to recap, and to point out those issues that are generally accepted and those that are controversial.

- Shareholders demand a higher return for riskier assets – **uncontroversial**.
- Risk-averters are wise to diversify – **uncontroversial**.

- The risk of securities (for example shares) has two elements: (a) unsystematic risk factors specific to firms which can be diversified away; and (b) systematic risk caused by risk factors common to all firms – **uncontroversial.**
- Investors will not be rewarded for bearing unsystematic risk – **uncontroversial.**
- Different shares have different degrees of sensitivity to the systematic risk elements – **uncontroversial.**
- Systematic risk is measured by beta which, in practice, is calculated as the degree of co-movement of a security's return with a market index return – **highly controversial.** As we will see later, some researchers believe beta has no effect on the level of returns earned on shares (that is, there is no relationship, and the SML does not exist); others believe that beta is one of a number of systematic risk factors influencing share returns.
- Beta, as calculated by examining past returns, is valid for decision making concerned about the future – **controversial.**

Technical problems with the CAPM

There are two issues that need to be addressed if the CAPM is to be a valid and useful tool in the commercial world. First, the CAPM has to be workable from the technical point of view. Second, the users have to be reassured that the CAPM, through its emphasis on beta, does accurately describe the returns witnessed on shares and securities. This second issue has been examined in scores of marketplace studies. The results of some of them are discussed in the next section; here we concentrate on the technical problems.

Measuring beta

The mathematics involved in obtaining a historic beta are straightforward enough; however it is not clear whether it is more appropriate to use weekly or monthly data, or whether the observation period should be three, five or ten years. (Some people observe market and share returns over a mere 30 days!) Each is likely to provide a different estimate of beta. Even if this issue is resolved, the difficulty of using a historic measure for estimating a future relationship is very doubtful. Betas tend to be unstable over time. This was discovered as long ago as the early 1970s. Both Blume and Levy carried out extensive testing and discovered that the beta for a share tends to change from one period to another. In recent years Glaxo's beta varied from less than zero (a negative beta!) to more than 1.6. For the first edition of this book Marks and Spencer's beta was obtained from Datastream. They used data for the five years to 1997 and M&S's beta was 0.95. A mere three years later Datastream calculated (based on the five years to 2000) its value at less than half that, at 0.44. For this edition the beta is 0.64. For Sainsbury's the change is even more dramatic: 0.60 in 1997, 0.19 in 2000, 0.8 in 2003 and 1.19 in 2007. Blume also showed that betas tended to change towards a value of 1 over time (M&S and Sainsbury's are exceptions, perhaps). The explanation he offered for this is that high-risk firms' new projects tend to have less extreme risk characteristics than existing projects. One potential explanation for the shifting betas is that the risk of the security changes – firms change the way they operate and the markets they serve. A company that was relatively insensitive to general market change two years ago may now be highly responsive, for example. But, can you really say that the risk of M&S's and Sainsbury's business has changed? Alternatively, the explanation may lie in measurement error – large random errors cause problems in producing comparable betas from one period to another. To add to this problem there is a wide variety of market indices (e.g. FT All-Share, FTSE-100) to choose from when calculating the historical covariability of a share with the market (its beta).

Ex ante *theory with* ex post *testing*

Applications of the CAPM tend to be focused on the future, for example deciding whether a share will provide a sufficiently high return to compensate for its risk level. Thus, it is investors' *expectations* that drive share prices. The CAPM follows this **ex ante** (before the event) line of reasoning; it describes *expected* returns and *future* beta. However, when it comes to testing the theory, we observe what has already occurred – these are **ex post** observations. There is usually a large difference between investors' expectations and the outcome. Therefore when we obtain, say, the risk premium for the market from historical data (*ex post*) we may be making an error in assuming that this is the appropriate rate today for calculating the required rate of return for an input to our *ex ante* (forward looking) analysis of say an investment project. **Exhibit 8.23** describes some of the difficulties caused by having to use *ex post* data for *ex ante* purposes.

Exhibit 8.23

Equity beta

FT

The theories of the ancient Greeks can be difficult to apply in the real world. Beta, one of modern finance's 'Greeks', is essential to calculate a company's cost of equity (COE), used to discount future earnings. It measures a stock's non-diversifiable risk, or sensitivity to market moves; shares with a beta of two move twice as far as the market. Unfortunately, beta statistics were wildly distorted by the dotcom bubble. In response, many analysts resorted to plugging gut-instinctive guesses into Nobel prize winning COE models.

Getting beta right matters. Assume current interest rates, and that equities return 3 per cent over bonds annually. A beta of one – that is, risk in line with that of the market – implies a COE of about 8 per cent. A beta of two means a COE of 11 per cent. Applied to a typical stream of earnings, the two discount rates generate at least a 50 per cent difference in net present value.

Ideally risk measures are forward looking. In the case of beta, investors must rely on historical data over, say, the last five years. That is the problem; until recently, this period included the internet bubble, when the volatile and overvalued telecommunications, media and technology sectors comprised up to half of the S&P 500. Since the market as a whole must have a beta of one, the betas of other sectors slumped. McKinsey reckons that US food stocks' observed beta reached zero, ridiculously implying that they had the same risk as Treasuries.

From a low of 0.6, the five-year beta of non-TMT sectors has recovered to about 1, according to McKinsey. That means classical COE formulae produce 'sensible' answers again. Still, the episode is a reminder that orthodox financial theory, which assumes that markets are efficient, breaks down if they are mispriced. Indeed, with a quarter of the FTSE 100 now comprised of mining and energy, deciding whether today's market conditions are sensible remains, as ever, a subjective affair.

Source: *Financial Times*, 4 September 2006, Lex column, p. 16.

The market portfolio is unobtainable

Roll's (1977) criticism of the CAPM as untestable, because the benchmark market indices employed, such as the FTSE All-Share Index, are poor substitutes for the true market portfolio, strikes at the heart of the CAPM. If the beta being used to estimate returns is constructed from an inferior proxy then the relationship revealed will not be based on the theoretically true CAPM. Even if all the shares in the world were included in the index this would exclude many other relevant assets, from stamp collections to precious metals.

One-period model

Investments usually involve a commitment for many years, whether the investment is made by a firm in real assets or by investors purchasing financial assets. However the CAPM is based on parameters measured at one point in time. Key variables such as the risk-free rate of return might, in reality, change.

A strict interpretation of the CAPM would insist on the use of the 3-month Treasury bill rate of return sold by a reputable government to investors. But sticking to the strict rule can lead to nonsense results. For example, in 2003 US Treasury bill rates fell to as low as 1 per cent. If this is used for r_f the required rate of return for an average risk-level US share is about 6 per cent (1 + 1(5) = 6%). For shares or projects within firms with a beta of 0.4 some analysts (and, it would seem, some textbook writers) would ask for a return of around 3 per cent (1 + 0.4(5) = 3%). This is less than individuals can get on savings accounts put at very low risk! This is odd given that many of these firms are investing in projects with lives of 5–15 years, not three months. Furthermore this was at a time when lending to the government could gain you return of 4.5 per cent, if you lent for 5 years or more. The practical solution is to use long-term government bond rates for r_f – more on this in Chapter 19.

Unrealistic assumptions

The CAPM is created on the foundation of a number of assumptions about the behaviour of investors and the operation of capital markets. Here are some of them:

- Investors are rational and risk averse.
- Investors are able to assess returns and standard deviations. Indeed they all have the same forecasts of returns and risk because of the free availability of information.
- There are no taxes or transaction costs.
- All investors can borrow or lend at the risk-free rate of interest.
- All assets are traded and it is possible to buy a fraction of a unit of an asset.

Clearly some of these assumptions do not reflect reality. But then, that is the way of economic modelling – it is necessary to simplify in order to explain real-world behaviour. In a sense it is not of crucial importance whether the assumptions are realistic. The important consideration is whether the model describes market behaviour. If it has some degree of predictive power about real-world relationships then it would be reasonable to overlook some of its technical problems and absurd assumptions.

Does the CAPM work in practice?

Researchers have sidestepped or ignored the technical and theoretical problems to try to see if taking on higher risk, as measured by beta, is rewarded by higher return, as described by the CAPM. More significantly, they have tried to establish if beta is the *only* factor influencing returns.

Empirical research carried out in the twenty years or so following the development of the CAPM tended to support the model. Work by Black *et al.* (1972) and Fama and MacBeth (1973), amongst dozens of others,[7] demonstrated that risk when measured by beta did have an influence on return. Eugene Fama and James MacBeth, for instance, allocated all the shares listed on the New York Stock Exchange between 1935 and 1966 to 20 portfolios. Over a five-year period monthly returns on specific shares and the market index were observed to calculate each share's beta. The shares were then allocated to portfolios. Portfolio 1 contained the 5 per cent of shares with the lowest betas. Portfolio 2 consisted of the second-lowest 5 per cent of shares as measured by their betas, and so on. Then a comparison was made for each subsequent four-year period between the calculated betas and the rate of return earned on each portfolio. If beta explained returns completely then the expectation is that the graphical plot points of beta and returns would be described by a straight line. The results did not show a perfect relationship. However, the plot points were generally placed around a market line and Fama and MacBeth felt able to conclude that 'there seems to be a positive trade off between returns and risk'.

While the early empirical work helped to spread the acceptance of the CAPM a few nagging doubts remained because, in general, the results gave only limited support to the notion that beta completely explains returns. An overview of these studies (presented in diagram form in **Exhibit 8.24**) gives the following conclusions. First, the intercept value for the Security Market Line (SML) tends to be higher than the risk-free rate of return, r_f; perhaps this indicates other risk factors at play, or perhaps investors expected to be compensated for accepting unsystematic risk. Second, the slope of the SML is much flatter than theory would imply – that is, low-risk shares tend to show rates of return higher than theory would suggest and high beta shares show lower returns than the CAPM predicts. Third, when individual shares are examined, the R^2 (coefficient of determination) of the characteristic line is low, suggesting that systematic risk as measured by beta is only a very small part of the explanation of the overall variability in share returns. Unsystematic risk and other types of systematic risk have far more significant effects on returns.

Work carried out in more recent years has generally caused more problems for the CAPM. For example Fischer Black (1993) discovered major differences in the strength of the beta-return relationship in the period 1931–65 compared with the period 1966–91. Ironically, up until the time of the development of the CAPM in the mid-1960s, the model seems to work reasonably well; but

---

[7] See References and Further Reading list at the end of this chapter for empirical studies.

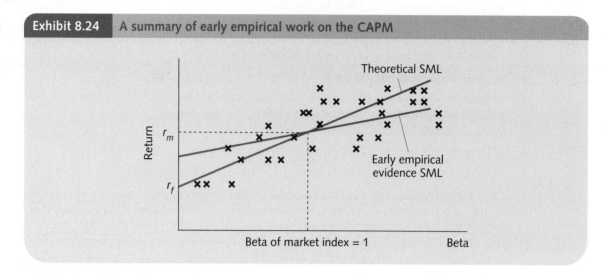

Exhibit 8.24 A summary of early empirical work on the CAPM

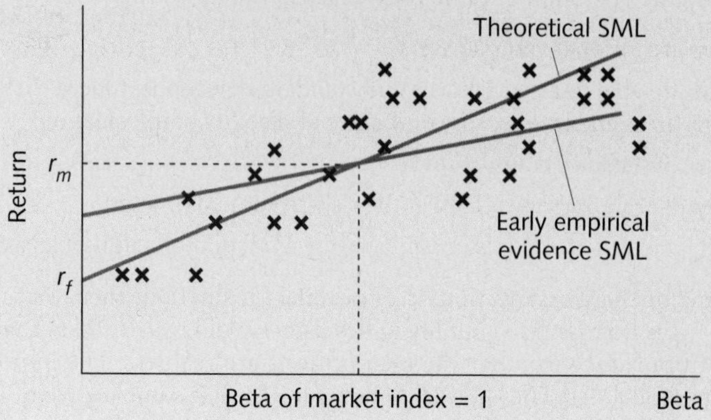

following its development and subsequent implementation the relationship breaks down. In his paper published in 1993 Black simulates a portfolio strategy that investors might adopt. The shares of quoted US companies (on the New York Stock Exchange) are allocated on an annual basis to 10 categories of different beta levels. Each year the betas are recalculated from the returns over the previous 60 months. The first investment portfolio is constructed by hypothetically purchasing all those shares within the top 10 per cent of beta values. As each year goes by the betas are recalculated and shares that are no longer in the top 10 per cent are sold and replaced by shares which now have the highest levels of beta. The second portfolio consists of the 10 per cent of shares with the next highest betas and this is reconstituted each year.

If ten portfolios with different levels of beta are created it should be possible to observe the extent to which beta risk is related to return in the period after formation. The relationship shown in **Exhibit 8.25** is not exactly as described by the SML for these ten portfolios held over the period 1931–91. The plot points are not placed precisely on the SML but it would be reasonable to conclude that higher-beta portfolios produce higher returns than lower-beta portfolios. The portfolio with a beta of 1.52 produces a return above the risk-free rate of 17 per cent per annum compared with 9 per cent for a portfolio having a beta of only 0.49. Also note that if a regression line is fitted to the observed data its shape would be flatter than the SML passing through the market portfolio plot point.

Exhibit 8.25 Beta and returns, 1931–91

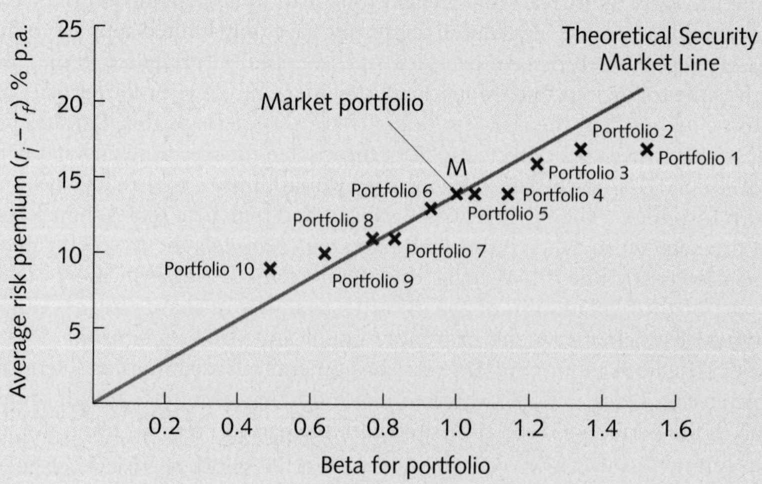

Source: Data derived from Black, F. (1993) 'Beta and return', *Journal of Portfolio Management*, 20, Fall, pp. 8–18.

The problems start when the data are split into two time periods. The pre-1965 data confirm a risk-return relationship roughly corresponding to the CAPM but with a flatter line. However, the post-1965 data (in **Exhibit 8.26**) show a complete absence of a relationship. Both the high-beta portfolio and the low-beta portfolio show average annual returns over the risk-free rate of 6 per cent.

A further blow to the CAPM came with the publication of Eugene Fama and Kenneth French's (1992) empirical study of US share returns over the period 1963–90. They found 'no reliable relation between β, and average return'.[8] They continue:

> The asset-pricing model of Sharpe (1964), Lintner (1965), and Black (1972) [the CAPM] has long shaped the way academics and practitioners think about average returns and risk . . . In short, our tests do not support the most basic prediction of the SLB model, that average stock returns are positively related to market *βs* . . . Our bottom-line results are: (a) *β* does not seem to help explain the cross-section of average stock returns, and (b) the combination of size and book-to-market equity [does].

Fama and French's later (2006) paper reports that higher beta did not lead to higher returns over the 77 years to 2004.

In other words, beta has not been able to explain returns whereas two other factors have. A firm's total market value has had some effect on returns: the larger the firm (market capitalisation), the lower the return. Also the ratio of the firm's book (balance sheet) value to its market value (total value of all shares issued) has had some explanatory power: if book value is high *vis-à-vis* market value, then returns tend to be higher.[9] This particular onslaught on the CAPM has caused great consternation and reaction in the academic world.

Another line of attack has come from Burton Malkiel (1990) who found that the returns on US mutual funds (collective investments similar to unit trusts in the UK) in the 1980s were unrelated to their betas. Louis Chan and Josef Lakonishok (1993) breathed a little life into the now dying

Exhibit 8.26 Beta and returns, 1966–91

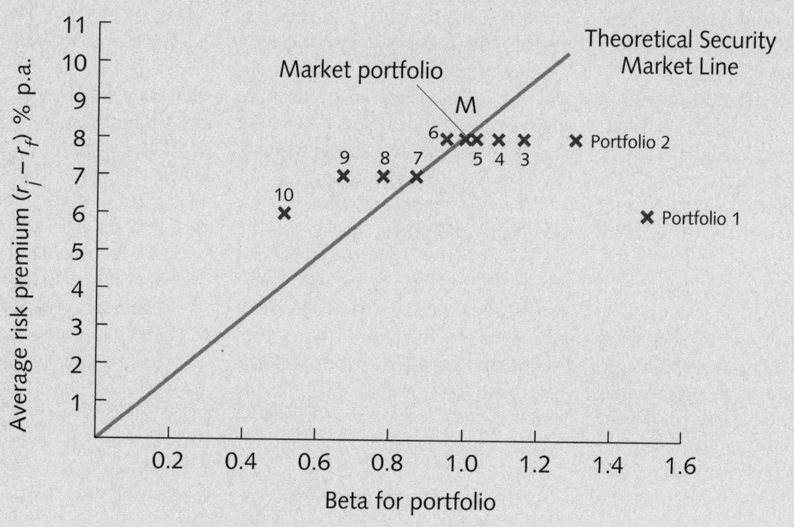

Source: Data derived from Black, F. (1993) 'Beta and Return', *Journal of Portfolio Management*, 20, Fall, pp. 8–18.

[8] There is some controversy over their interpretation of the data, but nevertheless this is a very serious challenge to the CAPM.

[9] In Fama and French's subsequent writing they describe size and book-to-market ratio as risk factors believing the market to be efficient at pricing shares. Other researchers (e.g. Daniel and Titman 1997, 2006) see these factors as elements that are not properly priced by investors, i.e. they underprice small companies and those with a high book value relative to market value. These shares subsequently produce high returns as investors slowly positively reappraise them. See Chapter 14 for a discussion on share mispricing.

beta. They looked at share returns over the period 1926–91 and found a faint pulse of a relationship between beta and returns, but were unable to show statistical significance because of the 'noisy' data. More vibrant life can be witnessed if the share return data after 1982 are excluded – but, then, shouldn't it work in all periods? They also argued that beta may be a more valid determinant of return in extreme market circumstances, such as a stock market crash, and therefore should not be written off as being totally 'dead'.

Beta has been brought to its knees by the punches delivered by American researchers; it was kicked again while it was down by the damaging evidence drawn from the European share markets. For example, Albert Corhay and co-researchers Gabriel Hawawini and Pierre Michel (1987) found that investors in shares trading in the United States, the United Kingdom and Belgium were not compensated with higher average returns for bearing higher levels of risk (as measured by beta) over the 13-year sample period. Investors in shares trading on the Paris Stock Exchange were actually penalised rather than rewarded, in that they received below-average rates of return for holding shares with above-average levels of beta risk. Rouwenhorst, Heston and Wessels (1999), however, found some relation between beta and returns in 12 European countries. Strong and Xu (1997) show that UK shares during the period 1973–92 displayed evidence consistent with a *negative* relationship between average returns and beta!

Exhibit 8.27

The time has come for the CAPM to RIP

FT

Tony Tassell The long view

Few theories are more influential or important in driving financial markets as [sic] the inelegantly named capital asset pricing model. Too bad it does not appear to work very well.

The CAPM, as it is widely known, is a cornerstone of modern financial market analysis, studied like a rosary by analysts and executives at business school. Most financial directors use it to assess everything from the viability of a new project to their cost of capital. Most stock market analysts consider it an essential tool.

But it has faced increasing criticism in recent years as unworkable in the real world, even from luminary market academics such as Harry Markowitz who laid the groundwork for the CAPM with research in 1950s on efficient portfolios.

James Montier, analyst at Dresdner Kleinwort, says CAPM has become the financial theory equivalent of Monty Python's famous dead parrot sketch. He says the model is empirically bogus – it does not work in any way, shape or form. But like the shopkeeper who insists to a customer with a dead parrot in the sketch that the bird is merely resting, financial markets are in denial.

'The CAPM is, in actual fact, Completely Redundant Asset Pricing (CRAP),' he says.

Some of the most damning evidence came from an exhaustive 2004 study by Eugene Fama and Kenneth French, the academics who helped develop the efficient markets theory in the early 1970s, that argued stocks are always correctly priced as everything that is publicly known about the stock is reflected in its market price.

The study looked at all stocks on the New York Stock Exchange, the American Stock Exchange and Nasdaq from 1923 to 2003. As Montier states, the study shows CAPM woefully underpredicts the returns to low beta stocks and massively overstates the returns to high beta stocks. 'Over the long run there has been essentially no relationship between beta and return,' he says.

Fama and French themselves concluded that while CAPM, was a fine theoretical tour de force, its empirical track record was so poor that its use in 'applications' was probably invalid. In others words, CAPM is a fine theory but useless in the real world.

A similar study of the 600 largest US stocks by Jeremy Grantham, the value investor, last year yielded similar results. It showed from 1969 to the end of 2005, the lowest decile of beta stocks – notionally the lowest risk – outperformed by an average 1.5 per cent a year. The highest beta stocks, or the riskiest, actually underperformed by 2.7 per cent a year.

Markowitz himself noted that the CAPM is like studying 'the motions of objects on Earth under the assumption that the Earth has no air'.

'The calculations and results are much simpler if this assumption is made. But at some point, the obvious fact that on Earth, cannonballs and feathers do not fall at the same rate should be noted,' he says.

Grantham says the flaws in the CAPM are probably inconvenient enough for the academic financial establishment to want to ignore it. But there ought to be more debate, particularly in using beta as a risk benchmark.

Montier cites a quote from legendary investor Ben Graham: 'What bothers me is that authorities now equate the beta with the concept of risk. Price variability, yes; risk, no. Real investment risk is measured not by the per cent a stock may decline in price in relation to the general market in a given period but by the danger of a loss of quality and earning power through economic changes or deterioration in management.'

Source: Financial Times, 10/11 February 2007, p. 24 of FT Money. Reprinted with permission.

In emerging markets Rouwenhorst (1999) finds no statistically significant evidence that high beta shares outperform low beta shares.

It is plain that even if the CAPM is not dead it has been severely wounded. Beta may or may not have strong explanatory power for returns. That debate will rage for many years yet. What we can conclude from the evidence presented is that there appears to be more to risk than beta.

Exhibit 8.27 describes the mood of scepticism now surrounding the CAPM.

Factor models

The capital asset pricing model assumes that there is a single factor influencing returns on securities. This view has been difficult to sustain over recent years given the empirical evidence and theoretical doubts. It also seems to defy common sense; for example, it seems reasonable, and is observed in practice, that the returns on a share respond to industry or sector changes as well as to the general market changes.

Multi-factor models are based on the notion that a security's return may be sensitive to a variety of factors. Using these models the analyst attempts to first identify the important influences within the business and financial environment, and second, measure the degree of sensitivity of particular securities to these factors. We will see how this works by considering a one-factor model and building from there.

A one-factor model

Let us assume that we believe the main influence on the returns of shares in Rose plc (*see* **Exhibit 8.28**) is the economy-wide inflation rate. To test this hypothesis we have gathered data for the past six years.

Exhibit 8.28 Returns on Rose and changes in a single potential explanatory factor

Year	Inflation (%)	Return on a share in Rose plc (%)
1	4	22.5
2	3.4	22.5
3	3.1	20.0
4	5.0	32.5
5	2.6	21.25
6	2.2	12.5

The fitted line in **Exhibit 8.29** has a positive slope of 5, indicating a positive relationship between Rose's returns and inflation. The relationship is not perfect (in that the plot points do not lie on the line), indicating that there are other influences on the return.

The kind of one-factor model shown in Exhibit 8.29 can be expressed in mathematical form:

$$r_j = a + b F_1 + e$$

where:

r_j = return on share j

a = intercept term when the Factor F_1 is zero

F_1 = the factor under consideration

b = the sensitivity of the return to the factor

e = error term caused by other influences on return, e.g. unsystematic risk

In the example shown in Exhibit 8.29 the expected return on a share in Rose is given by

$$r_j = 5 + 5 \times F_1$$

Exhibit 8.29 Rose plc returns and inflation

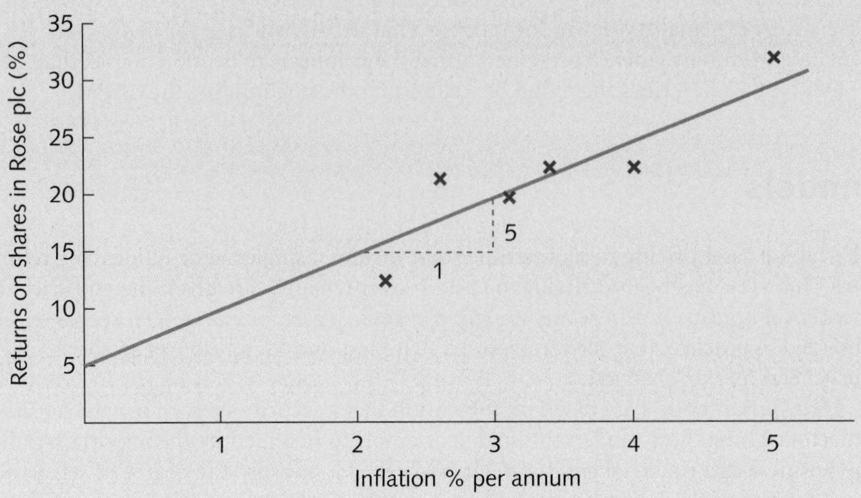

so, if inflation is 1 per cent the expected return on Rose will be 10 per cent; if it is 2 per cent, Rose is expected to return 15 per cent.

(Strictly speaking, many factor models focus on only the unexpected part of the change in F_1, F_2 etc. because returns on share j over a period are not going to respond to expected changes in F_1 or F_2 because in an efficient market the share would already have moved to the new level at the start of the period in anticipation.)

Of course, the CAPM is a type of one-factor model where F_1 is defined as the equity risk premium and b equates to beta (representing sensitivity to the determining factor):

$$r_j = a + b\,F_1 + e$$

In the CAPM: $a = r_f$, $b = \beta$, $F_1 = (r_m - r_f)$. Thus:

$$r_j = r_f + \beta\,(r_m - r_f) + e$$

However, the useful characteristic of this factor model is that it permits F_1 to be any one of a number of explanatory influences, and does not restrict the researcher or practitioner to the market index premium.

An investment in Rose is an investment in a single company's shares; therefore both systematic and unsystematic risk will be present – or in the language of factor models, *factor risk* and *non-factor risk*. By diversifying, an investor can eliminate non-factor risk. Most factor model analysis takes place under the assumption that all non-factor (unsystematic) risk can be ignored because the investors are fully diversified and therefore this type of risk will not be rewarded with a higher return.

A two-factor model

The returns on Rose may be influenced by more than simply the general inflation rate. Perhaps the price of oil products has an effect. A two-factor model can be represented by the following equation:

$$r_j = a + b_1\,F_1 + b_2\,F_2 + e$$

where:
- F_1 = inflation rate
- b_1 = sensitivity of j to inflation rate growth
- F_2 = price of oil
- b_2 = sensitivity of j to price of oil

To establish the slope values of b_1 and b_2 as well as a, a multiple regression analysis could be carried out. The relationship of the returns on Rose and the influencing factors can no longer be represented by a two-dimensional graph. The level of return in any one period is determined by the following formula, which has been constructed on the assumption that for every (unexpected) \$1 on the price of oil return increases by 0.3 of a percentage point and every (unexpected) 1 per cent increase in inflation generates an extra 5 per cent of return . . .

$$r_j = a + b_1 F_1 + b_2 F_2$$
$$r_j = 3 + 5 F_1 + 0.3 F_2$$

Multi-factor models

No doubt the reader can think of many other systematic risk factors that might influence the returns on a share, ranging from GDP growth to the exchange rate. These relationships have to be presented in a purely mathematical fashion. So, for a five-factor model the equation could look like this:

$$r_j = a + b_1 F_1 + b_2 F_2 + b_3 F_3 + b_4 F_4 + b_5 F_5 + e$$

where F_3 might be, say, the industrial group that firm j belongs to, F_4 is the growth in national GDP and F_5 is the size of the firm. This particular share will have a set of sensitivities (b_1, b_2, b_3, b_4 and b_5) to its influencing factors which is likely to be different from the sensitivity of other shares, even those within the same line of business.

The arbitrage pricing theory

As the CAPM has come under attack the arbitrage pricing theory (APT) has attracted more attention (at least in the academic world) since it was developed by Stephen Ross in 1976. In similar fashion to the CAPM it assumes that investors are fully diversified and therefore factor risks (systematic risks) are the only influence on long-term returns. However, the systematic factors permissible under the APT are many and various, compared with the CAPM's single determining variable. The returns on a share under the APT are found through the following formula:

$$\text{Expected returns} = \text{risk-free return} + \beta_1(r_1 - r_f) + \beta_2(r_2 - r_f) + \beta_3(r_3 - r_f) + \beta_4(r_4 - r_f) \ \ldots + \beta_n(r_n - r_f) + e$$

where β_1 stands for the security's beta with respect to the first factor, β_2 stands for the security's beta with respect to the second factor, and so on. The terms in brackets are the risk premiums f or each of the factors in the model – $(r_1 - r_f)$ is the risk premium for the first factor for a security whose beta with respect to the first factor is 1 and whose beta with respect to all other factors is zero. Notice that the $(r_1 - r_f)$ etc. are the extra percentage annual returns on a share for bearing this type of risk. This is different from F_1, F_2, etc. above, which relate to, say, the unexpected change in the price of oil which may be expressed in dollars per barrel, or GDP growth, as change year on year.

Arbitrage pricing theory does not specify what will be systematic risk factors, nor does it state the size or the sign (positive or negative) of the 'βs'. Each share or portfolio will have a different degree of sensitivity to each of the risk factors that happen to be included in the model tested.

Researchers have tried to identify the most frequently encountered systematic risk factors. Some studies have shown these to be changes in the macroeconomic environment such as inflation, interest rates, industrial production levels, personal consumption and money supply. This seems to make sense given that future profits are likely to be influenced by the state of the economy. All firms are likely to react to a greater or lesser extent to changes in those macroeconomic variables. Also, most firms will respond in the same way. For instance, if the economy is growing strongly then most firms' profits will rise; therefore these factors cannot be diversified away.

However, some firms will be more sensitive to changes in the factors than others – this is measured by the 'βs'. Each of these risk factors has a risk premium because investors will only accept the risk if they are adequately rewarded with a higher return. It is the sum of these risk premiums when added to the risk-free rate that creates the return on a particular share or portfolio.

A major problem with the APT is that it does not tell us in advance what the risk factors are. In practice there have been two approaches to find these. The first is to specify those factors thought most likely to be important and then to test to see if they are relevant. The drawback here is that it is rather *ad hoc* and there will always be the nagging doubt that you failed to test some of the crucial factors. The second approach employs a complex statistical technique that simultaneously determines from a mass of factors which are relevant in a data set, as well as their coefficients.

Empirical research has demonstrated the value of the APT in highlighting where there is more than one factor influencing returns. Unfortunately there is disagreement about the key variables as the identified factors vary from study to study. This lack of specificity regarding the crucial factors has meant that the APT has not been widely adopted in the investment community despite its intuitive appeal. Investors are generally left to themselves to discover the risk factors if they can. Even if they are able to identify relevant factors and the degree of sensitivity is carefully worked out, the analyst is forced to recognise that the outcomes only explain past returns. The focus of most investors and business people is on the future and so judgement is needed to make these models valuable in a predictive role. Using historical information in a mechanical fashion to predict future returns may produce disappointing results.

The three-factor model

Fama and French (1996) have developed a three-factor model based on their previous work which showed that smaller companies produce higher returns than larger companies, and those with lots of net assets compared to the market value of the company outperform those with few net assets as a proportion of share market value of the firm. They interpreted size and the book-to-market value ratio as risk factors that require compensation in the form of higher returns (rather than share traders temporarily irrationally underpricing small companies and those with high book-to-market values – *see* Chapter 14 for this alternative view). In their model returns are determined by the risk-free rate plus:

- the excess return on a broad market portfolio $(r_m - r_f)$;
- the difference between the return on a portfolio of small shares (companies with a small market capitalisation) and the return on a portfolio of large shares (SMB, small minus big);
- the difference between the return on a portfolio of high book-to-market shares and the return on a portfolio of low book-to-market shares (HML, high minus low).

$$\text{Expected return} = \text{risk-free rate} + \beta_1(r_m - r_f) + \beta_2(\text{SMB}) + \beta_3(\text{HML})$$

The model is attempting to pick up systematic risk factors not captured by the simple CAPM. In the Fama and French model, as well as being influenced by the general risk premium for shares $(r_m - r_f)$, the average small share is taken to be more risky than the average large share and so offers an additional risk premium, SMB. Also the share with a high balance sheet (book) value per share relative to the market value of each share is assumed to be more risky than a share with a low book value compared with the share price, and so offers a risk premium, HML. Fama and French tested this model on US shares and concluded that 'the model is a good description of returns' (Fama and French 1996). Other researchers say that returns may rise for smaller companies or high book-to-market ratio companies but this may not be due to risk compensation but merely inefficient share pricing.

To make the model useful you need to establish the risk premium associated with each factor $(r_m - r_f)$, (SMB) and (HML). For the purposes of illustration let us assume that the risk premium on the market portfolio $(r_m - r_f)$ is 5 per cent and the annual risk premium for a small company share compared with a large company share is 2 per cent and the extra return received on a share with a high book-to-market ratio compared with a low book-to-market ratio is 3 per cent.

These are the risk premiums for averagely sensitive shares. Individual shares are more or less sensitive to the fluctuations in the returns on the three factors.

So, if we take the shares of an imaginary company, A, with a high sensitivity to market movements ($r_m - r_f$), they will be observed to have a high β_1, say, 1.5. If the sensitivity to size (SMB) is small (in fact, negative) then β_2 will be, say, –0.02. If the sensitivity to HML is 0.25 then:

$$\begin{aligned}\text{Expected risk premium} &= \beta_1(r_m - r_f) + \beta_2(\text{SMB}) + \beta_3(\text{HML})\\ &= 1.5(5) - 0.02(2) + 0.25(3)\\ &= 8.21\%\end{aligned}$$

If the risk-free rate of return is 4 per cent the expected return is 12.21 per cent.

Arbitrage pricing theory and the three-factor model show promise but our quest to find an easy and workable model of risk and return is not yet over. Perhaps it will be useful to step back from high academic theory and observe the techniques that some market practitioners use to see if they have greater predictive power.

An alternative approach to the risk-return relationship

Our forefathers, long before the development of the APT and the CAPM, had to grapple with the problem of quantifying risk. Perhaps some of these more traditional approaches based on commonsense risk influences provide greater insight and predictive power than the fancy theoretical constructs. For example, you do not need knowledge of high finance to realise that a firm that has a large amount of borrowing relative to its equity base will be subject to more risk than one with a lower level of borrowing (assuming all other factors are the same). Furthermore, if the geared-up firm is in a particularly volatile industry it will be subject to even more risk.

Russell Fuller and Wenchi Wong (1988) carried out an investigation to see which of three approaches to measuring risk had the most predictive power over the rate of return witnessed on shares. The first two are now very familiar to us; they are beta and standard deviation. The third is a traditional risk measure called the Value Line Safety Rank. Under this popular US system shares are placed into one of five categories. A ranking of 1 indicates the lowest risk and a ranking of 5 indicates the highest. Two major sub-categories of risk are combined to produce the final ranking:

a the *price stability index*: this is merely the standard deviation of the share returns measured over the most recent five-year period; and

b the *financial strength rating*: this is an amalgam of risk factors which include, amongst others, debt-coverage ratios (a measure of proportion of profit absorbed by interest), fixed-charge coverage, accounting methods, the quick ratio (proportion of liquid short-term assets to short-term liabilities) and company size.

The Value Index Line Investment Survey provides a weekly advisory service for US shares. It reviews 1,700 shares and places them into the five risk categories for subscribers to enable them to make investment decisions. Fuller and Wong looked at the returns over the period 1974–85. To make the comparison between the alternative risk measures easier the shares were also placed in five beta categories (rank of 1 = lowest beta, rank of 5 = highest beta) and in five standard deviation categories (1 = lowest, 5 = highest). The results are presented in **Exhibit 8.30**. The safety ranks show a strong positive relationship between risk and return. Standard deviation also shows a strong relationship, but beta is shown as having a very low correlation with the returns. These observations led to the conclusion that 'Safety rank is the most powerful explanatory risk measure, sigma rank [standard deviation] the second most powerful; beta rank is a distant third'. This evidence has not helped the revival of the CAPM.

Exhibit 8.30 Return on shares categorised by risk measured in three ways, 1974–85

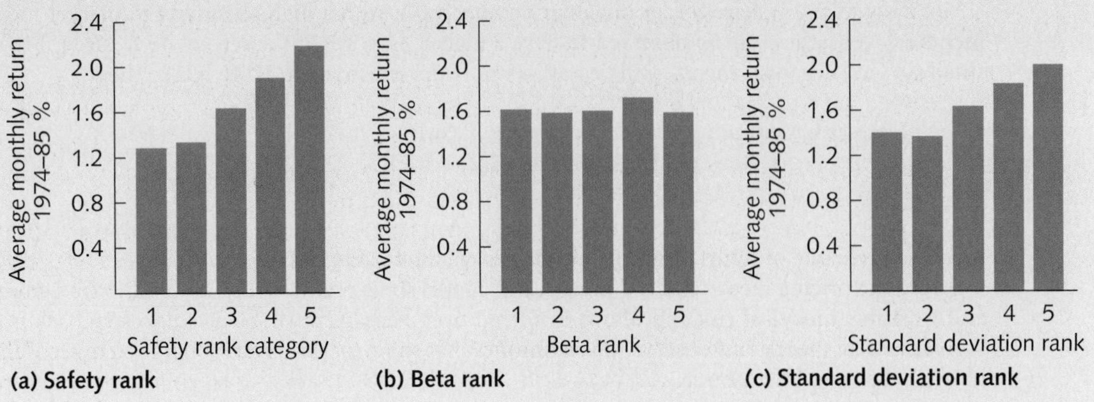

Source: Fuller, R. and Wong, G.W. (1988) 'Traditional versus Theoretical Risk Measures', *Financial Analysts Journal*, 44, March–April, pp. 52–7. Copyright 1988, Association for Investment Management and Research®. Reproduced and republished from *Financial Analysts Journal* with permission from the Association for Investment Management and Research.

Project appraisal and systematic risk

Senior managers are generally aware that the returns on their company's shares are set at a particular level by the collective buying and selling actions of shareholders adjusting the share price. They are further aware that adjustment continues until the investors are content that the prospective returns reflect the riskiness of the share. What determines the systematic risk of a share is the underlying activities of the firm. Some firms engage in high-risk ventures and so shareholders, in exchange for accepting the possibility of a large loss, will expect a high return. Other firms undertake relatively safe activities and so shareholders will be prepared to receive a lower return.

The overall risk and return on the equity finance of a firm is determined by the portfolio of projects and their associated systematic risk. If a firm undertook an additional capital investment which had a much higher degree of risk than the average in the existing set then it is intuitively obvious that a higher return than the normal rate for this company will be required. On the other hand, if an extraordinarily low-risk activity is contemplated this should require a lower rate of return than usual.

Situations of this type are illustrated in **Exhibit 8.31** for a representative all-equity financed firm. Given the firm's normal risk level the market demands a return of 15 per cent. If another project were started with a similar level of risk then it would be reasonable to calculate NPV on the basis of a discount rate of 15 per cent. This is the opportunity cost of capital for the sharehold-

Exhibit 8.31 Rates of return for projects of different systematic risk levels

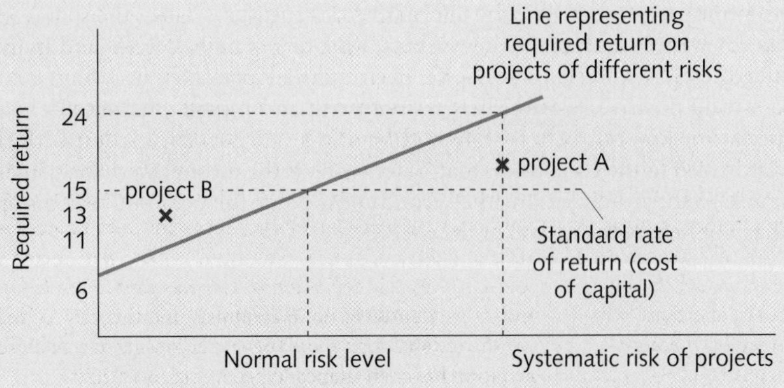

ers – they could obtain 15 per cent by investing their money in shares of other firms in a similar risk class. If, however, the firm were to invest in project A with a risk twice the normal level, management would be doing their shareholders a disservice if they sought a mere 15 per cent rate of return. At this risk level shareholders can get 24 per cent on their money elsewhere. This sort of economic decision making will result in projects being accepted when they should have been rejected. Conversely project B, if discounted at the standard rate of 15 per cent, will be rejected when it should have been accepted. It produces a return of 13 per cent when all that is required is a return of 11 per cent for this risk class. It is clear that this firm should accept any project lying above the sloping line and reject any project lying below this line.

The rule taught in Chapter 2 that a firm should accept any project that gives a return greater than the firm's opportunity cost of capital now has to be refined. This rule can only be applied if the marginal project has the same risk level as the existing set of projects. Projects with different risk levels require different levels of return.

While the logic of adjusting for risk is impeccable a problem does arise when it comes to defining risk. The traditional approach, before the use of the CAPM, was to exercise judgement. It was, and still is, popular to allocate projects to three or more categories (low, medium and high) rather than to precisely state the risk level. Then in the 1960s the CAPM presented a very precise linear relationship between beta risk as measured by the covariance of returns against the market index. Calculating the historical beta for a share quoted on a stock market is relatively straightforward because the analyst has access to share return data to construct the characteristic line. However the estimation of the risk on a *proposed* project that is merely one part of a firm's suite of activities is more problematic. A suggested solution is to use the beta values of quoted firms in a similar line of business. Thus if the new project were in food retailing, the betas from all the firms in the food retailing industry could be averaged to establish an estimate of this project's beta. Adjustments might have to be made to this to allow for differences in the riskiness of the average peer group firms and this particular project but the fundamental techniques will not change.

The doubts surrounding the CAPM have led to a questioning of this approach. An alternative is to factor in a range of macroeconomic influences. Here we would try to estimate the sensitivity of the project's cash flows to changes in the economy such as GDP, inflation and industrial output. Some projects will be highly sensitive to macroeconomic forces and so will be regarded as more risky, others will be relatively stable. It is possible that an amalgamation of all three approaches – judgement, the CAPM and factor analysis – might provide the most robust methodology in practice, even if it will be criticised on theoretical grounds.

Sceptics' views – alternative perspectives on risk

David Dreman, an experienced investor, does not have a great deal of respect for the financial economists' models. The following is a quotation from his book, *Contrarian Investment Strategies: The Next Generation*, pp. 297–311:

> **What is risk?**
>
> What then is risk? To the academics who built the efficient market hypothesis (EMH) and modern portfolio theory (MPT) the answer is obvious. Risk is an A-B-C commodity. According to this theory, investors are risk-averse: they are willing to take more risk for higher payoffs and will accept lower returns if they take less risk. A simple but elegant theory.
>
> How does one measure risk? That too is simple . . . The greater the volatility of a stock or portfolio, whether measured by standard deviation or beta, the greater the risk. A mutual fund of common stock that fluctuates more than the market is considered to be more risky and has a higher beta. One that fluctuates less is less risky and has a lower beta. How did these professors know that investors measured risk strictly by the volatility of the stock? They didn't, nor did they do any research to find out, other than the original studies of the correlation between volatility and return, with results which were mixed at best. The academics simply declared it as fact. Importantly, this definition of risk was easy to use to build complex market models, and that's what the professors wanted to do. Economists find this view of risk compelling, if not obsessional, because it is the way the rational man *should* behave according to economic theory . . . Whether unrealistic or not, an entire generation has been trained to believe risk is volatility.
>
> . . .

In the first place it has been known for decades that there is no correlation between risk, as the academics define it, and return. Higher volatility does not give better results, nor lower volatility worse . . . The lack of correlation between risk and return was not the only problem troubling academic researchers. More basic was the failure of volatility measures to remain constant over time, which is central to both the efficient market hypothesis and modern portfolio theory. Although beta is the most widely used of all volatility measures, a beta that can accurately predict future volatility has eluded researchers since the beginning. The original betas constructed by Sharpe, Lintner, and Mossin were shown to have no predictive power, that is, the volatility in one period had little or no correlation with that in the next. A stock could pass from violent fluctuation to lamb like docility.

. . .

Fama and French found that stocks with low betas performed roughly as well as stocks with high betas. Fama stated that 'beta as the sole variable in explaining returns on stocks . . . is dead.'* Write this on the tombstone: 'What we are saying is that over the last 50 years, knowing the volatility of an equity doesn't tell you much about the stock's return'. Yes, make it a large stone, maybe even a mausoleum.

. . .

Beta gives the appearance of being a highly sophisticated mathematical formula, but is constructed while looking into the rearview mirror. It takes inputs that seemed to correlate with volatility in the past, then states it will work again in the future. This is not good science. Because some variables moved in step with volatility for a number of years, does not mean they initiated it. Most often, such correlations are sheer coincidence.

I wrote almost two decades ago that betas, built as they were on spurious correlations with past inputs, were unlikely to work in the future. This is precisely what happened.

This is not just ivory tower stuff, as we've seen. Beta and other forms of risk measurement decide how hundreds of billions of dollars are invested by pension funds, and other institutional investors. High betas are no-nos while the money manager who delivers satisfactory returns with a low-beta portfolio is lionized.

. . .

We have seen that risk, as the academics defined it, was eventually rejected by efficient market types themselves. Higher volatility did not provide the promised returns, nor lower volatility lower results. This leads us back to square one.

. . .

What then is a better way of measuring your investment risk? . . .

. . .

A realistic definition of risk recognizes the potential loss of capital through inflation and taxes, and would include at least the following two factors:

1 The probability that the investment you choose will preserve your capital over the time you intend to invest your funds.
2 The probability the investments you select will outperform alternative investments for this period.

These measures of risk tell us the probabilities that we will both maintain our purchasing power and do better than alternative investments for the period we chose. Unlike the academic volatility measures, these risk measures look to the appropriate time period in the future – 5, 10, 15, 20, or 30 years – when the funds will be required. Market risk may be severe in a period of months or even for a few years, but . . . it diminishes rapidly over longer periods.

* *See* Eric N. Berg, 'Market Place: A study shakes confidence in volatile-stock theory', *New York Times*, 18 Feb. 1992, p. 3.

Warren Buffett, the world's richest man (or the second richest, depending on the relative performance of the shares of Microsoft and Buffett's company, Berkshire Hathaway), has little respect for the CAPM, as the following extract indicates. Note that these comments come from a man who started with very little capital and made all his money by selecting company shares for purchase:

In our opinion, the real risk that an investor must assess is whether his aggregate after-tax receipts from an investment (including those he receives on sale) will, over his prospective holding period, give him at least as much purchasing power as he had to begin with, plus a modest rate of interest on that initial stake. Though this risk cannot be calculated with engineering precision, it can in some cases be judged with a degree of accuracy that is useful. The primary factors bearing upon this evaluation are:

1 The certainty with which the long-term economic characteristics of the business can be evaluated;
2 The certainty with which management can be evaluated, both as to its ability to realize the full potential of the business and to wisely employ its cash flows;
3 The certainty with which management can be counted on to channel the rewards from the business to the shareholders rather than to itself;
4 The purchase price of the business;
5 The levels of taxation and inflation that will be experienced and that will determine the degree by which an investor's purchasing-power return is reduced from his gross return.

These factors will probably strike many analysts as unbearably fuzzy, since they cannot be extracted from a data base of any kind. But the difficulty of precisely quantifying these matters does not negate their importance nor is it insuperable. Just as Justice Stewart found it impossible to formulate a test for obscenity but nevertheless asserted, 'I know it when I see it', so also can investors – in an inexact but useful way – 'see' the risks inherent in certain investments without reference to complex equations or price histories.

Is it really so difficult to conclude that Coca-Cola and Gillette possess far less business risk over the long-term than, say, *any* computer company or retailer? Worldwide, Coke sells about 44% of all soft drinks, and Gillette has more than a 60% share (in value) of the blade market. Leaving aside chewing gum, in which Wrigley is dominant, I know of no other significant businesses in which the leading company has long enjoyed such global power.

Moreover, both Coke and Gillette have actually increased their worldwide shares of market in recent years. The might of their brand names, the attributes of their products, and the strength of their distribution systems give them an enormous competitive advantage, setting up a protective moat around their economic castles. The average company, in contrast, does battle daily without any such means of protection. As Peter Lynch says, stocks of companies selling commodity-like products should come with a warning label: 'Competition may prove hazardous to human wealth.'

The competitive strengths of a Coke or Gillette are obvious to even the casual observer of business. Yet the beta of their stocks is similar to that of a great many run-of-the-mill companies who possess little or no competitive advantage. Should we conclude from this similarity that the competitive strength of Coke and Gillette gains them nothing when business risk is being measured? Or should we conclude that the risk in owning a piece of a company – its stock – is somehow divorced from the long-term risk inherent in its business operations? We believe neither conclusion makes sense and that equating beta with investment risk also makes no sense.

The theoretician bred on beta has no mechanism for differentiating the risk inherent in, say, a single-product toy company selling pet rocks or hula hoops from that of another toy company whose sole product is Monopoly or Barbie. But it's quite possible for ordinary investors to make such distinctions if they have a reasonable understanding of consumer behavior and the factors that create long-term competitive strength or weakness. Obviously, every investor will make mistakes. But by confining himself to a relatively few, easy-to-understand cases, a reasonably intelligent, informed and diligent person can judge investment risks with a useful degree of accuracy.

Buffett, W. (1993) Letter accompanying the Annual Report for Berkshire Hathaway Inc. for 1993.

Benjamin Graham, the father of security analysis is equally scathing of the focus on short-term price movements as the form of risk. He taught his students (e.g. Warren Buffett) to examine the potential for loss over many years and even to welcome volatility as it gave people the chance to buy into good companies when the market was being unreasonably pessimistic. In his book *The Intelligent Investor* he wrote:

We should like to point out that the words 'risk' and 'safety' are applied to securities in two different senses, with a resultant confusion in thought.

A bond is clearly proved unsafe when it defaults its interest or principal payments. Similarly, if a preferred stock or even a common stock is bought with the expectation that a given rate of dividend will be continued, then a reduction or passing of the dividend means that it has proved unsafe. It is also true that an investment contains a risk if there is a fair possibility that the holder may have to sell at a time when the price is well below cost.

Nevertheless, the idea of risk is often extended to apply to a possible decline in the price of a security, even though the decline may be of a cyclical and temporary nature and even though the holder is unlikely to be forced to sell at such times. . . . But we believe that what is here involved is not a true risk in the useful sense of the term. The man who holds a mortgage on a building might have to take a substantial loss if he were forced to sell it at an unfavorable time. That element is not taken into account in judging the safety or risk of ordinary real-estate mortgages, the only criterion being the certainty of punctual payments. In the same way the risk attached to an ordinary commercial business is measured by the chance of its losing money, not by what would happen if the owner were forced to sell . . .

. . .

[T]he bona fide investor does not lose money merely because the market price of his holdings declines; hence the fact that a decline may occur does not mean he is running a true risk of loss. If a group of well-selected common-stock investments shows a satisfactory overall return, as measured through a fair number of years, then this group investment has proved to be 'safe'. During that period its market value is bound to fluctuate, and as likely as not it will sell for a while under the buyer's cost. If that fact makes the investment 'risky', it would then have to be called both risky and safe at the same time. This confusion may be avoided if we apply the concept of risk solely to a loss of value which either is realised through actual sale, or is caused by a significant deterioration in the company's position – or more frequently perhaps, is the result the payment of an excessive price in relation to the intrinsic worth of the security.

Many common stocks do involve risks of such deterioration. But it is our thesis that a properly executed group investment in common stocks does not carry any substantial risk of this sort and that therefore it should not be termed 'risky' merely because of the element of price fluctuation. But such risk is present if there is danger that the price may prove to have been clearly too high by intrinsic-value standards – even if any subsequent severe market decline may be recouped many years later.

Concluding comments

So, where does all this grand theory leave people of a more practical persuasion, who simply want a tool that will help them to make better investment decisions? It is clear that we are far from the end of the road of discovery in this area. We have not yet reached *the* answer. However, the theoretical and empirical work has helped to clarify some important matters. The distinction between systematic and unsystematic risk is an important one. It seems reasonable to focus on the former when describing the relationship between risk and return. It also seems reasonable that one of the systematic risk factors is the general movement of the securities market.

Investors' buying and selling actions have given us two benchmarks by which to judge returns; if the investment is without systematic risk then the risk-free rate of return, approximated by the returns on government-issued securities, gives us the marker at the lower end of risk spectrum; we also have a revealed demand for a risk premium of around 5 per cent for investors accepting a risk level equivalent to that on the average ordinary share. The problem is that we cannot unequivocally, given the recent empirical evidence, draw a straight line between these two plot points with beta values placed on the x-axis. The relationship appears to be far more complex – the 'x-axis' probably consists of numerous risk factors. Investors appear to demand additional reward for accepting risk related to a range of macroeconomic and other influences causing variability of return, ranging from the growth of GDP to the level of oil prices.

Nevertheless a finding of sorts emerges: higher risk, however defined, requires higher return. Therefore, for a company trying to estimate the rate of return a shareholder will require from a project, it is right that the estimate is calculated after taking account of some measure of systematic risk. If the project has a systematic risk which is lower than that on the average share then it would seem sensible that the returns attributable to shareholders on this project should be somewhere between the risk-free rate and the risk-free rate plus, say, 5 per cent. If the project has a systematic risk greater than that exhibited by shares generally then the returns required for shareholders will be more than the risk-free rate plus, say, 5 per cent.

The tricky part is calculating the systematic risk level. In the heyday of the CAPM this was simple: beta was all that was necessary. Today we have to allow for a multiplicity of systematic risk factors. Not unnaturally, many business people shrug their shoulders at the prospect of such a burdensome approach and fall back on their 'judgement' to adjust for the risk of a project. In practice it is extremely difficult to state precisely the riskiness of a project – we are dealing with future uncertainties about cash flows from day-to-day business operations subject to sudden and unforeseen shocks. The pragmatic approach is to avoid precision and simply place each proposed project into one of three risk categories: low, medium or high. This neatly bypasses the complexities laid on by the theorists and also accurately reflects the fact that decisions made in the real world are made with less than complete knowledge. Mechanical decision making within the firm based on over-simplistic academic models is often a poor substitute for judgement recognising the imperfections of reality. Analogously, informed judgement about unquantifiable factors such as strength of competitive position and quality of management is a very important part of successful stock market investment.

Having been so critical of the theoretical models we have to be careful not to 'throw out the baby with the bathwater'. The academic debate has enabled us to ask the right questions and to focus on the key issues when enquiring what it is we should be doing to enhance shareholder value. It has also enabled a greater understanding of price setting in the financial markets and insight into the behaviour of investors.

The road is long and winding but the vistas revealed along the way provide enlightenment, if only of the kind captured in the following phrase: 'The fool says he is knowledgeable and has the answers, the wise man says he has much to learn.'

Key points and concepts

- Risky securities, such as shares quoted on the London Stock Exchange, have produced a much higher average annual return than relatively risk-free securities. However, the annual swings in returns are much greater for shares than for Treasury bills. **Risk and return** are positively related.
- **Total risk** consists of two elements:
  - **systematic risk** (or market risk, or non-diversifiable risk) – risk factors common to all firms;
  - **unsystematic risk** (or specific risk, or diversifiable risk).
- **Unsystematic risk can be eliminated by diversification**. An efficient market will not reward unsystematic risk.
- **Beta** measures the covariance between the returns on a particular share with the returns on the market as a whole.
- The **Security Market Line (SML)** shows the relationship between risk as measured by beta and expected returns.
- The equation for the **capital asset pricing model** is:

  $$r_j = r_f + \beta_j (r_m - r_f)$$
- The slope of the characteristic line represents beta:

  $$r_j = \alpha + \beta_j r_m + e$$
- **Some examples of the CAPM's application**:
  - portfolio selection;
  - identifying mispriced shares;
  - measuring portfolio performance;
  - rate of return on firm's projects.
- **Technical problems with the CAPM**:
  - measuring beta;
  - *ex ante* theory but *ex post* testing and analysis;
  - unobtainability of the market portfolio;
  - one-period model;
  - unrealistic assumptions.
- **Early research** seemed to confirm the **validity of beta** as *the* measure of risk influencing returns. **Later work cast serious doubt** on this. Some researchers say beta has no influence on returns.
- **Beta is not the only determinant of return**.

- **Multi-factor models** allow for a variety of influences on share returns.
- Factor models refer to diversifiable risk as **non-factor risk** and non-diversifiable risk as **factor risk**.
- **Major problems with multi-factor models** include:
  - the difficulty of finding the influencing factors;
  - once found, the influencing factors only explain past returns.
- The **Arbitrage Pricing Theory (APT)** is one possible multi-factor model:

  Expected returns = risk-free return + $\beta_1(r_1 - r_f) + \beta_2(r_2 - r_f) + \beta_3(r_3 - r_f) + \beta_4(r_4 - r_f) \ldots + \beta_n(r_n - r_f) + e$
- Fama and French have developed a **three-factor model**:

  Expected return = risk-free rate + $\beta_1(r_m - r_f) + \beta_2(\text{SMB}) + \beta_3(\text{HML})$
- **Traditional commonsense based measures of risk** seem to have more explanatory power over returns than beta or standard deviation.
- Projects of differing risks should be appraised using different discount rates.

Appendix 8.1 Note on arithmetic and geometric means

To understand the difference between arithmetic and geometric means, consider the case of an investment that only has capital gains and losses (there are no dividends).

At Time 0 the investment is worth £100. One year later (Time 1) it has risen to £200, an annual rate of return of 100 per cent. In the next year the investment falls back to £100, a loss of 50 per cent for the year. In the third year the value rises to £130, a 30 per cent gain.

The arithmetic average annual rate of return is 26.67 per cent:

+ 100%	
− 50%	
+ 30%	
80%	80/3 = 26.67%

The arithmetic mean is the average of the annual returns. The geometric mean, on the other hand, is the compound annual return.

The geometric mean is the rate at which the beginning sum grows through the period of study. It depends on the initial and final values for the investment and not necessarily on any intermediate values.

So for our example:

Geometric annual rate of return

$$= \sqrt[n]{(1 + \text{the first return})(1 + \text{the second return})(1 + \text{the third return})} - 1$$

$$= \sqrt[3]{(1 + 1.0)(1 + [-0.5])(1 + 0.3)} - 1$$

$$= 0.0914 \text{ or } 9.14\%$$

Alternatively:

$$F = P(1 + r)^n$$

$$r = \sqrt[n]{(F/P)} - 1$$

$$= \sqrt[3]{(130/100)} - 1$$

$$= 0.0914 \text{ or } 9.14\%$$

For one-year periods arithmetic and geometric means will be identical. But over longer periods the geometric return is always less than the average returns (except when individual yearly returns are the same).

When examining past returns the geometric mean is more appropriate. However, for short-term forward-looking decisions the historic arithmetic mean is the more appropriate because it represents the mean of all the returns that may possibly occur over the investment holding period. For long-term forward-looking decisions the geometric mean is the more appropriate:

> Those who use the arithmetic mean argue that it is much more consistent with the mean-variance framework of the CAPM and a better predictor of the premium in the next period. The geometric mean is justified on the grounds that it takes into account compounding and that it is a better predictor of the average premium in the long term.
>
> (Damodaran (1999) p. 69.)

So, if the future-oriented decision is a short-term one (one year) then the arithmetic mean-based risk premium is appropriate. If the future-oriented decision is for more than one year then the geometric mean is more appropriate.

References and further reading

Adedeji, A. (1997) 'A test of the CAPM and the Three Factor Model on the London Stock Exchange', paper presented to the British Accounting Association Northern Accounting Group 1997 Annual Conference, 10 September 1997, Loughborough University.
Evidence of beta's poor relationship with returns.

Arnott, R. and Bernstein, P. (2002) 'What risk premium is normal?', *Financial Analysts Journal*, March/April.
Argues that investors were lucky to get a high equity premium in the past.

Barclays Capital *The Equity Gilt Study*. London: Barclays.
Annual reports on security returns. Excellent data and discussion.

Black, F. (1972) 'Capital market equilibrium with restricted borrowing', *Journal of Business* (July), pp. 444–55.
Showed how the CAPM changes when there is no risk-free asset or investors face restrictions on, or extra cost of, borrowing.

Black, F. (1993) 'Beta and return', *Journal of Portfolio Management*, 20, Fall, pp. 8–18.
Estimating the relationship between beta and return on US shares, 1926–91. Relationship is poor after 1965.

Black, F., Jensen, M.C. and Scholes, M. (1972) 'The Capital Asset Pricing Model: some empirical tests', in M. Jensen (ed.), *Studies in the Theory of Capital Markets*. New York: Praeger.
Early empirical work supporting the CAPM.

Blake, D. (2000) *Financial Market Analysis*, 2nd edn. Chichester: John Wiley & Sons.
A thorough treatment of asset pricing models – for the mathematically able.

Blume, M.E. (1971) 'On the assessment of risk', *Journal of Finance*, 26(1), March, pp. 1–10.
Betas change over time.

Blume, M.E. (1975) 'Betas and their regression tendencies', *Journal of Finance*, 30(3), June, pp. 785–95.
Betas tend to 1 over time.

Blume, M. and Friend, I. (1973) 'A new look at the Capital Asset Pricing Model', *Journal of Finance*, March, pp. 19–33.
The evidence in this paper seems to require a rejection of the capital asset pricing theory as an explanation of the observed returns on all financial assets.

Bower, D.H., Bower, R.S. and Logue, D.E. (1986) 'A primer on arbitrage pricing theory', in J.M. Stern and D.H. Chen (eds), *The Revolution in Corporate Finance*. Oxford: Basil Blackwell.
Well-written introduction to APT. Suitable for the beginner.

Brealey, R.H., Myers, S.C. and Allen, F. (2006) *The Principles of Corporate Finance*, 8th edn. Boston: McGraw-Hill.
A well-respected and time-honoured introductory finance text.

Chan, A. and Chui, A.P.L. (1996) 'An empirical re-examination of the cross-section of expected returns: UK evidence', *Journal of Business Finance and Accounting*, 23, pp. 1435–52.
In explaining returns beta is unimportant.

Chan, L.K.C. and Lakonishok, J. (1993) 'Are the reports of beta's death premature?', *Journal of Portfolio Management*, 19, Summer, pp. 51–62. Reproduced in S. Lofthouse (ed.), *Readings in Investment*. Chichester: John Wiley & Sons (1994).
Readable discussion of the CAPM's validity in the light of some new evidence.

Chi-Hsiou Hung, D., Shackleton, M. and Xu, X. (2004) 'CAPM, higher co-moment and factor models of UK stock returns', *Journal of Business Finance and Accounting*, 31 (1–2), January/March, pp. 87–112

The authors claim to have evidence which might revive beta in some circumstances. Higher maths required.

Cochrane, J.H. (2001) *Asset Pricing*. Princeton, NJ, and Oxford: Princeton University Press.

Advanced level.

Corhay, A., Hawawini, G. and Michel, P. (1987) 'Seasonality in the risk-return relationship: some international evidence', *Journal of Finance*, 42, pp. 49–68.

Evidence on the validity of the CAPM in the UK, France, Belgium and the USA. Not good news for the CAPM.

Damodaran, A. (1999) *Applied Corporate Finance: A User's Manual*. New York: John Wiley & Sons.

A writer prepared to address the difficult practical issues rather than stay on the (often barren) high ground of theory – easy to read as well!

Daniel, H. and Titman, S. (1997) 'Evidence on the characteristics of cross-sectional variation in common stock returns', *Journal of Finance*, Vol 52, pp. 1–33.

Points out that Fama and French's empirical results are also consistent with mispricing-based (behavioural) models.

Daniel, H. and Titman, S. (2006) 'Market reactions to tangible and intangible information', *Journal of Finance*, 61 (4), pp. 1605–43.

Disputes the interpretation that high returns to high book-to-market companies are due to these firms being in financial distress.

Dhrymes, P.J., Friend, I. and Gultekim, N.B. (1984) 'A critical reexamination of the empirical evidence on the arbitrage pricing theory', *Journal of Finance*, 39, June, pp. 323–46.

Attacks APT as not being markedly superior to the CAPM in explaining relevant empirical evidence.

Dimson, E., Marsh, P. and Staunton, M. (2002) *Triumph of the Optimists: 101 Years of Global Investment Returns*. Princeton, NJ, and Oxford: Princeton University Press.

Fascinating new evidence on risk premiums.

Dimson, E., Marsh, P. and Staunton, M. (2006) The Cap Worldwide Equity Premium: a smaller puzzle (April 7, 2006) EFA 2006 Zurich meetings papers available at SSRN: http://ssrn.com/abstract=891620

Equity risk premiums for 17 countries over 106 years – average 4 per cent. But authors suggest that currently investors expect a premium of around 3–3½ per cent. Easy to follow.

Dimson, E., Marsh, P., and Staunton, M. (2008) *Global investment returns yearbook 2007*. ABN AMRO.

A source of data on security (shares, bonds, etc.) returns – expensive to buy.

Dreman, D. (1998) *Contrarian Investment Strategies: The Next Generation*. New York: John Wiley & Sons.

A down-to-earth discussion of investment and the nature of risk and return.

Elton, E.J., Gruber, M.J. and Mei, J. (1994) 'Cost of capital using arbitrage pricing theory: a case study of nine New York utilities', *Financial Markets, Institutions and Instruments*, 3, August, pp. 46–73.

Interesting application.

Elton, E.J., Gruber, M.J., Brown, S.J. and Goetzmann, W.N. (2007) *Modern Portfolio Theory and Investment Analysis*, 7th edn. New York: Wiley.

Detailed but clear description of the CAPM, APT and empirical evidence.

Fama, G. and French, K. (1992) 'The cross-section of expected stock return', *Journal of Finance*, 47, June, pp. 427–65.

The relationship between beta and return is flat. Size and book-to-market equity ratio are better predictors of share returns.

Fama, E.F. and French, K.R. (1993) 'Common risk factors in the returns on stocks and bonds', *Journal of Financial Economics*, 33, pp. 3–56.

Three-factor model.

Fama, E.F. and French, K.R. (1995) 'Size and book-to-market factors in earnings and returns', *Journal of Finance*, 50(1), March, pp. 131–55.

The relationship of stock prices, size and book-to-market equity with earnings behaviour.

Fama, E.F. and French, K.R. (1996) 'Multifactor explanations of asset pricing anomalies', *Journal of Finance*, 50(1), March, pp. 55–84.

The three-factor model is discussed.

Fama, E.F. and French, K.R. (2002) 'The equity premium', *Journal of Finance*, 57(2), April, pp. 637–59.

A new look at judging the prospective equity risk premiums taking account of the lucky surprise US investors in equity had over the period 1951 to 2000.

Fama, E.F. and French, K.R. (2006) 'The Value premium and the CAPM', *Journal of Finance*, LXI (5) October, pp. 2163–85.

Higher returns for high book-to-market ratio and price-earnings ratio shares for US (and 14 other countries). The return premium is not explained by CAPM beta.

Fama, E.F. and MacBeth, J. (1973) 'Risk, return and equilibrium: empirical test', *Journal of Political Economy*, May/June, pp. 607–36.

Early empirical research. Shares on the NYSE grouped by beta and subsequent return is compared.

Friend, I. and Blume, M. (1970) 'Measurement of portfolio performance under uncertainty', *American Economic Review*, September, pp. 561–75.

A discussion of the usefulness of market-line theory and its ability to explain market behaviour.

Friend, I., Westerfield, R. and Granito, M. (1978) 'New evidence on the Capital Asset Pricing model', *Journal of Finance*, 33, June, pp. 903–20.
Empirical testing of the CAPM.

Fuller, R.J. and Wong, G.W. (1988) 'Traditional versus theoretical risk measures', *Financial Analysts Journal*, 44, March–April, pp. 52–7. Reproduced in S. Lofthouse (ed.), *Readings in Investment*. Chichester: John Wiley & Sons (1994).
A comparison of three explanatory models describing the relationship between risks and returns – the CAPM, standard deviation and Value Line Safety Rank. Value Line is best.

Graham, B. (1973, 2003) *The Intelligent Investor*. Revised edition with commentary by Jason Zweig. New York: Harper Business.
Widely regarded as the best book ever written on investment principles.

Haugen, R.A. (2001) *Modern Investment Theory*, 5th edn. Prentice Hall.
Contains a more detailed consideration of CAPM and APT.

Lakonishok, J. and Shapiro, A.C. (1984) 'Stock returns, beta, variance and size: an empirical analysis', *Financial Analysts Journal*, 40, July–August, pp. 36–41.
Technical paper.

Lakonishok, J. and Shapiro, A.C. (1986) 'Systematic risk, total risk and size as determinants of stock market returns', *Journal of Banking and Finance*, 10, pp. 115–32.
Technical paper.

Levy, H. (1978) 'Equilibrium in an imperfect market: a constraint on the number of securities in the portfolio', *American Economic Review*, September, pp. 643–58.
The CAPM cannot be accepted since it performs quite poorly in explaining price behaviour.

Levy, R.A. (1971) 'On the short-term stationarity of beta coefficients', *Financial Analysts Journal*, November–December, pp. 55–62.
Betas change over time.

Lintner, J. (1965) 'The valuation of risky assets and the selection of risky investments in stock portfolios and capital budgets', *Review of Economics and Statistics*, February, 47, pp. 13–37.
Major contributor to the development of CAPM theory.

Lowenstein, L. (1991) *Sense and Nonsense in Corporate Finance*. Reading, MA: Addison Wesley.
A sceptic's view of finance theory.

Macqueen, J. (1986) 'Beta is dead! Long live Beta!', in J.M. Stern and D.H. Chen (eds), *The Revolution in Corporate Finance*. Oxford: Basil Blackwell.
Entertaining, easy-to-read introduction to the CAPM. The main argument is somewhat dated given the 1990s evidence.

Malkiel, B.G. (1990) *A Random Walk Down Wall Street*. New York: W.W. Norton & Co.
A fascinating guide to financial markets.

Markowitz, H.M. (2005) 'Market efficiency: a theoretical distinction and so what?' *Financial Analysts Journal*, September/October, pp.17–30.
'I ... show here that the conclusion that expected returns are linear functions of beta does not hold when real-world limits on permitted portfolio holdings are introduced into CAPM. This discussion will call into question the frequent use of beta in risk adjustment'.

Mehra, R. (2003) 'The equity premium puzzle?' Why is it a puzzle? *Financial Analysts Journal*, 59, pp. 54–69.
High returns on shares relative to risk-free investments may well continue.

Mehra, R. and Prescott, E.C. (1985) 'The Equity Premium: A Puzzle', *Journal of Monetary Economics*, 15, pp. 145–61.
Investors in shares appear to have received an excessively high return relative to risk-free securities.

Mehra, R. and Prescott, E. (2006) 'The equity premium: what have we learned in 20 years?' in R. Mehra (ed.) *Handbook of Investments: Equity risk premium* in the Handbook of Economics and Finance Series. Amsterdam: Elsevier.
An overview of the debate on the equity risk premium.

Miles, D. and Timmermann, A. (1996) 'Variations in expected stock returns: evidence on the pricing of equities from a cross-section of UK companies', *Economica*, 63, pp. 369–82.
Beta has no relationship with UK share returns.

Mossin, J. (1966) 'Equilibrium in a capital asset market', *Econometrica*, 34, October, pp. 768–83.
Important early paper – technical.

Myers, S.C. (1996) 'Fischer Black's contributions to corporate finance', *Financial Management*, 25(4), Winter, pp. 95–103.
Acceptance of the CAPM: disillusionment expressed.

Nichols, N.A. (1993) 'Efficient? Chaotic? What's the New Finance?', *Harvard Business Review*, March–April, pp. 50–8.
Highly readable account of the 1990s disillusionment with the CAPM and market efficiency theory.

Reinganum, M.R. (1982) 'A direct test of Roll's conjecture on the firm size effect', *Journal of Finance*, 37, pp. 27–35.
Small firms' shares earn higher average rates of return than those of large firms, even after accounting for beta risk.

Ritter, J.R. and Chopra, N. (1989) 'Portfolio rebalancing and the turn-of-the-year effect', *Journal of Finance*, 44, pp. 149–66.
Empirical study investigating the 'January effect' for share returns. Makes use of beta.

Roll, R. (1977) 'A critique of the Asset Pricing Theory's tests: Part 1: On past and potential testability of the theory', *Journal of Financial Economics*, 4 March, pp. 129–76.
Important, theoretical attack on CAPM testing methods.

Roll, R. and Ross, S.A. (1980) 'An empirical investigation of the Arbitrage Pricing Theory', *Journal of Finance*, 35, December, pp. 1073–103.
Testing of APT leads to at least three, possibly four, factors generating returns.

Roll, R.W. and Ross, S.A. (1983) 'Regulation, the Capital Asset Pricing Model and the Arbitrage Pricing Theory', *Public Utilities Fortnightly*, 111, 26 May, pp. 22–8. Reproduced in S. Lofthouse (ed.), *Readings in Investment*. Chichester: John Wiley & Sons (1994).
Summary of the CAPM and outline guide to APT. Argues against the CAPM in favour of APT.

Rosenberg, B. and Rudd, A. (1986) 'The corporate uses of Beta', in J.M. Stern and D.H. Chew (eds), *The Revolution in Corporate Finance*. Oxford: Basil Blackwell.
Using the CAPM to find discount rate for projects. Incorporates other risk factors: growth, earnings variability, leverage and size. Easy-to-read article aimed at the novice.

Ross, S.A. (1974) 'Return, risk and arbitrage', in I. Friend and J.L. Bicksler (eds), *Risk and Return in Finance*. New York: Heath Lexington.
The arbitrage pricing theory – the early days.

Ross, S.A. (1976) 'The arbitrage theory of capital asset pricing', *Journal of Economic Theory*, 13, December, pp. 341–60.
Originator of the APT.

Ross, S.A., Westerfield, R.W. and Jaffe, J. (2004) *Corporate Finance*, 7th edn. Boston: McGraw Hill.
Good chapter on the APT.

Rouwenhorst, K.G. (1999) 'Local return factors and turnover in emerging stock markets', *Journal of Finance*, 54, August, pp. 1439–64.
Share returns are related to size of company and value characteristics, but not beta.

Rouwenhorst, K.G., Heston, S. and Wessels, R.E. (1999) 'The role of beta and size in the cross-section of European stock returns', *European Financial Management*, 4.
Some evidence of relation between beta and share returns in 12 countries.

Sharpe, W.F. (1964) 'Capital asset prices: a theory of market equilibrium under conditions of risk', *Journal of Finance*, 19, September, pp. 425–42.
Pioneering paper – technical.

Sharpe, W.F., Alexander, G.J. and Bailey, J.V. (1999) *Investments*, 6th edn. Upper Saddle River, NJ: Prentice-Hall.
Chapters 10, 11 and 12 give a clear exposition of the CAPM, factor models and APT.

Shiller, R.J. (2000) *Irrational Exuberance*. Princeton NJ: Princeton University Press.
A brilliantly timed and argued book describing the extent to which investors got carried away in the late 1990s.

Siegal, J.J. (2005) 'Perspectives on the equity risk premium', *Financial Analysts Journal*, Nov./Dec., pp. 61–73.
Discusses in an easy-to-read manner, the difficulties in fixing on a precise equity risk premium, and the 'equity premium puzzle'.

Stein, J.C. (1996) 'Rational capital budgeting in an irrational world', *Journal of Business*, 69, pp. 429–55.
A theoretical attempt to incorporate irrationality in share pricing (e.g. overoptimistic pricing of low book-to-market ratio shares) into a beta model. Beta is then 'hobbled', rather than dead.

Strong, N. and Xu, X.G. (1997) 'Explaining the cross-section of UK expected stock returns', *British Accounting Review*, 29(1), pp. 1–23.
More evidence of the poor relationship between beta and returns.

Treynor, J. (1965) 'How to rate management of investment funds', *Harvard Business Review*, January–February.
Early theory.

Case study recommendations

Please see www.pearsoned.co.uk/arnold for case study synopses.

- Deutsche Bank: Discussing the equity risk premium. Authors: George Chacko, Peter Hecht, Vincent Dessain, Anders Sjoman. (2005) Harvard Business School.

Self-review questions

1 Outline the difference between systematic and unsystematic risk.

2 Explain the meaning of beta.

3 State the equation for the security market line.

4 If a share lies under the security market line is it over- or under-valued by the market (assuming the CAPM to be correct)? What mechanism will cause the share return to move towards the security market line?

5 What problems are caused to the usefulness of the CAPM if betas are not stable over time?

6 What influences the beta level for a particular share?

7 Describe how the characteristic line is established.

8 What are the fundamental differences between the CAPM and the APT?

9 Is the firm's existing cost of capital suitable for all future projects? If not, why not?

10 List the theoretical and practical problems of the CAPM.

11 Discuss the potential problems with the implementation of the arbitrage pricing theory.

12 In 2000, 2001 and 2002 the return on UK shares was less than the return on UK Government bonds. Why don't we take the most recent returns for $r_m - r_f$ in the CAPM rather than the long-term historical average $r_m - r_f$?

Questions and problems

myfinancelab — **Questions with an icon are also available for practice in MyFinanceLab with additional supporting resources.**

1 Company X has a beta value of 1.3, the risk-free rate of return is 8 per cent and the historic risk premium for shares over the risk-free rate of return has been 5 per cent. Calculate the return expected on shares in X assuming the CAPM applies. ?

2 'Last year I bought some shares. The returns have not been as predicted by the CAPM.' Is this sufficient evidence to reject the CAPM?

3 Share A has a beta of 2, share B has a beta of 0.5 and C a beta of 1. The riskless rate of interest is 7 per cent and the risk premium for the market index has been 5 per cent. Calculate the expected returns on A, B and C (assuming the CAPM applies). ?

4 The risk-free return is 9 per cent, Company J has a beta of 1.5 and an expected return of 20 per cent. Calculate the risk premium for the market index over the risk-free rate assuming J is on the security market line. ?

5 Shares in M and N lie on the security market line.

	Share M	Share N
Expected return	18%	22%
Beta	1	1.5
(assume the CAPM holds)		

a What is the riskless rate of return and the risk premium on the market index portfolio?
b Share P has an expected return of 30 per cent and a beta of 1.7. What is likely to happen to the price and return on shares in P?
c Share Q has an expected return of 10 per cent and a beta of 0.8. What is likely to happen to the price and returns on a share in Q?

?

6 Explain from first principles the CAPM and how it may be used in financial markets and within a firm for determining the discount rate used in project appraisal. Why might you have doubts about actually using the model?

7 The directors of Frane plc are considering a project with an expected return of 23 per cent, a beta coefficient of 1.4 and a standard deviation of 40 per cent. The risk-free rate of return is 10 per cent and the risk premium for shares generally has been 5 per cent. (Assume the CAPM applies.)

a Explain whether the directors should focus on beta or the standard deviation given that the shareholders are fully diversified.
b Is the project attractive to those shareholders? Explain to the directors unfamiliar with the jargon of the CAPM the factors you are taking into account in your recommendation.

?

8 The risk-free rate of return is 7 per cent and the annual premium received on shares over Treasury bills has been 5 per cent. A firm is considering the following investments (the CAPM applies):

Project	Beta	Expected return (%)
1	0.6	10
2	0.9	11
3	1.3	20
4	1.7	21

a Which projects should be accepted?
b Why doesn't the firm simply use its overall discount rate of 13 per cent for all project appraisal?

?

9 True or false?

a A £1,000 investment in the market portfolio combined with a £500 investment in the risk-free security will have a beta of 2.
b The risk premium on the market portfolio of shares has always been 5 per cent.
c The CAPM states that systematic risk is the only factor influencing returns in a diversified portfolio.
d Beta has proved to be an excellent predictor of share returns over the past thirty years.
e Investors expect compensation for risk factors other than beta such as macroeconomic changes.
f The arbitrage pricing theory assumes unsystematic risk as a key input factor.

?

10 Mr Gill has inherited the following portfolio:

Share	Share price	No. of shares	Beta
ABC plc	£1.20	20,000	0.80
DEF plc	£2.00	10,000	1.20
GHI plc	£1.80	20,000	1.10

a What is the beta on this portfolio?

b If the risk-free rate of return is 6.5 per cent and the risk premium on shares over Treasury bills has been 5 per cent what is the expected return on this portfolio over the next year?

c Why might the outcome be significantly different from the expected return? **?**

11 'The arbitrage pricing theory has solved all the problems of estimating the relationship between risk and return.' Do you agree? Explain your reasoning.

myfinancelab ***Now retake your diagnostic test for Chapter 8 to check your progress and update your study plan.***

Assignments

1 Find out your firm's beta from published sources and calculate the rate of return expected from your firm's shares on the assumption that the CAPM holds.

2 Investigate how systematic risk factors are taken into account when setting discount rates for projects of different risk levels in a firm you know well. Write a report detailing how this process might be improved.

PART 4

Sources of finance

CHAPTER 9

Stock markets

LEARNING OUTCOMES

An appreciation of the rationale and importance of a well-organised stock market in a sophisticated financial system is a necessary precursor to understanding what is going on in the world around us. To this end the reader, having read this chapter, will be able to:

- describe the scale of stock market activity around the world and explain the reasons for the widespread adoption of stock exchanges as one of the foci for a market-based economy;
- explain the functions of stock exchanges and the importance of an efficiently operated stock exchange;
- give an account of the stock markets available to UK firms and describe alternative share trading systems;
- demonstrate a grasp of the regulatory framework for the UK financial system;
- be able to understand many of the financial terms expressed in the broadsheet newspapers (particularly the *Financial Times*);
- outline the UK corporate taxation system.

myfinancelab ***Complete your diagnostic test for Chapter 9 now to create your personal study plan***

Case study 9.1 **Using the stock market both to create wealth and to treat disease**

Oxford BioMedica

Alan and Sue Kingsman started an Oxford University-backed company called Oxford BioMedica in 1995. This company develops technologies to treat diseases including cancer, cystic fibrosis, Parkinson's disease and AIDS using gene therapy. The aim is to replace faulty genes.

Alan and Sue are biochemistry academics who lacked the finance needed for future research and development. They raised seed finance in June 1996 (small amounts of start-up money) and then raised £5.1bn by floating on the Alternative Investment Market (AIM) in December 1996. Later AIM shareholders bought another £23.6m of shares from the company which was then used to ramp up research.

Oxford BioMedica was upgraded to the Official List of the London Stock Exchange in April 2001 following a successful £35.5m fund-raising. In 2003 a further £20.4 million was raised through a rights issue (selling more shares to existing shareholders) followed by £30.1m in 2005. The company has a number of products in trial. TroVax® is an anti-cancer vaccine. MetXia® is a gene therapy for breast cancer. It also has gene therapy approaches to Parkinson's disease (ProSavin®) and loss of eyesight (RetinoStat®). It is even testing a way of treating spinal injuries through gene therapy (a virus carries a gene to injured nerves; the gene makes the cells receptive to body chemicals that stimulate the growth of nerve connections). In 2004 the Christopher Reeve Foundation (the paralysed Superman actor, who died in October 2004) gave a grant to King's College to explore the use of Innurex in spinal cord injuries.

The company has never made a profit, but shareholders are willing to wait. The potential rewards are huge, running into billions of pounds if successful treatments are created. The rewards to patients could be beyond price.

Sources: Based on various articles in the *Financial Times* and *Investors Chronicle*, and Oxford BioMedica's website.

Introduction

This chapter is concerned with the role and value of stock markets in the modern economy. It also looks more specifically at the workings of the London Stock Exchange. Imagine the difficulties Sue and Alan Kingsman would have getting their venture off the ground in a world without some form of market where long-term risk capital can be raised from investors, and where those investors are able to sell on their holdings to other risk takers whenever they wish. There would certainly be a much smaller pool of money made available to firms with brilliant ideas and society would be poorer.

Stock exchanges around the world

Stock exchanges are markets where government and industry can raise long-term capital and investors can buy and sell securities. Stock exchanges[1] grew in response to the demand for funds to finance investment and (especially in the early days) ventures in overseas trade. The risky sea-voyage trading businesses of the sixteenth, seventeenth and eighteenth centuries often required the raising of capital from large numbers of investors. Until the Napoleonic Wars the Dutch capital markets were pre-eminent, raising funds for investment abroad and loans for governments and businesses, and developing a thriving secondary market in which investors could sell their financial securities to other investors. This transferability of ownership of financial assets was an important breakthrough for the development of sophisticated financial systems. It offered the investor liquidity, which encouraged the flow of funds to firms, while leaving the capital in the business venture untouched.

The Napoleonic Wars led to a rapid rise in the volume of British government debt sold to the public. Trading in this debt tended to take place in coffee houses in London and other cities. Much

[1] Stock exchange and stock market will be used interchangeably. Bourse is an alternative word used particularly in Continental Europe.

of the early industrialisation was financed by individuals or partnerships, but as the capital requirements became larger it was clear that **joint-stock enterprises** were needed, in which the money of numerous investors was brought together to give joint ownership with the promise of a share of profits. Canal corporations, docks companies, manufacturing enterprises, railways and insurance companies were added to the list of firms with shares and bonds traded on the London Stock Exchange in the first half of the nineteenth century.

The second major breakthrough was the introduction of **limited liability** for shareholders in 1855.[2] This meant that the owners of shares were not responsible for the debts of the firm – once they had handed over the money to purchase the shares they could not be called on to contribute any further, regardless of the demands of creditors to a failed firm. This encouraged an even greater flow of funds into equity (ownership) capital and aided the spectacular rise of Victorian Britain as an economic powerhouse. Similar measures were taken in other European and North American countries to boost the flow of funds for investment. Outside the Western economies the value of a stock exchange was quickly recognised – for example, Bombay and Johannesburg opened stock markets in the nineteenth century.

Today the important contribution of stock exchanges to economic well-being has been recognised from Moldova to Botswana. There are now over 100 countries with officially recognised exchanges and many of these countries have more than one exchange. **Exhibit 9.1** focuses on the share trading aspect of a number of these markets. Shares will be the main concern of this and the following chapter, but it is important to note that stock markets often do much more than trade shares. Many also trade government debt securities and a wide array of financial instruments issued by firms, for example corporate bonds, convertibles, preference shares, warrants and eurobonds. (These will be examined in later chapters.) In Exhibit 9.1 **total** (or **market**) **capitalisation** is the total value, at market prices, of all the shares in issue of the companies quoted on the stock market.

The past 20 years have been a dynamic period for global financial markets. The shift in political and economic philosophies and policies towards free markets and capitalism produced a growing demand for capital. Following the successful example of the West and the 'Tiger' economies of Asia, numerous emerging markets promoted stock exchanges as a major pillar of economic progress. The liberalisation and the accelerating wave of privatisation pushed stock markets to the forefront of developing countries' tools of economic progress. The collapse of communism and the adoption of pro-market policies led to the rise of share exchanges in dozens of former anti-capitalist bastions. Even countries which still espouse communism, such as China and Vietnam, now have thriving and increasingly influential stock exchanges designed to facilitate the mobilisation of capital and its employment in productive endeavour, with – 'horror-of-horrors' to some hard-line communists – a return going to the capital providers. In the emerging countries alone there are now over 26,000 companies quoted on stock exchanges. The total value of all companies quoted on all the stock exchanges in the world amounts to more than £25,000 billion.

Clearly stock markets are an important element in the intricate lattice-work of a modern and sophisticated society. Not only are they a vital meeting place for investors and a source of investment capital for businesses, they permit a more appropriate allocation of resources within society – that is, a more optimum mix of goods and services produced to satisfy people.

There has been a remarkable increase in the number of officially recognised stock exchanges around the globe in the last five to ten years. Even Africa has 21 exchanges, one-half of which were opened in the past 12 years.

China is a wholehearted convert to the virtues of stock markets. Over 20 million[3] Chinese hold shares in over 1,400 companies quoted either on the stock exchange in Shanghai or on the one in Shenzhen. The former president of China, Jiang Zemin, no less, spoke with the fervour of the recent convert, describing them as a vital component of a modern economy.

Traditionally many European countries, such as France and Germany, were less focused on equity capital markets than the Anglo-Saxon economies (the UK, the USA, Australia, etc.), but this is starting to change. Privatisation and a greater concern for generating shareholder value is leading to an increasing appreciation of equity markets. **Exhibit 9.2** shows that, in France, shares are seen as having a role in the provision of pensions and in encouraging employees to take an interest in their company's profitability.

Thailand too is keen to develop an 'equity culture' – *see* **Exhibit 9.3**.

---

[2] The first limited liability law was introduced in the USA in 1811.

[3] There are over 80 million Chinese investor accounts. However, many investors use a number of pseudonyms to purchase shares so it is thought that, in reality, there are only about 20 million shareholders.

Exhibit 9.1 Stock exchanges around the world

Column 1: Total capitalisation of domestic equities, £bn (approx.).
Column 2: Number of domestic firms listed.
Column 3: Number of foreign firms listed.

Argentina	25	101	5	India:				OMX	560	765	26
Australia	550	1751	78	Mumbai	409	4796	0	Peru	20	189	32
Austria	92	96	17	NSE India	387	1156	0	Philippines	34	238	2
Bermuda	2	16	38	Indonesia	69	344	0	Poland	75	253	12
Brazil	355	347	3	Iran	18	320	0	Singapore	192	461	247
Canada	850	3790	52	Ireland	82	59	11	Slovenia	8	100	0
Chile	88	244	2	Israel	81	602	4	South Africa			
China:				Italy	513	284	27	(Jo'burg)	356	359	30
Shanghai	458	842	0	Japan:				Sri Lanka	4	237	0
Shenzhen	114	579	0	Osaka	92	466	1	Switzerland	606	256	92
Colombia	28	94	0	Tokyo	2307	2391	25	Taiwan	298	688	5
Cyprus	8	141	0	Korea	417	1689	0	Thailand	70	518	0
Egypt	47	595	0	Luxembourg	40	36	224	Turkey	81	316	0
Euronext	1854	954	256	Malaysia	117	1021	4	UK	1900	2913	343
Germany	819	656	104	Malta	2	14	0	USA:			
Greece	104	288	2	Mauritius	2	62	1	American (Amex)	140	492	100
Hong Kong	837	1165	8	Mexico	175	132	203	NASDAQ	1933	2812	321
Hungary	21	41	0	New Zealand	23	151	31	New York	7200	1829	451
				Norway	140	195	34				

Data include listed and small company markets (e.g. AIM). Global total capitalisation: £25,000 bn.
Note that the statistics were compiled in December 2006. Since then the New York Stock Exchange (NYSE) has merged with the Euronext market (comprising the Paris, Amsterdam, Brussels and Portuguese exchanges).

Sources: World Federation of Exchanges: www.worldexchanges.org.

Exhibit 9.2

France joins the stakeholder revolution

FT

The popularity of employee shareholding schemes at French companies is establishing an equity culture

says Samer Iskandar

. . . Gérard Mestrallet, Suez Lyonnaise's chairman, is aiming to raise the share of the group's capital held by its 120,000 employees from less than 1 per cent to more than 5 per cent. Staff at Vivendi, Suez Lyonnaise's main domestic rival, increased their stake in the company from 2.5 per cent to more than 4 per cent in a similar scheme this year.

Equity investment has been relatively unpopular in France where, until recently, money market [short-term lending] funds benefited from favourable tax treatment . . .

The fiscal [tax] treatment of shares, relative to bonds, has been gradually relaxed by Dominique Strauss-Khan, finance minister, in an attempt both to tackle the country's pensions shortfall (by encouraging personal investment) and to encourage 'productive investment' – investment leading to job creation.

Analysts are optimistic that the growing popularity of employee shareholding schemes will play a significant role in establishing an 'equity culture' in continental Europe – and in France, in particular. . . .

Source: *Financial Times*, 21 May 1999, p. 35. Reprinted with permission.

Exhibit 9.3 Thai Stock Exchange

A market appeals to the sceptical masses

FT

Thailand wants to build an 'equity culture', especially among the young. But doubts about the standards of corporate governance mean it faces an uphill struggle

says Amy Kazmin

During the recent school break, 15-year-old Soramon Prasirtphun spent three days at the Thai stock exchange.

It is all part of a campaign to create an 'equity culture' in Thailand, where less than 1 per cent of Thailand household savings are invested in stocks [shares]. As exchange officials struggle to breathe new life into a market valued at less than half of its 1994 all-time high, they say that attracting new money – and expanding the narrow domestic investor base – is crucial if the exchange is to be a viable venue for companies to raise capital . . .

A new Bt30m ($660,000) television advertising blitz contends that, like lighting a match, buying a diamond or growing a bonsai tree, investing in stocks can bring benefits if it is done properly . . .

Thailand's equity market has always been a secondary part of the country's story of economic growth. As elsewhere in Asia, Thailand's boom during the 1980s and early 1990s was largely financed by corporate debt: Thais entrusted about 95 per cent of their savings into banks.

Although plenty of companies listed on the exchange during the growth years, many offerings were driven more by a desire for the status of being listed than by a real need for capital. Often, only small amounts of equity in family-run companies were sold and most controlling shareowners continued to view their companies as private domains, even if they were listed.

But since the Asian crisis, Thai banks have shunned new lending, focusing instead on digging themselves out from beneath a pile of bad loans. That has put the spotlight on the need to strengthen the equity market as a forum for raising capital. Investors, too, are looking for new things to do with their savings, given the historically low deposit rates at banks now flush with unwanted liquidity.

Source: *Financial Times*, 21 May 2001, p. 11. Reprinted with permission.

It can be seen from Exhibit 9.1 that the dominant financial centres form a 'golden triangle' in three different time zones: USA, London and Tokyo. America is the largest source of equity capital, providing over one-third of the world's total, but the finance raised is split between three exchanges. The New York Stock Exchange (NYSE) (now merged with Euronext to form NYSE Euronext) is the largest in terms of market capitalisation. However, the NASDAQ (National Association of Securities Dealers Automated Quotations) market has more companies listed, but its market capitalisation is much less. The laggard is the American Stock Exchange. In terms of domestic company share trading the NYSE is the world leader. However, in terms of trading in non-domestic (foreign) shares, London is pre-eminent. This is shown in **Exhibit 9.4**.

European stock exchanges

In Europe the trend is for stock exchanges to merge together or to form alliances. This is being encouraged by the major financial institutions which desire a seamless, less costly way of trading shares across borders. The ultimate ambition for some visionaries is a single highly liquid equity

Exhibit 9.4 Domestic and foreign equity turnover on major exchanges, 2006

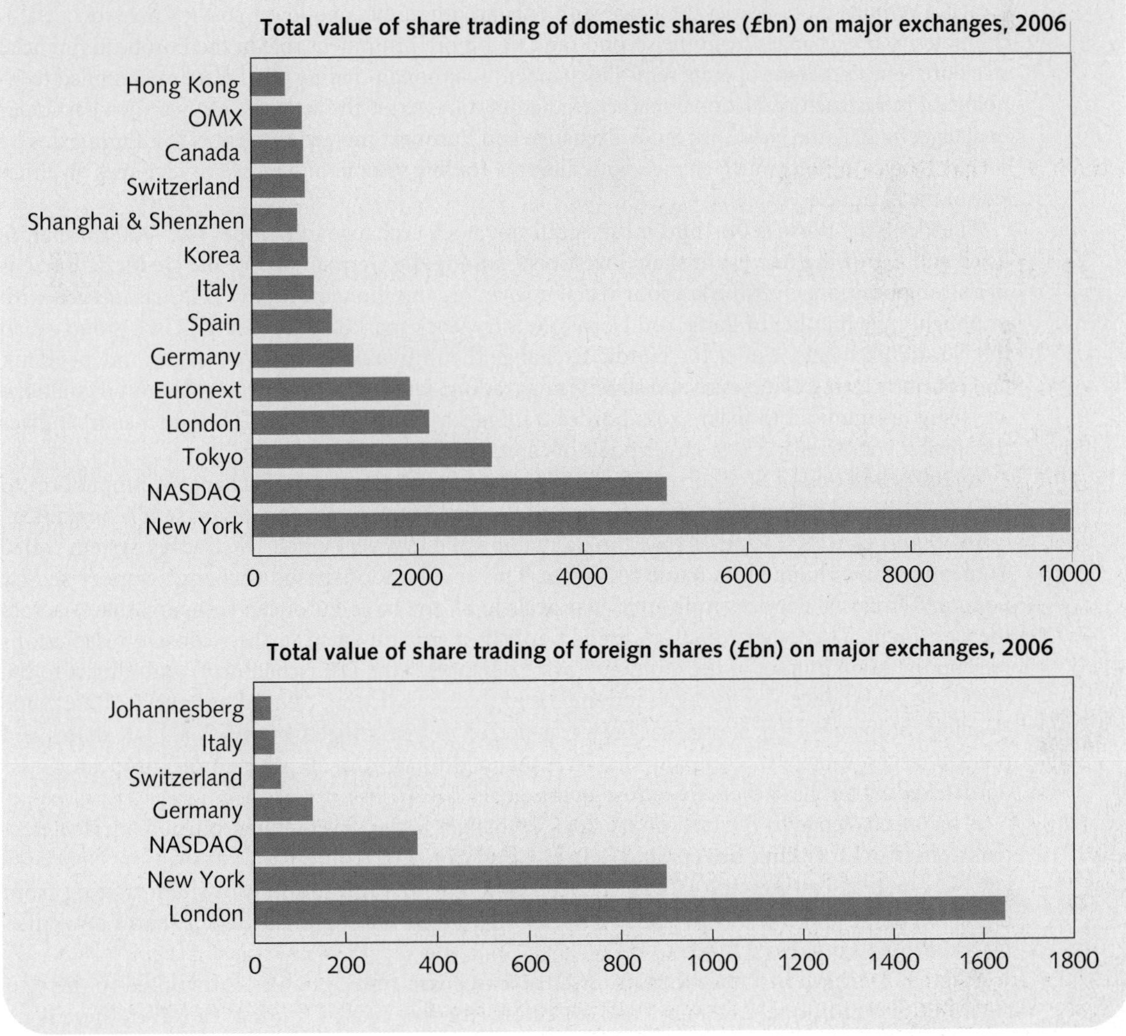

Source: World Federation of Exchanges, www.world-exchanges.org

Note: The New York Stock Exchange has now merged with Euronext.

market allowing investors to trade and companies to raise capital, wherever it suits them. Ideally there would be no distortions in share price, costs of trading or regulation as investors cross from one country to another. Whether it is necessary to merge Europe's disparate stock exchanges to achieve frictionless pan-European trading is a matter that is currently hotly debated. Some argue that the absence of a single securities market damages the EU's competitive position *vis-à-vis* the huge, streamlined and highly liquid US capital market. Furthermore, they say, it prevents European companies and investors enjoying the full benefits of the euro.

On the other hand the cost of actually trading shares in Europe is extremely low. The major costs (90 per cent) arise in the processing of the transaction *after* the deal is done ('the **back office**'). These clearing and settlement activities (*see* later in the chapter for a definition) are often carried out by organisations separate from the exchanges. The critics of the drive to merge argue that what is needed is pan-European transaction processing rather than one giant stock exchange. This has started to happen, but is frequently blocked because exchanges usually favour the clearing and settlement organisations that they own. Pan-European share trading is likely to remain expensive because of differing laws and taxes.

Whatever the long-run outcome of the current arguments the state of play as in late 2007 is as shown in **Exhibit 9.5**.

The most significant move toward integration has been the merger of the Brussels, Amsterdam, Paris and Portuguese markets to form Euronext. It is the largest market in the Eurozone with a market capitalisation of over £1,850 billion, only slightly lower than that for London. The merger creates a genuine cross-border exchange with enhanced liquidity and lower cost for investors. It also promotes four exchanges from the second rank to a more prominent role in the European financial structure. The exchanges operate semi-independently, although trading takes place on a unified technological infrastructure. National market regulators still oversee the activities of their own particular exchange. In 2007 the New York Stock Exchange and Euronext merged to form NYSE Euronext. The merger has yet to effect much change, with different trading systems and regulatory regimes on either side of the Atlantic.

The Deutsche Börse is the third most significant stock exchange in Europe. With 760 companies listed and a growing interest in share investment among the German people the Deutsche Börse is in a strong position. Over the last four years or so an organisation known as OMX has merged with or bought up a number of Baltic and Nordic country stock markets. They are held in a group called the Nordic Exchange. Under the Nordic Exchange the individual exchanges remain independent, and continue listing companies and supervising trading. However, the general rules and regulations are being harmonised to make cross-border trading simpler and cheaper. The larger market gives the smaller countries access to larger pools of capital and improves liquidity.

In 2007 the London Stock Exchange (LSE) merged with the Italian Exchange. Competition to the LSE in the UK is developing from an exchange called PLUS, which focuses on small companies.

In 2000 the Swiss stock exchange took a major stake in a very small UK trading system called Tradepoint and changed its name to Virt-x. This is a London-based exchange, supervised by London's Financial Services Authority, that deals in all the large European company shares across the Continent. The issuers of shares traded on Virt-x remain listed in their chosen jurisdictions (e.g. on the Main Market of the London Stock Exchange or the Deutsche Börse) and subject to the corporate governance and listing requirements of that jurisdiction. All trading in Swiss **blue chips** (leading companies), e.g. Nestlé, has been transferred to Virt-x together with 2,000 UK shares and the 250 largest European company shares. It planned to capture 20 per cent of European cross-border trading but has never come close to this goal.

A major challenge to the traditional stock exchanges is the development of sophisticated electronic networks linking buyers and sellers of shares. Electronic Communication Networks (ECNs), such as Instinet and Island, have taken a considerable amount of share trading from NASDAQ and the NYSE in the USA. Some 30 per cent of trading in NASDAQ shares now takes place outside its organised market.

So far ECNs have had little impact on European share trading. This is attributed to the efficiency of the traditional exchanges and, therefore, the low cost of trading. However, there is no room for complacency: Paul Walker-Duncalf, head of dealing in Europe of Merrill Lynch Investment Managers, said: 'It makes little difference where we trade. Most exchanges look the

Exhibit 9.5 Stock exchanges in Europe

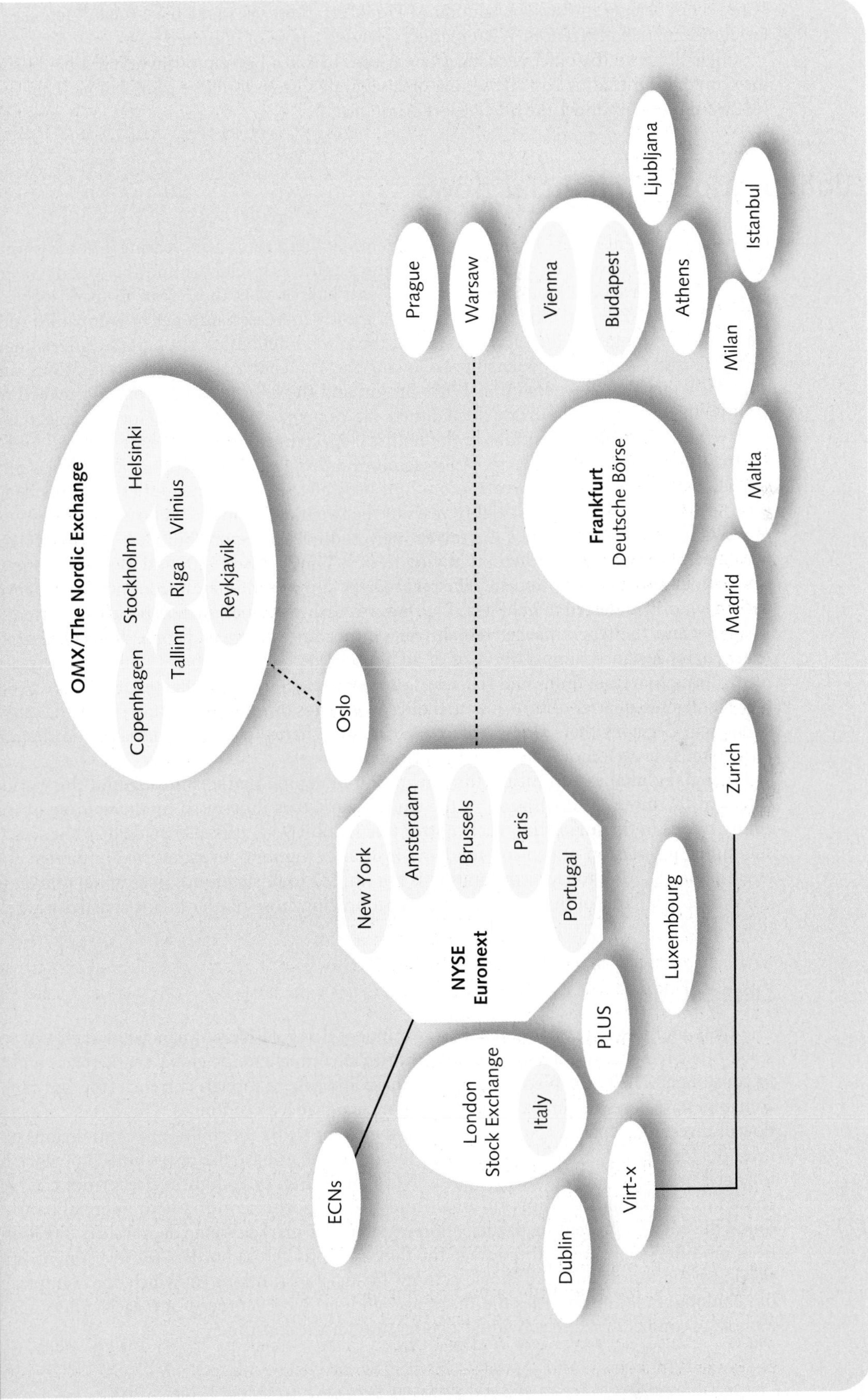

same. If I'm dealing in Paris, or London or Frankfurt, there are just a few visual differences and a few minor market differences. What matters is having a pool of liquidity.'[4]

A new threat to the older exchanges has arisen. In 2007 a group of investment banks thought they could lower trading costs by setting up a separate system for large transactions. They are currently building this under the title Project Turquoise.

Globalisation of financial flows

Over the last twenty years of the twentieth century there was an increasing emphasis on share (equity) finance and stock exchanges. An 'equity culture' spread around the world. Given that stock markets have been around for centuries, what happened in those years to spark such a widespread interest? The first explanation is that a greatly increased number of companies sought a stock market quotation for their shares and there were deliberate attempts by governments to stimulate interest in share ownership. Following the Thatcher and Reagan privatisations, and the push for wider share ownership in 1980s Britain and the USA, hundreds of state-owned or privately held companies worldwide floated their shares on stock exchanges. Governments the world over, regardless of their position on the political spectrum, promoted share markets and other financial markets as enabling tools for economic progress. The issue of new shares globally reached over £200 billion per year. Secondly, it became apparent that equities had provided good long-term returns over the first eighty years of the twentieth century – returns significantly ahead of inflation and those on bonds. So, increasingly, those with responsibility for providing pensions decades from now concentrated on buying shares. Thirdly, the 1980s and 1990s was one of the best periods ever for share returns. The bull market stimulated interest from millions of investors who previously preferred to hold less risky, lower-return securities, such as bonds.

Shares and the stock market remain very important for many people across the globe. In America, for instance, almost one-half of all households now own shares (either directly or indirectly through mutual funds and self-select pension funds). In Australia, the level of ownership is higher still. One-quarter of British households own shares directly. The equity culture has grown so strongly in Germany that over 12 million people hold shares. The Scandinavian countries and the Netherlands are even more 'equitised' than Germany.

Financial globalisation means the integration of capital markets throughout the world. The extent of the internationalisation of the equity markets is illustrated by the volume of foreign equity trades in the major financial centres (*see* Exhibit 9.4). It is also evident in the fact that a substantial proportion of pension fund and insurance fund money is invested in foreign equities (*see* Chapter 1). Also, today a corporation is not limited to raising funds in a capital market where it is domiciled. Three of the major elements encouraging cross-border financial activity are shown in **Exhibit 9.6**.

Deregulation

The 1980s and 1990s was a period when government deregulation of financial markets was seen as a way of enabling financial and corporate entities to compete in the global marketplace and benefit consumers. The limits placed on the purchase and sale of foreign currency (**foreign exchange controls**) have been eliminated or lowered in most advanced economies. This has encouraged the flow of investment capital. Cartel-like arrangements for fixing the minimum commissions paid by investors for buying and selling shares have been eroded, as have the restrictions on ownership of financial firms and brokers by foreigners. Now, more than ever, domestic securities can be purchased by individuals and institutional funds from another country. Commercial banks have found the barriers preventing participation in particular markets being demolished. Tax laws have been modified so as not to discourage the flow of funds across borders for investment, and the previously statutorily enforced 'single-activity' financial institutions (in which, for example, banks did banking, building societies did mortgage lending) have ventured into each others' markets, increasing competition and providing a better deal for the consumer.

[4] *Financial Times Special Report on World Stocks and Derivative Exchanges*, 28 March 2001.

Exhibit 9.6 Globalisation of financial flows

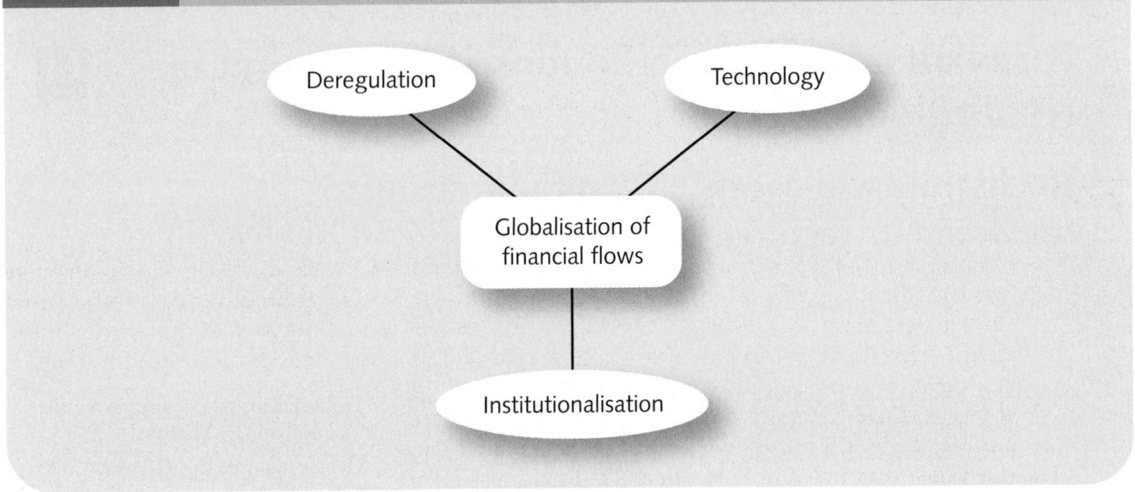

Technology

The rapid transmission of vast quantities of financial information around the globe has transformed the efficiency of financial markets. Securities can be monitored, analysed and dealt in on hundreds of share, bond, commodity and derivative exchanges at the touch of a button from almost anywhere in the world. The combination of powerful computers and extensive telecommunication networks allows accelerated integration, bringing with it complex trading strategies and enormous daily capital flows.

Institutionalisation

Forty years ago most shares were owned by individuals. Today, the markets are dominated by financial institutions (pension funds, insurance companies, hedge funds, the 'mutual funds' such as unit and investment trusts and private equity funds (*see* Chapter 10)). Whereas the individual, as a shareholder, tended to be more parochial and to concentrate on national company shares, the institutions have sufficient knowledge and strength to seek out the rewards from overseas investments. They also appreciate the diversification benefits which accrue due to the low level of correlation of returns between some financial markets (*see* Chapter 7).

Why do companies list their shares on more than one exchange?

There are hundreds of companies which pay for the privilege of having their shares listed for trading on stock exchanges in other countries instead of, or as well as, on their local exchange. Exhibit 9.1 shows that the most popular secondary listings locations are the USA and the UK. There are also substantial numbers of foreign shares listed on most of the northern European exchanges, as well as on those of Canada, Australia, Japan, Mexico, Switzerland and Singapore. This dual or triple listing can be a costly business and the regulatory environment can be stringent so there must be some powerful motivating factors driving managers to globalise their investor base. For Vodafone the costs and hassle of listing in three countries – the UK, the USA and Germany – must be thought provoking, as the cost of maintaining a listing on one market runs into hundreds of thousands of pounds per year. Here are some reasons for listing abroad:

- ***To broaden the shareholder base*** By inviting a larger number of investors to subscribe for shares it may be possible to sell those shares for a higher price and thus raise capital more cheaply (that is, a lower return will be required per £ invested). *See* the cases of Hochschild and Heiner Kamps (*see* **Exhibit 9.7**).

Exhibit 9.7

Peruvian miner lists in London in an attempt to regain global glories

FT

Hochschild will use its £270m fundraising to transcend its regional status

By Kevin Morrison

Hochschild Mining, the Peruvian-based silver miner that is one of the latest foreign mining companies to list on the London Stock Exchange, has a lot of work ahead in its strategy to once again become a global mining company.

In a step towards achieving its global ambitions, the Lima-based group raised £270m in London.

Hochschild is one of the world's top 20 silver miners and has a relatively small gold mine operation.

'If you look at the history of Hochschild, we were one of the first global mining companies' says Roberto Dañino, the deputy chairman of Hochschild and former prime minister of Peru. 'Then we became a regional player and now we want to become a global-player again.'

Mr Dañino says Hochschild plans to spend more than £200m of the float proceeds to expand three existing mines in Peru and to develop fully another four silver projects in Mexico, Argentina and Peru.

Hochschild has a market value of about £1.1bn, which qualifies it for entry into the FTSE 250.

Mr Dañino says it chose London over New York because the city had become the main global centre.

'We might have initially got a higher valuation in New York but I think in the medium term London will give us a higher valuation than what we could have got elsewhere,' he says.

Heiner Kamps chasing after the 'money on the Thames'

Heiner Kamps, the German bread baking and café entrepreneur, plans to float the core of a new food retailing empire on Aim next week and is eager to trumpet the advantages of doing so, writes Gerrit Wiesmann in Frankfurt.

'London is the main market,' the man who once listed a bakery chain in Germany told the FT. 'You can talk about Frankfurt as long as you like but you're not going to change the fact that all the money sits on the Thames.'

Source: *Financial Times*, 9 November 2006, p. 28. Reprinted with permission.

- ***The domestic stock exchange is too small or the firm's growth is otherwise constrained*** Some companies are so large relative to their domestic stock markets that they have no choice but to obtain equity finance from abroad. Ashanti Goldfields, the Ghanaian gold-mining company, was privatised in April 1994. It was valued at about \$1.7 billion, which was more than ten times the capitalisation of the Accra stock market. A listing in London was a great success and the company expanded its activities in other African countries – it listed in New York, Toronto, Zimbabwe, Ghana and London. Indian companies can raise money on a global basis and escape restrictions placed on them in India by listing in London (*see* **Exhibit 9.8**).
- ***To reward employees*** Many employees of foreign-owned firms are rewarded with shares in the parent company. If these shares are locally listed these share-ownership plans can be better managed and are more appealing to employees.
- ***Investors in that particular market may understand the firm better*** This point is illustrated with the case of KarstadtQuelle (**Exhibit 9.9**).
- ***To raise awareness of the company*** For example, Picsel listed on the Tokyo Stock Exchange as well as in London (*see* **Exhibit 9.10**).
- ***Discipline*** This is illustrated through the example of Chinese companies (*see* **Exhibit 9.11**). The value of stock market discipline has reached the heart of a previously totalitarian centrally controlled economy. Not only have Chinese companies seen the benefit of tapping capitalistic share capital, they have also been made aware of the managerial rigour demanded by stock markets and their investors. Many Russian companies have also listed in London to gain respectability through the enforcement by Western investors of good corporate governance and transparency of information (they have also listed in London to gain some protection against arbitrary actions by the Russian government).

Exhibit 9.8

Indian groups check out AIM

By Amy Yee in New Delhi

Dozens of Indian companies are keen to list on alternative global stock exchanges such as London's Alternative Investment Market (AIM) as they seek to boost valuations, sidestep India's regulatory hurdles and avoid stringent US rules.

'More than 30 companies have asked us to help them list on AIM. There has been an explosion in the number of inquiries,' said Vishesh Chandiok, director of international business at Grant Thornton India.

He estimated that at least a dozen smaller Indian companies would list on overseas stock markets in the next 12 months.

Such alternative markets, once geared toward smaller local companies, are becoming increasingly attractive to international investors.

'Some companies are driven by poor liquidity in home markets; others seek the opportunity to gain access to a larger investor base,' wrote Grant Thornton in its global new markets report released this week. 'Some are attracted to the regulatory structure of international markets.'

Interest is especial keen among Indian companies from sectors such as real estate, infrastructure, information technology, pharmaceuticals and energy.

Although real estate and infrastructure are booming sectors in India, they are new areas that the Indian stock market 'doesn't know now to value', said Mr Chandiok, because they tended to book revenue differently than conventional industries.

Emerging industries including property, biotech and alternative energy 'are more developed outside India so they get better investor perception', said Mr Chandiok. 'Overseas markets are in better position to value, assign and subscribe.'

Source: Financial Times, 1 September 2006, p. 22. Reprinted with permission.

Exhibit 9.9

KarstadtQuelle eyes London

German group aims to tap larger market Subsidiary Thomas Cook lists today

By Gerrit Wiesmann and Roger Blitz

KarstadtQuelle, the German retail and tourism group, is considering listing its shares in London because investors there understand its business better than in Frankfurt.

'London has more educated investors in retail and leisure,' chief executive Thomas Middelhoff told the Financial Times as Thomas Cook, KarstadtQuelle's subsidiary travel business, prepared to float on the UK stock market today.

Mr Middelhoff signalled that the parent company could seek a secondary listing in London after its restructuring over the past two years.

'You have more opportunities here than in Germany,' the former chief executive of media group Bertelsmann said.

Some big German companies such as Deutsche Telekom are listed in London for image as much as financial reasons.

KarstadtQuelle seems to be leading a charge of smaller groups that want to tap a larger financial market.

The listing of Thomas Cook on the London Stock Exchange follows a merger with the UK's MyTravel. KarstadtQuelle will hold a 52 per cent stake in Europe's second-largest travel group, which will have a market capitalisation of £3.15bn, sales of nearly £9bn and 19m customers.

With more companies to compare it with in London and a bigger pool of analysts to rate it, KarstadtQuelle's shares could rise above €40 from today's price of about €25 per share in Frankfurt, Mr Middelhoff said.

He stressed that Frankfurt would remain an important market for KarstadtQuelle shares but the company had long set its sights on wooing and serving a growing number of investors from the US and the UK. The company plans to change its name to Ancandor in September.

Source: Financial Times, 19 June 2007, p. 19. Reprinted with permission.

Exhibit 9.10

Picsel proposes listing in London and Tokyo

FT

By Andrew Bolger, Scotland Correspondent

Picsel Technologies, one of Scotland's most successful start-up companies, is preparing to seek a dual listing on the London and Tokyo stock exchanges.

The Glasgow-based company, which provides software to many of the world's leading mobile phone manufacturers, has appointed Morgan Stanley and Daiwa Securities as advisers for the IPO, which it hopes to achieve in 12 to 18 months.

Mr Khand said. 'We want to dual list in Tokyo as well as London because a lot of our customers are there and the Japanese are very responsive to technology stocks.'

Mr Khand said that, in addition to mobile phone manufacturers, Picsel was working closely with network and content providers as well as advertisers who were becoming increasingly excited about the potential of gaining access to consumers whose tastes could be individually targeted.

Picsel originally had raised \$21m of equity financing, mainly from Asian venture capital funds, and another \$30m of non-equity investment from the government of Malaysia, where it has an operation.

It has just completed a pre IPO fundraising round in which it received a further, \$46m.

Source: Financial Times, 1 November 2006, p. 22.

Exhibit 9.11 'We need the discipline of the market.'

HK is China's preferred stock market

FT

By Geoff Dyer in Shanghai

A leading Chinese government official said yesterday that state-owned companies would benefit more from listing first on overseas stock markets such as Hong Kong rather than on the mainland exchanges in Shanghai and Shenzhen.

Li Rongrong, chairman of the State-owned Assets Supervision and Administration: Commission (Sasac), which manages the state's corporate assets, defended the policy of floating large companies overseas, saying that international exchanges had more rigorous corporate governance standards, which would improve the performance of state-owned groups.

His comments underline the way Hong Kong is cementing its position as the preferred equity market for leading Chinese companies, at the expense of Shanghai, despite strong opposition from mainland investors and some politicians to Sasac's listing strategy.

'The overseas markets are more regulated and Chinese companies can benefit and learn to fine-tune corporate structure and governance,' he said at a press conference in Beijing. The domestic market would benefit because companies would be in stronger shape if they later listed on the mainland.

Source: Financial Times, 23 December 2005. Reprinted with permission.

- ***To understand better the economic, social and industrial changes occurring in major product markets.*** This is illustrated by the Toyota article (*see* **Exhibit 9.12**).

The importance of a well-run stock exchange

A well-run stock exchange has a number of characteristics. It is one where a '**fair game**' takes place; that is, where it is not possible for some investors and fund raisers to benefit at the expense of other participants – all players are on 'a level playing field'. It is a market which is well regulated

Exhibit 9.12

Toyota to list in New York and London

FT

Toyota, Japan's third-largest company by market capitalisation, plans to list its shares in New York and London this month.

The issue is aimed at attracting international investors, meeting the needs of the increasingly global industry and boosting Toyota's image, said Yuji Araki, senior managing director.

The move is the latest in a series of global offers by Japanese companies, which are aimed at increasing the international element of their shareholder base . . .

Mr Araki said the company decided to list in New York and London not only to increase its investor base but also to be able to judge whether Toyota's performance met western standards.

'If they don't, we will have to change ourselves', he said.

Listing in the two cities would also help Toyota sense the changes in foreign stock markets more quickly and from those changes, the economic, social and industrial changes occurring in those markets, Mr Araki said.

Foreigners own a relatively low proportion of Toyota – just 8.8 per cent. But Mr Araki emphasised that the company had no fixed target for foreign shareholders . . .

In addition to New York, Toyota decided to list in London because 'in order to attract international investors it is essential to list in London', he added . . .

However, over the next two to three years, changes would be introduced in Japanese reporting requirements, which would bring them much closer to SEC standards, Mr Araki said.

Source: Michiyo Nakamoto and Paul Abrahams, *Financial Times*, 8 September 1999, p. 26. Reprinted with permission.

to avoid abuses, negligence and fraud in order to reassure investors who put their savings at risk. It is also one on which it is reasonably cheap to carry out transactions. In addition, a large number of buyers and sellers are likely to be needed for the efficient price setting of shares and to provide sufficient liquidity, allowing the investor to sell at any time without altering the market price. There are six main benefits of a well-run stock exchange.

1 *Firms can find funds and grow*

Because investors in financial securities with a stock market quotation are assured that they are, generally, able to sell their shares quickly, cheaply and with a reasonable degree of certainty about the price, they are willing to supply funds to firms at a lower cost than they would if selling was slow, or expensive, or the sale price was subject to much uncertainty. Thus stock markets encourage investment by mobilising savings. As well as stimulating the investment of domestic savings, stock markets can be useful for attracting foreign savings and for aiding the privatisation process.

2 *Allocation of capital*

One of the key economic problems for a nation is finding a mechanism for deciding what mixture of goods and services to produce. An extreme solution has been tried and shown to be lacking in sophistication – that of a **totalitarian directed economy** where bureaucratic diktat determines the exact quantity of each line of commodity produced. The alternative method favoured in most nations (for the majority of goods and services) is to let the market decide what will be produced and which firms will produce it.

An efficiently functioning stock market is able to assist this process through the flow of investment capital. If the stock market was poorly regulated and operated then the mis-pricing of shares and other financial securities could lead to society's scarce capital resources being put into sectors which are inappropriate given the objective of maximising economic well-being. If, for instance, the market priced the shares of a badly managed company in a declining industrial sector at a high level then that firm would find it relatively easy to sell shares and raise funds for further investment in its business or to take over other firms. This would deprive companies with better prospects and with a greater potential contribution to make to society of essential finance.

To take an extreme example: imagine the year is 1910 and on the stock market are some firms which manufacture horse-drawn carriages. There are also one or two young companies which have taken up the risky challenge of producing motor cars. Analysts will examine the prospects of the two types of enterprise before deciding which firms will get a warm reception when they ask for more capital in, say, a rights issue. The unfavoured firms will find their share prices falling as investors sell their shares, and will be unable to attract more savers' money. One way for the older firm to stay in business would be to shift resources within the firm to the production of those commodities for which consumer demand is on a rising trend.

A more recent transfer of finance is discussed in **Exhibit 9.13**. A dramatic shift in resources occurred in the late 1990s as financial markets supplied hundreds of billions of dollars to high-technology industries.

3 *For shareholders*

Shareholders benefit from the availability of a speedy, cheap secondary market if they want to sell. Not only do shareholders like to know that they can sell shares when they want to, they may simply want to know the value of their holdings even if they have no intention of selling at present. By contrast, an unquoted firm's shareholders often find it very difficult to assess the value of their holding.

Exhibit 9.13

Rebuilt by Wall Street

FT

The US's dynamic stock market has directed resources into high-tech industries, giving the economy a huge advantage that other countries must strive to match

says David Hale

The stock market boom has been part of a much larger process of reallocation of global resources resulting from the end of the cold war, the increasing role of information technology in the economy, and the leadership of US companies in utilising this technology . . .

There has been a dramatic improvement in the ability of small companies in the technology sector to obtain capital. In 1999 initial public offerings raised $69.2bn, compared with a previous peak of $49.9bn in 1996 and a grand total of $350.8bn since 1989. Second, the ability of small companies to go public has encouraged a dramatic expansion of the US venture capital industry. It raised funds at an annualised rate of $25bn during the first half of 1999, nearly twice as much as during all of 1998. About 66 per cent of the funds were placed in the information technology sector while 73 per cent of the IT component was placed with internet companies.

As a result, the technology share of the US stock market has expanded from 10 per cent in the early 1990s to about 33 per cent today. The US technology sector now has a market capitalisation of over $3,000bn, compared with $350bn for the entire global mining industry . . .

As a result of the dramatic changes in the composition of the US stock market and the surge of IPO activity, the US economy has been able to reallocate resources on a large scale from traditional industries to new high-growth sectors linked to IT and the internet. But the impact of the technology revolution is also increasingly apparent in the real economy. Spending on research and development in the US has rebounded to 2.7 per cent of GDP after declining to 2.4 per cent during the mid-1990s. The number of patents issued during 1989 was about 140,000 – 29 per cent higher than during 1997 and 55 per cent higher than during 1990 . . .

The information technology share of output has increased to 5.8 per cent from 3.3 per cent in 1992 . . .

It would have been difficult for the US to finance the rapid growth of the IT sector without a buoyant stock market because companies in this field need equity capital, not debt finance . . .

The main lesson of the US experience of the late 1990s is that a dynamic stock market can be a valuable national asset for mobilising capital and reallocating resources from low- to high-growth sectors.

Source: Financial Times, 25 January 2000, p. 22.

Founders of firms may be particularly keen to obtain a quotation for their firms. This will enable them to diversify their assets by selling a proportion of their holdings. Also, venture capital firms which fund unquoted firms during their rapid growth phase often press the management to aim for a quotation to permit the venture capitalist to have the option of realising the gains made on the original investment, or simply to boost the value of their holding by making it more liquid.

4 *Status and publicity*

The public profile of a firm can be enhanced by being quoted on an exchange. Banks and other financial institutions generally have more confidence in a quoted firm and therefore are more likely to provide funds at a lower cost. Their confidence is raised because the company's activities are now subject to detailed scrutiny. The publicity surrounding the process of gaining a quotation may have a positive impact on the image of the firm in the eyes of customers, suppliers and employees and so may lead to a beneficial effect on their day-to-day business.

5 *Mergers*

Mergers can be facilitated better by a quotation. This is especially true if the payments offered to the target firm's shareholders for their holdings are shares in the acquiring firm. A quoted share has a value defined by the market, whereas shares in unquoted firms are difficult to assess.

The stock exchange also assists what is called 'the **market in managerial control**'. That is a mechanism in which teams of managers are seen as competing for control of corporate assets. Or, to put it more simply, mergers through the stock market permit the displacement of inefficient management with a more successful team. Thus, according to this line of reasoning, assets will be used more productively and society will be better off. This 'market in managerial control' is not as effective as is sometimes claimed (it tends to be over-emphasised by acquiring managers) (*see* Chapter 23 for further discussion).

6 *Improves corporate behaviour*

If a firm's shares are traded on an exchange, the directors may be encouraged to behave in a manner conducive to shareholders' interests. This is achieved through a number of pressure points. For example, to obtain a quotation on a reputable exchange, companies are required to disclose a far greater range and depth of information than is required by accounting standards or the Companies Acts. This information is then disseminated widely and can become the focus of much public and press comment. In addition, investment analysts ask for regular briefings from senior managers and continuously monitor the performance of firms. Before a company is admitted to the Stock Exchange the authorities insist on being assured that the management team are sufficiently competent and, if necessary, additional directors are appointed to supplement the board's range of knowledge and skills. Directors are required to consult shareholders on important decisions, such as mergers, when the firm is quoted. They also have to be very careful to release price-sensitive information in a timely and orderly fashion and they are strictly forbidden to use inside information to make a profit by buying or selling the firm's shares.

The London Stock Exchange

The London Stock Exchange (LSE) started in the coffee houses of eighteenth-century London where the buying and selling of shares in joint stock companies took place. In 1773 the volume of trade was sufficiently great for the brokers to open a subscription room in Threadneedle Street. They called the building the Stock Exchange.[5] During the nineteenth century, over twenty other stock exchanges were formed in the rapidly expanding industrial towns of Britain. They amalgamated in 1973 to become a unified Stock Exchange. All of the old trading floors of the regional exchanges and in London, where market members would meet face to face to exchange shares, are now obsolete. Today, there is no physical marketplace. The dealing rooms of the various finance

[5] It moved in 1801 to Capel Court and in 1972 back to Throgmorton Street.

houses are linked via telephone and computer, and trading takes place without physical contact. Having abandoned **floor trading** in 1986 the LSE found itself with an overly large building. In 2004 it finally moved within the City's square mile to Paternoster Square next to St Paul's Cathedral.

Securities traded

The volume of trade has expanded enormously in recent years. **Exhibit 9.14** indicates the types of securities sold on the Exchange. There are five types of *fixed-interest securities* traded in London: gilts, local authority bonds, foreign government bonds, sterling corporate bonds and Eurobonds. The government bond or 'gilts' market (lending to the UK government) is big, with an annual turnover in the secondary market of £3,508 billion in 2007. In that year the UK government raised £60 billion through selling gilt-edged securities. Sterling bonds issued by companies (corporate bonds) comprise a relatively small market – just a few billion. Specialist securities, such as warrants, are normally bought and traded by a few investors who are particularly knowledgeable in investment matters. (Warrants are discussed in Chapter 10.) During 2007, 2025 new Eurobonds were listed in London by UK companies, raising a total of £166 billion.

In addition foreign governments raised £5.6 billion by selling bonds on the LSE.

The Specialist Fund Market was launched in 2007. It creates a market in single strategy hedge funds and private equity funds for institutional investors (not for individuals, who may be less aware of the risks of investing in these funds).

There has been the rapid development of the **depositary receipt** market over the last ten years. These are certificates which can be bought and sold, which represent evidence of ownership of a company's shares held by a depositary. Thus, an Indian company's shares could be packaged in, say, groups of five by a depositary (usually a bank) which then sells a certificate representing the bundle of shares. The depositary receipt can be denominated in a currency other than the corporation's domestic currency and dividends can be received in the currency of the depositary receipt (say, pounds) rather than the currency of the original shares. These are attractive securities for sophisticated international investors because they may be more liquid and more easily traded than the underlying shares. They may also be used to avoid settlement, foreign exchange and foreign ownership difficulties which may exist in the company's home market. From the company's point

Exhibit 9.14 Types of financial securities sold on the London Stock Exchange

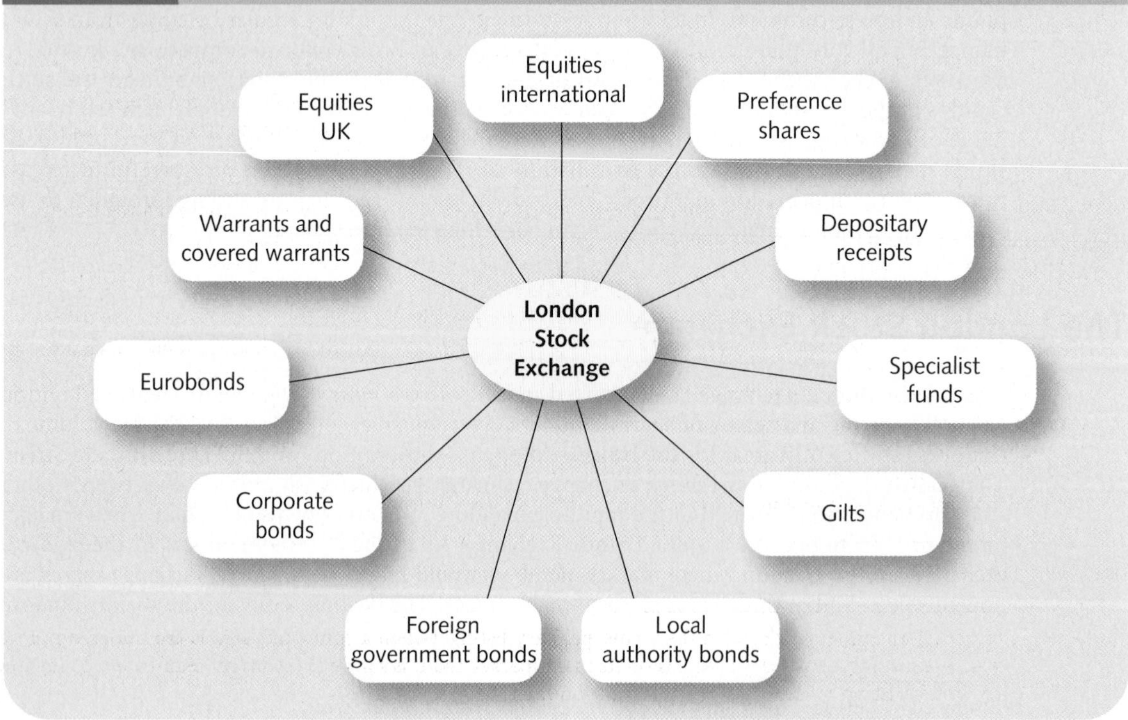

of view depositary receipts are attractive because they allow a market in the company's shares (even though they are wrapped up in a depositary receipt) permitting fund raising and the other benefits of a listing on a regulated global capital market without the company needing to jump the regulatory hurdles necessary to join the Main Market (Official List) in London. **Exhibit 9.15** discusses depositary receipts.

Our main concern in this chapter is with the market in ordinary shares and it is to this we now turn. The London Stock Exchange is both a **primary market** and a **secondary market**. The primary market is where firms can raise new finance by selling shares to investors. The secondary market is where existing securities are sold by one investor to another.[6]

Exhibit 9.15

A capital idea for emerging economies

FT

Joanna Chung on an increasingly popular means of getting access to foreign investors

A growing number of emerging market companies are choosing to raise capital from international investors through issues of depositary receipts.

Depositary receipts are increasingly popular because they give companies, particular [sic] those from developing markets, a simple and effective way to attract a broader range of investors than is possible locally.

'For emerging market companies, they are a very important security because many investors don't necessarily have the same kind of access to emerging economies as they do to developed ones,' says Nancy Lissemore, managing director and global head of depositary receipt services at Citigroup, the US bank.

'Intitutional investors can easily buy the ordinary shares sold in Western European markets, but it is more difficult and complex to do in emerging markets.'

A depositary receipt represents ownership of a given number of a company's shares and can be listed and traded independently of the underlying stock, in a different jurisdiction.

DRs enable investors to trade equities of companies listed in markets that are hard to access directly without, for instance, setting up a custodian or going through a local broker. They also appeal to investors because of the availability of widespread price information and lower transaction costs.

Global depositary receipts (GDRs) are usually listed in London and Luxembourg, while American depositary receipts (ADRs) are the US-listed equivalents. But offerings do occur elsewhere: for instance, last month saw the first ever GDR listing on the Singapore stock exchange.

In the past two years, the proportion of GDRs issued in the depositary receipt market has increased, with many companies from emerging markets choosing London for raising capital.

Bankers say the popularity of DRs is likely to grow among emerging market issuers because, although local stock exchanges are developing fast, they remain less developed than markets such as London.

'Some companies look at the size of their offering and decide that their home market is too small and too illiquid to absorb a significant amount of the offering. That is one reason you continue to see a trend of emerging market companies doing a dual, listing using GDRs,' says Ms Lissemore.

GDRs have typically come from fast-growing markets including Russia, South Korea, Taiwan. and India. Two of the biggest were done by Rosneft, the Russian oil group, and Lotte Shopping of South Korea.

The issuing of primary shares requires the company to meet the stringent corporate governance standards and disclosure requirements expected of UK-listed companies, or to explain why they do not. In contrast, GDRs require adherence to local standards and leave it more open to interpretation as to how they compare with UK rules.

Primary listers in London have to appoint a sponsor – which guides them through the intricacies of obtaining a listing and acts as a liaison between the company and the UK Listing Authority – and comply with all the UK listing rules over and above the EU prospectus rules.

Few foreign companies seek a primary listing. Only one company from the former Soviet Union, Kazakhmys, the mining group from Kazakhstan, currently has a primary listing.

GDRs in London are listed on the main market or the stock exchange regulated Professional Securities Market. They are sold only to professional investors and are not included in key indices.

Source: Financial Times, 30 May 2007, Corporate Finance Section, p. 2. Reprinted permission.

[6] Confusion can arise here with the terms 'primary listing' (when a company's shares are traded on more than one market its primary listing is on its main market and it is subject to stringent regulations there) and 'secondary listing' where the shares are traded outside its main market.

The primary market (equities)

Large sums of money flow from the savers in society via the Stock Exchange to firms wanting to invest and grow. In 2007 there were over 1,100 UK companies on the Main Market and 129 UK companies on the techMARK (also run by the London Stock Exchange). There were also over 1,600 companies on the Exchange's market for smaller and younger companies, the Alternative Investment Market (AIM). During 2007, UK-listed firms raised new capital amounting to £182 billion by selling equity and fixed interest securities on the LSE. Included in this figure was £7.6 billion raised by companies coming to the Stock Exchange for the first time by selling shares. Companies already quoted on the Main Market (Official List of LSE) sold a further £8.4 billion of shares through events such as rights issues and other securities such as bonds. AIM companies sold £16.2 billion of shares. UK companies also raised money by selling convertible bonds, debentures, loans and preference shares (*see* Chapters 10 and 11 for discussion on these securities and **Exhibit 9.16** for a summary of the money raised by UK companies).

Exhibit 9.16 Money raised by UK companies, 1999–2006

	New companies issuing shares		Other issues of shares and other securities		Eurobonds		AIM	
	No. of Co.'s	Money raised (£m)	No. of issues	Money raised (£m)	No. of issues	Money raised (£m)	No. of new companies joining AIM	Money raised* (£m)
1999	106	5,353	895	9,916	1,022	85,515	96	933
2000	172	11,399	897	13,978	1,012	100,556	265	3,073
2001	113	6,921	869	14,824	935	83,342	162	1,128
2002	59	5,081	764	11,696	815	86,657	147	975
2003	32	2,444	618	4,920	1,096	118,755	146	2,095
2004	55	3,431	697	8,801	1,170	127,508	294	4,656
2005	84	5,966	781	8,945	1,099	148,309	399	8,942
2006	77	8,415	675	15,244	1,500	216,495	338	15,678
2007	73	7,613	474	8,356	2,025	165,924	197	16,184

* Includes non-UK companies

Source: London Stock Exchange, www.londonstockexchange.com. Reproduced courtesy of London Stock Exchange plc.

Each year there is great interest and excitement inside dozens of companies as they prepare for flotation. The year 2007 was a watershed year for 73 UK companies which joined the Main Market and 197 which joined AIM. The requirements for joining the Main Market are stringent. The listing particulars should give a complete picture of the company; its trading history, financial record, management and business prospects. It should (normally) have at least a three-year trading history and has to make at least 25 per cent of its ordinary shares publicly available (*see* Chapter 10 for more detail). Given the costs associated with gaining a listing, it may be surprising to find that the total value of the ordinary shares of the majority of quoted companies is less than £100 million (*see* **Exhibit 9.17**).

The LSE is clearly an important source of new finance for UK corporations and for companies around the world. However, it is not the most significant source. The most important source of funds is generally from within the firm itself (**internal finance**). This is the accumulated profits retained within the firm and not distributed as dividends. In an average year retained profits account for about one-half of the new funds for UK firms.

These retained earnings are also equity capital because this is money that belongs to shareholders – they have merely allowed companies to use it within the business rather than paying it out to the owners. Thus the amount of equity capital devoted to a firm can grow to be worth millions of pounds largely through the retention of profits, despite the fact that it might have raised only a few thousands by selling shares to investors at its start. The sale of ordinary shares rarely accounts for a

Exhibit 9.17 Distribution of UK companies by equity market value at July 2007

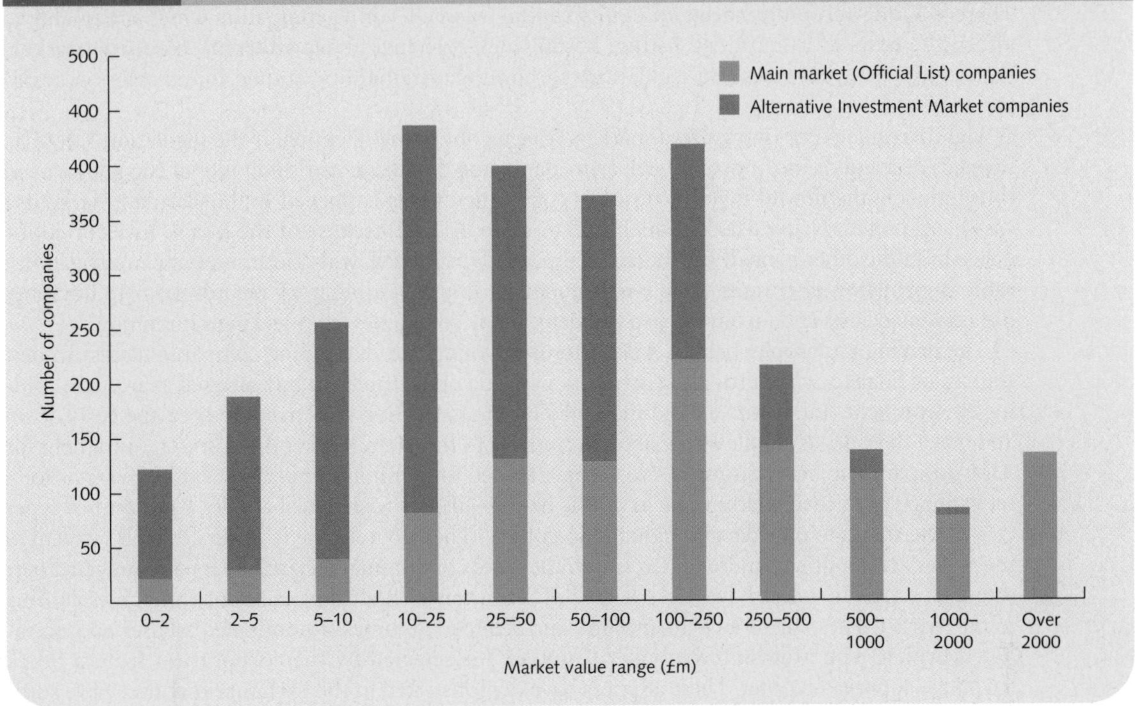

Source: www.londonstockexchange.com, statistics section. Reproduced courtesy of London Stock Exchange plc.

significant proportion of capital raised (it is usually less than 15 per cent of funds raised). Following retained earnings, bank loans are often very important for companies, but this does vary significantly. The sale of bonds and preference shares combined generally accounts for less than 5 per cent of new capital put into UK companies.

The secondary market in equities

The LSE operates and regulates a secondary market for the buying and selling of UK shares between investors in which an average of over 600,000 bargains, worth over £16 billion, were completed in an average day in 2007. In addition to these domestic equities a similar value of foreign shares were traded on a typical day. The secondary market turnover far exceeds the primary market sales. This high level of activity ensures a liquid market enabling shares to change ownership speedily, at low cost and without large movements in price – one of the main objectives of a well-run exchange.

The UK equity markets available to companies

The Main Market (Official List)

Companies wishing to be listed have to sign a **Listing Agreement** which commits directors to certain high standards of behaviour and levels of reporting to shareholders. This is a market for medium and large established firms with a reasonably long trading history. The costs of launching even a modest new issue runs into hundreds of thousands of pounds and therefore small companies are unable to justify a full main market listing. The regulations and the process of floating on the Main Market are discussed in Chapter 10.

The Alternative Investment Market (AIM)

There is a long-recognised need for equity capital by small, young companies which are unable to afford the costs of full Official listing. Many stock exchanges have **alternative equity markets** that set less stringent rules and regulations for joining or remaining quoted (often called '**second-tier markets**').

Lightly regulated or unregulated markets have a continuing dilemma. If the regulation is too lax scandals of fraud or incompetence will arise, damaging the image and credibility of the market, and thus reducing the flow of investor funds to companies. (This happened to the German market for small companies, **Neuer Markt**, which had to close in 2002 because of the loss in investor confidence.) On the other hand, if the market is too tightly regulated, with more company investigations, more information disclosure and a requirement for longer trading track records prior to flotation, the associated costs and inconvenience will deter many companies from seeking a quotation.

The driving philosophy behind **AIM** is to offer young and developing companies access to new sources of finance, while providing investors with the opportunity to buy and sell shares in a trading environment run, regulated and marketed by the LSE. Efforts are made to keep the costs down and make the rules as simple as possible. In contrast to the Main Market there is no requirement for AIM companies to be a minimum size, to have traded for a minimum period of three years or for a set proportion of their shares to be in public hands – if they wish to sell a mere 1 per cent or 5 per cent of the shares to outsiders then that is acceptable. They do not have to ensure that 25 per cent of the shares are in public hands (that is, not in the hands of dominant shareholders or connected persons). However, investors have some degree of reassurance about the quality of companies coming to the market. These firms have to appoint, and retain at all times, a nominated adviser and nominated broker. The **nominated adviser ('nomad')** is selected by the corporation from a Stock Exchange approved register. These advisers have demonstrated to the Exchange that they have sufficient experience and qualifications to act as a 'quality controller', confirming to the LSE that the company has complied with the rules. Unlike with Official List companies there is no pre-vetting of admission documents by the UK Listing Authority (or the Exchange) as a lot of weight is placed on the nominated advisers' investigations and informed opinion about the company.

Nominated brokers have an important role to play in bringing buyers and sellers of shares together. Investors in the company are reassured that at least one broker is ready to trade or do its best to match up buyers and sellers. The adviser and broker are to be retained throughout the company's life on AIM. They have high reputations and it is regarded as a very bad sign if either of them abruptly refuses further association with a firm. AIM companies are also expected to comply with strict rules regarding the publication of price-sensitive information and the quality of annual and interim reports. Upon flotation an '**AIM admission document**' is required; this is similar to a prospectus required for companies floating on the Main Market, but less detailed (see Chapter 10). The admission documentation even goes so far as to state the directors' unspent convictions and all bankruptcies of companies where they were directors. The LSE charges companies an annual fee of £4,535 to maintain quotation on AIM. If to this is added the cost of financial adviser's, brokers' and of management time spent communicating with institutions and investors the annual cost of being quoted on AIM runs into tens of thousands of pounds. This can be a deterrent for some companies.

However, there are cost savings compared with the Main Market. The flotation prospectus is less detailed and therefore cheaper. The annual expense of managing a quotation is less. For example AIM companies do not have to disclose as much information as companies on the Main Market. Price-sensitive information will have to be published but normally this will require only an electronic message from the adviser to the Exchange rather than a circular to shareholders. AIM companies are not bound by the Listing Rules administered by the UKLA but instead are subject to the AIM rules, written and administered by the LSE.

Note also that there are tax advantages for shareholders investing in AIM companies via venture capital trusts and the Enterprise Investment Scheme (*see* Chapter 10) or through the reduction in inheritance tax for some investors.

Offsetting the cost advantages AIM has over the Official List is the fact that the higher level of regulation and related enhanced image, prestige and security of Official List companies means that equity capital can usually be raised at a lower required rate of return (the shares can be sold for more per unit of projected profit). However, as **Exhibit 9.18** illustrates, AIM has pretty high standards of regulation anyway.

Exhibit 9.18

A mixed message for wondering naughty nomads

FT

Martin Dickinson
LOMBARD

LSE censures Aim participants

Success can breed laxity, so the London Stock Exchange yesterday tried to send a message to the market that it would not tolerate sloppy standards on Aim, the market for smaller companies.

It publicly censured Durlacher, the stockbroker that has since merged with Panmure Gordon, for its role as a nominated adviser, or nomad, to Prestbury Holdings, an Aim traded financial services company.

And it announced simultaneously that it had privately censured three other Aim companies and one nominated adviser for breaches of the rules covering press leaks, delay in issuing statements and incorrect advice to a client. In two cases it also fined companies – £5,000 and £10,000.

The market could certainly do with a reminder of the need for good behaviour. Aim's success is due to the fact it is lightly regulated (by the Exchange itself rather than the Financial Services Authority), which has attractions for young companies. But the market also benefits from London's generally high standards of regulation and information disclosure.

To safeguard its reputation those standards need to be carefully policed. The LSE knows this. It has recently doubled the core regulatory team that keeps an eye on nomads – which are responsible not only for bringing companies to Aim but keeping an eye on them thereafter.

However, the terms of the LSE's censure of Durlacher – the first public one it has ever issued – hardly seem designed to strike terror into a naughty nomad.

In the middle of a private fundraising, Prestbury found its financial performance was likely to fall significantly short of market expectations and provided Durlacher with a draft announcement on May 18 2004. Yet the announcement was not released until May 26, after completion of the fundraising, and a day after a sharp fall in Prestbury's share price, which continued to drop.

Durlacher had advised that it was permissible for the company to delay making a negative trading announcement, pending completion of an imminent private fundraising.

Such a delay goes so obviously against the known rules that companies must issue market sensitive statements without delay that it is surprising to find the LSE describing Durlacher's advice as 'given in good faith'. Without access to the Exchange's information on the case, it is impossible to know what extenuating circumstances it found. A censure was clearly deserved, but does its tone really send the right message?

Source: *Financial Times*, 9 August 2005, p. 18. Reprinted with permission.

AIM is not just a stepping-stone for companies planning to graduate to the Official List. It has many attractive features in its own right. Indeed, many Official List companies have moved to AIM in recent years. Also, as Exhibit 9.16 shows, over 300 new companies each year have joined the market in recent years, compared with fewer than 100 joining the main market.

techMARK

At the end of 1999, at the height of high technology fever, the London Stock Exchange launched a 'market-within-a-market' called **techMARK**. This is part of LSE's Main Market and is therefore technically not a separate market. It is a grouping of technology companies on the LSE. One of the reasons for its creation was that many companies lacking the minimum three-year account history required to join the Main Market had relatively high market values and desired the advantages of being on a prestigious market. The LSE relaxed its rule and permitted a listing if only one year of accounts are available for techMARK companies. This allowed investors to invest through a well-regulated exchange in companies at an early stage of development, such as Freeserve and lastminute.com. The LSE does insist that all companies joining techMARK have at least 25 per cent of their shares in a **free float** (in public hands).

PLUS

Companies that do not want to pay the costs of a flotation on one of the markets run by the LSE (these costs can range from £100,000 to £1m just for getting on the market in the first place) and the ongoing annual costs could go for a '**secondary market trading facility**' on PLUS. By having their shares quoted on **PLUS** companies provide a service to their shareholders, allowing them to buy and sell shares at reasonable cost. It also allows the company to gain access to capital, for example by selling more shares, without submitting to the rigour and expense of a quotation on LSE.

PLUS (originally called OFEX) was set up by broker J.P. Jenkins in 1995 and is now owned by **PLUS-Markets Group**. There is an annual fee of £5,000. When companies join the market there are also advisers' fees of around £20,000. If new capital is raised fees can climb above £100,000. PLUS companies are generally very small and often brand-new, but there are some long-established and well-known firms also trading on PLUS, such as Thwaites and Arsenal Football Club.

A number of competing market makers make a market in a company's shares by giving two prices to brokers who enquire about a share: the price at which it is willing to buy and a price at which it is willing to sell (see discussion on 'quote-driven' trading later in this chapter). The spread between these prices is normally a maximum of around 5 per cent. Having competing market makers improves the position for investors considerably, leading (hopefully) to greater liquidity and a small difference between the price an investor can sell to a market maker and the buying price from a market maker.

PLUS is now a Recognised Investment Exchange (RIE – *see* p. 349) under the law. Investors must note that the companies on PLUS are not subject to the same rigorous rules as those of the LSE's Main Market or AIM. PLUS is described as a 'prescribed market', which means that companies have to adhere to its code of conduct; for example insider trading by directors is prohibited; companies raising fresh capital on PLUS must have a Corporate Adviser (e.g. a stockbroker, accountant or lawyer); PLUS insists on seeing a prospectus produced to raise funds for companies or when first gaining a listing and expects this to comply with certain minimum standards as laid down in law.

There are over 200 companies with a combined market capitalisation of around £1,800m paying for a PLUS quotation. The secondary market can be relatively illiquid.

In addition to its own list of companies, PLUS also provides an alternative trading facility for hundreds of companies quoted on the LSE. It plans to offer an alternative secondary market trading facility for thousands of shares listed on other stock markets.

PLUS is often seen as a nursery market for companies that eventually grow big enough for AIM or Main Market. Despite this many companies are happy to remain on PLUS for many years and have no desire to increase their costs by moving up to the LSE markets. Indeed, some companies have come off AIM and joined PLUS.

Tasks for stock exchanges

Traditionally, exchanges perform the following tasks in order to play their valuable role in a modern society:

- Supervision of trading to ensure fairness and efficiency
- The authorisation of market participants such as brokers and market makers
- Creation of an environment in which prices are formed efficiently and without distortion (**price discovery** or **price formation**). This requires not only regulation of a high order and low transaction cost but also a liquid market in which there are many buyers and sellers, permitting investors to enter or exit quickly without moving the price.

- Organisation of the **settlement** of transactions (after the deal has been struck the buyer must pay for the shares and the shares must be transferred to the new owners)
- The regulation of the admission of companies to the exchange and the regulation of companies on the exchange
- The dissemination of information, e.g. trading data, prices and company announcements. Investors are more willing to trade if prompt and complete information about trades, companies and prices is available.

In recent years there has been a questioning of the need for stock exchanges to carry out all these activities. In the case of the LSE the settlement of transactions was long ago handed over to CREST (discussed later in this chapter). In 2001 the responsibility for authorising the listing of companies was transferred to the UK Listing Authority arm of the Financial Services Authority (the principal UK regulator). In 2002 the LSE's Regulatory News Service (which distributes important company announcements) was told that it will have to compete with other distribution platforms outside the LSE's control. Listed companies are now able to choose between competing providers of news dissemination platforms. Despite all this upheaval the LSE still retains an important role in the distribution of trading and pricing information. In response to some of these changes, and the threat to its position as the leading European stock exchange, from the competitive actions of other exchanges, the LSE went through a modernisation process: in 2000 it ceased to be an organisation owned by its members (a few hundred market makers, brokers and financial institutions) to become a company with shares. In 2001 it floated this company on its own Official List so anyone can now own a portion of the LSE. This move also makes mergers with other stock exchanges easier – not least, because the vested interests of the old members will not weigh so heavily in any future deal; shareholder value will be placed ahead of, say, market makers' loss of business.

Trading systems

Quote-driven systems

Following the stock market reforms known as 'Big Bang' in 1986, the LSE adopted a **quote-driven system**. At the centre of this system were about 40 market makers who posted on the computerised system called **SEAQ (Stock Exchange Automated Quotation)** the prices at which they were willing to trade shares. These competing market makers fed in two prices. The **'bid' price** is the price at which they are willing to buy. The **'offer' price** is the price at which they will sell. Thus, for Tesco, one market maker might quote the bid–offer prices of 335p–338p, while another quotes 336p–339p. The spread between the two prices represents a hoped-for return to the market maker.

The SEAQ computer gathered together the bid–offer quotes from all the market makers that make a market in that particular share. These competing quotations were then available to brokers and other financial institutions linked up to the SEAQ system. For frequently traded shares, such as those of Tesco, there were 15–20 market makers willing to 'make a book' in those shares. For an infrequently traded share there may be only two or three market makers willing to quote prices.

Exhibit 9.19 shows what a broker would see if linked up to the LSE's SEAQ system. What happens when you, as an investor, telephone your broker to buy shares is this: when you mentioned the company name the broker immediately punched into his/her computer the company code. So within a second of your mentioning your interest in the company the broker has on his/her screen all the prices that different market makers are willing to pay as well as all the prices they are willing to sell the shares for. A typical SEAQ screen is shown for the company ABC. This screen shows that nine market makers are offering prices in ABC. The fact that there are a relatively large number of competing organisations willing to quote prices indicates that ABC is a large company with a liquid secondary market in its shares. The 'bid' price is the price at which the market maker is willing to buy. So, in the case of the market maker PQR the bid price is 105p (bottom left of Exhibit 9.19). The 'offer' price is the price at which the market makers are willing to sell – PQR offers these shares at 110p. It can be confusing and time consuming for the broker to look at all the prices to find the best current rates. Fortunately he/she does not have to do this as the screen displays a

Exhibit 9.19 Typical SEAQ screen

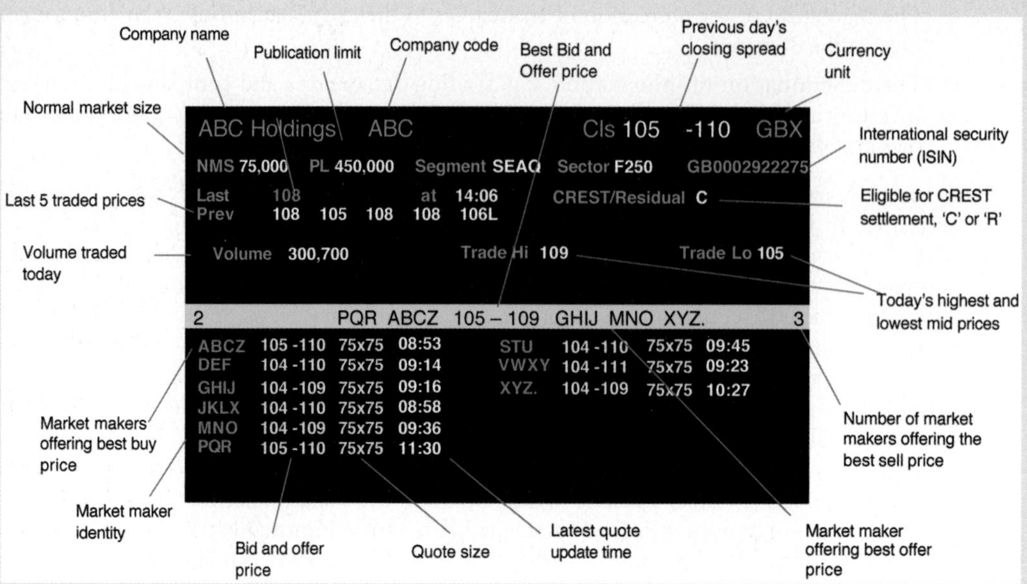

Source: Reproduced courtesy of London Stock Exchange plc.

'yellow strip' above the market makers' prices, which provides the identity of the market makers offering the best bid and offer prices (these are called **touch prices**). It is the price in the yellow strip that the broker will immediately report to you over the telephone. In the case of ABC you will be told 105–109. So, if you were happy with 109p you would then instruct your broker to buy, say, 1,000 shares.

The market makers are obliged to deal (up to a certain number of shares) at the price quoted, but they have the freedom to adjust prices after deals are completed. The investor or broker (on behalf of an investor) is able to see the best price available on their computer terminals linked up to SEAQ and is able to make a purchase or sale.

Transactions may be generally completed by the broker speaking to the market maker on the telephone but an increasing number of trades are completed electronically (through a network called Retail Service Provider). All trades are reported to the central electronic computer exchange and are disseminated to market participants (usually within three minutes) so that they are aware of the price at which recent trades were completed (*see* **Exhibit 9.20**).

The underlying logic of the quote-driven system is that through the competitive actions of numerous market makers, investors are able to buy or sell at any time at the best price. A problem arises for some very small or infrequently traded firms. Market makers are reluctant to commit capital to holding shares in such firms, and so for some there may be only one market maker's quote, for others there may be none. The LSE introduced **SETSqx** (Stock Exchange Electronic Trading Service – quotes and crosses) as a trading platform for less liquid shares. On SETSqx a single market maker's quote can be displayed if a market maker is interested in quoting price.[7] An investor wanting to trade with a market maker can do so in the normal way (as described under the SEAQ system). However, investors (usually via brokers) connected to the system can also put onto the system's screen display for that company an order for shares stating a price at which they would like to trade, either to sell or to buy – particularly useful if there are no market makers in that share. If someone else on the system likes the displayed price they can phone the originator and a deal is done. This may still leave some orders for trades unexecuted (i.e. no one phones up and trades at the advertised price). To cope with this, or to trade shares anonymously, throughout

[7] Market makers who register with the LSE that they are willing to make a market in a company's shares are obliged to offer two-way prices at all times in those shares.

Exhibit 9.20 The SEAQ quote-driven system

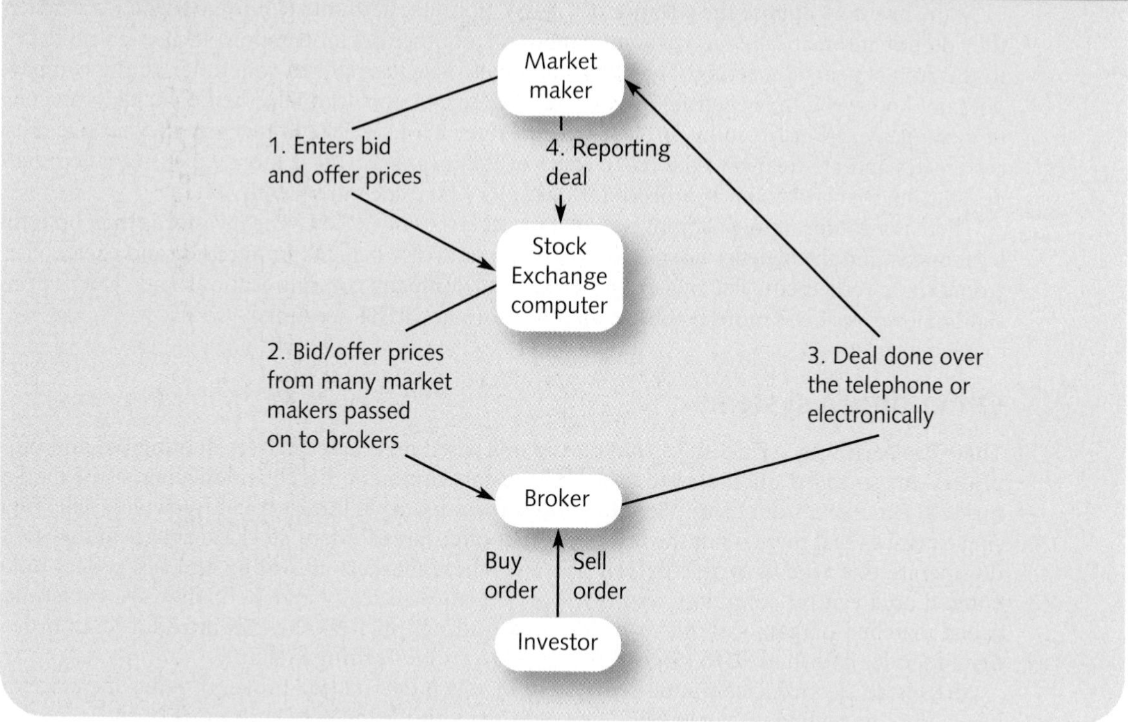

the day there are auctions in which investors make bids and the system matches up buyers and sellers.[8] The LSE transferred all the SEAQ shares to SETSqx at the end of of 2007. However, by then only the smallest of companies were left on the SEAQ system. The medium and large companies were all traded under the SETS system – see next page. With SEAQ shares now on SETSqx the typical screen for a company will show more than one market maker's prices.

When a trade has been completed and reported to the Exchange it is necessary to **clear the trade**. That is, the Exchange ensures that all reports of the trade are reconciled to make sure all parties are in agreement as to the number of shares traded and the price. The Exchange also checks that the buyer and seller have the cash and securities to do the deal. Also the company registrar is notified of the change in ownership. Later the transfer of ownership from seller to buyer has to take place: this is called **settlement**.

In 2001 the exchange moved to 'three-day rolling settlement' (Trading day +3, or T+3), which means that investors normally pay for shares three working days after the transaction date. Prior to 1996 the transfer of shares involved a tedious paper-chase between investors, brokers, company registrars, market makers and the Exchange. The new system, called **CREST** provides an electronic means of settlement and registration.

Under the CREST system shares are usually held in the name of a nominee company rather than in the name of the beneficial owner (i.e. the individual or organisation that actually bought them). Brokers and investment managers run these **nominee accounts**.

So your broker would hold your shares electronically in their nominee account and would arrange settlement through their membership of the CREST system. There might be dozens of investors with shares held by a particular nominee company. The nominee company appears as the registered owner of the shares as far as the company (say Sainsbury or BT) is concerned. Despite this, the beneficial owners will receive all dividends and the proceeds from the sale of the shares via the nominee company. One reason for this extra layer of complexity in the ownership and dealing of shares is that the nominee holdings are recorded in electronic form rather than in the form of a piece of paper (the inelegant word used for the move to electronic records is '**dematerialisation**'). Thus, if a purchase or sale takes place a quick and cheap adjustment to the

---

[8] These auctions take place at 8 a.m., 11 a.m., 3 p.m. and 4.35 p.m.

electronic record is all that is needed. Investors have no need to bother with share certificates. It is hoped that eventually one-day settlement can be achieved.

Many investors oppose the advance of CREST nominee accounts because under such a system they do not automatically receive annual reports and other documentation, such as an invitation to the annual general meeting. They also potentially lose the right to vote (after all the company does not know who the beneficial owners are). Those investors who take their ownership of a part of a company seriously can insist on remaining outside of CREST. In this way they receive share certificates and are treated as the real owners of the business. This is more expensive when share dealing, but that is not a great concern for investors who trade infrequently.

There is a compromise position: personal membership of CREST. The investor is then both the legal owner and the beneficial owner of the shares, and also benefits from rapid (and cheap) electronic share settlement. The owner will be sent all company communications and retain voting rights. However, this is more expensive than the normal CREST accounts.

Order-driven systems

There has been some criticism of trading systems based on market makers quoting bid and offer prices – the so-called 'quote-driven systems'. Investors comment that the middleman's (the market maker's) cut comes from them. Wouldn't it save them money if buyers could trade with sellers at a single price so that there is not the loss of the bid–offer spread? Many stock exchanges in the world do operate this type of **'order-driven' system**. These markets allow buy and sell orders to be entered on a central computer, and investors are automatically matched (they are sometimes called matched-bargain systems or order book trading). In 1997 the LSE introduced an order-driven service known as **SETS (Stock Exchange Electronic Trading System)**.

SETS is an electronic computerised system in which dealers (via brokers)[9] enter the prices at which they are willing to buy or sell. They can then wait for the market to move to the price they set as their limit. Alternatively they can instruct brokers to transact immediately at the best price currently available on the order book system. The LSE SETS computer does not simply act as a price-information system – as the SEAQ did – it executes the trades.

SETS derives market prices like this: Buyers and sellers enter a price limit at which they are willing to deal as well as the quantity of shares they want to trade. These prices are displayed anonymously to the entire market. An example of prices and quantities is shown in the lower half of **Exhibit 9.21** – a reproduction of a SETS screen as seen by brokers. The buy orders are shown on the left and the sell orders on the right. So, we can observe for the company ABC's shares someone (or more than one person) has entered that they are willing to buy 400 shares at a maximum price of 519p (bottom line on screen). Someone else has entered that they would like to sell 50,000 shares at a minimum price of 529p. Clearly the computer cannot match these two orders and neither of these two investors will be able to trade. They will either have to adjust their **limit prices** or to wait until the market moves in their favour.

As we travel up the screen we observe a closing of the gap between the prices buyers are willing to pay and the offering price of sellers. On the fifth line from the bottom we see that buyers want 20,000 shares at 524p whereas sellers are prepared to accept 525p for 10,000 shares. Now we are getting much closer to a match. Indeed if we look above the yellow strip we can see the price where buyers and sellers were last matched – the 'last traded price' is $524^1/_2$ p. These screens are available to market participants at all times and so they are able to judge where to pitch their price limits. For example if I was a buyer of 5,000 shares entering the market I would not be inclined to offer more than 525p given the current state of supply and demand. On the other hand if I was a seller of 5,000 shares I would recognise that the price offered would not have to fall below 524p to attract buyers. If however I was a buyer of 80,000 shares rather than just 5,000 I have two options: I could set a maximum price of 525p in which case I would transact for 10,000 immediately but would leave the other 70,000 unfilled order in the market hoping for a general market price decline; alternatively, I could set my limit at 526p in which case I could transact with those investors prepared to sell at 525p, $525^1/_2$ p and 526p. The unfilled orders of the sellers at 526p (81,900 – 80,000) are carried forward on SETS.

[9] Many brokers also offer institutional and individual investors desk-top direct market access systems allowing them to submit their own buy and sell orders – these now account for over 40 per cent of trading.

Exhibit 9.21 A SETS screen

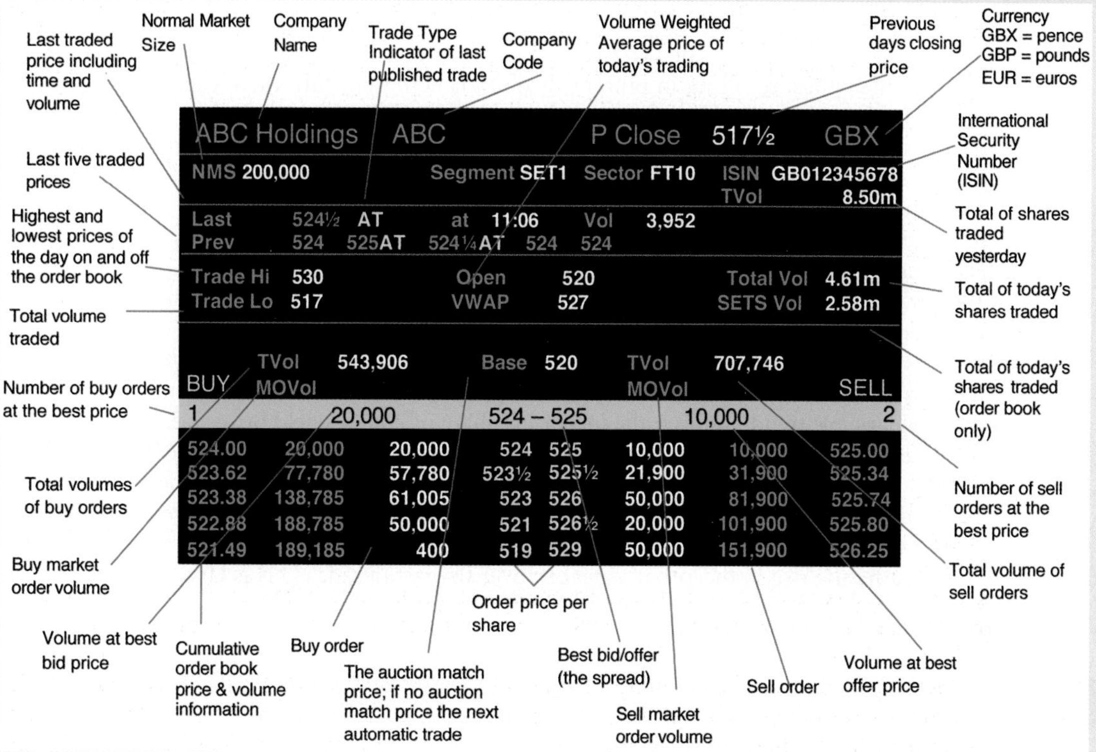

Source: Reproduced courtesy of London Stock Exchange plc.

Supporters of the quote-driven system say that a major problem with the order-driven system is that there may be few or no shares offered at prices close to a market clearing rate and so little trade can take place. In other words the market can be very illiquid. There may be times when no sellers are posting sensible prices and other times when buyers are scarce. The quote-driven system is more liquid because market makers who make a book in a company's shares continously offer prices and are obliged to trade at the price shown. By way of counter-criticism, it is alleged there have been times when it has been difficult to contact market makers on the telephone to trade at the prices they show on SEAQ – they don't pick up the telephone! So this system is not always as liquid as the market makers like to claim. In 2007 SETs was modified so that market makers can now post prices on the system.

Thus it offers a **continuous order book** with **automatic execution**, but also has market makers providing continuous bid and offer prices for many shares.[10] It is thought that by having the two systems combined there will be tighter bid–offer spreads, greater transparency of trades and improved liquidity.

Now more than one half of UK quoted shares are traded on SETS. These are the more liquid shares, leaving the smaller companies on SETSqx.

For SETS shares the London Stock Exchange has delegated clearing to the **LCH.Clearnet** and **SIS x-clear**. These competing clearers become the counter-party in every SETS transaction. They are **Central Counter-party (CCP) clearing houses**. This means that they act as the buyer to every seller and the seller to every buyer, thus guaranteeing that shares will be delivered against payment and vice versa. It also means that investors can trade anonymously. A further advantage is that investors can **'net' their trades**. So if one part of the investing institution has bought 1 million shares while another has sold 1.5 million the trades are paired so that settlement is for only 500,000 shares.

---

[10] If a market maker registers that they are willing to make a market in a SETS share they are obliged to offer two-way prices at all times.

The ownership of UK quoted shares

There has been a transformation in the pattern of share ownership in Britain over the last four decades (*see* **Exhibit 9.22**). The tax-favoured status of pension funds made them a very attractive vehicle for savings, resulting in billions of pounds being put into them each year. Most of this money used to be invested in equities, making pension funds the most influential investing group on the stock market. However, in the last decade pension funds have been taking money out of quoted shares and placing it in other investments such as bonds and venture capital. Insurance companies similarly rose in significance, increasing their share of quoted equities from 10 per cent to about one-quarter by the 1990s. The group which decreased in importance is ordinary individuals holding shares directly. They used to dominate the market, with 54 per cent of quoted shares in 1963. By the late 1980s this had declined to about 20 per cent, and has gone as low as 13 per cent.

Investors tended to switch from direct investment to collective investment vehicles. They gain benefits of diversification and skilled management by putting their savings into unit and investment trusts or into endowment and other savings schemes offered by the insurance companies. The most remarkable trend has been the increasing share of equities held by overseas investors: only 7 per cent in 1963, but 40 per cent in 2006. This increase partly reflects international mergers where the new company is listed in the UK. Also foreign companies sometimes float their UK subsidiaries but hold on to a large shareholding. It also reflects an increasing tendency of investors to buy shares in overseas markets.

Also note the rise in the 'other' category over the last decade. This is largely due to the rising importance of hedge funds and venture capital companies.

Exhibit 9.22 Share ownership of UK shares, distribution by sector (quoted shares) (%)

Sector	1963	1975	1989	1997	2006
Individuals	54	38	21	17	13
Pension funds	6	17	31	22	13
Insurance companies	10	16	19	24	15
Rest of the world	7	6	13	28	40
Unit trusts, investment trusts	–	–	7	5	4
Others – banks, public sector, other financial institutions, charities (+ unit and inv. trusts prior to 1989)	23	24	10	5	16

Source: Office for National Statistics, *Share Ownership*, 2006. Reproduced by permission of the Controller of HMSO and the Office for National Statistics. www.statistics.gov.uk.

In 1980 only three million UK individuals held shares. After the privatisation programme, which included British Gas, British Telecom and TSB, the figure rose to nine million by 1988. By 1991 the flotations of Abbey National, the water companies and regional electricity companies had taken the numbers to 11 million. The stampede of building societies to market in 1997 produced a record 16 million individual shareholders. Although the mode of investment has changed from direct to indirect, Britain remains a society with a deep interest in the stock market. Very few people are immune from the performance of the Exchange. The vast majority have a pension plan or endowment savings scheme, an individual savings account (ISA) or a unit trust investment. Some have all four.

Regulation

Financial markets need high-quality regulation in order to induce investors to place their trust in them. There must be safeguards against unscrupulous and incompetent operators. There must be an orderly operation of the markets, fair dealing and integrity. However, the regulations must not be so restrictive as to stifle innovation and prevent the markets from being competitive internationally.

London's financial markets have a unique blend of law, self-regulation and custom to regulate and supervise their members' activities. The Financial Services and Markets Act 2000 created the present structure, which puts supervisory power over a very wide range of financial service market activity in the hands of the **Financial Services Authority** (FSA). The FSA supervises all the UK's **wholesale** (large amounts) and **retail financial markets** directed at individuals – *see* **Exhibit 9.23**. With regard to the stock markets: it supervises exchanges, clearing houses and settlement houses. It also conducts market surveillance and monitors transactions on eight **Recognised Investment Exchanges** (RIEs). The recognised exchanges work with the FSA to protect investors and maintain the integrity of markets. Much of the monitoring and enforcement is delegated to the RIEs. The London Stock Exchange, LSE, for example, vets new stockbrokers and tries to ensure compliance with LSE rules, aimed at making sure members (e.g. market makers and brokers) act with the highest standards of integrity, fairness, transparency and efficiency. It monitors market makers' quotations and the price of actual trades to ensure compliance with its dealing rules. It is constantly on the lookout for patterns of trading that deviate from the norm with the aim of catching those misusing information (e.g. insider dealing), creating a false or misleading impression to the disadvantage of other investors or some other market-distorting action. The LSE in partnership with the FSA also requires companies to disseminate all information that could significantly affect their share prices.

Outside the FSA structure there are numerous ways in which the conduct of firms and financial institutions is put under scrutiny and constraint. The media keep a watchful stance – always looking to reveal stories of fraud, greed and incompetence. There is legislation prohibiting insider dealing, fraud and negligence. Companies Acts regulate the formation and conduct of companies and there are special Acts for building societies, insurance companies and unit trusts. The **Competition Commission** (CC) and the **Office of Fair Trading** (OFT) attempt to prevent abuse of market power. The **Panel on Takeovers and Mergers** determines the manner in which acquisitions are conducted for public companies (*see* Chapter 23). In addition European Union regulations are an increasing feature of corporate life. Accountants also function, to some extent, as regulators helping to ensure companies do not misrepresent their financial position. In addition any member of the public may access the accounts of any company easily and cheaply at **Companies House** (or via Companies House's website or the postal system). **The Serious Fraud Office** (SFO) investigates cases of serious or complex fraud.

Understanding the figures in the financial pages

Financial managers and investors need to be aware of what is happening on the financial markets, how their shares are affected and which measures are used as key yardsticks in evaluating a company. The financial pages of the broadsheet newspapers, particularly the *Financial Times*, provide some important statistics on company share price performance and valuation ratios. These enable comparisons to be made between companies within the same sector and across sectors. **Exhibit 9.24** shows extracts from two issues of the *Financial Times*. The information provided in the Monday edition is different from that provided on the other days of the week.

Indices

Information on individual companies in isolation is less useful than information set in the context of the firm's peer group, or in comparison with quoted companies generally. For example, if Tesco's shares fall by 1 per cent on a particular day, an investor might be keen to learn whether the market as a whole rose or fell on that day, and by how much. The *Financial Times* (FT) joined forces with the Stock Exchange (SE) to create **FTSE International** in November 1995, which has taken over the calculation (in conjunction with the Faculty and Institute of Actuaries) of a number of **equity indices**. These indicate the state of the market as a whole or selected sectors of the market and consist of 'baskets' of shares so that the value of that basket can be compared at different times. Senior managers are often highly sensitive to the relative performance of their company's share price. One reason for this is that their compensation package may be linked to the share price and in extreme circumstances managers are dismissed if they do not generate sufficiently high relative returns.

Exhibit 9.23 Financial service industry regulation

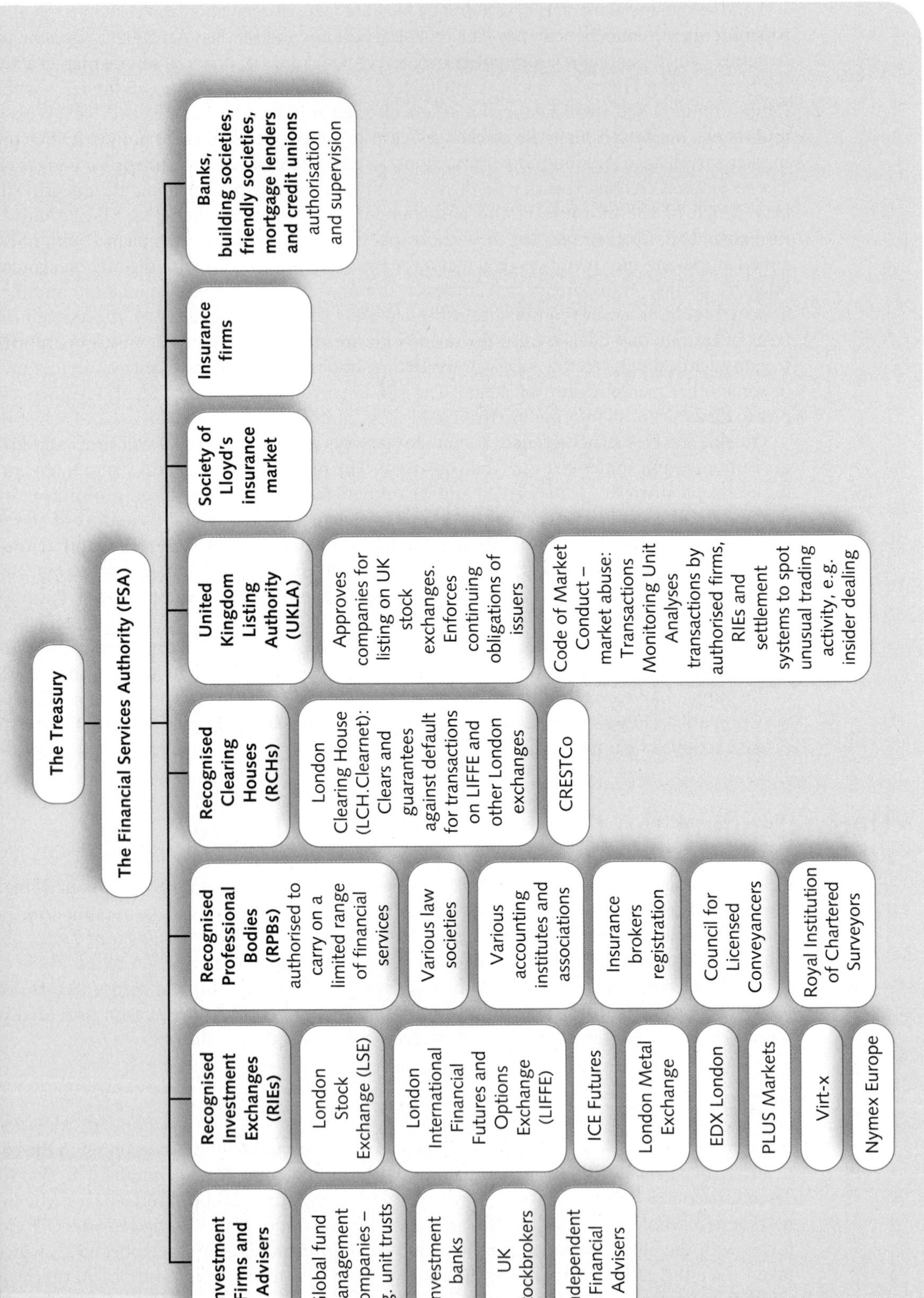
The Treasury
The Financial Services Authority (FSA)
Investment Firms and Advisers
Global fund management companies – e.g. unit trusts
Investment banks
UK stockbrokers
Independent Financial Advisers
Recognised Investment Exchanges (RIEs)
London Stock Exchange (LSE)
London International Financial Futures and Options Exchange (LIFFE)
ICE Futures
London Metal Exchange
EDX London
PLUS Markets
Virt-x
Nymex Europe
Recognised Professional Bodies (RPBs) authorised to carry on a limited range of financial services
Various law societies
Various accounting institutes and associations
Insurance brokers registration
Council for Licensed Conveyancers
Royal Institution of Chartered Surveyors
Recognised Clearing Houses (RCHs)
London Clearing House (LCH.Clearnet): Clears and guarantees against default for transactions on LIFFE and other London exchanges
CRESTCo
United Kingdom Listing Authority (UKLA)
Approves companies for listing on UK stock exchanges. Enforces continuing obligations of issuers
Code of Market Conduct – market abuse: Transactions Monitoring Unit Analyses transactions by authorised firms, RIEs and settlement systems to spot unusual trading activity, e.g. insider dealing
Society of Lloyd's insurance market
Insurance firms
Banks, building societies, friendly societies, mortgage lenders and credit unions authorisation and supervision

Exhibit 9.24 London Share Service extracts: Aerospace and Defence

Market price: *This is the mid-price (midway between the best buying and selling prices) quoted at 4.30 p.m. on the previous day.*

Change in closing price on Thursday compared with previous trading day.

The highest and lowest prices during the previous 52 weeks.

FRIDAY SEPTEMBER 7 2007

	Notes	Price	Chng	52 week High	52 week Low	Yld	P/E	Vol '000s
AEROSPACE & DEFENCE								
BAE SYS	✠†	448	+250	471.25	368.75	2.7	19.7	17,710
7¾pCvPf		170	–	221.50	110	4.6	–	15
Chemring	♣†	£19.87	+0.29	£21.66	£13.20	0.9	19.8	110
Cobham		196.25	+0.50	224.50	168	1.9	17.1	4,458
Hampson		168.25xd	+0.25	195	124	0.5	24.4	32
Meggitt	♣†	310	+3	338.25	248.47	2.4	18.6	2,089
QinetiQ		175.75	+0.25	218.50	161.25	2.1	18.7	1,075
Rolls-Ryc	†	501.50	+4	579	408.74	1.9	13.0	6,810
Thales €	♣	£27.29	+0.05	£31.81	£22.46	2.2	10.4	435
UltraElc	♣†	£11.61xd	–0.07	£12.78	972.50	1.7	20.0	325
UMECO	♣	576	+1	670	425	2.7	20.4	81
VT		579	+9.50	648	432.75	2.0	21.9	2,193

MONDAY SEPTEMBER 10 2007

	Notes	Price	W'K% Chng	Div	Div cov.	MCap £m	Last xd	City line
AEROSPACE & DEFENCE								
BAE SYS	✠†	454	–1.8	11.90	1.9	15,924.8	18.4	1890
7¾pCvPf		170	....	7.75	0	452.2	22.11	5174
Chemring	♣†	£18.90	–5.8	18.40	5.4	616.5	4.7	2116
Cobham		198	–1.5	3.75	3.1	2,246.4	30.5	2627
Hampson		168xd	–2.3	0.90	7.6	160.0	5.9	2817
Meggitt	♣†	305.50	–4	7.59	2.2	2,002.2	14.3	3331
QinetiQ		172.75	–2.9	3.65	2.6	1,141.0	1.8	3384
Rolls-Ryc	†	484.25	–5.2	9.59	4.0	8,812.2	7.3	3853
Thales €	♣	£26.99	–4.1	€0.87	2.6	5,318.1	31.5	2249
UltraElc	♣†	£11.48xd	–2.3	19.30	3.0	777.7	22.8	1363
UMECO	♣	588	+0.5	15.50	1.8	280.9	4.7	4929
VT		567	–1	11.85	2.2	993.1	20.6	4874

FT

Price/earnings ratio (PER): Share price divided by the company's earnings (profits after tax) per share in the latest twelve-month period. A much examined and talked about measure (see Chapter 20):

$$PER = \frac{\text{share price}}{\text{earnings per share}}$$

Share price change over the previous week.

The dividend paid in the company's last full year – it is the cash payment in pence per share.

Dividend yield: The gross dividend divided by the current share price expressed as a percentage:

$$\frac{\text{dividend per share}}{\text{current share price}} \times 100$$

Volume of trade in those shares that day.

Market capitalisation is calculated by multiplying the number of shares issued by their market price.

Ex-dividend date is the last date on which the share went ex-dividend (new buyers of the shares will not receive the recently announced dividend after this date, 20th June in this case.

City line: up-to-the-second share prices available by telephone (call 0906 843 0000 plus 4-digit code).

Dividend cover: Profit after tax divided by the gross dividend payment, or earnings per share divided by dividend per share:

$$\text{Dividend cover} = \frac{\text{earnings per share}}{\text{gross dividend per share}}$$

Source: The Times, 7 September 2007, and *Financial Times*, 10 September 2007. Reprinted with permission.

To calculate the indices shown in **Exhibit 9.25** each component share contributes to the index level. However, the shares do not have an equal weight in calculating the average. Rather, the average is derived by weighting each share by the size of the company; by its market capitalisation. Thus a 2 per cent movement in the share price of a large company has a greater effect on an index than a 2 per cent change in a small company's share price.[11] The characteristics of some of these indices are as follows.

- ***FTSE 100*** The 'Footsie™' index is based on the 100 largest companies (generally over £2bn market capitalisation). Large and relatively safe companies are referred to as '**blue chips**'. This index has risen six-fold since it was introduced at the beginning of 1984 at a value of 1,000. This is the measure most watched by investors. It is calculated in real time (every 15 seconds) and so changes can be observed throughout the day. The other international benchmarks are: for the USA, the **Dow Jones Industrial average (DJIA) (30 share) index**, the **Standard and Poors 500 index** and the **NASDAQ Comp.**; for the Japanese market the **Nikkei 225 index**; for France the **CAC-40**; for Hong Kong the **Hang Seng index** and for Germany the **Dax index**. For Europe as a whole there is **FTSEurofirst 300** and DJ **Euro Stoxx 50** and for the world **FTSE All World**.
- ***FTSE All-Share*** This index is the most representative in that it reflects the average movements of nearly 700 shares representing 98 per cent of the value of the London market. This index is broken down into a number of industrial and commercial sectors, so that investors and companies can use sector-specific yardsticks, such as those for mining or chemicals. Companies in the FTSE All-Share index have market capitalisations (roughly) above £40m. It is an aggregation of the FTSE 100, FTSE 250 and the FTSE SmallCap.

Exhibit 9.25 FTSE Actuaries Shares Indices

FTSE Actuaries Share Indices

Produced in conjunction with the Faculty and Institute of Actuaries

UK series

www.ft.com/equities

FT

	£ Stlg Sep 10	Day's chge%	Euro Index	£ Stlg Sep 7	£ Stlg Sep 6	Year ago	Actual yield%	Cover	P/E ratio	Xd adj. yld	Total Return
FISE 100 (100)	6134.1	−0.9	7032.0	6191.2	6313.3	5850.8	3.21	2.74	11.34	169.09	3537.83
FTSE 250 (250)	10974.18	−1.2	12581.2	11107.7	11330.8	9523.1	2.16	2.84	16.31	185.79	6046.15
FTSE 250 ex Inv Co (219)	11478.4	−1.2	13158.5	11621.0	11850.9	9927.1	2.22	2.97	15.19	198.00	6401.85
FTSE 350 (350)	3225.1	−1.0	3697.2	3256.5	3320.9	3033.2	3.06	2.75	11.88	83.70	3786.81
FTSE 350 ex Inv Co (319)	3213.9	−1.0	3684.3	3245.1	3309.1	3024.8	3.08	2.77	1174	84.00	1938.81
FTSE 350 Higher Yield (79)	3827.8	−0.6	4388.1	3850.0	3918.6	3707.8	4.12	2.19	11.08	132.93	4167.59
FTSE 350 Lower Yield (271)	2523.9	−1.4	2893.4	2559.2	2615.1	2299.8	1.91	4.06	12.88	42.27	2209.50
FTSE SmallCap (324)	3799.54	−0.7	4355.69	3827.02	3851.25	3444.49	1.90	1.96	26.93	54.84	4143.07
FTSE SmallCap ex Inv Co (224)	3641.79	0.7	4174.85	3665.92	3681.28	3350.17	2.22	2.14	21.11	60.62	4073.15
FTSE All-Share (674)	3173.22	−1.0	3637.69	3203.80	3265.70	2980.65	3.02	2.74	12.10	81.11	3775.67
FTSE All-Share ex Inv Co (543)	3156.84	−1.0	3618.92	3187.32	3249.04	2969.47	3.06	2.76	11.86	81.80	1937.31
FTSE All-Share ex Multinationals (609)	1172.36	−1.0	1113.90	1184.53	1211.82	1115.54	3.09	2.87	11.29	32.37	1508.41
FTSE Fledgling (225)	4442.92	−0.6	5093.25	4468.37	4474.22	3885.92	1.96	0.48	80.00	59.14	6287.93
FTSE Fledgling ex Inv Co (127)	5550.99	−0.6	6363.50	5585.74	5585.48	4743.95	2.20	0.01	80.00	81.65	7765.28
FTSE All Small (549)	2537.13	−0.7	2908.49	2555.00	2569.58	2289.51	1.90	1.77	29.69	36.25	3545.70
FTSE All-Small ex Inv Co (351)	2578.39	−0.7	2955.80	2595.39	2605.30	2355.55	2.22	1.95	23.14	42.44	3661.60
FTSE AIM All-Share (1176)	1104.1	−0.4	1265.8	1108.1	1109.4	1020.4	0.56	1.35	80.00	7.76	1083.03
FTSE Sector Indices											
Oil & Gas (22)	7973.42	−0.5	9140.52	8016.83	8112.63	7582.74	3.01	2.90	11.46	184.73	4807.31
Of & Gas Producers (15)	7653.80	−0.5	8774.11	7695.66	7789.86	7320.70	3.05	2.90	11.32	179.74	4752.37
Oil Equipment & Services (7)	13285.71	−0.4	15230.37	13342.17	13311.61	8831.92	0.83	4.28	28.12	93.64	7967.66
Basic Materials (21)	5934.58	−1.7	6803.25	6039.43	6252.92	4321.01	1.43	7.56	9.25	80.47	4699.45
Chemicals (7)	4645.97	−0.3	5326.02	4658.59	4700.94	3304.67	1.76	2.31	24.51	78.05	3260.37
Forestry & Paper (1)	5562.36	−0.2	6376.54	5574.11	5665.20	–	–	–	–	58.25	4432.84
Industrial Metals (0)	–	–	–	–	–	–	–	–	–	–	–
Mining (3)	18522.99	1.9	21234.25	18879.62	19596.79	13655.24	1.42	8.17	8.65	250.09	7635.39
Industrials (145)	2954.96	−1.0	3387.48	2984.96	3034.94	2497.17	2.12	2.57	18.38	43.02	2339.72

Source: *Financial Times*, 11 September 2007. Reprinted with permission.

[11] The weighting for some shares is reduced if a high proportion of the shares are held not in a free float but in the hands of people closely connected with the business, e.g. directors, major shareholders.

- ***FTSE 250*** This index is based on 250 firms which are in the next size range after the top 100. Capitalisations are generally between £250 million and £2 billion. (It is also calculated with investment trusts excluded.)
- ***FTSE 350*** This index is based on the largest 350 quoted companies. It combines the FTSE 100 and the FTSE 250. This cohort of shares is also split into two to give high and low dividend yield groups. A second 350 index excludes investment trusts.
- ***FTSE SmallCap*** This index covers companies (324 of them in September 2007) included in the FTSE All-Share but excluded from the FTSE 350, with a market capitalisation of about £40 million to £250 million.
- ***FTSE Fledgling*** This includes companies listed on the Main Market but too small to be in the FTSE All-Share Index.
- ***FTSE AIM All-Share*** Index of all AIM companies (except those with a low free float and low liquidity).
- ***FTSE All-small*** Combines companies in FTSE SmallCap with those in the FTSE Fledgling (549 companies in September 2007).

The indices in the first column in Exhibit 9.25 are price indices only (share price movements only are reflected in the indices). The final column, 'Total return', shows the overall performance with both share price rises and dividends reinvested in the portfolio.

Taxation and corporate finance

Taxation impacts on financial decisions in at least three ways.

1. ***Capital allowances*** At one time it was possible for a firm to reduce its taxable profit by up to 100 per cent of the amount invested in certain fixed assets. So if a firm made a profit of £10m, and in the same year bought £10m worth of approved plant and equipment, the Inland Revenue would not charge any tax because the capital allowance of £10m could be subtracted from the profit to calculate taxable profit. The idea behind this generosity was to encourage investment and thus stimulate economic growth. Today, the type of expenditure subject to 100 per cent capital allowances is very restricted and the capital allowance is generally 25 per cent of the value of the investment in the first year and 25 per cent on a declining balance for subsequent years.

   Capital allowances in project appraisal were discussed in Chapter 5.
2. ***Selecting type of finance*** The interest paid on borrowed capital can be used to reduce the taxable profit and thus lower the tax bill. On the other hand, payments to shareholders, such as dividends, cannot be used to reduce taxable profit. This bias against share capital may have some impact on the capital structure decision – see Chapter 21.
3. ***Distribution of profit*** Companies pay corporation tax on profits nine months after the end of the accounting period (except very large companies which pay quarterly instalments earlier than that). The profits are calculated after all costs have been deducted, including interest but excluding dividends. The proportion of taxable profit paid to the tax authorities is 28 per cent if taxable profit exceeds £1,500,000, and 21 per cent[12] where it is less than £300,000 (a sliding scale applies between £300,000 and £1.5 million).

   Standard-rate taxpayers (those with a marginal tax rate of 22 per cent on normal income) are liable to pay 10 per cent income tax on dividends. The rate of income tax on dividends for higher rate taxpayers is 32.5 per cent. The 10 per cent rate is deemed to be paid by the company when it pays corporation tax. Therefore, standard-rate taxpayers do not have to pay tax on dividends received. The higher-rate taxpayer can offset the 10 per cent tax paid against the total tax they are due to pay on dividends.

[12] This will rise to 22 per cent in 2009.

Concluding comments

Stock markets are major contributors to the well-being of a modern financially sophisticated society. They have great value to a wide variety of individuals and institutions. For savers they provide an environment in which savings can be invested in real productive assets to yield a return both to the saver and to society at large. The powerful pension and insurance funds rely on a well-regulated and broadly based stock exchange to enable the generation of income for their members. The mobilisation of savings for investment is a key benefit of a well-run exchange; so too is the improved allocation of scarce resources in society, and this results in a more satisfying mixture of goods and services being produced. The stock market has a part to play in directing investment to those parts of the economy which will generate the greatest level of utility for consumers. If people want cars rather than horse-drawn transport then savings will be directed to permit investment in factories and production lines for cars. If they demand word processors rather than typewriters then the computer firm will find it easier to raise fresh finance than will the typewriter firm.

Companies value stock markets for their capacity to absorb new issues of financial securities permitting firms to expand, innovate and produce wealth. Entrepreneurs can reap the rewards of their efforts by having access to a flourishing secondary share market and employees can be rewarded with shares which become more appealing because they can be quickly priced by examining reports in the financial press on market prices. Managers often acknowledge the disciplinary benefits of a stock market which insists on high levels of information disclosure, integrity, competence and the upholding of shareholder interests. Governments are aware of the range of social benefits listed above and so should value an exchange on these grounds alone. However, they also see more direct advantages in a fit and proper market. For example, they are able to raise finance to cover the difference between taxes and expenditure, and they are able to tap the market in privatisations and thereby not only fill government coffers but encourage wider share ownership and allow the market to pressurise managers to run previously state-owned businesses in a more efficient manner.

Having gained some background knowledge of the workings of the London Stock Exchange, we now need to turn to the question of how equity funds are actually raised on the Main Market of the LSE and on AIM. The next chapter will examine this. It will also describe sources of equity finance available to firms which are not quoted.

Key points and concepts

- **Stock exchanges** are markets where government and industry can raise long-term capital and investors can buy and sell securities.
- **Two breakthroughs in the rise of capitalism**:
  - thriving secondary markets for securities;
  - limited liability.
- **Over 100 countries now have stock markets**. They have grown in significance due to:
  - disillusionment with planned economies combined with admiration for Western and the 'tiger' economies;
  - recognition of the key role of stock markets in a liberal pro-market economic system.
- The **largest** domestic stock markets are in the USA, Japan and the UK. The **leading international equity market** is the London Stock Exchange.
- The **globalisation** of equity markets has been driven by:
  - deregulation;
  - technology;
  - institutionalisation.

- Companies **list on more than one exchange** for the following reasons:
  - to broaden the shareholder base and lower the cost of equity capital;
  - the domestic market is too small or the firm's growth is otherwise constrained;
  - to reward employees;
  - investors in particular markets may understand the firm better;
  - to raise awareness of the company;
  - to discipline the firm and learn to improve performance;
  - to understand better the economic, social and industrial changes occurring in major product markets.
- **A well-run stock exchange**:
  - allows a 'fair game' to take place;
  - is regulated to avoid negligence, fraud and other abuses;
  - allows transactions to take place cheaply;
  - has enough participants for efficient price setting and liquidity.
- **Benefits** of a well-run stock exchange:
  - firms can find funds and grow;
  - society can allocate capital better;
  - shareholders can sell speedily and cheaply. They can value their financial assets and diversify;
  - increase in status and publicity for firms;
  - mergers can be facilitated by having a quotation. The market in managerial control is assisted;
  - corporate behaviour can be improved.
- The **London Stock Exchange** regulates the trading of **equities** (domestic and international) and **debt instruments** (e.g. gilts, corporate bonds and Eurobonds, etc.) and **other financial instruments** (e.g. warrants, depositary receipts and preference shares).
- The **primary market** is where firms can raise finance by selling shares (or other securities) to investors.
- The **secondary market** is where existing securities are sold by one investor to another.
- **Internal funds** are generally the most important source of long-term capital for firms. **Bank borrowing** varies greatly and **new share or bond issues** account for a minority of the funds needed for corporate growth.
- LSE's **Main Market** is the most heavily regulated UK exchange.
- The **Alternative Investment Market (AIM)** is the lightly regulated exchange designed for small, young companies.
- **techMARK** is the sector of the Official List focused on technology-led companies. The rules for listing are different for techMARK companies than for other OL companies.
- **PLUS** provides a share trading facility for companies, less costly than the LSE.
- Stock exchanges undertake most or all of the following **tasks** to play their role in a modern society:
  - supervise trading;
  - authorise market participants (e.g. brokers, market makers);
  - assist price formation;
  - clear and settle transactions;
  - regulate the admission of companies to and companies on the exchange;
  - disseminate information.
- A **quote-driven** share trading system is one in which **market makers** quote a bid and an offer price for shares. An **order-driven** system is one in which investors' buy and sell orders are matched without the intermediation of market makers.
- The **ownership of quoted shares** has shifted from dominance by individual shareholders in the 1960s to dominance by institutions, many of which are from overseas.

- **High-quality regulation** generates confidence in the financial markets and encourages the flow of savings into investment.
- The **Financial Services Authority** is at the centre of UK financial regulation.
- **Dividend yield**:

$$\frac{\text{Gross dividend per share}}{\text{Share price}} \times 100$$

- **Price-earnings ratio (PER)**:

$$\frac{\text{Share price}}{\text{Earnings per share}}$$

- **Dividend cover**:

$$\frac{\text{Earnings per share}}{\text{Gross dividend per share}}$$

- **Taxation** impacts on financial decisions in at least three ways:
  - capital allowances;
  - selecting type of finance;
  - corporation tax.

References and further reading

Arnold, G. (2004) *The Financial Times Guide to Investing.* Harlow: FT Prentice Hall.
Contains more information on the financial markets.

Brett, M. (2003) *How to Read the Financial Pages.* 5th edn. London: Random House Business Books.
An easy to read jargon-buster. Chapter 6 is particularly relevant.

Levine, R. and Zervos, S. (1996a) 'Capital control liberalisation and stock market development', *World Bank Policy Research Working Paper* No. 1622. Washington, DC: World Bank.
Some useful data.

Levine, R. and Zervos, S. (1996b) 'Stock markets, banks and economic growth', *World Bank Policy Research Working Paper.* Washington, DC: World Bank.
Background information with a worldwide perspective.

London Stock Exchange Website.
An excellent overview of the role and activities of the LSE. Great graphics and illustrations.

Office for National Statistics (2006) *Share Ownership: A Report on Ownership of Shares as at 31st December 2006.* Norwich: HMSO.
The ONS is a great source of statistics – free on the internet.

Roberts, R. (2007) *The City: A Guide to London's Global Financial Centre.* 2nd edn. London: The Economist Newspaper/Profile Books.
An easy to read and up-to-date guide to the UK's financial sector.

Vaitilingam, R. (2006) *The Financial Times Guide to Using the Financial Pages.* 5th edn. London: FT Prentice Hall.
Excellent introduction to the mysteries of the financial pages.

Valdez, S. (2007) *An Introduction to Global Financial Markets.* 5th edn. London: Macmillan Palgrave.
Chapter 7 discusses, in an easy-to-read fashion, many of the topics covered in this chapter.

Websites

ADUFN www.adufn.com
Companies House www.companieshouse.gov.uk
CREST ww.euroclear.co.uk
Financial Services Authority www.fsa.gov.uk
Financial Times www.ft.com

FTSE International www.ftse.com
Hemmington Scott www.hemscot.com
Investors Chronicle www.investorschronicle.co.uk
London Clearing House, LCH.Clearnet www.lchclearnet.com
London Stock Exchange www.londonstockexchange.com
Morgan Stanley Capital www.MSCI.com
NASDAQ www.nasdaq.com
NYSE Euronext www.euronext.com or www.nyse.com
Office of National Statistics www.statistics.gov.uk
PLUS Markets Group www.plusmarketsgroup.com
Proshare Investment clubs www.proshareclubs.co.uk
World Federation of Exchanges www.world-exchanges.org

Video presentations

Chief executives and finance directors describe their current policy on raising funds on Cantos.com (www.cantos.com) – this is free to view.

Self-review questions

1 Name the largest (by volume of share turnover on the secondary market) share exchanges in the USA, Europe and Asia.

2 What is a depositary receipt and why are they created?

3 Explain why finance has been 'globalised' over the past 20 years.

4 What are the characteristics of, and who benefits from, a well-run exchange?

5 What securities, other than shares, are traded on the London Stock Exchange?

6 Why is a healthy secondary market good for the primary share market?

7 Explain the acronyms AIM, NASDAQ, SETS, RIE and FSA.

8 What is the most important source of long-term finance for companies generally?

9 Why has it been necessary to have more share exchanges than simply the Main Market of the London Stock Exchange in the UK?

10 Why is a nominated adviser appointed to a firm wishing to join AIM?

11 Why might you be more cautious about investing in a company listed on PLUS, than a company on the Main Market of the London Stock Exchange?

12 What is CREST?

13 What have been the main trends in UK share ownership over the past 30 years?

14 Explain the following: FTSE 100, FT All-Share, FTSE Fledgling.

Questions and problems

myfinancelab **Questions with an icon are also available for practice in MyFinanceLab with additional supporting resources.**

1 'Stock markets are capitalist exploitative devices giving no benefit to ordinary people.' Write an essay countering this argument.

2 Describe what a badly run stock exchange would be like and explain how society would be poorer as a result.

3 Many countries, for example Peru and Germany, are encouraging small investors to buy quoted shares. Why are they doing this?

4 Explain why firms obtain a share listing in countries other than their own.

5 Describe the trading systems of the London Stock Exchange and outline the advantages and disadvantages of the alternative methods of trading shares.

6 In the USA some firms have bypassed the formal stock exchanges and have sold their shares directly to investors over the internet (e.g. Spring Street Brewing). What advantages are there to this method of raising funds compared with a regulated exchange? What are the disadvantages, for firms and shareholders?

7 Discuss some of the consequences you believe might follow from the shift in UK share ownership over the past 30 years.

8 Describe the network of controls and restraints on the UK financial system to prevent fraud, abuse, negligence, etc.

9 Frame-up plc is considering a flotation on the Official List of the London Stock Exchange. The managing director has asked you to produce a 1,000-word report explaining the advantages of such a move.

10 Collasus plc is quoted on the London Stock Exchange. It is a large conglomerate with factories and sales operations in every continent. Why might Collasus wish to consider obtaining additional quotations in other countries?

11 'The City is still far too clubby and gentlemanly. They are not rigorous enough in rooting out wrongdoing. What we need is an American type of system where the government takes a lead in setting all the detailed rules of behaviour.' Consider the advantages and disadvantages of a self-regulatory system so decried by this speaker.

myfinancelab **Now retake your diagnostic test for Chapter 9 to check your progress and update your study plan.**

Assignments

1 Carry out a comparative study in your firm (or any quoted firm) using information provided by the *Financial Times*. Compare PERs, dividend yields, dividend cover and other key factors, with a peer group of firms and the stock market as a whole. Try to explain the differences.

2 If your firm has made use of the stock market for any reason, put together a report to explain the benefits gained and some estimate of the costs of membership.

CHAPTER 10

Raising equity capital

LEARNING OUTCOMES

By the end of this chapter the reader will have a firm grasp of the variety of methods of raising finance by selling shares and understand a number of the technical issues involved. More specifically the reader should be able to:

- contrast equity finance with debt and preference shares;
- explain the admission requirements and process for joining the Main Market of the London Stock Exchange and for the AIM;
- describe the nature and practicalities of rights issues, scrip issues, vendor placings, open offers and warrants;
- give an account of the options open to an unquoted firm wishing to raise external equity finance;
- explain why some firms become disillusioned with quotation, and present balanced arguments describing the pro's and con's of quotation.

myfinancelab ***Complete your diagnostic test for Chapter 10 now to create your personal study plan***

Case study 10.1 To float or not to float? ...

Some firms are keen to float on the London Stock Exchange . . .

Dunelm Mill, a very successful retailer of curtains and bedding, floated its shares in a new issue (or initial public offering, IPO) on the main market of the London Stock Exchange in 2006. 'The IPO represents the logical next step in the company's development' said Will Adderley, Chief Executive. 'It will significantly raise Dunelm's profile and will help support the business in the next stage of our growth.'[1] It was also hoped that the float would bring some free advertising and 'the discipline of being listed will make us stronger.'[2] It was Will's mother, Jean, and his father Bill who started selling curtains on Leicester market in 1979. They opened their first shop in 1984 in the same city. They now have 82 stores, but plan to move to 150 which will require a considerable amount of capital. Jean, having retired in 2001, sold a 30 per cent stake in the business on flotation to institutional investors (pocketing £103m), retaining a 7.5 per cent stake, while Bill, a non-executive director, will keep his 50 per cent in a business worth £340m.

Some firms are desperate to leave the London Stock Exchange . . .

Bernard Matthews, **Richard Branson**, **Alan Sugar**, **Andrew Lloyd Webber** and **Anita and Gordon Roddick** have demonstrated deep dissatisfaction with their companies' quotation. Mr Branson floated the Virgin Group in 1986, then bought it back in 1988. Lord Lloyd Webber bought back his Really Useful Theatre Group in 1990 four years after floating. Alan Sugar had made plain his dislike of the City and its ways, and was particularly annoyed when investors rejected his 1992 offer to buy the Amstrad group for £175m. Bernard Matthews concluded that his turkey business was paying too high a price for a quotation and so he bought back the company in 2000. Anita Roddick, co-founder of Body Shop which floated in 1984, for many years made no secret of her desire to free herself of the misunderstanding and constraints imposed by City Folk, who she once described as 'pin-striped dinosaurs'.

And some firms are content to raise equity finance without being quoted on an exchange.

Professor Steve Young, a specialist in information engineering at Cambridge University, became a millionaire by commercialising speech recognition software in the early 1990s. His project proceeded very nicely without a stock market quotation.

Initially his invention was licensed to a US company by Cambridge University. In 1995 the business was further developed by the creation of a UK company, half of which was owned by the US company. The other half was jointly held by the university, Professor Young and fellow academic Phil Woodland.

To grow further they needed 'venture money'. First, the US and UK companies combined and then the merged group took $3m from Amadeus Capital Partners (venture capitalists). By 1999, with 60 staff, the company, Entropic, was in need of more equity capital. Venture capitalists offered $20m, but here the story takes a strange twist. Young thought that it would be wise to have some of the shares bought by corporate investors. Microsoft was approached; they said they were not interested in making small corporate investments. A few weeks later, however, Microsoft telephoned and offered to buy the whole company instead. The deal is secret, but is thought to be worth tens of millions of pounds. Professor Young has returned to full-time academia a richer man and grateful for the existence of venture capital funds.

Sources: [1] *Financial Times*, 22 September 2006, p. 22. 'Dunelm founders in £120m windfall' by Philip Stafford; [2] *The Independent*, 22 September 2006, p. 52. 'Couple to cash in £120m from retail empire that grew out of market stall' by Susie Mesure; Bernard Matthews, etc.: based on *Financial Times*, 1 November 1995 and 17 May 2000; Prof. Young: based on *Financial Times*, 14 June 2001.

Introduction

There are many ways of raising money by selling shares, this chapter looks at the most important. It considers the processes that a firm would have to go through to gain a quotation on the Main Market of the London Stock Exchange (LSE) and raise fresh equity finance. We will examine the tasks and responsibilities of the various advisers and other professionals who assist a company like Dunelm to present itself to investors in a suitable fashion.

A firm wishing to become quoted may, in preference to the Main Market (Official List), choose to raise finance on the Alternative Investment Market (AIM), where the regulations and the costs are lower.

In addition to, or as an alternative to, a 'new issue' on a stock market, which usually involves raising finance by selling shares to a new group of shareholders, a company may make a rights issue, in which existing shareholders are invited to pay for new shares in proportion to their present holdings. This chapter explains the mechanics and technicalities of rights issues as well as some other methods, such as placings and open offers.

It is necessary to broaden our perspective beyond stock markets, to consider the equity finance-raising possibilities for firms which are not quoted on an exchange. There are over one million limited liability companies in the UK and only 0.2 per cent of them have shares traded on the recognised exchanges. For decades there has been a perceived financing gap for small and medium-sized firms which has to a large extent been filled by the rapidly growing venture capital/private equity industry, which has supplied share and debt capital to thousands of companies on fast-growth trajectories, such as the company established by Professor Young.

Many, if not most, companies are content to grow without the aid of either stock markets or venture capital. For example J.C. Bamford (JCB) which manufactures earth-moving machines, has built a large, export award winning company, without needing to bring in outside shareholders. This contentedness and absence of a burning desire to be quoted is reinforced by the stories which have emerged of companies which became disillusioned with being quoted. The pressures and strains of being quoted are considered by some (for example Philip Green, owner of Arcadia (Burtons, Top Shop, etc.) and BHS) to be an excessively high price to pay for access to equity finance. So to round off this chapter we examine some of the arguments advanced against gaining a quotation and contrast these with the arguments a growing company might make for joining a market.

What is equity capital?

Ordinary shares

Ordinary shares represent the equity share capital of the firm. The holders of these securities share in the rising prosperity of a company. These investors, as owners of the firm, have the right to exercise control over the company. They can vote at shareholder meetings to determine such crucial matters as the composition of the team of directors. They can also approve or disapprove of major strategic and policy issues such as the type of activities that the firm might engage in, or the decision to merge with another firm. These ordinary shareholders have a right to receive a share of dividends distributed as well as, if the worst came to the worst, a right to share in the proceeds of a liquidation sale of the firm's assets. To exercise effective control over the firm the shareholders will need information; and while management are reluctant to put large amounts of commercially sensitive information which might be useful to competitors into the public domain, they are required to make available to each shareholder a copy of the annual report.

There is no agreement between ordinary shareholders and the company that the investor will receive back the original capital invested. What ordinary shareholders receive depends on how well the company is managed. To regain invested funds an equity investor must either sell the shares to another investor (or in rare circumstances to the company – firms are now allowed to repurchase their own shares under strict conditions) or force the company into liquidation, in which case all assets are sold and the proceeds distributed. Both courses of action may leave the investor with less than originally invested. There is a high degree of discretion left to the directors in proposing an annual or semi-annual dividend, and individual shareholders are often effectively powerless to influence the income from a share – not only because of the risk attached to the trading profits which generate the resources for a dividend, but also because of the relative power of directors in a firm with a disparate or divided shareholder body.

Debt

Debt is very different from equity finance. Usually the lenders to the firm have no official control; they are unable to vote at general meetings and therefore cannot choose directors and determine major strategic issues. However, there are circumstances in which lenders have significant influence. For instance, they may insist that the company does not exceed certain liquidity or solvency ratio levels (*see* negative covenants in Chapter 11, p. 427), or they may take a charge over a particular building as security for a loan, thus restricting the directors' freedom of action over the use and disposal of that building. Debt finance also contrasts with equity finance in that it usually requires regular cash outlays in the form of interest and the repayment of the capital sum. The firm will be obliged to maintain the repayment schedule through good years and bad or face the possibility of action being taken by the lender to recover their money by forcing the firm to sell assets or liquidate.

Disadvantages of ordinary shares for investors

The main disadvantage for investors holding ordinary shares compared to other securities is that they are the last in the queue to have their claims met. When the income for the year is being distributed others, such as debt holders and preference shareholders, get paid first. If there is a surplus after that, then ordinary shareholders may receive a dividend. Also when a company is wound up, employees, tax authorities, trade creditors and lenders all come before ordinary shareholders. Given these disadvantages there must be a very attractive feature to ordinary shares to induce individuals to purchase and keep them. The attraction is that if the company does well there are no limits to the size of the claim equity shareholders have on profit. There have been numerous instances of investors placing modest sums into the shares of young firms who find themselves millionaires. For example, if you had bought $1,000 shares in Google in 1999, your holding would now be worth millions.

Advantages and disadvantages of share issues

From the company's point of view there are two significant advantages of raising finance by selling shares rather than borrowing more:

1 ***Usually there is no obligation to pay dividends*** So when losses are made the company does not have the problem of finding money for a dividend. Equity acts as a kind of shock absorber.

2 ***The capital does not have to be repaid*** Shares do not have a redemption date, that is, a date when the original sum invested is repaid to the shareholder. The requirement to repay debt capital put into the business can put a severe strain on cash flow, to the point where there is a danger of the firm not being able to survive. By always having equity capital kept in the business it again acts as a shock absorber in bad times.

There are, however, disadvantages of this form of finance.

1 ***High cost*** The cost of issuing shares is usually higher than the cost of raising the same amount of money by obtaining additional loans. There are two types of cost. First, there are the direct costs of issue such as the costs of advice from a merchant bank and/or broker, and the legal, accounting and prospectus costs, etc. These costs can absorb up to 10 to 25 per cent of the amount of money raised. Secondly, and by far the most important, there is the cost represented by the return required to satisfy shareholders, which is greater than that on safer securities such as bonds issued by the firm. Equity holders demand a greater rate of return because they recognise that investing in a firm via equity is more risky because interest on debt is paid out before dividends are paid even if that means there is nothing left to pay the shareholders a dividend. Also, if the the firm goes into liquidation, the holders of a debt type of financial security are paid back before shareholders receives anything. Thus, we say that debt holders '**rank**' higher than equity holders for annual payouts and liquidation proceeds. (*See* Chapter 19 on cost of capital).

2 ***Loss of control*** Entrepreneurs sometimes have a difficult choice to make – they need additional equity finance for the business and are unable to borrow more but dislike the notion of inviting external equity investors to buy shares. The choice is sometimes between slow/no growth or

dilution of the entrepreneurs' control. External equity providers may impose conditions such as veto rights over important business decisions and the right to appoint a number of directors. In many instances, founders take the decision to forgo expansion in order to retain control.

3 ***Dividends cannot be used to reduce taxable profit*** Dividends are paid out of after-tax earnings, whereas interest payments on loans are tax deductible. This affects the relative costs to the company of financing by issuing interest-based securities and financing through ordinary shares. When a company pays interest the tax authorities regard this as a cost of doing business and therefore it can be used to reduce the profit subject to tax. This lowers the effective cost to the firm of servicing the debt. Thus to the attractions of the low required return on debt we must add the benefit of tax deductibility. The effect of tax deductibility of interest is shown later in this chapter (in the section on preference shares).

Authorised, issued and par values

When a firm is created the original shareholders will decide the number of shares to be *authorised* (the **authorised capital**).[1] This is the maximum amount of share capital that the company can issue (unless shareholders vote to change the limit). In many cases firms do not issue up to the amount specified. For example, Green plc has authorised capital of £5m, split between £1m of preference shares and £4m of ordinary shares. The company has issued all of the preference shares (at par) but the issued ordinary share capital is only £2.5m, leaving £1.5m as **authorised but unissued ordinary share capital**. This allows the directors to issue the remaining £1.5m of capital without being required to ask shareholders for further permission (subject to the rights issue or placing rules – see later in chapter).

Shares have a **stated par value**, say 25p or 5p. This **nominal value** usually bears no relation to the price at which the shares could be sold or their subsequent value on the stock market. So let us assume Green has 10 million ordinary shares issued, each with a par value of 25p (£2.5m total nominal value divided by the nominal price per share, 25p = 10m shares); these were originally sold for £2 each, raising £20m, and the present market value is £3.80 per share.

The par value has no real significance[2] and for the most part can be ignored. However, a point of confusion can arise when one examines company accounts because issued share capital appears on the balance sheet at par value and so often seems pathetically small. This item has to be read in conjunction with the **share premium account**, which represents the difference between the price received by the company for the shares and the par value of those shares. Thus, in the case of Green the premium on each share was 200p – 25p = 175p. The total share premium in the balance sheet will be £17.5m.

Limited companies, plcs and listed companies

Limited liability means that the ordinary shareholders are only liable up to the amount they have invested or have promised to invest in purchasing shares. Lenders and other creditors are not able to turn to the ordinary shareholder should they find on a liquidation that the company, as a **separate legal 'person'**, has insufficient assets to repay them in full. This contrasts with the position for a partner in a **partnership** who will be liable for all the debts of the business to the point where personal assets such as houses and cars can be seized to be sold to pay creditors.

Private companies, with the suffix 'Limited' or '**Ltd**', are the most common form of company (over 95 per cent of all UK companies). The less numerous, but more influential, form of company is a **public limited company** (or just public companies). These firms must display the suffix '**plc**'. The private company has no minimum amount of share capital and there are restrictions on the

---

[1] Note that not all businesses are incorporated, that is, set up as a separate legal 'person' with its own constitution (memorandum and articles of association), limited liability and ability to issue shares. Many businesses are set up in an unincorporated fashion, e.g. sole trader or partnership, in which one, two or more people share risks and profits. Each partner is liable for the debts and business actions of the others, to the full extent or his/her resources.

[2] Except that it shows proportional voting and income rights.

type of purchaser who can be offered shares in the enterprise, whereas the plc has to have a minimum share capital of £50,000 but is able to offer shares to a wide range of potential investors. Not all public companies are quoted on a stock market. This can be particularly confusing when the press talks about a firm 'going public' – it may have been a public limited company for years and has merely decided to 'come to the market' to obtain a quotation. Strictly speaking, the term 'listed' should only be applied to those firms on the Official List (i.e. those accepted by the UK Listing Authority – most of which are on the Main Market of the London Stock Exchange) but the term is used rather loosely and shares on AIM are often referred to as being quoted or listed.

Preference shares

Preference shares usually offer their owners a fixed rate of dividend each year, unlike ordinary shares which offer no regular dividend. However, if the firm has insufficient profits the amount paid would be reduced, sometimes to zero. Thus, there is no guarantee that an annual income will be received, unlike with debt capital. The dividend on preference shares is paid before anything is paid out to ordinary shareholders – indeed, after the preference dividend obligation has been met there may be nothing left for ordinary shareholders. Preference shares are attractive to some investors because they offer a regular income at a higher rate of return than that available on fixed interest securities, e.g. bonds. However this higher return also comes with higher risk, as the preference dividend ranks after bond interest, and upon liquidation preference holders are further back in the queue as recipients of the proceeds of asset sell-offs.

Preference shares are part of shareholders' funds but are not equity share capital. The holders are not usually able to benefit from any extraordinarily good performance of the firm – any profits above expectations go to the ordinary shareholders. Also preference shares usually carry no voting rights, except if the dividend is in arrears or in the case of a liquidation.

Advantages to the firm of preference share capital

Preference share capital has the following advantages to the firm.

1. ***Dividend 'optional'*** Preference dividends can be omitted for one or more years. This can give the directors more flexibility and a greater chance of surviving a downturn in trading. Although there may be no legal obligation to pay a dividend every year the financial community is likely to take a dim view of a firm which missed a dividend – this may have a deleterious effect on the ordinary share price as investors become nervous and sell (dividends cannot be paid to ordinary shareholders before preference dividend arrears are cleared).
2. ***Influence over management*** Preference shares are an additional source of capital which, because they do not (usually) confer voting rights, do not dilute the influence of the ordinary shareholders on the firm's direction. Thus, a family-run or small company wishing to raise shareholder capital may do so using preference shares, thereby retaining voting control.
3. ***Extraordinary profits*** The limits placed on the return to preference shareholders mean that the ordinary shareholders receive all the extraordinary profits when the firm is doing well (unless the preference shares are 'participating' – *see* below).
4. ***Financial gearing considerations*** There are limits to safe levels of borrowing. Preference shares are an alternative, if less effective, shock absorber to ordinary shares because of the possibility of avoiding the annual cash outflow due on dividends. In some circumstances a firm may be prevented from raising finance by borrowing as this increases the risk of financial distress (*see* Chapter 21), and the shareholders may be unwilling to provide more equity risk capital. If this firm is determined to grow by raising external finance, preference shares are one option.

Disadvantages to the firm of preference share capital

Preference share capital also has disadvantages to the firm.

1 ***High cost of capital*** The higher risk attached to the annual returns and capital cause preference shareholders to demand a higher level of return than debt holders.

2 ***Dividends are not tax deductible*** Because preference shares are regarded as part of shareholders' funds the dividend is regarded as an appropriation of profits. Tax is payable on the firm's profit before the deduction of the preference dividend. In contrast, lenders are not regarded as having any ownership rights and interest has to be paid whether or not a profit is made. This cost is regarded as a legitimate expense reducing taxable profit. In recent years preference shares have become a relatively unpopular method of raising finance because bonds and bank loans, rival types of long-term finance, have this tax advantage. This is illustrated by the example of companies A and B. Both firms have raised £1m, but Company A sold bonds yielding 8 per cent, Company B sold preference shares offering a dividend yield of 8 per cent. (Here we assume the returns are identical for illustration purposes – in reality the return on preference shares might be a few percentage points higher than that on bonds.) *See* **Exhibit 10.1**.

Exhibit 10.1 Preference shares versus bonds

	Company A	Company B
Profits before tax, dividends and interest	200,000	200,000
Interest payable on bonds	80,000	0
Taxable profit	120,000	200,000
Tax payable @ 30% of taxable profit	36,000	60,000
	84,000	140,000
Preference dividend	0	80,000
Available for ordinary shareholders	84,000	60,000

Company A has a lower tax bill because its bond interest is used to reduce taxable profit, resulting in an extra £24,000 (£84,000 – £60,000) being available for the ordinary shareholders.

Types of preference shares

There are a number of variations on the theme of preference share. Here are some features which can be added:

- ***Cumulative*** If dividends are missed in any year the right to eventually receive a dividend is carried forward. These prior-year dividends have to be paid before any payout to ordinary shareholders.
- ***Participating*** As well as the fixed payment, the dividend may be increased if the company has high profits. (Usually the additional payment is a proportion of any ordinary dividend declared.)
- ***Redeemable*** These have a finite life, at the end of which the initial capital investment will be repaid. Irredeemables have no fixed redemption date.
- ***Convertibles*** These can be converted at the holder's request into ordinary shares at specific dates and on pre-set terms (for example, one ordinary share for every two preference shares). These shares often carry a lower yield (dividend as a proportion of share price) since there is the attraction of a potentially large capital gain.
- ***Variable rate*** A variable dividend is paid. The rate may be linked to general interest rates, e.g. LIBOR (*see* Chapter 11) or to some other variable factor.

Some unusual types of shares

In addition to ordinary shares and preference shares there are other, more unusual, types of shares.

1 **Non-voting shares** or **reduced voting shares** are sometimes issued by family-controlled firms which need additional equity finance but wish to avoid the diluting effects of an ordinary share issue. These shares are often called **'A' shares** or **'B' shares** (or N/V) and usually get the same dividends, and the same share of assets in a liquidation, as the ordinary shares. The issue of non-voting or reduced voting shares is contentious, with many in the City saying that everyone who puts equity into a company should have a vote on how that money is spent: the 'one share one vote' principle. On the other hand, investors can buy 'non-voters' for less than 'voters' and thereby gain a higher dividend yield. Also, without the possibility of issuing non-voting shares, many companies would simply prefer to forgo expansion. Around one-third of Europe's largest businesses fail to observe the one share one vote principle. The Ford family own a mere 3.75 per cent of the shares. However, when the motor company joined the NYSE in 1956 the family's shares were converted into a special class that guaranteed 40 per cent of the voting power, no matter how many ordinary shares are in issue. When Google floated in 2004 Larry Page and Sergey Brin, the founders, held 'B' shares each with ten times as many votes per share as the 'A' shares issued to other investors. In the UK there are few companies with reduced voting rights.

2 **Deferred ordinary shares** rank lower than **ordinary shares** for an agreed rate of dividend, so in a poor year the ordinary holders might get their payment while deferred ordinary holders receive nothing. **Preferred ordinary shares** usually rank ahead of ordinary shares for both income and capital. Many have a right to a fixed dividend or share of profits. They carry votes and are different from preference shares.

3 **Golden shares** are shares with extraordinary special powers, for example the right to block a takeover. The UK government holds golden shares in a number of privatised firms, e.g. BAE Systems and Rolls Royce. Golden shares are also useful if a company wishes to preserve certain characteristics it possesses (*see* **Exhibit 10.2**).

Exhibit 10.2

Golden share will corner Nottingham Forest buyer

FT

The owners of Nottingham Forest, the cash-strapped Premiership football club which has put itself up for sale, will retain a golden share after the club has been acquired by one of three potential buyers.

The golden share, which will be unique in football, will place tight restrictions on Forest's ultimate buyer. The most significant dictates that 80 per cent of revenues from transfer fees must be reinvested in new players.

This is aimed at deterring the club from selling players to get out of financial trouble.

The new owners will also be prevented from selling the club for five years, and will not be allowed to change the name or the colour of the team's red shirts.

If the new owners breach any of the rules, control of the club will automatically revert to Forest's current shareholders.

Mr Lance Darlaston, Forest's financial controller, said the golden share was designed to protect the integrity and traditions of the 131-year-old club.

'This reflects the fact that our structure is based upon a private club, with 209 shareholders owning one share each. The golden share is being put into the memorandum of the articles of association to protect those rights against abuse,' he says.

Source: Patrick Haverson, *Financial Times*, 25 November 1996, p. 23. Reprinted with permission.

Floating on the Main Market (Official List)

To 'go public' and become a listed company is a major step for a firm. The substantial sums of money involved can lead to a new, accelerated phase of business growth. Obtaining a quotation is not a step to be taken lightly; it is a major legal undertaking. The **United Kingdom Listing Authority, UKLA** (part of the Financial Services Authority)[3] rigorously enforces a set of demanding rules and the directors will be put under the strain of new and greater responsibilities both at the time of flotation and in subsequent years. As the example of RHM shows (*see* **Exhibit 10.3**), new issues can produce a greater availability of equity finance to fund expansion and development programmes. It may also allow existing shareholders to realise a proportion of their investment and for employees to be rewarded through share reward schemes. In addition it can 'raise the profile' of a company both in the financial world and in its product markets, which may give it a competitive edge.

Exhibit 10.3

Flotation price of 275p set for RHM

FT

By Maggie Urry

The flotation price of RHM, the food group whose brands include Hovis, Mr Kipling, Sharwoods and Bisto, was set at 275p yesterday. The closing price valued the company at slightly more than £lbn.

The offer raised £475m gross for RHM and £118m for Doughty Hanson, the private equity group.

Ian McMahon, chief executive, sold 500,000 shares in the offer and is set to receive £1.38m while retaining 2m shares worth £5.85m at yesterday's close. Andrew Allner, finance director, sold 200,000 shares for £550,000 and has kept 800,000, worth £2.34m. Paul Wilkinson, who retired as chief executive early in 2003, sold his entire 1.88m shareholding in the sale, worth £5.16m.

Source: Financial Times, 20 July 2005, p. 22. Reprinted with permission.

Prospectus

To create a stable market and encourage investors to place their money with companies the UKLA tries to minimise the risk of investing by ensuring that the firms which obtain a quotation abide by high standards and conform to strict rules. For example the directors are required to prepare a detailed **prospectus** ('**Listing Particulars**') to inform potential shareholders about the company. This may contain far more information about the firm than it has previously dared to put into the public domain. Even without the stringent conditions laid down by the UKLA the firm has an interest in producing a stylish and informative prospectus. A successful flotation can depend on the prospectus acting as a marketing tool as the firm attempts to persuade investors to apply for shares.

The content and accuracy of this vital document is the responsibility of the directors. Contained within it must be three years of audited accounts, details of indebtedness and a statement as to the adequacy of working capital. Statements by experts are often required: valuers may be needed to confirm the current value of property, engineers may be needed to state the viability of processes or machinery and accountants may be needed to comment on the profit figures. All major contracts entered into in the past two years will have to be detailed and a description of the risks facing the firm provided. Any persons with a shareholding of more than 3 per cent have to be

[3] Responsibility for governing admission to listing, the continuing obligations of issuers, the enforcement of those obligations and suspension and cancellation of listing was transferred from the LSE to the UKLA in 2000. However, companies also need to be admitted to trading by the Exchange.

named. A mass of operational data is required, ranging from an analysis of sales by geographic area and category of activity, to information on research and development and significant investments in other companies.

The **Listing Rules** state that the expected market value of the company's shares is to be at least £700,000 to allow for sufficient dealings to take place. However, this is an absurdly small number in this day and age. Given that the cost of advisers to the new issue will be at least £500,000 it is rarely worth floating on the Main Market unless the market capitalisation is at least £10m.

Conditions and responsibilities imposed

All companies obtaining a full listing must ensure that at least 25 per cent of their share capital is in public hands, to ensure that the shares are capable of being traded actively on the market. If a reasonably active secondary market is not established, trading may become stultified and the shares may become illiquid. 'Public' means people or organisations not associated with the directors or major shareholders.

Directors may find their room for discretion restricted when it comes to paying dividends. Stock market investors, particularly the major institutions, tend to demand regular dividends. Not only do they usually favour consistent cash flow, they also use dividend policy as a kind of barometer of corporate health (*see* Chapter 22). This can lead to pressure to maintain a growing dividend flow, which the unquoted firm may not experience.

There is also a loss of some privacy and autonomy, e.g. greater disclosure of directors' salaries and other remuneration, responding to the demands of a wider range of shareholders.

There are strict rules concerning the buying and selling of the company's shares by its own directors. The Criminal Justice Act 1993 and the **Model Code for Director Dealings** have to be followed. Directors are prevented from dealing for a minimum period (normally two months) prior to an announcement of regularly recurring information such as annual results. They are also forbidden to deal before the announcement of matters of an exceptional nature involving unpublished information which is potentially price sensitive. These rules apply to any employee in possession of such information. When directors do buy or sell shares in their company they are required to disclose these dealings publicly.[4]

Suitability

The UKLA tries to ensure that the 'quality of the company' is sufficiently high to appeal to the investment community. The management team must have the necessary range and depth, and there must be a high degree of continuity and stability of management over recent years. Investors do not like to be over-reliant on the talents of one individual and so will expect a team of able directors and managers, and – preferably – a separation of the roles of chief executive and chairman. They also expect to see an appropriately qualified finance director.

The UKLA usually insists that a company has a track record (in the form of accounting figures) stretching back at least three years. However this requirement has been relaxed for scientific research-based companies and companies undertaking major capital projects. In the case of scientific research-based companies there is the requirement that they have been conducting their activity for three years even if no revenue was produced. Some major project companies, for example Eurotunnel, have been allowed to join the market despite an absence of a trading activity or a profit record. Companies can be admitted to the techMARK, part of the Official List, with only one year of accounts.

Another suitability factor is the timing of the flotation. Investors often desire stability, a reasonable spread of activities and evidence of potential growth in the core business. If the underlying product market served by the firm is going through a turbulent period it may be wise to delay the flotation until investors can be reassured about the long-run viability.

---

[4] This disclosure rule applies to the buying and selling of financial instruments that derive their value from share price movements such as contracts for difference (see *The Financial Times Guide to Investing* (Arnold (2004)) for a description).

Other suitability factors are a healthy balance sheet, sufficient working capital, good financial control mechanisms and clear accounting policies.

The issuing process

The issuing process involves a number of specialist advisers (discussed below). The process is summarised in **Exhibit 10.4**.

The sponsor

Given the vast range of matters that directors have to consider in order to gain a place on LSE's Official List (the 'main market') it is clear that experts are going to be required to guide firms through the complexities. The key adviser in a flotation is the **sponsor**. This may be an investment bank, stockbroker or other professional adviser. Directors, particularly of small companies, often first seek advice from their existing professional advisers, for example accountants and lawyers. These may have the necessary expertise (and approval of the UKLA – see www.fsa.gov.uk/ukla for a list of approved sponsors) themselves to act for the company in the flotation or may be able to recommend a more suitable sponsor. Sponsors have to be chosen with care as the relationship is likely to be one which continues long after the flotation. For large or particularly complex issues investment banks are employed, although experienced stockbrokers have been used. The UKLA requires sponsors to certify that a company has complied with all the regulatory requirements and to ensure that all necessary documentation is filed on time.

The sponsor (sometimes called the **issuing house**) will first examine the company and the aspirations of the management team to assess whether flotation is an appropriate corporate objective by taking into account its structure, strategy and capital needs. The sponsor will also comment on the composition of the board and the calibre of the directors. The sponsor may even recommend supplementation with additional directors if the existing team do not come up to the quality expected. Sponsors can be quite forceful in this because they do not want to damage their reputation by bringing a poorly managed company to market. The sponsor will draw up a timetable, which can be lengthy – sometimes the planning period for a successful flotation may extend over two years. There are various methods of floating, ranging from a placing to an offer for sale (discussed later) and the sponsor will advise on the most appropriate. Another important function is to help draft the prospectus and provide input to the marketing strategy. Throughout the process of flotation there will be many other professional advisers involved and it is vital that their activities mesh into a coherent whole. It is the sponsor's responsibility to co-ordinate the activities of all the other professional advisers.

Paying underwriters

Shortly before the flotation the sponsor will have the task of advising on the best price to ask for the shares, and, at the time of flotation, the sponsor will usually underwrite the issue. Most new issues are underwritten, because the correct pricing of a new issue of shares is extremely difficult. If the price is set too high, demand will be less than supply and not all the shares will be bought. The company is usually keen to have certainty that it will receive money from the issue so that it can plan ahead. To make sure it sells the shares it buys a kind of insurance called underwriting. In return for a fee the underwriter guarantees to buy the proportion of the issue not taken up by the market. An investment bank sponsoring the issue will usually charge a fee of 2–4 per cent of the issue proceeds and then pays part of that fee, say 1.25–3.0 per cent of the issue proceeds, to sub-underwriters (usually large financial institutions such as pension funds and banks) who each agree to buy a certain number of shares if called on to do so. In most cases the **underwriters** do not have to purchase any shares because the general public are keen to take them up. However, occasionally they receive a shock and have to buy large quantities. As well as co-ordinating the UKLA's listing process the sponsor will apply to the Exchange to have the company's securities admitted to trading on its markets. The LSE has its own set of admission and disclosure standards which are designed to sit alongside the UKLA's Listing Rules.

Exhibit 10.4 The issuing process for the Main Market (Official List)

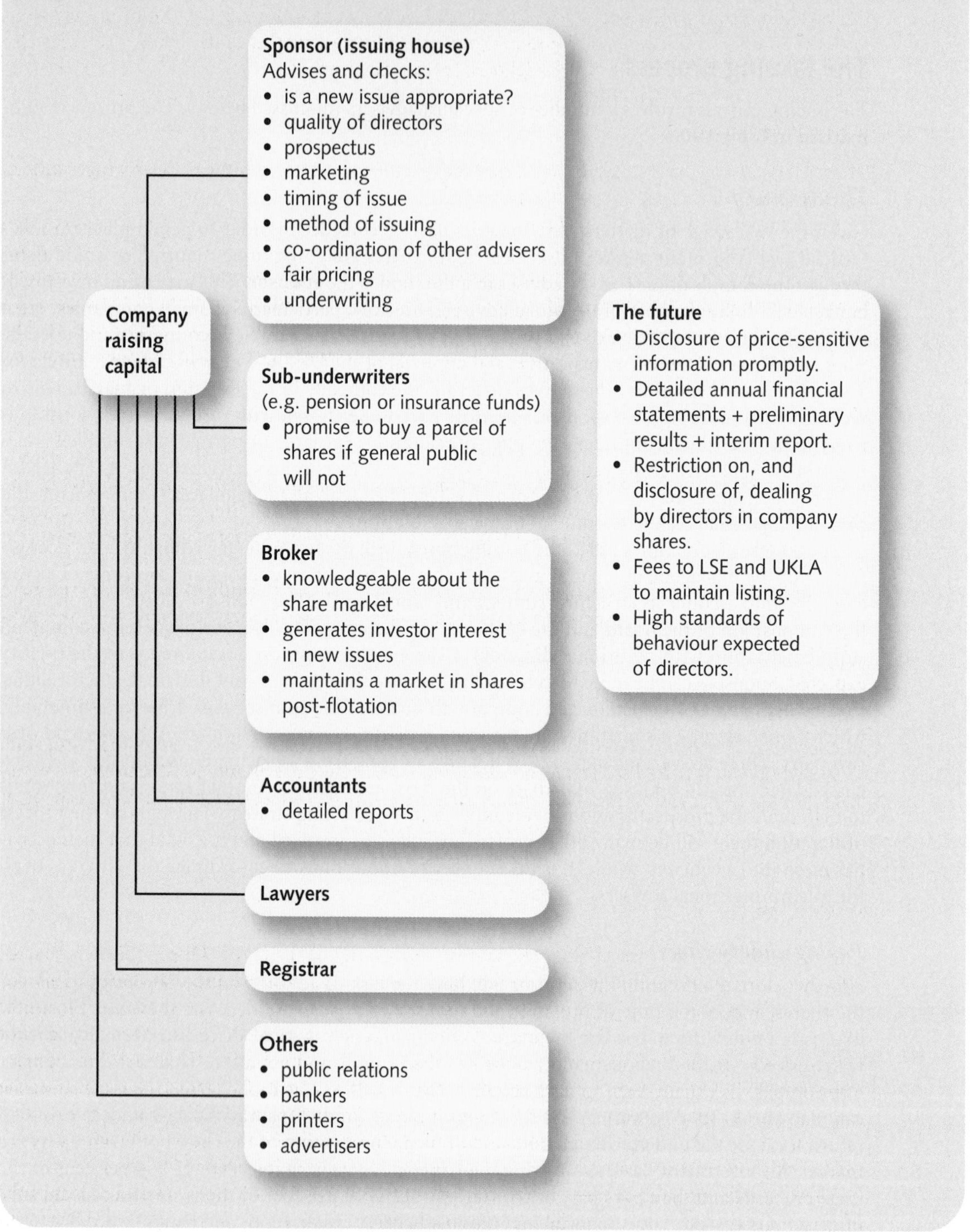

Company raising capital
Sponsor (issuing house)
Advises and checks:
• is a new issue appropriate?
• quality of directors
• prospectus
• marketing
• timing of issue
• method of issuing
• co-ordination of other advisers
• fair pricing
• underwriting
Sub-underwriters
(e.g. pension or insurance funds)
• promise to buy a parcel of shares if general public will not
Broker
• knowledgeable about the share market
• generates investor interest in new issues
• maintains a market in shares post-flotation
Accountants
• detailed reports
Lawyers
Registrar
Others
• public relations
• bankers
• printers
• advertisers
The future
• Disclosure of price-sensitive information promptly.
• Detailed annual financial statements + preliminary results + interim report.
• Restriction on, and disclosure of, dealing by directors in company shares.
• Fees to LSE and UKLA to maintain listing.
• High standards of behaviour expected of directors.

The corporate broker

When a **broker** is employed as a sponsor the two roles can be combined. If the sponsor is, say, an investment bank the UKLA requires that a broker is also appointed. However, most investment banks also have corporate broking arms and so can take on both roles. Brokers play a vital role in advising on share market conditions and the likely demand from investors for the company's shares. They also represent the company to investors to try to generate interest. When debating issues such as the method to be employed, the marketing strategy, the size of the issue, the timing or the pricing of the shares the company may value the market knowledge the broker has to offer. Brokers can also organise sub-underwriting and in the years following the flotation may work with the company to maintain a liquid and properly informed market in its shares. They may also help raise additional money through rights issues, for example.

Accountant

The **reporting accountant** in a flotation has to be different from the company's existing auditors, but can be a separate team in the same firm.

The accountant will be asked by the sponsor to prepare a detailed report on the firm's financial controls, track record, financing and forecasts (the **'long form' report**). Not all of this information will be included in the prospectus but it does serve to reassure the sponsor that the company is suitable for flotation. Accountants may also have a role in tax planning from both the company's viewpoint and that of its shareholders. They also investigate working capital requirements. The UKLA insists that companies show that they have enough working capital for current needs and for at least the next 12 months.

Lawyers

All legal requirements in the flotation preparation and in the information displayed in the prospectus must be complied with. Examples of other legal issues are directors' contracts, changes to the articles of association, re-registering the company as a plc, underwriting agreements and share option schemes.

Lawyers also prepare the 'verification' questions which are used to confirm that every statement in the prospectus can be justified as fact. Directors bear the ultimate responsibility for the truthfulness of the documents.

Registrars

The record on the ownership of shares is maintained by **registrars** as shares are bought and sold. They keep the company's register and issue certificates. There are about two dozen major registrars linked up to CREST through which they are required to electronically adjust records of ownership of company shares within two hours of a trade.

After flotation

The UKLA insists on listed companies having '**continuing obligations**'. One of these is that all **price-sensitive information** is given to the market as soon as possible and that there is 'full and accurate disclosure' to all investors at the same time. Information is price sensitive if it might influence the share price or the trading in the shares. Investors need to be sure that they are not disadvantaged by market distortions caused by some participants having the benefit of superior information. Public announcements will be required in a number of instances, for example: the development of major new products; the signing of major contracts; details of an acquisition; a sale of large assets; a change in directors or a decision to pay a dividend. The website www.investegate.co.uk shows all major announcements made by companies going back many years.

Listed companies are also required to provide detailed financial statements within six months of the year-end. Firms usually choose to make **preliminary profit announcements** based on unaudited results for the year a few weeks before the audited results are published. **Interim reports** for the first half of each accounting year are also required (within four months of the end of the half-year). The penalty for non-compliance is suspension from the Exchange.

Other ongoing obligations include the need to inform the market about director dealings in the company's shares. The UKLA and the Exchange also encourage high standards of corporate governance, some of which are contained in the Combined Code on Corporate Goverance (*see* Chapter 1). While these standards of behaviour are encouraged they are not required by the UKLA. However, if a company does not comply it must explain why not in the annual reports.

New issue statistics

The number of companies joining the Main Market and AIM varies greatly from one year to the next. But as **Exhibit 10.5** shows, the numbers are large and have not fallen below 175 per annum. Note that the AIM now attracts far more companies than the Main Market. The average amount raised by new issues is generally in the range £60m to £100m for the Main Market companies. For AIM the range used to be around £3–£10m but recently it has climbed significantly.

Methods of issue

The sponsor will look at the motives for wanting a quotation, at the amount of money that is to be raised, at the history and reputation of the firm and will then advise on the best method of issuing the shares. There are various methods, ranging from a full-scale offer for sale to a relatively simple introduction. The final choice often rests on the costs of issue, which can vary considerably. Here are the main options:

Offer for sale

The company sponsor offers shares to the public by inviting subscriptions from institutional and individual investors. Sometimes newspapers carry a notice and an application form. However, most investors will need to contact the sponsor or the broker to obtain an application form. Publications such as *Investors Chronicle* show the telephone numbers to call for each company floating. Also details of forthcoming flotations are available at www.londonstockexchange.com, and www.hemscot.com. Normally the shares are offered at a fixed price determined by the company's directors and their financial advisers. A variation of this method is an **offer for sale by tender**. Here investors are invited to state a price at which they are willing to buy (above a minimum reserve price). The sponsor gathers the applications and then selects a price which will dispose of all the shares – the strike price. Investors bidding a price above this will be allocated shares at the strike price – not at the price of their bid. Those who bid below the strike price will not receive any shares. This method is useful in situations where it is very difficult to value a company, for instance, where there is no comparable company already listed or where the level of demand may be difficult to assess. Leaving the pricing to the public may result in a larger sum being raised. On the other hand it is more costly to administer and many investors will be put off by being handed the onerous task of estimating the share's value. (This happened in the case of Google.com in 2004 which received fewer applications than expected in a type of auction system.)

Exhibit 10.5 Equity finance raised by UK companies through the new issue market, 2000–2007

Year	Main Market number	Main Market money raised (£m)	Main Market average (£m)	AIM number	AIM money raised (£m)	AIM average (£m)
2000	172	11,399	66	265	1,754	6.6
2001	113	6,922	61	162	593	3.7
2002	59	5,082	86	147	490	3.3
2003	32	2,445	76	146	1,095	7.5
2004	55	3,431	59	294	2,776	9.4
2005	84	5,966	71	399	8,942	22.4
2006	77	8,415	109	338	15,678	46.4
2007	73	7,613	104	197	16,184	82.2

Source: *London Stock Exchange*: www.londonstockexchange.com. Reproduced courtesy of London Stock Exchange plc.

Introduction

Introductions do not raise any new money for the company. If the company's shares are already quoted on another stock exchange or there is a wide spread of shareholders, with more than 25 per cent of the shares in public hands, the Exchange permits a company to be 'introduced' to the market. This method may allow companies trading on AIM to move up to the Main Market or for foreign corporations to gain a London listing. This is the cheapest method of flotation since there are no underwriting costs and relatively small advertising expenditures. When Carlton and Granada came together to form ITV plc in 2003 they were permitted to float the new company by way of an introduction as both component companies already had a wide spread of investors and these people merely swapped their old shares for shares issued by ITV plc.

Offer for subscription

An **offer for subscription** is similar to an offer for sale, but it is only partially underwritten or not underwritten at all. This method is used by new companies which state at the outset that if the share issue does not raise a certain minimum the offer will be aborted. This is a particularly popular method for new investment trusts – if the fund managers do not raise enough to create a large investment company which will be able to pay them large ongoing management fees, then they abandon the whole idea (*see* Chapter 1 for a description of investment trusts).

Placing

In a **placing**, shares are offered to the public but the term 'public' is narrowly defined. Instead of engaging in advertising to the population at large, the sponsor or broker handling the issue sells the shares to institutions it is in contact with, such as pension and insurance funds. The costs of this method are considerably lower than those of an offer for sale. There are lower publicity costs and legal costs. A drawback of this method is that the spread of shareholders is going to be more limited. To alleviate this problem the Stock Exchange does insist on a large number of placees holding shares after the new issue.

In the 1980s the most frequently used method of new issue was the offer for sale. This ensured a wide spread of share ownership and thus a more liquid secondary market. It also permitted all investors to participate in new issues. Placings were only permitted for small offerings (< £15m) when the costs of an offer for sale would have been prohibitive. Today any size of new issue can be placed. As this method is much cheaper and easier than an offer for sale, companies have naturally switched to placings so there are now few offers for sale.

Intermediaries offer

Another method which is often combined with a placing is an **intermediaries offer**. Here the shares are offered for sale to financial institutions such as stockbrokers. Clients of these intermediaries can then apply to buy shares from them.

Reverse takeover

Sometimes a larger unquoted company makes a deal with a smaller quoted company whereby the smaller company 'takes over' the larger firm by swapping newly created shares in itself for the shares in the unquoted firm currently held by its owners. Because the quoted firm creates and issues more new shares itself than it had to start with the unquoted firm's shareholders end up with the majority of the shares in the newly merged entity. They therefore now control a quoted company. The only task remaining is to decide on a name for the company – frequently the name of the previously unquoted company is chosen. A reverse takeover is a way for a company to gain a listing/quotation without the hassle of an official new issue.

Eddie Stobart gained a quotation through a reverse takeover (see **Exhibit 10.6**).

Exhibit 10.6

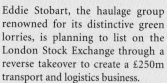

Eddie Stobart drives on to LSE

Business agrees to reverse takeover

Westbury link-up to form £250m group

By Chris Bryant

Eddie Stobart, the haulage group renowned for its distinctive green lorries, is planning to list on the London Stock Exchange through a reverse takeover to create a £250m transport and logistics business.

The group has agreed to be acquired by Westbury Property Fund, the listed commercial property, port and rail operator for £137.7m in cash and shares, continuing a trend towards consolidation and scale in the logistics industry.

The merged entity, called Stobart Group, will combine Eddie Stobart's 900-vehicle haulage fleet with Westbury's port and rail assets, to create a transport and logistics business with net assets of more than £250m. It also plans to acquire O'Connor, a rail freight handling business.

William Stobart, a son of the founder, who owns 27 per cent of the group and Andrew Tinker, who owns the other 73 per cent, together expect to hold 28.5 per cent of the enlarged group in the same proportions and would respectively become chief executive and chief operating officer.

They also intend to acquire Westbury's commercial property portfolio through WADI Properties, a separate wholly owned company, for £142m in cash and assumed debt, completing what is in effect an asset swap.

Source: Financial Times, 16 August 2007, p. 16. Reprinted with permission.

Book-building

Selling new issues of shares through **book-building** is a popular technique in the USA. It is starting to catch on in Europe as **Exhibit 10.7** demonstrates. Under this method the financial advisers to an issue contact major institutional investors to get from them bids for the shares over a period of eight to ten working days. The investors' orders are sorted according to price, quantity and other factors such as 'firmness' of bid (e.g. a '**strike bid**' means the investor will buy a given number of shares within the initial price range; leaving it to others to set the price, a '**limit bid**' means the investor would buy a particular quantity at a particular price). These data may then be used to establish a price for the issue and the allocation of shares.

Failure to float

Severe disruption can result if a company which planned to gain a quotation finds that circumstance forces the new issue to be scrapped. In the article 'Back to the start' (*see* **Exhibit 10.8**), it can be seen that one effect of an aborted float is the demoralisation of employees who had anticipated a rise in future monetary compensation through share options to supplement their income as well as an outlet for their stored wealth in the company's shares. Growth plans often have to be cut back and venture capital backers are annoyed at not having an easy exit route.

Timetable for a new issue (initial public offering, IPO)

The various stages of a new share issue will be explained using the example of the flotation of Sports Direct on the main market in 2007. This timetable is set out in **Exhibit 10.9**.

Exhibit 10.7

Booking the bids in the power sale

FT

This morning at 8.30 precisely, a small room on the second floor of a City office building will erupt in a flurry of activity as the international sale of the government's remaining 40 per cent stake in the UK's two big power generators – National Power and PowerGen – kicks off.

The 'book-building room' – the nerve centre of the operation – resembles the bridge of the Starship Enterprise, with a wall of computer screens displaying colour graphics that chart the progress of the sale by the minute. Thick blinds shield the action from inquisitive eyes.

Share orders from institutional investors across the globe will arrive here over the next week, indicating how much money they are prepared to invest at specific prices. The book-building period for the £4bn sale, one of Europe's largest privatisations this year, ends on March 3 at 5pm. The international offer price and allocation will be agreed over the weekend, and trading in the partly-paid shares begins on March 6.

Book-building, which has been used in previous UK privatisations, allows the Treasury to compile a comprehensive picture of the strength of institutional demand for the shares over a range of prices. The aim is to ensure that the shares will be spread across a wide range of high-quality investors.

The share offer, totalling about £4bn, is structured in two parts: a UK public offer, targeted at UK retail investors, and two separate international tender offers (one for shares in National Power and one for shares in PowerGen) aimed at institutional investors in the UK and around the world.

Roadshows for the international offer began last week, with both companies conducting separate roadshows in financial centres throughout Europe and the US.

The offers are being marketed through a syndicate of 17 investment banks with BZW and Kleinwort Benson acting as joint global co-ordinators and bookrunners.

The book-building process starts in the 'inputting room', where nine fax machines spew out forms detailing investors' orders. These show: how many shares in each company investors are willing to buy at what price, how much they would pay for a combination of shares in both at a ratio determined by the Treasury ('sector bid'), and whether the bid is firm or indicative.

The price and quality of investors' bids is crucial as it affects their final allocation. The Treasury will favour bids by investors considered to be likely buyers or holders of shares in the aftermarket; bids made at an early stage of the offer period; firm bids; bids at specific price levels (rather than market-relative or strike-price bids); and sector bids.

All the information is entered into a computer system by one of 15 input clerks and transmitted to the book-building room, where 24 screens throw up an instant graphic analysis of the data, highlighting strengths and weaknesses of distribution as the sale proceeds.

One monitor might show the build-up in demand for both companies over time. Another illustrates the value of demand at any given price. A pie chart represents the value of demand by country, and a bar chart shows it by syndicate member.

Yet another breaks down the orders into six different categories of investor quality, ranging from very serious, long-term investors to highly speculative accounts looking to play the deal over the very short term.

Source: Conner Middelmann, *Financial Times*, 21 February 1995. Reprinted with permission.

Exhibit 10.8

Back to the start

FT

Private companies in the UK are having a miserable time trying to float. Business owners are not only having to swallow the disappointment of lower valuations, but in some cases the abandonment of planned share sales.

Given the market's recent unpredictability most private company shareholders will recognise that a flotation can be 'pulled' easily. Nevertheless, those who have done it say the disappointment has to be addressed early after a decision to postpone or cancel has been taken.

'We addressed all the issues in advance,' says John Hannah, managing director of New Look, the west of England-based retailer that has opened more than 250 shops in the last 25 years. 'We consider the motivation and aspirations of all our staff to make sure morale is maintained.'

The contingency plan New Look developed gave senior executives a profits-related bonus scheme to replace the share options they would have received on flotation.

Exhibit 10.8 continued

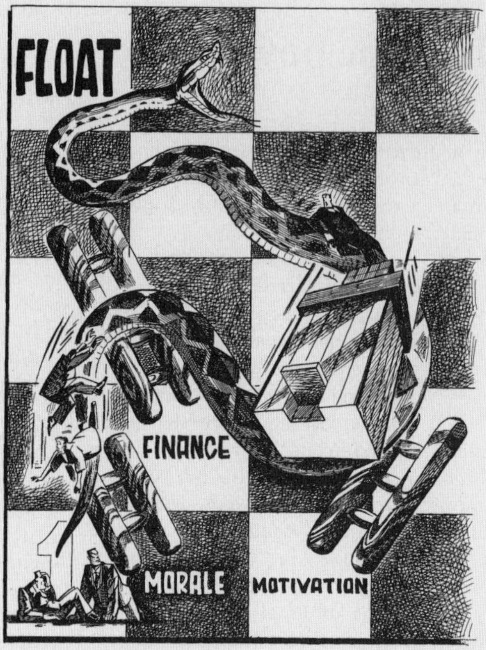

Computer Management Group, one of Europe's largest private computer services groups, had a bigger problem. With a float planned for the spring, the company's advisers decided to pull the issue after McDonnell Information Systems – a computer service business in loosely related markets – issued two profit warnings shortly after coming to the market last year.

The scope for disappointment was great because of the large shareholder base. Since the company was formed 30 years ago, staff have spent £14m buying shares and reducing the stake of founder and chairman, Douglas Gorman, from 40 per cent to 15 per cent.

CMG shares have been tradeable on one day a year. A stock market quote would have greatly increased liquidity – and indeed was the prime reason for the float. CMG communicated with its employees and shareholders immediately after the issue was pulled and followed the letters with staff meetings at offices in the UK, the Netherlands and Germany.

Many companies coming to the market are, like CMG, seeking a quotation as an exit route for investors. But highly geared companies or those needing capital to maintain their growth have a more difficult problem to manage. Century Inns, which runs a cash generative chain of 300 pubs, postponed its flotation on February 7, the day after the Office of Fair Trading launched a surprise inquiry into the wholesale beer trade.

Hit by events beyond its control, Century Inns is facing a limited number of options. 'We will try to do as much of the business plan as we can given the capital constraints,' says Alistair Arkley, chief executive.

Those constraints are dictated by the way the Century Inns' buy-out from Bass in 1991 was structured. Century's bill for interest, debt repayment and the dividends it pays its venture backers has swallowed more than 75 per cent of the £23m cash it has generated over the last three years.

Century Inns will consequently have only £1m a year to spend on its estate instead of the £3.5m available had the float gone ahead.

On the other hand, cash generative businesses which decide to postpone a float but which are not desperate to reduce debt can also expect a welcome from the banks.

'The banking markets are quite positive about supporting businesses' capital expenditure,' says Michael Guthrie, founder of Brightreasons which owns the Pizzaland restaurant chain.

Guthrie postponed the Brightreasons flotation last year after the new issues market softened. He has since raised bank debt to supplement cash flow and says he has been able to continue expanding according to plan.

'In motivational terms, people were disappointed and wanted to be in the public arena,' says Guthrie. 'But I am not entirely shocked; I feel more concerned about the troops that are not so experienced.'

With the stock market in its current mood there are strong financial reasons for postponing a flotation and handling the resulting disappointment.

Source: Richard Gourlay, *Financial Times*, 21 February 1995. Reprinted with permission. Illustration © Jo Cummings. Reproduced with permission.

Sports Direct

Pre-launch

Mike Ashley started Sports Direct (Sports World and Lillywhites), the major sportswear retailer, by opening one shop at the age of 18. By the time he had reached 43 in 2007 the company had 465 shops and revenue of £1.2bn, and Mr Ashley decided to float it on the Main Market of the LSE. He floated because he thought by doing so he could achieve the company's ambitious goal of being 'the leading, most profitable retailer in the world'. It would raise its profile and allow acquisitions of other companies.

He intended to sell 43 per cent of his shares to other investors on gaining a quotation, raising around £1bn to go into his bank account, while holding on to the other 57 per cent of the company's shares. He appointed himself deputy executive chairman. This is quite an unusual post given that chairmen are usually independent and non-executive, who are there to make sure the executive directors are operating the company in the best interests of all shareholders.

Exhibit 10.9 Timetable of an offer for sale and a placing

Time relative to Impact Day	*1–2 years*	*Several weeks (usually 12–24 weeks)*	*A few days*	*IMPACT DAY*		*A few days*	*2 days to 2 weeks for offer for sale*	*2 weeks or so for an offer for sale*
Stage	Pre-launch publicity.	Sponsor and other advisers consider details such as drawing up accountant s report, price and method of issue. Also obtain underwriting, etc.	Pathfinder prospectus • to Press; • to major investors. No price	Prospectus published. Price announced in a fixed-price sale offer or placing.	Investors apply and send payments.	Offer closes.	Allotment.	Admission to the Exchange and dealing begins.
Dates for Sports Direct (placing)	January & February 2007	Late 2006 & early 2007	14 February: price range of 250p to 310p is announced.	27 February: a price is given: 300p.				2 March: first formal dealings.

Normally there would be a lot of publicity about a company a year or so before the actual float. But Mike Ashley is not someone who is very comfortable with publicity – he had shunned the spotlight for 25 years. Despite this, in February 2007 we started to read in the press about the company and the story of the remarkable growth of Mike Ashley's empire. Merrill Lynch did its best to talk up the company's prospects. We heard about Ashley's fearsome buying acumen and power, the company's record of consistent growth and wisdom of the 'pile it high sell it cheap' strategy.

Technicalities

Merrill Lynch was appointed global coordinator, **bookrunner** and sponsor of the float; Citigroup and Credit Suisse were **co-lead managers**.

To strengthen the management team Simon Bentley, former chairman and chief executive of Blacks Leisure, was appointed in 2007 as a director, as was Chris Bulmer, former human resources director at Whitbread. David Richardson, finance director of Whitbread, was appointed non-executive chairman on the date of flotation. The executive management team was headed by Dave Forsey, who started as a Saturday boy when he was 18.

In February the directors went on a '**roadshow**' – they made presentations to institutional investors at various locations. Roadshows are important not just for marketing the issue, but because they allow sponsors to gather information from investors, such as their opinions of the company and its valuation.

Pathfinder prospectus

On 14 February the **pathfinder prospectus** was published and the price range was set at 250p to 310p, valuing the group at £1.8bn to £2.2bn. This is not a firm expectation of the sale price, but a 'test the water' type of price announcement. As a result of the book-building period through late February the book builders (Merrill Lynch etc.) built up a good picture of what demand was likely to be at different prices. In fact by 20 February the IPO had been 'more than covered' meaning that enough indicative offers had been received to sell the shares somewhere within the price range.

Impact day

The full prospectus is published on **impact day**, together with the price. For Sports Direct on 27 February the price was set at 300p, valuing the company at £2.16bn.

Offer closes

In an offer for sale, up to two weeks is needed for investors to consider the offer price and send in payments. There is a fixed cut-off date for applications. In the case of a placing/book-building the time needed is much shorter as the share buyers have already indicated their interest to the sponsors and managers and transactions can be expedited between City institutions.

Allotment

Investors applied for more than twice the number of shares available. The shares are allocated by the sponsors in a placing/book-building depending on commitments made in the book-building process. In an offer for sale allocation can be achieved in a number of different ways. A **ballot** means that only some investors receive shares (recipients are selected at random). In a **scaledown** applicants generally receive some shares, but fewer than they applied for. A cut-off point might be used in which applicants for large quantities are excluded.

Dealing begins

Formal dealing in the shares through the Stock Exchange started at 8 a.m. on 2 March. Formal dealing means on the Exchange after the shares have been allocated. However, deals had been made between investing institutions in an informal market from 27 February – buying and selling shares they believed they were to receive. The shares traded below the placing price, at 281p on 27 February, causing investors to lose 6.3 per cent in the first day of (informal) trading. Mike Ashley sold his shares for £929m. In the following six months the shares tumbled to under 130p.

How does an AIM flotation differ from one on the Official List?

AIM's rules are kept as relaxed as possible to encourage a wide variety of companies to join and keep costs of membership and capital raising to a minimum. However it is felt necessary to have some vetting process for firms wishing to float on AIM. This policing role was given to nominated advisers who are paid a fee by the company to act as an unofficial 'sponsor' in investigating and verifying its financial health. When the cost of the nominated advisers' time is added to those of the Stock Exchange fees, underwriters, accountants, lawyers, printers and so on, the (administrative) cost of capital raising can be as much as 10–37 per cent of the amount being raised. AIM was designed so that the minimum cost of joining was in the region of £40,000–£50,000. But, as **Exhibit 10.10** shows, it has now risen so that frequently more than £500,000 is paid. Most of the additional cost is for raising funds by selling shares rather than just joining AIM, which costs about £100,000 to £200,000, for nomads etc. The nominated advisers' fees have risen because they now incur more investigatory costs due to the emphasis put on their policing role by the Stock Exchange.

The cost of flotation on AIM (or the Main Market) varies significantly depending on the nature of the company and whether new capital is being raised, but a 'typical' breakdown for a company raising finance by selling shares might be as set out in **Exhibit 10.11**.

Exhibit 10.10

Cost of Aim flotations rises, especially for the minnows

FT

David Blackwell

The cost of raising money on Aim increased last year in spite of the reduction in the number of flotations from 519 to 462.

You might expect that competition among more than 80 nominated advisers (nomads) chasing fewer potential candidates would keep the lid on the cost of fees.

However, according to a survey by UHY Hacker Young, the accountancy firm, and Trowers & Hamlins, a City law firm, only the handful of companies raising more than £20m enjoyed a fall in the average costs as a percentage of funds raised.

The survey, which looked at the proportion of costs over funds raised in the last quarter of both 2005 and 2006, shows that an Aim flotation makes sense for the bigger companies. Costs accounted for 4.9 per cent of their total funds raised last year.

However, the costs remain the same when smaller amounts are raised. So the survey shows that for amounts between £10m and £20m, the costs rose from 10.1 to 10.9 per cent of the total; for between, £2m and £10m from 15.4 per cent to 18.1 per cent; and for anything less than £2m from 23.6 per cent to a punitive 37.3 per cent.

Part of the reason for the increase in costs is the growing number of companies joining Aim from overseas.

Only recently, as last week's column pointed out, have nomads started to employ private investigation firms almost as a matter of course when dealing with clients from emerging markets.

The survey was also carried out well before the launch of the London Stock Exchange's first rule book for nomads.

The LSE might claim the rules are merely 'codification of best practice' – but nomads are well aware that part of the reason for their introduction is to enable the LSE to be more rigorous with disciplinary action. Due diligence practices will inevitably be more strictly applied, with a knock-on effect on fees.

It is therefore indicative of the growing importance of Aim that small companies are still prepared to bear the costs.

One of the latest is NetDimensions, a Hong Kong-based software publisher that is raising £3m through a placing and expects to have a market capitalisation of about £15m. The company provides the learning and performance management software used by global corporations to train their workforces.

Jay Shaw, NetDimensions founder and chief executive, cites as one of the main reasons for floating on Aim the ability to use 'the enhanced profile from being a public company to continue to increase our market share'.

He described the due diligence carried out as 'very thorough – they checked every single transaction over the past eight years. When I hear Aim described as a casino, I think – that's not the Aim we listed on.'

Source: Financial Times, 27 April 2007. Reprinted with permission.

Exhibit 10.11 Typical costs associated with an AIM (and Main Market) company selling shares worth £20m

	£
Underwriters	400,000–1m
Financial adviser	200,000–400,000
Legal expenses	200,000–400,000
Accounting	100,000–300,000
Listing fees	< 20,000
Printing, public relations, etc	< 100,000
	1,020,000–2,220,000

Companies floating on AIM need to be public limited companies and have accounts conforming to UK and other recognised international accounting standards. They need to produce a prospectus (or AIM document) but this is less detailed than the prospectus for a Main Market quotation and therefore cheaper. The real cost savings come in the continuing annual expense of managing the quotation. For example, AIM companies do not have to disclose as much information as companies on the Main Market. Price-sensitive information will have to be published but normally this will require only an electronic message from the adviser to the Exchange rather than a circular to shareholders.

Main Market companies often complain that they are required to obtain shareholder approval for taking over another company[5] if the target is more than one-quarter its size. Issuing letters and accompanying information often costs over £100,000 on each occasion. The burden is lessened on AIM because a company only has to consult shareholders when it doubles in size through acquisition.

The costs of new issues

There are three types of cost involved when a firm makes an issue of equity capital:

- administrative/transaction costs;
- the equity cost of capital;
- market pricing costs.

The first of these has already been discussed earlier in this chapter. For both the Main Market and AIM the costs as a proportion of the amount raised can be anywhere between 5 per cent and 37 per cent depending on the size of issue, and the method used (*see* **Exhibit 10.12**).

Some idea of the transaction costs associated with flotation are given in the example of Servocell on which about £0.8m was spent (*see* **Exhibit 10.13**).

The second cost is not something to be discussed in detail here – this can be left to Chapter 19. However, we can say that shareholders suffer an opportunity cost. By holding shares in one company they are giving up the use of that money elsewhere. The firm therefore needs to produce a rate of return for those shareholders which is at least equal to the return they could obtain by investing in other shares of a similar risk class. Because ordinary shareholders face higher risks than debt or preference shareholders the rate of return demanded is higher. If the firm does not produce this return then shares will be sold and the firm will find raising capital difficult.

The market pricing cost is to do with the possibility of underpricing new issues. It is a problem which particularly affects offers for sale at a fixed price and placings. The firm is usually keen to have the offer fully taken up by public investors to make sure it can finance its planned growth. To have shares left with the underwriters gives the firm a bad image because it is perceived to have had an issue which 'flopped'. Furthermore, the underwriters, over the forthcoming months, will

[5] Shareholder approval is also required for disposal of a substantial asset.

Exhibit 10.12 Costs of new issues

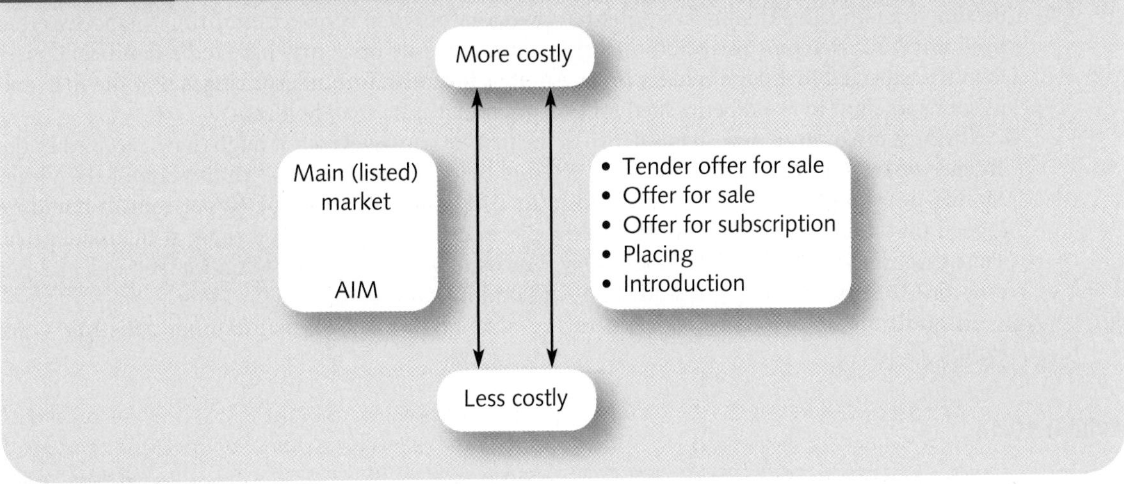

Exhibit 10.13

Aim augments the arduous process of listing

FT

David Blackwell

Servocell – which has a market capitalisation of about £23m – is the sort of company that Aim was set up to accommodate. It makes electromechanical locking mechanisms, which are increasingly used for electronic access systems. Bell Lawrie, its nomad, expects it to become profitable for the first time this year on sales of £5.5m.

Mr Powell was a founder director of Servocell, which was spun out of PowerBreaker in 1997. He described it as a high-tech company, burning lots of cash, which needed further funds to realise its potential.

He emphasised the need for the company to decide to float well before it required 'stay alive' money. The process started with gathering the team together – nomad, broker, legal and financial advisers, public relations team and an expanded board, including non executive directors.

He spoke of months of work on the admission document, which was only 75 pages but required 17 re-drafts.

The process of pitching to potential investors, he said, made BBC television's *Dragons' Den* look like *Play School*, and sleep became a fond memory. Yet in spite of all the work, nothing was certain until impact day, which for Servocell arrived on March 20 at $54\frac{1}{2}$p a share.

The company raised £5.5m before expenses, and £4.7m net. 'Don't look at the, size of the fee', said Mr Powell 'Look at what we have achieved.'

Then the trouble started, he said – a heavier workload, the demands of investors, preparation of the first accounts as a public company.

Nevertheless, Mr Powell described Aim as 'brilliantly clever' in terms of a light regulatory touch that 'does not intrude on normal daily operations'. He also found that being listed made a big difference to perceptions of the company by customers overseas although they did not really understand what Aim was.

Source: *Financial Times*, 2 February 2007, p. 22. Reprinted with permission.

try to offload their shares and this action has the potential to depress the price for a long time. The sponsor also has an incentive to avoid leaving the underwriters with large blocks of shares. The sponsoring organisation consists of people who are professional analysts and dealmakers and an issue which flops can be very bad for their image. It might indicate that they are not reading the market signals correctly and that they have overestimated demand. They might have done a poor job in assessing the firm's riskiness or failed to communicate its virtues to investors. These bad images can stick, so both the firm and the sponsor have an incentive to err on the side of caution and price a little lower to make sure that the issue will be fully subscribed.[6] A major problem in

[6] It has also been suggested that when sponsors are underwriters they have an additional incentive to price the shares cheaply as this reduces the risk of being required to buy the shares. If they do buy them, they then obtain them at a good price.

establishing this discount is that in an offer for sale the firm has to decide the price two weeks before the close of the offer. In the period between impact day and first trading the market may decline dramatically. This makes potential investors nervous about committing themselves to a fixed price. To overcome this additional risk factor the issue price may have to be significantly less than the expected first day's trading price. Another incentive for underpricing is that the firm and its sponsors want to avoid being sued for overpricing by irate shareholders.

Giving a discount to new shares deprives the firm of money which it might have received in the absence of these uncertainties, and can therefore be regarded as a cost.[7] In the case of the Virgin Mobile flotation in 2004 the shares moved to a first-day premium of 10 per cent. It could be argued that the existing shareholders sold a piece of the business too cheaply at the issue price. This is not untypical with average first-day returns of 4.4 per cent for Main Market and 11.2 per cent for AIM shown in a recent study (City of London *et al.* 2006).

In addition to the issue costs there are also high costs of maintaining a listing – *see* **Exhibit 10.14**.

Exhibit 10.14

Professional expenses prove a deterrent to maintaining stock market exposure

FT

But costs of public-to-private deals can also be considerable

Bertrand Benoit reports

Ask Richard Johnson, chief executive of Wyko, what the industrial distribution and maintenance group gained in 10 years on the stock market and the answer is likely to be short.

Launched with a market value of about £50m in 1989, the group was performing honorably until investors began to pull out from the small company sector last year.

In less than six months, its shares fell from 190p to 64p. 'This happened as we were considering a £60m acquisition,' Mr Johnson says. 'But with a p/e of 5, we had suddenly become vulnerable to a takeover.'

Unable to expand in a market where size increasingly mattered, Wyko put an end to its turbulent relationship with the Stock Exchange last week by going private in a management buy-out valuing it at £92.2m, a 30 per cent discount to its peak price.

This is not an isolated case. So far this year, nearly 40 companies have pulled out of the exchange, against 25 last year and a mere seven in 1997.

Although linked to the size of the company, the expense typically amounts to £250,000 a year. Businesses meeting the minimum requirements imposed by the exchange pay a lot less. However, Roy Hill, chief executive of Liberfabrica, the book manufacturer bought by a trade buyer this month, claims his company will save up to £400,000 a year in City-associated costs.

These include fees paid to stockbroker, registrars, lawyers, merchant banker and financial PR company, as well as the exchange fee and the auditing, printing and distribution of accounts.

Another problem has been the low rating experienced by some of the smaller companies that have virtually disappeared from investors' radar screens. As institutions have grown increasingly reluctant to invest in small caps, brokers have stopped following many of them, thus hastening share price declines.

'Some institutions have stopped investing in companies with a market capitalisation below £100m,' says Penny Freer, head of smaller companies research at Crédit Lyonnais in London. 'Some smaller companies that deliver good results may end up with a single digit p/e.'

For Tony Fry, partner at KPMG Transaction Services, 'being on the stock market is all about getting access to funding, if you are barred from such access, then the attraction disappears'.

In addition to the venture capital funding that can facilitate acquisitions, managers have been lured into public-to-private deals by the chance of raising their stake in the business. In a typical MBO backed by a private equity house, managers can end up owning up to 20 per cent of the bidding vehicle. One banker calculates that the value of

[7] Underpricing is discussed in detail in Jenkinson and Ljungquist (2001).

Exhibit 10.14 continued

such a stake can grow 10 times if the company is later sold for twice the price of the buy-out.

But because MBOs are highly geared operations, the risks involved are equally considerable. The same managers could lose all their investment if the company were sold below the original offer price.

Nor are the financial costs associated with a public-to-private transaction negligible. According to Richard Grainger, managing director at Close Brothers, the advisory firm, fees paid to bankers, registrars, venture capital funds and PR firms, can amount to 4 or 5 per cent of the purchase price.

The time spent in putting transactions together can also be consuming. 'The negotiations are so absorbing and involve so many parties that it can be very easy for management to take their eyes off the ball, especially if they do not have first class advisers,' says Mr Johnson, whose MBO of Wyko was concluded after seven months of talks.

In some instances, these efforts prove fruitless, as at Liberfabrica, whose management team was outbid by a trade buyer. Mr Hill reckons that £500,000 in fees was wasted in the exercise.

Source: Financial Times, 31 August 1999, p. 18. Reprinted with permission.

The cost of listing

Listed

Estimated annual cost of listing for a company with a market capitalisation of around £100m

Stockbroker	**£20,000 to £25,000**
Financial PR	**£20,000 to £25,000**
Financial reports and accounts	**around £30,000**
Registrars	**£5,000 to £25,000**
High profile merchant bank	**around £50,000**
Solicitors	**around £50,000**
Other costs	**around £50,000**
Total (per year)	**£250,000 to £350,000**

Private

Estimated cost of going private for a company with a purchase price of around £100m

Advisors to the bidders	**around 1% of purchase price**
Lawyers to the bidders	**£100,000 to £200,000**
Due diligence account	**£100,000 to £400,000**
Market report due diligence	**£30,000 to £50,000**
Stamp duty	**around 0.5% of purchase price**
Printers	**£15,000 to £20,000**
Receiving banks	**£10,000 to £15,000**
Takeover panel fee	**around £25,000**
Funders fee	**2% to 3% of purchase price**
Total	**£3,780,000 to £5,210,000**

Source: Financial Times, 31 August 1999, p. 18, Bertrand Benoit. Reprinted with permission. Industry estimates for figures.

Rights issues

A **rights issue** is an invitation to existing shareholders to purchase additional shares in the company. This is a very popular method of raising new funds. It is easy and relatively cheap (compared with new issues). Directors are not required to seek the prior consent of shareholders, and the London Stock Exchange will only intervene in larger issues (to adjust the timing so that the market does not suffer from too many issues in one period). The UK has particularly strong traditions and laws concerning **pre-emption rights**. These require that a company raising new equity capital by selling shares first offers those shares to the existing shareholders. The owners of the company are entitled to subscribe for the new shares in proportion to their existing holding. This will enable them to maintain the existing percentage ownership of the company – the only difference is that each slice of the company cake is bigger because it has more financial resources under its control.

The shares are usually offered at a significantly discounted price from the market value of the current shares – typically 10–20 per cent. Shareholders can either buy these shares themselves or sell the 'right' to buy to another investor. For further reassurance that the firm will raise the anticipated finance, rights issues are usually underwritten by institutions.

An example

Take the case of the imaginary listed company Swell plc with 100 million shares in issue. It wants to raise £25m for expansion but does not want to borrow it. Given that its existing shares are quoted on the stock market at 120p, the new rights shares will have to be issued at a lower price to appeal to shareholders because there is a risk of the market share price falling in the period between the announcement and the purchasing of new shares. (The offer must remain open for shareholders to get their applications in for at least three weeks.) Swell has decided that the £25m will be obtained by issuing 25 million shares at 100p each. Thus the ratio of new shares to old is 25:100. In other words, this issue is a 'one-for-four' rights issue. Each shareholder will be offered one new share for every four already held. The discount on these new shares is 20p or 16.7 per cent. The market price of Swell shares will not be able to stay at 120p after the rights issue is complete. The **ex-rights price** is the price at which the shares should theoretically sell after the issue. This is calculated as follows:

Four existing shares at a price of 120p	480p
One new share for cash at 100p	100p
Value of five shares	580p
Value of one share ex-rights 580p/5	116p

An alternative way of viewing this is to focus on the worth of the firm before and after the rights. Prior to the issue the total capitalisation of the firm was £120m (£1.20 × 100 million shares). The rights issue put another £25m into the company but also created 25 million additional shares. A company that was previously valued at £120m which then adds £25m of value to itself in the form of cash should be worth £145m. This company now has 125 million shares; therefore each share is worth £1.16 (disregarding stock market fluctuations and revaluations of the company):

$$\frac{\text{Total market capitalisation}}{\text{Total shares available}} = \frac{£145\text{m}}{125\text{m}} = £1.16$$

The shareholders have experienced a decline in the price of their old shares from 120p to 116p. A fall of this magnitude necessarily follows from the introduction of new shares at a discounted price. However the loss is exactly offset by the gain in share value on the new rights issue shares. They cost 100p but have a market price of 116p. This can be illustrated through the example of Sid, who owned 100 shares worth £120 prior to the rights announcement. Sid loses £4 on the old shares – their value is now £116. However, he makes a gain of £4 on the new shares:

Cost of rights shares (25 × £1)	£25
Ex-rights value (25 × £1.16)	£29
Gain	£4

What if a shareholder does not want to take up the rights?

As owners of the firm all shareholders must be treated in the same way. To make sure that some shareholders do not lose out because they are unwilling or unable to buy more shares the law requires that shareholders have a third choice, other than to buy or not buy the new shares. This is to sell the rights on to someone else on the stock market (**selling the rights nil paid**). Take the case of impoverished Sid, who is unable to find the necessary £25. He could sell the rights to subscribe for the shares to another investor and not have to go through the process of taking up any of the shares himself. Indeed, so deeply enshrined are pre-emption rights that even if the shareholder does nothing the company will sell his rights to the new shares on his behalf and send the proceeds to him.[8] Thus, Sid would benefit to the extent of 16p per share or a total of £4 (if the market price stays constant) which adequately compensates for the loss on the 100 shares he holds. But the extent of his control over the company has been reduced – his percentage share of the votes has decreased.

[8] For companies whose shares are not quoted on a recognised stock exchange it may be difficult to sell the rights to another investor.

The value of a right on one new share is:

Theoretical market value of share ex-rights – subscription price = 116p – 100p = 16p

The value of a right on one old share in Swell is:

$$\frac{\text{Theoretical market value of share ex-rights – subscription price}}{\text{No. of old shares required to purchase one new share}}$$

$$= \frac{116 - 100}{4} = 4\text{p}$$

Ex-rights and cum-rights

Shares bought in the stock market which are designated **cum-rights** carry with them to the new owner the right to subscribe for the new shares in the rights issue. After a cut-off date the shares go **ex-rights**, which means that any purchaser of old shares will not have the right to the new shares; they remain with the former shareholder.

The price discount decision

It does not matter greatly whether Swell raises £25m on a one-for-four basis at 100p or on a one-for-three basis at 75p per share, or on some other basis (*see* **Exhibit 10.15**).

Exhibit 10.15 Comparison of different rights bases

Rights basis	Number of new shares (m)	Price of new shares (p)	Total raised (£m)
1 for 4	25	100	25
1 for 3	33.3	75	25
1 for 2	50	50	25
1 for 1	100	25	25

As Exhibit 10.15 shows, whatever the basis of the rights issue, the company will receive £25m and the shareholders will see the price of their old shares decrease, but this will be exactly offset by the value of the rights on the new shares. However, the ex-rights price will change. For a one-for-three basis it will be £108.75:

Three shares at 120p	360p
One share at 75p	75p
Value of four shares	435p
Value of one share (435/4)	108.75p

If Swell chose the one-for-one basis this would be regarded as a **deep-discounted rights issue**. With an issue of this sort there is only a minute probability that the market price will fall below the rights offer price and therefore there is almost complete certainty that the offer will be taken up. It seems reasonable to suggest that the underwriting service provided by the institutions is largely redundant here and that the firm can make a significant saving. Yet 95 per cent of all rights issues are underwritten,[9] usually involving between 100 and 400 sub-underwriters. The underwriting fees used to be a flat 2 per cent of the offer. Of this the issuing house received 0.5 per cent,

[9] Breedon and Twinn (1996).

the broker received 0.25 per cent and the sub-underwriter 1.25 per cent. However, fees have fallen recently and can now be as little as 0.75 per cent for low-risk deep-discounted issues.

When the press talks glibly of a rights offer being 'very attractively priced for shareholders' they are generally talking nonsense. Whatever the size of the discount, the same value will be removed from the old shares to leave the shareholder no worse or better off. Logically value cannot be handed over to the shareholders from the size of the discount decision. Shareholders own all the company's shares before and after the rights issue – they can't hand value to themselves without also taking value from themselves. Of course, if the prospects for the company's profits rise because it can now make brilliant capital expenditures, which lead to dominant market positions, then the value of shares will rise – for both the old and the new shares. But this is value creation that has nothing to do with the level of the discount.

Case study 10.2 Cookson: a very troubled rights issue

The industrial material manufacturer Cookson announced on 19 July 2002 that it intended to raise £277.5m from a rights issue. The company needed the money to pay off its rapidly accumulating debt (a **rescue rights issue**). It was to be an 8 for 5 issue, that is, 8 new shares would be sold at 25 pence for every 5 shares currently held. Prior to the announcement the share traded at 52p and Cookson took the bold decision not to underwrite the issue, saving about £4m; at 25p it was deeply discounted.

If the old shares remained at 52p then the theoretical ex-rights price is 35p:

5 old shares at 52p	260p
8 new shares at 25p	200p
	460p
Theoretical ex-rights price: 460p/13	= 35p

However, the shares did not remain at 52p. On the announcement, they immediately fell to 33p as investors took the issue to be a sign of great problems at Cookson. Worse was to come a week later when the price of the old share moved to 20p.

Shareholders were now being asked to pay 25p for new shares when the company's shares can be bought on the Exchange for less. Obviously no one would want to support the issue in these circumstances. If the issue had been underwritten then the underwriter would have been obliged to buy the new shares at 25 pence and Cookson would have been guaranteed the money it so badly needed. The next few weeks were a tense time for the managers.

Fortunately, by the time the offer closed in late August the shares had risen to $29\frac{3}{4}$p. Almost 92 per cent of the shares on offer were taken up by existing shareholders; the remainder were placed with institutions.

Exercise Premier Foods

To consolidate the knowledge gained from the rights issue section it is suggested that it be applied to the case of Premier Food's one-for-one issue.

Premier Foods planned to raise a sum of money equivalent to 60 per cent of its stock market value through a rights issue in 2006. This was to provide the funds needed to purchase the UK and Irish operations of Campbell's Soup. One new share was offered for each existing share held at 185p. The existing shares traded at 310p.

Calculate the following on the assumption that the market price of an old share in Premier Foods is 310p:

- **a** the ex-rights price;
- **b** the value of a right of a new share;
- **c** the value of a right of an old share;
- **d** the amount a holder of £8,000 worth of shares could receive if the rights were sold.

Other equity issues

Some companies argue that the lengthy procedures and expense associated with rights issues (for example, a minimum three-week offer period) frustrate directors' efforts to take advantage of opportunities in a timely fashion. Firms in the USA have much more freedom to bypass pre-emption rights. They are able to sell blocks of shares to securities houses for distribution elsewhere in the market. This is fast and has low transaction costs. If this were permitted in the UK there would be a concern for existing shareholders: that is, they could experience a **dilution** of their voting power and/or the shares could be sold at such a low price that a portion of the firm is handed over to new shareholders too cheaply.

The UK authorities have produced a compromise. Here firms must obtain shareholders' approval through a **special resolution** (a majority of 75 per cent of those voting) at the company's annual general meeting or at an extraordinary general meeting to waive the pre-emption right. Even then the shares must not be sold to outside investors at more than a 5 per cent discount to the share price (except in an issue with a 'clawback' provision – see next section). This is an important condition. It does not make any difference to existing shareholders if new shares are offered at a deep discount to the market price as long as they are offered to them. If external investors get a discount there is a transfer of value from the current shareholders to the new. *See* **Exhibit 10.16** for the dangers to shareholders when pre-emption rights are removed or weak.

Exhibit 10.16

Call to tighten Asian rules on dilution

FT

Regulators are being pressed to address the abuse of pre-emption rights

Says Steve Johnson

Regulators in Hong Kong and other Asian markets are being urged to tighten legislation to protect investors from being diluted against their will.

Hermes, which manages the BT Pension Scheme, tabled resolutions against the boards of 15 Asian companies in its battle to protect its clients' ownership interests.

Most were based in Hong Kong, but Hermes also voted against companies in Singapore and Taiwan.

F&C Asset Management has also opposed a swathe of Hong Kong companies that it sees as abusing the territory's lack of statutory pre-emption rights.

Under Hong Kong's listing rules, companies only need to win a simple majority at a shareholder meeting to approve issuance of up to 20 per cent of additional stock, at a discount of up to 20 per cent.

This stock does not have to be offered to all existing shareholders, meaning minority investors can be heavily diluted at a deeply discounted rate, and also potentially opening the door to stakeholding by a preferred large shareholder.

'You get a potential dilution in your ownership of the company without having the opportunity to prevent that dilution. There is also the issue of creeping control where a large shareholder achieves a majority holding through that process,' said Colin Melvin, head of corporate governance at Hermes.

The situation contrasts sharply with that in the UK, where a 75 per cent majority is needed to approve a waiver of pre-emption rights, and the maximum issuance is limited to 5 per cent a year or 7.5 per cent in a three-year period, at a maximum discount of 5 per cent.

Karina Litvack, head of governance at F&C, said its fund managers were 'not best pleased' in December when a hedge fund controlled by George Soros bought a stake in Taishin Financial Holdings, a Taiwanese credit card company, at a 19 per cent discount to market price, an offer not extended to existing investors.

Source: Financial Times, 2 April 2007, FT Fund Management, p. 1. Reprinted with permission.

Placings and open offers

In placings, new shares from companies already quoted on the stock market are sold directly to a narrow group of external investors. The institutions, wearing their hat of existing shareholders, have produced guidelines to prevent abuse, which normally only allow a placing of a small proportion of the company's issued share capital (a maximum of 5 per cent in a single year and no more than 7.5 per cent is to be added to the company's equity capital over a rolling three-year period) in the absence of a *clawback*. Under **clawback** existing shareholders have the right to reclaim the shares as though they were entitled to them under a rights issue. They can buy them at the price they were offered to the external investors. With a clawback the issue becomes an '**open offer**'. The major difference compared with a rights issue is that if they do not exercise this clawback right they receive no compensation for a reduction in the price of their existing shares – there are no nil-paid rights to sell.

Exhibit 10.17 describes a placing.

Exhibit 10.17

Corus raises £300m for revival

FT

Troubled Anglo-Dutch steel group says share issue will help it to compete in Europe and plans more cost cuts

By Rebecca Bream

Corus, the Anglo-Dutch steelmaker, raised £307m yesterday through a well-received share issue . . .

Shares in the company rose 6p to 32p following the equity placement, which is designed to strengthen Corus's balance sheet and provide funding for its UK restructuring plan and further productivity initiatives . . .

Corus issued more than 1.3bn new shares – five for 12 – at 23.5p, a discount of 9.6 per cent on Monday's closing price. Analysts said that most buyers were existing investors but, because Corus chose an open share offer instead of a rights issue, it offered a relatively slim discount.

Cazenove and Lazard were joint sponsors and Hoare Govett was joint broker . . .

Source: Financial Times, 13 November 2003, p. 25. Reprinted with permission.

Acquisition for shares

Shares are often issued to purchase businesses or assets. This is usually subject to shareholder approval.

Vendor placing

If a company wishes to pay for an asset such as a subsidiary of another firm or an entire company with newly issued shares, but the vendor does not want to hold the shares, the purchaser could arrange for the new shares to be bought by institutional investors for cash. In this way the buyer gets the asset, the vendors (for example shareholders in the target company in a merger or takeover) receive cash and the institutional investor makes an investment.

There is usually a clawback arrangement for a **vendor placing** (if the issue is more than 10 per cent of market capitalisation of the acquirer). Again, the price discount can be no more than 5 per cent of the current share price.

Bought deal

Instead of selling shares to investors companies are sometimes able to make an arrangement with a securities house whereby it buys all the shares being offered for cash. The securities house then sells the shares on to investors included in its distribution network, hoping to make a profit on the deal. Securities houses often compete to buy a package of shares from the company, with the highest bidder winning. The securities house takes the risk of being unable to sell the shares for at least the amount that they paid. Given that some of these bought deals are for over £100m, these securities houses need substantial capital backing. Bought deals are limited by the 5 per cent pre-emption rules.

Scrip issues

Scrip issues do not raise new money: a company simply gives shareholders more shares in proportion to their existing holdings. The value of each shareholding does not change, because the share price drops in proportion to the additional shares. They are also known as **capitalisation issues** or **bonus issues**. The purpose is to make shares more attractive by bringing down the price. British investors are thought to consider a share price of £10 and above as less marketable than one in single figures. So a company with shares trading at £15 on the Exchange might distribute two 'free' shares for every one held – a two-for-one scrip issue. Since the amount of money in the firm and its economic potential is constant the share price will theoretically fall to £5.

With a scrip issue there will be some adjustment necessary to the balance sheet. If we suppose that the pre-scrip issued share capital was £200m (25p par value × 800m shares) and the profit and loss account reserves accumulated from previous years amounted to £500m, then after the two-for-one scrip issue the issued share capital figure rises to £600m (25p par value × 2,400m shares) and the profit and loss account reserve (revenue reserve) falls to £100m. Thus £400m of profit and loss reserves are 'capitalised' into issued share capital.

A number of companies have an annual scrip issue while maintaining a constant dividend per share, effectively raising the level of profit distribution. For example, if a company pays a regular dividend of 20p per share but also has a one-for-ten scrip, the annual income will go up by 10 per cent. (A holder of 10 shares who previously received 200p now receives 220p on a holding of 11 shares.) Scrip issues are often regarded as indicating confidence in future earnings increases. If this new optimism is expressed in the share price it may not fall as much as theory would suggest.

Scrip dividends are slightly different: shareholders are offered a choice between receiving a cash dividend or receiving additional shares. This is more like a rights issue because the shareholders are making a cash sacrifice if they accept the scrip shares. Shareholders are able to add to their holdings without paying stockbrokers' commission.

A **share split** (**stock split**) means that the nominal value of each share is reduced in proportion to the increase in the number of shares, so the book total nominal value of shares remains the same. So, for example, a company may have one million shares in issue with a nominal value of 50p each. It issues a further one million shares to existing shareholders with the nominal value of each share reducing to 25p, but total nominal value remains at £500,000. Of course, the share price will halve – assuming all else is constant. **Exhibit 10.18** presents a sceptic's view on share splits.

If the share price goes too low, say 15p, a company may decide to **consolidate** its shares. This is the opposite of a split: the number of shares is reduced and the nominal value of each remaining share rises. If the nominal (par) value is 5p the company could consolidate on the basis of five shares for one. Every five 5p nominal share would be replaced by a 25p nominal share, which would then trade in the market at 75p: 15p × 5 (or slightly more if investors are more attracted to shares within a normal price range).

Exhibit 10.18

Stock splits: time to query decades of dogma

FT

By John Authers

Let's take this opportunity to question one time-honoured ritual of equity investing: stock splits. What is the point of them?

Stock splits are meant to keep a share price at a manageable level. A two-for-one stock split involves replacing every outstanding share with two and making no other changes. It is a complicated operation (although not wildly expensive: it generally costs up to $1m for a large company), whose only effect is to halve the nominal price shares.

The habit is ingrained. General Electric's share price at the end of 1935 was $38.25. Exactly 70 years later, it was $35.05. According to research by a group of academics from the University of California at Los Angeles, Cornell University and the University of Chicago, GE would by this point have traded at $10,094.40, had it never paid stock dividends or split its stock.

No constituent of the Dow Jones Industrial Average has a share price of less than $19, or more than $95.

In the UK, people like the nominal price of their shares to be even lower. Prices are quoted in pence, not pounds. No constituent of the FTSE 100 has a share price of more than 2680p, or less than 310p.

There are obvious disadvantages. Splits get in the way of comparisons of share price performance over time (although decent data providers can overcome this).

Sometimes they are self-defeating. Lucent Technologies probably wished it had not bothered to keep its share price 'manageable' level after it was caught up in the collapse of the internet bubble. For years, until its merger with Alcatel of France last year), its share price stood at about $2. It almost always had the highest volume of shares traded on the New York Stock Exchange.

This is important, because stock exchanges and other intermediaries charge fees based on the number of shares traded, rather than on the amount of money that changes hands. So splitting stock increases costs for investors. The researchers from Cornell and elsewhere found that GE investors would have saved 99 per cent in brokerage commissions if the company had not split its stock. About 5bn GE shares traded in 2005, so this is equivalent, they say, to about $100m – big money, even for big investors.

Are there good reasons for this? None stand up to examination. One is that there might be an 'optimal' trading range, at which individual investors can afford to buy a round number of shares. But this should logically at least have risen with inflation, so that average nominal prices now would be ten times their level of the 1930s. And in any case, individuals mostly now hold stocks through mutual funds, which don't find high share prices a deterrent.

A final argument is that a low share price, despite the attendant costs, signals to investors that a company is of high quality. But a low share price can be embarrassing. And the researchers found splits tend to come just as earnings have peaked – not a time when companies need to send out positive signals.

So has anybody had the nerve to go against the orthodoxy? They have, and their identity is revealing. Warren Buffett, the world's most successful investor, has never seen the point of stock splits. A share of Berkshire Hathaway, his main investment vehicle, will cost you $100,000. This has not harmed demand for the stock over the long term. Beyond the Buffett empire, the two highest share prices belong to the Chicago Mercantile Exchange (which has been as high as $593) and Google (which has been as high as $513), the two most successful stock market debutants of this century. Neither has felt any need to bring its share price down to a lower level, and neither has been punished for this by investors.

So this is one case where questioning faith leads to a surprising result. Despite a century of dogma, companies should not split their stock, and investors should not reward them when they do.

Source: *Financial Times*, 7 April 2007, p. 16. Reprinted with permission.

Warrants

Warrants give the holder the right to subscribe for a specified number of shares at a fixed price during or at the end of a specified time period. If a company has shares currently trading at £3 it might choose to sell warrants, each of which grants the holder the right to buy a share at, say, £4 over the next five years. If by the fifth year the share price has risen to £6 the warrant holders could exercise their rights and then sell the shares immediately, realising £2 per share, which is likely to be a considerable return on the original warrant price of a few pence. Warrants are frequently attached to bonds, and make the bond more attractive because the investor benefits from a relatively safe (but low) income on the bond if the firm performs in a mediocre fashion, but if the firm does very well and the share price rises significantly the investor will participate in some of the extra returns through the 'sweetener' or 'equity kicker' provided by the warrant.

There is no requirement for investors to hold warrants until exercised or they expire. There is an active secondary market on the London Stock Exchange.

Equity finance for unquoted firms

We have looked at some of the details of raising money on the Stock Exchange. In the commercial world there are thousands of companies which do not have access to the Exchange. We now consider a few of the ways that **unquoted firms** can raise equity capital.

The financing gap

Small companies usually rely on retained earnings, capital injections from the founder family and bank borrowing for growth. More mature companies can turn to the stock market to raise debt or equity capital. In between these two, it is suggested, lies a **financing gap**. The intermediate businesses are too large or too fast growing to ask the individual shareholders for more funds or to obtain sufficient bank finance, and they are not ready to launch on the stock market.

These companies may be frustrated in their plans to exploit market opportunities by a lack of available funds. To help fill this gap there has been the rapid development of the private equity industry over the past 20 years. Currently there are 10,000 UK companies with three million employees (one in six of the non-government workforce) financed by private equity money. The tremendous growth of private equity capital has to a large extent plugged the financing gap which so vexed politicians and business people alike in the 1970s and early 1980s.

Business angels (informal venture capitalists)

Business angels are wealthy individuals, generally with substantial business and entrepreneurial experience, who usually invest between £10,000 and £250,000 primarily in start-up, early stage or expanding firms. About three-quarters of business angel investments are for sums of less than £100,000 and the average investment is £25,000–£30,000. The majority of investments are in the form of equity finance but they do purchase debt instruments and preference shares. These companies will be years away from obtaining a quotation or being advanced enough for a sale to other companies or investors, so in becoming a business angel the investor accepts that it may be difficult to dispose of their shares, even if the company is progressing nicely. They also accept a high degree of risk of complete failure – which happens in about one in three cases. They usually do not have a **controlling shareholding** and they are willing to invest at an earlier stage than most formal venture capitalists. (They often dislike the term business angel, preferring the title **informal venture capitalist**.) They are generally looking for entrepreneurial companies which have high aspirations and potential for growth. A typical business angel makes one or two investments in a three-year period, often in an investment syndicate (with an 'archangel' leading the group). They generally invest in companies within a reasonable travelling distance from their homes because most like to be 'hands-on' investors, playing a significant role in strategy and management – on average angels allocate 10 hours a week to their investments. Most angels take a seat on the board.[10] Business angels are patient investors willing to hold their investment for at least a five-year period.

The main way in which firms and angels find each other is through friends and business associates, although there are a number of formal networks. *See* British Venture Capital Association at www.bvca.co.uk for a list of networks.[11]

---

[10] Nevertheless, many business angels (generally those with investments of £10,000–£20,000) have infrequent contact with the company.

[11] Other useful contacts: British Business Angels Association, www.bbaa.org; National Business Angels Network (NBAN), (or gateway 2 investment) www.g2i.org; Angel Bourse, www.angelbourse.com; Fisma, www.fisma.org; VCR Directory, www.vcrdirectory.co.uk; Octopus Ventures, www.katalystventures.com; Hotbed, www.hotbed.uk.com; Beer & Partners, www.beerandpartners.com; Cavendish Management Resources, www.cmrworld.com; Development Capital Exchange, www.dcxworld.com; Department For Business Enterprise and Regulatory Reforms, www.berr.gov.uk.

Angel network events are organised where entrepreneurs can make a pitch to potential investors, who, if they like what they hear in response to their questions, may put in tens of thousands of pounds. Prior to the event the network organisers (or a member) generally screen the business opportunities to avoid time wasting by the no-hopers. To be a member of a network investors are expected either to earn at least £100,000 per year or to have a net worth of at least £250,000 (excluding main residence). If an investor has a specialist skill to offer, for example he/she is an experienced company director or chartered accountant, membership may be permitted despite a lower income or net worth.

Entrepreneurs need to be aware that obtaining money from informal venture capitalists is no easy task – the rejection rate runs at over 90 per cent; but following rejection the determined entrepreneur has many other angel networks to try.

Returns to business angel investments are often negative. However, they can be spectacular; the angels who put €2m into Skype multiplied their money by 350 times when the company was sold to eBay for €2.1 billion in 2005.

Many business angel deals are structured to take advantage of tax breaks such as those through enterprise investment schemes, EIS, which offer income tax relief and capital gains tax deferral (*see* later in this chapter).

Exhibit 10.19 descibes what a business angel is looking for.

Exhibit 10.19

A wing and a prayer

FT

Investor likes to contribute more than just his money to small businesses

Writes Monica Porter

Vanish Patel belongs to one of those astute and successful Indian business families expelled from Uganda by Idi Amin in 1972. He was four years old when his family arrived in London with a mere £100. His father opened a newsagent's in Hackney ('What else do you do when your name is Patel?') and in time Vanish went on to study IT and work as an IT consultant for some of the City's major blue chip companies.

He also spent hours each evening 'investigating fast growing companies on the stock market' and buying carefully-chosen stocks and shares. That proved so lucrative that in 2000, aged 32, he set himself up an independent property investor, and the following year, as a sideline, he became a business angel.

'I've made eight angel investments so far, totalling around £300,000', he says. 'The smallest amount I've invested has been £10,000, the largest £100,000. The businesses have been in a variety of sectors – media, software, retail – and although a few have been start-ups, most have been at the early growth stage. I prefer to invest in an actual business rather than an idea.'

Over the years he has built up an extensive network of 'introducers' – accountants, solicitors, bank managers, business consultants – who refer business plans to him, and he reads one plan per day.

'Each year I select about 20 to review in detail, make investment offers on five, and eventually do business with two. I spend around 10 hours a week on business angel activities.'

He always applies the same general criteria in choosing which businesses are right for him. Does he understand the business, and the sector? Does he like the management team? Will the business model scale? Does the business have a clear exit plan?

'I stay away from lone entrepreneurs because teams will always outperform individuals and from lifestyle businesses [businesses which are only run to support the owner/manager], as they leave the investor nothing to sell. I always expect to exit a business within a few years, when it floats on the stock market, and sell my share for a healthy profit.'

Geographical convenience is another factor: 'I wouldn't invest in a business in Scotland, for example, as it would be too far to visit. And it's important for me to actually go to the office, get a feel for it, see if there's a buzz.'

With each business, he does more than just invest some capital. 'I also bring to the table my contacts and my knowledge of business, finance and marketing. I take an active part for the first six months or so giving it one or two days a month – then a more passive role as the business moves forward.' He generally makes his investments as part of a small syndicate of angels who are well-

Exhibit 10.19 continued

known to him through business angel networks, and together they will typically acquire 10 per cent to 40 per cent in a business.

Half of his angel investments so far have failed. In the worst case he went against his instincts and put £25,000 into a lone entrepreneur's free-distribution directory of west London estate agents. 'There was no team and the entrepreneur didn't have the skills required to find and lead the team of capable and committed people needed to make the business work.'

But another £25,000 investment – in an online advertising business – has been highly rewarding. 'In 2001 it had five people and was turning over £10,000 a month. Now it has 80 people and a monthly turnover of £1m, and is still growing at 100 per cent per annum. I've already had offers of half-a-million pounds for my 1 per cent share, but I'll hold on to it for another two or three years, when I expect it to float. My share should then generate close to a £1m.'

He says the company's achievement is due to its 'dynamic' management, who, even in the early days when shareholders' meetings were held in a Brick Lane curry house, 'would think nothing of picking up the phone and talking to Microsoft.'

Vanish Patel describes the ideal business angel as someone with a passion for business and the ability to recognise talent and commitment in business executives. He should also have a good understanding of numbers and not worry about risking his capital or waiting five years before seeing a return. In other words someone rather like him.

'It's not about having a good batting average,' he remarks, 'but finding the big winners – the businesses that will grow a hundredfold.'

For light relief he acts as advisor to the BBC TV series The Dragons' Den, finding aspiring entrepreneurs to pitch their business ideas to the show's hard-nosed financiers. 'I find them a few mad people and plonkers, because they make for entertaining TV. And believe me, there are plenty out there to choose from...'

Source: *Financial Times*, 29/30 April 2006, FT Money, p. 6. © Monica Porter. Reprinted with permission.

Case study 10.3 describes a successful business angel investment.

Case study 10.3

The value of honesty and patience

FT

Paul Tyrrell on the relationship behind a company producing radiation monitors

Peter Doughty describes his company's core technology as, in simple terms, 'a 2lst-century Geiger counter'. In fact, Radiation Watch's Direct Dose Detection technology (D3) is far more accurate and versatile. 'But it enables people to grasp what we are about.'

D3 can measure any type of radiation – alpha, beta, gamma or X-rays (the Geiger counter measures only the first two accurately). Crucially, it can also distinguish between the isotopes that create any radiation it detects, making it ideal for security applications since it can provide vital early intelligence about hazardous materials. Other key markets include health physics, instrumentation and environmental monitoring.

Mr Doughty expects a handheld unit incorporating D3 to retail for only $2,000, while the nearest equivalent system costs about $20,000. Most of Radiation Watch's income will come, initially at least, from licensing.

Mr Doughty and three co-founders met in 2001 when they were recruited by a high-technology start-up, iXimaging, during its commercialisation phase. The dotcom crash meant it failed to secure necessary additional funding. In May 2003, Mr Doughty and colleagues decided to start their own business.

The team believed their combined experience and expertise – in a range of disciplines at companies such as IBM, Infineon, Nortel, Hewlett Packard and Mitsubishi – would enable them to penetrate the market for radiological measurement. They developed the D3 demonstrator technology using their own money, proved the concept and looked for business angels. They were backed by Professor Ian Page, a technologist who runs venture capital company Seven Spires Investments.

Mr Doughty says six 'major blue-chip companies' are conducting formal evaluations of products based on D3 technology, and some have announced related product launches. Volume production is expected to begin shortly.

The founder

Peter Doughty, 48, spent 17 years at Hewlett-Packard, in senior roles in its data storage division.

I knew from the outset that we would need external capital. We [the four co-founders] had to spend around £lm of our own money simply proving our concept and generating initial customer interest.

▶

By the time we met Ian Page we had several business angels lined up to provide us with the £450,000 we needed to complete the product development and to begin setting up our sales and marketing operations. We decided to go with Ian for several reasons. First, it is easier to deal with one person and easier to enter institutional funding rounds with a simple shareholding structure. Second, his company Seven Spires, had about £25m behind it, and a stated desire to stick with the business through subsequent rounds of investment. We liked the sound of this 'patient capital' – usually, VCs only want to know about the exit.

The third reason was Ian himself. He was very honest with us from the beginning, saying: 'I am an investor first and foremost. You can't rely on any added value that I might be able to give.'

However, he did have considerably more to offer because of his background and knowledge set – he is a prominent technologist as well as a prominent entrepreneurial academic – and we have benefited from that added value.

Aside from his helpful dialogue with the rest of the board, he has given us access to some powerful networks. For example, we would never have been able to recruit Lord Freeman [a junior cabinet minister in John Major's government] as chairman without him.

The only significant disagreement we have had was over how much of his money we should take in the initial funding round. Obviously, one of the biggest dilemmas for a founder is how much equity to give away in return for cash – you want to wait as long as possible to minimise dilution, but can't afford to leave it too late and end up with cash flow problems. I wanted to give away less, he wanted to buy more.

He didn't manage to persuade me at the time, but he was right. It transpired that I couldn't enter the second funding round in February 2005 at the stage of development I wanted. Even so, we managed as planned to raise another £2m. Seven Spires remained undiluted, and we brought in two prominent high-net worth individuals.

The extra investors had a superb level of understanding of what it meant to be a high-tech start up, and what is needed to build value. They also had track records of continued investment in their businesses. Most VCs impose very burdensome terms and conditions, but we managed to put a deal together that didn't carry most of those constraints.

The backer

Professor Ian Page, 57, is the business development manager of angel investment fund Seven Spires Investments, based in Oxford. A visiting professor at Imperial College, London, he has more than 20 years of academic experience in computing and electronic engineering. He is also the founder of Oxford University spin-out company Celoxica, which develops design systems for electronic engineers.

Peter Doughty and I met through the Thames Valley Investment Network, a networking club run by Oxford Innovation. It meets nearly every month and generally has about 30 attendees – a mix of angels, VCs and third-party service providers – who get to hear about six elevator pitches and then network over a buffet.

The first thing that struck me about Peter was that he was clearly at ease speaking in public and well in command of his facts. His experience in Hewlett Packard had prepared him well for this. When I talked to him and the other members of his team, I felt their business was very cohesive. Being a technologist myself, I pressed them as hard as I could on the technological details and they gave only convincing answers.

They also revealed up-front that they had been involved in a company that had failed. This impressed me, and not only because they were honest enough to talk about it. I have a somewhat 'Californian' attitude to failure. It is very helpful for a management team to know what failure is like, as they are then more likely, I believe, to avoid the most common failure modes seen in early stage companies. Their previous failure, in a different but related area, had 'derisked' the business proposition substantially.

Another reason for my interest was that, as a business angel myself, I had once invested in a sensor company that failed. Based on that experience, I felt that the important thing about their D3 sensor technology was its potential as a platform for other things – chemical and biological threat detection, for example.

Peter felt the same way from the start. He could see the big picture and was making sure everything he did was scalable. I saw immediately this strategy could play especially well in the homeland security market.

Seven Spires prefers to invest in high-tech companies that we believe can scale to a market capitalisation in excess of \$100m (£56.6m), even though they are still at pre-production stage – sometimes even pre-prototype. We derisk each investment by making sure it has the right intellectual property, team and routes to market. One of the ways I do this is by getting external validation from world-class scientists; in the case of Radiation Watch, this was a top physics professor.

I offered to fund the company over two funding rounds, because I believed in the idea and my fund had deep enough pockets. However, Peter wanted to take an initial sum, do a bit of work and then raise another round at a higher valuation. My experience told me he was being too optimistic, but he stuck to his guns.

He perhaps now agrees with me, because when it came to the second round he had not yet attracted a customer order or significant interest.

At the time I had a business partner whose view was that we should not invest in Radiation Watch again until it saw a significant 'external event'. This cost the team time and forced them on to the open market for funding. They managed to attract this funding, as it happens, from other angels who had invested in Celoxica, and Seven Spires maintained its stake from the first round. They did raise the amount they wanted, but it took them longer than expected.

Nevertheless, customers now seem to be desperate for the product: one senior homeland security official in the US recently said to Peter: 'If half of what you're telling me about this device is true, then you're two, years ahead of anything in the US.'

Source: *Financial Times*, 1 February 2006, p. 14. Reprinted with permission.

Private equity/Venture capital

The distinction between venture capital and private equity is blurry. Some use private equity to define all unquoted company equity investment, others confine 'private equity' to management buy-outs and the like of companies already well established, leaving '**venture capital**' for investment in companies at an early stage of development with high growth potential. Venture capital is a medium- to long-term investment and can consist of a package of debt and equity finance. Venture capitalists take high risks by investing in the equity of young companies often with a limited (or no) track record. Many of their investments are into little more than a management team with a good idea – which may not have started selling a product or even developed a prototype. It is believed, as a rule of thumb in the venture capital industry, that out of ten investments two will fail completely, two will perform excellently and the remaining six will range from poor to very good.

As we discussed in Chapter 8, high risk goes with high return. Venture capitalists therefore expect to get a return of between five and ten times their initial equity investment in about five to seven years. This means that the firms receiving equity finance are expected to produce annual returns of at least 26 per cent. Alongside the usual drawbacks of equity capital from the investors' viewpoint (last in the queue for income and on liquidation, etc.), investors in small unquoted companies also suffer from a lack of liquidity because the shares are not quoted on a public exchange. There are a number of different types of venture capital (although these days the last three will often be separated from VC and grouped under the title 'private equity' – *see* later in the chapter):

- ***Seedcorn*** This is financing to allow the development of a business concept. Development may also involve expenditure on the production of prototypes and additional research.
- ***Start-up*** A product or idea is further developed and/or initial marketing is carried out. Companies are very young and have not yet sold their product commercially.
- ***Other early-stage*** Funds for initial commercial manufacturing and sales. Many companies at this stage will remain unprofitable.
- ***Expansion (Development or growth)*** Companies at this stage are on to a fast-growth track and need capital to fund increased production capacity, working capital and for the further development of the product or market. Professor Steve Young's company Entropic (*see* Case study 10.1 at the beginning of the chapter) provides an example of this.
- ***Management buy-outs (MBO)*** Here a team of managers make an offer to their employers to buy a whole business, a subsidiary or a section so that they own and run it for themselves. Large companies are often willing to sell to these teams, particularly if the business is underperforming and does not fit with the strategic core business. Usually the management team have limited funds of their own and so call on private equity funds capitalists to provide the bulk of the finance.
- ***Management buy-ins (MBI)*** A new team of managers from outside an existing business buy a stake, usually backed by a private equity fund.
- ***Public-to-private (PTP)*** The management of a company currently quoted on a stock exchange may return it to unquoted status with the assistance of private equity finance being used to buy the shares.

Venture capital firms are less keen on financing seedcorn, start-ups and other early-stage companies than expansions, MBOs, MBIs and PTPs. This is largely due to the very high risk associated with early-stage ventures and the disproportionate time and costs of financing smaller deals. To make it worthwhile for a VC organisation to consider a company the investment must be at least £250,000 – the average investment is about £5m – and it is difficult to find venture capitalists willing to invest less than £2m.

Because of the greater risks associated with the youngest companies, the VC funds may require returns of the order of 50–80 per cent per annum. For well-established companies with a proven product and battle-hardened and respected management the returns required may drop to the high 20s. These returns may seem exorbitant, especially to the managers set the task of achieving them, but they have to be viewed in the light of the fact that many VC investments will turn out to be failures and so the overall performance of the VC funds is significantly less than these figures suggest. In fact the British Private Equity and Venture Capital Association which represents 'every major source of venture capital in the UK' reports that returns on funds are not excessively high. The overall long-term net returns to investors for venture funds raised between 1996 and 2006 measured to the end of 2006 was actually negative.[12] (*See* **Exhibit 10.20**.)

Exhibit 10.20

Haunted by the cost of dotcom crashing

FT

Low returns compared with private equity, have 'broken' European venture capital, write **Peter Smith** and **Martin Arnold**

The legacy of disastrous investments during the dot-com boom, when investors lost millions in companies such as Boo.com, the online retailer, haunts the UK venture capital industry.

Private equity sells itself on the basis that it outperforms the public markets. But the figures mask highly variable results.

Statistics this month from the BVCA trade body, which represents the UK private equity and venture capital industry, underline the weak returns. Over three, five and 10 years, venture capital has dramatically, underperformed all other parts of private equity and the FTSE All-Share.

Over three years, venture capital is up 3.5 per cent, compared to an average return of 31.3 per cent in all classes of UK private equity taken together and 17.2 per cent for the FTSE All-Share. On a 10-year view venture capital – investing in smaller, more speculative start-ups with high growth potential – has shown a negative return of 1.1 per cent, compared with 18.7 per cent for all private equity and a 7.9 per cent rise in the FTSE All-Share. Such figures help explain why investors have deserted venture capital in droves, with many preferring to put their capital into large buy outs.

'What happened in 1999 and 2000 was that a lot of inexperienced managers lost a lot of money,' a seasoned venture capital executive said. 'The weight of those losses are impossible for the industry to overcome when you look at the aggregate numbers.'

A leading buy-out executive told the Financial Times: 'Venture capital in Europe is broken.'

The European executive said the returns on venture capital deals were

Private equity and venture capital funds

1996 vintage funds onwards	Number of funds	Internal rate of return (% p.a.) 3 years	5 years	10 years
Venture	89	3.5	–4.8	–1.1
Small MBO	21	13.4	8.7	6.5
Mid MBO	96	28.0	17.7	13.2
Large MBO	31	37.1	27.3	22.2
Total 1996 onwards funds	237	31.3	21.1	17.1
Total all funds	391	31.3	20.9	18.7

Source: BVCA/PwC

[12] British Venture Capital Association, www.bvca.co.uk.

Exhibit 10.20 continued

much more varied than big buy-outs, pushing many leading groups to focus exclusively on bigger deals. And the profits from big buy-out deals were a 'much more stable base', he said.

As venture capital is relatively labour-intensive, requiring a large number of people working on dozens of deals to achieve the same level of returns as just one big buy-out deal, groups are deciding it is not worth pursuing.

Carlyle and 3i both do big and venture capital deals but operate under separate managements. But the fund manager said he could diversify his own portflio by picking the 'best-of-breed' firms from the venture capital and the buy-out sectors.

Another problem is that the exit markets – a sale to a rival private equity house, trade buyer or public market flotation – have been weak for venture capital.

It has been difficult to sell or float lossmaking companies even if they offer high growth characteristics.

Where there have been successes in venture capital, the businesses have often already been built to profitability. Cambridge Silicon Radio, a listed wireless chip designer business worth £1bn, was profitable at the operating level by the time it floated in 2004.

'It takes longer [to get a company to profitability] and that means you have to go for a fewer number [sic] of higher quality businesses,' the seasoned executive said. 'And that will narrow the field for those who are willing to play in this area.'

Source: Financial Times, 22 May 2007, p. 23. Reprinted with permission.

There are a number of different types of private equity providers, although the boundaries are increasingly blurred as a number of funds now raise money from a variety of sources. The **independents** can be firms, funds or investment trusts, either quoted or private, which have raised their capital from more than one source. The main sources are pension and insurance funds, but banks, corporate investors and private individuals also put money into these VC funds. **Captives** are funds managed on behalf of a parent institution (banks, pension funds, etc.). **Semi-captives** invest funds on behalf of a parent and also manage independently raised funds.

Exhibit 10.21 describes how an independent private fund is established and managed.

Exhibit 10.21

Limits are put to the test

FT

Peter Smith takes a look at a wonder of 21st century capitalism and explains how it all works

The private equity model at its core boils down to two activities – raising capital and investing it in companies.

In theory, the big attraction to investors is that private equity outperforms other asset classes. Private equity also has a role providing 'change capital' whether in restructuring, re-energising or refocusing an existing business, or fostering innovation via ventures or start-ups.

The starting point for most firms is for an individual or group of individuals to set up a limited liability partnership (LLP) and raise capital from a group of investors. The LLP has a limited life, often 10 years, and is a closed-end fund.

A plan is pitched to investors via in-house investor relations teams or by external placement agents.

This document will set out the fund's investment strategy, and describe in detail how the private equity manager defines the fund's focus and why it expects to invest profitability. It will set out the track record of the private equity manager and cover a range of terms and conditions.

Individual private equity funds vary in size, ranging from a few million dollars for venture capital funds to the more than $10bn raised by industry titans such as Blackstone, Carlyle, Kohlberg Kravis Roberts and Texas Pacific Group.

The private equity managers that run LLPs are known as the general partners (GPs), while investors are known as limited partners (LPs). LPs include US state pension schemes, historically the most important source of capital in the industry, institutional investors including banks and insurance companies, university endowments and high net worth individuals.

To date, private equity has not been easily accessed by retail investors, although in the UK there are some quoted private equity groups, notably 3i.

The fund comes into being at the time of its 'first close'.

This happens after a specified minimum amount of capital has been secured. The first close is an important milestone as it mean expressions of interest from LPs are converted into firm commitments allowing funds to be drawn down and invested at the discretion of the GP.

Exhibit 10.21 continued

Private equity manager sets up fund

1: Commitment for funds from investors (eg pension funds) to PE Fund
2: Annual management fees from fund to manager
3: Investment made by fund into 'Newco' buying target company (management also invests)
4: May include direct company investment by limited partners
5: Interest paid on loanstock element of investment either six monthly or annually, may be rolled up and repaid as capital on exist
6: Capital repaid on exist
7: Fund capital disributed as released from exited investments
8: Carried interest (bonus) paid to general partner when fund achieves hurdle rate of return

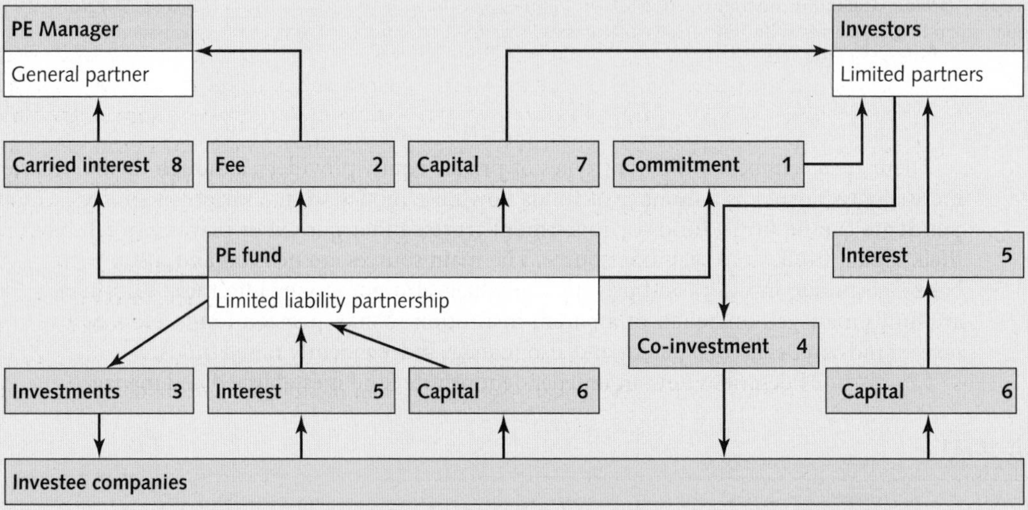

A number of subsequent 'closes' can then be held until the final close, when the fund's capital-raising programme ends.

The first part of the fund's life is the investment phase, which starts from the date of the first close and normally lasts for up to five years – although it can be shorter depending on how quickly the capital is deployed.

Both GPs and LPs do not want too much exposure to an individual deal, so are unlikely to devote more than 10 per cent of the fund's total committed capital to any one transaction. Diversification is important because private equity is a high risk, high reward endeavour.

In the case of buy-out firms, the GP will use capital drawn down from the fund together with a debt finance package to fund individual deals.

Deals may be financed with one part of equity from the fund with three or four parts of debt.

There may also be opportunities for LPs to invest additional capital in certain deals via direct 'co-invest' arrangements.

Buy-out firms normally look to take a controlling equity position in their investee companies, with stakes also held by the executives who run these businesses on their behalf.

Once under its ownership, the company could be restructured or expanded with bolt on acquisitions.

However, there are often variations, particularly in venture capital.

For example venture capital deals are often 100 per cent equity financed because it is difficult or impossible to raise debt finance for companies with little financial track record.

It is also more common for venture capital groups to back their portfolio companies for longer periods than three to five years.

Private equity firms only buy companies to sell or harvest them three to five years or more after initial investment. The aim is to make a profit on the equity.

Capital is recouped from investee companies by selling them to corporate buyers or to another private equity firm and from initial public offerings.

The private equity firm might also see a return of capital via a refinancing – whereby an investee company takes on a new and often heavier debt burden with some of the proceeds from the fresh debt package used to pay the backers a dividend.

GPs generate income and profits from two sources – they charge fees on the capital they manage and they hope to generate carried interest – a form of profit once performance hurdles are met.

Carried interest that flows to the GPs is normally based on the performance of the entire fund rather than on individual deals.

As a rule of thumb, once the fund has returned to investors the capital

Exhibit 10.21 continued

drawn from them, plus management and other fees, the subsequent profits are split.

The ratio is 80 per cent to LPs and 20 per cent to the GPs.

The GPs also charge management fees that range from 1 to 2.5 per cent. Management fees are more lucrative to the GPs in years one to five when the fund is being invested.

However, they persist in the second half of a fund's life on a stepped down basis at something like half or three quarters of the headline first five years rate.

The GPs also charge a variety of fees for portfolio company monitoring, transaction and advisory fees.

Some funds have deal-by-deal carried interest, while others generate profits for the GPs once all funds drawn from the LPs have been repaid and a hurdle rate is passed.

The hurdle rate returns to the LPs the cost of various fees that the GPs have previously charged. The GPs should be chiefly motivated by rewards generated from carried interest.

Source: *Financial Times*, 24 April 2007, p. 11. Reprinted with permission.

For the larger investments, particularly MBOs and MBIs, the private equity fund may provide only a fraction of the total funds required. Thus, in a £50m buyout the venture capitalist might supply (individually or in a syndicate with other private equity funds), say, £15m in the form of share capital (ordinary and preference shares). Another £20m may come from a group of banks in the form of debt finance. The remainder may be supplied as mezzanine debt – high-return and high-risk debt which usually has some rights to share in equity values should the company perform well (*see* Chapter 11). In the case of Alliance Boots (*see* **Exhibit 10.22**), of the £12.95 billion that was needed to buy this company and provide it with capital for expansion, 30.3 per cent (£3.93 billion) was equity, 63.3 per cent long-term debt (£8.2 billion) and 6.3 per cent short-term debt (£820m).

Private equity firms generally like to have a clear target set as the eventual '**exit**' (or '**take-out**') date. This is the point at which the private equity fund can recoup some or all of the investment.

Exhibit 10.22

Boots chief to pocket £6.5m if retailer sold

FT

Pessina and KKR share voting rights
Pension obligations to be protected

By Elizabeth Rigby, Paul J Davies and Andrew Taylor

Richard Baker, chief executive of Alliance Boots, will pocket £6.5m through the exercise of share options he has accrued in three-and-a-half years at the helm of the retail and drugs wholesaler, should the company get taken private.

Under the terms of the offer, Mr Pessina and Kohlberg Kravis Roberts will always retain equal half share in the voting rights over the group's strategy and business.

This is in spite of the fact that each party will initially own less than one-third of the equity in the group and will have the option to sell further portions of their holdings without losing any of their voting rights.

Mr Pessina, who helped create the business through the £7.8bn merger of Alliance Unichem and Boots last August, will step up to executive, chairman from his current deputy position.

He will control his share of the equity through a vehicle known as ASP, which will hold £1.27bn of his current 15 per cent stake in the business after he has cashed in about £500m worth of shares in the deal.

KKR and ASP will initially hold 32.32 per cent of the new company, but can later sell on some of their stakes after the deal is completed.

The remaining 35.4 per cent of the equity in the new group, worth £1.39bn which will carry no voting rights whatsoever, will be held by a consortium of banks and later syndicated to institutional investors in a co-operative sale that includes the assent of KKR and ASP.

The remaining £8.2bn of funds will be provided for by debt and a revolving credit facility of £820m, supplied by the consortium of banks.

Source: *Financial Times*, 10 May 2007, p. 20. Reprinted with permission.

Many exits are achieved by a sale of the company to another firm, '**corporate acquisition**' or '**trade sale**', but a popular method is a flotation on a stock market. Alternative exit routes are for the company to repurchase its shares (often accompanied by a general recapitalisation of the firm – more debt taken on) or for the private equity firm to sell the holding to an institution such as an investment trust or to another private equity group ('a **secondary buyout**').

Venture capital funds are rarely looking for a controlling shareholding in a company and are often content with a 20 or 30 per cent share. However, MBO funds usually take most of the shares of a company because the investee company is so large that the management team can only afford a small proportion of the shares. The fund may also provide money by the purchase of convertible preference shares which gives it rights to convert to ordinary shares – which will boost its equity holding and increase the return if the firm performs well. It may also insist, in an initial investment agreement, on some widespread powers. For instance, the company may need to gain the private equity/venture capitalist's approval for the issue of further securities, and there may be a veto over acquisition of other companies. Even though their equity holding is generally less than 50 per cent the venture capital funds frequently have special rights to appoint a number of directors. If specific negative events happen, such as a poor performance, they may have the right to appoint most of the board of directors and therefore take effective control. More than once the founding entrepreneur has been aggrieved to find him/herself removed from power. (Despite the loss of power, they often have a large shareholding in what has grown to be a multi-million pound company.) They are often sufficiently upset to refer to the fund which separated them from their creation as 'vulture capitalist'. But this is to focus on the dark side. When everything goes well, we have, as they say in the business jargon, 'a win-win-win situation': the company receives vital capital to grow fast, the venture capitalist receives a high return and society gains new products and economic progress.

The private equity firm can help a company with more than money. They usually have a wealth of experience and talented people able to assist the budding entrepreneur. Many of the UK's most noteworthy companies were helped by the VC industry, for example Waterstones bookshops, Oxford Instruments (and in America: Google, Apple and Sun Microsystems).

Venture capital is most powerful in the United States and in other Anglo-Saxon economies. Indeed, some would go so far as to say Silicon Valley would not exist without it (*see* **Exhibit 10.23**).

Exhibit 10.23

Founding father and mentor of digital age

FT

Obituary: Eugene Kleiner (1923–2003), Venture capitalist

Eugene Kleiner, who fled his native Austria ahead of the Nazis and later founded what became perhaps the world's most admired venture capital firm, has died . . .

As part of the team at Shockley Labs that launched the digital age by putting multiple transistors on a silicon chip, Kleiner moved from his engineering career to launch Kleiner, Perkins, Caulfield & Byers in 1972.

The Menlo Park firm, started with a then-record $8m, quickly became one of the best-known investors in technology, providing initial funding for Tandem Computer – bought years later by Compaq Computer – Genentech, America Online, Amazon.com and more than 300 other companies.

'They didn't just hand money to entrepreneurs,' Kleiner's son, Robert, said on Tuesday. 'They really mentored, and that was quite different than the type of thing you saw with investment banking.'

Kleiner left Vienna with his family in 1938 as the German occupation began. After serving in the US Army, he used the GI bill to earn a bachelor of science degree in mechanical engineering from Brooklyn Polytechnic.

In 1956, Kleiner left a job at Western Electric to join a band of engineers working for Nobel Prize-winner William Shockley at his transistor lab in Palo Alto near Stanford University. A year later, Kleiner and seven colleagues decided to strike out on their own. Using $3,500 of their own money, the eight developed a way to manufacture multiple transistors on a single silicon wafer.

Unsure how to proceed, the entrepreneurs turned to Hayden Stone, the New York investment firm. A junior employee at the firm named Arthur Rock persuaded wealthy industrialist and inventor Sherman Fairchild to set up a subsidiary called Fairchild Semiconductor. That company began Silicon Valley's long love affair with chips, transforming a

Exhibit 10.23 continued

region previously known for fruit orchards into a ground for cutting-edge technologies. The inventions made possible by chips – including desktop computers, cellular phones and hand-held organisers – drove much of the nation's productivity boom from the 1960s. . .

The engineers who started at Fairchild peeled off over the years to form most of the large chip companies in the valley, including National Semiconductor and Intel.

Not long after helping to finance Intel, Kleiner began to feel he was ready to move on from engineering. In 1972, he told Bay Area investment banker Sandy Robertson that he wanted to open a venture capital firm. Robertson introduced him to Thomas Perkins, who had run the computer business of Hewlett-Packard and also was interested in starting a venture firm.

'Sandy said you are the same kind of guys, you really ought to get together,' Perkins recalled on Tuesday. 'Neither of us wanted to combine, and it was reluctantly and only as a courtesy to Sandy Robertson that we got together for breakfast at the Hyatt Rickey's in Palo Alto.'

Kleiner Perkins invested in some companies that did terribly, including a manufacturer of a combination snowmobile and motorcycle. But its leaders formalised the venture capital field when it was very young, and Kleiner is credited with crafting a number of maxims. Among them: 'Never sell unless there are two buyers', and 'There is a time when panic is the correct response'.

By 1997, the partnership had backed companies whose combined stock market value topped $100bn.

Source: Financial Times, 4 December 2003, p. 33. Reprinted with permission.

Private equity categories

As share investment outside of stock markets has grown it has become differentiated. The main categories are shown in **Exhibit 10.24**. The title overarching all these activities is private equity. Private equity is defined as medium- to long-term finance provided in return for an equity stake in potentially high-growth unquoted companies. In this more differentiated setting the term venture capital is generally confined to describing the building of companies from the ground floor, or at least from a very low base. Management buyouts and buyins of established businesses (already off the ground floor) has become a specialist task, with a number of dedicated funds. Many of these funds are formed as private partnerships by wealthy individuals, a high proportion of which are American owned. However, there are funds available to small investors, such as 3i, that still conduct traditional VC business and MBOs and MBIs. The small investor can buy shares in these stock market listed funds. They are frequently classified as Private Equity Investment Trusts (PEITs).[13] The disadvantage of PEITs is the absence of tax benefits. This is where the **Venture Capital Trusts (VCTs)** and the **Enterprise Investment Scheme (EIS)** come in. They both offer significant tax breaks to investors in small unquoted companies – *see* next section. Finally, some funds have specialised in providing financial and professional support to quoted companies that wish to leave the stock market – public-to-private deals.

Exhibit 10.24 Private equity and its component parts

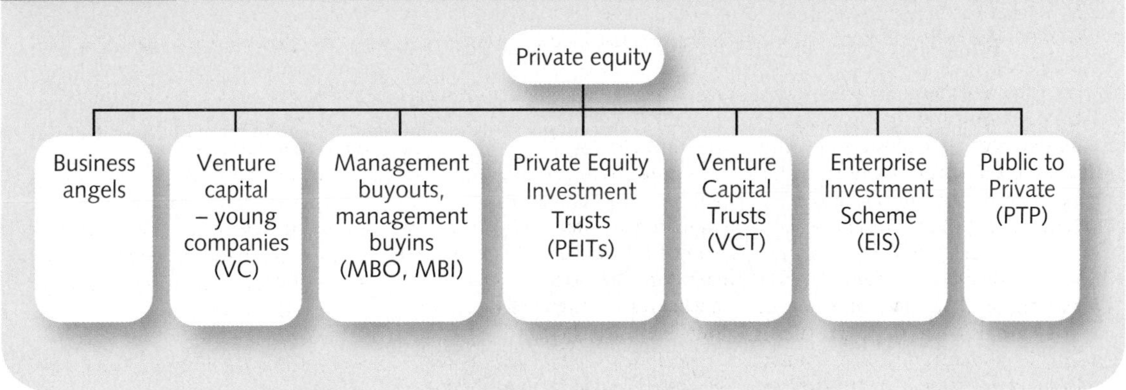

[13] More details on these are available from www.ipeit.com, www.bvca.co.uk and www.theaic.co.uk.

Venture Capital Trusts (VCTs)

It is important to distinguish between venture capital trusts, an investment vehicle introduced in 1995 to encourage investment in small and fast-growing companies which have important tax breaks, and two other types of venture capital organisations: Private Equity Investment Trusts (PEITs) which are standard investment trusts with a focus on more risky developing companies, and venture capital funds (described above).

The tax breaks for investors putting money into VCTs include an immediate relief on their current year's income at 30 per cent (by putting £10,000 into a VCT an investor will pay £3,000 less tax, so the effective cost is only £7,000). The returns (income and capital gains) on a VCT are free of tax. Investors can place up to £200,000 each per year into VCTs. These benefits are only available to investors buying new VCT shares who hold the investment for five years. The VCT managers can only invest in companies with gross assets less than £7m and the maximum amount a VCT is allowed to put into each unquoted company's shares is limited to £1m per year. ('Unquoted' for VCT is used rather loosely and includes AIM and PLUS companies.) A maximum of 15 per cent of the VCT fund can be invested in any one company. Up to half of the fund's investment in qualifying companies can be in the form of loans. VCTs are quoted on the London Stock Exchange.

These trusts offer investors a way of investing in a broad spread of small firms with high potential, but with greater uncertainty, in a tax-efficient manner. They thus provide on alternative source of equity capital.

VCTs have been used to raise money to promote bands – *see* **Exhibit 10.25**.

Enterprise Investment Scheme (EIS)

Another government initiative to encourage the flow of risk capital to smaller companies is the Enterprise Investment Scheme. Income tax relief at 20 per cent is available for investments of up to £400,000 made directly (no need for a fund manager as with VCTs) into qualifying company

Exhibit 10.25

Ingenious set to fund new bands to tune of £30m

FT

By Andrew Edgecliffe-Johnson, Media Editor

Investors will able to invest directly in a portfolio of new bands after Ingenious Media launched a £30m venture capital trust to provide independent artist and repertoire financing.

Its launch of Ingenious Music VCT 2 came as it announced the first investment from its earlier £15m music VCT, which will provide £300,000 of financial backing to a band called The Heights, funding their recording costs, tour plans, videos and album marketing expenses.

Ingenious claimed that, if it raised the full £45m from the two VCTs, it would become the largest independent provider of artist & repertoire investment in the UK.

Ingenious is working with some of the four large music companies and smaller independent labels. The investment in The Heights will be through a joint venture with Channelfly, operator of a chain of clubs at which acts including Franz Ferdinand and the Kaiser Chiefs first came to prominence.

Source: *Financial Times*, 17 January 2006, p. 24. Reprinted with permission.

shares. There is also capital gains tax relief, and losses within EISs are allowable against income tax. Investment under EIS means investing when the company issues shares, not the purchase of shares in the secondary market. The tax benefits are lost if the investments are held for less than three years. Investors are not allowed to hold more than 30 per cent of the shares in any company. To raise money from this source the firm must have been carrying out a 'qualifying activity' for three years – this generally excludes financial investment and property companies. The company must not be quoted on LSE's Main Market and the most it can raise under the EIS in any one year is usually £1m. The company must not have gross assets worth more than £7m. Funds which invest in a range of EIS companies are springing up to help investors spread risk.

Corporate venturing and incubators

Larger companies sometimes foster the development of smaller enterprises. This can take numerous forms, from joint product development work to an injection of equity finance. The small firm can thereby retain its independence and yet contribute to the large firm: perhaps its greater freedom to innovate will generate new products which the larger firm can exploit to the benefit of both. Intel uses **corporate venturing** to increase demand for its technology by, for example, investing in start-up companies in China. Shell uses it to promote innovation. BT established a venture unit to harvest value from its 14,000 patents and 2,500 unique inventions.

Another example of corporate venturing is described in **Exhibit 10.26**.

Incubators are places where a start-up company not only will gain access to finance, but will be able to receive support in many forms. This may include all humdrum operational managerial tasks being taken care of (e.g. accounting, legal, human resources), business planning, the supply of managers for various stages of the company's development, property management, etc. As a result the entrepreneurial team can concentrate on innovation and grow the business, even if they have no prior managerial experience.

Exhibit 10.26

GSK's venture capital funds steps up European focus

FT

By Andrew Jack

GlaxoSmithKline, the UK-based pharmaceutical group, is stepping up the European focus of its in-house venture capital fund in a sign of the growing capacity of the region's biotechnology companies to challenge their US rivals.

Deborah Harland, recently appointed as the first ever European-based principal for SR1, GSK's fund, projected that Europe could supply a third of its investments within two years.

Her strategy will be presented to senior GSK executives this week as SR1 details two new investments, one in the UK and another in a life sciences fund based in the Netherlands and Germany.

The actions come at a time when the European biotech sector has been demonstrating fresh vigour, with increased interest by venture capital funds and a series of recent licensing deals and acquisitions with larger pharmaceutical companies.

They also reflect increasing efforts by large, long-established pharmaceutical companies to stimulate research with external researchers that could lead to future partnerships to help boost their own lines of new medicines.

The fund has invested about $300m (£170m) in 120 companies over 20 years, of which about one-fifth has been in Europe but the vast majority in the US, with a strong biotech entrepreneurial tradition.

SR1 typically invests a maximum of $5m in any one investment initially, with another $15m in follow up support. It does not seek any pre-emption rights for GSK with promising projects, but hopes to increasingly align its projects with ones that are of interest to the parent company.

Source: Financial Times, 24 April 2006, p. 22. Reprinted with permission

Government sources

Some local authorities have set up VC-type funds in order to attract and encourage industry. Large organisations with similar aims include the Scottish Development Agency and the Welsh Development Agency. Equity, debt and grant finance may be available from these sources.

Disillusionment and dissatisfaction with quotation

Appendix 10.1 contains a number of newspaper articles about companies which either are dissatisfied with being quoted on a stock exchange or have never been quoted and feel no need to join. A reading of these will provide a wider understanding of the place of stock markets, their importance to some firms and how many companies are able to expand and produce wealth without them.[14] Some of the main points are summarised in **Exhibit 10.27**. The arguments are taken directly from numerous articles (only some of which are reproduced here) and do not necessarily represent reasoned scientific argument.

Exhibit 10.27 Arguments for and against joining a stock exchange

For

- Access to new capital for growth.
- Liquidity for existing shareholders.
- Discipline on management to perform.
- Able to use equity to buy businesses.
- Allows founders to diversify.
- Borrow more easily or cheaply.
- Can attract better management.
- Forces managers to articulate strategy clearly and persuasively.
- Succession planning may be made easier – professional managers rather than family.
- Increased customer recognition.
- Allow local people to buy shares.
- Share incentive schemes are more meaningful.

Against

- Dealing with 'City' folk is time consuming and/or boring.
- City is short-termist.
- City does not understand entrepreneurs.
- Stifles creativity.
- Focus excessively on return on capital.
- Empire building through acquisitions on a stock exchange – growth for its own sake (or for directors) can be the result of a quote.
- The stock market undervalues entrepreneur's shares in the entrepreneur's eyes.
- Loss of control for founding shareholders.
- Strong family-held companies in Germany, Italy and Asia where stock markets are used less.
- Examples of good strong unquoted companies in UK: Bamford, Rothschilds, Littlewoods.
- Press scrutiny is irritating.
- Market share building (and short-term low profit margins) are more possible off exchange.
- The temptation of over-rapid expansion is avoided off exchange.
- By remaining unquoted, the owners, if they do not wish to put shareholder wealth at the centre of the firm's purpose, don't have to (environment or ethical issues may dominate).
- Costs of maintaining a quote, e.g. SE fees, extra disclosure costs, management time.

[14] You might like to consult the first, second and third editions of this book for additional articles.

Concluding comments

There are a number of alternative ways of raising finance by selling shares. The advantages and problems associated with each method and type mean that careful thought has to be given to establishing the wisest course of action for a firm, given its specific circumstances. Failure here could mean an unnecessary loss of control, an unbalanced capital structure, an excessive cost of raising funds or some other destructive outcome. But getting the share question right is only one of the key issues involved in financing a firm. The next chapter examines another, that of long-term debt finance.

Key points and concepts

- **Ordinary shareholders** own the company. They have the rights of control, voting, receiving annual reports, etc. They have no rights to income or capital but receive a residual after other claimants have been satisfied. This residual can be very attractive.
- **Debt capital holders** have no formal control but they do have a right to receive interest and capital.
- **Equity** as a way of financing the firm:

Advantages	*Disadvantages*
1 No obligation to pay dividends – 'shock absorber'. **2** Capital does not have to be repaid – 'shock absorber'	**1** High cost: **a** issue costs; **b** required rate of return. **2** Loss of control. **3** Dividends not tax deductible.

- **Authorised share** capital is the maximum amount permitted by shareholders to be issued.
- **Issued share** capital is the amount issued (sold) expressed at par value.
- **Share premium** The difference between the sale price and par value of shares.
- **Private companies** Companies termed 'Ltd' are the most common form of limited liability company.
- **Public limited companies** (plcs) can offer their shares to a wider range of investors, but are required to have £50,000 of share capital.
- **Preference shares** offer a fixed rate of return, but without a guarantee. They are part of shareholders' funds but not part of the equity capital.

Advantages to the firm	*Disadvantages to the firm*
1 Dividend 'optional'. **2** Usually no influence over management. **3** Extraordinary profits go to ordinary shareholders. **4** Financial gearing considerations.	**1** High cost of capital relative to debt. **2** Dividends are not tax deductible.

- **Types of preference share:** cumulative, participating, redeemable, convertible.
- **Ordinary shares** rank higher than **deferred ordinary shares** for dividends. Preferred ordinary shares rank higher than ordinary shares
- **Golden shares** have extraordinary special powers.
- **To float on LSEs Main Market** of the London Stock Exchange the following are required:
  - a prospectus;
  - an acceptance of new responsibilities (e.g. dividend policy may be influenced by exchange investors; directors' freedom to buy and sell may be restricted);
  - 25 per cent of share capital in public hands;

▶

- that the company is suitable;
- usually three years of accounts;
- competent and broadly based management team;
- appropriate timing for flotation;
- a sponsor;
- a corporate broker;
- underwriters (usually);
- accountants' reports;
- lawyers;
- registrar.

- **Following flotation on the Main Market:**
  - greater disclosure of information;
  - restrictions on director share dealings;
  - annual fees to LSE;
  - high standards of behaviour.
- **Methods of flotation:**
  - offer for sale;
  - offer for sale by tender;
  - introduction;
  - offer for sale by subscription;
  - placing;
  - intermediaries' offer;
  - reverse takeover.
- **Book-building** Investors make bids for shares. Issuers decide price and allocation in light of bids.
- **Stages in a flotation:**
  - pre-launch publicity;
  - decide technicalities, e.g. method, price, underwriting;
  - pathfinder prospectus;
  - launch of public offer – prospectus and price;
  - close of offer;
  - allotment of shares;
  - announcement of price and first trading.
- **The Alternative Investment Market (AIM) differs** from the Main Market in:
  - nominated advisers, not sponsors;
  - lower costs;
  - no minimum capitalisation, trading history or percentage of shares in public hands needed;
  - lower ongoing costs.
- **Costs of new issues:**
  - administrative/transaction costs;
  - the equity cost of capital;
  - market pricing costs.
- **Rights issues** are an invitation to existing shareholders to purchase additional shares.
- **The theoretical ex-rights price** is a weighted average of the price of the existing shares and the new shares.
- The **nil paid rights** can be sold instead of buying new shares.
- **Value of a right on a new share:**

  Theoretical market value of share ex-rights – Subscription price

- **Value of a right on an old share:**

$$\frac{\text{Theoretical market value of share ex-rights} - \text{Subscription price}}{\text{Number of old shares required to purchase one new share}}$$

- **The pre-emption right** can be bypassed in the UK under strict conditions.
- **Placings** New shares sold directly to a group of external investors. If there is a *clawback* provision, so that existing shareholders can buy the shares at the same price instead, the issue is termed an **open offer**.
- **Acquisition for shares** Shares are created and given in exchange for a business.
- **Vendor placing** Shares are given in exchange for a business. The shares can be immediately sold by the business vendors to institutional investors.
- **Scrip issues** Each shareholder is given more shares in proportion to current holding. No new money is raised.
- **Warrants** The holder has the right to subscribe for a specified number of shares at a fixed price at some time in the future. Warrants are sold by the company, which is committed to selling the shares if warrant holders insist.
- **Business angels** Wealthy individuals investing £10,000 to £250,000 in shares and debt of small, young companies with high growth prospects. Also offer knowledge and skills.
- **Private equity/Venture capital (VC)** Finance for high-growth-potential unquoted firms. Sums: £250,000 minimum, average £5m. Some of the investment categories of VC are:
  - seedcorn;
  - start-up;
  - other early-stage;
  - expansion (development);
  - management buyouts (MBO): existing team buy business from corporation;
  - management buyins (MBI): external managers buy a stake in a business and take over management;
  - Public-to-private (PTP).
- **Rates of return** demanded by VC range from 26 per cent to 80 per cent per annum depending on risk.
- **Exit** ('take-out') is the term used by private equity/venture capitalists to mean the method of selling a holding. A popular method is a trade sale to another organisation. Stock market flotation, own-share repurchase and sale to an institution are other possibilities.
- Venture capitalists often strike **agreements** with entrepreneurs to give the venture capitalists **extraordinary powers** if specific negative events occur, e.g. poor performance.
- **Venture Capital Trusts (VCTs)** are special tax-efficient vehicles for investing in small unquoted firms through a pooled investment.
- **Enterprise Investment Scheme (EIS)** Tax benefits are available to investors in small unquoted firms willing to hold the investment for three years.
- **Corporate venturing** Large firms can sometimes be a source of equity finance for small firms. **Incubators** provide finance and business services.
- **Government agencies** can be approached for equity finance.
- **Being quoted has significant disadvantages**, ranging from consumption of senior management time to lack of understanding between the City and directors and the stifling of creativity.

Appendix 10.1 Reasons for and against floating

Exhibit 10.27

Your Move bosses make small fortune

FT

By Jim Pickard, Property Correspondent

The entrepreneurs who two years ago led a management buy-out of Your Move, the estate agency, from Aviva, the insurance group, are set to realise a small fortune with the £211m flotation of the business, now called LSL Property Services.

Six executives put just £1m into the £42m management buy-out of Your Move in July 2004.

Five of them are to reap a total of £18m from the sale of shares in the initial public offering while keeping another £52m of shares, or about a quarter of the business.

The sixth executive, Andy Mohum-Smith, is selling his entire £12m stake and retiring.

Barclays Private Equity, which backed the buy-out, will sell £45m of shares and keep a 29 per cent stake.

Your Move made losses for 18 years after it was founded in 1985.

In 2000, while part of Aviva, it made a loss of £40m.

Shortly after, Simon Embley, now chief executive, was hired to turn the business round.

When Aviva disposed of Your Move in 2004, along with E.surv, a surveying business, it recorded a book loss of £100m.

Since then, however, the business has improved to report an operating profit of £14m on turnover of £134.9m in the year to December 31 2005. In the six months to June 30, it reported operating profit of £10.2m on turnover of £91.3m.

After the buy-out, Your Move added 130 branches by buying rival Reeds Rains for an estimated £22m.

The combined business is now the third-largest estate agency in the UK with 322 owned branches and 85 other branches, all under the Your Move and Reeds Rains brands.

Source: Financial Times, 17 November 2006, p. 18. Reprinted with permission.

Exhibit 10.28

Virgin accepts defeat with Victory delist

FT

By Tom Braithwaite

Sir Richard Branson's Virgin Group plans to delist Victory Corporation, its struggling cosmetics and jewellery subsidiary, to cut costs and restructure the business

Shares in Victory, a retail group, have fallen 91 per cent in the past five years, hurt by consistently poor trading. They closed on Wednesday, at 46p, about 20 per cent lower than the 58p a share at which they listed on the AIM market 10 years ago.

In 1998, only two years after listing Victory, Virgin admitted that floating start-up companies was not the right way for the group to proceed. The retailer, which has also sold clothing, will become a part of Sir Richard's roster of companies, which includes Virgin Atlantic, the airline, and Virgin Rail, the train operator.

Virgin has gradually increased its stake in the group from an initial 12.8 per cent to 88.7 per cent before yesterday's announcement, as it tried to support the flagging business. It has subscribed for additional capital and guaranteed borrowing.

Virgin said the delisting would save about £300,000 a year in listing and brokers fees and allow Victory to concentrate on improving selling channels, using television and internet rather than stores.

Source: Financial Times, 24 November 2006, p. 18. Reprinted with permission.

Exhibit 10.29

Praise the company that stays public, for it does good work

FT

By Stefan Stern

I know what you're thinking: 'Why am I working in such a transparent business… a public company, making $1m or $2m and getting beaten up all the time? Why not run a private business?'

OK, so perhaps not all of you are thinking in precisely those terms. But the sentiment – outlined by David Rubenstein, co-founder of the Carlyle private equity group, in a recent interview in Business Week – may be widely held. Who needs to be filing quarterly reports and worrying every moment what analysts (or the press) may have got hold of? Why not just get your head down, run the business and earn some serious money?

Certainly, the conventional wisdom at the start of 2007 is that all the fun is being had in private business. Henry Silverman, former chief executive of the now-broken-up leisure and real estate conglomerate Cendant, told the New York Times recently: 'There is no reason to be public company any more.'

From a CEO's point of view you can see what he means. When Robert Nardelli left Home Depot earlier this month, his humiliation at the hands of shareholders was complete. Even if he did walk away with a consoling $210m in his back pocket, the damage to his reputation was considerable. Hedge fund manager Leon Cooperman declared: 'I think it will be a long time before Bob Nardelli gets involved in a public company again.'

There seems to be a dreadful inevitability about the phenomenon of private equity at the moment. No company's future – not even Pearson's, the owner of this newspaper – can be discussed without the possibility of a private equity bid being raised. Public markets are suddenly too boring. Why not wade into the deep and enticing pools of capital on offer at the private equity firms?

Freed from the intrusive gaze of institutional shareholders, it is said, management can take the bold and radical steps needed to turn businesses round without being penalised by investors in the short term. Relatively low interest rates allow companies to borrow cheaply while dramatically cutting costs. This sort of thinking informed Sir Philip Green's 2004 bid for the British retailer Marks and Spencer when he offered M&S investors £4 a share to take the company private.

Turning down Sir Philip's offer now looks like one of the better decisions those shareholders have ever made (current M&S share price: flirting with the £7 mark). What M&S has shown is that it is entirely possible for public companies to execute a recovery if the right leadership is in place and if investors give managers the time they need to deliver.

Just a few steps down the UK high street from your nearest M&S, you might find a branch of Debenhams, another retailer that has, unlike M&S experienced private equity ownership in the past few years (2003–2006) prior to being floated again last year.

Here the story is rather different. Debenhams' temporary owners did very well out of the deal, selling off valuable properties and issuing huge dividends to themselves. But having rejoined the stock market in May, the company's performance has been disappointing. And Debenhams' share price has slipped from 195p at flotation to about 170p today.

Running a public company is a huge responsibility. It is also a noble and worthwhile task. At a time when some are questioning the very legitimacy of business, the ethical public company is the key exhibit in the case for the defence: a big, transparent and responsible citizen.

Had Stuart Rose, the M&S boss, chosen to lead the company turnaround for private owners, he might now be tens of millions of pounds richer. But M&S would most likely be a smaller and less distinguished company. It would also almost certainly not have committed to spending £200m over the next five years in an attempt to become 'carbon neutral'.

Given that private equity owners often seek nothing more than the most rapid return possible to the stock market, you have to wonder whether this form of ownership can lay claim to any special virtues at all.

Managers should be stewards of their companies, not merely their semi-detached financial engineers. To illustrate the difference, consider people who think 'home' and people who think 'house' about the place where they live, says Mark Goyder, director of the London-based think-tank Tomorrow's Company. If you think 'home' there is an assumption of continuity. 'Money is spent that cannot be recovered in the event of an early sale but adds to the individual character of that home,' he says.

'Others, particularly those who expect to be moving on again in a few years, make a much simpler pay-back calculation. They accept what they inherit by way of carpets and colour schemes and avoid spending on the longer term, knowing that their time will soon come to sell.'

Source: Financial Times, 23 January 2007, p. 10. Reprinted with permission.

Exhibit 10.30

JCB's reasons to be private

FT

Paul Betts

To float or not to float? Sir Anthony Bamford has no hesitation in answering. 'Yes, we have looked at it but for a company like JCB with only a few family shareholders it is not a satisfactory option. We either stay private or sell 100 per cent; and I have no intention of doing that.'

He admits this makes his company somewhat singular: a privately owned, successful British-based manufacturer that is a global brand.

Started in the Midlands in 1945, JCB is now the UK's biggest privately owned manufacturer and the world's fourth largest maker of construction machinery, exporting nearly 75 per cent of its products to 140 countries. Its yellow backhoe loaders have become part of the landscape and of the language...

So why has JCB grown as a private manufacturing company in the UK when so many others have disappeared? Sir Anthony says the company has remained focused on its business, growing organically in its niche construction, industrial and agricultural equipment markets, relying on its own cash rather than borrowing and adopting a 'simple long-term strategy led by product and innovation'.

Floating the company would have spoilt this. 'If we were a public company we would probably have had to diversify because analysts and stockbrokers would have said we were in a very cyclical industry. They would have . . . pushed us into doing things we shouldn't.'

Companies float for several reasons, he says. 'They have lots of shareholders who want to cash in. But we don't. Or they need more capital and, again, we don't. Or they want to have paper to buy other businesses – but we have stuck to organic growth.' . . .

Sir Anthony recalls an old anecdote involving his father and Donald Stokes, then boss of Leyland: 'They were standing side by side in the men's room in the Dorchester Hotel in London, when Stokes asked my father if he would sell the business for £20m. My father said No. He offered £22m, then £25m with Leyland shares that he claimed were bound to go up in value. Thank goodness, my father said he was not selling. When the shares collapsed we would have been left with barely £1m.'

And that would have been curtains for what was to become a lonely flagship of British engineering in today's global market.

Source: Financial Times, 4 February 2003. Reprinted with permission.

Exhibit 10.31

Ferrari chief keen for IPO to drive growth

FT

By Paul Betts in Maranello

Luca di Montezemolo, Ferrari's chairman, is keen to see the sports car and racing company launch a public offering on the stock market.

He told the Financial Times this would help fund Ferrari's expansion into entertainment, including the development of Ferrari theme parks. It also wants to step up its retailing activities and further develop its Maserati car business.

To launch an initial public offer, Mr Montezemolo needs the approval of Ferrari's main shareholder, the Italian Fiat automotive group with 90 per cent of the company. The other 10 per cent is held by Piero Lardi-Ferrari, son of the company's founder.

In a leaked document following a recent board meeting, Fiat said it was contemplating a possible Ferrari IPO within the framework of a programme to cut its €6bn debt...

Ferrari had always relied on its own financial resources and would continue to do so. But at some later stage, an IPO would help raise fresh resources for new developments, he explained.

An IPO would also help develop Maserati...

Source: Financial Times, 18 March 2002, p. 25. Reprinted with permission.

Exhibit 10.32

This Lord is not for turning Haymarket over

FT

Michael Heseltine tells Emiko Terazono that he has no intention of selling or floating the magazine publisher

It is common for Westminster *habitué* Lord Heseltine to receive lunch invites from Mayfair-based private equity executives and investment bankers these days.

The Tory peer is the executive chairman of Haymarket, the UK's biggest privately owned magazine publisher, and the prospect of a possible sale of a float is enough to have City financiers and cash-rich financial sponsors filling his diary

'I'll tell them the business is not for sale, and then say "if you still want me for lunch, I'll come"', he smiles.

The 73-year old Lord Heseltine is determined to keep the company he created in 1959 within the family.

From the outfit started with the Directory of Opportunities for Graduates, it has expanded into an international publishing group with 100 titles in 28 languages.

'The disciplines applied by the stock market are not always good. You have to report quarterly and you are judged by the share value that may have nothing to do with you.

'You are forced to make relatively short-term decisions. We don't have, to make those sort of decisions. Instead of shareholders, we have a very supportive bank,' he says.

The publisher recorded a 12 per cent fall in pre-tax profit to £8.6m because of product launches and international and digital investments on a 17 per cent rise in revenues to £229m in 2005.

An important incentive for staff is the profit share scheme, although Lord Heseltine complains that staff incentive schemes at private companies are not as tax-efficient as those found at public companies.

Source: Financial Times, 8 June 2006, p. 18. Reprinted with permission.

Exhibit 10.33

Monsoon chief to try to take group private

FT

By Elizabeth Rigby, Retail Correspondent

Peter Simon, the founder and chairman of Monsoon, is attempting to take the clothing chain private by trying to buy the 24.6 per cent stake of the company that he does not own.

It is the second time in less than two years that Mr Simon has tried to increase his share in the company he floated in 1999.

Mr Simon has long been uncomfortable running the company he founded in 1974 under the public gaze.

He has refused to pay dividends or appoint independent non-executive directors – choosing to put his brother on the board instead.

'He hates running Monsoon as a public company,' the company said.

'He dislikes the costs and the criticism he receives and the restrictions it places on him. He feels that the growth strategy for the business – not paying a dividend and investing heavily in expansion – is something that does not fit with being a public company.'

Source: Financial Times, 23/24 July 2005, p. M1. Reprinted with permission.

Exhibit 10.34

Private equity demands only the best

Ian Armitage

FT

Everyone wants a job in private equity, or so it seems. Recent surveys, including one in this newspaper, suggest that not only are executives increasingly being offered the chance to join companies owned by private equity, but that many are hitting the phones in search of the opportunity to run their own business and make a pile.

The opportunity is certainly there. The ever-reliable statistics from the British Venture Capital Association state that the private equity community has £5.3bn invested in 1,300 companies in the UK. They all need a lot of management.

Personally I am not at all surprised that a growing number of executives would rather work for a business in the private equity sector than for a quoted company. The attractions are considerable. First, there is a great deal of job satisfaction. Private equity-backed companies work towards clear and stretching three- to five-year goals. You should never see the moving of goal-posts that might occur under the pressure to deliver short-term benefits.

Then there is direct accountability. The investors always sit on the board. They are well informed and, as directors, ultimately share responsibillty for success and failure of the enterprise alongside executives. Moreover, their reward and interests are aligned with management via the effect on their funds. Believe me, shared responsibility and motivation make us act and think like owners. We can be a demanding and sometimes difficult bunch of people but most managers whom I have worked with consider this a lot better than having to deal with numerous, faceless, institutional investors who will ignore you or slate you behind your back and wash their hands of all responsibility. Or, for that matter, better, than company placemen with no real interest in the business, its customers or staff.

Finally, managers are attracted to work with our industry by the financial rewards for success. It is no secret that private equity firms want to share their capital gains with management teams, rewards that can often run into many millions. Certainly they earn more than they would from the sum of salary, bonus and options they might get in the normal corporate world.

But before you all conclude that the pavements are made of gold allow me to state the obvious. The reason that private equity firms reward their successful managers so highly is that they want to be able to pick the very best talent out there, to give them the best chance of a great return for their investors. We really want to work with only the top 20 per cent of managers. The rest will tend to get stopped at the gate or their tenure will prove to be brief.

Many are called and few are chosen. What are we looking for among these special people? The first is the easiest to identify – a verifiable record of performance. We look for people with track records of making money, for making a positive difference, for out-competing their peer group. Best of all are people with a record of success that precisely matches the job in hand.

The next item is attitude. It is easy to underestimate but it nearly always makes the difference in our deals where we are attempting to capitalise on change, which normally goes hand in hand with surmounting obstacles. So we look for someone who likes hard work, who has passion for the business, its customers and its people. Someone who is self-confident and intellectually honest in the sense that all facts are friendly. We want to pick a person who wants to make a big capital gain. Relationships that work between us and those who run businesses are invariably open, direct, two-way and honest. These take time to work on and for trust to be built.

It would be comforting to believe that people with good track records are in plentiful supply; the facts are that they are rare and that they make all the difference. Indeed, as we know that we will face increasing pressure on our investment returns, it is safe to assume that the better European private equity firms will continue to scour the globe for the best managers they can find. Remember that our business is a people business and it is about allocating capital. Simply put, we ought to put our capital to work behind people who can make better returns than we can.

So how do we find these people? More than half of them come with the companies we buy. It is a key part of our due diligence, the most important part, to evaluate the management team and decide whether they will flourish in a private equity backed investment. The rest we find via headhunters and through our networks of friends and acquaintances. Our desire to strengthen teams remains undimmed as we know we must sell on a better team than we found when we bought the business. So if you have the right profile and track record do not feel obliged to call us or fill in a form sooner or later we will find you.

The private equity sector has been depicted by some parts of the media as a sure bet lottery ticket, a four year financial escalator that transforms modest journeymen into yacht owners. Do not be deceived. Our industry offers no one a free ride. It is all about performance.

The writer is chief executive of HG Capital

Source: *Financial Times*, 28 September 2005, p. 19. Reprinted with permission.

Exhibit 10.35

Chairman complains of City's short-termism

C&W wants impatient investors to sign up to a strategy that it hopes will come good in 2009

writes Mark Odell

Cable and Wireless management appears to have had enough of the 'short-termism' of the City and is, instead, wishing it were in private hands.

That seems to be the view of Richard Lapthorne as the chairman sought to give his embattled management room to deliver on a strategy to turn round the ailing UK business.

Mr Lapthorne is asking investors to sign up to a strategy that will not deliver until 2009. As part of this, he has scrapped short-term future guidance for the UK business. 'I was trying to give the management cover for doing the right thing rather than feeling exposed if they miss a target,' he said.

Yesterday, Richard Lapthorne lamented the City's short-termism, recalling the battle that Rolls-Royce had with the City when investors refused to buy into management's three- to four-year view of the business.

Eventually, he says, the UK engineering group delivered as promised.

To illustrate his point Mr Lapthorne suggested that Cable and Wireless could be better off in private hands. 'I think the market complains about private equity buyers when they only have themselves to blame,' he said.

Analysts are sceptical. They point out that the cash generation of the UK business, which accounts for about half of group revenues, is nowhere near as strong as that of some of the medium-sized European incumbent operators.

Source: Financial Times, 9 November 2005, p. 22. Reprinted with permission.

Exhibit 10.36

The Dalek invasion stumbles on the corporate ladder

Jonathan Guthrie

Private equity operators have a reputation in some quarters of business akin to that of the Daleks: mechanistic, invasive and not blessed with a sense of humour. They roll into companies in which they have acquired a majority stake brandishing their calculators as implacably as a Dalek's sink plunger while screaming tinnily: 'Exterminate costs! Exterminate costs!'

In Suffolk last week, Edward Atkin, chairman and main shareholder in Cannon Avent, a baby equipment manufacturer, proudly showed me machines printing logos on feeder bottles in an opulent eight colours. He claimed such indulgences – which he said contributed to the value of a brand supporting 1,000 jobs – would disappear rapidly following any buy-out backed by private equity. 'Those Smart Alecs would double their money in 24 months, but ruin the company,' he said. 'They would make a terrific profit at first, by outsourcing production to China, but over time the business would deteriorate.'

Despite the hostility of owner-managers such as Mr Atkin, private equity specialists are swarming all over British business, aided by an ability to climb stairs, obstacles that render many boardrooms inaccessible to marauding Daleks. My dog-eared list of the 100 largest private businesses in the UK shows about 40 are controlled by private equity houses. Over five years the number of people working for private equity-backed companies has jumped 23 per cent to about 2.9m, a striking 16 per cent of the private sector workforce. When Sir Ronald Cohen, founder of Apax, launched his first fund in 1981, venture capital was an arcane US concept. These days it permeates all levels of British life, from CVC and 3i bidding for the Daily Telegraph, to Carlyle planning to float Qinetiq, a business which was once part of the Ministry of Defence.

The growth of private equity results partly from defects in the stock market. Public company bosses benefit from a bewildering plethora of incentives. But it is the prospect of

Exhibit 10.36 continued

becoming a multi-millionaire quickly, via a successful buy-out, that really gets them sweating corporate assets. Direct communication between executives and a few private equity investors makes restructuring easier, while sparing the business from damaging shareholder panics. Private equity has made inroads into other forms of company ownership too – for example, in buying up businesses private owners would once have handed on to their children.

Private equity investments in the UK are estimated to be worth £100bn, a tidy sum even when the main market and Aim are capitalised at £2,300bn. And private equity has been growing, while the nominal value of those markets is the same now as it was at the end of 1998.

Time to learn Dalek? Perhaps not. Private equity is not the all-conquering force it sometimes appears. Although only 20 per cent of exits are via flotations, these set the tone for other forms of disposal. The two-year hiatus in UK new issues has left private equity houses bloated with assets, making it harder for them to raise new funds.

A report published by KPMG this year concluded that realisations would have to triple in 2004 to purge the gouty patient. Progress has been disappointing since then, despite the revival of new issues, says Oliver Tant, global head of private equity at KPMG. The KPMG report meanwhile confirmed that write-offs – for which read 'failed investments' – were close to becoming the predominant form of exit. In private equity, as in any other maturing industry, competition is reducing the scope for profits. Today, 10-year returns average 14 per cent, compared with a figure closer to 20 per cent eight years ago…

By now tears prompted by the plight of private equity executives will be welling in the eyes of more sensitive readers. Wipe them away. Successful venture capitalists enjoy big rewards and there are few tougher cookies in the biscuit tin. Andrew Palmer, founder of the New Covent Garden Soup Company, says any entrepreneur raising private equity 'should keep £100,000 in reserve in case you need to sue your backers. Otherwise you will be dead. They are experts in negotiating and tying up small print. They will say [an advantageous] clause is needed "just to protect investors", but don't you believe it'.

Sharing control of a business is generally odious for the bootstrapping entrepreneur. But for the career executive, private equity, via the buy-out, has created an invigorating opportunity to run a business free from the bureaucracy imposed by a big company.

One example is Peter Hatherly, finance director of Accantia, maker of Lil-lets tampons and Simple soap, bought out from Smith & Nephew for £140m in 2000. Accantia was backed first by ABN Amro, then by Duke Street Capital. Mr Hatherly says the key to harmony is for management to choose private equity investors whose objectives match their own, to deliver on targets and to 'manage expectations carefully'. He says: 'You need to be very transparent and avoid giving your backers any shocks.' That rules out printing logos in eight colours on all your products, I guess.

Source: *Financial Times*, 15 June 2004, p. 17. Reprinted with permission.

Exhibit 10.37

Climbing aboard the flight from flotation

FT

Philip Coggan

Farewell to the stock market. Hardly a week goes by without some smaller company announcing that it is in talks about a bid from its founding shareholders or from venture capital groups. By contrast, the new issues calendar looks fairly moribund.

The appeal of a stock market listing seems to be wearing thin. In large part, of course, this is because of three years of falling share prices. There was no shortage of listing applicants four years ago when you could float a brick on the world's stock markets.

Nowadays, however, entrepreneurs fret that the market does not give their shares an appropriate rating. They tire of being cross-questioned by impertinent shareholders about the details of their strategy and the minutiae of their accounts. Life will be better, they feel, outside the public gaze.

They may find that this is an illusion. Venture capital groups can be hard taskmasters. After all, they have large and illiquid stakes and tightly defined return targets. They will be even more attentive to detail than the likes of Fidelity and State Street.

Nevertheless, this flight from quotation does raise some important issues about the future of the stock market. There are more than 2,000 quoted companies in the UK. But the largest 100 companies in the FTSE 100 index comprise more than 80 per cent of the value of the market; while the Hoare Govett Smaller Company index, which covers the smallest 10 per cent of the main market by value, contains 1,284 constituents.

In other words, the vast bulk of investor attention focuses on a very small proportion of the market by number. The minnows of the market are often too tiny to be noticed by the big institutional investors; many

Exhibit 10.37 continued

would not look at a business valued at less than £100m. By the same token, they would be unlikely to attract the attention of investment bank analysts; it would not be worth the analysts' time, given the small amount of business such a company would be likely to generate . . .

What then is the point of such small companies being on the market? The theory of stock markets is that they add value by allowing companies to raise new capital, so they can expand. But many quoted companies joined the market, and had their best chance to raise capital, years ago. A lack of serious institutional or analytical interest means that it would be very hard for them to raise new equity capital in current markets.

A few small companies will always be able to exploit their listing. But these are likely to be businesses in fast-growing industries or, at least, businesses that are able to *convince* investors they are fast-growing. If they are engineering companies from the UK Midlands or the US Midwest, they have no hope.

In the 1990s, a stock market listing was probably of considerable use to companies in terms of attracting employees, because of the ability to grant stock options to new hires. But since the dotcom bubble burst in 2000, options have become less alluring than cold, hard cash.

A quotation still allows the founders to convert their equity into cash. For many, this must be the biggest remaining attraction of a listing.

But the private route gives the entrepreneur another two bites of the cherry. First, the value of his or her existing holdings is increased by the bid premium, financed by the helpful venture capitalist. Then there is the chance to bring the company back to market again, at a much higher valuation, in a few years' time.

Such a strategy presupposes, of course, that the market will be willing to give the company a second chance. For some businesses, that may not be plausible. Increasingly, venture capitalists are looking to trade buyers, or even other venture capitalists, to give them an exit route.

That creates a dilemma. For the last decade, free market enthusiasts have been lecturing the continental Europeans and the Japanese that their system of bank financing for the corporate sector was fatally flawed. The relationship was too cosy, they argued, allowing inefficient managements to stay in charge. In contrast, the Anglo-Saxon model allowed shareholders to replace dud executives via the takeover mechanism.

But does a market-based alternative really work, if the participants in the market are simply not interested in a large number of companies? The stock market's primary function is no longer to raise capital for the corporate sector; indeed in the US and the UK, companies have often been *returning* capital in recent years via share buy-backs. Instead, the stock market exists as a savings vehicle for the private sector and as a means for investment bankers to get rich. The ability to trade shares is valued far more highly than the ability to raise capital.

The pressure to consolidate in the fund management industry will only accelerate this process. As fund management companies get larger, the size of their minimum stake increases and their interest in smaller companies accordingly diminishes.

It is possible that a new system could emerge, with the largest companies freely traded on the stock market and the next tier owned by specialised groups such as venture capitalists that could afford longer term investment horizons. But that depends on there being enough exit routes for investors – an endless game of 'pass the parcel' among venture capitalists is not sustainable.

Somebody needs to fund those smaller companies that are not involved in technology or the fashionable industry of the moment. Although smallcap shares have rallied strongly this year, the quoted stock markets do not appear to be up to the job.

Source: Financial Times, 6/7 September 2003, p. M28. Reprinted with permission.

Exhibit 10.38

Enjoying life out of the spotlight

FT

The decision to stay away from the market can reap its own dividend – especially during a downturn

writes Alex Skorecki

Was there ever a better time to be a private company? While the publicly listed ones have been having a terrible time, with share prices enduring their worst bear market for 60 years and managers under harsh scrutiny from shareholders, private companies have been able to laugh from the sidelines.

Des Gunewardena, chief executive of retailer and restaurant owner Conran, says there has certainly been a change of attitude. 'Over the last 10 years I must have had 50 calls from journalists asking why Conran doesn't go public. But in the last year it has been quite the opposite. Now I'm being asked what it's like not to have to feel the pressure.'

Private companies, especially the sort that stay private in the long term, have distinct advantages. Although they forgo the opportunity to raise capital from equity markets, they are also free from the pressure to make short-term investment decisions to satisfy the demands of shareholders.

They can be an inscrutable lot. The US agricultural group Cargill, the world's biggest private company, operates from an obscure headquarters deep in the heart of Minnesota. The message is clear: we value our privacy.

One thing they agree on is how good it is not to have shareholders banging on the door. Sir Anthony Bamford, chairman of JCB, the construction equipment maker, says: 'When we went into America, it was 13 years before we made a profit. If we had been a public company, that would never have passed muster.'

But private companies are no more immune to downturn than the rest. 'Our business is not fashionable at the moment,' Sir Anthony admits.

The view from the private boardroom has changed little in 20 years. The stress, as ever, is on the advantages of taking the long-term view and of being in full control.

Mr Gunewardena says: 'Being private means we are able to develop and manage the business in ways we want as opposed to the way external shareholders want.'

He adds: 'When times get tough we can take the view [that] we want to maintain quality rather than worry about preserving the short-term bottom line. So we don't cut back on flowers or cleaning in our restaurants.'

Something private companies are less vocal about is the advantage of not needing to disclose their financial position to competitors. 'Take the two engineering companies Fluor and Bechtel,' says Eli Talmor, professor of accounting at London Business School. 'Bechtel can look at the profit margins of Fluor – but not vice versa.'

John Lewis, the UK retailer, is not a typical private company. Legally it is a trust, although since 1925 it has described itself as a partnership. But many of the same perspectives apply. Paul Burden, the communications director, says the poor markets have strengthened their view that 'the absence of conventional equity is more of an advantage than a handicap for us'.

Inability to raise capital on equity markets has never been a disadvantage, he says. 'Banks and bondholders have proved more than willing to lend to us on good terms.' And he does not report any cash shortages. 'Don't forget that retail is a highly cash-generative business to be in.'

Graham Wellesley, chief executive of financial trading group IFX – which he took public through a reverse takeover of Zetters, the pools group – still hankers after the freedoms he left behind. 'We could allow the revenues to be much more lumpy. We could take the chance of making a loss one year if none of our bets came off. But if all of them did, we'd be printing money.'

Poor markets have almost killed off the creation of new public companies. But the flow in the reverse direction – from public to private – has also diminished, contrary to what might be expected. Figures from Dealogic, a data provider, for the US and western Europe show that in 1999 there were 128 public-to-private deals while last year there were 88.

The explanation is that in 1999 the technology bubble was driving down the value of old economy companies, encouraging them to quit the markets. Now the boot is on the other foot but those same technology companies that flourished briefly during the boom burn cash quickly and have a much slimmer hope of going private. Many have simply been wound up.

The power to generate cash is obviously crucial. It is no coincidence that many of the big private names, such as Aldi of Germany, Ikea of Sweden and John Lewis of the UK, are retailers.

David Forbes of investment bankers NM Rothschild specialises in public-to-private deals. He reckons the downturn has changed attitudes about being private. 'It is more than just a short-term blip. The sophistication of private markets has grown,' he says.

Mr Forbes says the liquidity issue has become more important for fund managers, making them less inclined to invest in medium-sized public companies. Many who thought they were going to get investor interest and capital from their listing have been disappointed. 'The discount for illiquidity has changed quite markedly,' he says.

Exhibit 10.38 continued

Of course there are disadvantages to being a private company, otherwise there would surely be more among the ranks of the world's leading companies. One is that it is harder to build up trusting relationships. As Prof Talmor of LBS says: 'How do you convince your supplier? As a public company, it is easier for banks to get information on you. You are embraced by the stock exchange; you can't be that bad.'

Ultimately, staying private is a lot about control. As Mr Gunewardena says: 'We like running the business. With a public company, you have to take on board somebody else's views.

'We target profits. But we also seek longer-term value for our business. . . In the main we are driven by profit and cash – cash becomes even more important, if anything. But we do not necessarily pursue the project which will make most money.'

Culture also plays a big role: Germans, for instance, have different views from Americans. 'In Germany, to be private is normal,' says Prof Talmor. 'It is a failure if I have to ask another to come on board.' Of Europe's 50 biggest private companies, half are German.

Cargill may be the biggest in the world but in the US it ranks only 19th among all companies in terms of revenue. In terms of earnings it is not even in the top 100. The private road, as Mr Gunewardena hints, does not always make the most money.

Source: Financial Times, 23 January 2003, p. 13. Reprinted with permission.

References and further reading

Arnold, G. (2004) *The Financial Times Guide to Investing.* Harlow: Financial Times Prentice Hall.

An introduction to financial markets including the new issue market.

Breedon, F. and Twinn, I. (1996) 'The valuation of sub-underwriting agreements for UK rights issues', *Bank of England Quarterly Bulletin*, May, pp. 193–6.

A discussion of the mystery of apparently high underwriting fees for rights issues.

British Private Equity and Venture Capital Association, London (www.bvca.co.uk).

Variety of paper publications and online material which give an insight into a variety of aspects of venture capital.

Campbell, K. (2003) *Smarter Ventures: A Survivor's Guide to Venture Capital Through the New Cycle.* Harlow: Financial Times Prentice Hall.

Practical advice for entrepreneurs and venture capitalists.

City of London/London Stock Exchange/Oxera (2006) 'The cost of capital: an international comparison' (available for download: www.londonstockexchange.com).

Compares various costs associated with raising capital on stock markets.

European Private Equity and Venture Capital Association (www.evca.com).

Displays various useful publications.

Jenkinson, T. and Ljungquist, A. (2001) *Going Public: The Theory and Evidence on How Companies Raise Equity Finance.* 2nd edn. Oxford: Clarendon.

A detailed and accessible description of the new issue market internationally.

Levis, M. (1990) 'The winner's curse problem, interest costs and the underpricing of initial public offerings', *Economic Journal*, 100, March, pp. 76–89.

Underpricing for some issues is explained by fear on the part of uninformed investors, plus the cost of interest between application for shares and return of cheques in oversubscribed issues.

Ljungquist, A. (2004) 'IPO underpricing' in Exckbo, E. (ed.) *Handbook of Corporate Finance,* Vol. 1, Elsevier. New York.

Reviews the literature on IPO unerpinning.

London Stock Exchange (2004) *A Practical Guide to Listing on the London Stock Exchange.*

Available at www.londonstockexchange.com. A clear and succinct guide to the essential issues.

Marsh, P. (1994) 'Underwriting of rights issues: a study of the returns earned by sub-underwriters from UK rights issues', *Office of Fair Trading Research Paper No. 6.*

Conclusion: underwriting fees are excessive given the risk borne in rights issues.

Mason, C. and Harrison, R. (1997) 'Business angels – heaven-sent or the devil to deal with?' in Birley, S. and Muzyka, D.F. (eds) *Mastering Enterprise*, London: Pitman Publishing/Financial Times.

Easy-to-read summary of business angel activity in the UK.

Ritter, J.R. (2003) 'Differences in European and American IPO markets', *European Financial Management*, 9, pp. 421–34.

IPO discounting evidence in 38 countries.

Torstila, S. (2003) 'The clustering of IPO gross spreads: international evidence', *Journal of Financial and Quantitative Analysis*, 38, pp. 673–94.

Shows underwriting costs and other data.

Zider, B. (1998) 'How venture capital works', *Harvard Business Review*, November–December, pp. 131–9.

An easy-to-read account of the mechanisms of venture capital funding.

Websites

Angel Bourse www.angelbourse.com
Association of Corporate Treasurers www.treasurers.org
Beer & Partners www.beerandpartners.com
British Private Equity and Venture Capital Association www.bvca.co.uk
British Business Angels Association www.bbaa.org
Business Links www.businesslinks.gov.uk
Cavendish Management Resources www.cmrworld.com
CREST www.crestco.co.uk
Department for Business, Enterprise and Regulatory Reform www.berr.gov.uk
Development Capital Exchange www.dcxworld.com
Enterprise zone www.theenterprisezone.co.uk
Exemplas www.exem,plas.com
European Private Equity and Venture Capital Association www.evca.com
Financial Express www.investegate.co.uk
Financial Services Authority www.fsa.gov.uk
Fisma www.fisma.org
Hemscot www.hemscot.com
Hotbed www.hotbed.uk.com
Initiative for private equity investment trusts www.ipeit.com
Investors Chronicle www.investorschronicle.com
London Clearing House, LCH. Clearnet www.lchclearnet.com
London Stock Exchange www.londonstockexchange.co.uk
National Business Angels Network (or gateway 2 investment) www.g2i.org
Octopus Ventures www.katalystventures.com
Private Equity Intelligence www.prequin.com
UCR Directory www.ucrdirectory.co.uk
United Kingdom Listing Authority www.fsa.gov.uk/ukla

Video presentations

Chief Executives and finance directors describe their current policy on raising funds on Cantos.com (www.cantos.com) – this is free to view.

Case study recommendations

Please see www.pearsoned.co.uk/arnold for case study synopses

- How venture capitalists evaluate potential venture opportunities. Authors: Michael J. Roberts and L. Barley (2004) Harvard Business School.
- 3i Group plc. Authors: Josh Lerner, Feldon Hardymon and Ann Leamon. (2003) Harvard Business School.
- ONSET Ventures. Authors: Michael J Roberts, Nicole Tempest (1998) Harvard Business School
- Nestle and Alcon – the value of a listing Authors: Mihir A. Desai, Vincent Dessain and Anders (2004) Sjoman Publisher: Harvard Business School.

Self-review questions

1 What is equity capital? Explain the advantages to the firm of raising capital this way. What are the disadvantages?

2 Distinguish between authorised and issued share capital.

3 What is the par value of a share, and what is the share premium?

4 Are all plcs quoted? Describe both terms.

5 What is a preference share and why might a company favour this form of finance?

6 What would be the characteristics of a cumulative redeemable participating convertible preference share?

7 Why are non-voting shares disliked by the City investing institutions?

8 Why does the United Kingdom Listing Authority impose stringent rules on companies floating on LSE's Main Market?

9 Outline the contents of a prospectus in a new issue on LSE's Main Market.

10 How might the working lives of directors change as a result of their company gaining a quotation?

11 What does a sponsor have to do to help a company float?

12 Describe the role of each of the institutions and professional organisations that assist a company in floating on LSE's Main Market.

13 What are an offer for sale by tender and an introduction of a new issue? Which is the cheaper method of flotation?

14 List the differences between a flotation on AIM and LSE's Main Market.

15 What are, and why do the UK authorities insist upon, pre-emption rights?

16 Why are placings subject to strict rules concerning the extent of price discount?

17 What adjustments need to be made to a balance sheet after a scrip issue?

18 Suggest circumstances when a firm may find the selling of warrants advantageous.

19 What do business angels bring to a firm?

20 What are the following: MBO, MBI, PTP, a venture capital fund, seedcorn?

Questions and problems

myfinancelab **Questions with an icon are also available for practice in MyFinanceLab with additional supporting resources.**

For questions marked with an asterisk* answers are given in the Lecturer's Guide and the lecturer's part of the website www.pearsoned.co.uk/arnold

1 (*Examination level*) Bluelamp plc has grown from a company with £10,000 turnover to one with a £17m turnover and £1.8m profit in the last five years. The existing owners have put all their financial resources into the firm to enable it to grow. The directors wish to take advantage of a very exciting market opportunity but would need to find £20m of new equity capital as the balance sheet is already over-geared (i.e. has high debt). The options being discussed, in a rather uninformed way, are flotation on the Main Market of the London Stock Exchange, a flotation on the Alternative Investment Market and venture capital. Write a report to enlighten the board on the merits and disadvantages of each of these three possibilities.

2 In what circumstances would you advise a company to float on the Alternative Investment Market (AIM) in preference to the Main Market of the London Stock Exchange?

3 Checkers plc is considering a flotation on the Main Market of the London Stock Exchange. Outline a timetable of events likely to be encountered which will assist management planning.

4 Describe the three costs associated with gaining a flotation on a stock exchange by selling shares to new shareholders.

5 Discuss the merits and problems of the pre-emption right for UK companies.

6 Explain why failure to carry through a plan to raise capital by floating on the London Stock Exchange Main Market might be highly disruptive to a firm.

7 There are a number of different methods of floating a company on the new issue market of the London Stock Exchange Main Market (e.g. offer for sale). Describe these and comment on the ability of small investors to buy newly issued shares.

8* Mahogany plc has an ordinary share price of £3 and is quoted on the Alternative Investment Market. It intends to raise £20m through a one-for-three rights issue priced at £2.

a What will the ex-rights price be?
b How many old ordinary shares were in circulation prior to the rights issue?
c Patrick owns 9,000 shares and is unable to find the cash necessary to buy the rights shares. Reassure Patrick that he will not lose value. How much might he receive from the company?
d What is the value of a right on one old share?
e What do the terms cum-rights and ex-rights mean?
f Advise Mahogany on the virtues of a deep-discounted rights issue. ?

9 Venture capital funds made a negative internal rate of return on investments in the ten years up to the end of 2006. Describe the role of venture capitalists in the UK economy and comment on the rates of return they generally intend to achieve.

10 Examine the articles in Appendix 10.1 and write an essay advocating the case for avoiding flotation on a recognised investment exchange.

11 Write an essay advocating the case for flotation on a recognised investment exchange.

12 The shareholders of Yellowhammer plc are to offer a one-for-four rights issue at £1.50 when its shares are trading at £1.90. What is the theoretical ex-rights price and the value of a right per old share? **?**

13 Explain the function of a prospectus in a new share issue.

14 What are the main advantages and disadvantages of raising finance through selling (a) ordinary shares, and (b) preference shares?

15 Discuss the main features of venture capital and explain the dangers to an unwary management.

16 Explain placings and offers for sale for new issues and comment on the reasons for the increased use of placings.

17 If business angels are not connected with divine intervention in business matters, seedcorn capital is not something to do with growing food and a captured fund is not theft, what are they and how might they assist a company?

18 If par values are not something to do with golf, public to private is not something to do with sexual modesty and a pathfinder prospectus is not something to do with scouting, what are they? Explain the context in which these terms are used.

19 (*Examination level*) Imagine that AM Paper (*see* **Exhibit 10.39**) have appointed you as adviser to the board of directors. The directors have asked you to explain the relative merits and disadvantages of listing on the Main Market of the London Stock Exchange and continuing to be financed by the venture capital. Write an essay to inform them.

Exhibit 10.39

AM Paper to examine options for a sale

FT

HSBC private equity may sell stake as Lancashire-based group heads for 'rapid growth'

AM Paper, the Lancashire-based soft tissues manufacturer, has appointed JP Morgan, the investment bank, to examine options that could lead to a sale.

HSBC Private Equity, which owns 54 per cent of AM, said AM was heading for rapid growth and had to consider ways of financing this.

HSBC may sell its stake to another venture capital investor, in a deal that might value the group at £200m–£250m.

Alan Murphy, AM's founder, stands to gain more than £50m if he sells his 27 per cent stake. It is understood Mr Murphy raised about £100m when he sold part of the business in a restructuring in 1997. AM's other managers own the remaining 19 per cent.

'HSBC Private Equity has received a number of approaches from organisations looking to acquire our investment or form strategic alliances,' said Phil Goodwin, HSBC's director in Manchester. 'We are considering these approaches along with all the other options available, that might include a future listing of the business or a bond issue.'

The private equity firm invested £40m in the company in 1997 as part of a £145m debt and equity package. It put in a further £20m to fund expansion last year . . .

Mr Goodwin said HSBC was delighted with its investment in the group so far, and it was 'far from clear' which route would be taken 'if indeed HSBC decides to realise its investment'. He added it was too early to say what value might be put on the business.

Steve Sealey, chief executive, said yesterday HSBC had been 'very supportive' in its involvement with the group.

'We feel that it is time to look at our options as to how to achieve future growth,' he added.

Source: Sheila Jones and Richard Rivlin, *Financial Times*, 21 May 1999, p. 24. Reprinted with permission.

myfinancelab *Now retake your diagnostic test for Chapter 10 to check your progress and update your study plan.*

Assignment

Consider the equity base of your company, or one you are familiar with. Write a report outlining the options available should the firm need to raise further equity funds. Also consider if preference share capital should be employed.

CHAPTER 11

Long-term debt finance

LEARNING OUTCOMES

An understanding of the key characteristics of the main categories of debt finance is essential to anyone considering the financing decisions of the firm. At the end of this chapter the reader will be able to:

- explain the nature and the main types of bonds, their pricing and their valuation;
- describe the main considerations for a firm when borrowing from banks;
- give a considered view of the role of mezzanine and high-yield bond financing as well as convertible bonds, sale and leaseback, securitisation and project finance;
- demonstrate an understanding of the value of the international debt markets;
- explain the term structure of interest rates and the reasons for its existence.

myfinancelab *Complete your diagnostic test for Chapter 11 now to create your personal study plan*

Introduction

The concept of borrowing money to invest in real assets within a business is a straightforward one, yet in the sophisticated capital markets of today with their wide variety of financial instruments and forms of debt, the borrowing decision can be bewildering. Should the firm tap the domestic bond market or the Eurobond market? Would bank borrowing be best? If so, on what terms, fixed or floating rate interest, a term loan or a mortgage? And what about syndicated lending, mezzanine finance and high-yield bonds? The variety of methods of borrowing long-term finance is infinite. This chapter will outline the major categories and illustrate some of the fundamental issues a firm may consider when selecting its finance mix. As you can see from the extract from the annual accounts of GlaxoSmithKline (**Exhibit 11.1**) a firm may need knowledge and understanding of a great many different debt instruments. The terms loan stock, medium-term notes, and commercial paper mentioned in the extract are explained in this chapter. Lease finance and overdrafts are examined in Chapter 12.

Exhibit 11.1 Loans and other borrowings for GlaxoSmithKline plc, 2006 and 2005

	2006 £m	2005 £m
Short-term borrowings:		
6.125% US$ Notes 2006	–	291
2.375% US$ Medium Term Note 2007	255	–
Commercial paper	–	576
Bank loans and overdrafts	410	249
Other loans	11	46
Obligations under finance leases	42	38
	718	1,200
Long-term borrowings:		
2.375% US$ US Medium Term Note 2007	–	283
3.375% € European Medium Term Note 2008	671	689
4.875% € European Medium Term Note 2008	494	502
3.25% € European Medium Term Note 2009	338	342
3.00% € European Medium Term Note 2012	503	510
4.375% US$ Medium Term Note 2014	719	825
4.00% € European Medium Term Note 2025	497	503
5.25% £ European Medium Term Note 2033	977	976
5.375% US$ US Medium Term Note 2034	253	288
Loan stock	10	11
Bank loans	1	3
Other loans and private financing	212	256
Obligations under finance leases	97	83
	4,772	5,271

Long-term borrowings

Loans due after one year are repayable over various periods as follows:

	2006 £m	2005 £m
Between one and two years	1,202	317
Between two and three years	366	1,224
Between three and four years	26	354
Between four and five years	7	9
After five years	3,171	3,367
	4,772	5,271

Source: GlaxoSmithKilne Annual Report 2006.

Some fundamental features of debt finance

Put at its simplest, **debt** is something that has to be repaid. Corporate debt repayments have taken the form of interest and capital payments as well as more exotic compensations such as commodities and shares. The usual method is a combination of a regular interest, with capital (principal) repayments either spread over a period or given as a lump sum at the end of the borrowing. Debt finance is less expensive than equity finance, due to the lower rate of return required by finance providers, lower transaction costs of raising the funds (for example arrangement fees with a bank or the issue costs of a bond) and the tax deductibility of interest. The lower required returns arise because investors recognise that investing in a firm via debt finance is less risky than investing via shares. It is less risky because interest is paid out before dividends are paid so there is greater certainty of receiving a return than there would be for equity holders. Also, if the firm goes into liquidation, the holders of a debt type of financial security are paid back before shareholders receive anything.

Offsetting these plus-points for debt are the facts that lenders do not, generally, share in the value created by an extraordinarily successful business and there is an absence of voting power – although debt holders are able to protect their position to some extent through rigorous lending agreements.

There are dangers associated with raising funds through debt instruments. Creditors are often able to claim some or all of the assets of the firm in the event of non-compliance with the terms of the loan. This may result in liquidation. Institutions which provide debt finance often try to minimise the risk of not receiving interest and their original capital. They do this by first of all looking to the earning ability of the firm, that is, the pre-interest profits and cash flows in the years over the period of the loan. As a back-up they often require that the loan be secured against assets owned by the business, so that if the firm is unable to pay interest and capital from profits the lender can force the sale of the assets to receive their legal entitlement. The matter of security has to be thought about carefully before a firm borrows capital. It could be very inconvenient for the firm to grant a bank a **fixed charge** on a specific asset – say a particular building – because the firm is then limiting its future flexibility to use its assets as it wishes. For instance, it will not be able to sell that building, or even rent it without the consent of the bank or the bondholders.

Bonds

A **bond** is a long-term contract in which the bondholders lend money to a company. In return the company (usually) promises to pay the bond owners a series of interest payments, known as **coupons**, until the bond matures. At **maturity** the bondholder receives a specified principal sum called the **par** (**face** or **nominal**) value of the bond. This is usually £100 in the UK and $1,000 in the USA. The time to maturity is generally between seven and 30 years although a number of firms, for example Disney, IBM and Reliance of India, have issued 100-year bonds.

Bonds may be regarded as merely IOUs (I owe you) with pages of legal clauses expressing the promises made. Most corporate bonds are sufficiently **liquid** (many transactions, so able to sell/buy at low cost without moving the price) to be *listed* on the London Stock Exchange and other exchanges in Europe, but the majority of *trading* occurs in the over-the-counter (OTC) market directly between an investor and a bond dealer. Access to a secondary market means that the investor who originally provided the firm with money does not have to hold on to the bond until the maturity date (the **redemption date**). However, because so many investors buy and then hold to maturity rather than trade in and out bonds generally have very thin secondary markets compared with shares. The amount the investor receives in the secondary market might be more or less than what he/she paid. For instance, imagine an investor paid £99.80 for a bond which promised to pay a coupon of 9 per cent per year on a par value of £100 and to pay the par value in seven years. If one year after issue interest rates on similar bonds are 20 per cent per annum no one will pay £99.80 for a bond agreement offering £9 per year for a further six years plus £100 on the redemption date. We will look at a method for calculating exactly how much they might be willing to pay later in the chapter.

These **negotiable** (that is tradable in a secondary market) instruments come in a variety of forms. The most common is the type described above with regular (usually semi-annual) fixed coupons and a specified redemption date. These are known as **straight**, **plain vanilla** or **bullet bonds**. Other bonds are a variation on this. Some pay coupons every three months, some pay no coupons at all (called **zero coupon bonds** – these are sold at a large discount to the par value and the investor makes a capital gain by holding the bond), some bonds do not pay a fixed coupon but one which varies depending on the level of short-term interest rates (**floating-rate** or **variable-rate bonds**), some have interest rates linked to the rate of inflation. In fact, the potential for variety and innovation is almost infinite. Bonds issued in the last few years have linked the interest rates paid or the principal payments to a wide variety of economic events, such as the price of silver, exchange-rate movements, stock market indices, the price of oil, gold, copper – even to the occurrence of an earthquake. These bonds were generally designed to let companies adjust their interest payments to manageable levels in the event of the firm being adversely affected by some economic variable changing. For example, a copper miner pays lower interest on its finance if the copper price falls. Sampdoria, the Italian football club, issued a €3.5m bond that paid a higher rate of return if the club won promotion to the 'Serie A' division (2.5 per cent if it stayed in Serie B, 7 per cent if it moved to Serie A). If the club rose to the top four in Serie A the coupon would rise to 14 per cent.

Debentures and loan stocks

The most secured type of bond is called a **debenture**. They are usually secured by either a fixed or a floating charge against the firm's assets. A fixed charge means that specific assets are used as security which, in the event of default, can be sold at the insistence of the debenture bondholder and the proceeds used to repay them. Debentures secured on property may be referred to as **mortgage debentures**. A **floating charge** means that the loan is secured by a general charge on all the assets of the corporation (or a class of the firm's assets such as inventory or debtors). In this case the company has a high degree of freedom to use its assets as it wishes, such as sell them or rent them out, until it commits a default which 'crystallises' the floating charge. If this happens a **receiver** will be appointed with powers to dispose of assets and to distribute the proceeds to the creditors. Even though floating-charge debenture holders can force a **liquidation**, fixed-charge debenture holders rank above floating-charge debenture holders in the payout after insolvency.

The terms bond, debenture and **loan stock** are often used interchangeably and the dividing line between debentures and loan stock is a fuzzy one. As a general rule debentures are secured and loan stock is unsecured but there are examples which do not fit this classification. If liquidation occurs the unsecured loan stockholders rank beneath the debenture holders and some other categories of creditors such as the tax authorities. In the USA the definitions are somewhat different and this can be confusing. There a debenture is an unsecured bond and so the holders become general creditors who can only claim assets not otherwise pledged. In the USA the secured form of bond is referred to as the mortgage bond and unsecured shorter-dated issues (less than 15 years) are called **notes**.

Bonds are often referred to collectively as **fixed-interest securities**. While this is an accurate description for many bonds, others do not offer *regular* interest payments that are *fixed* amounts. Nevertheless they are all lumped together as fixed interest to contrast these types of loan instrument with equities that do not carry a promise of a return (Warren Buffett, the financialist, uses the term 'fixed maturity securities').

Trust deeds and covenants

Bond investors are willing to lower the interest they demand if they can be reassured that their money will not be exposed to a high risk. This reassurance is conveyed by placing risk-reducing restrictions on the firm. A **trust deed** sets out the terms of the contract between bondholders and the company. The **trustees** ensure compliance with the contract throughout the life of the bond and have the power to appoint a receiver. The loan agreement will contain a number of **affirmative covenants**. These usually include the requirements to supply regular financial statements, interest and principal payments. The deed may also state the fees due to the lenders and details of what procedures are to be followed in the event of a technical **default**, for example non-payment of interest.

In addition to these basic covenants are the **negative (restrictive) covenants**. These restrict the actions and the rights of the borrower until the debt has been repaid in full. Some examples are:

- ***Limits on further debt issuance*** If lenders provide finance to a firm they do so on certain assumptions concerning the riskiness of the capital structure. They will want to ensure that the loan does not become more risky due to the firm taking on a much greater debt burden relative to its equity base, so they limit the amount and type of further debt issues – particularly debt which is higher ('**senior debt**') ranking for interest payments and for a liquidation payment. **Subordinated debt** – with low ranking on liquidation – is more likely to be acceptable.
- ***Dividend level*** Lenders are opposed to money being taken into the firm by borrowing at one end, while being taken away by shareholders at the other. An excessive withdrawal of shareholder funds may unbalance the financial structure and weaken future cash flows.
- ***Limits on the disposal of assets*** The retention of certain assets, for example property and land, may be essential to reduce the lenders' risk.
- ***Financial ratios*** A typical covenant here concerns the **interest cover**, for example: 'The annual pre-interest pre-tax profit will remain four times as great as the overall annual interest charge'. Other restrictions might be placed on working capital ratio levels, and the debt to net assets ratio. In the case of Photobition the interest cover threshold is 3.25 – *see* **Exhibit 11.2**.

While negative covenants cannot provide completely risk-free lending they can influence the behaviour of the management team so as to reduce the risk of default. The lenders' risk can be further reduced by obtaining guarantees from third parties (for example **guaranteed loan stock**). The guarantor is typically the parent company of the issuer.

Repayments

The principal on many bonds is paid entirely at maturity. However, there are bonds which can be repaid before the final redemption date. One way of paying for redemption is to set up a **sinking fund** that receives regular sums from the firm which will be sufficient, with added interest, to redeem the bonds. A common approach is for the company to issue bonds where it has a range of dates for redemption; so a bond dated 2012–2016 would allow a company the flexibility to repay a part of the principal in cash over four years. Another way of redeeming bonds is for the issuing firm to buy the outstanding bonds by offering the holder a sum higher than or equal to the amount originally paid. A firm is also able to purchase bonds on the open market.

Some bonds are described as '**irredeemable**' as they have no fixed redemption date. From the investor's viewpoint they may be irredeemable but the firm has the option of repurchase and can effectively redeem the bonds.

Exhibit 11.2

Photobition cautions on covenants

FT

Photobition, the Surrey-based graphics business, admitted yesterday it could breach banking covenants over the level of its interest cover if US advertising spending continued to slow down.

The company, which also reported a sharp fall in half-year profits, said net debt has risen to $103.5m (£77.3m) after a number of US acquisitions . . .

Analysts forecast that cover might fall to 2.43 times at the year-end in June, below the required minimum of 3.25.

'If they breach the bank covenants, they will be at the mercy of debt holders,' said one analyst. 'They could have to renegotiate their debt, or make some form of debt-equity conversion. They might also resort to a rights issue.'

Source: Florian Gimbel, *Financial Times*, 28 February 2001, p. 28. Reprinted with permission.

Bond variations

Bonds which are sold at well below the par value are called **deep discounted bonds**, the most extreme form of which is the zero coupon bond. It is easy to calculate the rate of return offered to an investor on this type of bond. For example, if a company issues a bond at a price of £60 which is redeemable at £100 in eight years the annualised rate of return (r) is:

$$60(1 + r)^8 = 100$$

$$r = \sqrt[8]{\frac{100}{60}} - 1 = 0.066 \text{ or } 6.6\%$$

(Mathematical tools of this kind are explained in Appendix 2.1 to Chapter 2 (see page 78 onwards)).

These bonds are particularly useful for firms with low cash flows in the near term, for example firms engaged in a major property development which will not mature for many years.

A major market has developed over the past two decades called the floating-rate note (FRN) market (also called the variable-rate note market). Two factors have led to the rapid growth in FRN usage. First, the oscillating and unpredictable inflation of the 1970s and early 1980s caused many investors to make large real-term losses on fixed-rate bonds as the interest rate fell below the inflation rate. As a result many lenders became reluctant to lend at fixed rates on a long-term basis. This reluctance led to floaters being cheaper for the issuer because it does not need to offer an interest premium to compensate the investor for being locked into a fixed rate. Secondly, a number of corporations, especially financial institutions, hold assets which give a return that varies with the short-term interest rate level (for example bank loans and overdrafts) and so prefer to have a similar floating-rate liability. These instruments pay an interest that is linked to a benchmark rate – such as the **LIBOR (London Inter-Bank Offered Rate** – the rate that banks charge each other for borrowed funds). The issuer will pay, say, 70 basis points (0.7 of a percentage point) over six-month LIBOR. The coupon is set for (say) the first six months at the time of issue, after which it is adjusted every six months; so if LIBOR was 5 per cent, the FRN would pay 5.7 per cent for that particular six months. (There are LIBOR rates for various lengths of time, for example, lending/borrowing between high reputation banks for a few hours (overnight LIBOR), or three months.)

There are many other variations on the basic vanilla bond, two of which will be examined later – high-yield bonds and convertible bonds. We now turn to another major source of long-term debt capital – bank borrowing.

Bank borrowing

An alternative to going to the capital markets to raise money via a public bond issue or a private bond placement is to borrow directly from a bank. In this case a tradable security is not issued. The bank makes the loan from its own resources and over time the borrowing company repays the bank with interest. Borrowing from banks is attractive to companies for the following reasons.

- ***Administrative and legal costs are low*** Because the loan arises from direct negotiation between borrower and lender there is an avoidance of the marketing, arrangement, regulatory and underwriting expenses involved in a bond issue.
- ***Quick*** The key provisions of a bank loan can be worked out speedily and the funding facility can be in place within a matter of hours.
- ***Flexibility*** If the economic circumstances facing the firm should change during the life of the loan banks are generally better equipped – and are more willing – to alter the terms of the lending agreement than bondholders. Negotiating with a single lender in a crisis has distinct advantages. Bank loans are also more flexible in the sense that if the firm does better than originally expected a bank loan can often be repaid without penalty. Contrast this with many bonds with fixed redemption dates, or hire purchase/leasing arrangements with fixed terms.
- ***Available to small firms*** Bank loans are available to firms of almost any size whereas the bond market is for the big players only.

Factors for a firm to consider

There are a number of issues a firm needs to address when considering bank borrowing.

Costs

The borrower may be required to pay an **arrangement fee**, say 1 per cent of the loan, at the time of the initial lending, but this is subject to negotiation and may be bargained down.[1] The interest rate can be either fixed or floating. If it is floating then the rate will generally be a certain percentage above the banks' **base rate** or LIBOR. Because the borrowing corporation is not as safe as a high quality bank taking out the borrowing in the interbank market a corporation will pay say 1 per cent (or 100 basis points) more than LIBOR if it is in a good bargaining position. In the case of base-rate-related lending the interest payable changes immediately the bank announces a change in its base rate. This moves irregularly in response to financial market conditions, which are heavily influenced by the **Bank of England** in its attempt to control the economy. For customers in a poorer bargaining position offering a higher-risk proposal the rate could be 5 per cent or more over the base rate or LIBOR. The interest rate will be determined not only by the riskiness of the undertaking and the bargaining strength of the customer but also by the degree of security for the loan and the size of loan – economies of scale in lending mean that large borrowers pay a lower interest rate. A generation ago it would have been more normal to negotiate fixed-rate loans but most loans today are 'variable rate'.

Floating-rate borrowings have advantages for the firm over fixed-rate borrowings:

- If interest rates fall the cost of the loan falls.
- At the time of arrangement fixed rates are usually above floating rates (to allow for lenders' risk of misforecasting future interest rates).
- Returns on the firm's assets may go up at times of higher interest rates and fall at times of lower interest rates, therefore the risk of higher rates is offset. For example, a bailiff firm may prosper in a high interest rate environment.

However floating rates have some disadvantages:

- The firm may be caught out by a rise in interest rates if, as with most businesses, its profits do not rise when interest rates rise. Many have failed because of a rise in interest rates at an inopportune time.
- There will be uncertainty about the precise cash outflow impact of the interest. Firms need to plan ahead; in particular, they need to estimate amounts of cash coming in and flowing out, not least so that they can pay bills on time. Fixed rates contribute to greater certainty on cash flows.

Security

When banks are considering the provision of debt finance for a firm they will be concerned about the borrower's competence and honesty. They need to evaluate the proposed project and assess the degree of managerial commitment to its success. The firm will have to explain why the funds are needed and provide detailed cash forecasts covering the period of the loan. Between the bank and the firm stands the classic gulf called '**asymmetric information**' in which one party in the negotiation is ignorant of, or cannot observe, some of the information which is essential to the contracting and decision-making process. The bank is unable to assess accurately the ability and determination of the managerial team and will not have a complete understanding of the market environment in which they propose to operate. Companies may overcome bank uncertainty to some degree by providing as much information as possible at the outset and keeping the bank informed of the firm's position as the project progresses.

The finance director and managing director need to consider both the quantity and quality of information flows to the bank. An improved flow of information can lead to a better and more

[1] And indeed the firm should always try, where possible, to negotiate terms each year, or as and when the financial position of the company improves.

supportive relationship. Firms with significant bank financing requirements to fund growth will be well advised to cultivate and strengthen understanding and rapport with their bank(s). The time to lay the foundations for subsequent borrowing is when the business does not need the money, so that when loans are required there is a reasonable chance of being able to borrow the amount needed on acceptable terms.

Another way for a bank to reduce its risk is to ensure that the firm offers sufficient **collateral** for the loan. Collateral provides a means of recovering all or the majority of the bank's investment should the firm fail. If the firm is unable to meet its loan obligations then holders of fixed-charge collateral can seize the specific asset used to back the loan. Also, on liquidation, the proceeds of selling assets will go first to the secured loan holders, including floating-charge bank lenders. Collateral can include stocks, debtors and equipment as well as land, buildings and marketable investments such as shares in other companies. In theory banks often have this strong right to seize assets or begin proceedings to liquidate. In practice they are reluctant to use these powers because the realisation of full value from an asset used as security is sometimes difficult and such draconian action can bring adverse publicity. Banks are careful to create a margin for error in the assignment of sufficient collateral to cover the loan because, in the event of default, assigned assets usually command a much lower price than their value to the company as a going concern. A quick sale at auction produces bargains for the buyers of liquidated assets and usually little for the creditors.

Another safety feature applied by banks is the requirement that the firm abide by a number of loan covenants which place restrictions on managerial action in a similar fashion to bond covenants (*see* section on bonds earlier in this chapter).

Finally, lenders can turn to the directors of the firm to provide additional security. They might be asked to sign **personal guarantees** that the firm will not default. Personal assets (such as homes) may be used as collateral. This erodes the principle of limited liability status and is likely to inhibit risk-taking productive activity. However for many smaller firms it is the only way of securing a loan and at least it demonstrates the commitment of the director to the success of the enterprise.[2]

Repayment

A firm must carefully consider the period of the loan and the repayment schedules in the light of its future cash flows. It could be disastrous, for instance, for a firm engaging in a capital project which involved large outlays for the next five years followed by cash inflows thereafter to have a bank loan which required significant interest and principal payments in the near term. For situations like these **repayment holidays** or **grace periods** may be granted, with the majority of the repayment being made once cash flows are sufficiently positive.

It may be possible for a company to arrange a **mortgage-style repayment schedule** in which monthly payments from the borrower to the lender are constant throughout the term.

A **term loan** is a business loan with an original maturity of more than one year and a specified schedule of principal and interest payments. It may or may not be secured and has the advantage over the overdraft of not being repayable at the demand of the bank at short notice (*see* Chapter 12). The terms of the loan are usually tailored to the specific needs of the individual borrower and these are capable of wide variation. A proportion of the interest and the principal can be repaid monthly or annually and can be varied to correspond with the borrower's cash flows. It is rare for there to be no repayment of the principal during the life of the loan but it is possible to request that the bulk of the principal is paid in the later years. Banks generally prefer **self-amortising term loans** with a high proportion of the principal paid off each year. This has the advantage of reducing risk by imposing a programme of debt reduction on the borrowing firm.

The repayment schedule agreed between bank and borrower is capable of infinite variety – four possibilities are shown in **Exhibit 11.3**.

The retail and investment banks are not the only sources of long-term loans. Insurance companies and other specialist institutions such as 3i will also provide long-term debt finance.

---

[2] Indeed, when the author recently contacted a number of banks to negotiate a loan for a company he controls, the corporate loan officers were all amazed at his cheek in not accepting a personal guarantee clause – 'but we normally get a personal guarantee, it is just standard practice', they declared. Don't accept this line if you have a strong business plan and strong financial structure.

Exhibit 11.3 Examples of loan repayment arrangements

£10,000 borrowed, repayable over four years with interest at 10% p.a. (assuming annual payments, not monthly)

(a)	Time period (years)	1	2	3	4
	Payment (£)	3,155	3,155	3,155	3,155
(b)	Time period (years)	1	2	3	4
	Payment (£)	1,000	1,000	1,000	11,000
(c)	Time period (years)	1	2	3	4
	Payment (£)	0	0	0	14,641
(d)	Time period (years)	1	2	3	4
	Payment (£)	0	1,000	6,000	6,831

Syndicated loans

For large loans a single bank may not be able or willing to lend the whole amount. To do so would be to expose the bank to an unacceptable risk of failure on the part of one of its borrowers. Bankers like to spread their lending to gain the risk-reducing benefits of diversification. They prefer to participate in a number of syndicated loans in which a few banks each contribute a portion of the overall loan. So, for a large multinational company loan of, say, £500m, a single bank may provide £30m, with perhaps 100 other banks contributing the remainder. The bank originating the loan will usually manage the syndicate and is called the **lead manager** (there might be one or more lead banks). This bank (or these banks) may invite a handful of other banks to co-manage the loan who then persuade other banks to supply much of the funding. That is, they help the process of forming the syndicate group of banks in the general syndication. The managing bank also underwrites much of the loan while inviting other banks to underwrite the rest – that is, guaranteeing to provide the funds if other banks do not step forward.[3] Syndicated loans are available at short notice and can be provided discreetly (helpful if the money is to finance a merger bid, for example). Syndicated loans generally offer lower returns than bonds, but as they rank above most bonds on liquidation payouts there is less risk. The loans carry covenants similar to those on bond agreements. The volume of new international syndicated loans now runs into hundreds of billions of pounds per year.

Exhibit 11.4 provides more on the syndicated loan market. Credit ratings are discussed in the next section.

Credit rating

Firms often pay to have their bonds and other loans rated by specialist **credit-rating** organisations. The debt rating depends on the likelihood of payments of interest and/or capital not being paid (that is, default) and on the extent to which the lender is protected in the event of a default (an estimate is made of the likelihood of recouping money in the event of insolvency or bankruptcy, the recoverability of the debt). UK government gilts have an insignificant risk of default whereas unsecured subordinated corporate loan stock has a much higher risk. We would expect that firms in stable industries and with conservative accounting and financing policies and a risk-averse business strategy would have a low risk of default and therefore a high credit rating.

[3] The term 'mandated lead arranger' or MLA is often used for the managing bank(s). Also 'book runner' or 'bookrunner group' indicates those who solicit interest in the loan from lenders and gather offers of support. They gradually 'build a book' – a list of confirmed buyers. They do the syndication.

Exhibit 11.4

Deutsche's exclusive deal with Invensys shatters cosy world of syndicated loans

FT

Charles Batchelor

The habitual calm of the syndicated loan market was shattered recently when Deutsche Bank won the exclusive mandate to arrange the £2.7bn refinancing of Invensys, the struggling British engineering group.

A transaction of this size would normally have been shared between a group of banks, most probably those that had built up a long-term relationship with the company.

The Invensys restructuring involved an equity issue and a bond, as well as £1.65bn of loans. The bond encountered some resistance from investors and had to be trimmed in size. But it was the loan part of the deal that generated most controversy.

Normally urbane bankers choked on their lattes at the thought of a rival excluding them from helping to manage such a potentially profitable business. Many refused to subscribe for the loan, leaving Deutsche Bank struggling to find a home for £1bn of the total. Disappointed competitors gleefully conjured up visions of 'train wrecks' and other disasters.

Deutsche Bank failed to place any of the £1bn loan by its original deadline – though the remaining £650m went to institutions as planned. Deutsche was left with the funds on its own books and will attempt to trickle it out into the market over time.

'We hope they don't get too much of a nose bleed,' said one rival. 'But a little blood would be nice.'

Loan market bankers normally like to think of themselves as inhabiting a more gentlemanly world than their counterparts in bonds. Lending is frequently made on a 'relationship' basis to long-standing corporate clients. Deals can take weeks or months to put together, compared with the frenzy of the bond markets, where billions can be placed in a matter of hours.

This picture undoubtedly masks rivalries as intense as those elsewhere in the corporate finance market. But it is true that syndication involves a degree of co-operation between competing institutions.

The syndicated loan business may garner fewer headlines but it is a crucial part of international capital markets. It has been at least twice the size of the global bond market for most of the past decade, although growing enthusiasm among European companies for bonds is reducing that lead.

Much of the lending is at uncommercial rates because the banks hope to win other, more profitable, business – such as mergers and acquisitions, cash management or foreign exchange dealings – from their clients.

But companies only have a limited amount of business to dole out. They find it irksome trying to reward all of their relationship banks, while the banks often find that 'soft' loan terms are no guarantee that other business will come their way . . .

Although Deutsche Bank will bear the cost of keeping the Invensys loan on its own books, it will have captured a large part of the total of £108m of fees paid for the refinancing.

Some people expect solo deals of this type to become more common as the the big investment banks put their balance sheets to work to win new business . . .

To win fees and earn a place in the league tables that are such an important marketing tool, banks have been pressing for admission to deal management groups. Telecom Italia's recent €6.5bn loan involved no fewer than 12 'mandated lead arrangers', of which seven were also 'bookrunners'. Sharing fees among so many participants reduces the banks' earnings.

In reality, many of the banks involved will have had little to do. But the inflation of titles is devaluing the banks' traditional role and undermining issuers' perception of banking expertise. Going it alone or cosying up to competitors: both have their price.

Source: Financial Times, 10/11 April 2004, p. M21. Reprinted with permission.

Companies with a high total debt burden, a poor cash flow position, in a worsening market environment causing lower and more volatile earnings, will have a high default risk and a low credit rating. The leading organisations providing credit ratings are Moody's, Standard & Poor's (S&P) and Fitch. The highest rating is AAA or Aaa (triple-A rated). Such a rating indicates very high quality. The capacity to repay interest and principal is extremely strong. Single A indicates a strong capacity to pay interest and capital but there is some degree of susceptibility to impairment as economic events unfold. BBB indicates adequate debt service capacity but vulnerability to adverse economic conditions or changing circumstances. B and C rated debt has predominantly speculative characteristics. The lowest is D which indicates the firm is in default. Ratings of BBB – (or Baa3 for Moody's) or above are regarded as '**investment grade**' – this is important because many institutional investors are permitted to invest in investment grade bonds only (*see* **Exhibit 11.5**). Bonds rated below this are called **high-yield** (or **junk**) **bonds**. Generally, the specific loan is rated

Exhibit 11.5 A comparison of Moody's, Standard & Poor's and Fitch's rating scales

Standard & Poor's	Moody's	Fitch's	Grades	
AAA	Aaa	AAA	Prime, maximum safety	Investment grade bonds
AA+	Aa1	AA+	High grade, high quality	
AA	Aa2	AA		
AA–	Aa3	AA–		
A+	A1	A+	Upper medium	
A	A2	A		
A–	A3	A–		
BBB+	Baa1	BBB+	Lower medium	
BBB	Baa2	BBB		
BBB–	Baa3	BBB–		
BB+	Ba1	BB+	Speculative	Non-investment grade, high-yield or 'junk' bonds
BB	Ba2	BB		
BB–	Ba3	BB–		
B+	B1	B+	Highly speculative	
B	B2	B		
B–	B3	B–		
CCC+	Caa1	CCC+	Substantial risk	
CCC	Caa2	CCC	In poor standing	
CCC–	Caa3	CCC–		
CC	Ca	CC	Extremely speculative	
C	C	C	May be in default	
D		D	Default	

rather than the borrower. If the loan does not have a rating it could be that the borrower has not paid for one, rather than implying anything sinister.

The rating and re-rating of bonds is followed with great interest by borrowers and lenders and can give rise to some heated argument. Credit ratings are of great concern to the borrowing corporation because bonds with lower ratings tend to have higher costs – *see* **Exhibit 11.6** (reinsurance is the insurance of selected risks accepted by other insurance companies).

Exhibit 11.6

Munich Re swings S&P opinion

FT

By Ivar Simensen in London

Munich Re's efforts to improve its capital base were finally rewarded by Standard & Poor's yesterday, nearly three years after the German reinsurance company lost its prized AA-credit rating.

S&P changed to positive from stable the outlook on Munich Re's A+ rating and said it could upgrade the rating by the end of the year. A return to AA territory could bring to an end a dispute between the reinsurer and the rating agency that has lasted since Munich Re was downgraded in August 2003.

The positive outlook reflected the 'significant progress the group has made in strengthening its underwriting, pricing and risk-management processes,' S&P said yesterday.

The world's second largest reinsurer has reduced its risk profile in recent years by selling equity stakes in companies such as Allianz and fully integrated American Re, its US subsidiary.

'They have understood our approach and we see their priorities better,' said a spokesman for Munich Re yesterday.

The rating agency downgraded Munich Re to A+ from AA- in August 2003, when billions of euros in tax charges contributed to losses at the group.

The downgrade provoked a strong response at the time from Munich Re, which said it had already committed itself to boosting its capital base ▶

Exhibit 11.6 continued

through a combination of retained earnings and a possible equity rights issue. Clement Booth, a Munich Re board member, said its commitment had 'apparently been rejected' by S&P.

Credit ratings are particularly important to reinsurers as they not only dictate the cost of financing the business in the capital markets but the perceived financial strength also affects the company's ability to attract new underwriting business.

Munich Re made regaining a AA- rating a top priority, and some company insiders expected an upgrade within a year.

A €4bn ($5bn) rights issue in the autumn of 2003 helped boost the capital base but two seasons of costly hurricanes in the US weighed on the company's earnings in 2004 and 2005 and kept the company waiting for the rating agency to act.

S&P said yesterday it would conclude a review of Munich Re's reserve losses and risk management in the fourth quarter and that a satisfactory conclusion, combined with continued earnings improvement, could lead to a rating upgrade.

A return to AA territory could give Munich Re a boost ahead of the crucial autumn run-up to policy renewals in January.

Source: *Financial Times*, 28 June 2006, p. 28. Reprinted with permission.

The *Financial Times* shows credit ratings daily in the tables titled 'Global Investment Grade' and 'High Yield and Emerging Market Bonds'. **Exhibit 11.7** shows some examples drawn from these tables. The ratings shown are for September 2007 and will not necessarily be applicable in future years because the creditworthiness and the specific debt issue can change significantly in a short period.

Exhibit 11.7 Examples of ratings on bonds in Sept. 2007

	Currency of borrowing	S&P	Moody's	Fitch
Eurohypo	€	AAA	Aaa	AAA
Toyota	Yen	AAA	Aaa	–
Du Pont	US$	A	A2	A
HBOS	£	AA	Aa1	AA+
J.P. Morgan	US$	A+	Aa3	A+
Daimler Chrysler	£	BBB	Baa1	BBB+
Repsol	€	BBB	Baa1	BBB+
General Motors	US$	BB+	Ba1	BB+
Philippines	US$	BB–	B1	BB
Fiat Financial	€	–	Ba1	BBB–
Ecuador	US$	CCC	Caa2	CCC

Source: *Financial Times*, 21 September 2007, p. 35. Reprinted with permission.

Exhibit 11.8 describes how some companies are taking on more debt relative to their equity base, accepting lower credit ratings, to enhance shareholder wealth. (Capital structure, the debt-to-equity balance is discussed in Chapter 22.)

Exhibit 11.9 shows the proportion of bonds that have defaulted 1, 2, 3, 4 and 5 years over the period 1990–2006. Notice the large differences in default rates between the ratings. When examining data on default rates it is important to appreciate that default is a wide-ranging term, and could refer to any number of events from a missed payment to bankruptcy. For some of these events all is lost from the investor's perspective. For other events a very high percentage, if not all, of the interest and principal is recovered. Hickman (1958) observed that defaulted publicly held and traded bonds tended to sell for 40 cents on the dollar. This average recovery rate rule-of-thumb seems to have held over time – in approximate terms – with senior secured bank loans returning over 60 per cent and subordinated bonds under 30 per cent.

Exhibit 11.8

Weighing up the debt balancing act

FT

Private equity may use borrowing to maximise returns for shareholders, but the practice is much rarer among listed companies

writes Chris Hughes

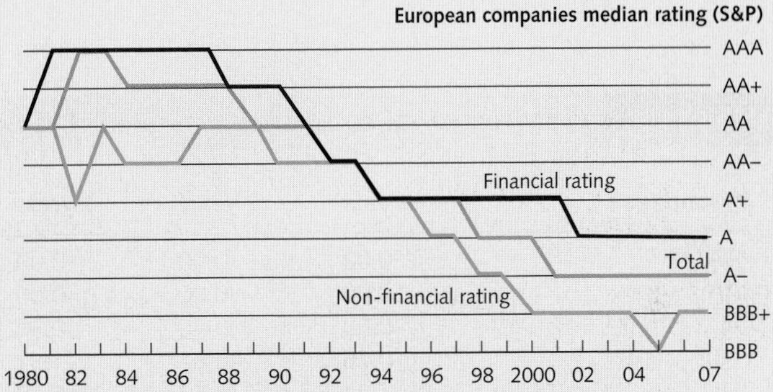

Private equity firms have demonstrated that loading a company with debt can help maximise returns for shareholders – even if its credit rating plummets to 'junk' status. But few listed UK companies seem willing to take on debt with any gusto.

The rising ambition of buy-out groups – shown in KKR's £9.7bn approach for Alliance Boots last week – has pushed some companies to take on more debt as a defence tactic against a takeover, sometimes pre-emptively.

Marks and Spencer, for example, sacrificed its single-A credit rating by gearing up as part of its fight against an approach from entrepreneur Sir Philip Green in 2004.

But such instances are sporadic. And in recent years, only two UK companies – Hilton, now the Ladbrokes betting group, and Rank, the leisure business – have deliberatly pushed their credit rating to junk, defined as BB+ or lower.

Standard & Poor's, the credit-rating agency, says average credit ratings in Europe are in decline because companies are generally taking on more debt.

But the UK lags behind this trend. Gearing – a measure of company debt in relation to equity – is at record low among British companies, according to Collins Stewart.

This resistance to increased debt is pronounced among larger UK companies. FTSE-100 companies seems to cherish high 'investment-grade' credit ratings of BBB- and higher. Banks and insurers benefit from a strong rating since this provides savers with confidence. But there are also 21 non-financial companies rated in the A range or higher in the FTSE-100. This is in spite of many companies funnelling billions of pounds to investors through share buy-back programmes or rasing dividends, as Scottish and Southern Energy did last week.

'In the current environment, there are not many sectors where you need an A rating,' says Chris Dinwoodie, head of corporate ratings in Europe for S&P.

This fondness for an A rating is potentially bad for shareholder. Debt is cheap, so shrinking a company's equity by taking on more debt can generate higher returns for equity investors.

While companies with lower credit ratings pay interest at higher rates, reflecting their increased risk, the cost is not that much higher.

Moreover, returns are boosted by tax relief on interest.

Private equity's business model exploits these very benefits.

True, too much debt can be a bad thing. Morgan Stanley recently warned investors against public companies that have imitated private equity. It found that those with a low ratio of operating profit to interest and other charges suffered below-average future earnings growth.

All the same, it is strange that all these A-rated UK companies have not embraced the private equity business model more.

'Some companies prefer to maintain an A rating to cushion them against any future economic or market shock, but others are finding it hard to justify, particularly given a marginal difference in the cost of funding from A- to BBB+,' says Mr Dinwoodie.

Neil Darke, analyst at Collins Stewart, says: 'The larger companies feel they can afford to maintain a lazy balance sheet because they are bid-proof.

Chief executives earn bigger salaries for running larger companies, so they have little incentive to shrink the equity by taking on more debt.'

There are some sector-specific factors. Utility companies may suspect that regulators would claw back any additonal returns generated by greater leverage. For its part, Centrica, the gas utility, has hinted that it may take on more debt if it expands overseas through cash-funded acquisitions.

The mining sector is awash with cash because it is at the peak of its business cycle. A spokesman for BHP Billiton says: 'You have to think of the balance sheet in the longer term, and ask what is going to be efficient through the cycle.'

Rio Tinto has said it is looking for acquisitions, which could absorb

Exhibit 11.8 continued

excess cash. But some analysts fear miners are building war chests that could fund an ill-disciplined acquisition spree at the top of the cycle.

Oil executives defend their lowly geared balance sheets by pointing to ExxonMobil, the oil company that generates the industry's best returns, in spite of having no debt.

The pharamaceutical sector is similarly bloated. Astra-Zeneca, which needs to acquire new drugs to flesh out its pipeline, has almost $6bn of net cash.

'We have to accept we can't hold it forever', says a spokesman. 'The flexibility of a strong balance sheet could be a key strategic advantage to us.'

But could it be, as Mr Darke suggests, that A-rated companies suffer from inertia and conservativism?

Reckitt Benckiser, the consumer goods company, vigorously denies this.

'In the real world, it is not as simple as saying more debt is good. We have a low tax benefit from taking on more debt,' says a spokesman.

'We do not sit around thinking, "what is the right credit rating?"'

Source: *Financial Times*, 12 March 2007, p. 21. Reprinted with permission.

Exhibit 11.9 Global corporate finance average cumulative default rates: 1990–2006

Percentage	1 year	2 years	3 years	4 years	5 years
'AAA'	0.00	0.00	0.00	0.00	0.00
'AA'	0.00	0.00	0.00	0.03	0.06
'A'	0.03	0.16	0.32	0.48	0.73
'BBB'	0.26	0.87	1.61	2.53	3.47
'BB'	1.24	3.64	5.78	7.82	9.84
'B'	1.47	3.66	6.16	8.59	11.16
'CCC' to 'C'	22.93	30.72	35.64	41.63	43.41
Investment grade	0.10	0.34	0.64	0.96	1.31
High yield	2.94	5.75	8.25	10.74	12.72
All corporates	0.61	1.27	1.89	2.51	3.04

Source: Fitch ratings global corporate finance 2006 transition and default study (www.fitchratings.com).

Mezzanine finance and high-yield (junk) bonds

Mezzanine debt is a loan offering a high return with a high risk. It may be either unsecured or secured but ranking behind senior loans for payment of interest and capital. This type of debt generally offers interest rates two to nine percentage points more than that on senior debt and frequently gives the lenders some right to a share in equity values should the firm perform well. It is a kind of **hybrid finance** ranking for payment below straight debt but above equity – it is thus described alternatively as *subordinated*, *intermediate* or *low grade*. One of the major attractions of this form of finance for the investor is that it often comes with equity warrants (*see* Chapter 10) or share options attached which can be used to obtain shares in the firm – this is known as an '**equity kicker**'. These may be triggered by an event such as the firm joining the stock market.

Mezzanine finance tends to be used when bank borrowing limits are reached and the firm cannot or will not issue more equity. It is more expensive than bank borrowing, but is cheaper (in terms of required return) than would be available on the equity market; and it allows the owners of a business to raise large sums of money without sacrificing control. It is a form of finance which permits the firm to move beyond what is normally considered acceptable debt : equity ratios (gearing or leverage levels).

Crucially, unlike most bank loans, which usually involve annual repayments, mezzanine is often like an interest-only mortgage with no capital repayments until the end of the loan. Also mezzanine lenders, which are often specialist funds rather than banks, are usually prepared to lend against the company's prospects in terms of expected cash flows, rather than insisting on security (collateral), as banks tend toward.

Bonds with high-risk and high-return characteristics are called high-yield (junk) bonds (they are rated below investment grade by rating agencies with ratings of Bs and Cs). These may be bonds which started as apparently safe investments but have now become riskier ('**fallen angels**') or they may be bonds issued specifically to provide higher-risk finance instruments for investors. This latter type began its rise to prominence in the USA in the 1980s and is now a market with over $100bn issued per year. The rise of the US junk bond market meant that no business was safe from the threat of takeover, however large – *see* **Case study 11.1** on Michael Milken.

Case study 11.1 The junk bond wizard: Michael Milken

While studying at Wharton Business School in the 1970s Michael Milken came to the belief that the gap in interest rates between safe bonds and high-yield bonds was excessive, given the relative risks. This created an opportunity for financial institutions to make an acceptable return from junk bonds, given their risk level. At the investment banking firm Drexel Burnham Lambert, Milken was able to persuade a large body of institutional investors to supply finance to the junk bond market as well as provide a service to corporations wishing to grow through the use of junk bonds. Small firms were able to raise billions of dollars to take over large US corporations. Many of these issuers of junk bonds had debt ratios of 90 per cent and above – for every $1 of share capital $9 was borrowed. These gearing levels concerned many in the financial markets. It was thought that companies were pushing their luck too far and indeed many did collapse under the weight of their debt. The market was dealt a particularly severe blow when Michael Milken was convicted, sent to jail and ordered to pay $600m in fines. Drexel was also convicted, paid $650m in fines and filed for bankruptcy in 1990. The junk bond market was in a sorry state in the early 1990s, with high levels of default and few new issues. However, it did not take long for the market to recover.

The high-yield bond is much more popular in the USA than in Europe because of the aversion (constrained by legislation) to such instruments in the major financial institutions. The European high-yield bond market is in its infancy. The first high-yield bonds denominated in European currencies were issued as recently as 1997 when Geberit, a Swiss/UK manufacturer, raised DM 157.5m by selling 10-year bonds offering an interest rate which was 423 basis points (4.23 per cent) higher than the interest rate on a 10-year German government bond (bund). Since then there have been hundreds of issues. However, the European high-yield market remains about one-quarter the size of the US one but it is growing rapidly.

Mezzanine finance is usually a private form of debt (e.g. loan), rather than a publicly traded bond form of debt. However mezzanine notes are sometimes issued which are tradable in a secondary market. Mezzanine finance (and **second lien** loans – whose owners by definition would be in line behind senior secured creditors in a liquidation) has proved to be particularly useful to managers involved in a management buyout (MBO) which by necessity requires high levels of debt, that is, **leveraged buyouts (LBOs)**. A typical LBO would have a financial structure as follows:

- 50–60 per cent from senior bank or other debt providers;
- 25–30 per cent from subordinated debt – for example, mezzanine finance, unsecured low-ranking bonds and/or preference shares;
- 10–25 per cent equity.

Fast-growing companies also make use of mezzanine finance and junk bonds. They have been particularly attractive sources for cable television companies, telecommunications and some media businesses which require large investments in the near term but also offer a relatively stable profits flow in the long term. Mezzanine loans have the advantage over bonds in flexibility on exit. That is, high yield bonds typically have a life of five to seven years, making it expensive to repay early. Mezzanine does not carry large penalties for early repayment.

Mezzanine financing and high-yield bonds have been employed by firms 'gearing themselves up' to finance merger activity, and also for **leveraged recapitalisations**. For instance, a firm might have run into trouble, defaulted and its assets are now under the control of a group of creditors, including bankers and bondholders. One way to allow the business to continue would be to persuade the creditors to accept alternative financial securities in place of their debt securities to bring the leverage (financial gearing) to a reasonable level. They might be prepared to accept a mixture of shares and mezzanine finance. The mezzanine instruments permit the holders to receive high interest rates in recognition of the riskiness of the firm, and they open up the possibility of an exceptionally high return from warrants or share options should the firm get back to a growth path. The alternative for the lenders may be a return of only a few pence in the pound from the immediate liquidation of the firm's assets.

Mezzanine finance/junk bond borrowing usually leads to high debt levels resulting in a high fixed cost imposition on the firm. This can be a dangerous way of financing expansion and therefore the use of these types of finance has been criticised. On the other hand, some commentators have praised the way in which high gearing and large annual interest payments have focused the minds of managers and engendered extraordinary performance (*see* Chapter 21). Also, without this finance, many takeovers, buyouts and financial restructurings would not take place. As **Exhibit 11.10** makes clear, Mezzanine and high yield bond finance has grown significantly in recent years.

Exhibit 11.10

Mezzanine is starting to stake its claim

Explosion in leveraged buy-outs leads to a surge in deals

writes David Oakley

A funny thing happened a couple of weeks ago when the European High Yield Association held its first annual gathering staged in recognition of the spectacular growth in junk rated corporate bonds.

The main theme of the event was – as the name suggests – supposed to be 'bonds'. But one of the main talking points was the rise of loans – and the threat these pose to high yield as an alternative way to raise money. In one of the key debates, BNP Paribas produced figures that showed how so-called mezzanine finance (one subset of loans) have recently been outpacing the growth of high-yield corporate bonds in Europe.

This is in spite of the record issuance of the latter, and the fact that until three years ago mezzanine was a slow-moving backwater.

The number of mezzanine deals has doubled since 2003 when the market for subordinated debt began to take off according to BNP, driven by the explosion in leveraged buy-outs from private equity. The dollar amount of European buy-outs exceeded US buy-outs in 2005 and is set to do so again this year, BNP said.

Richard Howell, co-head of leveraged finance at Lehman Brothers

In number of transactions, mezzazine issuance is outpacing high-yield issuance in Europe
European issuance (number of deals)

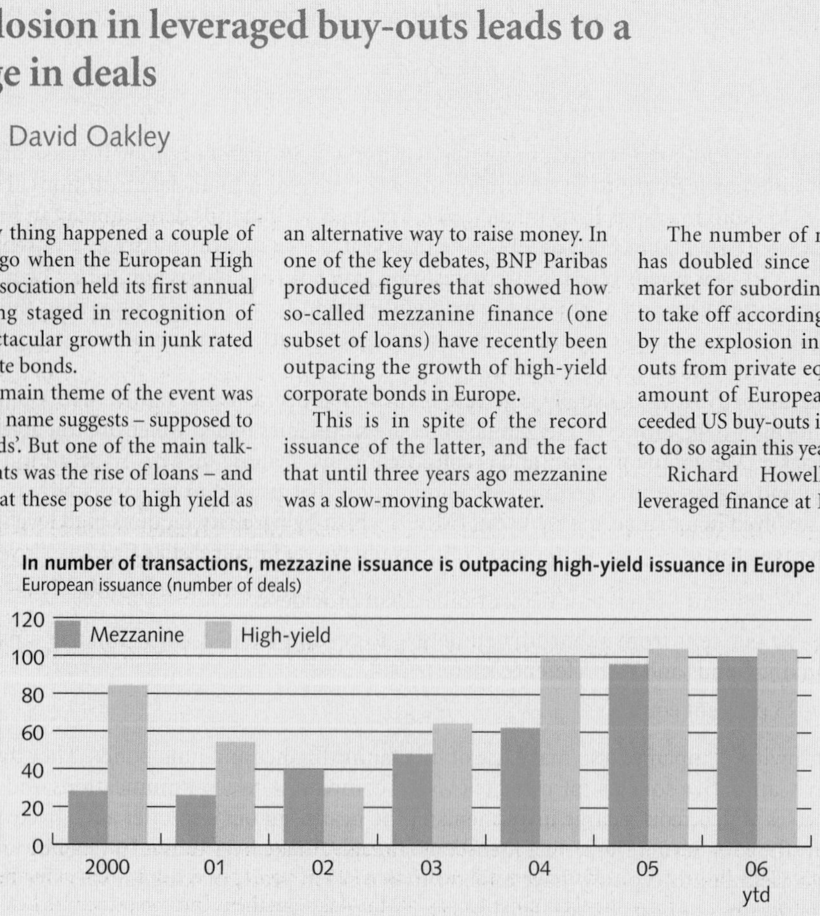

Exhibit 11.10 continued

in Europe, said: 'Mezzanine is almost exclusively a leveraged buy-out product whereas high yield is also increasingly issued by mainstream corporates.

'In Europe, high yield continues to grow. Mezzanine has outpaced that growth because of a substantial influx of new investors into the space in the last two years.'

The average spread – or the premium paid over government bonds, the safest form of debt – for mezzanine loans over the past three months to September was 902 basis points compared with about 300bp for a BB-rated junk bond or 600bp for a CCC– rating, the lowest, on the scale before default, BNP said.

Investors also like the flexibility that these loans offer. Matthew Naber, head of European loans syndication at Morgan Stanley, said: 'For the issuer, the advantage of mezzanine is that you get call flexibility, at the expense of additional yield. You can refinance mezzanine after a year or two at a minimal cost. A 10-year high-yield bond is often non-callable for five years.'

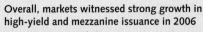

Overall, markets witnessed strong growth in high-yield and mezzanine issuance in 2006

European issuance (€bn)

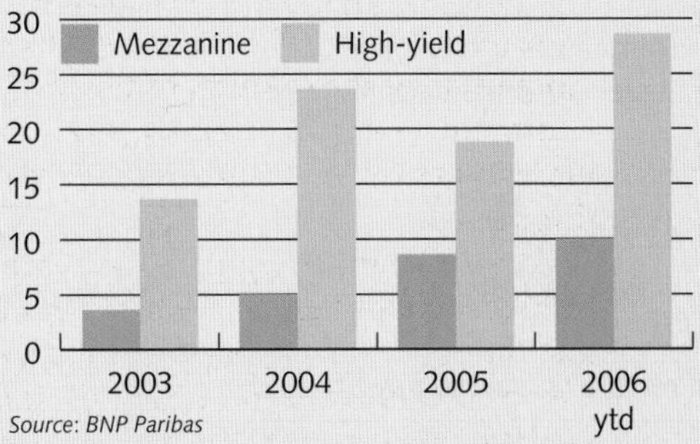

Source: BNP Paribas

For a corporate looking to raise more than €1bn, high yield is the better bet as there is a larger investor base. Mr Howell said: 'For the very largest LBOs, high yield is essential. Below these, however, sponsors have a genuine choice between high yield or mezzanine.'

So who is better off when the credit cycle turns? Opinion is divided, but bankers believe mezzanine might be the wiser option, in terms of recovery. 'High yield is typically unsecured while mezzanine has second ranking security. It's higher up the pecking order when it comes to getting your money back,' said one banker

Source: *Financial Times*, 16 November 2006, p. 43. Reprinted with permission

Financing a leveraged buyout

If the anticipated cash flows are reasonably stable then a highly leveraged buyout may give an exceptional return to the shareholders. Take the case of Sparrow, a subsidiary of Hawk plc (*see* **Exhibit 11.11**). The managers have agreed a buyout price of £10m, equal to Sparrow's assets. They are able to raise £1m from their own resources to put into equity capital and have borrowed £9m. The debt pays an interest rate of 14 per cent and the corporate tax rate is 25 per cent (payable one year after year-end). Profits before interest and tax in the first year after the buyout are expected to be £1.5m and will grow at 25 per cent per annum thereafter. All earnings will be retained within the business to pay off debt.

In the first few years the debt burden absorbs a large proportion of the rapidly increasing profits. However, it only takes six years for the entire debt to be retired. The shareholders then own a business with assets of over £10m, an increase of over tenfold on their original investment. The business is also producing a large annual profit which could make a stock market flotation attractive, in which case the value of the shares held by the management will probably be worth much more than £10m.[4]

Financial innovators have developed an even more risky form of debt, the pay-in-kind note or loan (PIK) – see **Exhibit 11.12**.

[4] This example is designed to show the effect of leverage. It does lack realism in a number of respects; for example it is unlikely that profits will continue to rise at 25 per cent per annum without further investment. This can be adjusted for – the time taken to pay off the debt lengthens but the principles behind the example do not alter.

Exhibit 11.11 Sparrow – Profit and Loss Account and Balance Sheet (£000s)

	Years					
	1	2	3	4	5	6
Profit before interest and taxes (after depreciation)	1,500	1,875	2,344	2,930	3,662	4,578
Less interest	1,260	1,226	1,144	999	770	433
	240	649	1,200	1,931	2,892	4,145
Tax	0	60	162	300	483	723
Profits available to pay off debt	240	589	1,038	1,631	2,409	3,422

Balance Sheet		Year					
	Opening	1	2	3	4	5	6
Equity	1,000	1,240	1,829	2,867	4,498	6,907	10,329
Debt	9,000	8,760	8,171	7,133	5,502	3,093	0
Assets	10,000	10,000	10,000	10,000	10,000	10,000	10,329

Notes: Past tax liabilities have been accepted by Hawk. Money set aside for depreciation is used to replace assets to maintain £10m of assets throughout. Also depreciation equals capital allowances used for tax purposes.

Exhibit 11.12

Deferred return: risky investment?

FT

Gillian Tett explains the prosaic reality behind a market growing in popularity

When Weetabix, the UK food company owned by Lion Capital, a private equity group, raised £130m with a so-called 'payment in kind' note in September, one public relations executive in London was baffled.

'What is payment in kind?' he quipped. 'Do you get paid in Weetabix?'

Sadly, the reality is rather more prosaic. Though the principle behind payment-in-kind (PIK) notes has [sic] existed in financial markets for years, the PIK market has really emerged in Europe only in the past 18 months, with some €3bn of such instruments issued so far. They take their name from the fact that PIK notes or loans do not pay out at the coupon date of the bond or loan. Instead, they pay out in the form of *more* bonds or loans.

It means that, in practical terms, the returns an investor receives from a PIK note are deferred for several years, until the issuer can either redeem the notes or the term of the instrument ends.

That obviously makes these instruments risky, since if the issuer fails, the investor may never get any return. Moreover, PIK notes are usually deeply subordinated in the capital structure – meaning that investors holding them receive payments only after other creditors in the case of default. Consequently, the risk can be so high that some investment bankers argue that PIKs are better viewed as quasi-equity – rather than a form of debt.

Nevertheless, investors are usually well compensated for these risks, at least compared with other debt instruments (although, they obviously do not have the potential upside enjoyed by true equity holders). According to research by Credit Suisse, PIK notes have typically been issued in Europe in recent months at a spread of about 800 to 900 basis points over Libor in the past couple of years. That means these instruments pay investor implied interest rates in the law teens, and sometimes even high teens.

Since this debt is obviously very costly compared with other instruments, PIKs carry few attractions for mainstream companies. However, there is often a strong incentive for private equity groups to fund their investments by issuing PIKs. For if they can defer cash repayments to

Exhibit 11.12 continued

investors for a few years, this frees cash to turn a business around – and if the restructured company is later successfully floated (or sold), then there should easily be enough cash to redeem the PIKs.

Investors purchasing the PIK notes have hitherto had a strong incentive to buy. The main buyers are a small pool of hedge funds, many US in origin. These have been hungry to find high-yielding assets – and investing in PIK notes has allowed them to enjoy high returns.

Source: Financial Times, 27 September 2006, Special Report: Corporate Finance, p. 2. Reprinted with permission.

Convertible bonds

Convertible bonds (or convertible loan stocks) carry a rate of interest in the same way as vanilla bonds, but they also give the holder the right to exchange the bonds at some stage in the future into ordinary shares according to some prearranged formula.[5] The owner of these bonds is not obliged to exercise this right of conversion and so the bonds may continue until redemption as interest-bearing instruments. Usually the **conversion price** is 10–30 per cent greater than the existing share price. So if a £100 bond offered the right to convert to 40 ordinary shares the conversion price would be £2.50 (that is, £100/40) which, given the current market price of the shares of, say, £2.20, would be a **conversion premium** of:

$$\frac{2.50 - 2.20}{2.20} = 0.136 \text{ or } 13.6\%$$

Venture Production, a North Sea oil explorer, issued covertible bonds in July 2005. The issue raised £29m. The bonds are to be redeemed in 2010 if they have not been converted before this and were issued at a par value of £100. The coupon was set at 4.25 per cent and the conversion price was at 474p per share. From this information we can calculate the **conversion ratio**:

$$\text{Conversion ratio} = \frac{\text{Nominal (par) value of bond}}{\text{Conversion price}} = \frac{£100}{£4.74} = 21.1 \text{ shares}$$

Each bond carries the right to convert to 21.1 shares, which is equivalent to paying 474p for each share at the £100 par value of the bond.

Unusually, in this particular case, if the bonds are not converted or redeemed then the holder will receive 110 per cent of par value rather than simply the par value in October 2010, to give a total yield to maturity (the properly calculated rate of return – *see* next section) of 5.904 per cent.

The conversion price was set at a premium of 16 per cent over the ordinary share price at the time of pricing which was 408p ((474–408)/408 = 16%). At the time of the issue many investors may have looked at the low interest rate on the convertible and said to themselves that although this was greater than the dividend yield on shares (3 per cent) it was less than that on conventional bonds, but offsetting this was the prospect of capital gains made by converting the bonds into shares. If the shares rose to, say, £6 each £100 bond could be converted to 21.1 shares worth $21.1 \times £6 = £126.6$.

The value of a convertible bond (also called an '**equity-linked bond**') rises as the value of the underlying ordinary shares increases, but at a lower percentage rate. The value could be analysed as a 'debt portion' (which depends on the discounted value of the coupons) and an 'equity portion' (the right to convert is an equity option). If the share price rises above the conversion price the investor may exercise the option to convert if he/she anticipates that the share price will at least be maintained and the dividend yield is higher than the convertible bond yield. If the share price rise is seen to be temporary the investor may wish to hold on to the bond.

[5] Alternatively they may be convertible into preference shares.

Exhibit 11.13 Summary of convertible bond technical jargon

- **Conversion ratio** This gives the number of ordinary shares into which a convertible bond may be converted:

$$\text{Conversion ratio} = \frac{\text{Nominal (par) value of bond}}{\text{Conversion price}}$$

- **Conversion price** This gives the price of each ordinary share obtainable by exchanging a convertible bond:

$$\text{Conversion price} = \frac{\text{Nominal (par) value of bond}}{\text{Number of shares into which bond may be converted}}$$

- **Conversion premium** This gives the difference between the conversion price and the market share price, expressed as a percentage:

$$\text{Conversion premium} = \frac{\text{Conversion price} - \text{Market share price}}{\text{Market share price}} \times 100$$

- **Conversion value** This is the value of a convertible bond if it were converted into ordinary shares at the current share price:

$$\text{Conversion value} = \text{Current share price} \times \text{Conversion ratio}$$

The right to convert may specify a specific date or several specific dates over, say, a four-year period, or any time between two dates. Most convertible bonds are unsecured but as Exhibit 11.14 on Greenhills shows, this is not always the case – a good thing for Hunter Ground.

Exhibit 11.14 Secured convertible debentures

Greenhills

The first AIM-traded company to go into receivership was Greenhills, the restaurant operator. A major investor, Hunter Ground, appointed administrative receivers on 4 December 1996. Hunter Ground held secured convertible debentures from Greenhills worth £506,000.

Source: Investors Chronicle, 20 December 1996, p. 11. Reprinted with kind permission of the *Investors Chronicle*.

Advantages to the company of convertible bonds

Convertible bonds have the following advantages to the company.

1 ***Lower interest than on a similar debenture*** The firm can ask investors to accept a lower interest on these debt instruments because the investor values the conversion right. This was a valuable feature for many dot.com companies in the late 1990s. Companies such as Amazon and AOL could pay 5–6 per cent on convertibles – less than half what they would have paid on straight bonds.

2 ***The interest is tax deductible*** Because convertible bonds are a form of debt the coupon payment can be regarded as a cost of the business and can therefore be used to reduce taxable profit.

3 ***Self liquidating*** When the share price reaches a level at which conversion is worthwhile the bonds will (normally) be exchanged for shares so the company does not have to find cash to pay off the loan principal – it simply issues more shares. This has obvious cash flow benefits. However the disadvantage is that the other equity holders may experience a reduction in earnings per share and dilution of voting rights.

4 ***Fewer restrictive covenants*** The directors have greater operating and financial flexibility than they would with a secured debenture. Investors accept that a convertible is a hybrid between debt and equity finance and do not tend to ask for high-level security, impose strong operating restrictions on managerial action or insist on strict financial ratio boundaries – notwithstanding the case of Greenhills. Many Silicon Valley companies with little more than a web-portal and a brand have used convertibles because of the absence of a need to provide collateral or stick to asset : borrowing ratios.

5 ***Underpriced shares*** A company which wishes to raise equity finance over the medium term but judges that the stock market is temporarily underpricing its shares may turn to convertible bonds. If the firm does perform as the managers expect and the share price rises, the convertible will be exchanged for equity.

6 ***Cheap way to issue shares*** Graham and Harvey (2001) found that managers favoured convertibles as an inexpensive way to issue 'delayed' equity. Equity is raised at a later date without the high costs of rights issues etc.

7 ***Available finance when straight debt and equity are not available*** Some firms locked out of the equity markets (e.g. because of poor recent performance) and the straight debt markets because of high levels of indebtedness may still be able to raise money in the convertible market. Firms use convertible debt 'to attract investors unsure about the riskiness of the company' (Graham and Harvey (2001)).

Advantages to the investor

The advantages of convertible bonds to the investor are as follows.

1 They are able to wait and see how the share price moves before investing in equity.

2 In the near term there is greater security for their principal compared with equity investment, and the annual coupon is usually higher than the dividend yield.

The bonds sold may not give the right to conversion into shares of the issuers, but shares of another company held by the issuer – *see* the cases of Hutchison Whampoa, Telecom Italia and France Telecom in **Exhibit 11.15**. Note that the term 'exchangeable bond' is probably more appropriate in these cases.

Exhibit 11.15

Brakes applied to convertible bond market

FT

Rebecca Bream

The European convertible bond market kicked off the year with the most active period for new issues that many can remember...

The first quarter saw €13.8bn of European equity-linked issuance, up almost 50 per cent from the first quarter of 2000's figure of €9.2bn. This compares to about €37bn of convertible issuance globally, and a 16 per cent decrease of issuance in the US...

In January Hong Kong conglomerate Hutchison Whampoa sold $2.65bn of bonds exchangeable into shares of Vodafone, the UK mobile phone operator. Hutchison had been gradually divesting its stake in the UK group since completing a $3bn exchangeable bond deal last September.

This was followed at the end of the month by Telecom Italia which sold €2bn of bonds exchangeable into shares of subsidiaries Telecom Italia Mobile and Internet operator Seat.

In February France Telecom sold €3.3bn of bonds exchangeable into shares of Orange, completed at the same time as the mobile unit's IPO, and one of the biggest exchangeable bond deals ever sold in Europe.

The deals were helped along by the fact that money had flowed into dedicated convertible bond funds at the end of 2000, both buy-and-hold accounts and arbitrage-driven hedge funds, and investor demand outstripped supply.

Source: Financial Times, 6 April 2001, p. 35. Reprinted with permission.

Valuing bonds

Bonds, particularly those which are traded in secondary markets such as the London Stock Exchange, are priced according to supply and demand. The main influences on the price of a bond will be the general level of interest rates for securities of that risk level and maturity. If the coupon is less than the current interest rate the bond will trade at less than the par value of £100. Take the case of an irredeemable bond with an annual coupon of 8 per cent. This financial asset offers to any potential purchaser a regular £8 per year for ever (i.e. 8 per cent of the par value of £100). When the bond was first issued general interest rates for this risk class may well have been 8 per cent and so the bond may have been sold at £100. However interest rates change over time. Suppose that the rate demanded by investors is now 10 per cent. Investors will no longer be willing to pay £100 for an instrument that yields £8 per year. The current market value of the bond will fall to £80 (£8/0.10) because this is the maximum amount needed to pay for similar bonds given the current interest rate of 10 per cent. If the coupon is more than the current market interest rate the market price of the bond will be greater than the nominal (par) value. Thus if market rates are 6 per cent the irredeemable bond will be priced at £133.33 (£8/0.06).

Notice the inverse relationship between the price of a bond and the rate of return offered on it.

The formula relating the price of an irredeemable bond, the coupon and the market rate of interest is:

$$P_D = \frac{i}{k_D}$$

where P_D = price of bond
i = nominal annual interest (the coupon rate × nominal (par) value of the bond)
k_D = market discount rate, annual return required on similar bonds

Also:

$$V_D = \frac{I}{k_D}$$

where V_D = total market value of all of the bonds of this type
I = total annual nominal interest of all the bonds of this type

We may wish to establish the market rate of interest represented by the market price of the bond. For example, if an irredeemable bond offers an annual coupon of 9.5 per cent and is currently trading at £87.50, with the next coupon due in one year, the rate of return is:

$$k_D = \frac{i}{P_D} = \frac{9.5}{87.5} = 0.1086 \text{ or } 10.86\%$$

Redeemable bonds

A purchaser of a redeemable bond buys two types of income promise: first the coupon, second the redemption payment. The amount that an investor will pay depends on the amount these income flows are worth when discounted at the rate of return required on that risk class of debt. The relationships are expressed in the following formulae:

$$P_D = \frac{i_1}{1 + k_D} + \frac{i_2}{(1 + k_D)^2} + \frac{i_3}{(1 + k_D)^3} + \ldots + \frac{R_n}{(1 + k_D)^n}$$

and:

$$V_D = \frac{I_1}{1 + k_D} + \frac{I_2}{(1 + k_D)^2} + \frac{I_3}{(1 + k_D)^3} + \ldots + \frac{R^*_n}{(1 + k_D)^n}$$

where i_1, i_2 and i_3 = nominal interest per bond in years 1, 2 and 3 up to n years
I_1, I_2 and I_3 = total nominal interest in years 1, 2 and 3 up to n years
R_n and R^*_n = redemption value of a bond, and total redemption of all bonds in year n, the redemption or maturity date

The worked example of Blackaby illustrates the valuation of a bond when the market interest rate is given.

Worked example 11.1 Blackaby plc

Blackaby plc issued a bond with a par value of £100 in September 2008, redeemable in September 2014 at par. The coupon is 8 per cent payable annually in September. The facts available from this are:

- the bond might have a par value of £100 but this may not be what investors will pay for it;
- the annual cash payment will be £8 (8 per cent of par);
- in September 2014, £100 will be handed over to the bondholder (in the absence of default).

Question 1

What is the price investors will pay for this bond at the time of issue if the market rate of interest for a security in this risk class is 7 per cent?

Answer

$$P_D = \frac{8}{1 + 0.07} + \frac{8}{(1 + 0.07)^2} + \frac{8}{(1 + 0.07)^3} + \ldots + \frac{8}{(1 + 0.07)^6} + \frac{100}{(1 + 0.07)^6}$$

P_D = £8 annuity for 6 years @ 7 per cent = 4.7665 × 8 = 38.132

plus $\frac{100}{(1 + 0.07)^6}$ = 66.634

£104.766

Question 2

What is the bond's value in the secondary market in September 2011 if interest rates rise by 200 basis points (i.e. for this risk class they are 9 per cent) between 2008 and 2011? (Assume the next coupon payment is in one year.)

Answer

P_D = £8 annuity for 3 years @ 9 per cent = 2.5313 × 8 = 20.25

plus $\frac{100}{(1 + 0.09)^3}$ = 77.22

£97.47

Again, note that as interest rates rise the price of bonds falls.

If we need to calculate the rate of return demanded by investors from a particular bond when we know the market price and coupon amounts, we can compute the internal rate of return. For example Bluebird plc issued a bond many years ago which is due for redemption at par of £100 in three years. The coupon is 6 per cent and the market price is £91. The rate of return now offered in the market by this bond is found by solving for k_D:

$$P_D = \frac{i_1}{1+k_D} + \frac{i_2}{(1+k_D)^2} + \frac{R_n + i_3}{(1+k_D)^3}$$

$$91 = \frac{6}{1+k_D} + \frac{6}{(1+k_D)^2} + \frac{106}{(1+k_D)^3}$$

To solve this requires the skills learned in calculating internal rates of return in Chapter 2. At an interest rate (k_D) of 9 per cent, the right side of the equation amounts to £92.41. At an interest rate of 10 per cent the right-hand side of the equation amounts to £90.05. Using linear interpolation:

Interest rate	9%	?	10%
Value of discounted cash flows	£92.41	£91	£90.05

$$k_D = 9\% + \frac{92.41 - 91}{92.41 - 90.05} \times (10 - 9) = 9.6\%$$

This is the yield-to-maturity or YTM discussed in the next section.

An Excel spreadsheet version of this calculation is available at www.pearsoned.com/arnold.

The two types of interest yield

There are two types of yield for fixed-interest securities. The **income yield** (also known as the **flat yield**, **interest yield** and **running yield**) is the gross (before tax) interest amount divided by the current market price of the bond expressed as a percentage:

$$\frac{\text{Gross interest (coupon)}}{\text{Market price}} \times 100$$

Thus for a holder of Bluebird's bonds the interest yield is:

$$\frac{£6}{£91} \times 100 = 6.59\%$$

This is a gross yield. The after-tax yield will be influenced by the investor's tax position.

Net interest yield = Gross yield $(1 - T)$,

where T = the tax rate applicable to the bondholder

The income yield is not the true rate of return available to the investor should he/she buy it because it fails to take into account the capital gain over three years to the expiry of the bond.

At a time when interest rates are higher than 6.59 per cent it is obvious that any potential purchaser of Bluebird bonds in the market will be looking for a return other than from the coupon. That additional return comes in the form of a capital gain over three years of £100 – £91 = £9. A rough estimate of this annual gain is (9/91) ÷ 3 = 3.3 per cent per year. When this is added to the interest yield we have an approximation to the second type of yield, the **yield to maturity** (also called the **redemption yield**). The yield to maturity of a bond is the discount rate such that the present value of all the cash inflows from the bond (interest plus principal) is equal to the bond's current market price. The rough estimate of 9.89 per cent (6.59% + 3.3%) has not taken into account the precise timing of the investor's income flows. When this is adjusted for, the yield to maturity is 9.6 per cent – the internal rate of return calculated above. Thus the yield to maturity includes both coupon payments and the capital gain or loss on maturity.

In the *Financial Times'* bond tables the column headed '**bid yield**' is the yield to maturity given the current bid price (traders quote bid and offer prices, the bid is the price at which market makers will buy from investors, the offer price is what an investor would pay to buy). Examples of these tables are shown later in the chapter, on page 455. It is important to note that many investors sell their bonds before the redemption date. The price received depends on market conditions. If general interest rates have risen over the holding period then a capital loss or a smaller gain than would occur if market interest rates were constant will be experienced, which will have a depressing effect on the rate of return received even though coupons may have been paid during the time the bonds were owned. For example, if an investor bought Bluebird bonds at £91 and sold them one year later when the required rate of return on two-year bonds of this risk level in the market is 10 per cent, instead of receiving the original 9.6 per cent yield to maturity he/she will only achieve a rate of return of 8.86 per cent over the year of holding, viz:

$$\text{Market value of bond after 1 year} = \frac{6}{1+0.1} + \frac{106}{(1+0.1)^2} = 93.06$$

Thus the return to our investor is:

$$91 = \frac{93.06+6}{1+r} \qquad r = 8.86\%$$

Semi-annual interest

The example of Bluebird given above is based on the assumption of annual interest payments. This makes initial understanding easier and reflects the reality for many types of bond, particularly internationally traded bonds. However UK companies usually issue domestic sterling bonds with semi-annual interest payments. A bond offering a coupon of 9 per cent would pay £4.50 halfway through the year and the remainder at the end. The rate of return calculation on these bonds is slightly more complicated. For example, Redwing plc has an 11 per cent bond outstanding which pays interest semi-annually. It will be redeemed in two years at £100 and has a current market price of £96, with the next interest payment due in six months. The yield to maturity on this bond is calculated as follows:

Cash flows

Point in time (years)	0.5	1	1.5	2.0	2.0
Cash flow	£5.5	£5.5	£5.5	£5.5	£100

The nominal interest rate over a six-month period is 5.5 per cent (11%/2):

$$96 = \frac{5.50}{1+k_D/2} + \frac{5.50}{(1+k_D/2)^2} + \frac{5.50}{(1+k_D/2)^3} + \frac{5.50}{(1+k_D/2)^4} + \frac{100}{(1+k_D/2)^4}$$

At a rate of 6 per cent for $k_D/2$ the right-hand side equals:

5.50 × 4-period annuity @ 6% = 5.50 × 3.4651	=	19.058
plus $\frac{100}{(1+0.06)^4}$	=	79.209
		£98.267

At a rate of 7 per cent for $k_D/2$ the right-hand side equals:

$$5.50 \times 4\text{-period annuity @ } 7\% = 5.50 \times 3.3872 = 18.630$$

$$\text{plus } \frac{100}{(1+0.07)^4} = \frac{76.290}{\pounds 94.920}$$

The IRR of the cash flow equals:

$$6\% + \frac{98.267 - 96}{98.267 - 94.92} \times (7 - 6) = 6.68\%$$

The IRR needs to be converted from a half-yearly cash flow basis to an annual basis:

$$(1 + 0.0668)^2 - 1 = 0.1381 \text{ or } 13.81\%$$

Exhibit 11.16 describes how the bond markets have been used to pay for immunisation programmes in developing countries. The interest and principal will be paid using money from future aid budgets of wealthy countries. Tapping the bond markets allows the project to get under way in the near term when the need is greatest. The upfront funding of mass vaccination, as opposed to long drawn-out schemes, increases their effectiveness by 25 per cent (after financing costs) and bulk buying lowers costs.

Exhibit 11.16

New bond raises $1bn for child jabs

FT

By Joanna Chung in London

An innovative bond aimed at financing child immunisation in some of the world's poorest countries yesterday raised $lbn after attracting demand from a wide range of investors, including central banks, religious groups and rock stars.

The new bond, issued by the International Finance Facility for Immunisation (IFFIm), allows vaccination and immunisation schemes to go ahead immediately with investors' money, which will be repaid in the future by government aid payments.

The five-year AAA-rated bond has a 5 per cent annual coupon and was priced yesterday to yield a premium of 31 basis points over the five-year US Treasury bond, the lower end of the initial price guidance set on Monday of between 30bp and 33bp over US Treasuries.

The inaugural bond, which met about $1.75bn worth of demand, is expected to be the first in a series of issues aimed at raising about $4bn over the next 10 years.

Alan Gillespie, chairman of IFFIm, said yesterday: 'The bond has caught the market's imagination and it paves the way forward. I would expect us to be back in the market in about a year's time.'

The money will be used to strengthen health systems and boost the uptake of existing and innovative vaccines for children via the Gavi Alliance (formerly the Global Alliance for Vaccines and Immunisation).

The UK, France, Italy, Spain, Sweden, Norway, Brazil and South Africa, together with the Bill and Melinda Gates Foundation have pledged future years' development assistance.

Thirty-five per cent of the bond issued yesterday was taken up by central banks and official institutions, 25 per cent by fund managers, 23 by pension funds, 8 per cent by retail investors, 6 per cent by banks and the remainder by corporations and insurance companies.

Gordon Brown, the UK chancellor, who has championed the scheme, marked the event with a ceremony yesterday.

The UK Treasury said the first six bonds would go to Pope Benedict XVI, the Archbishop of Canterbury, the Chief Rabbi, the Muslim Council of Britain, the Hindu Forum of Britain and the Network of Sikh Organisations. It also said that Bono and Bob Geldof, rockers-turned-activists, would buy bonds. Each bond has a face value of $1,000.

Goldman Sachs began helping to structure the bond in 2002 and advised the UK Treasury, which came up with the idea. Goldman Sachs acted as financial adviser on a pro-bono basis but it and Deutsche Bank will collect standard fees for the bond sale, which amount to 0.1 per cent of the amount raised, or about $lm.

Source: Financial Times, 8 November 2006, p. 45. Reprinted with permission.

International sources of debt finance

Larger and more creditworthy companies have access to a wider array of finance than small firms. These companies can tap the **Euromarkets** which are informal (unregulated) markets in money held outside its country of origin. For example there is a large market in **Eurodollars**. These are dollar credits (loans) and deposits managed by a bank not resident in the USA. This has the distinct advantage of transactions not being subject to supervision and regulation by the authorities in the USA. So, for example, an Italian firm can borrow dollars from a Spanish bank in the UK and the US regulatory authorities have no control over the transaction. There is a vast quantity of dollars held outside the USA and this money is put to use by borrowers. The same applies to all the major currencies – the money is lent and borrowed outside its home base and therefore is beyond the reach of the domestic regulators. Today it is not unusual to find an individual holding a dollar account at a UK bank – a **Eurodeposit account** – which pays interest in dollars linked to general dollar rates. This money can be lent to firms wishing to borrow in Eurodollars prepared to pay interest and capital repayments in dollars. There are large markets in **Euro Swiss Francs**, **Eurosterling**, **Euroyen** and many other currencies.[6] The title 'Euro' is misleading as this market is not limited to the European currencies or European banks (and is unconnected with the European single currency, the euro). The title came about because the modern market was started when the former Soviet Union transferred dollars from New York to a French bank at the height of the cold war in 1957. The cable address happened to be EUROBANK. This was long before the currency called the euro was conceived. Nowadays, there is daily **Eurosecurities** business transacted in all of the major financial centres. To add a little precision: '**Eurocurrency**' is short-term (less than one year) deposits and loans outside the jurisdiction of the country in whose currency the deposit/loan is denominated; '**Eurocredit**' is used for the market in medium- and long-term loans in the Euromarkets.

The companies which are large enough to use the Eurosecurities markets are able to put themselves at a competitive advantage *vis-à-vis* smaller firms. There are at least four advantages:

- The finance available in these markets can be at a lower cost in both transaction costs and rates of return.
- There are fewer rules and regulations such as needing to obtain official authorisation to issue or needing to queue to issue, leading to speed, innovation and lower costs.
- There may be the ability to hedge foreign currency movements. For example, if a firm has assets denominated in a foreign currency it can be advantageous to also have liabilities in that same currency to reduce the adverse impact of exchange-rate movements (*see* Chapter 25).
- National markets are often not able to provide the same volume of finance. The borrowing needs of some firms are simply too large for their domestic markets to supply. To avoid being hampered in expansion plans large firms can turn to the international market in finance.

For these internationally recognised firms there are three sources of debt finance:

a the domestic or national market;

b the financial markets of other countries which make themselves open to foreign firms – the **foreign debt market**;

c the Eurosecurities market which is not based in any one country and is not therefore regulated by any country.

Thus, for example, there are three bond markets available to some firms – as shown in **Exhibit 11.17**.

[6] Just to confuse everybody traders in this market often refer to all types of Eurocurrency, from Eurosterling to Euro-yen as Euro-dollars, and do not reserve the term for US dollars.

Exhibit 11.17 Bond markets

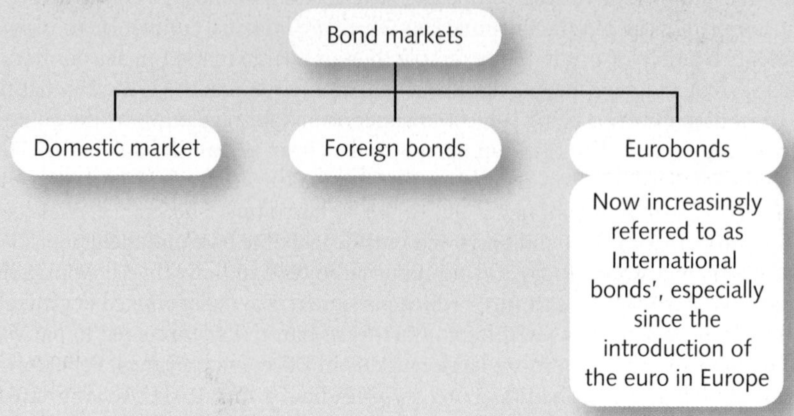

Foreign bonds

A **foreign bond** is a bond denominated in the currency of the country where it is issued when the issuer is a non-resident. For example, in Japan bonds issued by non-Japanese companies denominated in yen are foreign bonds. (The interest and capital payments will be in yen.) Foreign bonds have been given some interesting names: foreign bonds in Tokyo are known as **Samurai bonds**, foreign bonds issued in New York and London are called **Yankees** and **Bulldogs** respectively. The Netherlands allows foreigners to issue Rembrandt bonds and in Spain Matador bonds are traded. Foreign bonds are regulated by the authorities where the bond is issued. These rules can be demanding and an encumbrance to companies needing to act quickly and at low cost. The regulatory authorities have also been criticised for stifling innovation in the financial markets. The growth of the less restricted Eurobond market has put the once dominant foreign bond market in the shade.

Eurobonds (international bonds)

Eurobonds are bonds sold outside the jurisdiction of the country of the currency in which the bond is denominated. So, for example, the UK financial regulators have little influence over the Eurobonds denominated in sterling issued in Luxembourg, even though the transactions (for example interest and capital payments) are in pounds. Bonds issued in US dollars in Paris are outside the jurisdiction of the US authorities. They are medium- to long-term instruments. Eurobonds are not subject to the rules and regulations which are imposed on foreign bonds, such as the requirement to issue a detailed prospectus.[7] More importantly they are not subject to an **interest-withholding tax**. In the UK most domestic bonds are subject to a withholding tax by which basic rate income tax is deducted before the investor receives interest. Interest on Eurobonds is paid gross without any tax deducted – which has attractions to investors keen on delaying, avoiding or evading tax. Moreover, Eurobonds are **bearer bonds**, which means that the holders do not have to disclose their identity – all that is required to receive interest and capital is for the holder to have possession of the bond. In contrast, UK domestic bonds are registered, which means that companies and governments are able to identify the owners.

Despite the absence of official regulation, the International Capital Markets Association (ICMA), a self-regulatory body, imposes some restrictions, rules and standardised procedures on Eurobond issue and trading.

[7] Although new EU rules mean that a prospectus is required if the bond is marketed at retail (non-professional) investors.

Eurobonds are distinct from euro bonds, which are bonds denominated in euros and issued in the eurozone countries. Increasingly people differentiate between the two by calling old-fashioned Eurobonds 'International bonds', leaving the title 'euro' for the currency introduced in 1999. Of course, there have been euro-denominated bonds issued outside the jurisdiction of the authorities in the euro area. These are euro Eurobonds.

The development of the Eurobond (international bond) market

In the 1960s many countries, companies and individuals held surplus dollars outside of the USA. They were reluctant to hold these funds in American banks under US jurisdiction. There were various reasons for this. For example, some countries, particularly the former Soviet Union and other communist bloc countries of the cold war era, thought their interests were best served by using the dollars they had on the international markets, away from the powers of the US authorities to freeze or sequestrate (seize) assets. More recently this sort of logic has applied to countries such as Iran. Also in the 1960s the American authorities had some very off-putting tax laws and created a tough regulatory environment in their domestic financial markets. These encouraged investors and borrowers alike to undertake transactions in dollars outside the USA. London's strength as a financial centre, the UK authorities' more relaxed attitude to business, and its position in the global time zones, made it a natural leader in the Euro markets. The first Eurobond was issued in the early 1960s and the market grew modestly through the 1970s and then at a rapid rate in the 1980s. By then the Eurodollar bonds had been joined by bonds denominated in a wide variety of currencies. The market was stimulated not only by the tax and anonymity benefits, which brought a lower cost of finance than for the domestic bonds, but also by the increasing demand from transnational companies and governments needing large sums in alternative currencies and with the potential for innovatory characteristics. It was further boosted by the recycling of dollars from the oil-exporting countries.

In 1979 less than $20bn worth of bonds were issued in a variety of currencies. As can be seen from **Exhibit 11.18** the rate of new issuance is now around $2,000bn a year, with a total amount outstanding (bonds issued but not yet repaid) of over $19,000bn. In any one year approximately 30–40 per cent of new bonds are denominated in dollars. Euro-denominated issues account for more than one-half of issues. Even though the majority of Eurobond trading takes place through London, sterling is not one of the main currencies, and what is more, it tends to be large US and other foreign banks located in London which dominate the market.

Exhibit 11.18 International bond and notes

Type	Amounts outstanding $bn	Net issues, $bn	
	June 2007	2005	2006
Total issues	19,773	1,800	2,615
Floating rate	6,611	666	1,290
Straight fixed rate	12,809	1,154	1,319
Equity-related	353	-20	6

Source: Bank for International Settlements (BIS) Quarterly Review, September 2007 (www.bis.org).

Types of Eurobonds

The Eurobond market has been extraordinarily innovative in producing bonds with all sorts of coupon payment and capital repayment arrangements (for example, the currency of the coupon changes half-way through the life of the bond, or the interest rate switches from fixed to floating rate at some point). We cannot go into detail here on the rich variety but merely categorise the bonds into broad types.

1 ***Straight fixed-rate bond*** The coupon remains the same over the life of the bond. These are usually paid annually, in contrast to domestic bond semi-annual coupons. The redemption of these bonds is usually made with a 'bullet' repayment at the end of the bond's life.

2 ***Equity related*** These take two forms:

   a *Bonds with warrants attached* Warrants are options which give the holder the right to buy some other asset at a given price in the future. An equity warrant, for example, would give the right, but not the obligation, to purchase shares. There are also warrants for commodities such as gold or oil, and for the right to buy additional bonds from the same issuer at the same price and yield as the host bond. Warrants are detachable from the host bond and are securities in their own right, unlike convertibles.

   b *Convertibles* The bondholder has the right (but not the obligation) to convert the bond into ordinary shares at a preset price.

3 ***Floating-rate notes (FRNs)*** These have a variable coupon reset on a regular basis, usually every three or six months, in relation to a reference rate, such as LIBOR. The size of the spread over LIBOR reflects the perceived risk of the issuer. The typical term for an FRN is about five to 12 years.

Within these broad categories all kinds of 'bells and whistles' (features) can be attached to the bonds, for example **reverse floaters** – the coupon declines as LIBOR rises; **capped bonds** – the interest rate cannot rise above a certain level; *zero coupon* – a capital gain only is offered to the lender.

Many bonds have '**call back features**' under which the issuer may buy the bond back after a period of time has elapsed, say five years, at a price specified when the bond was issued. A '**put**' **feature** gives the bondholder the right, but not the obligation, to sell the bond back to the issuer (usually at par value) on designated dates.

The majority of Eurobonds (more than 80 per cent) are rated AAA or AA although those rated below BBB– are issued. Denominations are usually $1,000, $5,000 or $10,000 (or similar large sums in the currency of issue).

Corporations account for a relatively small proportion of the international bond market. The biggest issuers are the banks. Issues by governments ('sovereign issues') and state agencies in the public sector account for less than 10 per cent of issues. Also represented are international agencies such as the World Bank, the International Bank for Reconstruction and Development and the European Investment Bank.

Issuing Eurobonds

With Eurobonds a bank (lead manager or book runner) or group of banks acting for the issuer invite a large number of other banks or other investors to buy some of the bonds.[8] The managing group of banks is responsible for underwriting the issue and it may enlist a number of smaller institutions to use their extensive contacts to sell the bonds (the selling group or syndicate). Exhibit 9.16 on p. 338 in Chapter 9 gave some idea of the relative importance of the Eurobond market to UK-listed firms – in recent years the amount raised on the international market is greater than that raised through domestic debt and equity issues.

Eurobonds are traded on the secondary market through intermediaries acting as market makers. Most Eurobonds are listed on the London or Luxembourg stock exchanges but the market is primarily an over-the-counter one, that is, most transactions take place outside a recognised exchange. Most deals are conducted using the telephone, computers, telex and fax, but there are a number of electronic platforms for trading eurobonds. The extent to which electronic platforms will replace telephone dealing is as yet unclear. It is not possible to go to a central source for price information. Most issues rarely trade. Those that do are generally private transactions between investor and bond dealer and there is no obligation to inform the public about the deal. **Exhibit 11.19** presents the advantages and disadvantages of Eurobonds.

[8] Alternatively in a 'bought deal' the lead manager agrees to buy the entire issue at a specific price and yield. He then tries to sell it on in the market.

Exhibit 11.19 Advantages and drawbacks of Eurobonds as a source of finance for corporations

Advantage	*Drawback*
1 Large loans for long periods are available.	1 Only for the largest companies – minimum realistic issue size is about £50m.
2 Often cheaper than domestic bonds. The finance provider receives the interest without tax deduction and retains anonymity and therefore supplies cheaper finance. Economies of scale also reduce costs.	2 Because interest and capital are paid in a foreign currency there is a risk that exchange-rate movements mean more of the home currency is required to buy the foreign currency than was anticipated.
3 Ability to hedge interest rate and exchange-rate risk.	3 The secondary market can be illiquid.
4 The bonds are usually unsecured. The limitations placed on management are less than those for a secure bond.	
5 The lower level of regulation allows greater innovation and tailor-made financial instruments.	

To conclude the discussion of Eurobonds we will consider a few examples and deal with some of the jargon. **Exhibit 11.20** describes the first Eurobond from 40 years ago by Autostrade, a company that continues to make use of this financial market.

Exhibit 11.20

Autostrade returns to bond market after 40-year gap

FT

By Charles Batchelor and Ivar Simensen

Autostrade, the Italian motorway operator that launched the Eurobond market in 1963, is to return to the bond market this month after a gap of more than 40 years.

The company yesterday revealed plans for a bond issue worth up to €6.5bn (£4.5bn) to pay off bank loans and finance a 10-year investment programme. It would be by far the largest corporate bond offering in Europe this year – ahead of issues by Britain's Network Rail and Telecom Italia.

'We go to the market once every 40 years,' joked Luca Bettonte, who was born in the year the market started and has been finance director of Autostrade since November.

'This will give us a financial structure more adapted to the needs of the group,' he added.

Autostrade is expected to issue bonds in both euros and sterling following roadshows in continental Europe, the UK and US.

It was in July 1963 that the motorway group issued a $15m (£9m), 15-year bond, creating a market that was to wrest control of non-US bond issues from the American investment banks and cement London's position as an international financial centre.

European banks had been relegated to an underwriting role by the US banks that managed these issues – and hence earned much lower fees.

Siegmund Warburg, founder of SG Warburg – now part of UBS, the Swiss bank group – led negotiations with regulators in the UK and elsewhere to issue bonds that soaked up the large offshore dollar pool created by recurrent US balance of payments deficits.

The fledgling market received a crucial boost just $2^1/_2$ weeks after the Autostrade issue when President John F. Kennedy announced an interest equalisation tax.

The president's aim was to improve the US balance of payments but the result was to increase the cost of US borrowing by European issuers.

The Eurobond market has gone from strength to strength, gaining further impetus from the creation of the euro in 1999, and euro-denominated issues last year

▶

Exhibit 11.20 continued

overtook international dollar-denominated bonds.

The funds raised 40 years ago were intended for Finsider, the nationalised Italian steel manufacturer. Autostrade – then also state-owned – had a more favourable tax position and so was used as a channel for the funds.

Now a publicly listed company, Autostrade is 62 per cent owned by Schema Ventotto, a holding company in which the Benetton family has a 60 per cent stake.

The new issue will be managed by Barclays Capital, Caylon, Goldman Sachs, Invercaixa Valores, Mediobanca and UBM.

Source: *Financial Times*, 13 May 2004, p. 21. Reprinted with permission.

The *Financial Times* publishes a table showing a selection of secondary-market bid prices of actively traded international bonds (*see* **Exhibit 11.21**). This gives the reader some idea of current market conditions and rates of return demanded for bonds of different maturities, currencies and riskiness. The FT has another table, showing similar information for high yield and emerging-market (less financially mature economies, e.g. Argentina) bonds.

Euro medium-term notes and domestic medium-term notes

By issuing a note a company promises to pay the holders a certain sum on the maturity date, and in many cases a coupon interest in the meantime. These instruments are typically unsecured and may carry floating or fixed interest rates. **Medium-term notes (MTN)** have been sold with a maturity of as little as nine months and as great as 30 years, so the term is a little deceiving. They can be denominated in the domestic currency of the borrower (MTN) or in a foreign currency (**Euro MTN**). MTNs normally pay an interest rate above LIBOR, usually varying between 0.2 per cent and 3 per cent over LIBOR.

An MTN programme stretching over many years can be set up with one set of legal documents. Then, numerous notes can be issued under the programme in future years. A programme allows greater certainty that the firm will be able to issue an MTN when it needs the finance and allows issuers to bypass the costly and time-consuming documentation associated with each stand-alone note (bond). The programme can allow for bonds of various qualities, maturities, currencies or type of interest (fixed or floating). Over the years the market can be tapped at short notice in the most suitable form at that time, e.g. US dollars rather than pounds, or redemption in three years rather than in two. It is possible to sell in small denominations, e.g. $5m, and on a continuous basis, regularly dripping bonds into the market. Banks charge a '**commitment fee**' (around 10 to 15 basis points) for keeping open the option to borrow under an MTN programme, even if the company chooses not to do so in the end. Management fees will also be payable to the syndication of banks organising the MTN facility.

The success of a MTN programme depends on the efficiency of the lead manager and the flexibility of the issuer to match market appetite for lending in particular currencies or maturities with the issuer's demands for funds. The annual cost of running an MTN programme, excluding credit rating agency fees, can be around £100,000. GlaxoSmithKline's current outstanding MTNs are shown at the start of the chapter.

Eurocommercial paper and domestic commercial paper[9]

The issue and purchase of **commercial paper** is one means by which the largest commercial organisations can avoid paying the bank intermediary a middleman fee for linking borrower and lender. Commercial paper promises to the holder a sum of money to be paid in a few days. The

---

[9] This topic and the previous one do not sit perfectly in a chapter on long-term finance, but they help to give a more complete view of the Euromarkets.

Exhibit 11.21

Global Investment Grade

FT

Sep 20	Red date	Coupon	Ratings S*	M*	F*	Bid price	Bid yield	Day's chge yield	Mth's chge yield	Spread vs Govts
US $										
CIT Group	02/08	3.50	AA	Aa1	AA+	99.31	5.48	–0.06	–0.31	+1.69
Goldman Sachs	01/08	4.13	AA–	Aa3	AA–	99.52	5.66	–0.13	–0.20	+1.78
Citigroup	02/08	3.50	AA	Aa1	AA+	99.31	5.48	–0.06	–0.31	+1.69
Canada	11/08	5.25	n/a	Aaa	AAA	100.64	4.63	+0.12	–0.23	+0.54
DaimlerChrysler	09/09	7.20	BBB+	Baa1	A–	103.25	5.40	+0.03	–0.03	+1.31
Wal Mart	08/09	6.88	AA	Aa2	AA	103.40	4.95	–0.18	–0.18	+0.95
Philipps Petr	05/10	8.75	A–	A1	A–	110.51	4.52	–0.09	–0.08	+0.48
Unilever	11/10	7.13	A+	A1	A+	105.64	5.13	+0.12	–0.10	+0.99
JP Morgan	02/11	6.75	A+	Aa3	A+	105.09	5.08	–	–0.01	+1.03
France Telecom	03/11	7.75	A–	A3	A–	108.95	4.89	–0.03	–0.17	+0.84
Italy	09/23	6.88	A+	Aa2	AA–	113.52	5.59	+0.13	+0.02	+0.92
Deutsche Tel	07/13	5.25	A–	A3	A–	98.10	5.64	–0.23	–0.06	+1.42
DaimlerChrysler	01/31	8.50	BBB+	Baa1	A–	123.65	6.51	+0.04	–0.04	+1.67
Gen Motors	11/31	8.00	BB+	Ba1	BB+	106.00	7.46	–	–	+2.23
Euro										
BAT Int Fin	02/09	4.88	BBB+	Baa1	A–	99.81	5.00	+0.28	+0.49	+0.91
Mannesman Fin	05/09	4.75	A–	Baa1	A–	99.76	4.89	+0.29	+0.38	+0.81
Deutsche Fin	07/09	4.25	AA	Aa1	AA–	99.80	4.36	–0.22	+0.15	+0.28
Repsol Int Fin	05/10	6.00	BBB	Baa1	BBB+	103.13	4.69	+0.06	–0.16	+0.47
YEN										
Toyota Motor	06/08	0.75	AAA	Aaa		99.85	0.96	–	+0.10	+0.38
KFW Int Fin	03/10	1.75	AAA	Aaa	AAA	102.03	0.93	+0.02	–0.05	+0.10
Chubu Elec	07/15	3.40	NR	Aa2	AA–	113.15	1.52	≠0.03	–0.03	–
£										
HBOS	04/08	6.38	AA	Aa1	AA+	99.55	7.05	+0.96	+0.78	+1.63
Network Rail	03/09	4.88	AAA	Aaa	AAA	98.96	5.54	+0.06	–0.15	+0.31
Boots	05/09	5.50	BB–	B2	BBB	94.85	8.73	+0.03	+0.13	+3.52
France Telecom	03/11	7.50	A–	A3	n/a	103.72	6.28	+0.07	+0.05	+1.11

Redemption date: February 2008

Gross (before deduction of tax) yield to maturity

Spread to the government bond rate (in this case US). The extent to which the rate of interest (bid yield or yield to maturity or redemption yield) is greater than that on a government bond of the same length of time to maturity (in this case 0.84%)

Issuer

Coupon as a percentage of per value

Credit ratings

Bond price with par value set at 100

US $ denominated bonds NY close; all other London close *S Standard & Poor's, M – Moody's, F – Fitch.

Source: Reuters

Source: *Financial Times*, 21 September 2007, p. 35. Reprinted with permission.

lender buys these short-term IOUs, with an average life of about 40 days (normal range 30–90 days, but can be up to 270 days), and effectively lends money to the issuer. Normally these instruments are issued at a discount rather than the borrower being required to pay interest – thus the face value (amount paid on redemption) will be higher than the amount paid for the paper at issuance. Large corporations with temporary surpluses of cash are able to put that money to use by lending it directly to other commercial firms at a higher rate of effective interest than they might have received by depositing the funds in a bank. This source of finance is usually only available to the most respected corporations with the highest credit ratings, as it is usually unsecured lending. Standard & Poor's and Moody's use a different grading system for short-term instruments (e.g. A–1 or Prime–1 are the highest ratings). The main buyers, such as money market mutual funds, are often restricted to having the bulk of their portfolios in the form of 'tier-one' rated issues – top ratings from credit rating agencies. Tier-two and tier-three issues do exist, but the demand is very limited.

While any one issue of commercial paper is short term it is possible to use this market as a medium-term source of finance by '**rolling over**' issues. That is, as one issue matures another one is launched. A **commercial paper programme** (a **revolving underwriting facility**) can be set up by a bank whereby the bank (or a syndicate of banks) underwrites a specified sum for a period of five to seven years. The borrower then draws on this every few weeks or months by the issue of commercial paper to other lenders. If there are no bids for the paper the underwriting bank(s) buys the paper at a specified price. **Eurocommercial paper** is issued and placed outside the jurisdiction of the country in whose currency it is denominated.

Project finance

A typical project finance deal is created by an industrial corporation providing some equity capital for a separate legal entity to be formed to build and operate a project, for example an oil pipeline, an electricity power plant. The **project finance loan** is then provided as bank loans or through bond issues direct to the separate entity. The significant feature is that the loan returns are tied to the cash flows and fortunes of a particular project rather than being secured against the parent firm's assets. For most ordinary loans the bank looks at the credit standing of the borrower when deciding terms and conditions. For project finance, while the parent company's (or companies') credit standing is a factor, the main focus is on the financial prospects of the project itself.

To make use of project finance the project needs to be easily identifiable and separable from the rest of the company's activities so that its cash flows and assets can offer the lenders some separate security. Project finance has been used across the globe to finance power plants, roads, ports, sewage facilities, telecommunications networks and much more. A few recent examples are given in **Exhibit 11.22**.

Project finance has grown rapidly over the last 25 years. Globally, about £50bn is lent in this form per year. A major stimulus has been the development of oil prospects. For the UK, the North Sea provided a number of project finance opportunities. Many of the small companies which developed fields and pipelines would not have been able to participate on the strength of their existing cash flow and balance sheet, but they were able to obtain project finance secured on the oil or fees they would later generate.

There is a spectrum of risk sharing in project finance deals. At one extreme there are projects where the parent firm (or firms) accepts the responsibility of guaranteeing that the lenders will be paid in the event of the project producing insufficient cash flows. This is referred to as **recourse finance** because the lenders are able to seek the 'help' of the parent. At the other extreme, the lenders accept an agreement whereby, if the project is a failure, they will lose money and have no right of recourse to the parent company. If the project's cash flows are insufficient the lenders only have a claim on the assets of the project itself rather than on the sponsors or developers.

Between these two extremes there might be deals whereby the borrower takes the risk until the completion of the construction phase (for example, provides a completion guarantee) and the lender takes on the risk once the project is in the operational phase. Alternatively, the commercial firm may take some risks such as the risk of cost overruns and the lender takes others such as the risk of a government expropriating the project's assets.

Exhibit 11.22

Project finance has funded . . .

A liquefied natural gas project in Qatar

The biggest project-financed facility ever begun is being built in Qatar. Qatargas, the state-controlled energy firm, joined with Exxon and raised $7.6bn from 57 investors in 2005 to build a gas freezing and storage plant. The gas will then be shipped to the UK in tankers. Not only does forming a separate project with a state-controlled company reduce political risk (*see* below) but it can also open doors to lenders in the country.

Developing an oil field

In 2006 Northern Petroleum agreed a €40m project financing facility with Standard Bank to develop a number of onshore oilfields in the Netherlands. Normally a project lender would insist on the sponsoring company or its contractors providing a guarantee that it will be paid back in the event of failure to complete the project construction. However, Standard Bank agreed that Northern Petroleum has the skills to project manage and to forgo the guarantee. In return the bank received options to buy 3 million shares in Northern Petroleum thus taking some extra reward if the company (project) performs well. (An option gives the right to buy shares at a price already agreed – say £3 when the current share price is £2. If the company does well the share might move to, say, £4 in which case the options become worth at least £1 each – Chapter 24 has more on options.)

A telephone infrastructure

In 2000 Hutchinson UK 3G raised £3bn by way of project finance to part-fund the building of the UK's fifth mobile network. This was three-year debt without recourse to shareholders.

Source: Based on *Financial Times*, 31 May 2006 and *Economist*, 8 January 2005, p. 52.

The sums and size of projects are usually large and involve a high degree of complexity and this means high transaction and legal costs. Because of the additional risk to the lenders the interest rates charged tend to be higher than for conventional loans. Whereas a well-known highly creditworthy firm might pay 20 basis points (0.20 per cent) over LIBOR for a 'normal' parent company loan, the project company might have to pay 100 basis points (1 per cent) above LIBOR.

Advantages of project finance

Project finance has a number of advantages.

1 ***Transfer of risk*** By making the project a stand-alone investment with its own financing, the parent can gain if it is successful and is somewhat insulated if it is a failure, in that other assets and cash flows may be protected from the effects of project losses. This may lead to a greater willingness to engage in more risky activities, which may benefit both the firm and society. Of course, this benefit is of limited value if there are strong rights of recourse.

2 ***Off-balance-sheet financing*** The finance is raised on the project's assets and cash flows and therefore is not recorded as debt in the parent company's balance sheet. This sort of off-balance-sheet financing is seen as a useful 'wheeze' or ploy by some managers – for example, gearing limits can be bypassed. However, experienced lenders and shareholders are not so easily fooled by accounting tricks.

3 ***Political risk*** If the project is in a country prone to political instability, with a tendency towards an anti-transnational business attitude and acts of appropriation, a more cautious way of proceeding may be to set up an arm's length (separate company) relationship with some risk being borne by the banking community, particularly banks in the host country. An example of political risk is given in **Exhibit 11.23**.

4 ***Simplifies the banking relationship*** In cases where there are a number of parent companies, it can be easier to arrange finance for a separate project entity than to have to deal with each of the parent companies separately.

5 ***Managerial incentives*** Managers of projects may be given an equity stake in the project if it is set up as a separate enterprise. This can lead to high rewards for exceptional performance.

Exhibit 11.23 'Regulatory risk' exists in many parts of the world ...

Enron

In 1995 the state of Maharashtra in India suddenly revoked the contract it had with Enron for the construction of a power project, creating major problems for Enron and its bankers.

Sale and leaseback

If a firm owns buildings, land or equipment it may be possible to sell these to another firm (for example a bank, insurance company or specialised leasing firm) and simultaneously agree to lease the property back for a stated period under specific terms. The seller receives cash immediately but is still able to use the asset. However the seller has created a regular cash flow liability for itself. For example, in a flagship deal Abbey National, the mortgage bank, sold its branch network and its Baker Street head office (221b Baker Street – the home of Sherlock Holmes) totalling 6.5m sq.ft. The 722 branches and head office will be occupied by Abbey National under leases as short as one year, and as long as 20. The objective was to obtain flexibility in accommodation so that the bank can change with its customers and with the industry. It allowed the firm to 'concentrate on banking rather than being property developers, which is not our job'.[10]

In 2007 Tesco completed a **sale and leaseback** for £650m with British Land. The initial rent is £29m per year (a yield of 4.5 per cent). The rents will rise by a rate linked to inflation with a maximum of 3.5 per cent per year. Most of the proceeds are to be used to pay for the opening of more Tesco stores. A number of other retailers have used their extensive property assets for sale and leaseback transactions so that they could plough the proceeds into further expansion.

In a number of countries the tax regime propels sale and leaseback transactions. For example, some property owners are unable to use depreciation and other tax allowances (usually because they do not have sufficient taxable profits). The sale of the asset to an organisation looking to reduce taxable profits through the holding of depreciable assets enables both firms to benefit. Furthermore, the original owner's subsequent lease payments are tax deductible.

A further advantage is thought to be the efficiency boost sale and leaseback gives to the firm because managers are made more aware of the value of the assets used in the business (*see* **Exhibit 11.24**).

A sale and leaseback has the drawback that the asset is no longer owned by the firm and therefore any capital appreciation has to be forgone. Also long lease arrangements of this kind usually provide for the rental payments to increase at regular intervals, such as every three or five years. Companies sometimes find that the leaseback arrangement eliminates the flexibility to move to cheaper premises. There are other factors limiting the use of sale and leaseback as a financial tool. Leasing can involve complex documentation and large legal fees, which often make it uneconomic to arrange leases for less than £20m. There is also a degree of inflexibility: for example, unwinding the transaction if, say, the borrower wanted to move out of the property can be expensive. Another disadvantage is that the property is no longer available to be offered as security for loans.

Securitisation

In the strange world of modern finance you sometimes need to ask yourself who ends up with your money when you pay your monthly mortgage, or your credit card bill or the instalment payment

[10] John Price, director of property, *Financial Times*, 20 October 2000, p. 27.

Exhibit 11.24

Property leasing link with market return discovered

FT

By Juliana Ratner

Companies that lease some of their property have better shareholder returns, according to new research.

The study of more than 5,000 UK-listed companies from 1989 to 2002 showed that investment in companies that lease between 60 and 80 per cent of the property had a 71 per cent greater return than an investment in all the companies in the study.

Companies that lease 65 per cent of their real estate have the highest market-value-to-book-value ratio compared with those that lease all or own all of their property, according to a study by the Cass Business School in London, commissioned by Donaldsons, the property adviser.

The market appears to punish companies that own all of their property because too much capital is tied up in real estate, and also does not favour those that lease all of their property, because landlords jump to the front of a queue in the event of bankruptcy, said Meziane Lasfer, professor of finance at Cass.

One of the more surprising results of the study is that companies that lease more property are more efficient, because they see their rental payments move through the profit and loss accounts and are more aware of their costs, Mr Lasfer said.

Turnover growth is also affected by whether a company lets or owns its property. The average rate of turnover growth increases to more than 31 per cent for companies that lease all of their property, versus 15 per cent for those that own all of it. 'Leased property is treated as an expense so companies try to wring maximum efficiencies from it to justify that expense,' said Keith Martin, head of corporate division at Donaldsons. 'All too often property owned by a company is taken for granted and treated as a free good.'

Source: Financial Times, 3 November 2003, p. 2. Reprinted with permission.

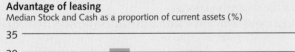

Advantage of leasing

Median Stock and Cash as a proportion of current assets (%)

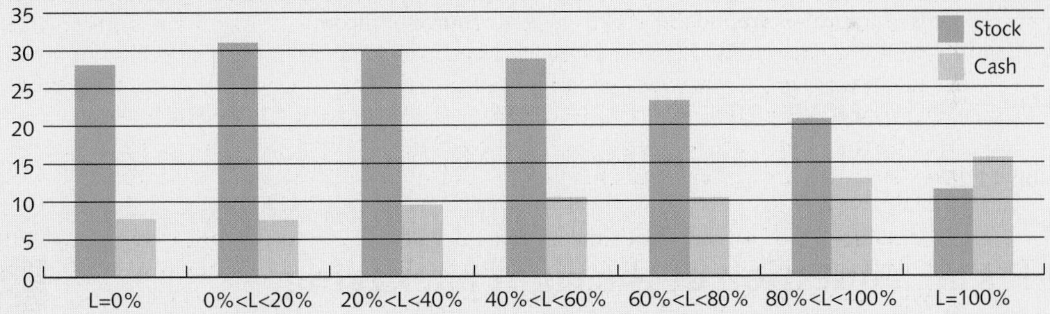

Source: Donaldsons

L = leased

on your car. In the old days you would have found that it was the organisation you originally borrowed from and whose name is at the top of the monthly statement. Today you cannot be so sure because there is now a thriving market in repackaged debt. In this market, a mortgage lender, for example, collects together a few thousand mortgage 'claims' it has (the right of the lender to receive regular interest and capital from the borrowers); it then sells those claims in a collective package to other institutions, or participants in the market generally. This permits the replacement of long-term assets with cash (improving liquidity and gearing) which can then be used to generate more mortgages. It may also allow a profit on the difference between the interest on the mortgages and the interest on the bonds. The borrower is often unaware that the mortgage is no longer owned by the original lender and everything appears as it did before, with the mortgage company acting as a collecting agent for the buyer of the mortgages. The mortgage company usually raises this cash by selling **asset-backed securities (ABS)** to other institutions (the 'assets' are the claim on interest and capital) and so this form of finance is often called **asset securitisation**. These asset-backed securities may be bonds sold into a market with many players. Usually a '**special purpose vehicle**' **(SPV)** or '**special purpose entity**' **(SPE)** is created separate from the originator of mortgages etc. The bonds sold are secured against the assets of the SPV (e.g. mortgage claims). This separates the creditworthiness of the assets involved from the general credit of the company.

Asset backed securitisation involves the pooling and repackaging of relatively small, homogeneous and illiquid financial assets into liquid securities.

The sale of the financial claims can be either 'non-recourse', in which case the buyer of the securities from the mortgage firm or the lender to the SPV (e.g. bond holder) bears the risk of non-payment by the borrowers, or with recourse to the mortgage lender.

Securitisation has even reached the world of rock. Iron Maiden issued a long-dated $30m asset-backed bond securitised on future earnings from royalties. It followed David Bowie's $55m bond securitised on the income from his earlier albums and Rod Stewart's $15.4m securitised loan from Nomura.

Tussauds has securitised ticket and merchandise sales, Keele University has securitised the rental income from student accommodation and in 2006 Arsenal securitised £260m future ticket sales at the Emirates Stadium. Loans to Hong Kong taxi drivers have been securitised, as have the cash flows from UK funeral fees.

Securitisation is regarded as beneficial to the financial system, because it permits banks and other financial institutions to focus on those aspects of the lending process where they have a competitive edge. Some, for example, have a greater competitive advantage in originating loans than in funding them, so they sell the loans they have created, raising cash to originate more loans. Securitisation was at the heart of the financial turmoil in 2007 when US sub-prime (poor quality) mortgage borrowers failed to repay in substantial numbers. Mortgage-backed bonds of SPVs plummeted in value, the asset-backed bond market froze and the businesses model of lending to households expecting to sell bonds backed with a bunch of mortgages (à la Northern Rock) became untenable as no one would buy the securitised bonds.

Exhibit 11.25 describes the securitisation of Dunkin' Donuts' royalties received from its hundreds of franchises around the world – a steady source of income.

Exhibit 11.25

It's all a question of the right packaging

FT

Richard Beales on fresh ways to isolate a company's income streams and cut its financing costs

In a corporate securitisation, assets and related cash flows are carved out from a business into special purpose entities (SPEs) and repackaged. Debt is then raised against the SPEs alone.

'Securitisation isolates a cash flow and insulates it from extraneous events,' says Ted Yarbrough, head of global securitised products at Citigroup.

Depending on the credit quality and the quantum of borrowing, part or all the debt may be highly rated, and there is sometimes a low-rated or unrated subordinated slice of debt as well. This is not, however, an off-balance sheet financing method – the assets and debt within the SPEs are consolidated in the company's financial statements.

A financing structured this way can achieve higher credit ratings than the business on its own. This partly reflects the structural aspects – for example, the fact that the SPEs can survive a bankruptcy of the umbrella group – and partly the fact that the securities issued are often 'wrapped', or guaranteed, by highly-rated bond

Exhibit 11.25 continued

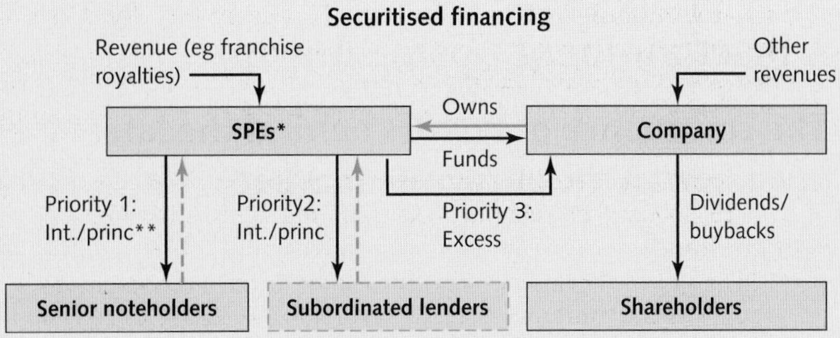

* Special purpose entitles owning franchise agreements, brands etc.
** Often guaranteed by bond insurer in return for additional fee

insurers such as Ambac, Figic or MBIA in return for a fee.

This is a complex and costly exercise, but can result in much cheaper debt. Once established, a securitisation can be tapped again later if a business grows.

Sometimes securitisation is best suited to part of a business rather than the whole. When applied to an entire business, as with Dunkin' Brands or Domino's, the new financing typically replaces all traditional debt.

While a securitisation does involve financial constraints, they can be fewer and less onerous than with traditional bank and bond debt. Managers would, for example, have greater flexibility to pay dividends or buy back stock.

This reflects the fact that financiers in a securitisation look only to the specific assets and cash flows held within the SPEs. But Eric Hedman, analyst at Standard & Poor's in New York, notes there can be a trade-off in terms of operational flexibility. 'Prior to the securitisation, Dunkin' was an owner operator. Now, the company is no longer the franchisor, there's an SPE. Any new store agreement is for the benefit of the securitisation.' The company's management also does not have sole discretion over advertising spending, for example.

And the Dunkin' Donuts brand is no longer owned by the company. 'The sign on the wall says "Copyright DD IP Holder LLC". That's a bankruptcy-remote SPE set up for the benefit of noteholders [in the securitisation]', Mr Hedman says.

This kind of shift might not suit all managers. But for some executives – particularly those focused on maximising cash returns to shareholders – such considerations can be outweighed by the financial benefits.

Source: *Financial Times*, 25 July 2007, p. 2. Reprinted with permission.

The term structure of interest rates

Until now we have assumed that the annual interest rate on a debt instrument remained the same regardless of the length of time of the loan. So, if the interest rate on a three-year bond is 7 per cent per year it would be 7 per cent on a five-year bond of the same risk class. However, it is apparent that lenders in the financial markets demand different interest rates on loans of differing lengths of time to maturity – that is, there is a **term structure of the interest rates**. Three of these relationships are shown in **Exhibit 11.26** for lending to the UK, German and US governments. Note that default risk remains constant along one of the lines; the reason for the different rates is the time to maturity of the bonds. Thus a one-year German government bond has to offer about 3.75 per cent whereas a 20-year bond offered by the same borrower gives about 3.88 per cent.

An upward-sloping yield curve occurs in most years (as shown for German Bunds in **Exhibit 11.26**) but occasionally we have a situation where short-term interest rates (lending for, say, one year) exceed those of long-term interest rates (say, a 20-year bond). A downward-sloping term structure (yield curve inversion) is shown in **Exhibit 11.26** for both UK and US government bonds.

Three main hypotheses have been advanced to explain the shape of the yield curve:

a the expectation hypothesis;

b the liquidity-preference hypothesis; and

c the market-segmentation hypothesis.

Exhibit 11.26

A brief moment upside down

FT

The confluence of factors behind the latest yield inversion in the eurozone market

Joanna Chung

Something remarkable happened in the eurozone government bond market yesterday.

The yield curve – a line chart plotting the yields paid out by different bonds against the dates at which they mature – inverted for the first time in more than six years. That is, the yield on 10-year Bunds fell below the yield on the two-year paper.

The inversion was not dramatic – one basis point separated two- and 10-year yields – and it was brief, with the curve returning to its more conventional shape soon afterwards. But the move was significant nonetheless.

The last time in inversion occurred, analysts say, was August 2000 in the aftermath of the dotcom crash.

Since December last year, the European Central Bank has been raising interest rates and investors have been selling shorter-dated bonds, pushing yields higher, Jean-Claude Trichet, the ECB president, has indicated in recent comments that monetary tightening is likely to continue.

But cash-rich investors, including pension funds and central banks, have, for a variety of reasons, continued to pour money into longer-dated assets, pushing longer-dated yields lower.

Some market participants say that a eurozone yield curve inversion has been overdue, not least because the UK curve is fully inverted and the US curve, as measured by the gap between two- and 10-year yields, has been inverted for most of the year.

A global financial system awash with liquidity and strong demand from Asian central banks and others – with huge reserves to invest – has helped keep long-term rates low.

In the UK, structural and regulatory shifts have also played a role.

They have created an almost insatiable appetite from pension funds for longer-dated bonds. Long-dated yields in the UK have been on a downward trajectory for years and the UK yield curve has been inverted to varying degrees since the mid-1990s – completely so since last October.

In the eurozone, an additional factor has been falling supply, with improving economies prompting some governments to trim issuance.

Normally, yield curves slope upwards because investors require a higher yield to compensate them for the greater risk and uncertainty of investing over a longer term.

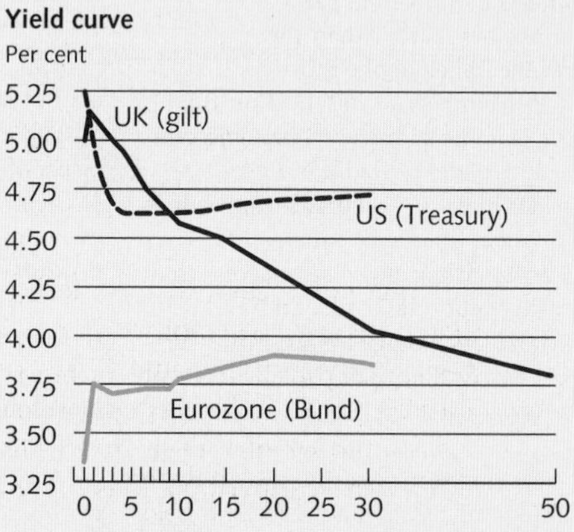

Source: Merrill Lynch

When the curve inverts or slopes downwards, however, it implies that investors believe growth will slow and inflationary pressures will weaken. They believe the central bank will be forced to cut interest rates to prop up a softening economy and head off the possibility of recssion.

*Note from Glen Arnold: *Using the benchmark yield curve as an example of term structures of interest rates may offend theoretical purity but it is a handy approximate measure and helps illustrate this section.*

Source: *Financial Times*, 10 November 2006, p. 41. Reprinted with permission.

The expectations hypothesis

The **expectations hypothesis** focuses on the changes in interest rates over time. To understand the expectations hypothesis you need to know what is meant by a '**spot rate of interest**'. The spot rate is an interest rate fixed today on a loan that is made today. So a corporation, Hype plc, might issue one-year bonds at a spot rate of, say, 8 per cent, two-year bonds at a spot rate of 8.995 per cent and three-year bonds at a spot rate of 9.5 per cent. This yield curve for Hype is shown in **Exhibit 11.27**. The interest rates payable by Hype are bound to be greater than for the UK government across the yield curve because of the additional default risk on these corporate bonds.

Exhibit 11.27 The term structure of interest rates for Hype plc at time 2008

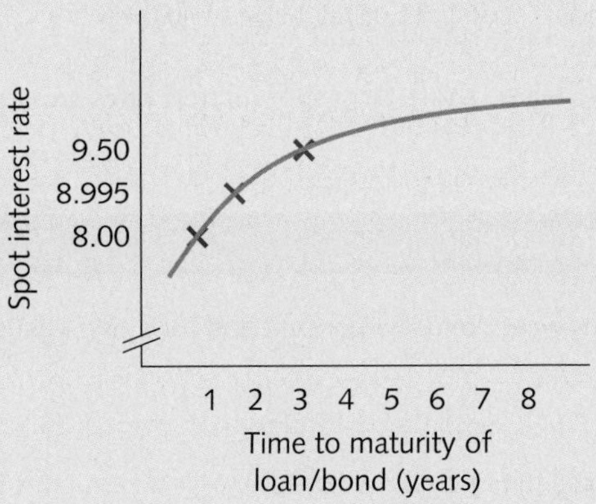

Spot rates change over time. The market may have allowed Hype to issue one-year bonds yielding 8 per cent at a point in time in 2008 but a year later (time 2009) the one-year spot rate may have changed to become 10 per cent. If investors expect that one-year spot rates will become 10 per cent at time 2009 they will have a theoretical limit on the yield that they require from a two-year bond when viewed from time 2008. Imagine that an investor (lender) wishes to lend £1,000 for a two-year period and is contemplating two alternative approaches:

1 Buy a one-year bond at a spot rate of 8 per cent; after one year has passed the bond will come to maturity. The released funds can then be invested in another one-year bond at a spot rate of 10 per cent, expected to be the going rate for bonds of this risk class at time 2009.
2 Buy a two-year bond at the spot rate at time 2008.

Under the first option the lender will have a sum of £1,188 at the end of two years:

$$£1,000\ (1 + 0.08) = £1,080$$

followed by $£1,080\ (1 + 0.1) = £1,188$

Given the anticipated change in one-year spot rates to 10 per cent the investor will only buy the two-year bond if it gives the same average annual yield over two years as the first option of a series of one-year bonds. The annual interest required will be:

$$£1,000\ (1 + k)^2 = £1,188$$

$$k = \sqrt{(1,188/1,000)} - 1 = 0.08995 \text{ or } 8.995 \text{ per cent}$$

Thus, it is the expectation of spot interest rates changing which determines the shape of the yield curve according to the expectation hypothesis.

Now consider a downward-sloping yield curve where the spot rate on a one-year instrument is 11 per cent and the expectation is that one-year spot rates will fall to 8 per cent the following year. An investor considering a two-year investment will obtain an annual yield of 9.49 per cent by investing in a series of one-year bonds, viz:

$$£1,000\ (1.08)\ (1.11) = £1,198.80$$

With this expectation for movements in one-year spot rates, lenders will demand an annual rate of return of 9.49 per cent from two-year bonds of the same risk class.

$$k = \sqrt{(1198.8/1{,}000)} - 1 = 0.0949 \text{ or } 9.49\% \text{ per year}$$

$$\text{or } \sqrt{(1.08)(1.11)} - 1 = 0.0949$$

Thus in circumstances where short-term spot interest rates are expected to fall, the yield curve will be downward sloping.

Worked example 11.2 Spot rates

If the present spot rate for a one-year bond is 5 per cent and for a two-year bond 6.5 per cent, what is the expected one-year spot rate in a year's time?*

Answer

If the two-year rate is set to equal the rate on a series of one-year spot rates then:

$$(1 + 0.05)(1 + x) = (1 + 0.065)^2$$

$$x = \frac{(1 + 0.065)^2}{1 + 0.05} - 1 = 0.0802 \text{ or } 8.02\%$$

*In the financial markets it is possible to agree now to lend money in one year's time for, say, a year (or two years or six months, etc.) at a rate of interest agreed at the outset. This is a 'forward'.

The liquidity-preference hypothesis

The expectation hypothesis does not adequately explain why the most common shape of the yield curve is upward sloping. The **liquidity-preference hypothesis** helps explain the upward slope by pointing out that investors require an extra return for lending on a long-term basis. Lenders demand a premium return on long-term bonds compared with short-term instruments because of the risk of misjudging future interest rates. Putting your money into a ten-year bond on the anticipation of particular levels of interest rates exposes you to the possibility that rates will rise above the rate offered on the bond at some point in its long life. Thus, if five years later interest rates double, say because of a rise in inflation expectations, the market price of the bond will fall substantially, leaving the holder with a large capital loss. On the other hand, by investing in a series of one-year bonds, the investor can take advantage of rising interest rates as they occur. The ten-year bond locks in a fixed rate for the full ten years if held to maturity. Investors prefer short-term bonds so that they can benefit from rising rates and so will accept a lower return on short-dated instruments. The liquidity-preference theory focuses on a different type of risk attaching to long-dated debt instruments other than default risk – a risk related to uncertainty over future interest rates. A suggested reinforcing factor to the upward slope is that borrowers usually prefer long-term debt because of the fear of having to repay short-term debt at inappropriate moments. Thus borrowers increase the supply of long-term debt instruments, adding to the tendency for long-term rates to be higher than short-term rates.

Note that the word liquidity in the title is incorrectly used – but it has stuck so we still use it. Liquidity refers to the speed and ease of the sale of an asset. In the case of long-term bonds (especially government bonds) sale in the secondary market is often as quick and easy for short-term bonds. The premium for long bonds is compensation for the extra risk of capital loss; 'term premium' might be a better title for the hypothesis.

The market-segmentation hypothesis

The **market segmentation hypothesis** argues that the debt market is not one homogeneous whole, that there are, in fact, a number of sub-markets defined by maturity range. The yield curve is therefore created (or at least influenced) by the supply and demand conditions in each of these sub-markets. For example, banks tend to be active in the short-term end of the market and pension funds to be buyers in the long-dated segment. If banks need to borrow large quantities quickly they will sell some of their short-term instruments, increasing the supply on the market and pushing down the price and raising the yield. On the other hand pension funds may be flush with cash and may buy large quantities of 20-year bonds, helping to temporarily move yields downward at the long end of the market. At other times banks, pension funds and the buying and selling pressures of a multitude of other financial institutions will influence the supply and demand position in the opposite direction. The point is that the players in the different parts of the yield curve tend to be different. This hypothesis helps to explain the often lumpy or humped yield curve.

A final thought on the term structure of interest rates

It is sometimes thought that in circumstances of a steeply rising yield curve it would be advantageous to borrow short term rather than long term. However this can be a dangerous strategy because long-term debt may be trading at a higher rate of interest because of the expected rise in short-term rates and so when the borrower comes to refinance in, say, a year's time, the short-term interest rate is much higher than the long-term rate and this high rate has to be paid out of the second year's cash flows, which may not be convenient.

Concluding comments

So far this book has taken a fairly detailed look at a variety of ways of raising money by selling shares and has examined the main methods of raising funds through long-term debt. The decision to raise equity or debt finance is neither simple nor straightforward. In the next chapter we consider a wider array of financial sources and types, from leasing to factoring. Knowledge of these will enable the finance manager or other executives to select and structure the different forms of finance to maximise the firm's potential. Topics covered later in the book draw on the knowledge gained in Chapters 10, 11 and 12 to permit informed discussion of such crucial questions as: What is the appropriate mixture of debt and equity? How is the cost of various forms of finance calculated? How can the risk of certain forms of finance (for example a floating-interest-rate term loan) be reduced?

Key points and concepts

- **Debt finance has a number of advantages** for the company:
  - it has a lower cost than equity finance:
    a lower transaction costs;
    b lower rate of return;
  - debt holders generally do not have votes;
  - interest is tax deductible.
- **Drawbacks of debt**:
  - Committing to repayments and interest can be risky for a firm, ultimately the debt-holders can force liquidation to retreive payment;
  - the use of secured assets for borrowing may be an onerous constraint on managerial action;
  - covenants may further restrict managerial action.
- A **bond** is a long-term contract in which the bondholders lend money to a company. A straight 'vanilla' bond pays regular interest plus the capital on the redemption date.
- Debentures are generally more secure than **loan stock** (in the UK).

- A **trust deed** has **affirmative covenants** outlining the nature of the bond contract and **negative** (restrictive) **covenants** imposing constraints on managerial action to reduce risk for the lenders.
- A **floating rate note (FRN)** is a bond with an interest rate which varies as a benchmark interest rate changes (e.g. LIBOR).
- **Attractive features of bank borrowing**:
  - administrative and legal costs are low;
  - quick;
  - flexibility in troubled times;
  - available to small firms.
- **Factors for a firm to consider with bank borrowing**:

  Costs
  - fixed versus floating;
  - arrangement fees;
  - bargaining on the rate.

  Security
  - asymmetric information;
  - collateral;
  - covenants;
  - personal guarantees.

  Repayment arrangements:

  Some possibilities:
  - grace periods;
  - mortgage style;
  - term loan.
- A **syndicated loan** occurs where a number of banks (or other financial institutions) each contribute a portion of a loan.
- A **credit rating** depends on **a** the likelihood of payments of interest and/or capital not being paid (i.e. default); and **b** the extent to which the lender is protected in the event of a default.
- **Mezzanine debt** and **high-yield bonds** are forms of debt offering a high return with a high risk. They have been particularly useful in the following:
  - management buyouts (MBOs), especially leveraged management buyouts (LBOs);
  - fast-growing companies;
  - leveraged recapitalisation.
- **Convertible bonds** are issued as debt instruments but they also give the holder the right to exchange the bonds at some time in the future into ordinary shares according to some prearranged formula advantages:
  - lower interest than on debentures;
  - interest is tax deductible;
  - self liquidating;
  - few negative covenants;
  - shares might be temporarily underpriced;
  - cheap way to issue shares;
  - an available form of finance when straight debt and equity are not.
- A bond is **priced** according to general market interest rates for risk class and maturity:

  Irredeemable:

  $$P_D = \frac{i}{k_D}$$

Redeemable:

$$P_D = \frac{i_1}{1 + k_D} + \frac{i_2}{(1 + k_D)^2} + \frac{i_3}{(1 + k_D)^3} + \ldots + \frac{R_n}{(1 + k_D)^n}$$

- The **interest (flat) yield** on a bond is:

$$\frac{\text{Gross interest (coupon)}}{\text{Market price}} \times 100$$

- The **yield to maturity** includes both annual coupon returns and capital gains or losses on maturity.
- The **Euromarkets** are informal (unregulated) markets in money held outside the jurisdiction of the country of origin of the currency.
- A **foreign bond** is a bond denominated in the currency of the country where it is issued when the issuer is a non-resident.
- A **Eurobond** is a bond sold outside the jurisdiction of the country of the currency in which the bond is denominated.
- A **project finance** loan is provided as a bank loan or bond finance to an entity set up separately from the parent corporation to undertake a project. The returns to the lender are tied to the fortunes and cash flows of the project.
- **Sale and leaseback** Assets are sold to financial institutions or another company which releases cash. Simultaneously, the original owner agrees to lease the assets back for a stated period under specified terms.
- **Securitisation** Relatively small, homogeneous and liquid financial assets are pooled and repackaged into liquid securities which are then sold on to other investors to generate cash for the original lender.
- The **term structure of interest rates** describes the manner in which the same default risk class of debt securities provides different rates of return depending on the length of time to maturity. There are three hypotheses relating to the term structure of interest rates:
  - the expectations hypothesis;
  - the liquidity-preference hypothesis;
  - the market-segmentation hypothesis.

References and further reading

To keep up to date and reinforce knowledge gained by reading this chapter I can recommend the following publications: *Financial Times, The Economist, Corporate Finance Magazine,* (London: Euromoney) *Bank of England Quarterly Bulletin, Bank for International Settlements Quarterly Review* (www.bis.org), *The Treasurer* (a monthly journal), *The Treasurer's Handbook* (by the Association of Corporate Treasurers) and *Finance and Leasing Association* (FLA) *Annual Report* (www.fla.org.uk.)

Arnold, G. and Smith, M. (1999) *The European High Yield Bond Market: Drivers and Impediments.* London: Financial Times Finance Management Report.

A comprehensive exploration of the potential of the junk bond market in Europe – a history of the US market is also given.

Blake, D. (2000) *Financial Market Analysis.* 2nd edn. Chichester: John Wiley & Sons.

A technical and detailed examination of long-term debt markets.

Brealey, R.A., Cooper, I.A. and Habib, M.A. (2001) 'Using project finance to fund infrastructure investments', in D.H. Chew (ed.) *The New Corporate Finance.* 3rd edn. New York: McGraw Hill Irwin.

A more detailed treatment of project finance.

Brett, M. (2003) *How to Read the Financial Pages.* 5th edn. London: Random House: Business Books.

An easy-to-read introductory text on the debt markets.

Brigham, E.F. (1966) 'An analysis of convertible debentures: Theory and some empirical evidence', *Journal of Finance,*

March, pp. 35–54.
Valuation of convertibles and the major factors influencing price. Evidence that most firms issue convertibles to raise equity finance.

Buckle, M. and Thompson, J. (2004) *The UK Financial System*. 4th edn. Manchester: Manchester University Press.
The Eurosecurities markets are discussed clearly and concisely. There are useful sections on the domestic bond market and the term structure of interest rates.

Buckley, A. (2004) *Multinational Finance*. 5th edn. Harlow: Financial Times Prentice Hall.
Some additional detail on some of the issues discussed in this chapter – easy to read.

Chew, D.H. (ed.) (2001) *The New Corporate Finance*. 3rd edn. New York: McGraw Hill Irwin.
A collection of articles, written in an easy-to-read style, describing US debt markets.

City of London/London Stock Exchange/Oxera (2006) The cost of capital: an international comparison (available from www.londonstockexchange.com). Contains an excellent easy-to-read description of the trading of bonds and costs of listings.

Eiteman, D.K., Stonehill, A.I. and Moffett, M.H. (2003) *Multinational Business Finance*. 10th edn. Reading, Mass: Addison Wesley.
Some useful, easy-to-follow material on international debt markets.

Fabozzi, F.J. (2003) *Bond Markets, Analysis and Strategies*. 5th edn. Harlow: Financial Times Prentice Hall.
A detailed yet accessible description of bonds with a US bond market focus.

Graham, J.R. and Harvey, C.R. (2001) 'The theory and practice of corporate finance: evidence from the field', *Journal of Financial Economics*, Vol. 60, Issues 2–3, May, pp. 187–243.
US survey of corporate use of debt.

Hickman, B.G. (1958) 'Corporate bond quality and investor experience', *National Bureau of Economic Research*, 14, Princeton.
Early research into the returns and default rates on bonds.

Hicks, J.R. (1946) *Value and Capital: An Inquiry into some Fundamental Principles of Economic Theory*. 2nd edn. Oxford: Oxford University Press.
Liquidity-preference hypothesis to explain the term structure of interest rates.

Lutz, F.A. and Lutz, V.C. (1951) *The Theory of Investment in the Firm*. Princeton, NJ: Princeton University Press.
Expectations hypothesis of the term structure of interest rates.

Pilbeam, K. (2005) *International Finance*. 3rd edn. London: Macmillan Business.
An introductory treatment of debt markets.

Valdez, S. (2007) *An Introduction to Global Financial Markets*. 5th edn. London: Palgrave Macmillan.
Easy-to-read background on international bond markets and banking.

Websites

Association of Corporate Treasurers www.treasurers.org
Bank for International Settlements www.bis.org
Bank of England www.bankofengland.co.uk
The Economist www.economist.com
Financial Times www.ft.com
Fitch ratings www.fitchratings.com
International Capital Market Association www.icma-group.co.uk
Moody's www.moodys.com
Standard & Poor's www.standardandpoors.com

Video presentations

Chief executives and financial directors describe their current policy on raising funds on Cantos.com (www.cantos.com) – this is free to view.

Case study recommendations

Please see www.pearsoned.co.uk/arnold for case study synopses

- Aluminium Bahrain (Alba). The Pot Line 5 Expansion Project Authors: Benjamin C. Esty, Aldo Sesia, Jr. (2005) Harvard Business School.
- An overview of project finance – 2004 Update. Authors: Benjamin C. Esty and Aldo Sesia, Jr (2005) Harvard Business School.
- Petrolera Zuata. Authors: Benjamin C. Esty and Mathew Mateo Millet (1998) Harvard Business School.
- Poland's A2 Motorway. Authors: Benjamin C. Esty, and Michael Kane (2001) Harvard Business School.
- Why study large projects? Author: Benjamin C. Esty (2003) Harvard Business School.

Self-review questions

1 What are the relative advantages and drawbacks of debt and equity finance?

2 Explain the following (related to bonds):

a Par value.
b Trustee.
c Debenture.
d Zero coupon bond.
e Floating-rate note.

3 The inexperienced finance trainee at Mugs-R-Us plc says that he can save the company money on its forthcoming issue of ten-year bonds. 'The rate of return required for bonds of this risk class in the financial markets is 10 per cent and yet I overheard our merchant banking adviser say, "We could issue a bond at a coupon of only 9 per cent." I reckon we could save the company a large sum on the £100m issue.' Do you agree with the trainee's logic?

4 In what circumstances would you recommend borrowing from a bank rather than a capital market bond issue?

5 What are the fundamental considerations to which you would advise a firm to give thought if it were contemplating borrowing from a bank?

6 Is securitisation something to do with anti-criminal precautions? If not, explain what it is and why firms do it.

7 In what ways does the tax regime encourage debt finance rather than equity finance?

8 Why does convertible debt carry a lower coupon than straight debt?

9 What is meant by asymmetric information in the relationship between banker and borrower?

10 What is a syndicated loan and why do banks join so many syndicates?

11 What are the differences between a domestic bond, a Eurobond and a foreign bond?

12 What is the credit rating on a bond and what factors determine it?

13 Why do bond issuers accept restrictive covenants?

14 What are high-yield bonds? What is their role in financing firms?

15 What is a bearer bond?

16 What is a debenture?

17 What is the difference between a fixed-rate and a floating-rate bond?

Questions and problems

myfinancelab **Questions with an icon are also available for practice in MyFinanceLab with additional supporting resources.**

Answers to questions marked with an asterisk are to be found in the Lecturer's Guide.

1 Imagine that the market yield to maturity for three-year bonds in a particular risk class is 12 per cent. You buy a bond in that risk class which offers an annual coupon of 10 per cent for the next three years, with the first payment in one year. The bond will be redeemed at par (£100) in three years.

a How much would you pay for the bond?
b If you paid £105 what yield to maturity would you obtain? ?

2 A £100 bond with two years to maturity and an annual coupon of 9 per cent is available. (The next coupon is payable in one year.)

a If the market requires a yield to maturity of 9 per cent for a bond of this risk class what will be its market price?
b If the market price is £98, what yield to maturity does it offer?
c If the required yield to maturity on this type of bond changes to 7 per cent, what will the market price change to? ?

3 a If the government sold a 10-year gilt with a par value of £100 and an (annual) coupon of 9 per cent, what price can be charged if investors require a 9.5 per cent yield to maturity on such bonds?
b If yields to maturity on bonds of this risk class fall to 8.5 per cent, what could the bonds be sold for?
c If it were sold for £105, what yield to maturity is the bond offering?
d What is the flat yield on this bond if it is selling at £105? ?

An Excel spreadsheet version of these calculations is available at www.pearsoned.com/arnold

4 The price of a bond issued by C & M plc is 85.50 per cent of par value. The bond will pay an annual 8.5 per cent coupon until maturity (the next coupon will be paid in one year). The bond matures in seven years.

a What will be the market price of the bond if yields to maturity for this risk class fall to 7.5 per cent?
b What will be the market price of the bond if yields to maturity for this risk class rise to 18 per cent? ?

5 A zero coupon bond with a par value of £100 matures in five years.

a What is the price of the bond if the yield to maturity is 5 per cent?
b What is the price of the bond if the yield to maturity is 10 per cent? ?

6 Bond 1 has an annual coupon rate of 6 per cent and Bond 2 has an annual coupon of 12 per cent. Both bonds mature in one year and have a par value of £100. If the yield to maturity on bonds of this risk class is 10 per cent at what price will the bonds sell? Assume that the next coupons are due in one year's time. ?

7* You are considering three alternative investments in bonds. The bonds have different times to maturity, but carry the same default risk. You would like to gain an impression of the extent of price volatility for each given alternative change in future interest rates. The investments are:

i A two-year bond with an annual coupon of 6 per cent, par value of £100 and the next coupon payment in one year. The current yield to maturity on this bond is 6.5 per cent.
ii A ten-year bond with an annual coupon of 6 per cent, a par value of £100 and the next coupon payable in one year. The current yield to maturity on this bond is 7.2 per cent.
iii A 20-year bond with an annual coupon of 6 per cent, a par value of £100 and the next coupon due in one year. The current yield to maturity on this bond is 7.7 per cent.

a Draw an approximate yield curve.
b Calculate the market price of each of the bonds.
c Calculate the market price of the bonds on the assumption that yields to maturity rise by 200 basis points for all bonds.
d Now calculate the market price of the bonds on the assumption that yields to maturity fall by 200 basis points.
e Which bond price is the most volatile in circumstances of changing yields to maturity?
f Explain the liquidity-preference theory of the term structure of yields to maturity. ?

An Excel spreadsheet version of this calculations is available at www.pearsoned.com/arnold.

8 What are the factors that explain the difference in yields to maturity between long-term and short-term bonds?

9 Find the current yield to maturity on government securities with maturities of one year, five years and ten years in the *Financial Times*. How has the yield curve changed since 2006 as shown in the chapter? What might account for this shift?

10 If the yield to maturity on a two-year zero coupon bond is 13 per cent and the yield to maturity on a one-year zero coupon bond is 10 per cent what is the expected spot rate of one-year bonds in one year's time assuming the expectations hypothesis is applicable? ?

11 If the yield to maturity on a one-year bond is 8 per cent and the expected spot rate on a one-year bond, beginning in one year's time, is 7 per cent what will be the yield to maturity on a two-year bond under the expectations hypothesis of the term structure of interest rates? ?

12 In 2006 the term structure of interest rates for UK government securities was downward sloping whereas in many other years it is upward sloping. Explain how these curves come about with reference to the expectations, liquidity and market-segmentation hypotheses.

13 Iris plc borrows £50m at 9.5 per cent from Westlloyds bank for five years. What cash flows will the firm have to find if the interest and principal are paid in the following ways?

a All interest and capital is paid at the end of the period.
b Interest only is paid for each of the years (at the year-ends); all principal is paid at the end.
c £10m of the capital plus annual interest is paid on each anniversary date. ?

14 What factors should a firm consider when borrowing from a bank?

15 'Convertibles are great because they offer a lower return than straight debt and we just dish out shares rather than having to find cash to redeem the bonds' – executive at Myopic plc. Comment on this statement as though you were a shareholder in Myopic.

16 Lummer plc has issued £60m 15-year 8.5 per cent coupon bonds with a par value of £100. Each bond is convertible into 40 shares of Lummer ordinary shares, which are currently trading at £1.90.

a What is the conversion price?
b What is the conversion premium?
c What is the conversion value of the bond?

17 Explain the following terms and their relevance to debt-finance decision makers:

a Negative covenant.
b Conversion premium.
c Collateral.
d Grace periods.

18 Outline the main advantages and disadvantages of fixed and floating interest rates from the borrowing company's perspective.

19 (*Examination level*) Flying High plc plans to expand rapidly over the next five years and is considering the following forms of finance to support that expansion.

a A five-year £10m floating-rate term loan from MidBarc Bank plc at an initial annual interest of 9 per cent.
b A five-year Eurodollar bond fixed at 8 per cent with a nominal value of US$15m.
c A £10m convertible bond offering a yield to redemption of 6 per cent and a conversion premium of 15 per cent.

As the financial adviser to the board you have been asked to explain each of these forms of finance and point out the relative advantages and drawbacks. Do this in report form.

20 'We avoid debt finance because of the unacceptable constraint placed on managerial actions.' Explain what this executive means and suggest forms of long-term borrowing which have few constraints.

myfinancelab **_Now retake your diagnostic test for Chapter 11 to check your progress and update your study plan._**

Assignments

1 Review the long-term debt instruments used by a company familiar to you. Consider the merits and drawbacks of these and explain alternative long-term debt strategies.

2 Write a report for the senior management of a company you know well explaining your views on the wisdom of using some of the firm's assets in a sale and leaseback transaction.

CHAPTER 12

Short-term and medium-term finance

LEARNING OUTCOMES

This chapter is largely descriptive and so it would be an achievement merely to understand the nature of each form of finance. However we will go further, and explore the appropriate use of these sources in varying circumstances. Specifically the reader should be able to:

- describe, compare and contrast the bank overdraft and the bank term loan;
- show awareness of the central importance of trade credit and good debtor management and be able to analyse the early settlement discount offer;
- explain the different services offered by a factoring firm;
- consider the relative merits of hire purchase and leasing;
- describe bills of exchange and bank bills and their uses.

Introduction

Short-term and medium-term finance is presented in this textbook as the third major category of funding. This is not meant to imply that the forms of finance described in this chapter are any less important than the first two (equity and long-term debt finance). Indeed, for many firms, especially smaller ones, a combination of overdrafts and loans, trade credit, leasing and hire purchase make up the greater part of the funding needs. Large companies have access to stock markets, bond markets and syndicated loan facilities. These are often closed to the smaller firm, so, in order to achieve their expansion programmes, they turn to the local banks and the finance houses as well as their suppliers for the wherewithal to grow. The giants of the corporate world have access to dozens of different types of finance, but they also value the characteristics, cheapness and flexibility of the forms discussed here.

The definitions of short-term and medium-term finance are not clear-cut. Usually finance which is repayable within a year is regarded as short, whereas that due for repayment between one and seven years is taken to be medium. But these cut-offs are not to be taken too seriously. Quite often an overdraft facility, which is due for repayment in, say, six months or one year, is regularly 'rolled over' and so may become relied upon as a medium- or even long-term source of funds. Leasing, which is usually classified as a medium-term source, can be used for periods of up to 15 years in some circumstances, in others it is possible to lease assets for a period of only a few weeks, for example, a computer or photocopier. The forms of finance we will examine in this chapter are listed in **Exhibit 12.1**.

Exhibit 12.1 The main forms of short-term and medium-term future

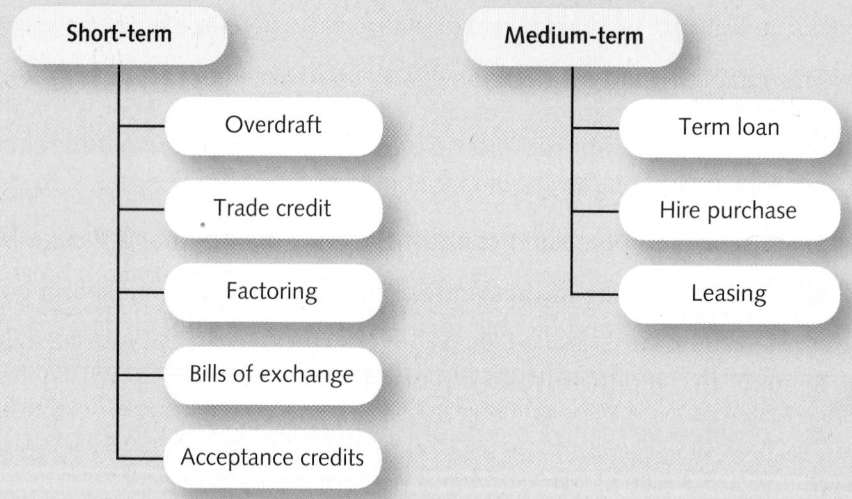

Bank sources

For most companies and individuals banks remain the main source of externally (i.e. not retained earnings) raised finance. Total bank lending outstanding to the small business sector in the UK is £30bn–£50bn per year. In the early 1990s the most common form of bank borrowing was the overdraft facility. As we shall see there has been a remarkable shift, so that now the term loan has come to dominate.

Overdraft

Usually the amount that can be withdrawn from a bank account is limited to the amount put in. However, business and other financial activity often requires some flexibility in this principle, and it is often useful to make an arrangement to take more money out of a bank account than it contains – this is an **overdraft**.

An overdraft is a permit to overdraw on an account up to a stated limit.

Overdraft facilities are usually arranged for a period of a few months or a year and interest is charged on the excess drawings.

Advantages of overdrafts

Overdrafts have the following advantages.

1 ***Flexibility*** The borrowing firm is not asked to forecast the precise amount and duration of its borrowing at the outset but has the flexibility to borrow up to a stated limit. Also the borrower is assured that the moment the funds are no longer required they can be quickly and easily repaid without suffering a penalty.

2 ***Cheapness*** Banks usually charge two to five percentage points over base rate (or LIBOR) depending on the creditworthiness, security offered and bargaining position of the borrower. There may also be an **arrangement fee** of, say, 1 per cent of the facility. However, many banks have dropped arrangement fees completely to attract borrowers. These charges may seem high but it must be borne in mind that overdrafts are often loans to smaller and riskier firms which would otherwise have to pay much more for their funds. Large and well-established borrowers with low gearing and plenty of collateral can borrow on overdraft at much more advantageous rates. A major saving comes from the fact that the banks charge interest on only the daily outstanding balance. So, if a firm has a large cash inflow one week it can use this to reduce its overdraft, temporarily lowering the interest payable, while retaining the ability to borrow more another week.

Drawbacks of an overdraft

A major drawback to an overdraft is that the bank retains the right to withdraw the facility at short notice. Thus a heavily indebted firm may receive a letter from the bank insisting that its account be brought to balance within a matter of days. This right lowers the risk to the lender because it can quickly get its money out of a troubled company; this allows it to lower the cost of lending. However, it can be devastating for the borrower and so firms are well advised to think through the use to which finance provided by way of an overdraft is put. It is not usually wise to use the money for an asset which cannot be easily liquidated; for example, it could be problematic if an overdraft is used for a bridge-building project which will take three years to come to fruition.

The age-old convention of attaching the right of the bank to withdraw the overdraft facility to a loan agreement was flouted by NatWest in 2000. (*See* **Exhibit 12.2**.)

Another major consideration for the borrower is the issue of security. Banks usually take a fixed charge (on a specific asset) or a floating charge ('floats' over the general assets of the firm). Alternatively, or in addition, the bank may require a personal guarantee of the directors or owners of the business. When Sir Richard Branson borrowed from Lloyds TSB the bank took shares owned by Sir Richard in Virgin Atlantic as security. Note also that, unusually, a three-year overdraft facility was arranged (*see* **Exhibit 12.3**).

Exhibit 12.2

NatWest deletes overdraft clause

FT

Campaigners for small companies claimed a victory yesterday after NatWest bank abolished its right to remove a customer's overdraft at a moment's notice.

NatWest said it would turn current industry practice on its head by deleting the 'repayable on demand' clause from its small business overdrafts.

The bank said it would end the uncertainty faced by SMEs by ensuring that a three, six or twelve month overdraft meant exactly that. The conditions will apply to both secured and unsecured overdrafts.

Source: Jim Pickard, *Financial Times*, 21 November 2000, p. 6. Reprinted with permission.

Exhibit 12.3

Branson wins £17m loan facility increase

FT

Sir Richard Branson can borrow a further £17m from Lloyds TSB under a loan facility backed by Virgin Group's controlling stake in Virgin Atlantic, the prize of his business empire.

Virgin said yesterday it had mortgaged his 51 per cent stake in the Virgin Atlantic in exchange for a £67m three-year facility from Lloyds.

Sir Richard's group has already used £50m of the overdraft facility on new businesses, including US and Australian mobile phone ventures and the acquisition of a chain of South African health clubs.

Source: Francesco Guerrera and Thorold Barker, *Financial Times*, 12 June 2001, p. 26. Reprinted with permission.

Conditions of lending

A bank will generally examine the following factors before lending to a firm:

1 ***Cash flow projections*** A healthy set of projected cash flows will usually be required showing sufficient profitability and liquidity to pay off the overdraft at the end of the agreed period.

2 ***Creditworthiness*** This goes beyond examining projected future cash flows and asset backing and considers important factors such as character and talents of the individuals leading the organisation.

3 ***The amount that the borrower is prepared to put into the project*** or activity, relative to that asked from the bank. If the borrower does not show commitment by putting their money into a scheme banks can get nervous and stand-offish.

4 ***Security*** The back-up of specific assets or a charge over a large body of general assets will help to reassure a lender that it will be repaid one way or another. Bankers may look at a firm or a project on two levels. First, they might consider a 'liquidation analysis' in which they think about their position in a scenario of business failure. Secondly, they will look at a firm or project on the assumption that it is a 'going concern', where cash flows rather than assets become more important.

Overdrafts are particularly useful for seasonal businesses because the daily debit-balance interest charge and the absence of a penalty for early repayment mean that this form of finance can be cheaper than a loan. Take the case of Fruit Growers plc (*see* Worked example 12.1).

The risk of a sudden withdrawal of an overdraft facility for most firms is very slight: banks do not generate goodwill and good publicity by capriciously and lightly cancelling agreed overdrafts. The high street banks came in for strong criticism in the early 1990s: 'In 1993 the best that could

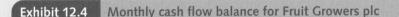

Worked example 12.1 Fruit Growers plc

The management of Fruit Growers plc are trying to decide whether to obtain financing from an overdraft or a loan. The interest on both would be 10 per cent per year or 2.5 per cent per quarter. The cash position for the forthcoming year is represented in **Exhibit 12.4**.

Exhibit 12.4 Monthly cash flow balance for Fruit Growers plc

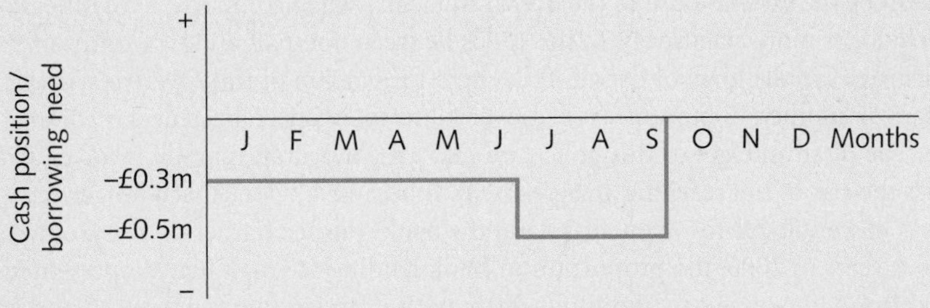

Option 1 A loan for the whole year

A loan for the whole year has the advantage of greater certainty that the lending facility will be in place throughout the year. A total loan of £500,000 will be needed, and this will be repaid at the end of the year with interest. At the beginning of the year Fruit Growers' account is credited with the full £500,000. For the months when the business does not need the £500,000 the surplus can be invested to receive a return of 2 per cent per quarter – *see* **Exhibit 12.5**.

Exhibit 12.5 Cost of a loan for the whole year

Interest charged 500,000 × 10%	=	£50,000
Less interest receivable when surplus funds earn 2% per quarter		
January–June 200,000 × 4%	=	£8,000
October–December 500,000 × 2%	=	£10,000
Total cost of borrowing	=	£32,000

Option 2 An overdraft facility for £500,000

An overdraft facility for £500,000 has the drawback that the facility might be withdrawn at any time during the year. However it is cheaper, as **Exhibit 12.6** shows.

Exhibit 12.6 Cost of an overdraft facility for £500,000

1st quarter (J, F & M) 300,000 × 2.5%	=	£7,500
2nd quarter (A, M & J) 300,000 × 2.5%	=	£7,500
3rd quarter (J, A & S) 500,000 × 2.5%	=	£12,500
4th quarter (O, N & D)	=	£0
Total cost of borrowing	=	£27,500

Note: We will ignore the complications of compounding intra-year interest.

be said about the relationship between banks and their small firm customers was that both sides were in a state of armed neutrality' (Howard Davies, Deputy Governor of the Bank of England, 1996). They were said to have failed to lower interest rates to small firms to the same extent as general base rates (a charge of which the Bank of England said they were not guilty), of not supporting start-ups, of having excessive fees, of being too ready to close down a business and being too focused on property-based security backing rather than looking at the cash flows of the proposed activity.

A number of these areas of contention have been addressed and matters are said to be improving (although many small business owners would disagree). One particular problem with UK lending was said to be the excessive use of the overdraft facility when compared with other countries which used term loans more extensively. In the 1980s between one-half and two-thirds of bank lending to small firms was in the form of overdrafts. A high proportion of these were rearranged at the end of each year for another 12 months ('rolled over') and so, in effect, became a medium-term source of finance. The disadvantages of this policy are that each overdraft renewal involves arrangement fees as well as the risk of not reaching an agreement. It became obvious that a longer-term loan arrangement was more suitable for many firms and the banks pushed harder on this front. As a result, over the dozen years to 2006, the proportion of bank lending to small firms represented by overdrafts declined from 49 per cent to about one-fifth, with term lending rising to 80 per cent. Also small companies have increasingly made use of a wider range of sources of finance, such as leasing and factoring so that the proportion of external finance accounted for by traditional bank borrowing has fallen from 60 per cent to about 50 per cent.

Term loans

A **term loan** is a loan of a fixed amount for an agreed time and on specified terms. These loans are normally for a period of between three and seven years, but the period can range from one to 20 years. The specified terms will include provisions regarding the repayment schedule. If the borrower is to apply the funds to a project which will not generate income for perhaps the first three years it may be possible to arrange a grace period during which only the interest is paid, with the capital being paid off once the project has a sufficiently positive cash flow. Other arrangements can be made to reflect the pattern of cash flow of the firm or project: for example a **'balloon' payment structure** is one when only a small part of the capital is repaid during the main part of the loan period, with the majority repayable as the maturity date approaches. A **'bullet'** repayment arrangement takes this one stage further and provides for all the capital to be repaid at the end of the loan term.

Not all term loans are drawn down in a single lump sum at the time of the agreement. In the case of a construction project which needs to keep adding to its borrowing to pay for the different stages of development, an **instalment arrangement** might be required with, say, 25 per cent of the money being made available immediately, 25 per cent at foundation stage and so on. This has the added attraction to the lender of not committing large sums secured against an asset not yet created. From the borrower's point of view a **drawdown arrangement** has an advantage over an overdraft in that the lender is committed to providing the finance if the borrower meets prearranged conditions, whereas with an overdraft the lender can withdraw the arrangement at short notice.

The interest charged on term loans can be at either fixed or floating rates. The fixed rate is generally at a higher rate of interest than the floating rate at the time of arrangement because of the additional risk to the lender of being unable to modify rates as an uncertain future unfolds. In addition, the borrower may pay an arrangement fee which will largely depend on the relative bargaining strength of the two parties.

A term loan often has much more accompanying documentation than an overdraft because of the lengthy bank commitment. This will include a set of obligations imposed on the borrowing firm such as information flows to the bank as well as **financial gearing** (debt to equity ratio) and liquidity ratio (availability of funds to meet claims) constraints. If these financial ratio limits are breached or interest and capital is not paid on the due date the bank has a right of termination, in which case it could decide not to make any more funds available, or, in extreme cases, insist on the repayment of funds already lent. Banks are unlikely to rush into declaring default, seizing assets and liquidating a firm because, even if they take such draconian action, they may not get much of their funds back, and the adverse publicity is a disincentive. Instead they will often try to reschedule or restructure the finance of the business (e.g. grant a longer period to pay). In addition to either a fixed or floating charge over the small firm's assets banks usually insist on guarantees from third parties.

Small Firms Loan Guarantee (SFLG)

Many small businesses face difficulty in growing because banks are reluctant to lend when there are few assets in the business to act as collateral for a loan. Fresh equity finance is an alternative, but many owners have put in as much as they can. They may be reluctant to sell ownership capital to outsiders, such as business angels, even if the business is sufficiently well advanced to attract funds from outside the founding family. Thus we have, through lack of finance, the stultification of otherwise vibrant businesses.

The UK government is sufficiently disturbed by this to support a scheme designed to encourage the banks to lend to small businesses with a workable business proposal, but lacking security. The SFLG is a joint venture between the Department for Business, Enterprise and Regulatory Reform (BERR) and approved lenders under which 75 per cent of the value of SFLG loans to these companies are guaranteed to be paid from the SFLG fund should the company fail. Note that the banks provide the finance (rather than the SFLG), but receive a guarantee from a government-backed fund that they will get most of their money back should the worst happen to the borrower. The SFLG helped Waterstone's, Coffee Republic and Body Shop set up.

Naturally, companies will fail from time to time and so the SFLG pays out regularly to the banks. The government has chosen not to provide this money from its own coffers, but it requires every business receiving a guarantee to pay an extra 2 per cent interest on SFLG loans outstanding each year into the fund.

The loans can be for any amount, with a minimum of £5,000 and a maximum of £250,000. The loans are for periods of up to 10 years and they are available to sole traders and partnerships as well as limited companies. If there are assets in the business then these will be used as security against the loan and will be confiscated first before any drawdown of the guarantee is made. There are a few restrictions:

- Businesses must be less than 5 years old and with a turnover of less than £5.6m.
- Some sectors are excluded, e.g. agriculture, banking, authors, betting.
- Only loans from approved lenders are permitted.
- Businesses can only apply if, in the lender's opinion, there is not enough security for conventional lending.

The lending decision is still in the hands of the bank so they still decide terms such as interest rates, repayment holidays (grace periods), arrangement fees or length of loan. However, there is an extra layer of bureaucracy, as the borrower also has to gain approval from the Small Business Service of the BERR. The Federation of Small Businesses argues that many opt for a simpler form of credit, that is using credit card borrowing. Over one-half of small and medium-sized businesses use a company credit card – most pay off the amount outstanding each month. Apparently credit card finance is valued for its flexibility, speed and ease.

The SFLG is currently under review – for an update see www.dti.gov.uk.

Trade credit

Perhaps the simplest and the most important source of short-term finance for many firms is **trade credit**. This means that when goods or services are delivered to a firm for use in its production they are not paid for immediately. These goods and services can then be used to produce income before the invoice has to be paid.

The writer has been involved with a number of small business enterprises, one of which was a small retail business engaged in the selling of crockery and glassware – Crocks. Reproduced as **Exhibit 12.7** is an example of a real invoice (with a few modifications to hide the identity of the supplier). When we first started buying from this supplier we, as a matter of course, applied for trade credit. We received the usual response, that the supplier requires two references vouching for our trustworthiness from other suppliers that have granted us trade credit in the past, plus a reference from our bankers. Once these confidential references were accepted by the supplier they granted us normal credit terms for retailers of our type of product, that is, 30 days to pay from the date of delivery. One of the things you learn in business is that agreements of this kind are subject to some flexibility. We found that this supplier does not get too upset if you go over the 30 days and pay around day 60: the supplier will still supply to the business on normal credit terms even if you do this on a regular basis.

Exhibit 12.7 A typical invoice

Supplier XYZ plc
54 West Street, Sussex

Invoice number 501360
Date 29/02/98

Invoice address
Crocks
Melton Mowbray
Leics
LE13 1XH

Branch address
Crocks
Grantham
Lincolnshire

INVOICE

Account	Customer order No.	Sales order	Carrier	AEP	Despatch No.	Due date	Page
TO2251	81535	TO1537		090	000067981	28/03/98	1

Item	Part code	Description	Unit of sale	Quantity despatched	Unit price	%	Amount	VAT code
1	1398973	Long glass	each	12	0.84	0.00	10.08	0
2	12810357	Tumbler	each	12	0.84	0.00	10.08	0
3	1395731	Plate	each	60	1.10	0.00	66.00	0
4	1258732	Bowls	each	30	4.23	0.00	126.90	0
5	1310102	Cup	each	1	4.24	0.00	4.24	0
		VAT 0: 217.30 @ 17.5%						

Note our settlement terms:
$2\frac{1}{2}$% discount may be deducted for payment within 14 days of invoice date; otherwise due 30 days strictly nett.

Nett goods	217.30
Charges	0.00
VAT	38.03
	255.33

Each time supplies were delivered by this firm we had to make a decision about when to pay. Option 1 is to pay on the 14th day to receive $2\frac{1}{2}$ per cent discount (see note at the bottom of the invoice). Option 2 is to take 60 days to pay. (Note: with Option 1 the $2\frac{1}{2}$ per cent deduction is on the 'nett goods' amount, which is the value of the invoice before value added tax (VAT) is added, that is £217.30.)

Option 1

$$£217.30 \times 0.025 = £5.43$$

So, we could knock £5.43 off the bill if we paid it 14 days after delivery. This looks good but we do not yet know whether it is better than the second option.

Option 2

This business had an overdraft, so if we could avoid taking money from the bank account the interest charge would be less. How much interest could be saved by taking an additional 46 days (60 – 14) to pay this invoice? Assuming the annual percentage rate (APR) charged on the overdraft is 10 per cent the daily interest charge is:

$$(1 + \mathrm{d})^{365} = 1 + i$$

$$d = \sqrt[365]{(1 + i)} - 1$$

$$= \sqrt[365]{(1 + 0.1)} - 1 = 0.00026116$$

where

d = daily interest, and i = annual interest

Interest charge for 46 days:

$$(1 + 0.00026116)^{46} - 1 = 0.01208 \text{ or } 1.208\%$$

If we go for the early settlement discount and pay on day 14 we would have to borrow £255.33 minus the discount of £5.43 over a 46-day period at 10 per cent per annum interest:

$$(255.33 - 5.43) \times 0.01208 = £3.02$$

Thus £3.02 interest is saved by delaying payment to the sixtieth day, compared with a saving of over £5 on the option of paying early.[1] In this particular case taking extended trade credit is not the cheapest source of finance; it is cheaper to use the overdraft facility.

Many suppliers to our business did not offer a discount for early settlement. This gives the impression that trade credit finance is a free source of funds and therefore the logical course of action is to get as much trade credit as possible. The system is therefore open to abuse. However, the corrective to that abuse is that a supplier will become tired of dealing with a persistent late payer and will refuse to supply, or will only supply on a basis of payment in advance. Another point to be borne in mind is that gaining a bad reputation in the business community may affect relationships with other suppliers.

Advantages of trade credit

Trade credit has the following advantages.

1 ***Convenient/informal/cheap*** Trade credit has become a normal part of business in most product markets.

---

[1] An alternative approach that is generally sufficiently accurate is:

$$\text{Interest rate for } n \text{ days} = \frac{i}{365} \times (n)$$

2 ***Available to companies of any size*** Small companies, especially fast-growing ones, often have a very limited range of sources of finance to turn to, and banks frequently restrict overdrafts and loans to the asset backing available. It is important to note that trade credit is a vital source of finance for the largest companies in the world as well as the smallest. For example, Tesco and Asda typically have over twice as much owing to suppliers at any one time as the value of all the goods on their shelves – more than £2.2bn for Tesco and £1.5bn for Asda. The suppliers don't just provide food etc.; they supply much of the money needed for the rest of Tesco's and Asda's operations.

Factors determining the terms of trade credit

Tradition within the industry

Customs have been established in many industries concerning the granting of trade credit. Individual suppliers may be unwise to step outside these traditions because they may lose sales. **Exhibit 12.8** shows the number of days it takes firms in the listed industries to pay their bills.

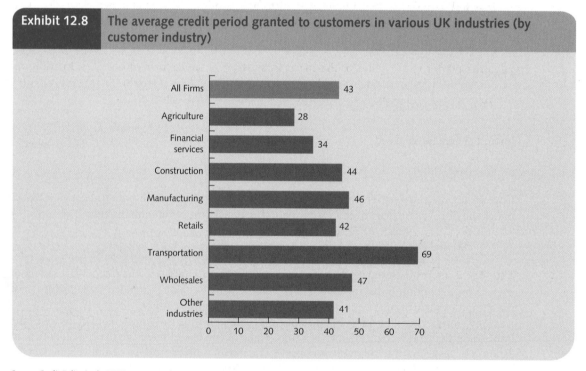

Exhibit 12.8 The average credit period granted to customers in various UK industries (by customer industry)

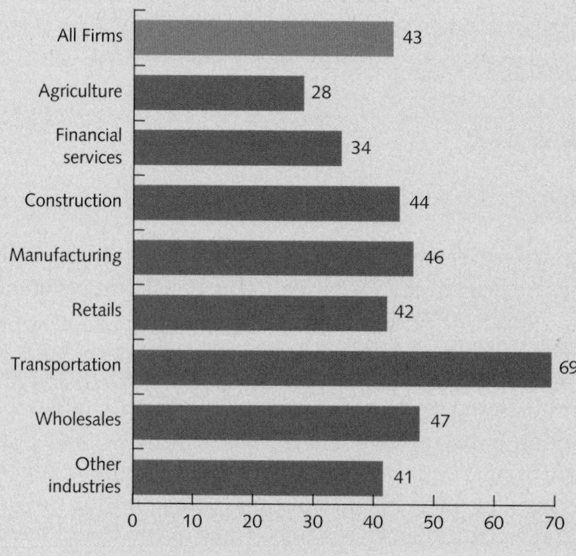

Source: Credit Policy in the UK Economy, Credit Management Research Centre, Leeds University Business School, April 2005 (also at www.payontime.co.uk)

Bargaining strength of the two parties

If the supplier has numerous customers, each wanting to purchase the product in a particular region, and the supplier wishes to have only one outlet then it may decide not to supply to those firms which demand extended trade credit. On the other hand, if the supplier is selling into a highly competitive market where the buyer has many alternative sources of supply credit might be used to give a competitive edge.

Product type

Products with a high level of turnover relative to stocks are generally sold on short credit terms (say, 10 days rather than 40 days), for example food. The main reason is that these products usually sell on a low profit margin and the delay in payment can have a large impact on the profit margin.

Credit standing of individual customers

A less risky customer may be granted long periods to pay and a higher credit rating – *see* next page.

Trade debtor management

Trade credit is a two-edged sword for businesses. Firms usually benefit from being granted credit by their suppliers but because of the necessity of providing credit to their customers they are burdened with additional costs. To gain a true appreciation of trade credit we need to examine the subject from the other side of the fence and ask: 'What considerations does the credit provider have to take into account?'

Trade debtors are the sales made on credit as yet unpaid.

The management of debtors[2] involves a trade-off (*see* **Exhibit 12.9**). On the one hand, the more generous a company is in allowing its customers to delay payment, the greater the sales. Trade credit as well as offering cheap finance to customers, sends a signal of supplier reputation and financial health (Wilson and Summers, 2002). On the other hand, longer credit terms impose costs of financing those goods and services until they are paid for. There may also be a strain on the company's liquidity with a large proportion of the company's assets tied up in debtors (typically one-quarter to one-third of the company's assets are in the form of debtors). In addition there is the risk of the customer defaulting on the payment and there are also the sometimes considerable costs of administering an effective debtor management system.

Exhibit 12.9 The debtor trade-off

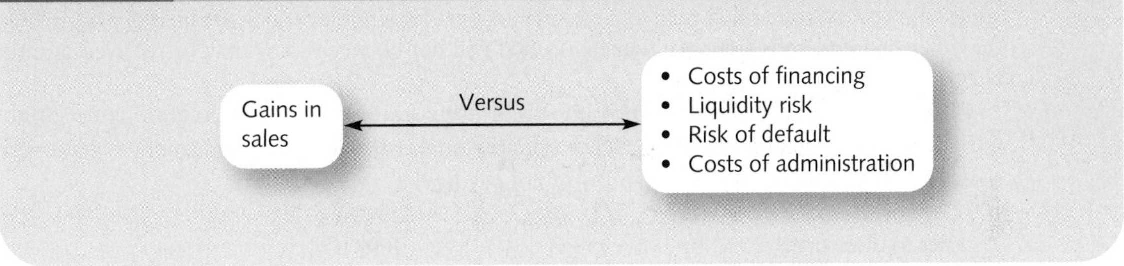

The solution to the debtor trade-off is to compare the incremental returns from a more accommodating credit stance with the incremental costs. The following points are relevant in trade credit management.

Credit (debtor) policy

The first issue in the management of trade debtors is to decide whether to grant credit at all. Credit is not inevitable; many businesses, for example service-based organisations, from hairdressers to vehicle repairers, choose not to offer any credit. Some compromise and offer credit on sales above a certain value, say £100. If a firm decides that it is in its best interest to allow delayed payment then it needs to set up a system of rules and guidelines which will amount to a debtor policy.

Assessing credit risk

Granting credit is, in effect, the granting of a loan. It is important to assess the probability of either delayed payment or complete failure to pay. Information to make this judgement can come from a

[2] In the USA trade debt is termed receivables or accounts receivable.

variety of sources. First, the customer's accounts could be examined. (All limited liability companies in the UK are required to submit their accounts to Companies House and these are then available for inspection by anyone.) An analysis of the accounts could give some idea of the liquidity and solvency of the customer as well as its trading performance and growth trajectory. Much of this type of public information is now held in electronic form and can be quickly accessed, for example through FAME (Financial Analysis Made Easy). If the credit provider does not wish to become involved in the detail of credit checking it could employ a credit reporting agency (such as Dun and Bradstreet) which uses accounting information combined with knowledge of the problems other companies have had with the customer and special enquiries to rate creditworthiness. In addition to trade references from existing suppliers and bank references the debtor management department could canvass the opinion and impressions of the salespeople. This can be a rich source of anecdotal evidence, as they are the individuals who are most likely to meet the customer in the work environment.

If the customer has been buying from an organisation for some time then that organisation will have a set of records on which to base an assessment of risk. Using this information, and keeping the corporate 'eyes and ears' open in day-to-day dealings for signs of customers experiencing liquidity problems, the supplier can take risk-reducing action early. For example, if a customer has gradually increased the length of time between delivery and payment and the sales team report that the customer's shops are looking understocked, the firm might move the customer from 30-day credit period terms to payment on delivery ('cash on delivery', COD).

Many companies allocate customers to different risk classes and treat each category differently. Some customers are allowed 60 days, while others are only permitted 10 days. Special discounts are available to some and not to others. Certain small, poorly capitalised companies present particular problems to the supplying firm as it is faced with the difficult choice of whether or not to sell. The first order from a company like this might be valued at only £1,000, the profit on which is only, say, £200. But the supplier has somehow to estimate the lost sales and profits for all future years if it refuses credit on this first purchase. These could mount up to a large present value. In addition, a lost customer will turn to a competitor firm for supplies and assist their expansion. On the other hand, there is a chance that the £1,000 will not be received or may be received months after the due date.

Once customers have been classified into risk categories it is possible to decide whether or not to trade with particular types of firms. For example, suppose that a group of customers have been assessed to have a one in eight probability of not paying:

Sales to these firms	100,000
Less bad debts (1/8 × 100,000)	–12,500
Income from sales	87,500
Costs of production, distribution, etc.	–80,000
Incremental profit	£7,500

Given the present costs of production and creditworthiness of the customers it is worthwhile selling goods on credit to these firms. However, a careful watch will have to be placed on firms of this risk class as their position can deteriorate rapidly.

Assessing credit risk is an area of management which relies less on numerical frameworks than on sound and experienced judgement. There are two rules to bear in mind:

1 ***Focus effort on the most risky*** Some sales are to large, safe, regular customers with a good reputation for prompt payment. Do not put large resources into monitoring these accounts. Concentrate time and effort on the problematic customers.

2 ***Accept some risk: it may lead to greater profit*** The minimisation of bad debt is not the key objective. Customers less than perfectly safe may have to be accepted to make sales and generate profit. For example, a relatively risky small customer may be granted credit in the hope that one day it will become large and established.

Agreeing terms

Having decided to sell on credit to a particular firm the supplier has to agree the precise details with the customer. This is going to be heavily influenced by the factors discussed earlier: industry tradition, bargaining strength, product type and credit standing. Firms usually adopt terms which require payment in a number of days from the invoice date or the delivery date (in theory these should be close together). An alternative system requires payment on or before the last day of the month following the date of invoice. Thus goods delivered on 5 August are paid for on 30 September. This approach can lead to almost two months' credit and customers quickly appreciate the advantage of making sure deliveries are made at the start of each month. Payment is usually by means of a cheque, but increasingly direct bank transfers are used, where the customer's bank automatically pays a certain number of days after receiving notification from the supplier. Sainsbury's has a system that both automatically pays and deducts a discount for early settlement – *see* **Exhibit 12.10**.

Exhibit 12.10

Sainsbury changes payment system in bank deal

FT

by Elizabeth Rigby

J Sainsbury has joined forces with Morgan Stanley to establish a new payment system allowing small suppliers to receive their cash within a few days of the supermarket approving their invoices, instead of waiting 45 days.

Britain's third-biggest supermarket announced its scheme – thought to be the first of its kind within the grocery sector – at a suppliers' conference yesterday.

Under the scheme, Morgan Stanley will act as a lender to suppliers, giving them early cash settlements for invoices approved by Sainsbury for a small interest rate payment, calculated against the supermarket's credit rating.

Sainsbury said that, under current interest rate terms, a supplier owed £100 would receive £99.30 after five days. Under the old system, suppliers put in invoices for goods, only then to wait 45 days before being paid.

Sainsbury used to pay suppliers on average within 21 days of submitting invoices – a very short lead-time in the industry – but moved it to a 45-day period in the middle of last year.

Within the new system, suppliers will be able to view their invoices, debit notes, remittance advices and payment dates, making it easier for them to predict cash flow.

Source: *Financial Times*, 24 November 2006, p. 20. Reprinted with permission.

Customers are generally given credit limits, that is, a maximum amount that can be outstanding at any one time. For example, suppose a customer has taken delivery of five consignments of goods over a three-week period from one supplier amounting to £2,000, which is equal to its credit limit with that supplier. That firm will be refused any more deliveries until it has paid off some of its arrears.

Goods are normally sold under a contract whereby the supplier can take repossession should the buyer fail to pay. This has the advantage that the supplier avoids becoming a lowly general creditor of the company and therefore being way down the pecking order in a liquidation. If the goods are perishable the supplier may grant only short credit terms because of the absence of good collateral.

The size of the orders may influence the terms of credit. Customers ordering small quantities are more expensive to manage than those that place large orders and therefore their credit period may be less generous.

Collecting payment

An effective administration system for debtors must be established. The firm needs clearly defined procedures and the customers need to be informed and/or warned that they are expected to conform to certain rules. Some profitable companies go bankrupt because they fail to collect the cash from customers that is vital to sustain production and satisfy their own creditors. The following list sets out some elements of a good system.

- ***Be strict with the credit limit*** Insist on payment for previous orders before dispatching more goods if the credit limit is breached.
- ***Send invoices promptly*** Ensure that there is no delay between delivery of the goods and dispatch of the invoice, so that the customer is made aware of the due date for payment as early as possible.
- ***Systematically review debtors*** One measure useful in reviewing debtors is the average collection period (ACP) (alternatively called the debtor collection period or debtor days). For example, if a firm has £1.5m of outstanding debtors and an annual turnover of £20m, the average collection period is:

$$\frac{\text{Debtors outstanding}}{\text{Average daily sales}} = \frac{1{,}500{,}000}{20{,}000{,}000/365} = 27 \text{ days}$$

Note that if sales are seasonal the 'acceptable' ACP may vary through the year. Another guide to aid decision making and prompt action is the ageing schedule. The total debtor figure is broken down to show how long invoices have been outstanding. An example is shown in **Exhibit 12.11**.

Exhibit 12.11 An ageing schedule

Period account has been outstanding (days)	Total debtors (%)
0–29	42
30–59	40
60–89	10
90–119	6
120+	2

- ***Slow payers have to be chased*** Any good system will call for a response immediately a debtor has failed to pay on time. This does not mean jumping to court action to recover the debt. There will be a sequence of actions before the drastic involvement of lawyers. **Exhibit 12.12** shows a typical sequence.

A balance has to be struck when pressing for payment between the effort, expense and lost goodwill on the one hand and the cost of financing the loan to a customer (and the growing risk of non-payment) on the other. The gain from receiving payment one day earlier is:

$$d = \sqrt[365]{(1+i)} - 1 \text{ multiplied by the amount}$$

where d = daily interest and i = annual cost of capital.

Exhibit 12.12 Stages in payment collection – an example

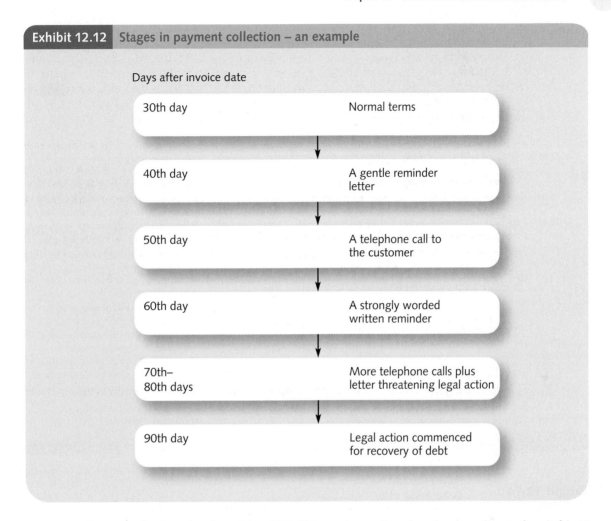

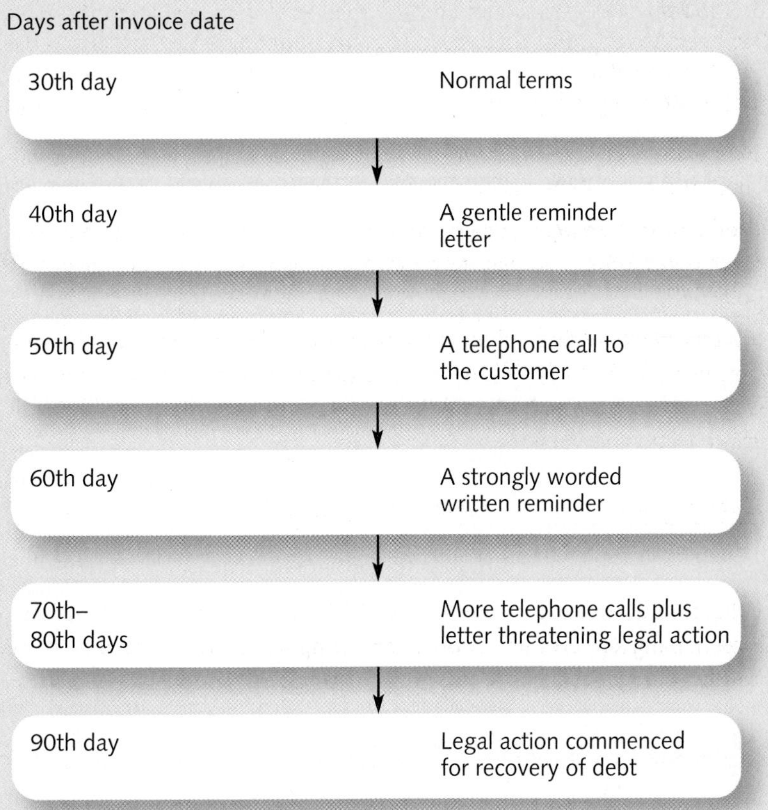

For example, the gain of receiving £100,000 one day earlier when the annual cost of capital is 12 per cent is:

$$d = \sqrt[365]{(1 + (0.12)} - 1 = 0.000310538$$

$$£100{,}000 \times 0.000310538 = £31.05$$

Despite improved credit controls late payment of bills is still a serious problem with a typical delay (beyond the normal 31 days) of 49 days for smaller firms, 31 days for medium-sized firms and 16 days for larger firms chasing payment in 2006. **Exhibits 12.13** and **12.14** provide some more ideas on how to speed up payment.

Cash discounts are used as part of the collecting system due to the benefits they give *if* they stimulate early settlement. Early settlement reduces the cost of carrying the loan. Also, the longer an account remains unpaid the greater the risk of eventual default, the greater the strain on liquidity and the costs of administering the debtors' ledger. The level of discount has to be considered very carefully as the effective cost can be extremely high.

Exhibit 12.13

'Cheques in the post' take up 11.5m hours

FT

by Jonathan Moules

The UK's 4m small and medium-sized companies spend a total of 11.5m hours every week chasing unpaid invoices, according to a survey.

The research, commissioned by GMAC Commercial Finance, corporate funding specialists, found that on average companies with turnovers between £350,000 and £10m spent 2.9 hours a week trying to get bills paid.

Nick Goulding, chief executive of the Forum of Private Business, an employers' group, said: 'That is precious time that should be spent running and growing the business.

'Late payment reduces cash flow, which is vital for financial health and can be the difference between making or breaking a business.'

The Small Business Service, a government agency, estimates that at any one time small businesses are owed £17bn by their debtors and about 10,000 companies fail each year as a direct result of late payment.

Nick Wilson, a professor at Leeds University's credit management research facility and a director of Credit-scorer.com, said that the figures probably underestimated the impact late payment had on companies because it ignored the effect on cash flow. 'The most damaging element is the uncertainty about payment, not the time taken to get it,' he said. 'It may force you to renegotiate your overdraft or seek additional financing.'

The key to controlling late payments was to have good credit management practices, Prof Wilson said. These included knowing who companies were dealing with, making sure that they understood the payment terms in advance and making sure they were proactive in chasing money when it was due. 'A little bit of effort up front saves a lot of time down the line.'

Companies now have a legal right to charge interest at 8 per cent above the base rate on debts due from businesses and public-sector bodies. However, Prof Wilson said the legal threat had tended to encourage large companies to negotiate longer payment periods with their smaller suppliers rather than pushing them to settle their bills promptly.

Source: *Financial Times*, 24 May 2005, p. 3. Reprinted with permission.

Exhibit 12.14

How to avoid late payment problems

FT

- Check new customers' creditworthiness before drawing up a contract
- Refuse orders, or obtain payment in advance, if a customer has an unacceptable payment record
- Set strict credit limits and stick to them
- Agree unambiguous written contracts and terms and conditions of trading with your customers
- Involve the salesforce in negotiating the payment terms to ensure that these are agreed with customer from the outset
- Initiate and maintain close contact with your customers, particularly with the person responsible for paying your account
- Make regular credit checks on your existing customers
- Put a 'stop' on supplies to customers who are not paying and use their desire for further supplies as a spur to payment
- If all else fails, place the debt in the hands of a debt collection agency or a solicitor who specialises in debt collection
- Lastly, remember to thank those customers who do pay on time

Source: Better Payment Practice Group and quoted in Jonathan Moules, *Financial Times*, 29 June 2004, p. 3. Reprinted with permission.

Take the case of a firm that normally collects debts after 40 days which introduces a 3 per cent discount for payment on the tenth day. If customers took advantage of this, the cost on an annual basis would be:

Discount over 30 days is: $\frac{3}{100-3} = 0.0309278$ or 3.09% for a 30-day period

The number of 30-day periods per year is: $\frac{365}{30} = 12.167$

The annual interest rate is:

$$(1.0309278)^{12.167} - 1 = 44.9\%$$

The effective cost of the discount is very large and has to be offset against the improved cash flow, lowered bad debt risk, lowered liquidity risk, administration costs and increased sales. The use of the cash discount has been further complicated by the fact that some customers abuse the system and take the discount even if they delay payment beyond the specified time.

Another way of encouraging payment at the contracted time is to make it clear that interest will be charged on overdue accounts. Suppliers are often reluctant to use this method as it has the disadvantage of creating resentment and blank refusals to pay the interest.

Firms that grant trade credit need to establish a policy on what to do when an invoice is highly unlikely to be paid, that is, it becomes a bad debt. In many cases there comes a stage when it is better to cease pursuing a debtor than to incur any more expense. The firm will need to work out a set of criteria for deciding when to write off a bad debt.

Integration with other disciplines

Customers sometimes see a glimpse of the conflict between the objectives of the sales team and the finance departments of suppliers. Sales representatives go out of their way to find new customers and to gain large orders from existing clients only to find that head office has vetoed the opening of a new account or is enforcing a strict credit limit. The sales personnel often spend years cultivating a relationship which can be seriously damaged by the harsh actions of the debtor collection department, ranging from unpleasant letters to court action. On the other hand, the debtor management department may complain that the sales representatives offer the customer excessively generous terms for the customer's risk class in order to meet a monthly sales target. Such conflicts need careful handling. Inter-function communication will help, as will an ethos of shareholder wealth enhancement with rewards and penalties directed at that goal in all departments.

Factoring

Factoring (or '**invoice finance**') companies provide three services to firms with outstanding debtors, the most important of which, in the context of this chapter, is the immediate transfer of cash. This is provided by the factor on the understanding that when invoices are paid by customers the proceeds will go to them. Factoring is increasingly used by companies of all sizes as a way of meeting cash flow needs induced by rising sales and debtor balances. About 80 per cent of factoring turnover is handled by the clearing bank subsidiaries, e.g. HSBC Invoice Finance, Lloyds TSB and Royal Bank of Scotland Corporate Banking. However, there are dozens of smaller factoring companies. Three closely related services are offered by factors. These are the provision of finance, sales ledger administration and credit insurance.

1 The provision of finance

At any one time a typical business can have a fifth or more of its annual turnover outstanding in trade debts: a firm with an annual turnover of £5m may have a debtor balance of £1m. These large sums create cash difficulties which can pressurise an otherwise healthy business. Factors step in to provide the cash needed to support stock levels, to pay suppliers and generally aid more profitable trading and growth. The factor will provide an advanced payment on the security of outstanding invoices. Normally about 80 per cent of the invoice value can be made available to a firm immediately (with some factors this can be as much as 90 per cent). The remaining 20 per cent is transferred from the factor when the customer finally pays up. Naturally the factor will charge a fee and interest on the money advanced. The cost will vary between clients depending on sales volume, the type of industry and the average value of the invoices. The charge for finance is comparable with overdraft rates (1.5–3 per cent over base rate). As on an overdraft the interest is calculated on the daily outstanding balance of the funds that the borrowing firm has transferred to their business account. Added to this is a service charge that varies between 0.2 per cent and 3 per cent of invoiced sales. This is set at the higher end if there are many small invoices or a lot of customer accounts or the risk is high. **Exhibit 12.15** shows the stages in a typical factoring transaction. First, goods are delivered to the customer and an invoice is sent. Second, the supplier sells the right to receive the invoice amount to a factor in return for, say, 80 per cent of the face value now. Third, some weeks later the customer pays the sum owing, which goes to the factor and finally, the factor releases the remaining 20 per cent to the supplier less interest and fees.

Factors frequently reject clients as unsuitable for their services. The factor looks for 'clean and unencumbered debts' so that it can be reasonably certain of receiving invoice payments. It will also want to understand the company's business and to be satisfied with the competence of its management.

Exhibit 12.15 Stages in a factoring deal

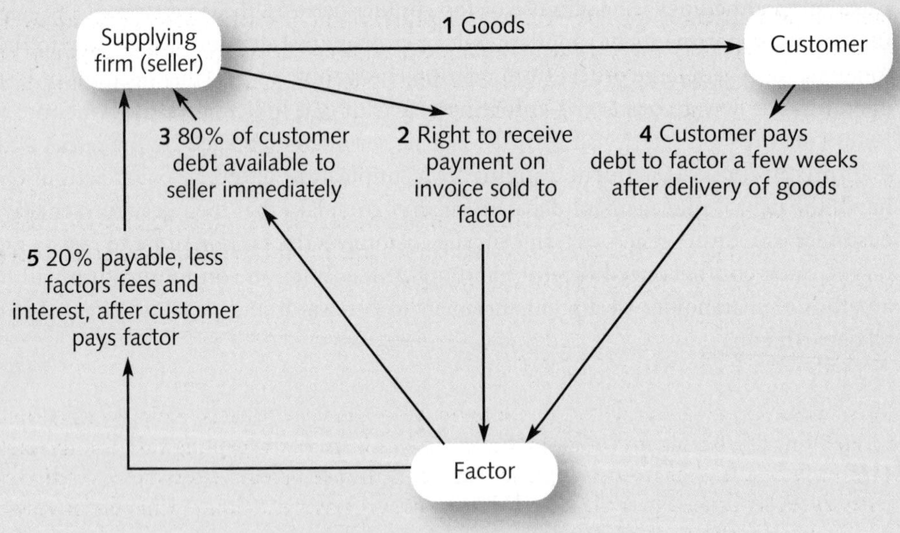

Exhibit 12.16 shows how a factor might calculate the amount to be advanced.

This form of finance has some advantages over bank borrowing. The factor does not impose financial ratio covenants or require fixed asset backing. Also the fear of instant withdrawal of a facility (as with an overdraft) is absent as there is usually a notice period. The disadvantages are the raised cost and the unavailability of factoring to companies with many small-value transactions. Also, some managers say it removes a safety margin. Instead of spending frugally while waiting for customers to pay, they may be tempted to splurge the advance.

Exhibit 12.16

Amount available from a factor

A supplying firm has £1,000,000 of outstanding invoices, £40,000 are so old that the factor will not consider them, £60,000 are rejected as poor quality or are export sales and £30,000 are subject to a dispute between the supplier and the customer. The factor is prepared to advance 80 per cent of suitable invoices:

Total invoices		£1,000,000
Less:		
Debts excessively old	£40,000	
Non-approved	£60,000	
In dispute	£30,000	
		(130,000)
		£870,000

The amount the factor is willing to provide to the supplier immediately is 80 per cent of £870,000, or £696,000 (69.6 per cent of total invoices).

2 Sales ledger administration

Companies, particularly young and fast-growing ones, often do not want the trouble and expense of setting up a sophisticated system for dealing with the collection of outstanding debts. For a fee (0.75–2.5 per cent of turnover) factors will take over the functions of recording credit sales, checking customers' creditworthiness, sending invoices, chasing late payers and ensuring that debts are paid. The fees might seem high, say £100,000 for a firm with a turnover of £5m, but the company avoids the in-house costs of an administrative team and can concentrate attention on the core business. Moreover, factors are experienced professional payment chasers who know all the tricks of the trade (such as 'the cheque is in the post' excuse) and so can obtain payment earlier. With factoring, sales ledger administration and debt collection generally come as part of the package offered by the finance house, unlike with invoice discounting (*see* below).

3 Credit insurance

The third service available from a factor is the provision of insurance against the possibility that a customer does not pay the amount owed. The charge for this service is generally between 0.3 per cent and 0.5 per cent of the value of the invoices.

Recourse and non-recourse

Most factoring arrangements are made on a **non-recourse** basis, which means that the factor accepts the risk of non-payment by the customer firm. For accepting this risk the factor will not only require a higher return but also want control over credit assessment, credit approval and other aspects of managing the sales ledger to ensure payment. Some firms prefer **recourse factoring** in which they retain the risk of customer default but also continue to maintain the relationship with their customers through the debt collection function without the sometimes overbearing intervention of the factor. With confidential invoice factoring the customer is usually unaware that a factor is the ultimate recipient of the money paid over, as the supplier continues to collect debts, acting as an agent for the factor.

Invoice discounting

Firms with an annual turnover under £10m typically use factoring (with sales ledger administration), whereas larger firms tend to use **invoice discounting**. Here invoices are pledged to the finance house in return for an immediate payment of up to 90 per cent of the face value. The supplying company guarantees to pay the amount represented on the invoices and is responsible for collecting the debt. The customers are generally totally unaware that the invoices have been discounted. When the due date is reached it is to be hoped that the customer has paid in full. Regardless of whether the customer has paid, the supplying firm is committed to handing over the total invoice amount to the finance house and in return receives the remaining 10 per cent less service fees and interest. Note that even invoice discounting is subject to the specific circumstances of the client agreement and is sometimes made on a non-recourse basis.

The finance provider usually only advances money under invoice discounting if the supplier's business is well established and profitable. There must be an effective and professional credit control and sales ledger administration system. Charges are usually lower than for factoring because the sales ledger administration is the responsibility of the supplying company. Fees are 0.2 per cent to 0.8 per cent of company sales plus interest comparable with business overdraft rates. Invoice discounting has the advantage over factoring of maintaining the relationship between customer and supplier without the intervention of a finance house. Thus customer records are kept confidential, the customer does not get nervous about its supplier using a factor – often seen (usually wrongly) as a desperate act, indicating financial troubles – and is not excessively pressurised by a forceful debt collector.

Exhibit 12.17 illustrates the importance of factoring to a packaging company.

Exhibit 12.17

Vital factor in surviving slump for SMEs

FT

Invoice discounting is increasingly used to help survive cashflow problems. But it is not suitable for everyone

says Fergal Byrne

In 1991, as recession took hold, Jitu Shukla, managing director of Shukla Packaging, reached the end of his tether. For months, he had struggled to get customers to pay outstanding invoices. That and a change in the production base of the Watford-based wrapping paper and accessories company, requiring 50 per cent advance payment on international production, meant cashflow was becoming critical.

'I was spending all my time chasing debtors [across England] and I was increasingly stressed,' says Mr Shukla. 'Customers were delaying their payments by 15–20 days on average and we were heading for a cashflow crisis.'

His experience is not unusual. In an economic downturn companies can see their payment terms extended by 10–15 days, to potentially disastrous effect, says Philip Mellor, senior analyst at D&B, the business information group. Mr Mellor says that for many smaller businesses, debtor payment after 70 days can wipe out the profit margin.

With his bank manager increasingly nervous about the size of the company's overdraft, Mr Shukla opted for full-service factoring plus credit insurance from Lombard, now part of Royal Bank of Scotland Commercial Services. He worried about how his clients might react but it was a risk worth taking because otherwise the business might fail.

While factoring was relatively rare in the UK then, today some 30,000 companies use it in some form. 'Factoring is a powerful way for companies to make their assets work harder,' says Andrew Pepper, a partner at accountancy firm BDO Stoy Hayward. 'Factors generally advance some 80–90 per cent of a company's debtor ledger compared to a figure of, say, 50 per cent for overdrafts. Factoring is particularly useful for a growing company as the size facility increases as your turnover does.'

For Mr Shukla, the decision to factor receivables was crucial. '[It] transformed the liquidity position of the company. And it has allowed me to focus my attention where it mattered – building relationships with our customers, vital during a downturn, and on new product development.'

Factoring is not suitable for every business. It is unlikely to be offered in sectors such as construction and engineering, where payments are made over extended periods.

Factoring is usually more suitable for companies suffering an adverse cash cycle rather than dealing with bad payers – Shukla Packaging suffered both. Unless a company chooses credit insurance – less than

▶

Exhibit 12.17 continued

10 per cent do – factoring cannot eliminate bad debts. It may, in some cases, exacerbate the underlying problem, says John Anglin, a business adviser working at Entrust, a local enterprise agency in the north-east of England. 'I have seen companies in serious financial trouble when they have had to pay advances back to the factors – money that had already been spent – when a customer defaulted,' he says.

For Mr Shukla, taking out credit insurance with the factoring saved his business when greetings card company Athena collapsed less than a year later, accounting for almost 40 per cent of his receivables.

Shukla's customers tend to pay the factors quicker than they paid Shukla Packaging but this is not always the case. Mike Savich, managing director of steel company Magnemag, found his customers were paying the factoring company later than when he ran his own debtors ledger. This has been a growth constraint as Magnemag was unable to factor new invoices until outstanding invoices were paid.

The cost of the credit management and bill collection service performed by Royal Bank of Scotland Commercial Services has varied between 1–2 per cent of total invoices, which Mr Shukla says 'is a fraction of the cost of hiring a sales ledger clerk and a credit controller to chase debts throughout the UK, not to mention the possible legal costs'.

The interest rate on the company's factoring advances is lower than the rate on its overdraft, which Mr Shukla attributes to the factoring company's better understanding of the underlying business, helping it make a more accurate risk assessment than the bank. But some companies have seen their working capital position deteriorate when the bank has reduced the overdraft facility dramatically, says Eddy Weatherall, of the Independent Banking Advisory Service.

Both the decision to factor and the choice of factoring company need careful consideration. Mr Savich says his factoring contract was long, with lots of legal detail. 'Many companies simply do not have the expertise or the time to fully assess the nature of the deal,' says Mr Savich. 'And it can be difficult to unwind later.'

Source: *Financial Times*, 24 January 2002, p. 12. Reprinted with permission.

Hire purchase

With **hire purchase** the finance company buys the equipment that the borrowing firm needs. The equipment (plant, machinery, vehicles, etc.) belongs to the hire purchase (HP) company. However, the finance house allows the 'hirer' firm to use the equipment in return for a series of regular payments. These payments are sufficient to cover interest and contribute to paying off the principal. While the monthly instalments are still being made the HP company has the satisfaction and security of being the legal owner and so can take repossession if the hirer defaults on the payments. After all payments have been made the hirer becomes the owner, either automatically or on payment of a modest option-to-purchase fee. Nowadays, consumers buying electrical goods or vehicles have become familiar with the attempts of sales assistants to sell an HP agreement also so that the customer pays over an extended period. Sometimes the finance is provided by the same organisation, but more often by a separate finance house. The stages in an HP agreement are as in **Exhibit 12.18**, where the HP company buys the durable good which is made available to the hirer firm for immediate use. A series of regular payments follows until the hirer owns the goods.

Some examples of assets that may be acquired on HP are as follows.

- Plant and machinery
- Business cars
- Commercial vehicles
- Agricultural equipment
- Hotel equipment
- Medical and dental equipment
- Computers, including software
- Office equipment

There are clearly some significant advantages of this form of finance, given the fact that hire purchase together with leasing has overtaken bank loans as a source of finance for business purchases up to £100,000. The main advantages are as follows.

1 ***Small initial outlay*** The firm does not have to find the full purchase price at the outset. A deposit followed by a series of instalments can be less of a cash flow strain. The funds that the company retains by handing over merely a small deposit can be used elsewhere in the business for productive investment. Set against this are the relatively high interest charges (high relative to the rates a large firm can borrow at but can be relatively low for a small firm) and the additional costs of maintenance and insurance.

Exhibit 12.18 The hire purchase sequence

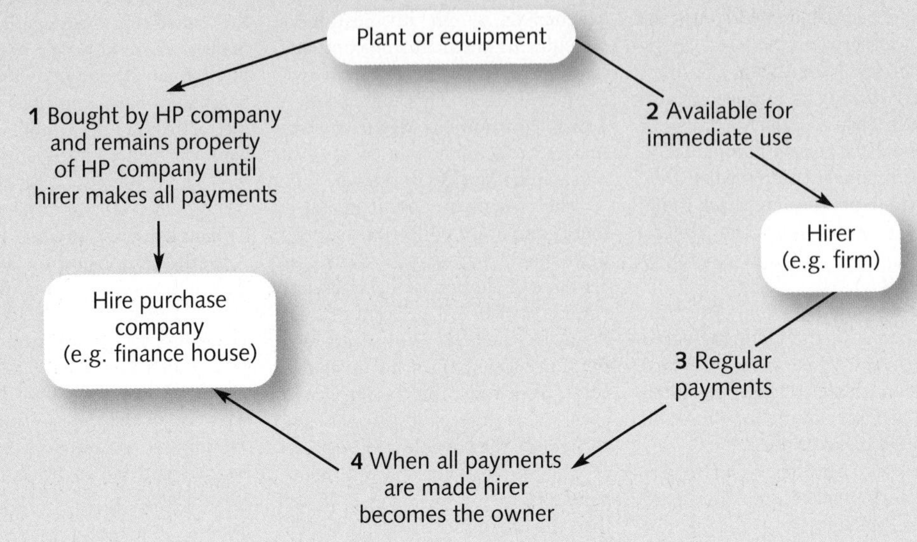

2 ***Easy and quick to arrange*** Usually at point of sale allowing immediate use of the asset.
3 ***Certainty*** This is a medium-term source of finance which cannot be withdrawn provided contractual payments are made, unlike an overdraft. On the other hand the commitment is made for a number of years and it could be costly to terminate the agreement. There are also budgeting advantages to the certainty of a regular cash outflow.
4 ***HP is often available when other sources of finance are not*** For some firms the equity markets are unavailable and banks will no longer lend to them, but HP companies will still provide funds as they have the security of the asset to reassure them.
5 ***Fixed-rate finance*** In most cases the payments are fixed throughout the HP period. While the interest charged will not vary with the general interest rate throughout the life of the agreement the hirer has to be aware that the HP company will quote an interest rate which is significantly different from the true annual percentage rate. The HP company tends to quote the **flat rate**. So, for example, on a £9,000 loan repayable in equal instalments over 30 months the flat rate might be 12.4 per cent. This is calculated by taking the total payments made over the two and a half years and dividing by the original £9,000. The monthly payments are £401.85 and therefore the total paid over the period is £401.85 × 30 = £12,055.50. The flat interest is:

$$\sqrt[2.5]{(12{,}055.50/9{,}000)} - 1 = 0.1240 \text{ or } 12.4\%$$

This would be the true annual rate if the entire interest and capital were repaid at the end of the thirtieth month. However, a portion of the capital and interest is repaid each month and therefore the annual percentage rate (APR) is much higher than the flat rate. As a rough rule of thumb the APR is about double the flat rate. To calculate the APR more accurately annuity tables can be used. The present value (PV) is given as £9,000, the regular payments are £401.85 and we need to find the (monthly) interest rate which makes these 30 future inflows, when discounted, the same as the initial outflow.

$$\text{Present value} = \text{annuity} \times \text{annuity factor}$$

$$9{,}000 = 401.85 \times \text{annuity factor (af)}$$

$$\text{af} = \frac{9{,}000}{401.85} = 22.3964$$

Look along the 30 payments row of the annuity table (*see* Appendix III) to find the interest rate which corresponds with an annuity factor of 22.3964. This is very nearly 2 per cent per month. An interest rate of 2 per cent per month is equivalent to an annual percentage rate of 26.8 per cent, viz.:

$$(1 + m)^{12} = 1 - i$$
$$i = (1 + m)^{12} - 1$$
$$i = (1 + 0.02)^{12} - 1$$
$$i = 0.268 \text{ or } 26.8\%$$

If the writer's experience in buying a car on HP is anything to go by, obtaining the annual percentage rate (APR) from the sales representative is not easy – they tend to be much more interested in talking about the flat rate and emphasising the affordability of the monthly payments. The point is that you need to know the APR in order to compare alternative sources of finance. (Some HP providers are prepared to offer the option of variable rates, which rise and fall with general short-term interest rates, on longer-term agreements.)

6 ***Tax relief*** The hirer qualifies for tax relief in two ways:
   a The asset can be subject to a writing-down allowance (WDA) on the capital expenditure. For example, if the type of asset is eligible for a 25 per cent WDA and originally cost £10,000 the using firm can reduce its taxable profits by £2,500 in the year of purchase; in the second year taxable profits will be lowered by £7,500 × 0.25 = £1,875. If tax is levied at 30 per cent on taxable profit the tax bill is reduced by £2,500 × 0.30 = £750 in the first year, and £1,875 × 0.3 = £562.50 in the second year. Note that this relief is available despite the hirer company not being the legal owner of the asset.
   b Interest payments (an element of the monthly instalment) are deductible when calculating taxable profits.

The tax reliefs are valuable only to profitable companies. Many companies do not make sufficient profit for the WDA to be worth having. This can make HP an expensive form of finance. An alternative form of finance which circumvents this problem (as well as having other advantages) is leasing.

Leasing

Leasing is similar to HP in that an equipment owner (the **lessor**) conveys the right to use the equipment in return for regular rental payments by the equipment user (the lessee) over an agreed period of time. The essential difference is that the **lessee** does not become the owner – the leasing company retains legal title.[3] Subsidiaries of clearing banks dominate the UK leasing market, but many of the world's biggest leasing companies are owned by vehicle manufacturers.

Exhibit 12.19 shows that a typical lease transaction involves a firm wanting to make use of an asset approaching a finance house which purchases the asset and rents it to the lessee.

It is important to distinguish between operating leases and finance leases.

Operating lease

Operating leases commit the lessee to only a short-term contract or one that can be terminated at short notice. These are certainly not expected to last for the entire useful life of the asset and so the finance house has the responsibility of finding an alternative use for the asset when the lessee no longer requires it. Perhaps the asset will be sold in the second-hand market, or it might be leased to another client. Either way the finance house bears the risk of ownership. If the equipment turns

[3] However, with many finance leases, after the asset has been leased for the great majority of its useful life (value), the lessee may have the option to purchase it.

Exhibit 12.19 A leasing transaction

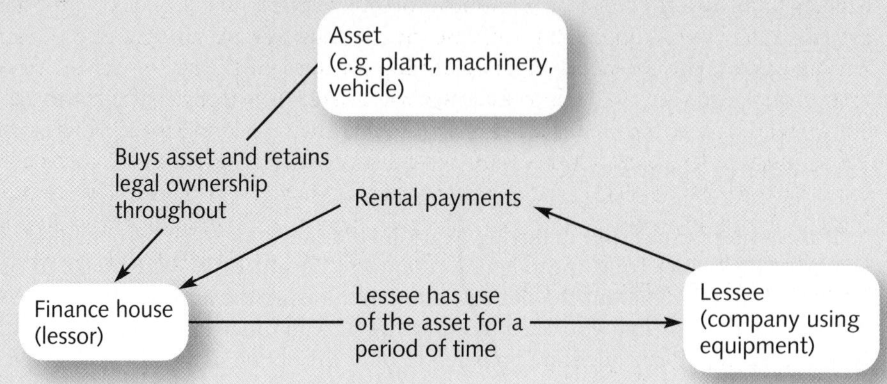

out to have become obsolete more quickly than was originally anticipated it is the lessor that loses out. If the equipment is less reliable than expected the owner (the finance house) will have to pay for repairs. Usually, with an operating lease, the lessor retains the obligation for repairs, maintenance and insurance. It is clear why equipment which is subject to rapid obsolescence and frequent breakdown is often leased out on an operating lease. Photocopiers, for example, used by a university department are far better leased so that if they break down the university staff do not have to deal with the problem. In addition the latest model can be quickly installed in the place of an outdated one. The most common form of operating lease is contract hire. These leases are often used for a fleet of vehicles. The leasing company takes some responsibility for the management and maintenance of the vehicles and for disposal of the vehicles at the end of the contract hire period (after 12 to 48 months).

Operating leases are also useful if the business involves a short-term project requiring the use of an asset for a limited period. For example, building firms often use equipment supplied under an operating lease (sometimes called plant hire). Operating leases are not confined to small items of equipment. There is a growing market in leasing aircraft and ships for periods less than the economic life of the asset, thus making these deals operating leases. Many of Boeing's and Airbus's aircraft go to leasing firms – *see* **Exhibit 12.20** about Boeing selling to International Lease Finance Corporation which will then lease the aircraft to Eos.

Exhibit 12.20

Eos to launch transatlantic fights

FT

By Kevin Done

Eos, the world's first all-business airline, said yesterday it would launch its first transatlantic flights between New York and London on October 18.

The carrier, which has been formed by a team of US aviation entrepreneurs led by David Spurlock, a former senior executive of British Airways, is planning to launch a daily flight between New York's JFK and London Stansted airports.

Mr Spurlock, a former management consultant at Boston Consulting and director of strategy at BA between 1997 and 2001, said the group had secured $85m in equity funding from private equity groups including Golden Gate Capital, Sutter Hill Ventures, and Maveron, a venture capital firm co-founded by Howard Schultz of Starbucks.

It is leasing its initial three aircraft from **International Lease Financial Corporation** with a fleet of three single-aisle Boeing 757s, with 48 seats rather than the 228 seats of an all-economy class configuration.

Source: Financial Times, 4 October 2005, p. 22. Reprinted with permission.

Finance lease

Under a **finance lease** (also called a **capital lease** or a **full payout lease**) the finance provider expects to recover the full cost (or almost the full cost) of the equipment, plus interest, over the period of the lease. With this type of lease the lessee usually has no right of cancellation or termination. Despite the absence of legal ownership the lessee will have to bear the risks and rewards that normally go with ownership: the lessee will usually be responsible for maintenance, insurance and repairs and suffer the frustrations of demand being below expectations or the equipment becoming obsolete more rapidly than anticipated. Most finance leases contain a primary and a secondary period. It is during the primary period that the lessor receives the capital sum plus interest. In the secondary period the lessee pays a very small 'nominal', rental payment. If the company does not want to continue using the equipment in the secondary period it may be sold second-hand to an unrelated company.

Advantages of leasing

The advantages listed for hire purchase also apply to leasing: small initial outlay, certainty, available when other finance sources are not, fixed-rate finance and tax relief. There is an additional advantage of operating leases and that is the transfer of obsolescence risk to the finance provider.

The tax advantages for leasing are slightly different from those for HP. The rentals paid on an operating lease are regarded as tax deductible and so this is relatively straightforward. However, for finance leases the tax treatment is linked to the modern accounting treatment. This is designed to prevent some creative accounting which under the old system allowed a company to appear to be in a better gearing (debt/equity ratio) position if it leased rather than purchased its equipment. In the old days a company could lower its apparent gearing ratio and therefore improve its chances of obtaining more borrowed funds by leasing. Take the two companies X and Y, which have identical balance sheets initially, as shown in **Exhibit 12.21**.

Exhibit 12.21 Off-balance sheet financing

Initial balance sheet for X and Y

Shareholders' funds (net assets)	£1,000,000
Debt capital	£1,000,000
Total assets	£2,000,000

Now if X borrows a further £1m to buy equipment, while Y leases £1m of equipment the balance sheets appear strikingly different under the old accounting rules.

	Company X	Company Y
Shareholders' funds (net assets)	1,000,000	1,000,000
Debt capital	2,000,000	1,000,000
Total assets	3,000,000	2,000,000

Company X has a debt/equity ratio of 200 per cent whereas Y has obtained the use of the asset 'off-balance sheet' and so has an apparent gearing ratio of only 100 per cent. A superficial analysis of these two firms by, say, a bank lender, may lead to the conclusion that Y is more capable of taking on more debt. However, in reality Y has a high level of fixed cash outflow commitments stretching over a number of years under the lease and is in effect highly geared. Furthermore,

Company Y could also show a higher profit to asset ratio despite the fact that the underlying economic position of each firm is almost identical.

Today (under International Accounting Standard 17) finance leases have to be '**capitalised**' to bring them on to the balance sheet. The asset is stated in the balance sheet and the obligations under the lease agreement are stated as a liability. Over subsequent years the asset is depreciated and, as the capital repayments are made to the lessor, the liability is reduced. The profit and loss account is also affected: the depreciation and interest are both deducted as expenses.

The tax authorities apply similar rules and separate the cost of interest on the asset from the capital cost. The interest rate implicit in the lease contract is tax deductible in the relevant year. The capital cost for each year is calculated by allocating rates of depreciation (capital allowances) to each year of useful life.

These new rules apply only to finance leases and not to operating leases. A finance lease is defined (usually) as one in which the present value of the lease payments is at least 90 per cent of the asset's fair value (usually its cash price). This has led to some bright sparks engineering leasing deals which could be categorised as operating leases and therefore kept off-balance sheets – some are designed so that 89 per cent of the value is paid by the lessee. However, the authorities are fighting back as Exhibit 12.22 shows.

Exhibit 12.22

Companies' balance sheets set to get a new lease of life

FT

IASB proposals could signal a shake-up of accounting methods

writes Jeremy Grant

At a congressional hearing in Washington last year, Sir David Tweedie, chairman of the International Accounting Standards Board, drew laughter when he said one of his ambitions was 'actually flying in an aircraft that's on an airline's balance sheet before I die.'

He has long been frustrated by the ability of airlines to run their fleets using certain types of leases whose costs do not have to be fully reflected in their financial statements – preventing investors from seeing the full extent of an airline's debt profile.

But last week, the world's accounting standard-setters signalled an end to this smoke-and-mirrors approach to lease accounting, heralding the first overhaul of the accounting treatment in the multibillion-dollar leasing business since the 1970s.

The IASB, which sets global accounting rules, and its US counterpart, the Financial Accounting Standards Board, met to work out new rules that would force not only airlines, but also retailers, restaurant chains and other users of commercial leases to bring lease assets on to their balance sheets for the first time.

Take Continental Airlines. At the end of 2005, the airline operated 622 aircraft, of which 477 were leased. Long-term debt recorded on Continental's balance sheet was $5bn.

But it also disclosed $11bn in future payments under operating leases for the lifetime of those leases. If this were brought on-balance sheet, Continental's debt could more than double.

With debt off-balance sheet, investors cannot easily see how much capital an airline or retailer is employing, nor the sources of financing for that capital.

Change is coming after a Securities and Exchange Commission report into off-balance sheet financing that discouraged structures 'motivated primarily and largely by accounting and reporting considerations, rather than economics.'

Tom Jones, vice-chairman of the IASB, says: 'There is generally a feeling that lease accounting is very old and not very effective. There's a suspicion that leasing standards have been so carved-up that it's relatively easy to keep stuff off-balance sheet. It's high time standard-setters looked to see if they're appropriate.'

Leasing is an important source of finance, allowing airlines to operate aircraft without owning them, and retailers similarly to operate stores. Under a capital, or finance lease, a company records a liability for rental payments but also records an asset for the property or equipment it is leasing.

But current so-called FAS 13 rules include four criteria that leases can be structured to avoid. This turns the lease into an operating lease – and

▶

Exhibit 12.22 continued

thus is placed off-balance sheet. Critics say this does not reflect the full extent of the liability that the lessee has taken on. They say operating leases are really a type of long-term debt and this obligation should be reflected on the balance sheet. Companies with a large volume of leases are likely to resist change because bringing leases on to the balance sheet could skew the leverage and financial return ratios that affect market valuations and their ability to borrow. Bank loan covenants may also have to be changed.

The Equipment Leasing and Finance Association challenges the idea that the right to use equipment under a lease should be represented in financial statements as an asset, because the lessee has no control over the asset – to sell it, for example.

Kenneth Bentsen, ELFA president, says a 'true lease' is one where a party agrees to provide an asset for use by another party in return for some consideration. However, that consideration does not amortise the cost of the asset the same way as if that asset had been purchased through a loan.

'We think there are some basic tenets that need to he adhered to. There is a clear difference in many cases between a pure operating lease and a true debt instrument where there is a transfer of ownership. That's a significant economic difference,' he says.

As for the airlines, banks that lend to them and Wall Street credit analysts have been aware of the on-balance sheet implications of their operating lease liabilities for years, according to Phil Baggaley, airline analyst at Standard & Poor's.

'Credit analysts are already capitalising off-balance sheet leases and, to a large extent, the equity analysts are – and certainly the banks that lend to them are,' he says. Such analysts typically estimate an airline's operating lease liabilities by plugging the future off-balance sheet lease payments that are listed in the notes to financial statements into financial models.

But accountants say that these future payment figures do not represent the current value of leases, and until such information is brought on to the balance sheet such modelling is too vague to be of real use to investors.

FASB and IASB are expected next year to produce a draft proposal for public comment. A final document would emerge in 2009.

Additional reporting by Barney Jopson in London.

Source: Financial Times, 21 February 2007, p. 28. Reprinted with permission.

A very important tax advantage can accrue to some companies through leasing because of the legal position of the asset not belonging to the lessee. Companies that happen to have sufficient profits can buy assets and then reduce their taxable profits by writing off a proportion of the assets' value (say 25 per cent on a reducing balance) against income each year. However, companies with low profits or those which make a loss are unable to exploit these investment allowances fully and the tax benefit can be wasted. But if the equipment is bought by a finance company with plenty of profits, the asset cost can be used to save on the lessor's tax. This benefit can then be passed on to the customer (the lessee) in the form of lower rental charges. This may be particularly useful to start-up companies and it has also proved of great value to low- or no-profit privatised companies. For example, the railway operating companies often make losses and have to be subsidised by the government. They can obtain the services of rolling stock (trains, etc.) more cheaply by leasing from a profit-generating train-leasing company than by buying. Another advantage is that the leasing agreement can be designed to allow for the handing back of the vehicles should the operating licence expire or be withdrawn (as the train-operating licences are – after seven years or so).

To buy or to lease?

A comparison of the relative costs of leasing through a finance lease and purchase through a bank loan is in practice a very complicated calculation. It is necessary to allow for the cost of capital and the tax treatment of alternative sources of finance. These, in turn, depend on the precise circumstances of the company at the time. It is further complicated by the timing of the tax payments and reliefs, by who pays for maintenance and the potential for a residual value of the asset at the end of the primary lease period. Added to all of that is the problem that the tax rules change frequently and so a method of calculation applicable at one time is quickly out of date. The point is that a proper comparison requires highly specialised knowledge and so is beyond the scope of this book. However, if a few simplifying assumptions are made the general principles can be conveyed easily. The simplifying assumptions are:

a Taxation does not exist.

b There is no value in the asset at the end of the lease period.

c The cost of capital applicable to the equipment is the same as the term loan interest rate; this is only valid if investors regard the lease and the bank loan as being perfect substitutes for each other with respect to the capital structure (gearing, etc.) and the riskiness of the cash flows.

Armed with these assumptions we can assess whether it is better for The Quissical Games Company to lease or to buy.

Worked example 12.2 Quissical Games Company

The Quissical Games Company needs £10m of equipment to increase its production capacity. A leasing company has offered to purchase the equipment and lease it to Quissical for three annual lease payments of £3.8m, with the first payable immediately, the second at the beginning of the second year and the third at the beginning of the third year. The equipment will have a three-year useful life at the end of which it will have a zero scrap value. A bank has offered to lend £10m on a three-year term loan at a rate of interest of 10 per cent p.a. Which form of finance should Quissical accept?

This problem may be analysed on an incremental cash flow basis, that is, focusing on the differences in the cash flows – as shown in Exhibit 12.23.

Exhibit 12.23 Quissical's lease versus buy decision (£m)

	Points in time (yearly intervals)		
	0	1	2
Lease rentals	–3.80	–3.80	–3.80
Cash flows associated with buy option	10.00		
Incremental cash flows (lease vs. buy)	+6.20	–3.80	–3.80
Present value of incremental cash flows at 10%	+6.20	–3.4545	–3.1405
Net present value	–0.395		

The cash flows associated with the lease option have a present value which is £395,000 more than £10m when discounted at 10 per cent and therefore the lease is the more expensive method of finance.

Of course, in reality the tax payments are likely to have a significant impact on the relative merits of a bank loan and leasing finance, but this depends on Quissical's tax position, the time delay in paying tax, the current tax rates, the capital allowance permitted and so on.

Exhibit 12.24 demonstrates the extent to which the availability of lease finance affects the working lives of millions of people even in the poorest countries on earth, where it is seen as playing an important role in lifting people out of poverty.

Bills of exchange

A **bill** is a document which sets out a commitment to pay a sum of money at a specified point in time. The simplest example is an ordinary bank cheque which has been dated two weeks hence. The government borrows by selling **Treasury bills** which commit it to paying a fixed sum in, say, three months. Local authorities issue similar debt instruments, as do commercial organisations in the form of commercial bills (discussed in Chapter 11).

Exhibit 12.24

IFC extends leasing aid to Vietnam

FT

The International Finance Corporation, the private sector arm of the World Bank, has announced its first foray in Vietnam's financial sector – the establishment of a leasing company to enable small and medium-sized companies to procure capital goods.

On the surface the $15m loan and $750,000 equity investment looks modest. However, the corporation has been promoting leasing as one of the quickest, cheapest and most flexible ways of supporting business in emerging economies, where businesses desperately need machinery, office and plant equipment.

The IFC is planning to sign a joint venture deal on November 12 to set up the first leasing company in Egypt.

The new Vietnamese company, Vietnam International Leasing Company (VILC), is expected to write leases of $25,000–$30,000 for smaller or micro enterprises and $100,000–$150,000 for medium-sized companies. IFC says VILC will have 'a strong impact on Vietnam's financial sector by extending and improving credit delivery and introducing new financial products to the local market to encourage capital formation and investment'...

IFC has been working closely with governments, advising them on leasing regulations, recruiting sponsors and technical partners and investing in new leasing companies.

An IFC paper, issued in August, said one-eighth of the world's private investment was financed through leasing. Its share is soaring; in some countries it provides as much as one-third of the private investment.

IFC has helped set up leasing companies in over half of the developing countries. In August it provided $5.6m in financing to help establish Uzbek Leasing International, the first specialised leasing company in Uzbekistan.

The corporation also helps leasing companies, in which it has equity, to expand. Last March it guaranteed a local currency loan of $3m equivalent for the Industrial Development Leasing Company of Bangladesh, established in 1986.

IFC's involvement allows the company to borrow locally for a longer period than otherwise would be possible.

IFC's first leasing venture was in 1977 in Korea. The Korea Development Leasing Corporation is now the world's fifth largest leasing industry.

Source: Nancy Dunne, *Financial Times*, 1 November 1996, p. 5. Reprinted with permission.

Bills of exchange are mainly used to oil the wheels of overseas trade. They have a long history helping to promote international trade, particularly in the nineteenth and twentieth centuries. The seller of goods to be transported to a buyer in another country frequently grants the customer a number of months in which to pay. The seller will draw up a bill of exchange (called a '**trade acceptance**' in international trade) – that is, a legal document is produced showing the indebtedness of the buyer. The bill of exchange is then forwarded to, and accepted by the customer, which means that the customer signs a promise to pay the stated amount and currency on the due date. The due date is usually 90 days later but 30, 60 or 180 days bills of exchange are not uncommon. The bill is returned to the seller who then has two choices, either to hold it until maturity, or to sell it to a bank or discount house (the bill is discounted). Under the second option the bank will pay a lower amount than the sum to be received in, say, 90 days from the customer. The difference represents the bank's interest.

For example, if a customer has accepted a bill of exchange which commits it to pay £200,000 in 90 days the bill might be sold by the supplier immediately to a discount house or bank for £194,000. After 90 days the bank will realise a profit of £6,000 on a £194,000 asset, an interest rate of 3.09 per cent ((6,000/194,000) × 100) over 90 days. This gives an approximate annual rate of:

$$(1.0309)^4 - 1 = 0.1296 = 12.96\%$$

Through this arrangement the customer has the benefit of the goods on 90 days credit, the supplier has made a sale and immediately receives cash from the discount house amounting to 97 per cent of the total due. The discounter, if it borrows its funds at less than 12.9 per cent, turns in a healthy profit. The sequence of events is shown in **Exhibit 12.25**.

Bills of exchange are normally only used for transactions greater than £75,000. The effective interest rate charged by the discounter is a competitive 1.5 per cent to 4 per cent over interbank

Exhibit 12.25 The bill of exchange sequence

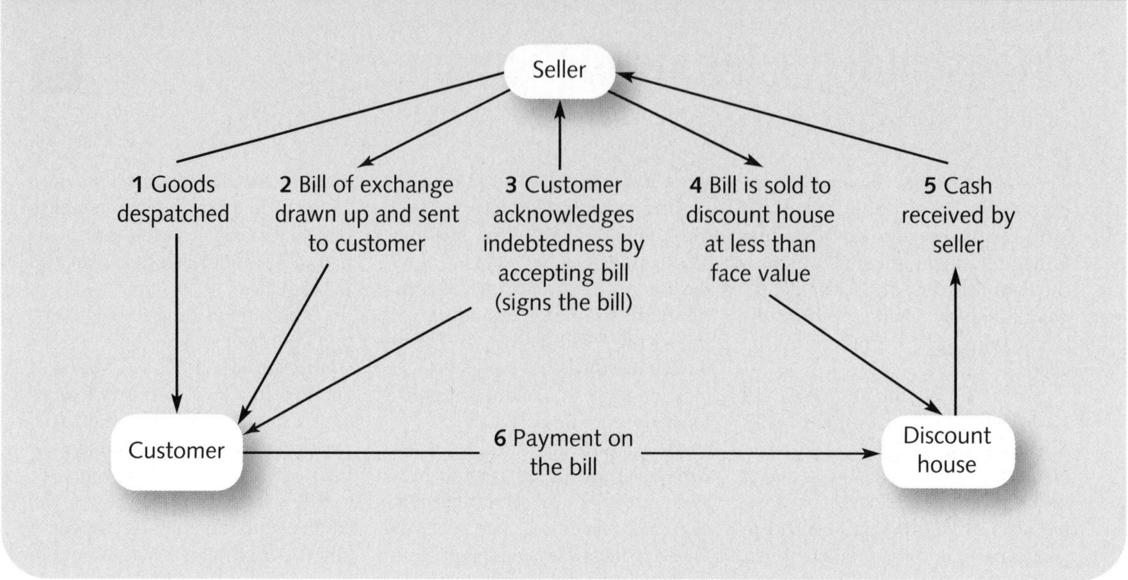

lending rates (for example, LIBOR) depending on the creditworthiness of the seller and the customer. The bank has recourse to both of the commercial companies: if the customer does not pay then the seller will be called upon to make good the debt. This overhanging credit risk can sometimes be dealt with by the selling company obtaining credit insurance. Despite the simplification of Exhibit 12.25 many bills of exchange do not remain in the hands of the discounter until maturity but are traded in an active secondary market (the money market). Note also that not all bills of exchange are a form of temporary finance. Some are '**sight drafts**', that is, payable on demand without a delay of a few days (as with '**time drafts**' or '**term drafts**').

Acceptance credits (bank bills or banker's acceptance)

In the case of **acceptance credits** the company which is in need of finance requests the drawing up of a document which states that the signatory will pay a sum of money at a set date in the future. This is 'accepted' by a bank rather than by a customer. (Simultaneously the company makes a commitment to pay the accepting bank the relevant sum at the maturity date of the bill.) This bank commitment to pay the holder of the acceptance credit can then be sold in the money markets to, say, another bank (a discounter) by the firm to provide for its cash needs. (Alternatively an importing company could give the acceptance credit to its overseas supplier in return for goods – and the supplier can then sell it at a discount if required.) The acceptance credit is similar to a bill of exchange between a seller and a buyer, but now the organisation promising to pay is a reputable bank representing a lower credit risk to any subsequent discounter. These instruments therefore normally attract finer discount rates than a trade bill. When the maturity date is reached the company pays the issuing bank the value of the bill, and the bank pays the ultimate holder of the bill its face value.

The company does not have to sell the acceptance credit immediately and so can use this instrument to plug finance gaps at opportune times. There are two costs of bank bill finance.

1 The bank charges acceptance commission for adding its name to the bill.
2 The difference between the discount price and the acceptance credit's due sum.

These costs are relatively low compared with those on overdrafts and there is an ability to plan ahead because of the longer-term commitment of the bank. Unfortunately this facility is only available in hundreds of thousands of pounds and then only to the most creditworthy of companies. **Exhibit 12.26** summarises the acceptance credit sequence.

Exhibit 12.26 An acceptance credit sequence

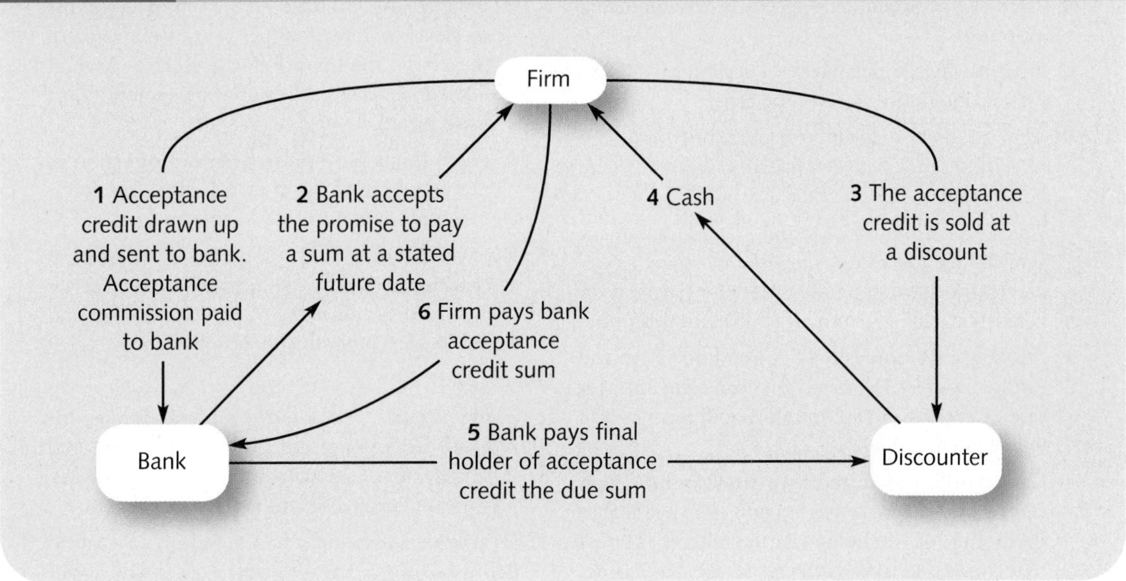

Concluding comments

The modern corporation has a rich array of alternative sources of funds available to it. Each organisation faces different circumstances and so the most appropriate mixture will change from one entity to another. Of the dozens of forms of finance discussed in this chapter and Chapters 10 and 11 any organisation is unlikely to select more than five or six. However, the knowledge gained by reading these chapters and considering the relative merits of each type will, it is hoped, lead to a more informed choice and contribute to the achievement of the firm's objective. The quick revision sheet that follows, covering the sources of finance, shows how far we have come (*see* **Exhibit 12.27**).

Exhibit 12.27 Some of the types of finance available to the firm

Equity

1 **Ordinary shares** Owners of the firm. Full rights to vote at general meetings. Entitled to dividend and surplus on liquidation. High risk – residual income.

2 **Deferred ordinary shares** Ordinary shares rank for payment of an agreed rate of dividend before deferred ordinary shares receive anything.

3 **Non-voting shares** Used to raise equity finance without losing control over the firm.

4 **Founders' shares** Dividends paid only after all other categories of equity shares have received fixed rates of dividend.

5 **Share warrants** Entitlement to buy a stated number of shares at a specific price up to a certain date. Often attached to loan stocks.

Preference shares

No voting rights (usually), except in liquidation. Entitled to a fixed and relatively certain dividend. Priority over ordinary shares in dividends and liquidation. Types:

- cumulative – if dividend is missed it is carried over and paid when firm is sufficiently profitable;
- participating – some or all of the dividend is related to corporate performance;
- redeemable – a fixed maturity date for capital repayment;
- convertible – can be converted into ordinary shares at a specific rate and price;
- variable rate – dividend depends on movements in benchmark, e.g. LIBOR.

Retained profits and reserves

The most important source of finance. Funds reinvested from previous years' profits.

Long-term debt

1 **Debenture (secured loan stock/bond)** A legal document showing the right to receive interest and a capital repayment. Often tradable (negotiable). Types:

▶

- 'fixed-charge debenture'– specific asset nominated as security;
- 'floating-charge debenture' – security is all the present and future assets of the firm;
- 'zero coupon' – no interest paid, but there is a large difference between initial payment for the bond and redemption value.

2 **Unsecured loan stock/bond** Legal document showing right to receive interest and capital repayment. Low down in pecking order for payment on liquidation. Rate of return higher than for debenture.

3 **Floating-rate note (FRN)** A bond on which the rate of interest is linked to short-term interest rates, e.g. three- or six-month London Interbank Offered Rate, LIBOR.

4 **Convertible unsecured loan stock/bond** Loan stock which can be converted into equity capital at the option of the holder. Lower rate of interest than for debentures. Interest is tax deductible. Often self-liquidating.

5 **Bank loan** Term lending at fixed or floating rates (1–6 per cent above base rate). Arrangement fees at, say, 1 per cent of loan. Usually secured – guarantees by directors or charge over assets. Covenants usually required – e.g. target interest cover ratios or limits on further borrowing. Types:

- 'Bullet' loan – one final payment of capital.
- 'Balloon' loan – low repayments in early periods followed by high repayment rate in later period.
- 'Mortgage' style – regular repayment of equal amount.
- 'Grace periods' often available with low or no repayment.

6 **Syndicated lending** A group of banks provide a large loan.

Medium-term

1 **Bank loans** As above except period is one to seven years.

2 **Medium-term notes (MTNs)** A promise to pay a certain sum on a named date. Unsecured. Maturity: 9 months–20 years. Sold on to the financial markets usually as part of a series under an MTN programme. Fixed, floating or zero interest rates.

3 **Floating rate notes (FRNs)** Promissory notes with a floating interest rate, e.g. linked to LIBOR. Used particularly in the Euromarkets.

4 **Leasing** An equipment owner conveys the right to use the equipment in return for rental payments over an agreed period. Avoids up-front lump-sum payment. Available when other sources exhausted. Tax advantages.

- Finance (capital) lease – covers entire useful life of asset (or at least 90 per cent of the value of the asset); the finance house receives back at least 90 per cent of the outlay plus interest over lease period.
- Operating lease – only covers a proportion of the useful life of the asset, e.g. plant hire, photocopier, cars.

5 **Hire purchase** An HP company purchases an asset which is used by the hirer, who after a series of payments becomes the owner. Convenient and available when other finance is not.

Short-term

1 **Trade credit** Delaying payment for goods received. Very important source, convenient and informal. Not necessarily free: consider opportunity cost of losing discount for early settlement.

2 **Overdraft** Allowing a bank account to go into debit position. Easy to arrange, flexible, but repayable on demand.

3 **Factoring** Raising funds on the security of the company's debts. Services available:

- Provision of finance – factor advances up to 90 per cent of value of debts. When invoices are paid the remaining 10 per cent less charges is paid to firm by factor. Fee plus interest at 1.5–3 per cent over base.
- Sales ledger administration, dispatching invoices and ensuring bills are paid. Fee: 0.75 to 2.5 per cent.
- Credit insurance.
- Confidential invoice factoring – customer is unaware that the debts have been sold. Customer sends payment to supplier, not to factor.

4 **Invoice discounting** Stages:

   1 Firm sends invoice to finance house (FH) and firm guarantees that invoice will be paid.

   2 FH pays up to 90 per cent of invoice amount to firm.

   3 Three months later (say) the firm collects debt from customer and pays FH.

   Cost: 1–6 per cent over base.

5 **Deferred tax payments** Interval between earning of profits and payment of taxes produces cash availability.

6 **Commercial paper** Paper (a legal document expressing loan terms) with a maturity of seven days to nine months.

7 **Bill of exchange** A buyer sends a promise to pay a sum of money at a future date to a supplier. The

bill can then be sold before the set date to a bank or discount house for cash. Useful for overseas trade. (Analogy: post-dated cheque.)

8 **Acceptance credit (bank bills)** A bank promises to pay out the amount of a bill at a future date. The firm then sells the bill. On maturity the bank pays the holder and the firm pays the bank.

9 **Revolving underwriting facility (RUF)** A bank underwrites the borrower's access to funds at a specified rate in the short-term financial markets throughout an agreed period.

10 **Revolving credit facility** A firm is able to borrow from a bank(s) up to a fixed amount for, say, 5 years. The borrower may repay, say, after 2 years, but already has agreement to reborrow up to the stated limit in the remaining 3 years.

Other

1 **Mezzanine finance and high-yield bonds** High-yielding loan or bond, usually with equity warrants attached. Low security/high risk. Useful for restructuring, buyouts and leveraged takeovers. Interest rate 2 to 9 per cent over LIBOR. Usually no secondary market. Types:

- strip financing – the firm obtains a variety of different types of mezzanine, with different costs, maturity and risk;
- stepped interest – lower repayments early on;
- junior mezzanine – ranking below senior mezzanine;
- high-yield (junk) bonds – high-risk bonds.

The definition of mezzanine can be stretched to preference shares and convertible loans subordinate to the secured debt.

2 **Private equity/Venture capital** Funding for new businesses or MBOs, etc. Specialist funds and banks are principal suppliers. High failure rate, therefore high return required. Finance provider is usually looking for exit route in five to ten years.

3 **Sale and leaseback** Sale of property, etc. to investment institution and then renting back.

4 **Mortgaging property** Available from insurance companies, investment companies and pension funds.

5 **Euromarkets** Informal (unregulated) markets in money (deposits and lending) held outside its country of origin.

6 **Eurobonds** International bonds sold outside the jurisdiction of the country of the currency in which the issue is denominated. No formal regulatory framework. Interest paid before tax. Usually bearer bonds. Usually cheaper than domestic bonds. Large sums available.

7 **Securitisation** A package of financial claims, e.g. the right to receive payments from 1,000 households for 25 years, is sold. Assets securitised include: commercial paper, mortgages, car loans, credit card receivables and export credits.

8 **Export finance** Documentary Letters of Credit. The purchaser's (importer's) bank undertakes to pay the exporter. Also overdraft, loans, acceptance credits.

9 **Forfaiting** A bank purchases a series of sales invoices or promissory notes from an exporting company given to it by an importer. Usually the importer's bank guarantees the invoices.

10 **Project finance** Medium-term borrowing for a particular purpose. The bank's security is the project itself, e.g. North Sea oil projects.

Key points and concepts

- **Overdraft** A permit to overdraw on an account up to a stated limit.

  Advantages:
  - flexibility;
  - cheap.

  Drawbacks:
  - bank has right to withdraw facility quickly;
  - security is usually required.

- **A bank usually considers the following before lending:**
  - the projected cash flows;
  - creditworthiness;
  - the amount contributed by borrower;
  - security.

- **Term loan** A loan of a fixed amount for an agreed time and on specified terms, usually one to seven years.
- **Trade credit** Goods delivered by suppliers are not paid for immediately.
- The **early settlement discount** means that taking a long time to pay is not cost free.
- **Advantages of trade credit:**
  - convenient, informal and cheap;
  - available to companies of any size.
- **Factors determining the terms of trade credit:**
  - tradition within the industry;
  - bargaining strength of the two parties;
  - product type;
  - credit standing of individual customers.
- **Trade debtors** are sales made on credit as yet unpaid. The management of debtors requires a trade-off between increased sales and costs of financing, liquidity risk, default risk and administration costs.
- **Debtor management** requires consideration of the following:
  - credit policy;
  - assessing credit risk;
  - agreeing terms;
  - collecting payment;
  - integration with other disciplines.
- **Factoring companies** provide at least three services:
  - providing finance on the security of trade debts;
  - sales ledger administration;
  - credit insurance.
- **Invoice discounting** is the obtaining of money on the security of book debts. Usually confidential and with recourse to the supplying firm. The supplying firm manages the sales ledger.
- **Hire purchase** is an agreement to hire goods for a specified period, with an option or an automatic right to purchase the goods at the end for a nominal or zero final payment.

  The main advantages:
  - small initial outlay;
  - certainty;
  - available when other sources of finance are not;
  - fixed-rate finance;
  - tax relief available.
- **Leasing** The legal owner of an asset gives another person or firm (the lessee) the possession of that asset to use in return for specified rental payments. Note that ownership is not transferred to the lessee.
- **An operating lease** commits the lessee to only a short-term contract, less than the useful life of the asset.
- **A finance lease** commits the lessee to a contract for the substantial part of the useful life of the asset.
- **Advantages of leasing:**
  - small initial outlay;
  - certainty;
  - available when other finance sources are not;
  - fixed rate of finance;

- tax relief (operating lease: rental payments are a tax-deductible expense; finance lease: capital value can be written off over a number of years; interest is tax deductible. Capital allowance can be used to reduce tax paid on the profit of a finance house, which then passes on the benefit to the lessee);
- avoid danger of obsolescence with operating lease.

- **Bills of exchange** A trade bill is the acknowledgement of a debt to be paid by a customer at a specified time. The legal right to receive this debt can be sold prior to maturity, that is discounted, and thus can provide a source of finance.

- **Acceptance credit** A financial institution or other reputable organisation accepts the promise to pay a specified sum in the future to a firm. The firm can sell this right, that is discount it, to receive cash from another institution.

References and further reading

International Accounting Standards Board (2007) IAS17 Leases.
Details on the accounting regulations.

Bank of England, www.bankofengland.co.uk.
Numerous useful publications on sources of finance for businesses.

Berry, A. *et al.* (1990) 'Leasing and the smaller firm', The Chartered Association of Certified Accountants, Occasional Research Paper No. 3.
Empirical evidence on the use of leasing by small firms – discussion of the influences leading to the decision to lease.

Better Payment Practice Group (1998) 'Better payment practice' (www.payontime.co.uk).
Some practical advice for those granting trade credit and those accepting trade credit.

Buckley, A. (2004) *Multinational Finance.* 5th edn. Harlow: FT Prentice Hall.
Contains some easy-to-follow descriptions of types of finance available to firms.

Clark, T.M. (1978) *Leasing.* Maidenhead: McGraw-Hill.
Old but still useful – easy to read.

Credit Management Research Centre, Leeds University Business School (2005) Credit policy in the UK economy. Prepared for the Small Business Service (www.payontime.co.uk).
Full of facts and figures on trade credit.

Drury, J.C. and Braund, S. (1990) 'The leasing decision: A comparison of theory and practice', *Accounting and Business Research*, Summer, pp. 179–91.
Survey evidence on the reasons why companies choose to lease assets.

Finance and Leasing Association (FLA) Annual Report. London: FLA.
Gives some insight into HP and leasing in the UK, www.fla.org.uk.

James, A.N.G. and Peterson, P.P. (1984) 'The leasing puzzle', *Journal of Finance*, September.
An investigation of the extent to which leases displace debt. An economic modelling approach.

Maness, T.S. and Zietlow, J.T. (1993) *Short-term financial management.* St Paul, MN: West Publishing Company.
Debtor management is explained in greater detail than in this chapter.

Ross, S.A., Westerfield, R.W. and Jaffe, J. (2004) *Corporate Finance.* 6th international edn. New York: McGraw-Hill.
Chapter 29 considers debtor management.

Wilson, N. and Summers, B. (2002) 'Trade credit terms offered by small firms: survey evidence and empirical analysis', *Journal of Business Finance and Accounting* 29 (3) and (4), April/May, pp. 317–51.
Useful UK survey data and disccussion.

Websites

Bank of England www.bankofengland.co.uk
Better Payments Practice Group www.payontime.co.uk
British Bankers Association www.bba.org.uk

Companies House. www.companieshouse.gov.uk
Department for Business, Enterprise and Regulatory Reform www.berr.gov.uk
Dun and Bradstreet www.dbuk.dnb.com
Factors and Discounters Association www.factors.org.uk
Federation of Small Businesses www.fsb.org.uk
Finance and Leasing Association www.fla.org.uk
International Accounting Standards Board www.iasb.org
National Statistics www.statistics.gov.uk

Video presentations

Chief executives and fianance directors describe their current policy on raising funds on Cantos.com (www.cantos.com/cantos) – this is free to view.

Case study recommendations

Please see www.pearsoned.co.uk/arnold for case study synopses

- Cartwright Lumber. Author: Thomas R. Piper (2004) Harvard Business School.
- Health Development Corporation. Author: Richard S. Ruback (2003) Harvard Business School.

Self-review questions

1 What are the essential differences between an overdraft and a term loan?

2 What do banks take into account when considering the granting of an overdraft or loan?

3 Describe a circumstance in which an overdraft is preferable to a term loan from the borrower's point of view.

4 'Taking a long time to pay suppliers' invoices is always a cheap form of finance.' Consider this statement.

5 What are the main determinants of the extent of trade credit granted?

6 In assessing whether to grant trade credit to a customer what would you take into account and what information sources would you use?

7 Discuss the advantages and disadvantages of offering an early settlement discount on an invoice from the supplier's point of view.

8 What are the main features of a good debtor collection system?

9 What is hire purchase and what are the advantages of this form of finance?

10 Explain the difference between the flat rate of interest on a hire purchase agreement quoted by a sales representative and the annual percentage rate.

11 How does hire purchase differ from leasing?

12 Explain the terms 'operating lease' and 'finance lease'.

13 How can lease finance be used to create off-balance-sheet debt? How are leases accounted for today?

14 What are the tax advantages of leasing an asset?

15 What is a bill of exchange and what does discounting a bill mean?

16 For what type of firms are acceptance credits useful?

Questions and problems

myfinancelab **Questions with an icon are also available for practice in MyFinanceLab with additional supporting resources.**

For questions marked with an asterisk, the answers are provided in the Lecturer's Guide.

1 Ronsons plc, the jewellery retailer, has a highly seasonal business with peaks in revenue in December and June. One of Ronsons' banks has offered the firm a £200,000 overdraft with interest charged at 10% p.a. (APR) on the daily outstanding balance, with £3,000 payable as an arrangement fee. Another bank has offered a £200,000 loan with a fixed interest rate of 10% p.a. (APR) and no arrangement fee. Any surplus cash can be deposited to earn 4% APR. The borrowing requirement for the forthcoming year is as follows:

Month	J	F	M	A	M	J	J	A	S	O	N	D
£000s	0	180	150	180	200	0	150	150	180	200	200	0

Which offer should the firm accept? ?

2 Snowhite plc has taken delivery of 50,000 units of Dwarf moulds for use in its garden ornament business. The supplier has sent an invoice which states the following:

'*£50,000 is payable if the purchaser pays in 30 days. However, if payment is within 10 days, a 1 per cent discount may be applied.*'

Snowhite has an unused overdraft facility in place, on which interest is payable at 12 per cent annual percentage rate on the daily outstanding balance. If Snowhite paid after 10 days the overdraft facility would have to be used for the entire payment.

a Calculate whether to pay on the 30th day or on the 10th day, on the basis of the information provided.

b Despite the 30-day credit limit on the contract Snowhite is aware that it is quite normal in this industry to pay on the 60th day without incurring a penalty legally, financially or in terms of reputation and credit standing. How does this alter your analysis? ?

3 (*Examination level*) Gordons plc has an annual turnover of £3m and a pre-tax profit of £400,000. It is not quoted on a stock exchange and the family owning all the shares have no intention of permitting the sale of shares to outsiders or providing more finance themselves. Like many small and medium-sized firms, Gordons has used retained earnings and a rolled-over overdraft facility to finance expansion. This is no longer seen as adequate, especially now that the bank manager is pushing the firm to move to a term loan as its main source of external finance.

You, as the recently hired finance director, have been in contact with some financial institutions. The Matey hire purchase company is willing to supply the £1m of additional equipment the firm needs. Gordons will have to pay for this over 25 months at a rate of £50,000 per month with no initial deposit.

The Helpful leasing company is willing to buy the equipment and rent it to Gordons on a finance lease stretching over the four-year useful life of the equipment, with a nominal rent thereafter. The cost of this finance is virtually identical to that for the term loan, that is, 13 per cent annual percentage rate.

Required

Write a report for the board of directors explaining the nature of the four forms of finance which may be used to purchase the new equipment: hire purchase, leasing, bank term loan and overdraft. Point out their relative advantages and disadvantages.

4 The Biscuit company has taken delivery of £10,000 of flour from its long-established supplier. Biscuit is in the habit of paying for flour deliveries 50 days after the invoice/delivery date. However things are different this time: the supplier has introduced an early settlement discount of 2 per cent if the invoice is paid within 10 days. The rate of interest being charged on Biscuit's overdraft facility is 11 per cent per annum. You may assume no tax to avoid complications.

Required

Calculate whether Biscuit should pay on the 10th day or the 50th day following the invoice date. **?**

5* The Snack company is considering buying £30,000 of new kitchen equipment through a hire purchase agreement stretching over 18 months. £10,000 is paid as a deposit and the hire purchase company will require 18 monthly payments of £1,222.22 each to pay for the £20,000 borrowed, before the ownership of the equipment is transferred to the snack company. The rate of interest the Snack company would pay on an overdraft is 10 per cent per annum.

Required

a Calculate the annual percentage rate paid on the hire purchase contract.
b Discuss the relative merits and drawbacks of the two forms of finance mentioned in the question. **?**

6 The Cable Company sells its goods on six months' credit which until now it has financed through term loans and overdrafts. Recently factoring firms have been pestering the managing director, saying that they can offer him immediate cash and the chance to get rid of the hassle of collecting debts. He is very unsure of factoring and has requested a report from you outlining the main features and pointing out the advantages and hazards. Write this report.

7 A small firm is considering the purchase of a photocopier. This will cost £2,000. An alternative to purchase is to enter into a leasing agreement known as an operating lease, in which the agreement can be terminated with only one month's notice. This will cost £60 per month. The firm is charged interest of 12 per cent on its overdraft.

Required

Consider the advantages and disadvantages of each method of obtaining the use of a photocopier.

8 Write an essay with the title: 'Small firms find it more difficult to raise finance than larger firms'.

9 (*Examination level*) A factoring company has offered a one-year agreement with Glub Ltd to both manage its debtors and advance 80 per cent of the value of all its invoices immediately a sale is invoiced. Existing invoices will be eligible for an immediate 80 per cent cash payment.

The annual sales on credit of Glub are £6m spread evenly through the year, and the average delay in payment from the invoice date is at present 80 days. The factoring company is confident of reducing this delay to only 60 days and will pay the remaining 20 per cent of invoice value to Glub immediately on receipt from the customer.

The charge for debtor management will be 1.7 per cent of annual credit turnover payable at the year-end. For the advance payment on the invoices a commission of 1 per cent will be charged plus interest applied at 10 per cent per annum on the gross funds advanced.

Glub will be able to save £80,000 during this year in administration costs if the factoring company takes on the debtor management. At the moment it finances its trade credit through an overdraft facility with an interest rate of 11 per cent.

Required

Advise Glub on whether to enter into the agreement. Discuss the relative advantages and disadvantages of overdraft, factoring and term loan financing. **?**

10 Acorn presently sells on 60 days' credit. Is it financially attractive for a customer to accept a 1.5 per cent discount for payment on the 14th day, given an annual percentage rate of interest of 9 per cent, or continue to take 60 days with no discount? **?**

11 (*Examination level*) Extracted data from Penguin plc's last accounts are as follows:

	£m
Annual sales	21
Profits before interest and tax	2
Interest	0.5
Shareholder funds	5
Long-term debt	4
Debtors	2.5
Stocks	2
Trade creditors	5
Bank overdraft	4

A major supplier to Penguin offers a discount of 2 per cent on all future supplies if payment is made on the seventh day following delivery rather than the present 70th day. Monthly purchases from this supplier amount to a regular £0.8m.

Penguin pays 15 per cent annual percentage rate on its overdraft.

Required

a Consider what Penguin should do with respect to this supplier.

b Suggest steps that Penguin could take to improve the balance sheet, profit and loss and cash flow position. **?**

12* (*Examination level*) Oxford Blues plc has standard trade terms requiring its customers to pay after 30 days. The average invoice is actually paid after 90 days. A junior executive has suggested that a 2.5 per cent discount for payment on the 20th day following the invoice date be offered to customers.

It is estimated that 60 per cent of customers will accept this and pay on the 20th day, but 40 per cent will continue to pay, on average, on the 90th day.

Sales are £10m per annum and bad debts are 1 per cent of sales.

The company's overdraft facility costs 14 per cent per annum.

The reduced collection effort will save £50,000 per annum on administration and bad debts will fall to 0.7 per cent of turnover.

Required

a Should the new credit terms be offered to customers?

b What are the main considerations you would give thought to in setting up a good credit management system?

?

13 What sources of information would you access to assess the creditworthiness of a customer? What systems would you install to try to obtain prompt payment?

14 Explain some of the reasons for the growth in the hire purchase and leasing industry round the world over the past two decades.

15 Explain why a loss-making company is more likely to lease an asset than to buy it.

myfinancelab *Now retake your diagnostic test for Chapter 12 to check your progress and update your study plan.*

Assignments

1 Consider some of the items of equipment that your firm uses and investigate the possibility of alternative methods of financing/obtaining the use of those assets. Write a report outlining the options with their advantages and disadvantages, fully costed (if possible) and make recommendations.

2 Investigate the debtor management policy of a firm with which you are familiar. Write a report contrasting current practice with what you consider to be best practice. Recommend action.

3 If a firm familiar to you is at present heavily reliant on bank finance, consider the relative merits of shifting the current balance from overdraft to term loans. Also consider the greater use of alternative forms of short-term or medium-term finance.

4 Obtain a representative sample of recently paid invoices. Examine the terms and conditions, calculate the benefit of paying early and recommend changes in policy if this seems appropriate.

CHAPTER 13

Treasury and working capital management

LEARNING OUTCOMES

This chapter covers a wide range of finance issues, from cheque clearance to optimum inventory models. Matters such as the use of derivatives to reduce interest rate risk or foreign exchange risk have entire chapters devoted to them later in the book and so will be covered in a brief fashion here to give an overview. By the end of this chapter the reader should be able to:

- describe the main roles of a treasury department and the key concerns of managers when dealing with working capital;
- comment on the factors influencing the balance of the different types of debt in terms of maturity, currency and interest rates;
- show awareness of the importance of the relationship between the firm and the financial community;
- demonstrate how the treasurer might reduce risk for the firm, perhaps through the use of derivative products;
- understand the working capital cycle, the cash conversion cycle and an inventory model.

myfinancelab *Complete your diagnostic test for Chapter 13 now to create your personal study plan*

Introduction*

The last few chapters have been concerned with describing the various types of finance available and the markets on which they trade. This is valuable knowledge, but it is not enough to run an organisation efficiently. We need decision makers who are knowledgeable about the markets and instruments so that they can help guide the firm in selecting the appropriate balance in sourcing finance, and can take steps to reduce the risk associated with that finance. As well as dealing with major financial moves treasurers help with many small and short-term finance-related decisions. Despite being individually small and often routine, they are collectively extremely important for the well-being of the firm and the achievement of its goals. This chapter provides a brief overview of the role of the corporate treasurer, which includes involvement in many long-term decisions, but, because other chapters cover issues such as financial gearing or mergers, its main focus is on the shorter-term management of working capital. Working capital decisions are usually handled by line managers, but specialists, such as accountants or treasurers, may assist.

An example of the sort of question that needs to be addressed in this area is, what should the organisation do with any temporary surplus cash? Should it merely be deposited in a bank account or should the firm be more adventurous and try to obtain a higher return by placing the funds in the money market? But then, what about the increased risk and loss of liquidity associated with some forms of lending?

Another area for action is the creation of a system which does not allow cash to lie idle or be unnecessarily tied up in, say, inventories of partially finished goods or debtors. The firm, naturally, has to put money into these areas to permit production and gain sales, but this should be kept at an optimum level, bearing in mind that money has an opportunity cost. The estimation of that optimum is far from easy. For instance, managers know that raw material and work-in-progress inventory are needed at a sufficiently high level to prevent the problems associated with running out of stock, for example through production stoppages and lost sales, but they do not want to incur the excessive costs of storage, deterioration and interest charges associated with warehouses full of stock piled up to prevent all risks of a stock-out. The difficult management task is to strike a balance of risks and costs and work out a policy for appropriate stock levels and reordering.

The quality of day-to-day interaction with banks, shareholders and other finance providers is also vitally important. Thought and time have to be devoted to cultivating these relationships. Any one encounter with, or information flow to, these backers may be regarded as insignificant, but cumulatively an image of a business is created in the minds of some very influential people. Ideally that image needs to be professional and purposeful and to show a sound grasp of the competitive positioning and potential of the firm. A poor image can lead to increased cost of funds, the blocking of expansion and, in extreme cases, the removal of managers.

There are some other fundamental financing problems where the knowledge and experience of the corporate treasurer may also be drawn upon. For example, how does the firm obtain a balance between short-term and long-term borrowing, and how could the firm finance a merger?

The treasurer is additionally given the task of managing the risk associated with interest rate and exchange rate change. So a UK firm may sell £1m of goods to a Canadian importer on six months' credit invoiced in dollars. What the UK firm does not know is the quantity of sterling it will receive when in six months it converts the dollars into pounds. The treasury department will have a range of approaches available to remove the uncertainty and reassure other managers that the export deal will be a profitable one. Similarly, skilled individuals within the treasury will be able to hedge interest rate risk; that is, make arrangements which reduce the potential for interest rate movements to impact adversely on the firm.

---

*I am grateful to Martin O'Donovan and James Lockyer of the Association of Corporate Treasurers for making some valuable suggestions for improvement of this chapter.

These and many other duties involve small, short-term decisions in the main, but can make or break a company. *The Economist* described the treasury function as 'the financial engine room of companies',[1] meaning that these decisions do not necessarily have the grandeur and broad sweep of the decisions made on the bridge of the corporate ship but they are vital to maintaining its progress. This becomes all too tragically apparent when things go wrong in the engine room and companies founder due to poor working capital management, to running out of cash despite high profits or to losing a fortune on the derivative markets.

The need for good treasury management and working capital management has been with us ever since business began. They both focus on liquid resources (cash flow) and they both take into account risk. Few businesses, even the simplest, can afford to ignore the importance of the efficient planning and control of cash resources while allowing for risk. In small and medium-sized firms both functions will usually be undertaken by the chief accountant and his/her team. As firms grow it usually becomes necessary to appoint specialist staff skilled in treasury while maintaining a team dedicated to helping to ensure high-quality **working capital** decisions.

Working capital can be defined as the difference between current assets and current liabilities.

Working capital thus means net current assets, or net current liabilities (if current liabilities exceed current assets). It is the investment a company makes in assets which are in continual use and are turned over many times in a year. Working capital encompasses the following:

- Short-term resources:
  - inventory;
  - debtors;
  - investments (marketable securities);
  - cash.

Less:

- Short-term liabilities:
  - trade creditors;
  - short-term borrowing;
  - other creditors repayable within a year.

The main areas of treasury and working capital management

Treasurers carry out a wide range of activities, from raising long-term finance to reducing interest rate risk. **Exhibit 13.1** shows the main issues addressed by treasurers or by line managers dealing with inventory, debtors, creditors and cash resources.

The way in which the organisation is structured, and roles assigned to individuals to undertake these kinds of decisions, vary tremendously but the fundamental questions and the need for action remain. These are illustrated in Exhibit 13.1, where the overarching groups of issues to be addressed are shown. The first two, financing and risk management, are usually in the domain of the specialist treasury department, in collaboration with other senior managers, in large multinational firms. The third, working capital and liquidity management, will require some input from the treasury team, especially for the investment of temporary cash, but many of these issues will be examined by line managers with the assistance of the finance and accounting team. The areas of responsibilities covered by either the treasurer or the **financial controller** (the head of the group concerned more with accounting issues rather than finance) will be unique for every firm, and the list in Exhibit 13.1 is far from exhaustive, but at least it provides a framework for considering the myriad decisions in this area.

[1] *The Economist*, 16 November 1996, p. 131.

Exhibit 13.1 The main areas of treasury and working capital management

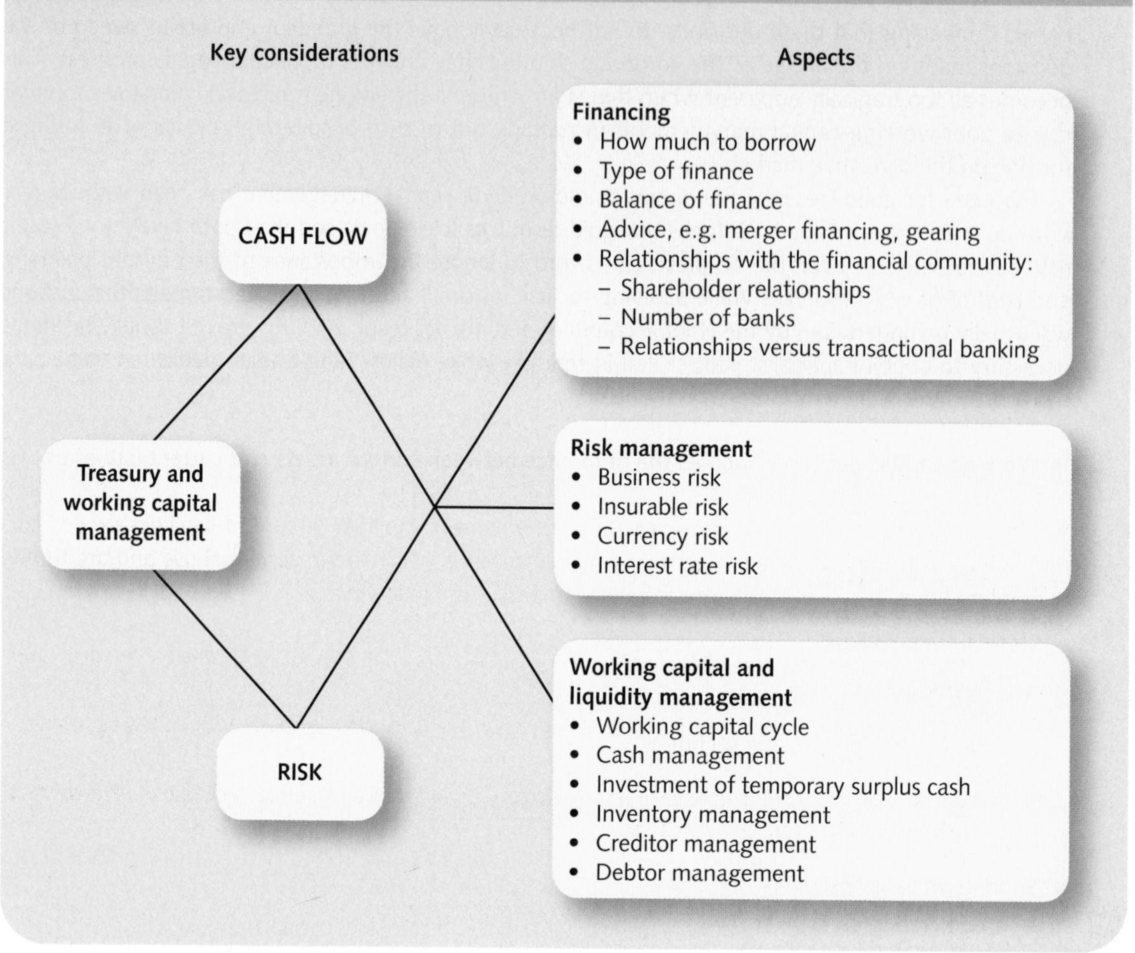

Exhibit 13.1 provides a guide for progress through this chapter but it must be noted that treasurers (leaving to one side the working capital specialists for the moment) must have knowledge of, and contribute toward, a wider range of corporate issues than those in Exhibit 13.1. The Association of Corporate Treasurers regard as key topics those listed in **Exhibit 13.2**.

Case study 13.1 gives some insight into the importance of the treasury department to one of the largest firms in the world, Cadbury Schweppes (Chapters 24 and 25 explain the terms and techniques discussed in the article).

The former treasurer at Glynwed International plc (now Aga Foodservice Group plc), Christopher Purser, put quite a heavy emphasis on investor relations when describing the purpose of his job:[2] 'To plan, organise and control the Glynwed International group's cash and borrowings so as to optimise interest and currency flows and minimise the cost of funds. To plan and execute communications programmes to enhance investors' confidence in Glynwed International's performance in the stock markets.' He lists five primary job accountabilities:

1 Manage the Group's cash and currency flows so as to:
   – minimise interest paid;
   – maximise interest earned;
   – minimise foreign currency exposure.

2 Ensure that sufficient funds are available at acceptable rates to meet the Group's cash flow requirements internationally.

---

[2] Given at a special lecture at Aston Business School, 'The Purpose of a Treasurer', 13 February 1997.

Exhibit 13.2 Corporate treasury subjects

Capital markets and funding
- Equity
- Debt capital markets
- Bank lending
- Trade finance
- Asset & project finance
- Credit ratings

Corporate financial management
- Capital structure
- Corporate strategy
- Business valuation
- Investment appraisal
- Regulation and law
- Accounting and reporting
- Taxation

Treasury operations and controls
- Treasury organisation
- Policy and objectives
- Control and reporting
- Technology and systems
- The treasury professional

Cash and liquidity management
- Cash management
- Short term liquidity
- Cashflow forecasting
- Payment and clearing systems

Risk management
- Managing risk
- Business and operational risk
- FX risk
- Interest rate risk
- Commodity risk
- Credit risk
- Pensions risk
- Exotic risks

Source: Reprinted with kind permission of the Association of Corporate Treasurers (www.treasurers.org).

3 Control, monitor and report the level of the Group's borrowings against available facilities and budgets.

4 Ensure that key financial analysts, fund managers and investors are aware of the Group's financial objectives and performance.

5 Ensure that investors' confidence in the Group is enhanced through knowledge of and contact with the Group's top management.

Case study 13.1 Cadbury Schweppes' treasury risk management

Treasury Risk Management

We are exposed to market risks arising from our international business. Derivative financial instruments are utilised to lower funding costs, to diversify sources of funding, to alter interest rate exposures arising from mismatches between assets and liabilities or to achieve greater certainty of future costs.

(i) Liquidity Risk

We seek to achieve a balance between certainty of funding even at difficult times for the markets or ourselves and a flexible, cost-effective borrowings structure. The policy, therefore, seeks to ensure that at a minimum all projected net borrowing needs are covered by committed facilities. Also, the objective for debt maturities is to ensure that the amount of debt maturing in any one year is not beyond our means to repay and refinance. To this end the policy provides that at least 75% of year end net debt should have a maturity of one year or more and at least 50%, three years or more. Committed but undrawn facilities are taken into account for this test.

(ii) Interest Rate Risk

We have an exposure to interest rate fluctuations on our borrowings and manage these by the use of interest rate swaps, cross currency interest rate swaps and forward rate agreements. The objectives for the mix between fixed and floating rate borrowings are set to reduce the impact of an upward change in interest rates while enabling benefits to be enjoyed if interest rates fall. Thus the policy sets minimum and maximum levels of the total of net debt and preferred securities permitted to be at fixed rates in various time bands, ranging from 50% to 100% for the period up to six months, to 0% to 30% when over five years.

Case study 13.1 Continued

(iii) Currency Risk

We operate internationally giving rise to exposure from changes in foreign exchange rates, particularly the US dollar. We do not hedge translation exposure and earnings because any benefit obtained from such hedging can only be temporary.

We seek to relate the structure of borrowings to the trading cash flows that service them and our policy is to maintain broadly similar fixed charge cover ratios for each currency bloc. Also, the ratio for any currency bloc may not fall below two times in any calendar year. This is achieved by raising funds in different currencies and through the use of hedging instruments such as swaps.

We also have transactional currency exposures arising from our international trade. Our policy is to take forward cover for all forecasted receipts and payments for as far ahead as the pricing structures are committed, subject to a minimum of three months' cover.

Source: Cadbury Schweppes, Report and Accounts 2005.

Financing

Obtaining the most appropriate mixture of finance is likely to be of great importance to most firms. In this section we first examine the most appropriate forms of borrowing in terms of maturity of that borrowing, for example a short-term overdraft or a 20-year loan, as well as considering the question of the currency of the borrowing and the choice of fixed or floating interest rates; secondly, we look at retained earnings as a source of finance; and thirdly, we consider the more 'strategic' type of financing issues for which a treasurer might be called upon to give advice. There follows a commentary on the importance of maintaining good relationships with the financial community.

Is it better to borrow long or short?

Once a company has decided to raise funds by borrowing, it then has to decide whether to raise the money through:

a short-term debt – a loan which has to be repaid within, say, one year;

b medium-term debt; or

c long-term debt – where the loan is paid over a 7-, 25- or even 100-year period.

There are a number of factors to be taken into consideration in making a decision of this nature.

- ***Maturity structure*** A company will usually try to avoid having all of its debts maturing at or near the same date. It could be disastrous if the firm was required to repay loan capital on a number of different instruments all within, say, a six-month period. Even if the firm is profitable the sudden cash outflow could lead to insolvency.

  Most companies include a breakdown of length of time to maturity of their debts in their annual report. The profile for Vodafone is shown in **Exhibit 13.3** (taken from the accounts for 2006).
- ***Costs of issue/arrangement*** It is usually cheaper to arrange an overdraft and other one-off short-term finance than long-term debt facilities, but this advantage is sometimes outweighed by the fact that if funds are needed over a number of years short-term debt has to be renewed more often than long-term debt. So over, say, a 20-year period, the issuing and arrangement costs of short-term debt may be much greater than for a 20-year bond.
- ***Flexibility*** Short-term debt is more flexible than long-term debt. If a business has fluctuations in its needs for borrowed funds, for example if it is a seasonal business, then for some months it does not need any borrowed funds, whereas at other times it needs large loans. A long-term loan may be inefficient because the firm will be paying interest even if it has surplus cash. True,

Exhibit 13.3 An example of a company conscious of the necessity for a range of maturity dates for debt – Vodafone plc

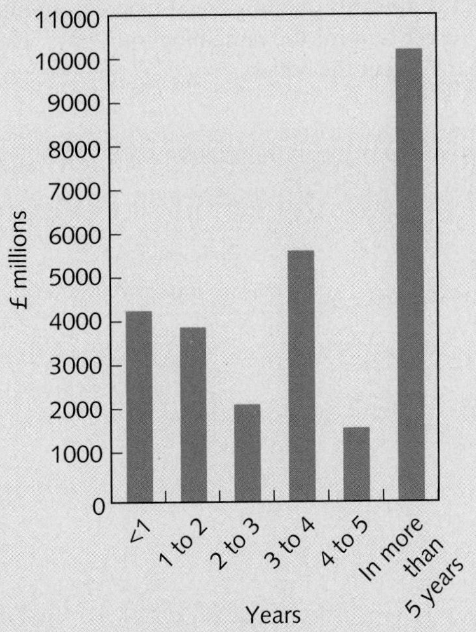

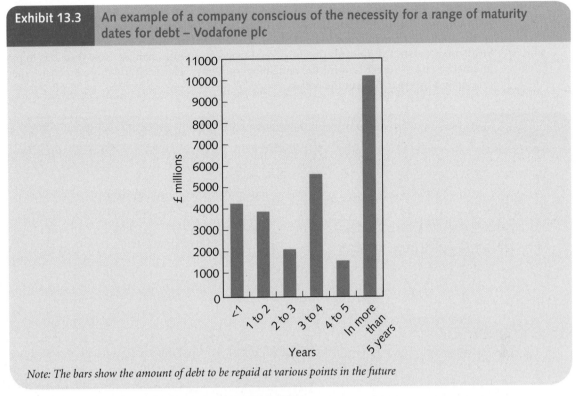

Note: The bars show the amount of debt to be repaid at various points in the future

(*Source:* Based on Vodafone Annual Report and Accounts 2006.)

the surplus cash could be invested but the proceeds are unlikely to be as great as the cost of the loan interest. It is cheaper to take out short-term loans or overdrafts when the need arises which can be paid back when the firm has high cash inflows.

- ***The uncertainty of getting future finance*** If a firm is investing in a long-term project which requires borrowing for many years it would be risky to finance this project using one-year loans. At the end of each year the firm has to renegotiate the loan or issue a new bond. There may come a time when lenders will not supply the new money. There may, for example, be a change in the bank's policy or a reassessment of the borrower's creditworthiness, a crisis of confidence in the financial markets or an imposition of government restrictions on lending. Whatever the reason, the project is halted and the firm loses money.

  Thus, to some extent, the type of project or asset that is acquired determines the type of borrowing. If the project or asset is liquid and short term then short-term finance may be favoured. If it is long term then longer-term borrowing gives more certainty about the availability of finance, and (possibly) the interest rate.

- ***The term structure of interest rates*** The yield curve is described in Chapter 11. There it is stated that it is usual to find interest rates on short-term borrowing which are lower than on long-term debt. This may encourage managers to borrow on a short-term basis. In many circumstances this makes sense. Take the case of Myosotis plc, which requires £10m of borrowed funds for a ten-year project. The corporate treasurer expects long-term interest rates to fall over the next year. It is therefore thought unwise to borrow for the full ten years at the outset. Instead the firm borrows one-year money initially with the expectation of replacing the loan at the end of the year with a nine-year fixed-rate loan at the then reduced rate.

  However, there are circumstances where managers find short-term rates deceptively attractive. For example, they might follow a policy of borrowing at short-term rates while the yield curve is still upward sloping, only switching to long-term borrowing when short-term rates rise above long-term rates. Take the case of Rosa plc, which wishes to borrow money for five years and faces the term structure of interest rates shown in the lower line of **Exhibit 13.4**. If it issued one-year bonds the rate of return paid would be 7 per cent. The returns required on four-year and five-year bonds are 8 per cent and 8.3 per cent respectively. The company opts for a one-year bond with the expectation of issuing a four-year bond one year later. However by the time the financing has to be replaced, 365 days after the initial borrowing, the entire yield curve has shifted upwards due to general macroeconomic changes. Now Rosa has to pay an interest rate of 10 per cent for the remaining four years. This is clearly more expensive than arranging a five-year bond at the outset.

Exhibit 13.4 **A shifting yield curve affects the relative cost of long- and short-term borrowing – the example of Rosa plc**

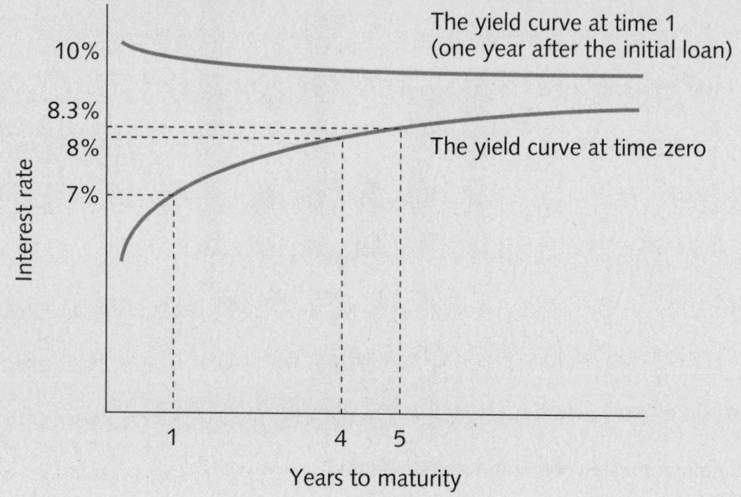

The case of Rosa shows that it can be cheaper to borrow long at low points in the interest rate cycle despite the 'headline' interest charge on long-term debt being greater than on short-term loans.[3]

The article in **Exhibit 13.5** discusses the problem of being too reliant on short-term debt as well as the willingness of companies to pay a higher interest rate to obtain longer-term debt.

To 'match' or not to 'match'?

Firms usually come to the conclusion that there is a need for an appropriate mixture of debt finance with regard to length of time to maturity: some short-term borrowing is desirable alongside some long-term borrowing. The major factors which need to be taken into account in achieving the right balance are: **a** cost (interest rate, arrangement fee, etc.) and **b** risk (of not being able to renew borrowings, of the yield curve shifting, of not being able to meet a sudden outflow if the maturity is bunched, etc.). Some firms follow the '**matching' principle**, in which the maturity structure of the finance matches the maturity of the project or asset. Here fixed assets and those current assets which are needed on a permanent basis (for example cash, minimum inventory or debtor levels) are financed through long-term sources, while current assets whose financing needs vary throughout the year are financed by short-term borrowings. Examples of the latter type of asset might be stocks of fireworks at certain times of the year, or investment in inventories of chocolate Easter eggs in the spring.

Thus there are three types of asset which need to be financed:

- fixed assets;
- permanent current assets;
- fluctuating current assets.

[3] There are ways of locking in interest rates in years 2, 3, 4 and 5 through the use of derivatives – *see* Chapter 24.

Exhibit 13.5

Pay now, live later is the new mantra of borrowing

Many companies are opting to face big bills in order to extend the terms of their loans

says Aline van Duyn

AOL Time Warner last week replaced $6bn (£4.2bn) of short-term debt with long-dated bonds, at a stroke adding millions of dollars to its annual interest payments.

Far from being unusual, the internet and media company's bond-financing exercise – the proceeds of which were used to repay bank loans and commercial paper – is just the latest example of a company choosing to pay higher interest in order to obtain debt with longer-dated maturities, usually between three and 30 years.

Whilst the economics of such transactions would have seemed unattractive to finance officers only six months ago, many now feel that they cannot afford not to lengthen their debt profile and diversify their funding.

Since the collapse of energy group Enron last year, investors and analysts have started to scrutinise company balance sheets more closely and debt markets have become more volatile.

'The greater volatility in the short-term capital markets has led treasurers to be more conservative with regard to funding,' said Ray Murphy, treasurer at AOL Time Warner.

The periodic closure of the commercial paper market to large global companies when concerns about their credit worthiness have surfaced has pushed company liquidity into focus for bond and equity investors – and the rating agencies – both in the US and Europe.

Tyco, Global Crossing, Qwest and ABB are just some examples of companies that have had billions of dollars wiped off their valuations amid concerns about access to short-term funds. A lack of liquidity affects both sentiment and a company's credit-worthiness, and can result in sharp cuts in credit ratings.

'The debt and equity markets have proved that they will punish companies which have an over-reliance on short-term liquidity sources rather than a more balanced reliance on longer-term liquidity sources,' says Andrew Cooley, head of debt capital markets at Bank of America Securities in Europe.

Bankers argue that it would have been worthwhile for these companies and others in similar situations to pay higher rates of interest in order to secure longer-term funds and avoid a short-term liquidity crunch . . .

'In a booming environment, commercial paper and bank lines are easily available,' says May Busch, head of corporate debt at Morgan Stanley. 'Now, companies realise the dangers when the availability of credit is suddenly reduced. Terming out debt is like buying an insurance policy, and is now seen worth paying for.'

Source: *Financial Times*, 9 April 2002, p. 23. Reprinted with permission.

A firm taking the maturity matching approach is considered to be adopting a moderate stance. This is shown in **Exhibit 13.6**, where a rising level of total assets is financed principally through increases in long-term finance applied to fixed assets and permanent current assets. The fluctuating current assets, such as those related to seasonal variations, are financed with short-term funds.

A more aggressive approach is represented in **Exhibit 13.7**. This entails more risk because of the frequent need to refinance to support permanent current assets as well as fluctuating current assets. If the firm relied on an overdraft for this it would be vulnerable to a rapid withdrawal of that facility. If stocks and cash are reduced to pay back the overdraft the firm may experience severe disruption, loss of sales and output, and additional costs because of a failure to maintain the minimum required working capital to sustain optimum profitability.

The low-risk policy is to make sure that long-term financing covers the total investment in assets. If there are times of the year when surplus cash is available this will be invested in short-term instruments. This type of policy is shown in **Exhibit 13.8**.

Many managers feel much happier under the conservative approach because of the lower risk of being unable to pay bills as they arise. However, such a policy may not be in the best interests of the owners of the firm. The surplus cash invested in short-term securities is unlikely to earn a satisfactory return relative to the cost of the long-term funds. In all likelihood shareholders would be better off if the firm reduced its long-term financing, by returning cash to shareholders or paying off some long-term loans.

Exhibit 13.6 Moderate financing policy stance – the matching principle

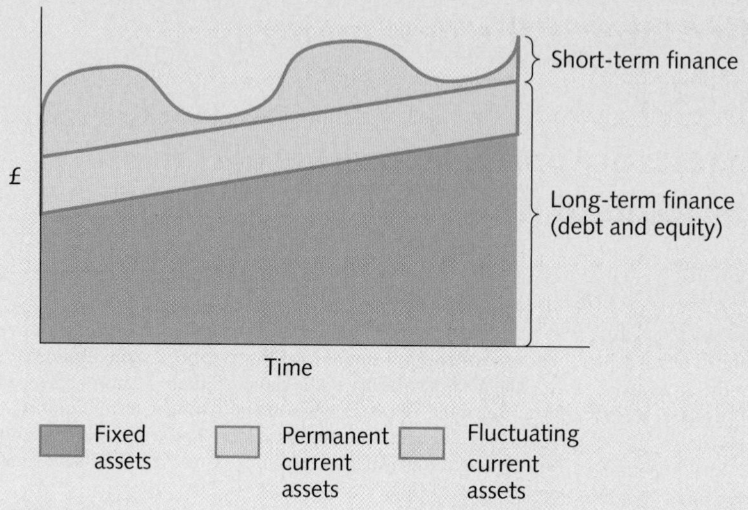

Exhibit 13.7 An aggressive financing policy

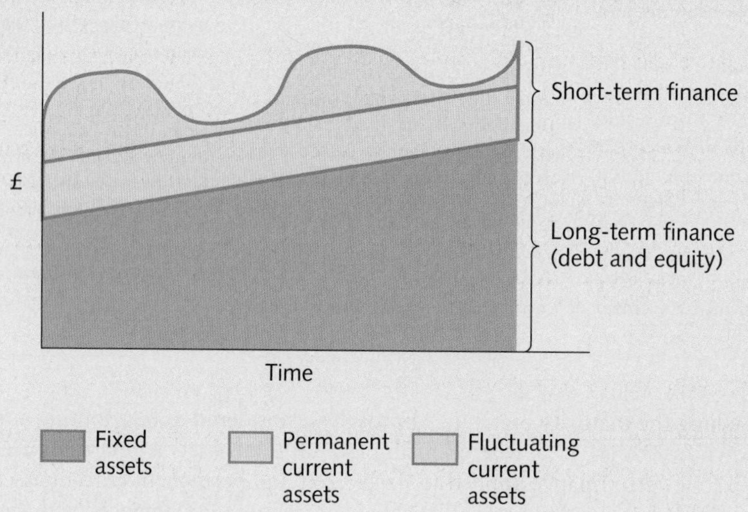

There is no sound theoretical formula to help decide the balance between long- and short-term finance but many managers seem to follow a policy of matching the maturity of their assets and liabilities, thereby accepting a modest level of risk while avoiding excessive amounts of surplus investible funds. However, this is far from universally accepted: for example, Microsoft had over $34bn of cash and short-term investments in 2006.

The currency of borrowing

Deciding on the maturity structure of the firm's debt is one aspect of the financing decision. Another is selecting the currency in which to borrow. For transnational firms it is common to find borrowing in the currency of the country where the funds are to be invested (as described by Cadbury Schweppes on page 518). This can reduce exposure to foreign exchange rate changes. For

Exhibit 13.8 A conservative financing policy

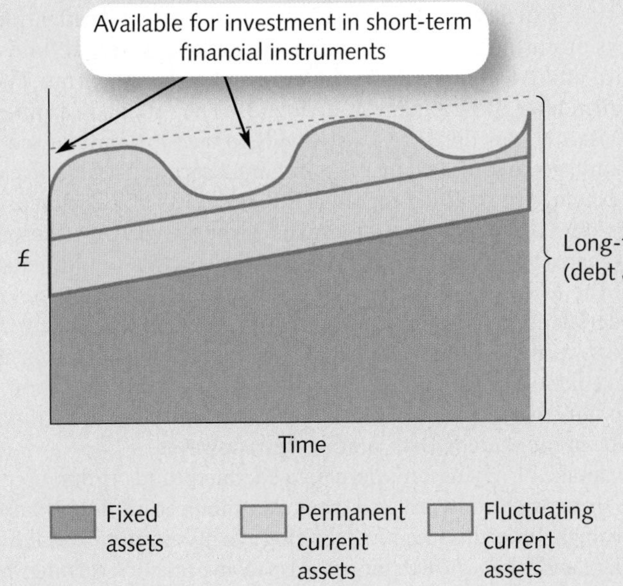

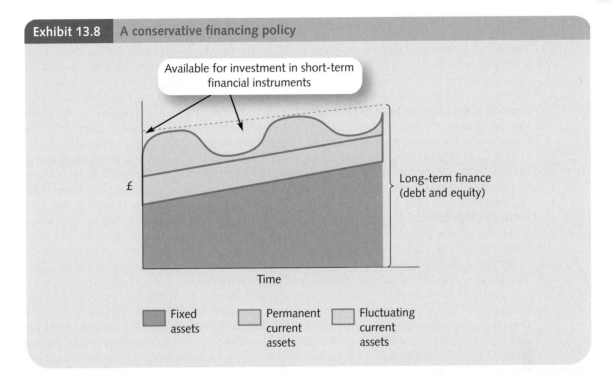

example, suppose that Union Jack plc borrows £100m to invest in the USA. It exchanges the £100m into $150m at the exchange rate of $1.5 to the pound. The net cash flows in subsequent years are expected to be $30m per annum. If the exchange rate remained constant Union Jack would therefore receive £20m per year to pay for the financing costs and produce a surplus. However, if the rate of exchange moved to $2 for every pound the annual cash inflow in sterling terms would be merely £15m.[4] The project is producing £5m less than originally anticipated despite generating the same quantity of dollars, and this is insufficient as a rate of return for Union Jack. The risk attached to this project can be reduced by ensuring that the liabilities are in the same currency as the income flow. So if Union Jack borrows $150m to invest in the project, even though the exchange rate may move to $2 : £1 the project remains viable. Currency risk is considered in more detail in Chapter 25.

The interest rate choice

Another consideration for the debt portfolio is the balance to be struck between fixed and floating interest-rate borrowings. In many circumstances it is thought advisable to have a mixture of the two types of borrowing. If all the borrowings are floating rate then the firm is vulnerable to rising interest rates. This often happens at the most unfortunate times: for example, at the start of recessions interest rates are usually high at the same time as sales are in decline.

Industries with high fixed-cost elements, which need a large volume of sales to maintain profitability, may be particularly averse to floating-rate borrowing as this may add to their cost base and create an additional source of risk. Even if they have to pay more for fixed-rate borrowing initially, the directors may sleep better knowing that one element of risk has been eliminated.

On the other hand, if all borrowing is fixed rate the firm is unable to take advantage of a possible decline in interest rates. Other aspects of the debate about fixed or floating rates were considered in Chapter 12.

[4] Assume no hedging in the derivative or money markets.

Retained earnings as a financing option

Internally generated funds from previous years' profits are the most important source of long-term finance for the typical firm, and yet it is so easily overlooked while attention is focused on the more glamorous ways of raising funds in the financial markets. **Internal funds** typically account for between one-third and two-thirds of the capital invested by UK firms. These are the profits retained within the firm after the payment of dividends. The retained earnings level is therefore the inverse of the decision to pay dividends. The dividend decision is discussed in Chapter 22. We now consider the advantages and disadvantages of retained earnings as a source of finance.

One significant advantage of **retained earnings** is that there is no dilution of the existing shareholders' share of corporate control or share of returns. If the alternative of raising long-term funds by selling additional shares to outside shareholders were taken this would reduce the proportionate shareholdings of the existing owners. Even a rights issue might alter the relative position of particular shareholders if some chose not to take up their rights. Secondly, retaining earnings avoids the issuing costs associated with new shares or bonds and the arrangement fees on bank loans. Thirdly, management may value the fact that, in contrast to the position with a new equity or debt issue, they do not have to explain in such detail the use to which the funds will be put. This 'advantage' may not be in the shareholders' best interest, however.

A potential disadvantage of relying on internally generated funds is that they are limited by the firm's profits. Some firms wish to invest and grow at a much faster rate than would be possible through retained earnings. Indeed, some biotechnology firms are not expected to have profits for many years and yet have ambitious growth targets. Also, using retained earnings means reducing the dividend payout. Shareholders, on the whole, like to receive a steadily rising dividend stream. They may not be willing to forgo this simply because the management have a large number of projects in which they wish to invest. Retained earnings also have the drawback of being uncertain as they fluctuate with the ups and downs of the company's fortunes. Depending on this source of finance alone carries the risk of not being able to obtain finance at a vital stage in an investment programme.

Perhaps the most serious problem associated with retained earnings is that many managers regard them as essentially 'free capital'. That is, there is no cost to this capital – no opportunity cost of using these funds. This can encourage firms to invest to a greater extent than can be justified by the availability of positive NPV projects. There can be a resulting diminution of shareholders' wealth as the firm expands beyond a profitable size or diversifies into new areas, or acquires other firms. Forcing firms to raise funds externally subjects them to periodic scrutiny by critically minded investors who ask for a thorough justification. (*See* Chapters 15 to 23 on shareholder value.)

Retained earnings are not free. Shareholders, by allowing the firm to keep profits within the business, are making a significant sacrifice. They are forgoing dividends which could be invested in other financial securities. These other financial securities, for example shares in other firms of the same risk class, would have given a return. Thus shareholders have an opportunity cost and so the return required on retained earnings is the same as for any equity capital invested at that level of risk.

The treasurer at a strategic level

Treasurers may be asked to advise on matters of great significance to the future direction of the firm. For example, the decision to merge with another firm or to purchase a major business (**a trade purchase**) will require some assessment of the ability of the organisation to finance such activity. The treasurer will be able to advise on the sources of finance available, the optimum mixture and the willingness of the financial community to support the initiative. In a similar fashion a treasurer could help with disposals of subsidiaries.

Their knowledge of financial markets may permit treasurers to advise on the course of interest rates and exchange rates and so may aid vital decisions such as whether to establish a manufacturing facility or begin a marketing campaign in another country (*see* Chapters 24 and 25). Forecasting interest and exchange rates is notoriously difficult and even the greatest so-called experts frequently predict the future erroneously, and yet the treasurer may be the only person in the company able to make an informed guess.

Another major area of concern is the total amount of borrowing a firm should aim for. If it does not borrow at all then it will be losing the advantage of cheap finance. On the other hand, high levels of borrowing increase the chances of financial distress and the firm could be liquidated. Striking the appropriate balance is important and the treasurer may have some input in this area. Chapter 21 is devoted to the question of how much to borrow.

Relationships with the financial community

Neglecting to engender good relationships with shareholders, banks and other financial institutions can result in severe penalties for the firm. The typical treasurer and chief financial officer of a corporation will spend a great deal of time communicating with major finance providers on a weekly, or even a daily basis.

There will be a planned and sustained effort to maintain mutual understanding between shareholders and the organisation. The treasurer might be asked to create a detailed and up-to-date picture of who the shareholders are and then to follow through with a high-quality flow of information to enable shareholders to better appreciate the firm and its strategy in order to sustain their commitment. In the absence of informative communication to fill in gaps in their knowledge, shareholders may imagine all kinds of problems. If they are kept informed they are more likely to be supportive when the firm asks for additional finance, or asks for patience in times of difficulty, or appeals for the rejection of a merger bid. The point could be put even more simply: the shareholders own the firm and therefore both desire and deserve comprehensive information about its progress.

We turn now to banking relationships. Most firms make use of the services of more than one bank. A multinational firm may use over 100 banks. For example, Monsanto, the US chemical company, is proud of the fact that it has managed to cut the number down to 150 – it used to have 336. One reason for using so many banks is that large international firms have complex financial issues to deal with and any one bank may not have all the requisite skills and infrastructure to cope with them. Also banks have a tendency to join syndicates to make large loans to firms – an example here is Eurotunnel with 225 banks. In addition, some companies operate in dozens of countries and so may value the local network of the domestic banks in each of those markets.

The relationship between banks and large corporations differs. Some corporate treasurers, in an attempt to cut costs and boost investment returns, insist on banks competing with each other to offer the lowest-cost services. The provision of credit, the arrangement of bonds, notes, loans and commercial paper are put out to tender, as are the foreign exchange and cash management services. This competitive method is called '**transactional banking**'. However, there are drawbacks to this mercenary approach. Banks start to view these companies as one-off service takers interested in low cost only, and do not attempt to become knowledgeable about the firms. This leads to complaints from corporations that banks are unable to provide more tailored advice and services which so many of them need. When crises arise firms find banks deserting them and this often poses a threat to their existence. The lack of two-way knowledge means a greater tendency to pull out of a difficult situation rather than help develop imaginative plans for regeneration. Also, maintaining contact with more than 100 bankers can be very costly if the treasury system is not to become chaotic.

More often the emphasis is on '**relationship banking**' in which there is much more intimacy, with corporations being open with their banks and attempting to nurture a long-term relationship. As a result the quality of tailored service and the volume of consultancy type advice from banks improves. The banks are frequently willing to supply finance at a low interest rate as a loss leader so that they can pick up fee-based work later. *See* **Exhibit 13.9** for an article illustrating the benefits of relationship banking.

Exhibit 13.9

Relationship banking: Why Barcap's loyalty paid off

FT

Despite endless lip-service paid to the importance of building long-term corporate relationships, many see investment banks as the ultimate fair-weather friends of companies, interested only when the future is bright and lucrative deals are on offer, writes Louisa Mitchell.

But the story of ABB's return to centre stage in the capital markets is proof that relationship banking is not quite dead – and, from time to time, it can pay off handsomely for everyone.

Since ABB's near collapse in 2002, Barclays Capital – to cite one example – has stuck with ABB, resulting in a relationship that has helped ABB's recovery and Barcap's revenues.

Now that operating performance has improved, the depth of Barcap's relationship with ABB has put it in a strong position to offer the engineering group tailored solutions for restructuring its balance sheet.

'We have a lot of dialogue with different banks,' says Michel Demaré, ABB's executive vice president and chief financial officer.

'But, if a bank understands our priorities and can structure solutions without us having to look at lots of complicated products that are not relevant, then that is a great help.'

The efficiency of the process does not just benefit ABB.

Banks that try 'ambulance-chasing' deals rarely win against those who endeavour to develop longer-term relationships with companies.

Also, the effort involved in catching up is huge, not to mention expensive, not least because it often means footing the cost of flying in high-ranking executives to show commitment to the client at the last minute.

Of course, it has been good business for Barcap.

By being present as ABB turned itself around, Barcap has generated investment banking fees every step of the way.

Relationship banking means sticking with a client through thick and thin. But the upside if that, if things work out, the strategy can lead to a profitable stream of business.

'We began our discussions with ABB on the early conversion and exchange offer over nine months before the deal was launched,' says Douglas Decker, head of equity-linked origination at Barclays Capital, who has been involved in talks with the company for the past five years.

'In the end, we are able to structure a deal that suited ABB and which was fairly priced for bondholders, because we understood ABB's objectives and we knew the investor base well because of our prior involvement with the convertible bond.'

Source: Financial Times, 28 June 2006, Special Report: Corporate Finance, p. 4. Reprinted with permission.

Risk management

Running a business naturally entails taking risks – it is what business activity is about. Satisfactory profits rarely emerge from a risk-eliminating strategy; some risk is therefore inevitable. However, it is up to managers of firms to select those risks the business might take and those which it should avoid. Take a company like GlaxoSmithKline which accepts high risks in its research and development programme. Should it also take a risk with exchange rates when it receives money from sales around the world, or should it try to minimise that particular type of risk? Risk reduction is often costly. For example, insurance premiums may be payable or transaction costs may be incurred in the derivative markets. Given the additional cost burden managers have to think carefully about the benefits to be derived from reducing or eliminating risk. There are at least three reasons firms sacrifice some potential profits in order to reduce the impact of adverse events.

- ***It helps financial planning*** Being able to predict future cash flows, at least within certain boundaries, can be advantageous and can allow the firm to plan and invest with confidence. Imagine trying to organise a business if the future cash flows can vary widely depending on what happens to the currency, the interest rate or the price of a vital raw material input.
- ***Reduce the fear of financial distress*** Some events can disrupt and damage a business to the point of threatening its existence. For example, massive claims have been made against firms involved in the production of asbestos. If it had not been for the passing on of this risk to the insurance companies many more of these firms would now be liquidated. A similar logic applies to the insurance of supertankers against an ocean oil spillage. By limiting the potential damage inflicted on firms, not only will the managers and shareholders benefit, but other finance providers, such as banks, will have greater confidence which will lower the cost of capital.

- ***Some risks are not rewarded*** It is possible to reduce risk in situations where there are no financial rewards for accepting that extra risk. For example, if British Airways contracted to buy a dozen aircraft from Boeing for delivery over the next ten years and had to pay in dollars as each aeroplane was completed it would have to accept the risk of a recession in international flights and numerous other risks, but, in the sophisticated foreign exchange markets of today, at least it can eliminate one risk. It does not have to live with any uncertainty about the cost of the aeroplanes in terms of sterling because it could make an arrangement with a bank at the outset to purchase the required number of dollars for a specified number of pounds at set dates in the future. (This is a **forward agreement**.) British Airways would then know precisely how many pounds will be needed to buy the dollars to pay Boeing in each year of the next decade (*see* Chapter 25 for more currency risk-hedging strategies).

There are many different types of risk that a commercial organisation has to deal with. We will discuss the four most important: business risk, insurable risk, currency risk and interest-rate risk.

Business risk

Many of the risks of operating in a competitive business environment have to be accepted by management to a greater or lesser extent. Sales may fall because of, say, recession, or innovative breakthroughs by competitors. Costs may rise because of, say, strong union power or government-imposed tariffs. For some of these risk elements there is little that management can do. However in many areas management can take positive action to reduce risk. For example consider a bakery company heavily dependent on buying in wheat. The managers are likely to be worried that the price of wheat may rise over the forthcoming months, thereby making their operations unprofitable. On the other hand farmers may be worried by the possibility of wheat falling in price. Both would value certainty. One way of achieving this is for the baker and farmer to enter into a wheat **forward agreement**, in which the baker agrees to take delivery of wheat at a later date at a price which is agreed today. Both sides now know exactly how much the wheat will be sold for and so can plan ahead.

There are other ways of reducing business risk. For example, firms are often faced with a choice between two machines. The first is highly specialised to a particular task, for example, turning out a particular component. The second, slightly more expensive machine can turn out the same component, but can also be used in a more flexible fashion to switch production to other components. The option to use the machine in alternative ways can sometimes have a high value and so it is worthwhile paying the extra initial set-up costs and even higher production costs.

Consider also an electricity generator contemplating the construction of a power plant. The installation of a coal-fired station would be £100m. This would leave the generator dependent on coal price movements for future profitability. An alternative power plant can be switched from coal to gas but costs an additional £30m. The value of the option to switch is then for the management to evaluate and weigh against the extra cost of construction.

Likewise, a car production line may be more expensive if it is to be capable of being used for a number of different models. But the option to use the facility for more than one type of car reduces the firm's risk by making it less dependent on one model. These are examples of real options, which were considered in Chapter 6.

Insurable risk

Many risks encountered by business can be transferred, through the payment of a premium, to insurance companies. These include factory fires, pollution damage and accidental damage to vehicles and machinery. Insurance companies are often better able to bear risk than ordinary commercial firms. The reasons for this are the following:

- experience in estimating probabilities of events and therefore 'pricing' risk more efficiently;
- knowledge of methods of reducing risk. They can pass on this knowledge to the commercial firms which may obtain lower premiums if they take precautionary measures;
- ability to *pool* risks, in other words, to diversify risk. The chance of an accident occurring in one firm is highly uncertain, but the probability of a particular proportion of a portfolio of insurance policies making a claim is fairly predictable.

Insurance can be an expensive option because of the tendency for insurance companies to charge for much more than the probability of having to pay out. For example, if there was a one in a hundred chance of your £10,000 car being stolen in a year and never recovered then for every 100 cars insured the insurance company will expect one £10,000 claim per year. The insurance premium to each owner to cover this specific type of risk would, justifiably, be slightly over £100 (£10,000/100), to allow for a modest profit. However, in reality, the premium may be much more than this. The insurance company is likely to have to bear significant administrative costs in setting up the policy in the first place and then dealing with subsequent claims. Anyone who has had to communicate with an insurance company quickly becomes aware of the mountain of paperwork they generate annually. Insurance companies also have to charge premiums sufficiently high to cover the problems of '**adverse selection**'. Put it this way: you may be a sensible car owner, be cautious about where you park your car, never leave the doors unlocked and live in a good part of town, but many of the other purchasers of theft insurance may be less fastidious and fortunate. The grouping together of good and bad risks tends to increase the cost of insurance to relatively good policyholders. This is made worse for the good policyholders by the increased tendency of those in high-risk situations to buy insurance.

The third boost to insurance premiums comes from '**moral hazard**' (the encouragement of bad behaviour) which causes holders of insurance to be less careful than they might otherwise be – the 'It's all right, don't worry, it's insured' syndrome. An extreme example of moral hazard has been created with the 'new-for-old' policies for electrical items in which a brand-new HDTV for example, is provided should the old one suffer accidental damage – some have been tempted to 'accidentally' drop the TV!

These three additional costs may push insurance premiums beyond acceptable levels for a firm. In some cases large corporations have taken the bold decision to bear many insurable risks. They may still pay insurance premiums to safeguard against major events which threaten the continuance of the firm but accept routine risks themselves such as machine breakdown, accidents at work, etc. There seems little point in paying premiums just to receive a regular, but lower, inflow in return. The treasurer may have an important role in deciding which risks to insure and which to accept in-house.

Currency risk

Another major area of responsibility for the corporate treasurer is in the management of risk which arises because exchange rates move. Take the case of Acarus plc which has sold electrical goods to an Australian importer on six months' credit. The importer is sent an invoice requiring payment of A$20m. The current exchange rate is two Australian dollars to one pound so if currency rates do not change in six months Acarus will receive £10m. If the exchange moves to A$1.80 : £1 then Acarus will receive £11.11m, and will be very pleased with the extra £1.11m of income. However matters might turn out worse than expected. Say the rate of exchange moved to A$2.20 : £1. Then Acarus would receive only £9.09m. If the management team are risk averse they may say to themselves, 'While we like the possibility of making additional profit on the deal this is more than outweighed by the downside risk of making less than £10m'. There are various ways of ensuring that Acarus receives at least £10m and an entire chapter (Chapter 25) is devoted to the subject of exchange-rate risk management. Here we will have just a taster. One of the possibilities is for Acarus to buy an option giving the firm the right but not the obligation to exchange A$20m for sterling at a rate of A$2 : £1 in six months. If the dollar appreciates against the pound to A$1.80 then Acarus would choose not to exercise the option – to let it lapse – and then exchange the A$20m for £11.11m in the spot market in six months' time. Alternatively, if the dollar falls against sterling Acarus would insist on exercising the option to receive £10m rather than exchanging at the spot rate of A$2.20 : £1 and therefore achieving a mere £9.09m. By purchasing the option Acarus ensures that the lowest amount it will receive is £10m and the upside potential is unrestrained. However, it would need to pay a hefty premium to the option seller for passing on this risk – perhaps 2 to 4 per cent of the amount covered. The difficult part is weighing the cost of risk-reducing action against the benefit.

Interest-rate risk

Future interest rates cannot be predicted with any degree of accuracy. If a company has large amounts of floating-rate debt it could be vulnerable to interest-rate rises. Alternatively, a company with large fixed-rate debt could have to face living with regret, and higher debt costs than necessary, if interest rates fall.

There is a wide variety of arrangements and financial products which enable a treasurer to reduce the firm's exposure to the vicissitudes of interest rates. Chapter 24 explores a number of them. Here we examine one of the weapons in the treasurer's armoury – the **cap**.

Ace plc wishes to borrow £20m to finance a major expansion. It does so at a floating rate of LIBOR plus 150 basis points. LIBOR is currently 8 per cent and therefore Ace pays a rate of 9.5 per cent. This loan is a large sum relative to Ace's capital base and profits, and the management are concerned that if LIBOR rises above 10 per cent the firm will get into serious financial difficulty. To avoid this Ace purchases a **cap agreement** by which a bank promises to pay any interest charge above a LIBOR of 10 per cent. Thus, if two years later LIBOR rises to 11 per cent, without the cap Ace would pay 12.5 per cent. However, Ace can call upon the bank which made the **cap agreement** to pay the extra 1 per cent. Ace's effective interest charge cannot go beyond a total of 10 per cent + 1.5 per cent = 11.5 per cent. What is more, Ace can benefit if interest rates fall because rates are linked to a variable LIBOR at any rate below the cap. The premium charged by the bank for this form of interest-rate insurance can be quite substantial but there are ways of offsetting this cost, for example by simultaneously selling a floor, but consideration of this will have to wait until Chapter 24. Suffice to say, the judicious management of interest-rate risk can be an important part of the treasurer's job description.

Working capital management

A firm needs to invest in order to thrive. Major long-term investments in a new factory or new machinery are part of that investment. Another necessary element for expansion is additional resources devoted to current assets. Higher levels of output call for extra inventories of raw materials and work in progress (WIP) (partially finished goods). More sales volume often means that additional credit is granted to customers so that the investment in debtors (receivables) increases. Greater sales usually means more inventory held in the form of finished goods. Also, a higher level of general business activity usually requires greater amounts of cash to oil the wheels. Some of the additional investment in inventories, debtors and cash may come from long-term sources of finance but in most cases short-term sources such as trade credit or a bank overdraft will cover much of the increased need.

The working capital cycle

The upper, circular, part of **Exhibit 13.10** shows the **working capital cycle** for a typical firm. (This chain of events applies to the typical manufacturing firm rather than service businesses, which often miss one or two stages.) It starts with the investment in raw material inventories which are then used in the production process and thereby become partially completed products. Eventually finished goods are produced which are held in inventory until sold. Some of these goods are sold for cash and others are sold on credit, with the customer paying days or weeks later. At each stage of the process expenditure is necessary on labour and other operational inputs. Helping to ease the cash burden of this cycle are suppliers, who provide credit.

The lower half of the diagram in Exhibit 13.10 shows non-working capital cash flows. These are generally infrequent events, involving large sums on each occasion and are of a long-term nature. They will not be considered any further in this chapter.

Money tied up in any stage in the working capital chain has an opportunity cost. In addition there are costs associated with storage and/or administration. The combined costs can be considerable and it is the art of good working capital management to so arrange the affairs of the business as to obtain a balance between the costs and benefits through raising or lowering stocks, cash, debtors and creditors to their optimum levels.

Exhibit 13.10 A typical working capital cycle and other cash flows

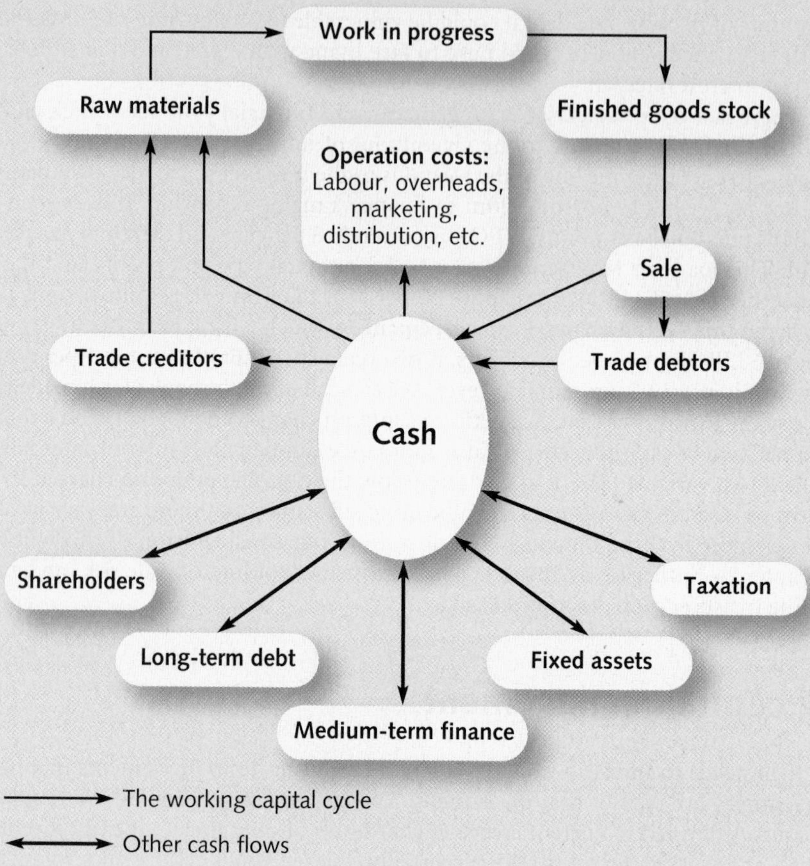

The amount invested by the average large UK firm in current assets is about 80 per cent of the amount devoted to fixed assets. The size and significance of working capital investment means that the success of an organisation may depend upon the wise implementation of well thought-out policies.

Cash-conversion cycle

The working capital cycle can be expressed in terms of the length of time between the acquisition of raw materials and other inputs and the inflow of cash from the sale of goods. As can be seen from **Exhibit 13.11** this involves a number of intermediate stages.

The **cash-conversion cycle** focuses on the length of time between the company's outlay on inputs and the receipt of money from the sale of goods. For manufacturing firms it is the average time raw materials remain in stock, plus the time taken to produce the company's output, plus the length of time finished goods stay within the company as a form of inventory, plus the time taken for debtors to pay, less the credit period granted by suppliers. The shorter this cycle the fewer resources the company needs to tie up. The cash-conversion cycle can be summarised as the stock-conversion period plus the debtor-conversion period less the credit period granted by suppliers – *see* **Exhibit 13.12**.

The cash-conversion cycle can be calculated approximately using the terms set out in **Exhibit 13.13**.

The cash-conversion cycle can, perhaps, be better understood when some numbers are attached. The figures given in **Exhibit 13.14** can be used to illustrate it.

Exhibit 13.11 The cash-conversion cycle as part of the working capital cycle

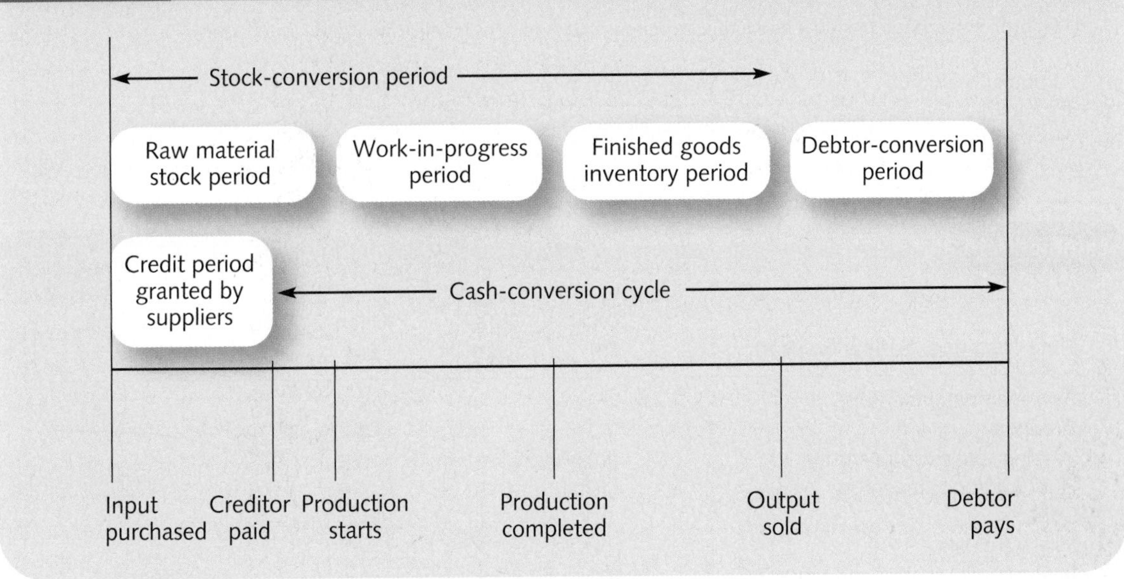

Exhibit 13.12 Summary of cash-conversion cycle

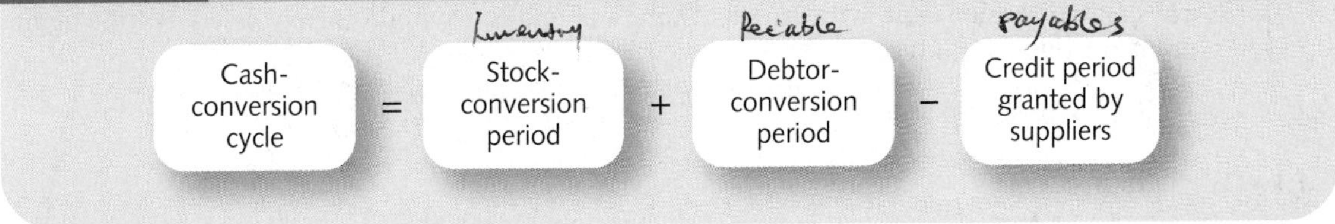

Exhibit 13.13 Calculation of cash-conversion cycle

- **Raw materials stock period** The average number of days raw materials remain unchanged and in stock:

$$\text{Raw materials stock period} = \frac{\text{Average value of raw materials stock}}{\text{Average usage of raw materials per day}} = X \text{ days}$$

Less

- **Average credit period granted by suppliers** The average length of time between the purchase of inputs and the payment of them:

$$\text{Credit period} = \frac{\text{Average level of creditors}}{\text{Purchases on credit per day}} = X \text{ days.}$$

Add

- **Work-in-progress period** The number of days to convert raw materials into finished goods:

$$\text{Work-in-progress period} = \frac{\text{Average value of work in progress}}{\text{Average cost of goods sold per day}} = X \text{ days}$$

Add

- **Finished goods inventory period** The number of days finished goods await delivery to customers:

$$\text{Finished goods inventory period} = \frac{\text{Average value of finished goods in stock}}{\text{Average cost of goods sold per day}} = X \text{ days}$$

Add

- **Debtor-conversion period** The average number of days to convert customer debts into cash:

$$\text{Debtor-conversion period} = \frac{\text{Average value of debtors}}{\text{Average value of sales per day}} = X \text{ days}$$

Exhibit 13.14 Figures invented in order to calculate a cash-conversion cycle

Time (year end, as flow for year)	20X1 £m	20X2 £m	Mean £m	Per day during 20X2 £
Raw materials inventory	22	24	23	
Creditors	12	14	13	
Work-in-progress inventory	10	11	10.5	
Finished goods inventory	9	10	9.5	
Debtors	30	32	31	
Sales (annual)	150	170	–	465,753
Raw material usage (annual)	100	116	–	317,808
Cost of goods sold (annual)	130	146	–	400,000

The cash-conversion cycle is the length of time a pound is tied up in current assets. For the figures given in Exhibit 13.14 it is:

$$\text{Raw materials stock period} = \frac{23{,}000{,}000}{317{,}808} = 72 \text{ days}$$

$$\textit{Less} \text{ creditor period*} = \frac{13{,}000{,}000}{317{,}808} = -41 \text{ days}$$

$$\text{Work-in-progress period} = \frac{10{,}500{,}000}{400{,}000} = 26 \text{ days}$$

$$\text{Finished goods inventory period} = \frac{9{,}500{,}000}{400{,}000} = 24 \text{ days}$$

$$\text{Debtor-conversion period} = \frac{31{,}000{,}000}{465{,}753} = 67 \text{ days}$$

$$\text{Cash-conversion cycle} = 148 \text{ days}$$

* This is simplified to the creditor period on a single input, raw materials – there will be other inputs and creditors in most firms.

After observing the length of time money is invested in working capital the management of the firm are likely to try to think of ways of shortening the cash-conversion cycle – so long as such shortening does not excessively damage operations. A number of actions could be taken: debtor levels could be cut by changing the conditions of sale or being more forceful in the collection of old debts; inventory levels can be examined to see if overstocking is occurring and whether the production methods can be altered to process and sell goods more quickly; perhaps creditors could be pushed into granting more credit. If these actions can be carried out without any adverse impact on costs or sales, then they should be implemented.

An extreme form of reducing the cash-conversion cycle is achieved by supermarkets. They sell goods and receive payment from customers *before* they have to pay suppliers – *see* **Exhibit 13.15**.

Exhibit 13.15

FT

Cash benefit: how big supermarkets fund expansion by using suppliers as bankers

Examining the accounts of multinational retailers shows the increasing extent to which they draw on trade creditors to provide working capital for their stores

write John Plender, Martin Simons and Henry Tricks

Power wielded by the big supermarkets is in most countries a source of growing political concern, not least in relation to their treatment of suppliers and smaller competitors. In particular, Wal-Mart Stores of the US and Britain's Tesco are noted for commanding positions in their domestic markets and super-efficient global management of their supply chains.

Yet any attempt to establish how far suppliers are being squeezed is hampered by what the Office of Fair Trading, the UK competition watchdog, has called 'a climate of apprehension among suppliers' that prevents them from coming forward as a source of information.

A Financial Times investigation has sought to address the gap by looking at supermarkets' balance sheets filed at Companies House in London. Combined with their publicly available accounts, these provide a remarkable insight into the activities of both UK and non-UK companies.

The results show that the extraordinarily efficient management of working capital by Tesco and Asda, the UK subsidiary of Wal Mart, has resulted in suppliers providing large and increasing amounts of finance, which has helped fund Tesco's and Asda's growth.

At Tesco the five-year increase in payments owed to creditors was £2.2bn, compared with a £0.7bn increase in stocks, leaving £1.5bn to finance the business. At Asda trade creditors were up £0.7bn while stocks rose by £0.2bn, yielding a net cash benefit of £0.5bn over the period.

Working capital in a conventional business is the amount required to finance stock and debtors after deducting the credit made available by suppliers. But food retailing is different, in that stock is turned into cash at the check-out counters long before suppliers have to be paid. Debtors are relatively insignificant and creditors exceed stock by a considerable margin. So there is a negative working capital requirement. Trade credit can end up providing finance for investment in fixed assets.

The result is a virtuous circle that has permitted £2bn to be released to help finance a combined £12bn of capital investment in Tesco and Asda over the past five years. For every £1bn of extra sales, these retailers have attracted roughly £100m of extra creditor finance – with Tesco, much, larger than the Wal Mart subsidiary, demonstrating how much size pays.

In effect, suppliers have acted as surrogate bankers to the two groups

How the supermarkets manage working capital

Trade creditors as a % of retail stock (peak years highlighted)

	2000	2001	2002	2003	2004
Wm Morrison	288	301	**362**	343	264
J Sainsbury	167	194	187	165	**255**
Tesco	189	201	196	203	**216**
Tesco Stores UK	200	202	199	**219**	n/a
Asda (Wal-Mart UK)	163	196	209	**262**	206
Wal-Mart group (US)	71	69	69	72.5	**74**
Alliance UniChem	138	148	149	159	**163**
John Lewis Partnership	89.5	**95.5**	88	72.5	88.5
Waitrose	n/a	**169**	153	128	150
Marks and Spencer	44	**61.5**	55.5	53	57.5
Boots	56	57	**59**	58.5	51

Source: Company accounts, FT analysis

Year-end nearest to Dec

Exhibit 13.15 continued

on a remarkable scale, contributing growing amounts of finance in a period when cash flow from depreciation covered only one-third of the combined investment outlay. This has reduced Tesco's and Asda's need for bank finance and support from the capital markets (or in Asda's case, its US parent) while mitigating balance-sheet strain.

In general, the supermarkets' increased reliance on trade credit will come at the expense of suppliers' balance sheets, because an increase in creditors must be matched by an increase in debtors elsewhere in the system: every credit has a debit.

Efficient management of the supermarkets' balance sheets, especially when conducted with the skill apparent at Wal Mart and Tesco, has been hugely beneficial for their shareholders and consumers. The numbers suggest that management of working capital by the two big retailers is in the top rank by global standards and has been an important contributor to their success in recent years.

Martin Simons consults on comparative corporate performance

Source: *Financial Times*, 7 December 2005, p. 19. Reprinted with permission.

The difficult decisions come when reducing the cash-conversion cycle entails costs as well as benefits – then a careful evaluation and balancing of cost and benefits is needed. These will be considered later in the chapter.

Exhibit 13.16 provides a brief overview of the tension with which managers have to cope. If there is too little working capital, it results in inventories, finished goods and customer credit not being available in sufficient quantity. On the other hand, if there are excessive levels of working capital, the firm has unnecessary additional costs: the cost of tying up funds, plus the storage, ordering and handling costs of being overburdened with stock. Running throughout is the risk of being temporarily short of that vital lifeblood of a business – cash (that is, suffering a liquidity risk).

Exhibit 13.16 Working capital tension

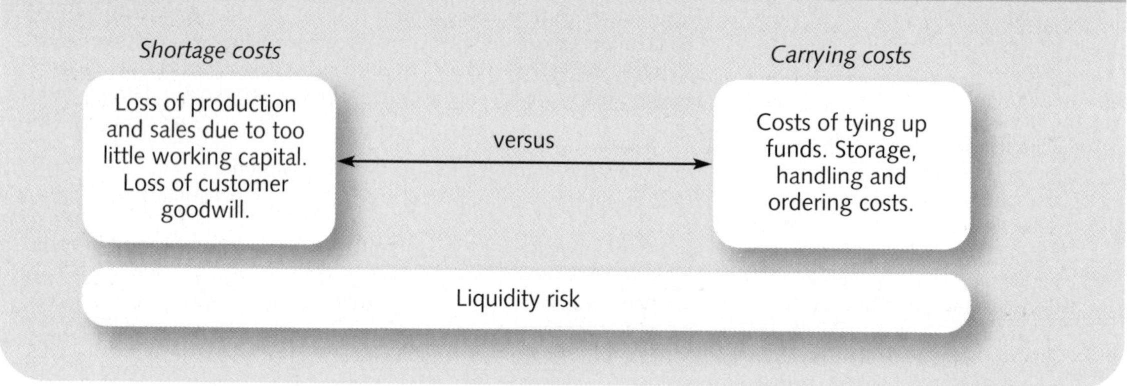
Shortage costs
Loss of production and sales due to too little working capital. Loss of customer goodwill.
versus
Carrying costs
Costs of tying up funds. Storage, handling and ordering costs.
Liquidity risk

The dynamics of working capital

The level of activity of an organisation is likely to have an impact on the investment needed in working capital. Take a company with annual sales of £10m and the working capital periods set out in **Exhibit 13.17**.

As the level of sales increases there are three possible types of impact on the level of working capital (if we exclude the theoretical fourth possibility of a decline):

1 The investment in working capital increases in proportion to the increase in sales because the conversion periods remain constant.

2 A disproportionate rise in working capital is experienced. The conversion periods may be lengthened because of longer credit granted to customers to increase sales or higher raw materials, WIP and finished goods inventory to support the increased activity. These moves may make logical

Exhibit 13.17 Working capital periods

Stock-conversion period (raw material + work-in-progress + finished goods periods)	2 months
Debtor-conversion period	1.5 months
Creditor period	1 month

Assuming that the input costs are 60 per cent of sales the working capital investment will be £1,750,000:

Stock	60% × £10m	× 2/12	1,000,000
Debtors	£10m	× 1.5/12	1,250,000
Creditors	60% × £10m	× 1/12	–500,000
			£1,750,000

business sense in order to generate more sales and avoid stock-out costs, or they may be a result of poor working capital management. Much depends on the environment and the economics of the business concerned.

3 Working capital increases at a slower rate than the sales volume.

These three possibilities are shown in **Exhibit 13.18**. What emerges from Exhibit 13.18 is that even though remarkable strides are made in limiting the rise in working capital as a proportion of sales in the third scenario, the firm will still have to find additional finance to invest in this area. If it fails to do so the firm may cease production due to an inability to pay for day-to-day expenses. This is a situation of overtrading, considered later in this chapter.

Exhibit 13.18 Working capital changes when sales rise by 50 per cent

Conversion periods	*Possibility 1*		*Possibility 2*		*Possibility 3*	
Stock	Constant @ 2 months		Increase to 3 months		Decrease to 1½ months	
Debtors	Constant @ 1½ months		Increase to 2 months		Decrease to 1 month	
Creditor	Constant @ 1 month		Increase to 1½ months		Decrease to ½ month	
		£m		£m		£m
Stock	60% × £15m × 2/12 =	1.5	60% × £15m × 3/12 =	2.25	60% × £15m × 1½/12 =	1.125
Debtors	£15m × 1½/12 =	1.875	£15m × 2/12 =	2.50	£15m × 1/12 =	1.250
Creditors	60% × £15m × 1/12 =	–0.750	60% × £15m × 1½/12 =	–1.125	60% × £15m × ½/12 =	–0.375
Working capital investment		2.625		3.625		2.0
Absolute increase		0.875		1.875		0.25
Percentage increase over £1.75m		50%		107%		14%

Working capital policies

Exhibit 13.19 shows three alternative policies for working capital as sales rise. The top line represents a relatively relaxed approach with large cash or near-cash balances, more generous customer credit and/or higher inventories. This may be a suitable policy for a firm operating in a relatively uncertain environment where safety (or buffer) stocks of raw materials, work in progress and finished goods are needed to avoid production stoppages and lost sales due to stock-outs. Customers may demand longer to pay and suppliers are less generous with credit. The aggressive stance is more likely to be taken in an environment of greater certainty over future flows which permits working capital to be kept to relatively low levels. Here the firm would hold minimal safety stocks of cash and inventories and/or would be able to press customers for relatively early settlement while pushing trade creditors to increase the time interval between receipt and payment for inputs. The aggressive policy approach will exhibit a shorter cycle for cash conversion.

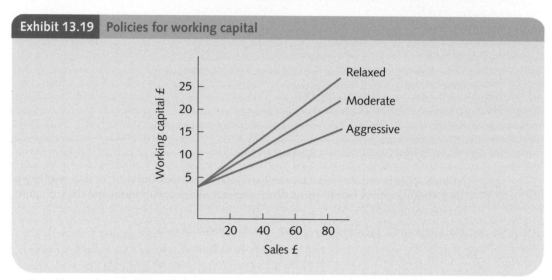

Exhibit 13.19 Policies for working capital

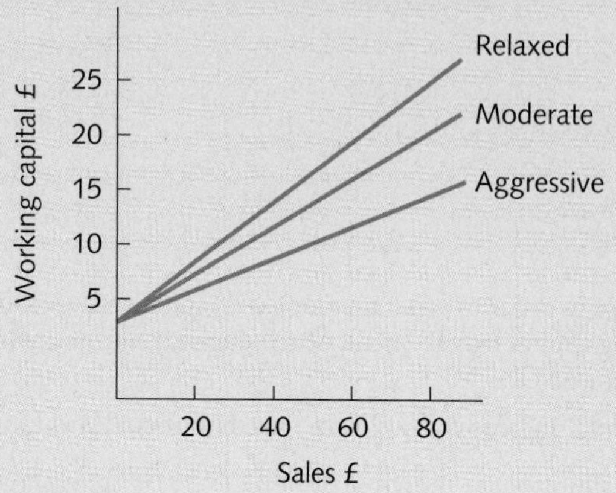

Note: The numbers are illustrative and do not imply a 'normal' relationship between sales and current assets.

Overtrading

A firm operating in a particular business environment and with a given level of activity will have certain levels of working capital needs. For example, a manufacturing firm with a stable level of annual sales will aim to invest an optimum amount in stocks and trade debtors. If sales should rise, by, say, 50 per cent, then it is likely that stocks of raw materials, WIP and finished goods will rise and the money devoted to support additional debtors will also increase. Perhaps the rise in investment in working capital will need to be more than 50 per cent, or perhaps the economics of the firm means that a lower proportionate rise in working capital is needed for each increase in total activity. Whatever the particular circumstance of each firm it is likely that additional working capital resources will be needed to permit judicious expansion without the fear of **overtrading**.

Overtrading occurs when a business has insufficient finance for working capital to sustain its level of trading.

A business is said to be overtrading when it tries to engage in more business than its working capital will allow. It could be that too much money is tied up in stocks and trade debtors, and cash is not coming in quickly enough to meet debts as they fall due. It could be that the firm failed to obtain sufficient equity finance when it was established to support its trading level, or it could be that the managers are particularly bad at managing the working capital resources that they have. The most common cause of overtrading (or under-capitalisation) is a failure to match increases in turnover with appropriate increases in finance for working capital.

It may seem odd that a firm could suffer from an increase in the demand for its products, but in the harsh world of business it is perfectly possible for a firm to double its sales, and its profits, and yet become insolvent. Managers can be sorely tempted by the lure of new sales opportunities and lead the firm to rapid expansion, believing that the additional revenue will more than cover the extra investment needed in working capital to pay day-to-day bills. However, this sometimes does not work out because of the time delays involved in receiving cash from customers and the necessity to precede turnover increases with large payments for inventory, labour and other costs.

Thus the firm could find itself unable to pay short-term bills while at the same time anticipating great prosperity in the long run. This sort of problem arose in a number of information technology businesses in the UK early this century as turnover doubled or tripled in a year. Take the case of (fictional) Bits and Rams Ltd which in 2006 had a turnover of £2m and a profit of £200,000:

	£000
Turnover	2,000
Cost of goods sold	1,800
Profit	200

All costs are variable for Bits and Rams and debtors generally take two and a half months to pay. Inventories for two months' worth of costs of sales are held and trade creditors are paid one and a half months after delivery.

In 2007 sales doubled but the company came close to collapse because it could not pay suppliers and the labour force on time. The cash flows for 2007 are as shown in **Exhibit 13.20**.

Exhibit 13.20 Cash flow for Bits and Rams Ltd

	£000
Turnover	4,000
Cost of goods sold	3,600
Profit	+400
Additional investment in debtors (2,000 × $2\frac{1}{2}$/12)	–417
Additional investment in inventories (1,800 × 2/12)	–300
Tax bill from previous year's trading	–67
Increase in trade creditors (1,800 × $1\frac{1}{2}$/12)	+225
Cash flow	–159

If Bits and Rams is unable to finance this large increase in working capital it could find itself insolvent. Even if it manages to avoid the worst fate management may have to engage in short-term crisis management to overcome the cash shortage (for example selling assets, chasing late payers) which is likely to distract them from the more important task of creating long-term shareholder wealth.

In an overtrading situation if it is not possible to increase the capital base of a firm, by borrowing finance or selling shares, and the management have done all they can to tighten up working capital management (for example, by reducing stock levels) then the only option left open is likely to be to reduce activity. This can be a very painful prescription psychologically for managers as they have to turn down profitable business.

Why is cash important?

Exhibit 13.10 shows the centrality of cash in the operations of firms. Many firms do not have stocks, particularly in the service sector, while others do not have debtors or creditors, but all have to use cash. So what is it about cash which causes all firms to need it? There are three categories of motives ascribed to the holding of cash:

1 ***Transaction motive*** Cash is often needed to pay for wages, buy materials and fixed assets, to pay taxes, service debts and for a host of other day-to-day transactions. This cash is necessary because the daily cash inflows do not match the cash outflows and so cash is needed to act as a buffer to permit activity to continue. This is particularly important in seasonal businesses or where long credit periods are granted to customers.

2 ***Precautionary motive*** The forecasting of future cash flows is subject to error. The more vulnerable cash flows are to unpredictable shocks the greater the cash balance needed to act as a

safety stock. Future cash flows can vary from those originally anticipated for a wide variety of reasons, for example a sales shortfall, a strike or the failure of a supplier.

3 ***Speculative motive*** This simply means that any unexpected profitable opportunities can be taken immediately, for example, to purchase a competitor firm quickly when a fleeting opportunity presents itself.

Operating cash is money held for operating purposes which is earning below-market interest rates because the firm needs quick access to it on a regular basis. So money held in cheque accounts is considered cash even if it is not in the form of the 'foldable stuff', because the interest earned on it is low due to the convenience of account withdrawals. Thus the firm deliberately makes an interest rate sacrifice to hold cash either in currency or in an easily accessible account.

Exhibit 13.21 shows the trade-off management have to take into account when considering the levels of cash to maintain. (Note that in many firms it is the fluctuations in the overdraft that provide the cash.)

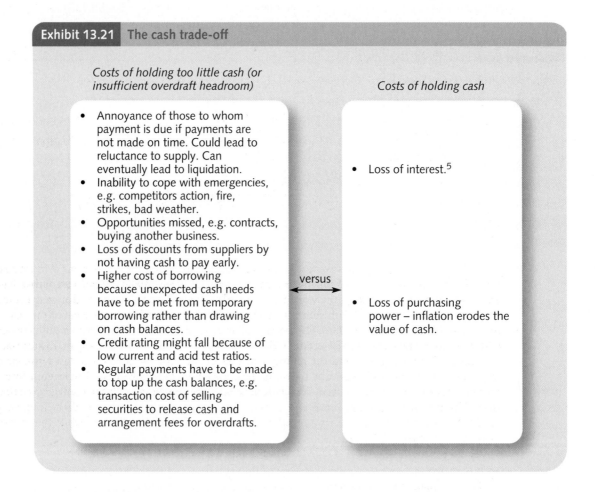

Exhibit 13.21 The cash trade-off

Costs of holding too little cash (or insufficient overdraft headroom)		*Costs of holding cash*
• Annoyance of those to whom payment is due if payments are not made on time. Could lead to reluctance to supply. Can eventually lead to liquidation. • Inability to cope with emergencies, e.g. competitors action, fire, strikes, bad weather. • Opportunities missed, e.g. contracts, buying another business. • Loss of discounts from suppliers by not having cash to pay early. • Higher cost of borrowing because unexpected cash needs have to be met from temporary borrowing rather than drawing on cash balances. • Credit rating might fall because of low current and acid test ratios. • Regular payments have to be made to top up the cash balances, e.g. transaction cost of selling securities to release cash and arrangement fees for overdrafts.	versus ⟷	• Loss of interest.[5] • Loss of purchasing power – inflation erodes the value of cash.

Cash management models

Models have been developed which attempt to set cash levels at a point, or within a range, which strikes the best balance between the costs outlined in Exhibit 13.21. All these models suffer from being over-simplistic and are heavily dependent on the accuracy of the inputs. There is also a danger of managers using them in a mechanical fashion, and neglecting to apply the heavy dose of judgement needed to allow for the less easily quantified variables ignored by the models.

[5] If an overdraft is used it is the excess cost of borrowing on overdraft as opposed to borrowing elsewhere.

Baumol's cash model

Baumol's model assumes that the firm operates in a steady state environment where it uses cash at a constant rate which is entirely predictable. Take the case of Cypressa plc which pays out £100,000 per week and receives a steady inflow of £80,000. The firm will have a need for additional cash of £20,000 per week. (This may sound like a disastrous pattern at first glance. However, it could be that Cypressa is highly profitable but has these cash flow shortages for the forthcoming months because of large capital expenditure. Eventually there will be a large cash inflow.) If it has a beginning cash balance of £80,000 then the pattern of cash balances over time will be as shown in **Exhibit 13.22**. It takes four weeks for the initial balance to be reduced to zero. At the end of Week 4 the cash balance is topped up to £80,000 by the firm, say, borrowing or selling some of its holdings of securities such as Treasury bills. Both of these actions involve costs. Let us say that the arrangement fees on £80,000 of borrowing or the transaction costs of selling £80,000 of Treasury bills are £500.

Exhibit 13.22 Cash balances for Cypressa plc with Baumol's model assumptions

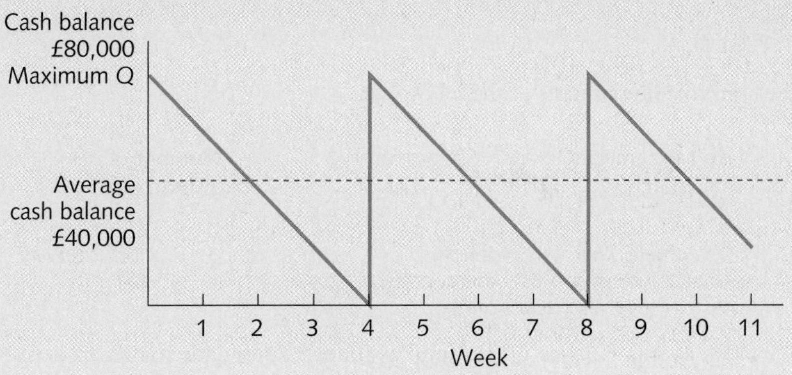

In **Baumol's cash model** the average amount of cash on hand and therefore earning no interest (an opportunity cost) is half of the maximum cash balance. If we denote the maximum cash balance as Q, the average cash balance is $Q/2$ = £40,000. The firm has the task of deciding on the most appropriate level of Q. For example instead of £80,000 it could raise the level of the maximum cash balance to £120,000, in which case the average cash balance incurring an opportunity cost of forgoing interest would be £60,000. However, this would also mean a saving on the transaction costs of arranging for a loan or selling securities because this would happen less frequently. Instead of every four weeks new finance would be drawn upon every six weeks. The forgone interest opportunity cost of having large cash holdings has to be compared with the lower transaction costs. This is shown in **Exhibit 13.23**, where, as the amount of cash held is increased, the frequency (and therefore the transaction cost) of selling securities or borrowing declines while the cost of interest forgone rises.

We have the following factors to help establish the position of Q^* mathematically:

Q = maximum cash balance
$Q/2$ = average cash balance
C = transaction costs for selling securities or arranging a loan
A = total amount of new cash needed for the period under consideration; this is usually one year
K = the holding cost of cash (the opportunity cost equal to the rate of return forgone)

Exhibit 13.23 Finding the optimum cash balance

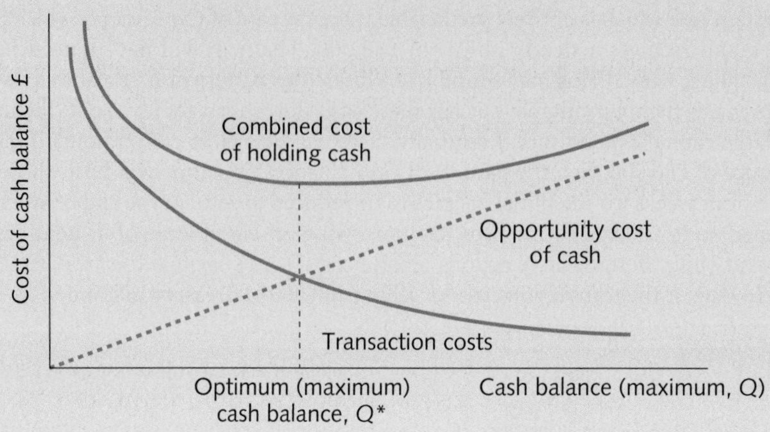

The total cost line consists of the following:

$$\text{Average amount tied up} \times \text{Opportunity cost} + \text{Number of transactions} \times \text{Cost of each transaction}$$

$$\frac{Q}{2} \times K + \frac{A}{Q} \times C$$

The optimal cash balance Q^* is found as follows (the mathematics to derive this are beyond the scope of this book – the derivative of the above total cost function is set to zero):

$$Q^* = \sqrt{\frac{2CA}{K}}$$

If we assume the interest rate forgone, *K*, is 7 per cent then, given that the annual need for cash is (£20,000 × 52) = £1,040,000 for Cypressa, the optimal amount to transfer into cash on each occasion is:

$$Q^* = \sqrt{\frac{2 \times £500 \times £1{,}040{,}000}{0.07}} = £121{,}890$$

Given the assumptions of the model Cypressa should replenish its cash balances when they reach zero to the extent of £121,890.

We can also calculate the number of times replenishment will take place each year:

$$A/Q^* = £1{,}040{,}000 \,/\, £121{,}890$$

that is, between eight and nine times per year.

Larger firms often find it worthwhile to buy and sell securities to adjust cash balances almost every day of the year. Take the case of a firm with an annual turnover of £2bn which pays £600 transaction costs every time it deals in the money market to, say, purchase Treasury bills. If the annual rate of return on money market instruments is 7 per cent, or 0.0185 per cent per day, then the daily interest on £5.5m (approximately one day's turnover) is £1,018 and it makes sense to lend for one day as the interest received outweighs the transaction costs. Sticking strictly to Baumol's model the firm should deal in £5.86m quantities or 342 times per year – let's say, every day:

$$Q^* = \sqrt{\frac{2 \times £600 \times £2{,}000{,}000{,}000}{0.07}} = £5.86\text{m}$$

The basic model demonstrated here could be modified to cope with the need for a safety stock of cash to reduce the probability of cash shortages in a less than certain world. One drawback of the model is its inapplicability when finance is provided by way of an overdraft. If the drawdown of additional cash from an overdraft has no transaction cost, the whole issue boils down to ensuring that the overdraft limit is not exceeded.

Some considerations for cash management

Create a policy framework

It is advisable for frequent and routine decisions to establish a set of policies. This will enable simpler and quicker decisions to be taken at lower levels in the organisation. Such a policy framework needs to retain some flexibility so that exceptional circumstances can bring forth a more detailed consideration. The framework should also be capable of change as the environment changes.

Plan cash flows

Good cash management requires good planning. Management need to know when cash is likely to be in surplus (so that it can be invested) and when it is necessary to borrow. Cash budgets allow for forward planning. For example, the company represented in **Exhibit 13.24** with a constant monthly cash outflow and an undulating cash inflow has six months of the year when effort has to be devoted to investing surplus cash and six months for financing a cash shortfall. The volume and length of time of those surpluses or deficits need to be known in advance to obtain the best terms and select the most appropriate instruments. For example if £10m is available for investment over three months perhaps a portfolio of commercial and Treasury bills will be purchased; if only £10,000 is available for seven days an interest-bearing bank account might be best. Companies that do not expect a surplus at any time in the forthcoming months but rely on an overdraft facility will still need to plan ahead to ensure that the overdraft limit is not breached. If there is to be an exceptional cash need for a few months perhaps an increased overdraft limit will have to be negotiated.

Exhibit 13.24 Cash planning

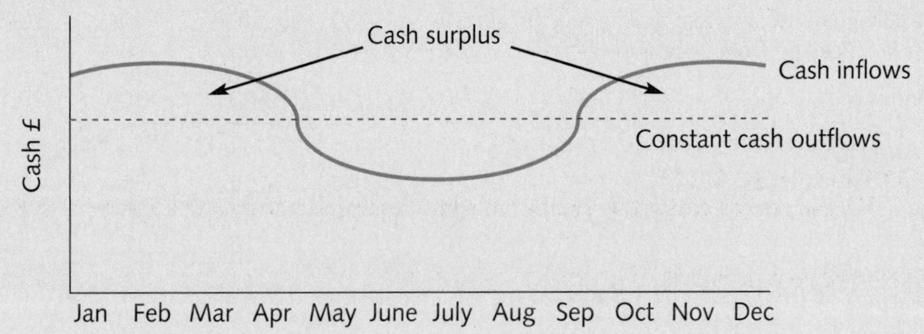

The cash budget is an estimate of cash inflows and outflows at fixed intervals over a future period.

Cash budgets may be drawn up on a quarterly, monthly, weekly or daily basis. Generally a monthly budget for the next year plus a more detailed daily budget for the forthcoming month will be drawn up.

Exhibit 13.25 shows the sales for Cedrus plc over the next six months. Cedrus is a manufacturer of nutcrackers and so has a peak in its sales in December. One-third of sales in any month are paid for in the month of delivery, with the remainder paid one month later.

Exhibit 13.25 Cedrus plc sales

		Sales £000s	
	Total	**Paid for in month of delivery**	**Paid for 1 month later**
August	90	30	60
September	90	30	60
October	120	40	80
November	150	50	100
December	600	200	400
January	60	20	40

Note: Sales on credit outstanding at the end of July are £60,000.

Cedrus maintains a constant level of output through the year and so builds up stocks in the autumn and early winter. During October an old machine tool will be replaced at a cost of £100,000 payable upon installation. Also, in the November edition of a glossy food and drink magazine the range of nutcrackers will be promoted, costing the firm a further £50,000. In January £150,000 tax will be payable. At the beginning of August the cash balance will be a positive £50,000.

To calculate the cash budget we can split the problem into three stages:

1 Show the inflows from sales when the cash is actually received rather than when the sale is recorded.

2 List the cash outflows in the month of occurrence.

3 Display the opening cash balance for each month less the cash surplus (or deficit) generated that month to show a closing cash balance (*see* **Exhibit 13.26**).

Exhibit 13.26 Cedrus plc cash budget

£000s	**Aug**	**Sep**	**Oct**	**Nov**	**Dec**	**Jan**
Cash inflows						
Sales (delivered and paid for in same month)	30	30	40	50	200	20
Sales (cash received from prior month's sales)	60	60	60	80	100	400
Total inflows	90	90	100	130	300	420
Cash outflows						
Payments for materials	50	50	55	55	55	55
Wages	20	20	22	25	30	22
Rent	10	10	10	10	10	10
Other expenses	10	10	11	9	10	11
New machine			100			
Advertising				50		
Tax						150
Total outflows	90	90	198	149	105	248
Balances						
Opening cash balance for month	50	50	50	(48)	(67)	128
Net cash surplus (deficit) for month (i.e. inflows minus outflows)	0	0	(98)	(19)	195	172
Closing cash balance	50	50	(48)	(67)	128	300

Cedrus is likely to need some borrowing facility to cover its cash shortfall in October and November. For the other four months the management will have to give thought to the best use of surplus cash. Perhaps some will be paid out in the form of dividends, some used to repay long-term debt and some deposited to earn interest. Having considered the projected cash flows the management might also consider ways of boosting net cash inflows by shortening the cash-conversion cycle, for example holding less stock or offering early settlement discount to customers.

Two additional points need to be made about the use of cash budgets in practice. First, the figures represent the most likely outcome and do not allow for the risk of variability from these 'best guesses'. It is more sensible to examine a range of possible outcomes to gain a realistic picture of what might happen and the range of the cash needs. The projection of sales is particularly problematic and yet it has a profound impact on the budget. Secondly, the figures shown are the cash position at the end of each month. It is possible that cash needs or surpluses are much larger than these during some parts of the month.

Control cash flows

Many large firms have operations in a number of regions in one country or in a range of countries. Unilever, for example, manufactures and sells all over the world. To operate effectively Unilever has numerous bank accounts so that some banking transactions can take place near to the point of business. Sales receipts from America will be paid into local banks there, likewise many operating expenses will be paid for with funds drawn from those same banks. The problem for Unilever is that some of those bank accounts will have high inflows and others high outflows, so interest could be payable on one while funds are lying idle or earning a low rate of return in another. Therefore, as well as taking advantage of the benefit of having local banks carry out local transactions, large firms need to set in place a co-ordinating system to ensure that funds are transferred from where there is surplus to where they are needed.

Also, many payments are made centrally, such as dividends, taxes, bond interest, major new investments, and so an efficient mechanism is needed to funnel money to the centre.

Another aspect of good cash management is to try to reduce the level of cash balances needed by ensuring that cash outflows occur at the same time as cash inflows. This is known as **cash flow synchronisation**. For example, some firms insist on customer payment at the end of the month and pay their own suppliers at the same time. The reduced cash balances mean lower bank loans and therefore higher profit.

Managers can make use of the cash budget as a control device by regularly comparing the outcome with the original plan for a period. If there is a substantial deviation then this might prompt enquiries and action to correct any problems.

Management should also consider using the delays in the cheque-clearing system rather than becoming victims of them. There is often a substantial delay between the time that a cheque is written and the time that the ultimate recipient can use the money. In the UK it generally takes between two and four days to clear a cheque and, as **Exhibit 13.27** shows, this is only one of the causes of delay.

Some firms are able to take advantage of this delay to boost their cash balances. Take a firm which writes, on average, cheques for £1,000 per day, where the managers know from experience that these cheques generally take five days to clear (that is, for the cheque to be received, paid into a bank account and for the cash to be drawn from the bank account). This means that the cheque book balance will be £5,000 less than the bank balance. If the firm also receives cheques of £1,000 per day from customers and takes three days to deposit and clear cheques, its cheque book balance will be £3,000 more than its bank balance. In total there will be a *net float* of £2,000 due to the delay in processing cheques. For large firms the float can run into millions of pounds and the resulting interest savings can be very large. If BT, with a turnover of £19.5bn per year, can obtain its money one day earlier, the cash balance will increase by £53m.

The *float* is the difference between the cash balance shown on the firm's cheque book and the bank account. The size of the float depends on the firm's ability to slow the cash transfer on cheques written and to accelerate the crediting of bank accounts with cheques received. Some firms are much more efficient at this than others and are capable of running accounts which are positive at the bank but are negative on the cheque book for lengthy periods.

Exhibit 13.27 The delays in clearing a cheque

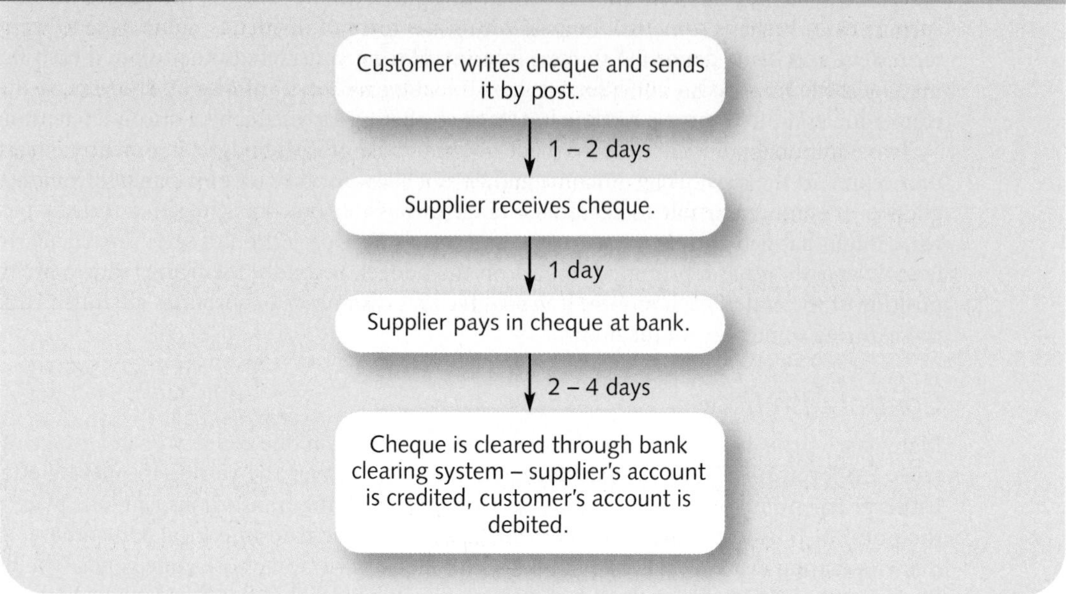

The banking system has responded to the growing need to speed up the transfer of money from one firm to another. For example, the **CHAPS** system in the UK (Clearing House Automated Payments System) permits same-day payment (in sterling and euros) and **CHIPS** (Clearing House Interbank Payment System), a computerised network, enables the electronic transfer of international dollar payments. These systems provide two benefits to the larger firms which use them. First, there is greater certainty as to when money will be received, and secondly, they can reduce the time that money is in the banking system.

Companies can take other action to create a beneficial float. They could bank frequently to avoid having cheques remaining in the accounts office for more than a few hours. They could also encourage customers to pay on time, or even in advance of the receipt of goods and services, by using the **direct debit** system through which money is automatically transferred from one account to another on a regular basis. Many UK consumers now pay for gas, telecommunications and electricity via a monthly direct debit. In return they often receive a small discount. From the producer's viewpoint this not only reduces the float but also avoids the onerous task of chasing late payers. Also retailers now have terminals which permit **electronic funds transfer at the point of sale** (EFTPOS) – money taken from customers' accounts electronically using a debit card.

For larger companies, with separate divisions, branches, offices or subsidiaries, each with their own bank accounts and cash inflows and outflows, most banks offer an automated pooling of balances into one master account. This may be done on a purely notional basis (if proper cross-guarantees and set-off agreements are in place). With notional pooling no cash is moved but interest is charged (paid) on the combined balance.

Inventory management

The form of inventory varies from one firm to another. For a construction firm it may consist of bricks, timber and unsold houses, while for a retailer it is goods bought in for sale but as yet unsold.

The quantity of inventory held is determined by factors such as the predictability of sales and production (more volatility may call for more safety stocks), the length of time it takes to produce and the nature of the product. On the last point, note that a dairy company is likely to have low stock levels relative to sales because of the danger of deterioration, whereas a jeweller will have large inventories to offer greater choice to the customer. Manufacturers with lengthy production cycles such as shipbuilders will have proportionately higher inventories than, say, a fast food chain.

Firms have the difficult task of balancing the costs of holding inventories against the costs which arise from having low inventory levels. The costs of holding inventories include the lost interest on the money tied up in stocks as well as additional storage costs (for example, rent, secure and temperature-controlled warehousing), insurance costs and the risk of obsolescence. The costs of holding low stock levels fall into two categories. First, a low stock level calls for frequent reordering. Each order involves administration costs (office employees' time, paperwork, etc.) and the physical handling of the goods (warehouse employees' time). Secondly, in a world of uncertainty there is a risk of stock-outs when production is halted for want of raw materials or WIP and/or sales are lost because of inadequate stocks of finished goods. Stock-out costs can be considerable; in the short term sales and profits fall, and in the long run customer goodwill is lost. These costs are shown in **Exhibit 13.28**.

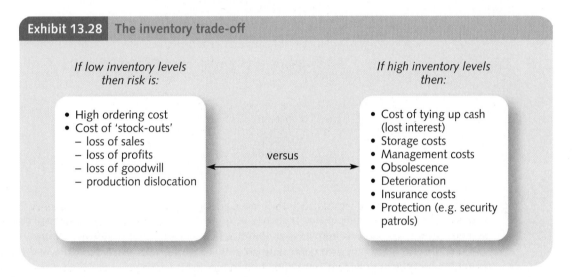

Exhibit 13.28 The inventory trade-off

If low inventory levels then risk is:

- High ordering cost
- Cost of 'stock-outs'
  - loss of sales
  - loss of profits
  - loss of goodwill
  - production dislocation

versus

If high inventory levels then:

- Cost of tying up cash (lost interest)
- Storage costs
- Management costs
- Obsolescence
- Deterioration
- Insurance costs
- Protection (e.g. security patrols)

Inventory management modelling in a world of certainty

If the usage and delivery of stock can be predicted accurately management are likely to avoid stock-out costs and need only concern themselves with achieving the optimal balance between ordering costs (the first point in the left box of Exhibit 13.28) and 'holding costs' (the right box of Exhibit 13.28). Given a steady usage of raw materials we can calculate the optimum size of order to be placed with suppliers. **Exhibit 13.29** shows a gradual rundown of stock levels until zero stock is reached, at which time there is an instant replenishment – taking stock back to the maximum level, Q. Each time stock is reordered there are ordering costs and so the firm naturally wishes to reduce this to a minimum, but on the other hand if it reorders very infrequently the average stock levels, $Q/2$, will be high and the holding costs will be excessive.

Exhibit 13.29 Stock levels over time in a predictable environment

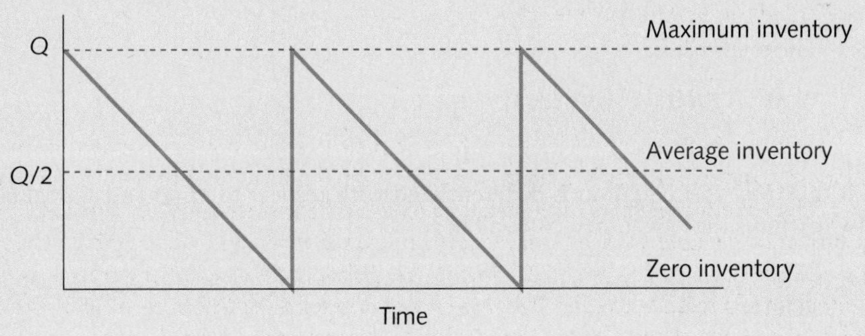

The holding costs are assumed to rise in proportion to the rise in the quantity ordered on each occasion (because of the rise in the average stock level) in **Exhibit 13.30**.

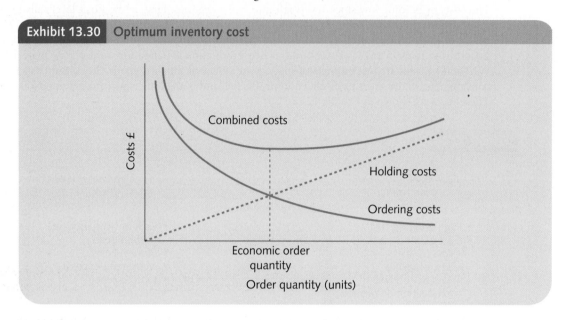

Exhibit 13.30 Optimum inventory cost

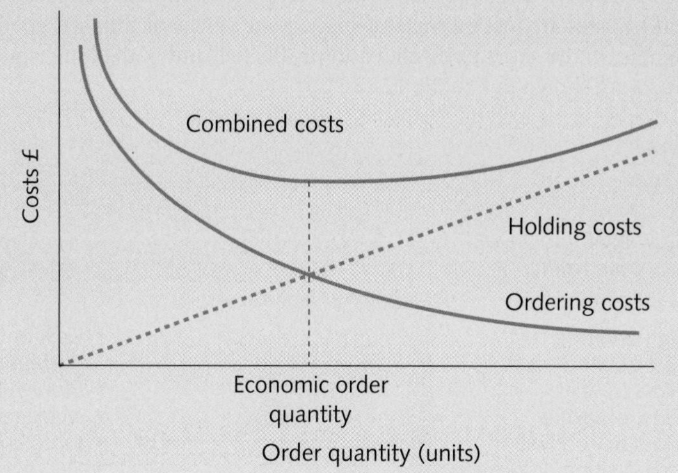

The ordering costs decline as the frequency of ordering declines and large orders are made on each occasion. There is an economic order quantity, EOQ, which minimises the combined costs.

If *C* is the cost of placing each order, *A* is the annual usage of the inventory items, and *H* is the cost of holding one unit of stock for one year then:

The annual ordering costs = Number of orders per year × Cost of each order

$$= A/Q \times C$$

$$\text{or } \frac{AC}{Q}$$

and:

The cost of holding stock = Average stock level (in units) × Cost of holding each unit per year

$$= Q/2 \times H$$

$$\text{or } \frac{HQ}{2}$$

The total cost is:

$$\frac{AC}{Q} + \frac{HQ}{2}$$

If this total cost equation is differentiated with respect to EOQ and set equal to zero the EOQ which gives the lowest total cost will be:

$$\text{EOQ} = \sqrt{\frac{2AC}{H}}$$

Worked example 13.1 Wicker plc

Wicker plc uses 20,000 units per year of a particular item of stock. It costs £28 for each order and the cost of holding each of the units is £1.20. What is the economic order quantity?

Answer

$$EOQ = \sqrt{\frac{2 \times 20{,}000 \times 28}{1.20}} = 966 \text{ units}$$

Each order will be for 966 units, which will cost an annual total of:

$$\frac{AC}{Q} = \frac{HQ}{2}$$

$$= (20{,}000 \times 28)/966 + (1.20 \times 966)/2 = £1{,}159.31$$

(This excludes the amount paid to the supplier for the particular inventory.)

The EOQ model used above has failed to take account of two types of risk:

1 There may be uncertainty over the time it takes for an order to be delivered. That is, the 'lead time' is neither 0 (as assumed in Exhibit 13.29 where instant delivery takes place) nor necessarily predictable.

2 The rate at which inventory is used may not be as shown in Exhibit 13.29 – demand may be subject to fluctuations and the overall annual demand may be impossible to predict with accuracy.

To cope with these two risk elements the company will hold buffer (or safety) stocks. These buffer stock levels can be calculated by weighing up the costs of stock-outs and the cost of holding additional inventories. This can be done in complicated mathematical fashion using probability distribution and sophisticated statistics, but for most firms a more pragmatic approach is adopted, with some estimate of uncertainty gained by subjective assessment defining the most appropriate buffer level. Consider first a firm which has to wait one week between reordering and the delivery of stock. For now we will assume that the weekly usage is stable and certain at 2,000 units per week and that the lead time is predictable. The economic order quantity is set at 8,000 units. To avoid having any stock-outs this firm will need to reorder when the stock levels fall to 2,000 units. This is shown in **Exhibit 13.31**.

Exhibit 13.31 Inventory level pattern when there is a delay between order and delivery

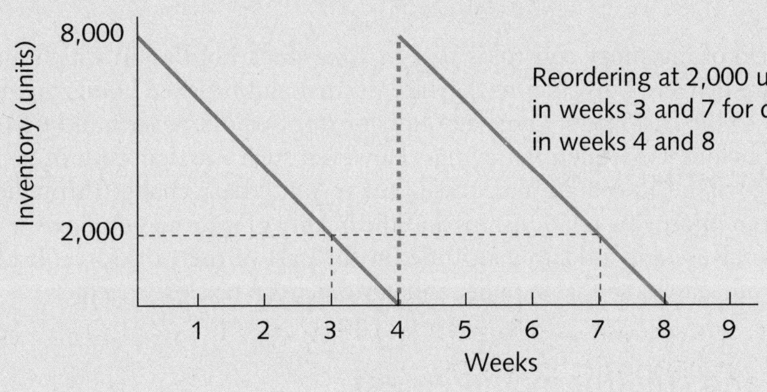

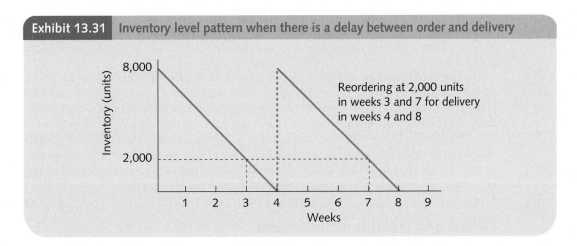

Now assume uncertainty over the lead time – it may be one week or it may be two – it is impossible to be precise because of the unreliability of the supplier. The firm will need to have a maximum inventory holding of 10,000 units with an EOQ of 8,000 units as shown in **Exhibit 13.32**.

Exhibit 13.32 Inventory level pattern when there is uncertainty over the lead time

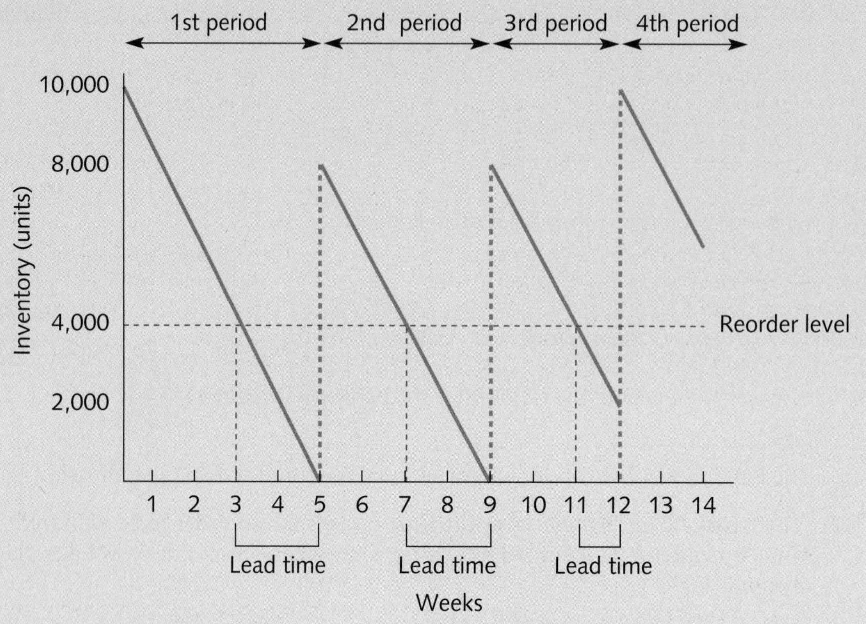

The firm has to ensure a maximum inventory level of 10,000 units just in case the supplier takes two weeks to deliver. Given the usage rate of 2,000 units per week the reorder level is set at 4,000 units and so in the first period, at the end of the third week, 8,000 units are ordered. It so happens that the supplier is slow with this order and delivery does not take place until the end of the fifth week. Again in the second period the supplier takes two weeks but the reorder level of 4,000 was reached in the seventh week and so the firm does not run out of stock. In the third period stocks are reordered at the end of the eleventh week and this time the supplier delivers one week later, resulting in total stocks rising to 10,000.

Another major element of uncertainty is on the demand side: the usage rate of the stock. The company may decide to increase the buffer stock to a higher level to prevent costly stock-outs due to the unpredictability of the firm's production or sales flow. The mathematics to allow for the extra layer of risk are beyond the scope of this book, and anyway many of the elements such as loss of customer goodwill or idle time of some of the workforce are difficult to quantify in most cases. As in so many areas of finance, managerial judgement comes to the fore in setting acceptable buffer stocks.

One form of inventory control is ***just-in-time* stock holding** in which materials and work in progress are delivered just before they are needed and finished goods are produced just before being sent to the customers. Large amounts of stock would never build up in such a system and there are obvious consequential savings. However, such a system cannot be introduced in isolation. There will be a need, in many cases, for revolutionary change throughout the organisation ranging from improving relationships and the quality of information flows to suppliers to a 'right-first-time' culture and a flexible attitude on the part of the workforce. It may even require the relocation of factories so that supplier and customer can be close together.

Debtor and creditor management

Trade credit is both a source and a use of finance. Chapter 12 dealt with the management of trade debtors and creditors. Here we will focus on a summary of the trade-off a firm has to consider when judging whether to accept trade credit. This is shown in **Exhibit 13.33**.

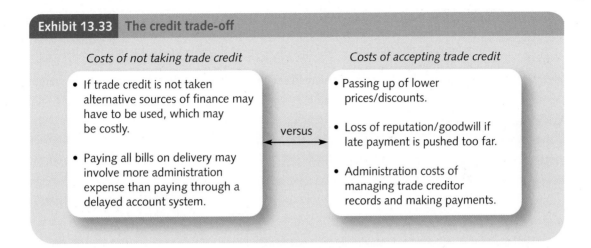

Exhibit 13.33 The credit trade-off

Costs of not taking trade credit

- If trade credit is not taken alternative sources of finance may have to be used, which may be costly.
- Paying all bills on delivery may involve more administration expense than paying through a delayed account system.

versus

Costs of accepting trade credit

- Passing up of lower prices/discounts.
- Loss of reputation/goodwill if late payment is pushed too far.
- Administration costs of managing trade creditor records and making payments.

Investment of temporary surplus funds

Most companies generate occasional cash surpluses which need to be kept within the business to be used at a later date. In the meantime opportunities should be taken to generate a return on these funds by following the treasurer's maxim 'never let cash lie idle'.

Short-term cash surpluses arise for a number of reasons and for varying periods of time. If a business is seasonal or cyclical there may be a build-up of cash in certain periods. For example, in 2007 Motorola was heavily criticised for having $10.7bn in near-cash financial instruments. Some of the shareholding critics would have preferred the company to pay out this money to them. The management, however, argued that the industry is a cyclical one and they need large cash or near-cash balances in good times in order to maintain product development and capital spending through a downturn in profits.

Firms also build up cash reserves to be able to meet large outflow events such as major asset purchases, dividends, tax bills or bond redemptions. In addition, some firms may have sold an asset or raised fresh borrowing but have yet to direct that money to its final use. Alternatively, cash could be in surplus due to surprisingly good control of working capital. Sometimes cash builds up because the business is highly profitable and the management choose to hold on to it. In 2007 Microsoft was generating cash at a rate of around $3bn per quarter, totalling $34bn.

Senior management, in partnership with the treasurer, need to consider carefully what proportion of surplus cash is permanent and therefore available for dividends or to repay debt and what proportion is really temporary.

The objective

A treasurer will set as an objective the maximisation of return from temporarily surplus cash, but this is subject to the constraints imposed by risk. One of those risk elements is the possibility of not having cash available at the right time to fund working capital – this is **liquidity risk**, i.e. not being able to sell the investment and raise cash quickly. There is a requirement to ensure that investments are sufficiently liquid to match anticipated cash flow needs and that there is a reserve (a safety margin) to provide a buffer against unpredictable events. Funds invested in a commercial bill may not be available for a three-month period whereas money placed in a 'sight' bank account can be withdrawn at very short notice. There is a price to pay for this degree of flexibility: keeping other factors constant, the rate of return on a more liquid financial asset is less than that on a less liquid one.

Another consideration for the treasurer is the risk of default (**credit risk**). This is the risk that the borrower will be unable to meet the interest and principal payments. Lending to the UK government (for example, buying Treasury bills) carries a minute default risk whereas investment in shares or corporate bonds can carry significant risk of non-payment.

Another risk factor is **event risk**. This is the probability that some events such as a change in capital structure (leverage) of the borrower will occur which will increase the risk of default. **Valuation risk** (or **price risk**) occurs because of the possibility that when the instrument matures or is sold in the market the amount received is less than anticipated. It could be that interest rates have risen unexpectedly, which will depress bond prices, or the investing firm may have to pay a penalty for early redemption. **Inflation risk** is the probability of a reduction in purchasing power of a sum of money.

The treasurer has the task of balancing return and acceptable risk when investing temporarily surplus funds, as shown in Exhibit 13.34.

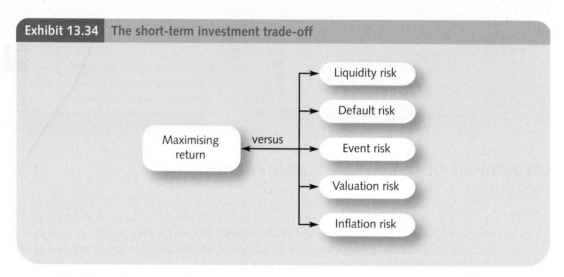

Exhibit 13.34 The short-term investment trade-off

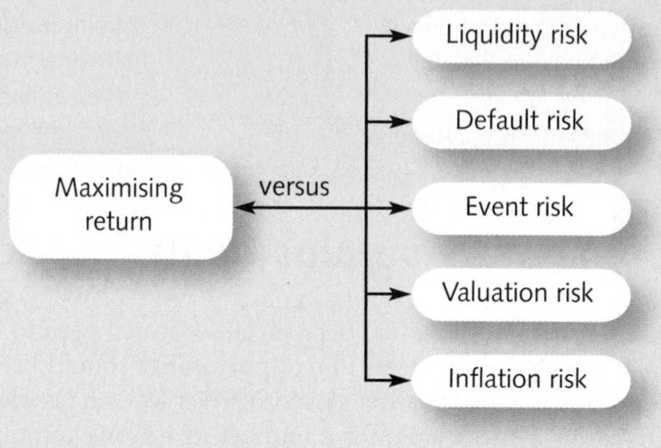

Investment policy

There are three crucial areas in which senior management need to set policy guidelines for treasurers:

1 ***Defining the investable funds*** Just how much of the firm's cash is to be available to invest is often a difficult decision. Subsidiaries will require minimum working capital and so cash has to be allocated to the units by the centre. But subsidiaries often lack the specialised personnel and economies of scale to carry out effective surplus cash investment so this is best done from the centre. It is therefore necessary to have policies and mechanisms for transferring cash between the central treasury and the operating units. The centre will need to provide sufficient cash to the subsidiaries to avoid liquidity risk, that is, a shortage of cash to pay day-to-day bills. This is likely to be uppermost in the minds of subsidiary managers whereas the treasurer will want to keep a tight rein to ensure cash is not being kept idle. This tension needs clever resolution.

2 ***Acceptable investment*** The treasurer may be permitted a wide range of investments, from bank deposits to futures and options. Alternatively there may be limits placed on the type of investment. For example, foreign shares may be excluded because of the valuation risk and the risk of exchange rates moving adversely. Perhaps all derivative instruments are banned except for the purpose of hedging.

3 ***Limits on holdings*** Within the acceptable range of instruments it may be necessary to set maximum acceptable holdings. This may be in terms of total monetary amount or as a proportion of the total investable funds. For example, the treasurer may not be permitted to invest more than 30 per cent of funds in the Euromarkets.

Investment choice

The range of instruments open to the treasurer is large. Some idea of this can be gained by examining the money market table published daily in the *Financial Times*, one of which is reproduced in Exhibit 13.35. Descriptions of the instruments are given in Exhibit 13.36.

The extent of marketability (or ability to sell in the secondary market) influences the interest paid. If you, as an investor, are unable to liquidate your investment before six months have passed, you are likely to insist on a higher return than if you could sell the financial security to another investor at any stage to retrieve your funds. The treasurer has not only a range of instruments to choose from but also a range of maturities, from overnight deposits to one-year commitments. It is also necessary to consider carefully the tax implications of each investment decision as well as the foreign exchange risk if non-sterling investments are made. One crucial final point is that the treasurer has to consider the administrative complexity and specialist skills needed to understand and use appropriately some of the more exotic instruments.

Exhibit 13.35

UK interest rates

FT

Mar 7	Over-night	7 days notice	One month	Three months	Six months	One year
Interbank Sterling	$5\frac{11}{32} - 5\frac{3}{16}$	$5\frac{11}{32} - 5\frac{9}{32}$	$5\frac{7}{16} - 5\frac{11}{32}$	$5\frac{17}{32} - 5\frac{7}{16}$	$5\frac{21}{32} - 5\frac{9}{16}$	$5\frac{3}{4} - 5\frac{21}{32}$
BBA Sterling	$5\frac{1}{4}$	$5\frac{11}{32}$	$5\frac{7}{16}$	$5\frac{17}{32}$	$5\frac{5}{8}$	$5\frac{23}{32}$
Sterling CDs			$5\frac{13}{32} - 5\frac{5}{16}$	$5\frac{1}{2} - 5\frac{13}{32}$	$5\frac{21}{32} - 5\frac{19}{32}$	$5\frac{13}{16} - 5\frac{23}{32}$
Treasury Bills			$5\frac{13}{32} - 5\frac{11}{32}$	$5\frac{1}{2} - 5\frac{7}{16}$		
Bank Bills			$5\frac{13}{32} - 5\frac{11}{32}$	$5\frac{1}{2} - 5\frac{7}{16}$		
†Local authority deps.		$5\frac{3}{8} - 5\frac{1}{4}$	$5\frac{3}{8} - 5\frac{5}{16}$	$5\frac{1}{2} - 5\frac{7}{16}$	$5\frac{19}{32} - 5\frac{17}{32}$	$5\frac{11}{16} - 5\frac{5}{8}$
Discount Market deps.	$5\frac{5}{16} - 5\frac{1}{4}$	$5\frac{3}{8} - 5\frac{9}{32}$				

Note: The lower rate quoted is the rate applicable to lenders, the higher rate is payable by borrowers.
Source: *Financial Times*, 8 March 2007. Reprinted with permission.

Exhibit 13.36 Some of the investments available to a corporate treasurer

'Sight' deposit at a bank, e.g. current account	Instant withdrawal – highly liquid but low (no) interest rate.
Deposit account (Time deposit) at a bank	Some notice is required to withdraw funds.
Interbank lending: (a) In sterling (b) In foreign currencies	Banks and others with a very high credit rating borrow from each other at these interest rates. The second rate shown applies if you are lending, the other (higher) rate applies if you, as a bank, are borrowing. LIBOR is the offer rate (the cost of borrowing if you are a top quality bank borrower in sterling). Lenders into the market do not need to be highly rated.
Certificate of deposit (CD) (also, confusingly, called 'time deposit')	A company agrees to lock away a sum (e.g. £500,000) in a bank deposit for a period of between seven days and five years (usually three or six months). The bank provides the company with a certificate of deposit stating that the bank will pay interest and the original capital to the holder. This is now a valuable instrument and the company can sell this to release cash. The buyer of the CD will receive the deposited money on maturity plus interest. Result: the bank has money deposited for a set period and the original lender can obtain cash by selling CD at any time.
Treasury bills	Sold by the government at a discount to face value to provide an effective yield. Tradable in the secondary market.
Bank bills (acceptance credits) – *see* Chapter 12	A bill accepted by a bank. The bank is committed to pay the amount on the bill at maturity. A company with surplus cash could invest in such a bill.
Local authority deposits or notes	Lending to a local authority (local government).
Discount market deposits	A deposit normally repayable at call (on demand) or made for a very short term with a London discount house.

▶

Money market funds	The firm invests in the money market fund which itself invests in short-term tradable paper, such as Treasury bills or bank bills. The pooling and portfolios effects mean that many market funds can offer good rates, an AAA credit rating and same-day liquidity.
Gilts	Purchase of UK government bonds, usually in the secondary market.
Corporate bonds	Secondary-market purchases of bonds issued by other firms.
Eurobonds, FRN, EMTN	Lending on an international bond – *see* Chapter 11.
Eurocurrency	Short-term wholesale money market deposits made in a currency outside the jurisdiction of the authorities of that currency.
Commercial paper	Unsecured promissory note: usually 60 days or less to maturity – *see* Chapter 11.
Shares	*See* Chapters 9 and 10.
Derivatives (futures, swaps, options, etc.)	*See* Chapter 24.

Concluding comments

Considering the complexity of modern finance it is not surprising that treasury management has become a profession in its own right. The efficient management of short-term assets and liabilities gives the competitive edge needed for a firm to survive and thrive.

This chapter has highlighted the core issues in treasury and working capital management but, in all truth, it has only skimmed the surface. One major question left untouched is whether to centralise the treasury function. The oil group, Shell, has chosen to centralise its treasury functions, so that today, despite Shell businesses operating in 145 countries, its cash and foreign exchange needs are handled by treasury operations in only three centres: London, Houston and Singapore. They handle 70,000 internal and external transactions worth over US$3,000bn per annum. The operating companies that make up Shell are able to use the central treasury for foreign exchange and money market deals. In this way the best rates can be achieved on the market due to economies of scale and netting (combining subsidiary balances and simply dealing with the net amounts), control over risk levels can be exercised, skills can be concentrated and advantage can be taken of the sophisticated computerised treasury management systems. The argument against centralisation is that this can be bureaucratic, inflexible and slow to respond to the immediate needs of the operating managers in far-flung places.

Another fundamental question is whether the treasury should act as a risk minimiser or a profit maximiser. Many companies make use of the derivative markets both to hedge (reduce risk) foreign exchange and interest rates, and for 'trading' purposes to try to make gains. Most firms, for example Pearson, are adamant that their treasury should not speculate: 'The treasury department is not a profit centre' (*Pearson plc Governance and Financial Statements, 2005*). The danger with instructing the treasury to act as a profit centre is that the managers may be tempted to take excessive risks. There have been some spectacular and well-publicised losses made by members of treasury teams. The embarrassment to ostensibly staid and low-risk firms such as Procter & Gamble (US$100m+ lost) can be considerable.

Key points and concepts

- **Working capital** is net current assets or net current liabilities.
- In deciding **whether to borrow long or short** a company might consider the following:
  - maturity structure of debt;
  - cost of issue or arrangement;
  - flexibility;
  - the uncertainty of getting future finance;
  - the term structure of interest rates.
- Firms often strive to **match** the maturity structure of debt with the maturity structure of assets. However a more **aggressive financing policy** would finance permanent short-term assets with short-term finance. A more **conservative policy** would finance all assets with long-term finance.
- Firms need to consider the **currency in which they borrow**.
- A balance needs to be struck between **fixed and floating** interest-rate debt.
- Don't forget **retained earnings** as a financing option:

  Advantages
  - No dilution of existing shareholders' returns or control
  - No issue costs
  - Managers may not have to explain use of funds (dubious advantage for shareholders)

  Disadvantages
  - Limited by firm's profits
  - Dividend payment reduced
  - Subject to uncertainty
  - Regarded as 'free capital'
- **Treasurers** help decision making at a **strategic level**:

  e.g. mergers, interest and exchange-rate changes, capital structure.
- **Good relationships need to be developed with the financial community**.

  This requires effort – often the treasurer makes a major contribution:
  - flow of information;
  - number of banks;
  - transaction banking versus relationship banking.
- Some of the **risks** which can **be reduced or avoided** by a firm:
  - business risk;
  - insurable risk;
  - currency risk;
  - interest-rate risk.
- The **working capital cycle** flows from raw materials, to work in progress, to finished goods stock, to sales, and collection of cash, with creditors used to reduce the cash burden.
- The **cash-conversion cycle** is the length of time between the company's outlay on inputs and the receipt of money from the sale of goods. It equals the stock-conversion period plus the debtor-conversion period minus the credit period granted by suppliers.
- **Working capital tension** Too little working capital leads to loss of production, sales and goodwill. Too much working capital leads to excessive costs of tying up funds, storage, handling and ordering costs.
- **Working capital policies:**
  - relaxed – large proportional increases in working capital as sales rise;
  - aggressive – small proportional increases in working capital as sales rise.

- **Overtrading** occurs when a business has insufficient finance for working capital to sustain its level of trading.
- The **motives for holding cash:**
  - transactional motive;
  - precautionary motive;
  - speculative motive.
- **Baumol's cash management model:**

$$Q^* = \sqrt{\frac{2CA}{K}}$$

- **Some considerations for cash management:**
  - create a policy framework;
  - plan cash flows, e.g. cash budgets;
  - control cash flows.
- **Inventory management** requires a balance of the trade-off between the costs of high inventory (interest, storage, management, obsolescence, deterioration, insurance and protection costs) against ordering costs and stock-out costs.
- An **economic order quantity** in a world of certainty can be found:

$$EOQ = \sqrt{\frac{2AC}{H}}$$

  With uncertainty buffer stocks may be needed.
- In **investing temporarily surplus cash** the treasurer has to consider the trade-off between return and risk (liquidity, default, event, valuation and inflation). Investment policy considerations:
  - defining the investable funds;
  - acceptable investments;
  - limits on holdings.

References and further reading

Ball, M., Brady, S. and Olivier, C. (1995) 'Getting the best from your banks', *Corporate Finance*, July, pp. 26–47.
Fascinating insight into the world of high finance.

Baumol, W.J. (1952) 'The transactions demand for cash: An inventory theoretic approach', *Quarterly Journal of Economics*, November, pp. 545–56.
Cash model is presented.

Brigham, E.F., Gapenski, L.C. and Ehrhardt, M.C. (2001) *Financial Management: Theory and Practice.* 10th edn. Fort Worth, TX: Dryden Press.
More detailed treatment of working capital issues.

Churchill, N.C. and Mullins J.W. (2001) 'How fast can your company afford to grow?', *Harvard Business Review*, May.
An easy-to-read guide to avoid overtrading.

Collier, P., Cooke, T. and Glynn, J. (1988) *Financial and Treasury Management.* Oxford: Heinemann CIMA series.
Good coverage of the essential elements of treasury management.

Corporate Finance. Monthly journal. London: Euromoney.
Provides insight into high-level corporate finance issues of a practical nature.

Eiteman, D.K., Stonehill, A.I. and Moffett, M.H. (2007) *Multinational Business Finance.* 11th edn. Reading, MA: Addison Wesley.
Chapter 22 discusses many of the additional considerations with regard to working capital, cash and treasury management faced by a multinational enterprise.

Howells, P. and Bain, K. (2004) *Financial Markets and Institutions.* 4th edn. Harlow: Financial Times Prentice Hall.
Includes a useful chapter introducing money market instruments.

Maness, T.S. and Zietlow, J.T. (1993) *Short-Term Financial Management.* St Paul, MN: West Publishing.
A more detailed consideration of many of the issues discussed in this chapter.

Miller, M.N. and Orr, D. (1966) 'A model of the demand for money by firms', *Quarterly Journal of Economics*, August, pp. 413–35.
A more sophisticated model than Baumol's.

Tirole, J. (2006) *The Theory of Corporate Finance.* Princeton, NJ: Princeton University Press.
Chapter 5 takes a highly theoretical/algebraic approach to the question of whether to borrow long or short.

The Treasurer (a monthly journal). London: Euromoney.
Up-to-date consideration of Treasurer matters.

The Treasurers Handbook. London: Association of Corporate Treasurers.
An annual publication. A useful reference work with articles from practitioners.

Westerman, W., and von Eije, H. (2005) 'Multinational cash management in Europe towards centralisation and disintermediation: the Philips case', *Management Finance*, 31(10), pp. 65–74.
An easy-to-follow description of changes in Philips' cash management across 60 currencies in recent years.

Websites

Association of Corporate Treasurers www.treasurers.org
Financial Times www.ft.com

Video presentations

Chief executives and finance directors describe their current policy on raising funds on Cantos.com (w3.cantos.com/cantos) – this is free to view.

Case study recommendations

Please see www.pearsoned.co.uk/arnold for case study synopses

- Dell's working capital. Authors: Richard S. Ruback and Aldo Sesia Jr. (2003). Harvard Business School.
- Toy World, Inc. Author: W. Carl Kester (1996). Harvard Business School.
- Crystal Meadows of Tahoe, Inc. Author: William J. Bruns Jr. (1993) Harvard Business School.

Self-review questions

1 Why do firms hold cash?

2 Why do firms need to make short-term financial investments?

3 Explain what is meant by liquidity risk, event risk and valuation risk.

4 What are the strengths and weaknesses of Baumol's cash management model?

5 Describe the advantages and disadvantages of retained earnings as a source of finance.

6 What are the main considerations when deciding whether to borrow long or short?

7 What are the main areas of risk a treasurer might help to manage?

8 What are relationship banking and transactional banking?

9 Describe the working capital cycle and the cash-conversion cycle.

10 What is overtrading?

11 Why do insurance companies exist?

12 What is an 'aggressive' working capital policy?

13 What is the 'float' in cash management?

14 What is a certificate of deposit?

15 What does it mean to 'make the treasury a profit centre'?

16 What are the main areas of 'control' of cash?

17 What is a cash budget?

18 What is the economic order quantity?

Questions and problems

myfinancelab ***Questions with an icon are also available for practice in MyFinanceLab with additional supporting resources.***

Answers to questions marked with an asterisk are to be found only in the Lecturer's Guide.

1 Tollhouse plc has a large overdraft which is expected to continue. Its annual sales are £10m, spread evenly through the year – the same amount in each week. The interest rate on the overdraft is 11 per cent. The present policy is to pay into the bank the weekly receipts from customers each Friday. However, a new director has raised the question of whether it would be better to pay in on Mondays as well as Fridays

especially in the light of the fact that Monday mornings' receipts are three times the level of those of the other days of the working week. No cash is received on Saturdays or Sundays. It costs £35 each time money is paid into the bank account and all daily cash inflows arrive before the regular paying-in time of 3 p.m. Ignore taxation and consider which of the following four policies is the best for Tollhouse:

a Continue to pay in on Fridays.
b Pay in on Mondays and Fridays.
c Pay in every day of the week.
d Pay in on Mondays and another selected day.

Also discuss ways of reducing the 'float' of a company. ?

2 As the treasurer of Stokes plc you have been asked to write a report putting forward ideas for the use of temporarily surplus cash. These funds will be available for varying periods – from one week to four months.

Describe the main considerations or trade-offs for short-term cash management. Choose any four of the potential investment instruments, describe them and outline their advantages and disadvantages.

3* Rounded plc, a new retail business, has projected sales as follows:

	£m		£m		£m
Jan.	1.3	May	2.0	Sept.	2.0
Feb.	1.5	June	2.2	Oct.	1.8
March	1.6	July	2.3	Nov.	1.9
April	1.5	Aug.	2.0	Dec.	3.0

One-third of sales are for cash, one-third is received one month after the sale, and one-third is received two months after the sale. The cash balance at the beginning of January is £500,000.

A major investment in new shops will cost £2m in cash in May. Stock (items purchased for sale and sold) costs one-half of sales and is purchased and paid for in the same month it is sold.

Labour and other costs amount to £300,000 per month, paid for as incurred. Assume no tax is payable in this year.

Required

a Show the monthly cash balance for the first year.
b Recommend action to be taken based on these cash balances. ?

4 Bluebond uses 300,000 units of raw material per year. It costs £200 to process and receive delivery of this stock regardless of the size of order. It also costs £10 per year to hold a unit for a year. Assuming complete certainty over demand and instantaneous delivery when an order is made, what is the economic order quantity? How many orders will be made per year and what is the total inventory cost of this raw material? ?

5 Blackwide uses 10,000 items of stock per year. It costs £7 to hold an item of stock for a year and the reorder costs are £50 regardless of quantity.

a Find the economic order quantity in a completely certain world with instantaneous replenishment of stock.
b Determine the total inventory cost for this item and the number of orders per year.
c If there was a certain delay in delivery of this item from the time of order of one week, at what level will stock be reordered?
d If the delay between order and delivery can vary from one week to two weeks what is the maximum inventory holding if no stock-outs are to occur?
e What other factors might need to be allowed for in the real world of business? ?

6* Numerical example of treasury investment:

As the treasurer of a firm you anticipate the following cash position which will require either short-term borrowing or investment:

Cash flow forecast for an 11-day period

Opening balance £11,000,000

Day	Net cash flow	Cumulative
1.3.x1	−5,000,000	6,000,000
2.3.x1	−5,000,000	1,000,000
3.3.x1	−6,000,000	−5,000,000
4.3.x1	0	−5,000,000
5.3.x1	+20,000,000	+15,000,000
6.3.x1	−3,000,000	+12,000,000
7.3.x1	−2,000,000	+10,000,000
8.3.x1	+1,000,000	+11,000,000
9.3.x1	0	+11,000,000
10.3.x1	− 500,000	+10,500,000
11.3.x1	+2,000,000	+12,500,000

The interest rates available are:

	Borrowing rate	Lending rate
Interbank overnight	5.75%	5.5%
Interbank seven-day	5.88%	5.67%
Time deposit (seven-day)		5%
Sight deposit at bank		4%
Borrowing on overdraft	7%	

Describe how you would manage the firm's money over this 11-day period.
What are the risks inherent in your plan of action?

?

7 (*Examination level*) You have been asked to prepare a cash budget for Whitborrow plc for the next three months, October, November and December. The managers are concerned that they may not have sufficient cash to pay for a £150,000 investment in equipment in December. The overdraft has reached its limit of £70,000 at the present time – the end of September. Sales during September were a total of £400,000, of which £55,000 was received in cash, £165,000 is expected to be paid in October, with the remainder likely to flow in during November. Sales for the next three months are expected to be:

	Total sales	Cash sales	Credit sales
October	450,000	90,000	360,000
November	550,000	110,000	440,000
December	700,000	140,000	560,000

There is a gross profit margin of 40 per cent on sales. All costs (materials, labour and other) are paid for on receipt. Only 20 per cent of customer sales are expected to be paid for in the month of delivery. A further 70 per cent will be paid after one month and the remainder after two months. Labour and other costs amount to 10 per cent of sales. Debtor levels at the end of September are £400,000 and the investment in stock is £350,000.

Required

a Prepare a cash budget for October, November and December, and state if the firm will be able to purchase the new equipment.

b Recommend action that could be taken to improve the working capital position of Whitborrow. **?**

8* Silk plc invests surplus cash in a range of money-market securities which earn a rate of return of 8 per cent per annum. It tries to hold the smallest cash balances possible while permitting the business to operate. For the next year there will be a need for cash taken from near-cash investments (money market investments) of £40,000 per week. There is a fixed cost of liquidating these securities of £200 regardless of amount (a combination of broker's fees and administration costs). Should Silk draw on these funds every week or at some other interval? Calculate the optimum level of cash balance. **?**

9 It costs £20 in administration expenses and fees every time Davy Ltd pays funds into the bank to reduce its large overdraft on which it is charged 10 per cent annual percentage rate (APR). The company receives net cash from operations of £10,000 per week. How often should Davy pay into the bank? **?**

10 Captain plc buys 100,000 widgets per year at a cost of £15 per widget for use in its production process. The cost of holding one widget in stock, in terms of interest, security, insurance, storage, etc. is £1.20 per year. The cost of reordering and taking delivery of widgets is £250 regardless of the size of the order.

Required

a Calculate the economic order quantity and the total cost of inventory management on the assumption that usage is predictable and even through the year and ordering and delivery of widgets is simultaneous.

b What buffer stock would you suggest if the firm is determined never to have a stock-out and the supplier of Widgets sometimes delivers one week and sometimes three weeks after an order? **?**

11 Christopher Purser said that Glynwed plc's treasury department had as one of its responsibilities to 'Manage the group's cash and currency flows so as to:

- minimise interest paid;
- maximise interest earned;
- minimise currency exposure risk'.

What do you understand by this statement?

12 'I run this business the way I want to. Shareholders and bankers are told once a year how we performed but I will not give them details or meet regularly with them. We have a business to run. Bankers should be treated like any supplier – make them compete to provide the lowest cost service and put everything out to tender and let them bid for each scrap of work.'

Consider this statement by a finance director and relate it to the efforts many treasurers and finance directors make in their relationships with finance providers.

13 (*Examination level*) Reraser plc has grown fast and has recently appointed you as its corporate treasurer. You have been asked by the board to write a report pointing out the ways in which the treasurer's department can help the firm to manage its various risks. Write this report.

14 Explain why firms sometimes have temporarily surplus funds. What considerations are relevant when choosing the type of financial instrument to be purchased with these funds?

15 Calumnor plc's board of directors is concerned that it may have an imbalance in its debt profile. You have been asked to write a report pointing out the main considerations in achieving the right mixture of debt.

16 (*Examination level*) 'The treasurer sits up there in his office, earning a salary three times my level, playing with his computer all day. At least I produce something useful for the firm' – a statement by a shopfloor worker.
Try to persuade this worker that the treasurer contributes to the well-being of the firm by illustrating the activities a typical treasurer might undertake (you do not have to justify the relative salary levels).

17 Describe the motives for holding cash. Why is it useful for a firm to draw up cash budgets?

18 (*Examination level*) Describe the cash conversion cycle and suggest ways of making it smaller.

19 'How can we go bankrupt if we have a full order book and sales rising by 100 per cent per year. Don't be ridiculous.' Explain to this incredulous managing director the problem of overtrading and possible solutions to it.

20 Explain the tension managers have to cope with when judging the correct level of working capital. Also describe the alternative approaches to funding business growth.

21 What are the costs of holding too little or too much cash? Describe what is meant by a policy framework for cash management, planning of cash flow and control of cash flow.

22 Companies go bankrupt if they get working capital management badly wrong. Describe two ways in which this might happen.

23* Rubel plc has the following figures:

	£000s	
	20X1	20X2
Year end figures		
Finished goods inventory	50	55
Work-in-progress inventory	40	38
Raw material inventory	100	110
Debtors	300	250
Creditors	150	160
During the year		
Sales (per annum)	1,000	1,200
Cost of goods sold (per annum)	600	650
Raw material purchases and usage (per annum)	500	550

Calculate the cash-conversion cycle during 20X2.

?

24 Texas plc, a large manufacturer of windscreen wipers, holds 100 days' stock. This contrasts with the 50 days' stock held by its main competitor. Describe what might explain this difference and suggest solutions to any problem areas.

25* (Examination level) Sheetly plc has an overdraft of £500,000 which the directors are alarmed about. Their concern is further aroused by the fact that in July a tax demand for £200,000 will be payable. Also the company expects to pay for replacement vehicles at a cost of £150,000 in August. The present time is the beginning of May and the figures in the table are projected for the next six months.

	May £000	June £000	July £000	Aug £000	Sept £000	Oct £000
Anticipated sales	1,100	1,150	900	800	1,300	1,200
Purchases (materials)	800	810	660	600	950	850
Labour	100	110	90	90	110	100
Rent	50	50	50	50	50	50
Other costs	40	50	60	45	50	60

For each month's sales 30 per cent of the cash is received in the month of sale, 40 per cent is received one month later, with the remainder coming in two months after sale. Debtors at the beginning of May are £200,000 and it is expected that of this, £120,000 will be received in May and £80,000 in June.

Suppliers of materials grant one month's credit and at the beginning of May these suppliers were owed £820,000. All other costs are paid for as incurred.

Required

a Draw up a cash flow forecast for the next six months showing the monthly overdraft if Sheetly continues to rely on this source of finance.

b Suggest ways in which working capital management policy could be altered to reduce the cash flow strain over the forthcoming months.

c Consider the following alternatives to the overdraft and describe their advantages *vis-à-vis* the overdraft:

- factoring;
- hire purchase;
- leasing.

?

myfinancelab

Now retake your diagnostic test for Chapter 13 to check your progress and update your study plan.

Assignments

1 Select an item of stock held by a firm familiar to you and estimate the total cost of holding one unit of that type of inventory for one year. Also obtain some estimate of the cost of placing and receiving an order from the supplier of that stock and the annual usage. Calculate the economic order quantity and appropriate buffer quantity under various assumptions concerning factors which are subject to uncertainty.

2 Consider the working capital cycle of a firm you know well. Try to estimate the length of time money is tied up in each stage. Suggest ways of improving the efficiency of working capital management.

3 If your firm does not yet have a designated treasurer write a report pointing out the value of such a role and recommend whether such an appointment should be made or other, less specialised managers should continue to carry out treasury-type functions.

4 Examine the annual reports of six large quoted UK firms and note the role of the treasury by reading the text and between the lines.

CHAPTER 14

Stock market efficiency

LEARNING OUTCOMES

By the end of this chapter the reader should be able to:

- discuss the meaning of the random walk hypothesis and provide a balanced judgement of the usefulness of past price movements to predict future share prices (weak-form efficiency);
- provide an overview of the evidence for the stock market's ability to take account of all publicly available information including past price movements (semi-strong efficiency);
- state whether stock markets appear to absorb all relevant (public or private) information (strong-form efficiency);
- outline some of the behavioural-based arguments leading to a belief in inefficiencies;
- comment on the implications of the evidence for efficiency for investors and corporate management.

Introduction

The question of whether the stock market is efficient in pricing shares and other securities has fascinated academics, investors and businessmen for a long time. This is hardly surprising: even academics are attracted by the thought that by studying in this area they might be able to discover a stock market inefficiency which is sufficiently exploitable to make them very rich, or at least, to make their name in the academic community. In an **efficient market** systematic undervaluing or overvaluing of shares does not occur, and therefore it is not possible to develop trading rules which will 'beat the market' by, say, buying identifiable underpriced shares, except by chance. However, if the market is inefficient it regularly prices shares incorrectly, allowing a perceptive investor to identify profitable trading opportunities.[1] This is an area of research where millions have been spent trying to find 'nuggets of gold' in the price movements of securities. A small amount of this money has been allocated to university departments, with the vast majority being spent by major securities houses around the world and by people buying investment advice from professional analysts offering to 'pick winners'. Money has also been taken from the computer literati paying for real-time stock market prices and analytical software to be piped into their personal computer, and by the millions of buyers of books which promise riches beyond imagining if the reader follows a few simple stock market trading rules.

They do say that a fool and his money are soon parted – never was this so true as in the world of stock market investment with its fringe of charlatans selling investment potions to cure all financial worries. This chapter may help the reader to discern what investment advice is, and is not, worth paying for. But this is too limited an ambition; the reader should also appreciate the significance of the discovery that for most of the people and for most of the time the stock market correctly prices shares given the information available (and it is extremely difficult to make more than normal returns). There are profound implications for business leaders and their interaction with the share markets, for professional fund managers, and for small investors.

What is meant by efficiency?

In an efficient capital market, security (for example shares) prices rationally reflect available information.

The **efficient market hypothesis (EMH)** implies that, if new information is revealed about a firm, it will be incorporated into the share price rapidly and rationally, with respect to the direction of the share price movement and the size of that movement. In an efficient market no trader will be presented with an opportunity for making a return on a share (or other security) that is greater than a fair return for the risk associated with that share, except by chance. The absence of abnormal profit possibilities arises because current and past information is immediately reflected in current prices. It is only new information that causes prices to change. News is by definition unforecastable and therefore future price changes are unforecastable. Stock market efficiency does not mean that investors have perfect powers of prediction; all it means is that the current share price level is an unbiased estimate of its true economic value based on the information revealed.

Market efficiency does not mean that share prices are equal to true value at every point in time. It means that the errors that are made in pricing shares are unbiased; price deviations from true value are random. Fifty per cent of efficiently priced shares turn out to perform better than the market as a whole and 50 per cent perform worse; the efficient price is unbiased in the statistical sense. So if Marks and Spencer's shares are currently priced at £7 it could be, over the next five

[1] Even though this discussion of the efficient markets hypothesis is set within the context of the equity markets in this chapter, it must be noted that the efficient pricing of financial and real assets is discussed in many contexts; from whether currencies are efficiently priced vis-à-vis each other to the pricing of commodities, bonds, property and derivative instruments.

years, that we discover they were grossly overpriced at £7, or that events show them to be under-priced at £7. Efficiency merely means that there is an equal chance of our being too pessimistic at £7 as being too optimistic. The same logic applies to shares on high or low price-earnings ratios (PERs). That is, shares with low PERs should be no more likely to be overvalued or undervalued than shares with high PERs. Both groups have an equal chance of being wrongly priced given future economic events on both the upside and the downside.

In the major stock markets of the world prices are set by the forces of supply and demand. There are hundreds of analysts and thousands of traders, each receiving new information on a company through electronic and paper media. This may, for example, concern a technological breakthrough, a marketing success or a labour dispute. The individuals who follow the market are interested in making money and it seems reasonable to suppose that they will try to exploit quickly any potentially profitable opportunity. In an efficient market the moment an unexpected, positive piece of information leaks out investors will act and prices will rise rapidly to a level which gives no opportunity to make further profit.

Imagine that BMW announces to the market that it has a prototype electric car which will cost £10,000, has the performance of a petrol-driven car and will run for 500 miles before needing a low-cost recharge. This is something motorists and environmentalists have been demanding for many years. The profit-motivated investor will try to assess the value of a share in BMW to see if it is currently underpriced given the new information. The probability that BMW will be able successfully to turn a prototype into a mass market production model will come into the equation. Also the potential reaction of competitors, the state of overall car market demand and a host of other factors have to be weighed up to judge the potential of the electric car and the future returns on a BMW share. No analyst or shareholder is able to anticipate perfectly the commercial viability of BMW's technological breakthrough but they are required to think in terms of probabilities and attempt to make a judgement.

If one assumes that the announcement is made on Monday at 10 a.m. and the overwhelming weight of investor opinion is that the electric car will greatly improve BMW's share returns, in an efficient market the share price will move to a higher level within seconds. The new higher price at 10.01 a.m. is efficient but incorporates a different set of information to that incorporated in the price prevailing at 10 a.m. Investors should not be able to buy BMW shares at 10.01 a.m. and make abnormal profits except by chance.

Most investors are too late

Efficiency requires that new information is rapidly assimilated into share prices. In the sophisticated financial markets of today the speedy dissemination of data and information by cheap electronic communication means that there are large numbers of informed investors and advisers. These individuals are often highly intelligent and capable of fast analysis and quick action, and therefore there is reason to believe many stock markets are efficient at pricing securities. However, this belief is far from universal. Thousands of highly paid analysts and advisers maintain that they can analyse better and act more quickly than the rest of the pack and so make abnormally high returns for their clients. There is a well-known story which is used to mock the efficient market theoreticians:

A lecturer was walking along a busy corridor with a student on his way to lecture on the efficient market hypothesis. The student noticed a £20 note lying on the floor and stooped to pick it up. The lecturer stopped him, saying, 'If it was really there, someone would have picked it up by now'.

With such reasoning the arch-advocates of the EMH dismiss any trading system which an investor may believe he has discovered to pick winning shares. If this system truly worked, they say, someone would have exploited it before and the price would have already moved to its efficient level.

This position is opposed by professional analysts: giving investment advice and managing collective funds is a multi-billion pound industry and those employed in it do not like being told that most of them do not beat the market. However, a *few* stock pickers do seem to perform extraordinarily well on a consistent basis over a long period of time. There is strong anecdotal evidence that some people are able to exploit inefficiencies – we will examine some performance records later.

What efficiency does not mean

To provide more clarity on what efficiency is, we need to deal with a few misunderstandings held by people with a little knowledge (a dangerous thing):

- **Efficiency means that prices do not depart from true economic value** This is false. At any one time we would expect most shares to deviate from true value, largely because value depends on the future, which is very uncertain (*see* Chapter 20 on share valuation). However, under the EMH we would expect the deviations to be random.
- **You will not come across an investor beating the market in any single time period** This is false because you would expect, in an efficient market, that approximately one-half of shares bought subsequently outperform. So, many investors, unless they buy such a broad range of shares that their portfolio tracks the market, would outperform. Note that, under the EMH, this is not due to skill, but simply caused by the randomness of price deviations from true economic value.
- **No investor following a particular investment strategy will beat the market in the long term** This is false simply because there are millions of investors. In a completely efficient market, with prices deviating in a random fashion from true value, it is likely that you could find a few investors who have outperformed the market over many years. This can happen because of the laws of probability; even if the probability of your investment approach beating the market is very small, the fact that there are millions of investors means that, purely by chance, a few will beat the market. Unfortunately, it is very difficult to investigate whether a long-term outperformance is luck or evidence against the EMH. We look at the performance of someone who has consistently outperformed for more than fifty years, Warren Buffett, later in the chapter. Some people believe his success is due to luck in an efficient market, others put it down to superior share-picking ability – you will have to make up your own mind.

Types of efficiency

Efficiency is an ambiguous word and we need to establish some clarity before we go on. There are three types of efficiency:

1. ***Operational efficiency*** This refers to the cost, speed and reliability of transactions in securities on the exchange. It is desirable that the market carries out its operations at as low a cost as possible, speedily and reliably. This may be promoted by creating as much competition between market makers and brokers as possible so that they earn only normal profits and not excessively high profits. It may also be enhanced by competition between exchanges for secondary-market transactions.
2. ***Allocational efficiency*** Society has a scarcity of resources (that is, they are not infinite) and it is important that we find mechanisms which allocate those resources to where they can be most productive. Those industrial and commercial firms with the greatest potential to use investment funds effectively need a method to channel funds their way. Stock markets help in the process of allocating society's resources between competing real investments. For example, an efficient market provides vast funds for the growth of the electronics, pharmaceuticals and biotechnology industries (through new issues, rights issues, etc.) but allocates only small amounts for slow-growth industries. Exhibit 14.1 discusses the importance of the financial markets in allocating society's scarce resources.
3. ***Pricing efficiency*** It is pricing efficiency that is the focus of this chapter, and the term 'efficient market hypothesis' applies to this form of efficiency only. In a pricing-efficient market the investor can expect to earn merely a risk-adjusted return from an investment as prices move instantaneously and in an unbiased manner to any news.

The black line in Exhibit 14.2 shows an efficient market response to BMW's (fictional) announcement of an electric car. The share price instantaneously adjusts to the new level. However, there are four other possibilities if we relax the efficiency assumption. First, the market could take a long time to absorb this information (under-reaction) and it could be only after the tenth day that the

Exhibit 14.1

Investors are taking the lead to help save the planet

Douglas Ferrans and Peter Scales

Climate change is one of the most serious issues facing the planet. This poses risks and opportunities to which investors and companies must respond.

Tackling climate change will hinge on the investment decisions made by institutional investors. Pension funds, insurance companies and other institutional investors hold approximately half of the shares listed on the London Stock Exchange. Other big markets around the world have similar concentrations of ownership.

How quickly these institutions move their investments from high-carbon to low-carbon companies will, to a large extent, determine our success in mitigating global warming. These investors' decisions will turn on assessments of the longevity of oil and gas fields; the ownership and control of energy supplies; the effectiveness of any regulations to control carbon emissions; the profitability of emerging low-carbon technologies and carbon capture techniques; and the willingness of consumers to change their lifestyles.

Until recently, many investors had been unconvinced that climate change would affect their returns significantly. This indifference is passing as the consensus on the severity of global warming hardens. This shift in attitude is demonstrated by today's launch of the Institutional Investors Group on Climate Change's statement on global warming. In total, 15 institutional investors managing assets worth £850bn have signed the statement. It is the strongest call to date from investors for urgent and effective action by policymakers and companies to address the threats posed by rising greenhouse gas emissions. Moreover, it calls for all parties to work together to develop appropriate policy solutions.

The pension fund signatories pledge to incorporate climate change considerations into how they appoint, evaluate and reward their asset managers. In future managers will be required to address climate change issues in investment research, analysis and decision-making.

This statement is one of the most important contributions made by institutional investors to the climate change debate. It recognises that investment decisions taken now will have big impact on current and future global greenhouse gas emissions and the world's climate. It also recognises the uncomfortable reality that current investment decision-making and share ownership overlooks the risks and opportunities presented by climate change.

Douglas Ferrans is chief executive of Insight Investment, HBOS's asset management arm. Peter Scales is chief executive of the London Pension Fund Authority and chairs the Institutional Investors Group on Climate Change

Source: *Financial Times*, 4 October 2006, p. 17.

share price approaches the new efficient level. This is shown in Line 1. Secondly, the market could anticipate the news announcement – perhaps there have been leaks to the press, or senior BMW management has been dropping hints to analysts for the past two weeks. In this case the share price starts to rise before the announcement (Line 2). It is only the unexpected element of the announcement that causes the price to rise further on the announcement day (from point A to point B). A third possibility is that the market overreacts to the new information (Line 3); the 'bubble' deflates over the next few days. Finally, the market may fail to get the pricing right at all and the shares may continue to be underpriced for a considerable period (Line 4).

The value of an efficient market

It is important that share markets are efficient for at least three reasons.

1 ***To encourage share buying*** Accurate pricing is required if individuals are going to be encouraged to invest in private enterprise. If shares are incorrectly priced many savers will refuse to invest because of a fear that when they come to sell the price may be perverse and may not represent the fundamental attractions of the firm. This will seriously reduce the availability of funds to companies and inhibit growth. Investors need to know they are paying a fair price and that they will be able to sell at a fair price – that the market is a 'fair game'.

Exhibit 14.2 New information (an electric car announcement by BMW) and alternative stock market reactions – efficient and inefficient

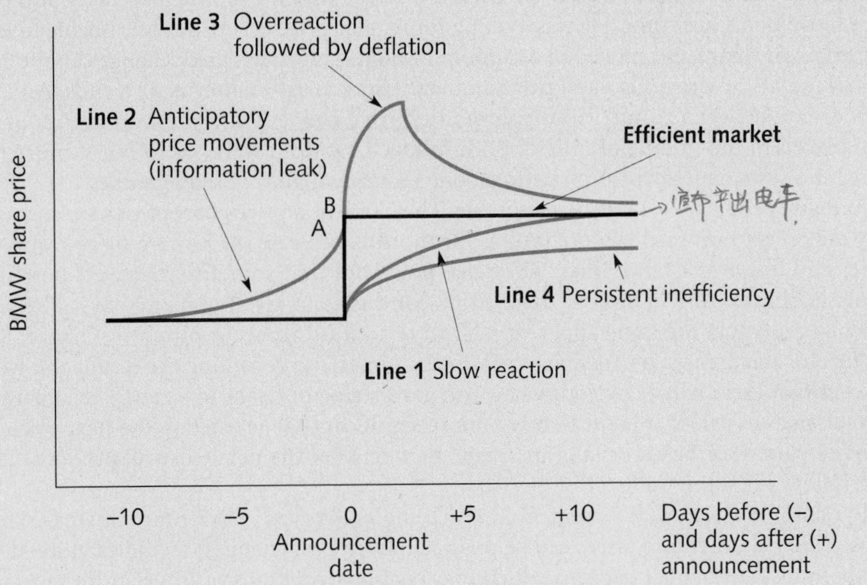

2 ***To give correct signals to company managers*** In Chapter 1 it was stated, for the purposes of this book, that the objective of the firm was the maximisation of shareholder wealth. This can be represented by the share price in an efficient market. Sound financial decision making therefore relies on the correct pricing of the company's shares. In implementing a shareholder wealth-enhancing decision the manager will need to be assured that the implication of the decision is accurately signalled to shareholders and to management through a rise in the share price. It is important that managers receive feedback on their decisions from the share market so that they are encouraged to pursue shareholder wealth strategies. If the share market continually gets the pricing wrong, even the most shareholder-orientated manager will find it difficult to know just what is required to raise the wealth of the owners.

In addition share prices signal the rate of return investors demand on securities of a particular risk class. If the market is inefficient the risk–return relationship will be unreliable. Managers need to know the rate of return they are expected to obtain on projects they undertake. If shares are wrongly priced there is a likelihood that in some cases projects will be wrongly rejected because an excessively high cost of capital (discount rate) is used in project appraisal. In other circumstances, if the share prices are higher than they should be the cost of capital signalled will be lower than it should be and projects will be accepted when they should have been rejected.

Correct pricing is not just a function of the quality of the analysis and speed of reaction of the investment community. There is also an onus placed on managers to disclose information. Shares can only be priced efficiently if all relevant information has been communicated to the market. Managers neglect this issue at their peril.

3 ***To help allocate resources*** Allocational efficiency requires both operating efficiency and pricing efficiency. If a poorly run company in a declining industry has highly valued shares because the stock market is not pricing correctly then this firm will be able to issue new shares, and thus attract more of society's savings for use within its business. This would be wrong for society as the funds would be better used elsewhere.

Random walks

Until the early 1950s it was generally believed that investment analysis could be used to beat the market. In 1953 Maurice Kendall presented a paper which examined security and commodity price movements over time. He was looking for regular price cycles, but was unable to identify any. The prices of shares, etc. moved in a random fashion – one day's price change cannot be predicted by looking at the previous day's price change. There are no patterns or trends. An analogy has been drawn between security and commodity price changes and the wanderings of a drunken man placed in the middle of a field. Both follow a **random walk**, or to put it more technically, there is no systematic correlation between one movement and subsequent ones.

To many people this is just unacceptable. They look at a price chart of a share and see patterns; they may see an upward trend running for months or years, or a share price trapped between upper and lower resistance lines. They also point out that sometimes you get persistent movements in shares; for example a share price continues to rise for many days. The statisticians patiently reply that the same apparent pattern or trends can occur purely by chance. Readers can test this for themselves: try tossing a coin several times and recording the result. You will probably discover that there will be periods when you get a string of heads in a row. The apparent patterns in stock market prices are said to be no more significant for predicting the next price movement than the pattern of heads or tails are for predicting what the next toss will produce. That is, they both follow a random walk.

To reinforce this look at **Exhibit 14.3**, which shows two sets of price movements. Many chartists (those who believe future prices can be predicted from past changes) would examine these and say that both display distinct patterns which may enable predictions of future price movements. One of the charts follows the FTSE 100 index each week over a two-year period. The other was generated by the writer's six-year-old son. He was given a coin and asked to toss it 110 times. Starting at a value of 100, if the first toss was a head the 'weekly return' was 4 per cent, if a tail it was –3 per cent. Therefore the 'index' for this imaginary share portfolio has a 50 : 50 chance of ending the first week at either 104 or 97. These rules were applied for each of the imaginary 110 weeks. This chart has a positive drift of 1 per cent per week to imitate the tendency for share indices to rise over time. However, the price movements within that upward drift are random because successive movements are independent.

Dozens of researchers have tested security price data for dependence. They generally calculate correlation coefficients for consecutive share price changes or relationships between share prices at intervals. The results show a serial correlation of very close to zero – sufficiently close to prevent reliable and profitable forecasts being made from past movements.

Why does the random walk occur?

A random walk occurs because the share price at any one time reflects all available information and it will only change if new information arises. Successive price changes will be independent and prices follow a random walk because the next piece of news (by definition) will be independent of the last piece of news. Shareholders are never sure whether the next item of relevant information is going to be good or bad – as with the heads and tails on a coin there is no relationship between one outcome and the next. Also, there are so many informed market traders that as soon as news is released the share price moves to its new rational and unbiased level.

We can see how an efficient market will not permit abnormal profits by examining **Exhibit 14.4**. Here a chartist at time A has identified a cyclical pattern. The chartist expects that over the next six months the share price will rise along the dotted line and is therefore a 'buy'. However, this chartist is not the only participant in the market and as soon as a pattern is observed it disappears. This happens because investors rush to exploit this marvellous profit opportunity. As a result of the extraordinary buying pressure the price immediately rises to a level which gives only the normal rate of return. The moment a pattern becomes discernible in the market it disappears under the weight of buy or sell orders.

Exhibit 14.3 Charts showing the movements on the FT 100 share index and a randomly generated index of prices. Which is which?

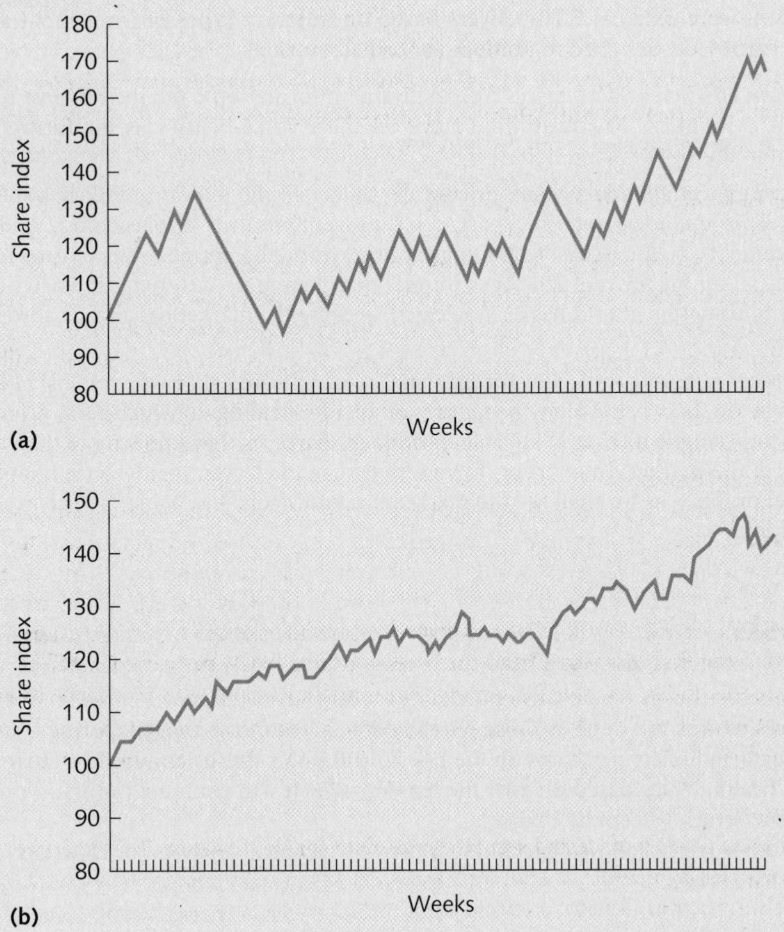

Exhibit 14.4 A share price pattern disappears as investors recognise its existence

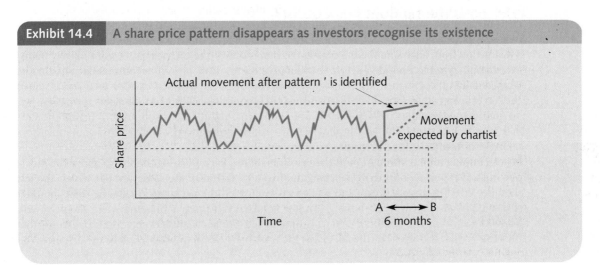

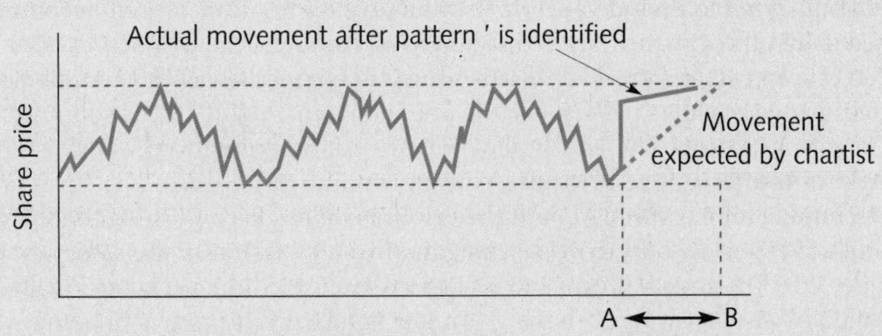

The three levels of efficiency

Economists have defined different levels of efficiency according to the type of information which is reflected in prices. Fama (1970) produced a three-level grading system to define the extent to which markets were efficient.[2] These were based on different types of investment approaches which were supposedly designed to produce abnormal returns.

1 ***Weak-form efficiency*** Share prices fully reflect all information contained in past price movements. It is pointless basing trading rules on share price history as the future cannot be predicted in this way.

2 ***Semi-strong form efficiency*** Share prices fully reflect all the relevant publicly available information. This includes not only past price movements but also earnings and dividend announcements, rights issues, technological breakthroughs, resignations of directors, and so on. The semi-strong form of efficiency implies that there is no advantage in analysing publicly available information after it has been released, because the market has already absorbed it into the price.

3 ***Strong-form efficiency*** All relevant information, including that which is privately held, is reflected in the share price. Here the focus is on **insider dealing**, in which a few privileged individuals (for example directors) are able to trade in shares, as they know more than the normal investor in the market. In a strong-form efficient market even insiders are unable to make abnormal profits – as we shall see the market is acknowledged as being inefficient at this level of definition.

Weak-form tests

If weak-form efficiency is true a naive purchase of a large, broadly based portfolio of shares typically produces returns the same as those purchased by a '**technical analyst**' poring over historical share price data and selecting shares on the basis of trading patterns and trends. There will be no mechanical trading rules based on past movements which will generate profits in excess of the average market return (except by chance).

Consider some of the following techniques used by technical analysts (or **chartists**) to identify patterns in share prices.

A simple price chart

A true chartist is not interested in estimating the intrinsic value of shares. A chartist believes that a chart of the price (and/or volume of trading data) is all that is needed to forecast future price movements. Fundamental information, such as the profit figures or macroeconomic conditions, is merely a distraction from analysing the message in the chart. One of the early chartists, John Magee, was so extreme in trying to exclude any other influences on his 'buy' or 'sell' recommendations that he worked in an office boarded up so that he was not aware of the weather. **Exhibit 14.5** shows one of the best known patterns to which chartists respond – it is called a head and shoulders formation.

A head and shoulders pattern like the one shown in Exhibit 14.5 is supposed to herald the start of a major price drop. The left shoulder is formed, according to the chartists, by some investors taking profits after a large price rise, causing a minor price drop. The small fall encourages new buyers, hoping for a continuation of the price rally. They keep pushing the shares above the previous high, but prices soon drift down again, often to virtually the same level at which the left shoulder's decline ended. It drops to a support level called the neckline. Finally the right shoulder is formed by another wave of buying (on low volume). This peters out, and when the prices fall below the neckline by, say, 3 per cent, it is time to sell. Some chartists even go so far as to say that they can predict the extent of the fall below the neckline – this is in proportion to the distance AB.

[2] Fama (1991) slightly changed the definitions later but the original versions have the virtues of elegance and simplicity.

Exhibit 14.5 The 'head and shoulders' pattern

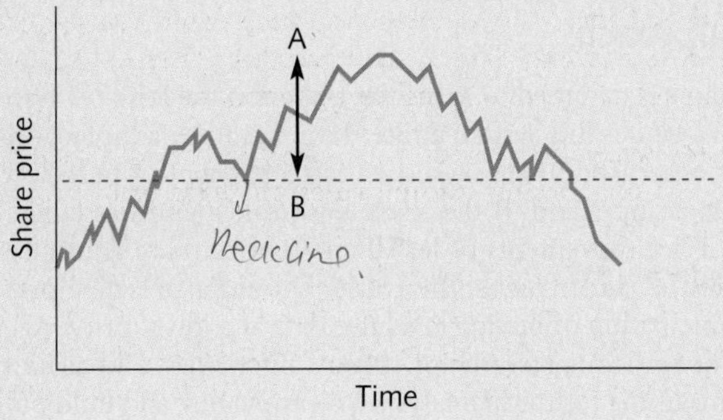

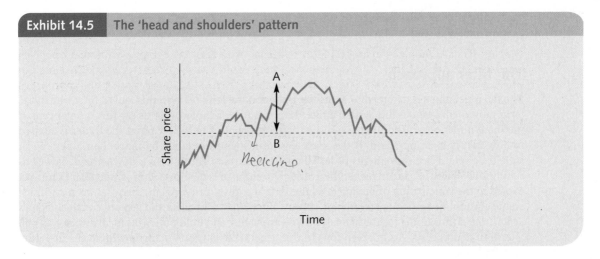

Exhibit 14.6 provides another chart with a pattern, where the share price trades between two trend lines until it achieves 'breakout' through the 'resistance line'. This is a powerful 'bull signal' – that is, the price is expected to rise significantly thereafter.

Exhibit 14.6 A 'line and breakout' pattern

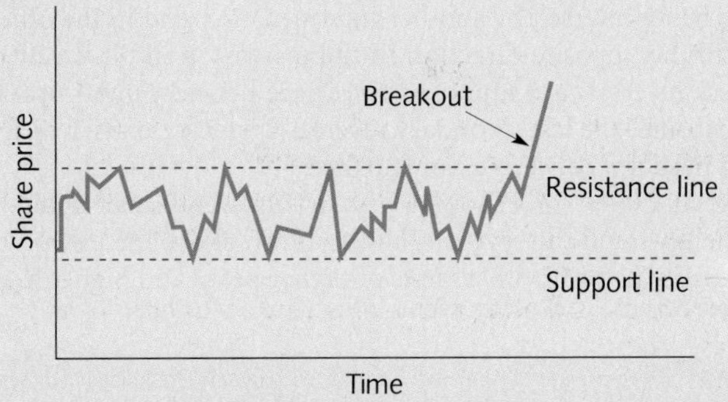

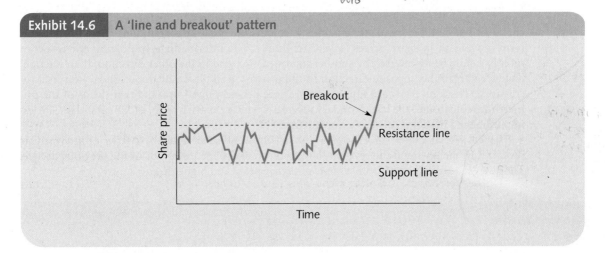

Chartists have a very serious problem in that it is often difficult to see a new trend until after it has happened. Many critical voices say that it is impossible for the chartist to act quickly enough on a buy or sell signal because competition among chartists immediately pushes the price to its efficient level. To overcome this, some traders start to anticipate the signal, and buy or sell before a clear breakthrough is established. This leads other traders to act even earlier, to lock themselves into a trade before competition causes a price movement. This, it is argued by EMH proponents, will lead to trends being traded away and prices adjusting to take into account all information regarding past price movements, leading us back to the weak form of stock market efficiency.

In academic studies modern high-powered computers have been used to simulate chartist trades. Researchers were instructed to find the classic patterns chartists respond to, ranging from 'triple tops' and 'triple bottoms' to 'wedges' and 'diamonds'.[3] The general result was that they found that a simple buy and hold strategy of a broadly based portfolio would have performed just as well as the chartist method, after transaction costs. Dawson and Steeley (2003), for example, found after examining UK share data that 'economic profits arising from the predictive ability of the technical patterns are unlikely to materialise'. However, some academic studies found evidence

[3] For explanations of these terms, the reader is referred to one of the populist 'how to get rich quickly' books.

suggesting trading rules that led to superior returns – see Park and Irwin (2007) for a survey of technical analysis studies.[4]

The filter approach

The filter technique is designed to focus the trader on the long-term trends and to filter out short-term movements. Under this system a filter level has to be adopted – let us say this is 5 per cent. If the share under observation rises by more than 5 per cent from its low point the trader is advised to buy, as it is in an up-trend. If the share has peaked and has fallen by more than 5 per cent it should be sold. Price movements of less than 5 per cent are ignored. In a down-trend, as well as selling the share the trader owns, the trader should also 'sell short', that is, sell shares not yet owned in the anticipation of buying at a later date at a lower price. Again, there has been a considerable amount of academic research of various filter rules, and again the general conclusion goes against the claims of the technical analysts – a simple buy and hold policy performs at least as well after transaction costs. Again exceptions to this general conclusion are turning up in the literature – *see* Park and Irwin (2007).

The Dow theory

Charles Dow, co-founder and editor of the *Wall Street Journal*, developed, along with others, the Dow theory in the early part of the twentieth century. According to the theory the stock market is characterised by three trends. The primary trend is the most important and refers to the long-term movement in share prices (a year or more). The intermediate trend runs for weeks or months before being reversed by another intermediate trend in the other direction. If an intermediate trend is in the opposite direction to the primary trend it is called a secondary reversal (or reaction). These reversals are supposed to retrace between one-third and two-thirds of the primary movement since the last secondary reversal. Tertiary trends, which last for a few days, are less important and need not concern us any further.

The left part of **Exhibit 14.7** shows a primary up-trend interrupted by a series of intermediate reversals. In the up-trend the reversals always finish above the low point of the previous decline. Thus we get a zigzag pattern with a series of higher peaks and higher lows.

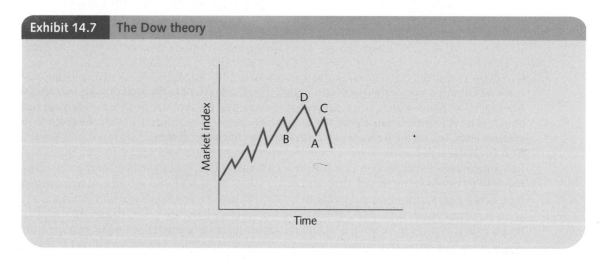

Exhibit 14.7 The Dow theory

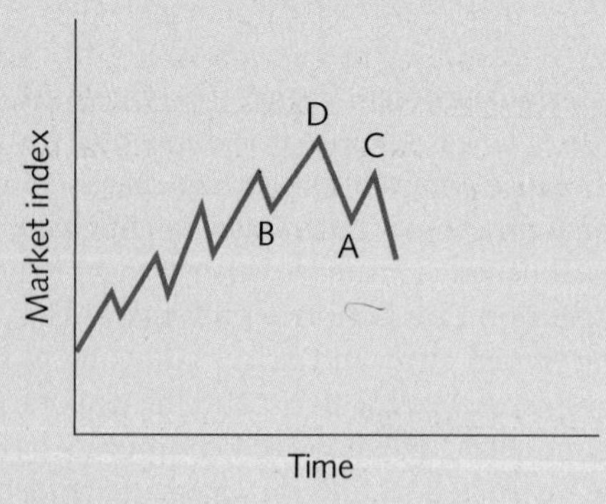

The primary up-trend becomes a down-trend (and therefore a sell signal) when an intermediate downward movement falls below the low of the previous reversal (A compared with B) and the next intermediate upward movement does not manage to reach the level of the previous intermediate upward spike (C compared with D).

[4] Their earlier working paper contains a lot more detail should you wish to pursue this.

In practice there is a great deal of subjectivity in deciding what is, or is not, an intermediate trend. Also primary trends, while relatively easy to identify with hindsight, are extremely difficult to identify at the moment they occur. The verdict of some academic researchers is that a simple buy and hold strategy produces better returns than those produced by the Dow theory, others show more positive results (e.g. Brown *et al.* 1998).

Moving averages

Examining the history of share prices and applying specific simple trading rules will produce abnormal returns according to Brock *et al.* (1992). They found that if investors (over the period 1897 to 1986) bought the 30 shares in the Dow Jones Industrial Average when the short-term moving average of the index (the average over, say, 50 days) rises above the long-term moving average (the average over, say, 200 days) they would have outperformed the investor who simply bought and held the market portfolio. Investors would also have achieved abnormal performance if they bought when a share 'broke out' from the trading range. 'However, transaction costs should be carefully considered before such strategies can be implemented' (Brock *et al.* 1992). A number of subsequent studies have found good performances (after transaction costs) from following rules based on moving average price charts (see Park and Irwin, 2007).

Other strategies

Technical analysts employ a vast range of trading rules. Some, for example, advise a purchase when a share rises in price at the same time as an increase in trading volume occurs. More bizarrely, other investors have told us to examine the length of women's dresses to get a prediction of stock market moves. Bull markets are apparently associated with short skirts and bear markets (falling) with longer hemlines! Some even look to sunspot activity to help them select shares.

A decade or so ago the conclusion from the academic studies on weak-form efficiency was that overwhelmingly the evidence suggested that stock markets correctly incorporated all past price and volume information into current share prices. That is, it is unlikely that you could achieve an extraordinary high return (for the risk level) by identifying patterns in charts, etc. (However, there were many studies that showed profitable technical trading strategies in the commodity and currency markets.)

This conclusion now needs to be revised in the light of dozens of recent rigorous academic studies into the profitability of 'technical analysis' in shares, as well as further studies into commodities and currency trading. The majority of these indicate that extraordinary high returns are achievable (see Park and Irwin, 2007). Note, though, that much of the evidence is disputed. For instance, other academics claim that some of the studies suffer from a number of methodological flaws: data snooping (using the same data to test for a variety of trading strategies and eventually finding one that works in that data set); selecting the trading rule *after* the period under study; inadequate allowance for extra risk and transaction costs. So this remains a field of intellectual endeavour that is wide open for future enterprising researchers to improve on the research techniques to help us grope towards a conclusion on the profitability of technical trading strategies.

Return reversal

We now turn to a group of studies that seem to indicate that the market might consistently fail to price properly. The first area of research concerns the phenomenon of **return reversal**. That is, shares that have given the highest returns over the previous three to five years (the 'winners') generally go on to underperform the stock market over the subsequent three to five years. Those shares that performed worst over a number of years (the 'losers') then, on average, show returns significantly higher than the market over the next three to five years.

De Bondt and Thaler (1985) selected portfolios of 35 US shares at three-year intervals, between 1933 and 1980. These portfolios contained the shares that had given the worst returns over a three-year period. The performances of these portfolios were then compared with the market as a whole over the subsequent three years. They found that these shares outperformed the market by an average of 19.6 per cent in the next 36 months. Their explanation is that the market had overreacted to the bad news and undervalued the shares. Moreover, when portfolios of shares which had risen the most in the prior three years were constructed and followed for a further three years, they underperformed the market by 5 per cent. De Bondt and Thaler claim: 'Substantial weak form market inefficiencies are discovered', in their analysis. Chopra *et al.* (1992) carried out a more detailed study and concluded: 'In portfolios formed on the basis of prior five-year returns, extreme prior losers outperform extreme prior winners by 5–10 per cent per year during the subsequent five years'.

Arnold and Baker (2007) investigated the return reversal phenomenon in UK shares. Our results show a stronger return reversal effect than that displayed in US shares. Every January between 1960 and 1998 we calculated for every share on the London Share Price Data (LSPD) its prior five-year return (capital gains plus dividends). The LSPD contains all the shares listed on the London Stock Exchange for the period 1975 to 2002. Before 1975 it contains share returns for a random one-third sample. Shares were ranked (an average of over 950 companies each January) in order of their five-year performance. They were then split into ten equal-sized groups (deciles) with group 1 containing the worst performers ('losers') over the prior five years, group 2 the next worst and so on, to group 10 (the 'winners'). We then imagined buying each of the portfolios of shares and holding them for various periods up to 60 months. Returns, relative to the market index, were recorded. We found that the loser shares (on average, over 39 portfolio formations, 1960–98) outperformed the winner shares by 14 per cent per year when held for five years. Furthermore, the 39 loser portfolios outperformed the market index by an average of 8.9 per cent per year over a five-year holding period.

Exhibit 14.8 shows some of the results. The lines trace the cumulative return for each of the ten portfolios after allowing for the return on the market. The horizontal line at '0' represents the market return re-based to zero throughout. The loser portfolios outperform the market by 53 per

Exhibit 14.8 Cumulative market-adjusted returns for UK share portfolios constructed on the basis of prior five-year returns

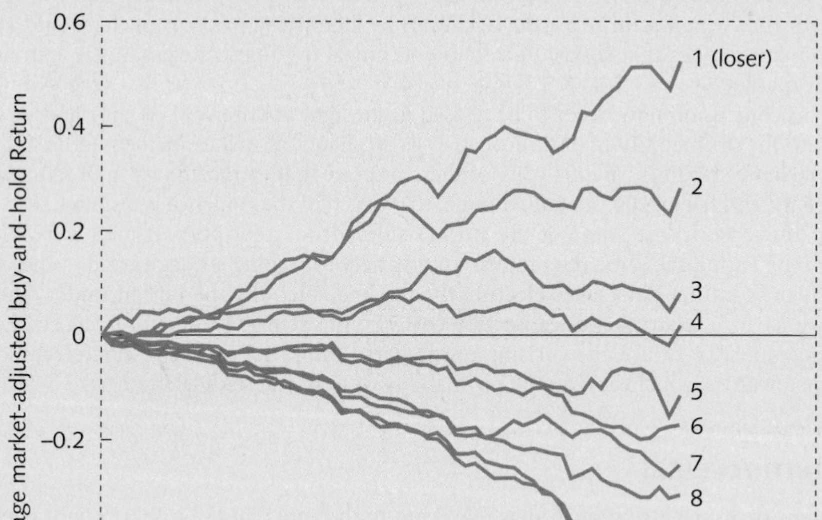

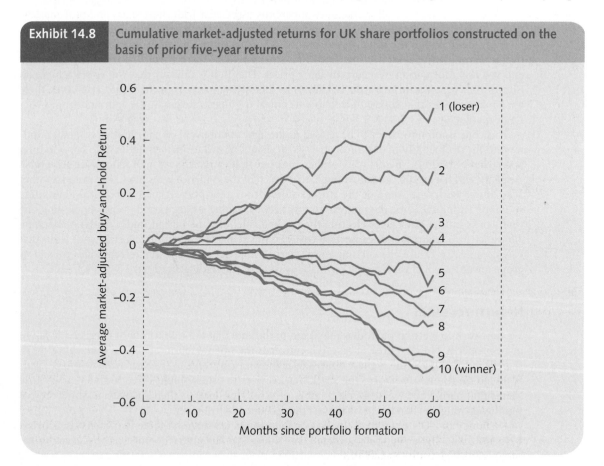

A figure of 0.4 should be interpreted as a cumulative return of 40% after allowance for the market return

Source: Arnold and Baker (2007).

cent over five-year holding periods, or 8.9 per cent per year; whereas the winner portfolio, on average over 39 tests, underperforms the market by 47 per cent. Remarkably, all the other portfolios are in the 'right' order: 2 is above 3, 3 above 4, and so on. This lends considerable support to the view that investors overreact to poor news (e.g. declining profits) coming from 'bad' companies and good news coming from the stars, because the greatest extent of return reversal is in the most extreme prior-period return-ranked portfolios. The **overreaction hypothesis** states that investors push the losers down too far, and push the winners up too much, failing to allow sufficiently for the potential of losers to pick themselves up, and for the winners to make a mistake and fall off their pedestals, or, at least, to perform less well than expected. **Exhibit 14.9** shows the difference in five-year test-period performance between the losers and the winners (losers minus winners) for each of the 39 portfolio formations separately. There are very few occasions when those companies considered star performers go on to generate better returns for investors than those widely regarded as the 'dogs'.

Exhibit 14.9 **Market-adjusted buy-and-hold five-year test-period returns for loser minus winner strategies for each of the 39 portfolio formations**

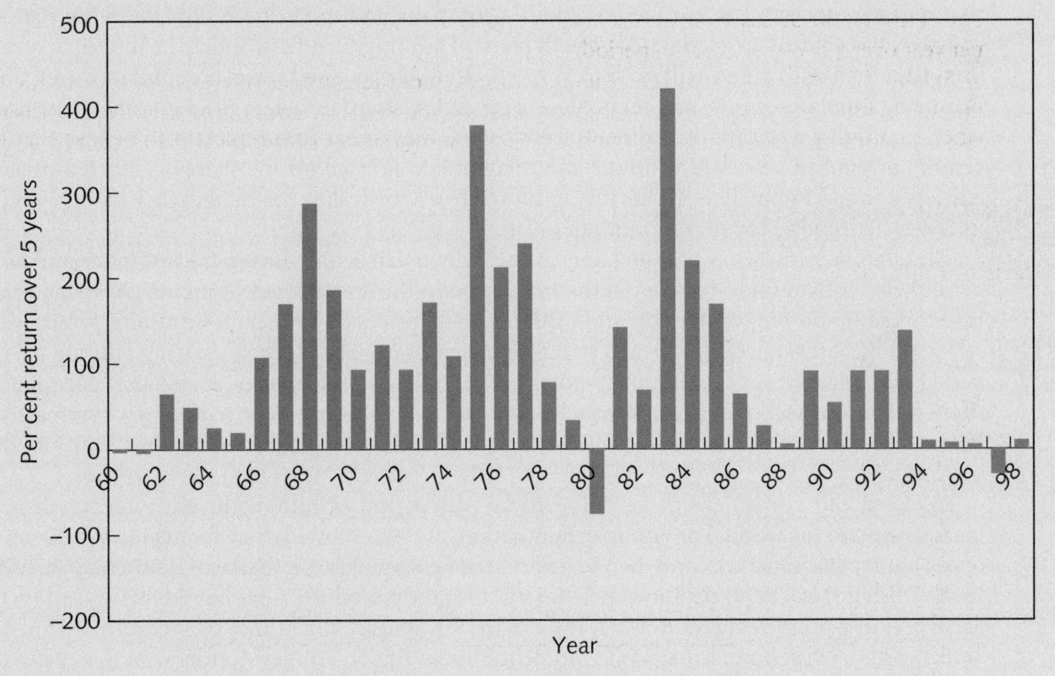

The five-year test period returns for each loser-winner strategy are assigned to the year of formation.

Source: Arnold and Baker (2007).

It might be thought that the results are explained by investors in loser shares taking on more risk than investors in winners. The study tests risk in six ways and failed to explain the outperformance as a result of losers being more risky. The CAPM-beta of losers, for example, is shown to be less than that for winners. In a further study (Arnold and Xiao, 2007) an even better performance was achieved by selecting only those loser companies with strong financial variables such as positive cash flow, improving gearing (using financial strength variables found to indicate abnormal share returns by Piotrosky (2000)).

Price (return) momentum

Many professional fund managers and private investors follow a price momentum strategy when choosing shares. That is, they buy shares which have risen in recent months and sell shares that have fallen. The first major academic study in this area was by Jegadeesh and Titman (1993) who found that if you bought US shares that had performed well in the past few months while selling shares that had performed poorly you would generate returns significantly exceeding those on the general market index for investment periods of three, six, nine and 12 months. For example, a strategy that selects shares on their past six-month returns and holds them for six months, realises a compounded return above the market of 12.01 per cent per year on average. Note that these results at first seem diametrically opposed to those of the return reversal, because the best strategy is to buy winners. However, the key to understanding the results and relating it to investor behaviour is to realise that return reversal is a long-term phenomenon stretching over many years, whereas price momentum strategists look only to the returns over the prior three, six, nine or 12 months to select their extreme winners – and they do not hold for more than one year.[5]

Two explanations for price momentum are debated in the literature (apart from the view that the returns are explained by risk differences). The first is that investors underreact to new information. So, if a company has reported large increases in profits over the last six months the share price rises, but it does not rise enough fully to reflect all the new information. The argument runs that investors tend to 'anchor' beliefs about a company and so they are slow to realise that the company has entered an accelerated growth phase. They might, at first, anticipate it fizzling out, or even that the profit trend will go into reverse. However, as good news accumulates over time, increasing numbers of investors rerate the shares and push up the share price. On the other hand, when examining a stream of bad news from losers, they are at first reluctant to believe that the severity of the bad news will continue and therefore do not sell off the shares as much as market efficiency would imply. This means that as more news arrives they realise that they had previously underreacted, and so the share continues to fall.

The alternative theory is that investors are actually overreacting during the test (after purchase) period (rather than underreacting in the *ranking* period). After a series of months of rising prices investors jump on the bandwagon and push the share prices of winners to irrational levels, while selling off the losers unreasonably and so pushing their prices below the efficient level during the test period. The advocates of this argument point to the tendency of these winner and loser portfolios to show return reversal over the subsequent two years or so as proof of temporary overreaction. Perhaps both theories could have a role to play in explaining the price momentum effects found in share returns.

Jegadeesh and Titman's work was followed up with papers examining the phenomenon in stock markets around the world. For example, Rouwenhorst (1998) showed price momentum in 12 developed country stock markets, and then in a number of emerging stock markets (Rouwenhorst, 1999). In the UK Liu *et al.* (1999) demonstrated the effect for the period 1977–98, but doubt was cast on the likelihood that price momentum is a feature of the UK market at all times by the work of Hon and Tonks (2003), who showed that while momentum was a good strategy to follow in the 1980s and 1990s (which was mostly one long bull market) it produced poor returns in the previous two decades. To discover the extent to which price momentum is a reliable strategy, and whether it works better in bull or bear markets, Arnold and Shi (2005) tested the strategy over the period 1956 to 2001. Some of the results are shown in **Exhibit 14.10**. While over the whole study period, on average, winners outperform losers by up to 9.92 per cent per year the strategy is fairly unreliable. There are long periods when the losers outperform the winners – an average monthly return of less than zero on the chart. We found no significant performance difference between bull and bear markets.

Exhibit 14.11 shows that momentum trading has been taken to the extreme with computers used for automatic trades. Because it is so well known and many attempt to exploit it, perhaps the momentum phenomena will disappear under the weight of buy and sell orders (or is that £20 note still lying on the floor?).

---

[5] There are some theoretical explanations for the co-existence of return reversal and momentum e.g. Barberis *et al.* (1988), Daniel *et al.* (1998) and Hong and Stein (1999).

Exhibit 14.10 Price momentum

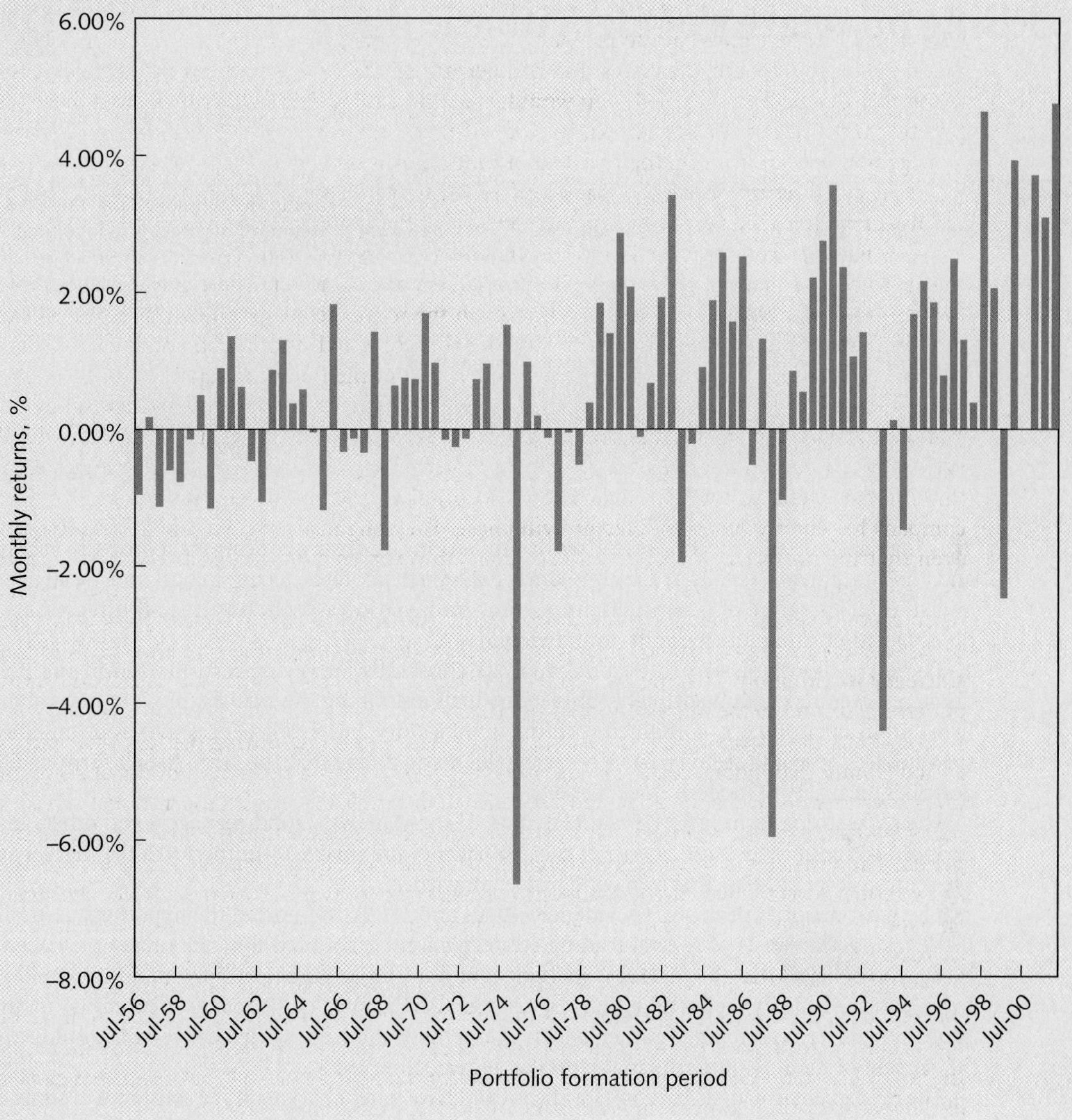

Portfolios are constructed on six-month prior-period returns and held for six months. Buy-and-hold monthly returns over the six months for the winner portfolio minus the loser portfolio. Each portfolio formation is shown separately.

Source: Arnold and Shi (2005).

Semi-strong form tests

The semi-strong form of efficiency has the greatest fascination for most researchers and practitioners. It focuses on the question of whether it is worthwhile expensively acquiring and analysing publicly available information. If semi-strong efficiency is true it undermines the work of millions of fundamental (professional or amateur) analysts whose trading rules cannot be applied to produce abnormal returns because all publicly available information is already reflected in the share price.

Fundamental analysts try to estimate a share's true value based on future business returns. This is then compared with the market price to establish an over- or under-valuation. To estimate the intrinsic value of a share the fundamentalists gather as much relevant information as possible.

Exhibit 14.11

Rising popularity of algorithmic trade

FT

By Phillip Stafford

Many in the stock market put the increase in the number of wild share price movements down to the growth of computer-driven trading.

Many hedge funds and proprietary trading desks at leading investment banks run sophisticated software applications, sometimes known as 'sniffers', which screen equities looking for momentum, effectively 'sniffing' out trading patterns.

'The software doesn't care what the stock is,' a trader at a leading broker says of his company's product.

'It doesn't look at anything else, such as price/ earnings ratios, it can just look at momentum in stocks.'

When a hedge fund or prop trader then submits their interest in a particular stock, it appears on electronic order books, and the sheer volume of the order is soon noticed.

Thus, orders to buy or sell shares attract similar orders, fuelling a virtuous or vicious circle that causes very dramatic share price movements.

Source: *Financial Times*, 23 April 2007, p. 19. Reprinted with permission.

This may include macroeconomic growth projections, industry conditions, company accounts and announcements, details of the company's personnel, tax rates, technological and social change and so on. The range of potentially important information is vast, but it is all directed at one objective: forecasting future profits and dividends.

There are thousands of professional analysts constantly surveying information in the public domain. Given this volume of highly able individuals examining the smallest piece of news about a firm and its environment, combined with the investigatory and investment activities of millions of shareholders, it would seem eminently reasonable to postulate that the semi-strong form of EMH describes the reality of modern stock markets.

The semi-strong form of EMH is threatening to share analysts, fund managers and others in the financial community because, if true, it means that they are unable to outperform the market average return except by chance or by having inside knowledge.

The great majority of the early evidence (1960s and 1970s) supported the hypothesis, especially if the transaction costs of special trading strategies were accounted for. The onus was placed on those who believed that the market is inefficient and misprices shares to show that they could perform extraordinarily well other than by chance. As **Exhibit 14.12** makes clear most of these professionals have performed rather poorly. Remember that simply by chance you would expect 50 per cent of them to outperform the market index before fees.

The fundamental analysts have not lost heart, and have fought back with the assistance of some academic studies which appear to suggest that the market is less than perfectly efficient. There are some anomalies which may be caused by mispricing. For example, small firm shares have performed abnormally well (for certain periods) given their supposed risk class, and 'value investing' seems to produce unexpectedly high returns.

We will now discuss *some* of the evidence for and against semi-strong efficiency.[6]

Information announcements

Many of the early studies investigated whether trading in shares immediately following announcements of new information (for example announcements on dividends or profit figures) could produce abnormal returns. Overwhelmingly the evidence supports the EMH, and excess returns are nil.

---

[6] This is an area with an enormous literature. The 'References and further reading' at the end of the chapter contain some of the EMH papers.

Exhibit 14.12

Fund managers

It does not always pay to follow the stars

Kate Burgess

FT

... Legal & General summarises much of the [fund management] data. It shows that over five years the FTSE All Share index outperformed 55 per cent of actively managed funds investing in UK shares – before fees. After high initial fees, just a quarter of funds managed to beat the index.

Investors would have made more money by backing the index and aiming for market returns than investing with most individual managers, says L&G. The chances of picking a UK fund that will continue to turn in an index-beating return over five years is considerably less than one in five. Of the 72 active funds that outperformed the index in 1998 just 31 active funds were still doing so in 2003.

The longer term statistics are just as bad. Of the 44 actively managed trusts with a 20-year performance history, eight outperformed the FTSE All-Share index, highlighting just how difficult it is to identify which trusts will be long-term winners, said the WM Company, which assesses performance.

Those funds that do outperform often do so because they are taking higher risks than other funds, say academics, and are unlikely to sustain that outperformance over successive years. If there is any evidence of persistent outperformance it is due to luck and momentum rather than judgement – that is, a fund holds a stock that produces a high return in one year and carries on to the next.

Once you adjust returns for risk that the managers have taken, the only evidence of consistency is on the downside – that is, poor managers systematically underperform benchmarks.

'Losers generally repeat, while winners do not necessarily repeat,' was the bleak summation reached by professors David Blake of Birkbeck College and Allan Timmerman of the University of California in a study for the Financial Services Authority ...

Source: Financial Times, 15/16 May 2004, p. M23. Reprinted with permission.

It has been discovered that most of the information in annual reports, profit or dividend announcements are reflected in share prices before the announcement is made. Ball and Brown (1968), for example, found that share prices start to drift upwards or downwards 12 months before the annual report is published. Most of the information contained within it is anticipated because investors receive information through press reports, statements and briefings by directors and interim reports and so on throughout the year. In the month the final report is produced less than 15 per cent of the information is unanticipated. The share price has already absorbed most of the relevant facts. The share price does tend to move by 10–15 per cent at the time of the announcement of the results, due to unanticipated information in the report. There is, therefore, some potential for investors to try to guess whether the new elements will be good or bad. But the direction of the movement is unpredictable (or unsystematic) and so there is an indication of efficiency. 'Over the entire six-month period after the announcement, investor returns . . . would have been close to zero. Thus, prices had incorporated the information released in annual earnings reports in a way that virtually eliminated future opportunities to profit from that news' (Ball, 2001).

However, the admittedly anecdotal evidence presented in **Exhibit 14.13** casts some doubt on the ability of investors to price in new information correctly.

Seasonal, calendar or cyclical effects

Numerous studies have identified apparent market inefficiencies on specific markets at particular times. One is the weekend effect, in which there appear to be abnormal returns on Fridays and relative falls on Mondays. The January effect refers to the tendency for shares to give excess returns in the first few days of January in the USA. Some researchers have found an hour of the day effect in which shares perform abnormally at particular times in the trading day. For example, the first 15 minutes have given exceptional returns, according to some studies.

Exhibit 14.13

Measuring the impact of IFRS

FT

Companies fear share price volatility due to new accounting standard

writes Barney Jopson

Cattles can count itself one of the unlucky few.

The consumer finance group took the stage last month to tell the market how it measured up under the new international accounting standards. But unlike peers who got through the experience unscathed, Cattles emerged battered and bruised. The group said its 2004 profits would have been 29 per cent lower under international accounting standards, catching the market off-guard and sending its shares tumbling 85 per cent on the day.

Cattles, however, was exceptional. At the end of last year, as companies geared up for the introduction of international accounting standards on January 1, there were dire warnings that a rush of unfamiliar numbers would befuddle investors and create market panic. Hedge funds even manoeuvred to take advantage of the stock price volatility.

The volatility has not emerged – yet. Although many analysts and investors are notoriously unprepared for international accounting standards, they are choosing to wait for extra information and give themselves more study time rather than succumb to knee-jerk reactions.

Cattles nonetheless demonstrated that when it comes to net income – still the City's favourite performance measure – companies must do as much as they can to prepare the market for significant swings.

The drop in profit stemmed from rules that required the company to book arrangement fees from loans later than it previously had. 'Our major investors are aware that this is just a different way, of adding up,' says Mark Collins, treasury and risk director at Cattles.

'The difficulty for other investors who don't have the opportunity to talk to management is that when profit is reduced they think it's gone away, when in fact it's only gone into the future.'

The company emphasised that its cash flow and risk profile were unaffected, a point later endorsed by Fitch, the credit ratings agency.

Anglo Irish Bank has said nothing about the impact of international accounting standards, but watched its stock fall about 5 per cent in two days last month after a report saying the rules would eat into its earnings

Source: *Financial Times*, 21 April 2005, p. 23. Reprinted with permission.

The problem for practical investment with placing too much importance on these studies is that the moment they are identified and publicised there is a good chance that they will cease to exist. Investors will buy in anticipation of the January effect and so cause the market already to be at the new higher level on 1 January. They will sell on Friday when the price is high and buy on Monday when the price is low, thus eliminating the weekend effect.

Even if the effects are not eliminated trading strategies based on these findings would be no more profitable than buying and holding a well-diversified portfolio. This is because of the high transaction costs associated with such strategies as, say, buying every Tuesday and selling every Friday. Also the research in this area is particularly vulnerable to the accusation of 'data-snooping'. Sullivan *et al.* (1999) claim to demonstrate that calendar effects are illusory and findings obtained merely the result of extensive mining of the data until an (apparent) relationship is found:

> Data-snooping need not be the consequence of a particular researcher's efforts. It can result from a subtle survivorship bias operating on the entire universe of technical trading rules that have been considered historically. Suppose that, over time, investors have experimented with technical trading rules drawn from a very wide universe – in principle thousands of parameterizations of a variety of types of rules. As time progresses, the rules that happen to perform well historically receive more attention and are considered 'serious contenders' by the investment community, and unsuccessful trading rules are more likely to be forgotten. After a long sample period, only a small set of trading rules may be left for consideration, and these rules' historical track records will be cited as evidence of their merits. If enough trading rules are considered over time, some rules are bound by pure luck, even in a very large sample, to produce superior performance even if they do not genuinely possess predictive power over asset

returns. Of course, inference based solely on the subset of surviving trading rules may be misleading in this context because it does not account for the full set of initial trading rules, most of which are likely to have underperformed.

Small firms

The searchers for inefficiency seemed to be on firmer ground when examining smaller firms. The problem is that the ground only appears to be firm until you start to build. A number of studies in the 1980s found that smaller firms' shares outperformed those of larger firms over a period of several decades (the **small firm effect**, small-capitalisation, or small-cap effects). This was found to be the case in the USA, Canada, Australia, Belgium, Finland, the Netherlands, France, Germany, Japan and Britain.[7] Dimson and Marsh (1986) put the outperformance of small UK firms' shares at just under 6 per cent per year. These studies caused quite a stir in both the academic and the share-investing communities. Some rational explanations for this outperformance were offered: for example, perhaps the researchers had not adequately allowed for the extra risk of small shares – particularly the risk associated with lower liquidity. In most of these studies beta is used as the measure of risk and there are now doubts about its ability to capture all the risk-return relationship (*see* Chapter 8). Besides, the results generally show lower betas for small companies. Some researchers have argued that small firms suffer more in recessions and so can be judged as more risky. Another explanation is that it is proportionately more expensive to trade in small companies' shares: if transaction costs are included, the net return of trading in small company shares comes down (but this does not explain the outperformance of a portfolio bought and held for a long period). There is also the issue of 'institutional neglect', by which analysts fail to spend enough time studying small firms, preferring to concentrate on the larger 100 or so. This may open up opportunities for the smaller investor who is prepared to conduct a more detailed analysis of those companies to which inadequate professional attention is paid.

The excitement about small companies' shares by investors and their advisers was much greater than in academe, but it was to end in tears. Investors who rushed to exploit this small firm effect in the late 1980s and early 1990s had their fingers burnt. As *The Economist*[8] put it: 'The supposedly inefficient market promptly took its revenge, efficiently parting investors from their money by treating owners of small stocks to seven years of under-performance.' This article refers to the US market but similar underperformance occurred on both the US and UK markets.

UK studies by Dimson, Marsh and Staunton (Dimson and Marsh 1999, Dimson *et al.* 2001, 2002) showed that smaller companies outperformed large companies by 5.2 per cent per annum between 1955 and 1988 (by 4.5 per cent for small companies and 9.0 per cent for very small (micro) companies). However, in the period 1989 to 1998 the return premium in favour of small companies went into reverse: large companies produced a return 7.0 per cent greater than small companies and 10.5 per cent for micro capitalisation companies – *see* **Exhibit 14.14**. (The research periods for the USA are 1926 to 1983, and then 1984 to 1998). The researchers show that this kind of reversal occurred in many different countries in the late 1980s and 1990s. Some people say that what happened was that following the early 1980s' academic studies so many funds were set up to buy small firms' shares that in 1986 and 1987 their prices were pushed up to unsustainable levels (they had 10 years of outperformance pushed into two). Indeed in the eight years to the end of 2006 small UK firms returned 172 per cent, beating the FTSE All-Share by 9 per cent per year. This return of the small cap effect is global: in a study of 22 countries for the period 2000–2006 small-caps outperformed substantially in most markets (see Dimson and Marsh (2007)).

[7] Key studies in the area are Banz (1981), Reinganum (1981), Keim (1983), Fama and French (1992), Dimson, *et al.* (2002) and the annual Hoare Govett Smaller Companies Index reports.

[8] *The Economist*, 26 March 1994.

Exhibit 14.14 The small-cap reversal in the United States and the United Kingdom

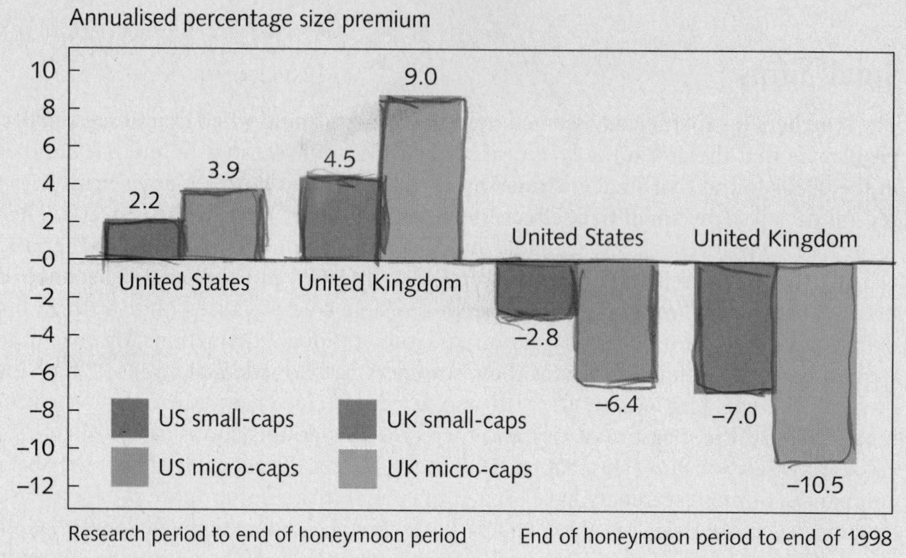

Source: Dimson, E., Marsh, P.R. and Staunton, M. (2002) *Triumph of the Optimists: 101 Years of Global Investment Returns*. Princeton, NJ: Princeton University Press.

Underreaction

Research evidence is building which shows that investors are slow to react to the release of information in some circumstances. This introduces the possibility of abnormal returns following the announcement of certain types of news. The first area of research has been into '**post-earnings-announcement drift**'. That is, there is a sluggish response to the announcement of unexpectedly good or unexpectedly bad profit figures. Bernard and Thomas (1989) found that **cumulative abnormal returns (CARs)** continue to drift up for firms that report unexpectedly good earnings and drift down for firms that report unexpectedly bad figures for up to 60 days after the announcement. (The abnormal return in a period is the return of a portfolio after adjusting for both the market return in that period and risk.) This offers an opportunity to purchase and sell shares after the information has been made public and thereby outperform the market returns. Shares were allocated to 10 categories of standardised unexpected earnings (SUE). The 10 per cent of shares with the highest positive unexpected earnings were placed in category 10. (The worst unexpected return shares were placed in category 1.) **Exhibit 14.15** shows that after the announcement the shares of companies in category 10 continue to provide positive CARs. Investors did not move the share price sufficiently to incorporate the new information in the earnings announcement on the day of the announcement. Those reporting bad surprises in earnings (the worst of which were in category 1) continued to show a falling return relative to the market in the period after the announcement day. Bernard and Thomas say that a strategy of buying shares in category 10 and selling shares in category 1 on the announcement day and selling (buying) 60 days later would have yielded an estimated abnormal return of approximately 4.2 per cent over 60 days, or about 18 per cent on an annualised basis. Similar results have been reported in studies by Foster *et al.* (1984), and Rendleman *et al.* (1982). These studies suggest that all the news is not properly priced into the shares at the time of announcement as would be expected under EMH.

The second area of research into underreaction relates to the repurchase of shares. Ikenberry *et al.* (1995) found that share prices rise on the announcement that the company will repurchase its own shares. This is to be expected as this is generally a positive piece of news. The suggestion of inefficiency arises because after the announcement the shares continue to provide abnormal

Exhibit 14.15 The cumulative abnormal returns (CAR) of shares in the 60 days before and the 60 days after an earnings announcement

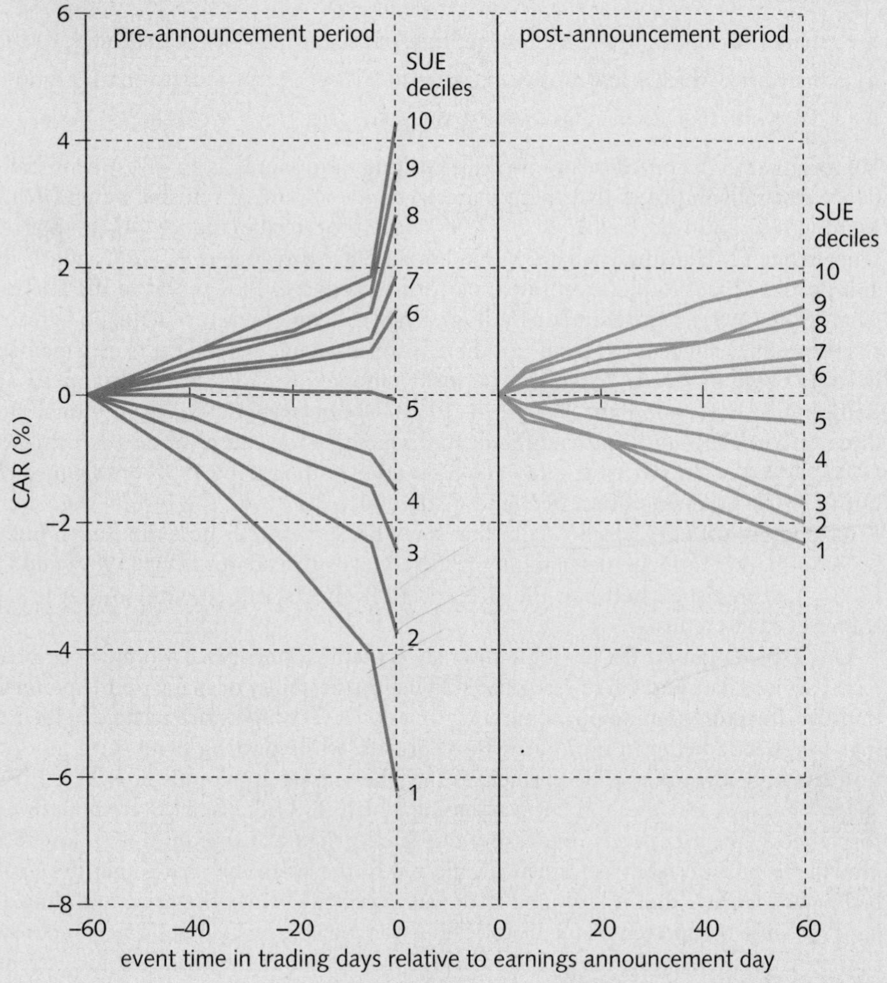

Note: The 10 per cent of shares with the most positive unexpected news continued to produce abnormal returns after the announcement day, whereas the 10 per cent with the worst news continued to produce negative abnormal returns cumulating to over 2 per cent.

Source: Bernard, V. and Thomas, J., 'Post-earnings-announcement drift: Delayed price response or risk premium?', *Journal of Accounting Research*, 27 (1989, Supplement), p. 10.

returns over the next few years. Thirdly, Michaely *et al.* (1995) found evidence of share price drift following dividend initiations and omissions. Fourthly, Ikenberry *et al.* (1996) found share price drift after share split announcements. Fifthly, Jegadeesh and Titman (1993) found that trading strategies in which the investor buys shares that have risen in recent months produce significant abnormal returns. Chan *et al.* (1996) confirm an underreaction to past price movements (a 'momentum effect') and also identify a drift after earnings surprises.

Value investing

There is a school of thought in investment circles that investors should search for 'value' shares. Different sub-schools emphasise different attributes of an undervalued share but the usual candidates for inclusion are:

- a share with a price which is a low multiple of the earnings per share (low P/E ratios or PERs);
- a share price which is low relative to the balance sheet assets (book-to-market ratio);
- a share with high dividends relative to the share price (high-yield shares).[9]

We turn first to the purchase of low price-earning ratio shares as an investment strategy. The evidence generally indicates that these shares generate abnormal returns. Basu (1975, 1977, 1983), Keim (1988) and Lakonishok *et al.* (1994) have produced evidence which appears to defy the semi-strong EMH, using US data. Mario Levis (1989), Gregory *et al.* (2001, 2003), and Anderson and Brooks (2006) found exceptional performance of low PER shares in the UK, and for Japan, Chan *et al.* (1991) report similar findings. The academic literature tends to agree that low PER shares produce abnormal returns but there is some dispute whether it is the small-size effect that is really being observed; when this factor is removed the PER effect disappears, according to Reinganum (1981) and Banz and Breen (1986). Doubts were raised because small firm shares are often on low PERs and so it is difficult to disentangle the causes of outperformance. Jaffe *et al.* (1989), based on an extensive study of US shares over the period 1951–86, claimed that there was both a price–earnings ratio effect and a size effect. However, the results were contradicted by Fama and French (1992), who claim that low PER shares offer no extra return but that size and book-to-market ratio are determining factors. On British shares Levis (1989) and Gregory *et al.* (2001) distinguished between the size and PER effects and concluded that low PERs were a source of excess returns.

One explanation for the low PER anomaly is that investors place too much emphasis on short-term earnings data and fail to recognise sufficiently the ability of many poorly performing firms to improve. Investors seem to put some companies on a very high price relative to their current earnings to reflect a belief in rapid growth of profits, while putting firms with modest growth on unreasonably low prices. The problem is that the market apparently consistently overprices the 'glamour' shares and goes too far in assigning a high PER because of overemphasis on recent performance, while excessively depressing the share prices of companies with low recent earnings growth. To put it crudely: so much is expected of the 'glamour' shares that the smallest piece of bad news (or news that is less good than was expected) brings the price tumbling. On the other hand, so little is expected of the historically poor performers that good news goes straight into a share price rise. What investors have failed to appreciate is the tendency for extreme profit and growth trends to moderate – 'to revert to the mean'. This was shown in research by Little as early as 1962. He described profit differences from one period to another as higgledy piggledy growth. Fuller *et al.* (1993) found that portfolios constructed from shares with low PERs showed lower profit growth than portfolios of high PERs shares in each of the eight years after portfolio formation. However, after three to four years the growth rate differences became very small. If investors were buying high PER shares because they expected high earnings growth for decades into the future (thus bidding up the price) they were frequently disappointed. On the other hand, investors buying low PER shares when the price is low because most investors believe the company is locked into low earnings growth found, after three or four years, that the earnings of these companies, on average grew at very nearly the same rate as the glamour shares. Dreman (1998) is a leading investor who has written on the tendency for investors to overreact and bid up glamour shares too far – while neglecting other companies.

The efficient market protagonists (e.g. Fama and French) have countered the new evidence of inefficiency by saying that the supposed outperformers are more risky than the average share and

---

[9] The doyen of the value investing school, Benjamin Graham, regarded the use of a single measure in isolation as a very crude form of value investing. In fact, he would condemn such an approach as not being a value strategy at all. *See Security Analysis* by Graham and Dodd (1934) and *The Intelligent Investor* (1973) by Graham (reprinted 2003).

therefore an efficient market should permit them to give higher returns. Lakonishok *et al.* (1994) examined this and found that low PER shares are actually less risky than the average.

Before everyone rushes out to buy low PER shares remember the lesson that followed the discovery of a small firm effect in the mid-1980s. In the case of the Gregory *et al.* (2003) study, the underpricing was observed over the period 1975 to 1993 – we do not know if it still exists.

Shares that sell at prices which are a low multiple of the net assets per share (i.e. high book-to-market ratio) seem to produce abnormal returns.[10] This seems odd because (as we discuss in Chapter 20) the main influence on most share prices is the discounted value of their future income flows. Take BSkyB which had a mere £47m of net assets in June 2007 and is valued in the stock market at over £12bn. Its assets are largely intangible and not adequately represented in a balance sheet. In other words, there is very little connection between balance sheet asset figures and share price for many shares. The causes of the results of the empirical studies remain largely unexplained. Fama and French (1992, 2006) suggest there may be a systematic difference between companies which have high or low book-to-market value ratios. That is, companies with high book-to-market ratios are more risky. However, company shares have high market price-to-book value for different reasons – for some the nature of their industrial sector means they have few balance sheet recordable assets, for some the share price has risen because of projections of strong earnings growth. It has been suggested that investors underprice some shares in an overreaction to a series of bad news events about the company, while overpricing other shares that have had a series of good news events. Thus, the book-to-market ratio rises as share prices fall in response to an irrational extrapolation of a bad news trend.

Many studies have concluded that shares offering a higher dividend yield tend to outperform the market.[11] Explanations have been offered for this phenomenon ranging from the fact that dividend income is taxed at a higher rate than capital gains and so those investors keen on after-tax income will only purchase high-yielding shares if they offer a higher overall rate of return, to the argument that investors are bad at assessing growth prospects and may underprice shares with a high dividend yield because many have had a poor recent history.

Two other value measures have been examined. The first is the share price to sales; high sales-to-price ratio firms perform better than low sales-to-price firms. Secondly, there is the cash flow (defined as profits after tax plus depreciation and amortisation) to price ratio. Lakonishok *et al.* (1994) showed a higher return to shares with a high cash flow to price ratio.

Bubbles

Occasionally financial and other assets go through periods of boom and bust. There are explosive upward movements generating unsustainable prices, which may persist for many years, followed by a crash. These **bubbles** seem at odds with the theory of efficient markets because prices are not supposed to deviate markedly from fundamental value.

The tulip bulb bubble (tulipmania) in seventeenth-century Holland is an early example in which tulip bulb prices began to rise to absurd levels. The higher the price went the more people considered them good investments. The first investors made lots of money and this encouraged others to sell everything they had to invest in tulips. As each wave of speculators entered the market the prices were pushed higher and higher, eventually reaching the equivalent of £30,000 in today's money for one bulb. But the fundamentals were against the investors and in one month, February 1637, prices collapsed to one-tenth of the peak levels (by 1739 the price had fallen to 1/200th of one per cent of its peak value).

The South Sea Bubble which burst in 1720 was a British share fiasco in which investors threw money at the South Sea Company on a surge of over-optimism only to lose most or all of it. The increase in share prices in the 1920s and before the 1987 crash have also been interpreted as

---

[10] For example Lakonishok *et al.* (1994), Chan *et al.* (1991), De Bondt and Thaler (1987), Rosenberg *et al.* (1985), Fama and French (1992, 2006), Capaul *et al.* (1993), Pontiff and Schall (1998), Reinganum (1988), Gregory *et al.* (2001, 2003) Dimson *et al.* (2002) and Lewellen (2004).

[11] For example Litzenberger and Ramaswamy (1979), Elton *et al.* (1983), Levis (1989), Morgan and Thomas (1998), Miles and Timmermann (1996), Dimson *et al.* (2002) and Lewellen (2004).

bubbles. Recently, the mania for telecoms, media and technology shares in the late 1990s has been identified as leading to a bubble. Many see property prices in 2007 in many countries as being determined largely by a bubble mentality (*see* Kindleburger (1996) for more on bubbles).

One explanation for this seemingly irrational behaviour of markets is what is called **noise trading** by naive investors. According to this theory there are two classes of traders, the informed and the uninformed. The informed trade shares so as to bring them towards their fundamental value. However, the uninformed can behave irrationally and create 'noise' in share prices and thereby generate bias in share pricing. They may be responding to frenzied expectations of almost instant wealth based on an extrapolation of recent price trends – perhaps they noted from the newspapers that the stock market made investors high returns over the past couple of years and so rush to get a piece of the action. This tendency to 'chase the trend' can lead to very poor performance because the dabbler in the markets often buys shares after a sharp rise and sells shares after being shocked by a sharp fall.

To reinforce the power of the uninformed investor to push the market up and up, the informed investor seeing a bubble developing often tries to get in on the rise. Despite knowing that it will all end in disaster for some the informed investor buys in the hope of selling out before the crash. This is based on the idea that the price an investor is willing to pay for a share today is dependent on the price the investor can sell for at some point in the future and not necessarily on fundamental value. Keynes (1936) as far back as the 1930s commented that share prices may not be determined by fundamentals but by investors trying to guess the value other investors will place on shares. He drew the analogy with forecasting the outcome of a beauty contest. If you want to win you are better off concentrating on guessing how the judges will respond to the contestants rather than trying to judge beauty for yourself. George Soros is an example of a very active (informed and successful) investor who is quite prepared to buy into an apparent irrational market move but makes every effort to get out before the uninformed investors. There is evidence that a number of hedge funds rode the technology share bubble in the late 1990s. They did not act as a correcting force returning prices to efficient levels, but reinforced the bubble in a destabilising way (*see* Brunnermeier and Nagel, 2004). Note that the term 'informed investor' does not equal professional investor. There are many professional fund managers and analysts who, on a close examination, fall into the category of ill-informed noise traders (*see* Arnold (2002) for more on the inadequacies of 'professional investors', also known as 'the oxymorons').

Comment on the semi-strong efficiency evidence

Despite the evidence of some work showing departures from semi-strong efficiency, for most investors most of the time the market may be regarded as efficient. This does not mean the search for anomalies should cease. The evidence for semi-strong efficiency is significant but not so overwhelming that there is no hope of outperformance for the able and dedicated.

While the volume of evidence of pockets of market inefficiencies is impressive, we need to be wary when placing weight on these results. Given the fact that there have been hundreds of researchers examining the data it is not a surprise that some of them find plausible looking statistical relationships indicating excess return opportunities. The research that actually gets published tends to be that which has 'found' an inefficiency. The research that does not show inefficiency receives much less publicity. Furthermore, the excess return strategies may be time specific and may not continue into the future.

On the other hand consider this: suppose that you discover a trading strategy that produces abnormal returns. You could publish it in a respected journal or you could keep it to yourself. Most would select the latter option because publishing may result in the elimination of the inefficiency and with it the chance of high investment returns. So there may be a lot of evidence of inefficiency that remains hidden and is being quietly exploited.

There is a strange paradox in this area of finance: in order for the market to remain efficient there has to be a large body of investors who believe it to be inefficient. If all investors suddenly believed that shares are efficiently priced and no abnormal profits are obtainable they would quite sensibly refuse to pay for data gathering and analysis. At that moment the market starts to drift away from fundamental value. The market needs speculators and long-term investors continually on the prowl for under- or overpriced securities. It is through their buying and selling activities that inefficiencies are minimised and the market is a fair game.

There are some investors who have rejected the strictures of the EMH and have achieved astonishingly good returns. Here are some of them.[12]

Peter Lynch

From May 1977 to May 1990 Peter Lynch was the portfolio manager of Fidelity's Magellan Fund. Over this 13-year period a $1,000 investment rose to be worth $28,000, a rate of return that is way ahead of the field at 29.2 per cent per annum. Furthermore, the fund's performance was consistent – in only two of those years did it fail to beat the S&P 500. The fund grew from an asset base of $18 million to one of more than $14 billion. It was not only the best-performing fund in the world; it also became the biggest. There were one million shareholders in 1990, when Lynch quit, at the age of 46, to devote more time to his family. His experiences as a young man gave him a sceptical eye to what was being taught on his MBA course at Wharton:

> It seemed to me that most of what I learned at Wharton, which was supposed to help you succeed in the investment business, could only help you fail . . . Quantitative analysis taught me that the things I saw happening at Fidelity couldn't really be happening. I also found it difficult to integrate the efficient market hypothesis . . . It also was obvious that the Wharton professors who believed in quantum analysis and random walk weren't doing nearly as well as my new colleagues at Fidelity, so between theory and practice, I cast my lot with the practitioners . . . My distrust of theorizers and prognosticators continues to the present day.[13]

John Neff

When John Neff managed the Windsor Fund, his investment philosophy emphasised the importance of a low share price relative to earnings. However, his approach required a share to pass a number of tests besides the price–earnings criteria. These additional hurdles turn his approach from simple low price–earnings investing to a sophisticated one. John Neff was in charge of the Windsor Fund for 31 years. It beat the market for 25 of those 31 years. He took control in 1964, and retired in 1995. Windsor was the largest equity mutual in the United States when it closed its doors to new investors in 1985. Each dollar invested in 1964 had returned $56 by 1995, compared with $22 for the S&P 500. The total return for Windsor, at 5,546.5 per cent, outpaced the S&P 500 by more than two to one. This was an additional return on the market of 3.15 percentage points a year after expenses. Before expenses the outperformance was 3.5 percentage points.[14] He was always on the lookout for out-of-favour, overlooked or misunderstood stocks. These nuggets of gold always stood on low price–earnings ratios. Not only that; their prospects for earnings growth were good. He believes that the market tends to allow itself to be swept along with fads, fashions and flavours of the month. This leads to overvaluation of those stocks regarded as shooting stars, and to the undervaluation of those which prevailing wisdom deems unexciting, but which are fundamentally good stocks. Investors become caught in the clutch of group-think and en masse ignore solid companies. Bad news tends to weigh more heavily than good news as the investor's malaise deepens. The way Neff saw it, if you could buy a stock where the negatives were largely known, then any good news that comes as a surprise can have a profoundly positive effect on the stock price. On the other hand if you buy into a growth story where great things are expected and built in to the price, the slightest hint of bad news can take the sizzle out of the stock.

Benjamin Graham

Benjamin Graham is regarded as the most influential of investment philosophers. Graham was the leading exponent of the value investing school of thought. Over 20 years (from 1936) the Graham-Newman Corporation achieved an abnormally high performance for its clients: 'The success of Graham-Newman Corporation can be gauged by its average annual distribution. Roughly

---

[12] These performances and the underlying investment philosophies are explored more fully in Arnold (2002).

[13] Lynch (1990), pp. 34–5.

[14] Neff (1999), pp. 62 and 71.

speaking, if one invested $10,000 in 1936, one received an average of $2,100 a year for the next twenty years and recovered one's original $10,000 at the end.'[15] Graham[16] in 1955 put a slightly different figure on it: 'Over a period of years we have tended to earn about 20 per cent on capital per year'. This is much better than the return available on the market as a whole. For example, Barclays Capital[17] show the annual average real (excluding inflation) rate of return on US stocks with gross income reinvested as 7.4 per cent for those years. Even if we add back average annual inflation of 3.8 per cent[18] to the Barclays' figures to make them comparable, the Graham-Newman figures are much better than the returns received by the average investor. According to Graham, market prices are not determined by any necessarily rational or mathematical relationship to fundamental factors (at least, not in the short run) 'but through the minds and decisions of buyers and sellers';[19] 'The prices of common stock are not carefully thought out computations, but the resultants of a welter of human reactions. The stock market is a voting machine rather than a weighing machine. It responds to factual data not directly, but only as they affect the decisions of buyers and sellers.'[20]

Plainly, he did not believe the efficient markets hypothesis:

> Evidently the processes by which the securities market arrives at its appraisals are frequently illogical and erroneous. These processes . . . are not automatic or mechanical, but psychological for they go on in the minds of people who buy and sell. The mistakes of the market are thus the mistakes of groups of masses of individuals. Most of them can be traced to one or more of three basic causes: exaggeration, oversimplification, or neglect.[21]

Warren Buffett and Charles Munger

Warren Buffett is the most influential investment thinker of our time; he is also the wealthiest. Charles Munger is Buffett's partner, both intellectually and in the running of one of the world's largest companies. They each started with very little capital. At first, they developed their investment philosophies independently. They were far away from each other, both in their investment approach and geographically (Munger in California and Buffett in Nebraska). Despite the different approaches to stock picking they each created highly successful fund management businesses before coming together. Buffett took managerial control of Berkshire Hathaway in 1965 when the book value per share was $19.46 (as measured at the prior year-end 30 September 1964). By year-end 2006 the book value, with equity holdings carried at market value, was $70,281 per share. The gain in book value over 42 years came to 21.4 per cent compounded annually. At this rate of return an investment of $100 becomes worth over $340,000 over 42 years. There are people who are multimillionaires today because in the 1960s or 1970s they invested a few thousand dollars in Berkshire Hathaway. Warren Buffett owns around 40 per cent of Berkshire Hathaway,[22] a company with a market capitalisation of over $200 billion (it was valued at a mere $20m in 1965). **Exhibit 14.16** shows the truly outstanding performance of Berkshire Hathaway. There have been only six years in which the rise in book value was less than the return on the S&P 500. It is even better than it looks – the S&P 500 numbers are pre-tax whereas the Berkshire numbers are after-tax!

Berkshire owns shares in publicly traded companies worth $62 billion. These holdings include approximately 12.6 per cent of American Express, 8.6 per cent of Coca-Cola, 3.27 per cent of Proctor & Gamble, 18 per cent of the *Washington Post* and 6.5 per cent of Wells Fargo. Some investors have been with Buffett long before he took control of Berkshire. An investor who placed $100 in one of his investment partnerships in the late 1950s, and placed it in Berkshire after the

---

[15] Train (1980), p. 98.
[16] Reproduced in Lowe (1999), p. 116.
[17] Barclays Capital, *Equity Gilt Studies* (published annually).
[18] Implicit price deflation for GNP. US Office of Business Economics, *The National Income and Product Accounts of the United States 1929–1965.*
[19] Graham and Dodd (1934), p. 12.
[20] Graham and Dodd (1934), p. 452.
[21] Graham and Dodd (1934), p. 585.
[22] He is gradually reducing his holding to give away his fortune mostly to his friends Bill & Melinda Gates' charity, assisting developing countries, particularly with medical aid.

Exhibit 14.16 Berkshire Hathaway's corporate performance vs. the S&P 500

	Annual percentage change		
Year	In per-share book value of Berkshire (1)	In S&P 500 with dividends included (2)	Relative results (1) – (2)
1965	23.8	10.0	13.8
1966	20.3	(11.7)	32.0
1967	11.0	30.9	(19.9)
1968	19.0	11.0	8.0
1969	16.2	(8.4)	24.6
1970	12.0	3.9	8.1
1971	16.4	14.6	1.8
1972	21.7	18.9	2.8
1973	4.7	(14.8)	19.5
1974	5.5	(26.4)	31.9
1975	21.9	37.2	(15.3)
1976	59.3	23.6	35.7
1977	31.9	(7.4)	39.3
1978	24.0	6.4	17.6
1979	35.7	18.2	17.5
1980	19.3	32.3	(13.0)
1981	31.4	(5.0)	36.4
1982	40.0	21.4	18.6
1983	32.3	22.4	9.9
1984	13.6	6.1	7.5
1985	48.2	31.6	16.6
1986	26.1	18.6	7.5
1987	19.5	5.1	14.4
1988	20.1	16.6	3.5
1989	44.4	31.7	12.7
1990	7.4	(3.1)	10.5
1991	39.6	30.5	9.1
1992	20.3	7.6	12.7
1993	14.3	10.1	4.2
1994	13.9	1.3	12.6
1995	43.1	37.6	5.5
1996	31.8	23.0	8.8
1997	34.1	33.4	0.7
1998	48.3	28.6	19.7
1999	0.5	21.0	(20.5)
2000	6.5	(9.1)	15.6
2001	(6.2)	(11.9)	5.7
2002	10.0	(22.1)	32.1
2003	21.0	28.7	(7.7)
2004	10.5	10.9	(0.4)
2005	6.4	4.9	1.5
2006	18.4	15.8	2.6
Average annual gain 1965–2006	21.4	10.4	11.0

Source: Berkshire Hathaway, Annual Report, 2006 (www.berkshirehathaway.com). Copyrighted material. Reprinted with permission.

partnership was dissolved, would find that investment worth more than \$2.8 million today. In the 13 years of the partnership funds (1957–69) investors made annual returns greater than that on Berkshire, at almost 30 per cent per year. The funds managed by the young Buffett outperformed the Dow Jones Industrial Average in every year and made money even when the market was sharply down. If you put the two phases of his career – first the partnership, then Berkshire – together then you have a quite remarkable performance record, one that, to my knowledge, has not been beaten.

Buffett is one of the three richest people in the world. Imagine being one of the lucky people to have trusted Buffett in the early days. It is what investors' dreams are made off. Apparently, the following conversation between two Berkshire shareholders was overheard at the annual meeting in 1996: 'What price did you buy at?' The reply: 'Nineteen,' says the first. 'You mean nineteen hundred?' 'No, nineteen.'[23] These shares are now worth \$136,000 each!

Warren Buffett said:

> I'm convinced that there is much inefficiency in the market . . . When the price of a stock can be influenced by a 'herd' on Wall Street with prices set at the margin by the most emotional person, or the greediest person, or the most depressed person, it is hard to argue that the market always prices rationally. In fact, market prices are frequently nonsensical . . . There seems to be some perverse human characteristic that likes to make easy things difficult. The academic world, if anything, has actually backed away from the teaching of value investing over the last 30 years. It's likely to continue that way. Ships will sail around the world but the Flat Earth Society will flourish.[24]

The question is: are these performances possible through chance? Just to muddy the waters, consider the following situation. You give dice to 100 million investors and ask them each to throw nine sixes in a row. Naturally most will fail, but some will succeed. You follow up the exercise with a series of interviews to find out how the masters of the die did it. Some say it was the lucky cup they use, others point to astrological charts. Of course we all know that it was purely chance that produced success but try telling that to the gurus and their disciples.

Warren Buffett has countered this argument – *see* **Exhibit 14.17**. It is very difficult to prove either way whether excellent stock picking performance is due to superior analysis in an inefficient environment or merely good fortune. Ultimately you have to make a subjective judgement given the weight of evidence.

Exhibit 14.17

The superinvestors of Graham-and-Doddsville

by Warren E. Buffett

Many of the professors who write textbooks . . . argue that the stock market is efficient: that is, that stock prices reflect everything that is known about a company's prospects and about the state of the economy. There are no undervalued stocks, these theorists argue, because there are smart security analysts who utilize all available information to ensure unfailingly appropriate prices. Investors who seem to beat the market year after year are just lucky. 'If prices fully reflect available information, this sort of investment adeptness is ruled out,' writes one of today's textbook authors. Well, maybe, but I want to present to you a group of investors who have, year in and year out, beaten the Standard & Poor's 500 stock index. The hypothesis that they do this by pure chance is at least worth examining. Crucial to this examination is the fact that these winners were all well known to me and pre-identified as superior investors, the most recent identification occurring over fifteen years ago. Absent this condition – that is, if I had just recently searched among thousands of records to select a few names for you this morning – I would advise you to stop reading right here. I should add that all these records have been audited. And I should further add that I have known many of those who have invested with these managers, and the checks received by those participants over the years have matched the stated records.

[23] Urry (1996), p. 1.
[24] Warren Buffett (1984).

Before we begin this examination, I would like you to imagine a national coin-flipping contest. Let's assume we get 225 million Americans up tomorrow morning and we ask them all to wager a dollar. They go out in the morning at sunrise, and they all call the flip of a coin. If they call correctly, they win a dollar from those who called wrong. Each day the losers drop out, and on the subsequent day the stakes build as all previous winnings are put on the line. After ten flips on ten mornings, there will be approximately 220,000 people in the United States who have correctly called ten flips in a row. They each will have won a little over $1,000.

Now this group will probably start getting a little puffed up about this, human nature being what it is. They may try to be modest, but at cocktail parties they will occasionally admit to attractive members of the opposite sex what their technique is, and what marvellous insights they bring to the field of flipping.

Assuming that the winners are getting the appropriate rewards from the losers, in another ten days we will have 215 people who have successfully called their coin flips 20 times in a row and who each, by this exercise, have turned one dollar into a little over $1 million. $225 million would have been lost; $225 million would have been won.

By then, this group will really lose their heads. They will probably write books on 'How I Turned a Dollar into a Million in Twenty Days Working Thirty Seconds a Morning'. Worse yet, they'll probably start jetting around the country attending seminars on efficient coin-flipping and tackling sceptical professors with, 'If it can't be done, why are there 215 of us?'

But then some business school professor will probably be rude enough to bring up the fact that if 225 million orangutans had engaged in a similar exercise, the results would be much the same – 215 egotistical orangutans with 20 straight winning flips.

I would argue, however, that there *are* some important differences in the examples I am going to present. For one thing, if (a) you had taken 225 million orangutans distributed roughly as the U.S. population is; if (b) 215 winners were left after 20 days; and if (c) you found that 40 came from a particular zoo in Omaha, you would be pretty sure you were on to something. So you would probably go out and ask the zookeeper about what he's feeding them, whether they had special exercises, what books they read, and who knows what else. That is, if you found any really extraordinary concentrations of success, you might want to see if you could identify concentrations of unusual characteristics that might be causal factors.

Scientific inquiry naturally follows such a pattern. If you were trying to analyse possible causes of a rare type of cancer – with, say, 1,500 cases a year in the United States – and you found that 400 of them occurred in some little mining town in Montana, you would get very interested in the water there, or the occupation of those afflicted, or other variables. You know that it's not random chance that 400 come from a small area. You would not necessarily know the causal factors, but you would know where to search.

I submit to you that there are ways of defining an origin other than geography. In addition to geographical origins, there can be what I call an *intellectual* origin. I think you will find that a disproportionate number of successful coin-flippers in the investment world came from a very small intellectual village that could be called Graham-and-Doddsville. A concentration of winners that simply cannot be explained by chance can be traced to this particular intellectual village.

Conditions could exist that would make even that concentration unimportant. Perhaps 100 people were simply imitating the coin-flipping call of some terribly persuasive personality. When he called heads, 100 followers automatically called that coin the same way. If the leader was part of the 215 left at the end, the fact that 100 came from the same intellectual origin would mean nothing. You would simply be identifying one case as a hundred cases. Similarly, let's assume that you lived in a strongly patriarchal society and every family in the United States conveniently consisted of ten members. Further assume that the patriarchal culture was so strong that, when the 225 million people went out the first day, every member of the family identified with the father's call. Now, at the end of the 20-day period, you would have 215 winners, and you would find that they came from only 21.5 families. Some naive types might say that this indicates an enormous hereditary factor as an explanation of successful coin flipping. But, of course, it would have no significance at all because it would simply mean that you didn't have 215 individual winners, but rather 21.5 randomly distributed families who were winners.

In this group of successful investors that I want to consider, there has been a common intellectual patriarch, Ben Graham. But the children who left the house of this intellectual patriarch have called their 'flips' in very different ways. They have gone to different places and bought and sold different stocks and companies, yet they have had a combined record that simply can't be explained by random chance. It certainly cannot be explained by the fact that they are all calling flips identically because a leader is signalling the calls to make. The patriarch has merely set forth the intellectual theory for making coin-calling decisions, but each student has decided on his own manner of applying the theory.

The common intellectual theme of the investors from Graham-and-Doddsville is this: they search for discrepancies between the *value* of a business and the *price* of small pieces of that business in the market. Essentially, they exploit those discrepancies without the efficient market theorist's concern as to whether the stocks are bought on

Monday or Thursday, or whether it is January or July, etc. Incidentally, when businessmen buy businesses – which is just what our Graham & Dodd investors are doing through the medium of marketable stocks – I doubt that many are cranking into their purchase decision the day of the week or the month in which the transaction is going to occur. If it doesn't make any difference whether all of a business is being bought on a Monday or a Friday, I am baffled why academicians invest extensive time and effort to see whether it makes a difference when buying small pieces of those same businesses. Our Graham & Dodd investors, needless to say, do not discuss beta, the capital asset pricing model, or covariance in returns among securities. These are not subjects of any interest to them. In fact, most of them would have difficulty defining those terms. The investors simply focus on two variables, price and value.

. . . I think the group that we have identified by a common intellectual home is worthy of study. Incidentally, despite all the academic studies of the influence of such variables as price, volume, seasonality, capitalization size, etc., upon stock performance, no interest has been evidenced in studying the methods of this unusual concentration of value-oriented winners.

I begin this study of results by going back to a group of four of us who worked at Graham-Newman Corporation from 1954 through 1956. There were only four – I have not selected these names from among thousands. I offered to go to work at Graham-Newman for nothing after I took Ben Graham's class, but he turned me down as overvalued. He took this value stuff very seriously! After much pestering he finally hired me. There were three partners and four of us at the 'peasant' level. All four left between 1955 and 1957 when the firm was wound up, and it's possible to trace the record of three.

The first example is that of Walter Schloss. Walter never went to college, but took a course from Ben Graham at night at the New York Institute of Finance. Walter left Graham-Newman in 1955 and achieved the record shown here over 28 years. [A compound rate of return of 21.3 per cent compared with a market return of 8.4 per cent from 1956 to 1984.]

. . . Walter has diversified enormously, owning well over 100 stocks currently. He knows how to identify securities that sell at considerably less than their value to a private owner. *And that's all he does* . . . He simply says, if a business is worth a dollar and I can buy it for 40 cents, something good may happen to me, and he does it over and over and over again. He owns many more stocks than I do – and is far less interested in the underlying nature of the business; I don't seem to have very much influence on Walter. That's one of his strengths; no one has much influence on him.

The second case is Tom Knapp, who also worked at Graham-Newman with me. Tom was a chemistry major at Princeton before the war; when he came back from the war, he was a beach bum. And then one day he read that Dave Dodd was giving a night course in investments at Columbia. Tom took it on a noncredit basis, and he got so interested in the subject from taking that course that he came up and enrolled at Columbia Business School, where he got the MBA degree. He took Dodd's course again, and took Ben Graham's course. Incidentally, 35 years later I called Tom to ascertain some of the facts involved here and I found him on the beach again. The only difference is that now he owns the beach!

In 1968 Tom Knapp and Ed Anderson, also a Graham disciple, along with one or two other fellows of similar persuasion, formed Tweedy, Browne Partners, and their investment results appear in Table 2 [showing an annual compound rate of return of 20 per cent compared with the market's return of 7 per cent, 1968–83]. Tweedy, Browne built that record with very wide diversification. They occasionally bought control of businesses, but the record of the passive investments is equal to the record of the control investments.

Table 3 describes the third member of the group who formed the Buffett Partnership in 1957. [Table 3, not reproduced here, shows a compound rate of 29.5 per cent against the market rate of 7.4 per cent, 1957–69.] The best thing he did was to quit in 1969. Since then, in a sense, Berkshire Hathaway has been a continuation of the partnership in some respects. There is no single index I can give you that I would feel would be a fair test of investment management at Berkshire. But I think that any way you figure it, it has been satisfactory.

Table 4 shows the record of the Sequoia Fund, which is managed by a man whom I met in 1951 in Ben Graham's class, Bill Ruane. [Table 4, not reproduced here, shows compound annual return of 17.2 per cent against a market return of 10 per cent, 1970–84.] After getting out of Harvard Business School, he went to Wall Street. Then he realized that he needed to get a real business education so he came up to take Ben's course at Columbia, where we met in early 1951. Bill's record from 1951 to 1970, working with relatively small sums, was far better than average. When I wound up Buffett Partnership I asked Bill if he would set up a fund to handle all our partners, so he set up the Sequoia Fund. He set it up at a terrible time, just when I was quitting.

He went right into the two-tier market and all the difficulties that made for comparative performance for value-oriented investors. I am happy to say that my partners, to an amazing degree, not only stayed with him but added money, with the happy result shown.

There's no hindsight involved here. Bill was the only person I recommended to my partners, and I said at the time that if he achieved a four-point-per-annum advantage over the Standard & Poor's, that would be solid performance. Bill has achieved well over that, working with progressively larger sums of money.

. . . I should add that in the records we've looked at so far, throughout this whole period there was practically no duplication in these portfolios. These are men who select securities based on discrepancies between price and value, but they make their selections very differently . . . The overlap among these portfolios has been very, very low. These records do not reflect one guy calling the flip and fifty people yelling out the same thing after him.

. . . A friend of mine who is a Harvard Law graduate . . . set up a major law firm. I ran into him in about 1960 and told him that law was fine as a hobby but he could do better. He set up a partnership quite the opposite of Walter's. His portfolio was concentrated in very few securities and therefore his record was much more volatile but it was based on the same discount-from-value approach [average annual compound rate of return of 19.8 per cent compared with market return of 5 per cent p.a., 1962–75]. He was willing to accept greater peaks and valleys of performance, and he happens to be a fellow whose whole psyche goes toward concentration, with the results shown [not reproduced]. Incidentally, this record belongs to Charlie Munger, my partner for a long time in the operation of Berkshire Hathaway. When he ran his partnership, however, his portfolio holdings were almost completely different from mine and the other fellows mentioned earlier.

Table 6 [not reproduced here] is the record of a fellow who was a pal of Charlie Munger's, another non-business school type – who was a math major at USC. He went to work for IBM after graduation and was an IBM salesman for a while. After I got to Charlie, Charlie got to him. This happens to be the record of Rick Guerin. Rick, from 1965 to 1983, against a compounded gain of 316 percent for the S&P, came off with 22,200 percent which, probably because he lacks a business school education, he regards as statistically significant.

One sidelight here: it is extraordinary to me that the idea of buying dollar bills for 40 cents takes immediately with people or it doesn't take at all. It's like an inoculation. If it doesn't grab a person right away, I find that you can talk to him for years and show him records, and it doesn't make any difference. They just don't seem able to grasp the concept, simple as it is. A fellow like Rick Guerin, who had no formal education in business, understands immediately the value approach to investing and he's applying it five minutes later. I've never seen anyone who became a gradual convert over a ten-year period to this approach. It doesn't seem to be a matter of IQ or academic training. It's instant recognition, or it is nothing.

. . . Stan Perlmeter . . . was a liberal arts major at the University of Michigan who was a partner in the advertising agency of Bozell & Jacobs. We happened to be in the same building in Omaha. In 1965 he figured out I had a better business than he did, so he left advertising. Again, it took five minutes for Stan to embrace the value approach. [Performance: 23 per cent p.a. compared with market return of 7 per cent 1966–83.]

Perlmeter does not own what Walter Schloss owns. He does not own what Bill Ruane owns. These are records made *independently*. But every time Perlmeter buys a stock it's because he's getting more for his money than he's paying. That's the only thing he's thinking about. He's not looking at quarterly earnings projections, he's not looking at next year's earnings, he's not thinking about what day of the week it is, he doesn't care what investment research from any place says, he's not interested in price momentum, volume, or anything. He's simply asking: What is the business worth?

. . . So these are . . . records of 'coin-flippers' from Graham-and-Doddsville. I haven't selected them with hindsight from among thousands. It's not like I am reciting to you the names of a bunch of lottery winners – people I had never heard of before they won the lottery. I selected these men years ago based upon their framework for investment decision-making. I knew what they had been taught and additionally I had some personal knowledge of their intellect, character, and temperament. It's very important to understand that this group has assumed far less risk than average; note their record in years when the general market was weak. While they differ greatly in style, these investors are, mentally, *always buying the business, not buying the stock*. A few of them sometimes buy whole businesses. Far more often they simply buy small pieces of businesses. Their attitude, whether buying all or a tiny piece of a business, is the same. Some of them hold portfolios with dozens of stocks; others concentrate on a handful. But all exploit the difference between the market price of a business and its intrinsic value.

I'm convinced that there is much inefficiency in the market. These Graham-and-Doddsville investors have successfully exploited gaps between price and value.

. . . In conclusion, some of the more commercially minded among you may wonder why I am writing this article. Adding many converts to the value approach will perforce narrow the spreads between price and value, I can only tell you that the secret has been out for 50 years, ever since Ben Graham and Dave Dodd wrote *Security Analysis*, yet I have seen no trend toward value investing in the 35 years that I've practiced it . . . There will continue to be wide discrepancies between price and value in the marketplace, and those who read their Graham and Dodd will continue to prosper.

Source: Warren Buffett (1984), An edited transcript of a talk given at Columbia University in 1984. Reproduced in *Hermes*, magazine of Columbia Business School, Fall 1984 and in both the 1997 and the 2003 reprints of Graham (1973).

Eugene Fama is perhaps the most well-known advocate of EMH, with a string of quantitative empirical papers to his name. And yet even he, is this 2002 newspaper interview (**Exhibit 14.18**) shows some doubts.

Exhibit 14.18

Forty years on, Fama holds to his big idea

FT

The Chicago based professor says his theory has stood the test of time

says Simon London

One of the biggest unanswered questions in financial economics is why Eugene Fama has yet to win the Nobel Prize. The University of Chicago business school professor coined the term 'efficient markets' with his 1963 doctoral thesis, pioneered empirical research into the behaviour of capital markets and, in the early 1990s, devised the 'three-factor model' that led to a whole new taxonomy of investment funds.

The passive fund management industry owes its rise to the insight that markets quickly and accurately assimilate new information, and cannot be beaten over the long term without the assumption of additional risk.

So, 40 years on, does Prof Fama believe more or less strongly in the efficiency of capital markets?

'I've never said that markets are totally efficient. I've always said that for most investors, most of the time, markets are efficient. For most corporate managers, markets are efficient – for all practical purposes.'

How, then, does he explain the extraordinary record of Warren Buffet, who has beaten the market with remarkable consistency? 'I think Warren Buffet is great. I am willing to believe that he wins, OK. But what he says is that he can pick an [undervalued] company once every couple of years. And he is the best. He says that for everything else, markets are efficient.

'Remember also that he doesn't just pick companies, he runs them. That is a different activity. No one would argue against the idea that, if you participate in these companies, you might be able to make them better or worse. It doesn't mean that the companies were inefficiently priced to begin with, just that something can be done to make them more attractive. If Warren Buffet can do it only once every couple of years, that is the best thing you can say about market efficiency.'

What about stock market bubbles and crashes? Surely, stocks cannot have been correctly priced on Monday morning if they are worth 30 per cent less by the end of the day? 'I don't know why these things happen so quickly', he concedes. 'We don't know enough about the way in which information gets assimilated into prices. But if you look at crashes, half of them turn out to be too small and half turn out to be too big.

'The 1987 crash was clearly too big because the market came back so quickly, the '29 crash was too small because the market carried on going down. They are both mistakes, but they are unbiased mistakes.'

In other words, stock market crashes don't have any statistical significance and there is no pattern that can be used as evidence against efficient markets.

Prof Fama's belief in market efficiency has been strengthened by the many inconclusive studies over the years attempting to disprove it: 'Today there are 10,000 finance academics looking for violations of one theory or another, including efficient markets. I think it has stood up very well.'

The fund management industry has a vested interest in undermining the idea that markets are efficient. Fees charged by active managers only make sense if investors believe they have good chance of beating the market indices.

The snag for active managers is that studies have failed to find real evidence of 'persistency' in the performance of managers who invest on the basis of either fundamental analysis of companies or technical analysis of market trends. 'The thing people can't deal with is that, if you look at the performance of active managers, there is nothing there,' says Prof Fama. According to efficient markets theory, the only way to beat, the market over the long term is to accept additional risk. Prof Fama's 'three-factor model,' published with Ken French of Dartmouth College in 1993, says the returns of any portfolio are determined by:

- The market risk of investing in equities rather than less volatile vehicles;
- Whether the stocks in the portfolio have growth or value characteristics;
- Whether the stocks are issued by large medium or small-cap companies.

According to the model, investors in small-cap value stocks should achieve the highest returns over the long term because they are adopting the most risk. But Prof Fama admits that the nature of these risks remains little understood.

'We don't claim that we totally understand what additional risks you are taking, particularly when it comes to size. But do you think that small firms have the same cost of capital as big firms? No, they have a higher cost of capital. This is the flip side of expected returns: We don't fully understand these mechanisms but we have observed the effect.'

Source: *Financial Times*, 3 June 2002, p. 4. Reprinted with permission.

Strong-form tests

It is well known that it is possible to trade shares on the basis of information not in the public domain and thereby make abnormal profits. The mining engineer who discovers a rich seam of silver may buy the company shares before the market is told of the likely boost to profits. The director who becomes aware of lost orders and declining competitive position may quietly sell shares to 'diversify his interests' or 'pay for school fees', you understand. The merchant banker who hears of a colleague assisting one firm to plan a surprise takeover bid for another has been known to purchase shares (or options) in the target firm. Stock markets are not strong-form efficient.

Trading on inside knowledge is thought to be a 'bad thing'. It makes those outside of the charmed circle feel cheated. A breakdown of the fair game perception will leave some investors feeling that the inside traders are making profits at their expense. If they start to believe that the market is less than a fair game they will be more reluctant to invest and society will suffer. To avoid the loss of confidence in the market most stock exchanges attempt to curb insider dealing. It was made a criminal offence in the UK in 1980 where **insider dealing** is considered to be, besides dealing for oneself, either counselling or procuring another individual to deal in the securities or communicating knowledge to any other person, while being aware that he or she (or someone else) will deal in those securities. The term 'insider' now covers anyone with sensitive information, not just a company director or employee. Most modern economies have rules on insider dealing and the EU has a directive on the subject. Despite the complex legislation and codes of conduct it is hard to believe that insider trading has been reduced significantly in the last two decades. It would appear that the lawyers have great difficulty obtaining successful prosecutions. Since 2001 the Financial Services Authority has had the power to fine insiders for 'market abuse' encompassing both insider dealing and attempts to manipulate the market, for example through misleading statements. This is under civil law rather than criminal law and therefore has a lower burden of proof. The article in **Exhibit 14.19** shows insider dealing is rife; it is very difficult to detect and to punish.

Exhibit 14.19

FT

FSA boss admits defeat

Insider dealing still rife despite efforts

Outgoing chief calls for more powers

By Peter Thai Larsen and Lina Saigol

When John Tiner last year identified cracking down on market abuse as one of the Financial Services Authority's main priorities, many observers questioned whether the regulator would really be able to stop insider dealing.

More than 12 months on, the sceptics appear to have been proved right. Though the FSA has scored some high profile successes – notably in its case against Philippe Jabre, the former star trader with GLG, the hedge fund – the flow of price-sensitive information into the market ahead of major announcements appears to be as steady as ever.

Mr Tiner acknowledged as much yesterday. In his last major speech to a City audience before he steps down as the FSA's chief executive this month, he set out the reasons for insider trading being so difficult to police.

'The perpetrators may be in a ring designed to disguise the identity of both the intermediaries and the beneficiaries, and some may operate from abroad. Market abuse can be a very sophisticated activity, where complex derivative transactions – which are not easily visible to the market or us – may be used. And the standards of evidence to prosecute successfully market abuse are high, and reliance on circumstantial evidence can seriously weaken a case.'

Mr Tiner was explaining why the FSA needs powers to offer people immunity from prosecution in return for their co-operation, similar to its counterparts at the US Securities and Exchange Commission.

At the same time, however, the regulator is also cracking down on market abuse by making the firms it

▶

Exhibit 14.19 continued

regulates act more responsibly with sensitive information.

In spite of the FSA's efforts to tackle the underlying causes of market abuse, there is still a widespread feeling that a few high profile scalps would be a more effective deterrent.

One trader at a City firm says: 'This review is a green light for insider traders. Unless the FSA introduces US style penalties, nothing will change.'

Source: Financial Times, 3 July 2007, p. 18. Reprinted with permission.

Another weapon in the fight against insiders is to raise the level of information disclosure: making companies release price-sensitive information quickly. The London Stock Exchange and the United Kingdom Listing Authority have strict guidelines to encourage companies to make announcements to the market as a whole as early as possible, on such matters as current trading conditions and profit warnings.

A third approach is to completely prohibit certain individuals from dealing in the company's shares for crucial time periods. For example, directors of quoted firms are prevented by the 'Model Code for Director Dealings' from trading shares for a minimum period (two months) before an announcement of regularly recurring information such as annual results. The Code also precludes dealing before the announcement of matters of an exceptional nature involving unpublished information which is potentially price sensitive. These rules apply to other employees in possession of price-sensitive information.

There is a grey area which stands between trading on inside knowledge and trading purely on publicly available information. Some investment analysts, though strictly outsiders, become so knowledgeable about a firm that they have some degree of superior information. Their judgement or guesstimates about future prospects are of a higher order than those of other analysts and certainly beyond anything the average shareholder is capable of. They may make regular visits to the company head office and operating units. They may discuss the opportunities and potential problems for the firm and the industry with the directors and with competitors' employees. Despite the strict rules concerning directors briefing one analyst better than the generality of shareholders it may be possible to 'read between the lines' and gather hints to give an informed edge. The hypothesis that there are some exceptional analysts has limited empirical backing and relies largely on anecdotal evidence and so this point should not be overemphasised. It is clear from previous sections of this chapter that the vast majority of professional analysts are unable to outperform the market.

Behavioural finance

There has been a forceful attack on the EMH by finance specialists drawing on a combination of human behavioural literature and their knowledge of markets. The EMH rests on the assumption that all investors are rational, or, even if there are some irrational investors, that the actions of rational informed investors will eliminate pricing anomalies through arbitrage. The **behavioural finance** proponents argue that investors frequently make systematic errors and these errors can push the prices of shares (and other financial securities) away from fundamental value for considerable periods of time.

This is a field of intellectual endeavour that is attracting increasing numbers of adherents as the evidence on apparent inefficiencies grows. Behavioural finance models offer plausible reasoning for the phenomena we observe in the pattern of share prices. They offer persuasive explanations for the outperformance of low PER, high dividend yield and low book-to-market ratio shares as well as the poor performance of 'glamour' shares. They can also be drawn on to shed light on both return reversal and momentum effects. In addition, behavioural science has a lot to offer when it comes to understanding stock market bubbles and irrational pessimism.

Many of the investors who made a fortune in the twentieth century have been saying all along that to understand the market you must understand the psychology of investors. In the 1960s, 1970s and even the 1980s, they were denounced as naive at best by the dyed-in-the-wool quantitative financial economist – the economists had 'scientific proof' of the market's efficiency. They insisted that even if investors were generally irrational the market had inherent mechanisms to arrive at the efficient price, leaving no abnormal returns to be had. The successful investors were merely lucky. Worse! They were lucky and had the nerve to go against the scientific 'evidence' and publicly declare that they believed that there are sound investment principles which permit outperformance.

The successful investors continued to believe in the irrationality and exploitability of markets despite the onslaught from many university economists who were characterised as believing that 'It might work in practice, but it'll never work in theory'. Eventually a growing band of respected academics provided theoretical and empirical backing to the behavioural view of financial markets. Now the debate has reached a fascinating point with high-quality modelling and empirical evidence on both sides.

The three lines of defence for EMH

To defend the EMH its adherents have three progressively stronger arguments which have to be surmounted if the behavioural finance advocates are to be able to attack the core.[25]

1 Investors are rational and hence value securities rationally.
2 Even if some investors are not rational, their irrationally inspired trades of securities are random and therefore the effects of their irrational actions cancel each other out without moving prices away from their efficient level.
3 If the majority of investors are irrational in similar ways and therefore have a tendency to push security values away from the efficient level this will be countered by rational arbitrageurs who eliminate the influence of the irrational traders on prices.

Under the first condition all investors examine securities for their fundamental value. That is, they calculate the present value of the future income flow associated with the security using an appropriate discount rate given the risk level (*see* Chapter 20). If any new information comes along which will increase future flows or decrease the discount rate then the price will rise to the new efficient level instantly. Likewise, bad news results in a lower efficient price. This barrier is easy to attack and demolish. It is plain from anecdotal evidence and from empirical study that the majority of share traders do not assess fundamental value – just ask those who were day-traders in the dotcom boom or those who buy on the basis of a tip from a friend, or a newspaper or broker.

The second barrier is more of a challenge. It accepts individual irrational behaviour but the result is collective rationality in pricing because the irrational trades are evenly balanced and so the effect is benign. This may explain the large volume of trades as irrational investors exchange securities with each other, but this does not lead to systematic inefficient pricing away from fundamental value. The key assumption to be attacked here is the absence of correlation in the actions of irrational investors. There is growing evidence that investors do not deviate from rationality randomly but there is a bias to deviate in the same way (that is, there is positive correlation between their deviations) and therefore they lead prices away from fundamental value. The next section of this chapter provides an outline of some of the psychological biases that are being studied to try to explain apparent inefficiencies in pricing.

The third argument says that the actions of rational arbitrageurs are strong enough to restore efficiency even in the presence of numerous investors making cognitive errors. **Arbitrage** is the act of exploiting price differences on the same security or similar securities by simultaneously selling the overpriced security and buying the underpriced security. If a security did become overpriced because of the combined actions of irrational investors, smart investors would sell this security (or if they did not own it, 'sell it short') and simultaneously purchase other 'similar securities' to hedge their risks. In a perfect arbitrage they can make a profit without any risk at all (and even without money). The arbitrageurs' selling action brings down the security's price to its fundamental value in the EMH. If a security became underpriced arbitrageurs would buy the security and, to hedge risk, would sell short essentially similar securities, lifting the price of the security to its efficient level.

[25] These three arguments are identified by Andrei Shleifer in his excellent book *Inefficient Markets* (2000).

The arbitrage argument is impressive and forms a strong bulwark against the financial behaviourists. However, there are some weaknesses. Shleifer (2000) points out a number of reasons why arbitrage does not work well in the real world and therefore prices are not returned to fundamental value. To be effective the arbitrageur needs to be able to purchase or sell a close-substitute security. Some securities, e.g. futures and options, usually have close substitutes, but in many instances there is no close substitute and so locking in a safe profit is not possible. For example, imagine that you, as a rational investor, discover that Unilever's shares are undervalued. What other security (securities) would you sell at the same time as you purchase Unilever's shares to obtain a risk-free return when the price anomaly is detected? If we were talking about the price of a tonne of wheat of the same quality selling on two different markets at different prices we could buy in the low-price market and simultaneously sell in the high-price market and make a profit (guaranteed without risk and probably without the need for capital) even if the price difference was only 10p. But what can you use in arbitrage trade that is the same as a Unilever share? Well, you might consider that Procter & Gamble shares are close enough and so you sell these short.[26] You expect that in six months the pricing anomaly will correct itself and you can close your position in Unilever by selling and close your position in P&G by buying its shares. But this strategy is far from the risk-free arbitrage of economists' ideal. You face the risk of other fundamental factors influencing the shares of Unilever and P&G (e.g. a strike, a product flop). You also face the risk that the irrational investors push irrationality to new heights. That is, the price does not gradually move towards the fundamental value over the next six months, but away from it. If this happens you lose money as a buyer of Unilever shares and have no offsetting gain on P&G shares. There is growing evidence of the problem of continued movement away from the fundamental value even after an anomaly has been spotted by arbitrageurs (e.g. Froot and Dabora (1999)). For anecdotal evidence we need only remember back to 1999 and the pricing of dotcom stocks where arbitrageurs sold at high prices only to see the price climb higher as thousands of ill-informed investors piled in. This type of risk facing the arbitrageur is called '**noise trader risk**' (De Long *et al.* (1990)) because it is the actions of the poorly informed investors that create noise in the price series; and this can get worse rather than better. So, in the real world 'with a finite risk-bearing capacity of arbitrageurs as a group, their aggregate ability to bring prices of broad groups of securities into line is limited' (Shleifer (2000), p. 14).

Trading in overvalued or undervalued shares and using imperfect substitutes to offset a position is termed 'risk arbitrage' and is a completely different kettle of fish from risk-free arbitrage.[27] Risk arbitrage entails a calculation of the statistical likelihood of the convergence of relative prices and does not deal with certainties.

Shleifer builds a behaviourally based model on the foundation of two observations of real-world markets.

1 Many securities do not have perfect, or even good, substitutes, making arbitrage risky.
2 Even if a good substitute is available arbitrage remains risky because of noise trader risk, and the possibility that prices will not converge to fundamental values quickly enough to suit the arbitrageur's time horizon.

---

[26] We are assuming that selling shares that you do not own (and therefore have to borrow) is easy and available to a large number of potential investors. However, in reality, borrowing shares is costly, often impossible and open to only a few institutional investors. Also your period of going short is usually only for days, weeks or a few months rather than years.

[27] Arbitrageurs face a number of risks.

a Fundamental risk: they may be wrong about perceived under- or overpricing.

b Noise trader risk: **i** Horizon risk: prices may revert to a correct level eventually, but the length of time needed may reduce the arbitrageurs' return to very little, e.g. if a 5 per cent underpricing is corrected in one month the annual rate of return is 79.6 per cent. If it takes two years the annual rate of return is under 2.5 per cent. **ii** Margin risk: arbitrageurs often borrow to buy into positions. If the market moves against them the lender may ask for more collateral or, in the derivatives market may ask for more margin (*see* Chapter 24). Arbitrageurs may not be able to meet these requirements and so may be forced to sell their positions at inconvenient times. **iii** Short covering risk: If the arbitrageur has borrowed shares to go short the lender may not be able to continue to supply shares for more than a few days, forcing the arbitrageur to liquidate the position prematurely.

He concludes that market efficiency will only be an extreme special case and financial markets in most scenarios are not expected to be efficient.

Some cognitive errors made by investors

Investors are subject to a variety of psychological tendencies that do not fit with the economists' 'rational man' model. This, it is argued, can lead to markets being heavily influenced by investor sentiment. The combination of limited arbitrage and investor sentiment pushing the market leads to inefficient pricing. Both elements are necessary. If arbitrage is unlimited then arbitrageurs will offset the herd actions of irrational investors so prices quickly and correctly move to incorporate relevant news. In the absence of investor sentiment prices would not move from fundamental value in the first place. Listed below are some of the psychological tendencies that are thought to impact on investors' buying and selling decisions and thus to create sentiment.

Overconfidence

When you ask drivers how good they are relative to other drivers research has shown that 65–80 per cent will answer that they are above average. Investors are as **overconfident** about their trading abilities as about their driving abilities. People significantly overestimate the accuracy of their forecasts. So, when investors are asked to estimate the profits for a firm one year from now and to express the figures in terms of a range where they are confident that the actual result has a 95 per cent chance of being within the projected range, they give a range that is far too narrow. Investors make bad bets because they are not sufficiently aware of their informational disadvantage. This line of research may help explain the underreaction effect. Investors experience unanticipated surprise at, say, earnings announcements because they are overconfident about their earnings predictions. It takes a while for them to respond to new information in the announcement (due to conservatism – *see* below) and so prices adjust slowly. This may contribute to price momentum and earnings momentum.

Overconfidence may be caused, at least in part, by **self-attribution bias**. That is, investors ascribe success to their own brilliance, but failures in stock picking to bad luck. Overconfidence may be a cause of **excessive trading** because investors believe they can pick winners and beat the market (Barber and Odean, 1999, 2000). Inexperienced investors are, apparently, *more* confident that they can beat the market than experienced investors.

Representativeness

Representativeness is the making of judgements based on stereotypes. It is the tendency to see identical situations where none exist. For example, if Michael is an extrovert, the life and soul of the party, highly creative and full of energy, people are more likely to judge that he is an advertising executive rather than a postman. Representativeness can be misleading. Michael is more likely to be a postman than an advertising executive, even though he 'sounds' to be typical of advertising executives: there are far more postmen than advertising executives. People overweight the representative description and underweight the statistical base evidence.

If there is a sharp decline in the stock market, as in 1987 or 2001, you will read articles pointing out that this is 1929 all over again. These will be backed up by a chart showing the index movement in 1929 and recent index movements. The similarities can be striking, but this does not mean that the Great Depression is about to be repeated, or even that share prices will fall for the next three years. The similarities between the two situations are superficial. The economic fundamentals are very different. Investors tend to give too much weight to representative observation (e.g. share price movements) and underweight numerous other factors.

Representativeness may help explain the return reversal effect. People look for patterns. If a share has suffered a series of poor returns investors assume that this pattern is representative for that company and will continue in the future. They forget that their conclusion could be premature and that a company with three bad years can produce several good profit figures. Similarly investors overreact in being too optimistic about shares that have had a lot of recent success. It may also explain why unit trusts and investment trusts with high past performance attract more of investors' capital even though studies have shown that past performance is a poor predictor of future performance – even poor-quality managers can show high returns purely by chance.

Conservatism

Investors are resistant to changing an opinion, even in the presence of pertinent new information. So, when profits turn out to be unexpectedly high they initially underreact. They do not revise their earnings estimates enough to reflect the new information and so one positive earnings surprise is followed by another positive earnings surprise.

Narrow framing

Investors' perceptions of risk and return are highly influenced by how the decision problems are framed. Many investors '**narrow frame**' rather than look at the broader picture. For example, an investor aged under 35 saving for retirement in 30 years pays too much attention to short-term gains and losses on a portfolio. Another investor focuses too much on the price movements of a single share, although it represents only a small proportion of total wealth. This kind of narrow framing can lead to an over-estimation of the risk investors are taking, especially if they are highly risk averse. The more narrow the investor's focus, the more likely he is to see losses. If the investor took a broad frame he would realise that despite short-term market fluctuations and one or two down years the equity market rises in the long term and by the time of retirement a well-diversified portfolio should be worth much more than it is today. Likewise, by viewing the portfolio as a whole the investor does not worry excessively about a few shares that have performed poorly. Benartzi and Thaler (1995) show evidence suggesting that framing errors cause investors to avoid equities in favour of risk-free government securities, thus missing out on the much better returns on equities. Investors evaluated the riskiness of shares on a time horizon that was too short, say once a year, or even once a month.

Ambiguity aversion

People are excessively fearful when they feel that they do not have very much information. On the other hand they have an excessive preference for the familiar on which they feel they have good information: as a result they are more likely to gamble. For example, **ambiguity aversion** may explain the avoidance of overseas shares despite the evidence of the benefits of international diversification.

Positive feedback and extrapolative expectations

Stock market bubbles may be, at least partially, explained by the presence of **positive-feedback traders** who buy shares after prices have risen and sell after prices fall. They develop **extrapolative expectations** about prices. That is, simply because prices rose (fell) in the past and a trend has been established investors extrapolate the trend and anticipate greater future price appreciation (falls). This tendency has also been found in house prices and in the foreign exchange markets. George Soros describes in his books (1987, 1998) his exploitation of this trend-chasing behaviour in a variety of financial and real asset markets. Here the informed trader (e.g. Soros) can buy into the trend thus pushing it along, further away from fundamental values, in the expectation that uninformed investors will pile in and allow the informed trader to get out at a profit. Thus the informed trader creates additional instability instead of returning the security to fundamental value through arbitrage.

Regret

Experimental psychologists have observed that people will forgo benefits within reach in order to avoid the small chance of feeling they have failed. They are overly influenced by the fear of feeling **regret**.

Confirmation bias

People desire to find information that agrees with their existing view. Information that conflicts is ignored. For example, in 2007 many people ignored the arguments suggesting property prices might fall.

Cognitive dissonance

If a belief has been held for a long time people continue to hold it even when such a belief is plainly contradicted by the evidence. People experience mental conflict when presented with evidence that their beliefs or assumptions are wrong, resulting in denial for a considerable period.

Availability bias

People may focus excessively on a particular fact or event because it is more visible, fresher in the mind or emotionally charged, at the expense of seeing the bigger picture. The bigger picture may incorporate soundly based probabilities. For example, following a major train crash, people tend to avoid train travel and use their cars more. However, the bigger picture based on the statistical evidence reveals that train travel is far safer than road transport. In financial markets, if some particularly high-profile companies in an industrial sector (e.g. IT) have produced poor results, investors might abandon the whole sector, ignoring the possibility that some excellent companies may be selling at low prices. They overweight the prominent news.

Miscalculation of probabilities

Experiments have shown that people attach too low a probability to likely outcomes and too high a probability to quite unlikely ones. Can this explain the low valuations of 'old economy' shares in the late 1990s as the technological revolution was in full swing? Did investors underestimate these companies' prospects for survival and their ability to combine the new technology with their traditional strengths? At the same time did investors overestimate the probability of all those dotcom start-ups surviving and becoming dominant in their segments?

Anchoring

When people are forming quantitative assessments their views are influenced by suggestion. So, for example, people valuing shares are swayed by previous prices. They **anchor** their changes in valuation on the value as suggested in the past. This may contribute to understanding post-earnings-announcement drift as investors make gradual adjustments to historic figures.

There is some meeting of the ways between the rational and the irrational schools of thought, so that investors are viewed as flawed rationalists rather than hopelessly irrational beings. These quasi-rational humans try hard to be rational but are susceptible to repeating the same old mistakes. They have memory limitations, cognitive limitations and emotional limitations.

William Sharpe, the Nobel laureate and developer of the CAPM, believes there is much to be gained by stepping outside economists' models and allowing for human behaviour – *see* **Exhibit 14.20**.

Misconceptions about the efficient market hypothesis

There are good grounds for doubting some aspects of the EMH and a reasoned debate can take place with advocates for efficiency and inefficiency stating their cases with rigorous argument and robust empirical methodology. However, the high-quality debate has sometimes been overshadowed by criticism based on one or more misunderstandings of the EMH. There are three classic misconceptions.

1 **Any share portfolio will perform as well as or better than a special trading rule designed to outperform the market** A monkey choosing a portfolio of shares from the *Financial Times* for a buy and hold strategy is nearly, but not quite, what the EMH advocates suggest as a strategy likely to be as rewarding as special inefficiency-hunting approaches. The monkey does not have the financial expertise needed to construct broadly based portfolios which fully diversify away unsystematic risk. A selection of shares in just one or two industrial sectors may expose the investor to excessive risk. So it is wrong to conclude from the EMH evidence that it does not matter what the investor does, and that any portfolio is acceptable. The EMH says that after first eliminating unsystematic risk by holding broadly based portfolios and then adjusting for the residual systematic risk, investors will not achieve abnormal returns.

Exhibit 14.20

Life at the Sharpe end of economic modelling

FT

The godfather of index funds says psychology will contribute to the next big breakthrough

writes Simon London

Prof Sharpe's [Bill Sharpe, the brains behind the Capital Asset Pricing Model] analysis of markets and finance has yet to come to rest and he has several answers as to where financial economics is heading. First, he argues that finance has become too obsessed with mathematics.

'We have got so intent on having elegant solutions to closed-form equations that we have tolerated some really stupid assumptions about people's preferences,' he says.

Linked to this, he wants financial economists to strive for a better understanding of how people really act.

Does that make Prof Sharpe a closet fan of behavioural finance, which tries to explain financial markets by looking at human psychology?

'I'm a fan of good behavioural finance. It is not a question of trying to show that people are irrational or throwing out all the models that involve rationality. The interesting thing is to find out what kinds of decisions people make under conditions of uncertainty if they know what they are doing.'

It is from this marriage of psychology and economics that Prof Sharpe expects the next breakthrough in finance. Fund managers, watch this space.

Source: *Financial Times*, 29 July 2002, p. 4. Reprinted with permission.

2 **There should be fewer price fluctuations** If shares are efficiently priced why is it that they move every day even when there is no announcement concerning a particular company? This is what we would expect in an efficient market. Prices move because new information is coming to the market every hour which may have some influence on the performance of a specific company. For example, the governor of the Bank of England may hint at interest rate rises, the latest industrial output figures may be released and so on.

3 **Only a minority of investors are actively trading, most are passive, therefore efficiency cannot be achieved** This too is wrong. It only needs a few trades by informed investors using all the publicly available information to position (through their buying and selling actions) a share at its semi-strong-form efficient price.

Implications of the EMH for investors

If the market is efficient there are a number of implications for investors. Even if it is merely efficient most of the time, for most participants a sensible working assumption is that pricing is based on fundamental values and the following implications apply.

1 **For the vast majority of people public information cannot be used to earn abnormal returns** (This refers to returns above the normal level for that systematic risk class.) The implications are that fundamental analysis is a waste of money and that so long as efficiency is maintained the average investor should simply select a suitably diversified portfolio, thereby avoiding costs of analysis and transaction. This message has struck a chord with millions of investors and thousands of billions of pounds have been placed with fund managers who merely replicate a stock market index (**index funds**) rather than try to pick winners in an actively managed fund. About 25 per cent of UK financial assets managed by professional investors (e.g. unit trusts) is in indexed funds. For the USA the figure is 35 per cent. It has been found that the active fund managers generally underperform the All Share Index – so do the 'trackers', but at least they have lower costs.

Another trend has been for small investors to trade shares through **execution-only brokers**. These brokers do not provide their clients with (nor charge them for) analysis of companies, 'hot tips' and suggestions for purchases. They merely carry out the client's buy or sell orders in the cheapest manner possible.

2 **Investors need to press for a greater volume of timely information** Semi-strong efficiency depends on the quality and quantity of publicly available information, and so companies should be encouraged by investor pressure, accounting bodies, government rulings and stock market regulation to provide as much as is compatible with the necessity for some secrecy to prevent competitors gaining useful knowledge.

3 **The perception of a fair game market could be improved by more constraints and deterrents placed on insider dealers**. Strong-form efficiency does not exist and so insiders can gain an unfair advantage.

Implications of the EMH for companies

The efficient market hypothesis also has a number of implications for companies.

1 **Focus on substance, not on short-term appearance** Some managers behave as though they believe they can fool shareholders. For example creative accounting is used to show a more impressive performance than is justified. Most of the time these tricks are transparent to investors, who are able to interpret the real position, and security prices do not rise artificially.

There are some circumstances when the drive for short-term boosts to reported earnings can be positively harmful to shareholders. For example, one firm might tend to overvalue its inventory to boost short-term profitability, another might not write off bad debts. These actions will result in additional, or at least earlier, taxation payments which will be harmful to shareholder wealth. Managers, aware that analysts often pay a great deal of attention to accounting rate of return, may, when facing a choice between a project with a higher NPV but a poor short-term ARR, or one with a lower NPV but higher short-term ARR, choose the latter. This principle of short-termism can be extended into areas such as research and development or marketing spend. These can be cut to boost profits in the short term but only at a long-term cost to shareholders.

One way to alleviate the short-term/long-term dilemma is for managers to explain why longer-term prospects are better than the current figures suggest. This requires a diligent communications effort.

2 **The timing of security issues does not have to be fine-tuned** Consider a team of managers contemplating a share issue who feel that their shares are currently underpriced because the market is 'low'. They opt to delay the sale, hoping that the market will rise to a more 'normal level'. This defies the logic of the EMH – if the market is efficient the shares are already correctly (unbiasedly) priced and the next move in prices is just as likely to be down as up. The past price movements have nothing to say about future movements.

The situation is somewhat different if the managers have private information that they know is not yet priced into the shares. In this case if the directors have good news then they would be wise to wait until after an announcement and subsequent adjustment to the share price before selling the new shares. Bad news announcements are more tricky – to sell the shares to new investors while withholding bad news will benefit existing shareholders, but will result in loss for the new shareholders. There are rules against withholding price sensitive information.

3 **Large quantities of new shares can be sold without moving the price** A firm wishing to raise equity capital by selling a block of shares may hesitate to price near to the existing share price. Managers may believe that the increase in supply will depress the price of the shares. This is generally not the case. In empirical studies (e.g. Scholes (1972)), if the market is sufficiently large (for example the London or New York Stock Exchange) and investors are satisfied that the new money will generate a return at least as high as the return on existing funds, the price does not fall. This is as we would expect in an efficient market: investors buy the new shares because of the return offered on them for their level of risk.[28] The fact that some old shares of the same

[28] Although some studies have shown a decrease in share price when the sale of shares is announced (e.g. *see* Smith (1986) for a list of studies).

company already exist and that therefore supply has risen does not come into the equation. The key question is: what will the new shares produce for their holders? If they produce as much as an old share they should be priced the same as an old share. If they are not, then someone will spot that they can gain an abnormal return by purchasing these shares (which will push up the price).

4 **Signals from price movements should be taken seriously** If, for instance, the directors announce that the company is to take over another firm and its share price falls dramatically on the day of the announcement this is a clear indication that the merger will be wealth destroying for shareholders – as the majority of mergers are (*see* Chapter 23). Managers cannot ignore this collective condemnation of their actions. An exception might be allowed if shareholders are dumping the shares in ignorance because the managers have special knowledge of the benefits to be derived from the merger – but then shouldn't the directors explain themselves properly?

Concluding comments

While modern, large and sophisticated stock markets exhibit inefficiencies in some areas, particularly at the strong-form level, it is reasonable to conclude that they are substantially efficient and it is rare that a non-insider can outperform the market. One of the more fruitful avenues of future research is likely to concern the influence of psychology on stock market pricing. We have seen how many of the (suggested) semi-strong inefficiencies, from bubbles to underpricing low PER shares, have at their base a degree of apparent 'non-rationality'.

Another line of enquiry is to question the assumption that all investors respond in a similar manner to the same risk and return factors and that these can be easily identified. Can beta be relied upon to represent all relevant risk? If it cannot, what are the main elements investors want additional compensation for? What about information costs, marketability limits, taxes and the degree of covariability with human capital returns for the investor (e.g. earnings from employment)? These are factors disliked by shareholders and so conceivably a share with many of these attributes will have to offer a high return. For some investors who are less sensitive to these elements the share which gives this high return may seem a bargain. A problem for the researcher in this field is that abnormal returns are calculated after allowance for risk. If the model used employs a risk factor which is not fully representative of all the risk and other attributes disliked by investors then efficiency or inefficiency cannot be established.

One way of 'outperforming' the market might be to select shares the attributes of which you dislike less than the other investors do, because they are likely to be underpriced for you – given your particular circumstances. Another way is through luck – which is often confused with the third way, that of possessing superior analytical skills.

A fourth method is through the discovery of a trading rule which works (but do not tell anybody, because if it becomes widespread knowledge it may stop working, unless it is based on some deep-seated psychological/cognitive error prevalent among investors). A fifth possibility is to be quicker than anyone else in responding to news – George Soros and his teams may fall into this category occasionally. The last, and the most trustworthy method, is to become an insider – the only problem with this method is that you may end up a different kind of insider – in prison.

To conclude: the equity markets are generally efficient, but the person with superior analytical ability, knowledge, dedication and creativity can be rewarded with abnormally high returns. However, for people who do not have these four qualities directed effectively at security analysis – the vast majority – it is dangerous to invest or make corporate decisions on the assumption that the share (currency and commodity) markets are inefficient, because most of the time they are efficient. Markets are inefficient in spots. Those spots are first of all difficult to identify, and then, once you think you have identified an area of inefficient pricing it has a tendency to fade away, or additional analysis shows it was not really there in the first place. Playing the game of trying to land yourself in an area of inefficiency is only to be played by the very skilful and knowledgeable. Most corporate managers and fund managers do not qualify.

Key points and concepts

- **In an efficient market security prices rationally reflect available information** New information is **a** rapidly and **b** rationally incorporated into share prices.
- **Types of efficiency**:
  - operational efficiency;
  - allocational efficiency;
  - pricing efficiency.
- **The benefits of an efficient market are**:
  - it encourages share buying;
  - it gives correct signals to company managers;
  - it helps to allocate resources.
- Shares, other financial assets and commodities generally move with a **random walk** – one day's price change cannot be predicted by looking at previous price changes. Security prices respond to news which is random.
- **Weak-form efficiency** Share prices fully reflect all information contained in past price movements.

  Evidence: mostly in support, but there are some important exceptions.
- **Semi-strong form efficiency** Share prices fully reflect all the relevant, publicly available information.

  Evidence: substantially in support but there are some anomalies.
- **Strong-form efficiency** All relevant information, including that which is privately held, is reflected in the share price.

  Evidence: stock markets are strong-form inefficient.
- **Insider dealing** is trading on privileged information. It is profitable and illegal.
- **Behavioural finance studies** offer insight into anomalous share pricing.
- **Implications of the EMH for investors**:
  - for the vast majority of people public information cannot be used to earn abnormal returns;
  - investors need to press for a greater volume of timely information;
  - the perception of a fair game market could be improved by more constraints and deterrents placed on insider dealers.
- **Implications of the EMH for companies**:
  - focus on substance, not on short-term appearances;
  - the timing of security issues does not have to be fine-tuned;
  - large quantities of new shares can be sold without moving the price;
  - signals from price movements should be taken seriously.

References and further reading

Abraham, A. and Ikenberry, D. (1994) 'The individual investor and the weekend effect', *Journal of Financial and Quantitative Analysis*, June.

An examination of a particular form of inefficiency.

Anderson, K. and Brooks, C. (2006) 'The long-term price–earnings ratio', *Journal of Business Finance and Accounting*, 33(7) & (8), pp.1063–86.

A PER effect with a difference – shows a high return to shares with a low share price relative to the previous eight years of earnings.

Arnold, G.C. (2002) *Valuegrowth Investing*. London: Financial Times Prentice Hall.

Brings together the insights from successful investors, finance theory and strategic analysis.

Arnold, G.C. and Baker, R.D. (2007) 'Return reversal in UK shares', Salford Business School Working Paper 107/07. Available at: www.mams.salford.ac.uk/mams/m/?s=14.

Shows evidence supporting the view that investors in shares with the worst recent five-year returns outperform in the subsequent five years (on average).

Arnold, G. and Shi, J. (2005) 'Profitability of momentum strategies in UK bull and bear market conditions', University of Salford Working Papers.

Momentum effects are present in bull and bear markets.

Arnold, G.C. and Xiao, Y. (2007) 'Financial statement analysis and the return reversal effect'. Salford Business School Working Paper 108/07 Available at: www.mams.salford.ac.uk/mams/m/?=14.

Shows evidence indicating that portfolios of 'loser' shares (those that give the lowest returns over five years) which also have strong financial variables (e.g. positive cash flow or improving financial gearing) outperform those with poor financial fundamentals.

Atkins, A.B. and Dyl, E.A. (1993) 'Reports of the death of the efficient markets hypothesis are greatly exaggerated', *Applied Financial Economics*, 3, pp. 95–100.

A consideration of some key issues.

Baba, N. and Kozaki, M. (1992) 'An intelligent forecasting system of stock prices using neural networks', *Proceedings of International Joint Conference on Neural Networks*, Baltimore, MD, vol. 1, pp. 371–7.

Evidence on a possible inefficiency.

Ball, R. (1995) 'The theory of stock market efficiency: Accomplishments and limitations', *Journal of Applied Corporate Finance*, Winter and Spring, pp. 4–17.

Interesting discussion.

Ball, R. (2001) 'The theory of stock market efficiency: accomplishments and limitations', in Chew, D.H. (ed.) *The New Corporate Finance*, 3rd edn. New York: McGraw-Hill Irwin.

An interesting overview of how far we have come in understanding the efficiency of stock markets.

Ball, R. and Brown, P. (1968) 'An empirical evaluation of accounting income numbers', *Journal of Accounting Research*, Autumn, pp. 159–78.

The stock market turns to other sources of information to value shares so that when the annual report is published it has little effect on prices.

Ball, R. and Kothari, S.P. (1989) 'Nonstationary expected returns: Implications for tests of market efficiency and serial correlation in returns', *Journal of Financial Economics*, 25, pp. 51–94.

Negative serial correlation in relative returns is due largely to changing relative risks and thus changing expected returns.

Ball, R., Kothari, S.P. and Shanken, J. (1995) 'Problems in measuring portfolio performance: An application to contrarian investment strategies', *Journal of Financial Economics*, May, vol. 38, pp. 79–107.

Performance measurement problems cast doubt on the overreaction study results.

Banz, R. (1981) 'The relationship between return and market value of common stock', *Journal of Financial Economics*, 9, pp. 3–18.

Important early paper on the small firm effect.

Banz, R.W. and Breen, W.J. (1986) 'Sample-dependent results using accounting and market data: Some evidence', *Journal of Finance*, 41, pp. 779–93.

A technical article concerned with the problem of bias when using accounting information (earnings). The bias in the data can cause the low PER effect.

Barber, B.M. and Odean, T. (1999) 'The courage of misguided convictions', *Financial Analysts Journal*, 55, November–December, pp. 41–55.

Investors who trade frequently perform worse than those who trade little. Support for over-confidence hypothesis.

Barber, B. and Odean, T. (2000) 'Trading is hazardous to your wealth: the common stock investment performance and individual investors', *Journal of Finance*, 55(2), April, pp. 773–806.

Investors who trade a lot perform worst.

Barberis, N., Shleifer, A. and Vishny, R.W. (1998) 'A model of investor sentiment', *Journal of Financial Economics*, 49, pp. 307–43.

A theoretical model based on behaviotral finance ideas in which investors believe at times that the market is trending and at other times it is mean-reverting (draws on representativeness and conservatism).

Barclays Capital (annual) *Equity Gilt Study*. London: Barclays Capital.

Important source of data on share and other security returns and risks.

Basu, S. (1975) 'The information content of price-earnings ratios', *Financial Management*, 4, Summer, pp. 53–64.
Evidence of a market inefficiency for low PER shares. However transaction costs, search costs and taxation prevent abnormal returns.

Basu, S. (1977) 'Investment performance of common stocks in relation to their price/earnings ratios: A test of the efficient market hypothesis', *Journal of Finance*, 32(3), June, pp. 663–82.
Low PER portfolios earn higher absolute and risk-adjusted rates of return than high PER shares. Information was not fully reflected in share prices.

Basu, S. (1983) 'The relationship between earnings' yield, market value and return for NYSE stocks – Further evidence', *Journal of Financial Economics*, June, pp. 129–56.
The PER effect subsumes the size effect when both variables are considered jointly.

Benartzi, S. and Thaler, R. (1995) 'Myopic loss aversion and the equity premium puzzle', *Quarterly Journal of Economics*, 110(1), pp. 73–92.
Narrow framing leads to unreasonable risk aversity and too little investment in equities.

Bernard, V. (1993) 'Stock price reaction to earnings announcements', in Thaler, R. (ed.) *Advances in Behavioural Finance*. New York: Russell Sage Foundation.
Sluggish response.

Bernard, V.L. and Thomas, J.K. (1989) 'Post-earnings-announcement drift: Delayed price response or risk premium?', *Journal of Accounting Research*, 27 (Supplement 1989), pp. 1–36.
A study showing slow reaction to unexpected earnings figures indicating inefficiency.

Black, F. (1986) 'Noise', *Journal of Finance*, 41(3), July, pp. 529–34.
A large number of small events is often a causal factor much more powerful than a small number of large events.

Blake, D. (2000) *Financial Market Analysis*, 2nd edn. Chichester: Wiley.
A more technical approach. Useful as an introduction to empirical research methodology in this area.

Bris, A. (2005) 'Do insider trading laws work?' *European Financial Management*, 11(3) pp. 267–312.
A study of the effect of the enforcement of insider trading laws across the world.

Brock, W., Lakonishok, J. and LeBaron, B. (1992) 'Simple technical trading rules and the stochastic properties of stock returns', *Journal of Finance*, 47, December, pp. 1731–64.
Some interesting evidence suggesting weak-form inefficiency.

Brown, S.J., Goetzmann, W.N. and Kumar, A. (1998) 'The Dow theory: William Peter Hamilton's track record reconsidered', *Journal of Finance*, 53(4), pp. 1311–33.
Some positive results for the Dow theory.

Brunnermeier, M.K. and Nagel, S. (2004) 'Hedge funds and the technology bubble', *Journal of Finance* LIX (5), October, pp. 2013–40.
Rational investors are not acting as arbitrageurs to return share prices to an efficient level – they reinforce inefficient pricing helping to destabilise.

Brusa, J., Liu, P. and Schulman, C. (2003) 'The weekend and "reverse" weekend effects: An analysis by month of the year, week of month, and industry', *Journal of Business Finance and Accounting*, 30(5) and (6), June/July, pp. 863–90.
Findings: weekend and reverse weekend effects are shown for US share indices.

Buffett, W.E. (1984) 'The superinvestors of Graham-and-Doddsville', an edited transcript of a talk given at Columbia University in 1984.
Reproduced in *Hermes*, the magazine of Columbia Business School, Fall 1984 and in the 1997 and 2003 reprints of Graham (1973).

Buffett, W.E. (2000) Letter to shareholders included with the 2000 Annual Report of Berkshire Hathaway Inc: www.berkshirehathaway.com.
High-quality thinking and writing from the world's most successful investor.

Capaul, C., Rowley, I. and Sharpe, W.F. (1993) 'International value and growth stock returns', *Financial Analysts Journal*, 49, January–February, pp. 27–36.
Evidence on returns from a book-to-market ratio strategy for France, Germany, Switzerland, the UK and Japan.

Chan, A. and Chen, A.P.L. (1996) 'An empirical re-examination of the cross-section of expected returns: UK evidence', *Journal of Business Finance and Accounting*, 23, pp. 1435–52.
High divided yields associated with high share returns.

Chan, L.K.C. and Lakonishok, J. (2004) 'Value and growth investing: review and update', *Financial Analysts Journal*, January/February, pp. 71–86.
An overview of the value versus growth empirical evidence plus some recent evidence.

Chan, L.K.C., Hamao, Y. and Lakonishok, J. (1991) 'Fundamentals and stock returns in Japan', *Journal of Finance*, 46, pp. 1739–64.
The book-to-market ratio and cash flow yield have influences on the returns. There is a weak size effect and a doubtful PER effect.

Chan, L.K.C. Jegadeesh, N. and Lakonishok, J. (1996) 'Momentum strategies', *Journal of Finance*, 51, December, pp. 1681–713.
Underreaction to both past share returns and earnings surprises.

Chew, D.H. (ed.) (1993) *The New Corporate Finance*. New York: McGraw-Hill.
Contains a number of easy-to-read articles on efficiency.

Chopra, N., Lakonishok, J. and Ritter, J.R. (1992) 'Measuring abnormal performance: Do stocks overact?', *Journal of Financial Economics*, 31, pp. 235–68.
Overreaction effect observed.

Clare, A. and Thomas, S. (1995) 'The overreaction hypothesis and the UK stock market', *Journal of Business Finance and Accounting*, 22(7), October, pp. 961–73.
Overreaction occurs, but it is a manifestation of the small firm effect.

Cuthbertson, K. (1996) *Quantitative Financial Economics*. Chichester: Wiley.
Contains a more rigorous mathematical treatment of the issues discussed in this chapter.

Daniel, K. and Titman, S. (1997) 'Evidence on the characteristics of cross sectional variation in stock returns', *Journal of Finance*, 52(1), March, p. 1–33.
The high returns to high book-to-market ratio shares and small market capitalisation shares is not a result of compensation for risk (opposing Fama and French's view and supporting the behavioural finance view).

Daniel, K., Hirshleifer, D. and Subrahmanyam, A. (1998) 'Investor psychology and security market under- and overreactions', *Journal of Finance*, 53(6), pp. 1839–85.
Behavioural explanation of inefficiencies. Under- and overreaction are due to the psychological biases of investor overconfidence and biased self-attributes.

Dawson, E.R. and Steeley, J.M. (2003) 'On the existence of visual technical patterns in the UK stock market', *Journal of Business Finance and Accounting*, 30(1) and (2), January–March, pp. 263–97.
Failure to find profitable trading rules based on technical patterns.

De Bondt, W.F.M. and Thaler, R.H. (1985) 'Does the stock market overreact?', *Journal of Finance*, 40(3), July, pp. 793–805.
An important paper claiming weak-form inefficiency.

De Bondt, W.F.M. and Thaler, R.H. (1987) 'Further evidence on investor overreaction and stock market seasonality', *Journal of Finance*, 42(3), pp. 557–81.
Overreaction effect observed.

De Long, J.B., Shleifer, A., Summers, L.H. and Waldmann, R.J. (1989) 'The size and incidence of the losses from noise trading', *Journal of Finance*, 44(3), July, pp. 681–96.
Noise trading by naive investors can lead to costs for society.

De Long, J.B., Shleifer, A., Summers, L.H. and Waldmann, R.J. (1990) 'Noise trader risk in financial markets', *Journal of Political Economy*, 98, pp. 703–38.
Discussing the risk that irrational ill-informed investors may push prices further away from fundamental value thus throwing the arbitrageurs' trading strategies.

Dimson, E. (ed.) (1988) *Stock Market Anomalies*. Cambridge: Cambridge University Press.
A collection of 19 important articles questioning stock market efficiency.

Dimson, E. and Marsh, P.R. (1986) 'Event study methodologies and the size effect: The case of UK press recommendations', *Journal of Financial Economics*, 17, pp. 113–42.
UK small firm shares outperformed those of larger firms.

Dimson, E. and Marsh P.R. (1999) 'Murphy's law and market anomalies', *Journal of Portfolio Management*, 25(2), pp. 53–69.
Small companies outperformed large companies until the 1980s, then they underperformed.

Dimson, E., and Marsh, P.R. (2007) 'The Hoare Govett smaller companies (HGSC) index report 2007'.
London: ABN AMRO and London Business School.
Data and commentary on the performance of companies of different sizes (market capitalization).

Dimson, E., Marsh, P.R. and Staunton, M. (2001) *The Millennium Book II: 101 Years of Investment Returns*. London: ABN AMRO and London Business School.
Shows returns on shares and other securities over the twentieth century. The section on small firms shows a reversal of the small-firm effect.

Dimson, E., Marsh, P.R. and Staunton, M. (2002) *The Triumph of the Optimists: 101 Years of Global Investment Returns*. Princeton, NJ: Princeton University Press.
An important study on market returns with a chapter on the small firm effect.

Dissanaike, G. (1997) 'Do stock market investors overreact?', *Journal of Business Finance and Accounting*, 24(1), January, pp. 27–49.
Buying poor-performing shares gives abnormal returns as they are underpriced due to investor overreaction (UK study).

Dreman, D. (1998) *Contrarian Investment Strategies: The next generation*. New York: Simon & Schuster.
A sceptic's view on efficiency.

Dreman, D. and Berry, M. (1995) 'Overreaction, underreaction, and the low P/E effect', *Financial Analysts Journal*, 51, July/August, pp. 21–30.
Overreaction and underreaction shown.

Economist, The (1992) 'Beating the market: Yes – it can be done', *The Economist*, 5 December.
Good survey of the evidence on the EMH and CAPM. Easy to read.

Elton, E.J., Gruber, M.J. and Rentzler, J. (1983) 'A simple examination of the empirical relationship between dividend yields and deviations from the CAPM', *Journal of Banking and Finance*, 7, pp. 135–46.
Complex statistical analysis leads to the conclusion: 'We have found a persistent relationship between dividend yield and excess returns.'

Elton, E.J., Gruber, M.J., Brown, S.J. and Goetzmann, W.N. (2003) *Modern Portfolio Theory and Investment Analysis*, 6th edn. New York: Wiley.
A more technical treatment than that in this chapter.

Fama, E.F. (1965) 'The behaviour of stock market prices', *Journal of Business*, January, pp. 34–106.
Leading early article that first defined market efficiency.

Fama, E.F. (1970) 'Efficient capital markets: A review of theory and empirical work', *Journal of Finance*, May, pp. 383–417.
A review of the early literature and a categorisation of efficiency.

Fama, E.F. (1991) 'Efficient capital markets II', *Journal of Finance*, 46(5), December, pp. 1575–617.
A review of the market efficiency literature with a strong bias in favour of the view that the market is efficient.

Fama, E.F. (1998) 'Market efficiency, long-term returns, and behavioural finance', *Journal of Financial Economics*, 49, September, pp. 283–306.
Anomalies are explained and efficiency is championed.

Fama, E.F. and French, K.R. (1988) 'Permanent and temporary components of stock prices', *Journal of Political Economy*, 96, pp. 246–73.
Useful.

Fama, E.F. and French, K.R. (1992) 'The cross-section of expected stock returns', *Journal of Finance*, 47, pp. 427–65.
An excellent study casting doubt on beta and showing size of company and book-to-market ratio affecting returns on shares.

Fama, E.F. and French, K.R. (1995) 'Size and book-to-market factors in earnings and returns', *Journal of Finance*, 50(1), pp. 131–55.
Higher returns to smaller companies and those with high book-to-market ratios. These are described as risk factors and so, it is argued, efficiency is maintained.

Fama, E.F. and French, K.R. (1996) 'Multifactor explanations of asset pricing anomalies', *Journal of Finance*, 50(1), March, pp. 55–84.
Efficiency is retained – size and book-to-market are risk factors.

Fama, E.F. and French, K.R. (1998) 'Value versus growth: The international evidence', *Journal of Finance*, 53(6), December, pp. 1975–99.
An average return on global portfolios of high and low book-to-market shares is 7.68 per cent per year. Explanation: additional distress risk.

Fama, E.F. and French, K.R. (2006) 'The value premium and the CAPM', *Journal of Finance*, LXI (5) October, pp. 2163–85.
Value shares (defined by low price-to-earning ratio or book-to-market ratio) outperform in the USA and in other countries – and they have lower betas.

Fama, E.F., Fisher, L., Jensen, M.C. and Roll, R. (1969) 'The adjustment of stock prices to new information', *International Economic Review*, 10(1), February, pp. 1–21.
Investigates the adjustment of share prices to the information which is implicit in share splits. Evidence of semi-strong EMH.

Fifield, S.G.M., Power, D.M. and Sinclair, C.D. (2005) 'An analysis of trading strategies in eleven European stock markets', *European Journal of Finance*, 11(6) pp. 531–48.
Investigates weak-form efficiency and finds inefficiency in less developed markets.

Firth, M.A. (1977a) 'An empirical investigation of the impact of the announcement of capitalisation issues on share prices', *Journal of Business Finance and Accounting*, Spring, p. 47.
Scrip issues in themselves have no impact on share prices. Evidence that the stock market is efficient.

Firth, M.A. (1977b) *The Valuation of Shares and the Efficient Markets Theory*. Basingstoke: Macmillan.
An early discussion of stock market efficiency.

Foster, G. (1979) 'Briloff and the capital markets', *Journal of Accounting Research*, 17, pp. 262–74.
An elegantly simple investigation of the effect of one man's pronouncement on stock market prices.

Foster, G., Olsen, C. and Shevlin, T. (1984) 'Earnings releases, anomalies, and the behaviour of security returns', *Accounting Review*, 59(4), October, pp. 574–603.
A delayed response of share prices to earnings surprise news.

Frazzini, A. (2006) 'The disposition effect and underreaction to news', *Journal of Finance*, LXI (4), August, pp. 2017–46.
Provides a behavioural finance explanation for post-announcement drift.

Froot, K.A. and Dabora, E. (1999) 'How are stock prices affected by the location of trade?', *Journal of Financial Economics*, 53, pp. 189–216.
Evidence of noise trader risk.

Fuller, R.J., Huberts, L.C. and Levinson, M.J. (1993) 'Returns to E/P strategies, higgledy-piggledy growth, analysts' forecast errors, and omitted risk factors', *Journal of Portfolio Management*, Winter, pp. 13–24.
Regression to the mean of earnings growth shown for US companies classified by PER.

Graham, B. (1973, revised 2003) *The Intelligent Investor*, revised edition, updated by Jason Zweig. New York: Harper Business Essentials.
The classic value investing book.

Graham, B. and Dodd, D. (1934) *Security Analysis*. New York: McGraw-Hill.
The foundation stone for value investors.

Gregory, A., Harris, R.D.F. and Michou, M. (2001) 'An analysis of contrarian investment strategies in the UK', *Journal of Business Finance and Accounting*, 28(9) and (10), November–December, pp. 1193–228.
Value shares outperform.

Gregory, A., Harris, R.D.F. and Michou, M. (2003) 'Contrarian investment and macroeconomic risk', *Journal of Business Finance and Accounting*, 30(1) and (2), January–March, pp. 213–55.

Grinblatt, M. and Han, B. (2005) 'Prospect theory, mental accounting and momentum', *Journal of Financial Economics*, 78, pp. 311–39.
Uses behavioural finance models to explain the momentum phenomenon in shares.

Harris, A. (1996) 'Wanted: Insiders', *Management Today*, July, pp. 40–1.
A short and thought-provoking article in defence of insider dealing.

Hawawini, G.A. and Michel, P.A. (eds) (1984) *European Equity Markets, Risk, Return and Efficiency*. Garland Publishing.
A collection of articles and empirical work on the behaviour of European equity markets.

Hawawini, G. and Klein, D.B. (1994) 'On the predictability of common stock returns: Worldwide evidence', in Jarrow, R.A., Maksinovic, V. and Ziembas, W.T. (eds) *Finance*. Amsterdam: North-Holland.
More evidence on inefficiency.

Hon, M.T. and Tonks, I. (2003) 'Momentum in the UK stock market', *Journal of Multinational Financial Management*, 13, pp. 43–70.
Momentum of share returns is not present in all periods of stock market history.

Hong, H. and Stein, J.C. (1999) 'A unified theory of underreaction, momentum trading and overreaction in asset markets', *Journal of Finance*, 54(6), pp. 2143–84.
Behavioural explanation of inefficiencies. A model in which information diffuses gradually across the investing population is used to provide an explanation for underreaction and then overreaction.

Ikenberry, D., Lakonishok, J. and Vermaelen, T. (1995) 'Market under reaction to open market share repurchases', *Journal of Financial Economics*, October–November, pp. 181–208.
Share price drift after share repurchase announcements.

Ikenberry, D., Rankine, G. and Stice, E. (1996) 'What do stock splits really signal?', *Journal of Financial and Quantitative Analysis*, 31, pp. 357–75.
Share price drift evidence.

Jaffe, J., Keim, D.B. and Westerfield, R. (1989) 'Earnings yields, market values and stock returns', *Journal of Finance*, 44, pp. 135–48. US data, 1951–86.
Finds significant PER and size effects (January is a special month).

Jegadeesh, N. and Titman, S. (1993) 'Returns to buying winners and selling losers: Implications for stock market efficiency', *Journal of Finance*, 48, March, pp. 65–91.
Holding shares which have performed well in the past generates significant abnormal returns over 3–12-month holding periods.

Jensen, M.C. (1968) 'The performance of mutual funds in the period 1945–64', *Journal of Finance*, 23, May, pp. 389–416.
Mutual funds were poor at predicting share prices and underperformed the market.

Kahnemann, D. and Tversky, A. (2000) *Choices, Values and Frames*. Cambridge: Cambridge University Press.
An important book on behavioural finance.

Kahneman, D., Slovic, P. and Tversky, A. (1982) *Judgment under Uncertainty: Heuristics and Biases*. Cambridge: Cambridge University Press.
A collection of classic articles on decision making which have strongly influenced the behavioural finance field.

Kamijo, K.-I. and Tanigawa, T. (1990) 'Stock price recognition – approach', *Proceedings of International Joint Conference on Neural Networks*, San Diego, CA, vol. 1, pp. 215–21.
Evidence on a potential inefficiency.

Kaplan, R. and Roll, R. (1972) 'Investor evaluation of accounting information: Some empirical evidence', *Journal of Business*, 45, pp. 225–57.
Earnings manipulation through accounting changes has little effect on share prices.

Keim, D.B. (1983) 'Size-related anomalies and stock return seasonality: Further empirical evidence', *Journal of Financial Economics*, 12, pp. 13–32.
Small-firm effect.

Keim, D.B. (1988) 'Stock market regularities: A synthesis of the evidence and explanations', in Dimson, E. (ed.) *Stock Market Anomalies*, Cambridge: Cambridge University Press, and in Lofthouse, S. (ed.) (1994) *Readings in Investment*, Chichester: Wiley.
A non-technical, easy to understand consideration of some evidence of market inefficiencies.

Keim, D.B. and Ziemba, W.T. (eds) (2000) *Security Market Imperfections in World Wide Equity Markets*. Cambridge: Cambridge University Press.
A collection of empirical articles on the evidence on efficiency.

Kendall, M. (1953) 'The analysis of economic time-series prices', *Journal of the Royal Statistical Society*, 96, pp. 11–25.
Classic founding article on random walks.

Keynes, J.M. (1936) *The General Theory of Employment, Interest and Money*. London: Harcourt, Brace and World.
A classic economic text with some lessons for finance.

Kindleberger, C.P. (1996) *Manias, Panics and Crashes: A History of Financial Crises*, 3rd edn. New York: Macmillan.
Study of the history of odd market behaviour.

Kothari, S.P., Shanken, J. and Sloan, R.G. (1995) 'Another look at the cross-section of expected stock returns', *Journal of Finance*, 50(1) March, pp. 185–224.
Apparent excess returns disappear if risk is allowed for.

Lakonishok, J., Shleifer, A. and Vishny, R. (1994) 'Contrarian investment extrapolation and risk', *Journal of Finance*, 49, pp. 1541–78.
Value share outperformance.

Lamont, O.A. and Thaler, R.H. (2003) 'Can the market add and subtract? Mispricing in tech price equity carve-outs', *Journal of Political Economy*, 111 (2 April), pp. 227–68.
Examples of odd pricing by the market: e.g. 3Com held a proportion of Palm's shares, yet 3Com was valued by the market at less than the Palm shareholding – a rational market?

La Porta, R. (1996) 'Expectations and the cross-section of stock returns', *Journal of Finance*, 51(5), December, pp. 1715–42.
'I show that investment strategies that seek to exploit errors in analysts' forecasts earn superior returns.'

La Porta, R., Lakonishok, J., Shleifer, A. and Vishny, R. (1997) 'Good news for value stocks: Further evidence on market efficiency', *Journal of Finance*, 52(2), pp. 859–74.
Earnings surprises are more positive for value shares: 'The evidence is inconsistent with risk-based explanation for the return differential.'

Lee, D.R. and Verbrugge, J.A. (1996) 'The efficient market theory thrives on criticism', *Journal of Applied Corporate Finance*, 9(1), pp. 3–11.
An overview of efficiency evidence.

Levis, M. (1989) 'Stock market anomalies: A reassessment based on UK evidence', *Journal of Banking and Finance*, 13, pp. 675–96.
Shows that strategies based on dividend yield, PE ratios and share prices appear to be as profitable as (if not more so than) a strategy of concentrating on firm size.

Lewellen, J. (2004) 'Predicting returns with financial ratios' *Journal of Financial Economics*, 74, pp. 209–35.
Evidence that higher returns are attainable by buying high dividend yield shares, high earnings–price ratio shares or high book to market value shares.

Little, I.M.D. (1962) 'Higgledy piggledy growth', *Institute of Statistics Bulletin*, 24(4), pp. 387–412.
Profit trends for companies are unreliable.

Liu, W., Strong, N. and Xu, X. (1999) 'The profitability of momentum investing', *Journal of Business Finance and Accounting*, 26(9) and (10), November–December, pp. 1043–91.
Following a price momentum strategy was profitable over the period 1977 to 1998.

Litzenberger, R.H. and Ramaswamy, K. (1979) 'The effect of personal taxes and dividends on capital asset prices: Theory and empirical evidence', *Journal of Financial Economics*, 7, pp. 163–95.
Technical paper with the conclusion: 'There is a strong positive relationship between dividend yield and expected return for NYSE stocks.'

Lofthouse, S. (2001) *Investment Management*, 2nd edn. Chichester: John Wiley & Sons.
Great for those interested in financial market investment. Transparently clear explanations of complex material.

Lofthouse, S. (ed.) (1994) *Readings in Investment*. Chichester: John Wiley & Sons.
A superb book for those keen on understanding stock market behaviour. A collection of key papers introduced and set in context by Stephen Lofthouse.

Lowe, J. (1997) *Warren Buffett Speaks*. New York: John Wiley & Sons.
Terrific quotations from Buffett.

Lowe, J. (1999) *The Rediscovered Benjamin Graham*. New York: John Wiley & Sons.
Some observations from the most respected practitioner/intellectual, compiled by Janet Lowe.

Lynch, P. (1990) *One Up on Wall Street* (with John Rothchild). New York: Penguin Books. (Originally published by Simon & Schuster, 1989.)
Fascinating insight into the world of stock picking. Presents sound investment principles.

Lynch, P. (1994) *Beating the Street* (with John Rothchild). New York: Simon & Schuster.
Revised version of 1993 hardback publication. Fascinating insight into the world of stock picking. Presents sound investment principles.

Malkiel, B.G. (1999) *A Random Walk Down Wall Street*. New York: W.W. Norton & Co.
A superb introduction to the theory and reality of stock market behaviour. A witty prose description of the arguments for and against EMH.

Martikainen, T. and Puttonen, V. (1996) 'Finnish days-of-the-week effects', *Journal of Business Finance and Accounting*, 23(7), September, pp. 1019–32.
There is evidence of a day-of-the-week effect in the cash and derivative markets.

Michaely, R., Thaler, R. and Womack, K. (1995) 'Price reaction to dividend initiations and omissions: Overreaction or drift?', *Journal of Finance*, 50, pp. 573–608.
Share price drift evidence.

Miles, D. and Timmerman, A. (1996) 'Variations in expected stock returns: evidence on the mispricing of equities from a cross-section of UK companies', *Economica*, 63, pp. 369–82.
Some interesting evidence and discussion.

Montier, J. (2002) *Behavioural Finance: Insights into Irrational Minds and Markets*. London: John Wiley & Sons.
A very good overview of the usefulness of developments in the decision-making under uncertainty literature in the real world of fund management. Written by a practising equity strategist.

Morgan, G. and Thomas, S. (1998) 'Taxes, dividend yields and returns in the UK equity market', *Journal of Banking and Finance*, 22, pp. 405–23.
High dividend yield is correlated with high returns.

Neff, J. (1999) *John Neff on Investing* (with S.L. Mintz). New York: John Wiley & Sons.
Decades of investing experience create a very interesting book to guide aspiring investors. Insight into investor/market behaviour.

Park, C-H. and Irwin, S.H. (2007) 'What do we know about the profitability of technical analysis?' *Journal of Economic Surveys*, 21 (4), pp. 786–826.

Examines a great array of literature testing weak form efficiency – the more recent evidence generally supports the technical analyst's view that the share, currency and commodity markets examined are inefficient in many ways.

Peters, E.E. (1991) *Chaos and Order in the Capital Markets.* New York: John Wiley & Sons.

A comprehensible account of chaos theory applied to market pricing. The evidence is not powerful enough to demolish the EMH.

Piotroski, J. D. (2000) 'Value investing: the use of historical financial statement information to separate winners from losers', *Journal of Accounting Research*, 38, Supplement, pp. 1–51.

Piotroski uses nine accounting variables (e.g. positive cash flow) to classify high book-to-market ratio shares into different categories of financial strength. He finds evidence that the market does not properly incorporate these financial strength factors because 'strong' company shares significantly outperform 'weak' company shares.

Pontiff, J. and Schall, L.D. (1998) 'Book-to-market ratios as predictors of market returns', *Journal of Financial Economics*, 49, pp. 141–60.

Book-to-market ratios predict market returns and small-firm excess returns.

Poterba, J.M. and Summers, L.H. (1988) 'Mean reversion in stock prices: Evidence and implications', *Journal of Financial Economics*, 22, pp. 27–59.

The idea that share returns eventually revert to the average.

Reinganum, M.R. (1981) 'Misspecification of capital asset pricing: Empirical anomalies based on earnings' yields and market values', *Journal of Financial Economics*, 9, pp. 19–46.

The PER effect disappears when size is simultaneously considered.

Reinganum, M.R. (1988) 'The anatomy of a stock market winner', *Financial Analysts Journal*, March–April, pp. 272–84.

More on inefficiencies due to low net assets.

Rendleman, R.J., Jones, C.P. and Latané, H.E. (1982) 'Empirical anomalies based on unexpected earnings and the importance of risk adjustments', *Journal of Financial Economics*, November, pp. 269–87.

Abnormal returns could have been earned by exploiting the slow response to unexpected earnings figures.

Ridley, M. (1993) 'Survey of the frontiers in finance', *The Economist*, 9 October.

A series of excellent easy-to-read articles on the use of mathematics for predicting share prices.

Roberts, H.V. (1959) 'Stock market "patterns" and financial analysis: Methodological suggestions', *Journal of Finance*, March, pp. 1–10.

Describes chance-generated price series to cast doubt on technical analysis.

Roll, R. (1981) 'A possible explanation for the small firm effect', *Journal of Finance*, September.

Interesting consideration of the issue.

Roll, R. (1994) 'What every CFO should know about scientific progress in financial economics: What is known and what remains to be resolved', *Financial Management*, 23(2) (Summer), pp. 69–75.

A discussion, in straightforward terms, of Roll's views on the state of play in the efficiency/inefficiency debate.

Rosenberg, B., Reid, K. and Lanstein, R. (1985) 'Persuasive evidence of market inefficiency', *Journal of Portfolio Management*, 11, Spring, pp. 9–16.

Reports the identification of two market inefficiencies.

Rouwenhorst, K.G. (1998) 'International momentum strategies', *Journal of Finance*, 53(1), February, pp. 267–84.

Price momentum evidence for 12 countries.

Rouwenhorst, K.G. (1999) 'Local return factors and turnover in emerging stock markets', *Journal of Finance*, 54(4), pp. 1439–63.

Emerging stock markets exhibit price momentum.

Schoenburg, E. (1990) 'Stock price prediction using neural networks', *Neurocomputing*, 2, pp. 17–27.

Some evidence of predictability.

Scholes, M. (1972) 'The market for securities: Substitution versus price pressure effects of information on share prices', *Journal of Business*, April, pp. 179–211.

Evidence that the issue of more shares does not depress share prices.

Shefrin, H. (2000) *Beyond Greed and Fear.* Boston, MA: Harvard Business School Press.

An important book in the field of the application of behavioural finance to inefficiency in the markets.

Shiller, R.J. (1981) 'Do stock prices move too much to be justified by subsequent charges in dividends?', *American Economic Review*, 71, pp. 421–36.

The volatility of US shares is too large to be explained by the volatility of dividends. Taken to be evidence of overreaction and investors' pursuit of fads and the herd.

Shiller, R.J. (2000) *Irrational Exuberance.* Princeton, NJ: Princeton University Press.

Behavioural finance applied to the bubble at the turn of the millennium.

Shivakumar, L. (2006) 'Accruals, cash flows and the post-earnings-announcement drift', *Journal of Business Finance and Accounting*, Jan–Mar, 33(1), pp. 1–25.

Earnings surprises cause post-earnings-announcement drift. However, if earnings are broken down into cash flow and accruals we find cash flows can predict future returns above and beyond that predicted by earnings alone.

Shleifer, A. (2000) *Inefficient Markets: An Introduction to Behavioural Finance.* Oxford: Oxford University Press.

A landmark presentation of the case for the impact of human (irrational) behaviour in financial markets.

Smith, C. (1986) 'Investment banking and the capital acquisition process', *Journal of Financial Economics*, 15, pp. 3–29.

Lists numerous studies that report a decrease in the share price when a share issue is announced.

Soros, G. (1987) *The Alchemy of Finance*. New York: John Wiley & Sons. (Reprinted in 1994 with a new preface and a new foreword.)

Provides insight into the investment approach of a highly successful investor.

Soros, G. (1995) *Soros on Soros*. New York: John Wiley & Sons.

Financial theory and personal reminiscence interwoven.

Soros, G. (1998) *The Crisis of Global Capitalism*. New York: Public Affairs.

More on market irrationality.

Sullivan, R., Timmermann, A. and White, H. (1999) 'Data-snooping, technical trading rule performance, and the bootstrap', *Journal of Finance*, 54(5), pp. 1647ff.

A demonstration of false inferences being drawn from data. Many technical trading rules that had been shown to 'work' in other academic studies are shown to be false when data snooping is eliminated.

'Symposium on some anomalous evidence on capital market efficiency' (1977). A special issue of the *Journal of Financial Economics*, 6, June.

Generally technical articles, but useful for those pursuing the subject in depth.

Thaler, R. (ed.) (1993) *Advances in Behavioural Finance*. New York: Russell Sage Foundation.

An important book in the growth of this developing discipline.

Thaler, R. H. (2005) *Advances in Behavioural Finance* Volume II. Princeton, NJ: Russell Sage Foundation.

An important collection of key papers in this young discipline.

Train, J. (1980) *The Money Masters*. New York: Harper Business (reprinted 1994).

Some insights into successful trading strategies.

Train, J. (1987) *The Midas Touch*. New York: Harper & Row.

Some insights into successful trading strategies.

Urry, M. (1996) 'The $45bn man makes his pitch', *Financial Times, Weekend Money*, 11/12 May, p. 1.

An article on Buffett.

US Office of Business Economics (1966) *The National Income and Product Accounts of the United States 1929–1965*. Washington: Government Printing Office.

West, K.D. (1988) 'Bubbles, fads and stock price volatility tests: A partial evaluation', *Journal of Finance*, 43(3), pp. 639–56.

A summary and interpretation of some of the literature on share price volatility. Noise trading by naive investors is discussed.

Xiao, Y. and Arnold, G. (2007) 'Testing Benjamin Graham's Net Current Asset Value Strategy in London'. Salford Business School Working Paper 109/07. Available at: www.mams.salford.ac.uk/mams/m/?s=14

Those shares listed on the London Stock Exchange in the period 1981 to 2005 with a net current asset value to market capitalisation ratio greater than 1.5 display significantly positive market-adjusted returns (annualised return up to 19.7 per cent per year) over five holding years. (Net current asset value is total current assets minus all liabilities – long and short liabilities.)

Case study recommendations

Please see www.pearsoned.co.uk/arnold for case study synopses

- Global equity markets. The case of Royal Dutch and Shell. Authors: Kenneth A. Froot and André. F. Perold (1997). Harvard Business School.
- The Harmonized savings plan at BP Amoco. Author: Luis M. Viceira (2000). Harvard Business School.
- Beta Management Co. Author: Michael E. Edelson (1993): Harvard Business School.

Self-review questions

1 Explain the three forms of market efficiency.

2 Does the EMH imply perfect forecasting ability?

3 What does 'random walk' mean?

4 Reshape plc has just announced an increase in profit of 50 per cent. The market was expecting profits to double. What will happen to Reshape's share price?

5 Can the market be said to be inefficient because some shares give higher returns than others?

6 What use is inside information in the trading of shares?

7 Why is it important for directors and other managers to communicate to shareholders and potential shareholders as much information as possible about the firm?

8 What are the implications of the EMH for investors?

9 What are the implications of the EMH for managers?

10 What are allocative, operational and pricing efficiency?

11 What are 'technical analysis' and 'fundamental analysis'?

Questions and problems

myfinancelab ***Questions with an icon are also available for practice in MyFinanceLab with additional supporting resources.***

1 Manchester United plc, the quoted football and leisure group, wins the cup and therefore can anticipate greater revenues and profits. Before the win in the final the share price was 640p.

a What will happen to the share price following the final whistle of the winning game?
b Which of the following suggests the market is efficient? (Assume that the market as a whole does not move and that the only news is the football match win.)
i The share price rises slowly over a period of two weeks to reach 700p.
ii The share price jumps to 750p on the day of the win and then falls back to 700p one week later.
iii The share price moves immediately to 700p and does not move further relative to the market.

2 If Marks & Spencer has a 1 for 1 scrip issue when its share price is 550p what would you expect to happen to its share price in theory (no other influences) and in practice?

3 (*Examination level*) 'The paradox of the efficient market hypothesis is that large numbers of investors have to disbelieve the hypothesis in order to maintain efficiency.' Write an essay explaining the EMH and explain this statement.

4 (*Examination level*) 'Of course the market is not efficient. I know lots of people from technical analysts to professional fundamental analysts who have made packets of money on the market.' Describe the terms 'technical' and 'fundamental analyst'. Explain how some individuals might generate a satisfactory return from stock market investment even if it is efficient.

5 (*Examination level*) It could be said that insufficient attention has been paid to psychological factors when explaining stock efficiency anomalies. Outline the efficient stock market hypothesis (EMH) and describe some of the evidence which casts doubts on the semi-strong level of the efficient market hypothesis for which psychological explanations might be useful.

6 (*Examination level*) The efficient market hypothesis, if true, encourages managers to act in shareholder wealth enhancing ways. Discuss this.

7 If the efficient market hypothesis is true an investor might as well select shares by sticking a pin into the *Financial Times*. Explain why this is not quite true.

8 Arcadura plc has been planning a major rights issue to raise £300m. The market has fallen by 10 per cent in the past four days and the investment bank adviser suggests that Arcadura wait another three or four months before trying to sell these new shares. Given that the market is efficient, evaluate the investment banker's suggestion.

9 Chartism and fundamental analysis are traditional methods used by stock market investors to make buy or sell decisions. Explain why modern finance theory has contributed to the growing popularity of share index funds which have a simple strategy of buying and holding a broadly based portfolio.

10 (*Examination level*) 'The world's well developed stock markets are efficient at pricing shares for most of the people most of the time.' Comment on this statement and explain what is meant by stock market efficiency.

11 (*Examination level*) The following statements are extracts from the detailed minutes taken at a Board meeting of Advance plc. This company is discussing the possibility of a new flotation on the main listed market of the London stock market.

Mr Adams (Production Director): 'I have been following the stock market for many years as a private investor. I put great value on patterns of past share prices for predicting future movements. At the moment my charts are telling me that the market is about to rise significantly and therefore we will get a higher price for our shares if we wait a few months. This will benefit our existing shareholders as the new shareholders will not get their shares artificially cheap.'

Mr Cluff: 'I too have been investing in shares for years and quite frankly have concluded that following charts is akin to voodoo magic, and what is more, working hard analysing companies is a waste of effort. The market cannot be predicted. I now put all my money into tracker funds and forget analysis. Delaying our flotation is pointless, the market might just as easily go down.'

Required

Consider the efficient stock markets theory and relate it to Mr Adams' and Mr Cluff's comments.

12 'A number of companies were put off flotation on the London Stock Exchange in 2008 because the market was too low.' Explain the efficient market hypothesis and assess the logic of such postponements.

13 The chief geneticist at Adams Horticultural plc has discovered a method for raising the yield of commercial crops by 20 per cent. The managing director will make an announcement to the Stock Exchange in one week which will result in a sharp rise in the share price. Describe the level of inefficiency this represents. Is the geneticist legally free to try to make money on the share price issue by buying now?

14 Rapid Growth plc has recently changed the methods of accounting for depreciation, stock and research and development, all of which have the effect of improving the reported profit figures. Consider whether the share price will rise as a result of these actions.

15 A famous and well-respected economist announces in a Sunday newspaper that the growth phase of the economy is over and a recessionary trend has begun. He bases his evidence on the results of a dozen surveys which have been conducted and made public by various economic institutes over the past three months. Should you sell all your shares? Explain the logic behind your answer with reference to the efficient market hypothesis.

16 Explain why professional and highly paid fund managers generally produce returns less than those available on a broadly based market index.

17 (*Examination level*) Describe the extent to which the evidence supports the efficient market hypothesis.

myfinancelab *Now retake your diagnostic test for Chapter 14 to check your progress and update your study plan.*

Assignment

Consider the actions of the directors of a stock-market quoted company you know well. Do they behave in such a way as to convince you they believe in the efficiency of the stock market? In what ways could they take steps to ensure greater efficiency of stock market pricing of the company's shares?

PART 5

Corporate value

CHAPTER

15

Value management

LEARNING OUTCOMES

This chapter demonstrates the rationale behind value-based management techniques. By the end of it the reader should be able to:

- explain the failure of accounts-based management (e.g. profits, balance sheet assets, earnings per share and accounting rate of returns) to guide value-maximising decisions in many circumstances;
- describe the four key drivers of value and the five actions to increasing value.

myfinancelab ***Complete your diagnostic test for Chapter 15 now to create your personal study plan***

Introduction

The first few chapters of this book linked together the objective of shareholder wealth maximisation and acceptance or otherwise of proposed projects. This required knowledge of the concepts of the time value of money and the opportunity cost of investors' funds placed into new investments. If managers are unable to achieve returns at least as high as those available elsewhere for the same level of risk then, as agents for investors, they are failing in their duty. If a group of investors place £1m in the hands of managers who subsequently generate annual returns of 10 per cent those managers would in effect be destroying value for those investors if, for the same level of risk, a 14 per cent return is available elsewhere. With a future project the extent of this value destruction is summarised in the projected negative NPV figure.

This technique, and the underlying concepts, are well entrenched throughout modern corporations. However, the full potential of their application is only now dawning on a few particularly progressive organisations. Applying the notion of opportunity cost of capital and focusing on the cash flow of *new projects* rather than profit figures is merely skimming the surface. Since the mid-1980s a growing band of corporations, ranging from Pepsi in the USA to Lloyds TSB bank in the UK, have examined their businesses, or parts of their businesses, in terms of the following questions:

- How much money has been (or will be) placed in this business by investors?
- What rate of return is being (or will be) generated for those investors?
- Is this sufficient given the opportunity cost of capital?

These questions can be asked about past performance or about future plans. They may be asked about the entire organisation or about a particular division, strategic business unit or product line. If a line of business does not create value on the capital invested by generating a return greater than the minimum required then managerial attention can be directed to remedying the situation. Ultimately every unit should be contributing to the well-being of shareholders.

The examination of an organisation to identify the sources of value may not seem particularly remarkable to someone who has absorbed the concepts discussed in Chapters 1 to 8, but to many managers steeped in the traditions of accounting-based performance measures such as profits, return on investment and earnings per share, they have revolutionary consequences.

The ideas themselves are not revolutionary or even particularly new. It is the far-reaching application of them to create a true shareholder-value-orientated company that can revolutionise almost everything managers do.

- Instead of ***plans*** drawn up in terms of accounting budgets, with their vulnerability to distortion and manipulation of 'profit' and 'capital investment', managers are encouraged to think through the extent to which their new strategies or operational initiatives will produce what shareholders are interested in: a discounted inflow of cash greater than the cash injected.
- Instead of being ***rewarded*** for meeting goals set in terms of accounting rates of return (and other 'non-value' performance measures, such as earnings per share and turnover) achieved in the short term, they are rewarded by the extent to which they contribute to shareholder value over a long time horizon. This can radically alter the incentive systems in most firms.
- Instead of directors accepting a low ***cash flow return on the value of assets tied up*** in a poorly performing subsidiary because the accounting profits look satisfactory, they are forced to consider whether greater wealth would be generated by either closure and selling off the subsidiary's assets or selling the operation to another firm which can make a more satisfactory return.
- There then follows a second decision: should the ***cash*** released be invested in other activities or be ***given back to shareholders*** to invest elsewhere in the stock market? The answers, when genuinely sought, can sometimes be uncomfortable for executives who prefer to expand rather than contract the organisation.

Dealing with such matters is only the beginning once an organisation becomes value based. Mergers must be motivated and evaluated on the criterion of the extent to which a margin above the cost of capital can be achieved given the purchase price. Strategic analysis does not stop at the point of often vague and woolly qualitative analysis, it goes on to a second phase of valuation of the strategies and quantitative sensitivity analysis. The decisions on the most appropriate debt levels and the dividend payout ratios have as their core consideration the impact on shareholder wealth. In the field of human resources, it is accepted that all organisations need a committed workforce. But committed to what? Shareholder value-based management provides an answer but also places an onus on managers to communicate, educate and convert everyone else to the process of value creation. This may require a shift in culture, in systems and procedures as well as a major teaching and learning effort.

Value-based management brings together the way in which shares are valued by investors with the strategy of the firm, its organisational capabilities and the finance function – *see* **Exhibit 15.1**.

Exhibit 15.1 Components of shareholder value-based management

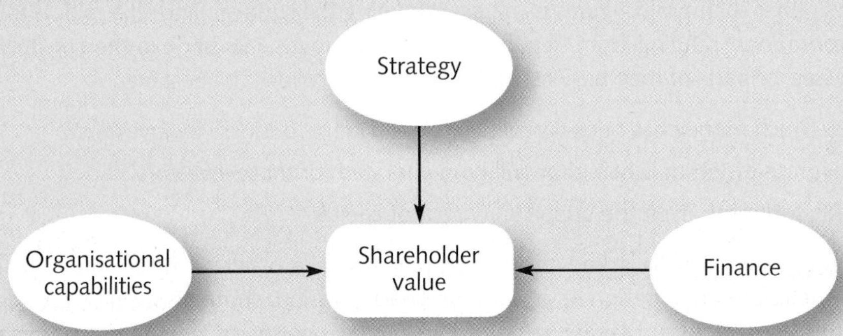

Value-based management is much more than a technique employed by a few individuals 'good with numbers'. The principles behind it must pervade the organisation; it touches almost all aspects of organisational life.

Value-based management is a managerial approach in which the primary purpose is long-run shareholder wealth maximisation. The objective of the firm, its systems, strategy, processes, analytical techniques, performance measurements and culture have as their guiding objective shareholder wealth maximisation.

The example of German companies (*see* **Exhibit 15.2**) shows that a switch to shareholder value-based management can have dramatic consequences.

Exhibit 15.2

The monoliths stir

FT

A wave of corporate restructuring is sweeping across Germany in response to the growing pressures of global competition

writes Haig Simonian

'Shareholder value' has become a driving force in German boardrooms. Conglomerates could once justify unwieldy structures, poor earnings and cross subsidisation between profitable and loss-making businesses by saying they were pursuing long-term goals. This stance tended to be compared favourably

Exhibit 15.2 continued

with the 'short termism' of industrial rivals in the UK or US.

The argument sometimes had merits, but it was also used as an excuse for inactivity. It has been harder to make the same claim in the face of rising shareholder pressure. This has partly come from German investors, but has been led by the US and UK institutions that have increasingly diversified investments outside their domestic stock market.

The pressure for improved profitability and consistency of dividends has led to greater pressure on operations within larger underperforming industrial groups. At Daimler-Benz, Mr Schrempp has required every business to make a return of 12 per cent on capital employed or face closure. Mr Esser of Mannesmann has set an internal target of 15 per cent return on capital for his group next year.

The demand for higher profits has forced many company chairmen to reassess the breadth of their activities. Not all have been as Draconian as Mr Schrempp, but there has been a widespread move to identify activities with the most potential, and try either to improve or to sell less promising ones.

'We have to think what is best for business, and of creating value for the shareholders,' says Mr Esser about Mannesmann's demerger plan . . .

Heinrich von Pierer, Siemens chairman, wants to shed the group's reputation for conservatism by divesting almost one-seventh of its businesses, with sales of about DM17bn. Earlier this year, he said three of its four loss making operations would break even within a year, and launched plans to float a number of subsidiaries. 'It's only in the past year that they have started to take shareholder value really seriously,' says Mr Berger.

Source: Financial Times, 28 September 1999, p. 25. Reprinted with permission.

Value creation and value destruction

We will start by taking a brief look at three companies. One has successfully created vast amounts of value for shareholders, one has destroyed shareholder value over a long period and one is trying to convert itself from a value destroyer to a value creator.

GlaxoSmithKline has been a terrific share to own. If you had bought £1,000 of shares in Glaxo in 1965 your holding would have grown to be over £2m by 2007. Ian White, pharmaceutical analyst at Robert Fleming, says of Glaxo, 'It had the combination of good commercial management, vibrancy and the drive to succeed, and the right products. You often get two of the three, but rarely the whole package.'[1] The return on Glaxo shares relative to the FTSE All-Share Index is shown in **Exhibit 15.3**.

Exhibit 15.3 GlaxoSmithKline total share return performance (dividends plus share price movements) compared with FTSE All-Share Index

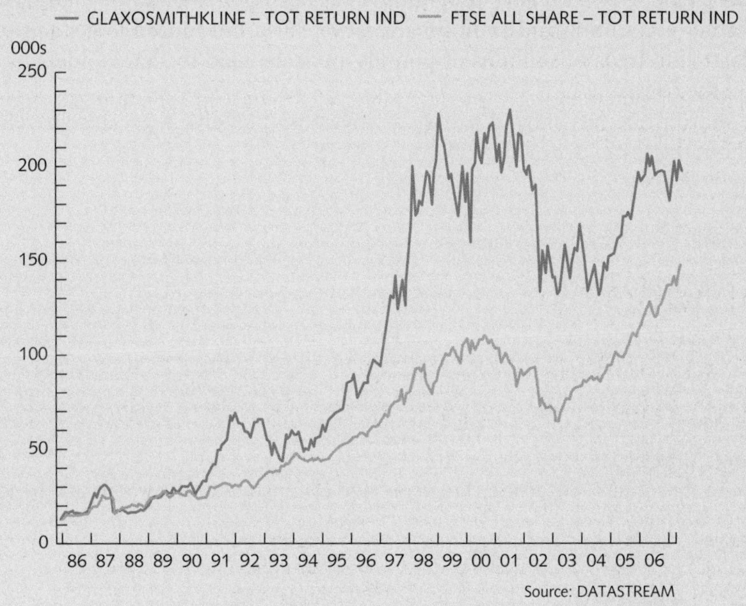

Source: DATASTREAM

[1] Quoted in *Investors Chronicle*, 26 July 1996, p. 20.

Take another company, the UK-based industrial firm T & N. In 1982 investors realised that T & N would suffer as a result of asbestosis-related litigation. During August of that year the market value of its shares fell to £37m as the shareholders realised that T & N would be forced to pay out vast sums to the victims of asbestosis. In November 1996 the company estimated that past and future compensation and other payments would amount to between £800m and £1.6bn.

> From where [the *Investors Chronicle*[2] asked] did a £37m basket case get £1.6bn? From its shareholders. Since 1986 T & N has issued around £700m of new equity via five rights issues, one placing and the 1987 takeover of AE . . . All this is to the good of the asbestosis sufferers, but it's a fair bet the shareholders who put it up aren't normally so generous with their donations to charity which is what in effect all T & N's capital raisings have been . . . The best course of action for T & N at any date in the 1980s would have been to hand the company over to the asbestos litigants lock, stock and barrel.

In 1998 what was left of T & N was taken over by the US company Federal Mogul.

Perhaps we can gain a glimpse of what shareholder value is by considering the 2006 crisis at the worldwide catering company Compass. Sir Roy Gardner was appointed chairman by shareholders to sort out the mess at this 40,000-employee company. Over the previous four years the share price had halved as the company suffered from one subsidiary after another reporting difficulties; there was even one subsidiary, which feeds UN peace-keepers around the globe, being investigated for corruption at the UN. In the UK catering businesses (e.g. supplying school dinners) there were many loss-making contracts, problems with suppliers and collapsing profit margins.

Sir Roy quickly identified poor decision-making processes; lack of controls to see what was going on in the business and direct action; poor control of working capital; and a flawed operational structure. He said, 'The previous management concentrated far too much on growing the business, through acquisition. They should have stopped and made sure what they had acquired delivered the expected results'.[3] The acquisition spree resulted in an odd collection of businesses often with little in common. For example, it owned a single hotel, the Strand Palace; 'We don't need one hotel and you have to ask yourself why have we got this'.[4]

A plan was formulated involving organisational restructuring, disposals and cost savings. The hotel was quickly sold. Select Service Partner, its travel concessions group, was sold for £1.8bn and the proceeds used to reduce its debt and pension deficit. Selecta, the European vending machine business, was sold in 2007 for £772.5m. Compass withdrew from one-third of the countries it operated in, bringing the total down to around 60. The pull-outs were from countries where little or no profit was being made and where operations were small. It also decided to cease the UN business.

'I will not rule out further disposals. At the end of the day it's about shareholder value. If there are businesses that are producing low returns we will consider divesting them,' Sir Roy said.[5] A new management performance programme has been put in place to change the operational culture. Tighter accounting and audit processes were also introduced to get a grip on where value is being lost. Hundreds of millions of pounds are to be paid to shareholders by buying back their shares in the company.

The share price has started to rise as investors perceive a greater shareholder value focus throughout the firm – *see* **Exhibit 15.4**.

---

[2] *Investors Chronicle*, 18 April 1997, p. 10.

[3] Quoted in *Financial Times* article, 'Problems kept coming out of the woodwork' by Salamander Davoudi, 19 January 2007, p. 19.

[4] Ibid., p. 19.

[5] Ibid., p. 19.

Exhibit 15.4 **Compass plc total share return performance (dividends plus share price movement) compared with the FTSE All-Share Index**

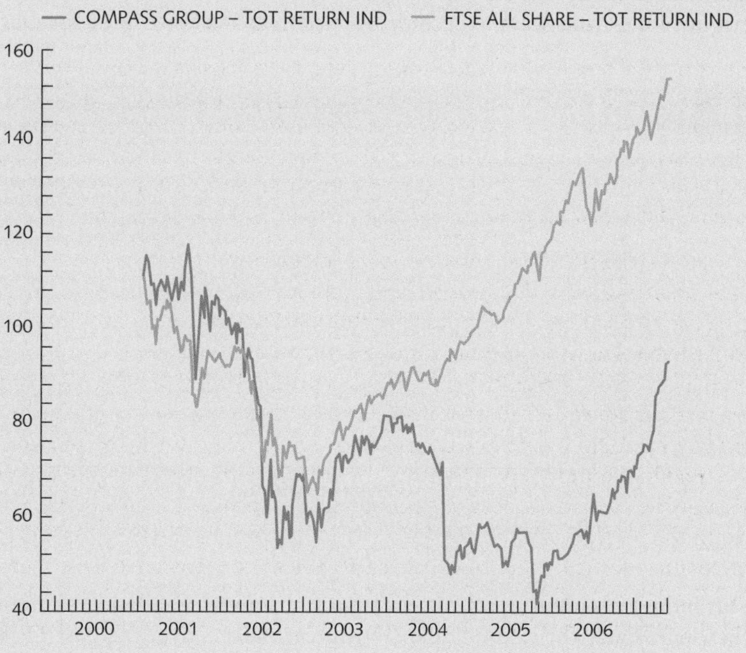

Source: Thomson Financial Datastream

The shareholder wealth-maximising goal

It is clear that many commercial companies put shareholder value in second or third place behind other objectives. So why should we feel justified in holding up shareholder wealth maximisation as the banner to follow? Isn't growth in sales or market share more worthy? And what about the return to the labour force and to society generally?

There follows a brief recap and extension of some of the comments made in Chapter 1 about the objectives of the firm that has responsibilities to shareholders in a competitive market environment.

There are several reasons why shareholder value is gaining momentum. One of these is the increasing threat of takeover by teams of managers searching for poorly managed businesses. Perhaps these individuals are at present running a competitor firm or are wide-ranging 'corporate raiders' ready to swoop on undermanaged firms in any industry which, through radical strategic change, divestiture and shifting of executive incentives, can create more value for shareholders.

The owners of businesses have a right to demand that directors act in their best interests, and are increasingly using their powers to remove the stewards of their savings if they fail to do their utmost. To feel truly safe in their jobs managers should aim to create as much wealth as possible.

Arguably society as a whole will benefit if shareholder-owned firms concentrate on value creation. In this way scarce resources can be directed to their most valuable uses. Maximising the productivity of resources enables high economic growth and higher standards of living.

Confusing objectives

Some managers claim that there are measures of performance that are synonymous with, or good proxies for, shareholder wealth – such as customer satisfaction, market share leadership or lowest-cost producer. These proxies are then set as '**strategic objectives**'. In many cases achieving these goals does go hand in hand with shareholder returns but, as **Exhibit 15.5** shows, the pursuit of these objectives can be taken too far. There is frequently a trade-off between shareholder value and these proxy goals. Taking market share as an example: it is apparent that for many firms increasing market share will bring greater economies of scale, create barriers to entry for potential competitors and help establish brand loyalty, amongst other benefits. This sort of situation is demonstrated by moving from A to Z in Exhibit 15.5. High market share is clearly an important factor in many industries but some firms seem to become trapped in an obsessive quest for market share.

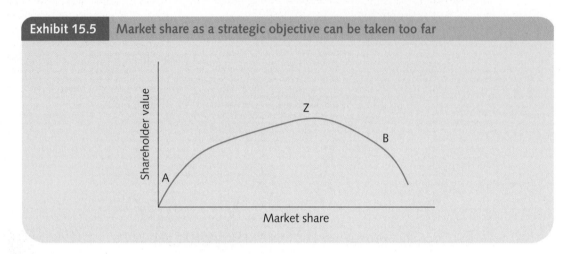

Exhibit 15.5 Market share as a strategic objective can be taken too far

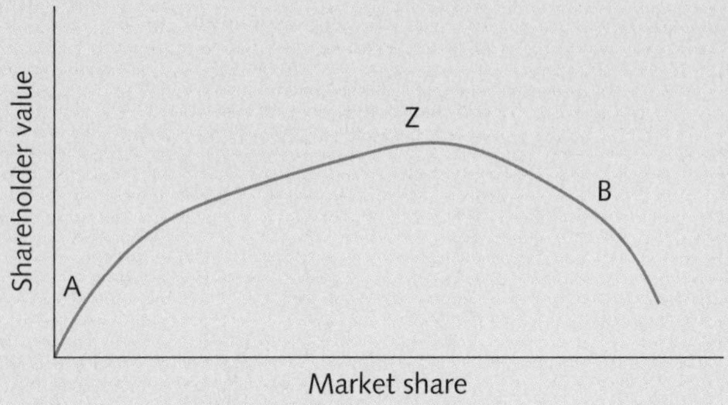

The car industry is notorious for its very poor returns to shareholders combined with addiction to market share data. For example the Detroit car makers over the past 15 years have displayed averaged returns on capital of less than 3 per cent per year. Perhaps some in the industry have taken matters too far and ended up at point B in Exhibit 15.5. Enormous investment in plant capacity, marketing and price promotions has created a situation where the risk-adjusted returns on the investment are lower than the optimum. **Exhibits 15.6** and **15.7** discuss the problems encountered by firms setting proxy goals.

Exhibit 15.6

Motorola falls victim to its own success

FT

The iconic Razr phone won millions of customers, yet its inventors now admit they got their strategy wrong

writes Paul Taylor

A few years ago, Nokia, the world's biggest mobile phone maker, stumbled badly. The Finnish company had been slow to recognise the demand for mid-market 'clamshell' phones and was caught with an ageing product portfolio that, unlike Motorola's slim, sleek Razr, failed to fire the imagination of consumers.

Nokia responded by undertaking a two year strategic makeover aimed at turning the company into the most nimble and efficient manufacturer of handsets in the business. The strategy worked and Nokia's market share and profitability started climbing again.

Now it is Motorola's turn to feel the pain, and analysts fear it may be just as tough for the world's second-largest handset maker to get back on track.

While Nokia was struggling, Motorola and chief executive Ed Zander rode the Razr wave, lifting market share from 14 per cent in 2003 to 22 per cent last year.

But the latest gains came at the expense of profit margins, forcing Mr Zander to acknowledge that the company's fourth-quarter results were 'unacceptable' and blaming miscalculations on pricing and product lineup.

'Motorola has become a victim of its own success,' said Madhu Babu, an analyst at First Global.

'The company's aggressive focus on increasing market share by making steep price cuts in the mid to high-end phones and selling more low-end phones had a negative impact on the operating margin and profitability of its handset business.

▶

Exhibit 15.6 continued

Profit margins in Motorola's phone division – which now accounts for a full two thirds of its revenues – shrank to 4.4 per cent in the fourth quarter from almost 12 per cent in the preceding three months.

Ed Zander and other key executives, including Casey Keller, a consumer goods industry veteran who joined Motorola as chief marketing officer in October, have acknowledged that the obsessive focus on gaining market share was a mistake. 'We need to get the balance between market share and margin right,' Mr Keller said in an interview. 'We cannot grow at the expense of driving premium products and margins down.'

At the same time, analysts believe Motorola must cut costs to compete with Nokia and other rivals, particularly in the fiercely competitive emerging markets – the new mobile phone battleground. Mr Zander has announced plans to cut Motorola's workforce by 3,500, but that may not be enough.

'The company must remove approximately $3–$5 (per handset) at costs from its low-end devices and gain traction in the higher ASP (average selling price) 3G market to offset pressure from a greater mix of shipments coming from low-end emerging markets,' Goldman Sachs said in a note to investors this month.

Source: Financial Times, 19 March 2007, p. 26. Reprinted with permission.

Exhibit 15.7

Non-financial measures just don't add up

FT

Executives are discovering that measuring intangibles is a poor way to judge a company's performance

writes Robert Bruce

Non-financial performance measurement was supposed to be the answer to management's woes. All those financial results were backward-looking and told you nothing about how the business was running. Only if intangibles such as employee loyalty and customer satisfaction were measured would companies boost shareholder value and investors gain a real understanding of what was happening.

But the experience of those who have poured their efforts into basing strategy on what non-financial measurement tells them suggests another story. Research by David Larcker, Ernst & Young professor of accounting at the Wharton School, suggests that companies are 'attempting to apply a seemingly endless set of measurement frameworks, models and laundry lists of measures being pushed by consultants'. In their frustration at not seeing the benefits they have been promised they are 'simply measuring an ever-increasing number of measures to avoid missing anything important'...

An example was the experience of a large fast-food chain. 'They thought that reducing employee turnover was the name of the game,' says Prof Larcker. 'So a series of costly initiatives was implemented, including anniversary bonuses. The theory was that if you retained staff this would create high satisfaction and motivation; that would improve customer service with a resulting effect on the bottom line. The system ran for several years 'but then someone said: "Before we write these cheques let's find out if it is working."' Proper statistical analysis showed it was achieving none of its goals.

Among other things, the fast-food chain found that, for example, only turnover among supervisors had any relation to financial performance and that the more profitable stores had higher overall employee turnover. This is the problem with non-financial measurement. Unlike financial measurement it has no rules to stick by. When Prof Larcker talked to the managers involved, they simply said that it stood to reason that employee retention had to make things more profitable.

'The idea of 100 per cent satisfied customers is very nice. But maybe 85 per cent is good enough and trying to reach 100 per cent is expensive. You could lose more by going for the 100 per cent,' says Prof Larcker...

Source: Financial Times, 29 March 2004, p. 10. Reprinted with permission.

Three steps of value

There are three steps to creating shareholder value – *see* **Exhibit 15.8**. First, create awareness of, and a genuine commitment to, a shareholder wealth-enhancing mission throughout the organisation. Second, put in place techniques for measuring whether value is being created at various organisational levels. And make sure everyone understands and respects the measures adopted. Third, ensure that every aspect of management is suffused with the shareholder value objective, from human resource management to research and development; from target setting to the allocation of resources.

Exhibit 15.8 The three steps of value-based management

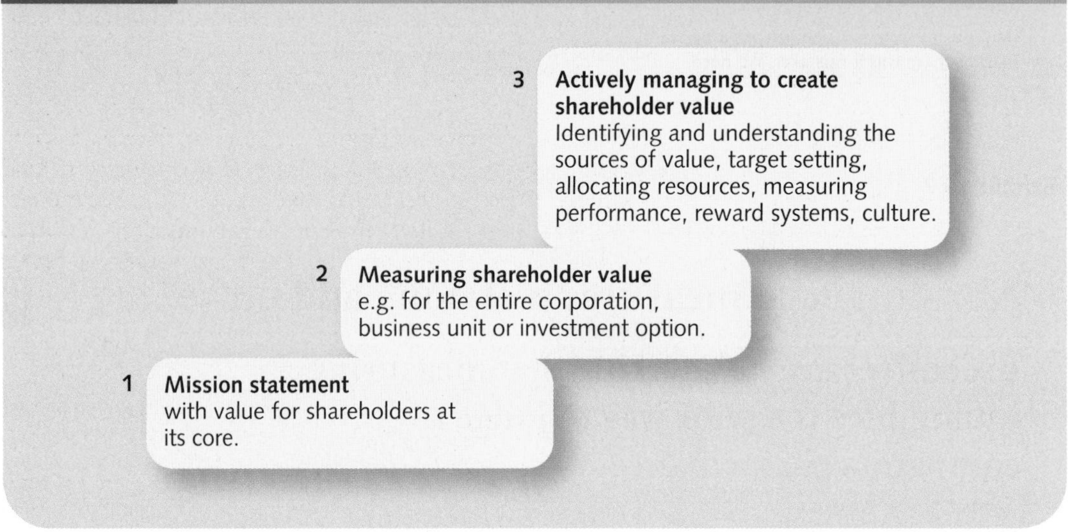
3 Actively managing to create shareholder value
Identifying and understanding the sources of value, target setting, allocating resources, measuring performance, reward systems, culture.
2 Measuring shareholder value
e.g. for the entire corporation, business unit or investment option.
1 Mission statement
with value for shareholders at its core.

It is clearly important to have a management team that both understand and are fully committed to shareholder value. To implement true shareholder wealth maximisation managers need to know how to measure the wealth-creating potential of their actions. Before turning to appropriate methods of evaluating value creation we will examine some of the more popular and increasingly dated measurement techniques used to guide (or misguide) a business.

Earnings-based management

The *Financial Times*'s Lex column expressed a view on the traditional accounting-based performance measure of earnings (profits) per share:

> How do you know a company is doing well? When earnings per share (eps) are growing rapidly, would be the standard reply. Eps is the main valuation yardstick used by investors; it has also become something of a fixation within companies. Rentokil, most famously among UK companies, has a target of boosting eps by at least 20 per cent a year . . . But eps is not a holy grail in determining how well a company is performing. This is not merely because management still have latitude in deciding what earnings to report; it is because eps growth says little about whether a company is investing shrewdly and managing its assets effectively. It may, for example, be possible to boost eps by stepping up the rate of investment. But unless the return on investment exceeds the cost of capital, a company will be destroying value.[6]

[6] *Financial Times*, 7 May 1996, Lex column.

There are many reasons why earnings can mislead in the measurement of value creation, some of which are:[7]

- accounting is subject to distortions and manipulations;
- the investment made is often inadequately represented;
- the time value of money is excluded from the calculation;
- risk is not considered.

Accounting numbers

In drawing up profit and loss accounts and balance sheets accountants have to make judgements and choose a basis for their calculations. They try to match costs and revenues. Unfortunately for the users of the resulting 'bottom line' figures, there can be many alternative approaches, which give completely different results and yet all follow accounting body guidelines.

Take the example of the identical companies X and Y. These have just started up and in the first three years annual profits before deducting depreciation of £3m are expected. Both companies invested their entire initial capital of £10m in plant and machinery. The accountant at X takes the view that the machinery has a useful life of ten years and that a 25 per cent declining balance depreciation is appropriate. The accountant at Y, after reviewing the information on the plant and machinery, is more pessimistic and judges that a seven-year life with straight-line depreciation more truly reflects the future reality. The first three years' profits are shown in **Exhibit 15.9**.

Exhibit 15.9 Companies X and Y: Profits for the first three years

		Years (£000s)	
	1	2	3
Company X			
Pre-depreciation profit	3,000	3,000	3,000
Depreciation	2,500	1,875	1,406
Earnings	500	1,125	1,594
Company Y			
Pre-depreciation profit	3,000	3,000	3,000
Depreciation	1,429	1,429	1,429
Earnings	1,571	1,571	1,571

The underlying economic position is the same for both company X and company Y, but in the first two years company X appears to be less profitable. Outside observers and management comparing the two companies may gain a distorted view of quality of stewardship and the potential of the firm. Investment decisions and incentive schemes based on profit figures can lead to sub-optimal decisions and behaviour. They may also lead to deliberate manipulation. There are several arbitrary accounting allocations that make comparisons and decisions difficult. These concern, for example, goodwill and provisions, extraordinary and exceptional items and the treatment of research and development expenditure.

Ignoring the investment money sacrificed

Examining earnings per share growth as an indicator of success fails to take account of the investment needed to generate that growth. Take the case of companies A and B (*see* **Exhibit 15.10**), both of which have growth in earnings of 10 per cent per year and are therefore equally attractive to an earnings-based analyst or manager.

---

[7] Rappaport (1998) and Cornelius and Davies (1997) go into more detail on these issues.

Exhibit 15.10 Companies A and B: Earnings

	Year (£000s) 1	2	3
Earnings of A	1,000	1,100	1,210
Earnings of B	1,000	1,100	1,210

To a value-oriented analyst A is much more interesting than B if we allow for the possibility that less additional investment is needed for A to create this improving profits pattern. For example, both firms need to offer credit terms to their customers: however B has to offer much more generous terms than A to gain sales; therefore it has to invest cash in supporting higher debtor balances. B is also less efficient in its production process and has to invest larger amounts in inventory for every unit increase in sales.

When B's accounts are drawn up the additional debtors and inventory are included as an asset in the balance sheet and do not appear as a cost element in the profit and loss account. This results in the costs shown in the profit and loss account understating the cash outflow during a period.

If we examine the cash flow associated with A and B (**Exhibit 15.11**) we can see immediately that A is generating more shareholder value (assuming the pattern continues and all other factors are the same).

Exhibit 15.11 illustrates the conversion from earnings to cash flow figures.

Exhibit 15.11 Companies A and B: Earnings and cash flow

	Company A £000s			Company B £000s		
Year	**1**	**2**	**3**	**1**	**2**	**3**
Profit (earnings)	1,000	1,100	1,210	1,000	1,100	1,210
Increase in debtors	0	20	42	0	60	126
Increase in inventory	0	30	63	0	50	105
Cash flow before tax	1,000	1,050	1,105	1,000	990	979
Percentage change		+5%	+5.2%		−1%	−1.1%

If B also has to invest larger amounts than A in vehicles, plant, machinery and property for each unit increase in sales and profit, the difference in the relative quality of the earnings growth will be even more marked.

Time value of money

It is possible for growth in earnings to destroy value if the rate of return earned on the additional investment is less than the required rate. Take the case of a team of managers trying to decide whether to make a dividend payment of £10m. If they retained the money within the business both earnings and cash flow would rise by £1,113,288 for each of the next ten years. Managers motivated by earnings growth might be tempted to omit the dividend payment. Future earnings would rise and therefore the share price would also rise on the announcement that the dividend would not be paid. Right? Wrong! Investors in this firm are likely to have a higher annual required rate of return on their £10m than the 2 per cent offered by this plan.[8] The share price will fall and shareholder value will be destroyed. What the managers forgot was that money has a time value and investors value shares on the basis of *discounted* future cash flows.

[8] A ten-year annuity of £1,113,288 per year for a £10m investment at time 0 has an effective annual rate of return of about 2 per cent.

It seems so obvious that a 2 per cent rate of return on invested money is serving shareholders badly. Yet how many companies do you know holding tens or hundreds of millions of pounds in cash rather than giving it back to shareholders to invest elsewhere? Certainly, it gives managers a greater sense of security to have all that cash around – how can the company be liquidated and they lose their jobs? – but shareholders would rather this money was used more effectively and any money that cannot be used to generate good returns should be handed back to shareholders. If earnings per share are rising what have the shareholders got to complain about, retort the managers? The thundering reply is: it is easy to increase earnings per share just by holding on to ever-larger quantities of money; what shareholders want is a return greater than the opportunity cost of capital (the time value of money) – the return available elsewhere for the same level of risk – *see* **Exhibit 15.12** for an example.

Exhibit 15.12

Silicon Valley is starting to return cash to investors

FT

By Richard Waters in San Francisco

When Dell, the US computer maker, said this month that it was buying back its shares at a faster rate and had set aside another $10bn (£5.2bn) for repurchases, it echoed an increasingly shareholder friendly message from the technology industry.

Stock market incentives may encourage a faster adjustment in thinking at tech companies than has been apparent so far.

Over the past year, the shares of technology companies that pay dividends have out performed those that do not by 10 per cent, according to Steve Milunovich, strategist at Merrill Lyrch.

But the Wall St message does not seem to have been loud or clear enough for many. Stock market inefficiencies are still encouraging many companies to hold more cash than they need, according to Rick Sherlund, software analyst at Goldman Sachs.

The interest income from cash holdings boosts earnings, yet technology investors, accustomed to studying revenue growth rather than balance sheets, may not have adjusted their thinking as growth rates have slowed.

Source: Financial Times, 14 March 2005, p. 21. Reprinted with permission.

A variation on the theme of growing eps by investing large sums is to acquire other companies. In the case of Vodafone (**Exhibit 15.13**) shareholders were worried that managers were incentivised to increase eps with insufficient attention being paid to the amount of investment required by shareholders to boost these accounting numbers.

Exhibit 15.13

Gent's latest package raises acquisition fear

FT

By Robert Budden, Telecommunications correspondent

Analysts and investors in Vodafone have started questioning some of the performance targets behind Sir Christopher Gent's latest bonus package.

They argue that the new targets could over-encourage the chief executive to pursue more acquisitions.

Attention is focusing on Sir Christopher's new 9m share options package, where the award of options is linked to earnings per share targets. To receive his total entitlement to the estimated 9m options, Sir Christopher must deliver challenging group eps growth of 15 per cent a year over and above retail price inflation.

Analysts said this top hurdle was tough, but warned it could encourage Sir Christopher to embark on more acquisitions to hit the eps targets. 'These targets include acquired eps,' said one analyst, 'so an easy way to grow eps would be to acquire companies on a lower multiple.'

Vodafone confirmed that if it were to take over companies trading on lower price earnings multiples

Exhibit 15.13 continued

this could boost its earnings per share figure and so trigger higher pay-outs. But this could jeopardise its other performance-based targets linked to factors such as share price performance or growth in average revenues per user . . .

'We would be wary of further acquisitions,' said one large shareholder.

'An acquisition strategy that fits in terms of extending their global footprint would have to be proved to be rapidly enhancing to shareholder value.'

Some analysts are also believed to be unhappy that Sir Christopher's share options are tied to eps 'before goodwill amortisation and exceptional items', because they fear this protects him against any future write-downs against acquisitions.

Source: Financial Times, 24 June 2002, p. 26. Reprinted with permission.

Ignoring risk

Focusing purely on the growth in earnings fails to take account of another aspect of the quality of earnings: risk. Increased profits that are also subject to higher levels of risk require a higher discount rate. Imagine a firm is contemplating two alternative growth options with the same expected earnings, of £100,000 per year to infinity. Each strategy is subject to risk but S has a wider dispersion of possible outcomes than T (*see* **Exhibit 15.14**).

Exhibit 15.14 Probabilities of annual returns on strategies S and T

	Strategy S		Strategy T	
	Outcome earnings (profits) £	**Probability**	**Outcome earnings (profits) £**	**Probability**
	–100,000	0.10	80,000	0.10
	0	0.20	90,000	0.15
	100,000	0.40	100,000	0.50
	200,000	0.20	110,000	0.15
	300,000	0.10	120,000	0.10
Expected outcome	£100,000		£100,000	

Investors are likely to value strategy T more highly than strategy S. Examining crude profit figures, either historic or projected, often means a failure to allow adequately for risk. In a value-based approach it is possible to raise the discount rate in circumstances of greater uncertainty – more on this in Chapter 19.

For an example of a real company growing earnings (profits carefully defined as before the deduction of interest, tax, depreciation and amortisation) but producing poor returns on invested capital we again turn to Vodafone – *see* **Exhibit 15.15**. Perhaps we should not focus exclusively on income over a few recent years. Perhaps this near-term sacrifice is worth it. Perhaps net cash flows will rocket once the basic infrastructure is in place. Perhaps.

Worked example 15.1 Earnings growth and value

Earnings and earnings per share growth can lead to higher shareholder value in some circumstances. In others it can lead to value destruction. Shareholder value will rise if the return obtainable on new investment is at least as great as the required rate of return for the risk class. Consider EPSOS plc, financed entirely with equity capital and with a required rate of return on that capital of 15 per cent (assume for simplicity that this is the optimal financial gearing level). To make the example simple we assume that EPSOS does not need to invest in higher levels of working capital if sales expand. EPSOS pays shareholders its entire earnings after tax every year and is expected to continue doing this indefinitely. Earnings and cash flow amount to £100m per year. (The amount charged as depreciation is just sufficient to pay for investment to maintain sales and profits.) The value of the company given the opportunity cost of shareholders' money of 15 per cent is £100m/0.15 = £666.67m.

	£m
Sales	300.00
Operating expenses	157.14
Pre-tax profit	142.86
Taxes @ 30 per cent	42.86
Profits and cash flow after tax	100.00

Now imagine that EPSOS takes the decision to omit this year's dividend. Shareholders are made poorer by £100m now. However, as a result of the additional investment in its operations for the next year and every subsequent year sales, earnings, eps and cash flows after tax will rise by 20 per cent. This is shown below.

	£m
Sales	360.00
Operating expenses	188.57
Pre-tax profit	171.43
Taxes @ 30 per cent	51.43
Profits and cash flow after tax	120.00

Earnings have grown by an impressive 20 per cent. Also value has been created. The extra £20m cash flow per annum stretching into the future is worth £20m/0.15 = £133.33m. This is achieved with a £100m sacrifice now. Here a growth in earnings has coincided with an increase in value: £33.33m of value is created.

Now consider a scenario in which sales growth of 20 per cent is achieved by using the £100m to expand the business, but this time the managers, in going for sales growth, push up operating expenses by 32 per cent. Earnings and cash flow increase by a respectable 6.81 per cent, but, crucially, value falls.

	£m
Sales	360.00
Operating expenses (157.14 × 1.32)	207.42
Pre-tax profit	152.58
Taxes @ 30 per cent	45.77
Profits and cash flow after tax	106.81

The incremental perpetual cash flow is worth a present value of £6.81m/0.15 = £45.4m. But the 'cost' of achieving this is the sacrifice of £100m of income now. Therefore overall shareholder value has been destroyed despite earnings and eps growth. It is surprising how often senior managers make this basic error.

Exhibit 15.15

Big feet, shrinking values, surreal numbers

John Plender

There was something faintly surreal about the accounts of telecom companies in the 1990s bubble, with their multiple definitions of profit and their customary invitation to ignore the bottom line loss. Now that the bubble has burst there is still a hint of surrealism about, as I found when thumbing through Vodafone's figures last week.

Vodafone is now the 13th largest company in the world measured by stock market capitalisation. The obvious pertinent question is whether, when Vodafone's managers talk of 'enlarging our footprint', they are employing a euphemism for size for size's sake or whether they are creating real value.

The preliminary announcement contains a welter of figures, including a loss for the year of £9.8bn. ('Once again we have delivered excellent results,' says Lord MacLaurin, the chairman.) Then you have operating profit before goodwill amortisation and exceptional items; adjusted earnings per share; earnings before interest, tax, depreciation and amortisation (ebitda); and free cash flow.

These numbers are more flattering. Understandably enough, they are also the ones on which Sir Christopher Gent, Vodafone's outgoing chief executive, chooses to dwell.

I emphasise that this is no criticism of Sir Christopher or Vodafone, which observes the normal reporting conventions, but of the conventions themselves. Despite the shareholder value movement, traditional disclosure is hopelessly deficient in explaining the efficiency with which companies deploy capital.

Ebitda, earnings per share, free cash flow and the rest mean nothing without adequate information on the capital used to generate them. Yet nobody has had the wit to ask the quoted companies to report routinely their weighted average cost of capital along with some sensible measure of return on capital.

For that you have to turn to a securities analyst like Mustapha Omar at brokers Collins Stewart. His figures will tell you that Vodafone's cash flow return on investment stopped covering its cost of capital in 2000. Given the wholesale destruction of value since then, he worries that Arun Sarin, the incoming chief executive, is already talking about those damned footprints again . . .

Forcing companies, analysts and investors to focus on whether a surplus is being earned over the cost of capital could do wonders for value creation.

Source: Financial Times, 2 June 2003, p. 22. Reprinted with permission.

Return on Capital Employed (ROCE) has failings

It is becoming clear that simply examining profit figures is not enough for good decision making and performance evaluation. Obviously the amount of capital invested has to be considered alongside the income earned. This was recognised long before the development of value-based management, as signified by the widespread use of a ratio of profits to assets employed. There are many variations on this theme: return on capital employed (ROCE), return on investment (ROI), return on equity (ROE) and accounting rate of return (ARR), but they all have the same root. They provide a measure of return as a percentage of resources devoted. The major problem with using these metrics of performance is that they are still based on accounting data. The profit figure calculations are difficult enough, but when they are combined with balance sheet asset figures we have a recipe for unacceptable distortion. The *Financial Times* puts it this way:

> Unfortunately, the crude figures for return on capital employed – operating profit/capital employed – that can be derived from a company's accounts are virtually useless. Here the biggest problem is not so much the reported operating profit as the figures for capital employed contained in the balance sheet. Not only are assets typically booked at historic cost, meaning they can be grossly undervalued if inflation has been high since they were acquired; the capital employed is also often deflated by goodwill write-offs. Once balance sheets have been shrunk, pedestrian profits translate into fabulous returns.[9]

Added to the list of problems is the issue of capitalisation. That is the extent to which an item of expenditure is written off against profits as an expense or taken on to the balance sheet and capitalised as an asset. For example, firms differ in their treatment of research and development;

[9] *Financial Times*, 7 May 1996, Lex column.

companies that spend significant sums on R&D and then have a policy of writing it off immediately are likely to have lower asset value than those that do not write it off against profits in the year of expenditure. Cross-company comparisons of profits/assets can therefore be very misleading.

Focusing on accounting rates of return can lead to short-termism. Managers who are judged on this basis may be reluctant to invest in new equipment, as this will raise the denominator in the ratio, producing a poor ARR in the short term. This can destroy value in the long run. Fast-growing companies needing extensive investment in the near term with the expectation of reaping rich rewards in the long term should not be compared with slow-growth and low-investing firms on the basis of ARR. **Exhibit 15.16** points out some problems associated with an excessive focus on profit-based measures for rewarding managers.

Exhibit 15.16

Strategy – the key issue suffering from neglect

FT

A change in thinking has produced an understanding that increasing value is what matters to corporate survival and growth

writes Robert Bruce

. . . Leaving fraud aside, the main reason for high-profile business failures has been inadequate strategy . . .

The issue is performance and how it is linked to profitability. No amount of regulation can remedy failures in this field.

Enron is a good example. In a report on enterprise governance published last month, the way that performance and strategy parted company is made clear. 'In some cases,' it says, 'performance incentives created a climate where employees would seek to generate profit at the expense of a company's stated standards of ethics and strategic goals. The case of Enron in the US illustrates this very clearly. The assessment of performance was ostensibly based on Enron's stated values of respect, integrity, communication and excellence. But employees soon learned that the only real performance measure was the amount of profits they could produce.'

The result was disaster. 'Performance measurement is very easy to talk about,' says Mr Tilley, 'but very challenging to put into place.' And linking it with profitability is often even harder. As the report says: 'Enron's emphasis on earnings growth and individual initiative meant that inexperienced managers were given too much leeway without the necessary controls to minimise failure.'

'The essential link,' says Bill Connell, chairman of the Professional Accountants In Business committee of the International Federation of Accountants, which sponsored the report, 'is that between performance and shareholder value'.

This is where the real change in thinking has occurred. 'Profitability is fine, but it may not be increasing value,' he says. As in the case of Enron, and many other recent corporate disasters, the idea of linking performance to profitability has increased the emphasis on the short-term . . .

'It needs to be balanced,' says Mr Connell. 'For example, a company should have 50 per cent of bonuses measured by strategic milestones from a full five-year strategic plan.'

The worst offender is often the main board of directors. These days, directors need to understand the balance between long-term and short-term actions, as well as their consequences.

'It is about getting the right performance matrix at the start,' says Mr Connell.

Otherwise the whole system develops a life of its own and the results are unintended disasters. Mr Connell recalls discovering at one organisation, for example, that bonuses were linked simply to sales without any profitability criteria.

The result was that everyone went for sales in greater and greater volume without a thought for more usual controls. 'They simply ended up with huge bad debts,' he says. But it does come back to the difficulty of measurement . . .

Source: Financial Times, 8 March 2004, p. 1. Reprinted with permission.

The superficial highlighting of eps and ARR

One of the most pervasive myths of our time is: 'But our shareholders do focus on eps and ARR, don't they?' – and it is easy to see why. Senior executives when talking with institutional shareholders and analysts often find the conversation reverting to a discussion of short-term earnings forecasts. If a merger is announced directors feel the need to point out in press releases that the result will not be 'earnings dilutive' in the forthcoming year.

This surface noise is deceiving. Intelligent shareholders and analysts are primarily interested in the long-term cash flow returns on shares. The earnings attributable to the next couple of years are usually an insignificant part of the value of a share. Over two-thirds of the value of a typical share is determined by income to be received five or more years hence (*see* Chapter 20 for these calculations). Knowledge of this or next year's earnings is not particularly interesting in itself. It is sought because it sheds light on the medium- and long-term cash flows.

There are hundreds of quoted companies that do not expect to produce any positive earnings at all in the next two to five years and yet these shares are frequently amongst the most highly valued in the market. There are dozens of biotechnology companies that have tapped shareholders for funds through rights issues and the like for years. Some have become massive concerns and yet have never made a profit or paid a dividend. The same applies to Internet companies, and, in the past it was true of satellite television operators (for example BSkyB) which have now reached the phase of high cash generation. **Exhibit 15.17** describes what investors are looking for.

Exhibit 15.17

Investment community piles on pressure for better returns

FT

Companies need increasingly to develop medium-term corporate strategies which will enable them to meet the rising expectations of those who provide their equity capital

Tapping into the booming liquidity of global capital markets is the corporate ideal – but the gatekeepers of that liquidity, the global investor and analyst communities, are basing their investment strategies on increasingly focused information. In this environment, the historical reporting model is living on borrowed time – investors, who typically base share price valuations on their forecasts of future cash flows, demand forward-looking information to feed into their valuation models.

Management is increasingly sensitive to the stark fact that the use of equity capital is not 'free' – it has been invested in the hope of earning a return. It is this required return . . . that defines the company's cost of equity capital. Management can only create value for shareholders if the company consistently generates a return on capital greater than its cost of capital . . .

For companies, the challenge must be to use this escalating value focus in their strategic planning, and in measuring performance. Once the internal systems are in place, the priority is to establish effective communication into the marketplace . . .

'Historical cost accounting measures are becoming less relevant, with more companies using value-based information and non-financial indicators to judge performance internally. Greater disclosure in these areas will allow investors to make more informed decisions on the potential future of companies.'

The international investment community is well aware of the limitations of annual reports, which provide emphasis on accounting profit – itself no real indicator of the creation of economic value . . .

Analysts and institutional investors focus much of their research on company strategy and the 'value platforms' underlying that strategy and recent surveys of investors' demand for, and use of, information confirm their desire for more forward-looking information, as well as the importance of drivers of future performance to their investment decisions.

Source: © Nigel Page, *Financial Times*, 10 December 1999, FT Director (special section), p. VIII. Reprinted with permission.

How a business creates value

Value is created when investment produces a rate of return greater than that required for the risk class of the investment. Shareholder value is driven by the four factors shown in **Exhibit 15.18**.

Exhibit 15.18 The four key elements of value creation

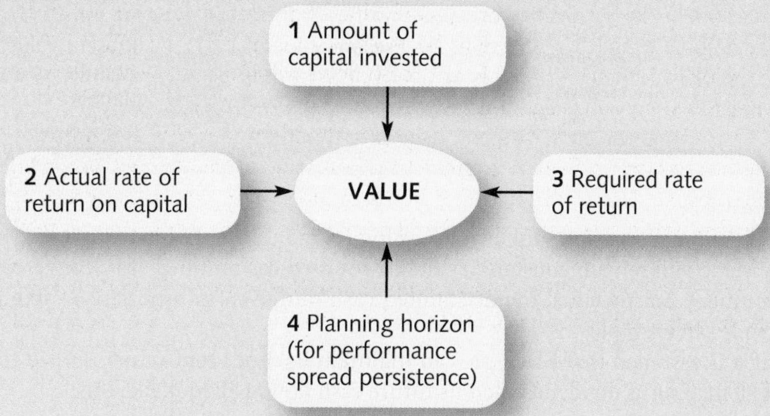

The difference between the second and third elements in Exhibit 15.18 creates the **performance spread**. The performance spread is measured as a percentage spread above or below the required rate of return, given the finance provider's opportunity cost of capital. Value is destroyed if 3 is greater than 2, and is created when 2 is greater than 3.

The absolute amount of value generated is determined by the quantity of capital invested multiplied by the performance spread. So, for example, if Black plc has a required rate of return of 14 per cent per annum and actually produces 17 per cent on an investment base of £1,000,000 it will create £30,000 of value per year:

$$\text{Annual value creation} = \text{Investment} \times (\text{Actual return} - \text{Required return})$$
$$= \text{I}\,(r - k)$$
$$= £1{,}000{,}000 \times (0.17 - 0.14) = £30{,}000$$

The fourth element in Exhibit 15.18 needs more explanation. It would be unreasonable to assume that positive or negative return spreads will be maintained forever. If return spreads are negative, presumably managers will (eventually) take the necessary action to prevent continued losses. If they fail to respond then shareholders will take the required steps through, say, sackings or the acceptance of a merger offer. Positive spreads arise as a result of a combination of the attractiveness of the industry and the competitive strength of a firm within that industry (*see* Chapter 16). High returns can be earned because of market imperfections. For example, a firm may be able to prevent competitors entering its market segment because of economies of scale, brand strength or legal exclusion through patents. However, most firms will sooner or later experience increased competition and reduced margins. The higher the initial performance spread the more attractive **market entry** seems to potential competitors (or substitute product developers). Examples of industries that were at one time extremely profitable and which were penetrated to the point where they have become highly competitive include personal computers and mobile phone manufacture.

In shareholder value analysis it is usually assumed that returns will, over time, be driven towards the required rate of return. Beyond some point in the future (the **planning horizon**) any new investment will, on average, earn only the minimum acceptable rate of return. Having said this, I do acknowledge that there are some remarkable businesses that seem to be able to maintain positive performance spreads for decades. Their economic franchises are protected by powerful barriers preventing serious competitive attack, e.g. Coca-Cola, Gillette. Warren Buffett calls such companies '**Inevitables**' because there is every reason to believe they will be dominating their industries decades from now – *see* Arnold (2002). If we leave Inevitables to one side, we see that for the majority of businesses their value consists of two components, as shown in **Exhibit 15.19**.

Exhibit 15.19 Corporate value

Corporate value = Present value of cash flows within planning horizon + Present value of cash flows after planning horizon

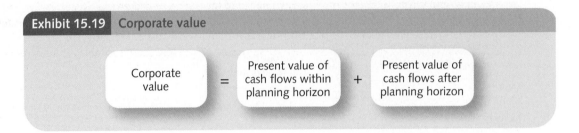

In the second period (after the planning horizon), even if investment levels are doubled, corporate value will remain constant, as the discounted cash inflows (to time zero) associated with that investment exactly equal the discounted cash outflows (to time zero) – Exhibit 17.2 on page 675 provides an example.

If it is assumed that Black plc can maintain its 3 per cent return spread for ten years and pays out all income as dividends then its future cash flows will look like this:

Years:	$1 \rightarrow 10$	$11 \rightarrow$ infinity
Cash flow:	£170,000	£140,000

The value of the firm is the discounted value of these cash flows.
The discounted cash flow within the planning horizon is:

$$£170{,}000 \times \text{Annuity factor (10 years, 14 per cent)} = £170{,}000 \times 5.2161 = £886{,}737$$

plus the discounted cash flow after the planning horizon:
First discounted to time 10: £140,000/0.14 = £1,000,000.
This is then discounted back 10 years to time zero:

$$\frac{1{,}000{,}000}{(1+0.14)^{10}} = £269{,}744$$

Value of the firm	£1,156,481
Less initial investment	(£1,000,000)
Value created	£156,481

An alternative approach: The value of the firm is equal to the initial investment in the firm (£1,000,000) plus the present value of all the values created annually.

Investment	+	Value created within planning horizon	+	Value created after planning horizon
£1,000,000	+	£30,000 × 5.2161	+	£1,000,000(0.14 – 0.14)
		£30,000 × Annuity factor (10 years, 14%)		
£1,000,000	+	£156,481	+	0 = £1,156,481

The five actions for creating value

Good growth occurs when a business unit or an entire corporation obtains a positive spread on the new investment capital. **Bad growth**, the bane of shareholders, occurs when managers invest in strategies that produce negative return spreads. This can so easily happen if the focus of attention is on sales and earnings growth. To managers encouraged to believe that their job is to expand the business and improve the bottom line, acceptance of the notion of bad growth in profits is a problem. But, as we have seen, it is perfectly possible to show growing profits on a larger investment base producing an incremental return less than the incremental cost of capital.

Exhibit 15.20 shows the options open to managers. This model can be applied at the corporate, business unit or product line level.

Exhibit 15.20 To expand or not to expand?

	Grow	Shrink
Positive performance spread	Value creation	Value opportunity forgone
Negative performance spread	Value destruction	Value creation

DaimlerChrysler refused to put more money into a business that produces negative performance spreads – Mitsubishi Motors – despite its desire to be a global manufacturer. It refused to allow bad growth – *see* **Exhibit 15.21**.

Exhibit 15.21

MMC reels as Daimler walks away

FT

By Davis Ibison in Tokyo and James Mackintosh in London

Investors in Mitsubishi Motors panicked yesterday after DaimlerChrysler, its biggest shareholder, abandoned the Japanese carmaker, sending the shares tumbling by a quarter, the maximum allowed under Tokyo stock exchange rules.

Daimler said righting the business would require a 'very, very high capital infusion'. The carmaker would not take part in a fundraising expected to top Y700bn (£3.6bn) because it did not believe it would get the returns it required, said Manfred Gentz, finance director.

The move ends a four-year venture for the German company, marred by police raids on MMC headquarters, cover-ups of potentially fatal vehicle flaws and crippling bad debts in the US. It also leaves Daimler little presence in the Asian mass market, endangering its goal of becoming a global manufacturer.

Daimler paid about €2.5bn for its 37 per cent stake in MMC four years ago. The possible loss of this adds to pressure on Jürgen Schrempp, chief executive and architect of the deal. Analysts said the company's share price would rise if he quit, but that was unlikely, as he appeared to have the support of Deutsche Bank, its largest shareholder.

Daimler shares rose as investors expressed relief at what appeared to be the end of its costly entanglement with Japan's only unprofitable carmaker. In New York late trading they were up 5 per cent at $45.45 . . .

Source: Financial Times, 24/25 April 2004, p. M1. Reprinted with permission.

It has already been demonstrated that overall Black plc produces a more than satisfactory return on investment. Now assume that the firm consists of two divisions: a clothing factory and a toy import business. Each business is making use of £500,000 of assets (at market value). The clothing division is expected to produce an 11 per cent return per annum over the next ten years whereas the toy division will produce a 23 per cent per annum return over the same period. After the ten-year planning horizon both divisions will produce returns equal to their risk-adjusted required return: for the clothing division this is 13 per cent and for the more risky toy division this is 15 per cent.

The cash flows are:

Year	1 → 10	11 → infinity
Clothing	£55,000	£65,000
Toys	£115,000	£75,000

The annual value creation within the planning horizon is:

$I \times (r - k)$

Clothing £500,000 × (0.11 – 0.13) = –£10,000

Toys £500,000 × (0.23 – 0.15) = +£40,000

Despite the higher return required in the toy division, it creates value (calculating required rates of return is covered in Chapter 19). For the next ten years a 15 per cent return is achieved plus a shareholder bonus of £40,000. This division could fit into the top left box of Exhibit 15.20. The management team may want to consider further investment in this unit so long as the marginal investment can generate a return greater than 15 per cent. To pass up positive return spread investments would be to sacrifice valuable opportunities and enter the top right box of Exhibit 15.20.

The clothing operation does not produce returns sufficient to justify its present level of investment. Growth in this unit would only be recommended if such a strategy would enable the division to somehow transform itself so as to achieve a positive spread. If this seems unlikely then the best option is probably a scaling down or withdrawal from the market. This will release resources to be more productively employed elsewhere, either within or outside the firm. Such shrinkage would create value by reducing the drag this activity has on the rest of the firm.

This line of thought can assist managers at all levels to allocate resources. At the corporate level knowledge of potential good-growth and bad-growth investments will help the selection of a portfolio of businesses. At the business unit level, product and customer groups can be analysed to assess the potential for value contribution. Lower down, particular products and customers can be ranked in terms of value. A simplified example of corporate level value analysis is shown in **Exhibit 15.22**.

In Exhibit 15.22, strategic business unit A (SBU_A) is a value destroyer due to its negative return spread. Perhaps there is over-investment here and shareholders would be better served if resources were transferred to other operations. SBU_B produces a small positive spread. However, it is only just managing this, and, in the uncertain world of business it may falter, so a managerial watchful eye will trained on it to ensure that it continues to produce positive performance spreads. SBU_C produces a lower return spread than SBU_E, but manages to create more value because of its higher future investment levels. Some businesses have greater potential than others for growth while maintaining a positive spread. For example, SBU_E might be a niche market player in fine china where greatly expanded activity would reduce the premium paid by customers for the exclusivity of the product – quickly producing negative spread on the marginal production. Strategic business unit C might be in mid-priced tableware competing on design where investment in the design and marketing teams might produce positive spread growth. Strategic business unit D is capable of high spreads over a long period producing the largest overall gain in value. Drugs with lengthy patent rights often produce high positive spreads for many years leading to high value creation over their lifetimes.

There are five actions available to managers to increase value. These are shown in the **value action pentagon** (**Exhibit 15.23**).

Exhibit 15.22 Value creation and Strategic Business Unit (SBU) performance spreads

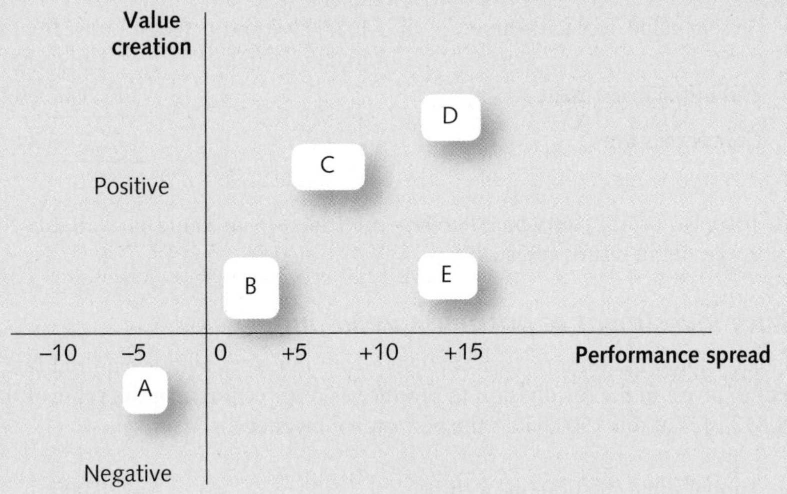

The five actions in the value action pentagon below could be applied to Black plc.

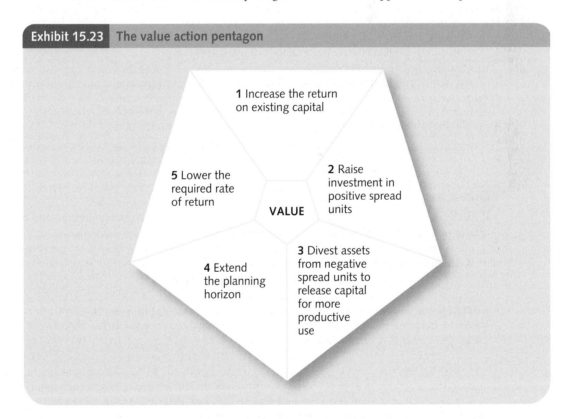

Exhibit 15.23 The value action pentagon

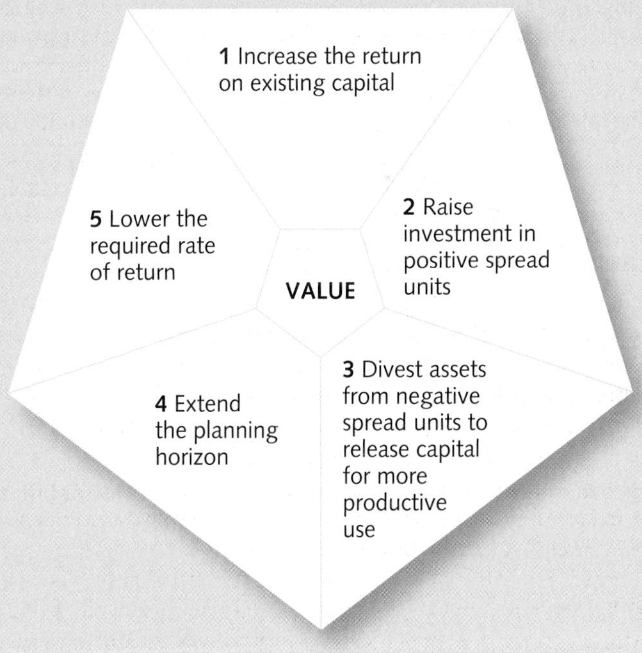

Increase the return on existing capital

The value of Black of £1,000,000 + £156,481 could be increased if the management implemented a plan to improve the efficiency of their existing operations. If the rate of return on investment for the firm as a whole over the next ten years is raised to 18 per cent then the firm's value rises to £1,208,644, viz:

Annual value creation	$= I \times (r - k)$	
	= £1,000,000 × (0.18 – 0.14)	
	= £40,000	
Present value over ten years	= £40,000 × Annuity factor (10 years, 14%)	
	= £40,000 × 5.2161 =	£208,644
plus initial investment		£1,000,000
Corporate value		£1,208,644

An increase of £52,163 (£1,208,644 – £1,156,481) in value is available for every 1 per cent improvement in return spread.

Raise investment in positive spread units

If Black could obtain a further £500,000 from investors with a required rate of return of 15 per cent to invest in the toy division to produce a 23 per cent return the value of the firm would rise to £1,847,242 (of this £500,000 is the new capital invested).

Annual value creation on clothing	=	–£10,000
Annual value creation on toys = £40,000 × 2	=	£80,000
		£70,000

Over ten years			
Clothing:	–£10,000 × Annuity factor (10 years, 13%)		
Toys:	£80,000 × Annuity factor (10 years, 15%)		
Clothing:	–£10,000 × 5.4262	=	–£54,262
Toys:	£80,000 × 5.0188	=	£401,504
			£347,242
plus the initial investment			£1,500,000
Corporate value			£1,847,242

Divest assets

If Black could close its clothing division, release £500,000 to expand the toy division and achieve returns of 23 per cent on the transferred investment then value increases dramatically:

Annual value creation	$= I \times (r - k)$	
	= £1,000,000 × (0.23 – 0.15)	
	= £80,000	
Present value over ten years	= £80,000 × Annuity factor (10 years, 15%)	
	= £80,000 × 5.0188 =	£401,504
plus initial investment		£1,000,000
Corporate value		£1,401,504

Extend the planning horizon

Sometimes there are steps that can be taken to exploit a competitive advantage over a longer period than originally expected. For example, perhaps the toy division could negotiate a long-term exclusive import licence with the supplier of an established premium-priced product, thus closing the door on the entry of competitors. If we suppose that the toy division will now produce a return spread of 23 per cent for a 15-year period rather than ten years the value of the company rises to £1,179,634, viz:

Annual value creation on clothing	=	–£10,000	
Annual value creation on toys	=	£40,000	
Present value over 10 years (clothing)			
	=	– £10,000 × Annuity factor (10 years, 13%)	
	=	–£10,000 × 5.4262	
	=	–£54,262	
Present value over 15 years (toys)	=	£40,000 × Annuity factor (15 years, 15%)	
	=	£40,000 × 5.8474 = £233,896	
Total value creation	=	£233,896 – £54,262 =	£179,634
plus initial investment			£1,000,000
Corporate value			£1,179,634

Lower the required rate of return

It may be possible to lower the required rate of return by adjusting the proportion of debt to equity in the capital structure (examined in Chapters 19 and 21) or by reducing business risk.[10] Suppose that Black can lower its required rate of return by shifting to a higher proportion of debt, so that the overall rate falls to 12 per cent. Then the value of the firm rises to £1,282,510.

Annual value creation	=	$I \times (r - k)$	
	=	1,000,000 × (0.17 – 0.12)	
	=	£50,000	
Present value over ten years	=	£50,000 × Annuity factor (10 years, 12%)	
Total value creation	=	£50,000 × 5.6502 =	£282,510
plus initial investment			£1,000,000
Corporate value			£1,282,510

(Many companies tend to borrow little. They finance their businesses almost entirely through equity (shareholders') money. The motivation is often to reduce the risk of financial distress. This may be due to a desire to serve the interests of shareholders, but more often it is because managers want to avoid financial distress for their own safety. They can become too cautious and forgo the opportunity of reducing the overall cost of capital (discount rate) by not using a higher proportion of cheaper debt finance.)

Concluding comments

The switch from management by accounting numbers to management using financial concepts such as value, the time value of money and opportunity cost is only just beginning. Some highly successful firms are leading the way in insisting that each department, business unit and project add value to shareholders' investment. This has required a re-examination of virtually all aspects of management, ranging from performance measurement systems and strategic planning to motivational schemes and training programmes. The rest of this part of the book builds on the basic principles behind value-based management discussed in this chapter.

---

[10] Business risk can be reduced by, for example, reducing operating gearing (that is, reducing the proportion of costs that are fixed thus lowering the break-even point – *see* Chapter 21); or by encouraging customers (e.g. through advertising) to regard your products as essential rather than discretionary; or by matching assets and liabilities better, in terms of maturity and currency (*see* Chapter 13).

Key points and concepts

- **Value-based management** is a managerial approach in which the primacy of purpose is long-run shareholder-wealth maximisation. The objective of the firm, its systems, strategy, processes, analytical techniques, performance measurement and culture have as their guiding objective shareholder-wealth maximisation.

- **Shareholder-wealth maximisation** is the superior objective in most commercial organisations operating in a competitive market for many reasons. For example:

  - managers not pursuing this objective may be thrown out (e.g. via a merger);
  - owners of the business have a right to demand this objective;
  - society's scarce resources can thereby be better allocated.

- **Non-shareholder wealth-maximising goals** may go hand in hand with shareholder value, for example market share targets, customer satisfaction and employee benefits. But, sometimes the two are contradictory and then shareholder wealth becomes paramount.

- **Earnings- (profit)-based management is flawed**:

  - profit figures are drawn up following numerous subjective allocations and calculations relying on judgement rather than science;
  - profit figures are open to manipulation and distortion;
  - the investment required to produce earnings growth is not made explicit;
  - the time value of money is ignored;
  - the riskiness of earnings is ignored.

- **Bad growth** is when the return on the marginal investment is less than the required rate of return, given the finance providers' opportunity cost of funds. This can occur even when earnings-based figures are favourable.

- **Using accounting rates of return** (ROCE, ROI, ROE, etc.) is an attempt to solve some of the problems associated with earnings or earnings per share metrics, especially with regard to the investment levels used to generate the earnings figures. However balance sheet figures are often too crude to reflect capital employed. Using ARRs can also lead to short-termism.

- **That shareholders are interested solely in short-term earnings and EPS is a myth** These figures are only interesting to the extent that they cast light on the quality of stewardship over fund providers' money by management and therefore give an indication of long-term cash flows. Evidence:

  - most of the value of a share is determined by income to be received five or more years hence;
  - hundreds of quoted firms producing zero or negative profits have high market values;
  - earnings changes are not correlated with share price changes; for example, earnings can fall due to a rise in R&D spending and yet share prices may rise;
  - the window-dressing of accounts (creative accounting) does not, in most cases, influence share prices.

- **Value is created** when investment produces a rate of return greater than that required for the risk class of investment.

- **Shareholder value is driven by four key elements**:

  1 Amount of capital invested.
  2 Required rate of return.
  3 Actual rate of return on capital.
  4 Planning horizon (for performance spread persistence).

- **Performance spread**

  Actual rate of return on capital – required return

  $r - k$

- **Corporate value**

= Present value of cash flows within planning horizon + Present value of cash flows after planning horizon

- **To expand or not to expand?**

	Grow	Shrink
Positive performance spread	Value creation	Value opportunity forgone
Negative performance spread	Value destruction	Value creation

- **The value action pentagon**

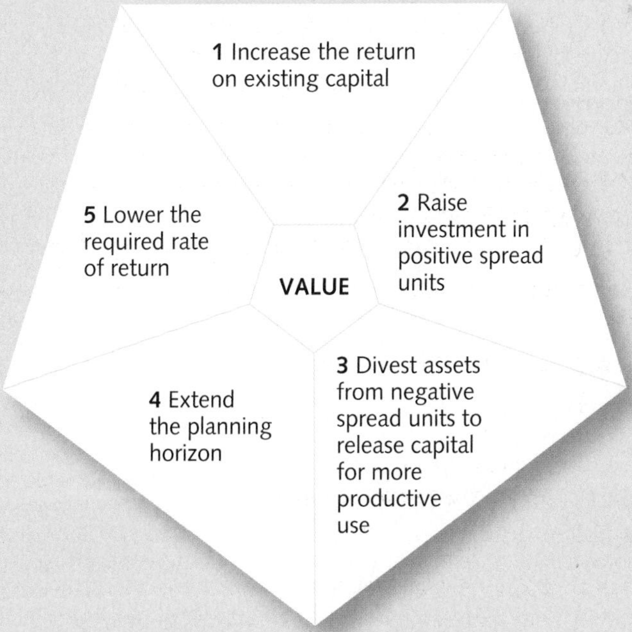

References and further reading

Arnold, G.C. (2002) *Valuegrowth Investing.* London: Financial Times Prentice Hall.

An investment book that considers corporate strategy and the potential for value creation.

Arnold, G.C. and Davies, M. (eds) (2000) *Value-Based Management.* London: John Wiley & Sons.

A collection of research monographs focuses on this emerging field.

Cornelius, I. and Davies, M. (1997) *Shareholder Value.* London: Financial Times: Financial Publishing.

A good account of value-based management and the metrics used.

Davies, M., Arnold, G.C., Cornelius, I. and Walmsey, S. (2000) *Managing For Shareholder Value.* London: Informa Publishing Group.

An introductory overview of VBM.

Investors Chronicle (1997) 'A week in the markets', 18 April, p. 10.

The value destruction by T & N is discussed.

McKinsey & Co. (Koller, T., Goedhart, M. and Wessels, D.) (2005) *Valuation.* 4th edn. New York: Wiley.

The management of value-based organisations and the principles behind the techniques are explained well.

McTaggart, J.M., Kontes, P.W. and Mankins, M.C. (1994) *The Value Imperative.* New York: Free Press.

A very good book showing the application of value-based techniques to strategy and other disciplines.

Pitman, B. (2003) 'heading for value', *Harvard Business Review*, April, pp. 41–6.

The former CEO and chairman describes clearly and succinctly the evolution of Lloyds Bank from a company without a clear objective to a focus on shareholder value, using return on equity relative to cost of equity to evaluate company operations and reward managers. The logic of a value focus led to 'we had to accept that it was all right to get smaller, to stay close to home, to focus on unglamorous products . . . getting rid of unprofitable customers, getting out of unprofitable markets'.

Rappaport, A. (1998) *Creating Shareholder Value.* (Revised and updated version.) New York: Free Press.

A landmark book. Presents an important value metric – shareholders' value analysis (SVA).

Reimann, B.C. (1989) *Managing for Value.* Oxford: Basil Blackwell.

Useful because it brings together strategy and value.

Stewart, G.B. (1991) *The Quest for Value.* New York: Harper Business.

Written by a founding partner in Stern Stewart and Co., the US consultancy which has so successfully promoted MVA and EVA. Some useful insights.

Stewart, G.B. (2001) 'Market Myths', in *The New Corporate Finance.* 3rd edn. Edited by Donald H. Chew, New York: McGraw-Hill/Irwin.

An easy-to-read discussion of the difficulties with accounting metrics and the triumphing of value principles.

Case study recommendation

Please see www.pearsoned.co.uk/arnold for case study synopses

- Harris Seafoods. Authors: William E. Fruhan Jr. and Willian A. Sahlman, (1993) Harvard Business School.

Self-review questions

1 In what ways are accounting-based performance measures inadequate for guiding managerial decisions?

2 Define value-based management.

3 What are the four key drivers of shareholder value creation?

4 What are the five actions available to increase value?

5 Describe at least three arguments for managers putting shareholder-wealth maximisation as the firm's objective.

6 Invent a mission statement and strategic objectives that comply with value-based management principles.

7 Outline the evidence against the popular view that shareholders judge managerial performance on the basis of short-term earnings figures.

8 What is 'good growth' and what is 'bad growth'?

9 In what circumstances would you reduce investment in a strategic business unit even if its profits are on a rising trend?

Questions and problems

myfinancelab **Questions with an icon are also available for practice in MyFinanceLab with additional supporting resources.**

The answers to questions marked with an asterisk are in the Lecturer's Guide only.

1 (*Examination level*) 'Thirty years ago we measured the success of our divisional managers on the basis of market share growth, sales and profits. In the late 1970s we switched to return on capital employed because the old system did not take account of the amount of capital invested to achieve growth targets. Now you are telling me that we have to change again to value-based performance metrics. Why?' Explain in the form of an essay to this chief executive what advantages value-based management has over other approaches.

2 Describe three of the ways in which accounts can be manipulated and distorted.

3 Gather some more data on T & N, GSK, and Compass from newspapers, industry sources, annual reports, etc. and give a more detailed account than that given in this chapter of the ways in which value was created or destroyed.

4 Shareholder value management has been described as a 'weird Anglo-American concept'. Describe this philosophy and consider whether it has applicability outside the Anglo-American world.

5 Do you feel comfortable with the notion that commercial organisations acting in a competitive environment should put shareholders' wealth creation as their first priority? If not, why not? Explain your reasoning.

6 'EPS (earnings per share) is not a holy grail in determining how well a company is performing': Lex column of the *Financial Times*, 7 May 1996. Describe and explain the reasons for dissatisfaction with eps for target setting and increasing performance.

7* Which of the following two companies creates more value, assuming that they are making the same initial investment?

Company A's projected profits

Year	Profit (£000s)
Last year	1,000
1 (forthcoming year)	1,000
2	1,100
3	1,200
4	1,400
5	1,600
6 and all subsequent years	1,800

Company B's projected profits

Year	Profit (£000s)
Last year	1,000
1 (forthcoming year)	1,000
2	1,080
3	1,160
4	1,350
5	1,500
6 and all subsequent years	1,700

Profits for both companies are 20 per cent of sales in each year. With company A, for every £1 increase in sales 7p has to be devoted to additional debtors because of the generous credit terms granted to customers. For B, only 1p is needed for additional investment in debtors for every £1 increase in sales. Higher sales also mean greater inventory levels at each firm. This is 6p and 2p for every extra £1 in sales for A and B respectively.

Apart from the debtor and inventory adjustments the profit figures of both firms reflect their cash flows. The cost of capital for both firms is 14 per cent.

?

8 Ready plc is financed entirely by equity capital with a required return of 13 per cent. Ready's business is such that as sales increase, working capital does not change. Ready currently has £10m in cash not needed for business operations that could be used to pay a dividend immediately. Under current policy, post-tax earnings (and free cash flow) of £10m per year are expected to continue indefinitely. All earnings in future years are expected to be paid out as dividends in the year of occurrence.

Calculate

a The value of the company before the current dividend is paid from the £10m of cash.

b The value of the company if the current dividend (time 0) is missed and the retained earnings are put into investments (with the same risk as current set of projects) yielding an extra £2m per year to infinity in addition to the current policy's earnings. What happens to earnings and cash flow? Is this good or bad investment?

c The value of the company if half of the current dividend is missed and the retained earnings are put into investment yielding £0.5m per year to infinity. What happens to earnings and cash flows? Is this good or bad investment?

?

9 What is the annual value creation of Sheaf plc which has an investment level of £300,000 and produces a rate of return of 19 per cent per annum compared with a required rate of return of 13 per cent? What is the performance spread?

Assuming that the planning horizon for Sheaf plc is 12 years, calculate the value of the firm. (Assume the investment level is constant throughout.) ?

10* Busy plc, an all equity-financed firm, has three strategic business units. The polythene division has capital of £8m and is expected to produce returns of 11 per cent for the next five years. Thereafter it will produce returns equal to the required rate of return for this risk level of 14 per cent. The paper division has an investment level of £12m and a planning horizon of 10 years. During the planning horizon it will produce a return of 22 per cent compared with a risk-adjusted required rate of return of 15 per cent. The cotton division uses £2m of capital, has a planning horizon of seven years and a required rate of return of 16 per cent compared with the anticipated actual rate of 17 per cent over the first seven years.

a Calculate the value of the firm.
b Draw a value-creation and strategic business unit performance spread chart.
c Develop five ideas for increasing the value of the firm. State your assumptions. ?

myfinancelab *Now retake your diagnostic test for Chapter 15 to check your progress and update your study plan.*

Assignment

Apply the four key elements of value creation, the 'expand or not to expand?' model and the value action pentagon to a firm you are familiar with. Write a report for senior executives.

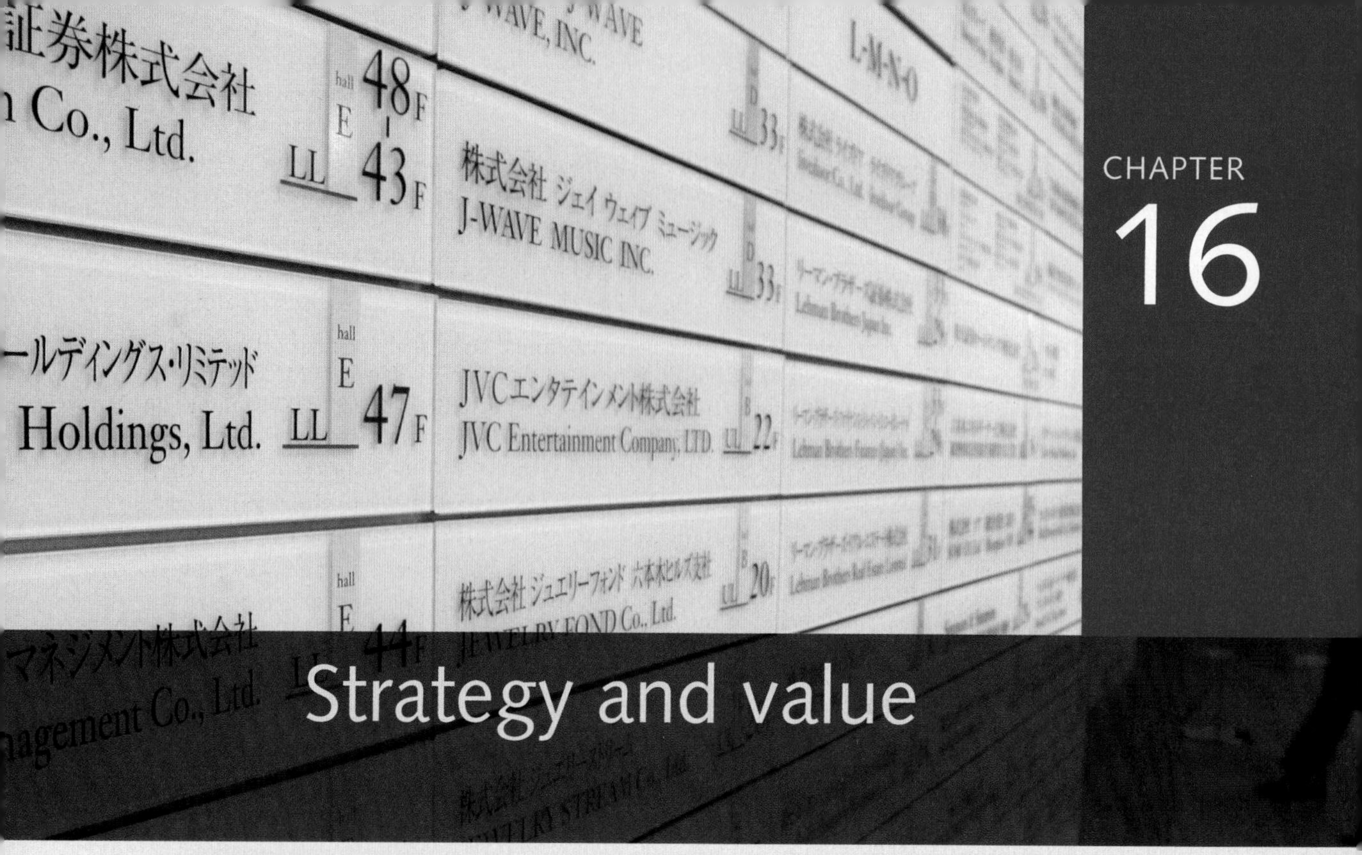

CHAPTER 16

Strategy and value

LEARNING OUTCOMES

By the end of this chapter the reader should be able to:

- explain the extent of the ramifications of value-based management;
- discuss the main elements to examine when evaluating alternative strategies for the business from a value perspective; map business activities in terms of industry attractiveness, competitive advantage within the industry and life-cycle stage and make capital allocation choices;
- describe a system for making strategic choices that requires both qualitative thinking and quantitative analysis;
- describe the four main tasks for the corporate centre (head office).

myfinancelab *Complete your diagnostic test for Chapter 16 now to create your personal study plan*

Introduction

The transforming of a corporation from one that is earnings based to one that is focused on value has profound effects on almost all aspects of organisational life. New light is cast on the most appropriate portfolio of businesses making up the firm, and on the strategic thrust of individual business units. Acquisition and divestment strategies may be modified to put shareholder wealth creation at centre stage. Capital structure (proportion of debt relative to equity capital) and dividend payout policy are predicated on the optimal approach from the shareholders' point of view, not by 'safety first' or earnings growth considerations. Performance measures, target setting and managerial compensation become linked to the extent that wealth is created rather than the vagaries of accounting numbers.

To unite the organisation in pursuit of wealth creation an enormous educational and motivational challenge has to be met. A culture change is often required so that everyone's goals, at all levels, ensure that value is created. Retraining and new reward systems are needed to help lift eyes from the short-term to long-term achievements. This chapter gives a taste of the pervading nature of value-based managerial thinking. Later chapters consider some specific aspects of value-based management such as the employment of metrics to gauge the extent of achievement in value terms, the way to calculate the opportunity cost of capital and the value to be destroyed or gained through mergers.

An overview of the application of value principles

Exhibit 16.1 summarises some of the most important areas where value-based management impacts on the firm. To describe them all fully would require a book as long as this one, so only a short discussion of some of the most important points is given.

The firm's objective

The firm has first to decide what it is that is to be maximised and what will merely be satisficed. In value management the maximisation of sales, market share, employee satisfaction, customer service excellence, and so on, are rejected as the objective of the firm. All of these are important and there are levels of achievement for each which are desirable in so far as they help the achievement of maximising shareholder wealth, but they are not *the* objective. It is important that there is clarity over the purpose of the firm and crystal-clear guiding principles for managers making strategic and operational decisions. Objectives stated in terms of a vague balance of interests are not appropriate for a commercial organisation in a competitive environment. The goal of maximising discounted cash flows to shareholders brings simplicity and direction to decision making.

Strategic business unit management

A **strategic business unit** (**SBU**) is a business unit within the overall corporate entity which is distinguishable from other business units because it serves a defined external market in which management can conduct strategic planning in relation to products and markets.

Large corporations often have a number of SBUs which each require strategic thought and planning. **Strategy** means selecting which product or market areas to enter/exit and how to ensure a good competitive position in those markets/products. Establishing a good competitive position requires a consideration of issues such as price, service level, quality, product features, methods of distribution, etc., but these issues are secondary to deciding which products to produce and which markets to enter or exit.

Exhibit 16.1 Value principles influence most aspects of management

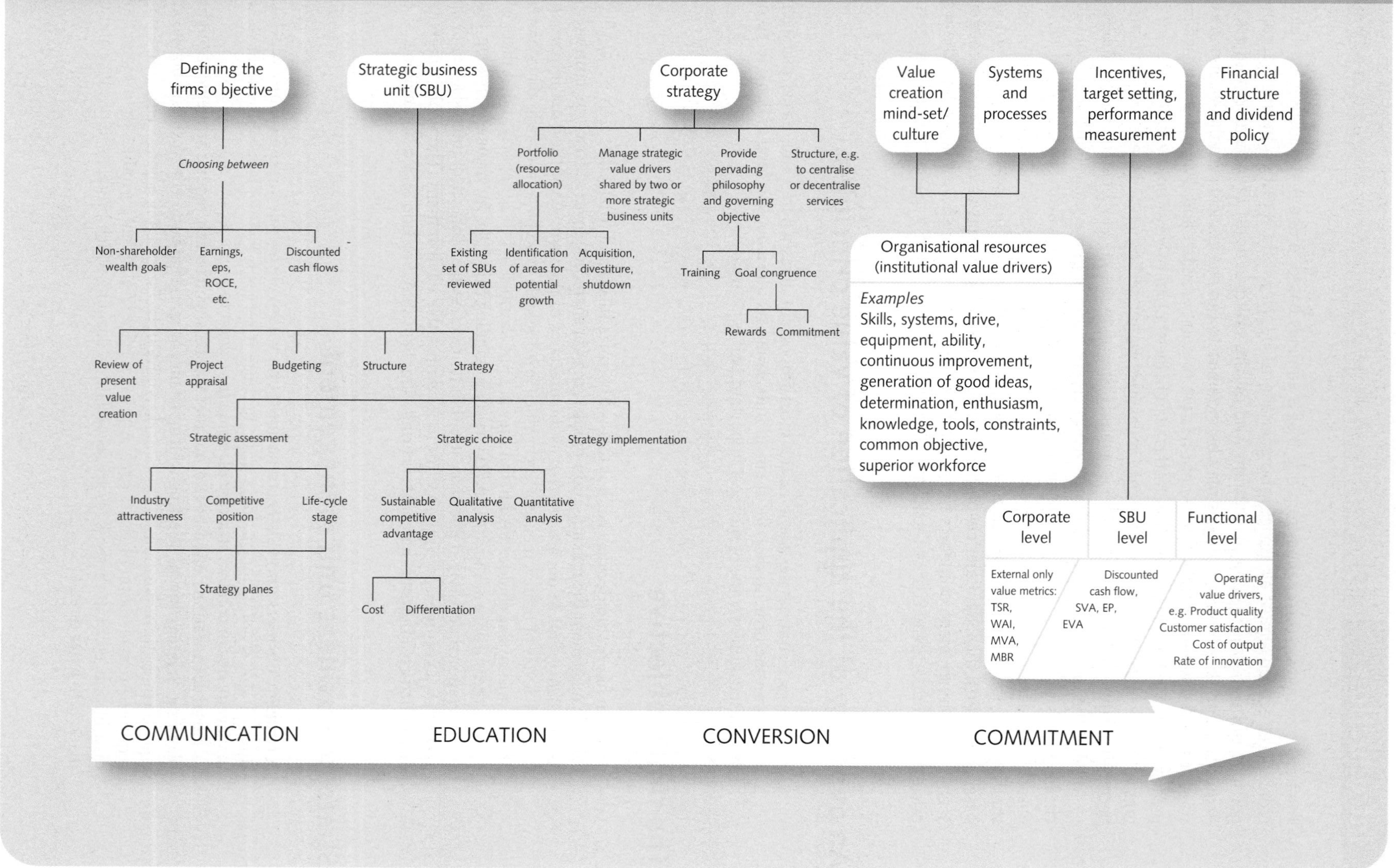

It is the managers of an SBU who are the individuals who come into regular contact with customers in the competitive market environment and it is important that SBU strategy be developed largely by those managers who will be responsible for its execution. By doing this, by harnessing these managers' knowledge and encouraging their commitment through a sense of 'ownership' of a strategy, the firm is more likely to prosper.

Before the creation of new strategic options it is advisable to carry out a review of the value creation of the present strategy. This can be a complex task, but an example will demonstrate one approach. Imagine that the plastic products division of Red plc is a defined strategic business unit with a separable strategic planning ability servicing markets distinct from Red's other SBUs. This division sells three categories of product, A, B and C to five types of customer, (a) UK consumers, (b) UK industrial users, (c) UK government, (d) European Union consumers and (e) other overseas consumers. Information has been provided showing the value expected to be created from each of the product/market categories based on current strategy. These are shown in **Exhibits 16.2** and **16.3**.

Product line C is expected to destroy shareholder value while absorbing a substantial share of the SBU's resources. Likewise this analysis has identified sales to UK industry and government as detrimental to the firm's wealth. This sort of finding is not unusual: many businesses have acceptable returns at the aggregate level but hidden behind these figures are value-destructive areas of activity. The analysis could be made even more revealing by showing the returns available for each product and market category; for example, product A in the UK consumer market can be compared with product A in the European market.

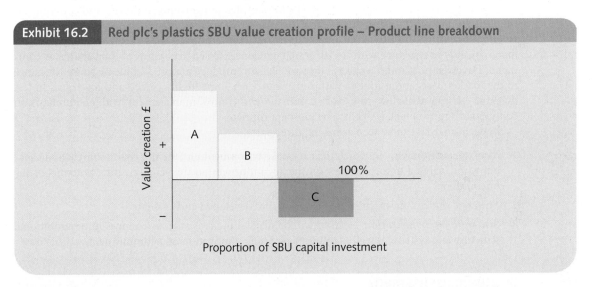

Exhibit 16.2 Red plc's plastics SBU value creation profile – Product line breakdown

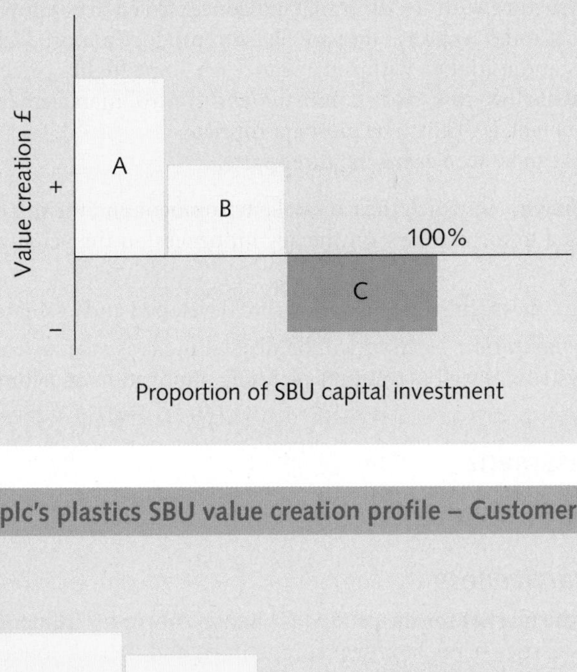

Exhibit 16.3 Red plc's plastics SBU value creation profile – Customer breakdown

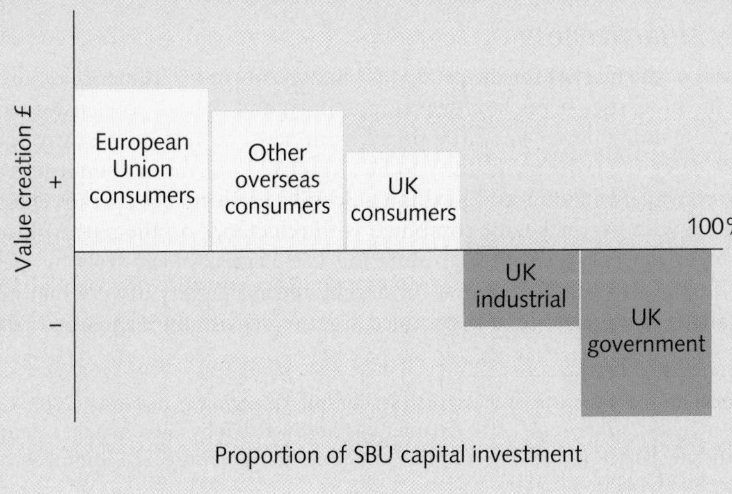

Warren Buffett, the financier, has made some pithy comments on the tendency for firms to fail to identify and root out value-destructive activities:

> Many corporations that consistently show good returns both on equity and on overall incremental capital have, indeed, employed a large portion of their retained earnings on an economically unattractive, even disastrous, basis. Their marvellous core businesses, however, whose earnings grow year after year, camouflage repeated failures in capital allocation elsewhere (usually involving high-priced acquisitions of businesses that have inherently mediocre economics). The managers at fault periodically report on the lessons they have learned from the latest disappointment. They then usually seek out future lessons. (Failure seems to go to their heads.)
>
> *Source*: Berkshire Hathaway 1984 Annual Report.© Warren Buffett. Reproduced with the permission of the author.

To get a clear line of sight from the customer to the shareholder many businesses need to build an entirely new fact base showing the full economic cost and cash flows associated with customers and product markets. Recognising that some activities are far more valuable than others prepares the ground for a shift of strategic resources. Attention can be directed at restructuring or eliminating value-destructive operations, while building up value-creative aspects of the business.

Furthermore, project appraisal, budgeting systems and the organisational structure of each SBU must be in harmony with the principle of value-based management. Project appraisal will be carried out using discounted cash flow techniques. Budgeting will not rely solely on accounting considerations, but will have value-based metrics (methods of measurement) as guides – some of which are described in the next chapter. The lines of decision-making authority and communication will be the most appropriate given the market environment in order to achieve greatest returns. For example, in a dynamic unpredictable market setting it is unwise to have a bureaucratic, hierarchical type structure with decision making concentrated at the top of long chains of command. Devolved power and responsibility are likely to produce a more flexible response to change in the marketplace, and initiative with self-reliance are to be highly prized and rewarded. In less dynamic environments low-cost, close command and control management, with an emphasis on continuous improvement, is likely to be most appropriate.

Strategic analysis can be seen as having three parts.

1. ***Strategic assessment*** – in which the external environment and the internal resources and capability are analysed to form a view on the key influences on the value-creating potential of the organisation.
2. ***Strategic choice*** – in which strategic options are developed and evaluated.
3. ***Strategic implementation*** – action will be needed in areas such as changes in organisational structure and systems as well as resource planning, motivation and commitment.

Strategic assessment

There are three primary strategic determinants of value creation.

1 Industry attractiveness

The **economics of the market** for the product(s) has an enormous influence on the profitability of a firm. In some industries firms have few competitors, and there is low customer buying power, low supplier bargaining power and little threat from new entrants or the introduction of substitute products. Here the industry is likely to be attractive in terms of the returns accruing to the existing players, which will on average exhibit a positive performance spread. Other product markets are plagued with over-capacity, combined with reluctance on the part of the participants to quit and apply resources in another product market. Prices are kept low by the ability of customers and suppliers to 'put the squeeze on' and by the availability of very many close-substitute products. Markets of this kind tend to produce negative performance spreads.[1] **Exhibit 16.4** shows

---

[1] For more detail on market attractiveness analysis consult *Valuegrowth Investing* (2002: Chapter 9) or *The Financial Times Guide to Investing* (2004: Chapter 14) both written by Glen Arnold or any major textbook on strategy. Michael Porter, whose 'five forces' is a very useful framework, is a leading writer in the field of strategy (Porter 1980, 1985).

the poor returns on invested capital in the car industry. Many of the companies in this industry have lost money on every car they have sold for most of the years of the past decade. Some have survived by owning profitable finance subsidiaries, others have survived with the help of government props or indulgent and over-optimistic shareholders: the directors seem to be able to persuade them that the next round of investment will bring revolutionary new models that will sweep the board and restore returns to greater than the cost of capital. However, year after year the return on capital for most major US and European car-makers is pathetic. It is difficult to see how, using Michael Porter's five forces analysis, this state of affairs is going to change. There is massive overcapacity as each country saves its car industry in any way it can. Contrary to popular belief barriers to entry are really quite small if you take a global perspective (look at the new car producers in China and India, or, in the 1980s, in South Korea and Brazil) which exacerbates the overcapacity problem. Customers have high bargaining power, especially the fleet buyers who can play one manufacturer off against another. Unions are usually strong in this industry, a factor which imposes heavy costs, not just on wages, but also on pensions and health care costs. Because the firms are competing fiercely, a boost to profit through an (expensively developed) innovation is short lived, as competitors quick emulate. All-in-all the car industry has bad economics. You can employ the best in the world, but if they are trying to move a sinking boat they will fail – the boat that managers get into is more important to shareholder returns than their skills as navigators.

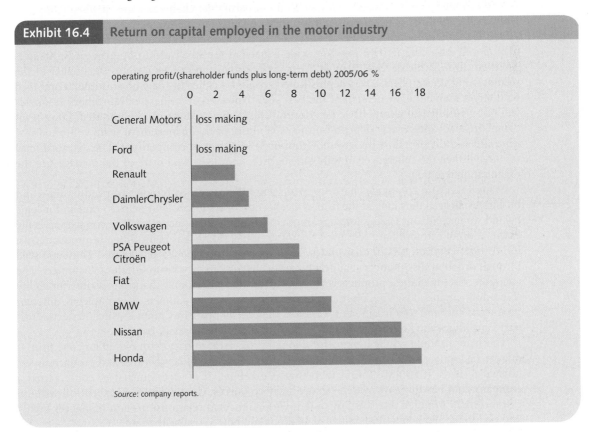

Exhibit 16.4 Return on capital employed in the motor industry

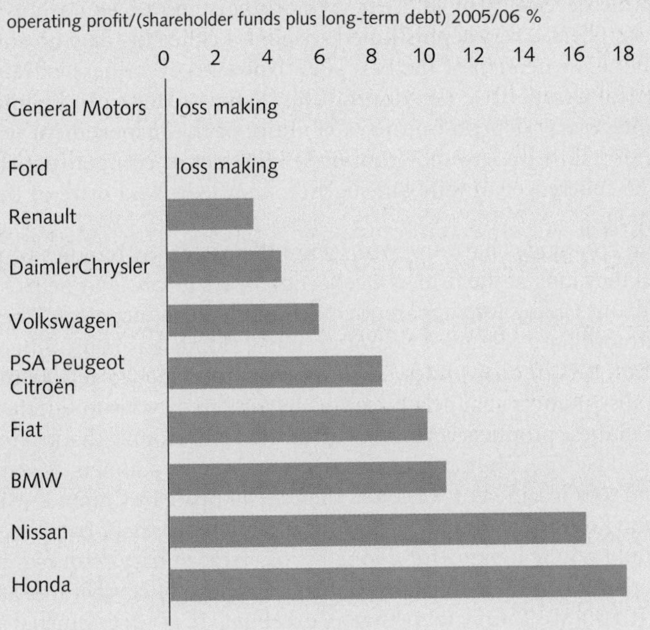

Source: company reports.

2 *The strength of resources*

Identifying a good industry is only the first step. Value-based companies aim to beat the average rates of return on capital employed within their industries. To beat the averages, companies need something special. That something special comes from the bundle of resources that the firm possesses. Most of the resources are ordinary. That is, they give the firm competitive parity. However, the firm may be able to exploit one or two extraordinary resources – those that give a competitive edge. An **extraordinary resource** is one which, when combined with other (ordinary) resources, enables the firm to outperform competitors and create new value-generating opportunities. Critical extraordinary resources determine what a firm can do successfully.

It is the ability to generate value for customers that is crucial for superior returns. High shareholder returns are determined by the firm either being able to offer the same benefits to customers as competitors, but at a lower price; or being able to offer unique benefits that more than outweigh the associated higher price.

Ordinary resources provide a threshold competence. They are vital to ensure a company's survival. In the food retail business, for example, most firms have a threshold competence in basic activities, such as purchasing, human resource management, accounting control and store layout. However, the large chains have resources that set them apart from the small stores: they are able to obtain lower-cost supplies because of their enormous buying power; they can exploit economies of scale in advertising and in the range of produce offered.

Despite the large retailers having these advantages it is clear that small stores have survived, and some produce very high returns on capital invested. These superior firms provide value to the customer significantly above cost. Some corner stores have a different set of extraordinary resources compared with the large groups: personal friendly service could be valued highly; opening at times convenient to customers could lead to acceptance of a premium price; the location may make shopping less hassle than traipsing to an out-of-town hypermarket. The large chains find emulation of these qualities expensive. If they were to try and imitate the small store they could end up losing their main competitive advantages, the most significant of which is low cost.

The extraordinary resources possessed by the supermarket chains as a group when compared with small shops are not necessarily extraordinary resources in the competitive rivalry *between* the chains. If the focus is shifted to the 'industry' of supermarket chains factors like economies of scale may merely give competitive parity – scale is needed for survival. Competitive advantage is achieved through the development of other extraordinary resources, such as the quality of the relationship with suppliers, a very sophisticated system for collecting data on customers combined with target marketing, ownership of the best sites. However, even these extraordinary resources will not give superior competitive position forever. Many of these can be imitated. Long-term competitive advantage may depend on the capabilities of the management team continually to innovate and thereby shift the ground from under the feet of competitors. The extraordinary resource is then the coherence, attitude, intelligence, knowledge and drive of the managers in the organisational setting.

Many successful companies have stopped seeing themselves as bundles of product lines and businesses. Instead they look at the firm as a collection of resources. This helps to explain the logic behind some companies going into apparently unconnected product areas. The connection is the exploitation of extraordinary resources. So, for example, Honda has many different product areas: motor boat engines, cars, motor-cycles, lawn mowers and electric generators. These are sold through different distribution channels in completely different ways to different customers. The common root for all these products is Honda's extraordinary resource that led to a superior ability to produce engines. Likewise, photocopiers, cameras and image scanners are completely different product sectors and sold in different ways. Yet, they are all made by Canon – which has extraordinary capabilities and knowledge of optics, imaging and microprocessor controls.

The analyst should not be looking for a long list of extraordinary resources in any one firm. If one can be found, that is good – it only takes one to leap ahead of competitors and produce supernormal returns. If two are found then that is excellent. It is very unusual to come across a company that has three or more extraordinary resources. Coca-Cola is an exception with an extraordinary brand, a distribution system with connected relationships and managers highly knowledgeable about anti-competitive regulations and how to deal with them.

The TRRACK system

To assist the thorough analysis of a company's extraordinary resource I have developed the **TRRACK system**. This classifies extraordinary resources into six categories – *see* **Exhibit 16.5**.

Notice that the vast majority of extraordinary resources are intangible. They are qualities that are carried within the individuals who make up organisations, or are connected with the interaction between individuals. They are usually developed over a long time rather than bought. These qualities cannot be scientifically evaluated to provide objective quantification. Despite our inability to be precise, these people-embodied factors are usually the most important drivers of value creation and we must pay most attention to them.

Exhibit 16.5 The TRRACK system

T Tangible
R Relationships
R Reputation
A Attitude
C Capabilities
K Knowledge

- ***Tangible*** Occasionally physical resources provide a sustainable competitive advantage. These are assets that can be physically observed and are often valued (or misvalued) in a balance sheet. They include real estate, materials, production facilities and patents. They can be purchased, but if they were easily purchased they would cease to be extraordinary because all competitors would go out and buy. There must be some barrier preventing other firms from acquiring the same or similar assets for them to be truly valuable in the long run. Microsoft's ownership of its operating system and other standards within the software industry gives it a competitive edge. McDonald's makes sure that it takes the best locations on the busiest highways, rather than settle for obscure secondary roads. Many smaller businesses have found themselves, or have made smart moves to ensure they are, the owners of valuable real estate adjacent to popular tourist sites. Pharmaceutical companies, such as Merck, own valuable patents giving some protection against rivalry – at least temporarily.
- ***Relationships*** Over time companies can form valuable relationships with individuals and organisations that are difficult or impossible for a potential competitor to emulate. Relationships in business can be of many kinds. The least important are the contractual ones. The most important are informal or implicit. These relationships are usually based on a trust that has grown over many years. The terms of the implicit contract are enforced by the parties themselves rather than through the court – a loss of trust can be immensely damaging. It is in all the parties' interests to co-operate with integrity because there is the expectation of reiteration leading to the sharing of collective value created over a long period. South African Breweries (SAB) has 98 per cent of the beer market in South Africa. It has kept out foreign and domestic competitors because of its special relationships with suppliers and customers. It is highly profitable. Most of South Africa's roads are poor and electricity supplies are intermittent. To distribute its beer it has formed some strong relationships. The truck drivers, many of whom are former employees, are helped to set up their small trucking businesses by SAB. Shebeens sell most of the beer. These are unlicensed pubs. Often, they are tiny – no more than a few benches. SAB cannot sell directly to the illegal shebeens. Instead it maintains an informal relationship via a system of wholesalers. SAB makes sure that distributors have refrigerators and, if necessary, generators. A new entrant to the market would have to develop its own special relationship with truck drivers, wholesalers and retailers. In all likelihood it would have to establish a completely separate and parallel system of distribution. Even then it would lack the legitimacy that comes with a long-standing relationship. Relationships between employees, and between employees and the firm, can give a competitive edge. Some firms seem to possess a culture that creates wealth through the co-operation and dynamism of the employees. Information is shared, knowledge is developed, innovative activity flows, rapid response to market change is natural and respect for all pervades. The quality of the relationships with government can be astonishingly important to a company. Defence contractors cultivate a special relationship with various organs of government. The biggest firms often attract the best ex-government people to take up directorships or to head liaison with government. Their contacts and knowledge of the inside workings of purchasing decisions, with the political complications, can be very valuable. A similar logic often applies to pharmaceutical companies, airlines and regulated companies.
- ***Reputation*** Reputations are normally made over a long period. Once a good reputation is established it can be a source of very high returns (assuming that all the necessary ordinary resources are in place to support it). With car hire in a foreign country the consumer is unable to assess quality in advance. Hertz provides certification for local traders under a franchise arrangement.

These local car hirers would see no benefit to providing an above-average service without the certification of Hertz because they would not be able to charge a premium price.[2] It is surprising how much more consumers are willing to pay for the assurance of reliable and efficient car hire when they travel abroad compared with the cost of hiring a car from an unfranchised local company. Companies pay a large premium to hire Goldman Sachs when contemplating an issue of securities or a merger. They are willing to pay for 'emotional reassurance'.[3] The CEO cannot be sure of the outcome of the transaction. If it were to fail the penalty would be high – executives may lose bonuses, and, perhaps their jobs, shareholders lose money. The CEO therefore hires the best that is available for such once-in-a-lifetime moves. The cost of this hand-holding is secondary. Once an adviser has a history of flawless handling of large and complex transactions it can offer a much more effective 'emotional comfort-blanket'[4] to CEOs than smaller rivals. This principle may apply to pension fund advisers, management consultants and advertising agencies as well as top investment bankers. Perhaps the most important manifestation of the importance of reputation is branding. Branded products live or die by reputation. A strong brand can be incredibly valuable.

- ***Attitude*** Attitude refers to the mentality of the organisation. It is the prevalent outlook. It is the way in which the organisation views and relates to the world. Terms such as disposition, will and culture are closely connected with attitude. Every sports coach is aware of the importance of attitude. The team may consist of players with the best technique in the business or with a superb knowledge of the game, they may be the fastest and the most skilful, but without a winning attitude they will not succeed. There must be a will to win. Attitude can become entrenched within an organisation. It is difficult to shake off a negative attitude. A positive attitude can provide a significant competitive edge. Some firms develop a winning mentality based on a culture of innovation, others are determinedly orientated towards customer satisfaction while some companies are quality driven. 3M has a pervasive attitude of 'having a go'. Testing out wild ideas is encouraged. Employees are given time to follow up a dreamed-up innovation, and they are not criticised for failing. Innovations such as 'Post-it' notes have flowed from this attitude. Canon has the attitude of *Tsushin* – 'heart-to-heart and mind-to-mind communication' between the firm and its customers. In this way trust is developed.
- ***Capabilities*** Capabilities are derived from the company's ability to undertake a set of tasks. The term 'skill' can be used to refer to a narrow activity or a single task. Capability is used for the combination of a number of skills.[5] For example, a company's capability base could include abilities in narrow areas such as market research, innovative design and efficient manufacturing that, when combined, result in a superior capability in new product development. A capability is more than the sum of the individual processes – the combination and co-ordination of individual processes may provide an extraordinary resource. Sony developed a capability in miniaturisation. This enabled it to produce a string of products from the Walkman to the Playstation.
- ***Knowledge*** Knowledge is the awareness of information, and its interpretation, organisation, synthesis and prioritisation, to provide insights and understanding. The retention, exploitation and sharing of knowledge can be extremely important in the achievement and maintenance of competitive advantage. All firms in an industry possess basic knowledge. For example, all publishers have some knowledge of market trends, distribution techniques and printing technology. It is not this common knowledge that I am referring to in the context of extraordinary resources. If a publisher builds up data and skills in understanding a particular segment of the market, say investments books, then its superior awareness, interpretation, organisation, synthesis, and prioritisation of information can create competitive advantage through extraordinary knowledge. The company will have greater insight than rivals into this segment of the market. There are two types of organisational knowledge. The first, *explicit* knowledge, can be formalised and passed on in

---

[2] Kay (1993).

[3] Martin, P. (1998) 'Goldman's goose', *Financial Times*, 11 August, p. 14. Explains why Goldman Sachs can charge a large amount for advice.

[4] Ibid.

[5] De Wit and Meyer (2004).

codified form. This is objective knowledge that can be defined and documented. The second, *tacit* knowledge, is ill-defined or undefined. It is subjective, personal and context specific. It is fuzzy and complex. It is hard to formalise and communicate. Examples of explicit knowledge include costing procedures written in company accounting manuals, formal assessment of market demand, customer complaint data and classification. Explicit knowledge is unlikely to provide competitive advantage: if it is easily defined and codified it is likely to be available to rivals. Tacit knowledge, on the other hand, is very difficult for rivals to obtain. Consider the analogy of a football player: explicit knowledge of tactics is generally available; what separates the excellent from the ordinary player is the application of tacit knowledge, e.g. what becomes an instinctive ability to recognise types of play and the appropriate response to them. Tacit knowledge is transmitted by doing; the main means of transferring knowledge from one individual to another is through close interaction to build understanding, as in the master–apprentice relationship.

If you would like to delve more deeply into competitive resource analysis there are fuller discussions in Arnold (2002: Chapter 10) and Arnold (2004: Chapter 15).

3 Life-cycle stage of value potential

A competitive advantage in an attractive industry will not lead to superior long-term performance unless it provides a *sustainable* competitive advantage and the economics of the industry *remains* favourable. Rival firms will be attracted to an industry in which the participants enjoy high returns and sooner or later competitive advantage is usually whittled away. The longevity of the competitive advantage can be represented in terms of a life cycle with four stages: development, growth, maturity and decline (*see* **Exhibit 16.6**). In the development phase during which competitive advantage (and often the industry) is established, perhaps through technological or service innovation, the sales base will be small. As demand increases a growth phase is entered in which competitive strength is enhanced by factors such as industry leadership, brand strength and patent rights. A lengthy period of competitive advantage and high return can be expected. Eventually the sources of advantage are removed; perhaps by competitor imitation, or by customers and suppliers gaining in bargaining power. Other possibilities pushing towards the maturity stage are technological breakthroughs by competitors able to offer a superior product, or poor management leading to a loss of grip on cost control. Whatever the reason for the reduction in the performance spread, the firm now faces a choice of three routes, two of which can lead to a repositioning on the life cycle; the third is to enter a period of negative performance spreads. The two positive actions are (**a**) to erect barriers and deterrents to the entry of firms to the industry. Barriers put in the path of the outsiders make it difficult for those insects to advance on your honey pot. Also, a clear

Exhibit 16.6 The life-cycle stages of value creation

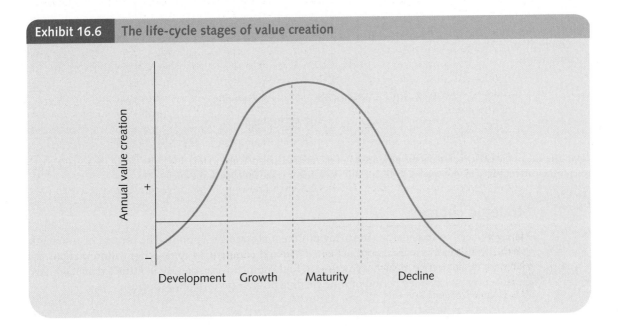

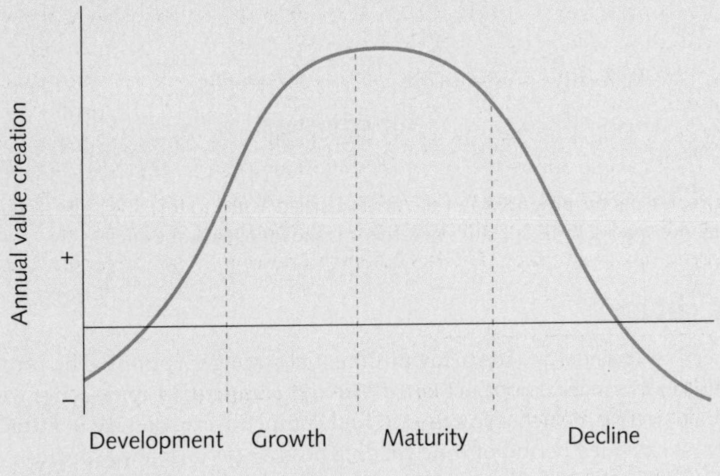

message could go out to the aspiring entrant that if they did dare to cross the threshold they will be subject to a massive retaliatory attack until they are driven out again, and (**b**) continually to innovate and improve the SBU's product offering so as to stay one step ahead of the competitors. An example of the simultaneous use of those two actions is provided by Microsoft. It is able to dominate the operating software market and the application market because of the network effect of its Office system being a standard system used throughout the world and because of its close working relationships with hardware producers; thus making life very difficult for any potential new entrant. It is also pumping billions into new products – it has thousands of software engineers. But even Microsoft will find its business units eventually fall into a terminal decline phase of value creation because of a loss of competitive advantage. When it does, even though it will be extremely difficult for it to do so, the company must withdraw from value-destructive activities and plough the capital retrieved into positive performance-spread SBUs.

Strategy planes

The three elements of strategic assessment can be summarised on a **strategy planes chart** like the one shown in **Exhibit 16.7** for Red plc which, besides the plastics SBU, also has a young Internet games division, a coal-mining subsidiary, a publishing group with valuable long-term copyrights on dozens of best sellers, a supermarket chain subject to increasingly intense competition in an over-supplied market and a small airline company with an insignificant market share. The strategy planes framework can be used at the SBU level or can be redrawn for product/customer segments within SBUs.

Exhibit 16.7 Strategy planes

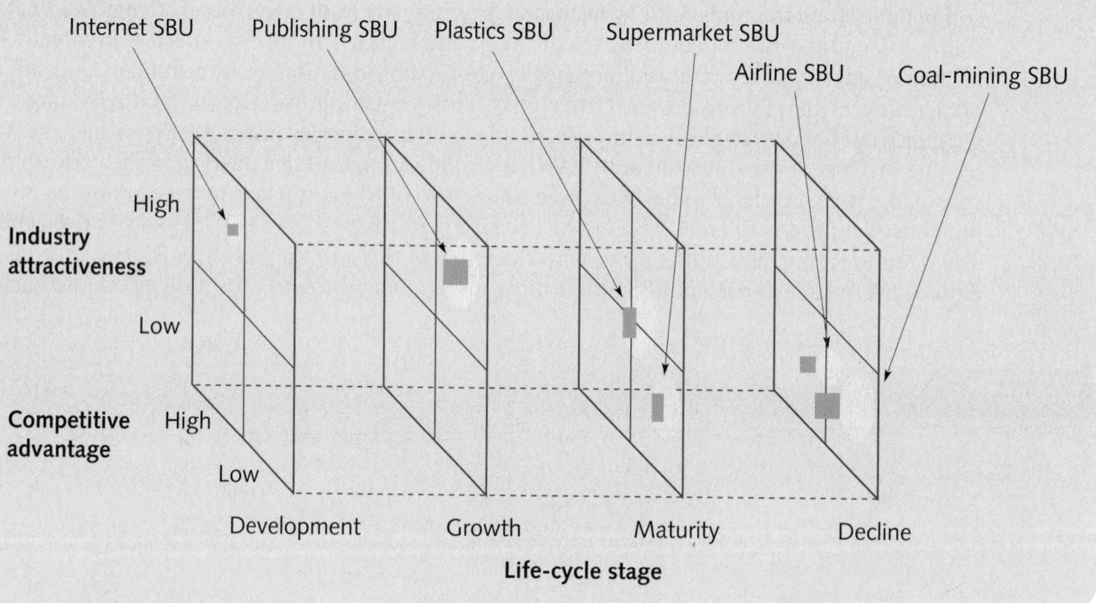

Note: The size of the circle represents the proportion of the firm's assets devoted to this SBU. The size of the rectangle represents the current performance spread. If the spread is negative it is shown outside the circle.

Strategic choice

Managers need to consider a wide array of potential strategic options. The process of systematic search for alternative market product entry/exit and competitive approaches within markets is a vital one. The objective of such a search is to find competitive advantage in attractive markets sustainable over an extended period of time yielding positive performance spreads.

There are two proven types of strategies to achieve sustainable competitive advantage:

- *A cost leadership strategy* – a standard no-frills product. The emphasis here is on scale economies or other cost advantages.
- *A differentiation strategy* – the uniqueness of the product/service offering allows for a premium price to be charged.

To fall between these two stools can be disastrous.

Once a sufficiently wide-ranging search for possible strategic directions has been conducted the options that come to the fore need to be evaluated. They are usually considered in broad descriptive terms using qualitative analysis with written reports and reflective thought. This qualitative thinking has valuable attributes such as creativity, intuition and judgement in the original formulation of strategic options, the assessment of their merits and in the subsequent reiterations of the process. The qualitative strategy evaluation is complemented by a quantitative examination for which accounting terms such as profit, earnings per share (eps), return on capital employed (ROCE) and balance sheet impact are traditionally used. This has the advantage of presenting the strategic plans in the same format that the directors use to present annual results to shareholders. However, these metrics do not accurately reflect the shareholder value to be generated from alternative strategic plans. The value-based metrics such as economic profit and discounted cash flow described in the next chapter are more appropriate.

Exhibit 16.8 shows the combination of qualitative assessment and quantitative analysis of strategic options. When a shortlist of high-value-creating strategies has been identified, sensitivity and scenario analysis of the kinds described in Chapter 6 can be applied to discover the vulnerability of the 'most likely' outcome to changes in the input factors such as level of sales or cost of

Exhibit 16.8 Strategy formulation and evaluation

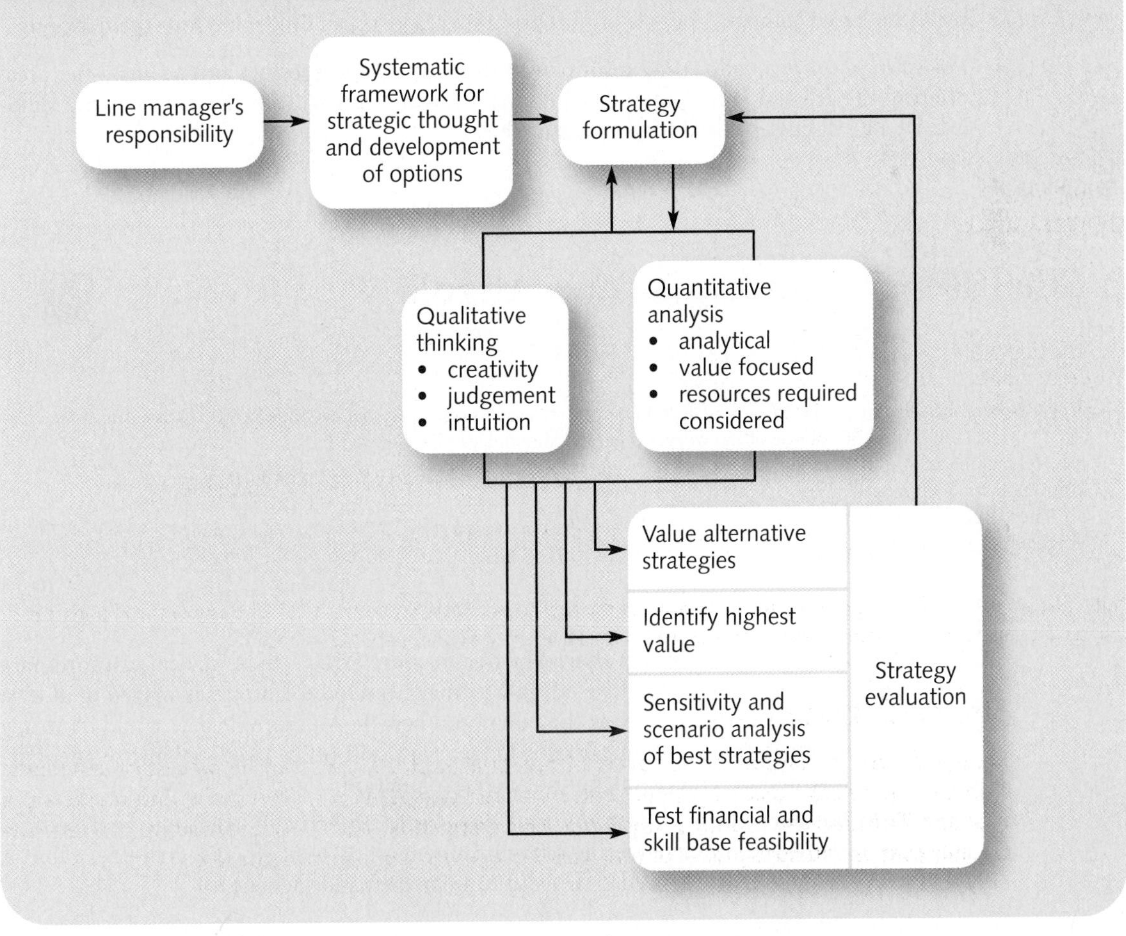

materials. The company also needs to consider whether it has the financial resources necessary to fund the strategy. The issues of finance raising, debt levels and dividend policy come into the equation at this point. Other aspects of feasibility include whether the organisation has the skill base necessary to provide the required quality of product or service, whether it is able to gain access to the required technology, materials, services and so on.

Strategy implementation

Making the chosen strategy work requires the planned allocation of resources and the reorganisation and motivation of people. The firm's switch to value-based principles has an impact on these implementation issues. Resources are to be allocated to units or functions if it can be shown that they will contribute to value creation after taking into account the quantity of resources used. Managers are given responsibilities and targets are set in accordance with value creation.

Corporate strategy

So far the firm has been described as consisting of a group of strategic business units. So where does the head office fit into this picture if each of these units has a separately identifiable market and is capable of independent strategic action?

We know that companies need to apply value-based principles to all their activities and so this must include the centre. Everything the head office does must create value for shareholders. This means there must be awareness of the quantity of assets used in each task and the return generated by those assets in that task. Many companies fail to think this through; head office costs spiral as new activities are taken to the centre to add to those traditionally carried out, without thought as to whether these tasks are (**a**) necessary, or (**b**) if necessary, most efficiently executed by the centre.

In a value-based company the role of the corporate centre (head office) has four main aspects:

1 ***Portfolio planning*** – allocating resources to those SBUs and product and/or customer areas offering the greatest value creation while withdrawing capital from those destroying value. Exhibit 16.9 discusses this kind of action at Shell.

Exhibit 16.9

Shell all but withdraws from Angola

FT

By Carola Hoyos

Royal Dutch/Shell, Europe's second-largest listed energy group, has all but bowed out of one of the world's biggest new oil regions, selling its stake in a key field in the waters off Angola for \$600m (£327m).

The company said: 'We don't have critical mass in Angola. The funds will be reinvested in other parts of the business where we believe higher returns for our shareholders can be achieved.'

Source: Financial Times, 10 April 2004, p. M5. Reprinted with permission.

2 ***Managing strategic value drivers shared by two or more SBUs*** – these crucial extraordinary resources, giving the firm competitive advantage, may need to be centrally managed or at least co-ordinated by the centre to achieve the maximum benefit. An example here could be strong brand management or technological knowledge. The head office needs to ensure adequate funding of these and to achieve full, but not over-exploitation.

3 ***Providing the pervading philosophy and governing objective*** – training, goal setting, employee rewards and the engendering of commitment are all focused on shareholder value. A strong lead from the centre is needed to avoid conflict, drift and vagueness.

4 ***The overall structure of the organisation*** needs to be appropriate for the market environment and designed to build value. Roles and responsibilities are clearly defined with clear accountability for value creation.

We can apply the principles of portfolio planning to Red plc. The corporate centre could encourage and work with the plastics division in developing ideas for reducing or eliminating the value losses being made on some of its products and markets – recall (from Exhibits 16.2 and 16.3 earlier in this chapter) that it is destroying value in product line C and in sales to UK industrial customers and the UK government. Once these have been fully evaluated head office could ensure that resources and other services are provided effectively to implement the chosen strategy. For example, if the highest value-creating option is gradually to withdraw capital from product line C and to apply the funds saved to product line A, the management team at C are likely to become demotivated as they reduce the resources under their command and experience lower sales (and profit) rather than, the more natural predisposition of managers, a rising trend. The centre can help this process by changing the targets and incentives of these managers away from growth and empire building towards shareholder value.

On the level of corporate-wide resource allocation, the directors of Red plc have a great deal of work to do. The publishing division is already creating high value from its existing activities and yet it is still in the early growth phase. The subsidiary management team believe that significant benefits would flow from buying rights to other novels and children's stories. By combining these with its present 'stable' it could enter more forcefully into negotiations with book retailers, television production companies wishing to make screen versions of its stories and merchandising companies intending to put the image of some of the famous characters on articles ranging from T-shirts to drink cans. This strategy will involve the purchase of rights from individual authors as well as the acquisition of firms quoted on the stock exchange. It will be costly and require a substantial shift of resources within the firm. But, as can be seen from **Exhibit 16.10**, the value created makes the change attractive.

The Internet division has been put on a tight rein in terms of financial resources for its first three years because of the high risk attached to businesses involved in speculative innovation in this market. However, the energetic and able managers have created a proven line of services that have a technological lead over competitors, a high market share and substantial barriers to entry in the form of copyrights and patents. The directors decide to expand this area.

Exhibit 16.10 Using strategy plane analysis. Red plc's shifting strategic plan

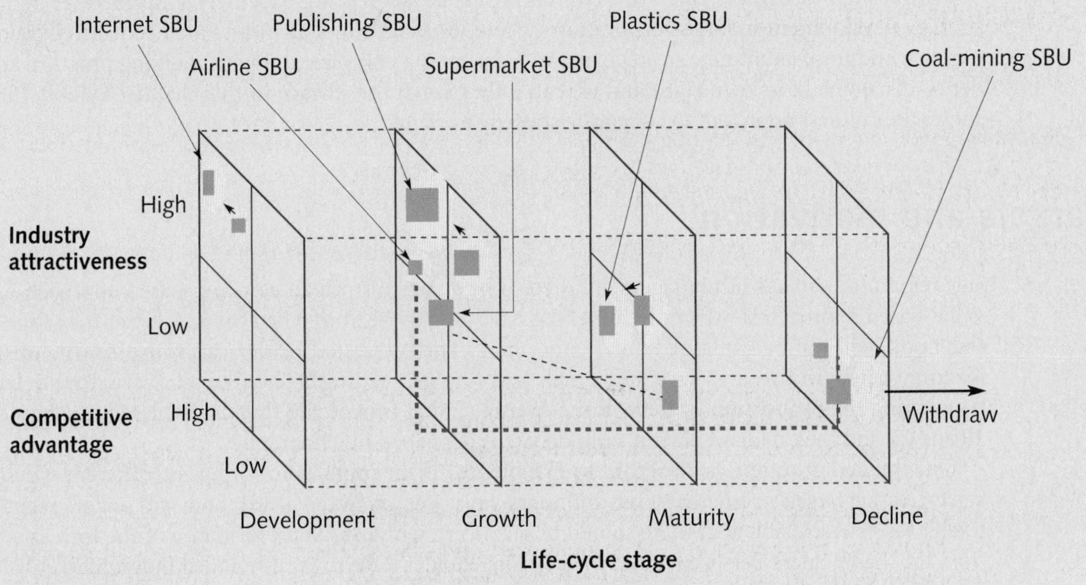

Note: The size of the circle represents the proportion of the firm's assets devoted to this SBU. The size of the rectangle represents the current performance spread. If the spread is negative it is shown outside the circle.

The plastics division as a whole is in a mature market with positive but gradually declining performance spreads. Here the strategic approach is to reduce the number of product lines competing on cost and transfer resources to those niche markets where product differentiation allows a premium price to be charged. The intention is to move gradually to a higher competitive advantage overall but accept that industry attractiveness will decline. Overall resources dedicated to this division will remain approximately constant, but the directors will be watching for deterioration greater than that anticipated in the current plan.

The supermarket division is currently producing a positive performance spread but a prolonged price war is forecast for the industry, to be followed by a shake-out, leading to a withdrawal of many of the current firms. Some directors are in favour of supporting this division vigorously through the troublesome times ahead in the expectation that when many of the weaker players have left the field, margins will rise to abnormally high levels – producing large performance spreads and high value in the long run. In terms of the value-creating life cycle this SBU would be shifted from the maturity strategy plane to the growth plane (shown in Exhibit 16.10). Other directors are not willing to take the risk that their firm will not be one of the survivors from the battle for market share. Furthermore, they argue that even if they do win, the enormous resources required, over the next five years, will produce a value return less than that on the publishing or Internet SBUs. Therefore, if financial resources are to be constrained, they should put money into these 'star' divisions.

The coal-mining division is haemorrhaging money. The industry is in terminal decline because of the high cost of coal extraction and the increasing tendency for the electricity-generating companies to source their coal needs from abroad. Moreover, Red is a relatively small player in this market and lacks the economies of scale to compete effectively. To add insult to injury a large proportion of the corporation's capital is tied up in the coal stockpiles required by the electricity firms. The decision is taken to withdraw from this industry and the best approach to achieve this is investigated – sale to a competitor or liquidation.

The airline operation has never made a satisfactory return and is resented by the managers in other divisions as a drain on the value they create. However, the recent deregulation of air travel and especially the opening up of landing slots at major European airports has presented an important new opportunity. Despite being one of the smallest operators and therefore unable to compete on price, it provides a level of service which has gained it a high reputation with business travellers. This, combined with its other major value driver, the strength of its marketing team, leads the divisional managers and the once sceptical directors to conclude that a sufficiently high premium ticket price can be charged to produce a positive performance spread. The new European rules enable the division to be placed on the growth plane as the spread is thought to be sustainable for some time.

The analysis in Exhibit 16.10 of Red's corporate strategy is an extremely simplified version of strategy development in large corporations where thousands of staff-hours are needed to develop, evaluate and implement new strategic plans. Strategy is a complex and wide-ranging practical academic discipline in its own right and we can only scratch the surface in this chapter. **Exhibit 16.11** shows the ruthless approach to corporate strategy by Sanyo.

Targets and motivation

The remaining aspects of management affected by a switch from an earnings-based approach to a value-based approach shown in Exhibit 16.1 have already been touched on and, given the scope of this book, will not be explained any further here. The interested reader can consult some of the leading writers in this area (*see* References and further reading). The financial structure debate concerning the proportion of debt in the overall capital mix of the firm is discussed in Chapters 19 and 21 and the dividend payout ratio debate is described in Chapter 22.

One final point to note with regard to Exhibit 16.1 is the importance of having different types of value-creating targets at different levels within the organisation. At the board room and senior executive level it seems reasonable that there should be a concern with overall performance of the firm as seen from the shareholders' perspective and so Total Shareholder Return, Wealth Added Index, Market Value Added and Market to Book Ratio (metrics described in Chapter 18) would be important guides to performance, and incentive schemes would be (at least partially) based upon them. Economic Profit,

Exhibit 16.11

The Japanese art of performance

FT

Sanyo has achieved record results and market dominance by adopting a rigorous GE-style investment strategy

writes Michiyo Nakamoto

Ask any Japanese business executive which company he or she considers a role model and the chances are high they will name General Electric.

While few companies in Japan have come anywhere near matching GE's impressive record, Sanyo Electric has been compared to the US conglomerate for a distinctly un-Japanese strategy: its habit of rapidly ditching businesses that fail to perform.

The consumer electronics maker has recently transformed itself from an industry also-ran, best known for its low prices, to a technology powerhouse focused on businesses where it has leadership in global markets.

Sanyo is the world's largest maker of digital still cameras, with a 30 per cent share of the market. It leads the global market in optical pick-ups – key components of CD and DVD players – with its 40 per cent share and has the top share in some 40 types of semiconductor. Sanyo's rechargeable batteries dominate the market and can be found in half the world's mobile phones . . .

Yukinori Kuwano, Sanyo's chief executive, has led the group's makeover alongside Satoshi Iue, chairman, and attributes Sanyo's recent success to its recent efforts to be selective about where it puts its resources.

'Our main aim [has been] to focus on products that we are number one in globally,' says a smiling Mr Kuwano. 'Unless you choose what to focus on you will not be able to survive.'

For many Japanese companies, this is easier said than done. Resistance to business closures is so strong that, even after a decade of restructuring, many electronics companies still retain unprofitable businesses that are not central to their overall strategy.

In contrast, Sanyo has adopted a system that rates its businesses according to margins and growth potential. Those offering low margins and low growth prospects become candidates for weeding out. 'It's easy to say "concentrate and select", but you need a standard for doing so,' says Mr Kuwano.

Once a business is identified as a 'loser' managers go through a lengthy process of debate about what to do with it. When, for instance, Sanyo decided it had to do something about a loss-making vending machine business that was number two in its market, managers considered several options, including an acquisition of one of its rivals, before deciding to sell the business to its leading competitor.

At the same time Sanyo led the market in rechargeable batteries. Since this was a promising sector it decided to bolster its position by acquiring Nippon Batteries' lithium ion battery business and Toshiba's nickel metal hydride business.

Sanyo has thus managed to streamline its businesses relatively quickly while ensuring staff clearly understand the rationale behind the decisions. Mr Kuwano says divisional leaders are given a final chance if their businesses fail the survival test. Charge-coupled devices were one such business, 'which died many times,' he says. That was before camera-equipped mobile phones, which use Sanyo's smaller-sized CCDs, became hugely popular . . .

Source: Financial Times, 18 May 2004, p. 12. Reprinted with permission.

Economic Value Added, Discounted Cash Flow and Shareholder Value Analysis are also useful guides for senior managers. These metrics are described and critically assessed in the next chapter.

Moving down the organisation, target setting and rewards need to be linked to the level of control and responsibility over outcomes. Strategic business unit performance needs to be expressed in terms of value metrics such as Discounted Cash Flow, Economic Profit and Economic Value Added. Outcomes here are usually under the control of divisional and other middle-ranking managers and so the reward system might be expressed in terms of achieving targets expressed in these metrics. At the operating level where a particular function contributes to value creation but the managers in that function have no control over the larger value centre itself, perhaps the emphasis should shift to rewarding high performance in particular operational value drivers such as throughput of customers, reduced staff turnover, cost of production, faster debtor turnover, etc. *See* **Case study 16.1**.

Key rule: All managers should agree to both short- and long-term targets. This counters the natural tendency in all of us to focus on short-term goals that might not be optimal in the long run.

Case study 16.1 Strategy, planning and budgeting at Lloyds TSB

Although business units are responsible for their own strategy development, the Lloyds TSB group provides guidelines on how strategy should be developed. . . . These unit plans are then consolidated into an aggregate plan for the value centre. The process undertaken is then subjected to scrutiny by the centre. The strategic planning process consists of five stages:

1 ***Position assessment***. Business units are required to perform a value-based assessment of the economics of the market in which the business operates and of the relative competitive position of the business within that market. Market attractiveness and competitive position must include a numerical rather than a purely qualitative assessment.
2 ***Generate alternative strategies***. Business units are required to develop a number of realistic and viable alternatives.
3 ***Evaluate alternative strategies***. Business units are required to perform shareholder value calculations in order to prioritise alternatives. Even if a potential strategy has a high positive net present value, this does not necessarily mean that it will be accepted. An assessment of project risk or do-ability is overlaid across the net present value calculations.
4 ***Agree chosen strategy with the centre***. Whilst it is perceived to be vital that the managers who best understand their business are given sufficient authority to develop strategies which they consider to be most appropriate, it is nevertheless considered equally important that there is a challenge mechanism at the centre to ensure that appropriate analyses have been performed and assumptions made are credible.
5 ***The chosen strategy becomes a contract***. Once the preferred strategy has been agreed with the centre, resource allocation and milestones are agreed. Budgetary performance targets are derived from the projections included within the strategic plan. Beyond this, however, business unit managers are free to choose whatever structures and performance indicators are considered to be relevant and appropriate.

Source: M. Davies (2000), 'Lessons from practice: VBM at Lloyds TSB', in G. Arnold and M. Davies (eds), *Value-Based Management*. Chichester: John Wiley & Sons.

Concluding comments

A commercial organisation that adopts value principles is one that has an important additional source of strength. The rigorous thought process involved in the robust application of these principles will force managers to review existing systems and product and market strategies and to bring an insistence on a contribution to shareholder value from all parts of the company. A firm that has failed to ask the right questions of its operating units or to use the correct metrics in measuring performance will find its position deteriorating *vis-à-vis* its competitors.

Key points and concepts

- **Switching to value-based management principles affects many aspects of the organisation**. These include:
  - strategic business unit strategy and structure;
  - corporate strategy;
  - culture;
  - systems and processes;
  - incentives and performance measurement;
  - financial policies.
- **A strategic business unit (SBU)** is a business unit within the overall corporate entity which is distinguishable from other business units because it serves a defined external market in which management can conduct strategic planning in relation to products and markets.

- **Strategy** means selecting which product or market areas to enter/exit and how to ensure a good competitive position in those markets or products.
- **SBU managers** should be involved in strategy development because **a** they usually have great knowledge to contribute, and **b** they will have greater 'ownership' of the subsequently chosen strategy.
- **A review of current SBU** activities using **value-creation profile charts** may reveal particular product or customer categories that destroy wealth.
- **Strategic analysis** has three stages:
  - strategic assessment;
  - strategic choice;
  - strategic implementation.
- **Strategic assessment** focuses on the three determinants of value creation:
  - industry attractiveness;
  - competitive resources;
  - life-cycle stage of value potential.
- **Competitive resource analysis** can be conducted using the **TRRACK system**:
  - Tangible
  - Relationships
  - Reputation
  - Attitude
  - Capabilities
  - Knowledge
- A company's SBU positions with regard to the three value-creation factors could be represented in a **strategy planes diagram**. The product and/or market segment within SBUs can also be shown on strategy planes.
- To make good **strategic choices** a wide search for alternatives needs to be encouraged.
- **Sustainable competitive advantage** is obtainable in two ways:
  - cost leadership;
  - differentiation.
- In the **evaluation of strategic options** both qualitative judgement and quantitative valuation are important. The shortlisted options can be tested in sensitivity and scenario analysis as well as for financial and skill-base feasibility.
- **Strategy implementation** is making the chosen strategy work through the planned allocation of resources and the reorganisation and motivation of people.
- The **corporate centre** has four main roles in a value-based firm:
  - portfolio planning;
  - managing strategic value drivers shared by SBUs;
  - providing and inculcating the pervading philosophy and governing objective;
  - structuring the organisation so that rules and responsibilities are clearly defined, with clear accountability for value creation.
- **Targets, incentives and rewards** should be based on metrics appropriate to the level of management within the firm as shown in **Exhibit 16.12**.

Exhibit 16.12

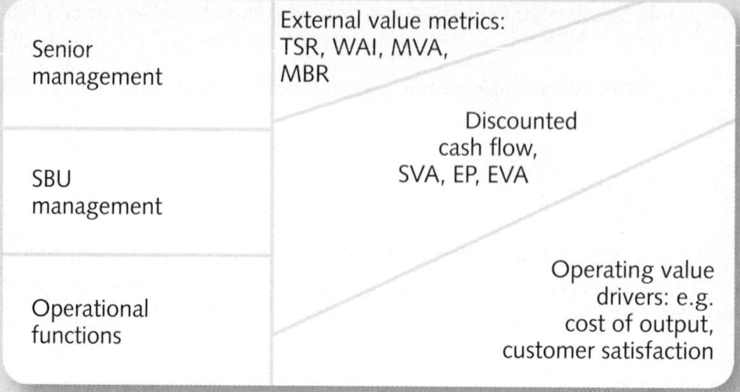

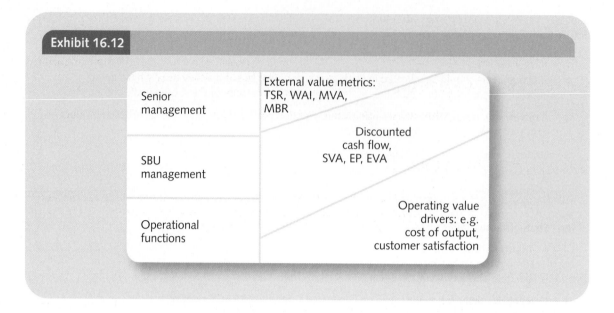

References and further reading

Arnold, G. (2002) *Valuegrowth Investing*. London: Financial Times Prentice Hall.
An integration of strategic analysis with equity market investment principles.

Arnold, G.C. (2004) *The Financial Times Guide to Investing*. London: Financial Times Prentice Hall.
Contains chapters on strategic evaluation of companies

Arnold, G.C. and Davies, M. (eds) (2000) *Value-Based Management*. Chichester: John Wiley.
A collection of research monographs describing practical and theoretical issues in this field.

Buffett, W. (1984) *Berkshire Hathaway Annual Report*. Omaha, NE: Berkshire Hathaway.
As with all reports by Buffett, this one is full of profound and witty insight. www.berkshirehathaway.com.

Collis, D.J. and Montgomery, C.A. (2005) *Corporate Strategy: A resource-based approach*. 2nd edn. New York: McGraw Hill.
A very important and easy-to-read book on the subject of resources of companies.

Cornelius, I. and Davies, M. (1997) *Shareholder Value*. London: Financial Times: Financial Publishing.
A good account of value-based management and the metrics used.

Davies, M. (2000) 'Lessons from Practice: VBM at Lloyds TSB', in G.C. Arnold and M. Davies (eds) *Value-Based Management*. Chichester: John Wiley & Sons.
Insights into a company making use of VBM principles.

Davies, M., Arnold, G.C., Cornelius, I. and Walmsley, S. (2001) *Managing for Shareholder Value*. London: Informa.
An overview of shareholder value management for practitioners.

De Wit, B. and Meyer, R. (2004) *Strategy: Process, Content, Context*. 3rd edn. Cincinnati, OH: South-Western College Publishers.
Some interesting sections in a very long book.

Johnson, G. and Scholes, K. (2006) *Exploring Corporate Strategy*. 7th edn. Harlow: Pearson Education.
A well-regarded introductory textbook to the strategic management of firms.

Kay, J. (1993) *Foundations of Corporate Success*. New York: Oxford University Press.
A study of corporate strategy.

McKinsey (Koller, T., Goedhart, M., and Wessels, D.) (2005) *Valuation*. 4th edn. New York: John Wiley & Sons.
The management of value-based organisations and the principles behind the techniques are explained well.

McTaggart, J.M., Kontes, P.W. and Mankins, M.C. (1994) *The Value Imperative*. New York: Free Press.
A very good book showing the application of value-based techniques to strategy and other disciplines.

Porter, M.E. (1980) *Competitive Strategy*. New York: Free Press.
One of the most important books on strategy ever written.

Porter, M.E. (1985) *Competitive Advantage*. New York: Free Press.
More valuable insight into strategic analysis.

Prahalad, C.K. and Hamel, G. (1990) 'The core competence of the corporation', *Harvard Business Review*, Vol. 68, No. 3, May–June, pp. 79–91.
A paper that led to increased interest in seeing the corporation as a collection of resources, some of which are extraordinary.

Rappaport, A. (1998) *Creating Shareholder Value*. Revised and updated edition. New York: Free Press.

A landmark book. Presents an important value metric – shareholder value analysis.

Reimann, B.C. (1989) *Managing for Value*. Oxford: Basil Blackwell.

Useful because it brings together strategy and value.

Stewart, G.B. (1991) *The Quest for Value*. New York: Harper Business.

Written by a founding partner in Stern Stewart & Co., the US consultancy, which has so successfully promoted MVA and EVA. Some useful insights.

Video presentations

Chief executives and finance directors describe their current thinking on the strategy they are pursuing (you can check on previous year's video presentation to see how consistent they are) on Cantos.com (www.cantos.com/cantos) – free to view.

Website

Stern Stewart www.sternstewart.com. Contains some useful additional literature.

Case study recommendation

Please see www.pearsoned.co.uk/arnold for case study synopses

- New World Development Co. Ltd: Diversify or Focus? Authors: Mary Ho, Su Han Chan and Ko Wang (2001) Centre for Asian Business Cases, School of Business, The University of Hong Kong (available via Harvard Business School case study website).

Self-review questions

1 List the main areas in which value principles have an impact on the managerial process. Write a sentence explaining each one.

2 What is an SBU and how can a value-creation profile chart be used to improve on an SBU's performance?

3 List the three stages of strategic analysis and briefly describe the application of value-based management ideas to each one.

4 Invent a company and show how the strategy planes diagram can be used to enhance shareholder wealth. Explain each dimension of the planes as you do so.

5 Briefly describe the main roles of the corporate centre in a value-led organisation.

Questions and problems

myfinancelab **Questions with an icon are also available for practice in MyFinanceLab with additional supporting resources.**

1 (*Examination level*) Imagine you are an expert on finance and strategy and have been asked by a large company with subsidiaries operating in a variety of industrial sectors to explain how the organisation might be changed by the adoption of value principles. Write a report to convince the managerial team that the difficulties and expense of transformation will be worth it.

2 In the form of an essay discuss the links between strategy and finance with reference to value-based management principles.

3 Payne plc has six SBUs engaged in different industrial sectors:

	Proportion of firm's capital	Annual value creation (£m)
1 Glass production	0.20	3
2 Bicycles retailing	0.15	10
3 Forestry	0.06	2
4 Electrical goods manufacture	0.20	5
5 Car retailing	0.25	–1
6 Road surfacing	0.14	–10

Make assumptions (and explain them) about the industry attractiveness and competitive position of Payne and its stage in the life-cycle of value potential. Place the SBUs on a strategy planes diagram. Explain and show how you would alter the portfolio of the company.

4 'The corporate centre in most firms is an expensive drag on the rest of the organisation.' Explain to this sceptical head of an SBU how the corporate centre can contribute to value creation.

myfinancelab **Now retake your diagnostic test for Chapter 16 to check your progress and update your study plan.**

Assignments

1 Identify an SBU in a company you know well. Conduct a value-based analysis and write a report showing the current position and your recommendations for change. Include in the analysis value-creation profile charts, strategy planes diagrams, sources of competitive advantage (value drivers) and qualitative evaluation of strategies.

2 Write a report for senior managers pointing out how incentive schemes within the firm should be changed to achieve goal congruence around shareholder wealth maximisation.

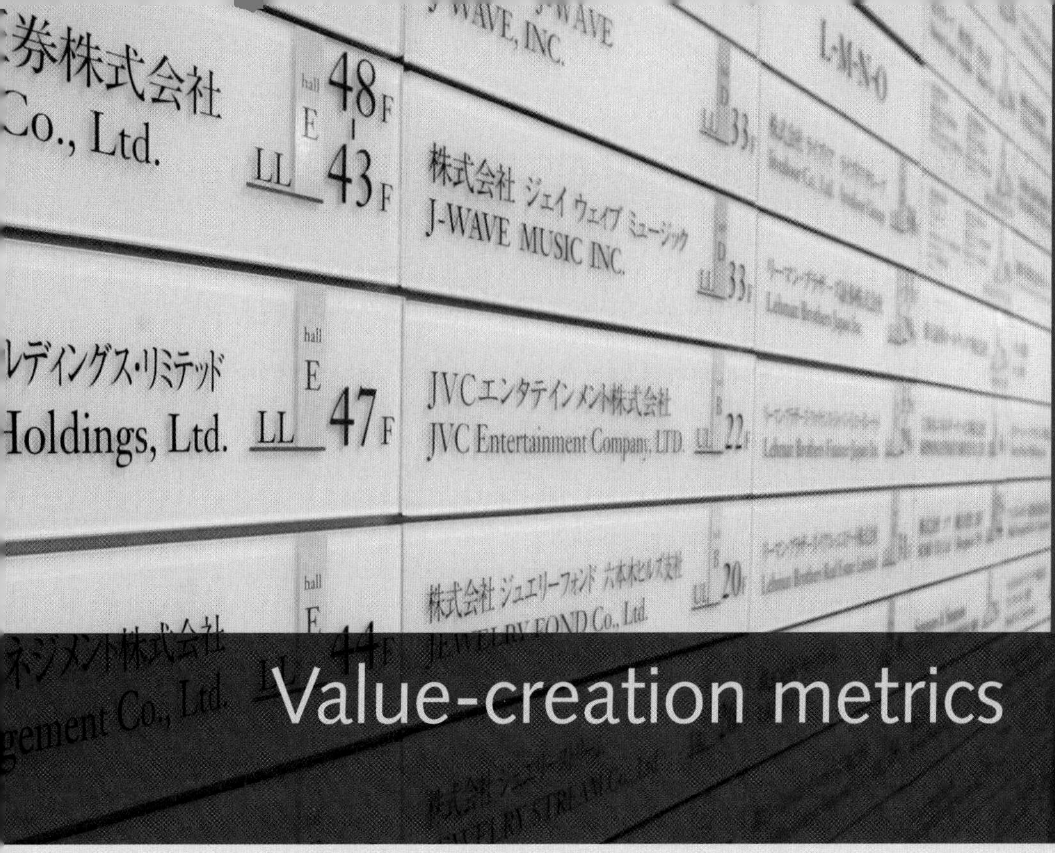

CHAPTER
17

Value-creation metrics

LEARNING OUTCOMES

By the end of this chapter the reader should be able to:

- describe, explain and use the following measures of value:
  - discounted cash flow
  - shareholder value analysis
  - economic profit;
- provide a brief outline of economic value added and cash flow return on investment (CFROI).

myfinancelab — *Complete your diagnostic test for Chapter 17 now to create your personal study plan*

Introduction

Managers at all levels need to establish plans for future actions. In drawing up these plans they need reliable measures of value to choose between alternative paths. The metrics discussed in this chapter are useful for this purpose.

Then, as strategic moves at both the corporate level and the business unit level unfold, managers need to monitor progress to see if they are still on track to create value. Again, these metrics can be useful. Targets can be set, and, as milestones are passed, incentive schemes can bestow a share of the value created on those responsible. The aim is to make sure every member of staff understands what value is, and each person becomes fully committed to creating it.

At each level of responsibility there should be knowledge of how much of the finance provider's cash has been used in an SBU, product line or project and the required rate of return on that capital. Everyone should know that extra rewards flow to those who help achieve returns above the required rate of return.

The metrics discussed in this chapter quantify the plan, targets and incentives to encourage high performance from the boardroom to the shopfloor. They can be used to judge the entire firm or just a small part of it.

Using cash flow to measure value

There are many measures of value promoted by different consultants. We discuss a number of them in this and the next chapter. There is hot debate between rival consultants as to which is the best for guiding managers seeking to create value. However they all agree that the measure that lies at the theoretical heart of all the others is discounted cash flow.

In Chapter 2 the value of an investment is described as the sum of the discounted cash flows (NPV). This principle was applied to the assessment of a new project: if the investment produced a rate of return greater than the finance provider's opportunity cost of capital it is wealth enhancing. The same logic can be applied to a range of different categories of business decisions, including:

- resource allocation;
- business unit strategies;
- corporate-level strategy;
- motivation, rewards and incentives.

Consider the figures for Gold plc in **Exhibit 17.1**. These could refer to the entire company. Alternatively the figures could be for a business unit predicated on the assumption of a particular strategy being pursued. Or they could be for a product line. (Note: to understand this chapter the reader needs the concepts and tools developed in Chapter 2 and its appendix. You may want to refresh your knowledge of basic discounted cash flow analysis before proceeding.)

In Exhibit 17.1 we start with forecasted profit figures and then make a number of adjustments to arrive at cash flow figures. This method is valuable because it reflects the corporate reality that forward estimates for business units are usually in the form of accounting budgets rather than cash flows, and managers need to know how to work from these numbers toward cash flow rather than starting from scratch to obtain reliable cash flow projections.

Profit figures are created after a number of deductions, such as depreciation, that do not affect the company's cash flow for the year. When an item is depreciated in the accounts profits are reduced but no cash is lost. It is only when capital items are paid for that cash actually flows out. To move towards cash flow we therefore add depreciation and other non-cash items that were deducted in calculating the future profit figures. Instead of depreciation we take away the amount that actually flows out each year for investment in fixed capital equipment such as factories, machinery and vehicles (fixed capital investment).

Exhibit 17.1 Gold plc forecast cash flows

Required rate of return = 12% per annum

Year	1	2	3	4	5	6	7	*8 and subsequent years*
	£	£	£	£	£	£	£	£
Forecast profits	1,000	1,100	1,100	1,200	1,300	1,450	1,600	1,600
Add book depreciation and other non-cash items (e.g. amortisation of goodwill)	500	600	800	800	800	800	800	800
Less fixed capital investment	−500	−3,000	−600	−600	−300	−600	−800	−800
Less additional investment in working capital*								
Inventory	50	−100	−70	−80	−50	−50	−50	0
Debtors	−20	−20	−20	−20	−20	−20	−20	0
Creditors	10	20	10	10	20	20	30	0
Cash	−10	−10	−10	−10	−10	−10	−10	0
Add interest previously charged to profit and loss account	100	150	200	200	200	200	200	200
Taxes	−300	−310	−310	−420	−450	−470	−550	−550
Cash flow	830	−1,570	1,100	1,080	1,490	1,320	1,200	1,250
Discounted cash flow	$\frac{830}{1.12}$	$-\frac{1,570}{(1.12)^2}$	$+\frac{1,100}{(1.12)^3}$	$+\frac{1,080}{(1.12)^4}$	$+\frac{1,490}{(1.12)^5}$	$+\frac{1,320}{(1.12)^6}$	$+\frac{1,200}{(1.12)^7}$	$+\frac{1,250}{0.12} \times \frac{1}{(1.12)^7}$
	741	−1,252	783	686	845	669	543	4,712

Note: * A positive figure for inventory, debtors and cash floats indicates cash released from these forms of investment. A negative figure indicates additional cash devoted to these areas. For creditors a positive figure indicates higher credit granted by suppliers and therefore a boost to cash flows.
An Excel spreadsheet version of this calculation is available at www.pearsoned.co.uk/arnold.

In drawing up the profit figures the accountant does not recognise the using up of shareholder's cash when inventory (e.g. raw materials stock) or debtors (granting credit to customers) are increased. The accountant observes one asset (cash in hand) being replaced by another (inventory, money owed by customers) and so there is no expense to deduct. However, the cash flow analyst sees cash being used for these items as the business grows and so makes an adjustment to the profit figures when deriving the cash flow numbers.

Similarly, if cash is tied up in cash floats to run the business (e.g. cash in the tills of a betting shop or food retailer) the fact that this cash is no longer available to shareholders needs to be recognised. So, if shareholders had to supply extra cash floats in a period this is deducted from the profit numbers when trying to get at cash flow.

Whether suppliers send input goods and services to this firm for payment on 'cash on delivery terms' or 'credit terms' the accountant, rightly, records the value of these as an expense, and deducts this from the profit and loss account, in the year of delivery and use. The cash flow analyst needs to make an adjustment here because the full amount of the expense may not yet have flowed out in cash. So, if creditor balances increase we need to recognise that the profit and loss account has overstated the outflow of cash. We need then to add back the extent to which the creditor amount outstanding has increased from the beginning of the year to the end to arrive at the cash flow figure.

We also add back the interest charged to profit because the 12 per cent discount rate already includes an allowance for the required return to lenders. To include a deduction for interest in calculating cash flow would be to double-count this element.

The cash flow figures at the bottom of the columns are sometimes referred to as '**free cash flow**'. That is, they represent the amount that is free to be paid out to the firm's investors (shareholders and debt holders). These amounts could be paid out without affecting future operating cash flows because the necessary investment for future growth in the form of fixed capital items and working capital (inventory, debtor, cash floats less trade credit) is already allowed for.

The total of the discounted cash flows provides us with a value of the SBU (or firm, etc.) after taking into account all the cash inflows/outflows and reducing those distant cash flows by the required rate of return (the opportunity cost of capital). This discount rate is based on a blend of the required return to shareholders' capital and the required return to debt holders' capital. Chapter 19 describes the logic behind the derivation of the discount rate, which is a weighted average of the required returns to equity and debt – the Weighted Average Cost of Capital or WACC.

By examining the discounted cash flow the SBU management and the firm's managing director can assess the value contribution of the SBU. The management team putting forward these projected cash flows could then be judged and rewarded on the basis of performance targets expressed in cash flow terms. On the other hand, the cash flows may refer to a particular product line or specific customer(s). At each of these levels of management a contribution to overall corporate value is expected.

The planning horizon[1] is seven years and so the present value of the future cash flows is:

Present value of cash flows within planning horizon	+	Present value of cash flows after planning horizon		
741 – 1,252 + 783 + 686 + 845 + 669 + 543	+	4,712		
£3,015	+	£4,712	=	£7,727

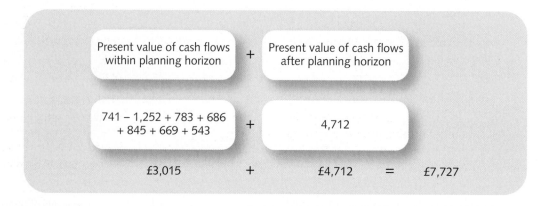

In analysis of this kind it is not unusual to find that most of the value arises after the planning horizon. However, bear in mind that it is the actions (strategic positioning, etc.) and the investments made within the planning horizon that creates the platform for these high post-planning-horizon free cash flows.

Note that in the case of Gold we have not shown a large initial cash outflow, unlike with the NPV calculations described in the first part of the book. This is to illustrate how you can use discounted cash flow analysis to analyse the future value (not *Net* present value) of an SBU, etc. that was established years before, and you do not have the start-up costs to consider – this type of analysis only considers the future cash inflows and outflows, not the bygone (sunk?) costs.

The value shown in the calculation based on one particular strategic direction (say, the result from Exhibit 17.1) can be compared with alternatives to see which is likely to provide the highest value. You could also conduct sensitivity and scenario analysis (*see* Chapter 6) to highlight areas of concern and in order that managerial attention may be directed to reduce the probability of a poor outcome.

[1] Discussed in Chapter 15.

Corporate value

If the SBU that we are valuing has other assets that are not used in the creation of operational free cash flow and those assets have a market value then we add this to the total of the discounted operational cash flow to arrive at the total firm value. For example, many firms hold portfolios of shares or bonds as investments with no connection to the firm's operations. The market value of these adds to the value of the firm derived from the operational free cash flow. Likewise, if a company owns an empty and unused factory which could be sold its value can be added to the total.

Corporate value (Enterprise value)	=	Present value of free cash flow from operations	+	Value of non-operating assets

Shareholder value from operations and total shareholder value

If the value of debt is deducted from the total present value from operations we derive the value belonging to shareholders from operations. So, if we assume that this SBU has £3,000 of debt the shareholder value before taking account of non-operating assets is £4,727.

Shareholder value from operations	=	Present value of free cash flow from operations	–	Debt
£4,727	=	£7,727	–	£3,000

The term 'debt' here extends beyond interest-bearing debt to finance lease obligations, underfunded pension plans and contingent liabilities.

If we now assume that this SBU has £800 of government bonds held as investments separate from operations and £600 of equity investment total shareholder value amounts to £6,127:

Total shareholder value	=	Shareholder value from operations	+	Value of non-operating assets
£6,127	=	£4,727	+	£1,400

Comparing the discounted free cash flows with alternatives

The figure of £4,727 is the shareholder value of all the future operating cash flows. An alternative course of action is to sell off the SBU's assets, either piecemeal or as a whole. We should compare these alternatives with the present value of continuing to own and run the business. The opportunity cost of following the strategy is the value of the best forgone alternative.

Real management is not about precise numbers – it's about what lies behind the numbers

By embarking on cash-flow-based analysis (or shareholder value analysis or economic profit analysis or economic value added analysis) the decision maker is forced to investigate and understand the underlying business. Only by thorough examination is he/she going to put reasonably realistic numbers into the future projection table. This means a knowledge of the competitive environment and the extraordinary resources that the firm possesses to produce high returns in its chosen industry(ies) – *see* Chapter 16. In other words, the decision maker needs to investigate the key '**value drivers**' in the company and the industry.

However, there is a trap here for the unwary and ill-informed. A manager lacking the intellectual tools, theoretical frameworks and facts to carry out high-quality strategic analysis will produce simplistic and misleading input numbers to the cash flow forecasts: GIGO – garbage in/garbage out.

Value-based management is not a mechanical discipline. It is not about inputting a few numbers to a computer program and then waiting until *the* answer pops out. It is a process requiring judgement every step of the way; it requires careful reflection on the results and their sensitivity to the input numbers. Deep thought is required to appreciate the impact of making slightly (or greatly) different judgements on the input variables; and in assessing the probabilities of variations occurring. Value-based management is a decision-making-in-a-haze-of-uncertainty discipline. How can it be otherwise if it is to be useful in the real world of unpredictability and vagueness? But it gives us a framework and the tools for navigating the best-judged route given these circumstances.

A premium is put on people who can exercise good judgement despite the imprecision – they are not paralysed by uncertainty. These people search for more data to try to see through the haze of the future. More data leads to thought and action designed to reduce the range of probable outcomes.

Investment after the planning horizon

After the planning horizon annual cash flows may well differ from the figure of £1,250 due to additional investment in fixed and working capital items but this will make no difference to present value as any new investment made (when discounted) will be the same as the discounted value of the future cash inflows from that investment. In other words, the company is able to earn merely the required rate of return from Year 8 onwards so no new investment can create value. For example, suppose that Gold raised additional funds of £1,000 and at time 9 (nine years from the present time) invested this in a project generating a perpetual annual net cash inflow of £120 starting at time 10. When these figures are discounted to time 0 the NPV is zero:

Present value of cash outflow $\frac{-£1,000}{(1.12)^9} = -360.61$

Present value of cash inflows $\frac{£120/0.12}{(1.12)^9} = +360.61$

Thus incremental investment beyond the planning horizon generates no incremental value and so can be ignored for value calculations.

The connection with stock market valuation

The kind of discounted cash flow analysis illustrated in Exhibit 17.1 is used by financial institutions to value shares. (In these cases interest paid to lenders is subtracted to determine the cash flow attributable to shareholders which is then discounted at the required return for shares of that risk class – not a weighted average cost of capital including the return to debt holders – *see* Chapter 20.) Given the emphasis by the owners of the firm on cash-flow generation it makes sense for managers, when evaluating strategies, projects, product lines and customers, to use a similar method.

Shareholder value analysis

Alfred Rappaport (1998) has taken the basic concept of cash flow discounting and developed a simplified method of analysis. In the example of Gold plc (*see* Exhibit 17.1) the component elements of the cash flow did not change in a regular pattern. For example, fixed capital investment was ten times as great in Year 2 as in Year 5. **Rappaport's shareholder value analysis** assumes relatively smooth change in the various cash flow elements from one year to the next as they are all taken to be related to the sales level. Rappaport's seven key factors that determine value are as set out in **Exhibit 17.2**.

Exhibit 17.2 Rappaport's value drivers

1 Sales growth rate
2 Operating profit margin
3 Tax rate
4 Fixed capital investment
5 Working capital investment
6 The planning horizon (forecast period)
7 The required rate of return

Rappaport calls the seven key factors value drivers, and this can be confusing given that other writers describe a value driver as a factor that provides some degree of competitive advantage. To distinguish the two types of value driver the quantitative seven listed in Exhibit 17.2 will be referred to as **Rappaport's value drivers**. To estimate future cash flows Rappaport assumes a constant percentage rate of growth in sales. The operating profit margin is a constant percentage of sales. Profit here is defined as profit before deduction of interest and tax, PBIT. The tax rate is a constant percentage of the operating profit. Fixed capital and working capital investment are related to the *increase* in sales.

So, if sales for the most recent year amount to £1,000,000 and are expected to continue to rise by 12 per cent per year, the operating profit margin on sales[2] is 9 per cent, taxes are 31 per cent of operating profit, the incremental investment in fixed capital items is 14 per cent of the *change* in sales, and the incremental working capital investment is 10 per cent of the *change* in sales, the cash flow for the next year will be as set out in **Exhibit 17.3**.

Using shareholder value analysis to value an entire company

Corporate value is the combined value of the debt portion and equity portion of the overall capital structure:

Corporate value = Debt + Shareholder value

[2] Operating profit margin on sales is sales revenue *less* cost of sales and all selling and administrative expenses before deduction of tax and interest.

Exhibit 17.3 Silver plc: Sales, operating profit and cash outflows for next year

Sales in year 1		
= Sales in prior year × (1 + Sales growth rate)		
	= 1,000,000 × 1.12	
		1,120,000
Operating profit		
= Sales × Operating profit margin		
	= 1,120,000 × 0.09	
		100,800
Taxes		
= Operating profit × 31%		
	= 100,800 × 0.31	
		−31,248
Incremental investment in fixed capital		
= Increase in sales × Incremental fixed capital investment rate		
	= 120,000 × 0.14	
		−16,800
Incremental investment in working capital		
= Increase in sales × Working capital investment rate		
	= 120,000 × 0.10	
		−12,000
Operating free cash flow		£40,752

The debt element is the market value of debt, such as long-term loans and overdrafts, plus the market value of quasi-debt liabilities, such as preference shares. In practical shareholder value analysis the balance sheet book value of debt is often used as a reasonable approximation to the market value.

The above equation can be rearranged to derive shareholder value:

Shareholder value = Corporate value – Debt

Rappaport's corporate value has three elements, due to his separation of the discounted cash flow value of marketable securities – these are assets not needed in operations to generate the business's cash flows – from the cash flows from operations (*see* **Exhibit 17.4**). The value of the marketable securities is expressed as their current market price.

Exhibit 17.4 Rappaport's corporate value

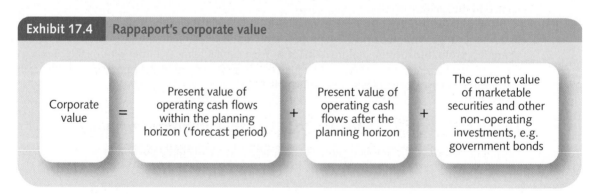

Corporate value = Present value of operating cash flows within the planning horizon ('forecast period) + Present value of operating cash flows after the planning horizon + The current value of marketable securities and other non-operating investments, e.g. government bonds

A closer look at depreciation and investment in fixed capital

Investment in plant, machinery, vehicles, buildings, etc. consists of two parts:

- Type 1. Annual investment to replace worn-out equipment and so on, leaving the overall level of assets constant.
- Type 2. Investment that adds to the stock of assets, presumably with the intention of permitting growth in productive capacity. This is called **incremental fixed-capital investment**.

A simplifying assumption often employed in shareholder value analysis is that the 'depreciation' figure in the profit and loss account is equal to the type 1 investment. This avoids the necessity of first adding back depreciation to operating profit figures and then deducting type 1 capital investment. It is only necessary to account for that extra cash outflow associated with incremental fixed capital investment.

Thus, **free cash flow** is the operating cash flow after incremental fixed and working capital investment; that which comes from the *operations* of the business. It therefore excludes cash flows arising from, say, the sale of shares by the company or bond issue. It also excludes payments of interest or dividends (*see* **Exhibit 17.5**).

Exhibit 17.5 Rappaport's free cash flow

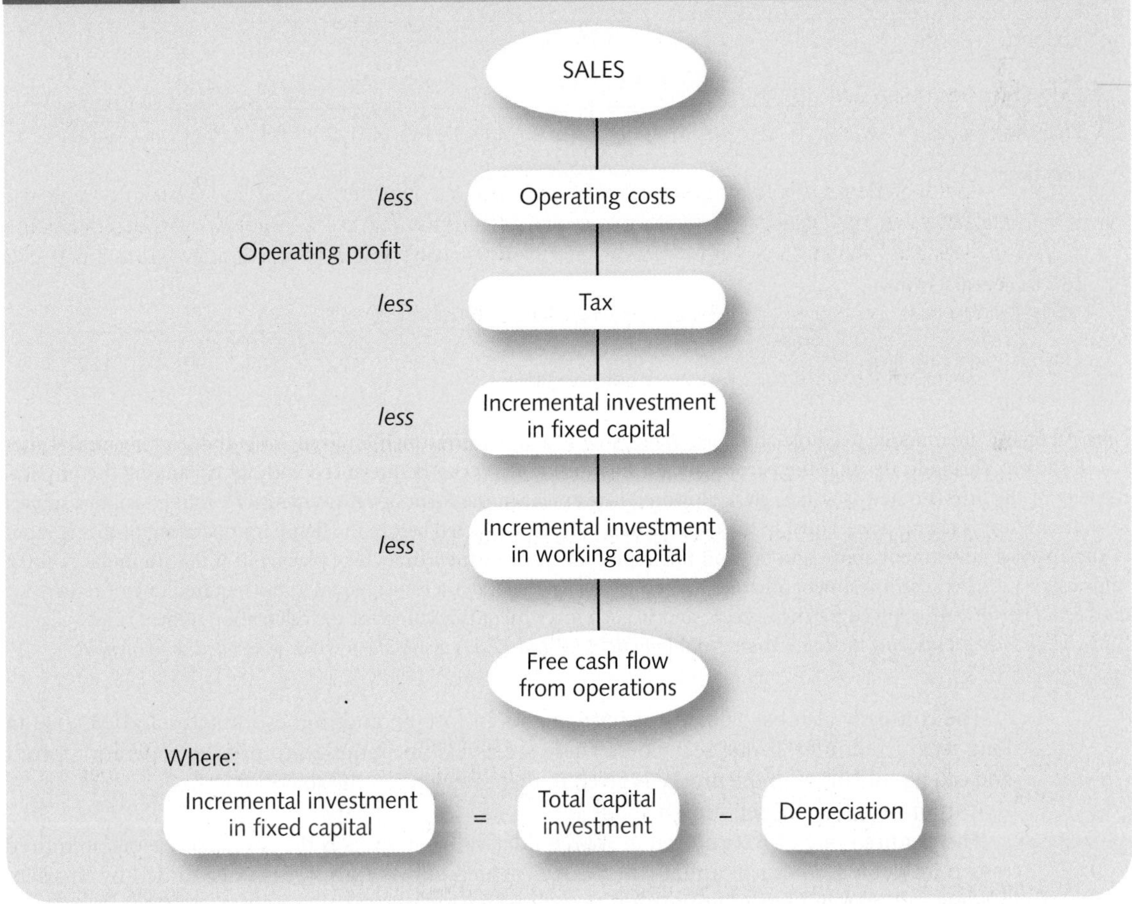

Illustration

We can calculate the shareholder value of Silver plc by using Rappaport's seven value drivers if we assume a planning horizon of eight years and a required rate of return of 15 per cent (*see* **Exhibits 17.6** and **17.7**).

Exhibit 17.6 Rappaport's value drivers applied to Silver plc

1	Sales growth	12% per year
2	Operating profit margin	9% of sales
3	Taxes	31% of operating profit
4	Incremental fixed capital investment	14% of the change in sales
5	Incremental working capital investment	10% of the change in sales
6	The planning horizon (forecast period)	8 years
7	The required rate of return	15% per year

Exhibit 17.7 An example of shareholder value analysis – cash flow calculation

Year	0	1	2	3	4	5	6	7	8	9 and subsequent years
£000s										
Sales	1,000	1,120	1,254	1,405	1,574	1,762	1,974	2,210	2,476	2,476
Operating profits		101	113	126	142	159	178	199	223	223
Less taxes		−31	−35	−39	−44	−49	−55	−62	−69	−69
Less incremental investment in fixed capital		−17	−19	−21	−24	−26	−30	−33	−37	0
Less incremental working capital investment		−12	−13	−15	−17	−19	−21	−24	−27	0
Operating free cash flow		41	46	51	57	65	72	80	90	154

Note: All figures are rounded to whole numbers. There is no additional investment in fixed assets and working capital after year 8 shown. This indicates that the perpetual cash flow of £154,000 can be produced without expanding the physical capacity of the firm (no new factories, etc.). However, investment in the form of replacement of existing facilities subject to wear and tear is taking place, equal to the depreciation amount deducted before the figure for operating profits is input to the analysis. Investment above and beyond this replacement investment may take place, but it has no impact on the value calculation because investment after the planning horizon generates a return equal to the required rate of return, i.e. there is no performance spread for these assets, and so such investment is ignored for the calculation of firm value.
An Excel spreadsheet showing the calculations from Exhibits 17.7 and 17.8 is available at www. pearsoned.co.uk/arnold

The company also has £60,000 of investments in foreign and domestic shares and £50,000 in long-term fixed interest rate securities. These are assets not required to produce operating profit and can be sold off with the proceeds given to their owners, i.e. the shareholders.

Corporate value is as set out in **Exhibit 17.8**.

The required rate of return used in shareholder value analysis is the weighted average required return on debt and equity capital (the WACC) which allows for a return demanded by the debt holders and shareholders in proportion to their provision of capital (*see* Chapter 19 for its calculation). This explains why cash flows before deduction of interest are discounted rather than just those attributable to shareholders: some of those cash flows will go to debt holders. The discounted cash flows derived in this way are then summed to give corporate value (sometimes called enterprise value). When debt, in this case £200,000, is deducted, shareholder value is obtained.

Exhibit 17.8 Corporate value

Present value of operating cash flows within the planning horizon (forecast period)	$\frac{41}{1.15} + \frac{46}{(1.15)^2} + \frac{51}{(1.15)^3} + \frac{57}{(1.15)^4} + \frac{65}{(1.15)^5} + \frac{72}{(1.15)^6} + \frac{80}{(1.15)^7} + \frac{90}{(1.15)^8}$	= 259
+		
Present value of operating cash flows after the planning horizon	$\frac{154}{0.15} = 1{,}027$	
	then discount result by eight years $\frac{1{,}027}{(1.15)^8}$	= 336
+		
The current value of marketable securities and other non-operating investments	60 + 50	= 110
	Corporate value	= 705
		or £705,000

Shareholder value = Corporate value – Debt
Shareholder value = £705,000 – £200,000 = £505,000

Again, this kind of analysis can be used at a number of different levels:

- whole business;
- division/SBU;
- operating unit;
- project;
- product line or customer.

Strategy valuation using shareholder value analysis

The quantitative evaluation of alternative strategies in terms of value creation can assist strategic choice. It is advisable when applying shareholder value analysis to a business unit or corporate-level strategy formulation and evaluation to consider at least four alternative strategic moves:

- a continuation of the current strategy – the '**base-case' strategy**;
- liquidation;
- a trade sale (selling the entire business to another firm) or spin-off (selling a business unit, while perhaps retaining a stake);
- a new operating strategy.

Imagine that Silver plc is involved in the production of plastic guttering for houses and the shareholder value figure of £505,000 represents the base-case strategy, consisting of relatively low levels of incremental investment and sales growing at a slow rate.

Alternatives

- The company has recently been approached by a property developer interested in purchasing the company's depot and offices for the sum of £400,000. Other assets (vehicles, inventory, machinery) could be sold to raise a further £220,000 and the marketable securities could be sold for £110,000. This liquidation would result in shareholders receiving £530,000 (£400,000 + £220,000 + £110,000 – £200,000). This liquidation option produces slightly more than the base-case strategy.

- The third possibility is a trade sale or spin-off. Companies can sell separable businesses to other firms or float off strategic business units or groups of SBUs on the stock market. In 2007 Cadbury Schweppes announced that it was to split itself into a confectionary company (the largest in the world, with a 10 per cent market share) and a soft drinks company mostly focused in the US. In the case of the fictional guttering firm, it is too small to obtain a separate quotation for component parts, and its operations are too well integrated to allow a trade sale of particular sections. However, in the past shareholders have been approached by larger competitors to discuss the possibility of a takeover. The three or four major industry players are trying to build up market share with the stated aim of achieving 'economies of scale and critical mass' and there is the distinct impression that they are being over-generous to selling shareholders in smaller firms – they are paying 'silly prices'. The management judge that if they could get a bidding war going between these domineering larger firms they could achieve a price of about £650,000 for shareholders.
- The fourth possibility involves an expansion into a new product area of multicoloured guttering. This will require large-scale investment but should result in rapidly rising sales and higher operating margins. The expected Rappaport value drivers are as set out in **Exhibit 17.9**. Note the increased investment in capital items. Also note the higher risk of this strategy compared with the base-case is reflected in the increased discount rate from 15 per cent to 16 per cent.

Exhibit 17.9 Rappaport's value drivers applied to an expansion of Silver plc

1	Sales growth	25% per year
2	Operating profit margin	11% of sales
3	Taxes	31% of operating profit
4	Incremental fixed capital investment	15% of the change in sales
5	Incremental working capital investment	10% of the change in sales
6	The planning horizon (forecast period)	8 years
7	The required rate of return	16% per year

The guttering firm's shareholder value under the new strategy is set out in **Exhibit 17.10**. This shows that there are lower cash flows in the first three years with this strategy compared with the base-case strategy because of the increased investment, yet the overall expected shareholder value rises from £505,000 to £1,069,000.

Sensitivity and scenario analysis

To make a more informed choice the directors may wish to carry out a sensitivity and scenario analysis. A worst-case and a best-case scenario could be constructed and the sensitivity to changes in certain variables could be scrutinised. For example, alternative discount rates and incremental investment in fixed capital rates could be examined for the multicoloured product strategy as shown in **Exhibit 17.11**.

One observation that may be made from Exhibit 17.11 is that even if the amount of incremental capital investment required rises to 20 per cent of the increase in sales and the discount rate moves to 17 per cent this strategy produces the highest value of all the four options considered. The management team may wish to consider the consequences and the likelihood of other variables changing from the original expected levels.

Exhibit 17.10 The guttering firm's shareholder value under the new strategy

Year	0	1	2	3	4	5	6	7	8	9 and subsequent years
£000s										
Sales	1,000	1,250	1,563	1,953	2,441	3,052	3,815	4,768	5,960	5,960
Operating profits		138	172	215	269	336	420	524	656	656
Less taxes		−43	−53	−67	−84	−104	−130	−162	−203	−203
Less incremental investment in fixed capital		−38	−47	−59	−73	−92	−114	−143	−179	0
Less incremental working capital investment		−25	−31	−39	−49	−61	−76	−95	−119	0
Operating free cash flow		32	41	50	63	79	100	124	155	453

Discounted cash flows within planning horizon

$$\frac{32}{1.16}+\frac{41}{(1.16)^2}+\frac{50}{(1.16)^3}+\frac{63}{(1.16)^4}+\frac{79}{(1.16)^5}+\frac{100}{(1.16)^6}+\frac{124}{(1.16)^7}+\frac{155}{(1.16)^8}=295$$

Discounted cash flow beyond planning horizon $\frac{453}{0.16}=2{,}831$, then $\frac{2{,}831}{(1.16)^8}$ $=864$

Marketable securities $=110$

Corporate value 1,269

Shareholder value = Corporate value − Debt
= £1,269,000 − £200,000
= £1,069, 000

Exhibit 17.11 Shareholder value for the guttering firm under different discount and capital investment rates

£000s		Discount rate		
		15%	16%	17%
Incremental fixed capital investment rates	15%	1,205	1,069	951
	20%	1,086	955	843

Targets, rewards and alignment of managerial effort

Following an initial shareholder value analysis it can be useful to break down each of the seven Rappaport value drivers into more detail. So, for example, if the operating profit margin is 20 per cent you could investigate what proportion of the 80 per cent of income from sales flows out in the form of wages, or material costs, or overheads, etc. This will permit focus of managerial attention. It also allows performance measures and targets to be more detailed. Thus, the production manager can be set targets in terms of raw material wastage and shopfloor employee efficiency. These operating targets can then be fed into the goal to improve the operating margin and the ultimate goal of shareholder wealth maximisation. Similarly, managers with responsibility for fixed and working capital investment can agree targets that are aligned with those of all the other managers in terms of being focused on value.

Another use of this analytical method: the value drivers (and their component parts) can be used to benchmark the company against competitors. So, if, for example, you find that your firm has the highest level of work-in-progress inventory per unit of sales you may want to see if there are efficiency gains to be made.

Problems with shareholder value analysis

There are some disadvantages to the use of shareholder value analysis:

- Constant percentage increases in value drivers lack realism in some circumstances, in others it is a reasonable simplification.
- It can be misused in target setting, for example if managers are given a specific cash flow objective for a 12-month period they may be dissuaded from necessary value-enhancing investment (i.e. using cash) in order to achieve the short-term cash flow target. Alleviate this problem by setting both short- and long-term targets. The short-term ones may show negative cash flows.
- Data availability – many firms' accounting systems are not equipped to provide the necessary input data. The installation of a new cash flow-orientated system may be costly.

Economic profit

Economic profit, EP (also called **residual income**), has an advantage over shareholder value analysis because it uses the existing accounting and reporting systems of firms by focusing on profit rather than cash flow information. This not only reduces the need to implement an overhaul of the data-collecting and reporting procedures but also provides evaluatory and performance measurement tools which use the familiar concept of profit. Thus, managers used to 'bottom line' figures are more likely to understand and accept this metric than one based on cash flow information.

Economic profit for a period is the amount earned by a business after deducting all operating expenses and a charge for the opportunity cost of the capital[3] employed.

There are two versions of economic profit.

1 The entity approach to EP

One version of EP is based on profit after tax is deducted but before interest is deducted. There are two ways to calculate this EP.

a ***The profit less capital charge method*** Here a charge for the use of capital equal to the invested capital multiplied by the return required by the share and debt holders (which is a weighted average cost of the debt and the equity, WACC) is deducted from the operating profits after tax:

Economic profit (Entity approach)	=	Operating profit before interest deduction and after tax deduction	–	Capital charge to cover both returns to shareholders and debt holders
Economic profit (Entity approach)	=	Operating profit before interest deduction and after tax deduction	–	Invested capital × WACC

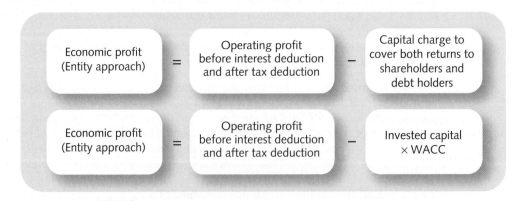

[3] The meaning of 'capital' here is different from its meaning in accounting. 'Capital' in accounting is a part of the shareholders' equity of the company ('capital issued', 'paid-in capital', etc.). 'Capital' in the present context means the sum of shareholders' equity (and of the borrowings of the company in the first version of EP)/, only some of which may be recognised in a balance sheet (see p. 686 for a discussion on 'invested capital').

b ***The 'performance spread' method*** The difference between the return achieved on invested capital and the weighted average cost of capital (WACC), i.e. the required rate of return, is the performance spread. This percentage figure is then multiplied by the quantity of invested capital to obtain EP:

$$\text{Economic profit (Entity approach)} = \text{Performance spread} \times \text{Invested capital}$$

$$\text{Economic profit (Entity approach)} = (\text{Return on capital} - \text{WACC}) \times \text{Invested capital}$$

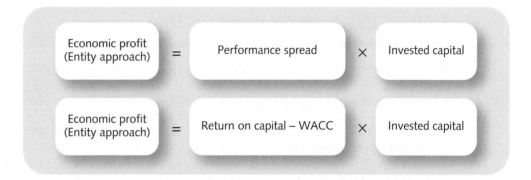

As can be seen from the following illustration either method leads to the same EP.

Illustration

EoPs plc has a weighted average cost of capital (required rate of return) of 12 per cent and has used £1,000,000 of invested capital (share and debt) to produce an operating profit before interest deduction and after tax of £180,000 during the past year.

Profit less capital charge approach

EP = Operating profits before interest and after tax – (Invested capital × WACC)
= £180,000 – (£1,000,000 × 0.12)
= £60,000

Performance spread approach

EP = (Return on capital – WACC) × Invested capital
= (18% – 12%) × £1,000,000
= £60,000

2 The equity approach to EP

The entity EP approach (described above), based on operating profit before the deduction of interest, calculates the surplus above the return to all the finance providers to the business entity including the debt holders. The alternative is the '**equity approach**'. With this, interest is deducted from the profit figure so we obtain the profit that belongs to the shareholders. Also the required return is the return demanded on the equity capital only. So, EP is the profit attributable to shareholders after a deduction for the implicit cost of employing shareholders' capital.

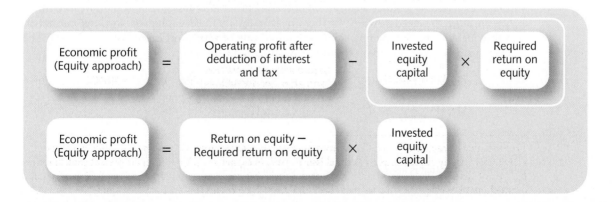

$$\text{Economic profit (Equity approach)} = \text{Operating profit after deduction of interest and tax} - (\text{Invested equity capital} \times \text{Required return on equity})$$

$$\text{Economic profit (Equity approach)} = (\text{Return on equity} - \text{Required return on equity}) \times \text{Invested equity capital}$$

Illustration

In the case of EoPs let us assume that one-half the £1,000,000 of capital is equity and the other half debt. The equity required rate of return is 15 per cent and the debt required rate of return is 9 per cent (i.e. £45,000 per year), therefore the weighted average cost of capital is 12 per cent (that is, $(15\% \times 0.5) + (9\% \times 0.5) = 12\%$).

Profit less capital charge approach

Deducting £45,000 of interest from the operating profit figure we have £135,000.

EP (equity) = Operating profits after interest and tax – (Invested equity capital × Required return on equity)
= £135,000 – (£500,000 × 0.15)
= £60,000

Performance spread approach

EP (equity) = (Return on equity – Required return on equity) × Invested equity capital
= (27% – 15%) × £500,000
= £60,000

The return on equity[4] is 27 per cent (£135,000/£500,000).

A short history of economic profit

The principles behind economic profit have a long antecedence. For at least a century economists have been aware of the need to recognise the minimum return to be provided to the finance provider as a 'cost' of operating a business. Enlightened chief executives have for decades, if not centuries, taken account of the amount of capital used by divisional managers when setting targets and measuring performance, with some sort of implicit, or explicit, cost being applied. David Solomons (1965) formalised the switch from return on capital employed (ROCE) and other accounting rates of return measures to 'the excess of net earnings over the cost of capital as the measure of managerial success'. But even he drew on practical innovation that had taken place in a number of large US companies.

Usefulness of economic profit

- A focus on EP rather than the traditional accounting profit has the advantage that every manager down the line is encouraged (rewarded) for paying close attention to the cost associated with using capital in a business unit, project, product line or the entire corporation. The introduction of EP targets has resulted in some dramatic reductions in money tied up wastefully in assets such as raw material stocks, and to significant reductions in requests for major fixed capital expenditure. Managers who are judged on profits may not be as keen to reduce capital employed as those judged on EP.
- Economic profit can be used to evaluate strategic options that produce returns over a number of years. For example, Spoe plc is considering the investment of £2,000,000 in a new division that is expected to produce a consistent operating profit after tax of £300,000 per year to infinity without the need for any further investment in fixed capital or working capital in subsequent years. The company has a required rate of return on capital of 13 per cent. The extra 'value' created on top of the initial investment of £2m is:

Economic profit (entity) per year = (Return on capital – WACC) × Invested capital
= (15% – 13%) × £2,000,000
= £40,000

[4] See p. 698 for an understanding of how the entity EP equity value may differ from the equity EP equity value, and the care that is needed when making these calculations.

Exhibit 17.12

The use of economic profit is becoming more widespread

For over two decades major US firms, including Walt Disney, Quaker Oats and AT&T, have been switching to using economic profit as a guiding concept. The focus of economic profit on the productive use of capital can have profound consequences. Roberto Goizueta, CEO of Coca-Cola, put the basic philosophy this way: 'We raise capital to make concentrate, and sell it at an operating profit. Then we pay the cost of that capital. Shareholders pocket the difference'.* Barclays Bank adopted the technique in 2000 declaring their aim to double economic profit every four years. In 2005 Barclays reported that it produced economic profit of £1.75bn (it used the equity method with 'average shareholders' equity for economic profit purposes' of £18,150m and cost of equity of 9.5 per cent). Cadbury Schweppes are very straightforward about their switch to value based management: 'Our objective is to maximise the value of Cadbury Schweppes for our shareowners. An important financial tool that helps us measure value is economic profit. Traditional ways of measuring performance, such as operating profit after tax or earnings per share, do not take into account the full cost of capital used to generate those profits. Capital is a combination of the funds provided by shareowners and money borrowed by Cadbury Schweppes. We only create value when we make a profit greater than the cost of capital invested. We define economic profit as operating profit less tax less a Capital Charge, where the capital charge is calculated by multiplying the money the business has tied up in capital by the weighted average cost of capital "WACC".' When Xerox adopted Six Sigma, an approach to problem solving developed by General Electric that emphasises small teams, measurement and economic return, it found a significant improvement. 'Six Sigma is very rigid and disciplined ... Every project is managed with economic profit metrics. There is none of the squishy stuff ... The learning process begins with taking out waste, working out where value gets added and where it does not', says Xerox manager Anne Mulcahy. *** (*Financial Times*, 23 September 2005, p. 13.)

Sources: *Quoted in Tully (1993), p. 93. ** www.cadburyschweppes.com.

The present value of this perpetuity is:

£40,000/0.13 = £307,692

This £307,692 is the additional value, in present terms, of economic profit. Of course, we can only call this value if we make the bold assumption that profit numbers bear a close resemblance to cash flow numbers (an assumption too frequently and too glibly made by consultant writers in this area). *See* below for challenges to this assumption.

To obtain the total value of this division we add to this the initial investment:

Value of new division = Present value of economic profit + Initial investment
= £307,692 + £2,000,000 = £2,307,692

Having expressed the new strategy in terms of EP, in implementing it we can set EP targets annually and grant rewards for achieving (exceeding) those targets.

- Economic profit has an advantage over shareholder value analysis in that it can be used to look back at how the firm (unit) has performed relative to the amount of capital used each year as well as creating future targets in terms of EP. Shareholder value analysis is generally used only in forward-looking mode. (Nevertheless, once the shareholder value analysis estimates have been made for a strategy it is possible to set interim targets, which, as time passes, are examined for deviation. So, in this sense it can be used in backward-looking mode, i.e. within a plan.) With EP it is possible to go to a firm and examine past performance from scratch, without the need for established EP targets within a plan.
- Economic profit per unit can be calculated: for example, economic profit per square foot or economic profit per unit of output. Economic profit sends a more powerful signal because it is expressed in absolute amounts of money generated for shareholders above the minimum required, e.g. £1.20 EP per unit sold, rather than a percentage, e.g. a profit margin of 14 per cent. Profit margins fail to allow for the size of the capital commitment.

Difficulties with economic profit

There are, however, some disadvantages to the use of economic profit.

1 ***The balance sheet does not reflect invested capital*** Balance sheets are not designed to provide information on the present economic value of assets being used in a business. Assets are generally recorded at original cost less depreciation, amortisation (reduction in intangibles) and depletion (e.g reduction in oil reserves). With or without inflation it does not take many years for these balance sheet values to deviate dramatically from the theoretically correct capital employed figures for most firms. Generally balance sheets significantly understate the amount of capital employed, and this understatement therefore causes EP to appear high. Moreover, many businesses invest in assets that never find their way to a balance sheet. For example, some firms pour vast sums into building up brand images and do so with the belief, often correct, that shareholders' money is being well invested, with the pay-off arising years later. Nevertheless, accounting convention insists on such expenditures being written off against profits rather than being taken into the balance sheet. The same problem applies to other investments such as business reputation and management training. The early theorists in value measurement suggested using current values of assets. Following them I would be tempted, depending on the circumstances, to use either (a) the sum of the resale value of individual assets, or (b) the replacement cost. Much depends on the objective of the analysis:

   - If the objective is to monitor past performance in terms of examining the efficiency with which money was invested the historic amount invested seems somewhat relevant as the 'capital' figure. However, there will be many circumstances where a distinctly unsatisfactory capital figure is derived from a balance sheet, e.g. when assets were acquired decades before the current period.
   - If you are monitoring current (this year) performance perhaps the current replacement value or the sum of the resale value of individual assets may be most useful. Sometimes the resale value is very low when the assets are highly specific with little secondary market. In such a case relying on the resale value alone would give an artificially low asset value. In other circumstances the replacement value is clearly way above the level at which any manager would actually replace and so a more informed decision can be made by using the sum of resale values as this figure represents the opportunity cost of using the assets this year.
   - If the asset value is needed to make future-oriented decisions about where to apply assets at present owned by the firm then the sum of the resale value of the individual assets would be most useful because this would capture the opportunity cost – the firm could sell off these assets as an alternative. The sunk costs associated with past investment are not relevant in such a decision and so balance sheet values are not very useful.
   - If the decision concerns the obtaining of new assets to implement a project/strategy then the cost of obtaining them is relevant.

   Note that we use the 'sum of the resale value of individual assets' rather than the current market value of all-the-assets-when-welded-together-as-a-coherent-whole for the corporation/SBU because to use the latter would eliminate any value by definition. For example, if a firm starts up with £1m of capital and a brilliant idea, immediately the strategy is put in place to exploit the idea the resale value of the firm as an operating entity rises to, say, £10m. That is, the resale value of the firm is equal to the initial capital plus the present value of the future cash flows or EP. The £10m current market value of all-the-assets-when-welded-together-as-a-coherent-whole includes £9m of value, but the value of the sum of the individual assets is in the region of £1m.

2 ***Manipulation and arbitrariness*** The difficulties caused by relying on accounting data are exacerbated by the freedom available to manipulate such figures as well as the degree of subjectivity involved in arriving at some of the figures in the first place. For example, if a business has sold goods on credit some customers are likely to fail to pay on the due date. The problem for the accountant (and managers) is to decide when to accept that particular debts will never be paid; is it after three months, six months or a year? Until they are declared 'bad debts' they are

recorded as an asset – perhaps they will turn out to be worth something, perhaps they won't. At each balance sheet date judgement is required to establish an estimate of the value of the debtor balance to the firm. Similar problems of 'flexibility' and potential for manipulation are possible with the estimate of the length of life of an asset (which has an effect on annual depreciation), and with R&D expenditure or inventory valuation.

Having a wide range of choices of treatment of key inputs to the profit and loss account and balance sheets makes comparability over time, and between companies, very difficult.

3 ***High economic profit and negative NPV can go together*** There is a danger of over-reliance on EP. For example, imagine a firm has become a convert to economic profit and divisional managers are judged on annual economic profit. Their bonuses and promotion prospects rest on good performance spreads over the next 12 months. This may prompt a manager to accept a project with an impressive EP over the short term whether or not it has a positive NPV over its entire life. Projects that produce poor or negative EPs in the first few years, for example biotechnology investments, will be rejected even if they will enhance shareholder wealth in the long term.

Also, during the life of a project managers may be given specific EP targets for a particular year. They may be tempted to ensure the profit target is met by cutting down on certain expenditures such as training, marketing and maintenance. The target will be achieved but long-term damage may be inflicted. The CEO of Siemens, Klaus Kleinfield was quoted in the *Financial Times* (6 November 2006, p. 24) saying that 'management pay is based on the "economic value added" each division provides against each year's budget. But a former senior director says this has led to a lack of investment in some parts of the business as managers look to earn as much as possible.'

A third value-destroying use of EP occurs when managers are demotivated by being set EP targets. For example, if managers have no control over the capital employed in their part of the business, they may become resentful of and cynical about value-based management if they are told nevertheless to achieve certain EP targets.

Care must be taken by external observers when examining the EP (or EVA) to judge performance, particularly in annual league tables. Misleading impressions are frequent over periods as short as one year because some firms that are on a high value-creating path often have years where EP is low (or nil). Then there are firms on a value-destructive path which report high current-year EP. It is only possible to judge performance over a number of years. When EP is used internally, however, it frequently does make sense to produce annual (or even six-monthly) EP figures to compare with a plan to see if the value-creation strategy is on target. Within the plan there will probably be periods of negative EP (e.g. in the start-up phase), as well as periods of high surpluses over the cost of capital.

4 ***Difficult to allocate revenues, costs and capital to business units, products, etc.*** To carry out EP analysis at the sub-firm level it is necessary to measure profit and capital invested separately for each area of the business. Many costs and capital assets are shared between business units, product lines and customers. It is very difficult in some situations to identify the proportion of the cost, debt or asset that is attributable to each activity. It can also be expensive. Consultants tend to be overoptimistic about the ability of accountants and managers to do this in a theory-compliant and precise manner.

Exhibit 17.13 describes the use of economic profit by a number of firms.

Exhibit 17.13

Profits: not what we accounted for

Economic profit paints a different picture from accounting profit

Alistair Blair

It's time for my annual evangelical on 'economic profit', the profit measurement that takes account of the cost of capital . . .

The general idea of economic profit is that you start with accounting profit (that's the concept you are already familiar with) and deduct what you might think of as 'interest on equity'. Interest on loans has, of course, already been deducted in arriving at accounting profit, and this is the same concept taken one stage further.

A company that does not earn at least the same on the capital invested in it as that capital would earn in a deposit account is difficult to take seriously. In fact, given that businesses are riskier than deposit accounts, the company should earn rather more. The hurdle to clear is, in fact, the 'cost of capital' – a figure that can be difficult to pin down, but starts at about 9 per cent for well-established companies and escalates for riskier companies.

Here's a real live example. Last year, HSBC reported profit after tax of \$6.2bn – up from \$5bn the year before. Earning \$6.2bn sounds impressive, but don't overlook the fact that HSBC has at least \$52bn of shareholder money at its disposal. You could do quite a lot with \$52bn. In fact, HSBC itself reckons that, if you had invested \$52bn in a global banking business, your reasonable expectations would be to earn \$6.05bn – and it owns up rather sheepishly to having earned an economic profit last year of just \$150m.

At Lloyds TSB, accounting profit suffers a smaller gouge from the cost of capital: the £1.8bn on the profit-and-loss account comes out at £820m after Lloyds recognises the obligations of running £8bn of shareholder capital. Mind you, it helps – in the comparison with HSBC – that Lloyds reckons its cost of capital is 9 per cent. HSBC uses a figure of 12.5 per cent. In fact it believes – quite reasonably – that current low interest rates reduce its actual cost of capital to 10 per cent, but it has historically used 12.5 per cent and continues to do so to aid comparability. If HSBC used 9 per cent, its economic profit would come out closer to \$2bn . . .

In other sectors, you'd be hard-pressed to find any company reporting its economic profit, although quite a few companies claim to use it internally. I had to suppress a smile when I read in ICI's annual report that 'economic profit is ICI's key internal financial measure'. It's no wonder that ICI doesn't report its economic profit: I'll bet you a pound to a penny that ICI hasn't made an economic profit in more than two of the past 20 years. Scottish & Newcastle and Tate & Lyle are also self-proclaimed advocates of economic profit, but neither deigns to share the figures with shareholders. Last year, Hanson made so much noise in its annual report about having adopted economic profit as a new mantra that I thought it might be on the verge of breaking new ground. But, this year, the subject didn't get a peep. Which is a bit of a pity, considering that 'economic profit measures the true value created for the business'.

Source: Investors Chronicle, 29 August 2003, p. 74. Reprinted with permission.

Economic value added (EVA®)

Economic value added, developed and trademarked by the US consultants Stern Stewart and Co., is a variant of EP that attempts to overcome some of the problems outlined above. Great energy has been put into its marketing and it is probably the most widely talked about value metric.

$$\text{EVA} = \text{Adjusted invested capital} \times (\text{Adjusted return on capital} - \text{WACC})$$

or

$$\text{EVA} = \text{Adjusted operating profits after tax} - (\text{Adjusted invested capital} \times \text{WACC})$$

The adjustments to profit and capital figures are meant to refine the basic EP.[5] Stern Stewart suggest that up to 164 adjustments to the accounting data may be needed. For example, spending on marketing and R&D helps build value and so if expenditure on these has been deducted in past years it is added back to the balance sheet as an asset (and amortised over the period expected to benefit from the expenditure). Goodwill on acquisitions previously written off is also returned and is expressed as an asset, thus boosting both profits and the balance sheet.

There are a number of difficulties with these adjustments – for example, over what period should these reconstituted 'assets' be amortised? After all they are not expected to be valuable forever; they often gradually (or suddenly) fail to maintain their contributions to the firm. Also should you add back 'assets' for, say, R&D expenditure that took place five years ago, ten years ago, or over the whole life of the firm?

EVA, like the generic EP, has the virtue of being based on familiar accounting concepts and it is arguably more accurate than taking ordinary accounting figures. However, critics have pointed out that the adjustments can be time consuming and costly, and many are based on decisions that are as subjective as the original accountant's numbers. There also remains the problem of poorly, if enthusiastically, implemented EVA reward systems producing results that satisfy targets for EVA but which produce poor decisions with regard to NPV. Furthermore, the problem of allocating revenue, costs and capital to particular business units and products is not solved through the use of EVA. Also the Stern Stewart definition of capital is 'the sum of all the cash that has been invested in a company's net assets over its life' (Stewart, 1991, p. 86). Imagine the difficulties in establishing this given that most invested 'cash' put in will be in the form of many years of retained earnings, which leads us back to the difficulties of accounting numbers and the dubiousness of making 'adjustments' to the raw numbers. Added to this problem is the issue of accepting this capital figure as relevant for many decisions. For example, in judging future strategic plans perhaps the opportunity cost of those assets (the sum of the individual resale values) would be more relevant than what was paid for them, much of which may have become a sunk cost years ago (*see* Chapter 3). So, if Eurotunnel is contemplating a new strategy in 2009 should its 'capital invested' figure be £9bn (its cost of building, etc.) when calculating projected annual EVAs? Of course not. What is relevant is the opportunity cost of capital – the value of those assets in their best alternative use today (2009), not the money invested in the 1980s. Likewise if you are monitoring managers' performance this year the historic cost of assets they are using may be totally irrelevant to the analysis of their efficiency, whereas the money that they could have raised through the alternative of selling off the assets rather than operating them, might be of enormous interest, as this may be the best alternative use.

Despite the outstanding problems companies are seeing benefits from introducing EVA:

> It's not rocket science, but it is good lingua franca that does indeed get everyone back to basics, makes them understand better the cash consequences of their own actions and, further, makes them address other departments' problems, not just their own. Within each of our businesses we don't incentivise, for example, the sales director on sales and we don't incentivise the finance director on cash generation. The whole management team is incentivised on EVA and that means they are all pulling in the same direction and have to liaise better.
>
> (Mike Ashton, finance director of BWI).[6]

At Brambles, the world's biggest supplier of pallets said that a big factor in the company's recovery has been the introduction of 'Brambles Value Added'. This concept – derived from economic value added – measures performance as profit minus the cost of capital and is used to evaluate investment, to report on performance and reward managers. 'The objective was to ensure that management had an absolute incentive to count capital employed as a cost of doing business' (David Turner, CEO of Brambles, quoted in the *Financial Times*, 27 December 2005, p. 13).

---

[5] Notice that EVA is derived from the entity EP rather than equity EP because the WACC contains an allowance for a return to all finance providers including debt holders. Therefore, the 'adjusted invested capital' is equity plus debt capital.

[6] Quoted in *Management Today*, January 1997, p. 45.

The use of EVA is spreading around the world. Sony, in Japan, has invited Stern Stewart to work with the company. In Germany Volkswagen has attempted to align managerial interests with those of shareholders by making up to 40 per cent of their annual bonuses dependent on achieving EVA targets – *see* **Exhibit 17.14** (excuse the confusion in the article on the meaning of 'E').

Vodafone reported some very impressive numbers, but according to **Exhibit 17.15** it produced a return less than its costs of capital.

Exhibit 17.14

VW to alter management focus

FT

By James Mackintosh, Motor Industry Editor, in Wolfsburg

Volkswagen, Europe's largest manufacturer of motor vehicles, is shaking up executive pay in an attempt to make managers more cautious about investment and increase loyalty to the group rather than the seven individual brands.

VW will base up to 40 per cent of this year's bonus on returns above the cost of capital, a big step in an industry renowned for destroying capital.

The move to earnings value added (EVA) measures to determine pay is part of an attempt by Bernd Pischetsrieder, chief executive, and Hans Dieter Pötsch, incoming finance director, to make managers think harder before making investments.

The group has abandoned return on sales targets in favour of measuring return on invested capital and is clamping down on investment and research and development spending, seen as out of control . . .

In addition to EVA, the bonus structure adds group performance measures to the individual and brand measures already used in an attempt to make the brands work with each other, rather than competing . . .

Last year VW made a return on invested capital of 7.4 per cent, below its 7.7 per cent cost of capital – equivalent to destroying €134m ($146m) of value. It paid an average bonus of €1.31m last year to the nine management board members.

To start with directors will have only 40 per cent of bonuses determined by EVA measures, a similar level to more junior managers. Base salary is unaffected. But Mr Pötsch said: 'Eventually a substantial part of payments will be based on EVA.'

Investment was already expected to fall, with more than €3bn cut from capital spending, 10 per cent of the 2002 five-year plan. Mr Pötsch said 'a similar amount' could be saved from the R&D budget . . .

Source: *Financial Times*, 1 September 2003, p. 24. Reprinted with permission.

Exhibit 17.15

Vodafone

FT

Up and up goes Vodafone's ebitda; down and down goes its share price. The story is a depressingly old one. Motivate executives by one performance measure and they will strain every sinew to meet it, but other statistics may go by the board.

That is shown up in an analysis by the consultancy Stern Stewart of Vodafone's recent performance. Vodafone's earnings before interest, tax, depreciation and amortisation have grown from £650m in the year to March 1997 to £9.9bn in the year to March 2002.

But in Stern Stewart's preferred measure of economic value added, the performance is pretty dire. In the years 1997–99, EVA was positive. But in the years to March 2000, 2001 and 2002, Vodafone had negative EVAs of £2.49bn, £12.02bn and £9.6bn respectively.

Of course, Stern Stewart has an interest in plugging EVA. Nevertheless, it measures a serious thing; the difference between the return on capital employed and the cost of capital. The EVA figures are the corollary of last week's massive goodwill write-off; clearly Vodafone has not realised an adequate return on acquisitions made in 1999 and 2000.

The enthusiasm for ebitda as a performance measure in the 1990s always seemed overblown and likely to encourage executives to take on excessive debt. But shareholders should always beware of relying on any one performance measure and should ensure that executives are never rewarded on the basis of one measure alone.

Source: *Financial Times*, 4 June 2002, p. 21. Reprinted with permission.

Cash flow return on investment (CFROI)

The CFROI approach is a more complicated version of the internal rate of return (IRR), except that it is used to judge whether a company has produced a satisfactory rate of return on capital in the past, rather than providing an evaluation of future investment. Thus, to calculate the CFROI for a strategic business unit you would need to obtain the amount of capital (including debt) that was devoted to it and then obtain the operating cash flows. After a few complicating adjustments you calculate the rate of return that causes cash outflows (including initial capital value) to equal cash inflows to arrive at the CFROI.

The promoters of this approach recommend that assets in the balance sheet be restated to their current price equivalent value to achieve a proper estimate of the sacrifice finance providers to the company made in the SBU (or product line, or entire company). Thus, for example, accumulated depreciation is added back to the balance sheet value for fixed assets. Inventory values and fixed asset values may be raised by the amount of inflation since purchase to be at 'current prices'. Goodwill from acquired companies previously written off is added back. The value of future lease obligations are also added back.

CFROI suffers from the same problems of IRR such as the tendency to favour projects with a high percentage gain over those with a high absolute gain in shareholder wealth – *see* Chapter 2.

There is a high degree of imprecision and arbitratriness in calculating the capital invested figure. For example how much of the previously written-off depreciation should you reinstate? Do you go back twenty years or only three years? The numbers included in CFROI are usually so suspect that a great deal of caution is needed in interpreting the outcomes.

It is also a relatively complicated method to use, particularly in circumstances where assets and costs are shared between SBUs, projects or product lines.

Concluding comments

This chapter has described a number of value-based metrics used to guide organisations. This is a field dominated by consultancy organisations each with a particular approach to sell. The foundation for all of them is discounted cash flow allowing for a suitable return on the money shareholders contribute to the business. I suggest that, rather than selecting one internal value metric, a better approach, for both strategic investment discussion and performance targeting and measurement, is to set both cash flow and economic profit targets. This would counter a number of problems raised by using each separately and would help to alleviate the tendency of managers to take action to achieve particular short-term targets at the expense of long-term wealth. However, when examining the resulting numbers, you should allow for the drawbacks of these approaches so that you do not use these metrics in an inappropriate, dysfunctional fashion.

Key points and concepts

- **Discounted cash flow** is the bedrock method underlying value management metrics. It requires the calculation of future annual free cash flows attributable to both shareholders and debt holders, then discounting these cash flows at the weighted average cost of capital.
- **Corporate value (Enterprise value)** equals present value of free cash flows from operations plus the value of non-operating assets.
- **Shareholder value from operations** equals present value of free cash flows from operations minus debt.
- **Total shareholder value** equals shareholder value of free cash flows from operations plus the value of non-operating assets.
- **Investment after the planning horizon does not increase value.**

- **Shareholder value analysis** simplifies discounted cash flow analysis by employing **(Rappaport's) seven value drivers**, the first five of which change in a consistent fashion from one year to the next.
- **Rappaport's seven value drivers**:

  1 Sales growth rate.
  2 Operating profit margin.
  3 Tax rate.
  4 Fixed capital investment.
  5 Working capital investment.
  6 The planning horizon.
  7 The required rate of return.

- **At least four strategic options should be considered** for a SBU or product and/or market segment:

  – base-case strategy;
  – liquidation;
  – trade sale or spin-off;
  – new operating strategy.

- **Merits of shareholder value analysis:**

  – easy to understand and apply;
  – consistent with share valuation;
  – makes value drivers explicit;
  – able to benchmark.

- **Problems with shareholder value analysis**:

  – constant percentages unrealistic;
  – can lead to poor decisions if misused;
  – data often unavailable.

- **Economic profit (EP)** is the amount earned after deducting all operating expenses *and* a charge for the opportunity cost of the capital employed. A major advantage over shareholder value analysis is that it uses accounting data.
- **The entity approach to EP**

  a The profit less capital charge method

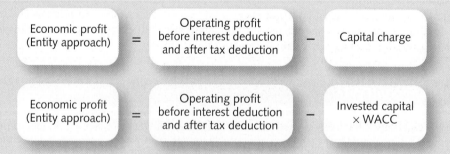

$$\text{Economic profit (Entity approach)} = \text{Operating profit before interest deduction and after tax deduction} - \text{Capital charge}$$

$$\text{Economic profit (Entity approach)} = \text{Operating profit before interest deduction and after tax deduction} - \text{Invested capital} \times \text{WACC}$$

b The 'performance spread' method

Economic profit (Entity approach) = Performance spread × Invested capital

Economic profit (Entity approach) = Return on capital − WACC × Invested capital

- **The equity approach to EP**

Economic profit (Equity approach) = Operating profit after deduction of interest and tax − (Invested equity capital × Required return on equity)

Economic profit (Equity approach) = Return on equity − Required return on equity × Invested equity capital

- **Usefulness of economic profit**:
  - Managers become aware of the value of the investment in an SBU, product line or entire business.
  - Can be used to evaluate strategic options.
  - Can be used to look back at past performance.
  - Economic profit per unit can be calculated.
- **Difficulties in using EP**:

  – the balance sheet does not reflect invested capital;
  – open to manipulation and arbitrariness;
  – high economic profit and negative NPV *can* go together;
  – problem with allocating revenues, costs and capital to business units.
- **Economic value added (EVA®)** is an attempt to overcome some of the accounting problems of standard EP.

  EVA = Adjusted invested capital × (Adjusted return on capital – WACC)

  or

  EVA = Adjusted operating profit after tax – (Adjusted invested capital × WACC)

References and further reading

Aggarwal, R. (2001) 'Using economic profit to assess performance: a metric for modern firms', *Business Horizons*, Jan/Feb, pp. 55–60.

A brief overview of the issues raised by implementing an EP–based programme.

Anderson, A.M., Bey, R.P. and Weaver, S.C. (2005) 'Economic Value Added® Adjustments: Much ado about nothing?' Working paper. Bethlehem, PA: Lehigh University.

Casts doubt on the usefulness of moving away from EP. EVA's adjustments from accounting income and capital do not make much difference to residual income.

Arnold, G.C. and Davies, M. (eds) (2000) *Value-Based Management*. London: John Wiley & Sons.

A collection of research monographs.

Barker, R. (2001) *Determining Value: Valuation models and financial statements*. Harlow: Financial Times Prentice Hall.

Provides a fairly detailed discussion of economic profit, EVA and shareholder value analysis and CFROI. Good if you are keen on model proofs and theoretical linkages between the metrics.

Davies, M. (2000) 'Lessons from Practice: VBM at Lloyds TSB', in Arnold, G.C. and Davies, M. (eds) *Value-Based Management*. London: John Wiley & Sons.

Insights into a company making use of VBM principles.

Davies, M., Arnold, G., Cornelius, I. and Walmsley, S. (2001) *Managing for Shareholder Value*. London: Informa.

An overview of shareholder value management for practitioners.

Martin, J.D. and Petty, J.W. (2000) *Value Based Management: Corporate response to the shareholder revolution*. Boston: Harvard Business School Press.

There are good chapters on free cash flow and CFROI.

McKinsey (Koller, T., Goedhart, M. and Wessel, D.) (2005) *Valuation*. 4th edn. New York: John Wiley & Sons.

The management of value-based organisations and the principles behind the techniques are explained.

McTaggart, J.M., Kontes, P.W. and Mankins, M.C. (1994) *The Value Imperative*. New York: Free Press.

Showing the application of value-based techniques to strategy and other disciplines.

Rappaport, A. (1998) *Creating Shareholder Value*. Revised and updated edition. New York: Free Press.

A landmark book. Presents an important value metric – shareholder value analysis.

Reimann, B.C. (1989) *Managing for Value*. Oxford: Basil Blackwell.

Useful because it brings together strategy and value.

Solomons, D. (1965) *Divisional Performance: Measurement and Control*. Reproduced (1983) Connecticut: M. Weiner Publishing.

An early formulation of residual income (economic profit).

Stern, J.M., Stewart, G.B. and Chew, D.H. (2001) 'The EVA® Financial Management System', in Chew, D.H. (ed.) *The New Corporate Finance*. New York: McGraw-Hill/Irwin.

The case for the use of EVA for motivating operating heads is presented in an easy-to-read fashion.

Stewart, G.B. (1991) *The Quest for Value*. New York: Harper Business.

Written by a founding partner in Stern Stewart & Co., the US consultancy, which has so successfully promoted MVA and EVA. Some useful insights.

Stewart, G.B. (2001) 'Market Myths', in Chew, D.H. (ed.) *The New Corporate Finance*. New York: McGraw-Hill/Irwin.

Advocating the value approach.

Tully, S. (1993) 'The real key to creating wealth', *Fortune*, 20 September, pp. 38–50.

The application of EVA to US corporations is described in an accessible style.

Wallace, J. S. (1997) 'Adopting residual income-based compensation plans: do you get what you pay for?' *Journal of Accounting and Economics*, 24, pp. 275–300.

Observes that firms which adapt economic profit for managerial incentive targets achieve a change in managerial actions (decreased new investment, sell-off of assets, raised share buy-backs and more intense asset utilisation).

Weaver, S.C. (2001) 'Measuring Economic Value Added®: a survey of the practices of EVA® proponents', *Journal of Applied Finance*, Fall/Winter, pp. 7–17.

Evidence that EVA is implemented in a variety of ways (different 'adjustments', different 'WACC' calculations).

Young, S.D. and O'Byrne, S.F. (2001) *EVA® and Value-based Management: A practical guide to implementation*. New York: McGraw-Hill.

An easy-to-follow description of EVA with a critical edge.

Website

Stern Stewart and Co. www.eva.com

Case study recommendations

Please see www.pearsoned.co.uk/arnold for case study synopses

- CITIC Tower II. Authors: Frederick Pretorius, Mary Ho and Lucy Fung (2002) Centre for Asian Business Cases (also available from Harvard Business School Case Study collection).
- The continuing transformation of Asahi Glass: Implementing EVA. Authors: Mihir A. Desai, Masako Egawa and Yanjun Wang (2004) Harvard Business School.

Self-review questions

1 List the stages in the conversion of profit and loss accounts to cash flow figures.

2 What is shareholder value analysis and what are the seven value drivers as described by Rappaport?

3 What is economic profit (EP)? Describe the alternative ways of measuring it.

4 Describe the relative merits and problems of shareholder value analysis and EP.

5 What are the alternatives when trying to establish a figure for the amount of capital devoted to a business?

Questions and problems

myfinancelab ***Questions with an icon are also available for practice in MyFinanceLab with additional supporting resources.***

Answers to questions marked with an asterisk are available in the Lecturer's materials.

1 Blue plc is a relatively small company with only one SBU. It manufactures wire grilles for the consumer market for cooker manufacturers and for export. Following a thorough investigation by the finance department and the heads of the customer lines some facts emerged about the returns expected in each of the customer sectors. The consumer sector uses £1m of the firm's capital and is expected to produce a return of 18 per cent on this capital, for the next five years, after which it will return the same as its risk-adjusted cost of capital (WACC), 15 per cent.

The cooker sales sector uses £2m of capital and will return 14 per cent per annum for seven years when its planning horizon ends. Its WACC is 16 per cent.

The export sector has a positive performance spread of 2 per cent over WACC for the next six years. The required rate of return is 17 per cent. From Year 7 the performance spread becomes zero. This division uses £1.5m of capital.

Required

a Calculate the annual (entity version) economic profit of each sector.

b What is the total value creation from each if you assume profit numbers equate to cash flow numbers?

c Display a value-creation profile chart and suggest possible action. ?

2* Apply shareholder value analysis to an all-equity firm with the following Rappaport value drivers, assuming that the last reported annual sales were £25m.

Sales growth rate	13%
Operating profit margin before tax	10%
Tax rate	31%
Incremental fixed capital investment (IFCI)	11% of the change in sales
Incremental working capital investment (IWCI)	8% of the change in sales
Planning horizon	4 years
Required rate of return	15%

Marketable securities amount to £5m and depreciation can be taken to be equal to the investment needed to replace worn-out equipment.

(*An Excel spreadsheet version of the answers to this question is available in the lecturer's section of the website www.pearsoned.co.uk/arnold*)

?

3* Regarding the answer obtained in Question 2 as the 'base-case' strategy, make a judgement on the best strategic option given the following:

– If the firm were liquidated the operating assets could be sold, net of the repayment of liabilities, for a total of £20m.
– If the firm separated its A division from its B division then A could be sold for £10m and the B division would have the following Rappaport value drivers:

Sales	15%
Operating profit margin before tax	12%
Tax rate	31%
Incremental fixed capital investment (IFCI)	13% of change in sales
Incremental working capital investment (IWCI)	10% of change in sales
Planning horizon	6 years
Required rate of return	14%

The B division had sales in the last year of £15m.

– If both divisions are retained and a new product differentiation strategy is attempted then the following Rappaport value drivers will apply:

Sales	18%
Operating profit margin before tax	12%
Tax rate	31%
Incremental fixed capital investment (IFCI)	15%
Incremental working capital investment (IWCI)	9%
Planning horizon	5 years
Required rate of return	17%

?

4* **a** Conduct sensitivity analysis on the shareholder value analysis of Question 2, changing the required rate of return to 14 per cent and 16 per cent, and changing the planning horizon to Year 5 and Year 6. Present the results in a table and comment on them briefly.

b Discuss the advantages and disadvantages of using shareholder value analysis.

?

5 Last year Tops plc (a firm financed entirely by equity) produced an accounting operating profit after tax of £5m. Its equity cost of capital is 14 per cent and the firm has £50m of capital. What was the economic profit?

?

6 Buit plc is trying to estimate its value under the current strategy. The managerial team have forecast the following profits for the next five years:

Year	1	2	3	4	5
	£m	£m	£m	£m	£m
Forecast profit	12	14	15	16	16

Depreciation of fixed capital items in each of the first two years is £2m. In each of the following three years it is £3m. This has been deducted before arriving at the profit figures shown above. In years 1, 2 and 3 capital expenditure will be £5m per year which both replaces worn-out assets and pays for fresh investment to grow the business. In the fourth and fifth year capital expenditure will be £3m.

The planning horizon is four years. Additional working capital will be needed in each of the next four years. This will be £1m in year 1, £1.2m in year 2, £1.5m in year 3 and £1.8m in year 4.

The company is partially financed by debt – it owes £20m – and partially by equity capital. The required rate of return (WACC) is 10 per cent.

The forecast profit figures include a deduction for interest of £1.2m per year, but do not include a deduction for tax, which is levied at 30 per cent of forecasted profits, payable in the year profits are made.

The company also owns a number of empty factories that are not required for business operations. The current market value of these is £16m.

Required

a Calculate the future cash flows for the company to an infinite horizon – assume year 5 cash flows apply to each year thereafter. Discount the cash flows and calculate the present value of all the cash flows.

b Calculate corporate value and shareholder value.

?

7 Mythier plc, in its first year, produced profits after deduction of tax but before deduction of interest of £1m. The amount invested by debt holders was £4m. Equity holders also invested £4m. Interest paid during the year was £0.24m and the weighted average cost of capital is 8 per cent, while the cost of equity capital is 10 per cent.

a Calculate economic profit using the entity approach.

b Calculate economic profit using the equity approach.

c Describe the advantages of using economic profit in the modern corporation.

d Explain the difficulties with economic profit.

?

8 Explain and contrast economic profit and shareholder value analysis.

myfinancelab *Now retake your diagnostic test for Chapter 17 to check your progress and update your study plan.*

Assignment

Conduct a value-based analysis and write a report for a company you know well. Show the current position and your recommendations for change. Include in the analysis value-creation profile charts, strategy planes diagrams, sources of competitive advantage (value drivers), qualitative evaluation of strategies, cash flow analysis, shareholder value analysis and EP.

Note to footnote 4, on page 684. *Further consideration of the entity and equity EP*

The entity EP and the equity EP give the same annual EP figures but can give different equity values if calculated with a WACC determined by the initial proportions of debt and equity (i.e. those amounts put into the business by shareholders and debt holders). This is apparent in the following illustration. (To be read after absorbing the fundamentals of the WACC in Chapter 19.) Valucrazee plc is set up with £50m from shareholders and £50m of debt capital. Equity at this risk level requires a rate of return of 20%, while debt requires 10%, therefore the WACC (based on initial proportions of debt and equity) = 15%. The company is expected to produce cash flow available for all the finance providers (i.e. before deduction of interest but after tax) of £25m per year to infinity.

Value under the entity approach

Annual EP = Profit after tax before interest – Capital × Required rate of return
Annual EP = £25m – (£100m × 15%) = £10m

Corporate value = Initial total capital + Present value of annual economic profit
Corporate value = £100m + £10m/0.15 = £166.67m

Equity value = Corporate value – Debt value = £166.67m – £50m = £116.67m

Value under the equity approach

Annual EP = Profit after tax and interest – Equity capital × Required rate of return
Annual EP = (£25m – £5m) – (£50m × 20%) = £10m

Equity value = Initial equity + Present value of annual equity economic profit
Equity value = £50m + £10m/0.20 = £100m

The reason for the £16.67m difference is that the surplus cash flow above the minimum required is discounted at different rates. In the first case the £10m surplus cash flow (which must all be attributable to shareholders as the debt holders are satisfied with the 'required rate of return' deduction) is discounted at 15%, whereas in the second case it is discounted at 20%.

To make the two equity values equal we need to follow the rule when calculating the WACC of using market value weights for debt and equity (i.e. what the total value of the shares in the company is after going ahead) rather than original book (balance sheet) values. The market value of debt remains the same if a value-enhancing project is accepted – that is, £50m. However, the market value of the equity is significantly higher than the amount first put in by the shareholders.

The annual cash flow to equity of £20m when discounted at 20% is £100m. Therefore, the weights used to calculate the WACC are:

Debt	£50m	Weight: £50m/£150m = 0.333
Equity	£100m	Weight: £100m/£150m = 0.667
Total capital	£150m	

WACC = $k_E W_E + k_D W_D$ = 0.2 × 0.667 + 0.1 × 0.333 = 16.67%

This changes the valuation under the entity approach:

Annual EP = Profit after tax before interest – Capital × Required rate of return
Annual EP = £25m – (£100m × 16.67%) = £8.33m

Corporate value = Initial total capital + Present value of annual economic profit
Corporate value = £100m + £8.33m/0.1667 = £150m
Equity value = Corporate value – Debt value = £150m – £50m = £100m (the same as under the equity approach)

Under the WACC-adjusted-for-market-value-of-equity approach we observe a fall in the annual EP when using the entity approach from £10m to £8.33m because we, correctly, require 20% return on two-thirds (£100m) of capital employed out of a total of £150m (at market values).

What is the practical manager to do? In theory you should be using the market value proportions of debt and equity that are optimal for your firm for all projects and SBUs and for valuing the entire firm. That is, the firm should have target levels of debt relative to the equity base that produces the lowest WACC (*see* Chapter 19).

The reality in most firms is that the optimum mix of debt and equity is unlikely to be known with any precision as the factors determining the optimum, at base, can only be quantified through subjective probability estimates, e.g. the chance of financial distress (*see* Chapter 21). So, it is reasonable to think of the optimum proportions of debt and equity as a range rather than a pinpoint percentage. For most firms the reasonable range is quite large. It could easily run from 50 : 50 gearing to 33 : 66 gearing. The advice to think in terms of a range for the WACC is reinforced by the many difficulties in other inputs to the WACC calculation, from the cost of equity (what is the risk premium? Is beta the appropriate adjustment for risk?) to the risk-free rate of return – *see* Chapter 19.

Given the complications with the WACC under the entity approach many analysts would simply plump for the equity approach in the first place.

CHAPTER 18

Entire firm value measurement

LEARNING OUTCOMES

By the end of this chapter the reader should be able to explain the following value metrics, pointing out their advantages and the problems in practical use:

- total shareholder return;
- wealth added index;
- market value added;
- excess return;
- market to book ratio.

myfinancelab *Complete your diagnostic test for Chapter 18 now to create your personal study plan*

Introduction

This chapter describes five 'market-based' measures of value performance. The feature that runs through all these measures is the focus on the stock market's valuation of the company. **Total shareholder return, TSR**, measures the rise or fall in the capital value of a company's shares combined with any cash payment, e.g. dividends, received by shareholders over particular periods of time, be it one year, three years or ten years. This gets to the heart of the issue for owners of companies – what return do I get on my shares from the activities of the managers hired to steward the resources entrusted to them? **The Wealth Added Index, WAI**,[1] examines the change in share values (capital gains plus dividends) after allowance for the required rate of return over the period of time examined.

Two other metrics, the Market Value Added, MVA,[2] and the Market to Book Ratio, MBR, also examine the current share price in the market (together with the value of debt). However, rather than track share return performance through time these metrics relate the current market values to the amount of capital put into the business by the share owners (and lenders) since its foundation. If the company's strategic and operational actions have been robust in the pursuit of shareholder value then the current market value of the equity and debt should be significantly greater than the amount placed in the directors' hands by the purchasers of shares, through the retention of profits and the lending of debt capital. If, however, the market currently values the shares and the debt at less than the amount put in we know for sure that value has been destroyed.

The observation of a positive difference between current valuation and amount injected may or may not mean value has been generated. This depends on whether the investment made by shareholders and debt holders produced a sufficient *rate* of return given the time period over which the money was held in the stewardship of the directors. So, for example, if a firm founded 15 years ago with £1m of shareholder capital and £1m of debt which paid out no dividends and received no more funds from finance providers is now valued at £3.56m for its shares and £1m for its debt, we need to know the required rate of return on equity for this risk class given the shareholders' opportunity cost to judge whether the annual rate of return of around 8.8 per cent is sufficient. (Chapter 19 discusses how to calculate required rates of return.) Excess Return, ER, is a modified MVA, allowing for this opportunity cost of capital over the period.

These five metrics can only be used for 'entire firm' assessment for a select group of companies – those with a stock market price quotation (around 3,000 companies in the UK, and fewer in many other countries). Also note that these metrics cannot be used for analysis of parts of the business, such as a strategic business unit, for the obvious reason that there is no share price for a section of a company.

The metrics discussed in the last chapter on the other hand, can be used both for disaggregated analysis and for the entire firm. So it makes sense to think in terms of there being at least nine whole-firm value metrics available. Furthermore, these should not be thought of as mutually exclusive. They are complementary if calculated and viewed with sufficient informed thought.

Total shareholder return (TSR)

Shareholders are interested in the total return earned on their investment relative to general inflation, a peer group of firms, and the market as a whole. **Total return** includes dividend returns and share price changes over a specified period. For one-period TSR:

$$\text{TSR} = \frac{\text{Dividend per share} + (\text{Share price at end of period} - \text{Initial share price})}{\text{Initial share price}} \times 100$$

[1] Wealth Added Index and WAI are both registered trademarks of the consulting firm Stern Stewart and Co.

[2] Market Value Added and MVA are both registered trademarks of the consulting firm Stern Stewart and Co.

Consider a share that rises in price over a period of a year from £1 to £1.10 with a 5p dividend paid at the end of the year. The TSR is 15 per cent.

$$\text{TSR} = \frac{d_1 + (\text{P}_1 - \text{P}_0)}{\text{P}_0} \times 100$$

$$\text{TSR} = \frac{0.05 + (1.10 - 1.00)}{1.00} \times 100 = 15\%$$

When dealing with multi-period TSRs we need to account for the dividends received in the interim years as well as the final dividend. The TSR can be expressed either as a total return over the period or as an annualised rate.

So, for example, if a share had a beginning price of £1, paid annual dividends at the end of each of the next three years of 9p, 10p and 11p and had a closing price of £1.30, the total average annual return (assuming dividends are reinvested in the company's shares immediately on receipt) is calculated via the internal rate of return (*see* Chapter 2 for an introduction to the IRR):

Time	0	1	2	3
Price/cash flow (p)	–100	9	10	11+130

$$-100 + \frac{9}{1+r} + \frac{10}{(1+r)^2} + \frac{141}{(1+r)^3} = 0$$

At:

$r = 19\%: -1.7037$

$r = 18\%: 0.6259$

$$\text{The internal rate of return} = 18 + \frac{0.6259}{0.6259 + 1.7037} = 18.27\%$$

The annualised TSR is 18.27 per cent.

The total shareholder return over the 3 years = $(1 + 0.1827)^3 - 1 = 65.4\%$.

TSRs for a number of periods are available from financial data organisations, such as Datastream and on most financial websites (e.g. www.advfn.com).

In **Exhibit 18.1** the TSRs of the ten largest UK companies are shown for one year and for five years. Some perform better over one year relative to the others in the group, others perform better over five years. The 'dividend yield plus capital gain' metric needs to be used in conjunction with a benchmark to filter out economy-wide or industry-wide factors. So, it would make sense to compare the TSR for Barclays with the TSR for the banking sector to be able to judge whether a particular performance is due to factors lifting the entire sector or is attributable to good management in the firm.

The TSR has taken off as a key performance measure. For example, HSBC say in the 2006 annual report that payment to directors will be increased if TSR over three years relative to a comparator group of 28 major banks is good. If HSBC's TSR is ranked at 15th or worse then no bonus payment is due, but if HSBC is 7th or better a large amount will flow to the directors. Between 7th and 15th a reduced amount is granted. It is now compulsory for UK quoted companies to include in their annual reports a five-year chart showing their total shareholder return compared with an appropriate index.

Exhibit 18.1 TSRs for the 10 largest UK quoted companies over one year and five years to September 2007

	TSR – 1 year %	TSR – 5 years %
BP	3	48
HSBC	7	43
Vodafone	40	80
GlaxoSmithKline	–6	10
Royal Bank of Scotland	17	17
Royal Dutch Shell	17	76
Barclays	29	53
Anglo American	34	301
HBOS	25	63
Astrazeneca	0	2

Source: Thomson Financial Datastream.

Thoughtful use of the TSR

There are four issues to be borne in mind when making use of the TSR:

1 ***Relate return to risk class*** Two firms may have identical TSRs and yet one may be subject to more risk due to the greater volatility of earnings as a result, say, of the economic cycle. The risk differential must be allowed for in any comparison. This may be particularly relevant in the setting of incentive schemes for executives. Managers may be tempted to try to achieve higher TSRs by taking greater risk.

2 ***TSR assumes efficient share pricing*** It is difficult to assess the extent to which share return out-performance is due to management quality and how much is due to exaggerated (or pessimistic) expectations of investors at the start and end of the period being measured. If the market is not efficient in pricing shares and is capable of being swayed by irrational optimism and pessimism then TSRs can be an unreliable guide to managerial performance. Even an efficient market often prices shares away from true economic value – it just does so in an unbiased manner.

3 ***TSR is dependent on the time period chosen*** A TSR over a three-year period can look very different from a TSR measured over a one-year or ten-year period. Consider the annual TSRs for company W in **Exhibit 18.2**. Measured over the last two years the TSR of company W is very good. However over five years a £1,000,000 investment grows to only £1,029,600, an annual rate of return of 0.6 per cent.

Exhibit 18.2 Annual TSRs for company W

	Annual TSR	Value of £1m investment made at the end of 2002
2003	+10%	£1,100,000
2004	–20%	£880,000
2005	–40%	£528,000
2006	+30%	£686,400
2007	+50%	£1,029,600

4 ***TSR is useless in the case of companies not quoted on a stock market (over 99 per cent of firms)***

TSRs must be used with caution. Fund managers are increasingly wary of using them in managerial incentive schemes because performance bonuses dependent on one-year TSRs may result in managers being rewarded for general stock market movements beyond their control – *see* **Exhibit 18.3**. Even worse would be the encouragement of the selective release of information to boost short-term TSR so that managers can trigger higher bonuses.

Exhibit 18.3

Investor warns companies on measures for executive pay

FT

By Tony Tassell

One of the country's leading institutional investors has warned companies to avoid using share price-based performance measures in setting executive pay.

Standard Life, which has about £70bn of assets under management and owns about 2 per cent of the UK stock market, said it would oppose pay packages solely based on share price-based performance targets such as total shareholder return – the share price movement of a company plus dividend payments.

The fund manager, one of the most activist in the UK market, said in its new corporate governance guidelines that pay schemes should be underpinned by challenging performance targets of underlying financial performance such as earnings. 'We expect executive bonus and share incentive schemes to use challenging performance conditions that are neither too easy nor too tough to achieve,' said Guy Jubb, head of corporate governance. 'We continue to have reservations about the use of total shareholder return and other share price performance schemes.'

Some shareholders believe share price-based targets are influenced too much by factors outside management control such as general stock market sentiment . . .

Source: *Financial Times*, 2 December 2003, p. 8. Reprinted with permission.

Wealth Added Index (WAI)[3]

The Wealth Added Index, promoted by consultant firm Stern Stewart, measures the increase in shareholders' wealth through dividends received and share capital gains (or losses) over a period of time, say five years, after deducting the 'cost of equity', defined as the return required for shares of that risk class. It thus addresses one of the key criticisms of TSR by checking whether an impressive-looking increase in market capitalisation has actually produced a return greater than the investors' opportunity cost given the length of time over which the growth in capitalisation is measured.

To calculate the WAI first observe the rise in market capitalisation (the market value of all the shares) over, say, five years. Deduct the rise that is due to the firm obtaining more money from shareholders in this period, for example from a rights issue. Then add back cash returned to shareholders in the form of dividends and share buy-backs. Then deduct the required return on the money shareholders committed to the company for the relevant period – this is the equity opportunity cost – *see* Chapter 19 for a discussion on how this might be calculated.

Under WAI analysis those companies whose share values grow more than the return required by investors create value. Those that return less than the required return destroy value. Take the case of Vodafone over the five years to September 2007 (*see* **Case study 18.1**).

[3] Wealth Added Index and WAI are both registered trademarks of the consulting firm Stern Stewart and Co.

Case study 18.1 Vodafone's wealth added index

(Analysis undertaken 18.9.07)

Vodafone had a market capitalisation of £61,685m on 18 September 2002. By 18 September 2007 this had grown to £88,291m. This seems an impressive rise, but we do not know yet whether shareholders put more money into the company in the intervening five years, nor whether the company had paid out vast sums to shareholders in the form of dividends and share buy-backs. Also, we do not know whether the gain is more than or less than the required rate of return given that these shares are risky. The WAI takes into account these factors.

To calculate the WAI we could consult the annual reports to establish the amount paid to the company by shareholders buying more shares. This is £802m over the five years. We could also examine the accounts to find the amounts paid to shareholders in dividends and share buy-backs. This is a very large sum because of the policy in 2004–6 of large buy-backs (£20,628m). Together with dividends shareholders received £31,278m.

If we used the CAPM to calculate the required rate of return we need to do some investigation. The 10-year UK government bond yield in September 2002 was 4.41 per cent (from Datastream) – we'll take this as our risk-free rate of return (*see* Chapter 19 for a discussion on this). Beta is more tricky because we ideally need to know the beta in 2002. We could search for a database which had historic betas, but given our scepticism about the validity of CAPM beta for risk adjustment we'll simply take 1.0 as the value (Datastream showed a beta of 1.12 in 2007). The equity risk premium can be taken as 5 per cent – *see* Chapter 8 for a discussion on this. Thus the rate of return over one year is

$r_i = r_f + \beta(\text{RP}) = 4.41 + 1(5) = 9.41\%$. Over five years: $(1 + 0.0941)^5 - 1 = 0.57$ or 57%.

	£m
Change in market capitalisation over five years	26,606
Less the rise due to additional money injected by shareholders	–802
Plus dividends, share buy-backs, etc.	31,278
Less required rate of return over five years £61,685 × 0.57	–35,160
Wealth Added Index	21,922

Thus Vodafone added wealth to shareholders above their required rates during this five-year period. However, to put this into perspective the total return (dividends + capital gains) on the UK stock market as a whole in the five years was over 100 per cent. Also, Vodafone's market capitalisation stood at over £90,000m in 2001.

Points to consider when using the WAI

- Stern Stewart rely on the CAPM to calculate the required return on share capital. There are serious problems with this – *see* Chapters 8 and 19 for a discussion.
- There is an assumption that stock markets price shares correctly given company prospects at both the start and end dates. The experience of the tech bubble around the turn of the millennium should have raised a doubt here, let alone the evidence of share mispricing in the academic literature (*see* Chapter 14). So, one has to be sceptical as to whether outperformance is due to managerial skill or market movements. Volatile markets can turn an apparent 'wealth creator' into a 'wealth destroyer' which may have little to do with managerial performance.
- Critics say that the WAI, in most circumstances, is no better than the use of an appropriately benchmarked TSR (i.e. benchmarked against a group of peers). Certainly, in a period of declining share prices (e.g. 2000–3) you will find that the vast majority of companies show depressingly negative WAI because the deduction of CAPM-required returns remains so high (usually between 8 per cent and 11 per cent per year). Comparing total return performance against peers (e.g. industry group) may be quicker, more informative and more just to the

managers. At the heart of the problem is the artificiality of requiring companies to achieve increases in market capitalisation above a theoretical minimum rate in all market conditions and regardless of whether all similar companies are experiencing an industry or market-wide shock.

- Because the WAI measures in cash terms rather than percentages the biggest companies appear at the top (and bottom) of the league tables, pushing out smaller companies with higher percentage rates of return on shareholders' capital.

Market Value Added (MVA)

Stern Stewart and Co. have also developed the concept of **Market Value Added (MVA)**. This looks at the difference between the total amount of capital put into the business by finance providers (debt and equity) and the current market value of the company's shares and debt. It provides a measure of how executives have performed with the capital entrusted to them. A positive MVA indicates value has been created. A negative MVA indicates value has been destroyed.

MVA = Market value – Invested capital

where:

Market value	=	Current value of debt, preference shares and ordinary shares.
Invested capital	=	All the cash raised from finance providers or retained from earnings to finance new investment in the business, since the company was founded. In practice, balance asset values (with a few adjustments) are used.

Managers are able to push up the conventional yardstick, total market value of the business, simply by investing more capital. The MVA, by subtracting capital injected or retained from the calculation, measures net value generated for shareholders.

Worked example 18.1 Illustration of MVA

MerVA plc was founded 20 years ago with £15m of equity finance. It has no debt or preference shares. All earnings have been paid out as dividends. The shares in the company are now valued at £40m. The MVA of MerVA is therefore £25m:

MVA = Market value – Capital
MVA = £40m – £15m = £25m

If the company now has a rights issue raising £5m from shareholders the market value of the firm must rise to at least £45m in order for shareholder wealth to be maintained. If the market value of the shares rose to only £44m because shareholders are doubtful about the returns to be earned when the rights issue money is applied within the business (that is, a negative NPV project) shareholders will lose £1m of value. This is summarised in the table below.

	Before rights issue	After rights issue
Market value	£40m	£44m
Capital	£15m	£20m
MVA	£25m	£24m

According to Stern Stewart if a company pays a dividend both the 'market value' and the 'capital' parts of the equation are reduced by the same amount, and MVA is unaffected. Imagine an all-equity financed company with an equity market value of £50m at the start of the year, which increased to £55m by the end of the year after generating £10m of post-tax profit in the year and the payment of a £6m dividend. The capital put into the firm by shareholders over the company's life by purchasing shares and retained earnings amounted to £20m at the start of the year, as shown in the table below.

	At start of year		At end of year
Market value	£50m		£55m
Capital	£20m	£20m	
	plus earnings	£10m	
	less dividend	–£6m	
			£24m
MVA	£30m		£31m

If the company had not paid the dividend then, according to Stern Stewart, both the market value and the capital rise by £6m and the MVA would remain at £31m, as shown in the next table.

	At start of year	At end of year
Market value	£50m	£61m
Capital	£20m	£30m
MVA	£30m	£31m

This dividend policy irrelevance argument is challenged in Chapter 22, where it is shown that increasing or decreasing the dividend may add value. The point to take from this section is that profits produced by the business are just as much part of the ownership capital as money raised through the sale of shares to owners at the foundation of the business or in later years. If £1 is to be retained rather than paid out to shareholders then market capitalisation should rise by £1 to avoid loss of shareholder value. If it does not then that £1 can be put to a better use outside of the firm.

A short cut

In the practical application of MVA analysis it is often assumed that the market value of debt and preference shares equals the book value of debt and preference shares. This permits the following version of the MVA, cutting out the necessity to obtain data for the debt levels (market value or balance sheet value) or the preference share values:

MVA = Market value of ordinary shares – Capital supplied by ordinary shareholders

Judging managerial performance by an MVA

The absolute level of MVA is perhaps less useful for judging performance than the change in MVA over a period. Alistair Blair, writing in *Management Today*,[4] is quite scathing about crude MVA numbers:

> An MVA includes years old and now irrelevant gains and losses aggregated on a pound-for-pound basis with last year's results and today's hope or despair, as expressed in the share price. Surely, what we are interested in is current performance, or if we're going to be determinedly historic, performance since the current top management team got its hands on the controls.

[4] Alistair Blair, *Management Today*, January 1997, p. 44.

What Alistair Blair seems to be proposing is that we convert an MVA into a period (say, five-year) measure of performance so we can isolate the value-creating contribution of a particular span of years under the leadership of a team of managers.

Points to consider when using an MVA

There are a number of issues to be borne in mind when using MVA.

- **Estimating the amount of cash invested** Measuring the amount of capital put into and retained within a business after it has been trading for a few years is fraught with problems. For example, does R&D expenditure produce an asset (i.e. become part of shareholders' funds) or is it an expense to be written off the profit and loss account? How do you treat goodwill on acquisitions? The accountants' balance sheet is not designed for measuring capital supplied by finance providers, but at least it is a starting point. Stern Stewart make use of a proxy measure called 'economic book value'. This is based on the balance sheet capital employed figure, subject to a number of adjustments. Critics have pointed out that these adjustments are rather arbitrary and complex, making it difficult to claim that economic book value equals the theoretically correct 'capital' in most cases.
- **When was the value created?** The fact that a positive MVA is produced is often of limited use when it comes to evaluating the quality of the current managers. For a company that is a few decades old the value drivers may have been put in place by a previous generation of directors and senior managers. The MVA measure can be considered crude in that it measures value created over the entire life of the firm but fails to pinpoint when it was created. Nor does it indicate whether value creation has stopped and the firm is living off accumulated fat in terms of strong market positions, patents, etc. Ideally we need to know whether new value-creating positions are being constructed rather than old ones being eroded.
- **Is the rate of return high enough?** It is difficult to know whether the amount of MVA generated is sufficiently in excess of capital used to provide a satisfactory return relative to the risk-adjusted time value of money. Positive MVA companies can produce poor rates of return. Take company B in Worked example 18.2. Firm B has a much lower rate of return on capital than A and yet it has the same MVA.
- **Inflation distorts the MVA** If the capital element in the equation is based on a balance sheet figure then during times of inflation the value of capital employed may be understated. If capital is artificially lowered by inflation *vis-à-vis* current market value for companies where investment took place a long time ago then the MVA will appear to be superior to that for a similar firm with recently purchased assets.
- **Trusting that the stock market prices shares correctly at all times** This is a very dubious assumption. It is not even required for pricing efficiency, which is based on the notion of there being no bias in the errors of pricing, not on the perfect pricing of all shares at all times – *see* Chapter 14.

Worked example 18.2

	A	B
MVA	£50m	£50m
Market value	£100m	£100m
Capital	£50m	£50m
Age of firm	3 years	30 years

Both firms have paid out profits each year as dividends, therefore the capital figure is the starting equity capital.

- **The MVA is an absolute measure** Judging companies on the basis of absolute amounts of pounds means that companies with larger capital bases will tend to be at the top (and bottom) of the league tables of MVA performance. Size can have a more significant impact on the MVA than efficiency. This makes comparison between firms of different sizes difficult. The market to book ratio, MBR, described below, is designed to alleviate this problem.
- **Two companies showing the same MVA can produce different levels of real wealth for shareholders** – *see* the example of AVerseM in the next section.

Excess return (ER)

Two of the major drawbacks of the MVA are illustrated in the case of AVerseM. This company was established five years ago with £10m of equity capital (assume no debt throughout the example). At that time equity put at this level of risk was required to produce a return of 10 per cent per year. The company made after-tax profits of £1m in its second year and £1m in its third year (zero in the other years). These profits were paid out as dividends in the year of occurrence. AVerseM now has a market capitalisation of £11m and is therefore showing a respectable MVA of £1m.

MVA = Market value – Invested capital
Invested capital = Original capital + Retained earnings = £10m + £0m
MVA = £11 – £10m = £1m

(Stern Stewart and Co. actually define capital as 'essentially a company's net assets (total assets less non-interest-bearing current liabilities)' Stewart (1991), p. 744) rather than strictly the amount of money put into the business by investors. They make three major groups of adjustments to the raw balance sheet numbers, such as adding the capital value of leases and adding back R&D expenses previously written off, to try to get closer to the amount put into the business by investors, but using balance sheet numbers for a firm that has operated for a number of years must be considered crude.]

If the original £10m put into AVerseM had been invested elsewhere to yield its required rate of return for the same risk, 10 per cent, today shareholders would hold an investment worth £16.1m:

$$10\,(1 + 0.1)^5 = £16.1\text{m}$$

Determining whether AVerseM has achieved shareholder wealth creation is far from clear with the MVA, even if we had a precise 'invested capital' figure. Notice how the MVA has ignored the value of dividends. If there was another company that also started with £10m of capital and has a current market capitalisation of £11m, but has made no profits and paid no dividends over the five years, it would also show an MVA of £1m, despite the fact that it has not generated as much wealth for shareholders as AVerseM.

Also notice that the time value of money is not allowed for (the third problem listed for the MVA). To cope with these two problems we could use **Excess Return, ER.**[5] This metric examines the amount of capital invested in previous years and then charges the company for its use over the years. It also credits companies for the returns shareholders can make from the money paid to them (e.g. as dividends) when re-invested in the market.

Excess return expressed in present value terms = Actual wealth expressed in present value terms – Expected wealth expressed in present value terms

[5] This method is promoted by Young and O'Byrne (2001) in their book.

Expected wealth is calculated as the value of the initial investment in present value terms if it had achieved the required rate of return over the time it has been invested in the business. So, for AVerseM this is £16.1m. (Of course, if AVerseM had raised more money from shareholders, in, say, the fourth year, through a rights issue, we would include that here too.)

Actual wealth is the present values of cash flows received by shareholders, plus the current market value of the shares. Each cash flow received in past years needs to be compounded up to the present.

Present value of dividends if the money received was invested at the required rate of return between receipt and present time	Received 3 years ago	£1m $(1 + 0.1)^3$ =	£1.331m
	Received 2 years ago	£1m $(1 + 0.1)^2$ =	£1.210m
Current market value of shares (market capitalisation)			£11.000m
	Actual wealth		£13.541m

Excess return = Actual wealth – Expected wealth
Excess return = £13.541 – £16.1m = –£2.559m

Value has been destroyed as the return achieved is less than 10 per cent per year.

Expected return suffers from many of the other drawbacks associated with the MVA, such as finding the figure for the capital injected by shareholders for a company that has traded for many years, faith that the market will price the shares correctly and the fact that because it is an absolute measure rather than a percentage it favours larger firms. There is also the difficulty of selecting the required rate of return (*see* Chapter 19).

Also if inflation turned out to be much higher than anticipated when the bulk of the capital was invested, ER will be distorted as nominal returns on the stock market rise, lifting current market value of shares.

Market to book ratio (MBR)

Rather than using the arithmetical difference between the capital raised and the current value, as in the MVA, the **MBR** is the market value divided by the capital invested. If the market value of debt can be taken to be the same as the book value of debt then a version of the MBR is the ratio of the market value of the company's ordinary shares to the amount of capital provided by ordinary shareholders (if preference share capital can be regarded as debt for the purpose of value-based management).

There is, of course, the problem of estimating the amount of capital supplied, as this is usually dependent on adjusted balance sheet net asset figures. For example, goodwill write-offs and other negative reserves are reinstated, as in the MVA. It is also suggested that asset values be expressed at replacement cost so that the MBR is not too heavily distorted by the effects of inflation on historic asset figures.

The rankings provided by the MBR and the MVA differ sharply. The largest companies dominating the MVA ranks generally have lower positions when ordered in terms of MBR.

Worked example 18.3 **Illustration of the MBR**

MaBaR plc has an equity market value of £50m, its book debt is equal to the market value of debt, and the capital contributed by ordinary shareholders amounts to £16m.

Market value	£50m
Capital	£16m
MVA	£34m
MBR £50m/£16m	= 3.125

MaBaR has turned every pound put into the firm into £3.125 (if the capital figure is money put into the firm).

The MBR suffers from the problems listed for the MVA, except for the issue of measuring in absolute amounts of money. An additional problem for the MBR is that care must be taken when using the MBR for performance measurement and target setting because if it is wrongly applied it is possible for positive NPV projects to be rejected in order for MBR to be at a higher level. Take the case of a company with an MBR of 1.75 considering fundraising to make an investment of £10m in a project estimated to produce a positive NPV of £4m. Its MBR will fall even though the project is shareholder wealth enhancing (*see* Worked example 18.4).

Worked example 18.4

		Before project		After project acceptance
Value of firm		£70m	(70 + 10 + 4)	£84m
Capital		£40m		£50m
MVA		£30m		£34m
MBR	70/40 =	1.75	84/50 =	1.68

The new project has an incremental MBR of 1.4 (14/10 = 1.4). This is less than the firm's original overall MBR of 1.75, which is therefore dragged down by the acceptance of the project. This effect should be ignored by managers motivated by shareholder wealth enhancement. They will focus on NPV.

Exhibit 18.4 **Summary table of market-based performance metrics**

	Merits	Problems
TSR	• Very easy to understand and calculate. • Not affected by the problems of having to rely on accounting balance sheet values. • Subjective and complex adjustments are avoided. • Not affected by relative size of firms. • Better able to identify when value is created than are the MVA and the MBR.	• Vulnerable to distortion by the selection of time period over which it is measured. • Need to express the TSR relative to a peer group to obtain impression of performance. • It fails to relate risk to the TSR. • Assumes stock market perfection in share pricing. • Useless for firms without a quotation.
WAI	• Relates return to risk class by allowing for opportunity cost of capital. • No need to make a (dubious) estimation of the amount of capital injected into a business from its balance sheet. • Better able to identify when value is created than the MVA and the MBR.	• There are doubts about the CAPM as the only method of calculating the required rate of return. • The assumption of stock market pricing perfection can be challenged. • In bear markets most companies show negative WAI for years, despite the management performing well against their sector or the market. • Useless for firms without a quotation. • Affected by relative size of firms – favours large firms.

	Merits	Problems
MVA	• Assesses wealth generated over entire business life. • Managers judged on the MVA have less incentive to invest in negative NPV projects than those judged on earnings growth. • Measures in absolute amounts of money.	• Many doubts about the validity of the capital invested figure used. • Excessive faith in the correct pricing of shares by stock markets. • Size of business not allowed for in inter-firm comparisons. • Do not know in which part of the firm's history the value was created. • Inflation can distort the MVA. • Do not know if rate of return obtained is higher or lower than the required rate of return given the opportunity cost of capital. • Two firms with the same MVA may have generated different levels of wealth for shareholders because the MVA fails to allow properly for dividends paid in previous years.
ER	• Allows for the time value of money on share holder money put into the business. • Gives credit for dividends received by shareholders. • Assesses wealth generated over the entire life of the firm. • Managers judged on an ER have less incentive to invest in negative NPV projects than those judged on earnings growth. • Measures in absolute amounts of money.	• Size of business not allowed for in inter-firm comparisons. Larger companies tend to produce the better ERs. • Excessive faith in the correct pricing of shares by stock markets. • There is difficulty in selecting the appropriate required rate of return, especially if inflation has varied considerably. • Useless for firms without a quotation for their shares.
MBR	• Assesses wealth generated over entire business life. • Measures in percentage terms and therefore allows comparison between firms of all sizes.	• Same problems as the MVA except it is not an absolute measure and therefore does not favour larger firms. • Over-reliance on the MBR for performance measurement and incentive schemes can lead to bad investment decisions. • Useless for those firms without a market quote for their shares.

Concluding comments

The TSR, WAI, MVA, ER and MBR should be seen not as competitors, but as complementary, especially as each has serious drawbacks. Relying on one indicator is unnecessarily restrictive. It is perfectly possible to use all these measures simultaneously and thereby overcome many of the weaknesses of each individually. And don't forget that the measures described in the previous chapter may be used alongside these in the assessment of value creation by the entire firm.

Key points and concepts

- **Total shareholder returns (TSR)**

  Single period:

$$\text{TSR} = \frac{\text{Dividend per share} + (\text{Share price at end of period} - \text{Initial share price})}{\text{Initial share price}}$$

  Multi-period:

  Allow for intermediate dividends in an internal rate of return calculation.

- **Wealth added index (WAI)**

  WAI = Change in market capitalisation over a number of years

Less net additional money put into business by investors after allowance for money returned to investors by dividends, etc.

Less required rate of return

- **Market value added (MVA)**

  MVA = Market value – Invested capital

  or, if the market value of debt (and preference shares) equals the book value of debt (and preference shares):

  Equity MVA = Ordinary shares' market value – Capital supplied by ordinary shareholders

- **Excess return (ER)**

  [Excess return expressed in present value terms] = [Actual wealth expressed in present value terms] – [Expected wealth expressed in present value terms]

  Expected wealth is calculated as the value of the initial investment (plus any other monies placed in the business by shareholders) in present value terms if it had achieved the required rate of return over the time it has been invested in the business. Actual wealth is the present values of cash flows received by shareholders, plus the current market value of the shares. Each cash flow received in past years needs to be compounded up to the present:

  Actual wealth = [Present value of dividends if the money received was invested at the required rate of return between receipt and present time] + [Current market value of shares (market capitalisation)]

- **Market to book ratio (MBR)**

$$\text{MBR} = \frac{\text{Market value}}{\text{Capital invested}}$$

  An alternative is the equity MBR:

$$\text{MBR} = \frac{\text{Market value of ordinary shares}}{\text{Amount of capital invested by ordinary shareholders}}$$

References and further reading

Stewart, G.B. (1991) *The Quest for Value.* New York: Harper Business.

Written by a founding partner in Stern Stewart and Co., the US consultancy which has so successfully promoted MVA and EVA®. Some useful insights.

Young, D.S. and O'Byrne, S.F. (2001) *EVA and value-based management: a practical guide to implementation.* New York: McGraw-Hill.

A useful overview of value-based management.

Website

Stern Stewart www.stern.stewart.com. Some useful additional literature.

Case study recommendation

Please see www.pearsoned.co.uk/arnold for case study synopses

- Amtelecom Group Inc. Authors: Craig Dunbar and Andrew Cogan (2004). Source: Richard Ivey School of Business/UWO. Also available at Harvard Business School case study website.

Self-review questions

1 What is the total shareholder return (TSR) and what are its advantages and problems as a metric of shareholder wealth creation?

2 Compare the metrics total shareholder return (TSR) and wealth added index (WAI).

3 Describe the metric market value added (MVA) and note the problems in its practical use.

4 Outline the market to book ratio (MBR) and state why it is superior to the MVA for some purposes.

5 Compare the value metrics market value added (MVA) and excess return (ER).

Questions and problems

myfinancelab ***Questions with an icon are also available for practice in MyFinanceLab with additional supporting resources.***

1 a Tear plc has not paid a dividend for 20 years. The current share price is 580p and the current share market index level is 3,100. Calculate total shareholder returns for the past three years, the past five years and the past ten years, given the following data:

Time before present	Share price (pence)	Share index
1 year	560	3,000
2 years	550	2,400
3 years	600	2,500
4 years	500	2,000
5 years	450	1,850
6 years	400	1,700
7 years	250	1,300
8 years	170	1,500
9 years	130	1,300
10 years	125	1,000

b Comment on the problems of total shareholders' returns as a metric for judging managerial performance.
c Calculate the wealth added index for ten and five years for Tear plc given the following assumptions:
- The required rate of return on shares of the same risk class as Tear plc, over both ten and five years, was 9 per cent per year.
- The company had 10 million shares in issue throughout the entire period.

d Discuss the advantages of the wealth added index compared with the total shareholder return. What are the difficulties in the practical use of the wealth added index?

?

2 Sity plc has paid out all earnings as dividends since it was founded with £15m of equity finance 25 years ago. Today its shares are valued on the stock market at £90m and its long-term debt has a market value and book value of £20m.

a How much market value added (MVA) has Sity produced?
b What is Sity's market to book ratio (MBR)?
c Given that another company, Pity plc, was founded with £15m of equity capital five years ago and has paid out all earnings since its foundation and is now worth (equity and debt) £110m (£90m equity, £20m debt), discuss the problems of using the MVA and the MBR for inter-firm comparison.
d Calculate the excess return (ER) for both Sity and Pity given that the required rate of return for Sity is 8 per cent per year and the required rate of return is 10 per cent per year for Pity. Sity has paid only two dividends: £2m was paid five years ago and £3m was paid three years ago. Pity has paid £2m in dividends at the end of every year since its foundation.
e Discuss the advantages and disadvantages in using the MVA and ER to judge managerial performance.

?

myfinancelab *Now retake your diagnostic test for Chapter 18 to check your progress and update your study plan.*

Assignment

Using data on a company you know well try to calculate the TSR, WAI, MVA, ER and MBR. Point out the difficult judgements you have had to make to calculate these figures.

CHAPTER 19

The cost of capital

LEARNING OUTCOMES

By the end of this chapter the reader should be able to:

- calculate and explain the cost of debt capital, both before and after tax considerations;
- describe the difficulties in estimating the equity cost of capital and explain the key elements that require informed judgement;
- calculate the weighted average cost of capital (WACC) for a company and explain the meaning of the number produced;
- describe the evidence concerning how UK companies actually calculate the WACC;
- explain the outstanding difficulties in this area of finance.

myfinancelab *Complete your diagnostic test for Chapter 19 now to create your personal study plan*

Introduction

Until this point a cost of capital (required rate of return) has been assumed for, say, a project or a business unit strategy, but we have not gone into much detail about how an appropriate cost of capital is calculated. This vital issue is now addressed.

The objective set for management in a value-based organisation is the maximisation of long-term shareholder wealth. This means achieving a return on invested money that is greater than shareholders could obtain elsewhere for the same level of risk. Shareholders (and other finance providers) have an opportunity cost associated with putting money into your firm. They could withdraw the money placed with you and invest it in a comparable company's securities. If, for the same risk, the alternative investment offers a higher return than your firm's shares, then as a management team you are destroying shareholder wealth.

The cost of capital is the rate of return that a company has to offer finance providers to induce them to buy and hold a financial security. This rate is determined by the returns offered on alternative securities with the same risk.

Using the correct cost of capital as a discount rate is important. If it is too high investment will be constrained, firms will not grow as they should and shareholders will miss out on value-enhancing opportunities. There can be a knock-on effect to the macroeconomy and this causes worry for politicians. For example the one-time President of the Board of Trade, Michael Heseltine, complained:

> Businesses are not investing enough because of their excessive expectations of investment returns . . . The CBI tells me that the majority of firms continue to require rates of return above 20 per cent. A senior banker last week told me his bank habitually asked for 30 per cent returns on capital.[1]

This chapter focuses on the question of how to measure the returns available on a variety of financial securities at different risk levels. This will provide the base for estimating the required rate of return for a particular enterprise.

A word of warning

Too often, academics and consultants give the impression of scientific preciseness in calculating a firm's cost of capital. The reality is that behind any final number generated lies an enormous amount of subjective assessment or, worse, opinion. Choices have to be made between competing judgements on a range of issues, including the appropriate risk premium, financial gearing level and risk measure. Good decision making comes from knowing the limitations of the input variables to the decision. Knowing where informed judgement has been employed in the cost of capital calculation is required to make value-enhancing decisions and thus assist the art of management. In short, the final number for the required rate of return is less important than knowledge of the factors behind the calculation and the likely size of the margin of error. Precision is less important than knowledge of what is a reasonable range.

The required rate of return

The capital provided to large firms comes in many forms. The main forms are equity and debt capital, but there are a number of hybrids, such as convertible bonds. When a finance provider chooses to supply funds in the form of debt finance, there is a deliberate attempt to reduce risk, e.g. by imposing covenants or requiring collateral. However, a lender to a corporation cannot expect to

[1] Quoted in Philip Coggan and Paul Cheeseright, *Financial Times*, 8 November 1994.

eliminate all risk and so the required rate of return is going to be above that of lending to a reputable state such as the USA or the UK. Placing your savings with the UK government by buying its bonds in return for the promise of regular interest and the payment of a capital sum in a future year is the closest you are going to get to risk-free lending. The rate of return offered on government bonds and Treasury bills is the bedrock rate that is used to benchmark other interest rates. It is called the risk-free rate of return, given the symbol r_f.

A stable well-established company with a relatively low level of borrowing and low-risk operations might have to pay a slightly higher rate of return on debt capital than the UK government. Such a company, if it issued a corporate bond with a high credit rating, would pay, say, an extra 100 basis points per year. This is described as the risk premium (RP) on top of the risk-free rate:

Then, the cost of debt capital, k_D, is:

$$k_D = r_f + RP$$

If the current risk free rate is 6 per cent, then $k_D = 7$ per cent.

If the firm has a high level of debt it may need to offer, say, 300 basis points above the risk-free rate. So the required return might be 9 per cent.

$$k_D = r_f + RP = 6 + 3 = 9\%$$

If the form of finance provided is equity capital then the investor is accepting a fairly high probability of receiving no return at all on the investment. On the other hand, if the firm performs well very high returns can be expected. It is the expectation of high returns that causes ordinary shareholders to accept high risk.

Different equities have different levels of risk, and therefore returns. A shareholder in Marks and Spencer is likely to be content with a lower return than a shareholder in, say, an internet start-up, or a company quoted on the Russian stock exchange. Thus we have a range of financial securities with a variety of risk and associated return (*see* **Exhibit 19.1**).

Exhibit 19.1 Risk–return – hypothetical examples

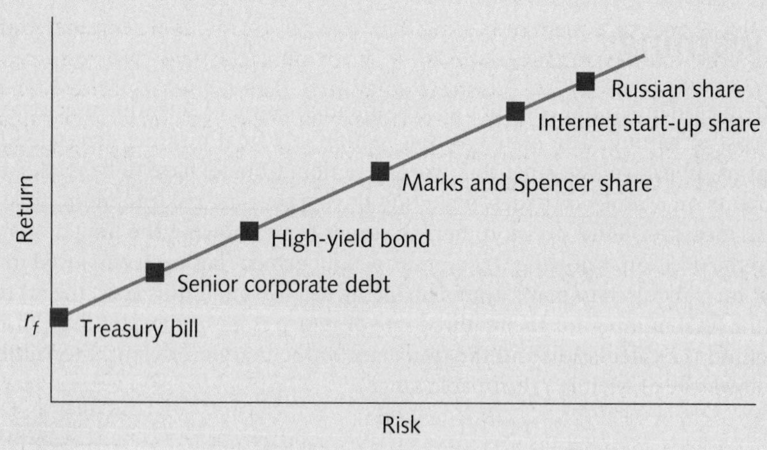

Two sides of the same coin

The issues of the cost of capital for managerial use within the business and the value placed on a share (or other financial security) are two sides of the same coin. They both depend on the level of return (*see* **Exhibit 19.2**). The holders of shares make a valuation on the basis of the returns they estimate they will receive. Likewise, from the firm's perspective, it estimates the cost of raising money through selling shares (or retaining earnings) as the return that the firm will have to pay to

Exhibit 19.2 Two sides of the same coin

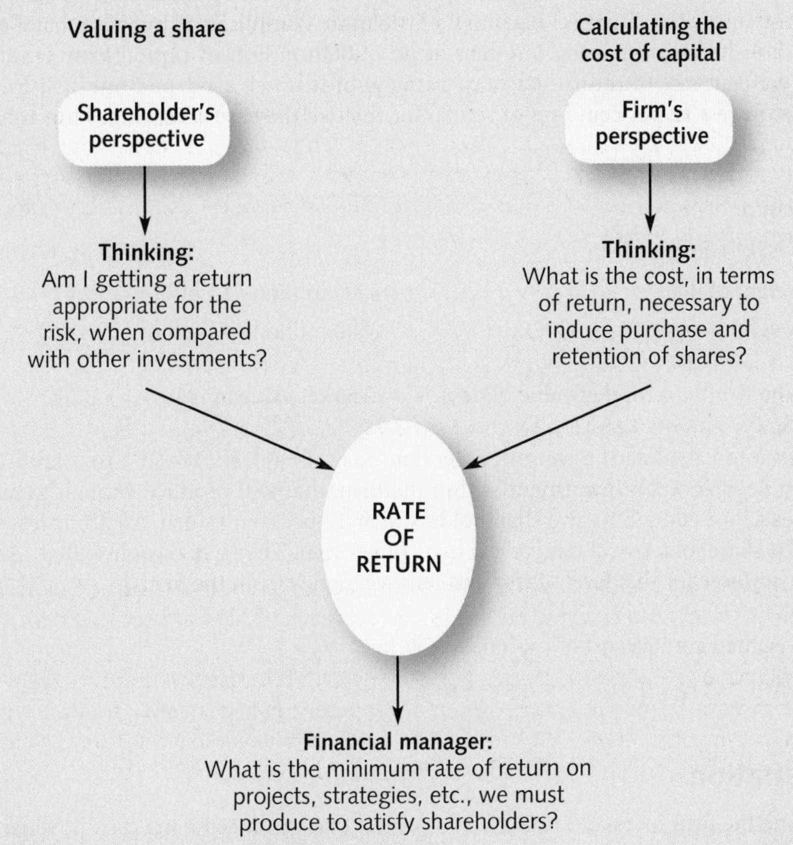

shareholders to induce them to buy and hold the shares. The same considerations apply to bondholders, preference shareholders and so on. If the future cash flowing from the form of finance is anticipated to fall from a previously assumed level then the selling price of the share, bond, etc. goes down until the return is at the level dictated by the returns on financial securities of a similar type and risk. If a company fails to achieve returns that at least compensate finance providers for their opportunity cost it is unlikely to survive for long.

The weighted average cost of capital (WACC)

We have established that firms need to offer returns to finance providers commensurate with the risk they are undertaking. The amount of return is determined by what those investors could get elsewhere at that risk level (e.g. by investing in other companies). If we take a firm that is financed entirely by share capital (and this is the optimal capital structure), then the required rate of return to be used in value analysis, e.g. a project or SBU appraisal, is the required return demanded by investors on the company's shares. However, this is only true if the new project (or division) has the same level of risk as the existing set of projects.

The stock market prices shares on the basis of the current riskiness of the firm. This is determined by the activities it undertakes. A company can be seen as merely a bundle of projects from the perspective of ordinary shareholders. If these projects are, on average, of high risk then the required return will be high. If the proposed project (or division) under examination has the same risk as the weighted average of the current set then the required return on the company's equity capital is the rate appropriate for this project (if the company received all its capital from shareholders and none from lenders). If the new project has a lower risk, the company-wide cost of capital needs to be adjusted down for application to this project.

If we are dealing with a company that has some finance in the form of debt and some in the form of equity the situation becomes a little more complicated. Imagine that a corporation is to be established by obtaining one-half of its £1,000 million of capital from lenders, who require an 8 per cent rate of return for an investment of this risk class, and one-half from shareholders, who require a 12 per cent rate of return for the risk they are accepting. Thus we have the following facts:

Cost of debt			$k_D = 8\%$
Cost of equity			$k_E = 12\%$
Weight of debt	$V_D/(V_D + V_E)$	£500 million / £1 billion	$W_D = 0.5$
Weight of equity	$V_E/(V_D + V_E)$	£500 million / £1 billion	$W_E = 0.5$

Where V_D = Market value of debt, V_E = Market value of equity

We need to calculate the **weighted average cost of capital** (**WACC**) to establish the minimum return needed on an investment within the firm, that will produce enough to satisfy the lenders and leave just enough to give shareholders their 12 per cent return. Anything less than this WACC and the shareholders will receive less than 12 per cent. They will recognise that 12 per cent is available elsewhere for that level of risk and remove money from the firm.

$$\text{Weighted average cost of capital, WACC} = k_E W_E + k_D W_D$$

$$\text{WACC} = (12 \times 0.5) + (8 \times 0.5) = 10\%$$

Illustration

Imagine the firm invested £100,000 in a project that produced a net cash flow per year of £10,000 to infinity (assuming a perpetuity makes the example simple), the first call on that cash flow is from the debt holders, who effectively supplied £50,000 of the funds. They require £4,000 per annum. That leaves £6,000 for equity holders – an annual return of 12 per cent on the £50,000 they provided. Thus an overall return of 10 per cent (the WACC) provides an 8 per cent return on the capital supplied by lenders and 12 per cent on the capital supplied by shareholders.

If things go well and a return of £11,000 (i.e. 11 per cent) is generated then debt holders still receive the contracted amount of £4,000, but the equity holders get a return significantly above the minimum they require, at 14 per cent return: £7,000 is left to pay out to shareholders on their £50,000 capital input to this project.

Of course, this example assumes that all new projects use the same proportions of debt and equity finance as the firm as a whole, that is 50 per cent of its capital comes from debt. The issue of whether you should use different types (or weights) of finance for different projects (say, borrow all the £100,000 for this particular project at 8 per cent) rather than use the 50 : 50 mixture is discussed later.

Lowering the WACC and increasing shareholder returns

Examining the WACC formula we see an apparently simple way of reducing the required rate of return, and thus raising the value of a project, division or the entire firm: change the weights in the formula in favour of debt. In other words, alter the capital structure of the firm by having a higher proportion of its capital in the form of cheaper debt – the jargon referring to levels of debt relative to equity capital is 'financial gearing' or 'leverage' (used in US).[2]

[2] More details of gearing definitions and types of gearing can be found in Chapter 21.

For example, if the company is expected to produce £100 million cash flow per year (to infinity), and its WACC is 10 per cent, its total corporate value ('enterprise' value that is, the value of the debt and equity) is:

£100 million / 0.10 = £1,000 million

Let us try to lower the WACC.

Imagine that instead of the firm being established with 50 per cent debt in its overall capital it is set up with 70 per cent debt. The proportion of total capital in the form of equity is therefore 30 per cent. *If* (a big if) the equity holders remain content with a 12 per cent return while the debt holders accept an 8 per cent annual return the WACC will fall, and the value of the firm will rise.

$$\text{WACC} = k_E \, W_E + k_D \, W_D$$
$$\text{WACC} = (12 \times 0.3) + (8 \times 0.7) = 9.2\%$$

Firm value = £100 million /0.092 = £1,086.96 million

Why don't all management teams increase the proportion of debt in the capital structure and 'magic up' some shareholder value? The fly in the ointment for many firms is that equity investors are unlikely to be content with 12 per cent returns when their shares have become more risky due to the additional financial gearing. The key question is: how much extra return do they demand? The financial economists and Nobel laureates Franco Modigliani and Merton Miller (MM) presented the case that in a perfect capital market (in which all participants such as shareholders and managers have all relevant information, all can borrow at the same rate of interest, etc.) the increase in k_E would exactly offset the benefit from the increase in the debt proportion; this would leave the WACC constant, so increasing the debt proportion does not add to shareholder value; the only factor that can add value is the improvement in the underlying performance of the business, i.e. its cash flows. According to this view (that there is no optimal capital structure that will maximise shareholder wealth) there is no point in adjusting the debt or equity proportions.

In this stylised world k_D remains at 8 per cent, but k_E moves to 14.67 per cent, leaving the WACC, firm value and shareholder value constant.

$$\text{WACC} = k_E \, W_E + k_D \, W_D$$
$$\text{WACC} = (14.67 \times 0.3) + (8 \times 0.7) = 10\%$$

However, there is hope for managers trying to improve shareholder wealth by adjusting the capital structure because in constructing a perfect world Modigliani and Miller left out at least two important factors: tax and financial distress.[3]

The benefit of tax

The first consideration is tax. A benefit of financing through debt is that the annual interest can be used to reduce taxable profit thus lowering the cash that flows out to the tax authorities. In contrast, the annual payout on equity (dividends) cannot be used to reduce the amount of profit that is taxed. The benefits gained from being able to lower the tax burden through financing through debt reduces the effective cost of this form of finance. (Note this reduction is only valid if the company is profitable and paying corporation tax.)

To illustrate: Firm A is a company in a country that does not permit interest to be deducted from taxable profit. Firm B is in a country that does permit interest to be deducted. In both companies the interest is 8 per cent on £500m. Observe the effect on the amount of profit left for distribution to shareholders in the table overleaf.

[3] Modigliani and Miller did not ignore tax and financial distress in their work, but did downplay them in the formulation of their early model.

	Firm A £m	Firm B £m
Profits before interest and tax	100	100
Interest		–40
Taxable profit	100	60
Amount taxed @ 30%	–30	–18
Interest	–40	
Amount available for distribution shareholders	30	42

The extra £12 million for Firm B reduces the effective cost of debt from 8 per cent to only 8 (1 – T), where T = the corporation tax rate, 30 per cent. The cost of debt capital falls to 8 (1 – 0.3) = 5.6, or £28 million on £500 million of debt. The taxman, by taking £12m less from the company purely because the tax rules allow the deductibility of interest from taxable profit, lowers the effective cost of the debt.

So including the '**tax shield**' effect, we find a reduction in the WACC that leads to an increase in the amount available for shareholders. In our example, if we assume tax on corporate profits at 30 per cent then the effective cost of debt falls to 5.6 per cent. This results in the WACC becoming 8.8 per cent.

k_{DBT} = Cost of debt before tax benefit = 8%
k_{DAT} = Cost of debt after tax benefit = 8 (1 – T) = 8 (1 – 0.30) = 5.6%

If we assume a 50 : 50 capital structure the WACC is:

$$\text{WACC} = k_E W_E + k_{DAT} W_D$$
$$\text{WACC} = (12 \times 0.5) + (5.6 \times 0.5) = 8.8\%$$

Investment project cash flows discounted at this lower rate will have a higher present value than if discounted at 10 per cent. Given that the debt holders receive only their contractual interest and no more, this extra value flows to shareholders.

Financial distress constrains gearing

The introduction of the tax benefit strongly pushes the bias towards very high gearing levels to obtain a lower WACC and higher value. However, we do not observe such extreme gearing very often in real-world companies. There are a number of reasons for this, the most important of which is the increasing risk to the finance providers (particularly equity capital holders) of financial distress and, ultimately, liquidation. (*See* Chapter 21 for more reasons and a more detailed discussion of capital structure.)

As gearing rises so does the probability of equity investors receiving a poor (no) return. So they demand higher expected returns to compensate. At first, the risk premium rises slowly, but at high gearing levels it rises so fast that it more than offsets the benefit of increasing debt in the capital structure. This is demonstrated in **Exhibit 19.3**, in which the WACC at lower levels of debt is primarily influenced by the increasing debt proportion in the capital structure, and at higher levels by the rising cost of equity (and eventually debt).

The conclusion drawn from the capital structure literature is that there is an optimal gearing level that achieves the lowest WACC and highest firm value. When companies are calculating their WACC they should use this target gearing ratio and not a gearing ratio they happen to have at the time of calculation.

So, if in our example the required return on equity rises from 12 per cent to 13 per cent when the proportion of the debt in the capital structure rises to 65 per cent from 50 per cent, and the effective rate of return payable on debt is 5.6 per cent after the tax shield benefit (i.e. remaining at 8 per cent before the tax benefit) then the WACC falls and the value available for shareholders rises.

Exhibit 19.3 Cost of capital with different capital structures (including consideration of the tax shield and finance distress).

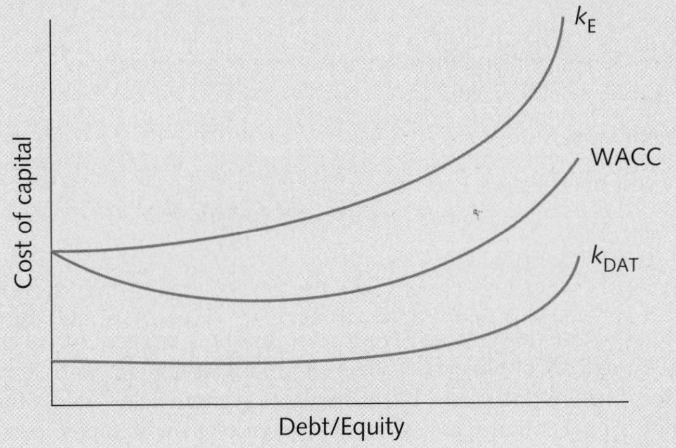

$$WACC = k_E W_E + k_{DAT} W_D$$
$$WACC = (13 \times 0.35) + (5.6 \times 0.65) = 8.19\%$$

Taking financial gearing too far

For this particular company we will assume that 65 per cent gearing is the optimum debt/equity ratio. If we go to 80 per cent debt we find this reduces shareholder wealth because the firm's projects (in aggregate) are now discounted at a higher rate of return (WACC), reducing their present value. The main reason the discount rate rises significantly is that the required return on shares rises to, say, 30 per cent as investors fear massive potential loss due to the large commitment of the firm to pay out interest whether or not the firm is doing well. The debt holders are also worried about increased financial distress risk – i.e. they might not receive their capital or interest – and so they increase their required rate of return to 10 per cent before the tax shield benefit, which is an effective cost to the firm of 7 per cent after allowing for the tax shield benefit.

$$WACC = k_E W_E + k_{DAT} W_D$$
$$WACC = (30 \times 0.2) + (7 \times 0.8) = 11.6\%$$

Worked example 19.1 **Poise plc**

The rate of return offered to debt holders of Poise plc before considering the benefit to shareholders of the tax shield, k_{DBT}, is 10 per cent, whereas the required return on equity is 20 per cent. The total amount of capital in use (equity + debt), V, is £2m. Of that, £1.4m represents the market value of its equity, V_E, and £600,000 equals the market value of its debt, V_D. These are the optimum proportions of debt and equity.

Thus:

k_{DBT} = 10%
k_E = 20%
V = £2m
V_E = £1.4m
V_D = £0.6m

The weight for equity capital is:

$$W_E = \frac{V_E}{V} = \frac{1.4}{2.0} = 0.7$$

The weight for debt is:

$$W_D = \frac{V_D}{V} = \frac{0.6}{2.0} = 0.3$$

The corporate tax rate is 30 per cent and therefore the after-tax cost of debt is:

$$k_{DAT} = k_{DBT}(1 - T)$$
$$k_{DAT} = 10(1 - 0.30) = 7\%$$

The weighted average cost of capital for Poise is:

$$\begin{aligned} WACC &= k_E W_E + k_{DAT} W_D \\ &= 20\% \times 0.7 + 7\% \times 0.3 \\ &= 16.1\% \end{aligned}$$

This is the rate of return Poise needs to achieve on new business projects if they are of the same risk as the average risk of the current set of projects. If the new projects are of higher or lower risk an adjustment needs to be made to the discount rate used – this is discussed in more detail later in the chapter.

If Poise is considering a project that requires an investment of £1m at Time 0 and then produces after-tax annual cash flows before interest payments of £161,000 as a perpetuity (i.e. it achieves a 16.1 per cent rate of return) then the net cost of satisfying the debt holders after the tax shield benefit is £21,000. (The debt holders supplied 30 per cent of the £1m invested, i.e. £300,000; and the cost to the firm of satisfying them is £300,000 × 7% = £21,000.)

The remainder of the annual cash flows go to the shareholders; so they receive £140,000 per year, which is a 20 per cent return on the £700,000 they supplied.

If the project produces a much lower annual cash flow of £100,000 (a rate of return of 10 per cent) then the debt holders still receive £21,000, leaving only £79,000 for the shareholders. These investors could have achieved a return of 20 per cent by investing in other companies at this level of risk. An annual return of £79,000 represents a mere 11.3 per cent return (£79,000/£700,000). Thus shareholders suffer a loss of wealth relative to the forgone opportunity.

An Excel spreadsheet version of these calculations is available at www.pearsoned.co.uk/arnold.

The *Financial Times* article in **Exhibit 19.4** makes use of the cost of capital concept.

Exhibit 19.4

Lex column – returns

FT

Corporate returns on capital should not, over time, exceed their cost of capital. That is the theory. Aside from the ticklish subject of defining the time period, the aggregate picture masks some stark sectoral differences.

Pharmaceuticals and biotechnology, for instance, have managed a median return on invested capital, excluding goodwill, of just over 20 per cent between 1963 and 2004, according to a McKinsey study. The sector managed to squeeze out even higher returns between 1995 and 2004. Software and services, household products and media are other types of businesses where returns are high, according to McKinsey. This is evidence of the power of brands, patents and product development.

Why do returns matter? High returns translate into stronger free cash flows since companies do not have to invest as much to generate sales and gross cash flows. This is an important reminder to investors fixated on growth. A company whose business generates returns below its cost of capital should usually make reversing this position its priority, rather than chasing new, marginal, projects in the name of growth.

But investors should not necessarily punish those companies or sectors with high existing returns that decide to ramp up investment – choosing to take on new projects with somewhat lower returns. For as long as the net present value of a project is positive, there is still something there to be mined for shareholders.

Source: Financial Times, 11 February 2006, p. 12. Reprinted with permission.

The cost of equity capital

A shareholder has in mind a minimum rate of return determined by the returns available on other shares of the same risk class. Managers, in order to maximise shareholder wealth, must obtain this level of return for shareholders from the firm's activities. If a company does not achieve the rate of return to match the investor's opportunity cost it will find it difficult to attract new funds and will become vulnerable to takeover or liquidation.

With debt finance there is generally a specific rate payable for the use of capital. In contrast, ordinary shareholders are not explicitly offered payments. However, there is an implicit rate of return that has to be offered to attract investors. It is the expectation of high returns that causes ordinary shareholders to accept high risk.

Investors in shares require a return that provides for two elements. First, they need a return equal to the risk-free rate (usually taken to be that on government securities). Secondly, there is the risk premium, which rises with the degree of systematic risk:

Rate of return on shares	=	Risk-free rate	+	Risk premium
k_E	=	r_f	+	RP

The risk-free rate gives a return sufficient to compensate for both impatience to consume and inflation (*see* Chapter 2).[4] To estimate the relevant risk premium on a firm's equity we generally take two steps.

- Stage one is to estimate the average extra return demanded by investors above the risk-free return to induce them to buy a portfolio of average-risk-level shares. We usually look back at the returns shareholders have *actually* received on average-risk shares above the risk-free return in the past and make the assumption that this is what they also demanded before the event, *ex ante* in the jargon,[5] and then make the further assumption that this is the extra rate that they demand on shares today. The average annual risk premium actually obtained by shareholders can only be calculated over an extended period of time (many decades) as short-term returns on shares can be distorted (they are often negative for a year, for example). The risk premium is expressed as the difference between the market return, r_m, and the risk-free return, r_f, that is $(r_m - r_f)$.
- The second stage is to adjust the risk premium for a typical (average-risk-level) share to suit the risk level for the particular company's shares under consideration. If the share is more risky than the average then $(r_m - r_f)$ is multiplied by a systematic risk factor greater than 1. If it is less risky it may be multiplied by a systematic risk factor of less than 1, say 0.8, to reduce the premium.

The capital-asset pricing model (CAPM)

In the forty years following the development of the CAPM, in practical cost of capital calculations, the risk premium has generally been adjusted by a beta based on the extent to which a share had moved when a market index moved (its covariance with the market), say over a five-year period:

$$k_E = r_f + \beta (r_m - r_f)$$

There are some fairly obvious problems with this approach; for example, does historic co-movement with the market index reflect future risk accurately? (*See* Chapter 8 for more

[4] This is assuming that future inflation is included in the projected cash flows. That is, we are using nominal cash flows and a nominal interest rate. An alternative method is to use real cash flows and a real discount rate (i.e. with inflation removed).

[5] An alternative is the 'forward looking approach' in which the analyst tries to obtain estimates of what extra future annual return investors require at this time for investing in an averagely risky share. There are some serious doubts about the subjective nature of the inputs to these calculations – the Gordon growth model, explained in the next section, is one such method.

problems.) But at least we have some anchor points for equity cost calculations. We have general acceptance that it is only systematic risk that is compensated for in the required returns. We also have an approximate figure for the historic risk premium on the average-risk share and thus, given a certain risk-free rate, we know roughly what rate of return is required for an average share – with rates on government securities at 5 per cent this would be around 9–10 per cent. We could also probably agree that the relative volatility of a share against the market index is some indicator of riskiness, and that therefore more variable shares should bear a higher risk premium. Despite this progress we are still left with some uncertainty over how to adjust the average risk premium for specific shares – beta is less than perfect.

The Gordon growth model method for estimating the cost of equity capital

The most influential model for calculating the cost of equity in the early 1960s (and one which is still used today) was created by Gordon and Shapiro (1956), and further developed by Gordon (1962). Suppose a company's shares priced at P produce earnings of E per share and pay a dividend of *d* per share. The company has a policy of retaining a fraction, *b*, of its earnings each year to use for internal investments. If the rate of return (discount or capitalisation rate) required on shares of this risk class is k_E then, under certain restrictive conditions, it can be shown that earnings, dividends and reinvestment will all grow continuously, at a rate of $g = br$, where *r* is the rate of return on the reinvestment of earnings, and we have:

$$P = \frac{d_1}{k_E - g}$$

(There is more on this formula in Chapter 20.)

Solving for k_E we have:

$$k_E = \frac{d_1}{P} + g$$

where d_1 is the dividend to be received next year.

That is, the rate of return investors require on a share is equal to the prospective dividend yield (d_1/P) *plus* the rate at which the dividend stream is expected to grow (*g*).

Gordon and Shapiro said that there are other approaches to the estimation of future dividends than the extrapolation of the current dividend on the basis of the growth rate explicit in *b* and *r*, so we can derive *g* in other ways and still the k_E formula remains valid.

A major problem in the practical employment of this model is obtaining a trustworthy estimate of the future growth rate of dividends to an infinite horizon. Gordon and Shapiro (1956) told us to derive this figure from known data in an objective manner, using common sense and with reference to the past rate of growth in a corporation's dividend. In other words a large dose of judgement is required. The cost of equity capital under this model is very sensitive to the figure put in for *g*, and yet there is no reliable method of estimating it for the *future*, all we can do is make reasoned estimates and so the resulting k_E is based merely on an informed guess. Using past growth rates is one approach, but it means that it is assumed that the future growth of the company's earnings and dividends will be exactly the same as in the past – often an erroneous supposition. Professional analysts' forecasts could be examined, but their record of predicting the future is generally a poor one – especially for more than two years ahead (remember this model requires us to estimate *g* for all future years, to an infinite horizon).

The cost of retained earnings

The most important source of long-term finance for most corporations is **retained earnings**. There are many large companies that rarely, if ever, go to their shareholders to raise new money, but rely on previous years' profits. There is a temptation to regard retained earnings as 'costless' because it was not necessary for the management to go out and persuade investors to invest by offering a rate of return.

However, retained earnings should be seen as belonging to the shareholders. They are part of the equity of the firm. Shareholders could make good use of these funds by investing in other firms and obtaining a return. These funds therefore have an opportunity cost. We should regard the cost of retained earnings as equal to the expected returns required by shareholders buying new shares in a firm. There is a slight modification to this principle in practice because new share issues involve costs of issuance and therefore are required to give a marginally higher return to cover the costs of selling the shares.

The cost of debt capital

The cost of debt is generally determined by the following factors:

- The prevailing interest rates.
- The risk of default (and expected rate of recovery of money lent in the event of default).
- The benefit derived from interest being tax deductible.

There are two types of debt capital. The first is debt that is traded, that is, bought and sold in a security market. The second is debt that is not traded.

Traded debt

In the UK bonds are normally issued by companies to lenders with a nominal value of £100. Vanilla bonds carry an annual coupon rate until the bonds reach maturity when the nominal or par value of £100 is paid to the lender (*see* Chapter 11 for more details). The rate of return required by the firm's creditors, k_D, is represented by the interest rate in the following equation which causes the future discounted cash flows payable to the lenders to equal the current market price of the bond P_D. We know the current price P_D of the bond in the market, the annual cash flow that will go to the lenders in the form of interest, i, and we know the cash to be received, R_n, when the bond is redeemed at the end of its life. The only number we don't yet have is the rate of return, k_D. This is found in the same way as the internal rate of return is found:

$$P_D = \sum_{t=1}^{t=n} \frac{i}{(1+k_D)^t} + \frac{R_n}{(1+k_D)^n}$$

where:

i = annual nominal interest (coupon payment) receivable from year 1 to year n;

R_n= amount payable upon redemption;

k_D= cost of debt capital (before the tax benefit).

$\sum_{t=1}^{t=n}$ means add up the results of all the $\frac{i}{(1+k_D)^t}$ from next year (year 1) to the t number of years of the bond's life.

For example, Elm plc issued £100m of bonds six years ago carrying an annual coupon rate of 8 per cent. They are due to be redeemed in four years for the nominal value of £100 each. The next coupon is payable in one year and the current market price of a bond is £93. The cost of this redeemable debt can be calculated by obtaining the internal rate of return, imagining that a new identical set of cash flows is being offered to the lenders from a new (four-year) bond being issued today. The lenders would pay £93 for such a bond (in the same risk class) and receive £8 per year for four years plus £100 at the end of the bond's life. Thus, the cash flows from the firm's perspective are:

Year	0	1	2	3	4
Cash flow	+£93	–£8	–£8	–£8	–£108

Thus the rate of return being offered is calculated from:

$$93 = \frac{8}{1 + k_D} + \frac{8}{(1 + k_D)^2} + \frac{8}{(1 + k_D)^3} + \frac{108}{(1 + k_D)^4}$$

With k_D at 11 per cent the discounted cash flow on the right hand side = 90.69.
With k_D at 10 per cent the discounted cash flow on the right hand side = 93.66.
Using linear interpolation the IRR can be found:

$$k_D = 10\% + \frac{93.66 - 93.00}{93.66 - 90.69}(11 - 10) = 10.22\%$$

Even though the bonds were once worth a total of £100m in the market, this is no longer their value because they are now selling at £93 each. The total market value of the bonds today, V_D, is calculated as follows:

$$V_D = £100\text{m} \times \frac{£93}{£100} = £93\text{m}$$

We are concerned with finding the cost to a company of the various types of capital it might use to finance its investment projects, strategic plans, etc. It would be wrong to use the coupon rate of 8 per cent on the bond for the cost of debt. This was the required rate of return six years ago (assuming the bond was sold for £100). A rate of 10.22 per cent is appropriate because this is the rate of return bond investors are demanding in the market today. The cost of capital is the best available return elsewhere for the bondholders for the same level of risk. Managers are charged with using the money under their command to produce a return at least equal to the opportunity cost. If the cash flows attributable to these lenders for a project or SBU are discounted at 8 per cent then a comparison of the resulting net present value of the investment with the return available by taking the alternative of investing the cash in the capital markets at the same risk is not being made. However, by using 10.22 per cent for the bond cost of capital we can compare the alternatives available to the lenders in the financial markets.

In the calculation for Elm plc taxation has been ignored and so the above calculation of 10.22 per cent should be properly defined as the cost of debt before tax, k_{DBT}. An adjustment is necessary to establish the true cost of the bond capital to the firm.

If T is the rate of corporate tax, 30 per cent, then the cost of debt after tax, k_{DAT}, is:

$$k_{DAT} = k_{DBT}(1 - T)$$
$$k_{DAT} = 10.22\,(1 - 0.30) = 7.15\%$$

A short cut

We have calculated the yield to redemption on a very simple bond from first principles, to illustrate the key elements. In reality, most bonds offer coupon payments every six months – this complicates the type of analysis shown above (*see* Chapter 11). However, yields to redemption on bonds of different risk classes are available commercially, which avoids effort. The *Financial Times* displays the yields ('bid yield') offered on a range of frequently traded bonds of various risk classes (*see* the tables, 'Global Investment Grade' and 'High Yield and Emerging Market Bonds'). Two useful websites for bond yields are *Investors Chronicle*: www.ic-community.co.uk/bonds and the Bondsonline Group, Inc.: www.bondsonline.com. These sources may not be able to provide the yield to redemption for the particular bond that interests you, but you can discover the rates payable for bonds of different credit ratings. So if you know or can estimate the credit rating of the company under examination you can obtain an approximate rate of return (before the tax shield benefit K_{DBT}).

Untraded debt

Most debt capital, such as bank loans, is not traded and repriced regularly on a financial market. We need to find the rate of interest that is the opportunity cost of lenders' funds – the current 'going rate' of interest for the risk class. The easiest way to achieve this is to look at the rate being offered on similar tradable debt securities.

Floating-rate debt

Most companies have variable-rate debt in the form of either bonds or bank loans. Usually the interest payable is set at a margin over a benchmark rate such as bank base rate or LIBOR. For practical purposes the current interest payable can be taken as the before-tax rate of return (k_{DBT}) because these rates are the market rates. There is a rational argument against this simple approach based on the difference between short- and long-term interest rates. For example, it may be that a firm rolls over a series of short-term loans and so in effect will be using this as long-term finance. In this case the theoretically correct approach is to use the long-term interest rate and not the current short-term rate because the former more accurately reflects what is likely to be required to be paid over the life of the loan.

The cost of preference share capital

Preference shares have some characteristics in common with debt capital (e.g. a specified annual payout of higher ranking than ordinary share dividends) and some characteristics in common with equity (dividends may be missed in some circumstances, and the dividend is not tax deductible) – *see* Chapter 10 for more details. If the holders of preference shares receive a fixed annual dividend and the shares are irredeemable the perpetuity formula may be used to value the security:

$$\mathrm{P_p} = \frac{d_1}{k_p}$$

where $\mathrm{P_p}$ is the price of preference shares, d_1 is the annual preference dividend, k_p is the investors' required rate of return.

Therefore, the cost of this type of preference share is given by:

$$k_p = \frac{d_1}{\mathrm{P_p}}$$

Hybrid securities

Hybrid securities can have a wide variety of features – e.g. a convertible bond is a combination of a straight bond offering regular coupons and an option to convert the bond to shares in the company. It is usually necessary to calculate the cost of capital for each of the component elements separately. This can be complex and is beyond the scope of this chapter.

Calculating the weights

Book (balance sheet) values for debt, equity and hybrid securities should not be used in calculating the weighted average cost of capital. Market values should be used. For example, a company might have raised £100m by selling £100 perpetual bonds, which promised annual coupons of £5 each without a definite cease date, when interest rates were 5 per cent. However if general interest rates rise to, say, 10 per cent for this risk class bonds offering £5 per year will not be attractive at £100 each, therefore the price will fall to £50 until they yield the required 10 per cent return. It is the £50m current market value figure that should be used in the weightings. The rationale for using market values is that we need to generate a return for the finance providers on the basis of their current contribution to the capital of the firm and in relation to the current opportunity cost – accounting values have little relevance to this. Investors in bonds right now are facing an opportunity cost of £50m (i.e. they could sell the bonds and release £50m of cash) so this is the figure that managers should see as the amount sacrificed by these finance providers, not the £100m that the bonds once traded at.

With equity capital it is correct to use the **market capitalisation** figure (current share price multiplied by number of shares issued to investors). This is the amount that current investors are sacrificing to invest in this company today – the shares could be sold in the marketplace at that value. The balance sheet value for equity shareholders' funds is not relevant. This is likely to be very different from the market capitalisation. Balance sheets consist of a series of historic accounting entries that bear little relation to the value placed on the shares by investors. Market capitalisation figures are available in Monday editions of the *Financial Times* for quoted companies. Most financial websites provide market capitalisation, e.g. www.londonstockexchange.com.

The WACC with three or more types of finance

The formula becomes longer, but not fundamentally more difficult, when there are three (or more) types of finance. For example, if a firm has preference share capital as well as debt and equity the formula becomes:

$$\text{WACC} = k_E W_E + k_{DAT} W_D + k_p W_P$$

where W_P is the weight for preference shares and,

$$W_E = \frac{V_E}{V_E + V_D + V_P} \quad W_D = \frac{V_D}{V_E + V_D + V_P} \quad W_P = \frac{V_P}{V_E + V_D + V_P}$$

The weight for each type of capital is proportional to market values – and, of course, $W_E + W_D + W_P$ totals to 1.0.

Classic error

Managers are sometimes tempted to use the cost of the latest capital raised to discount projects, SBUs, etc. This is wrong. Also they must not use the cost of the capital they might be about to raise to finance the project.

The latest capital raised by a company might have been equity at, say, 12 per cent, or debt at a cost of, say, 8 per cent. If the firm is trying to decide whether to go ahead with a project that will produce an IRR of 10.5 per cent the project will be rejected if the latest capital-raising exercise was for equity and the discount rate used was 12 per cent. On the other hand the project will be accepted if, by chance, the latest funds raised happen to be debt with a cost of 8 per cent. The WACC should be used for all projects – at least, for all those of the same risk class as the existing set of projects. The reason is that a firm cannot move too far away from its optimum debt-to-equity ratio level. If it does its WACC will rise. So, although it may seem attractive for a subsidiary manager to promote a favoured project by saying that it can be financed with borrowed funds and therefore it needs only to achieve a rate of return in low single figures it must be borne in mind that the next capital-raising exercise after that will have to be for equity to maintain an appropriate financial gearing level.

What about short-term debt?

Short-term debt should be included as part of the overall debt of the firm when calculating the WACC. The lenders of this money will require a return. However, to the extent that this debt is temporary or offset by cash and marketable securities held by the firm it may be excluded.

Finance and operating leases usually require fixed regular payments over lengthy periods of time incorporating an interest rate. These commitments are similar to bank loan obligations and so the capitalised value of the leases should be regarded as adding to the debt of the firm.

Applying the WACC to projects and SBUs

The overall return generated on the finance provided to a firm is determined by the portfolio of current projects. Likewise the risk (systematic) of the firm is determined by the collection of projects to which it is currently committed. If a firm made an additional capital investment that has a much higher degree of risk than the average in the existing set then it is intuitively obvious that a higher return than the normal rate for this company will be required. On the other hand if an extraordinarily low-risk activity is contemplated this should require a lower rate of return than usual.

Some multidivisional firms make the mistake of demanding that all divisions achieve the same rate of return. This results in low-risk projects being rejected when they should be accepted and high-risk projects being accepted when they should be rejected.

Exhibit 19.5 is drawn up for an all-equity financed firm, but the principle demonstrated applies to firms financed by a mixture of types of capital. Given the firm's normal risk level the market demands a return of 11 per cent. If another project is started with a similar level of risk then it would be reasonable to calculate NPV on the basis of a discount rate of 11 per cent. This is the opportunity cost of capital for the shareholders – they could obtain 11 per cent by investing their money in shares of other firms in a similar risk class. If, however, the firm invested in project A

Exhibit 19.5 Rates of return for projects of different systematic risk levels

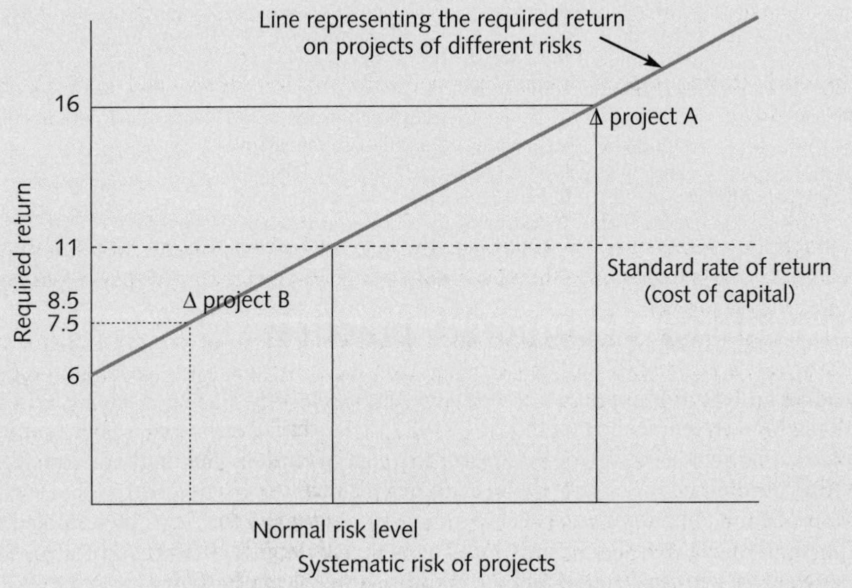

with a risk twice the normal level management would be doing their shareholders a disservice if they sought a mere 11 per cent rate of return. At this risk level shareholders can get 16 per cent on their money elsewhere. This sort of economic decision making will result in projects being accepted when they should have been rejected. Conversely project B if discounted at the standard rate of 11 per cent will be rejected when it should have been accepted. It produces a return of 8.5 per cent when all that is required is a return of 7.5 per cent for this risk class. It is clear that this firm should accept any project lying on or above the sloping line and reject any project lying below this line.

The rule discussed earlier (that a firm should accept any project that gives a return greater than the opportunity cost of capital) now has to be refined. This rule can only be applied if the marginal project has the same risk level as the existing set of projects. Projects with different risk levels require different levels of return.

Just how high the discount rate has to be is as much a matter for managerial judgement as one based on the measures of risk and return developed by theorists. The CAPM provides a starting point, a framework for thinking about risk premiums, but judging the viability of a project or division is still largely an art which requires experience and perceptive thought, not least because it is very difficult to quantify the likely risk of, say, an internet business. It may be possible to classify projects into broad categories, say, high, medium and low, but precise categorisation is difficult. What is clear is that the firm should not use a single discount rate for all its activities.

The article in **Exhibit 19.6** shows the use of WACC and a comment on the use of WACCs specific to projects.

Exhibit 19.6

BSkyB/triple play

Lex column

FT

'Uploads, downloads, save loads'. The advertising slogan for British Sky Broadcasting's new broadband offering makes it clear what customers can expect. But will Sky make any money out of its move into triple play?

The initial costs – £400m of operating profit to be invested over the next three years – are higher than expected and will prompt earnings downgrades. Sky is targeting a return on capital employed for broadband of 15 per cent by 2011, including the cost of acquiring the Easynet network. That return, however, shrinks to 10.5 per cent post tax, compared with Sky's group weighted average cost of capital (WACC), estimated at about 9 per cent. A WACC specific to the project would be higher still.

A new investment that does little more than meet its cost of capital in five years is hardly compelling – particularly given that Sky's assumptions on further price deflation in broadband provision may prove conservative.

Strategic necessity, however, not standalone economics, is the main reason for the push into broadband. Other telephony providers, including BT, are lining up to make inroads into the television market. Sky has unveiled a strong, cheaply priced product. It already has 8m existing pay-TV subscribers and the expertise to service them. Sky's target for 30 per cent of customers to take broadband by 2010 does not appear too ambitious.

Investing in broadband is the latest example of the rising cost of staying ahead of the pack. There is one thing Sky is guaranteed to have loads of: fierce competition.

Source: Financial Times, 19 July 2006, p. 20. Reprinted with permission.

Empirical evidence of corporate practice

Academic literature promotes forcefully the use of the WACC. But to what extent have UK firms adopted the recommended methods? In 1983 Richard Pike expressed a poor opinion of the techniques used by business people to select the cost of capital: 'the methods commonly applied in setting hurdle rates are a strange mixture of folk-lore, experience, theory and intuition'. In 1976 Westwick and Shohet reported that less than 10 per cent of the firms they studied used a WACC. The position changed significantly over the next two decades. Arnold and Hatzopoulos (2000), in a study of 96 UK firms, found that the majority now calculate a WACC – *see* **Exhibit 19.7**.

Exhibit 19.7 **Replies to the question: How does your company derive the discount rate used in the appraisal of major capital investments? (percentage of respondents)**

	Category of company			
Method used	Small (%)	Medium (%)	Large (%)	Composite (%)
WACC	41	63	61	54
The cost of equity derived from the capital asset pricing model is used	0	8	16	8
Interest payable on debt capital is used	23	8	1	11
An arbitrarily chosen figure	12	4	3	6
Dividend yield on shares plus estimated growth in capital value of share	0	0	3	1
Earnings yield on shares	3	0	0	1
Other	12	8	11	10
Blank	9	8	5	7

Source: Arnold and Hatzopoulos (2000).

Despite years of academic expounding on the virtues of the WACC and extensive managerial education, a significant minority of firms do not calculate a WACC for use in capital investment appraisal. Furthermore, as **Exhibits 19.8** and **19.9** show, many firms that calculate a WACC do not follow the prescribed methods. Further evidence of a light grasp of textbook procedure was demonstrated in some of the statements made by respondents: 'Above is a minimum [WACC]. A hurdle rate is also used which is the mid-point of the above [WACC] and the lowest rate of return required by venture capitalists' 'WACC + safety margin'.

Exhibit 19.8 **Method of calculating the weighted average cost of capital (percentage of respondents that use the WACC)**

	Category of company			
Method	Small (%)	Medium (%)	Large (%)	Composite (%)
Using the capital asset pricing model for equity and the market rate of return on debt capital	50	68	79	70
Cost of the equity calculated other than through the capital asset pricing model with the cost of debt derived from current market interest rates	50	32	18	29
Other	0	0	3	1

Source: Arnold and Hatzopoulos (2000).

Exhibit 19.9 If the weighted average cost of capital is used, then how are the weights defined? (percentage of respondents)

Method of defining weights	Category of company Small (%)	Medium (%)	Large (%)	Composite (%)
A long-term target debt and equity ratio	19	26	39	30
The present market values of debt and equity	44	47	42	44
Balance sheet ratios of debt and equity	37	26	19	26

Source: Arnold and Hatzopoulos (2000).

Gregory and Rutterford (1999) and Rutterford (2000) carried out a series of in-depth interviews with 18 FTSE 100 company finance directors or heads of corporate finance in 1996. All 18 estimate their weighted average cost of capital. They found that 14 of the companies made use of the capital asset pricing model to estimate the equity cost of capital, five used the dividend yield plus growth method (Gordon's growth model), four used the historic real rate of return on equity and five used more than one method.

Risk-free rate and betas used

In terms of the risk-free rate most firms (12 out of 14 using the CAPM) used the yield on UK government bonds – they generally chose a bond with a maturity of between seven and 20 years. The remainder used a real (excluding inflation) rate of interest. None used the Treasury bill rate.

Betas were sourced from financial databases, such as that of the London Business School, or from financial advisers – most firms used more than one source. Many interviewees felt that any fine-tuning of the beta estimate would have less impact on the k_E estimate than would the choice of the equity risk premium.

Risk premiums used

Two out of the 13 firms which estimated an equity risk premium chose a figure from a mid-1990s Barclays Capital Equity Gilt Study. This was based on a different time period from that of the study of Dimson, Marsh and Staunton described in Chapter 8. The Barclays studies published in the mid-1990s tracked returns from 1918 only rather than from January 1900 (the more recent Equity Gilt studies go back to 1900). The risk premium figures picked up by companies from these reports, at around 7.5 per cent, are much higher than that used earlier in this book. The other 11 firms chose a number in a narrow range of 4.5 per cent to 6 per cent. The firms concerned admitted that their estimates were a 'gut feel' choice 'that came from our planning manager. He's an MBA and a lot of his MBA work was on the cost of capital. 5 per cent is a figure he's plucked out of the air based on his experience and knowledge' (Company O: Gregory and Rutterford, 1999, p. 43). Alternatively, managers tended to rely on advice from their bankers that the current equity risk premium was lower than at any time in the past – this had the effect of reducing the WACC estimate by almost two percentage points (compared with using a risk premium of 7.5 per cent) in most cases. This intuitive approach has subsequently been borne out by the downward revision of historic risk premiums in empirical studies.

Cost of debt

All 11 firms that explicitly consider the cost of debt allow for the corporate tax rate to reduce the effective cost. All the companies used the cost of long-term debt. The majority chose to base the cost of debt on the cost of government debt and either take this as the cost of debt or add a credit risk premium. Three companies took the yield on their own outstanding bonds and the remainder chose a long-term bond yield 'based on experience'. 'We do not put in our real cost of debt. There are certain, for example tax driven, vehicles which give us actually quite a low cost of debt . . . So we tend to ignore those. That does build up a nice margin of safety within the target (cost of capital) of course' (Company C: Gregory and Rutterford, 1999, p. 46).

Debt/equity ratios

Ten out of 15 firms that calculated the WACC used a long-run target debt/equity ratio, five used the actual debt/equity ratio and one used both. For firms using a target ratio, this was taken as 20 per cent, 25 per cent or 30 per cent, and was at least as high as the current actual debt/equity ratio, in some cases substantially higher – one firm with a cash surplus nevertheless chose a ratio of 20 per cent.

Ten companies chose to estimate a nominal (including inflation) WACC (average value of 11.67 per cent). Five used a real (excluding inflation) WACC (average value of 8.79 per cent) and three used both a nominal and a real WACC. Rutterford (2000) comments: 'differences in data inputs for the equity risk premium (from 4 per cent to 7.5 per cent) and the choice of debt/equity ratio (from 0 per cent to 50 per cent) meant that the final WACC estimate was a fairly subjective estimate for each firm'.

Hurdle rates

Corporations seem to make a distinction between the WACC and the hurdle rate. Gregory and Rutterford found that the average *base* **hurdle rate** was 0.93 per cent higher than the average WACC. The base hurdle rate is defined as the rate for standard projects, before any adjustments for divisional differences in operating risk, financial risk or currency risk. Most of the firms had a range of hurdle rates, depending on the project or the risk factors.

However, there was no consensus among the firms on how to adjust the differential project risk. Fourteen out of 18 made some adjustment for different levels of risk, with nine of those 14 making some adjustment for country risk or foreign exchange risk as well as for systematic risk. Note, however, that in 17 out of 18 cases the adjustment was made to the base hurdle rate and not to the more theoretically appropriate WACC. There was a general impression of sophistication in attaining the WACC in the first place, followed by a rule-of-thumb-type approach when making risk adjustments: 'The comment I make in terms of the hurdle rates for investment purposes is that we do it relatively simplistically in terms of low risk, high risk, country-specific risk' (Company P: Gregory and Rutterford, 1999, p. 53). Methods range from adding two percentage point increments, to having two possible hurdle rates, say, 15 per cent and 20 per cent. Fifteen firms had premiums of 0 per cent to 8 per cent over the base hurdle rate, while three firms added more than 10 percentage points for the highest-risk projects.

Some way to go yet

Even when the textbook model is accepted a range of WACCs can be estimated for the same firm: 'for example, altering the choice of target debt/equity ratio or equity risk premium can have an impact of 2 per cent or more on the resulting WACC figure. Furthermore, little work has yet been done to extend the complex analysis for the firm's WACC to the divisional level' (Rutterford, 2000, p. 149). This lack of sophistication was confirmed in another study, carried out by Francis and Minchington (2000) which discovered that 24 per cent of firms (of varied sizes) used a divisional cost of capital that reflects the cost of debt capital only, thus significantly underestimating the cost of capital. Furthermore, 69 per cent did not use a different rate for different divisions to reflect levels of risk.[6]

---

[6] The method we use throughout the book is the 'post-tax approach' in which the cost of equity is calculated as a return required after tax deductions on returns and the cost of debt is after the tax shield effect. This is to be used when the cash flows of the project or company to be discounted are calculated after tax has been deducted. Alternatively the 'pre-tax approach' could be used in which the cost of equity is 'grossed up' by 1–T (T = corporation tax rate).

$$k_{\text{E pre-tax}} = \frac{k_{\text{E post-tax}}}{1 - \text{T}}$$

Then Post-tax WACC = Pre-tax WACC (1 – T).

This pre-tax WACC can be used for cash flows before a deduction for tax is made. Regulators, such as those for energy supply (Ofgem), often use a third WACC. This is called 'vanilla WACC'. The required return is set equal to a weighted average of post-tax cost of equity (e.g. normal CAPM calculation shown in this chapter) and pre-tax cost of debt. Tax is estimated and allowed for separately in a similar way as other elements of operating expenditure.

Implementation issues

How large is the equity risk premium?

To understand the controversy over the equity risk premium we need to appreciate that it can only ever be a subjective estimate. The reason for this is that we are trying to figure out how much additional annual return investors in an averagely risky share require above the risk-free rate today. When deciding this, investors are looking at the future, not the past. Each investor is likely to have a different assessment of the appropriate extra return compared with the risk-free investment. We need to assess the weighted average of investors' attitudes.

Using historical returns to see the size of the premium actually received may be a good starting point, but we must be aware that we are making a leap of faith to then assume that the past equity risk premium is relevant for today's analysis with its future focus. In using historic data we are making at least two implicit assumptions:

- There has been no systematic change in the risk aversion of investors over time.
- The index being used as a benchmark has had an average riskiness that has not altered in a systematic way over time.

Differing views

Some City analysts believe that things have changed so radically in terms of the risk of ordinary shares for a fully diversified investor that the risk premium is now very small – some plump for 2 per cent while extremists say that over the long run shares are no more risky than gilts, and therefore say that the premium is zero. To justify their beliefs they point to the conquest of inflation, the lengthening of economic cycles, the increased internationalisation of investment opportunities reducing portfolio volatility, the long bull market (an argument weakened recently) and the increasing supply of risk capital as ageing industrial societies start to save more for retirement.

Barclays Capital, by undertaking a more thorough analysis of historical return data on shares and government bonds, have recently dramatically revised the equity risk premium in their Equity Gilt studies from over seven percentage points greater than gilts to around 4 per cent. The Competition Commission tends to take a range of between 2.5 and 4.5 per cent for inclusion in cost of capital calculations for use in deciding a justifiable rate of return for a company. Ofcom uses 4.5 per cent (but considers a range of 4 per cent to 5 per cent as 'reasonable') as an input to the cost of capital calculation for regulated telecom and media companies. Ofwat (the UK water industry regulator) uses a range of between 4 and 5 per cent, but adds a premium of 0.2 per cent to 0.7 per cent if the company is small (this relates to the evidence that small companies outperform large companies (*see* Chapter 14) – some researchers put this down to additional risk carried by small firms resulting in investors demanding a higher return, rather than pricing inefficiency). Ofgem (the UK gas and electricity regulator) uses a range of 2.5 per cent to 4.5 per cent. The regulators calculate the amount of capital these firms are using and then allow prices charged to the consumer to be at a level which targets an appropriate rate of return (WACC) on the money invested in the business.[7]

An opinion

Equities have not become as safe as gilts. For equities the last two decades of the twentieth century were a charmed period. If long-term history is a guide shareholders will eventually learn the hard way that one can lose a great deal of money in stock markets. It is possible for returns to be negative for an entire decade or more. Turbulence and volatility will be as present in the twenty-first century as in the last. The prudent investor needs to examine a long period of time, in which rare, but extreme, events have disrupted the financial system (wars, depressions, manias and panics) to gain an impression of the risk of shares.

---

[7] An excellent discussion of the calculation of the cost of capital by regulators is to be found in Lockett, M. (2001), 'Calculating the Cost of Capital for the Regulated Electricity Distribution Companies', Aston University MBA Project Dissertation and in a later paper: Lockett, M. (2002), 'Calculating the cost of capital for the regulated electricity distribution companies', *Power Engineering Journal*, October, pp. 251–63. Also, the regulators' websites and publications often include a detailed discussion of the theory and practical difficulties of the calculation of the WACC as well as a justification of the rate they choose. Some excellent examples of these are listed in the Further Reading section.

What is clear is that obtaining the risk premium is not as scientific as some would pretend. The range of plausible estimates is wide and the choosing of 2 per cent rather than 4.4 per cent, or even 7.5 per cent, can have a significant effect on the acceptance or rejection of capital investment projects within the firm, or the calculation of value performance metrics. One of the respondents to the Arnold and Hatzopoulos survey expressed the frustration of practitioners by pointing out that precision in the WACC method is less important than to have reliable basic data: 'The real issue is one of risk premium on equity. Is it 2% or 8%?!'

The importance of and the difficulties of estimating the equity risk premium are considered by the economist John Kay in **Exhibit 19.10**.

Exhibit 19.10

The past is a poor guide to future share earnings

FT

John Kay

In the 20th century, returns on equities substantially exceeded returns on safer assets. The size of the difference depends on the time period, the country and the method of calculation. But estimates of the average long-run value of the equity premium are mostly in the range of 3 per cent to 8 per cent.

Equity investment is riskier than cash or bonds. But not that much riskier. If the average return were even 3 per cent higher, medium to long-term investment in equities would be almost certain to yield more: the risk would become negligible. In countries such as Britain and the US with large equity markets, 5 per cent or more of national income is needed to compensate people for worrying about the value of their stocks.

So why is the historic equity premium figure so high and will be as high in the future? Estimates of the prospective equity premium determine the cost of capital to business. Such estimates are central to every long-term economic decision – how to fund pensions, whether to build nuclear power stations, what to do about climate change.

Some explanations of historic levels of the equity premium imply that it will continue to be high in future. Perhaps there are many people who really need to be richly compensated to invest in equities. Even a small probability of large loss causes them great distress, or puts their job at risk. They invest a lot of emotional energy in turning nervously every morning to the share price pages of the Financial Times. They twitch over their BlackBerries in the airport lounge. They pay fees and commissions to financial advisers in generally unsuccessful pursuit of better returns.

If these are indeed the explanations, then the moral is to discipline yourself to avoid these traps. Accept that there are more important things to worry about than a falling stock market, recognise that daily share price movements are meaningless noise, restrict yourself to reviewing your portfolio only once a year. Stick with a few good stocks and take a cynical view of the claims of financial advisers. You will then gain most of the additional return from equity investment for little of the added cost.

But other explanations of the high equity premium offer less reassurance: they imply that the future cannot be like the past. If you examine figures at the higher end of estimates of the historic premium, you realise that they are arithmetically unsustainable: within a few decades, profits and dividends would absorb the whole of national income.

Perhaps the past century was just a very good time for equity investors. It was the age of inflation, in which real assets did better than nominal assets: the age of the large public corporation, in which big, professionally managed companies came into being and a regulatory framework was put in place that enabled small savers to trust business people with their money. Shareholders benefited from changes in the economic environment that will not happen again.

All historic analysis of investment performance suffers from survivor bias. Returns on the successful investments of the past are generally higher than you can expect on similar investments in the future. Investment managers advertise their best funds, not their dogs; unsuccessful hedge funds close. The equity markets of western Europe and the US are the bourses that remain open. People who put their money a century ago in Russian bonds, Chinese equities and Argentinian tramways lost most of it and there are today no analysts of these markets to tell the sorry tale.

Since none of these explanations is wholly convincing, the most plausible account of the equity premium paradox is that there is a bit of truth in all of them. That would imply that a future premium would be much lower than a historic premium, but still surprisingly high. But with real returns on indexed bonds below 2 per cent around the world and much lower in the UK, an equity premium at the low end of estimates of the historic range would offer a prospective real return on stocks below 5 per cent. That is a lot less than most people expect and many are counting on.

Source: Financial Times, 31 January 2006, p. 19. Reprinted with permission.

The three article excerpts in **Exhibit 19.11** show how WACC calculations make an enormous difference to consumers and managers of regulated industries. Note that the WACC numbers shown are 'real', that is, inflation has been removed (unlike the calculations we did above).

You need to add two percentage points or so inflation allowance to arrive at the 'post-tax nominal WACC' comparable with the method we have used in this chapter. Note also that the regulators are assuming a quite high level of borrowing with full tax shields which brings down the WACC. (The detailed rationale for these calculations is set out in reports posted on the websites of the regulators – well worth a read if you are pursuing this topic in depth.)

Exhibit 19.11

The practical use of the WACC

FT

Lex column – infrastructure returns

Successful regulation of monopolies consists of holding their feet to the fire but leaving them able to stand up afterwards. The latest pricing and investment regime proposed for the UK's electricity and gas transmission networks leaves the likes of National Grid uncomfortable but with their toes intact. Whether the implications are as agreeable across other infrastructure businesses is less clear.

Ofgem, the energy regulator, set a real post-tax rate of return for the transmission business of 4.4 per cent, 20 basis points above its original proposal. Besides the energy utilities, that concession yesterday spurred a positive reaction in the shares of water companies, which face their own review in 2009. Last time, Ofwat, the water watchdog, set a generous real return of 5.1 per cent.

Come 2009, Ofwat is likely to take its lead from Ofgem. Notwithstanding the extra 20bp allowed by Ofgem, the trend is downwards.

The UK's Civil Aviation Authority is expected to announce today a reduced cost of capital assumption for 2008–12 in the airports sector.

UK airports

Virgin Atlantic, the long-haul airline, yesterday called the UK's Civil Aviation Authority 'more of a lapdog than a watchdog'. The outburst followed the CAA's recommendation that the caps on how much regulated airports can charge airlines should rise by substantially more than inflation between 2008 and 2013. The CAA also proposed cutting the allowed real pre-tax rate of return BAA, the airports operator, makes on its regulated assets, from 7.75 per cent currently to 6.2 per cent for Heathrow and 6.7 per cent for Gatwick.

Squeals of protest were not limited to the airlines. Ferrovial, BAA's Spanish owner, also called the CAA's proposals 'unsatisfactory'. The response demonstrates the difficulties the regulator faces in balancing the need to incentivise the airports' owner to make the investment it believes ncessary, whilst pricing fairly for their customers, the airlines.

The job has got more difficult since Ferrovial's takeover of BAA this year. BAA plans £3.3bn of investment between 2008–2013, but the risk to this programme is greater now that its balance sheet has been geared up. To make sure the investment happens, the CAA could tie a greater proportion of revenues to the achievement of investment goals than it currently does. Yet, by doing so, it would create greater unpredictability about those revenues. That, in turn, would increase BAA's overall cost of capital, thus providing further temptation to defer investment.

Energy groups protest at Ofgem's price control plans

By Ed Crooks, Energy Editor

National Grid and other energy companies have protested to Ofgem, the gas and electricity regulator, after it announced only small concessions in its proposals for price control in gas distribution for the next five years.

Ofgem yesterday set out its revised plans for 2008–13, updating its previous proposals, published in May. A final decision will be taken in December.

National Grid said it was 'very disappointed' by the lack of movement from Ofgem.

The regulator plans to allow the gas distribution companies to spend about £1bn a year on replacement of infrastructure and new capital spending. That is a third higher than in the previous five-year period from 2002–7, but significantly less than the companies' plans, which add up to almost £1.2bn a year.

Companies want to invest more because the profits they are allowed to make are based on the size of their regulated asset base.

Ofgem has also tightened up its assumption of the cost of capital that the regulated companies will face, squeezing the returns they will be allowed to make.

In the previous five-year period, the assumed basic cost of capital was 5.25 per cent; in the next period that will be cut to 4.84 per cent.

Gas distribution is treated separately from the high-pressure transmission of gas across the country, which is owned by National Grid.

Sources: 1 *Financial Times*, 5 December 2006, p. 20; 2 *Financial Times*, 6 December 2006, p. 20; 3 *Financial Times*, 25 September 2007, p. 21. Reprinted with permission.

Which risk-free rate?

The risk-free rate is a completely certain return. For complete certainty two conditions are needed:

- The risk of default is zero.
- When intermediate cash flows are earned on a multi-year investment there is no uncertainty about reinvestment rates.

The return available on a zero coupon government bond which has a time horizon equal to the cash flow (of a project, an SBU, etc.) being analysed is the closest we are going to get to the theoretically correct risk-free rate of return.

Business projects usually involve cash flows arising at intervals, rather than all at the end of an investment. Theoretically, each of these separate cash flows should be discounted using different risk-free rates. So, for the cash flows arising after one year on a multi-year project, the rate on a one-year zero coupon government bond should be used as part of the calculation of the cost of capital. The cash flows arising in year five should be discounted on the basis of a cost of capital calculated using the five-year zero coupon rate and so on. However, this approach is cumbersome, and there is a practical alternative that gives a reasonable approximation to the theoretical optimum. It is considered acceptable to use a long-term government rate on all the cash flows of a project that has a long-term horizon. Furthermore, the return on a government bond with coupons, rather than a zero coupon bond, is generally taken to be acceptable.[8] The rule of thumb seems to be to use the return available on a reputable government security having the same time horizon as the project under consideration – so for a short-term project one should use the discount rate which incorporates the short-term government security rate, for a 20-year project use the 20-year government bond yield to maturity.

Note that the risk-free rate used depends on whether the future cash flows are expressed in nominal or real terms. If they are in nominal (money) terms then the risk-free rate should also include the inflation element. If the cash flows are in real terms then the r_f should exclude an allowance for inflation.[9]

How reliable is CAPM's beta?

There are many problems with the use of the capital asset pricing model's beta in the cost of equity capital calculation. We will consider two of them here.

The use of historic betas for future analysis

The mathematics involved in obtaining an historic beta are straightforward enough; however, it is not clear whether using weekly data is more appropriate than monthly, or whether the historical data on the returns on the market and the return on a particular share should be recorded over a one-, three-, five- or ten-year period. Each is likely to provide a different estimate of beta. Even if this is resolved the difficulty of using an historic measure for estimating a future relationship is very doubtful. Betas tend to be unstable over time. If the requirement is to compensate investors for the risk class of the share they hold surely we need a measure of risk that is not volatile, otherwise managers will be rejecting projects in one year that they accept in another purely because of the different time

---

[8] (See Ofcom (2005) for a justification)

[9] Lockett (2002) and the Competition Commission (2007) describe the increasingly popular approach of using the rate of return offered on a UK government index-linked gilt in a WACC calculation that is based on real rates of return and real cash flows. That is, with inflation removed from both. This would appear to be a method used by regulators such as Ofgem, Ofwat and the Competition Commission. This currently provides a figure of around 2 per cent as the required return in the absence of inflation or risk. However, this has fluctuated so wildly over the last 15 years (from 5 per cent to 1 per cent) that the Competition Commission (2007) and Ofcom (Wright *et al.* 2006) put little weight on the current real return offered on an index-linked gilt (around 2 per cent in Autumn 2007) and go for a rate of 2.5 per cent to 'strike a sensible balance' or 'to make an overall judgement based in the range of evidence'. In other words, they don't know what the future risk-free rate is, don't trust Autumn 2007's rate and adjust it towards the average for the last 15 years. So much for scientific precision. If you are conducting an analysis with actual projected cash flows (i.e. with inflation built into the assumptions) then you need to add an estimated inflation rate, which will take you back (approximately) to the rate on the conventional government bond of the same time to maturity.

period over which beta was measured (and whether weekly or monthly data are used). **Exhibit 19.12** gives an impression of the variability of the betas for some randomly selected UK firms (the same for each edition of this book) – some have been stable, while others have changed significantly.

Exhibit 19.12 Betas as measured for the five years to 1997, 2000, 2004 and 2007

	1997	2000	2004	2007
Barclays Bank	1.22	1.55	1.11	1.03
BT	0.91	0.94	1.62	0.94
GUS	0.59	0.39	0.97	n/a
Marks and Spencer	0.95	0.44	0.50	0.64
J. Sainsbury	0.60	0.19	0.80	1.04

Source: Thomson Financial Datastream.

One potential explanation for the shifting betas is that the risk of the security changes – firms change the way they operate and the markets they serve. A company that was relatively insensitive to general market change two years ago may now be highly responsive – but have the companies in Exhibit 19.12 really changed the nature (risk) of their businesses very much over these periods? I doubt it. Alternatively, the explanation may lie in measurement error – large random errors cause problems in producing comparable betas from one period to another. To add to this problem we have a wide variety of market indices (such as the FTSE 100, or the FTSE All-Share) to choose from when calculating the historical co-variability of a share with the market (its beta). The Competition Commission report (2007) gives some idea of the wide variety of betas that could be selected for the same company or project, in this case BAA, the owner of a number of UK airports. While BAA wanted the regulator to accept a beta between 1.97 and 2.52 (for Heathrow), the Civil Aviation Authority suggested between 1.13 and 1.26, while the Competition Commission said it was between 0.8 and 1.0. Remember: each of these used respectable financial arguments to support their beta estimates.

The breakdown in the relationship between beta and return

The fundamental point about the CAPM is that investors demand higher returns on shares that are more volatile relative to the market index. Investors require that a share with a beta of 1.5 should provide a higher return than a share with a beta of 1. Recent evidence has cast doubt on the strength of the relationship between CAPM's beta and return – *see* Chapter 8.

Fundamental beta

Instead of using historic betas calculated through a regression of the firm's returns against a proxy for the market portfolio (e.g. the FTSE 100) some analysts calculate a '**fundamental beta**'. This is based on the intuitive underpinning of the risk-return relationship: if the firm (or project) cash flows are subject to more (systematic) variability then the required return should be higher. What causes greater systematic variability? Three factors have been advanced.

1 **The type of business that the company (SBU or project) is engaged in** Some businesses are more sensitive to market conditions than others. The turnover and profits of **cyclical industries** change a great deal with macroeconomic fluctuations. So, for example, the sale of yachts, cars or designer clothes rises in a boom and crashes in decline. On the other hand, non-cyclical industries, such as food retailing or tobacco, experience less variability with the economic cycle. Thus, in a fundamental beta framework cyclical businesses would be allocated a higher beta than non-cyclical businesses – if the variability is systematic rather than specific to the firm. If the purchase of the product can be delayed for months, years or even indefinitely (i.e. it is discretionary) then the industry is more likely to be vulnerable to an economic downturn.

2 **Degree of operating gearing** If the firm has high fixed costs compared with variable costs of production its profits are highly sensitive to output (turnover) levels. A small percentage fall in sales can result in a large percentage change in profits. The higher variability in profit means that a higher beta should be allocated. (Chapter 21 discusses operating gearing.)

3 **Degree of financial gearing** If the company has high borrowings, with a concomitant requirement to pay interest regularly, then profits attributable to shareholders are likely to be more vulnerable to shocks. So the beta will rise if the company has higher financial gearing (leverage). The obligation to meet interest payments increases the variability of after-interest profits. In a recession profits can more easily turn into losses. Financial gearing exacerbates the underlying business risk.

The obvious problem with using the fundamental beta approach is the difficulty of deriving the exact extent to which beta should be adjusted up or down depending on the strength of the three factors.

Some thoughts on the cost of capital

Progress

There have been a number of significant advances in theory and in practice over the last forty years. No longer do most firms simply use the current interest rate, or adjust for risk in an entirely arbitrary manner. There is now a theoretical base to build on, both to determine a cost of capital for a firm, and to understand the limitations (or qualities) of the input data and economic modelling.

It is generally accepted that a weighted average of the costs of all the sources of finance is to be used. It is also accepted that the weights are to be based on market values (rather than book values), as market values relate more closely to the opportunity cost of the finance providers. Furthermore, it is possible that the WACC may be lowered and shareholder value raised by shifting the debt/equity ratio.

Even before the development of modern finance it was obvious that projects (or collections of projects, as firms are) that had a risk higher than that of investing in government securities require a higher rate of return. A risk premium must be added to the risk-free rate to determine the required return. However, modern portfolio theory has refined the definition of risk, so the analyst need only consider compensation (additional return) for systematic risk.

Outstanding issues

Despite the progress, considerable difficulties remain. Practitioners need to be aware of both the triumphs of modern financial theory as well as its gaps. The area of greatest controversy is the calculation of the cost of equity capital. In determining the cost of equity capital we start with the following facts.

- The current risk-free rate is the bedrock. It is acceptable to use the rate on a government bond with the same maturity as the project, SBU, etc.
- The return should be increased to allow for the risk of a share with average systematic risk. (Add a risk premium to the risk-free rate return.) As a guide, investors have received a risk premium of around 4–5 per cent for accepting the risk level equivalent to that on the average ordinary share over the past 100 years.
- A particular company's shares do not carry average equity risk, therefore the risk premium should be increased or decreased depending on the company's systematic risk level.

So, if the project or SBU under examination has a systematic risk which is lower than that on the average share it would seem sensible that the returns attributable to shareholders on this project should be somewhere between the risk-free rate and the risk-free rate plus, say, 5 per cent. If the project has a systematic risk greater than that exhibited by shares generally then the returns required for shareholders will be more than the risk-free rate plus, say, 5 per cent.

There is a major difficulty calculating the systematic risk level. In the heyday of the CAPM this was simple: beta was all you needed. Today we have to allow for the possibility that investors want compensation for a multiplicity of systematic risk factors. Not unnaturally many business people are unwilling to adopt such a burdensome approach and fall back on their 'judgement' to adjust for the risk of a project. In practice it is extremely difficult to state precisely the risk of a project – we are dealing with future uncertainties about cash flows from day-to-day business operations subject to sudden and unforeseen shocks. The pragmatic approach is to avoid precision and simply place each proposed project into one of three risk categories: low, medium or high. This neatly bypasses the complexities laid out by the theorists and also reflects the fact that decisions made in the real world are made with less than complete knowledge: mechanical decision making within the firm based on over-simplistic academic models is often a poor substitute for judgement that recognises the imperfections of reality.

One thing is certain: if anyone ever tells you that they can unequivocally state a firm's cost of capital to within a tenth of a percentage point, you know you are talking to someone who has not quite grasped the complexity of the issue.

Concluding comments

A firm that asks an unreasonably high rate of return will be denying its shareholders wealth-enhancing opportunities and ceding valuable markets to competitors. One that employs an irrationally low cost of capital will be wasting resources, setting managers targets that are unduly easy to reach and destroying wealth.

This chapter has described the academic foundations for calculating a company's cost of capital. It has also pointed out the practical difficulties of calculating real-world discount rates. The difficulties are severe, but please don't throw your hands up and conclude that the economists and finance theorist have taken us on a long, arduous road back to where we started. We are not at square one. We have a set of rules to provide a key management number. We now know that judgement is required at many stages in the process and where those particular points are. This allows us to view any number produced by our own calculations, or those of the finance team, with the required amount of reasoned scepticism. And, in making decisions on whether to invest in that new factory or close down a division we have some grasp of the degree to which there is room for error in the value calculation. This part of the book reinforces again that in this uncertain world we should think in terms of a range of possible outcomes, with all too imprecise subjective probabilities, not in terms of cut-and-dried pinpoint precision. The arguments in this chapter should, I hope, allow you to estimate the boundaries for the range of values you feel comfortable with. Returns falling below the acceptable range can be easily rejected, those with a good margin above are simple to make a decision about. Management at these extremes is survivable even for the humdrum executive. It is those projects that give returns lying in the middle that require insightful judgement that is the art of management: they call for leaders.

Key points and concepts

- **The cost of capital** is the rate of return that a company has to offer finance providers to induce them to buy and hold a financial security.
- The **weighted average cost of capital (WACC)** is calculated by weighting the cost of debt and equity in proportion to their contribution to the total capital of the firm:

  $$\text{WACC} = k_E W_E + k_{DAT} W_D$$

- **The WACC can be lowered** (or raised) by altering the proportion of debt in the capital structure:
- **Investors in shares** require a return, k_E, which provides for two elements:
  - a return equal to the risk-free rate; plus
  - a risk premium.

The most popular method for calculating the risk premium has two stages:

- estimate the average risk premium for shares ($r_m - r_f$); and:
- adjust the average premium to suit the risk on a particular share.

The CAPM using a beta based on the relative co-movement of a share with the market has been used for the second stage but other risk factors appear to be relevant.

- An alternative method for calculating the required rate of return on equity is to use the **Gordon growth model**:

$$k_E = \frac{d_1}{P} + g$$

- The **cost of retained earnings** is equal to the expected returns required by shareholders buying new shares in a firm.
- The **cost of debt capital**, k_D, is the current market rate of return for a risk class of debt. The cost to the firm is reduced to the extent that interest can be deducted from taxable profits:

$$k_{DAT} = k_{DBT}(1 - T)$$

- The **cost of irredeemable constant dividend preference share capital** is:

$$k_p = \frac{d_1}{P_p}$$

- The **weights in the WACC are based on market values**, not balance sheet values.
- For projects, etc. with similar risk to that of the existing set, use the WACC, which is based on the target debt to equity ratio. **Do not use the cost of the latest capital raised.**
- For projects, SBUs, etc. of a **different risk level from that of the firm**, raise or lower the discount rate in proportion to the risk.
- Companies use a mixture of theoretically correct techniques with rules of thumb to calculate hurdle rates of return.
- Calculating a cost of capital relies a great deal on judgement rather than scientific precision. But there is a theoretical framework to guide that judgement.
- **Difficulties remaining**:
  - estimating the equity risk premium;
  - obtaining the risk free rate;
  - unreliability of the CAPM's beta.
- **Fundamental beta** is based on factors thought to be related to systematic risk:
  - type of business;
  - operating gearing;
  - financial gearing.

References and further reading

Al-Ali, J. and Arkwright, T. (2000) 'An investigation of UK companies' practice in the determination, interpretation and usage of the cost of capital', *Journal of Interdisciplinary Economies*, 11, pp. 303–19.
Some interesting survey results.

Arnold, G.C. and Davies, M. (eds) (2000) *Value-Based Management*. London: John Wiley & Sons.
A collection of research monographs.

Arnold, G.C. and Hatzopoulos, P.D. (2000) 'The theory practice gap in capital budgeting: evidence from the United Kingdom', *Journal of Business Finance and Accounting*, 27(5) and (6), June/July, pp. 603–26.

Barclays Capital, *Equity Gilt Studies*. London: Barclays.
Annual publications which are an important source of data on historic returns.

Competition Commission (2007) BAA Ltd. A report on the economic regulation of London airport's companies (download from website).
Forget the title; this contains a very good discussion of the difficult judgements that need to be made to estimate the cost of capital.

Damodaran, A. (2002) *Investment Valuation*. New York: John Wiley & Sons.
Chapters 7 and 8 have some good material on the element required to calculate the WACC.

Damodaran, A. (2005) *Applied Corporate Finance: A User's Manual*. 2nd edn. New York: John Wiley & Sons.
A book prepared to deal with the difficult practical issues of WACC calculation and employment.

Dimson, E., Marsh, P. and Staunton, M. (2001) *The Millennium Book II: 101 Years of Investment Returns*. London: London Business School and ABN AMRO.
Fascinating new evidence on risk premiums.

Dimson, E., Marsh, P. and Staunton, M. (2002) *Triumph of the Optimists: 101 Years of Global Investment Returns*. Princeton, NJ: Princeton University Press.
Fascinating evidence on risk premiums.

Dimson, E., Marsh, P., and Staunton, M (2006) The worldwide equity premium: A smaller puzzle. Social Science Research Network (www.ssrn.com).
Provides an alternative view on how to calculate the equity risk premium. Arrives at a figure of 3 to 3.5 per cent (geometric mean) for the world index.

Francis, G. and Minchington, C. (2000) 'Value-based Metrics as Divisional Performance Measures', in Arnold, G.C. and Davies, M. (eds) *Value-Based Management*. Chichester: John Wiley & Sons.
Empirical evidence and discussion.

Gordon, M.J. (1962) *The Investment, Financing and Valuation of the Corporation*. Homewood, IL: Irwin.
Dividend growth model.

Gordon, M.J. and Shapiro, E. (1956) 'Capital equipment analysis: the required rate of profit', *Management Science*, III, pp. 102–10.
Dividend growth model.

Graham, J.R. and Harvey, C.R. (2001) 'The theory and practice of corporate finance: evidence from the field', *Journal of Financial Economics*, 60 (2–3), May, pp. 187–243.
A survey of US corporations: includes a section on how they calculate the WACC and its components.

Gregory, A. and Rutterford, J. (1999) 'The cost of capital in the UK: a comparison of industry and the city'. CIMA monograph, May.
Evidence on UK practice.

Lister R. (2005) 'Cost of capital: the case for the prosecution', *Investment Management and Financial Innovations*, 2, pp. 142–57,
Argues that the conventional method of calculating the WACC (as described in this chapter) is fundamentally flawed.

Lister, R. (2006) 'Cost of capital is beyond our reach', *Accountancy*, December, pp. 42–3.
Points out the difficulties in calculating the WACC and is spectical about our ability to overcome them.

Lockett, M. (2001) 'Calculating the Cost of Capital for the Regulated Electricity Distribution Companies', Aston University MBA Project.
A thorough analysis of the theoretical and practical issues.

Lockett, M. (2002) 'Calculating the cost of capital for the regulated electricity distribution companies', *Power Engineering Journal*, October, pp. 251–63.
An excellent summary of this issue with particular emphasis on regulated companies.

McLaney, E., Pointon, J., Thomas, M. and Tucker, J. (2004) 'Practitioners' perspectives on the UK cost of capital', *European Journal of Finance*, 10, April, pp. 123–38.
A survey of finance directors in 1997 provides some additional insight into how managers go about calculating the WACC.

Ofcom (2005) Ofcom's approach to risk in the assessment of the cost of capital (www.ofcom.org.uk).
Carefully takes the reader through the background finance theory and practical difficulties of calculating a WACC.

Ofgem (2004) Eletricity Distribution Price Control review: Background information on the cost of capital (www.ofgem.gov.uk).
Describes the key elements making up the WACC calculations used for some regulated companies.

Ogier, T., Rugman, J. and Spicer, L. (2004) *The real cost of capital*. London: FT Prentice Hall.
An easy-to-read introduction to the subject written by consultants.

Pike, R.H. (1983) 'A review of recent trends in formal capital budgeting processes', *Accounting and Business Research*, Summer, pp. 201–8.
Evidence of practitioner approaches.

Rutterford, J. (2000) 'The cost of capital and shareholder value', in Arnold, G.C. and Davies, M. (eds) *Value-Based Management*. Chichester: John Wiley & Sons.
Some fascinating evidence of UK practice.

Solomon, E. (1963) *The Theory of Financial Management*. New York: Columbia University Press.
The WACC presented for the first time.

Solomons, D. (1985) *Divisional Performance, Measurement and Control*. 2nd edn. (1st edn, 1965). Princeton, NJ: Markus Wiener Publishing.
An early use of the concept of economic profit.

Westwick, C.A. and Shohet, P.S.D. (1976) 'Investment Appraisal and Inflation', ICAEW Research Committee, Occasional Paper, No. 7.
Early evidence of techniques used in practice.

Wright, S., Mason, R., Satchell, S., Hari, K., and Baskaya, M. (2006) Smither's and Co.'s report on the cost of capital provided to Ofgem (www.ofgem.gov.uk).
Considers a number of the practical difficulties in estimating a WACC. It is remarkable how many 'judgements' need to be made along the way.

Websites

Bondsonline Group, Inc. www.bondsonline.com.
Competition Commission www.competition-commission.org.uk
Investors Chronicle www.ic-community.co.uk/bonds
Ofcom www.ofcom.org.uk
Ofgem www.ofgem.org.uk
London Stock Exchange www.londonstockexchange.com

Video presentations

Chief executives and finance directors discuss various financial issues on Cantos.com (www.cantos.com/cantos) – this is free to view.

Case study recommendations

Please see www.pearsoned.co.uk/arnold for case study synopses

- Lex Service plc: cost of capital. Authors: W. Carl Kester and Kendall Backstrand (1998) Harvard Business School.
- Pioneer Petroleum Corp. Author: Richard S. Ruback (2004) Harvard Business School.
- Marriott Corp.: The cost of capital. Author: Richard S. Ruback (1998) Harvard Business School.
- Cost of capital at Ameritrade. Authors: Mark Mitchell and Erik Stafford (2001) Harvard Business School.

Self-review questions

1 Explain the term 'the cost of capital'.

2 Explain how you might calculate the cost of equity capital.

3 Why can we not always take the coupon rate on a bond issued years ago as the cost of bond capital?

4 Describe the weighted average cost of capital and explain why a project SBU or product line should not be evaluated using the cost of finance associated with the latest portion of capital raised.

5 Should the WACC be used in all circumstances?

6 Explain two of the practical difficulties in calculating a firm's cost of capital.

Questions and problems

myfinancelab **Questions with an icon are also available for practice in MyFinanceLab with additional supporting resources.**

For those questions marked with an asterisk* the answers are given in the Lecturer's Guide.

1* (*Examination level*) Burgundy plc is financed through bonds and ordinary shares. The bonds were issued five years ago at a par value of £100 (total funds raised £5m). They carry an annual coupon of 10 per cent, are due to be redeemed in four years and are currently trading at £105.

The company's shares have a market value of £4m, the return on risk-free government securities is 8 per cent and the risk premium for an average-risk share has been 5 per cent. Burgundy's shares have a lower than average risk and its historic beta as measured by the co-movement of its shares and the market index correctly reflects the risk adjustment necessary to the average risk premium – this is 0.85. The corporate tax rate is 30 per cent. Burgundy has a net asset figure of £3.5m showing in its balance sheet.

Required

a Calculate the cost of debt capital.
b Calculate the cost of equity capital.
c Calculate the weighted average cost of capital.
d Should Burgundy use the WACC for all future projects and SBUs? Explain your answer. ?

2 (*Examination level*) Petalt plc wishes to carry out a shareholder value analysis for which it has gathered the information shown in the table below:

The managers do not yet know the cost of capital but do have the following information. The capital is in three forms:

1 A floating-rate bank loan for £1m at 2 per cent over bank base rate. Base rates are currently 9 per cent.
2 A 25-year vanilla bond issued 20 years ago at par (£100) raising £1m. The bond has an annual coupon of 5 per cent and is currently trading at £80. The next coupon is due in one year.
3 Equity capital with a market value of £2m.

Latest annual sales	£1m
Sales growth rate	10%
Operating profit margin before tax	10%
Tax rate on corporate profits	31%
Incremental fixed capital investment	17% of sales change
Incremental working capital investment	6% of sales change
Planning horizon	5 years

The rate of return available by purchasing long-term government securities is currently 6 per cent and the average risk premium for shares over the risk-free rate has averaged 5 per cent. Petalt's shares have an above-average risk and its historic beta as measured by the co-movement of its shares and the market index correctly reflects the risk adjustment necessary to the average risk premium – this is 1.3.

Required

a Calculate the cost of bond finance.
b Calculate the cost of equity finance.
c Calculate the weighted average cost of capital.

d Calculate shareholder value using Rappaport's method.
e Conduct sensitivity analysis on the calculated shareholder value by altering the operating profit margin and the number of years in the planning horizon. Show a table containing alternative profit margin assumptions and planning horizon assumptions. ?

An Excel spreadsheet version of these calculations is available at www.pearsoned.co.uk/arnold

3 (*Examination level*) Diversified plc is trying to introduce an improved method of assessing investment projects using discounted cash flow techniques. For this it has to obtain a cost of capital to use as a discount rate.

The finance department has assembled the following information:

- The company has an equity beta of 1.50, which may be taken as the appropriate adjustment to the average risk premium. The yield on risk-free government securities is 7 per cent and the historic premium above the risk-free rate is estimated at 5 per cent for shares.
- The market value of the firm's equity is twice the value of its debt.
- The cost of borrowed money to the company is estimated at 12 per cent (before tax shield benefits).
- Corporation tax is 30 per cent.

Assume: No inflation.

Required

a Estimate the equity cost of capital using the capital asset pricing model (CAPM). Create an estimate of the weighted average cost of capital (WACC).
b Comment on the appropriateness of using this technique for estimating the cost of capital for project appraisal purposes for a company with many subsidiaries in different markets.
c Given the difficulties in the calculation of WACC are companies justified in using using rules of thumb rather than theoretically precise methods? Explain the difficulties and describe the approximations used by business people. ?

4 The projected cash flows for a company to be established are £1m per year forever. The company will require £9m in capital to be viable and produce the £1m annual cash flows. The prospective directors suggest that they raise £2m by borrowing from a bank at a fixed rate of 6 per cent per year. The remaining £7m will come from an issue of shares. Shares with a similar systematic risk are currently offering an expected return of 11 per cent. This cautious level of borrowing suits the directors because their livelihood depends on the survival of the firm. The corporation tax rate is 30 per cent.

Required

a Calculate the WACC and the value of the enterprise (debt + equity value)
b If a higher level of financial gearing is targeted such that £5m of the capital comes from lenders and £4m comes from shareholders the required rates of return change. The debt holders now require 7 per cent per annum, whereas the equity holders expect a return of 16 per cent per year. Does this capital structure raise or lower the WACC and value of the firm?

An Excel spreadsheet version of these calculations is available at pearsoned.co.uk/arnold.

5 Triglass plc has three types of capital. The market capitalisation of its equity is £20m. These ordinary shares have a beta of 0.9, as measured over the past five years of monthly returns which may be taken as the appropriate adjustment to the average risk premium. The current risk free rate on government bonds is 4.5 per cent. The historic equity risk premium is 5 per cent per year. The market value of its irredeemable non-participating non-convertible preference shares is £5m and the rate of return being offered is 7.5 per cent per year. The debt of the firm amounts to £15m and costs 6.5 per cent per year before allowing for tax shield benefits. The corporation tax rate is 30 per cent. Calculate the WACC for Triglass plc.

An Excel spreadsheet version of these calculations is available at www.pearsoned.co.uk/arnold

myfinancelab **Now retake your diagnostic test for Chapter 19 to check your progress and update your study plan.**

Assignment

Calculate the weighted average cost of capital for a company or SBU of a company you know well. Explain those areas where you have made difficult judgements in deciding which numbers to use.

CHAPTER 20

Valuing shares

LEARNING OUTCOMES

By the end of this chapter the reader should be able to:

- describe the principal determinants of share prices and estimate share value using a variety of approaches;
- demonstrate awareness of the most important input factors and appreciate that they are difficult to quantify;
- use valuation models to estimate the value of shares when managerial control is achieved.

myfinancelab *Complete your diagnostic test for Chapter 20 now to create your personal study plan*

Introduction

Knowledge of the main influences on share prices is important from the perspective of two groups. The first group is managers, who, if they are to be given the responsibility of maximising the wealth of shareholders, need to know the factors influencing that wealth, as reflected in the share price of their own company. Without this understanding they will be unable to determine the most important consequence of their actions – the impact on share value. Managers need to appreciate share price derivation because their company's share price is one of the key factors by which they are judged. It is also useful for them to know how share prices are set if the firm plans to gain a flotation on a stock exchange, or when it is selling a division to another firm. In mergers an acquirer needs good valuation skills so as not to pay more than necessary, and a seller needs to ensure that the price is fair.

The second constituency for whom the ideas and models presented in this chapter will be of practical use is investors, who risk their savings by buying shares.

This chapter describes the main methods of valuing shares: net asset value, dividend valuation models, price-earnings ratio models and cash flow models. There is an important subsection in the chapter which shows that the valuation of shares is somewhat different when the size of the shareholding is large enough to give managerial control over the firm compared with the valuation when there is only a small holding providing a small minority stake.

Two skills are needed to be able to value shares. The first is analytical ability, to be able to understand and use mathematical valuation models. Second, and most importantly, good judgement is needed, because most of the inputs to the mathematical calculations are factors, the precise nature of which cannot be defined with absolute certainty, so great skill is required to produce reasonably accurate results. The main problem is that the determinants of value occur in the future, for example future cash flows, dividends or earnings.

The monetary value of an asset is what someone is prepared to pay for it. Assets such as cars and houses are difficult enough to value with any degree of accuracy. At least corporate bonds generally have a regular cash flow (coupon) and an anticipated capital repayment. This contrasts with the uncertainties associated with shares, for which there is no guaranteed annual payment and no promise of capital repayment.

The difficulties of share valuation are amply represented by the case of Amazon.com.

Case study 20.1 Amazon.com

Amazon floated in 1997 and it failed to make any profit at all for six years. For example, it lost over \$700m in 1999 and offered little prospect of profits in the near term. So, if you were an investor in early 2000 what value would you give to a company of this calibre? Anything at all? Amazingly, investors valued Amazon at over \$30 billion in early 2000 (more than all the traditional book retailers put together). The brand was well established and the numbers joining the online community rose by thousands every day. Investors were confident that Amazon would continue to attract customers and produce a rapid rate of growth in revenue. Eventually, it was thought, this revenue growth would translate into profits and high dividends. When investors had calmed down after taking account of the potential for rivalrous competition in this business and the fact that by 2001 Amazon was still not producing profits they reassessed the value of Amazon's likely future dividends. In mid-2001, they judged the company to be worth only \$4bn – it had run up losses of \$1.4bn in 2000, indicating that profits and dividends were still a long way off. However in 2007 the market capitalisation of the company almost reached the dizzying height of 2000 (at \$26 billion) as investors reacted to the rising profits and the optimistic messages.

Valuation using net asset value (NAV)

The balance sheet seems an obvious place to start when faced with the task of valuation. In this method the company is viewed as being worth the sum of the value of its net assets. The balance sheet is regarded as providing objective facts concerning the company's ownership of assets and obligations to creditors. Here fixed assets are recorded along with stocks, debtors, cash and other liquid assets. With the deduction of long-term and short-term creditors from the total asset figure we arrive at the **net asset value** (NAV).

An example of this type of calculation is shown in **Exhibit 20.1** for the publisher Pearson.

Exhibit 20.1 Pearson plc abridged balance sheet as at 31 December 2006

	£m
Fixed assets (Non-current)	4,543
Current assets	2,670
Non-current liabilities	(1,853)
Current liabilities	(1,690)
Other liabilities	(26)
Net assets	3,644
Total equity attributable to equity holders of the company	3,476
Minority interests	168
	3,644

Source: Pearson plc, Annual Review 2006.

The NAV of £3,644m (or more properly £3,476m when minority interests[1] are removed) of Pearson compares with a market value placed on all the shares when totalled of £7,000m (market capitalisation figures are available in Monday editions of the *Financial Times* or from most financial websites (e.g. www.advfn.com)). This great difference makes it clear that the shareholders of Pearson are not rating the firm on the basis of balance sheet net asset figures. This point is emphasised by an examination of **Exhibit 20.2**.

Exhibit 20.2 Net asset values and total capitalisation of some firms

Company (Accounts year)	NAV £m	Total capitalisation (market value of company's shares) £m
AstraZeneca (2006)	$15,416	41,326.6
BSky B (2006)	121	11,016
Bloomsbury (2006)	89	138
Cadbury Schweppes (2006)	3,696	14,166
Unilever (2006)	11,672	46,007
Vodafone (2006)	85,312	84,107

Source: Annual reports and accounts; www.advfn.com 7.5.07.

[1] The 'Total equity attributable to equity holders of the Company' is the net assets available to Pearson's shareholders rather than the total net assets available to both Pearson's shareholders and those that hold some of the shares in subsidiaries of Pearson.

Some of the firms listed in Exhibit 20.2 have a very small balance sheet value in comparison with their total market capitalisation. Vodafone, the exception, boosted its balance sheet by including a lot of intangible assets in the form of goodwill following acquisitions (£53m). Analysts may adjust values shown on balance sheets to replacement cost or realisable values e.g. a property asset bought 5 years ago and valued on the balance sheet at cost may be adjusted to its current market value. However, even with many alterations of this kind for most companies market value will remain a long way from NAV.

For most companies, investors look to the income flow to be derived from a holding. This flow is generated when the balance sheet assets are combined with assets impossible to quantify: these include the unique skills of the workforce, the relationships with customers and suppliers, the value of brands, the reservoir of experience within the management team, and the competitive positioning of the firms' products. Thus assets, in the crude sense of balance sheet values, are only one dimension of overall value – *see* **Exhibit 20.3**. Investors in the market generally value intangible, unmeasurable assets more highly than those which can be identified and recorded by accountants.

Exhibit 20.3 What creates value for shareholders?

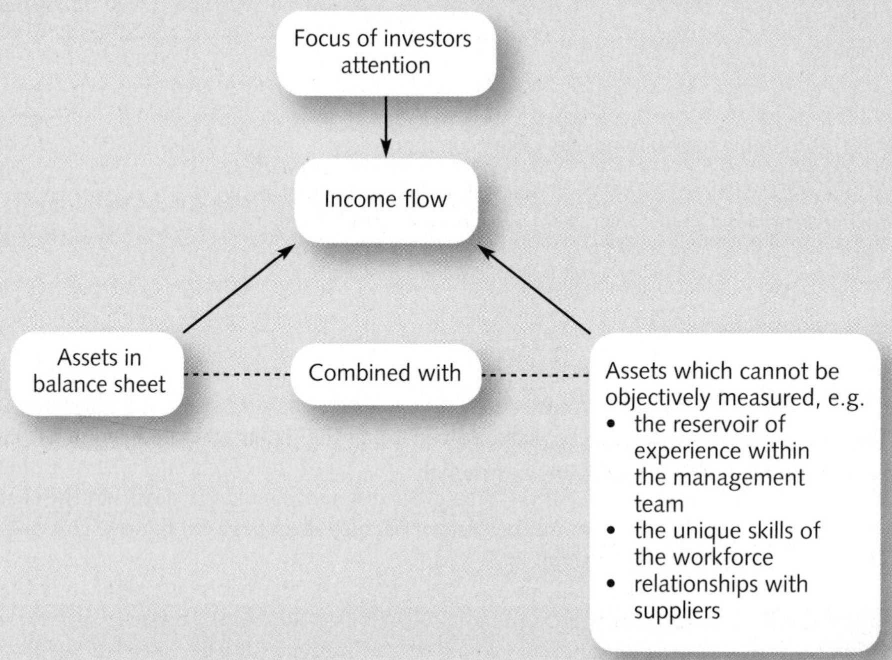

Criticising accountants for not producing balance sheets which reflect the true value of a business is unfair. Accounts are not usually designed to record up-to-date market values. Land and buildings are frequently shown at cost rather than market value; thus the balance sheet can provide a significant over- or under-valuation of the assets' current value. Plant and machinery is shown at the purchase price less a depreciation amount. Stock is valued at the lower of cost or net realisable value – this can lead to a significant underestimate, as the market value can appreciate to a figure far higher than either of these. The list of balance sheet entries vulnerable to subjective estimation, arbitrary method and even cynical manipulation is a long one: goodwill, provisions, merger accounting, debtors, intangible brand values and so on.

The slippery concept of balance sheet value is demonstrated in the article about Vodafone reproduced in **Exhibit 20.4**.

Exhibit 20.4

£300bn binge ends in severe hangover write-downs

FT

by Philip Stafford

The scale of Vodafone's £300bn binge on telecoms assets at the turn of the century can still be seen six years on, with the company announcing big write-downs of goodwill for a third successive year.

The £23.5bn write-down in the carrying value of goodwill, flagged earlier this year, is one of the largest corporate write-downs on record.

But it is the £101bn purchase of Germany's Mannesmann in 2000, and the Italian operations it partly inherited from the deal, that has caused the problems.

Broken down, Voafone ascribed a write-down value of £19.4bn for its assets in Germany, £3.6bn for its Italian operations and £515m for the assets in Sweden.

The latter had already had an impairment charge of £475m a year ago, and Vodafone has since sold the Swedish operation to Norway's Telenor Mobile.

Vodafone blamed the write-down on its revision of the longer-term prospects in the German and Italian markets, pointing to the tough price competition.

The markets have been a problem for several years, although the comparison is clouded by a change in accounting standards from UK GAAP to IFRS standards.

Under the old system, the German and Italian operations accounted for £10bn of Vodafone's £14.7bn asset write-down in 2005 and nearly £13bn of the £15.2bn write-down in 2004.

But the figures yesterday also included an impairment of £4.9bn relating to the impairment of goodwill for Vodafone Japan, the operation it sold to Softbank, the Japanese internet group, in March.

Vodafone broke into Japan with five deals in 2000 and 2001, includng buying stakes in Japan Telecom, the country's third-biggest telecoms operator, and J-Phone, the mobile operator.

It spent £7.9bn in the assets, making it the largest sum of foreign investment by a single company in Japanese history at the time.

Source: Financial Times, 31 May 2006, p. 21. Reprinted with permission.

When asset values are particularly useful

The accounts-based approach to share value is fraught with problems but there are circumstances in which asset backing is given more attention.

Firms in financial difficulty

The shareholders of firms in financial difficulty may pay a great deal of attention to the asset backing of the firm. They may weigh up the potential for asset sales or asset-backed borrowing. In extreme circumstances they may try to assess the break-up value. Here the **liquidation value** is key: what could be realised by selling the assets and paying off all liabilities. Liquidation value may or may not be close to NAV.

Takeover bids

In a takeover bid shareholders will be reluctant to sell at less than NAV even if the prospect for income growth is poor. A standard defensive tactic in a takeover battle is to revalue balance sheet assets to encourage a higher price.

When discounted income flow techniques are difficult to apply

For some types of company there is no straightforward way of employing income-flow-based methods:

1 ***Property investment companies*** are primarily valued on the basis of their assets. It is generally possible to put a fairly realistic up-to-date price on the buildings owned by such a company. These market values have a close link to future cash flows. That is, the future rents payable by tenants, when discounted, determine the value of property assets and thus the company. If higher rent levels are expected than were previously anticipated, chartered surveyors will place a

higher value on the asset, and the NAV in the balance sheet will rise, forcing up the share price. For such companies, future income, asset values and share values are all closely linked. However the value of a property investment company may be less than its NAV. Exhibit 20.5 describes two reasons for a discount to NAV: the capital gains tax the company would incur on the sale of its assets; and the cost of paying off high interest rate debt. Analysts also deduct the costs of remaining as a going concern (the present value of management costs and general overheads).

2 ***Investment trusts*** The future income of investment trusts comes from the individual shareholdings. The shareholder in a trust would find it extremely difficult to calculate the future income to be received from each of the dozens or hundreds of shares held. An easier approach is simply to take the current share price of each holding as representing the future discounted income. The share values are aggregated to derive the trusts' NAV and this has a strong bearing on the price at which the trust shares are traded.

3 ***Resource-based companies*** For oil companies, mineral extractors, mining houses and so on, the proven or probable reserves have a significant influence on the share price.

Exhibit 20.5

Canary Wharf reflects change of sentiment to unloved sector

FT

Juliana Ratner

This week's angry outburst from Canary Wharf shareholders – attacking the board for selling the development group too cheaply – shows how far sentiment has changed to the unloved property sector.

A year ago, UK property companies traded at an average 40 per cent discount to net asset value (NAV), a key measure of performance for UK property groups . . .

The discount has narrowed from 19 per cent to 16 per cent this year . . .

The shrinking discount has made obsolete triple-net asset value – a relatively new measure of what a buyer would have to pay to take a UK property company private. Now, investors are more confident of the value of their businesses as the market picks up and discounts narrow.

Triple-net asset value was first used as a valuation tool in 2000 when GE Real Estate and Hermes took MEPC private. It was, in effect, a way to drive down the price.

Triple-net is a liquidation value. It takes the company's net asset value as estimated by chartered surveyors, and deducts its investment portfolio's unbooked capital gains tax (CGT) liability. It also subtracts the cost of refinancing existing debt at current interest rates.

While investors, four years ago, were happy to sell at discounts to triple-net, they are no longer inclined to give that value away. The mood has changed because triple-net was probably not the most appropriate measure of MEPC's worth.

The buyers paid £1.9bn for MEPC. But the price had been reduced to allow the new owners to repay outstanding bonds. In fact, they retained the bonds and kept the difference in cost. Fancy footwork in asset disposals cut the expected CGT liability, enhancing further the returns for MEPC's new owners . . .

Increasingly, Canary Wharf's shareholders are concerned the board is asking them to sell at the wrong price and at the wrong time.

Morgan Stanley this month raised its offer to 292p, or £1.7bn, trumping a rival £1.6bn bid from Brascan, the Canadian group. Yet Morgan's offer is still well below the group's NAV of 344p as of June 31 and below 299p, which the company last autumn indicated was its triple-net. In addition, Canary Wharf in December sold two buildings, which it said would have increased the June NAV to 350p . . .

Source: Financial Times, 26 March 2004, p. 28. Reprinted with permission.

Valuation using income-flow methods

The value of a share is usually determined by the income flows that investors expect to receive in the future from its ownership. Information about the past is only of relevance to the extent that it contributes to an understanding of expected future performance. Income flows will occur at different points in the future and so they have to be discounted. There are three classes of income valuation model:

- dividend-based models;
- earnings-based models;
- cash-flow-based models.

The dividend valuation models

The **dividend valuation models** (**DVMs**) are based on the premise that *the market value of ordinary shares represents the sum of the expected future dividend flows, to infinity, discounted to present value.*

The only cash flows that investors ever receive from a company are dividends. This holds true if we include a 'liquidation dividend' upon the sale of the firm or on formal liquidation, and any share repurchases can be treated as dividends. Of course, an individual shareholder is not planning to hold a share forever to gain the dividend returns to an infinite horizon. An individual holder of shares will expect two types of return:

a income from dividends, and

b a capital gain resulting from the appreciation of the share and its sale to another investor.

The fact that the individual investor is looking for capital gains as well as dividends to give a return does not invalidate the model. The reason for this is that when a share is sold, the purchaser is buying a future stream of dividends, therefore the price paid is determined by future dividend expectations.

To illustrate this, consider the following: A shareholder intends to hold a share for one year. A single dividend will be paid at the end of the holding period, d_1 and the share will be sold at price P_1 in one year.

To derive the value of a share at time 0 to this investor (P_0), the future cash flows, d_1 and P_1, need to be discounted at a rate which includes an allowance for the risk class of the share, k_E.

$$P_0 = \frac{d_1}{1 + k_E} + \frac{P_1}{1 + k_E}$$

Worked example 20.1

An investor is considering the purchase of some shares in Willow plc. At the end of one year a dividend of 22p will be paid and the shares are expected to be sold for £2.43. How much should be paid if the investor judges that the rate of return required on a financial security of this risk class is 20 per cent?

Answer

$$P_0 = \frac{d_1}{1 + k_E} + \frac{P_1}{1 + k_E}$$

$$P_0 = \frac{22}{1 + 0.2} + \frac{243}{1 + 0.2} = 221\text{p}$$

The dividend valuation model to infinity

The relevant question to ask in order to understand DVMs is: Where does P_1 come from? The buyer at time 1 estimates the value of the share based on the present value of future income given the required rate of return for the risk class. So if the second investor expects to hold the share for a further year and sell at time 2 for P_2, the price P_1 will be:

$$P_1 = \frac{d_2}{1 + k_E} + \frac{P_2}{1 + k_E}$$

Returning to the P_0 equation we are able to substitute discounted d_2 and P_2 for P_1. Thus:

$$P_0 = \frac{d_1}{1 + k_E} + \frac{P_1}{1 + k_E}$$

$$P_0 = \frac{d_1}{1 + k_E} + \frac{d_2}{(1 + k_E)^2} + \frac{P_2}{(1 + k_E)^2}$$

If a series of one-year investors bought this share, and we in turn solved for P_2, P_3, P_4, etc., we would find:

$$P_0 = \frac{d_1}{1 + k_E} + \frac{d_2}{(1 + k_E)^2} + \frac{d_3}{(1 + k_E)^3} + \ldots + \frac{d_n}{(1 + k_E)^n}$$

Even a short-term investor has to consider events beyond his or her time horizon because the selling price is determined by the willingness of a buyer to purchase a future dividend stream. If this year's dividends are boosted by short-termist policies such as cutting out R&D and brand-support marketing the investor may well lose more on capital value changes (as other investors push down the share price when their forecasts for future dividends are lowered) than the gains in dividend income.

Worked example 20.2

If a firm is expected to pay dividends of 20p per year to infinity and the rate of return required on a share of this risk class is 12 per cent then:

$$P_0 = \frac{20}{1 + 0.12} + \frac{20}{(1 + 0.12)^2} + \frac{20}{(1 + 0.12)^3} + \ldots + \frac{20}{(1 + 0.12)^n}$$

$$P_0 = 17.86 + 15.94 + 14.24 + \ldots + \ldots +$$

Given this is a perpetuity there is a simpler approach:

$$P_0 = \frac{d_1}{k_E} = \frac{20}{0.12} = 166.67\text{p}$$

The dividend growth model

In contrast to the situation in the above example, for most companies dividends are expected to grow from one year to the next. To make DVM analysis manageable simplifying assumptions are usually made about the patterns of growth in dividends. Most managers attempt to make dividends grow more or less in line with the firm's long-term earnings growth rate. They often bend over backwards to smooth out fluctuations, maintaining a high dividend even in years of poor profits or losses. In years of very high profits they are often reluctant to increase the dividend by a large percentage for fear that it might have to be cut back in a downturn.[2] So, given management propensity to make dividend payments grow in an incremental or stepped fashion it seems that a

---

[2] For a discussion on the propensity for directors to keep to a steadily rising dividend policy *see* Chapter 22.

reasonable model could be based on the assumption of a constant growth rate. (Year to year deviations around this expected growth path will not materially alter the analysis.) See Worked examples 20.3 and 20.4 for the use of the constant dividend growth model.

Worked example 20.3 A constant dividend growth valuation: Shhh plc

If the last dividend paid was d_0 and the next is due in one year, d_1, then this will amount to d_0 (1 + g) where g is the growth rate of dividends.

For example, if Shhh plc has just paid a dividend of 10p and the growth rate is 7 per cent then:

d_1 will equal $d_0 (1 + g) = 10 (1 + 0.07) = 10.7$p
and
d_2 will be $d_0 (1 + g)^2 = 10 (1 + 0.07)^2 = 11.45$p

The value of a share in Shhh will be all the future dividends discounted at the risk-adjusted discount rate of 11 per cent:

$$P_0 = \frac{d_0 (1 + g)}{(1 + k_E)} + \frac{d_0 (1 + g)^2}{(1 + k_E)^2} + \frac{d_0 (1 + g)^3}{(1 + k_E)^3} + \ldots + \frac{d_0 (1 + g)^n}{(1 + k_E)^n}$$

$$P_0 = \frac{10 (1 + 0.07)}{1 + 0.11} + \frac{10 (1 + 0.07)^2}{(1 + 0.11)^2} + \frac{10 (1 + 0.07)^3}{(1 + 0.11)^3} + \ldots + \frac{10 (1 + 0.07)^n}{(1 + 0.11)^n}$$

Using the above formula could require a lot of time. Fortunately it is mathematically equivalent to the following formula which is much easier to employ. (This is called the Gordon growth model.)

$$P_0 = \frac{d_1}{k_E - g} = \frac{d_0 (1 + g)}{k_E - g} = \frac{10.7}{0.11 - 0.07} = 267.50\text{p}$$

Note that, even though the shortened formula only includes next year's dividend all the future dividends are represented. In using the model you are assuming the inclusion of all dividends stretching to an infinite horizon growing at a constant rate of g.

A further illustration is provided by the example of Pearson plc.

Worked example 20.4 Pearson plc

Pearson plc, the publishing, media and education group, has the following dividend history.

Year	Net dividend per share (p)
1996	16.1
1997	17.4
1998	18.8
1999	20.1
2000	21.4
2001	22.3
2002	23.4
2003	24.2
2004	25.4
2005	27.0
2006	29.3

The average annual growth rate, g, over this period has been:

$$g = \sqrt[10]{\frac{29.3}{16.1}} - 1 = 0.062 \text{ or } 6.2\%$$

If it is assumed that this historic growth rate will continue into the future (a big *if*) and 10 per cent is taken as the required rate of return, the value of a share can be calculated.

$$P_0 = \frac{d_1}{k_E - g} = \frac{29.3\ (1 + 0.062)}{0.1 - 0.062} = 819\text{p}$$

In the first four months of 2007 (around the time of the 2006 results announcement) Pearson's shares ranged as high as 925p and as low as 761p. So there were times when investors were more optimistic than we have been in the above analysis: perhaps they were anticipating a faster rate of growth in future than in the past or judged the risk to be less, thus lowering k_E. On other occasions investors were more pessimistic, perhaps seeing Pearson's shares as sufficiently risky to require a rate of return higher than 10 per cent per year or anticipating lower future profits and dividend growth.

An Excel spreadsheet version of this calculation for Pearson is avilable at: www.pearsoned.co.uk/arnold.

Non-constant growth

Firms tend to go through different phases of growth. If they have a strong competitive advantage in an attractive market they might enjoy super-normal growth for a while. Eventually, however, most firms come under competitive pressure and growth becomes normal. Ultimately, many firms fail to keep pace with the market environmental change in which they operate and growth falls to below that for the average company.

To analyse companies which will go through different phases of growth a two-, three- or four-stage model may be used. In the simplest case of two-stage growth the share price calculation requires the following:

1 Calculate each of the forecast annual dividends in the first period.
2 Estimate the share price at the point at which the dividend growth shifts to the new permanent rate.
3 Discount each of the dividends in the first period and the share price given in 2. Add all the discounted numbers to obtain the current value.

Worked example 20.5 Use of the two-stage growth model – Noruce plc

You are given the following information about Noruce plc.

The company has just paid an annual dividend of 15p per share and the next is due in one year. For the next three years dividends are expected to grow at 12 per cent per year. This rapid rate is caused by a number of favourable factors: for example an economic upturn, the fast acceleration stage of newly developed products and a large contract with a government department.

After the third year the dividend will grow at only 7 per cent per annum, because the main boosts to growth will, by then, be absent.

Shares in other companies with a similar level of systematic risk to Noruce produce an expected return of 16 per cent per annum.

What is the value of one share in Noruce plc?

Answer

Stage 1 Calculate dividends for the super-normal growth phase.

$d_1 = 15\ (1 + 0.12) = 16.8$

$d_2 = 15\ (1 + 0.12)^2 = 18.8$

$d_3 = 15\ (1 + 0.12)^3 = 21.1$

Stage 2 Calculate share price at time 3 when the dividend growth rate shifts to the new permanent rate.

$$P_3 = \frac{d_4}{k_E - g} = \frac{d_3\ (1 + g)}{k_E - g} = \frac{21.1\ (1 + 0.07)}{0.16 - 0.07} = 250.9$$

Stage 3 Discount and sum the amounts calculated in Stages 1 and 2.

$$\frac{d_1}{1 + k_E} = \frac{16.8}{1 + 0.16} = 14.5$$

$$+\frac{d_2}{(1 + k_E)^2} = \frac{18.8}{(1 + 0.16)^2} = 14.0$$

$$+\frac{d_3}{(1 + k_E)^3} = \frac{21.1}{(1 + 0.16)^3} = 13.5$$

$$+\frac{P_3}{(1 + k_E)^3} = \frac{250.9}{(1 + 0.16)^3} = 160.7$$

$$\underline{\underline{202.7\text{p}}}$$

An Excel spreadsheet version of this calculation for Noruce is available at www.pearsoned.co.uk/arnold.

What is a normal growth rate?

Growth rates will be different for each company, but for corporations taken as a whole dividend growth will not be significantly different from the growth in nominal gross national product (real GNP plus inflation) over the long run. If dividends did grow in a long-term trend above this rate then they would take an increasing proportion of national income – ultimately squeezing out the consumption and government sectors. This is, of course, ridiculous. Thus in an economy with inflation of 2 per cent per annum and growth of 2.5 per cent we might expect the long-term growth in dividends to be about 4.5 per cent. Also, it is unreasonable to suppose that a firm can grow its earnings and dividends forever at a rate significantly greater than that for the economy as a whole. To do so is to assume that the firm eventually becomes larger than the economy. There will be years, even decades, when average corporate dividends do grow faster than the economy as a whole and there will always be companies with much higher projected growth rates than the average for periods of time. Nevertheless the real GNP + inflation growth relationship provides a useful benchmark.

Companies that do not pay dividends

Some companies, for example Dell, Apple and Warren Buffett's Berkshire Hathaway, do not pay dividends. This is a deliberate policy as there is often a well-founded belief that the funds are better used within the firms than they would be if the money was given to shareholders. This presents an apparent problem for the DVM but the formulae can still be applied because it is reasonable to suppose that one day these companies will start to pay dividends. Perhaps this will take the form of a final break-up payment, or perhaps when the founder is approaching retirement he/she will start to distribute the accumulated resources. At some point dividends must be paid, otherwise there would be no attraction in holding the shares. Microsoft is an example of a company that did not pay a dividend for 28 years. However, in 2003 it decided it would start the process of paying out some of its enormous cash pile and paid a dividend. In 2004 it decided to pay a 'special dividend' on top of its now regular dividend amounting to a massive $32bn. Furthermore, it made a commitment to share at least $43bn with shareholders over the next four years in the form of share repurchases and its regular dividend.

Some companies do not pay dividends for many years due to regular losses. Often what gives value to this type of share is the optimism that the company will recover and that dividends will be paid in the distant future.

Problems with dividend valuation models

Dividend valuation models present the following problems.

1 They are highly sensitive to the assumptions. Take the case of Pearson above. If we change the growth assumption to 8 per cent and reduce the required rate of return to 9.5 per cent, the value of the share leaps to 2,110p.

$$P_0 = \frac{d_0 (1+g)}{k_E - g} = \frac{29.3\,(1+0.08)}{0.095-0.08} = 2{,}110\text{p}$$

As the growth rate converges on the required rate of return the value goes to infinity.

2 The quality of input data is often poor. The problems of calculating an appropriate required rate of return on equity were discussed in the previous chapter. Added to this is great uncertainty about the future growth rate, g, discussed below.

3 If g exceeds k_E a nonsensical result occurs. This is a problem for those who would use the model in a mechanical way by simply using the historic growth rate for g. However, in intelligent use of the model we replace the short-term super-normal growth rate plus the lower rate after the super-normal period with a g which is some weighted average growth rate reflecting the return expected over the long run. This is unlikely to result in a g more than one or two percentage points greater than the growth rate for the economy as a whole (because the largest weight will be given to the near term non-supernormal growth period, we may allow a growth rate slightly higher than the economy.) Alternatively, for those periods when g is greater than k, one may calculate the specific dividend amounts and discount them as in the non-constant growth model (e.g. the two-stage model). For the years after the super-normal growth occurs, the usual growth formula may be used – as we did for Noruce plc in Worked example 20.5.

The difficulties of using the DVMs are real and yet they are to be favoured, less for the derivation of a single number than for the understanding of the principles behind the value of financial assets that the exercise provides. They demand a disciplined thought process that makes the analyst's assumptions (about earnings and dividend growth, about reasonable required rates of return, etc.) explicit, thus allowing him or her to question the validility of any final number produced. The analyst is also made aware of the possibility of a range of values depending on the assumptions made.

Forecasting dividend growth rates – *g*

The most influential variable, and the one subject to most uncertainty, on the value of shares is the growth rate expected in dividends. Accuracy here is a much sought-after virtue. While this book cannot provide readers with perfect crystal balls for seeing future dividend growth rates, it can provide a few pointers.

Determinants of growth

There are three factors which influence the rate of dividend growth.

1 ***The quantity of resources retained and reinvested within the business*** This relates to the percentage of earnings not paid out as dividends. The more a firm invests the greater its potential for growth.

2 ***The rate of return earned on those retained resources*** The efficiency with which retained earnings are used will influence value.

3 ***Rate of return earned on existing assets*** This concerns the amount earned on the existing baseline set of assets, that is, those assets available before reinvestment of profits. This category may be affected by a sudden increase or decrease in profitability. If the firm, for example, is engaged in oil exploration and production, and there is a worldwide increase in the price of oil, profitability will rise on existing assets. Another example would be if a major competitor is liquidated, enabling increased returns on the same asset base due to higher margins because of an improved market position.

There is a vast range of influences on the future return from shares. One way of dealing with the myriad variables is to group them into two categories: at the firm and the economy level.

Focus on the firm

A dedicated analyst would want to examine numerous aspects of the firm, and its management, to help develop an informed estimate of its growth potential. These will include the following.

1. ***Strategic analysis*** The most important factor in assessing the value of a firm is its strategic position. The analyst needs to consider the attractiveness of the industry, the competitive position of the firm within the industry and the firm's position on the life cycle of value creation to appreciate the potential for increased dividends (*see* Chapter 16 and, for a fuller discussion, see Arnold (2002) or Arnold (2004)).
2. ***Evaluation of management*** Running a close second in importance for the determination of a firm's value is the quality of its management. A starting point for analysis might be to collect factual information such as the age of the key managers and their level of experience (particularly longevity with the company) and of education. But this has to be combined with far more important evaluatory variables which are unquantifiable, such as judgement, and even gut feeling about issues such as competence, integrity, intelligence and so on. Having honest managers with a focus on increasing the wealth of shareholders is at least as important for valuing shares as the factor of managerial competence. Investors downgrade the shares of companies run by the most brilliant managers if there is any doubt about their integrity – highly competent crooks can destroy shareholder wealth far more quickly than any competitive action: just ask the shareholders in WorldCom, Enron and Parmalat. (For a fuller discussion of the impact of managerial competence and integrity on share values *see* Arnold (2002).)
3. ***Using the historical growth rate of dividends*** For some firms past growth may be extrapolated to estimate future dividends. If a company demonstrated an annual growth rate of 6 per cent over the past ten years it might be reasonable to use this as a starting point for evaluating its future potential. This figure will probably have to be adjusted for new information such as new strategies, management or products – that is the tricky part.
4. ***Financial statement evaluation and ratio analysis*** An assessment of the firm's profitability, efficiency and risk through an analysis of accounting data can be enlightening. However, adjustments to the published figures are likely to be necessary to view the past clearly, let alone provide a guide to the future. Warren Buffett comments:

   > 'When managers want to get across the facts of the business to you, it can be done within the rules of accounting. Unfortunately when they want to play games, at least in some industries, it can also be done within the rules of accounting. If you can't recognise the differences, you shouldn't be in the equity-picking business.'[3]

   Accounts are valuable sources of information but they have three drawbacks: **a** they are based in the past when it is the future which is of interest, **b** the fundamental value-creating processes within the firm are not identified and measured in conventional accounts, and **c** they are frequently based on guesses, estimates and judgements, and are open to arbitrary method and manipulation.

   Armed with a questioning frame of mind the analyst can adjust accounts to provide a truer and fairer view of a company. The analyst may wish to calculate three groups of ratios to enable comparisons:

   a. Internal liquidity ratios permit some judgement about the ability of the firm to cope with short-term financial obligations – quick ratios, current ratios, etc.
   b. Operating performance ratios may indicate the efficiency of the management in the operations of the business – asset turnover ratio, profit margins, debtor turnover, etc.
   c. Risk analysis concerns the uncertainty of income flows – sales variability over the economic cycle, operational gearing (fixed costs as a proportion of total), financial gearing (ratio of debt to equity), cash flow ratios, etc.

---

[3] Warren Buffett seminar held at Columbia University Business School, 'Investing in equity markets', 13 March 1985, transcript, p. 23. Reproduced in Janet Lowe (1997).

Ratios examined in isolation are meaningless. It is usually necessary to compare with the industry, or the industry sub-group comprising the firm's competitors. Knowledge of changes in ratios over time can also be useful.

Focus on the economy

All firms, to a greater or lesser extent, are influenced by **macroeconomic changes**. The prospects for a particular firm can be affected by sudden changes in government fiscal policy, the central bank's monetary policy, changes in exchange rates, etc. Forecasts of macroeconomic variables such as GNP are easy to find (for example *The Economist* publishes a table of forecasts every week). Finding a forecaster who is reliable over the long term is much more difficult. Perhaps the best approach is to obtain a number of projections and through informed judgement develop a view about the medium-term future. Alternatively, the analyst could recognise that there are many different potential futures and then develop analyses based on a range of possible scenarios – probabilities could be assigned and sensitivity analysis used to provide a broader picture.

It is notable that the great investors (e.g. Benjamin Graham, Philip Fisher, Warren Buffett and Charles Munger) pay little attention to macroeconomic forecasts when valuing companies. The reason for this is that value is determined by income flows to the shareholder over many economic cycles stretching over decades, so the economists' projection (even if accurate) for this or that economic number for the next year is of little significance.

Another approach to estimating *g*

Some analysts use the following logic for estimating *g*: first, they assume that the only source of growth in earnings comes from using additional capital from retained earnings. In other words, *g* cannot rise due to changes in industry conditions, e.g. government changing permitted price levels, price of oil rising – the third point on page 760.

Second, assume that the historic return on equity capital (labelled r_E) as shown in the accounts is going to continue for every additional £1 of extra equity capital (retained from profits) for every future year.

Third, assume a constant retention ratio (labelled *b*) for all future years, i.e.

$$\frac{Earnings - Dividends}{Earnings},$$

then,

$$g = br_E$$

So, for example, if Slightly Unrealistic plc retains three-quarters of its earnings, $b = 0.75$. Over the past five years it has obtained a return on equity, given its equity capital base, of 10 per cent, and this will continue even for any expansion of the business operations.

The growth estimate is $g = br_E = 0.75 \times 0.10 = 7.5\%$ per year

The assumptions made may be challenges to your perception of the real world – you are right to be suspicious. However, this approach at least provides a starting point for estimating *g* – after all, some firms are able to invest in similar operations with each annual increment of retained earnings and produce similar rates of return to those achieved in the past. But it would be wrong to generalise from that.

You still need to make a judgement on the likely reasonable range of values for future *b*s and r_Es given the specific circumstances of the firm under consideration. Note that many (most?) companies cannot, year after year, simply open yet another factory or another retail outlet with their retained earnings and expect to obtain the same return on equity capital on the additional investment as they do on the existing assets.

The price-earnings ratio (PER) model

The most popular approach to valuing a share is to use the **price-to-earnings ratio (PER)**. The historic PER compares a firm's share price with its latest earnings (profits) per share. Investors estimate a share's value as the amount they are willing to pay for each unit of earnings. If a company produced earnings per share of 10p in its latest accounts and investors are prepared to pay 20 times historic earnings for this type of share it will be valued at £2.00. The historic PER is calculated as follows:

$$\text{Historic PER} = \frac{\text{Current market price of share}}{\text{Last year's earnings per share}} = \frac{200\text{p}}{10\text{p}} = 20$$

So, the retailer Next which reported earnings per share of 146p for the year to December 2006 with a share price of 2,394p in May 2007 had a PER of 16.4. PERs of other retailers are shown in Exhibit 20.6.

Exhibit 20.6 PERs for retailers

Retailer	PER
Alliance Boots	23.6
Debenhams	11.6
DSG International (previously Dixons)	17.5
HMV	10.5
JJB Sports	24.0
Kingfisher	21.6
Marks & Spencer	21.0
Next	16.4

Source: Financial Times, 5 May 2007.

Investors are willing to buy Next shares at 16.4 times last year's earnings compared with only 11.6 times last year's earnings for Debenhams. One explanation for the difference in PERs is that companies with higher PERs are expected to show faster growth in earnings in the future. Next may appear expensive relative to Debenhams based on historical profit figures but the differential may be justified when forecasts of earnings are made. If a PER is high investors expect profits to rise. This does not necessarily mean that all companies with high PERs are expected to perform to a high standard, merely that they are expected to do significantly better than in the past. Few people would argue that Marks & Spencer has performed, or will perform, well in comparison with Next over the past 5–10 years and yet it stands at a higher historic PER, reflecting the market's belief that Marks & Spencer has more growth potential from its low base than Next.

So, using the historic PER can be confusing because a company can have a high PER because it is usually a high-growth company or because it has recently had a reduction of profits from which it is expected soon to recover.

PERs are also influenced by the uncertainty of the future earnings growth. So, perhaps, DSG and Kingfisher might have the same expected growth rate but the growth at DSG is subject to more risk and therefore the market assigns a lower earnings multiple.

PERs over time

There have been great changes over the years in the market's view of what is a reasonable multiple of earnings to place on share prices. What is excessive in one year is acceptable in another. This is illustrated in Exhibit 20.7.

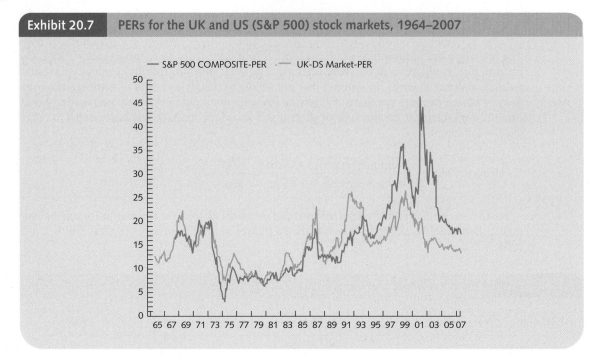

Exhibit 20.7 PERs for the UK and US (S&P 500) stock markets, 1964–2007

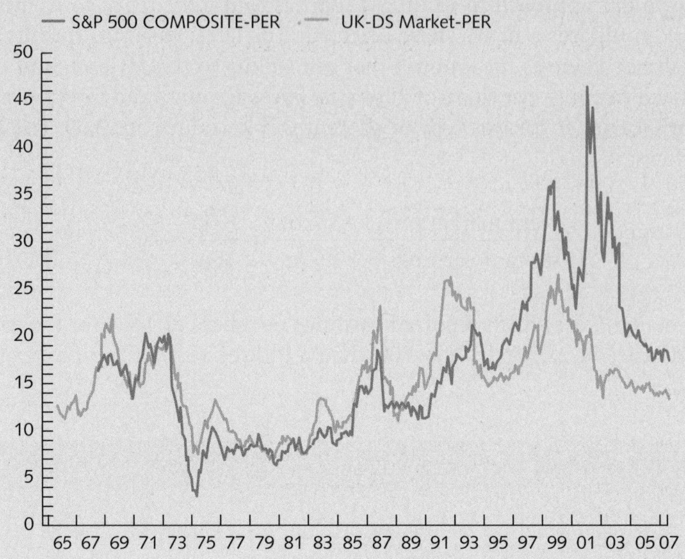

Source: Datastream.

The crude and the sophisticated use of the PER model

Some analysts use the **historical PER** (P_0/E_0), to make comparisons between firms without making explicit the considerations hidden in the analysis. They have a view of an appropriate PER based on current prevailing PERs for other firms in the same industry. So, for example, in 2007 Barclays with a PER of 13.6 may be judged to be priced correctly relative to similar firms – HBOS had a PER of 11.4, Lloyds TSB 13.3 and Royal Bank of Scotland 10.5. Analysing through comparisons lacks intellectual rigour. First, the assumption that the 'comparable' companies are correctly priced is a bold one. It is easy to see how the market could be pulled up (or down) by its own bootstraps and lose touch with fundamental considerations by this kind of thinking. A good example of this is the rise of telecommunication shares in the 1998–2000 bubble. Secondly, it fails to provide a framework for the analyst to test the important implicit input assumptions – for example, the growth rate expected in earnings in each of the companies, or the difference in required rate of return given the different risk level of each. These elements are probably in the mind of the analyst, but there are benefits in making these more explicit. This can be done with the more complete PER model which is forward looking and recognises both risk levels and growth projections.

The infinite dividend growth model can be used to develop the more complete PER model because they are both dependent on the key variables of growth, g (in dividends or earnings), and the required rate of return, k_E. The dividend growth model is:

$$P_0 = \frac{d_1}{k_E - g}$$

If both sides of the dividend growth model are divided by the expected earnings for the next year, E_1, then:

$$\frac{P_0}{E_1} = \frac{d_1/E_1}{k_E - g}$$

Note this is a ***prospective* PER** because it uses next year's earnings, rather than a historic PER, which uses E_0.

In this more complete model the appropriate multiple of earnings for a share rises as the growth rate, g, goes up; and falls as the required rate of return, k_E, increases. The relationship with the ratio d_1/E_1 is more complicated. If this payout ratio is raised it will not necessarily increase the PER because of the impact on g – if more of the earnings are paid out less financial resource is being invested in projects within the business, and therefore future growth may decline.

Worked example 20.6 Ridge plc

Ridge plc is anticipated to maintain a payout ratio of 48 per cent of earnings. The appropriate discount rate for a share for this risk class is 14 per cent and the expected growth rate in earnings and dividends is 6 per cent.

$$\frac{P_0}{E_1} = \frac{d_1/E_1}{k_E - g}$$

$$\frac{P_0}{E_1} = \frac{0.48}{0.14 - 0.06} = 6$$

The spread between k_E and g is the main influence on an acceptable PER. A small change can have a large impact. If we now assume a k_E of 12 per cent and g of 8 per cent the PER doubles.

$$\frac{P_0}{E_1} = \frac{0.48}{0.12 - 0.08} = 12$$

If k_E becomes 16 per cent and g 4 per cent then the PER reduces to two-thirds of its former value:

$$\frac{P_0}{E_1} = \frac{0.48}{0.16 - 0.04} = 4$$

Worked example 20.7 Whizz plc

You are interested in purchasing shares in Whizz plc. This company produces high-technology products and has shown strong earnings growth for a number of years. For the past five years earnings per share have grown, on average, by 10 per cent per annum.

Despite this performance and analysts' assurances that this growth rate will continue for the foreseeable future you are put off by the exceptionally high prospective price earnings ratio (PER) of 25.

In the light of the more complete forward-looking PER method, should you buy the shares or place your money elsewhere?

Whizz has a beta of 1.8 which may be taken as the most appropriate systematic risk adjustment to the risk premium for the average share (*see* Chapter 19).

The risk premium for equities over government bills has been 5 per cent over the past few decades, and the current risk-free rate of return is 7 per cent.

Whizz pays out 50 per cent of its earnings as dividends.

Answer

Stage 1 Calculate the appropriate cost of equity.

$$k_E = r_f + \beta\,(r_m - r_f)$$
$$k_E = 7 + 1.8\,(5) = 16\%$$

Stage 2 Use the more complete PER model.

$$\frac{P_0}{E_1} = \frac{d_1/E_1}{k_E - g} = \frac{0.5}{0.16 - 0.10} = 8.33$$

The maximum multiple of next year's earnings you would be willing to pay is 8.33. This is a third of the amount you are being asked to pay, therefore you will refuse to buy the share.

Prospective PER varies with g and k_E

If an assumption is made concerning the payout ratio, then a table can be drawn up to show how PERs vary with k_E and g – *see* **Exhibit 20.8**.

Exhibit 20.8 Prospective PERs for various risk classes and dividend growth rates

Assumed payout ratio $= \frac{d_1}{E_1} = 0.5$

Growth rate, g	Discount rate, k_E: 8	9	10	12
0	6.3	5.6	5.0	4.2
4	12.5	10.0	8.3	6.3
5	16.7	12.5	10.0	7.1
6	25.0	16.7	12.5	8.3
8	–	50.0	25.0	12.5

A payout ratio of 40–50 per cent of after-tax earnings is normal for UK shares.

Exhibit 20.9 A comparison of the crude PER and the more complete model

Crude PER, P_0/E_1

The assumptions here are implicit, e.g.

1 Valuation (P_0) consists of two parts:
  a value of earnings assuming no growth,
  b value of growth in earnings.

2 No explicit recognition of the need for different required rates of return (k_E) for shares in different risk classes.

The more complete model

$$\frac{P_0}{E_1} = \frac{d_1/E_1}{k_E - g}$$

Payout ratio
Superficially P_0 relative to E_1 could be raised by increasing payout ratio. However a lower retention ratio may reduce g to leave the overall value lower.

Growth rate, g
A complex composite of myriad influences on a firm's future growth of earnings and dividends, e.g.:
- proportion of profit retained;
- efficient use of resources;
- market opportunities;
- quality of management;
- strategy.

Required return for risk class, k_E related to risk class of share

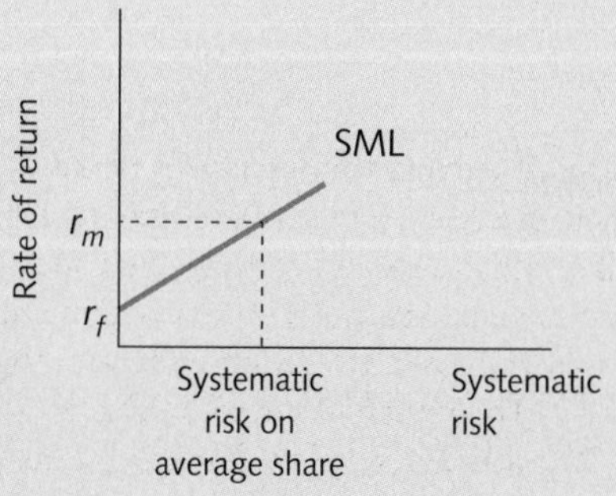

Note the influences on k_E: e.g. if prospective inflation rises, interest rates (probably) rise and SML shifts upwards thus increasing k_E (g will probably also rise). Also the risk profile of the firm may change with a new strategy, therefore altering k_E.

With the market propensity to focus on the future it can appear to provide strange valuations if historic relationships are examined. Take the case of Jefferson Smurfit, the Irish paper and packaging company which announced a fivefold jump in interim profits in August 1995 to IR£200.6m. The company was optimistic about its prospects, yet the consensus view on the stock exchange was that Jefferson Smurfit should be valued at a PER which was one-third of that for the average quoted firm, six compared with 18. The market was concerned about future earnings and was far less sanguine than the company. The Lex column of the *Financial Times* summed up the market view (*see* **Exhibit 20.10**).

Exhibit 20.10

Jefferson Smurfit

FT

The world's paper companies have a reputation for being like the Bible's Gadarene swine which, in a fit of madness, charged down a cliff. Paper groups are enjoying sharp increases in profitability, as shown by Jefferson Smurfit's interim results yesterday; but shareholders believe the industry will bring disaster on itself through over-investment in new capacity just as demand turns down. Hence, the sector's lowly ratings: Smurfit trades on little over six times next year's projected earnings; its US and European rivals trade on multiples of about seven or eight.

But, according to Smurfit, the industry is not about to repeat the destructive behaviour of previous cycles. New capacity is coming on stream less quickly than demand is growing. Some groups, notably Smurfit itself, have put plans for new plants on the back-burner. Instead, the industry has embarked on a wave of takeovers, since it is cheaper to buy old capacity than build new plants. Such consolidation is healthy since it should lead to a more disciplined market. A further healthy development is the trend, joined by Smurfit yesterday, for share buy-backs and large dividend increases. The more cash channelled into buy-backs, dividend increases and takeovers, the less will be left over for new capacity. While it is hard to believe that the industry's suicidal tendencies are permanently in check, current moves towards self-control are positive.

Source: Lex column, *Financial Times*, 24 August 1995. Reprinted with permission.

The pessimism of the *Financial Times* proved to be correct as overcapacity hit the industry again by 2003 – *see* **Exhibit 20.11**.

Exhibit 20.11

Paper groups see few signs of upturn

FT

By Nicholas George in Stockholm

Stora Enso and UPM-Kymmene, two of the world's largest paper producers, yesterday reported a sharp drop in third-quarter operating profits and said they saw only weak signs of economic recovery in Europe and North America.

Although the Finnish companies reckoned product prices were stabilising at low levels, overcapacity meant huge paper machines were being left to stand idle and the market was slow to accept price increases . . .

Source: *Financial Times*, 24 October 2003, p. 29. Reprinted with permission.

The more complete model can help explain the apparently perverse behaviour of stock markets. If there is 'good' economic news such as a rise in industrial output or a fall in unemployment the stock market often falls. The market likes the increase in earnings that such news implies, but this effect is often outweighed by the effects of the next stage. An economy growing at a fast pace is vulnerable to rises in inflation and the market will anticipate rises in interest rates to reflect this. Thus the r_f and the rest of the SML are pushed upward. The return required on shares, k_E, will rise, and this will have a depressing effect on share prices. The article reproduced in **Exhibit 20.12** expresses this well.

Exhibit 20.12

Why policymakers should take note

FT

One issue which always mystifies the novice investor is why the financial markets always react so joyously to bad economic news. A rise in unemployment or a fall in industrial production seems to be worth a point on bonds and a jump in the stock market index.

Experienced global investors explain patiently that the key determinant of short term financial market performance is interest rates. Slower growth prompts monetary authorities to lower rates; this in turn reduces corporate costs, reduces the appeal of holding cash, and in the case of falling long term yields, by lowering the rate at which future income streams are discounted, increases the present value of shares.

Conversely, of course, faster economic growth causes governments and central banks to fear higher inflation, prompting them to increase interest rates, with consequent adverse effects on share prices.

Source: Philip Coggan, 'Global Investors', *Financial Times*, 5 February 1996, p. 20. Reprinted with permission.

Valuation using cash flow

The third and most important income-based valuation method is cash flow. In business it is often said that 'cash is king'. From the shareholders' perspective the cash flow relating to a share is crucial – they hand over cash and are interested in the ability of the business to return cash to them. John Allday, head of valuation at Ernst and Young, says that discounted cash flow 'is the purest way. I would prefer to adopt it if the information is there.'[4]

The interest in cash flow is promoted by the limited usefulness of published accounts. Scepticism about the accuracy of earnings figures, given the flexibility available in their construction, prompts attempts to find a purer valuation method than PER.

The cash flow approach involves the discounting of future cash flows, that is, the cash generated by the business after investment in fixed assets and working capital to fully maintain its long-term competitive position and its unit volume, and to make investment in all new value-creating projects. To derive the cash flow attributable to shareholders, any interest paid in a particular period is deducted. The process of the derivation of cash flow from profit figures is shown in **Exhibit 20.13**.

An example of a cash flow calculation is shown in **Exhibit 20.14**. Note that the earnings figures for 2010 are very different from the cash flow because of the large capital investment in fixed assets – earnings are positive because only a small proportion of the cost of the new fixed assets is depreciated in that year.

There is a subtle assumption in this type of analysis. This is that all annual cash flows are paid out to shareholders rather than reinvested. If all positive NPV projects have been accepted using the money allocated to additional capital expenditures on fixed assets and working capital, then to withhold further money from shareholders would be value destructive because any other projects would have negative NPVs. An alternative assumption, which amounts to the same effect in terms of share value, is that any cash flows that are retained and reinvested generate a return that merely equals the required rate of return for that risk class; thus no additional value is created. Of course, if the company either knows of other positive-value projects at the outset or comes across them in future years, it should take them up. This will alter the numbers in the table and so a new valuation is needed.

The definition of cash flow used here (which includes a deduction of expenditure on investment in fixed and working capital to maintain long-term competitive position, unit volume, and to make investment all new value-creating projects) is significantly different from many accountants' and analysts' definitions of cash flow. They often neglect to allow for one or more of these factors. Be careful if you are presented with alternative cash flow numbers based on a different definition of cash flow.

---

[4] Quoted by Robert Outram (1997), p. 70.

Exhibit 20.13 Cash flow approach: one possibility

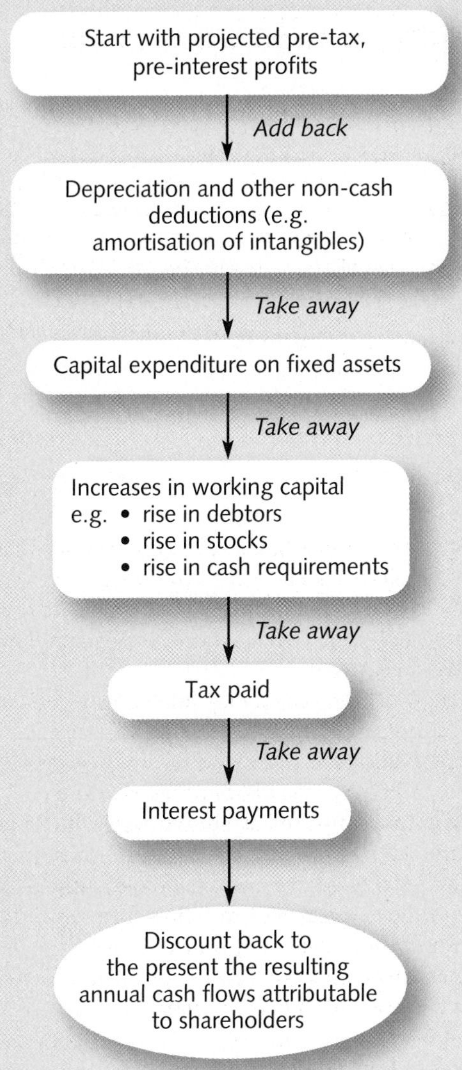

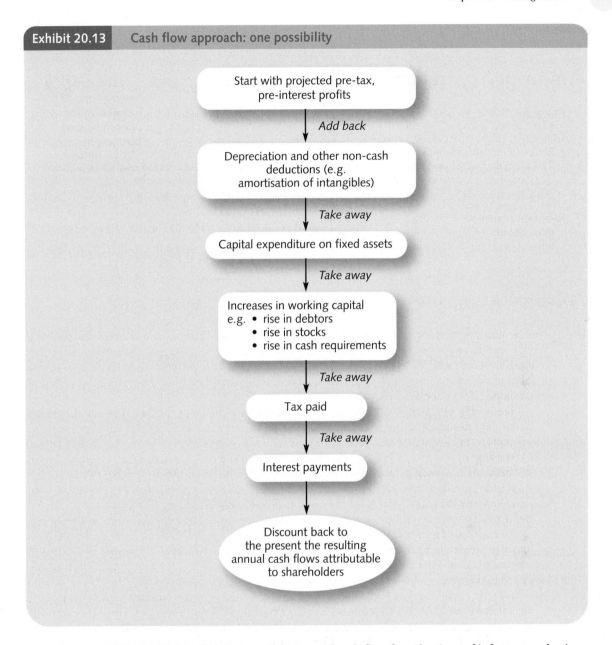

Exhibit 20.15 describes the use of discounted cash flow for valuations of infrastucture business (e.g. toll roads, water supply).

Exhibit 20.14 Cash flow-based share valuation

£m	2009	2010	2011	2012	2013	Estimated average annual cash flow for period beyond planning horizon 2014–infinity
Forecast pre-tax, pre-interest profits	+11.0	+15.0	+15.0	+16.0	+17.0	
Add non-cash items: depreciation, amortisation, etc.	+1.0	+2.5	+5.5	+4.5	+4.0	
Working capital increase (–) decrease (+)	+1.0	–0.5	0.0	+1.0	+1.0	
Tax (paid in year)	–3.3	–5.0	–5.0	–5.4	–5.8	
Interest on debt capital	–0.5	–0.5	–0.5	–0.6	–0.7	
Fixed capital investment	–1.0	–16.0	0.0	–1.2	–1.8	
Cash flow	+8.2	–4.5	+15.0	+14.3	+13.7	+14.0
Cash flow per share (assuming 100m shares)	8.2p	–4.5p	15p	14.3p	13.7p	14p
Discounted cash flow $k_E = 14\%$	$\frac{8.2}{1.14}$	$-\frac{4.5}{(1.14)^2}$	$+\frac{15}{(1.14)^3}$	$+\frac{14.3}{(1.14)^4}$	$+\frac{13.7}{(1.14)^5}$	$+\frac{14}{0.14} \times \frac{1}{(1.14)^5}$
Share value =	7.20	–3.5	+10.1	+8.5	+7.1	+51.9
						= 81.3p

An Excel spreadsheet version of this is available at www.pearsoned.co.uk/arnold.

Valuation using owner earnings

A simplified version of cash flow analysis is **owner earnings**. For shares, **intrinsic value** is the discounted value of the owner earnings that can be taken out of a business during its remaining life. These correspond with standard cash flow analysis shown in the last section except that we calculate a sustainable level of owner earnings for a typical year (subject to a steady growth) rather than lumpy cash flows for the future years. Future owner earnings are determined by the strength and durability of the economic franchise (attractiveness of the industry plus competitive position of the firm in the industry), the quality of management and the financial strength of the business. In the following analysis we make use of Warren Buffett's definition of owner earnings, but with the additional factor in **c** and **d** of 'investment in all new value-creating projects'.[5] Owner earnings are defined as:

a earnings after tax; *plus*

b depreciation, depletion, amortisation and certain other non-cash charges; *less*

[5] This form of analysis is set out in Arnold (2002).

Exhibit 20.15

Value model that ignores share prices

FT

For investors in infrastructure assets, discounted cash flow is the key

writes Peter Thal Larsen

The phrase infrastructure finance get used a lot, often with subtle but important differences in meaning. Nevertheless, the area is now sufficiently well established that it is possible to make some broad generalisations about how it works, and how it differs from other fields such as private equity.

To begin with, there is the heavy reliance on discounted cash flow modelling. While public investors still tend to rely heavily on multiples of earnings when picking stocks, most infrastructure analysts pride themselves on paying little attention to the price of something in the public markets.

Instead they attempt to model revenues, costs, investment requirements and cash flows for a particular business well into the future, and then work out what those cash flows are worth today. The final figure gives an indication of what an asset might be worth, and how much debt it can support. In both cases, the answer often differs significantly from the view of the stock market.

The most striking recent example of this was the auction of BAA, the British airport operator, which saw its share price double amid a fierce battle which was eventually won by Ferrovial of Spain. But infrastructure investors tend to stick with the DCF analysis, even after they have bought an asset.

Ultimately, the idea of infrastructure finance is to leave enough cash flow – after the investment needs of the business have been met and the debt has been paid off – to pay investors a dividend. 'Our product is yield,' says one senior executive.

Yet this does not always happen immediately. As the price of infrastructure assets has risen, returns have not ony declined, they have been pushed back. As a result, executives now acknowledge that some investments make little or no return in the first few years, but only begin to pay a healthy dividend later on, once some of the debt has been paid down.

There is also a suspicion that some infrastructure investors are gambling on being able to sell the business for more than they paid for it, or on refinancing the debt at better rates in the future, in order to provide their investors with a decent return.

For the bank that handles the investment, however, the picture may look significantly different. This is because many banks charge a series of fees to their investors on deals they have arranged. They might take an advisory fee, a fee for arranging the financing, and performance fees for managing the asset in the future.

A factor in the growth of infrastructure financing has been the availability of large amounts of cheap debt. Low interest rates and the willingness of lenders to reduce risk premiums have allowed infrastructure investors to borrow larger amounts on more favourable terms than ever before.

But this raises the question of what will happen to the business if interest rates rise. In an industry where returns are driven by assumptions based on long-term financial forecasts, even a small change in the cash flows can lead to dramatic changes in the projected returns.

Infrastructure executives argue that many of their investments have built-in hedges against inflation. Water companies and other utilities are subject to regular reviews by regulators. In which their prices are set according to inflation. The same is true for many toll roads.

However, these cannot protect investors from other shocks, such as a spike in the oil price, which could diminish road usage. Infrastructure groups argue that they subject their models to substantial stress tests before launching bids for concessions or companies, in order to see what would happen to their investments if things go differently than expected.

Source: Financial Times, 25 October 2006, Corporate Finance, p. 20. Reprinted with permission.

c the amount of expenditures for plant and machinery, etc. that a business requires to fully maintain its long-term competitive position and its unit volume and to make investment in all new value-creating projects; *less*

d any extra amount for working capital that is needed to maintain the firm's long-term competitive position and unit volume and to make investment in all new value-creating projects.

Thus, there are two types of investment. First, that which is needed to permit the firm to continue to maintain its existing competitive position at the current level of output. Secondly, investment in value-creating growth opportunities beyond the current position.

So, for example, Cotillo plc has reported earnings after tax for the most recent year of £16.3 million. In drawing up the income (profit and loss) account deductions of £7.4 million were made for depreciation and £152,000 for the amortisation of intangible assets, and £713,000 of goodwill was written off. It is estimated that an annual expenditure of £8.6 million on plant, machinery, etc. will be required for the company to maintain its long-term competitive position and unit volume. For the sake of simplicity we will assume that no further monies will be needed for extra working capital to maintain long-term competitive position and unit volume. Also, Cotillo has no new value-creating projects.

The trading record of Cotillo plc has been remarkably stable in the past and is unlikely to alter in the future. It is therefore reasonable to use the above figures for all the future years. This would result in estimated annual owner earnings of £15.965 million (*see* **Exhibit 20.16**).

Exhibit 20.16 Cotillo plc, owner earnings

		£000s
a	Reported earnings after tax	16,300
	Plus	
b	Depreciation, depletion, amortisation and other non-cash charges (7,400 + 152 + 713)	8,265
		24,565
	less	
c and d	Expenditure on plant, equipment, working capital, etc. required to maintain long-term competitive position, unit volume and investment in new projects	8,600
		15,965

The discounted value of this perpetuity = £159.65m, if we take the discount rate to be 10 per cent:

$$\text{Intrinsic value} = \frac{£15.965\text{m}}{0.10} = £159.65\text{m}$$

Intrinsic value is determined by the owner earnings that can be *taken out* of the business during its remaining life. Logically the management of Cotillo should pay out the full £15.965m each year to shareholders if the managers do not have investment projects within the firm that will generate returns of 10 per cent or more because shareholders can get 10 per cent return elsewhere for the same level of risk as holding a share in Cotillo. If the managers come across another project that promises a return of exactly 10 per cent shareholder wealth will be unchanged whether the company invests in this or chooses to ignore the project and continues with the payment of all owner earnings each year. If the management discover, in a future year, a value-creating project that will produce, say, a 15 per cent rate of return (for the same level of risk as the existing projects) then shareholders will welcome a reduction in dividends during the years of additional investment. The total value of discounted future owner earnings will rise and intrinsic value will be greater than £159.65m if such a project is undertaken.

Now let us assume that Cotillo has a series of new value-creating projects (i.e. generating returns greater than 10 per cent) in which it can invest. By investing in these projects owner earnings will rise by 5 per cent year on year (on the one hand owner earnings are decreased by the need for additional investment under **c** and **d**, but, on the other hand reported earnings are boosted under **a**, to produce a net 5 per cent growth). The intrinsic value becomes £335.26m, viz:

$$\text{Next year's owner earnings} = £15.965\text{m}\ (1 + g) = £15.965\text{m}\ (1 + 0.05) = £16.763\text{m}$$

$$\text{Intrinsic value} = \text{next year's owner earnings}/(k_E - g) = \frac{16.763}{0.10 - 0.05} = £335.26\text{m}$$

It is legitimate to discount owner earnings because they amount to that which can be paid out to shareholders after all value-creating projects are financed and payments have been made for the investment to maintain the firm's competitive position and unit volume. It would not be legitimate to discount conventional accounting earnings. These are much larger than dividends because part of these earnings is ploughed back into the business for capital items and working capital. Owner earnings are much smaller than conventional earnings, and are in general closer to the dividend level than the conventional earnings figure, much of which could not be paid out to shareholders without jeopardising the future income flows of the business.

EBITDA is classified by some commentators as a cash flow measure of value. There will be no promoting of EBITDA as a useful measure of valuation in this book, because it can lead to some very distorted thinking. EBITDA (pronounced e-bit-dah) became a very popular measure of a company's performance in the late 1990s. It was especially popular with managers of firms that failed to make a profit. EBITDA means **earnings before interest, taxation, depreciation and amortisation**. Managers liked to emphasise this measure in their communications to shareholders because large positive numbers could be shown. Some cynics have renamed it, '**E**arnings **B**efore **I** **T**ricked the **D**umb **A**uditor'.

If you run an internet company that makes a £100m loss and the future looks pretty dim unless you can persuade investors and bankers to continue their support, perhaps you would want to add back all the interest (say £50m), depreciation on assets that are wearing out or becoming obsolete (say £40m), and the declining value of intangible assets, such as software licences and goodwill amortisation of, say, £65m, so that you could show a healthy positive number on EBITDA of £55m. And if your loss seems to get worse from one year to the next as your acquisition strategy fails to pay off it is wonderfully convenient to report and emphasise a stable or rising EBITDA.

The use of EBITDA by company directors makes political spin doctors look amateurs by comparison. EBITDA is not covered by any accounting standards so companies are entitled to use a variety of methods – whatever shows the company in the best light, I guess.

In the real world directors (and valuers) cannot ignore (however much they would want to) the cost of using up and wearing out equipment and other assets or the fact that interest and tax need to be paid. Warren Buffett made the comment: 'References to EBITDA make us shudder – does management think the tooth fairy pays for capital expenditures?' (Warren Buffett, a letter to shareholders attached to the *Annual Report of Berkshire Hathaway Inc* (2000). Reprinted with kind permission of Warren Buffett. © Warren Buffett.)

Valuing unquoted shares

The principles of valuation are the same for companies with a quoted share price on an exchange and for unquoted firms. The methods of valuation discussed above in relation to shares quoted on an exchange may be employed, but there may be some additional factors to consider in relation to unquoted firms' shares.

1 ***There may be a lower quality and quantity of information*** The reporting statements tend to be less revealing for unquoted firms. There may also be a managerial reluctance to release information – or managers may release information selectively so as to influence price, for example, in merger discussions.
2 ***These shares may be subject to more risk*** Firms at an early stage in their life cycle are often more susceptible to failure than are established firms.
3 ***The absence of a quotation usually means the shares are less liquid***, that is, there is a reduced ability to sell quickly without moving the price. This lack of marketability can be a severe drawback and often investors in unquoted firms, such as venture capitalists, insist on there being a plan to provide an exit route within, say, five years, perhaps through a stock market float. But that still leaves a problem for the investor within the five years should a sale be required.

4 ***Cost of tying in management*** When a substantial stake is purchased in an unquoted firm, in order for the existing key managers to be encouraged to stay they may be offered financial incentives such as '**golden handcuffs**' which may influence value. Or the previous owner-managers may agree an '**earn-out**' clause in which they receive a return over the years following a sale of their shares (the returns paid to these individuals will be dependent on performance over a specified future period).

5 ***Owner/director compensation*** When considering a takeover price for an unquoted company the reported figures need to be examined carefully because it is often the case that the owner-directors have been over-paying themselves from company coffers. Therefore an upward adjustment is needed to the profit/cashflow numbers. On the other hand, owner-directors may have under-paid themselves and a takeover would mean their replacements would need to be paid considerably more.

Unquoted firms' shares tend to sell at significantly lower prices than those of quoted firms. The BDO Stoy Hayward Private Company Price Index (www.bdo.co.uk) shows that generally unquoted firms are sold at an average PER of under two-thirds that for quoted shares. However, as **Exhibit 20.17** shows, recent demand has been so strong that prices paid have risen.

Exhibit 20.17

Private companies catching up

Sarah Spikes

The UK's private companies, once seen as the ugly stepchildren of the business world, are catching up with their publicly traded rivals in terms of value, with private equity and hedge funds driving the trend, according to research by BDO Stoy Hayward, an accounting and business advice firm.

Private companies have recently changed hands at prices that show their market value is much closer to that of publicly traded companies than it was in 2004.

BDO said the explosion in funds available from private equity companies is one of the main reasons for the change. Private equity firms flush with cash have been targetting large mid-market companies in particular, said Jon Breach, corporate finance partner at BDO.

Source: Financial Times, 18 September 2006, p. 22. Reprinted with permission.

Unusual companies

Obtaining information to achieve accuracy with discounted income flow methods is problematic for most shares. But in industries subject to rapid technological innovation it is extraordinarily difficult. While discounted income flow remains the ultimate method of valuation some analysts use more immediate proxies to estimate value. (A less scientific-sounding description is 'rules of thumb'.) For example, Gerry Stephens and Justin Funnell, media and telecoms analysts at NatWest Markets, describe the approach often adopted in their sector:[6]

> Rather than DCF (discounted cash flow), people are often more comfortable valuing telemedia project companies using benchmarks that have evolved from actual market prices paid for similar assets, being based on a comparative measure or scale such as per line, per subscriber, per home or per pop (member of population). For example, an analyst might draw conclusions from the per-pop price that Vodaphone [sic] trades at to put a price on the float of Telecom Italia Mobile. The benchmark prices will actually have originated from DCF analysis and the price paid can give an element of objective validation to the implied subjective DCF.

This sort of logic has been employed in the valuation of internet companies. In their attempt to value future profits that were far from certain 'analysts' became more and more extreme in clutching at straws to value internet companies in the late 1990s – *see* **Exhibit 20.18**.

[6] Stephens and Funnell (1995), p. 20.

Exhibit 20.18

The internet revolution

FT

Lies, damned lies and web valuations

Internet fever gripped the world and led credulous investors to think dotcom companies were sure-fire winners. We show how scarce data, high hopes and fast-talking 'rock star' analysts fuelled a frenzy of speculation that eventually ended in tears

In a market where many internet companies had little in the way of revenues to show, let alone profits, their ability to attract the attention of growing online audience became one of the only ways of measuring their performance.

Investors began to focus on the number of unique users (the number of different people who visited its site) and page views (the number of web pages these visitors clicked on) claimed by a site.

Bob Davis, chief executive of Lycos, the US portal, defends the methods that have been developed for measuring internet audiences, while adding: 'It's working on being a science, but it isn't a science yet.' Of the audience numbers produced by such research, he adds: 'I wouldn't want to look at them on an absolute basis – but on a relative basis, they probably do a good job.' . . .

But companies did not always make it clear where they were using gross revenue, before subtracting cost of sales, and where they were referring to net revenue. Some omitted to point out how much of their advertising revenues derived from barter advertising with other websites, where money did not actually change hands. This backdrop of scarce data and high hopes provided an ideal environment for a number of quick-thinking, fast-talking analysts to make a name for themselves . . .

Indeed, credibility was sometimes conferred by the amount of press attention the stocks had generated. Internet analysts joked about a 'price-to-press-cuttings ratio'.

Source: *Financial Times*, 13 October 2000, p. 16. Reprinted with permission.

Other sectors difficult to value directly on the basis of income flow include: advertising agencies, where a percentage of annual billings is often used as a proxy; mobile phone operators, where ARPU (average revenue per user) is used; fund managers, where value of funds under management is used; and hotels, where star ratings may be combined with number of rooms and other factors such as revenue per room.

Managerial control and valuation

The value of a share can change depending on whether the purchaser gains a controlling interest in the firm. The purchase of a single share brings a stream of future dividends without any real influence over the level of those dividends. However, control of a firm by, say, purchasing 50 per cent or more of the shares, permits the possibility of changing the future operations of the firm and thus enhancing returns. A merger may allow economies of scale and other synergies, or future earnings may be boosted by the application of superior management skills.

The difference in value between a share without management control and one with it helps to explain why we often witness a share price rise of 30–50 per cent in a takeover bid battle. There are two appraisals of the value of the firm, both of which may be valid depending on the assumption concerning managerial control. **Exhibit 20.19** shows that extra value can be created by merging the operations of two firms.

Exhibit 20.19 is not meant to imply that the acquiring firm will pay a bid premium equal to the estimated merger benefits. The price paid is subject to negotiation and bargaining. The acquirer is likely to try to offer significantly less than the combined amount of the target firm's value 'as is' and the merger benefits. This will enable it to retain as much as possible of the increased value for itself rather than pass value on to the target shareholders. (*See* Chapter 23 for more detail.)

Exhibit 20.19 Value creation through merger

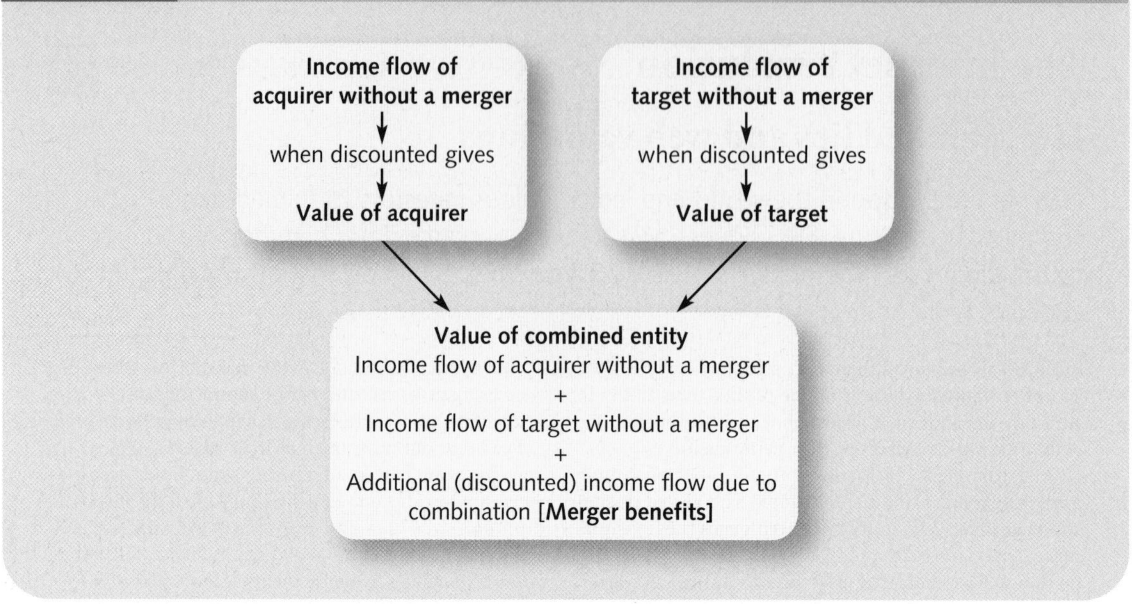

Valuation models and managerial control

The takeover of the British & Dutch steel producer, Corus, by India's Tata Steel in 2007 will provide a framework for illustrating possible use of the income flow model when managerial control is obtained. Tata Steel claimed that it could reduce costs at Corus by £178 m per year.

In the absence of a takeover the value of a share in either company is:

$$P_0 = \frac{d_1}{k_E - g}$$

This is where d_1 and g are generated by the existing structure and strategy.

Alternatively, we could examine the entire cash flow of the company (available to be paid out to shareholders after maintaining the firm's competitive position and unit volume and investing in all value-generating projects) rather than a single share.

$$V_E = \frac{C_1}{k_E - g_c}$$

where:

V_E = value of the entire share capital of the firm;

C_1 = total cash flows at time 1 expected to continue growing at a constant rate of g_c in future years.

If there is a new strategy the values in the equations change:

$$P_0 = \frac{d_1^*}{k_E - g^*}$$

or, for the entire cash flow:

$$V_E = \frac{C_1^*}{k_E - g_c^*}$$

d_1^*, C_1^*, g^*, g_c^* allow for the following:

- synergy;
- cutting out costs;
- tax benefits;
- superior management;
- other benefits (for example, lower finance costs, greater public profile, market power) less any additional costs.

Alternatively, a marginal approach could be adopted in which C_1^*, d_1^*, g^* and g_c^* are redefined as the *additional* cash flows and growth in cash flows due to changes in ownership. For example, let us assume that the annual earnings gain of £178m is obtained in Year 1 but does not increase thereafter. Therefore $g = 0$. Let us further assume that the required rate of return on an investment of this risk class is 10 per cent. Thus the present value of the efficiency gains is:

$$V_E = \frac{C_1^*}{k_E - g_c^*} = \frac{£178\text{m}}{0.10 - 0} = £1{,}780\text{m}$$

We could change the assumption to gain insight into the sensitivity of the added value figure. For example, if it is anticipated that the benefits will rise each year by 2 per cent (so they are £182m in Year 2 and £185m in Year 3, etc.) then the maximum bid premium will rise:

$$V_E = \frac{C_1^*}{k_E - g_c^*} = \frac{£178\text{m}}{0.10 - 0.02} = £2{,}225\text{m}$$

On the other hand, the management of Tata might have been carried away with the excitement of the bid battle and the £178m quoted might have come from hype or hubris, and, in fact, the difficulties of integration produce negative incremental cash flows. (*See* Chapter 23 for a discussion on the problems of post-merger integration, and hubris as a driver of merger activity.)

Allowing for real option values

The expected income flows to be received by shareholders are the foundation for share valuation. But what about companies that have no projected income flows? Take an oil company that has fallen on hard times. It has shut down all of its oil wells because the cost of extraction is greater than the current market price of oil. In fact the oil price would have to double to make it worthwhile reopening the wells. So there is little that the analyst can put into, say, a discounted cash flow calculation because the chances are that the company will never produce income again. However, this is not to say that there is no value. The company has the right but not the obligation to start taking oil from its wells when it wants to. This can be worth a lot of money, if an event happens, e.g. the price of oil triples.

The same logic applies to parts of a firm. There may be little prospect of the asset producing an income flow for the shareholders and yet there is value because of the existence of an option someday to implement the project should circumstances change. Thus to the value of identifiable income flows we should add the value of the collection of options that the firm may be holding, ranging from expansion options, delaying options to the option to quit. This area of finance is known as **contingent claim valuation**: cash flows are to some extent contingent on the occurrence or non-occurrence of some event and therefore the asset being valued is greater than the present value of the expected cash flows. BT owns thousands of patents some of which may be worth millions, if not billions, when the time is ripe. Indeed, we may discover at some point in the future that one or two of the inventions and innovations produced in the labs and currently hidden away in the vaults are worth more than all the currently projected cash flows on its existing business. We will not know until the contingent event happens (e.g. a complementary technological breakthrough) and the new business is created. Another example: if you were a song writer in the 1970s and you were smart you would have held on to the rights to use your music in any form. Even though you could not at that time value those rights for use in devices you could not even imagine (mobile phone ringtones, MP3 players, etc.) you did figure out that circumstances change and options to do something can suddenly become amazingly valuable.

Knowing that real options are important is one thing, valuing them is quite another. Most are very difficult to value. Be cautious: people can come up with very suspect numbers vulnerable to bias. Chapter 6 discusses real options.

Worked example 20.8 Thingamees

Big plc has made it clear to the widget industry that it is willing to sell its subsidiary, Little plc, a manufacturer of thingamees. You are a member of the strategy management team at Thingamees International plc, the largest producers of thingamees in the UK. Your firm is interested in acquiring Little and as a first step has obtained some information from Big plc.

Little plc Balance Sheet		**£m**
Fixed assets		10
Current assets		
Cash	0.5	
Stock	1.5	
Debtors	3.0	
		5
Current liabilities		(6)
Bank *loan*		(4)
Net assets		5

Trading record Year	**Total earnings, £m (owner earnings)**
2007	1.86
2006	1.70
2005	1.65
2004	1.59
2003	1.20
2002	1.14
2001	1.01

Additional information

By combining the logistical departments you estimate that transport costs could be lowered by £100,000 per annum, and two secretarial posts eliminated, saving £28,000 p.a.

The closure of Little's head office would save £400,000 p.a. in staffing and running costs, but would also mean an additional £250,000 of administration costs at Thingamees plc to undertake some crucial tasks. The office building is situated in a good location and would raise a net £5m if sold immediately. A potential liability not displayed in Little's balance sheet is a possible legal claim of £3m relating to an earlier disposal of an asset. The plaintiff and Little's board have not yet reached agreement (Little's board is adamant that there is no liability).

Your appraisal of Little's management team is that it is a mixed bunch – some good, some very bad. Profits could be raised by £500,000 per year if you could impose your will quickly and remove poor managers. However, if you have to take a more gradual 'easing out' approach, operating profits will rise by only £300,000 per year.

The problems connected with a quick transition are: a sacking left, right and centre may cause disaffection amongst the good managers, encouraging hostility, departures and **a** profits collapse, and **b** Big plc is keen that you provide a commitment to avoid large-scale redundancies.

Big, Little and Thingamees International all have a beta of 1.5, which is representative of the appropriate adjustment to the risk premium on the average share given the systematic risk. The risk-free rate of return is 8 per cent and the historical risk premium of share portfolios over safe securities has been 5 per cent.

The increased market power available to Thingamees International after purchasing Little would improve margins in Thingamees International's existing business to provide an additional £100,000 per annum.

Assume that tax is irrelevant.

Required

a Calculate the value of Little plc in its present form, assuming a continuation of its historic growth rate.
b Calculate the value of Little plc if you took it over but were unable to push for maximum management redundancies and Little continued with its historical growth rate for its profits (that is, the profits before merger benefits). Include the annual merger benefits assuming they are constant for all future years to an infinite horizon, that is, there is no growth in these.
c Calculate the value of Little plc on the assumption that you are able to push through the rapid management changes and the pre-acquisition earnings continue on their historic growth path. (Add on the annual merger savings assuming these are the same for every future year.)
d Discuss the steps you would take to get around the obstacles to profit maximisation.

Answers

a First calculate the required rate of return:

$$k_E = r_f + \beta (r_m - r_f)$$
$$= 8 + 1.5\ (5) = 15.5\%$$

Then calculate growth rate of cash flows:

$$g = \sqrt[6]{\frac{1.86}{1.01}} - 1 = 10.71\%$$

Then calculate the value of Little plc:

$$V_E = \frac{C_1}{k_E - g} = \frac{1.86\ (1 + 0.1071)}{0.155 - 0.1071} = £42.990\text{m}$$

The value of Little to its shareholders under its present strategy and managers is £42.990m.

b Calculate the present value of the future cash flows. These come in three forms.

i Those cash flows available immediately from selling assets, etc., less the amount due on a legal claim (taking the most conservative view):

Time 0 cash flows	
Sale of head office	£5m
less legal claim	£3m
	£2m

ii Merger benefit cash flow – constant for all future years:

	£m
Transport	0.100
Secretaries	0.028
Head office	0.150
Managerial efficiency	0.300
Market power	0.100
Boost to cash flow	0.678

This is a perpetuity which has a present value of:

$$\frac{0.678}{0.155} = £4.374\text{m}$$

iii The present value of Little under its existing strategy, £42.990m.

Add these values together:

i	£2.000m
ii	£4.374m
iii	£42.990m
Total value	£49.364m

c Value of business in existing form £42.990m

plus value of annual savings and benefits

$$\frac{678{,}000 + 200{,}000}{0.155} \quad £5.665\text{m}$$

plus Time 0 cash flows £2.000m

Total value £50.655m

Thingamees International now has a bargaining range for the purchase of Little. Below £42.99m the existing shareholders will be reluctant to sell. Above £50.665m, Thingamees may destroy value for its own shareholders even if all poor managers can be removed.

d Some ideas: one possible step to reduce risk is to insist that Big plc accepts all liability relating to the legal claim.

Another issue to be addressed in the negotiation phase is to avoid being hamstrung by redundancy commitments.

Also plan the process of merger integration. In the period before the merger explain your intentions to Little's employees. After the transfer do not alienate the managers and other employees by being capricious and secretive – be straight and honest. If pain is to be inflicted for the good of the firm, be quick, rational and fair, communicate and explain. (*See* Chapter 23 for more detail.)

Concluding comments

There are two points about valuation worth noting. First, going through a rigorous process of valuation is more important than arriving at *an* answer. It is the understanding of the assumptions and an appreciation of the nature of the inputs to the process which give insight, not a single number at the end. It is the recognition of the qualitative, and even subjective, nature of key variables in a superficially quantitative analysis that leads to knowledge about values. We cannot escape the uncertainty inherent in the valuation of a share – what someone is willing to pay depends on what will happen in the future – and yet this is no excuse for rejecting the models as unrealistic and impractical. They are better than the alternatives: guessing, or merely comparing one share with another with no theoretical base to anchor either valuation. At least the models presented in this chapter have the virtue of forcing the analyst to make explicit the fundamental considerations concerning the value of a share. As the sage of finance, Warren Buffett, says, 'Valuing a business is part art and part science'.[7]

The second point leads on from the first. It makes sense to treat the various valuation methods as complementary rather than rivals. Obtain a range of values in full knowledge of the weaknesses of each approach and apply informed judgement to provide an idea of the value region.

[7] Quoted by Adam Smith, 'The modest billionaire', *Esquire*, October 1988, p. 103. Reprinted in Janet Lowe (1997), p. 100.

Key points and concepts

- **Knowledge of the influences on share value** is needed by:

  a managers seeking actions to increase that value;
  b investors interested in allocating savings.

- **Share valuation requires a combination of two skills**:

  a analytical ability using mathematical models;
  b good judgement.

- The **net asset value (NAV)** approach to valuation focuses on balance sheet values. These may be adjusted to reflect current market or replacement values.

  Advantage: 'objectivity'.
  Disadvantages: – excludes many non-quantifiable assets;
  – less objective than is often supposed.

- **Asset values are given more attention in some situations**:

  – firms in financial difficulty;
  – takeover bids;
  – when discounted income flow techniques are difficult to apply, for example in property investment companies, investment trusts, resource-based firms.

- **Income flow valuation methods** focus on the future flows attributable to the shareholder. The past is only useful to the extent that it sheds light on the future.

- **The dividend valuation models (DVM)** are based on the premise that the market value of ordinary shares represents the sum of the expected future dividend flows to infinity, discounted to a present value.

- A **constant dividend valuation model**:

  $$P_0 = \frac{d_1}{k_E}$$

- The **dividend growth model**:

  $$P_0 = \frac{d_1}{k_E - g}$$

  This assumes constant growth in future dividends to infinity.

- **Problems with dividend valuation models**:

  – highly sensitive to the assumptions;
  – the quality of input data is often poor;
  – If g exceeded k_E a nonsensical result would occur, but then, on a long-term view, g would not exceed k_E.

- **Factors determining the growth rate of dividends**:

  – the quantity of resources retained and reinvested;
  – the rate of return earned on retained resources;
  – the rate of return earned on existing assets.

- **How to calculate *g*,** some pointers:

  a Focus on the firm:

  – evaluate strategy;
  – evaluate the management;
  – extrapolate historic dividend growth;
  – financial statement evaluation and ratio analysis.

  b Focus on the economy.

- **The historic price-earnings ratio (PER)** compared with PERs of peer firms is a crude method of valuation (it is also very popular):

$$\text{Historic PER} = \frac{\text{Current market price of share}}{\text{Last year's earnings per share}}$$

- **Historic PERs may be high for two reasons**:
  - the company is fast growing;
  - the company has been performing poorly, has low historic earnings, but is expected to improve.

  The linking factor is the anticipation of high future growth in earnings. Risk is also reflected in differences between PERs.

- The **more complete PER model**:

$$\frac{P_0}{E_1} = \frac{d_1/E_1}{k_E - g}$$

  This is a prospective PER model because it focuses on next year's dividend and earnings.

- The **discounted cash flow method**:

$$P_0 = \sum_{t=1}^{t=n} C/(1 + k_E)^t)$$

  For constant cash flow growth:

$$P_0 = \frac{C_1}{k_E - g_c}$$

- The **owner earnings model** requires the discounting of the company's future owner earnings which are standard expected earnings after tax plus non-cash charges less the amount of expenditure on plant, machinery and working capital needed for the firm to maintain its long-term competitive position and its unit volume and to make investment in all new value-creating projects.

- Additional factors to consider when **valuing unquoted shares**:
  - lower quality and quantity of information;
  - more risk;
  - less marketable;
  - may involve 'golden hand-cuffs' or 'earn-outs';
  - adjustment for over- or under-paying of director-owners.

- Some companies are extraordinarily **difficult to value**; therefore **proxies are used for projected cash flow**, such as:
  - telemedia valuations: multiply the number of lines, homes served or doors passed;
  - advertising agencies: annual billings;
  - fund managers: funds under control;
  - hotels: star ratings and bedrooms.

- **Control over a firm** permits the possibility of changing the future cash flows. Therefore a share may be more highly valued if control is achieved.

- **A target company could be valued on the basis of its discounted future cash flows**, e.g.:

$$V_E = \frac{C_1^*}{k_E - g_c^*}$$

- Alternatively the **incremental flows** expected to flow from the company under new management could be discounted to estimate the bid premium (d_1^*, C_1^* and g^* are redefined to be incremental factors only):

$$P_0 = \frac{d_1^*}{k_E - g^*} \text{ or } V_E = \frac{C_1^*}{k_E - g_c^*}$$

- **Real options** or **contingent claim values** may add considerably to a share's value.

References and further reading

Arnold, G.C. (1996) 'Equity and corporate valuation', in E. Gardener, E. and Molyneux, P. (eds), *Investment Banking: Theory and Practice.* 2nd edn. London: Euromoney.
A more succinct version of valuation methods.

Arnold, G. (2002) *Valuegrowth Investing.* London: Financial Times Prentice Hall.
An integration of strategic analysis with equity market investment principles.

Arnold, G. (2004) *The Financial Times Guide to Investing.* Prentice Hall.
An introduction to share valuation including guidance on industry and competitive position analysis.

Blake, D. (2000) *Financial Market Analysis.* 2nd edn. New York: John Wiley & Sons.
Chapter 6 contains a valuable discussion on share valuation.

Bodie, Z., Kane, A. and Marcus, A.J. (2005) *Investments.* 6th edn. New York: McGraw-Hill.
Contains a well-written chapter (18) on valuation models – easy to follow.

Damodaran, A. (2002) *Investment Valuation.* 2nd edn. New York: John Wiley & Sons.
Covers many aspects of share and company valuation at introductory and intermediate level.

Damodaran, A. (2005) *Applied Corporate Finance: A User's Manual.* 2nd edn. New York: John Wiley & Sons.
A good chapter on share valuation.

Gordon, M.J. (1962) *The Investment, Financing and Valuation of the Corporation.* Homewood, IL: Irwin.
An early statement of a dividend growth model.

Gordon, M.J. and Shapiro, E. (1956) 'Capital equipment analysis: the required rate of profit', *Management Science,* III, pp. 102–10.
Dividend growth model presented.

Lofthouse, S. (2001) *Investment Management.* 2nd edn. Chichester: John Wiley & Sons.
A practitioner assesses the theoretical models and empirical evidence on investment issues, including valuation. Very easy to follow.

Lowe, J. (1997) *Warren Buffett Speaks.* New York: John Wiley & Sons.
A knowledgeable, witty and wise financier's comments are collected and presented. An excellent antidote to theoretical purism.

McKinsey and Company (Koller, T., Goedhart, M. and Wessels, D) (2005). *Valuation.* 4th edn. New York: John Wiley & Sons.
Some valuation issues are presented in an accessible style.

Outram, R. (1997) 'For what it's worth', *Management Today,* May, pp. 70–1.

Rappaport, A. (1999) *Creating Shareholder Value.* New York: Free Press. Revised and updated.
Describes cash flow valuation models clearly.

Sharpe, W.F., Alexander, G.J. and Bailey, J.V. (1999) *Investments.* 6th edn. Upper Saddle River, NJ: Prentice-Hall.
A wider range of valuation issues is discussed in an accessible introductory style.

Solomon, E. (1963) *The Theory of Financial Management.* New York: Columbia University Press.
An early discussion of the Gordon and Shapiro dividend growth model.

Stephens, G. and Funnell, J. (1995) 'Take your partners . . .', *Corporate Finance,* London: Euromoney monthly journal, July.
Discusses the difficult issue of valuation of telemedia companies.

Websites

The Society of Share and Business Valuers www.ssbv.org
The Institute of Chartered Accountants www.icaew.co.uk
The Chartered Institute of Taxation www.tax.org.uk
American Society of Appraisers www.appraisers.org
Canadian Institute of Chartered Business Valuators www.cicbv.ca.

Case study recommendations

Please see www.pearsoned.co.uk/arnold for case study synopses

- Ryanair Holdings plc. Author: Mark T. Bradshaw (2005) Harvard Business School.
- Spyder Active Sports – 2004. Authors: Belen Villalonga, Dwight Crane and James Quinn (2005) Harvard Business School.
- Radio One, Inc. Authors: Richard Ruback and Pauline Fischer (2003) Harvard Business School.
- Liston Mechanics Corporation. Author: Marc Bertoneche (2005) Harvard Business School.

Self-review questions

1 What are the problems of relying on NAV as a valuation method? In what circumstances is it particularly useful?

2 Why do analysts obtain historic information on a company for valuation purposes?

3 Name the three types of future income flows which may be examined to value shares.

4 Explain why the dividend valuation model discounts all dividends to infinity and yet individual investors hold shares for a shorter period, making capital gains (and losses).

5 The dividend growth model takes the form:

$$P_0 = \frac{d_1}{k_E - g}$$

Does this mean that we are only valuing next year's dividend? Explain your answer.

6 What are the main investigatory routes you would pursue to try to establish the likely range of future growth rates for a firm?

7 What are the differences between the crude PER model and the more complete PER model?

8 Why do PERs vary over time, and between firms in the same industry?

9 What additional factors might you consider when valuing an unquoted share rather than one listed on a stock exchange?

10 Why might a share have a different value to someone who was able to exercise control over the organisation than to someone who had a small, almost powerless, stake?

Questions and problems

myfinancelab *Questions with an icon are also available for practice in MyFinanceLab with additional supporting resources.*

For questions marked by an asterisk, the answers are given in the Lecturer's Guide.

1 'Valuing shares is either a simple exercise of plugging numbers into mathematical formulae or making comparisons with shares in the same sector.' Explain the problems with this statement.

2 'Some companies do not pay dividends, in others the growth rate is higher than the required rate of return, therefore the dividend valuation models are useless.' Explain your reasons for agreeing or disagreeing with this statement.

3 Shades plc has the following dividend history:

Year	Dividend per share
Recently paid	21p
Last year	19p
Two years ago	18p
Three years ago	16p
Four years ago	14p
Five years ago	12p

The rate of return required on a share of this risk class is 13 per cent. Assuming that this dividend growth rate is unsustainable and Shades will halve its historic rate in the future, what is the value of one share? ?

4 ElecWat is a regulated supplier of electricity and water. It is expected to pay a dividend of 24p per share per year for ever. Calculate the value of one share if a company of this risk class is required to return 10 per cent per year. ?

5 Tented plc has developed a new tent which has had rave reviews in the camping press. The company paid a dividend of 11p per share recently and the next is due in one year. Dividends are expected to rise by 25 per cent per year for the next five years while the company exploits its technological and marketing lead. After this period, however, the growth rate will revert to only 5 per cent per year.

The rate of return on risk-free securities is 7 per cent and the risk premium on the average share has been 5 per cent. Tented is in a systematic risk class which means that the average risk premium should be adjusted by a beta factor of 1.5.

Calculate the value of one share in Tented plc. ?

6 (*Examination level*) The current share price of Blueberry plc is 205p. It recently reported earnings per share of 14p and has a policy of paying out 50 per cent of earnings in dividends each year. The earnings history of the firm is as follows:

Last reported	14p
One year ago	13p
Two years ago	12p
Three years ago	11p
Four years ago	10p
Five years ago	9p

The rate of growth in earnings and dividends shown in the past is expected to continue into the future. The risk-free rate of return is 6.5 per cent and the risk premium on the average share has been 5 per cent for decades. Blueberry is in a higher systematic risk class than the average share and therefore the risk premium needs to be adjusted by a beta factor of 1.2.

Required

a Calculate the historical price-earnings ratio.
b Calculate the future growth rate of dividends and earnings.
c Calculate the required rate of return on a share of this risk class.
d Use the more complete PER model to decide whether the shares at 205p are over- or under-priced.
e Describe and explain the problems of using the crude historic PER as an analytical tool.
f What additional factors would you need to allow for when valuing an unquoted share rather than one listed on a stock exchange?

?

7 (*Examination level*) The following figures are extracted from Tes plc's Annual Report and Accounts.

Balance sheet

	£m
Fixed assets	
Tangible assets	5,466
Investments	19
	5,485
Current assets	
Stocks	559
Debtors	80
Investments	54
Cash at bank and in hand	38
	731
Creditors: falling due within one year	(2,002)
Creditors: falling due after more than one year	(598)
Provisions for liabilities and charges	(22)
	3,594
Capital and reserves	
Called-up share capital	108
Share premium account	1,383
Other reserves	40
Profit and loss account	2,057
Equity shareholders' funds	3,588
Minority equity interests	6
	3,594

Dividend and earnings history	*Dividends per share*	*Earnings per share*
16 years ago	0.82p	3.51p
Most recent	9.60p	21.9p

The average risk premium over risk-free securities is 5 per cent. The risk-free rate of return is 6.25 per cent and Tes's beta of 0.77 represents the appropriate adjustment to the average risk premium.

Required

a Calculate a revised net asset value (NAV) for the Tes group assuming the following:
  - buildings are overvalued in the balance sheet by £100m;
  - 20 per cent of the debtors figure will never be collected;
  - the stock figure includes £30m of unsaleable stock;
  - 'Current investments' now have a market value of £205m.

b The total market capitalisation of Tes at the present time is £8bn. Provide some possible reasons for the great difference between the value that the market placed on Tes and the NAV.

c For what type of company and in what circumstances does NAV provide a good estimate of value?

d If you assume that the dividend growth rate over the past 16 years is unsustainable, and that in the future the rate of growth will average half the rate of the past, at what would you value one share using the dividend growth model?

e Give some potential explanatory reasons for the difference between the value given in (d) and the value placed on a share in the London Stock Market of 355p.

f Given the answer in (d) for share price, what is the *prospective* price-earnings ratio (PER) if future earnings grow at the same rate as future dividends?

g What would be the PER if, (i) $k = 14$, $g = 12$; (ii) $k = 15$, $g = 11$ and next year's dividend and earnings are the same as calculated in (d) and (f) and the payout ratio is the same for all future years?

h If you assumed for the sake of simplicity that all the long-term debt in the balance sheet is a debenture issued six years ago which is due for redemption three years from now at par value of £100, what is the weighted average cost of capital for this firm?

Other information

- The debenture pays a coupon of 9 per cent on par value.
- The coupons are payable annually – the next is due in 12 months.
- The debenture is currently trading at 105.50.
- The balance sheet shows the nominal value, not the market value.
- Tax is payable at 30 per cent (relevant to question (h) only).
- Use the capitalisation figure given in b for the equity weight.
- You can ignore short-term debt.

?

8* Lanes plc, the retail butchers, is considering the purchase of ten shops from Roberts plc, the conglomerate. The information gathered on the ten shops trading as a separate subsidiary company is as follows:

Balance sheet

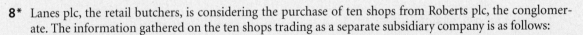

		£m
Fixed assets		2
Current assets		
Cash	0.1	
Stock	0.6	
Debtors	0.1	
		0.8
Current liabilities		(0.5)
Long-term loan		(1.0)
Net assets		1.3

Trading history

Year	Earnings (£m)
Last year	1.4
1 year ago	1.3
2 years ago	1.1
3 years ago	1.2
4 years ago	1.0
5 years ago	1.0

If the shops remain part of Roberts the earnings growth is expected to continue at the average historical rate to infinity.

The rate of return required on a business of this risk class is 13 per cent per annum.

Required

a Calculate the value of the shops to Roberts' shareholders.

b Lanes' management believe that the ten shops will be a perfect fit with their own. There are no towns in which they both trade, and economies of scale can be obtained. Suppliers will grant quantity discounts which will save £1m per annum. Combined transportation costs will fall by £200,000 per year and administration costs can be cut by £150,000 per year. These savings will remain constant for all future years. In addition, the distribution depot used by the ten shops could be closed and sold for £1.8m with no adverse impact on trading. Calculate the value of the ten shops to Lanes' shareholders on the assumption that the required return remains at 13 per cent and underlying growth continues at its historic rate.

?

9 (*Examination level*) Green plc is a conglomerate quoted on the main London market. The latest set of accounts has just been published. The balance sheet is summarised below.

Green plc	Balance Sheet	1 June 20X8
		£m
Fixed assets		
Tangible fixed assets		140
Investments		40
		180
Current assets		
Stocks	180	
Debtors	120	
Cash	30	
		330
Creditors (amounts falling due within one year)		(200)
Creditors (amounts falling due after more than one year)		(100)
Net assets		210

Other information

Dividend history								
20X0	20X1	20X2	20X3	20X4	20X5	20X6	20X7	20X8
5p (dividend per share)	5.3	6	6.2	7	7.5	8	8.5	9.2p

Green plc has demonstrated an equity beta of 1.3 over the past five years (and this can be taken as an appropriate adjustment factor to the average risk premium for shares over risk-free securities). The risk-free return is currently 6.5 per cent and the risk premium for equities over risk-free securities has averaged 5 per cent per annum.

Shares in issue: 300 million (constant for the last ten years).

Required

a Calculate a net asset value for each of Green's shares after adjusting the balance sheet for the following:
- tangible assets are worth £50m more than shown in the balance sheet;
- one-half of the debtors figure will never be collected; and
- in your judgement Green's directors have overestimated the stock value by £30m.

b Comment on some of the problems associated with valuing a share or a corporation using net asset value. For what type of company is net asset value particularly useful?

c Use a dividend valuation model to calculate the value of one share in Green plc. Assume that future dividend growth will be the same as the average rate for recent years.

d Calculate the weighted average cost of capital (WACC) for Green plc on the assumptions that the share price calculated in question c is the market share price and the entry 'Creditors (amounts falling due after more than one year)' consists entirely of a debenture issued at a total par value of £100m five years ago and this is the only liability relevant to the WACC calculation. The debenture will pay a coupon of 8 per cent in one year, followed by a similar coupon in two years from now. A final coupon will be paid in three years upon redemption of the debenture at par value. The debenture is currently trading in the secondary market at £103 per £100 nominal.

For the purpose of calculating the weighted average cost of capital the tax rate may be assumed to be 30 per cent.

?

10* (*Examination level*) You have been asked to carry out a valuation of Dela plc, a listed company on the main London market.

At the last year-end Dela's summarised balance sheet is as shown in Table 1.

Table 1 Dela 1, May 20X8

		£m
Fixed assets		300
Current assets		
Stocks	70	
Debtors	120	
Cash at bank	90	
		280
Liabilities		
Creditors: trade creditors falling due within one year		(400)
Creditors falling due after more than one year		(50)
Shareholders' funds (Net assets)		130

Table 2 Dela plc trading history

Year-end	Earnings per share (pence)	Dividend per share (pence)
20X8	20	10
20X7	18	9.5
20X6	17	9
20X5	16	8
20X4	13	7
20X3	12	6
20X2	10	5.5
20X1	10	5

Datastream has calculated a beta for Dela of 1.2 and this may be used as the appropriate adjustment to the risk premium on the average share. The risk-free rate of return on UK Treasury bills is 6.5 per cent and the latest study shows an annual equity risk premium over the yield on UK government bonds of 5 per cent for the past 100 years.

The impressive average annual growth in Dela's earnings and dividends over the last few years is likely to persist.

Additional information

- You have obtained an independent valuation of Dela's fixed assets at £350m.
- You believe that Dela has overstated the value of stocks by £30m and one-quarter of its debtors are likely to be uncollectable.
- There have been no new issues of shares in the past eight years.
- Dela has 1,000 million shares in issue.

Required

a Value Dela using the net asset value (NAV) method.

b Briefly explain why balance sheets generally have limited usefulness for estimating the value of a firm.

c Briefly describe two circumstances where balance sheet net asset values become very important for corporate valuation.

d Value one of Dela's shares using the dividend valuation model. (Assume the dividend of 10p has just been paid and the next dividend is due in one year.)

e What is the prospective price to earnings ratio (P/E ratio) given the share price in d?

f Calculate a weighted average cost of capital given that the balance sheet entry 'Creditors falling due after more than one year' consists entirely of the nominal value of a debenture issue and this is the only form of debt you need to consider for a WACC calculation. The debenture will be redeemed at par in three years, it carries an annual coupon of 8 per cent (the next payment will be in one year) and it is presently trading in the market at 96.50 per £100 nominal. The total nominal value is £50m.

Assume for the purpose of (f) that the shares are valued at your valuation in (d) and that Dela is taxed at a rate of 30 per cent.

?

myfinancelab — *Now retake your diagnostic test for Chapter 20 to check your progress and update your study plan.*

Assignments

1 Estimate the value of a share in your company (or one you know well) using the following approaches:

- net asset value;
- dividend valuation model;
- crude price-earnings ratio – comparing with peer firms;
- more complete price-earnings ratio model;
- cash flow model;
- owner earnings model.

In a report make clear your awareness of the sensitivity of the results to your assumptions.

2 If your company has recently acquired a business or is considering such a purchase obtain as much data as you can to calculate a possible bargain range. The upper boundary of this is fixed by the value of the business to your firm, given the implementation of a plan to change the future cash flows. The lower boundary is fixed by the value to the present owner.

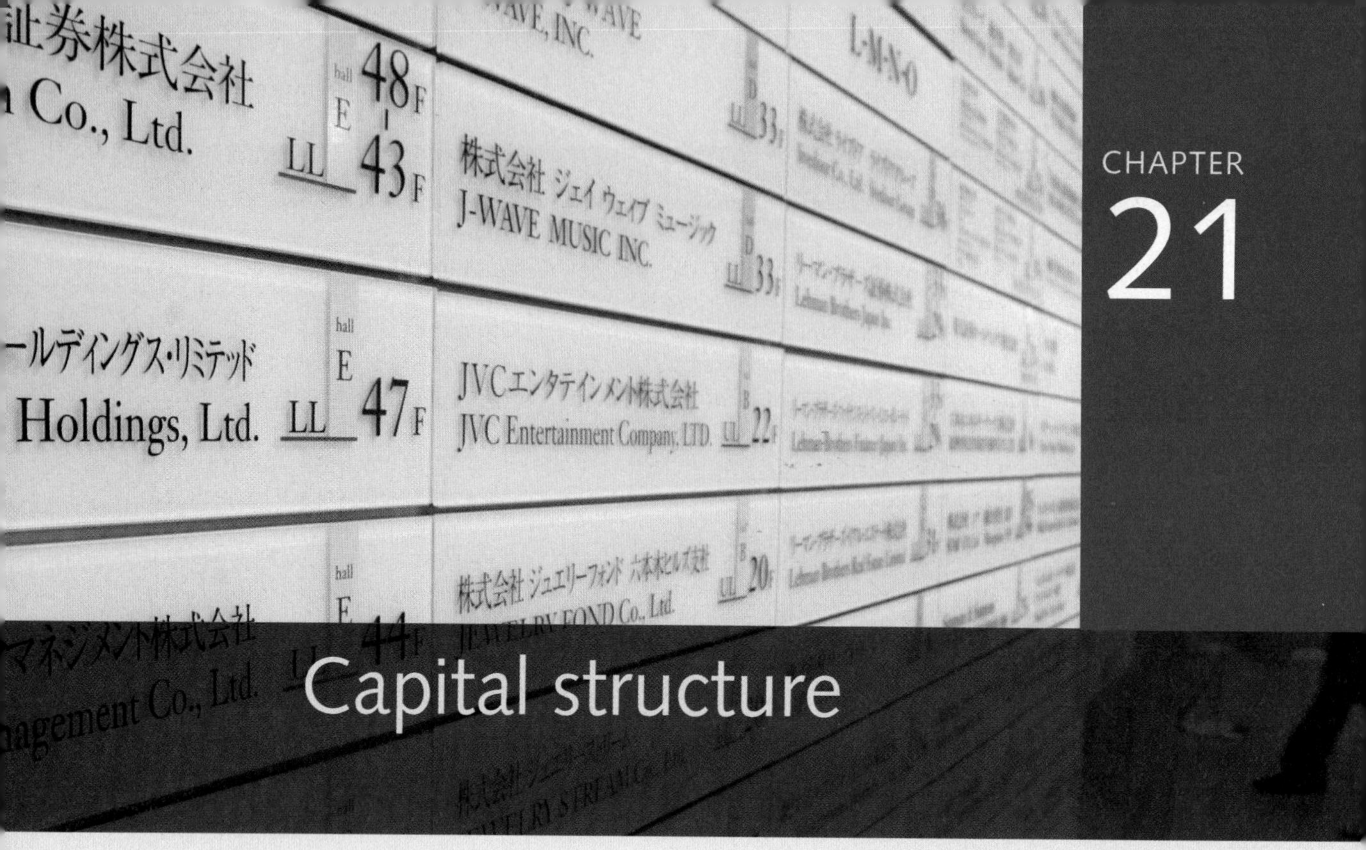

CHAPTER 21

Capital structure

LEARNING OUTCOMES

The level of debt relative to ordinary share capital is, for most firms, of secondary consideration behind strategic and operational decisions. However, if wealth can be increased by getting this decision right managers need to understand the key influences. By the end of the chapter the reader should be able to:

- discuss the effect of gearing, and differentiate business and financial risk;
- describe the underlying assumptions, rationale and conclusions of Modigliani and Miller's models, in worlds with and without tax;
- explain the relevance of some important, but often non-quantifiable, influences on the optimal gearing level question.

Introduction

Someone has to decide what is an appropriate level of borrowing for a firm given its equity capital base. To assist this decision it would be useful to know if it is possible to increase shareholder wealth by changing the gearing (debt to equity ratio) level. That is, if future cash flows generated by the business are assumed to be constant, can managers simply by altering the proportion of debt in the total capital structure increase shareholder value? If this is possible then surely managers have a duty to move the firm towards the optimal debt proportion.

The traditional view was that it would be beneficial to increase gearing from a low (or zero) level because the firm would then be financed to a greater extent by cheaper borrowed funds, therefore the weighted average cost of capital (WACC) would fall. The discounting of future cash flows at this lower WACC produces a higher present value and so shareholder wealth is enhanced. However, as debt levels rise the firm's earnings attributable to shareholders become increasingly volatile due to the requirement to pay large amounts of interest prior to dividends. Eventually the burden of a large annual interest bill can lead the firm to become financially distressed and, in extreme circumstances, to be liquidated. So the traditional answer to the question of whether there was an optimal gearing level was 'yes'. If the gearing level is too low, shareholder value opportunities are forgone by not substituting 'cheap' debt for equity. If it is too high the additional risk leads to a loss in shareholder value through a higher discount rate being applied to the future cash flows attributable to ordinary shareholders. This is because of the higher risk and, at very high gearing, the penalty of complete business failure becomes much more of a possibility.

Then, in the 1950s a theory was developed by Franco Modigliani and Merton Miller (1958) which said that it did not matter whether the firm had a gearing level of 90 per cent debt or 2 per cent debt – the overall value of the firm is constant and shareholder wealth cannot be enhanced by altering the debt to equity ratio. This conclusion was based on some major assumptions and required the firm to operate in a perfect world of perfect knowledge, a world in which individual shareholders can borrow and lend at the same rate as giant corporations, and in which taxation and cost of financial distress do not exist.

Later Modigliani and Miller (MM) modified the no-taxation assumption. This led to a different conclusion: the best gearing level for a firm interested in shareholder wealth maximisation is, generally, as high as possible. This was an astonishing result; it means that a company financed with £99m of debt and £1m of equity serves its shareholders better than one funded by £50m of debt and £50m of equity. Within academic circles thousands of hours of thinking and research time have been spent over the past four decades building on the MM foundations, and millions of hours of undergraduates' and postgraduates' precious time have been spent learning the intricacies of the algebraic proofs lying behind MM conclusions. Going through this process has its virtues: the models provide a systematic framework for evaluating the capital structure question and can lead to some rigorous thought within the confines of the models.

However, this chapter will not dwell on algebra (the interested reader is referred to some more advanced reading at the end of the chapter). Emphasis will be given to explanations which have been advanced to explain actual gearing levels. A conclusion will be drawn which fits neither the MM first conclusion, that there is not an optimal gearing level, nor their modified theory with taxes, in which there is an optimum at the most extreme level of debt.

A fundamental question for any chapter of this book is: does this subject have any relevance to the real world? Perhaps **Case Study 21.1** will help. As the case study shows senior managers frequently consider the balance between debt and ordinary share capital in a company's financial make-up.

Clearly there is a perception amongst directors, analysts and financial commentators that there is an optimal gearing level, or at least a range of gearing levels which help to maximise shareholder wealth and this lies at neither extreme of the spectrum.

Case study 21.1 The balance between debt and ordinary share capital

Whitbread (Beefeater, Costa Coffee, Premier Travel Inn, etc.) had already returned £400m to shareholders after disposing of Marriott UK when in 2005 it considered increasing its debt burden 'as part of a review of its capital structure'. According to the *FT* it was exploring ways of making its balance sheet more efficient: 'We've had a fairly conservative approach to the balance sheet', said Alan Parker, chief executive. 'We will be looking at a range of options to increase shareholder value'.[1] Similarly, David Finch, Chief Financial Officer of O_2, conceded that the company was 'not optimally financed at the moment' which could result in more cash being returned to shareholders.[2]

In the cases of Whitbread and O_2 the directors concluded that there was too much equity capital and too little debt and something had to be done about it. In the space of six years BT made first the decision that it had too much debt relative to its equity base and then that it had too little. In 2001 its management was in serious trouble. The company had accumulated debt of over £30bn following a worldwide acquisition spree and infrastructure investment (the 3G excitement). The net assets of the company were roughly half the debt level, at £14bn. City institutions were desperately concerned by the high level of debt. Sir Peter Bonfield, the chief executive, recognised that he had allowed the debt to rise too high. 'We identified the need to introduce new equity capital into the business to support the reduction in the unsustainable level of group debt'.[3] The company raised £5.9bn through a rights issue, sold off property, slashed investment and sold stakes in telecom businesses around the world. It also stopped paying a dividend. By mid 2007 the company had been so successful at reducing its debt (down to £8.1bn, or about one-third of the amount of equity capital in the business) that it pondered handing over £2bn to shareholders, financing this by raising its debt to £10bn 'to enhance returns to shareholders'.[4]

Bristol Water gave £51bn of cash to shareholders as part of a balance sheet restructuring in 2004. Then in 2005 it paid out a further £30m raising its borrowing levels again. 'Bristol Water was overcapitalised and it was time to do something for the shareholders',[5] said John Murray, representative of the largest shareholder. Moger Wooley, chairman, said 'we concluded that shareholders' interests were best served by increasing the capital efficiency of the group.'[6]

Debt finance is cheaper and riskier (for the company)

Financing a business through borrowing is cheaper than using equity. This is, first, because lenders require a lower rate of return than ordinary shareholders. Debt financial securities present a lower risk than shares for the finance providers because they have prior claims on annual income and in liquidation. In addition, security is often provided and covenants imposed.

A profitable business effectively pays less for debt capital than equity for another reason: the debt interest can be offset against pre-tax profits before the calculation of the corporation tax bill, thus reducing the tax paid.

Thirdly, issuing and transaction costs associated with raising and servicing debt are generally less than for ordinary shares.

There are some valuable benefits from financing a firm with debt. So why do firms tend to avoid very high gearing levels? One reason is financial distress risk. This could be induced by the requirement to pay interest regardless of the cash flow of the business. If the firm hits a rough patch in its business activities it may have trouble paying its bondholders, bankers and other creditors their entitlement. **Exhibit 21.1** shows that, as gearing increases, the risk of financial failure grows.

Note the crucial assumption in Exhibit 21.1 – if the returns to equity are constant, or do not rise much, the overall cost of finance declines. This is obviously unrealistic because as the risk of financial distress rises ordinary shareholders are likely to demand higher returns. This is an important issue and we will return to it after a discussion of some basic concepts about gearing.

---

[1] Quoted in Matthew Garrahan, 'Whitbread looks to extend debt', *Financial Times*, 15 June 2005.
[2] Quoted in Mark Odell, 'O_2 review could return more cash to investors', 21 July 2005, p. 21.
[3] BT Annual Report 2001.
[4] Andrew Parker, 'Resurgent BT planning £2bn share buy-back', *Financial Times*, 5/6 May 2007, p. 15.
[5] Quoted in Rebecca Bream, 'Bristol Water plans to return £50m cash' *Financial Times*, 22 July 2003.
[6] Quoted in Rebecca Bream, 'Bristol Water to deliver a £30m payback', *Financial Times*, 21/22 May 2005, p. M5.

Exhibit 21.1 At low gearing levels the risk of financial distress is low, but the cost of capital is high; this reverses at high gearing levels

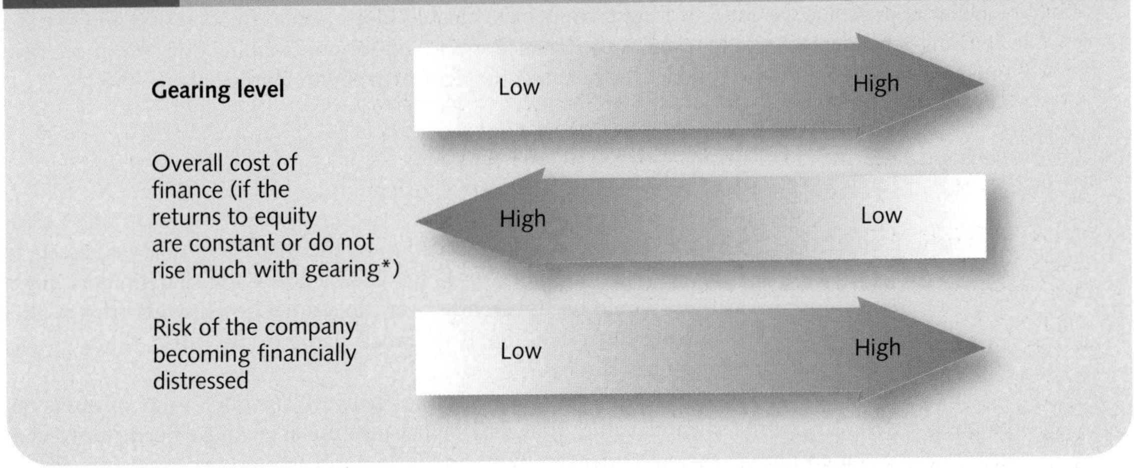

Note: *This assumption is considered in the text.

What do we mean by 'gearing'?

We need to avoid some confusion which is possible when using the word 'gearing'. First, we should make a distinction between operating gearing and financial gearing.

Operating gearing refers to the extent to which the firm's total costs are fixed. The profits of firms with high operating gearing, such as car or steel manufacturers, are very sensitive to changes in the sales level. They have high break-even points (the turnover level at which profits are achieved) but when this level is breached a large proportion of any additional sales revenue turns into profit because of the relatively low variable costs.

Financial gearing is the focus of this chapter and concerns the proportion of debt in the capital structure. Net income to shareholders in firms with high financial gearing is more sensitive to changes in operating profits.

Secondly, the terms gearing and leverage are used interchangeably by most practitioners, although leverage is used more in America.

Thirdly, there are many different ways of calculating financial gearing (to be called simply 'gearing' throughout this chapter). Financial analysts, the press and corporate managers usually measure gearing by reference to balance sheet (book) figures, but it is important to recognise that much of finance theory concentrates on the market values of debt and equity. Both book and market approaches are useful, depending on the purpose of the analysis.

There are two ways of putting into perspective the levels of debt that a firm carries – *see* Exhibit 21.2. ***Capital gearing*** focuses on the extent to which a firm's total capital is in the form of debt. ***Income gearing*** is concerned with the proportion of the annual income stream (that is, the pre-interest profits) which is devoted to the prior claims of debt holders, in other words, what proportion of profits is taken by interest charges.

Exhibit 21.2 A firm's financial gearing can be measured in two ways

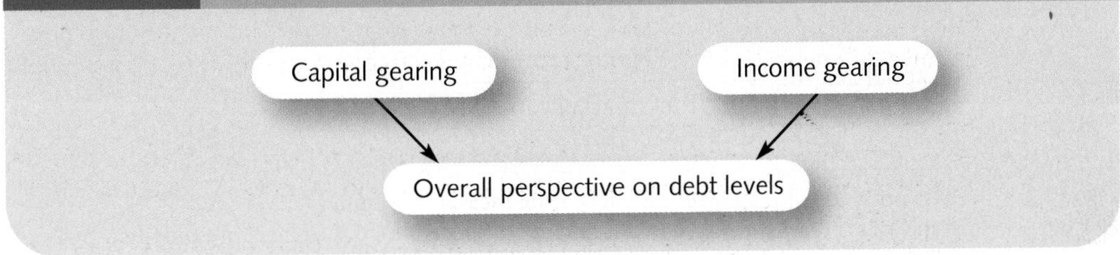

Capital gearing

There are alternative measures of the extent to which the capital structure consists of debt. One popular approach is the ratio of long-term debt to shareholders' funds (the debt to equity ratio). The long-term debt is usually taken as the balance sheet item 'amounts falling due after more than one year', and shareholders' funds is the net asset (or net worth) figure in the balance sheet.

$$\text{Capital gearing (1)} = \frac{\text{Long-term debt}}{\text{Shareholders' funds}}$$

This ratio is of interest because it may give some indication of the firm's ability to sell assets to repay debts. For example, if the ratio stood at 0.3, or 30 per cent, lenders and shareholders might feel relatively comfortable as there would be, apparently, over three times as many net (that is after paying off liabilities) assets as long-term debt. So, if the worst came to the worst, the company could sell assets to satisfy its long-term lenders.

There is a major problem with relying on this measure of gearing. The book value of assets can be quite different from the saleable value. This may be because the assets have been recorded at historical purchase value (perhaps less depreciation) and have not been revalued over time. It may also be due to the fact that companies forced to sell assets to satisfy creditors often have to do so at greatly reduced prices if they are in a hurry.[7]

Secondly, this measure of gearing can have a range of values from zero to infinity and this makes inter-firm comparisons difficult. The measure shown below puts gearing within a range of zero to 100 per cent as debt is expressed as a fraction of all long-term capital.[8]

$$\text{Capital gearing (2)} = \frac{\text{Long-term debt}}{\text{Long-term debt + Shareholders' funds}}$$

These ratios could be further modified by the inclusion of 'provisions', that is, sums set aside in the accounts for anticipated loss or expenditure, for example a bad debt or costs of merger integration. Deferred tax likewise may be included as an expected future liability.

The third capital gearing measure, in addition to allowing for long-term debt, includes short-term borrowing.

$$\text{Capital gearing (3)} = \frac{\text{All borrowing}}{\text{All borrowing + Shareholders' funds}}$$

Many firms rely on overdraft facilities and other short-term borrowing, for example commercial bills. Technically these are classified as short term. In reality many firms use the overdraft and other short-term borrowing as a long-term source of funds. Furthermore, if we are concerned about the potential for financial distress, then we must recognise that an inability to repay an overdraft can be just as serious as an inability to service a long-term bond.

To add sophistication to capital gearing analysis it is often necessary to take into account any cash (or marketable securities) holdings in the firm. These can be used to offset the threat that debt poses.

A measure of gearing which is gaining prominence is the ratio of debt to the total market value of the firm's equity.

$$\text{Capital gearing (4)} = \frac{\text{Long-term debt}}{\text{Total market capitalisation}}$$

---

[7] These problems also apply to capital gearing measures (2) and (3).

[8] To make this discussion easier to follow it will be assumed that there are only two types of finance: debt and ordinary shares. However, the introduction of other types of finance does not fundamentally alter the analysis.

This has the advantage of being closer to the market-value-based gearing measures (assuming book long-term debt is similar to the market value of the debt). It gives some indication of the relative share of the company's total value belonging to debt holders and shareholders.

It is plain that there is a rich variety of capital gearing measures and it is important to know which measure people are using – it can be very easy to find yourself talking at cross-purposes.

Income gearing

The capital gearing measures rely on the appropriate valuation of net assets either in the balance sheet or in a revaluation exercise. This is a notoriously difficult task to complete with any great certainty. Try valuing a machine on a factory floor, or a crate of raw material. Also the capital gearing measures focus on a worst case scenario: 'What could we sell the business assets for if we had to, in order to pay creditors?'

It may be erroneous to focus exclusively on assets when trying to judge a company's ability to repay debts. Take the example of a successful advertising agency. It may not have any saleable assets at all, apart from a few desks and chairs, and yet it may be able to borrow hundreds of millions of pounds because it has the ability to generate cash to make interest payments. Thus, quite often, a more appropriate measure of gearing is one concerned with the level of a firm's income relative to its interest commitments:

$$\text{Interest cover} = \frac{\text{Profit before interest and tax}}{\text{Interest charges}} \text{ or } \frac{\text{Operating cash flow}}{\text{Interest charges}}$$

The lower the **interest cover** ratio the greater the chance of interest payment default and liquidation. The inverse of interest cover measures the proportion of profits (or cash flow) paid out in interest – this is called income gearing.

The ratios considered above are now calculated for Cadbury Schweppes. The data in **Exhibit 21.3** and in the following calculations are taken from the Report and Accounts 2006.

Exhibit 21.3 Cadbury Schweppes balance sheet and profit figures

Consolidated Balance Sheet at 31 December 2006

	2006 £m
Assets	
Non-current assets	7,815
Current assets	
Inventories	728
Short-term investments	126
Trade and other receivables	1,186
Tax recoverable	36
Cash and cash equivalents	269
Derivative financial instruments	51
	2,369
Assets held for sale	22
Total assets	**10,233**

	2006 £m
Liabilities	
Current liabilities	
Trade and other payables	(1,588)
Tax payable	(239)
Short-term borrowings and overdrafts	(1,439)
Short-term provisions	(55)
Obligations under finance leases	(22)
Derivative financial instruments	(35)
	(3,378)
Non-current liabilities	
Trade and other payables	(30)
Borrowings	(1,810)
Retirement benefit obligations	(204)
Tax payable	(5)
Deferred tax liabilities	(1,050)
Long-term provisions	(18)
Obligations under finance leases	(33)
	(3,150)
Liabilities directly associated with assets classified as held for sale	(9)
Total liabilities	**(6,537)**
Net assets	**3,696**
Equity attributable to equity holders of the parent	**3,688**
Minority interest	**8**
Total equity	**3,696**
Profit before interest and taxation	£893m
Interest paid	£203m
Market capitalisation	£14,743m

Source: Cadbury Schweppes Report and Accounts 2006, *Financial Times*, 28 May 2007. © Cadbury Schweppes

We now calculate some ratios using the data in Exhibit 21.3 (there are alternatives to these which would be used by some analysts, e.g. including deferred tax liabilities or provisions):

$$\text{Capital gearing (1)} = \frac{\text{Long-term debt}}{\text{Shareholders' funds}} \times 100$$

$$= \frac{£1{,}810\text{m}}{£3{,}688\text{m}} \times 100 = 49\%$$

$$\text{Capital gearing (2)} = \frac{\text{Long-term debt}}{\text{Long-term debt} + \text{Shareholders' funds}} \times 100$$

$$= \frac{£1{,}810\text{m}}{£1{,}810\text{m} + £3{,}688\text{m}} \times 100 = 33\%$$

$$\text{Capital gearing (3)} = \frac{\text{All borrowing}}{\text{All borrowing + Shareholders' funds}} \times 100$$

$$= \frac{\pounds1{,}810\text{m} + \pounds1{,}439\text{m}}{\pounds1{,}810\text{m} + \pounds1{,}439\text{m} + \pounds3{,}688\text{m}} \times 100 = 47\%$$

$$\text{Capital gearing (4)} = \frac{\text{Long-term debt}}{\text{Total market capitalisation}} \times 100$$

$$= \frac{\pounds1{,}810\text{m}}{\pounds14{,}743\text{m}} \times 100 = 12\%$$

$$\text{Interest cover} = \frac{\text{Profit before interest and taxation}}{\text{Interest charges}}$$

$$= \frac{\pounds893\text{m}}{\pounds203\text{m}} = 4.4 \text{ times}$$

$$\text{Income gearing} = \frac{\text{Interest charges}}{\text{Profit before interest and taxation}} \times 100$$

$$= \frac{\pounds203\text{m}}{\pounds893\text{m}} = 23\%$$

The Lex column of the *Financial Times* commented on the most appropriate measures of gearing for modern industry (*see* **Exhibit 21.4**).

Exhibit 21.4

Goodbye gearing

FT

Lex column

Investors have long used balance-sheet gearing as the main yardstick of a company's indebtedness. In the past, this was appropriate as the balance sheet offered a reasonable guide to a company's value. But balance sheets are now scarcely relevant as a measure of corporate worth. As the world economy shifts from manufacturing to services, value is increasingly the product of human brains. Companies like Microsoft, Disney and Marks & Spencer owe their success to intellectual property, media creations and brands. Unlike physical property or machines, such products of the mind do not typically appear on balance sheets. Even in manufacturing, inflation and arbitrary depreciation policies make balance sheets a misleading guide to value.

If balance-sheet gearing is no longer useful, what yardsticks should be employed instead? One option is to look at interest cover – either operating profit or operating cash flow divided by interest payments. Such ratios measure how easy it is for companies to service their debts. Different levels of interest cover are appropriate for different types of company; clearly, cyclicals need higher ratios than utilities.

Another option is to divide a company's debt by its market capitalisation. Market capitalisation overcomes the inadequacies of balance-sheet measures of equity. But in other ways this ratio is similar to traditional gearing: a higher figure means shareholders' returns are more leveraged to the enterprise's underlying performance and so more risky. In future, debt/market capitalisation and interest cover will be Lex's preferred yardsticks.

Source: *Financial Times*, 9 October 1995. Reprinted with permission.

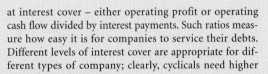

The effect of gearing

The introduction of interest-bearing debt 'gears up' the returns to shareholders. Compared with those of the ungeared firm the geared firm's returns to its owners are subject to greater variation than underlying earnings. If operating profits are high, the geared firm's shareholders will experience a more than proportional boost in their returns compared to the ungeared firm's shareholders. On the other hand, if operating profits turn out to be low the geared firm's shareholders will find their returns declining to an exaggerated extent.

The effect of gearing can best be explained through an example. Harby plc is shortly to be established. The prospective directors are considering three different capital structures which will all result in £10m of capital being raised.

1 All equity – 10 million shares sold at a nominal value of £1.
2 £3m debt (carrying 10 per cent interest) and £7m equity.
3 £5m debt (carrying 10 per cent interest) and £5m equity.

To simplify their analysis the directors have assigned probabilities to three potential future performance levels (*see* **Exhibit 21.5**).

Exhibit 21.5 Probabilities of performance levels

Customer response to firm's products	Income before interest*	Probability (%)
Modest success	£0.5m	20
Good response	£3.0m	60
Run-away success	£4.0m	20

* Taxes are to be ignored.

We can now examine what will happen to shareholder returns for each of the gearing levels.

Note, in **Exhibit 21.6**, what happens as gearing increases: the changes in earnings attributable to shareholders are magnified. For example, when earnings before interest rise by 500 per cent from £0.5m to £3.0m the returns on the 30 per cent geared structure rises by 1,200 per cent from 3 per

Exhibit 21.6 The effect of gearing

Customer response	Modest	Good	Run-away
Earnings before interest	£0.5m	£3.0m	£4.0m
All-equity structure			
Debt interest at 10%	0.0	0.0	0.0
Earnings available for shareholders	£0.5m	£3.0m	£4.0m
Return on shares	$\frac{£0.5m}{£10m} = 5\%$	$\frac{£3.0m}{£10m} = 30\%$	$\frac{£4.0m}{£10m} = 40\%$
30% gearing (£3m debt, £7m equity)			
Debt interest at 10%	£0.3m	£0.3m	£0.3m
Earnings available for shareholders	£0.2m	£2.7m	£3.7m
Return on shares	$\frac{£0.2m}{£7m} = 3\%$	$\frac{£2.7m}{£7m} = 39\%$	$\frac{£3.7m}{£7m} = 53\%$

50% gearing (£5m debt, £5m equity)			
Debt interest at 10%	£0.5m	£0.5m	£0.5m
Earnings available for shareholders	0.0	£2.5m	£3.5m
Returns on shares	$\frac{£0.0m}{£5m} = 0\%$	$\frac{£2.5m}{£5m} = 50\%$	$\frac{£3.5m}{£5m} = 70\%$

cent to 39 per cent. This magnification effect works in both positive and negative directions – if earnings before interest are only £0.5m the all-equity structure gives shareholders some return, but with the 50 per cent geared firm they will receive nothing. Harby's shareholders would be taking a substantial risk that they would have no profits if they opted for a high level of gearing.

The data for the ungeared and the 50 per cent geared capital structure are displayed in **Exhibit 21.7**. The direction of the effect of gearing depends on the level of earnings before interest. If this is greater than £1m, the return to shareholders is increased by gearing. If it is less than £1m, the return is reduced by gearing. Note that the return on the firm's overall assets at this pivot point is 10 per cent (£1m/£10m). If a return of more than 10 per cent (debt cost of capital) on assets is achieved, shareholders' returns are enhanced by gearing.

Exhibit 21.7 Changes in shareholder returns for ungeared and geared capital structures

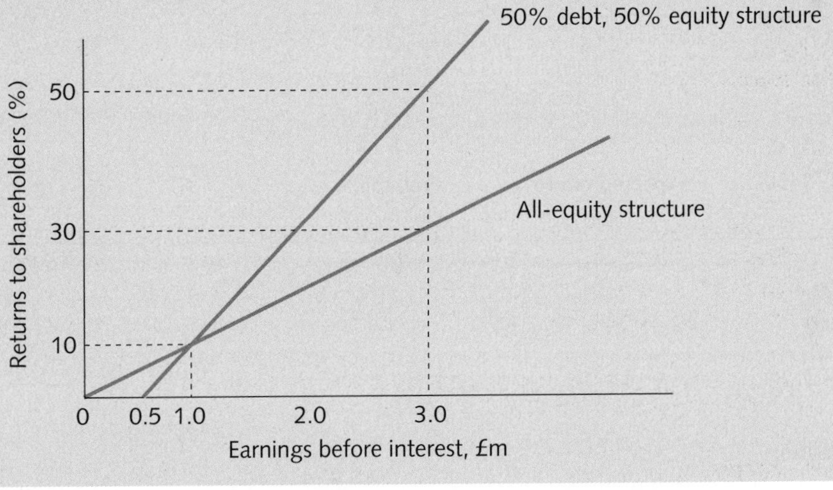

Expected returns and standard deviations for Harby plc

It makes intuitive sense to say that year-to-year variations in income will be greater for a more highly geared firm as it experiences good and bad trading years. We can be more precise for Harby if we calculate the standard deviation of the return to shareholders under the three gearing levels (*see* **Exhibit 21.8**).

As Exhibit 21.8 indicates, as the gearing levels rise for Harby, the expected return for shareholders also rises (from 27 per cent to 34.6 per cent to 44 per cent), but this is accompanied by a rising level of risk. Management have to weigh up the relative importance of the 'good' resulting from the increase in expected returns and the 'bad' from the wider dispersion of returns attributable to shareholders.

Exhibit 21.8 Expected returns and standard deviations of return to shareholders in Harby plc

All equity

Return, R (%)	Probability, p_i	Return × probability	
5	0.2	1	
30	0.6	18	
40	0.2	8	
		27	Expected return, $\bar{R}$ = 27%

Return, R (%)	Expected return, $\bar{R}$	Probability	$(\bar{R} - R)^2\ p_i$
5	27	0.2	96.8
30	27	0.6	5.4
40	27	0.2	33.8
			Variance σ^2 = 136.0
			Standard deviation σ = 11.7%

30% gearing

Return, R (%)	Probability, p_i	Return × probability	
3	0.2	0.6	
39	0.6	23.4	
53	0.2	10.6	
		34.6	Expected return, $\bar{R}$ = 34.6%

Return, R (%)	Expected return, $\bar{R}$	Probability	$(\bar{R} - R)^2\ p_i$
3	34.6	0.2	199.71
39	34.6	0.6	11.62
53	34.6	0.2	67.71
			Variance σ^2 = 279.04
			Standard deviation σ = 16.7%

50% gearing

Return, R (%)	Probability, p_i	Return × probability	
0	0.2	0	
50	0.6	30	
70	0.2	14	
		44	Expected return, $\bar{R}$ = 44%

Return, R (%)	Expected return, $\bar{R}$	Probability	$(\bar{R} - R)^2\ p_i$
0	44	0.2	387.2
50	44	0.6	21.6
70	44	0.2	135.2
			Variance σ^2 = 544.0
			Standard deviation σ = 23.3%

Business risk and financial risk

Business risk is the variability of the firm's operating income, that is, the income before interest. In the case of Harby this is found by examining the dispersion of returns for the all-equity capital structure. This dispersion is caused purely by business-related factors, such as the characteristics of the industry and the competitive advantage possessed by the firm within that industry. This risk will be influenced by factors such as the variability of sales volumes or prices over the business cycle, the variability of input costs, the degree of market power and the level of growth.

The business risk of a monopoly supplier of electricity, gas or water is likely to be significantly less than that for, say, an entrepreneurial company trying to gain a toehold in the internet optical switch market. The range of possible demand levels and prices is likely to be less for the utilities than for the high-tech firm. Business risk is determined by general business and economic conditions and is not related to the firm's financial structure.

Financial risk is the additional variability in returns to shareholders and the increased probability of insolvency that arises because the financial structure contains debt. In **Exhibit 21.9** the standard deviation gives the total risk. If a 50 per cent geared structure is selected the returns to shareholders would have a high dispersion, that is, a standard deviation of 23.3 per cent. Of this overall risk roughly half is caused by underlying business risk and half by financial risk. The increasing proportion of debt raises the firm's fixed financial costs. At high gearing levels there is an increased probability of the firm not only failing to make a return to shareholders, but also failing to meet the interest cost obligation, and thus raising the likelihood of insolvency.

Exhibit 21.9 Business and financial risk

Gearing (%)	Expected return to shareholders (%)	Standard deviation (total risk) (%)	Business risk (%)	Remaining total risk due to financial risk* (%)
0 (all-equity)	27	11.7	11.7	0
30	34.6	16.7	11.7	5
50	44	23.3	11.7	11.6

*This is a simplified representation of the relationship between total risk, financial risk and business risk. It should be: Variance of total risk = (Business risk standard deviation)^2 + (Financial risk standard deviation)^2. To be even more strict: we should be considering systematic risk rather than Standard deviation.

Firms with low business risk can take on relatively high levels of financial risk without exposing their shareholders to excessive total risk. The increased expected return more than compensates for the higher variability resulting in climbing share prices.

It is appropriate at this point to remember that, until now we have focused primarily on accounting values for debt and equity – book debt, net assets in the balance sheet, etc. In the models which follow the correct bases of analysis are the market values of debt and equity. This is because we are interested in the effect of the capital structure decision on share values in the marketplace, not on accounting entries.

The value of the firm and the cost of capital

Recall from Chapters 19 and 20 that the value of the firm is calculated by estimating its future cash flows and then discounting these at the cost of capital. For the sake of simplification we will assume, in the following theoretical discussion, that the future cash flows are constant and perpetual (at annual intervals to an infinite horizon) and thus the value of the firm is:

$$V = \frac{C_1}{\text{WACC}}$$

where:

V = value of the firm;
C_1 = cash flows to be received one year hence;
WACC = the weighted average cost of capital.

The same logic can be applied to cash flows which are increasing at a constant rate, or which vary in an irregular fashion. The crucial point is this: if the cash flows are assumed to be at a set level then the value of the firm depends on the rate used to discount those cash flows. If the cost of capital is lowered the value of the firm is raised.

What is meant by the value of the firm, V, is the combination of the market value of equity capital, V_E (total capitalisation of ordinary shares), plus the market value of debt capital, V_D.

$$V = V_E + V_D$$

Does the cost of capital (WACC) decrease with higher debt levels?

The question of whether the cost of capital decreases with higher debt levels is obviously crucial to the capital structure debate. If the WACC is diminished by increasing the proportion of debt in the financial structure of the firm then company value will rise and shareholders' wealth will increase.

The firm's cost of capital depends on both the return needed to satisfy the ordinary shareholders given their opportunity cost of capital, k_E, and the return needed to satisfy lenders given their opportunity cost of capital k_D. (We will ignore taxes for now.)

$$\text{WACC} = k_E W_E + k_D W_D$$

where:

W_E = proportion of equity finance to total finance;
W_D = proportion of debt finance to total finance.

If some numbers are now put into this equation, conclusions might be possible about the optimal debt level and therefore the value of the firm. If it is assumed that the cost of equity capital is 20 per cent, the cost of debt capital is 10 per cent, and the equity and debt weights are both 50 per cent, the overall cost of capital is 15 per cent.

$$\text{WACC} = (20\% \times 0.5) + (10\% \times 0.5) = 15\%$$

If it is further assumed that the firm is expected to generate a perpetual annual cash flow of £1m, then the total value of the firm is:

$$V = \frac{C_1}{\text{WACC}} = \frac{£1\text{m}}{0.15} = £6.667\text{m}$$

This whole area of finance revolves around what happens next, that is, when the proportion of debt is increased. So, let us assume that the debt ratio is increased to 70 per cent through the substitution of debt for equity. We will consider four possible consequences.

Scenario 1: The cost of equity capital remains at 20 per cent

If shareholders remain content with a 20 per cent return, the WACC decreases:

$$\text{WACC} = k_E W_E + k_D W_D$$
$$\text{WACC} = (20\% \times 0.3) + (10\% \times 0.7) = 13\%$$

If the cost of capital decreases, the value of the firm (and shareholder wealth) increases:

$$V = \frac{C_1}{\text{WACC}} = \frac{£1\text{m}}{0.13} = £7.69\text{m}$$

Under this scenario the debt proportion could be increased until it was virtually 100 per cent of the capital. The WACC would then approach 10 per cent (assuming that the cost of debt capital remains at 10 per cent).

Scenario 2: The cost of equity capital rises due to the increased financial risk to exactly offset the effect of the lower cost of debt

In this case the WACC and the firm's value remain constant.

$$\text{WACC} = k_E W_E + k_D W_D$$
$$\text{WACC} = (26.67\% \times 0.3) + (10\% \times 0.7) = 15\%$$

Scenario 3: The cost of equity capital rises, but this does not completely offset all the benefits of the lower cost of debt capital

Let us assume that equity holders demand a return of 22 per cent at a 70 per cent gearing level:

$$\text{WACC} = k_E W_E + k_D W_D$$
$$\text{WACC} = (22\% \times 0.3) + (10\% \times 0.7) = 13.6\%$$

In this case the firm, by increasing the proportion of its finance which is in the form of debt, manages to reduce the overall cost of capital and thus to increase the value of the firm and shareholder wealth.

$$V = \frac{C_1}{\text{WACC}} = \frac{£1\text{m}}{0.136} = £7.35\text{m}$$

Scenario 4: The cost of equity rises to more than offset the effect of the lower cost of debt

Here the equity holders are demanding much higher returns as compensation for the additional volatility and risk of liquidation. Let us assume that shareholders require a return of 40 per cent.

$$\text{WACC} = k_E W_E + k_D W_D$$
$$\text{WACC} = (40\% \times 0.3) + (10\% \times 0.7) = 19\%$$

$$V = \frac{C_1}{\text{WACC}} = \frac{£1\text{m}}{0.19} = £5.26\text{m}$$

The first of the four scenarios presented above is pretty unrealistic. If the amount of debt that a firm has to service is increased, the riskiness of the shares will presumably rise and therefore the shareholders will demand a higher return. Thus, we are left with the three other scenarios. It is around these three possibilities that the capital structure debate rumbles.

Modigliani and Miller's argument in a world with no taxes

The capital structure decision was first tackled in a rigorous theoretical analysis by the financial economists Modigliani and Miller in 1958. MM created a simplified model of the world by making some assumptions. Given these assumptions they concluded that the value of a firm remains constant regardless of the debt level. As the proportion of debt is increased, the cost of equity will rise just enough to leave the WACC constant. If the WACC is constant then the only factor which can influence the value of the firm is its cash flow generated from operations. Capital structure is irrelevant. Thus, according to MM, firms can only increase the wealth of shareholders by making good investment decisions. This brings us to MM's first proposition.

Proposition 1

The total market value of any company is independent of its capital structure

The total market value of the firm is the net present value of the income stream. For a firm with a constant perpetual income stream:

$$V = \frac{C_1}{\text{WACC}}$$

The WACC is constant because the cost of equity capital rises to exactly offset the effect of cheaper debt and therefore shareholder wealth is neither enhanced nor destroyed by changing the gearing level.

The assumptions

Before going any further, some of the assumptions upon which this conclusion is reached need to be mentioned.

1 There is no taxation.
2 There are perfect capital markets, with perfect information available to all economic agents and no transaction costs.
3 There are no costs of financial distress and liquidation (if a firm is liquidated, shareholders will receive the same as the market value of their shares prior to liquidation).
4 Firms can be classified into distinct risk classes.
5 Individuals can borrow as cheaply as corporations.

Clearly, there are problems relating some of these assumptions to the world in which we live. For now, it is necessary to suspend disbelief so that the consequences of the MM model can be demonstrated. Many of the assumptions will be modified later in the chapter.

An example to illustrate the MM no-tax capital structure argument

In the following example it is assumed that the WACC remains constant at 15 per cent regardless of the debt to equity ratio.

A company is shortly to be formed, called Pivot plc. It needs £1m capital to buy machines, plant and buildings. The business generated by the investment has a given systematic risk and the required return on that level of systematic risk for an all-equity firm is 15 per cent.

The expected annual cash flow is a constant £150,000 in perpetuity. This cash flow will be paid out each year to the suppliers of capital. The prospective directors are considering three different finance structures.

- **Structure 1** All-equity (1,000,000 shares selling at £1 each).
- **Structure 2** £500,000 of debt capital giving a return of 10 per cent per annum. Plus £500,000 of equity capital (500,000 shares at £1 each).
- **Structure 3** £700,000 of debt capital giving a return of 10 per cent per annum. Plus £300,000 of equity capital (300,000 shares at £1 each).

Exhibit 21.10 shows that the returns to equity holders, in this MM world with no tax, rises as gearing increases so as to leave the WACC and the total value of the company constant. Investors purchasing a share receive higher returns per share for a more highly geared firm but the discount rate also rises because of the greater risk, to leave the value of each share at £1.

Exhibit 21.10 Pivot plc capital structure and returns to shareholders

	Structure 1 £	Structure 2 £	Structure 3 £
Annual cash flows	150,000	150,000	150,000
less interest payments	0	50,000	70,000
Dividend payments	150,000	100,000	80,000
Return on debt, k_D	0	50,000/500,000 = 10%	70,000/700,000 = 10%
Return on equity, k_E	150,000/1m = 15%	100,000/500,000 = 20%	80,000/300,000 = 26.7%
Price of each share, $\frac{d_1}{k_E}$	$\frac{15\text{p}}{0.15}$ = 100p	$\frac{20\text{p}}{0.20}$ = 100p	$\frac{26.7\text{p}}{0.267}$ = 100p
WACC ($k_E W_E + k_D W_D$)	(15 × 1.0) + 0 = 15%	(20 × 0.5) + (10 × 0.5) = 15%	(26.7 × 0.3) + (10 × 0.7) = 15%
Total market value of debt, V_D	0	500,000	700,000
Total market value of equity, V_E	$\frac{150{,}000}{0.15}$ = 1m	$\frac{100{,}000}{0.2}$ = 0.5m	$\frac{80{,}000}{0.267}$ = 0.3m
Total value of the firm, $V = V_D + V_E$	£1,000,000	£1,000,000	£1,000,000

The relationship given in the tabulation in Exhibit 21.10 can be plotted as a graph (*see* **Exhibit 21.11**). Under the MM model the cost of debt remains constant at 10 per cent,[9] and the cost of equity capital rises just enough to leave the overall cost of capital constant.

Exhibit 21.11 The cost of debt, equity and WACC under the MM no-tax model

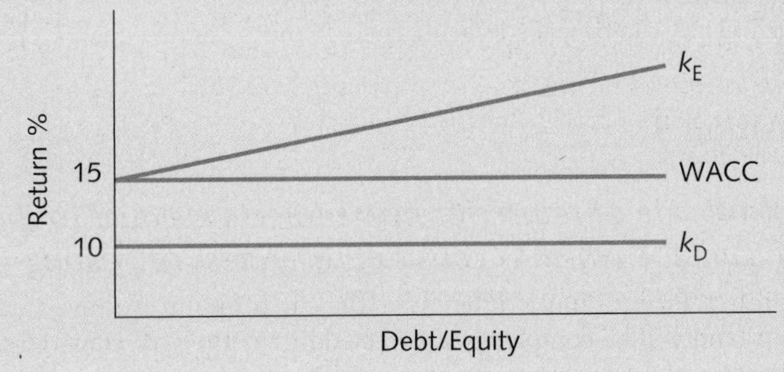

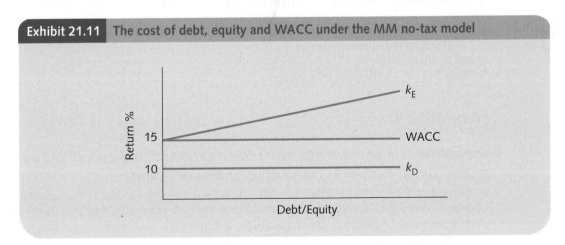

[9] An alternative scenario is also discussed in the MM 1958 paper in which the cost of debt rises at high gearing levels and the cost of equity declines at high gearing levels.

If the WACC is constant and cash flows do not change, then the total value of the firm is constant:

$$V = V_E + V_D = £1m$$

$$V = \frac{C_1}{WACC} = \frac{£150{,}000}{0.15} = £1m$$

This is presented in Exhibit 21.12.

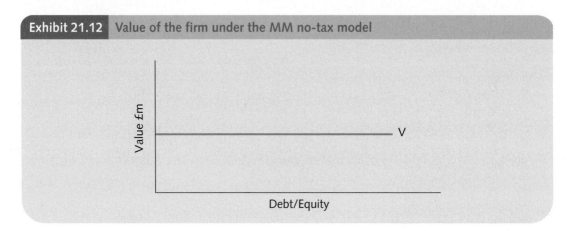

Exhibit 21.12 Value of the firm under the MM no-tax model

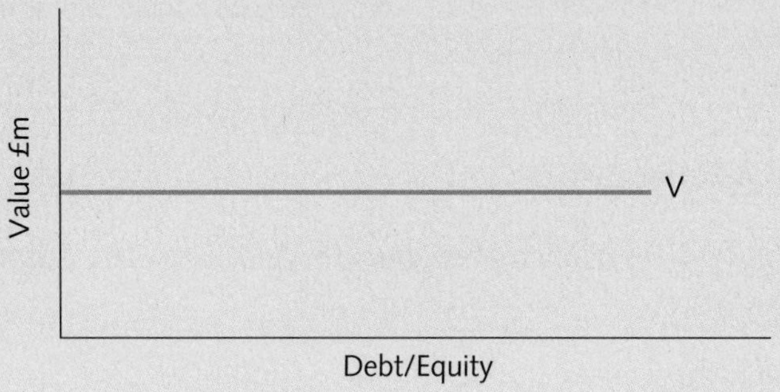

Pivot also illustrates the second and third propositions put forward by MM.

Proposition 2

The expected rate of return on equity increases proportionately with the gearing ratio

As shareholders see the risk of their investment increase because the firm is taking on increasing debt levels they demand a higher level of return. The geared firm pays a risk premium for financial risk. The increase in the cost of equity exactly offsets the benefit to the WACC of 'cheaper' debt. (Modigliani and Miller actually expressed Proposition 2 in a more technical way requiring a knowledge of the full theoretical proof to understand that 'the expected yield of a share of stock is equal to the appropriate capitalisation rate, ρ_k, for a pure equity stream in the class, plus a premium related to financial risk equal to the debt-to-equity ratio times the spread between ρ_k and r' (MM (1958), p. 271). ρ_k can be taken as being equal to our k_E, and r equals k_D.)

Proposition 3

The cut-off rate of return for new projects is equal to the weighted average cost of capital – which is constant regardless of gearing

MM expressed Proposition 3 differently: 'the cut-off point for investment in the firm will in all cases be ρ_k and will be completely unaffected by the type of security used to finance the investment. Equivalently, we may say, that regardless of the financing used, the marginal cost of capital to a firm is equal to the average cost of capital, which is in turn equal to the capitalisation rate for an unlevered stream in the class to which the firm belongs' (MM (1958), p. 288).

Worked example 21.1 Cost of equity capital for a geared firm that becomes an all-equity financed firm in a world with no taxes

Assume that the world is as described by MM, with no taxes, to answer the following.

What would the cost of equity capital be if the firm described below is transformed into being all-equity financed rather than geared?

$$\frac{\text{Market value of debt}}{\text{Market value of debt + Market value of equity}} = 0.40$$

k_D = 9% regardless of gearing ratio.
At a gearing level of 40%, k_E = 22%.

Answer

Calculate the weighted average cost of capital at the gearing level of 40 per cent.

$$\text{WACC} = k_E W_E + k_D W_D$$
$$\text{WACC} = (22 \times 0.6) + (9 \times 0.4) = 16.8\%$$

Under the MM no-tax model the WACC is constant at all gearing levels; therefore, at zero debt the required return to equity holders will be 16.8 per cent.

The capital structure decision in a world with tax

The real world is somewhat different from that created for the purposes of MM's original 1958 model. One of the most significant differences is that individuals and companies *do* have to pay taxes. MM corrected for this assumption in their 1963 version of the model – this changes the analysis dramatically.

Most tax regimes permit companies to offset the interest paid on debt against taxable profit. The effect of this is a tax saving which reduces the effective cost of debt capital.[10] (*See* Chapter 19 for a discussion of this.)

In the previous no-tax analysis the advantage of gearing up (a lower cost of debt capital) was exactly matched by the disadvantage (the increased risk for equity holders and therefore an increased k_E). The introduction of taxation brings an additional advantage to using debt capital: it reduces the tax bill. Now value rises as debt is substituted for equity in the capital structure because of the tax benefits (or tax shield). The WACC declines for each unit increase in debt so long as the firm has taxable profits. This argument can be taken to its logical extreme, such that the WACC is at its lowest and corporate value at its highest when the capital of the company is almost entirely made up of debt.

In **Exhibit 21.13** the cost of equity rises but the extent of the rise is insufficient to exactly offset the cheaper debt. Thus the overall cost of capital falls throughout the range of gearing. In a 30 per cent corporate tax environment a profitable firm's cost of debt falls from a pre-tax 10 per cent to only 7 per cent after the tax benefit (assuming continued firm profitability):

$$10\% (1 - T) = 10\% (1 - 0.30) = 7\%$$

For a perpetual income firm, the value is $V = C_1/\text{WACC}$. As the WACC falls, the value of the company rises, benefiting ordinary shareholders. *See* **Exhibit 21.14**.

The conclusion from this stage of the analysis, after adjusting for one real-world factor, is that companies should be as highly geared as possible.

---

10 Note that the required rate of return on debt is not lowered; rather, the cash outflow to the tax authorities is less, resulting in more being available for equity investors, thus the effective cost of debt is less.

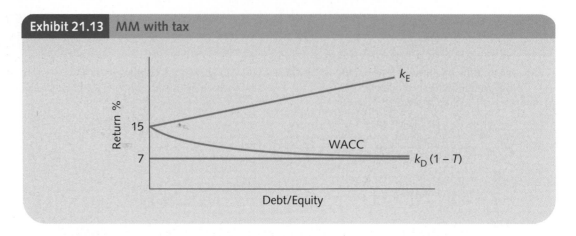

Exhibit 21.13 MM with tax

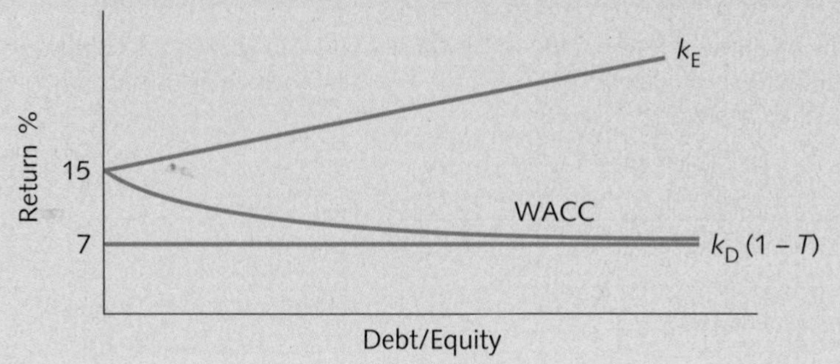

Exhibit 21.14 Value of the firm, MM with Tax

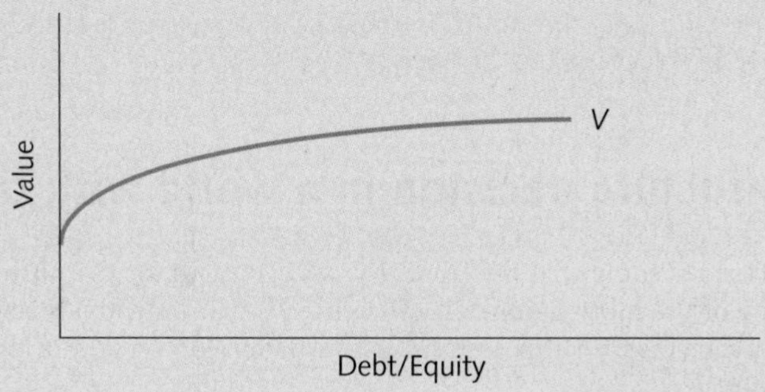

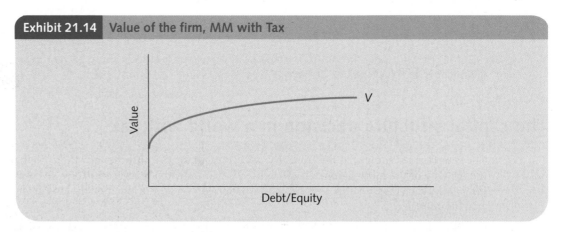

The article reproduced in **Exhibit 21.15** shows a company that has structured itself so that it can take on an extreme capital structure – Glas Cymru is financed entirely by debt. Note that this is possible only because the risk of financial distress has been substantially reduced. The bond offerings were eagerly taken up by lenders.

Exhibit 21.15

Glas Cymru launches bond campaign

FT

Water marketing drive in plan to raise £2bn for purchase of Dwr Cymru

by Aline van Duyn and Andrew Taylor

Glas Cymru, the self-styled 'Welsh people's company' which has agreed to buy the principality's water supplier, will today launch a £2bn bond marketing campaign to turn the company into the UK's first fully debt-financed water utility . . .

The bond issues, if successful, will reduce Glas Cymru's cost of capital to between 4 and 4.5 per cent, compared with a 6.5 per cent industry threshold set by the regulator.

Glas Cymru, a non-profit making company led by Lord Burns, former permanent secretary at the Treasury, will buy Dwr Cymru (Welsh Water) in return for taking on debts of £1.8bn. It will be fully debt financed and switch from shareholder ownership . . .

Bond investors in the water sector have seen prices on their holdings fall after rating downgrades following the regulatory price cuts and concern over diversification strategies.

The Glas Cymru deal aims to address these concerns by giving bondholders full control and ensuring that they are exposed purely to the water sector, which is a monopoly business with stable cash flows.

Exhibit 21.15 continued

Most of the bonds will be denominated in sterling, although euro and dollar tranches are also being considered. About £1bn worth of bonds will have a Triple A rating, the highest rating category, due to a guarantee from an insurance company.

Just under £700m worth will be rated A minus. About £250m is rated Triple B, with £100m worth of unrated bonds also sold.

The Glas Cymru structure is possible because the assets are bought for less than their regulatory asset value, giving a £150m cushion. Between now and the next regulatory price review in 2004–2005, Glas Cymru can lock in a lower cost of capital and accumulate the excess, boosting its reserves to £350m. It expects to tap the markets for £100m–£150m a year.

Source: Financial Times, 9 April 2001, p. 26. Reprinted with permission.

It is not inevitable that tax shields on debt will always be with us – *see* **Exhibit 21.16**.

Exhibit 12.16

Demands to cut corporate relief cause alarm

FT

Vanessa Houlder

The private equity industry and some influential businesses have reacted with alarm to calls from policy experts, economists and union officials for Gordon Brown, the chancellor, to reduce corporate tax relief for interest payments. Similar proposals in Denmark and Germany have already met ferocious opposition.

Critics of the disparity in the tax treatment of debt and equity finance – which economists agree is unjustified – have usually been drawn from academic circles. But recently there has been wider interest in reform, prompted by a debate over how best to level the playing field for corporate takeovers, improve the competitiveness of the tax system and reform the tax treatment of foreign dividends.

The recent growth in takeovers has highlighted the case for reducing the tax advantages of businesses backed by private equity and foreign-owned companies, which can borrow more heavily than quoted companies, which are often reluctant to damage their credit ratings.

Bill Dodwell of Deloitte, professional services companies, said: 'The problem is that the way debt financing works is that UK-headquartered companies pay more tax than overseas-headquartered companies which pay more tax than private-equity backed companies. The overriding question is: is that a sensible way to run a tax system?'

Last week the GMB union urged Mr Brown to end tax relief for interest payments on loans used by private equity groups to buy companies.

'This relief costs the exchequer hundereds of millions per annum, while giving debt unfair tax advantages over equity,' it said.

As well as protecting tax revenues, restricting interest relief could free up funds to reduce corporate tax rates, potentially improving the competitiveness of the tax system.

The Institute for Fiscal Studies, the think-tank, this month calculated that removing the tax breaks for the interest costs of non-fnancial companies would allow the British corporate tax rate to be reduced from 30 per cent to 20 per cent.

But whatever the theoretical merits of a sharp reduction in tax breaks on interest costs, there would be strong opposition from businesses that stand to lose out under the new regime.

The Oxford University Centre for Business Taxation concluded that 'At best, many companies would find it costly to change that structure. At worst, simply removing interest deductability may leave many companies unable to afford tax payments, and hence facing bankruptcy. This may be particularly true of smaller companies.'

Source: Financial Times, 12 February 2007, p. 2. Reprinted with permission.

Additional considerations

In the real world companies do not, generally, raise their debt-to-equity ratios to very high levels. This suggests that the models described so far are not yet complete. There are some important influences on capital structure not yet taken into account. As Stewart Myers[11] wrote, 'Our theories don't seem to explain actual financing behaviour, and it seems presumptuous to advise firms on optimal structure when we are so far from explaining actual decisions'.

We now turn to some additional factors which have a bearing on the gearing level.

Financial distress

A major disadvantage for a firm taking on higher levels of debt is that it increases the risk of **financial distress**, and ultimately liquidation. This may have a detrimental effect on both the equity holders and the debt holders.

Financial distress: where obligations to creditors are not met or are met with difficulty.

The risk of incurring the costs of financial distress has a negative effect on a firm's value which offsets the value of tax relief of increasing debt levels. These costs become considerable with very high gearing. Even if a firm manages to avoid liquidation its relationships with suppliers, customers, employees and creditors may be seriously damaged.

Suppliers providing goods and services on credit are likely to reduce the generosity of their terms, or even stop supplying altogether, if they believe that there is an increased chance of the firm not being in existence in a few months' time. Rover's troubles in 2005 were made more difficult by supplier nervousness – *see* **Exhibit 21.17**.

Exhibit 21.17

Rover's suppliers tighten terms

FT

■ Extended credit and late payment not available as companies guard against collapse ■ Carmaker keen to settle on time to keep goodwill

By James Mackintosh, Motor Industry Editor

Suppliers to MG Rover have tightened the terms under which they provide components and services to the troubled Birmingham carmaker to protect themselves againt its possible collapse.

Six large suppliers contacted by the Financial Times said they had shortened payment periods or were enforcing payment more strictly, reducing their exposure to the possible failure of a rescue deal with Shanghai Automotive Industry Corp, China's largest carmaker.

The stricter payment terms have left Rover without the benefit of late payment and extended credit available to more stable manufacturers.

'We are providing no leeway at all,' one of Rover's largest suppliers said.

However, none of the suppliers contacted was demanding cash upfront, a move which one said could force the company into liquidation by hurting its cashflow.

Source: Financial Times, 21 March 2005, p. 19. Reprinted with permission.

The situation may be similar with customers. Many customers expect to develop close relationships with their suppliers, and plan their own production on the assumption of a continuance of that relationship, for example motor manufacturers. If there is any doubt about the longevity of a

[11] Myers (1984), p. 575.

firm it will not be able to secure high-quality contracts. In the consumer markets customers often need assurance that firms are sufficiently stable to deliver on promises, for example package holiday companies taking bookings six months in advance. Exhibit 21.18 discusses the case of NTL (now Virgin Media) which lost 800 customers each day. Furthermore the cash shortage meant a cut in advertising to win new customers.

Exhibit 21.18

NTL lost 73,400 customers during rescue talks

FT

Falls in its three largest residential services underline fears over impact of restructuring

by Carlos Grande

NTL shed a net 73,400 UK customers in the three months to March 31 while it slashed spending and held urgent talks on the rescue plan forecast to cost it about $95m in advisers' fees and other charges to execute.

The falls were in its three largest residential services – telephony, cable television and dial-up internet – and in dual users . . .

The trend towards a shrinking UK-customer base is expected to continue until NTL emerges from Chapter 11 in September or October since it has taken an axe to advertising, some capital expenditure and other funding on winning new customers.

Barclay Knapp, chief executive, said: 'We remain on track to improve the state of our balance sheet.' . . .

Source: *Financial Times*, 12 June 2002, p. 21. Reprinted with permission.

Employees may become demotivated in a struggling firm as they sense increased job insecurity and few prospects for advancement. The best staff will start to move to posts in safer companies.

Bankers and other lenders will tend to look upon a request for further finance from a financially distressed company with a prejudiced eye – taking a safety-first approach – and this can continue for many years after the crisis has passed.

Bankers may also insist that managerial freedom to act be constrained. In 2003, for example, Waterford Wedgwood was told by its banks to reduce stock levels, to undertake no further capital expenditure other than what was already under way, to issue a high-yield bond to replace some of the bank debt, and not to pay an interim dividend.

Management find that much of their time is spent 'fire fighting' – dealing with day-to-day liquidity problems – and focusing on short-term cash flow rather than long-term shareholder wealth. Companies are often forced to sell off their most profitable operations in an attempt to raise cash. For instance, in 2003 Fiat put up for sale its most valuable businessess (e.g. Fiat Avio) to raise enough cash to allow it to continue producing cars.

The indirect costs associated with financial distress can be much more significant than the more obvious direct costs such as paying for lawyers and accountants and for refinancing programmes. Some of these indirect and direct costs are shown in Exhibit 21.19.

As the risk of financial distress rises with the gearing ratio shareholders (and lenders) demand an increasing return in compensation. The important issue is at what point does the probability of financial distress so increase the cost of equity and debt that it outweighs the benefit of the tax relief on debt? Exhibit 21.20 shows that there is an optimal level of gearing. At low levels of debt the major influence on the overall cost of capital is the cheaper after-tax cost of debt. As gearing rises investors become more concerned about the risk of financial distress and therefore the required rates of return rise. The fear of loss factor becomes of overriding importance at high gearing levels.

In the capital structure literature the balancing of the benefits of debt, such as the tax shield, with the costs of debt, such as distress costs, to achieve an optimal debt to equity ratio, is known as the **trade-off model**.

Exhibit 21.19 Costs of financial distress

Indirect examples	Direct examples
• Uncertainties in customers' minds about dealing with this firm – lost sales, lost profits, lost goodwill. • Uncertainties in suppliers' minds about dealing with this firm – lost inputs, more expensive trading terms. • If assets have to be sold quickly the price may be very low. • Delays, legal impositions, and the tangles of financial reorganisation may place restrictions on management action, interfering with the efficient running of the business. • Management may give excessive emphasis to short-term liquidity, e.g. cut R&D and training, lower credit terms are offered to customers, which impacts on the marketing effort. • Temptation to sell healthy businesses as this will raise the most cash. • Loss of staff morale, tendency to examine possible alternative employment, difficulty in recruiting talented people.	• Lawyers' fees. • Accountants' fees. • Court fees. • Management time.

Exhibit 21.20 The cost of capital and the value of the firm with taxes and financial distress, as gearing increases

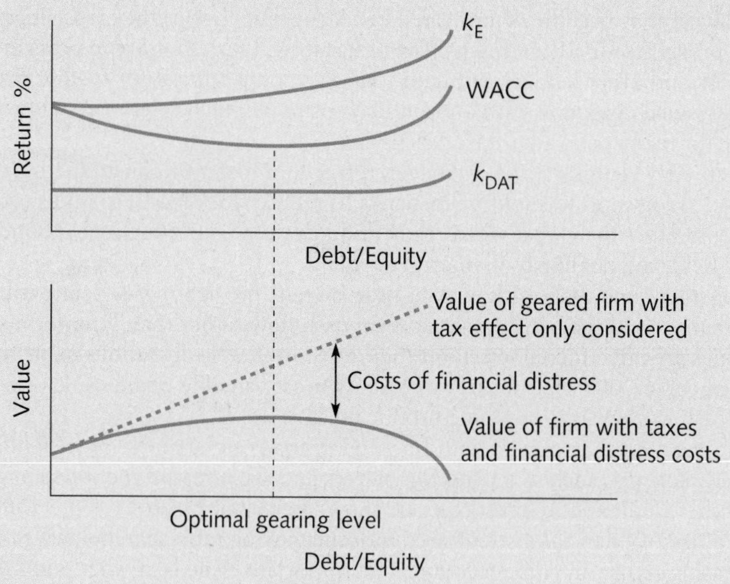

The article in **Exhibit 21.21** argues that some UK firms are undergeared and should follow private equity in taking on more debt. Despite the raised risk of distress it is claimed the weighted average cost of capital will fall – see chart in exhibit. (Enterprise value is the total of the equity market capitalisation plus borrowings.)

Exhibit 21.21

Pressure building for public companies to utilise private equity tactics

FT

Some institutional investors are questioning whether companies should put up more resistance to approaches from buy-out firms and use some of their typical methods to create value

Reporting by Kate Burgess, Chris Hughes, Jim Pickard, Peter Smith and Salamander Davoudi

The fightback against private equity is gathering support among punchy investors, who want public company executives to borrow some of the tricks of the trade.

Time and again, investors have seen private equity groups snap up publicly quoted assets, inject piles of debt, dispose of underperforming businesses and then sell the company back to investors.

Private equity firms often make companies perform by bringing in focused management who can take tough action because they are out of the public glare. But it does seem that many of the corporate finance techniques deployed by private equity could just as easily be used by public companies.

Weighted average cost of capital

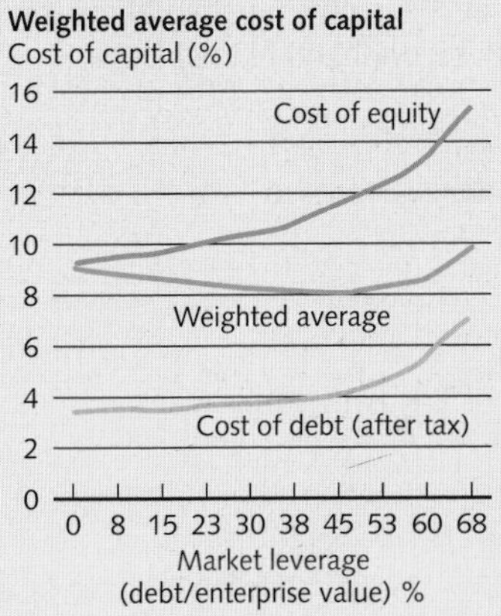

Some bosses have already woken up to the idea.

The most famliar tactic is to take on more debt. This can boost returns by cutting a company's tax bill because company profit is taxed after interest payments are deducted. Debt is cheaper than equity financing because creditors have a prior claim in assets if a company goes under, making it less risky.

The snag is that very high levels of debt can make the company more risky – increasing the cost of equity and debt financing.

Bankers say the trick is to take on just enough debt to reap the benefits, without going too far. This minimises the company's weighted average cost of capital – a blend of its cost of debt and cost of equity.

It is becoming more usual to see over-capitalised companies return cash to investors and take on more debt, especially when they are forced onto the defensive.

There are also a host of techniques available to UK companies with large freehold property portfolios.

One private equity tactic is to orchestrate a straight sale or sale and leaseback of property assets. This has been imitated by Christian Salvesen, the logistics group.

KPMG recently said sale and leasebacks were no longer the 'act of the desperate corporate'.

There is one main reason that more companies do not embrace these and other techniques beloved of private equity – conservatism at board level.

Bankers also say finance directors are often unaware of new forms of debt that make fewer demands on the company's cash flow.

There are also fears that now is a bad time to take on extra leverage – a view reinforced by the Bank of England's recent warning to companies to beware the rise of interest rates.

Some institutional investors are themselves divided over whether public companies should take on more debt. Tony Dalwood, head of public equities at SVG Advisers, says: 'There is great resistance from the public markets to put a large of amount of leverage on to a listed business.'

Source: *Financial Times*, 12 August 2006, p. 15. Reprinted with permission.

Some factors influencing the risk of financial distress costs

The susceptibility to financial distress varies from company to company. Here are some influences:

1. ***The sensitivity of the company's revenues to the general level of economic activity*** If a company's revenues are highly responsive to the ups and downs in the economy, shareholders and lenders may perceive a greater risk of liquidation and/or distress and demand a higher return in compensation for gearing compared with that demanded for a firm which is less sensitive to economic events.
2. ***The proportion of fixed to variable costs*** A firm which is highly operationally geared, and which also takes on high borrowing, may find that equity and debt holders demand a high return for the increased risk.
3. ***The liquidity and marketability of the firm's assets*** Some firms invest in a type of asset which can be easily sold at a reasonably high and certain value should they go into liquidation. This is of benefit to the financial security holders and so they may not demand such a high risk premium. A hotel chain, for example, should it suffer a decline in profitability, can usually sell hotels in a reasonably active property market. On the other hand investors in an advertising agency, with few saleable assets, would be less relaxed about rises in gearing.
4. ***The cash-generative ability of the business*** Some firms produce a high regular flow of cash and so can reasonably accept a higher gearing level than a firm with lumpy, highly uncertain and delayed cash inflows.

Exhibit 21.22 illustrates that the optimal gearing level for two example firms shifts depending on key characteristics of the underlying business.

Exhibit 21.22 The characteristics of the underlying business influences the risk of liquidation/distress, and therefore WACC, and the optimal gearing level

Characteristic	Food retailer	Steel producer
Sensitivity to economic activity	Relatively insensitive to economic fluctuations	Dependent on general economic prosperity
Operational gearing	Most costs are variable	Most costs are fixed
Asset liquidity	Shops, stock, etc., easily sold	Assets have few/no alternative uses. Thin secondhand market
Cash-generative ability	High or stable cash flow	Irregular cash flow
Likely acceptable gearing ratio	HIGH	LOW

Exhibit 21.23 shows a chart of the historic gearing levels of UK companies when market values are used.

Agency costs

Another restraining influence on the decision to take on high debt is the **agency cost** of doing so. Agency costs arise out of what is known as the 'principal–agent' problem. In most large firms the finance providers (principals) are not able to actively manage the firm. They employ 'agents' (managers) and it is possible for these agents to act in ways which are not always in the best interests of the equity or debt holders.

Agency costs are the direct and indirect costs of attempting to ensure that agents act in the best interest of principals as well as the loss resulting from failure to get them to act this way.

Exhibit 21.23

Bank puts assessment of risks into sharp focus

FT

Chris Giles and Peter Thal Larsen

In the Bank of England stress tests, the problem of rising global corporate debt levels also ranks as having the second highest impact on UK bank capital, if a crisis were triggered.

The Bank's message is highly nuanced, however. It is not saying that corporate leverage is currently at a level that threatens the financial system. Its analysis shows that UK company borrowing has fallen as a share of its market value over the past three years.

Rather, the Bank is concerned at the effect of this relative balance sheet health on incentives within and outside companies. The explosion of leveraged buy-outs might, according to Bank estimates, only have increased the average annual default probability of UK companies by 0.2 per centage points, but it has changed incentives in the system.

It argues that although leveraged buy-outs have affected only a small number of companies, the threat that they will become more widespread is encouraging other companies to increase their gearing by borrowing more.

'If these patterns continued, they would increase the vulnerability of global corporate balance sheets to a change in the future financial environment,' the report argues.

British companies gearing has risen since the 1990s ...

Private non-financial companies gearing ratio at market value (%)

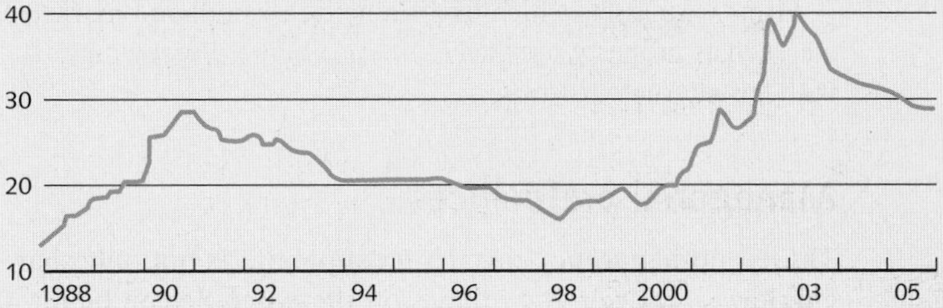

Source: *Financial Times*, 12 July 2006, p. 3. Reprinted with permission.

If management are acting for the maximisation of shareholder wealth debt holders may have reason to fear agency problems, because there may be actions which potentially benefit the owners at the expense of lenders. It is possible for lenders to be fooled or misled by managers. For example, management might raise money from bondholders, saying that this is low-risk lending (and therefore paying a low interest rate) because the firm has low gearing and the funds will be used for a low-risk project. In the event the managers invest in high-risk ventures, and the firm becomes more highly geared by borrowing more. As a result the original lenders do not receive a return sufficient for the level of risk and the firm has the benefit of low-interest financing.

Alternatively, consider a firm already in financial distress. From the shareholders' point of view there is little to lose from taking an enormous gamble by accepting very high-risk projects. If the gamble pays off the shareholders will win but the debt holders will gain no more than the obligatory fixed interest. If it fails, the shareholders are no worse off but the lenders experience default on their securities. Another temptation is for the shareholders to take large amounts out of a business through the payment of dividends when the managers become aware of a high chance of liquidation, leaving the debt holders with little to salvage.

The problem boils down to one of *information asymmetry* – that is, the managers are in possession of knowledge unavailable to the debt providers. One of the solutions is to spend money on monitoring. The lenders will require a premium on the debt interest to compensate for this additional cost. Also restrictions (covenants) are usually built into a lending agreement. For example, there may be limits on the level of dividends so that shareholders do not strip the company of cash. There may be limits placed on the overall level of indebtedness, with precise capital and income-gearing ratios. Managers may be restricted in the disposal of major assets or constrained in the type of activity they may engage in.

Extensive covenants imposed by lenders can be costly for shareholders because they reduce the firm's operating freedom and investment flexibility. Projects with a high NPV may be forgone because of the cautiousness of lenders. The opportunity costs can be especially frustrating for firms with high growth potential.

Thus agency costs include monitoring costs passed on as higher interest rates and the loss of value caused by the inhibition of managerial freedom to act. These increase with gearing, raising the implicit cost of debt and lowering the firm's value.[12]

There may also be a psychological element related to agency costs; managers generally do not like restrictions placed on their freedom of action. They try to limit constraints by not raising a large proportion of capital from lenders. This may help to explain why, in practice, we find companies generally have modest gearing levels.

Borrowing capacity

Borrowing capacity has a close connection with agency costs. Lenders prefer secured lending, and this often sets an upper limit on gearing. They like to have the assurance that if the worst happened and the firm was unable to meet its interest obligations they could seize assets to sell off in order that loans could be repaid. Thus, high levels of gearing are unusual because companies run out of suitable assets to offer as security against loans. So, the gearing level may not be determined by a theoretical, informed and considered management decision, but by the limits to total borrowing imposed by lenders.

Firms with assets which have an active secondhand market, and which do not tend to depreciate, such as property, are likely to have a higher borrowing capacity than firms that invest in assets with few alternative uses.

Managerial preferences

This is another agency cost. Liquidation affects not only shareholders, but managers and other employees. Indeed, the impact on these people can be far greater than the impact on well-diversified investors. It may be argued that managers have a natural tendency to be cautious about borrowing.

Pecking order

There is a '**pecking order**' for financing. Firms prefer to finance with internally generated funds. If a firm has potentially profitable investments it will first of all try to finance the investments by using the store of previous years' profits, that is, retained earnings. If still more funds are needed, firms will go to the capital markets. However, the debt market is called on first, and only as a last resort will companies raise equity finance. The pecking order of financing is in sharp contrast to the MM plus financial distress analysis (the 'trade-off model'), in which an optimal capital structure is targeted. Myers (1984, p. 581) puts it this way: 'In this story, there is no well-defined target debt–equity mix, because there are two kinds of equity, internal and external, one at the top of the pecking order and one at the bottom.'

One reason for placing new issues of equity at the bottom is supposedly that the stock markets perceive an equity issue as a sign of problems – an act of desperation. Myers and Majluf (1984) provide a theoretical explanation of why an equity issue might be bad news – managers will only issue shares when they believe the firm's shares are overpriced. In the capital structure literature the term '**adverse selection problem**' is used to convey the idea that managers are likely to act on their informational advantage over investors and so there is an extra degree of risk for equity investors because usually only those managers observing overpricing of their shares relative to the company's prospects would elect for a new share issue. Companies with underpriced shares would generally raise debt capital. This means that equity has 'an adverse selection premium' – a raised level of return required – making newly raised equity an expensive form of finance, thus only the desperate raise funds by selling shares. Bennett Stewart (1990, p. 391) puts it differently: 'Raising equity conveys

---

[12] On the other hand Jensen (1986) has argued that if managers have less free cash flow they are less likely to invest in negative NPV projects, and this restraint is better for shareholders.

doubt. Investors suspect that management is attempting to shore up the firm's financial resources for rough times ahead by selling over-valued shares.'[13]

There is an argument that firms do not try to reach the 'correct' capital structure as dictated by theory, because managers are following a **line of least resistance**. Internal funds are the first choice because using retained earnings does not involve contact with outside investors. This avoids the discipline involved in trying to extract investors' money. For example, the communication process required to raise equity finance is usually time consuming and onerous, with a formal prospectus, etc., and investors will scrutinise the detailed justifications advanced for the need to raise additional finance. It seems reasonable to suppose that managers will feel more comfortable using funds they already have in their hands. However, if they do have to obtain external financing then debt is next in the line of least resistance. This is because the degree of questioning and publicity associated with a bank loan or bond issue is usually significantly less than that associated with a share issue.

Another reason for a pecking order is that ordinary shares are more expensive to issue (in terms of administrative costs) than debt capital, which in turn is more expensive than simply applying previously generated profits. The costs of new issues and rights issues of shares can be very expensive, whereas retained earnings are available without transaction costs.

The pecking order idea helps to explain why the most profitable companies often borrow very little. It is not that they have a low target debt ratio, but because they do not need outside finance. If they are highly profitable they will use these profits for growth opportunities and so end up with very little debt and no need to issue shares.

Less profitable firms with many positive NPV projects to fund issue debt because they do not have internal funds sufficient for their capital investment programme and because debt is first in the pecking order of externally raised finance.

Exhibit 21.24 shows that rights issues (particularly 'rescue' rights issues designed to save the company from the danger of liquidation) can be viewed in a very negative light by financial markets.

Exhibit 21.24

Companies go back to basics in search for cash

FT

Rights issues are a trusted route to funds

says Arkady Ostrovsky

Two French groups yesterday joined the lengthening queue of cash-hungry European companies lining up to raise money from shareholders through rights issues.

Scor, the reinsurer, plans a capital increase of €400m (£251.2m) – equivalent to its market capitalisation – but the move was poorly received and the company's shares tumbled by a third. Meanwhile, Bouygues Telecom said it was looking to launch a rights issue to pay for its €619m licence to operate a third-generation mobile phone network.

Rights issues – offerings of new shares to existing shareholders on a pro-rata basis to their holdings – have been the most popular way for companies to raise money this year. Shareholders can either subscribe to a rights issue or reject it, depending on their view of the company's future. But when stock markets are tumbling and other sources of financing have dried up, it can be a life-and-death choice for a company.

'For a number of highly geared companies, bond markets have been, in effect, shut this year, the IPO market is dry and banks are reluctant to lend long-term money to indebted companies, so companies have no choice but to ask shareholders for money,' says James Renwick, European head of equity capital markets at UBS Warburg . . .

'Rights issues are the most basic way of raising money, which companies undertook before capital markets were properly developed. But when times get tough, companies go back to basics,' says Dante Roscini, global co-head of equity capital markets at Merrill Lynch . . .

▶

[13] Some theorists have taken the argument a step further: managers will want to issue debt even if their shares are currently over-valued. The logic is as follows: investors are aware that managers have an incentive to sell shares when they are over-priced and therefore take an equity issue as a bad signal. So, if management go ahead with the share sale the equity price will fall. To avoid this, managers choose to issue debt.

Exhibit 21.24 continued

'European companies are facing up to reality. Volatility is at record high levels and a rescue rights issue is likely to be the only way of restructuring balance sheets in the short to medium term,' says Mr Renwick . . .

There is little doubt that a rising level of rights issues is a sign of desperation on the part of many companies. But it is also the first step towards balance sheet restructurings and the reducing of debt, which, ultimately, should lead to the revival of equity capital markets.

Source: Financial Times, 1 October 2002, p. 23. Reprinted with permission.

Market timing

A counter argument to the reluctance to issue equity under the pecking order theory is the '**market timing theory**' (see Baker and Wurgler, 2002). Here gearing decreases when firms have the opportunity to issue shares at a high price ('over-priced') and increases when share values are low as firms buy in their shares (remember that gearing is measured by market values of debt and equity not balance sheet values). Thus gearing varies in response to opportunities to sell or buy shares not according to a trade-off theory rationale; and movement away from optimal gearing levels persist into the long term. In Baker and Wurgler's view there is no attempt at an optimal capital structure; market timing decisions just accumulate into a capital structure.

However, Alti (2006) shows that despite advantage being taken of high share prices the gearing ratio effect of this completely vanishes within two years (this study examined 'hot' initial public offerings): 'the results are consistent with the modified version of the traditional trade-off view of capital structure, one that includes market timing as a short term factor' (Alti, p. 1684). Also, Leary and Roberts (2005) show that Baker and Wurgler's market timing effects of gearing are more likely to be due to the high cost of regularly changing debt or equity levels (issue or redemption costs). Firms do move back toward the target debt–equity range but the high cost of issuance of debt and so on mean that this is gradual. Furthermore, Graham and Harvey's (2001) survey confirmed that the majority of firms have debt–equity ratio targets.

Financial slack

Operating and strategic decisions are generally the prime determinants of company value, not the financing decision. Being able to respond to opportunities as they fleetingly appear in business is important. If a firm is already highly geared it may find it difficult to gain access to more funds quickly as the need arises. **Financial slack** means having cash (or near-cash) and/or spare debt capacity. This slack can be extremely valuable and firms may restrict debt levels below that of the 'optimal' gearing level in order that the risk of missing profitable investments is reduced. Graham and Harvey (2001) show that 59 per cent of US companies deliberately restrict debt 'so we have enough internal funds available to pursue new projects when they come along'. This was the most important factor determining the debt levels of these firms, out-ranking tax deductibility of debt and risk of distress.

Financial slack is also valuable for meeting unforeseen circumstances. Managers may wish to be cautious and have a reserve of cash or spare borrowing capacity to cope with a 'rainy day'.

An interesting example of this is described by the treasurer of Pfizer, Richard Passov, who argued in a *Harvard Business Review* article (2003) that the reason Pfizer, Intel and other firms with high levels of investment in intangible assets have cash on their balance sheets and no borrowing is because they are subject to high business risk through their risky R&D programmes. This means that they cannot take the chance of having any financial risk at all. They have billions in cash as cushions to meet unforeseen shocks and allow the continuance of investment in potential winners, many of which may not be providing cash inflows for five years or more. They are concerned about the potential for financial distress either to halt promising investment or to force the hurried sale of expensive equity (i.e. selling a chunk of the company too cheaply) at a time of crisis.

Signalling

Managers and other employees often have a very powerful incentive to ensure the continuance of the business. They are usually the people who suffer most should it become insolvent. Because of this, it is argued, managers will generally increase the gearing level only if they are confident about the future. Shareholders are interested in obtaining information about the company's prospects, and changes in financing can become a signal representing management's assessment of future returns. Ross (1977) suggests that an increase in gearing should lead to a rise in share price as managers are **signalling** their increased optimism. Managers, therefore, need to consider the signal transmitted to the market concerning future income whenever it announces major gearing changes.

Control

The source of finance chosen may be determined by the effect on the control of the organisation. For example, if a shareholder with 50 per cent of a company's shares is unable to pay for more shares in a rights issue, he or she may be reluctant to allow the company to raise funds in this way, especially if shares are sold to a rival. This limits the range of sources of finance and may lead to a rise in debt levels. If we broaden the definition of control beyond shareholder voting rights, the article reproduced in **Exhibit 21.25** provides yet another incentive for keeping debt levels low.

Exhibit 21.25 An aversion to dependency on men's institutions

Matriarch in a waxed jacket

FT

Margaret Barbour enjoys undeserved obscurity. As the highest-earning business woman in Britain, she shuns publicity, believing renown based on her wealth would be misleading and dangerous.

In her eyes, her multi-million income is no more than a number on a balance sheet. Most of it is locked up in the assets of Barbour, the waxed jacket manufacturer.

When she took charge of the business in 1968, Barbour was no more than a tiny mail-order company, set up at the end of the last century to make oilskins for lighthouse men, and since developed as a manufacturer of motor cycle gear.

Today the company has nine factories, 800 employees and turnover of about £75m, compared with £500,000 in 1968.

She characterises her approach as the woman's way of doing business. 'The Barbour family has never lived in any great style,' she says, and the Barbour women have never required huge dividends. That has left the company with plenty of cash. It did once have some debt, after a sharp rise in demand in the early 1980s triggered a rapid expansion into more factories. But the loans are long since repaid.

An aversion to dependency on men's institutions is a recurring theme. She describes the textile and clothing industry associations as 'too male-dominated'. Barbour belongs to none of them.

Source: Jenny Luesby, *Financial Times*, 23 June 1997, p. 10. Reprinted with permission.

Tax exhaustion

Many companies do not have extremely high debt levels because their profits are not high enough to benefit from the tax shield.

Industry group gearing

Suppose you are a financial manager trying to decide on an appropriate gearing ratio and have absorbed all the above theories, ideas and models. You might have concluded that there is no precise formula which can be employed to establish the *best* debt to equity ratio for firms in all circumstances. It depends on so many specific, and often difficult to measure, factors. One must consider the tax position of the firm, the likelihood of financial distress, the type of business the firm is in, the saleability of its assets, the level of business risk and the 'psychology' of the market. (For example, are rights issues perceived as bad signals, and debt issues a sign of confidence, or not?)

Given all these difficulties about establishing the theoretically 'correct' gearing level that will maximise shareholder wealth, managers may be tempted simply to follow the crowd, to look at what similar firms are doing, to find out what the financial markets seem to regard as a reasonable level of gearing, and to follow suit.

Some further thoughts on debt finance

There are some intriguing ideas advanced to promote the greater use of debt in firms' capital structure. Three of them will be considered here.

Motivation

High debt will motivate managers to perform better and in the interests of shareholders. Consider this thought: if an entrepreneur (an owner-manager) wishes to raise finance for expansion purposes, debt finance is regarded as the better choice from the perspective of entrepreneurs and society. The logic works like this: if new shares are sold to outside investors, this will dilute the entrepreneur's control and thus the level of interest of the entrepreneur in the success of the business. The manager would now be more inclined to take rewards in the form of salary, perks and leisure rather than concentrating purely on returns to shareholders. The firm will be run less efficiently because less effort is provided by the key person.

Or consider this argument: Bennett Stewart believes that in firms without a dominant shareholder and with a diffuse shareholder base, a **recapitalisation** which substitutes debt for equity can result in the concentration of the shares in the hands of a smaller, more proactive group. These shareholders have a greater incentive to monitor the firm. (If managers are made part of this shareholder owning group there is likely to be a greater alignment of shareholders' and managers' interests.) Large quoted firms often have tens of thousands of shareholders, any one of whom has little incentive to go to the expense of opposing managerial action detrimental to shareholders' interests – the costs of rallying and co-ordinating investors often outweigh the benefits to the individuals involved. However, if the shareholder base was shrunk through the substitution of debt for equity, the remaining shareholders would have greater incentive to act against mismanagement. An extreme form of this switch to concentration is when a management team purchases a company through a leveraged buy-out or buy-in. Here a dispersed, divided and effectively powerless group of shareholders is replaced with a focused and knowledgeable small team, capable of rapid action and highly motivated to ensure the firm's success.

Reinvestment risk

High debt forces the firm to make regular payments to debt holders, thereby denying 'spare' cash to the managers. In this way the firm avoids placing a temptation in the manager's path which might lead to investment in negative NPV projects and to making destructive acquisitions. Deliberately keeping managers short of cash avoids the problem that shareholders' funds may be applied to projects with little thought to returns. If funds are needed, instead of drawing on a large pot held within the firm, managers have to ask debt and equity finance providers. This will help to ensure that their plans are subject to the scrutiny and discipline of the market.

The problem of managers over-supplied with money, given the limited profitable investment opportunities open to them, seems to be widespread, but specific examples are only clearly seen with hindsight. For example, in the 1990s GEC was a cash-rich company under Arnold Weinstock. New managers changed the name to Marconi and spent billions buying high-technology communication infrastructure companies working at the cutting edge, but with little in the way of certainty over the likely future demand for the services/goods they offered. Hope of a glorious future was all that was needed for the spending of the large pot of money (as well as additional borrowings). When demand projections were shown to be absurdly optimistic the company barely survived – shareholder value was destroyed on a massive scale.

The danger of poor investment decisions is at its worst in firms that are highly profitable but which have few growth opportunities. The annual surplus cash flow is often squandered on increasingly marginal projects within existing SBUs or wasted in a diversification effort looking to buy growth opportunities: unfortunately these often cost more than they are worth (*see* the evidence on merger failure in Chapter 23). It is far better, say Stewart (1990), Hart (1995), Jensen (1986) and others, that managers are forced to justify the use of funds by having to ask for it at regular intervals. This process can be assisted by having high debt levels which absorb surplus cash through interest and principal payments and deposit it out of the reach of empire-building, perk-promoting, lazy managers.

High debt can also bring with it covenants and monitoring that restrict managerial activities so as to reduce the risk of over-investment for both debt and equity-holders. Evidence for this benefit was found in emerging financial markets by Harvey *et al.* (2004).

Exhibit 21.16 provides some more examples of reinvestment risk.

Exhibit 21.26

A surplus of cash invariably leads to a shortage of sense

FT

Simon London

It is more than 30 years since Gulf Oil tried to buy Ringling Brothers Circus, but investors still get twitchy when companies hoard large amounts of cash. History shows that most chief executives put in charge of a company with billions in the bank are compelled to act like Coco the Clown.

There is plenty to be twitchy about. These days it is not only big oil companies that are generating more cash than they can invest with a straight face. The cost-cutting, outsourcing and restructuring of the last few years means that market leaders in most sectors are enjoying tremendous operational gearing: relatively modest revenue growth translates into substantial increases in earnings and, all things being equal, free cash flow.

At the last count, more than a third of the companies in the Standard & Poor's 500 index of US stocks had net cash on their balance sheets. The combined cash hoard: $650bn (£377bn), up from $329bn five years ago. The richest of them all is Microsoft, the world's largest software company, which has $40bn in the bank even after paying out $33bn last year to shareholders as a special dividend.

The good news is that really comical attempts at diversification are these days rarely a problem. Gulf Oil's proposed move from hydrocarbons into lion-taming was probably the high point (or, more accurately, the low point) of the fashion for conglomerate strategies. Today's managers have been educated to believe in focus. But they are no less vulnerable to cash-induced madness than their forebears – it is just that their madness is expressed in different ways.

Recall, if it is not too painful, the cash-fuelled acquisition binge that turned General Electric Company, once the pride of the UK electronics industry, into the listing hulk that is Marconi. A quick scan of the financial pages reveals the telltale signs of cash again burning holes in trouser pockets. Would Porsche have acquired a substantial stake in Volkswagen unless it had a few billion euros stashed in the corporate glove compartment?

Cash breeds not only slapstick action but also tragicomic inaction. General Motors might have been forced to produce cars people acually wanted to drive had it not been sitting atop a $29bn (as of 2003, now down to $19bn) cash pile. Sun Microsystsms might have been forced to concede that its technology strategy was a dud had its coffers not been filled to overflowing during the bubble years.

To be fair, there are some legitimate reasons for companies to keep what looks surplus cash in the bank. Managers operating in feast-or-famine industries can argue that a fat balance sheet helps them to survive lean years. Yes, carrying around the extra weight is inefficient. But it is less inefficient than teetering on the edge of bankruptcy during every downturn.

Then there are industries where success depends on persuading customers to make long-term commitments to products. In these circumstances, a rock-solid balance sheet is an invaluable marketing tool, without which customers and business partners will be reluctant to make 'co-investments' required to train employees or develop complementary products. Curiously, this was always Sun's main justification for maintaining a cash pile – which goes to show that surplus cash can be useful and harmful simultaneously.

Big bucks can also be an important weapon for companies engaged in 'wars of attrition' – long-term struggles where the enormous costs are justified by the potential for a

▶

Exhibit 21.26 continued

winner-takes-all outcome. Thus Microsoft's extreme cash riches might be justified because it allows the company to pitch its Xbox games console against Sony's PlayStation in an epic struggle for dominance of the world's living rooms.

The snag is that companies that can afford to fight wars of attrition tend to see everything in those terms. Thus Microsoft in the 1990s won what it thought was a war of attrition against Netscape for control of the internet browser market, only to find competition re-emerging in recent years in the form of Firefox, a browser developed by the open-source software community. The winner may not take all, after all.

A wider problem, notes Preston McAfee, professor of business, economics and management at the California Institute of Technology, is that cash-rich companies tend to rush to invest in new markets when it might be more sensible to hang back. 'The strategic value of delay is widely underappreciated,' he says.

John Roberts, professor of economics and management at Stanford Graduate School of Business, is sceptical of the idea that keeping cash on hand 'just in case' ever makes sense from a strategic perspective.

'Excess cash is good for tactics,' he says. 'But it is bad for strategy on all kinds of dimensions.'

Poster boy for this hair-shirted philosophy is BP's John Brown, who has committed the company to returning every last dollar of surplus cash flow to investors. BP will this year return roughly $20bn through its share buy-back programme as well as paying a hefty dividend.

Then again, as ever in management theory, every shining example yields a troublesome counter-example. Thus Toyota is not only the world's most profitable volume car manufacturer, one of the world's most respected companies and famed for its 'lean' approach to business, it also has $30bn in the bank – and not a clown or a contortionist in sight. That's (show) business.

Source: Financial Times, 30 November 2005, p. 13. Reprinted with permission.

Operating and strategic efficiency

'Equity is soft; debt is hard. Equity is forgiving; debt is insistent. Equity is a pillow; debt is a dagger.' This statement by Bennett Stewart (1990, p. 580) emphasises that operating and strategic problems and inefficiencies are less likely to be attended to and corrected with a capital base which is primarily equity. However, the managers of a highly geared company are more likely to be attuned to the threat posed by falling efficiency and profitability. The failing is the same under both a high equity and a high debt structure: it just seems more of a crisis when there is a large interest bill each month. The geared firm, it is argued, simply cannot afford to have any value-destructive activities (SBUs or product lines). Managers are spurred on by the pressing need to make regular payments, to reform, dispose or close – and quickly.

These are some of the arguments put forward in support of high debt, particularly in America in the era of massive **leveraged buy-outs** (**LBOs**), junk bonds and share repurchase programmes (in the 1980s and 1990s), and in 2006–7 when private equity firms took over well-known companies and gave them highly geared capital structures. They seem to make some sense but the downside of excessive debt must be balanced against these forcefully advanced ideas. Turning back to Exhibit 21.19, which shows the costs of financial distress, can help to give some perspective. In addition, many firms have found themselves crippled and at a competitive disadvantage because of the burden of high debt. For example Marconi is a shadow of its former self, as are Cable & Wireless and Vivendi Universal.

Exhibit 21.27 discusses the myth that firms should aim for a level of gearing that permits a high credit rating.

Exhibit 21.27

Highest scores may not be most efficient

FT

by Adrienne Roberts

Credit rating downgrades tend to be seen as a symptom of corporate illness, bringing to mind a host of 'fallen angels' such as WorldCom and Tyco.

But not all downgrades signal ill health. In recent years increasing numbers of finance directors have deliberately chosen to take a step or two down the credit curve.

Ratings advisers say the highest rating a company can achieve is not necessarily the 'right' one to pursue.

'Considering what the right rating is for you is linked to asking what your optimal capital structure is,' says May Busch, a managing director at Morgan Stanley in London. 'It's a question of determining the right amount of debt relative to equity, and more importantly relative to the operating cashflows which will be used to service that debt.'

Debt tends to be cheaper than equity (interest payments, unlike dividends, are tax-deductible) so increasing the amount of debt in the mix brings down a company's weighted average cost of capital.

Over the past decade US companies have focused increasingly on optimising their capital structures, moving down the ratings scale as their leverage increased.

European companies have followed suit in recent years, although the trend is not as far advanced.

In the mid-1990s the average European corporate rating was around AA on the Standard & Poor's scale and Aa2 from Moody's Investors Service. That is now about four notches lower, around A– and A3.

In the early 1980s about 25 US companies were rated triple A by Standard & Poor's. There are currently only seven, including Pfizer, Johnson & Johnson and General Electric.

Outside the US there are a handful of triple A names such as Nestlé and Novartis in Europe and Toyota in Japan.

Standard & Poor's ascribes the trend to investors' increasing tolerance for risk, 'coupled with companies shifting from historically conservative financial policies to a greater emphasis on shareholder returns'.

Unilever gave up triple A status with its $20.3bn debt-financed acquisition of Bestfoods in 2000. That decision took the group's rating down four notches from triple A to A+.

'If Unilever had said triple A was the only rating they would tolerate, it would have been too expensive to do the Bestfoods deal,' said Ms Busch. 'Instead they used this deal as an opportunity to adopt a more efficient capital structure and adjust leverage to optimise the company's ratings.'

There is a balancing act between leveraging up enough to achieve the company's strategic goals, but not taking on so much debt that credit ratings slump, pushing the company's cost of debt too high.

'Studies we've done have shown that, generally, the most efficient rating to have in terms of minimising weighted average cost of capital is a high triple B,' said Tom Crawley, head of credit research at Citigroup in London. 'That's deemed to be an efficient capital structure, because you work your equity harder and the increase in your cost of debt doesn't offset the benefit.'

But what a university professor might identify as the ideal capital structure is not always the mix companies choose, because other factors come into the decision.

'Having financial flexibility and achieving the company's strategic goals can override the theoretical optimal capital structure,' says Mr Crawley.

Mirco Bianchi, global head of ratings advisory services at UBS in London, says: 'Every segment has its own sweet spot depending on the way it operates, its financing needs and how much flexibility it needs.'

Consumer product companies, for example food and beverage producers, tend to aim for a higher rating than the pure industrials. The consumer sector's thin profit margins and large working capital financing

Rating it right

Corporate credit rating distributions (%)

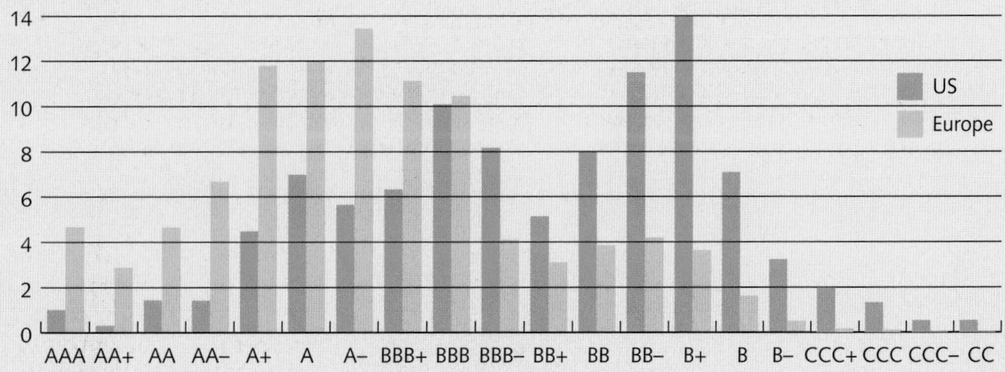

Source: Standard & Poors Global Fixed Income Research

▶

Exhibit 21.27 continued

needs often mean that companies need to keep their borrowing costs down in order to stay competitive.

Industrials tend to gravitate towards lower ratings because, for example, heavier capital investment requires more leverage.

Then again, a company which needs to go to the markets regularly to fund capital spending or acquisitions might need to maintain a credit rating above the mid-triple B level to ensure it has good market access throughout the business cycle.

Ultimately, argues Mr Bianchi, the right rating is a stable rating. 'Sometimes companies aim for too high a rating because they think investors will view them as a better company. But what is more important is sustainability. That is crucial for bond investors, but it is becoming increasingly important to equity investors too,' he says.

Source: Financial Times, 12 August 2003, p. 39. Reprinted with permission.

Concluding comments

The proportion of debt in the total capital of a firm can influence the overall cost of capital and therefore the value of the firm and the wealth of shareholders. If, as a result of increasing the gearing ratio, it is possible to lower the weighted average cost of capital, then all the future net cash flows will be discounted at a lower rate. It is generally observed that as gearing increases the WACC declines because of the lower cost of debt. This is further enhanced by the tax relief available on debt capital.

But as gearing rises the risk of financial distress causes shareholders (and eventually debt holders) to demand a greater return. This eventually rises to such an extent that it outweighs the benefit of the lower cost of debt, and the WACC starts to rise. This risk factor is difficult, if not impossible, to quantify and therefore the exact position and shape of the WACC curve for each firm remains largely unknown. Nevertheless, it seems reasonable to postulate there is a U-shaped relationship like that shown in **Exhibit 21.28**.

We cannot scientifically establish a best debt to equity ratio. There are many complicating factors which determine the actual gearing levels adopted by firms. These cloud the picture sufficiently for us to say that while we accept that the WACC is probably U-shaped for firms generally, we cannot precisely calculate a best gearing level.

This explains why there is such a variation in gearing levels. Some firms are under the influence of particular factors to a greater extent than other firms: some may have very low borrowing capacity, and others may have management keen on signalling confidence in the future; some may have very cautious management unwilling to borrow and a diffuse unco-ordinated shareholder body; some may be in very volatile product markets with high liquidation probabilities and others in stable industries with marketable tangible assets; other companies may be dominated by leaders steeped in the high gearing thinking of the 1980s and 1990s, believing that managers are better motivated and less likely to waste resources if the firm is highly indebted.

So, to the question of whether a firm can obtain a level of gearing which will maximise shareholder wealth the answer is 'yes'. The problem is finding this level in such a multifaceted analysis.

Exhibit 21.28 The WACC is U-shaped and value can be altered by changing the gearing level

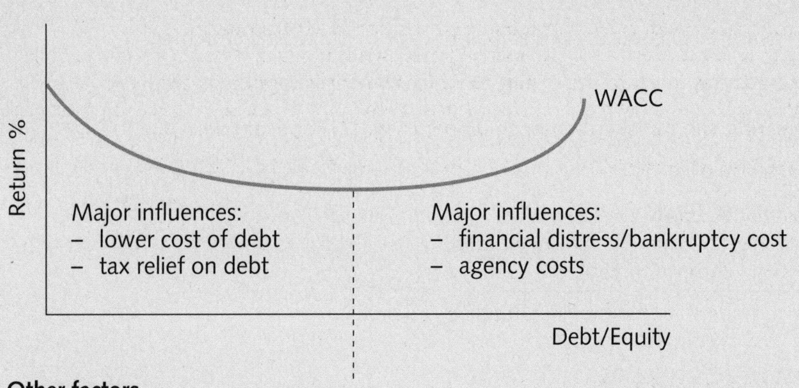

Other factors

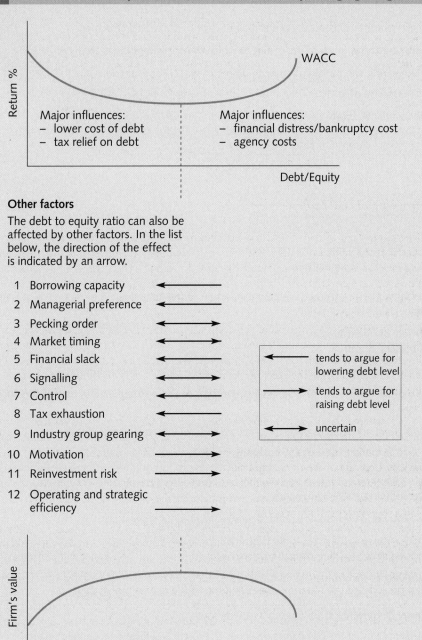

The debt to equity ratio can also be affected by other factors. In the list below, the direction of the effect is indicated by an arrow.

1	Borrowing capacity	←
2	Managerial preference	←
3	Pecking order	↔
4	Market timing	↔
5	Financial slack	←
6	Signalling	↔
7	Control	←
8	Tax exhaustion	←
9	Industry group gearing	↔
10	Motivation	→
11	Reinvestment risk	→
12	Operating and strategic efficiency	→

← tends to argue for lowering debt level

→ tends to argue for raising debt level

↔ uncertain

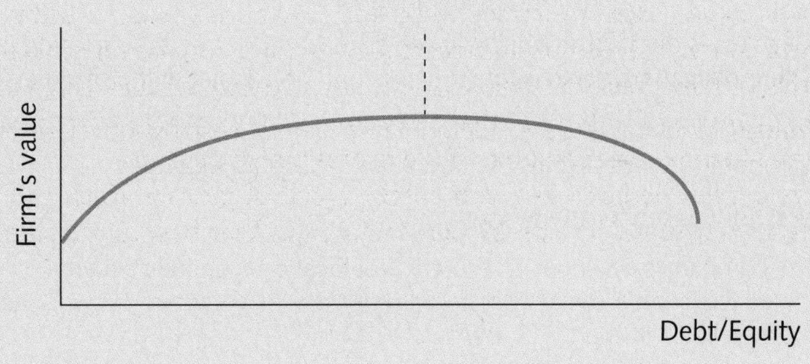

Key points and concepts

- **Financial gearing** concerns the proportion of debt in the capital structure.
- **Operating gearing** refers to the extent to which the firm's total costs are fixed.
- **Capital gearing** can be measured in a number of ways. For example:

  1 $\dfrac{\text{Long-term debt}}{\text{Shareholders' funds}}$

  2 $\dfrac{\text{Long-term debt}}{\text{Long-term debt + Shareholders' funds}}$

  3 $\dfrac{\text{All borrowing}}{\text{All borrowing + Shareholders' funds}}$

  4 $\dfrac{\text{Long-term debt}}{\text{Total market capitalisation}}$

- **Income gearing** is concerned with the proportion of the annual income stream which is devoted to the prior claims of debt holders.
- The **effect of financial gearing** is to magnify the degree of variation in a firm's income for shareholders' returns.
- **Business risk** is the variability of the firm's operating income (before interest).
- **Financial risk** is the additional variability in returns to shareholders due to debt in the financial structure.
- In **Modigliani and Miller's perfect no-tax world** three propositions hold true:
  1 The total market value of any company is independent of its capital structure.
  2 The expected rate of return on equity increases proportionately with the gearing ratio.
  3 The cut-off rate of return for new projects is equal to the weighted average cost of capital – which is constant regardless of gearing.
- In an **MM world with tax** the optimal gearing level is the highest possible.
- The **risk of financial distress** is one factor which causes firms to moderate their gearing levels. Financial distress is where obligations to creditors are not met, or are met with difficulty.
- The **indirect costs of financial distress**, such as deterioration in relationships with suppliers, customers and employees, can be more significant than the direct costs, such as legal fees.
- **Financial distress risk is influenced by the following**:
  – the sensitivity of the company's revenues to the general level of economic activity;
  – the proportion of fixed to variable costs;
  – the liquidity and marketability of the firm's assets;
  – the cash-generative ability of the business.
- **Agency costs** are the direct and indirect costs of ensuring that agents (e.g. managers) act in the best interests of principals (e.g. shareholders, lenders), for example monitoring costs, restrictive covenants, loss of managerial freedom of action and opportunities forgone.
- **Financial distress and agency costs eventually outweigh the lower cost of debt** as gearing rises causing the WACC to rise and the firm's value to fall. (The **'trade-off'** *theory*)
- **Borrowing capacity** is determined by the assets available as collateral – this restricts borrowing.
- There is often a **managerial preference** for a lower risk stance on gearing.

- **The pecking order** of finance:

  1 internally generated funds;
  2 borrowings;
  3 new issue of equity.

  The reasons for the pecking order:

  – equity issue perceived as 'bad news' by the markets;
  – line of least resistance;
  – transaction costs.

- **Market timing theory** is founded on the observation that firms tend to issue shares when their share price is high and repurchase shares when it is low. This leads to the idea of an absence of a movement towards an optimal capital structure in the short or long term. However, the evidence suggests that in the medium or long term firms do move towards a target optimal debt/equity ratio.
- **Financial slack** means having cash (or near-cash) and/or spare debt capacity so that opportunities can be exploited quickly (and trouble avoided) as they arise in an unpredictable world and to provide a contingency reserve – it tends to reduce borrowing levels.
- **Signalling** An increased gearing level is taken as a positive sign by the financial markets because managers would only take the risk of financial distress if they were confident about future cash flows.
- The source of finance chosen may be determined by the effect on the **control** of the organisation.
- **Tax exhaustion** (profit insufficient to take advantage of debt's tax shield benefit) may be a factor limiting debt levels.
- Managers may be tempted to adopt the **industry group gearing** level.
- It is suggested that high gearing **motivates** managers to perform if they have a stake in the business, or if a smaller group of shareholders are given the incentive to monitor and control managers.
- **Reinvestment risk** is diminished by high gearing.
- It is argued that **operating and strategic efficiency** can be pushed further by high gearing.

Appendix 21.1 Asset beta

The assets of a business contain only business systematic risk. However, the equity of a geared company has to bear both (**a**) business systematic risk, and (**b**) financial systematic risk due to the additional variability caused by borrowing. The business systematic risk remains constant regardless of gearing level. The equity systematic risk, however, rises with higher gearing

In the CAPM the beta of the equity (β_E) rises as the firm takes on higher gearing. Debt can also have a beta. That is, the returns to the lenders have a co-variability greater than zero with the market portfolio's returns. Both types of finance providers, debt and equity, bear risk – it is just that the shareholders bear a greater risk.

Imagine that an individual owned all the equity and all the debt of a firm. This person therefore bears all the risks. If these two holdings form this person's entire portfolio then the overall systematic risk is a weighted average of the two component betas (ignoring taxes).

$$\beta_{\text{portfolio}} = W_E\beta_E + W_D\beta_D = \beta_A$$

where
β_D = beta of debt
β_A = asset beta
W_E = proportion of total finance that is equity
W_D = proportion of total finance that is debt

So, if debt has a beta of 0.3 and equity a beta of 1.3 in a company with equal amounts of capital from debt and equity the overall beta for the firm, the asset beta, β_A, is:

$$\beta_A = (0.5 \times 1.3) + (0.5 \times 0.3) = 0.8$$

The asset beta is a weighted average of the beta values of the debt and equity that financed the assets. To be more accurate, the asset beta determines the equity beta and debt beta. Asset beta remains constant regardless of the gearing level because it is determined by the business systematic risk, which does not change with the debt level. So, if in the example above the company lowered its gearing from the position where debt accounts for half of the capital to the point where it accounts for only 25 per cent the systematic risk on both the equity and debt would decrease. Assuming that the debt beta falls to 0.2 we can work out the new equity beta:

$$\begin{aligned} \beta_A = 0.8 &= W_E\beta_E + W_D\beta_D \\ 0.8 &= 0.75\beta_E + (0.25 \times 0.2) \\ \beta_E &= 1 \end{aligned}$$

Note that both the debt and equity betas fall as a result of lower gearing but the asset beta remains the same.

If the borrowing is eliminated the asset beta equals the equity beta:

$$\begin{aligned} \beta_A &= 0.8 = 1 \times \beta_E + 0 \\ \beta_A &= \beta_E = 0.8 \end{aligned}$$

Asset beta is the equity beta of the ungeared company given its underlying business systematic risk.

It is often assumed that the beta of debt is zero. This makes usable the following formulae:

$$\beta_A = \beta_E \times W_E$$

and

$$\beta_E = \beta_A \times 1/W_E$$

or

$$\beta_E = \beta_A(1 + D/E)$$

where D = amount of borrowing
E = amount of equity finance

In this case equity beta rises in direct proportion to the gearing level.

If we now switch to a world where there are taxes, then (keeping the assumption of debt beta of zero) the tax shield on debt results in the following relationship:

$$\beta_E = \beta_A[1 + (1 - T)(D/E)]$$

where T = corporation tax rate.

The equity beta is reduced because the tax relief (shield) on debt capital effectively lowers the financial risk borne by the equity holders at all gearing levels.

Users of this formula should never forget the major assumption that the lenders bear no systematic risk (debt beta is zero). There is also the assumption that the CAPM is the right model for risk. If it is not the betas estimated may not reflect the true market risk exposure for the equity. In addition, the model excludes the possibility that β_E might rise in a non-linear fashion with gearing.

Perhaps the most useful point to make about asset beta analysis is that it is good to be aware that the beta obtained from commercial sources is an equity beta dependent on the gearing levels for the firms at the time that the beta was estimated. This gearing level may not be the gearing level applicable to WACC calculations and so some adjustment is needed. The equity beta can be *ungeared* by using the above formulae, and then calculated for a variety of gearing levels (if a few bold assumptions are made).

Appendix 21.2 Adjusted present value (APV)

In the adjusted present value approach the value of financial gearing is separated from the value of the firm (project) without debt. The APV is equal to the value of the firm or project at zero debt (the NPV) plus the present value of the benefits (costs) of debt financing.

APV = NPV + PV of effects of gearing.

Or,

APV = value with all equity financing + PV of the effects of gearing.

Start by calculating the NPV of a project (or firm) as though it was to be financed entirely by equity. For example, a project is being considered that will produce annual cash flows of £1m for every future year to infinity. The project's business risk is such that the appropriate discount rate for this all-equity financed project is 10 per cent. The initial investment required is £10.5m.

NPV = –£10.5m + £1m/0.1 = –£0.5m

Under this all-equity capital structure the project produces a negative NPV and the managers would be inclined to reject it.

Now consider the same project in the circumstances where one half of the firm's (and project's) finance is debt and one half is equity. The debt finance carries with it a tax shield due to the ability to reduce taxable profit, and therefore the amount of tax paid, by the amount of interest. In other words, interest payments on debt are tax deductible, while cash flows on equity have to be paid out of after-tax cash flows.

If we make a few assumptions we can value the tax shield. If the interest rate on the £5.25m of debt is 6 per cent, and the tax rate, T, on income is 30 per cent, the annual tax savings from being able to deduct interest from taxable profits are:

Annual interest on the debt $= k_D \times D$

$= 0.06 \times £5.25m =$ £315,000

Annual tax savings due to interest payments $= T \times k_D \times D$

$= 0.3 \times 0.06 \times £5.25m = £94{,}500$

If we make the following four assumptions we can calculate the present value of all the future tax savings due to interest payments:

- The debt remains at the same level forever, therefore the tax savings are a perpetuity.
- The discount rate to be used to obtain the present value of all the future tax savings is the interest rate on debt (because it reflects the riskiness of debt).
- The tax rate will be the same for all future periods.
- The company will always be in a tax-paying position. There are always annual taxable profits that can be decreased by the payment of interest.

In these circumstances the present value of the savings is:

Present value of tax savings due to debt $= \dfrac{Tk_D D}{k_D} = TD$

$= 0.3 \times £5.25m$

$= £1{,}575m$

Thus, the tax rate multiplied by the amount of debt gives us the present value of the effects of gearing in this simple case where there is only one effect of gearing: the tax shield benefit. We will introduce other effects later.

We can now add together the value of the project in the all-equity case and the value of the tax shield.

$$\begin{aligned} \text{APV} &= \text{value with all-equity finance} + \text{PV of the effects of gearing} \\ &= -£0.5\text{m} + £1.575\text{m} = £1.075\text{m} \end{aligned}$$

As a result of changing the financing structure the project generates positive value and should be accepted.

In separating the value of gearing the APV approach has the suggested advantage that we can more easily calculate overall value at a variety of debt levels than by using the WACC. For example, in a leveraged buy-out where there is rapid pay-down of the debt, so that the ratio changes from year to year, the APV provides a computationally easier way of calculating value than the WACC.

However, some caution is needed when employing the APV. It assumes, for instance, that the firm can fully benefit from the tax shield at all debt levels. In reality tax shields will often be unused and therefore not adding value because the firm is not paying taxes. There may be periods of the future when the company is not making profits. Also very high debt levels need very high taxable income to gain all the benefit from the deductibility of interest. The tax shield value may be much less than that calculated using the simple formula above.

In addition, to use the APV you need to be able to predict debt ratio levels for each of the future years with some considerable accuracy.

Most importantly, the APV formula used so far has ignored the disadvantages of higher debt. It implicitly assumes that the benefits of debt increase as the gearing level rises (as in MM's world with tax model). The logical extreme outcome of this would be to select a capital structure that was virtually all debt. In reality, there are some drawbacks of higher debt, the most important of which are financial distress, agency costs and loss of financial slack. So, the APV formula needs to be modified to allow for the disadvantages of debt:

$$\text{APV} = \begin{matrix}\text{Value with}\\ \text{all-equity}\\ \text{financing}\end{matrix} + \begin{matrix}\text{PV of tax}\\ \text{benefits of}\\ \text{debt}\end{matrix} - \begin{matrix}\text{PV of expected}\\ \text{disadvantages}\\ \text{of debt}\end{matrix}$$

At low levels of debt the tax benefits will outweigh the disadvantages. But at high gearing it will be the other way round and the APV will fall with an increasing proportion of debt.

In this more realistic model the valuation of the financially geared company at different debt levels is far more complex, not least because it is very difficult to put numerical values on the disadvantages. To add to the complexity, there are a number of other factors we should allow for: for example, the benefit of higher debt leading to more highly motivated managers, the benefit of government loan subsidies, the transaction costs of issuing debt.

References and further reading

Alti, A. (2006) 'How persistent is the impact of market timing on capital structure?' *Journal of Finance*, 61(4), August, pp. 1681–710.

Evidence from the US that 'market timing' of equity issues does affect gearing (because if shares are easy to sell in large volume firms take advantage of that fact – the firms studied are 'hot' IPO stocks). However, the effect is short-lived – 'at the end of the second year following the IPO, the impact of market timing on leverage completely vanishes'.

Anderson, R.C., Mansi, S.A. and Reeb, D.M. (2003) 'Founding family ownership and the agency cost of debt', *Journal of Financial Economics*, 68, pp. 263–85.

Evidence is presented that suggests that debt holders' agency worries are less in companies with family ownership of shares. Interest rates are less because the founding family better protects debt holders' interests, it is posited.

Baker, A. and Wurgler, J. (2002) 'Market timing and capital structure', *Journal of Finance*, 62(1), February, pp. 1–32.

Firms tend to issue equity when market values are high, and repurchase shares when market values are low. These actions influence the debt to equity ratio in the short, and, more surprisingly, over the long run. Thus 'capital structure is largely the cumulative outcome of past attempts to time the equity market. In this theory, there is no optimum capital structure, so market timing decisions just accumulate over time into the capital structure outcome.'

Bevan, A.A. and Danbolt, J. (2004) 'Testing for inconsistencies in the estimation of UK capital structure determinants', *Applied Financial Economics*, 14, pp. 55–66.
UK empirical evidence showing debt (relative to asset base) rises with company size, perhaps because larger firms have less financial distress and agency cost risk. Also more profitable companies have lower debt levels (pecking order theory support?). And companies with more tangible assets carry more debt (adverse selection and moral hazard lead lenders to demand collateral).

Booth, L., Aivazian, V., Demirgue-Kunt, A. and Maksimovic, V. (2001) 'Capital structures in developing countries', *Journal of Finance*, 61(1), February, pp. 87–130.
The same decision variables influence capital structure in developing and developed countries. This is especially true of pecking order factors, e.g. the more profitable the firm the lower the debt.

Brealey, R.H., Myers, S.C. and Allen, F. (2005) *Principles of Corporate Finance*. 8th edn. New York: McGraw-Hill.
A more detailed treatment of the theoretical material is provided.

Brierley, P. and Bunn, P. (2005) 'The determination of UK corporate capital gearing', *Bank of England Quarterly Bulletin*, Autumn, pp. 356–66.
Empirical evidence that UK companies' gearing is positively related to company size and negatively correlated with growth opportunities and the importance of intangible assets. Until 1995 highly profitable firms had low gearing but this changed after 1995.

Bunn, R. and Young, G. (2004) Corporate capital structure in the United Kingdom: determinants and adjustment. Bank of England Working Paper 226 (www.bankofengland.co.uk/wp/index.html).
Evidence that UK companies comply with the trade-off model by borrowing to take advantage of the tax benefits of debt, which they set against possible costs of over-indebtedness. Also companies adjust gearing through dividend payments, new equity issues and to a lesser extent lowering or raising capital investment.

Damodaran, A. (1999) *Applied Corporate Finance*. New York: John Wiley & Sons.
An accessible introduction to the practical estimation of optimum capital structure.

Donaldson, G. (1961) *Corporate debt policy and the determination of corporate debt capacity*. Boston: Harvard Graduate School of Business Administration.
A study of the financing practices of large corporations: discussion of pecking order theory. Proposes a measure of debt capacity based on distressed cashflow.

Donaldson, G. (1969) *Strategy for financial mobility*. Boston: Harvard University.
An early discussion of financial slack.

Fama, E.G. (1978) 'The effects of a firm's investment and financing decisions', *American Economic Review*, 68(3), June, pp. 272–84.
A development of the economic modelling approach.

Fama, E.F. and French, K.R. (2005) 'Financing decisions: who issues stocks?', *Journal of Financial Economics*, 76, pp. 549–82.
Evidence against the pecking order theory prediction that firms rarely issue equity.

Flannery, M.J. and Rangan, K.P. (2006) 'Partial adjustment toward target capital structures', *Journal of Financial Economics*, 79, pp. 469–506.
Provides evidence that US companies have target ratios of debt/equity and try to (fairly rapidly) move towards them – thus supporting the trade-off theory. The evidence provides only weak support for the pecking order theory or the idea that firms decrease gearing when their share price is high by issuing more shares (the 'market-timing theory').

Frank, M.Z. and Goyal, V.K. (2003) 'Testing the pecking order theory of capital structure', *Journal of Financial Economics*, 67, pp. 217–48.
Evidence contradictory to the pecking order model.

Graham, J.R. and Harvey, C.R. (2001) 'The theory and practice of corporate finance: evidence from the field', *Journal of Financial Economics*, 60(2–3), pp. 187–243.
Empirical evidence on capital structure decisions.

Harris, M. and Raviv, A. (1991) 'The theory of capital structure', *Journal of Finance*, 46, pp. 297–355.
A helpful review of the subject.

Hart, O. (1995) *Firms, Contracts and Financial Structure*. Oxford: Oxford University Press.
High debt helps to align the interests of owners and managers.

Harvey, C.R., Lins, K.V. and Roper, A.H. (2004) 'The effect of capital structure when expected agency costs are extreme', *Journal of Financial Economics*, 74, pp. 3–30.
Evidence that the issuance of debt (e.g. syndicated term loans, international bonds and Yankee bonds) that come with restrictive operational covenants and monitoring of firms reduces agency costs and information problems. In particular, overinvestment is reduced. The more intensive monitoring and the constraints serve shareholders well.

Jensen, M.C. (1986) 'Agency costs of free cashflow, corporate finance and takeovers', *American Economic Review*, 26 May, p. 323.
Discusses the problem of encouraging managers to pay to shareholders cash above that needed for all positive NPV projects.

Jensen, M.C. (1989) 'Eclipse of the public corporation', *Harvard Business Review*, September–October, pp. 61–74.
High debt levels impose a discipline on managers. In particular they are forced to distribute cash, reducing the potential waste of free cash flow investment. Also in LBOs managers are incentivised by becoming owners.

Journal of Economic Perspectives (1988) Fall.
A collection of review articles on MM propositions.

Kisgen, D.J. (2006) 'Credit ratings and capital structure', *Journal of Finance*, 61(3), June, pp. 1035–72.
US firms' capital struture decisions are influenced by credit ratings.

Korajczyk, R.A. and Levy, A. (2003) 'Capital structure choice: macroeconomic conditions and financial constraints', *Journal of Financial Economics*, 68, pp. 75–109.
Macroeconomic conditions affect capital structure.

Leary, M.T. and Roberts, M.R. (2005) 'Do firms rebalance their capital structures?', *Journal of Finance*, 60(6), December, pp. 2575–619.
Findings: 'We find that firms activity rebalance their leverage to stay within an optimal range. Our evidence suggests that the persistent effect of shocks on leverage observed in previous studies is more likely due to adjustment costs than indifference toward capital structure'.

Lowenstein, L. (1991) *Sense and Nonsense in Corporate Finance*. Reading, MA: Addison-Wesley.
A sceptical approach to the over-elaborate algebraic examination of financial structure.

Luehrman, T.A. (1997) 'Using APV: A better tool for valuing operations', *Harvard Business Review*, 75 (May–June), pp. 145–54.
An easy-to-read introduction to adjusted present value.

Marsh, P. (1982) 'The choice between equity and debt: An empirical study', *Journal of Finance*, 37, March, pp. 121–44.
Evidence that companies appear to have target debt levels. These targets are a function of company size, bankruptcy risk and asset composition.

Merton, R.C. (2005) 'You have more caital than you think', *Harvard Business Review*, November, pp. 1–10.
Argues that modern large firms can use derivatives to lower risk thus allowing a reduction in equity capital.

Miller, M.H. (1977) 'Debt and taxes', *Journal of Finance*, 32, May, pp. 261–75.
A further contribution to the theoretical debate – technical and US focused.

Miller, M.H. (1988) 'The Modigliani–Miller propositions after thirty years', *Journal of Economic Perspectives* (Fall). Also reproduced in Chew, D.H. (ed.) (2001) *The New Corporate Finance*. New York: McGraw-Hill. 3rd edn.
Miller muses on the original propositions and the debate over 30 years. He acknowledges the departure of real-world practice from the artificial world constructed for the models.

Miller, M.H. (1991) 'Leverage', *Journal of Finance*, 46, pp. 479–88.
An interesting article by a leader in the field.

Modigliani, F. and Miller, M.H. (1958) 'The cost of capital, corporation finance and the theory of investment', *American Economic Review*, 48, June, pp. 261–97.
The classic original economic modelling approach to this subject.

Modigliani, F. and Miller, M.H. (1963) 'Corporate income taxes and the cost of capital: A correction', *American Economic Review*, 53, June, pp. 433–43.
A technical account of the important correction to the 1958 article – allows for taxes.

Modigliani, F. and Miller, M.H. (1969) 'Reply to Heins and Sprenkle', *American Economic Review*, 59, September, pp. 592–5.
More on the economic model approach.

Myers, S.C. (1974) 'Interaction of corporate financing and investment decisions – implications for capital budgeting', *Journal of Finance*, 29 (March), pp. 1–25.
The adjusted present value method is developed in this article.

Myers, S.C. (1984) 'The capital structure puzzle', *Journal of Finance*, 39, July, pp. 575–82.
Easy-to-read consideration of capital structure theory – particularly of pecking order theory.

Myers, S. and Majluf, N. (1984). 'Corporate financing and investment decisions when firms have information investors do not have', *Journal of Financial Economics*, June, pp. 187–221.
Pecking order theory is advanced as an explanation for capital structure in practice.

Passov, R. (2003) 'How much cash does your company need?' *Harvard Business Review*, November, pp. 1–8.
Knowledge-based companies need low debt or net cash to allow ongoing investment without resort to the financial market where finance can be exorbitantly expensive or simply unavailable.

Ross, S. (1977) 'The determination of financial structure: The incentive-signalling approach', *Bell Journal of Economics*, 8, pp. 23–40.
The signalling hypothesis of debt increases is advanced.

Ross, S.A., Westerfield, R.W. and Jaffe, J. (2002) *Corporate Finance*. 6th edn. New York: McGraw-Hill.
More on the theoretical elements than in this chapter.

Shyam-Sunder, L. and Myers, S.C. (1999) 'Testing static trade off against pecking order models of capital structure', *Journal of Financial Economics*, 51, pp. 219–44.
Supporting evidence for the pecking order model.

Solomon, E. (1963) *The Theory of Financial Management*. New York: Columbia University Press.
An early discussion of the WACC.

Stern, J. (1998) 'The capital structure puzzle', *Journal of Applied Corporate Finance*, II(I), Spring, pp. 8–23.
A round-table discussion between Joel Stern, Stewart Myers and other capital structure specialists. It focuses particularly on managerial performance and incentives. There is also a discussion of financial slack by the Treasurer of Sears – very interesting.

Stewart, G.B. (1990) *The Quest for Value.* New York: Harper Business.
Chapter 13 is written in praise of capital structures with high debt levels.

Tirole J. (2006) *The Theory of Corporate Finance.* Princeton, NJ: Princeton University Press.
An algebraic/theoretical approach to the borrowing question.

Watson, R. and Wilson, N. (2002) 'Small and medium size enterprise financing: A note of some empirical implications of a pecking order', *Journal of Business Finance and Accounting*, 29(3) and (4) April/May, pp. 557–78.
A testing of the pecking order model in UK shares. Evidence found in support.

Welch, I. (2004) 'Capital structure and stock returns', *Journal of Political Economy*, 112(1), pp. 106–31.
A major influence on the gearing level is fluctuations in the equity market capitalisation raising or lowering the equity figure in the debt/equity ratio. Firms are slow to raise or pay off finance to counteract market capitalisation fluctuations. This is an 'inertia' explanation of capital structure.

Video presentations

Chief executives and finance directors describe their current policy on capital structure on Cantos.com (www.cantos.com/cantos) – this is free to view.

Case study recommendations

Please see www.pearsoned.co.uk/arnold for case study synopses

- Bed Bath and Beyond: the capital structure decision. Authors: Philip Gresh, Shannon Hennessy, Arthur Raviv and Timothy Thompson (2005). Kellogg School of Management. Also available from Harvard Business School case studies website.

Self-review questions

1 What was the traditional (pre-MM) view on optimal gearing levels?

2 Explain how debt finance is 'cheaper and riskier' for the firm.

3 Explain the terms operating gearing, financial gearing, capital gearing, income gearing.

4 What are business risk and financial risk?

5 Modigliani and Miller's original model resulted in three propositions. Describe them. Also, what are the major assumptions on which the model was built?

6 Describe how MM analysis changes if taxes are allowed into the model.

7 What is financial distress and how does it affect the gearing decision?

8 What are agency costs and how do they affect the gearing decision?

9 Describe the following ideas which are advanced to explain the low levels of gearing in some companies:

a Borrowing capacity.
b Managerial preferences.
c Pecking order.
d Financial slack.
e Control.

10 Some writers advocate the increased use of debt because of its beneficial effect on (**a**) managerial motivation, (**b**) reinvestment risk and (**c**) operating and strategic efficiency. Explain these ideas.

Questions and problems

myfinancelab ***Questions with an icon are also available for practice in MyFinanceLab with additional supporting resources.***

The answers to questions marked with an asterisk are in the Lecturers Guide.

1* Calculate and comment upon some gearing ratios for Vodafone plc.

Extracts from Vodafone Group plc Balance sheet and profit and loss account, 2007

	£m	£m
Non current assets		96,804
Current assets:		
Inventory	288	
Trade and other receivables	5,023	
Taxation recoverable	21	
Cash and cash equivalents	7,481	
		12,813
Current liabilities		(18,946)
of which:		
Short term borrowings	4,817	
Long term borrowings		(17,798)
Other Non-current liabilities		(5,580)
Net assets		67,293
Profit before interest and taxation (ignoring goodwill impairment)		9,200
Interest payable		(1,612)
Market capitalisation		93,300

Note: Assume net assets equal shareholder funds.

?

2 (*Examination level*) Eastwell plc is to be established shortly. The founders are considering their options with regard to capital structure. A total of £1m will be needed to establish the business and the three ways of raising these funds being considered are:

a Selling 500,000 shares at £2.00.
b Selling 300,000 shares at £2.00 and borrowing £400,000 with an interest rate of 12 per cent.
c Selling 100,000 shares at £2.00 and borrowing £800,000 at an interest rate of 13 per cent.

There are three possible outcomes for the future annual cash flows before interest:

Success of product	Cash flow before interest	Probability
Poor	£60,000	0.25
Good	£160,000	0.50
Excellent	£300,000	0.25

Note: Taxes may be ignored.

Required

a Calculate the expected annual return to shareholders under each of the capital structures.
b Calculate the standard deviation of the expected annual return under each of the capital structures.
c Calculate business risk and the additional risk due to financial risk and explain what these terms mean.
d Some writers have advocated the high use of debt because of the positive effect on managerial actions. Describe these ideas and consider some counter-arguments. ?

3 a (*Examination level*) Hose plc presently has a capital structure which is 30 per cent debt and 70 per cent equity. The cost of debt (i.e. borrowings) before tax shield benefits is 9 per cent and that for equity is 15 per cent. The firm's future cash flows, after tax but before interest, are expected to be a perpetuity of £750,000. The tax rate is 30 per cent.

Calculate the WACC and the value of the firm.

b The directors are considering the partial replacement of equity finance with borrowings so that the borrowings make up 60 per cent of the total capital. Director A believes that the cost of equity capital will remain constant at 15 per cent; Director B believes that shareholders will demand a rate of return of 23.7 per cent; Director C believes that shareholders will demand a rate of return of 17 per cent and Director D believes the equity rate of return will shift to 28 per cent. Assuming that the cost of borrowings before income taxes remains at 9 per cent, what will the WACC and the value of the firm be under each of the directors' estimates?

c Relate the results in question 3b to the capital structure debate. In particular draw on Modigliani and Miller's theory, financial distress and agency theory. ?

4 (*Examination level*) 'It is in management's interest to keep the financial gearing level as low as possible, while it is in shareholders' interests to keep it at a high level.' Discuss this statement.

5 (*Examination level*) In 1984 Stewart Myers wrote, 'our theories do not seem to explain actual financing behaviour', when referring to the capital structure debate. In what ways do the main MM economic models of gearing fail? Discuss some alternative explanations for the actual gearing levels of companies.

6 a (*Examination level*) Hickling plc has estimated the cost of debt and equity for various financial gearing levels:

Proportion of debt $\frac{V_D}{(V_D + V_E)}$	Required rate of return Debt, k_{DAT} %	Equity, k_E %
0.80	9.0	35.0
0.70	7.5	28.0
0.60	6.8	21.0
0.50	6.4	17.0
0.40	6.1	14.5
0.30	6.0	13.5
0.20	6.0	13.2
0.10	6.0	13.1
0.00	–	13.0

What is the optimal capital structure?

b Describe and explain the factors which might lead to a rise in the overall cost of capital for Hickling.

?

7 (*Examination level*) The managing director of your firm is thinking aloud about an appropriate gearing level for the company:

> 'The consultants I spoke to yesterday explained that some academic theorists advance the idea that, if your objective is the maximisation of shareholder wealth, the debt to equity ratio does not matter. However, they did comment that this conclusion held in a world of no taxes. Even more strangely, these theorists say that in a world with tax it is best to "gear-up" a company as high as possible. Now I may not know much about academic theories but I do know that there are limits to the debt level which is desirable. After listening to these consultants I am more confused than ever.'

You step forward and offer to write a report for the managing director both outlining the theoretical arguments and explaining the real-world influences on the gearing levels of firms.

8 (*Examination level*) Within a given industry, wide variations in the degree of financial gearing of firms are observed. What might explain this?

9 Given the following facts about Company X, what would the equity cost of capital be if it was transformed from its current gearing to having no debt, if Modigliani and Miller's model with no tax applied?

$$k_E = 30\%$$

$$k_D = 9\%$$

$$\frac{V_D}{(V_D + V_E)} = 0.6$$

?

myfinancelab **Now retake your diagnostic test for Chapter 21 to check your progress and update your study plan.**

Assignments

1 Obtain accounting and other information on a company of interest to you and calculate gearing ratios. Point out in a report the difficulties involved in this process.

2 Analyse a company you know well in the light of the various ideas, theories and models regarding capital structure. Write up your findings in a report, and include implications and recommendations for action.

CHAPTER 22

Dividend policy

LEARNING OUTCOMES

This area of finance has no neat over-arching theoretical model to provide a simple answer. However, there are some important arguments which should inform the debate within firms. By the end of this chapter the reader should be able to:

- explain the rationale and conclusion of the ideas of Miller and Modigliani's dividend irrelevancy hypothesis, as well as the concept of dividends as a residual;
- describe the influence of particular dividend policies attracting different 'clients' as shareholders, the effect of taxation and the importance of dividends as a signalling device;
- outline the hypothesis that dividends received now, or in the near future, have much more value than those in the far future because of the resolution of uncertainty and the exceptionally high discount rate applied to more distant dividends;
- discuss the impact of agency theory on the dividend decision;
- discuss the role of scrip dividends and share repurchase (buy-back).

myfinancelab *Complete your diagnostic test for Chapter 22 now to create your personal study plan*

'Dividend policy is often reported to shareholders, but seldom explained. A company will say something like, "Our goal is to pay out 40% to 50% of earnings and to increase dividends at a rate at least equal to the rise in the CPI."[1] And that's it – no analysis will be supplied as to why that particular policy is best for the owners of the business. Yet, allocation of capital is crucial to business and investment management. Because it is, we believe managers and owners should think hard about the circumstances under which earnings should be retained and under which they should be distributed.'

Source: Warren Buffett, a letter to shareholders attached to the *Annual Report of Berkshire Hathaway Inc* (1984). Reprinted with kind permission of Warren Buffett. © Warren Buffett.

Introduction

No one has more right to speak on dividend policy than Warren Buffett, who has become a multi-billionaire by putting his money where his mouth is and backing managers who agree with, and implement, his approach to management. After sixty years of observing managers his comments may be viewed as a sad indictment of the quality of managerial thought. On the central issue of whether to retain profits, or distribute them to shareholders to use elsewhere, there appears to be vagueness and confusion. He has suggested that the issue is addressed at a superficial level with the employment of simple rules of thumb and no analysis. This conclusion may or may not be unfair – this chapter is not designed to highlight managerial failings in the depth of thought department. What it can do, however, is point out the major influences on the level of the dividend decision in any one year. Some of these are fully 'rational' in the sense of the economist's model, others are less quantifiable, and stem more from the field of psychology.

The conclusion reached is that managers have to weigh up a range of forces – some pulling them in the direction of paying out either a high proportion of earnings or a low one; other forces pulling them to provide a stable and consistent dividend, and yet others pulling them to vary the dividend from year to year.

These are, of course, merely the range of forces influencing managers who are fully committed to shareholder wealth maximisation and thinking 'hard about the circumstances under which earnings should be retained'. If we admit the possibility that managers have other goals, or that they make little intellectual effort, the possible outcomes of the annual or semi-annual boardroom discussion on the dividend level can range widely.

Defining the problem

Dividend policy is the determination of the proportion of profits paid out to shareholders – usually periodically. The issue to be addressed is whether shareholder wealth can be enhanced by altering the *pattern* of dividends not the *size* of dividends overall. Naturally, if dividends over the lifetime of a firm are larger, value will be greater. So in the forthcoming analysis we will assume that:

a the underlying investment opportunities and returns on business investment are constant; and

b the extra value that may be created by changing the capital structure (the debt to equity ratio) is constant.

Therefore only the pattern of dividend payments may add or subtract value. For example, perhaps a pattern of high payouts in the immediate future, with a consequential reduction in dividend growth thereafter, may be superior to a policy of zero or small dividends now followed by more rapid growth over time.

Another aspect of the pattern question is whether a steady, stable dividend growth rate is better than a volatile one which varies from year to year depending on the firm's internal need for funds.

[1] The CPI, consumer price index, is the main US measure of inflation.

Some background

UK-quoted companies usually pay dividends every six months. In each financial year there is an ***interim* dividend** related to the first half-year's trading, followed by the ***final* dividend** after the financial year-end. The board of directors are empowered to recommend the final dividend level but it is a right of shareholders as a body to vote at the annual general meeting whether or not it should be paid. Not all companies follow the typical cycle of two dividends per year: a few pay dividends quarterly and others choose not to pay a dividend at all.

Dividends may only be paid out of **accumulated distributable profits** and not out of capital. This means that companies which have loss-making years may still pay dividends, but only up to the point that they have retained profits from previous years. This rule is designed to provide some protection to creditors by putting a barrier in the way of shareholders looking to remove funds from the firm, and thereby withdrawing the cushion of capital originally provided by shareholders. Further restrictions may be placed on the firm's freedom of action with regard to dividend levels by constraints contained in bond, preference share and bank-loan agreements.

The proportion of after-tax earnings paid as dividends varies greatly between firms, from zero to more than 100 per cent. The average for companies listed on the London Stock Exchange is usually around 40–50 per cent. However, in 2004 the payout ratio rose to about 70 per cent – *see* **Exhibit 22.1**.

Exhibit 22.1

Dividend payouts surge to new record

FT

by Henry Tricks

Dividend payments by listed UK companies surged 16 per cent last year to a record £52.3bn.

Morgan Stanley estimates the payout ratio has risen to about 70 per cent, its highest level since 1993.

Source: *Financial Times*, 2 April 2005, p. 1. Reprinted with permission.

Miller and Modigliani's dividend irrelevancy proposition

According to an important 1961 paper by Miller and Modigliani (MM), if a few assumptions can be made, dividend policy is irrelevant to share value. The determinant of value is the availability of projects with positive NPVs; and the pattern of dividends makes no difference to the acceptance of these. The share price would not move if the firm declared either a zero dividend policy or a policy of high near-term dividends. The conditions under which this was held to be true included:

1 There are no taxes.
2 There are no transaction costs; for example:
 a investors face no brokerage costs when buying or selling shares;
 b companies can issue shares with no transaction costs.
3 All investors can borrow and lend at the same interest rate.
4 All investors have free access to all relevant information.
5 Investors are indifferent between dividends and capital gains.

Given these assumptions, dividend policy can become irrelevant. For example, a firm which has plenty of positive NPV projects but nevertheless paid all profits each year as dividends would not necessarily be destroying shareholder wealth because in this ideal world any money paid out could quickly be replaced by having a new issue of shares.[2] The investors in these shares would willingly

[2] The complicating effect of capital structure on firms' value is usually eliminated by concentrating on all-equity firms.

pay a fair price because of their access to all relevant information. The shares can be issued by the firm without costs of underwriting or investment banks' fees, etc., and bought by the shareholders without brokers' fees or costs associated with the time spent filling in forms, etc. That is, there are no transaction costs.

If a company chose not to pay any dividends at all and shareholders required an income then this could be achieved while leaving the firm's value intact. '**Homemade dividends**' can be created by shareholders selling a portion of their shares to other investors – again, as there are no costs of transactions and no taxation the effect is identical to the receipt of cash in the form of an ordinary dividend from the firm.

Take the example of Belvoir plc, an all-equity company which has a policy of paying out all annual net cash flow as dividend. The company is expected to generate a net annual cash flow of £1m to an infinite horizon. Given the cost of equity capital is 12 per cent we can calculate the value of this firm using the dividend valuation model (with zero growth – *see* Chapter 20 for details).

$$P_0 = d_0 + \frac{d_1}{k_E} = £1\text{m} + \frac{£1\text{m}}{0.12} = £9.333\text{m}$$

This includes £1m of dividend due to be paid immediately, plus the £1m perpetuity.

Now suppose that the management have identified a new investment opportunity. This will produce additional cash flows of £180,000 per year starting in one year. However, the company will be required to invest £1m now. There are two ways in which this money for investment could be found. First, the managers could skip the present dividend and retain £1m. Second, the company could maintain its dividend policy for this year and pay out £1m, but simultaneously launch a new issue of shares, say a rights issue, to gain the necessary £1m.

It will now be demonstrated that in this perfect world, with no transaction costs, shareholder value will be the same whichever dividend policy is adopted.

What *will* increase shareholder value is the NPV of the project.

$$\text{NPV} = -£1\text{m} + \frac{£180{,}000}{0.12} = £500{,}000$$

The value of the firm is raised by £500,000, by the acceptance of the project and not because of the dividend policy. If the project is financed through the sacrifice of the present dividend the effect on shareholder wealth is:

Year	*0*	*1*	*2*	*3, etc.*
Cash flow to shareholders	0	1,180,000	1,180,000	1,180,000

$$\text{Shareholders' wealth} = \frac{1{,}180{,}000}{0.12} = £9.833\text{m}$$

Thus shareholders' wealth is increased by £500,000.

If the project is financed through a rights issue while leaving the dividend pattern intact the effect on shareholder wealth is the same – an increase of £500,000.

Year	*0*	*1*	*2*	*3, etc.*
Cash flow to shareholders				
Receipt of dividend	+ £1,000,000			
Rights issue	– £1,000,000			
	0	1,180,000	1,180,000	1,180,000

$$\text{Shareholders' wealth} = \frac{1,180,000}{0.12} = £9.833\text{m}$$

Shareholders' wealth is enhanced because £1m of shareholders' money is invested in a project which yields more than 12 per cent. If the incremental cash inflows amounted to only £100,000 then the wealth of shareholders would fall, because a 10 per cent return is insufficient given the opportunity cost of shareholders' money:

$$\frac{£1,100,000}{0.12} = £9.167\text{m}$$

If the new investment produces a 12 per cent return shareholders will experience no loss or gain in wealth. The critical point is that in this hypothetical, perfect world the pattern of dividend makes no difference to shareholders' wealth. This is determined purely by the investment returns. If a firm chose to miss a dividend for a year, because it had numerous high-yielding projects to invest in, this would not decrease share values, because the perfectly well-informed investors are aware that any cash retained will be going into positive NPV projects which will generate future dividend increases for shareholders. If a shareholder needs income this year he/she can sell a proportion of shares held to create a 'homemade dividend' confident in the knowledge that a fair price would be obtained in this perfect world, which takes into account the additional value from the project.

Dividends as a residual

Now we take another extreme position. Imagine that the raising of external finance (for example rights issues) is so expensive that to all intents and purposes it is impossible. The only source of finance for additional investment is earnings. Returning to the example of Belvoir, it is obvious that under these circumstances, to pay this year's dividend will reduce potential shareholder value by £500,000 because the new project will have to be abandoned.

In this world dividends should only be paid when the firm has financed all its positive NPV projects. Once the firm has provided funds for all the projects which more than cover the minimum required return, investors should be given the residual. They should receive this cash because they can use it to invest in other firms of the same risk class which provide an expected return at least as great as the required return on equity capital, k_E. If the firm kept all the cash flows and continued adding to its range of projects the marginal returns would be likely to decrease, because the project with the highest return would be undertaken first, followed by the one with the next highest return, and so on, until returns became very low.

In these circumstances dividend policy becomes an important determinant of shareholder wealth:

1 If cash flow is retained and invested within the firm at less than k_E, shareholder wealth is destroyed; therefore it is better to raise the dividend payout rate.

2 If retained earnings are insufficient to fund all positive NPV projects shareholder value is lost, and it would be beneficial to lower the dividend.

What about the world in which we live?

We have discussed two extreme positions so far and have reached opposing conclusions. In a perfect world the dividend pattern is irrelevant because the firm can always fund itself costlessly if it has positive NPV projects, and shareholders can costlessly generate 'homemade dividends' by selling some of their shares. In a world with no external finance the pattern of dividends becomes crucial to shareholder wealth, as an excessive payout reduces the take-up of positive NPV projects; and an unduly low payout means value destruction because investors miss out on investment opportunities elsewhere in the financial securities market.

In our world there are transaction costs to contend with. If a firm pays a dividend in order to keep to its avowed dividend pattern and then, in order to fund projects, takes money from shareholders through a rights issue, this is not frictionless: there are costs. The expense for the firm includes the legal and administrative cost of organising a rights issue or some other issue of shares; it may be necessary to prepare a prospectus and to incur advertising costs; underwriting fees alone can be as much as 2 per cent of the amount raised. The expense for the shareholder of receiving money with one hand only to give it back with the other might include brokerage costs and the time and hassle involved. Taxes further complicate the issue by imposing additional costs.

It is plain that there is a powerful reason why dividend policy might make some difference to shareholder wealth: the investment opportunities within the firm obviously have some effect. This may help to explain why we witness many young rapidly growing firms with a need for investment finance having a very low dividend (or zero) payouts, whereas mature 'cash cow' type firms choose a high payout rate.

The relationship between investment opportunity and dividend policy is a far from perfect one and there are a number of other forces pulling on management to select a particular policy. These will be considered after some more down-to-earth arguments from Warren Buffett (*see* **Exhibit 22.2**).

Exhibit 22.2 Buffett on dividends

Berkshire Hathaway Inc

'Earnings should be retained only when there is a reasonable prospect – backed preferably by historical evidence or, when appropriate by a thoughtful analysis of the future – *that for every dollar retained by the corporation, at least one dollar of market value will be created for owners* [italics in original]. This will happen only if the capital retained produces incremental earnings equal to, or above, those generally available to investors.'

Warren Buffett says that many managers think like owners when it comes to demanding high returns from subordinates but fail to apply the same principles to the dividend payout decision:

'The CEO of multi-divisional company will instruct Subsidiary A, whose earnings on incremental capital may be expected to average 5%, to distribute all available earnings in order that they may be invested in Subsidiary B, whose earnings on incremental capital are expected to be 15%. The CEO's business school oath will allow no lesser behaviour. But if his own long-term record with incremental capital is 5% – and market rates are 10% – he is likely to impose a dividend policy on shareholders of the parent company that merely follows some historic or industry-wide payout pattern. Furthermore, he will expect managers of subsidiaries to give him a full account as to why it makes sense for earnings to be retained in their operations rather than distributed to the parent-owner. But seldom will he supply *his* owners with a similar analysis pertaining to the whole company . . . shareholders would be far better off if earnings were retained only to expand the high-return business, with the balance paid in dividends or used to repurchase stock.'

Source: Warren Buffett, A letter to shareholders attached to the *Annual Report of Berkshire Hathaway Inc* (1984). Reprinted with kind permission of Warren Buffett. © Warren Buffett.

HMV (*see* **Exhibit 22.3**) is handing cash back to shareholders when it has cash surplus to requirements as that is 'the responsible thing to do'. Arc, on the other hand, has been criticised for holding on to cash that it cannot use for value-creating investments (*see* **Exhibit 22.4**)

Clientele effects

Some shareholders prefer a dividend pattern which matches their desired consumption pattern. There may be **natural clienteles** for shares which pay out a high proportion of earnings, and another clientele for shares which have a low payout rate. For example, retired people, living off their private investments, may prefer a high and steady income, so they would tend to be attracted to firms with a high and stable dividend yield. Likewise, pension funds need regular cash receipts to meet payments to pensioners.

Shareholders who need a steady flow of income could, of course, generate a cash flow stream by selling off a proportion of their shares on a regular basis as an alternative to investing in firms with a high payout ratio. But this approach will result in transaction costs (brokerage, market makers' spread and loss of interest while waiting for cash after sale). Also it is time consuming and inconvenient regularly to sell off blocks of shares; it is much easier to receive a series of dividend cheques.

Exhibit 22.3

Double boost for HMV shareholders

FT

by Sophy Buckley

HMV, the music, book and film retailer, is increasing the return to its shareholders with a 31 per cent jump in its interim dividend and a 12-month share buy-back programme that could be worth about £50m.

The group, which includes the Waterstone's book chain, said the moves reflected its confidence despite showing a degree of caution about slowing sales growth.

The shares dipped $3^1/_2$p to 251p as analysts shaved their profits forecasts.

Alan Giles, chief executive, said: 'We are very comfortable with the level of gearing in the business – if you talk to analysts most think we will be debt free by the end of this financial year.

'We can very comfortably fund £60m–£65m on our ongoing organic expansion and still have £50m plus left over. Obviously the responsible thing to do with that is to return it to shareholders.'

Source: Financial Times, 19 January 2005, p. 24. Reprinted with permission.

Exhibit 22.4

Arc agrees to hand back £50m

FT

by Astrid Wendlandt

Arc International has agreed to hand back £50m excess cash after arm-twisting by some of its largest shareholders.

The lossmaking chip designer yesterday announced plans to return to investors 17p a share in the first half of next year.

The move came after at least one institutional shareholder threatened to call an extraordinary meeting to remove management if their demands for a return of the cash were not heeded.

Mike Gulett, Arc chief executive, said: 'We decided that we had more cash than we needed and decided to give some of it back to increase shareholder value.'

However, some shareholders had been hoping to see Arc, which has £100m of cash, return at least £75m, or 25p a share. Yesterday, the shares closed up $^3/_4$p at 21p.

One of the company's largest shareholders said: 'It's been a battle to get 17p but they have not gone far enough. The board does not understand that shareholders would rather have the cash in their hands than sitting on the company's balance sheet.' . . .

Source: Financial Times, 23/24 November 2002, p. 13.

Furthermore, people often acknowledge self-control problems and so make rules for themselves, such as 'we will live off the income but never touch the capital' (Shefrin and Statman, 1984). They are afraid of starting down a slippery slope of selling off a proportion of shares each year in case they are tempted to over-indulge. Thus shares with high dividends are attractive because they give income without the need to dig into capital.

Another type of clientele is people who are not interested in receiving high dividends in the near term. These people prefer to invest in companies with good growth potential – companies which pay low dividends and use the retained money to invest in projects with positive NPVs within the firm. The idea behind such practices is that capital gains (a rising share price) will be the main way in which the shareholder receives a return. An example of such a clientele group might be wealthy middle-aged people who have more than enough income from their paid employment for their consumption needs. If these people did receive large amounts of cash in dividends now they would probably only reinvest it in the stock market. A cycle of receiving dividends followed by reinvestment is inefficient.

Thus, it seems reasonable to argue that a proportion of shareholders choose to purchase particular shares at least partially because the dividend policy suits them. This may place pressure on the management to produce a stable and consistent dividend policy because investors need to know that a particular investment is going to continue to suit their preferences. Inconsistency would result in a lack of popularity with any client group and would depress the share price. Management therefore, to some extent, target a particular clientele.[3]

The clientele force acting on dividend policy at first glance seems to be the opposite of the residual approach. With the clientele argument, stability and consistency are required to attract a particular type of clientele, whereas with the residual argument, dividends depend on the opportunities for reinvestment – the volume of which may vary in a random fashion from year to year, resulting in fluctuating retentions and dividends. Most firms seem to 'square this circle' by having a consistent dividend policy based on a medium- or long-term view of earnings and investment capital needs. The shortfalls and surpluses in particular years are adjusted through other sources of finance: for example, borrowing or raising equity through a rights issue in years when retained earnings are insufficient; paying off debt or storing up cash when retentions are greater than investment needs. There are costs associated with such a policy, for example the costs of rights issues, and these have to be weighed against the benefit of stability.

The clientele effect is often reinforced by the next factor we will examine, taxation. The consistent dividend pattern is encouraged by the information aspect of dividends – discussed after that.

Taxation

The taxation of dividends and capital gains on shares is likely to influence the preference of shareholders for receiving cash either in the form of a regular payment from the company (a dividend) or by selling shares (in the market to create homemade dividends or in a share buy-back – see later in the chapter). If shareholders are taxed more heavily on dividends than on capital gains they are more likely to favour shares which pay lower dividends. In the past, UK and US dividends were taxed at a significantly higher rate than that which applied to the capital gains made on the sale of shares for those shareholders subject to these taxes. However, in recent years, the difference has been narrowed significantly. In the UK capital gains are now taxed at 18 per cent. Capital gains have other tax advantages. Investors are allowed to make annual capital gains of £9,200 (in 2007–8) tax free. Furthermore, they only pay tax on realised gains (when the shares are sold). Therefore they can delay payment by continuing to hold the shares until they can, say, take advantage of a future year's capital allowance of £9,200.[4]

Elton and Gruber (1970) found evidence that there was a statistical relationship between the dividend policy of firms and the tax bracket of their shareholders – shareholders with higher income tax rates were associated with low-dividend shares and those with lower income tax rates with high-dividend shares.

Gordon Brown, then Chancellor, changed the tax system explicitly to encourage lower dividends and raise investment by firms. He said:

> The present system of tax credits encourages companies to pay out dividends rather than reinvest their profits. This cannot be the best way of encouraging investment for the long term. Many pension funds are in substantial surplus and at present many companies are enjoying pension holidays, so this is the right time to undertake long-needed reform. So, with immediate effect, I propose to abolish tax credits paid to pension funds and companies.[5]

Dividends as conveyors of information

Dividends appear to act as important **conveyors of information** about companies. An unexpected change in the dividend is regarded as a sign of how the directors view the future prospects of the firm. An unusually large increase in the dividend is often taken to indicate an optimistic view about future profitability. A declining dividend often signals that the directors view the future with some pessimism.

---

[3] The following researchers present evidence on the clientele effect: Elton and Gruber (1970), Pettit (1977), Lewellen, Stanley, Lease and Schlarbaum (1978), Litzenberger and Ramaswamy (1982), Shefrin and Statman (1984), Crossland, Dempsey and Moizer (1991), Graham and Kumar (2006) and Dhanani (2005).

[4] On the other hand, basic rate taxpayers only pay 10 per cent tax on dividends (higher rate taxpayers are charged 32.5 per cent).

[5] Gordon Brown, Chancellor of the Exchequer, Budget Speech, 2 July 1997.

The importance of the dividend as an information-transferring device occurs because of a significant market imperfection – **information asymmetry**. That is, managers know far more about the firm's prospects than do the finance providers. Investors are continually trying to piece together scraps of information about a firm. Dividends are one source that the investor can draw upon. They are used as an indicator of a firm's sustainable level of income. It would seem that managers choose a target dividend payout ratio based on a long-term earnings trend.[6] It is risky for managers' career prospects for them to increase the dividend above the regular growth pattern if they are not expecting improved business prospects. This sends a false signal and eventually they will be found out when the income growth does not take place.

It is the increase or decrease over the *expected* level of dividends that leads to a rise or fall in share price. This phenomenon is illustrated almost daily in the *Financial Times* as companies report falling profits but the market reacts by raising the share price because the company also signals confidence by raising the dividend by an unexpectedly large amount. **Exhibit 22.5** contains the comments of a respected investor. He certainly looks to dividends for signals.

Exhibit 22.5

Dividends can be the best reward

FT

John Lee

I have been a consistent fan of dividends for all my investing life and never deserted them as others did during the absurd years of internet madness.

When I learn of a company's results in my 8.15am daily broker's call, the first question I ask is about the dividend; for me the dividend decision usually says it all – it is a reflection of the results for the past year, the directors' view of the coming year and, very importantly, the financial strength/liquidity of the business.

Most boards recognise the importance of endeavouring to maintain if not increase dividends annually – providing more certainty for investors. Only the short-sighted cut their dividend unless they really have to.

A dividend yield also provides a prop to a share price and gives an annual return to investors when perhaps capital growth is hard to come by. Sometimes when talking to a chairman or chief executive after a poor trading statement, encourage them to maintain their dividend – often they express surprise that I need to question this as they have every intention of doing so.

Source: Financial Times, 2/3 December 2006, FT Money, p. 10. Reprinted with permission from J. Lee.

Generally company earnings fluctuate to a far greater extent than dividends. This smoothing of the dividend flow is illustrated in **Exhibit 22.6** where Cadbury Schweppes has shown a rise and a fall in earnings per share but a steadily rising dividend.

A reduction in earnings is usually not followed by a reduction in dividends, unless the earnings fall is perceived as likely to persist for a long time. Researchers, ever since Lintner's (1956) survey on managers' attitudes to dividend policy in the 1950s, have shown that directors are aware that the market reacts badly to dividend downturns and they make strenuous efforts to avoid a decline. By continuing the income stream to shareholders the management signal that a decline in earnings is temporary.

When times are good and profits are bounding ahead directors tend to be cautious about large dividend rises. To double or treble dividends in good years increases the risk of having to reduce dividends should the profit growth tail off and losing the virtue of predictability and stability cherished by shareholders.

---

6 Lintner (1956) observed this. It was also recorded in a 3i (1993) survey, in which 93 per cent of finance directors agreed with the statement that 'dividend policy should follow a long-term trend in earnings'. Baker, Powell and Veit (2002) found that more than 90 per cent of Nasdaq company managers surveyed agreed that a firm should avoid increasing its regular dividend if it expected to reverse the decision in a year or so and the firm should strive to maintain an uninterrupted record of dividend payments. Brav *et al.* (2005) say that 'managers express a strong desire to avoid dividend cuts'.

Exhibit 22.6 Cadbury Schweppes' earnings and dividends, thirteen-year record (pence per share)

Year	Earnings	Dividends
1994	16.1	7.5
1995	16.2	8.0
1996	16.9	8.5
1997	34.0	9.0
1998	17.1	9.5
1999	32.0	10.0
2000	24.8	10.5
2001	27.0	11.0
2002	27.4	11.5
2003	18.2	12.0
2004	23.3	12.5
2005	33.9	13.0
2006	31.6	14.0

Source: Cadbury Schweppes, *Report and Acccounts* 2003, 2006. Reprinted with permission.

Signals are funny things. A number of the large US technology companies started paying dividends for the first time in the years 2000–4. In many cases the share price fell. The reason: investors took the dividends as a signal that the companies had run out of growth opportunities.

Resolution of uncertainty

Myron Gordon (1963) argued that investors perceive that a company, by retaining and reinvesting a part of its current cash flow, is replacing a certain dividend flow to shareholders now with an uncertain more distant flow in the future. Because the returns from any reinvested funds will occur in the far future they are therefore subject to more risk and investors apply a higher discount rate than they would to near-term dividends. Thus the market places a greater value on shares offering higher near-term dividends. Investors are showing a preference for the early **resolution of uncertainty**. Under this model investors use a set of discount rates which rise through time to calculate share values; therefore the dividend valuation model becomes:

$$P_0 = \frac{d_1}{1 + k_{E1}} + \frac{d_2}{(1 + k_{E2})^2} + \ldots + \frac{d_n}{(1 + k_{En})^n} + \ldots$$

where:

$$k_{E1} < k_{E2} < k_{E3} \ldots$$

The dividends received in Years 2, 3 or 4 are of lower risk than those received seven, eight or nine years hence.

The crucial factor here may not be actual differences in risk between the near and far future, but *perceived* risk. It may be that immediate dividends are valued more highly because the investors' perception of risk is not perfect. They overestimate the risk of distant dividends and thus undervalue them. However, whether the extra risk attached to more distant dividends is real or not, the effect is the same – investors prefer a higher dividend in the near term than they otherwise would and shareholder value can be raised by altering the dividend policy to suit this preference – or so the argument goes.

There have been some impressive counter-attacks on what is described as the '**bird-in-the-hand fallacy**'. The riskiness of a firm's dividend derives from the risk associated with the underlying business and this risk is already allowed for through the risk-adjusted discount rate, k_E. To discount future income even further would be excessive. Take a company expected to produce a dividend per share of £1 in two years and £2 in ten years. The discount rate of, say, 15 per cent ensures that the £2 dividend is worth, in present value terms, less than the dividend received in two years, and much of this discount rate is a compensation for risk.

$$\text{Present value of £1 dividend} = \frac{£1}{(1.15)^2} = 75.6\text{p}$$

$$\text{Present value of £2 dividend} = \frac{£2}{(1.15)^{10}} = 49.4\text{p}$$

Alternatively, take a company which pays out all its earnings in the hope of raising its share price because shareholders have supposedly had resolution of uncertainty. Now, what is the next move? We have a company in need of investment finance and shareholders wishing to invest in company shares – as most do with dividend income. The firm has a rights issue. In the prospectus the firm explains what will happen to the funds raised: they will be used to generate dividends in the future. Thus shareholders buy shares on the promise of future dividends; they discount these dividends at a risk-adjusted discount rate determined by the rate of return available on alternative, equally risky investments, say, 15 per cent (applicable to *all* the future years). To discount at a higher rate would be to undervalue the shares and pass up an opportunity of a good investment.

Owner control (agency theory)

Many people take the view that UK firms pay out an excessive proportion of their earnings as dividends. The argument then runs that this stifles investment because of the lower retention rate.

However, set alongside this concern should go the observation that many firms seem to have a policy of paying high dividends, and then, shortly afterwards, issuing new shares to raise cash for investment. This is a perplexing phenomenon. The cost of issuing shares can be burdensome and shareholders generally pay tax on the receipt of dividends. One possible answer is that it is the signalling (information) value of dividends that drives this policy. But the costs are so high that it cannot always be explained by this. A second potential explanation lies with agency cost.

Managers (the agents) may not always act in the best interests of the owners. One way for the owners to regain some control over the use of their money is to insist on relatively high payout ratios. Then, if managers need funds for investment they have to ask. A firm that wishes to raise external capital will have its plans for investment scrutinised by a number of experts, including:

- investment bankers who advise on the issue;
- underwriters who, like investment bankers, will wish to examine the firm and its plans as they are attaching their good names to the issue;
- analysts at credit-rating agencies;
- analysts at stockbroking houses who advise shareholders and potential shareholders;
- shareholders.

In ordinary circumstances the firm's investors can only influence managerial action by voting at a general meeting (which is usually ineffective due to apathy and the use of proxy votes by the board), or by selling their shares. When a company has to ask for fresh capital investors can tease out more information and can examine managerial action and proposed actions. They can exercise some control over their savings by refusing to buy the firm's securities if they are at all suspicious of managerial behaviour. Of particular concern might be the problem of investment in projects with negative NPV for the sake of building a larger managerial empire (Easterbrook, 1984; Jensen 1986).

A more generous view, from the field of behavioural finance, is that managers are merely over-optimistic and over-confident about their ability to invest the money wisely.

From the viewpoint of lenders there is also an agency problem. Managers may pay out excessive dividends to shareholders to keep the money out of the reach of the lenders – particularly in the case of a company likely to fail. Thus lenders' agreements often restrict dividend payments.

Exhibit 22.7 discusses an implicit bargain in which companies return to investors capital they do not need, on the understanding that it will be returned to the company when it is needed.

Exhibit 22.7

Lurid acquisitions lose their edge as the retro dividend makes a comeback

FT

Shareholders are pushing companies to return surplus cash instead of pursuing the vagaries of capital appreciation

writes Henry Tricks

There was a fashion statement buried deep in French Connection's interim results yesterday that had nothing to do with fcuk, and everything to do with the dowdy world of dividends.

In an era of bare midriffs, the UK corporate sector is revisiting a fashion that dates back to a time when City gents wore bowler hats and bow ties.

After a long spell in the cold, the dividend is making a comeback. Bankers say there is such pressure on companies to hand back cash to shareholders that some are forsaking the lurid world of acquisitions as a result.

Yesterday, French Connection, the fashion retailer, showed its commitment to the dividend with a 20 per cent half-year increase – double the rate of earnings growth – in spite of headwinds in the UK high streets. Redrow, the housebuilder, also raised its dividend 20 per cent, pledging to do the same for the next three years even if the housing market cooled.

Merrill Lynch, meanwhile, said yesterday that for the second month running its monthly survey of 290 global fund managers showed more preferred companies to return cash than increase capital spending or improve balance sheets.

This represented a significant change from 2002 and 2003, which is as far back as Merrill's survey goes.

'It's a story that's still gathering momentum,' said David Bowers, Merrill's chief global investment strategist. 'The economy isn't strong enough to justify increased capex, but it isn't really weak enough to persuade companies to rebuild their balance sheets.'

The watershed for dividend payments started across the Atlantic this summer when Microsoft risked its established rating as a growth company by agreeing to pay \$32bn (£17.8bn) in a special dividend this year, and \$44bn in buy-backs and an enhanced dividend over the next four years . . .

Michael Tory, head of UK investment banking at Morgan Stanley, said the UK was far ahead of its continental European counterparts in getting the message.

The backdrop, he said, was the period of balance sheet repair that went on after the dotcom collapse, which had put much of corporate Britain on a sounder fiscal footing. However, the uncertain economic outlook, together with a more disciplined and selective approach towards mergers and acquisitions, meant companies had more surplus cash. This combination had intensified investor pressure to return cash, he said.

'The implicit bargain is that companies that are well managed and return capital they don't immediately need will be supplied if they do change their minds and need the capital back,' Mr Tory said.

In boardrooms, the debate about what to do with cash on the balance sheet is often tense. Returning it to shareholders is not the virile growth sport executives are used to. Often, non-executive directors will have to fight the shareholders' corner.

It is also feared that returning too much cash to shareholders can carry risks, however. Companies should not liquidate their cash balances to please investors if that jeopardises their ability to compete on the global stage . . .

Source: Financial Times, 15 September 2004, p. 25.

Scrip dividends

A **scrip dividend** gives shareholders an opportunity to receive additional shares in proportion to their existing holding instead of the normal cash dividend. The shareholders can then either keep the shares or sell them for cash. From the company's point of view scrip dividends have the advantage that *cash does not leave the company*. This may be important for companies going through difficult trading periods or as a way of adjusting the gearing (debt to equity) ratio. Shareholders may welcome a scrip dividend because they can increase their holdings without brokerage costs and other dealing costs.

An enhanced scrip dividend is one where the shares offered are worth substantially more than the alternative cash payout. Such an offer is designed to encourage the take-up of shares and is like a mini-rights issue.

Share buy-backs and special dividends

An alternative way to return money, held within the company, to the owners is to repurchase issued shares. In 2004 Marks & Spencer paid out £2.3bn by buying back shares. This was to raise the level of borrowings on its balance sheet – *see* **Exhibit 22.8** for a discussion of this and alternative ways of handing cash to shareholders.

Exhibit 22.8

The dilemma of how best to share the wealth

FT

Maggie Urry

Amid the blizzard of announcements from Marks & Spencer this week was the apparently welcome news that it was 'giving' £2.3bn to shareholders, reported widely as being 'worth' £1 per share . . .

But before M&S shareholders start spending, they need to read the detail.

Rather than paying a special dividend to all shareholders, investors will be invited to tender shares they would like to sell back to M&S and can specify the price they want to sell at, within a range set by the company.

M&S will work out the lowest possible price at which it can spend the full £2.3bn, and then cancel the shares it buys in the process.

Shareholders can benefit in two ways: either by selling some or all of their shares in the tender, or because the value of the shares they continue to hold should rise afterwards since the M&S pie will then be divided into fewer, bigger, slices.

The retailer is the latest in an increasing number of companies seeking to return cash to investors, mostly through share buybacks.

Graham Secker, equity strategist at Morgan Stanley, says this trend reflects the current strength of company balance sheets and their free cashflow generation . . .

But do shareholders really benefit from buybacks? In theory, yes. Buying in and cancelling shares – at the right price – enhances earnings per share. If the market then applies the same price/earnings ratio to the shares, investors will see the value of their stake rise.

In practice, though, it is not at all certain that the amount of money the company puts into the market through a buyback is equal to the increase in value shareholders enjoy. That is the sort of question academics can debate for hours. At the least, the expected share price gain can take months or even longer to materialise, and can never be disentangled from other market moving factors.

Further, not all investors want to receive their returns in the form of a higher share price, which can be reaped only on the sale of shares.

Some, such as pension funds, like a capital gain since they do not pay gains tax. Others prefer their return in the form of income, and would, given the choice, plump for a special dividend.

There is likely to be conflict between the interests of different types of shareholders, which companies must try to resolve.

J Sainsbury, which is returning 35p a share to its investors after selling its US grocery chain, thinks it has come up with a scheme that offers its shareholders a choice. It was approved by investors this week.

Investors could opt to take the 35p as a dividend – to be taxed as income – or a capital gain. If they pick the capital gain, they can then choose to take the money now or defer some or all of the gain to later tax years to make use of their annual gains tax exemptions.

The supermarket group thinks that is the fairest way to give the £680m to shareholders, and worth paying the extra administration costs involved. Critics say that the one choice shareholders do not have is not to participate at all.

Meanwhile Centrica, the gas and telephone group, which has agreed the sale of its AA business for £1.75bn, plans to return £1.5bn of that money to shareholders. It has decided to pay a £1bn special dividend, and use £500m to buy shares in the market.

Centrica argues that its shareholders' preference is for immediate income. Hence the special dividend, which is also the cheapest route for the company. The buy-back element gives the company some flexibility.

Investors in Vodafone, the mobile phone group, are being rewarded by 20 per cent dividend increases and a rolling buyback programme planned to total £3bn this year.

As more companies face the dilemma of how to return cash to shareholders, the debate of the best way of doing it is likely to grow. There does not yet seem to be a perfect, one-size-fits-all, solution that makes all investors happy. But then, as M&S knows, shareholders come in as many shapes and sizes as its customers do.

Source: *Financial Times*, 17/18 July 2004, p. M21. Reprinted with permission.

Buy-backs may also be a useful alternative when the company is unsure about the sustainability of a possible increase in the normal cash dividend. A stable policy may be pursued on dividends, then, as and when surplus cash arises, shares are repurchased. This two-track approach avoids sending an over-optimistic signal about future growth through underlying dividend levels.

A second possible approach to returning funds without signalling that all future dividends will be raised abnormally is to pay a **special dividend**. This is the same as a normal dividend but usually bigger and paid on a one-off basis.

Share repurchases are permitted under UK law, subject to the requirement that the firm gain the permission of shareholders as well as warrant holders, option holders or convertible holders. The rules of the London Stock Exchange (and especially the Takeover Panel) must also be obeyed. These are generally aimed at avoiding the creation of an artificial market in the company's shares.

A special dividend has to be offered to all shareholders. However a share repurchase may not always be open to all shareholders as it can be accomplished in one of three ways:

a purchasing shares in the stock market;

b all shareholders are invited to sell some or all of their shares;

c an arrangement with particular shareholders.

An alternative method of returning money to shareholders is via a 'B share scheme' – *see* the example of William Hill in **Exhibit 22.9**. Some shareholders pay lower tax if the B shares are taxed as capital gains rather than income.

Buy-backs and special dividends are growing in popularity but they are not always regarded as a 'good thing' – *see* **Exhibit 22.10**.

Exhibit 22.9

William Hill hands back £453m to investors

FT

by Matthew Garrahan, Leisure Industries Correspondent

The government's moves to scale back its controversial gambling bill has prompted bookmaker William Hill to give shareholders a £453m windfall.

Tom Singer, finance director, said the company saw 'fewer synergies' between betting and gambling operators under the bill so had decided to return funds to shareholders rather than wait for a substantial acquisition target.

William Hill's shares fell by 2.9 per cent yesterday to 597p despite the capital return – which is equivalent to 115p a share or 20 per cent of the group's market capitalisation.

The group is the latest in a series of companies to hand back cash to shareholders either through share buy backs, increased dividend payments or other forms of capital returns, including BP, Rio Tinto, Shell, HBOS and Marks and Spencer.

With William Hill having a strong cash position and not anticipating any big acquisitions the company said it could support a 'significantly higher amount of debt'.

It has secured a new £1.2bn facility and will have increased its net debt to about £900m once the capital has been returned to investors. David Harding, chief executive, said the company would be left with about £300m for acquisitions, should any arise.

Funds will be returned to investors via a B share scheme. Shareholders will be able to choose how they take the benefit, either by redeeming the new B shares for 115p, receiving an immediate 115p dividend or deferring redemption.

The amount returned to investors by William Hill since its float in 2002 will rise to £752m following the return of the capital.

Tom Singer, Hill's finance director, said the group had chosen the B share scheme instead of a more conventional special dividend because it was fair and gave investors more choice. 'Shareholders, when offered a choice, would usually be split 50–50 between taking the money as income or as a capital receipt,' he said.

'If you only offer a special dividend, you're going to upset the remaining 50 per cent.'

Source: Financial Times, 3 March 2005, p. 25. Reprinted with permission.

Exhibit 22.10

Shareholders taking a stand on handouts

FT

Despite record returns, investors are rebelling. Chris Hughes asks whether companies should continue with buy-backs

Investors used to be grateful when companies promised to return buckets full of cash. These days they seem to shrug their shoulders at corporate handouts. Many are even rebelling against the most common method of cash-return – the share buyback.

Last year was a record year for cash returns to investors, with UK companies funnelling £108bn their way, according to Morgan Stanley. That includes £46bn of share buy-backs, up from about £28bn in 2005.

But fashions are changing and share buy-backs by UK companies are expected to be only £23bn this year.

Buy-backs took off because they were a simple and flexible means of distributing cash generated by rising corporate profitability.

But buy-backs are not necessarily a good thing. They absorb cash that could be spent on higher annual dividend payments or capital expenditure.

If a company's stock is overvalued, the company wastes money buying it – just like any other investor. And to the extent that stock repurchases are good for the company's continuing investors, they are correspondingly bad for those who sell out during the buy-back.

Private shareholders have long opposed buy-backs because they think they cannot participate in them. This is a fallacy given that anyone can sell shares in the market during a buy-back and the price at which buy-backs are conducted is regulated.

At Royal Dutch Shell's annual meeting this week, a disgruntled shareholder drew applause when he thanked the oil company for stopping its share buy-back citing Morgan Stanley's research.

'You've returned £16.3bn in dividends and buy-backs. Thank you for my dividends, I have banked them,' he said. 'Tell me, how do I bank my buy-backs? . . . Where is [the money] exactly?'

Euan Sirling, investment director, UK equities at Standard Life, says: 'There can be value creation from buying back cheap shares. But if companies have a permanent increase in their cashflows, dividends are the best way to distribute this to shareholders. There is plenty of scope for UK companies to grow dividends from here.'

Other investors want cash to be spent on capital expeniture instead. Robert Waugh, head of UK equities at Scottish Widows Investment Partnership, says: 'Buy-backs can make sense at the right price, but we prefer good management to invest more in the business. At the moment most investment is going on expensive acquisitions.'

Neil Darke, analyst at Collins Stewart, has campaigned against ill-judged share buy-backs, arguing that investment banks advise companies to do buy-backs because their equity desks make easy commission from them. He says other means of capital return – such as special dividends or redeemable 'B' shares – are preferable, since they do not differentiate between selling and buying shareholders.

Top 20 companies by buy-back yield

	Buy-backs (£m)	Buy-back yield*
Psion	84	38.0
First Choice	200	26.1
Computacenter	75	15.5
Wetherspoon (JD)	79	13.9
Evolution	50	13.2
Biocompatibles	12	12.6
Enterprise Inns	388	12.6
Pennon	138	12.0
SurfControl	15	11.1
Rank	201	10.5
Hays	209	10.2
Burberry	192	9.8
Capita	245	9.0
Spirent Comms	42	8.6
Reuters	527	8.5
InterCont Hotels	307	8.4
Next	341	8.2
Vodafone	6,457	7.2
Anglo American	2,111	7.1
BP	8,155	6.7

* Buy-back to average market cap 2005 and 2006 results

Source: Morgan Stanley

But management at companies that have been buying back shares are quick to dismiss criticism.

Ted Tuppen, chief executive of Enterprise Inns, says investors seem to

UK companies total cash returns
By type (£bn)

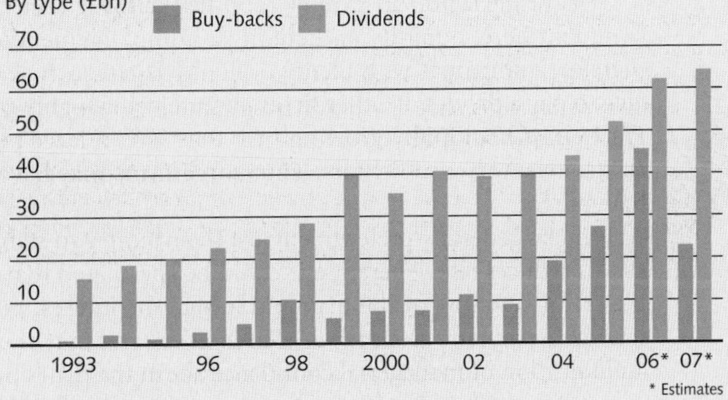

Source: Morgan Stanley

Exhibit 22.10 continued

prefer buy-backs because they do not trigger a taxable event like a dividend.

'When we asked our shareholders, the overwhelming response was that they preferred share buy-backs. But fashions change, and you get to a point when it's not earnings enhancing.'

Mr Tuppen says companies are not being cajoled into buy-backs by bankers, since it is possible to negotiate very low commission rates with brokers.

Jim Clarke, finance director of JD Wetherspoon, says: 'Most of our long-term large shareholders have said they see buy-backs creating more value than putting up dividends.'

So should companies continue buy-backs? It depends. Collins Stewart research has found that buy-backs trigger share price outperformance when the company also has a low valuation, a reputation for disciplined capital investment and a strong balance sheet.

Source: Financial Times, 19 May 2007, p. 16

A round-up of the arguments

There are two questions at the core of the dividend policy debate.

- ***Question 1*** Can shareholder wealth be increased by changing the pattern of dividends over a period of years?
- ***Question 2*** Is a steady, stable dividend growth rate better than one which varies from year to year depending on the firm's internal need for funds?

The answer to the first question is 'yes'. The accumulated evidence suggests that shareholders for one reason or another value particular patterns of dividends across time. But there is no neat, simple, straightforward formula into which we can plug numbers in order to calculate the best pattern. It depends on numerous factors, many of which are unquantifiable, ranging from the type of clientele shareholder the firm is trying to attract to changes in the taxation system.

Taking the residual theory alone the answer to Question 2 is that the dividend will vary from year to year because it is what is left over after the firm has retained funds for investment in all available projects with positive NPV. Dividends will be larger in years of high cash flow and few investment opportunities, and will be reduced when the need for reinvestment is high relative to internally generated cash flow. However, in practice, shareholders appear to prefer stable, consistent dividend growth rates. Many of them rely on a predictable stream of dividends to meet (or contribute to) their consumption needs. They would find an erratic dividend flow inconvenient. Investors also use dividend policy changes as an indication of a firm's prospects. A reduced dividend could send an incorrect signal and depress the share price.

There are so many factors influencing dividend policy that it is very difficult to imagine that someone could develop a universally applicable model which would allow firms to identify an optimal payout ratio. **Exhibit 22.11** shows the range of forces pulling managers towards a high payout rate, and other forces pulling towards a low payout rate. Simultaneously, there are forces encouraging a fluctuating dividend and other factors promoting a stable dividend.

Most of the factors in Exhibit 22.11 have already been explained, but there are two which need a comment here: liquidity and credit standing. Dividends require an outflow of cash from firms; therefore companies with plenty of liquid assets, such as cash and marketable securities, are more able to pay a dividend. Other firms, despite being highly profitable, may have very few liquid assets. For example, a rapidly growing firm may have a large proportion of its funds absorbed by fixed assets, inventory and debtors. Thus some firms may have greater difficulty paying cash dividends than others.

Lenders generally prefer to entrust their money to stable firms rather than ones that are erratic, as this reduces risk. Therefore it could be speculated that a consistent dividend flow helps to raise the credit standing of the firm and lowers the interest rates payable. Creditors suffer from information asymmetry as much as shareholders and may therefore look to this dividend decision for an indication of managerial confidence about the firm's prospects.

Exhibit 22.11 The forces pulling management in the dividend decision

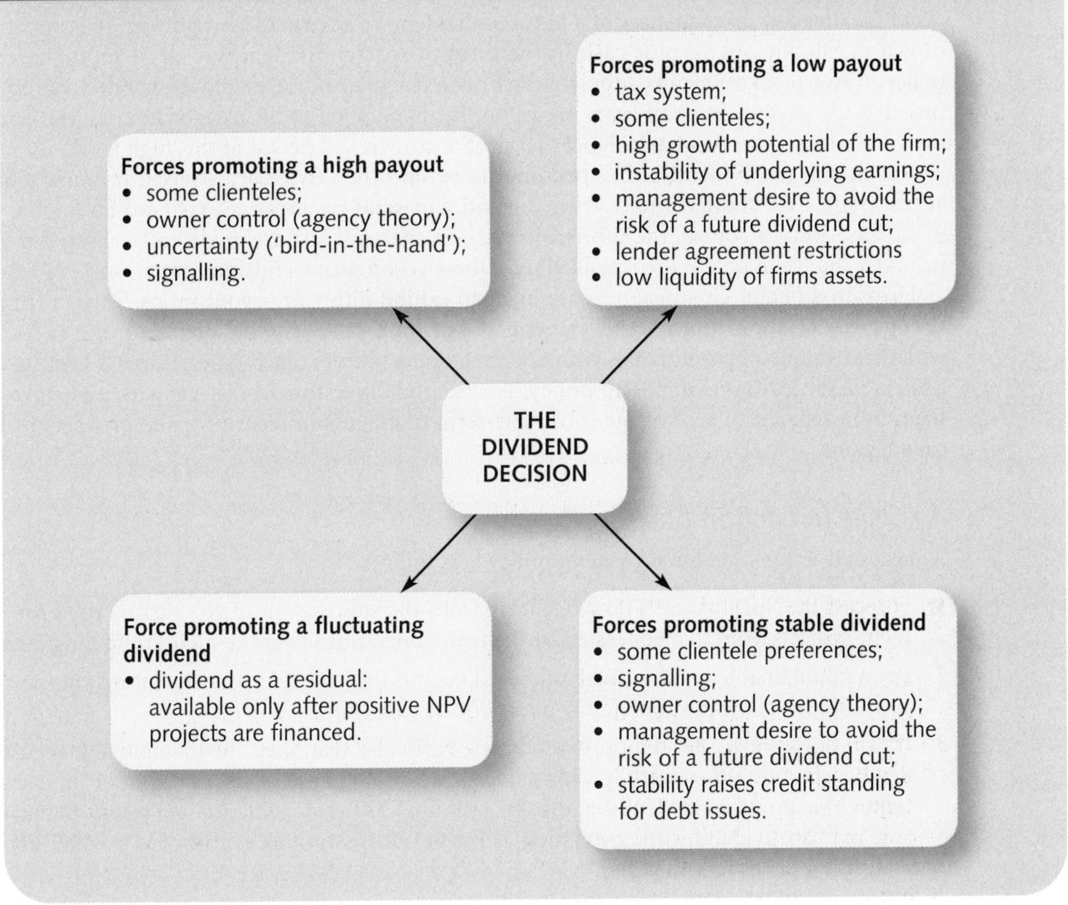
Forces promoting a low payout
• tax system;
• some clienteles;
• high growth potential of the firm;
• instability of underlying earnings;
• management desire to avoid the risk of a future dividend cut;
• lender agreement restrictions
• low liquidity of firms assets.
Forces promoting a high payout
• some clienteles;
• owner control (agency theory);
• uncertainty ('bird-in-the-hand');
• signalling.
THE DIVIDEND DECISION
Force promoting a fluctuating dividend
• dividend as a residual: available only after positive NPV projects are financed.
Forces promoting stable dividend
• some clientele preferences;
• signalling;
• owner control (agency theory);
• management desire to avoid the risk of a future dividend cut;
• stability raises credit standing for debt issues.

Concluding comments

This section considers a possible practical dividend policy, taking into account the various arguments presented in the chapter.

Most large firms forecast their financial position for a few years ahead. Their forecasts will include projections for fixed capital expenditure and additional investment in working capital as well as sales, profits, etc. This information, combined with a specified target debt to equity ratio, allows an estimation of medium- to long-term cash flows.

These companies can then determine a dividend level that will leave sufficient retained earnings to meet the financing needs of their investment projects without having to resort to selling shares. (Not only does issuing shares involve costs of issue but, as described in Chapter 21, investors sometimes view share issues as a negative omen.) Thus a ***maintainable regular dividend*** on a growth path is generally established. This has the virtue of providing some certainty to a particular clientele group and provides a stable background, to avoid sending misleading signals. At the same time the residual theory conclusions have been recognised, and (over, say, a five-year period) dividends are intended to be roughly the same as surplus cash flows after financing all investment in projects with a positive NPV. Agency costs are alleviated to the extent that managers do not, over the long run, store up (and misapply) cash flows greater than those necessary to finance high-return projects.

The future is uncertain and so companies may consider their financial projections under various scenarios. They may focus particularly on the negative possibilities. Dividends may be set at a level low enough that, if poorer trading conditions do occur, the firm is not forced to cut the dividend. Thus a margin for error is introduced by lowering the payout rate.

Companies that are especially vulnerable to macroeconomic vicissitudes, such as those in cyclical industries, are likely to be tempted to set a relatively low maintainable regular dividend so as to avoid the dreaded consequences of a reduced dividend in a particularly bad year. In years of plenty directors can pay out surplus cash in the form of special dividends or share repurchases. This policy of low regular payouts supplemented with irregular bonuses allows shareholders to recognise that the payouts in good years might not be maintained at the extraordinary level. Therefore they do not interpret them as a signal that profits growth will persist at this high level.

If a change in dividend policy becomes necessary then firms are advised to make a gradual adjustment, as a sudden break with a trend can send an erroneous signal about the firms' prospects. And, of course, the more information shareholders are given concerning the reasons behind a change in policy, the less likelihood there is of a serious misinterpretation.

Firms in different circumstances are likely to exhibit different payout ratios. Those with plentiful investment opportunities will, in general, opt for a relatively low dividend rate as compared with that exhibited by companies with few such opportunities. Each type of firm is likely to attract a clientele favouring its dividend policy. For example investors in fast-growth, high-investment firms are prepared to accept low (no) near-term dividends in return for the prospect of higher capital gains.

A suggested action plan

A suggested action plan for a dividend policy is as follows.

1. Forecast the 'surplus' cash flow resulting from the subtraction of the cash needed for investment projects from that generated by the firm's operations over the medium to long term.
2. Pay a maintainable regular dividend based on this forecast. This may be biased on the conservative side to allow for uncertainty about future cash flows.
3. If cash flows are greater than projected for a particular year, keep the maintainable regular dividend fairly constant (hopefully with stable growth), but pay a special dividend or initiate a share repurchase programme. If the change in cash flows is permanent, gradually shift the maintainable regular dividend while providing as much information to investors as possible about the reasons for the change in policy.

Key points and concepts

- **Dividend policy** concerns the pattern of dividends over time and the extent to which they fluctuate from year to year.
- UK-quoted companies generally pay dividends every six months – an **interim** and a **final**. They may only be paid out of accumulated profits.
- **Miller and Modigliani** proposed that, in a perfect world, the policy on dividends is irrelevant to shareholder wealth. Firms are able to **finance investments** from retained earnings or new share sales at the same cost (with no transaction costs). Investors are able to manufacture **'homemade dividends'** by selling a portion of their shareholding.
- In a world with **no external finance dividend policy should be residual**.
- In a world with some transaction costs associated with issuing dividends and obtaining investment finance through the sale of new shares, dividend policy will be **influenced by**, but not exclusively determined by, the **'dividends as a residual approach'** to dividend policy.
- The **clientele effect** is the concept that shareholders are attracted to firms that follow dividend policies consistent with their objectives. The clientele effect encourages stability in dividend policy.
- **Taxation** can influence the investors' preference for the receipt of high dividends or capital gains from their shares.
- **Dividends can act as conveyors of information**. An unexpected change in dividends is regarded as a **signal** of how directors view the future prospects of the firm.

- It has been argued (e.g. by Myron Gordon) that **investors perceive more distant dividends as subject to more risk**, therefore they prefer a higher near-term dividend – a 'bird in the hand'. This **'resolution of uncertainty'** argument has been attacked on the grounds that it implies an extra risk premium on the rate used to discount cash flows.
- The **owner control** argument says that firms are encouraged to distribute a high proportion of earnings so that investors can reduce the **principal–agent problem** and achieve greater goal congruence. Managers have to ask for investment funds; this subjects their plans to scrutiny.
- A **scrip dividend** gives the shareholders an opportunity to receive additional shares in proportion to their existing holding instead of the normal cash dividend.
- A **share repurchase** is when the company buys a proportion of its own shares from investors.
- A **special dividend** is similar to a normal dividend but is usually bigger and paid on a one-off basis.

References and further reading

Baker, H.K., Powell, G.E. and Veit E.T. (2002) 'Revisiting managerial perspectives on dividend policy', *Journal of Economics and Finance*, 26(3), pp. 267–83.
Evidence for avoidance of dividend cuts and the maintenance of dividend continuity.

Baker, M. and Wurgler, J. (2004) 'A catering theory of dividends', *Journal of Finance*, 59(3), June, pp. 1125–65.
'Managers give investors what they currently want.'

Black, F. (1976) 'The dividend puzzle', *Journal of Portfolio Management*, 2, pp. 5–8.
A consideration of the issue by a leading writer in the field.

Brav, A., Graham, J.R., Harvey, C.R. and Michaely, R. (2005) 'Payout policy in the 21st century', *Journal of Financial Economics*, 77, pp. 483–527.
A survey of US executives. Confirms Lintner's (1956) observation that perceived stability of future earnings affects dividend policy. Signalling is asymmetric, therefore firms are reluctant to cut dividend.

Brealey, R.H. (1986) 'Does dividend policy matter?', in Stern, J.M. and Chew, D.H. (eds), *The Revolution in Corporate Finance*. Oxford: Basil Blackwell.
Argues that dividend policy is irrelevant to wealth except that this is affected by taxes. Also acknowledges the information effect.

Brennan, M. (1971) 'A note on dividend irrelevance and the Gordon valuation model', *Journal of Finance*, December, pp. 1115–21.
A technical discussion of the opposing theories of MM and Gordon.

Crossland, M., Dempsey, M. and Moizer, P. (1991) 'The effect of cum- to ex-dividend changes on UK share prices', *Accounting and Business Research*, 22(85), pp. 47–50.
'Our statistical analysis provides evidence of the clientele effect in the UK stock market' – shareholders in the high-income, low capital gains tax bracket hold shares in high-growth companies and shareholders with low income and in the high capital gains tax bracket hold shares in low-growth companies.

Damodaran, A. (1999) *Applied Corporate Finance*, New York: Wiley.
Chapters 10 and 11 consider dividend policy in a practical exposition.

Dhanani, A. (2005) 'Corporate dividend policy: the views of British financial managers', *Journal of Business Finance and Accounting*, 32 (7) and (8), Sept/Oct, pp. 1625–72.
A survey of UK managers. Signalling and clienteles (with the influence of tax) are apparent.

Easterbrook, F.H. (1984) 'Two *agency-cost* explanations of dividends', *American Economic Review*, 74(4), September pp. 650–60.
Managers may act in their own self-interest. Agency cost explanation of dividends.

Elton, E.J. and Gruber, M.J. (1970) 'Marginal stockholder tax rates and the clientele effect', *Review of Economics and Statistics*, February, pp. 68–74.
Evidence is found which supports the clientele effect – shareholders in higher tax brackets prefer capital gains to dividend income.

Fama, E.F. and French, K.R. (2001) 'Disappearing dividends: changing firm characteristics or lower propensity to pay?' *Journal of Financial Economics*, 60(1), April, pp. 3–43.
Only 20.8 per cent of US quoted firms paid cash dividends in late 1990s.

Gordon, M.J. (1959) 'Dividends, earnings and stock prices', *Review of Economics and Statistics*, 41, May, pp. 99–105.
Discusses the relationship between dividends, earnings and share prices.

Gordon, M.J. (1963) 'Optimal investment and financing policy', *Journal of Finance*, May.
A refutation of the MM dividend irrelevancy theory based on the early resolution of uncertainty idea.

Graham, J.R. and Kumar, A. (2006) 'Do dividend clienteles exist? Evidence on dividend preferences of retail investors', *Journal of Finance* 61(3), June, pp. 1305–36.
Evidence for clienteles (e.g. older investors prefer high dividend yields). Also tax influences preferences of clienteles.

Grullon, G. and Michaely, R. (2002) 'Dividends, share repurchases, and the substitution hypothesis', *Journal of Finance*, 57(4), pp. 1649–84.
US companies have increasingly substituted share repurchases for dividends – tax considerations were a major reason.

Gustavo, G. and Roni, M. (2004) 'The information content of share repurchase programs', *Journal of Finance*, April, 59 (2), pp. 651–80.
Finds evidence consistent with free cash flow hypothesis of dividend policy.

Jagannathan, M., Stephens, C.P. and Weisbach, M.S. (2000) 'Financial flexibility and the choice between dividends and stock repurchases', *Journal of Financial Economics*, 57(3), September, pp. 355–84.
US study. Repurchases are pro-cyclical, dividends are steady. Repurchases used to distribute high temporary cash flows.

Jensen, M.C. (1986) 'Agency costs of free cash flow, corporate finance and takeovers', *American Economic Review*, 76, pp. 323–9.
Managers act in their own interests therefore increased dividends increase value of mature cash-generating companies.

Julio, B. and Ikenberry, D.L. (2004) 'Reappearing dividends', *Journal of Applied Corporate Finance*, 16(4), Fall, pp. 89–100.
A discussion of dividend policy of US firms.

Keane, S. (1974) 'Dividends and the resolution of uncertainty', *Journal of Business Finance and Accountancy*, Autumn.
Discusses the 'bird-in-the-hand' theory of dividend policy.

Koch, A.S. and Sun, A.X. (2004) 'Dividend changes and the persistence of past earnings changes', *Journal of Finance*, 59 (5), October, pp. 2093–116.
'Results confirm the hypothesis that changes in dividends cause investors to revise their expectations about the persistence of past earnings changes', thus dividend changes act as a signalling device.

Lewellen, W.G., Stanley, K.L., Lease, R.C. and Schlarbaum, G.G. (1978) 'Some direct evidence of the dividend clientele phenomenon', *Journal of Finance*, December, pp. 1385–99.
An investigation of the clientele effect.

Lintner, J. (1956) 'Distribution of income of corporations among dividends, retained earnings and taxes', *American Economic Review*, 46, May, pp. 97–113.
An empirical study and theoretical model of dividend policy practices.

Litzenberger, R. and Ramaswamy, K. (1982) 'The effects of dividends on common stock prices: tax effects or information effects?', *Journal of Finance*, May, pp. 429–43.
A technical paper which presents 'evidence consistent with the Tax-Clientele CAPM'.

Miller, M.H. and Modigliani, F. (1961) 'Dividend policy, growth and the valuation of shares', *Journal of Business*, 34, October, pp. 411–33.
In an ideal economy dividend policy is irrelevant – algebraic proofs.

Mougoué, M. and Rao, R.P. (2003) 'The information signalling hypothesis of dividends: Evidence from cointegration and causality tests', *Journal of Business Finance and Accounting*, 30(3) and (4), April/May, pp. 441–78.
Evidence consistent with the information-signalling hypothesis.

Nissim, D. and Ziv, A. (2001) 'Dividend changes and future profitability', *Journal of Finance*, 56(6), pp. 2111–33.
Strong support for the information content of dividends hypothesis.

Pettit, R.R. (1977) 'Taxes, transaction costs and clientele effects of dividends', *Journal of Financial Economics*, December.
Discusses the clientele effect.

Porterfield, J.T.S. (1965) *Investment Decisions and Capital Costs*. Upper Saddle River, NJ: Prentice-Hall.
Chapter 6 discusses the dividend decision in a readable fashion with an emphasis on theory.

Rozeff, M. (1986) 'How companies set their dividend payout ratios'. Reprinted in J.M. Stern and D.H. Chew (eds), *The Revolution in Corporate Finance*. Oxford: Basil Blackwell.
A discussion of the information effect of dividends, the agency problems, industry rules of thumb. Easy-to-follow arguments.

Shefrin, H.M. and Statman, M. (1984) 'Explaining investor preference for cash dividends', *Journal of Financial Economics*, 13, pp. 253–82.
Individuals impose a rule that prevents spending from capital: only dividends may be used for consumption, which cannot be boosted by selling shares. This is to impose discipline and reduce the need for willpower. Some of these individuals form a clientele for companies pursuing a high-dividend payout policy – particularly older people. Other investors prefer low payouts.

Solomon, E. (1963) *The Theory of Financial Management*. New York: Columbia University Press.
Chapter 11 contains an interesting early discussion of the dividend policy debate.

Tse, C-B, (2005) 'Use dividends to signal or not: An examination of the UK dividend payout patterns', *Managerial Finance*, 31(4), pp. 12–33.
'Some firms need to use dividends to signal but some do not need to. For example, a firm that has built up reputational capital can communicate directly with shareholders'.

3i (1993) 'Dividend Policy'. Reported in *Bank of England Quarterly Review* (1993), August, p. 367.
The most important factor influencing dividend policy is long-term profit growth. Cuts in dividends send adverse signals.

Video presentations

Chief executives and finance directors talk about this dividend portions on Cantos.com (www.cantos.com/cantos) – this is free to view.

Case study recommendations

Please see www.pearsoned.co.uk/arnold for case study synopses

- Dividend policy at Linear Technology Authors: Malcolm P. Baker, Alison Berkley Wagonfeld. (2004) Harvard Business School.
- Dividend policy at FPL Group, Inc (A). Authors: Benjamin Esty and Craig Schreiber (1995) Harvard Business School.

Self-review questions

1 What are the two fundamental questions in dividend policy?

2 Explain the main elements of MM's dividend irrelevancy hypothesis.

3 Explain the idea that dividends should be treated as a residual.

4 How might clientele effects influence dividend policy?

5 What is the effect of taxation on dividend payout rates?

6 What is meant by 'asymmetry of information' and 'dividends as signals'?

7 Explain the 'resolution of uncertainty' argument supporting high dividend payout rates. What is the counter-argument?

8 In what ways does agency theory influence the dividend debate?

9 When are share repurchases and special dividends particularly useful?

10 Outline a dividend policy for a typical fast-growth and high-investment firm.

Questions and problems

myfinancelab ***Questions with an icon are also available for practice in MyFinanceLab with additional supporting resources.***

1 (*Examination level*) 'These days we discuss the dividend level for about an hour a year at board meetings. It changes very little from one year to the next – and it is just as well if you consider what happened to some of the other firms on the stock exchange which reduced their dividend' – director of a large company.

Explain, with reference to dividend theory, how this firm may have settled into this comfortable routine. Describe any problems that might arise with this approach.

2 (*Examination level*) 'We believe managers and owners should think hard about the circumstances under which earnings should be retained and under which they should be distributed.'

Use the above sentence together with the following one written in the same letter to shareholders by Warren Buffett (1984), plus dividend policy theory, to explain why this is an important issue: 'Nothing in this discussion is intended to argue for dividends that bounce around from quarter to quarter with each wiggle in earnings or in investment opportunities.'

3 (*Examination level*) Sendine plc has maintained a growth path for dividends per share of 5 per cent per year for the past seven years. This was considered to be the maintainable regular dividend. However, the company has developed a new product range which will require major investment in the next 12 months. The amount needed is roughly equivalent to the proposed dividend for this year. The project will not provide a positive net cash flow for three to four years but will give a positive NPV overall.

Required

Consider the argument for and against a dividend cut this year and suggest a course of action.

4 (*Examination level*) Vale plc has the following profit-after-tax history and dividend-per-share history:

Year		Profit after tax £	Dividend per share
This year	(t_0)	10,800,000	5.4
Last year	($t-1$)	8,900,000	4.92
2 years ago	($t-2$)	6,300,000	4.48
3 years ago	($t-3$)	5,500,000	4.083
4 years ago	($t-4$)	3,500,000	3.71
5 years ago	($t-5$)	2,600,000	3.38

Two years ago the number of issued ordinary shares was increased by 30 per cent (at the beginning of the financial year $t-1$). Four years ago a rights issue doubled the number of shares (at the beginning of financial year $t-3$). Today there are 100 million ordinary shares in issue with a total market value of £190m. Vale is quoted on the Alternative Investment Market. Vale's directors are committed to shareholder wealth maximisation.

Required

a Explain the following dividend theories and models and relate them to Vale's policy:
   i dividends as a residual;
   ii signalling;
   iii clientele preferences.

b The risk-free return on government securities is currently 6.5 per cent, the risk premium for shares above the risk-free rate of return has been 5 per cent per annum and Vale is in a risk class of shares which suggests that the average risk premium of 5 should be adjusted by a factor of 0.9. The company's profits after tax per share are expected to continue their historic growth path, and dividends will remain at the same proportion of earnings as this year.

   Use the dividend valuation model and state whether Vale's shares are a good buying opportunity for a stock market investor.

?

5 (*Examination level*) Tesford plc has estimated net cash flows from operations (after interest and taxation) for the next five years as follows:

Year	Net cash flows £
1	3,000,000
2	12,000,000
3	5,000,000
4	6,000,000
5	5,000,000

The cash flows have been calculated before the deduction of additional investment in fixed capital and working capital. This amounts to £2m in each of the first two years and £3m for each year thereafter. The firm currently has a cash balance of £500,000 which it intends to maintain to cope with unexpected events. There are 24 million shares in issue. The directors are committed to shareholder wealth maximisation.

Required

a Calculate the annual cash flows available for dividend payments and the dividend per share if the residual dividend policy was strictly adhered to.

b If the directors chose to have a smooth dividend policy based on the maintainable regular dividend what would you suggest the dividends in each year should be? Include in your consideration the possibility of a special dividend or share repurchase.

c Explain why companies tend to follow the policy in b rather than a.

?

6 (*Examination level*) The retailers Elec Co. and Lighting are competitors in the electrical goods market. They are similar firms in many respects: profits per share have been very similar over the past 10 years, and are projected to be the same in the future; they both have (and have had) a 50 per cent debt to equity ratio; and they have similar investment needs, now and in the future. However they do differ in their dividend policies. Elec Co. pays out 50 per cent of earnings as dividends, whereas Lighting has adopted a stable dividend policy. This is demonstrated in the table.

Year	Elec Co.		Lighting	
	Earnings per share	Dividend per share	Earnings per share	Dividend per share
20×1	11p	5.5p	11p	5.5p
20×2	16p	8.0p	17p	6.25p
20×3	13p	6.5p	11p	7.11p
20×4	20p	10.0p	21p	8.1p
20×5	10p	5.0p	9p	9.2p
20×6	0	0	0	10.5p
20×7	15p	7.5p	17p	11.9p
20×8	25p	12.5p	24p	13.5p
20×9	30p	15.0p	31p	15.4p
20×10	35p	17.5p	35p	17.5p

The managing director of Elec Co. has asked you to conduct a thorough review of dividend policy and to try to explain why it is that Lighting has a market value much greater than Elec Co. (Both companies have, and have had, the same number of shares in issue.)

Write a report detailing the factors that influence dividend policy and recommend a dividend policy for Elec Co. based on your arguments.

7 (*Examination level*) Guff plc, an all-equity firm, has the following earnings per share and dividend history (paid annually).

Year	Earnings per share	Dividend per share
This year	21p	8p
Last year	18p	7.5p
2 years ago	16p	7p
3 years ago	13p	6.5p
4 years ago	14p	6p

This year's dividend has just been paid and the next is due in one year. Guff has an opportunity to invest in a new product, Stuff, during the next two years. The directors are considering cutting the dividend to 4p for each of the next two years to fund the project. However the dividend in three years can be raised to 10p and will grow by 9 per cent per annum thereafter due to the benefits from the investment. The company is focused on shareholder wealth maximisation and requires a rate of return of 13 per cent for its owners.

Required

a If the directors chose to ignore the investment opportunity and dividends continued to grow at the historical rate what would be the value of one share using the dividend valuation model?

b If the investment is accepted, and therefore dividends are cut for the next two years, what will be the value of one share?

c What are the dangers associated with dividend cuts and how might the firm alleviate them? ?

myfinancelab **Now retake your diagnostic test for Chapter 22 to check your progress and update your study plan.**

Assignments

1 Consider the dividend policy of your firm or one you know well. Write a report detailing the factors contributing to the selection of this particular policy. Make recommendations on the decision-making process, range of influences considered and how a change in policy could be executed.

2 Write a report which relates the dividend frameworks and theories discussed in this chapter to the evidence provided by the following UK companies.

Year	Marks & Spencer		Vodafone		AstraZeneca	
	Earnings (Pence per share)	Dividends (Pence per share)	Earnings	Dividends (Pence per share)	Earnings	Dividends (US cents per share)
1999	15	14.4	4	1.5	73	70.0
2000	11.4	9.0	2	1.5	130	70.0
2001	11.2	9.0	(16)	1.6	165	70.0
2002	16.3	9.5	(24)	1.7	164	70.0
2003	23.3	10.5	(14)	1.9	178	79.5
2004	24.7	11.5	(15)	2.3	218	94
2005	19.2	12.1	11	4.7	291	130
2006	31.4	14.0	(40)	6.9	386	172
2007	40.4	18.3	(10)	6.8	374	187

Note: figures in brackets indicate a loss.

CHAPTER 23

Mergers

LEARNING OUTCOMES

The study of mergers is a subject worthy of a textbook in its own right. This chapter provides an overview of the subject and raises the most important issues. By the end of the chapter the reader should be able to:

- describe the rich array of motives for a merger;
- express the advantages and disadvantages of alternative methods of financing mergers;
- describe the merger process and the main regulatory constraints;
- comment on the question: 'Who benefits from mergers?';
- discuss some of the reasons for merger failure and some of the practices promoting success.

myfinancelab *Complete your diagnostic test for Chapter 23 now to create your personal study plan*

Introduction

The topic of mergers is one of those areas of finance which attracts interest from the general public as well as finance specialists and managers. There is nothing like an acrimonious bid battle to excite the press, where one side is portrayed as 'David' fighting the bullying 'Goliath', or where one national champion threatens the pride of another country by taking over a key industry. Each twist and turn of the campaign is reported on radio and television news broadcasts, and, finally, there is a victor and a victim. So many people have so much hanging on the outcome of the conflict that it is not surprising that a great deal of attention is given by local communities, national government, employees and trade unionists. The whole process can become emotional and over-hyped to the point where rational analysis is pushed to the side.

This chapter examines the reasons for mergers and the ways in which they are financed. Then the merger process itself is described, along with the rules and regulations designed to prevent unfairness. A major question to be addressed is: Who gains from mergers? Is it shareholders, managers, advisers, society, etc.? Evidence is presented which suggests that in less than one half of corporate mergers do the shareholders of the acquiring firm benefit. To help the reader understand the causes of this level of failure the various managerial tasks involved in achieving a successful (that is, a shareholder wealth-enhancing) merger, including the 'soft' science issues, such as attending to the need to enlist the commitment of the newly acquired workforce, are discussed.

The merger decision

Expanding the activities of the firm through acquisition involves significant uncertainties. Very often the acquiring management seriously underestimate the complexities involved in merger and post-merger integration.

Theoretically the acquisition of other companies should be evaluated on essentially the same criteria as any other investment decision, that is, using NPV. As Rappaport states: 'The basic objective of making acquisitions is identical to any other investment associated with a company's overall strategy, namely, to add value'.[1]

In practice, the myriad collection of motivations for expansion through merger, and the diverse range of issues such an action raises, means that mergers are usually extremely difficult to evaluate using discounted cash flow techniques. Consider these two complicating factors.

1 The benefits from mergers are often difficult to quantify. The motivation may be to 'apply superior managerial skills' or to 'obtain unique technical capabilities' or to 'enter a new market'. The fruits of these labours may be real, and directors may judge that the strategic benefits far outweigh the cost, and yet these are difficult to express in numerical form.

2 Acquiring companies often do not know what they are buying. If a firm expands by building a factory here, or buying in machinery there, it knows what it is getting for its money. With a merger information is often sparse – especially if it is a hostile bid in which the target company's managers are opposed to the merger. In Chapter 20 it was stated that most of the value of many firms is in the form of assets which cannot be expressed on a balance sheet, for example the reservoir of experience within the management team, the reputation with suppliers and customers, competitive position and so on. These attributes are extremely difficult to value, especially from a distance, and when there is a reluctance to release information. Even the quantifiable elements of value, such as stock, buildings and free cash flow, can be miscalculated by an 'outsider'.

[1] Rappaport (1998), p. 138.

Definitions and semantics

Throughout this book the word **merger** is used to mean the *combining of two business entities under common ownership.*

Many people, for various reasons, differentiate between the terms merger, acquisition and takeover – for example, for accounting and legal purposes. However, most commentators use the three terms interchangeably, and with good reason. It is sometimes very difficult to decide whether a particular unification of two companies is more like a merger, in the sense of being the coming together of roughly equal-sized firms on roughly equal terms and in which the shareholders remain as joint owners, or whether the act of union is closer to what some people would say is an **acquisition** or **takeover** – a purchase of one firm by another with the associated implication of financial and managerial domination. In reality it is often impossible to classify the relationships within the combined entity as a merger or a takeover. The literature is full of cases of so-called mergers of equals which turn out to be a takeover of managerial control by one set of managers at the expense of the other.[2] Jürgen Schrempp, the chairman of DaimlerChrysler, shocked the financial world with his honesty on this point. At the time of the union of Chrysler with Daimler Benz in 1998 it was described as a merger of equals. However, in 2000 Schrempp said, 'The structure we have now with Chrysler [as a standalone division] was always the structure I wanted. We had to go a roundabout way but it had to be done for psychological reasons. If I had gone and said Chrysler would be a division, everybody on their side would have said: "There is no way we'll do a deal."'[3] Jack Welch, the well-respected industrialist, supports Schrempp: 'This was a buy-out of Chrysler by Daimler. Trying to run it as a merger of equals creates all kinds of problems . . . There is no such thing as a merger of equals . . . There has to be one way forward and clear rules.'[4] Lord Browne, chief executive of BP, following the mergers with Amoco and Arco, expressed strong views on this subject: 'There is a big cultural problem with mergers of equals . . . in the end there has to be a controlling strain from the two companies.'[5] This book uses the terms merger, acquisition and takeover interchangeably.

Economic and/or strategic definitions of mergers

Mergers have been classified into three categories: horizontal, vertical and conglomerate.

1 ***Horizontal*** In a **horizontal merger** two companies which are engaged in similar lines of activity are combined. Recent examples include the merger of the housebuilders George Wimpey and Taylor Woodrow and supermarkets Wm. Morrison and Safeway. One of the motives advanced for horizontal mergers is that economies of scale can be achieved. But not all horizontal mergers demonstrate such gains. Another major motive is the enhancement of market power resulting from the reduction in competition. Horizontal mergers often attract the attention of government competition agencies such as the Office of Fair Trading and the Competition Commission in the UK.

2 ***Vertical*** **Vertical mergers** occur when firms from different stages of the production chain amalgamate. So, for instance, if a manufacturer of footwear merges with a retailer of shoes this would be a (downstream) vertical merger. If the manufacturer then bought a leather producer (an upstream vertical merger) there would be an even greater degree of vertical integration. The major players in the oil industry tend to be highly vertically integrated. They have exploration subsidiaries, drilling and production companies, refineries, distribution companies and petrol stations. Vertical integration often has the attraction of increased certainty of supply or market outlet. It also reduces costs of search, contracting, payment collection, advertising, communication and co-ordination of production. An increase in market power may also be a motivation: this is discussed later.

---

[2] For example, *see* Cartwright and Cooper (1992); Buono and Bowditch (2003).
[3] Tim Burt and Richard Lambert, 'The Schrempp Gambit . . .', *Financial Times*, 30 October 2000, p. 26.
[4] Tim Burt, 'Steering with his foot to the floor', *Financial Times*, 26 February 2001, p. 12.
[5] David Buchan and Tobias Buck, 'Refining BP's management', *Financial Times*, 1 August 2002, p. 21.

3 ***Conglomerate*** A **conglomerate merger** is the combining of two firms which operate in unrelated business areas. For example, GE buys companies in areas as diverse as jet engines, financial services and medical imaging.

Some conglomerate mergers are motivated by risk reduction through diversification; some by the opportunity for cost reduction and improved efficiency. Others have more complex driving motivations – many of which will be discussed later.

Merger statistics

The figures in **Exhibit 23.1** show that merger activity has occurred in waves, with peaks in the early 1970s, late 1980s and late 1990s and 2004–6 – periods of rising stock market prices. The vast majority (over 95 per cent) of these mergers were agreed ('friendly'), rather than opposed by the target (acquired) firm's management ('hostile'). It is only a small, but often noisy, fraction which enter into a bid battle stage. In the late 1990s shares became a more important means of payment as the stock market boomed. In the first part of the 1980s merger boom (1985–7) ordinary shares tended to be the preferred method of payment. However, after the October 1987 stock market decline there was a switch to cash. There was a similar pattern in the early 1970s and in the early noughties: when share prices were on the rise (1970–2 and 1997–2000) shares were used most frequently. Following the collapse in 1973–4 and 2001–2 cash became more common.

On a worldwide scale merger activity grew dramatically through the 1990s. In the early part of the decade the value of companies merging rarely totalled more than \$400bn during a year. However, in 1999 and 2000 a staggering \$3,300bn and \$3,500bn respectively was achieved. This level of activity subsided but then picked up to be similar to its peak levels in 2007.

It is not entirely clear why merger activity has boom periods, but some relationships have been observed and ideas advanced: companies go through confident expansion phases **organically** (that is, by **internal growth**) and through acquisitions, as the economy prospers, and corporate profitability and liquidity are high; there is also a deregulation effect which allows increased innovation in financial markets, and access to finance, especially debt, permitting even the largest firms to be threatened with takeover; perhaps some managers become over-confident after a few good years, and, impatient with internal growth, decide to grow in big steps through acquisition. The hubris hypothesis and other managerial explanations of mergers are discussed in the next section.

Merger motives

Firms decide to merge with other firms for a variety of reasons. **Exhibit 23.2** identifies four classes of merger motives. This may not be complete but at least it helps us to focus.

Synergy

In the first column of Exhibit 23.2 we have the classic word associated with merger announcements – **synergy**. The idea underlying this is that the combined entity will have a value greater than the sum of its parts. The increased value comes about because of boosts to revenue and/or the cost base. Perhaps complementary skills or complementary market outlets enable the combined firms to sell more goods. Sometimes the ability to share sources of supply or production facilities improves the competitive position of the firm. Some of the origins of synergy are listed in the first column of the exhibit. Before discussing these we will look at the concept of synergy in more detail.

If two firms, A and B, are to be combined a gain may result from synergistic benefits to provide a value above that of the present value of the two independent cash flows:

$$PV_{AB} = PV_A + PV_B + \text{gains}$$

Exhibit 23.1 UK merger activity, 1970–2006 (UK firms merging with UK firms)

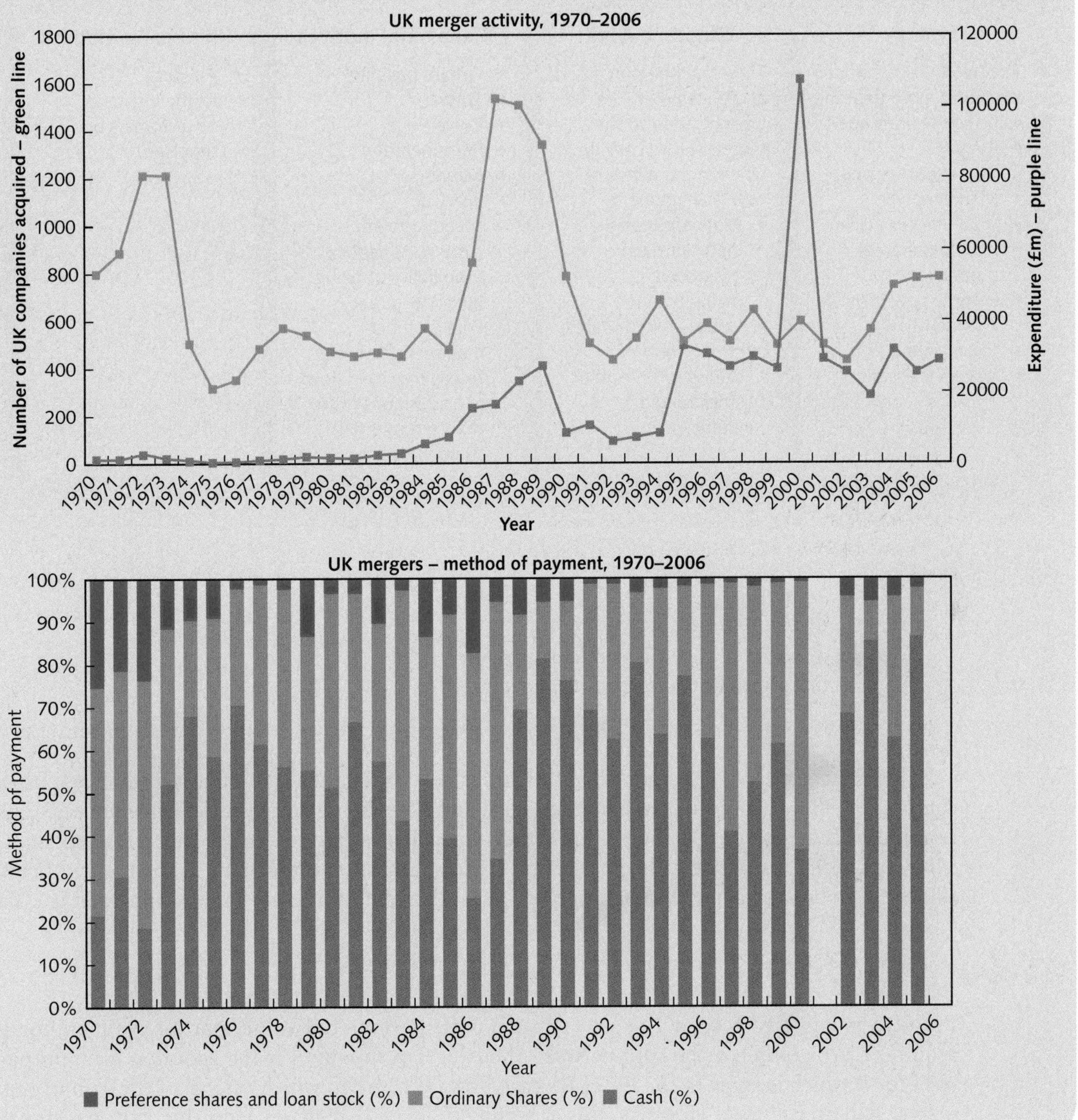

Note: The figures include all industrial and commercial companies (and financial institutions for 1995), quoted or unquoted, which reported the merger to the press (small private mergers are excluded).

Source: Office for National Statistics, *Financial Statistics*. © Crown Copyright. Reproduced by the permission of the Controller of HMSO and the Queen's Printer for Scotland.

Exhibit 23.2 Merger motives

Synergy	Bargain buying	Managerial motives	Third party motives
The two firms together are worth more than the value of the firms apart. • PV_{AB} = $PV_A + PV_B$ + gains • Market power • Economies of scale • Internalisation of transactions • Entry to new markets and industries • Tax advantages • Risk diversification.	Target can be purchased at a price below the present value of the targets future cash flow when in the hands of new management. • Elimination of inefficient and misguided management • Under-valued shares: strong form or semi-strong form of stock market inefficiency.	• Empire building • Status • Power • Remuneration • Hubris • Survival: speedy growth strategy to reduce probability of being takeover target • Free cash flow: management prefer to use free cash flow in acquisitions rather than return it to shareholders.	• Advisers • At the insistence of customers or suppliers.

where:

PV_A = discounted cash flows of company A;
PV_B = discounted cash flows of company B;
PV_{AB} = discounted cash flows of the merged firm.

Synergy is often expressed in the form 2 + 2 = 5.

Value is created from a merger when the gain is greater than the transaction costs. These usually comprise advisers' fees, underwriters' fees, legal and accounting costs, stock exchange fees, public relations bills and so on. So if we assume that A and B as separate entities have present values of £20m and £10m respectively, the transaction costs total £2m and the value of the merged firms is £40m (£42m before paying transaction costs), then the net (after costs) gain from merger is £10m:

£40m = £20m + £10m + gain

But who is going to receive this extra value? The incremental value may be available for the acquirer or the target, or be split between the two. If company A is the acquirer, it might pay a price for B which is equal to the PV of B's cash flows (£10m), in which case all of the gain from the merger will accrue to A. However, this is highly unlikely. Usually an acquiring firm has to pay a price significantly above the pre-bid value of the target company to gain control – this is called the **acquisition premium, bid premium** or **control premium.**

If it is assumed that before the bid B was valued correctly on the basis of its expected future cash flows to shareholders then the bid premium represents the transferring of some of the gains to be derived from the created synergy. For example, if A paid £15m for B then B's shareholders receive £5m of the gain. If A has to pay £20m to acquire B then A receives no gain.

In 2007 Barclays launched a takeover bid for ABN AMRO offering €68bn. Prior to the bidding period ABN AMRO was valued at €50bn (market capitalisation). Barclays expected to make 'annual pre-tax synergies of around €3.5bn by 2010 with about 80 per cent seen resulting from cost synergies and the rest from revenue benefits' (pre tax integration costs are expected to be €3.6bn).[6]

Also, note another possibility known as the '**winner's curse**' – the acquirer pays a price higher than the combined present value of the target and the potential gain. The winner's curse is illustrated by Scottish Power overpaying for PacifiCorp (*see* **Exhibit 23.3**).

[6] In the end Royal Bank of Scotland outbid Barclays to take over ABN AMRO

Exhibit 23.3

Electric shock as ScotPower pulls US plug

FT

The utility's long list of problems since taking over PacifiCorp reflect the difficulties involved in transatlantic takeovers

report Thomas Catan and Rebecca Bream

Scottish Power's surprise sale of its US arm is the latest example of a UK or US utility returning to its home market after being badly burnt abroad.

Scottish Power moved decisively into the US market in 1999 when it brought PacifiCorp for $10.9bn (£5.95bn) – $6.5bn for the equity plus the assumption of $4.4bn of debt.

It acquired one of the largest electricity generators in the western US. The Scottish company became far larger in the US, which seemed to hold the biggest promise, than it was in the UK.

But its prize has been dogged by a long list of problems ever since, including the California power crisis in 2000, regulatory problems, unhelpful weather and a falling US dollar. Yesterday it rid itself of the troubled unit, selling it to MidAmerica for $9.4bn ($5.1bn for the equity plus the assumption of $4.3bn of debt). It is taking a £927m hit in the process.

James Sparrow, Royal Bank of Scotland analyst, says: 'PacifiCorp has not been a successful acquisition, both operationally and financially.'

But if Scottish Power had a difficult time in the US, many American companies had an even worse experience in the UK market.

Many US utilities came to Britain after it deregulated its gas and electricity market, starting in the mid-1980s. But virtually none remain. Many, such as TXU of Texas and AES of Virginia, either exited the market or allowed their local operations to go bust.

Part of the problem was bad timing, analysts say. US utilities often overpaid for assets and were hit hard by a collapse of wholesale electricity prices in the late 1990s. But more broadly, companies often find it hard to replicate their success under sharply different regulatory environments.

'There have been very few cross-border utility acquisitions that you could say have been a shining success,' says another investment banker involved in yesterday's deal. 'Utilities are really very local businesses. And in the US they are very political because you're dealing with state governments. It helps if you're from that neck of the woods.'

Source: *Financial Times*, 22 May 2005, p. 23. Reprinted with permission.

Market power

One of the most important forces driving mergers is the attempt to increase **market power**. This is the ability to exercise some control over the price of the product. It can be achieved through either (**a**) monopoly, oligopoly or dominant producer positions, etc., or (**b**) collusion.

If a firm has a large share of a market it often has some degree of control over price. It may be able to push up the price of goods sold because customers have few alternative sources of supply. Even if the firm does not control the entire market, a reduction in the number of participating firms to a handful makes collusion easier. Whether openly or not, the firms in a concentrated market may agree amongst themselves to charge customers higher prices and not to undercut each other. The regulatory authorities are watching out for such socially damaging activities and have fined a number of firms for such practices, for example in the cement, vitamins and chemicals industries.

Market power is a motivator in vertical as well as horizontal mergers. Downstream mergers are often formed in order to ensure a market for the acquirer's product and to shut out competing firms. Upstream mergers often lead to the raising or creating of barriers to entry or are designed to place competitors at a cost disadvantage.

Even conglomerate mergers can enhance market power. For example, a conglomerate may force suppliers to buy products from its different divisions under the threat that it will stop buying from them if they do not comply. It can also support each division in turn as it engages in predatory pricing designed to eliminate competitors. Or it may insist that customers buy products from one division if they want products from another.

According to the European Commission, General Electric, in trying to merge with Honeywell, was attempting to put competitors at a disadvantage. In the end the Competition Commissioner blocked the bid, much to the annoyance of GE and US politicians, including George W. Bush – *see* **Exhibit 23.4**.

Exhibit 23.4

GE to face call for Gecas separation

FT

European Commission sees aircraft leasing arm as possible obstacle to Honeywell deal

by Deborah Hargreaves in Brussels

The European Commission is expected to press General Electric to separate the accounts and management of Gecas, its aircraft leasing arm, as a condition of giving the go-head to its $41bn (£29bn) deal to buy Honeywell.

The Commission is also believed to be looking for some divestment of part of Honeywell's avionics business and its regional jet engines business . . .

Gecas offers aircraft financing, leasing and fleet management. Brussels has been concerned about GE's ability to bundle products when offering equipment to airlines – for example, by offering a cheaper engine if an airline agrees to take Honeywell avionics – and its use of Gecas' market power to kit out airlines with GE products.

The Commission's statement of objections to the deal says: 'Gecas is therefore used by GE to influence the outcome of airlines' airframe purchasing decisions and act as a promoter of GE-powered airframes to the detriment of GE's engine manufacturer competitors and eventually results, through the use of its disproportionate power, in excluding competing engine sales.'

Gecas will specify the use of a GE engine in aircraft it wants to buy. Brussels is worried that the leasing arm will do the same for Honeywell's avionics and other aircraft equipment.

Source: *Financial Times*, 6 June 2001, p. 23. Reprinted with permission.

Economies of scale

An important contributor to synergy is the ability to exploit **economies of scale**. Larger size often leads to lower cost per unit of output. Rationalising and consolidating manufacturing capacity at fewer, larger sites can lead to economies of production utilising larger machines. Economies in marketing can arise through the use of common distribution channels or joint advertising. There are also economies in administration, research and development and purchasing.

Even with mergers of the conglomerate type managers claim achievable economies of scale. They identify savings from the sharing of central services such as administrative activities and accounting. Also the development of executives might be better at a large firm with a structured programme of training and access to a wider range of knowledgeable and experienced colleagues. Financial economies, such as being able to raise funds more cheaply in bulk, are also alluded to.

Many businesses possess assets such as buildings, machinery or people's skills which are not used to their full limits. For example, banks and building societies own high-street sites. In most cases neither the buildings nor the employees are being used as intensively as they could be. Hence we have one of the motivating forces behind bank and building society mergers. Once a merger is completed, a number of branches can be closed, to leave one rather than two in a particular location. Thus the customer flow to the remaining branch will be, say, doubled, with the consequent saving on property and labour costs.

Another synergistic reason for financial service industry mergers is the ability to market successful products developed by one firm to the customers of the other. Also when two medium-size banks or building societies become large, funds borrowed on the capital market are provided at a lower cost per unit of transaction and at lower interest rates.

Case study 23.1 on the oil industry demonstrates the importance of even greater size in an industry that already had giants.

Case study 23.1

Economies of scale in oil

Around the turn of the millennium there was a great deal of merger activity in the oil industry. Exxon and Mobil merged; as did Chevron and Texaco; Total, Fina and Elf; and BP, Amoco and Arco, to name a few. The financial markets encouraged the trend, seeing the benefits from economies of scale. Greater size allows the possibility of cutting recurring costs, particularly in overlapping infrastructure. It also means access to cheaper capital. However, the most important advantage it gives is the ability to participate in the difficult game of twenty-first-century exploration and production. The easily accessible oil of the world has long been tapped. Today's oil companies have to search in awkward places like the waters off West Africa and in China. The capital costs are enormous and risks are high. It is only very large companies that can put up the required money and absorb the risk of a series of failed explorations. In addition, bigger oil companies have more political clout in capitals around the world.

Occasionally firms present themselves to financial backers as 'industry consolidators', meaning that they perceive their industry as having too many companies with too much capacity chasing too little business. The logical actions are to reduce the output of the industry thus permitting prices to rise and/or to reduce the number of production sites to gain economies of scale. Industry returns on capital employed will rise to or above the required rates of return. A further boost comes from the selling-off of assets, e.g. closed warehouses might become trendy apartments, or a factory is sold to a company in another industry. Cadbury Schweppes pursues a policy of buying confectionery companies around the world, combining manufacturing, distribution and marketing and selling off surplus assets, gaining market power and economies of scale.

Internalisation of transactions

By bringing together two firms at different stages of the production chain an acquirer may achieve more efficient co-ordination of the different levels. The focus here is on the costs of communication, the costs of bargaining, the costs of monitoring contract compliance and the costs of contract enforcement. Vertical integration reduces the uncertainty of supply or the prospect of finding an outlet. It also avoids the problems of having to deal with a supplier or customer in a strong bargaining position. Naturally, the savings have to be compared with the extra costs which may be generated because of the loss of competition between suppliers – managers of units may become complacent and inefficient because they are assured of a buyer for their output.

Across Europe the heavy building materials industry is vertically integrated. The manufacturers of cement also own ready-mix concrete divisions and/or aggregates businesses. 'Cement represents the main cost item in the production of ready mix concrete, so there are powerful incentives for ready mix suppliers to secure access to supplies of cement to add to their existing supplies of aggregates.'[7]

Entry to new markets and industries

If a firm has chosen to enter a particular market but lacks the right know-how, the quickest way of establishing itself may be through the purchase of an existing player in that product or geographical market. To grow into the market organically, that is, by developing the required skills and market strength through internal efforts alone, may mean that the firm, for many years, will not have the necessary critical size to become an effective competitor. During the growth period losses may well be incurred. Furthermore, creating a new participant in a market may generate oversupply and excessive competition, producing the danger of a price war and thus eliminating profits. An example of a market-entry type of merger is Tata Steel's merger with Corus in 2007. As a result Tata quickly established a position as the leading steel producer in the UK, the Netherlands and a number of other countries without creating additional capacity.

[7] Charles Batchelor, 'Vertical integration sets building materials debate', *Financial Times*, 17 December 1999, p. 26.

Many small firms are acquired by large ones because they possess particular technical skills. The small firm may have a unique product developed through the genius of a small team of enthusiasts, but the team may lack the interest and the skills to produce the product on a large scale, or to market it effectively. The purchaser might be aware that its present range of products is facing a declining market or is rapidly becoming obsolescent. It sees the chance of applying its general managerial skills and experience to a cutting-edge technology through a deal with the technologically literate enthusiasts. Thus the two firms are worth more together than apart because each gains something it does not already have.

The large pharmaceutical companies frequently team up with biotechnology firms so that they can each draw on the strengths of the other – *see* **Exhibit 23.5**.

Exhibit 23.5

Valuing pharmas is not an exact science

FT

Big acquisition premiums may be perfectly justified

write Lisa Urquhart and Robert Orr

The prospect of Novartis paying what appears to be an eye-watering 100 per cent premium to the share price of NeuTec Pharma has again left some questioning why the market valuations for biotechnology companies bear little or no resemblance to what large pharmaceutical companies are prepared to pay for them.

Nick Lowcock, managing director at investment group Warburg Pincus, argues that, while there appears to be 'little art' in some of the valuations for biotechnology assets, prices are driven by the well-documented desire of big pharmaceutical companies to fill weakness in their own product pipelines.

'What we are seeing is that big pharma is starting to think about the relative costs to them of developing their own products and that appears to be getting more and more inefficient,' he says.

This inefficiency, says Alan McKay, lead healthcare partner at 3i, is leading to deals that are strategically driven rather than relying on what many would see as conventional analysis. 'If a company feels that they need a particular asset, they will pay to buy it,' he says.

What are not always clear to the outside market when big pharmaceutical companies come calling are their own internal valuations put on their targets.

Others in the industry point to how quickly 'hot' areas of research can emerge that can command high premiums, such as work on developing monoclonal antibodies that have created a number of blockbuster drugs, including Herceptin, the breast cancer treatment. Pfizer's $1.9bn (£1bn) deal for Vicuron, the anti-infectives business, reflects the growing annual worldwide spend on hospital acquired infections, now estimated at $1.5bn.

Andy Smith, investment manager at SV Life Sciences, says normal metrics such as net present value and discounted cash flows (DCF) are all used to value biotechnology companies. But the strategic value of some companies for some buyers can drive much headier premiums. 'If you use the DCF and net present value, you will often come out close to the share price,' he says. 'But, as a buyer, you are trying to prise future value away from shareholders and, to do that, you will have to pay a premium.'

Another explanation for what on the surface appear to be steep valuations is that the large timescales over which large pharmaceutical groups operate far exceed the much shorter time horizons of the equity market.

'Big pharma groups will look at assets in terms of the whole of the life of drug, which from inception to end could be 15 to 25 years,' says one investment banker. 'And if you consider this time-frame, which is even longer than investments from venture capital groups, it starts to look a a lot more reasonable.'

Samir Devani, biotechnology analyst at Nomura Code, highlights the 67 per cent proposed premium to be paid by AstraZeneca for Cambridge Antibody Technology. 'On the surface, the price tag looked very rich but AstraZeneca said that CAT would become its centre for biologics research. They weren't just paying for assets – they were paying for a platform to develop possibly hundreds of drugs.'

Source: Financial Times, 8 June 2006, p. 22. Reprinted with permission.

In the case of the merger between NTL, Telewest and Virgin mobile in 2006 the main motivations were to bring in the respected Virgin brand to replace the poor ones created by the cable companies and to tap customer service expertise.

Another reason for acquiring a company at the forefront of technology might be to apply the talent, knowledge and techniques to the parent company's existing and future product lines to give them a competitive edge. Many Chinese companies have this in mind when they buy western firms – *see* **Exhibit 23.6**.

Exhibit 23.6

Chinese companies acquire a taste for western targets

Hunger for technology has led some groups to hunt overseas

say James Mackintosh, Richard McGregor and Francesco Guerrera

FT

Chinese industry has been sucking in so much foreign cash to build new factories that it is easy to overlook the handful of acquisitions being made by the country's manufacturers.

But the trickle of small deals is rapidly growing into a stream of acquisitions as China's engineering, telecommunications equipment and white goods producers look for technical expertise and markets.

This month Shanghai Automotive Industry Corp, the country's largest carmaker, made a joint approach with Britain's MG Rover to buy a bankrupt car factory in Poland . . .

China's desire for foreign manufacturers is driven by three factors: to gain access to technology, to acquire research and development skills, and to find new markets . . .

Technology and R&D are by far the most important factors for the country's manufacturers, many of which have been reliant on foreign joint venture partners to provide fully engineered designs they can build . . .

Source: *Financial Times*, 19 October 2004, p. 20. Reprinted with permission.

Tax advantages

In some countries, if a firm makes a loss in a particular year these losses can be used to reduce taxable profit in a future year. More significantly, for this discussion about mergers, not only can past losses be offset against current profits within one firm in one line of business, past losses of an acquired subsidiary can be used to reduce present taxable profits of the parent company and thus lower tax bills. Thus there is an incentive to buy firms which have accumulated tax losses.

In the UK the rules are more strict. The losses incurred by the acquired firm before it becomes part of the group cannot be offset against the profits of another member of the group. The losses can only be set against the future profits of the acquired company. Also that company has to continue operating in the same line of business.

Risk diversification

One of the primary reasons advanced for conglomerate mergers is that the overall income stream of the holding company will be less volatile if the cash flows come from a wide variety of products and markets. At first glance the pooling of unrelated income streams would seem to improve the position of shareholders. They obtain a reduction in risk without a decrease in return.

The problem with this argument is that investors can obtain the same risk reduction in an easier and cheaper way. They could simply buy a range of shares in the separately quoted firms. In addition, it is said that conglomerates lack focus – with managerial attention and resources being dissipated.

A justification which is on more solid theoretical grounds runs as follows. A greater stability of earnings will appeal to lenders, thus encouraging lower interest rates. Because of the reduced earnings volatility there is less likelihood of the firm producing negative returns and so it should avoid defaulting on interest or principal payments. The other group that may benefit from diversification is individuals who have most of their income eggs in one basket – that is, the directors and other employees.

Bargain buying

The first column of Exhibit 23.2 deals with the potential gains available through the combining of two firms' trading operations. The second column shows benefits which might be available to an acquiring company which has a management team with superior ability, either at running a target's operations, or at identifying undervalued firms which can be bought at bargain prices.

Inefficient management

If the management of firm X is more efficient than the management of firm Y then a gain could be produced by a merger if X's management is dominant after the unification. Inefficient management may be able to survive in the short run but eventually the owners will attempt to remove them by, say, dismissing the senior directors and management team through a boardroom coup. Alternatively the shareholders might invite other management teams to make a bid for the firm, or simply accept an offer from another firm which is looking for an outlet for its perceived surplus managerial talent.

A variation on the theme is where the target firm does have talented management but they are directing their efforts in their own interests and not in the interests of shareholders. In this case the takeover threat can serve as a control mechanism limiting the degree of divergence from shareholder wealth maximisation.

Undervalued shares

Many people believe that stock markets occasionally underestimate the true value of a share. It may well be that the potential target firm is being operated in the most efficient manner possible and productivity could not be raised even if the most able managerial team in the world took over. Such a firm might be valued low by the stock market because the management are not very aware of the importance of a good stock market image. Perhaps they provide little information beyond the statutory minimum and in this way engender suspicion and uncertainty. Investors hate uncertainty and will tend to avoid such a firm. On the other hand, the acquiring firm might be very conscious of its stock market image and put considerable effort into cultivating good relationships with the investment community.

This line of thinking does not automatically reject semi-strong-form efficiency. This requires that share prices fully reflect all publicly available information. In many of these situations the acquiring firm has knowledge that goes beyond that which is available to the general public. It may be intimately acquainted with the product markets, or the technology, of the target firm and so can value the target more accurately than most investors. Or it may simply be that the acquirer puts more resources into information searching than anyone else. Alternatively the acquirer may be an insider, using private information, and may buy shares illegally.

Managerial motives

The reasons for merger described in this section are often just as rational as the ones which have gone before, except, this time, the rational objective may not be shareholder wealth maximisation.

One group which seems to do well out of merger activity is the management team of the acquiring firm.[8] When all the dust has settled after a merger they end up controlling a larger enterprise. And, of course, having responsibility for a larger business means that the managers *have* to be paid a lot more money. Not only must they have higher monthly pay to induce them to give of their best, they must also have enhanced pension contributions and myriad perks. Being in charge of a larger business and receiving a higher salary also brings increased status. Some feel more successful and important, and the people they rub shoulders with tend to be in a more influential class.

---

[8] For evidence on the monetary benefits to directors of expanding the firm, *see* Meeks and Whittington (1975), Firth (1991) and Conyon and Clegg (1994).

As if these incentives to grow rapidly through mergers were not enough, some people simply enjoy putting together an empire – creating something grand and imposing gives a sense of achievement and satisfaction. To have control over ever-larger numbers of individuals appeals to basic instincts: some measure their social position and their stature by counting the number of employees under them. Warren Buffett comments, 'The acquisition problem is often compounded by a biological bias: many CEOs attain their positions in part because they possess an abundance of animal spirits and ego. If an executive is heavily endowed with these qualities – which, it should be acknowledged, sometimes have their advantages – they won't disappear when he reaches the top. When such a CEO is encouraged by his advisors to make deals, he responds much as would a teenage boy who is encouraged by his father to have a normal sex life. It's not a push he needs.'[9]

John Kay points out that many managers enjoy the excitement of the merger process itself:

> For the modern manager, only acquisition reproduces the thrill of the chase, the adventures of military strategy. There is the buzz that comes from the late-night meetings in merchant banks, the morning conference calls with advisers to plan your strategy. Nothing else puts your picture and your pronouncements on the front page, nothing else offers so easy a way to expand your empire and emphasise your role.[10]

These first four managerial motives for merger – empire building, status, power and remuneration – can be powerful forces impelling takeover activity. But, of course, they are rarely expressed openly, and certainly not shouted about during a takeover battle.

Hubris

The fifth reason, hubris, is also very important in explaining merger activity. It may help particularly to explain why mergers tend to occur in greatest numbers when the economy and companies generally have had a few good years of growth, and management are feeling rather pleased with themselves.

Richard Roll in 1986 spelt out his hubris hypothesis for merger activity. **Hubris** means overweening self-confidence or, less kindly, arrogance. Managers commit errors of over-optimism in evaluating merger opportunities due to excessive pride or faith in their own abilities. The suggestion is that some acquirers do not learn from their mistakes and may be convinced that they can see an undervalued firm when others cannot. They may also think that they have the talent, experience and entrepreneurial flair to shake up a business and generate improved profit performance (*see* **Exhibit 23.7**).

Exhibit 23.7 Warren Buffett on hubris

On toads and princesses

'Many managements apparently were overexposed in impressionable childhood years to the story in which the imprisoned, handsome prince is released from the toad's body by a kiss from the beautiful princess. Consequently, they are certain that the managerial kiss will do wonders for the profitability of Company T(arget). Such optimism is essential. Absent that rosy view, why else should the shareholders of Company A(cquisitor) want to own an interest in T at the 2X takeover cost rather than at the X market price they would pay if they made direct purchases on their own? In other words, investors can always buy toads at the going price for toads. If investors instead bankroll princesses who wish to pay double for the right to kiss a toad, those kisses had better pack some real dynamite. We've observed many kisses, but very few miracles. Nevertheless, many managerial princesses remain serenely confident about the future potency of their kisses – even after their corporate backyards are knee-deep in unresponsive toads.'

Source: Warren Buffett, *Berkshire Hathaway Annual Report 1981*. Reprinted by kind permission of Warren Buffett. © Warren Buffett.

Note that the hubris hypothesis does not require the conscious pursuit of self-interest by managers. They may have worthy intentions but can make mistakes in judgement.

---

[9] Warren Buffett, *Berkshire Hathaway Annual Report 1984*.

[10] John Kay, 'Poor odds on the takeover lottery', *Financial Times*, 26 January 1996.

Survival

It has been noticed by both casual observers and empiricists that mergers tend to take place with a large acquirer and a smaller target. Potential target managements may come to believe that the best way to avoid being taken over, and then sacked or dominated, is to grow large themselves, and to do so quickly. Thus, mergers can have a self-reinforcing mechanism or positive feedback loop – the more mergers there are in an industry the more vulnerable management feel and the more they are inclined to carry out mergers – *see* **Exhibit 23.8**. Firms may merge for the survival of the management team and not primarily for the benefit of shareholders.[11]

Exhibit 23.8 The self-reinforcement effect of mergers

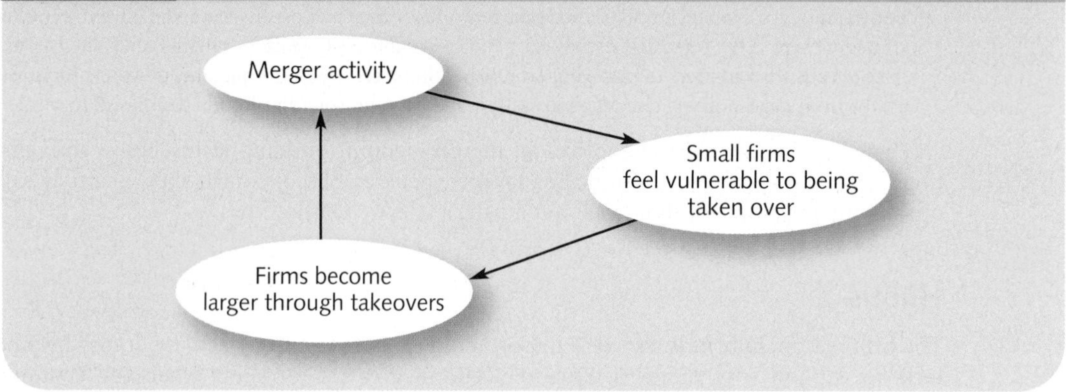

Free cash flow

Free cash flow is defined as cash flow in excess of the amount needed to fund all projects that have positive NPVs. In theory firms should retain money within the firm to invest in any project which will produce a return greater than the investors' opportunity cost of capital. Any cash flow surplus to this should be returned to shareholders (*see* Chapter 22).

However, Jensen (1986) suggests that managers are not always keen on simply handing back the cash which is under their control. This would reduce their power. Also, if they needed to raise more funds the capital markets will require justification concerning the use of such money. So instead of giving shareholders free cash flow the managers use it to buy other firms. Peter Lynch is more blunt: '[I] believe in the bladder theory of corporate finance, as propounded by Hugh Liedtke of Pennzoil: The more cash that builds up in the treasury, the greater the pressure to piss it away.'[12]

Third party motives

Advisers

There are many highly paid individuals who benefit greatly from merger activity.

Advisers charge fees to the bidding company to advise on such matters as identifying targets, the rules of the takeover game, regulations, monopoly references, finance, bidding tactics, stock market announcements and so on. Advisers are also appointed to the target firms.

Other groups with a keen eye on the merger market include accountants and lawyers. **Exhibit 23.9** gives some impression of the level of fees paid.

There is also the press, ranging from tabloids to specialist publications. Even a cursory examination of them gives the distinct impression that they tend to have a statistical bias of articles which emphasise the positive aspects of mergers. It is difficult to find negative articles, especially at the time of a takeover. They like the excitement of the merger event and rarely follow up with a

---

[11] *See* Louis (2004b) for an example in banking

[12] Lynch (1990), p. 204.

Exhibit 23.9 Advisers don't come cheap

A lucrative business for some

The amount of money spent on advisers during merger battles is truly astonishing.

In 2007 two groups were trying to take over the Dutch bank ABN AMRO. One was a consortium led by the Royal Bank of Scotland (the other was Barclays). The consortium's transactions costs were estimated at €660m. This was split between €175m for advisory fees plus a further €485m on expected expenses related to financing the offer (e.g. arrangement fees to advisers and banks for organising loans). Merrill Lynch alone, which advised the consortium and underwrote the financing, expected around €30m. Note: these are the costs to one of the bidders only. The costs to ABN AMRO and Barclays were also considerable.

When Mittal took over Arcelor in 2006, Goldman Sachs, Citigroup, Credit Suisse, Société Générale and HSBC shared more than $100m in fees. The investment banks involved in the takeover of O_2 by Telefónica received around £50m in fees in 2005 for advising on the deal plus payments related arranging the £18.5bn syndicated loan facility (thought to be hundreds of millions).

Investment bankers, lawyers and other advisers who worked on the 2004 merger between Santander Central Hispano and Abbey National are reported to have charged €179m (£121m). Bankers and lawyers advising on the 2004 bid battle for the UK landfill group Shanks initiated by Terra Firma picked up fees of about £23m representing a tenth of the £227.5m purchase price. Shanks' bill was a further £10m. Fees on smaller deals (like Shanks) are normally expected to be worth 3 to 4 per cent of the total sale value. For larger deals, e.g. Abbey which was sold for £8.5bn, they typically average between 0.125 per cent and 0.5 per cent of the value of the target.

considered assessment of the outcome. Also the press reports generally portray acquirers as dynamic, forward-looking and entrepreneurial.

It seems reasonable to suppose that professionals engaged in the merger market might try to encourage or cajole firms to contemplate a merger and thus generate turnover in the market. Some provide unsolicited reports on potential targets to try and tempt prospective clients into becoming acquirers.

Of course, the author would never suggest that such esteemed and dignified organisations would ever stoop to promote mergers for the sake of increasing fee levels alone. You may think that, but I could not possibly comment.

Suppliers and customers

In 2005 Rolls-Royce, the aircraft engine maker, called for consolidation of the aerospace parts sector. The company announced it would like to reduce the number of suppliers to as few as 40 companies, including 25 'first tier' suppliers (compared with 70 previously). This may lead to mergers amongst its suppliers. When Bosch merged with American Allied Signal and Lucas with Varity in the late 1990s there was pressure from the customers – the car producers. They were intent on reducing the number of car-parts suppliers and on putting more and more responsibility on the few remaining suppliers. Instead of buying in small mechanical parts from dozens of suppliers and assembling them themselves into, say, a braking system, the assemblers wanted to buy the complete unit. To provide a high level of service Bosch, which is skilled in electronics, needed to team up with Allied Signal for its hydraulics expertise. Similarly Lucas, which specialises in mechanical aspects of braking, needed Varity's electronic know-how. Ford announced that it was intent on reducing its 1,600 suppliers to about 200 and is 'even acting as marriage broker to encourage smaller suppliers to hitch-up with bigger, first-tier suppliers'.[13] These suppliers would then be world players with the requisite financial, technical and managerial muscle.

An example of suppliers promoting mergers is at the other end of the car production chain. Motor dealers in the UK in the late 1990s were sent a clear message from the manufacturers that a higher degree of professionalism and service back-up is required. This prompted a flurry of merger activity as the franchisees sought to meet the new standards.

[13] *The Economist*, 8 June 1996, pp. 92–3.

Exhibit 23.2 provided a long list of potential merger motives. This list is by no means complete. Examining the reasons for merger is far from straightforward. There is a great deal of complexity, and in any one takeover, perhaps half a dozen or more of the motives discussed are at play.

Financing mergers

Exhibit 23.1 showed the relative importance of alternative methods of paying for the purchase of shares in another company over three decades. The relative popularity of each method has varied considerably over the years but in most years cash is the most attractive option, followed by shares, and finally the third category, comprising mostly debentures, loan stocks, convertibles and preference shares.

The chart tends to give a slightly distorted view of the financial behaviour of acquiring firms. In many cases where cash is offered to the target shareholders the acquirer does not borrow that cash or use cash reserves. Rather, it raises fresh funds through a rights issue of shares before the takeover bid.

The chart may also be misleading in the sense that a substantial proportion of mergers do not fall neatly into the payment categories. Many are mixed bids, providing shareholders of the target firms with a variety of financial securities or offering them a choice in the consideration they wish to receive, for example cash or shares, shares or loan stock. This is designed to appeal to the widest range of potential sellers. For example, in 2006 NTL offered Virgin Mobile shareholders either 372p in cash, or 0.23245 NTL shares or 67p in cash plus 0.18596 NTL shares for each Virgin Mobile share.

Cash

One of the advantages of using cash for payment is that the acquirer's shareholders retain the same level of control over their company. That is, new shareholders from the target have not suddenly taken possession of a proportion of the acquiring firm's voting rights, as they would if the target shareholders were offered shares in the acquirer. Sometimes it is very important to shareholders that they maintain control over a company by owning a certain proportion of the firm's shares. Someone who has a 50.1 per cent stake may resist attempts to dilute that holding to 25 per cent even though the company may more than double in size.

The second major advantage of using cash is that its simplicity and preciseness give a greater chance of success. The alternative methods carry with them some uncertainty about their true worth. Cash has an obvious value and is therefore preferred by vendors, especially when markets are volatile.

From the point of view of the target's shareholders, cash has the advantage – in addition to being more certain in its value – that it also allows the recipients to spread their investments through the purchase of a wide-ranging portfolio. The receipt of shares or other securities means that the target shareholder either keeps the investment or, if diversification is required, has to incur transaction costs associated with selling the shares.

A disadvantage of cash to the target shareholders is that they may be liable for capital gains tax (CGT). This is payable when a gain is 'realised'. If the target shareholders receive cash for shares which have risen in value they may pay CGT. If, on the other hand, the target shareholders receive shares in the acquiring firm then their investment gain is not regarded as being realised and therefore no capital gains tax is payable at that time. The tax payment will be deferred until the time of the sale of the new shares – assuming an overall capital gain is made. (Note that some investment funds, e.g. pension funds, do not pay CGT and so this problem does not arise. Also, CGT can be reduced by tax-free allowances, and capital losses on other investments and so many shareholders will not consider CGT a burden.)

In certain circumstances the Takeover Panel insist on a cash offer or a cash alternative to an all-share offer.

One further consideration: borrowing cash that is then paid out for the target's shares may be a way of adjusting the financial gearing (debt to equity ratio) of the firm. On the other hand, the firm may already have high borrowings and be close to breaching loan covenants and so is reluctant to borrow more.

Shares

There are two main advantages to target shareholders of receiving shares in the acquirer rather than cash. First, capital gains tax can be postponed because the investment gain is not realised. Secondly, they maintain an interest in the combined entity. If the merger offers genuine benefits the target shareholders may wish to own part of the combined entity.

To the acquirer, an advantage of offering shares is that there is no immediate outflow of cash. In the short run this form of payment puts less pressure on cash flow. However the firm may consider the effect on the capital structure of the firm and the dilution of existing shareholders' positions – *see* **Exhibit 23.10**.

Exhibit 23.10

Vodafone's winning formula is now seen as a recipe for producing wrong numbers

FT

£113bn takeover was once hailed as a smart move. Not any more

says Dan Roberts

The end of the telecommunications investment bubble has put many of last year's takeovers and mergers under the spotlight.

Now attention is turning towards the biggest of them all – Vodafone's £113bn takeover of Mannesmann.

It had looked smart compared with deals struck by rivals such as British Telecommunications because it used highly-rated shares as currency rather than saddling Vodafone with unsustainable debt as a result of paying cash.

Assembling the world's biggest mobile phone company to provide mobile internet access seemed a winning formula.

But renewed scepticism about the growth potential of mobile internet services has led investors to question whether Mannesmann, and Vodafone's string of other acquisitions over the last 18 months, were worth the fourfold dilution of existing shareholders' holdings.

Vodafone shares have fallen 18 per cent since it produced its annual results on May 29, underperforming the sector as analysts have reduced forecasts. Its market capitalisation this week fell below £100bn – at the peak it was £270bn – with the shares at their lowest since October 1998.

Some of the pricing pressure reflects a share overhang, with recipients of Vodafone paper cashing in.

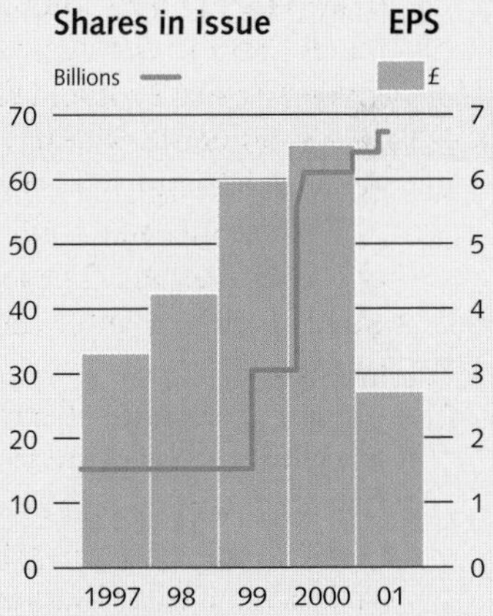

Source: Financial Times, 28 June 2001, p. 23. Reprinted with permission. Graphs: © Thomson Financial Datastream.

A second reason for the acquirer to use shares as the consideration is that the **price-earnings ratio (PER) game** can be played. Through this companies can increase their earnings per share (eps) by acquiring firms with lower PERs than their own. The share price can rise (under certain conditions) despite there being no economic value created from the merger.

Imagine two firms, Crafty plc and Sloth plc. Both earned £1m last year and had the same number of shares. Earnings per share on an historic basis are therefore identical. The difference between the two companies is the stock market's perception of earnings growth. Because Crafty is judged to be a dynamic go-ahead sort of firm with management determined to improve earnings per share by large percentages in future years it is valued at a high PER of 20.

Sloth, on the other hand, is not seen by investors as a fast-moving firm. It is considered to be rather sleepy. The market multiplies last year's earnings per share by only a factor of 10 to determine the share price – *see* **Exhibit 23.11**.

Exhibit 23.11 Illustration of the price to earnings ratio game – Crafty and Sloth

	Crafty	Sloth
Current earnings	£1m	£1m
Number of shares	10m	10m
Earnings per share	10p	10p
Price to earnings ratio	20	10
Share price	£2	£1

Because Crafty's shares sell at a price exactly double that of Sloth's it would be possible for Crafty to exchange one of its shares for two of Sloth's. (This is based on the assumption that there is no bid premium, but the argument that follows works just as well even if a reasonable bid premium is paid.)

Crafty's share capital rises by 50 per cent, from 10 million shares to 15 million shares. However eps are one-third higher. If the stock market still puts a high PER on Crafty's earnings, perhaps because investors believe that Crafty will liven up Sloth and produce high eps growth because of their more dynamic management, then the market capitalisation of Crafty increases and Crafty's shareholders are satisfied.

Each old shareholder in Crafty has experienced an increase in earnings per share and a share price rise of 33 per cent. Also, previously Sloth's shareholders owned £10m of shares in Sloth; now they own £13.33m of shares (*see* **Exhibit 23.12**).

Exhibit 23.12 Crafty after an all-share merger with Sloth

	Crafty
Earnings	£2m
Number of shares	15m
Earnings per share	13.33p
Price to earnings ratio	20
Share price	267p

This all seems rational and good, but shareholders are basing their valuations on the assumption that managers will deliver on their promise of higher earnings growth through operational efficiencies, etc. Managers of companies with a high PER may see an easier way of increasing eps and boosting share price. Imagine you are managing a company which enjoys a high PER. Investors in your firm are expecting you to produce high earnings growth. You could try to achieve this through real entrepreneurial and/or managerial excellence, for example by product improvement, achieving economies of scale, increased operating efficiency, etc. Alternatively you could buy firms with low PERs and not bother to change operational efficiency. In the long run you know that your company will produce lower earnings because you are not adding any value to the firms that you acquire, you are probably paying an excessive bid premium to buy the present earnings and you probably have little expertise in the new areas of activity.

However, in the short run, eps can increase dramatically. The problem with this strategy is that in order to keep the earnings on a rising trend you must continue to keep fooling investors. You have to keep expanding at the same rate to receive regular boosts. One day expansion will stop; it will be revealed that the underlying economics of the firms bought have not improved (they may even have worsened as a result of neglect), and the share price will fall rapidly. Here is another reason to avoid placing too much emphasis on short-term eps figures. The Americans call this the **bootstrap game**. It can be very lucrative for some managers who play it skilfully. However there can be many losers – society, shareholders, employees.

There are some significant dangers in paying shares for an aquisition, as Buffett makes clear in Exhibit 23.13.

Exhibit 23.13

Wealth for shareholders from mergers: the view of Warren Buffett

Our share issuances follow a simple basic rule: we will not issue shares unless we receive as much intrinsic business value as we give. Such a policy might seem axiomatic. Why, you might ask, would anyone issue dollar bills in exchange for fifty-cent pieces? Unfortunately, many corporate managers have been willing to do just that.

The first choice of these managers in making acquisitions may be to use cash or debt. But frequently the CEO's cravings outpace cash and credit resources (certainly mine always have). Frequently, also, these cravings occur when his own stock [shares] is selling far below intrinsic business value. This state of affairs produces a moment of truth. At that point, as Yogi Berra has said, 'You can observe a lot just by watching.' For shareholders then will find which objective the management truly prefers – expansion of domain or maintenance of owners' wealth.

The need to choose between these objectives occurs for some simple reasons. Companies often sell in the stock market below their intrinsic business value. But when a company wishes to sell out completely, in a negotiated transaction, it inevitably wants to – and usually can – receive full business value in whatever kind of currency the value is to be delivered. If cash is to be used in payment, the seller's calculation of value received couldn't be easier. If stock [shares] of the buyer is to be currency, the seller's calculation is still relatively easy: just figure the market value in cash of what is to be received in stock.

Meanwhile, the buyer wishing to use his own stock as currency for the purchase has no problems if the stock is selling in the market at full intrinsic value.

But suppose it is selling at only half intrinsic value. In that case, the buyer is faced with the unhappy prospect of using a substantially undervalued currency to make its purchase.

Ironically, were the buyer to instead be a seller of its entire business, it too could negotiate for, and probably get, full intrinsic business value. But when the buyer makes a partial sale of itself – *and that is what the issuance of shares to make an acquisition amounts to* – it can customarily get no higher value set on its shares than the market chooses to grant it.

The acquirer who nevertheless barges ahead ends up using an undervalued (market value) currency to pay for a fully valued (negotiated value) property. In effect, the acquirer must give up \$2 of value to receive \$1 of value. Under such circumstances, a marvelous business purchased at a fair sales price becomes a terrible buy. For gold valued as gold cannot be purchased intelligently through the utilization of gold – or even silver – valued as lead.

If, however, the thirst for size and action is strong enough, the acquirer's manager will find ample rationalizations for such a value-destroying issuance of stock. Friendly investment bankers will reassure him as to the soundness of his actions. (Don't ask the barber whether you need a haircut.)

A few favorite rationalizations employed by stock-issuing managements follow:

(a) 'The company we're buying is going to be worth a lot more in the future.' (Presumably so is the interest in the old business that is being traded away; future prospects are implicit in the business valuation process. If 2X is issued for X, the imbalance still exists when both parts double in business value.)

(b) 'We have to grow.' (Who, it might be asked, is the 'We'? For present shareholders, the reality is that all existing businesses shrink when shares are issued. Were Berkshire to issue shares tomorrow for an acquisition, Berkshire would own everything that it now owns plus the new business, but *your* interest in such hard-to-match businesses as See's Candy Shops, National Indemnity, etc. would automatically be reduced. If (1) your family owns a 120-acre farm and (2) you invite a neighbor with 60 acres of comparable land to merge his farm into an equal partnership – with you to be managing partner, then (3) your managerial domain will have grown to 180 acres but you will have ▶

permanently shrunk by 25% your family's ownership interest in both acreage and crops. Managers who want to expand their domain at the expense of owners might better consider a career in government.) . . .

There are three ways to avoid destruction of value for old owners when shares are issued for acquisitions. One is to have a true business-value-for-business-value merger, . . . Such a merger attempts to be fair to shareholders of *both* parties, with each receiving just as much as it gives in terms of intrinsic business value . . . It's not that acquirers wish to avoid such deals, it's just that they are very hard to do . . .

The second route presents itself when the acquirer's stock sells at or above its intrinsic business value. In that situation, the use of stock as currency actually may enhance the wealth of the acquiring company's owners . . .

The third solution is for the acquirer to go ahead with the acquisition, but then subsequently repurchase a quantity of shares equal to the number issued in the merger. In this manner, what originally was a stock-for-stock merger can be converted, effectively, into a cash-for-stock acquisition. Repurchases of this kind are damage-repair moves. Regular readers will correctly guess that we much prefer repurchases that directly enhance the wealth of owners instead of repurchases that merely repair previous damage. Scoring touchdowns is more exhilarating than recovering one's fumbles.

The language utilized in mergers tends to confuse the issues and encourage irrational actions by managers. For example, 'dilution' is usually carefully calculated on a pro forma basis for both book value and current earnings per share. Particular emphasis is given to the latter item. When that calculation is negative (dilutive) from the acquiring company's standpoint, a justifying explanation will be made (internally, if not elsewhere) that the lines will cross favorably at some point in the future. (While deals often fail in practice, they never fail in projections – if the CEO is visibly panting over a prospective acquisition, subordinates and consultants will supply the requisite projections to rationalize any price.) Should the calculation produce numbers that are immediately positive – that is, anti-dilutive – for the acquirer, no comment is thought to be necessary.

The attention given this form of dilution is overdone: current earnings per share (or even earnings per share of the next few years) are an important variable in most business valuations, but far from all-powerful.

There have been plenty of mergers, non-dilutive in this limited sense, that were instantly value-destroying for the acquirer. And some mergers that have diluted current and near-term earnings per share have in fact been value-enhancing. What really counts is whether a merger is dilutive or anti-dilutive in terms of intrinsic business value (a judgment involving consideration of many variables). We believe calculation of dilution from this viewpoint to be all-important (and too seldom made).

A second language problem relates to the equation of exchange. If Company A announces that it will issue shares to merge with Company B, the process is customarily described as 'Company A to Acquire Company B', or 'B Sells to A'. Clearer thinking about the matter would result if a more awkward, but more accurate description were used: 'Part of A sold to acquire B' or 'Owners of B to receive part of A in exchange for their properties'. In a trade, what you are giving is just as important as what you are getting . . .

Managers and directors might sharpen their thinking by asking themselves if they would sell 100% of their business on the same basis they are being asked to sell part of it. And if it isn't smart to sell all on such a basis, they should ask themselves why it is smart to sell a portion. A cumulation of small managerial stupidities will produce a major stupidity – not a major triumph. (Las Vegas has been built upon the wealth transfers that occur when people engage in seemingly-small disadvantageous capital transactions.) . . .

Finally, a word should be said about the 'double whammy' effect upon owners of the acquiring company when value-diluting stock issuances occur. Under such circumstances, the first blow is the loss of intrinsic business value that occurs through the merger itself. The second is the downward revision in market valuation that, quite rationally, is given to that now-diluted business value. For current and prospective owners understandably will not pay as much for assets lodged in the hands of a management that has a record of wealth-destruction through unintelligent share issuances as they will pay for assets entrusted to a management with precisely equal operating talents, but a known distaste for anti-owner actions. Once management shows itself insensitive to the interests of owners, shareholders will suffer a long time from the price/value ratio afforded their stock (relative to other stocks), no matter what assurances management gives that the value-diluting action taken was a one-of-a-kind event.

Source: Warren Buffett's Letter to Shareholders in the *Berkshire Hathaway Annual Report 1982*. Reprinted with permission. © Warren E. Buffett and Berkshire Hathaway Inc.

A disadvantage of using shares occurs when the acquirer is not quoted on a stock exchange. The target shareholders are unable to see a market price for the shares they receive. Also they will be unable to sell easily in a secondary market should they wish to do so.

Other types of finance

Alternative forms of consideration including debentures, loan stock, convertibles and preference shares are unpopular, largely because of the difficulty of establishing a rate of return on these securities which will be attractive to target shareholders. Also, these securities often lack marketability and voting rights over the newly merged company.

The merger process

The regulatory bodies

The **City Code on Takeovers and Mergers** ('**the Code**') provides the main governing rules for companies engaged in merger activity. The actions and responsibilities of quoted and unlisted public companies have been laid down over a period of more than 30 years. The Code was developed in a self-regulatory fashion by City institutions, notably the London Stock Exchange, the Bank of England, the investment institutions, companies, banks, and the accounting profession. It is administered on a day-to-day basis by the Panel Executive of the City Panel on Takeovers and Mergers ('the **Takeover Panel**'). The Panel has been designated as the supervisory authority to carry out certain regulatory functions under the Companies Act 2006 and the EU's Directive on Takeover Bids, and so the Panel's rules have been placed on a statutory footing.

Under company law directors are required to carry out their duty without prejudice in a fiduciary manner. That is, that they show trustworthy and faithful behaviour for the benefit of shareholders equally. The City Code adds to this by specifying standards of behaviour in merger situations.

The self-regulatory (with light-touch statutory back-up) approach is considered superior because it can provide a quick response in merger situations and be capable of regular adaptation to changed circumstances. Companies frequently try to bend or circumvent the rules and it is useful to have a system of regulation which is continually reviewed and updated as new loopholes are discovered and exploited. While the Panel may resort to law courts it rarely does so.

However, the Takeover Panel does have some powerful alternative sanctions. These range from public reprimands to the shunning of those who defy the Code by the regulated City institutions – the Financial Services Authority (FSA) requires that no regulated firm (such as a bank, a broker or an adviser) should act for client firms that seriously break the Panel's rules. Practitioners in breach of the Code may be judged not fit and proper persons to carry on investment business by the FSA so there is considerable leverage over the City institutions that might otherwise be tempted to assist a rule breaker. The Panel may give a ruling to restrain a person from acting in breach of the rules. It can also insist on compensation being paid. The FSA may also take legal action under market abuse legislation – e.g. when there is share price manipulation. In rare cases the Panel may temporarily remove share-voting rights for particular shareholders.

The fundamental objective of the Takeover Panel regulation is to ensure fair and equal treatment for all shareholders. The main areas of concern are:

- shareholders being treated differently, for example large shareholders getting a special deal;
- insider dealing (control over this is assisted by statutory rules);
- target management action which is contrary to its shareholders' best interests; for example, the advice to accept or reject a bid must be in the shareholders' best interest, not that of the management;
- lack of adequate and timely information released to shareholders;
- artificial manipulation of share prices; for example an acquirer offering shares cannot make the offer more attractive by getting friends to push up its share price;
- the bid process dragging on and thus distracting management from their proper tasks.

The **Office of Fair Trading** (**OFT**) also takes a keen interest in mergers to ensure that mergers do not produce 'a substantial lessening of competition'. The OFT has the power to clear a merger on competition grounds. A small minority of proposed mergers may, after an OFT initial screening, be followed by a **Competition Commission** (CC) investigation. The CC is the ultimate arbiter in deciding if a substantial lessening of competition is likely. It conducts full detailed investigations and can insist on major changes to the merged entity. For example Wm Morrison was required to sell a number of Safeway supermarkets following the merger in 2004.[14] A CC inquiry may take several months to complete, during which time the merger bid is put on hold. Currently (2007) there is some confusion as to where the jurisdiction boundaries of the OFT and the CC lie because competitors of the merging firms can ask a tribunal (the Competition Appeal Tribunal) to overturn a clearance by the OFT and insist on a CC referral thus casting doubt on the power of the OFT.

Another hurdle in the path of large intra-European Union mergers is their scrutiny by the European Commission in Brussels. This is becoming increasingly influential, but the Takeover Panel remains very powerful.

Pre-bid

Exhibit 23.14 shows the main stages of a merger. The acquiring firm usually employs advisers to help make a takeover bid. Most firms carry out mergers infrequently and so have little expertise in-house. The identification of suitable targets may be one of the first tasks of the advisers. Once these are identified there would be a period of appraising the target. The strategic fit would be considered and there would be a detailed analysis of what would be purchased. The product markets and types of customers could be investigated and there would be a financial analysis showing sales, profit and rates of return history. The assets and liabilities would be assessed and non-balance sheet assets such as employees' abilities would be considered.

If the appraisal stage is satisfactory the firm may approach the target. Because it is often cheaper to acquire a firm with the agreement of the target management, and because the managers and employees have to work together after the merger, in the majority of cases discussions take place which are designed to produce a set of proposals acceptable to both groups of shareholders and managers.

During the negotiation phase the price and form of payment have to be decided upon. In most cases the acquirer has to offer a bid premium. This tends to be in the range of 20 per cent to 100 per cent of the pre-bid price. The average is about 30–50 per cent. The timing of payment is also considered. For example, some mergers involve 'earn-outs' in which the selling shareholders (usually the same individuals as the directors) receive payment over a period of time dependent on the level of post-merger profits. The issue of how the newly merged entity will be managed will also be discussed – who will be chief executive? Which managers will take particular positions? Also the pension rights of the target firm's employees and ex-employees have to be considered, as does the issue of redundancy, especially the removal of directors – what pay-offs are to be made available?

If agreement is reached then the acquirer formally communicates the offer to the target's board and shareholders. This will be followed by a recommendation from the target's board to its shareholders to accept the offer.

If, however, agreement cannot be reached and the acquirer still wishes to proceed the interesting situation of a **hostile bid** battle is created. One of the first stages might be a '**dawn raid**'. This is where the acquirer acts with such speed in buying the shares of the target company that the raider achieves the objective of obtaining a substantial stake in the target before the target's management have time to react. The acquirer usually offers investors and market makers a price which is significantly higher than the closing price on the previous day. This high price is only offered to those close to the market and able to act quickly

An important trigger point for disclosure of shareholdings in a company, whether the subject of a merger or not, is the 3 per cent holding level. If a 3 per cent stake is owned then this has to be declared to the company. This disclosure rule is designed to allow the target company to know who is buying its shares and to give it advance warning of a possible takeover raid. The management can then prepare a defence and present information to shareholders should the need arise.

If a company builds up a stake of more than 30 per cent the Takeover Panel rules usually oblige it to make a cash bid for all of the target company's shares (or a share offer with a cash alternative) at the highest price paid in the previous 12 months. A 30 per cent stake often gives the owner a

[14] This was actually negotiated between the OFT and Morrisons following the Competition Commission's ruling.

Exhibit 23.14 The merger process

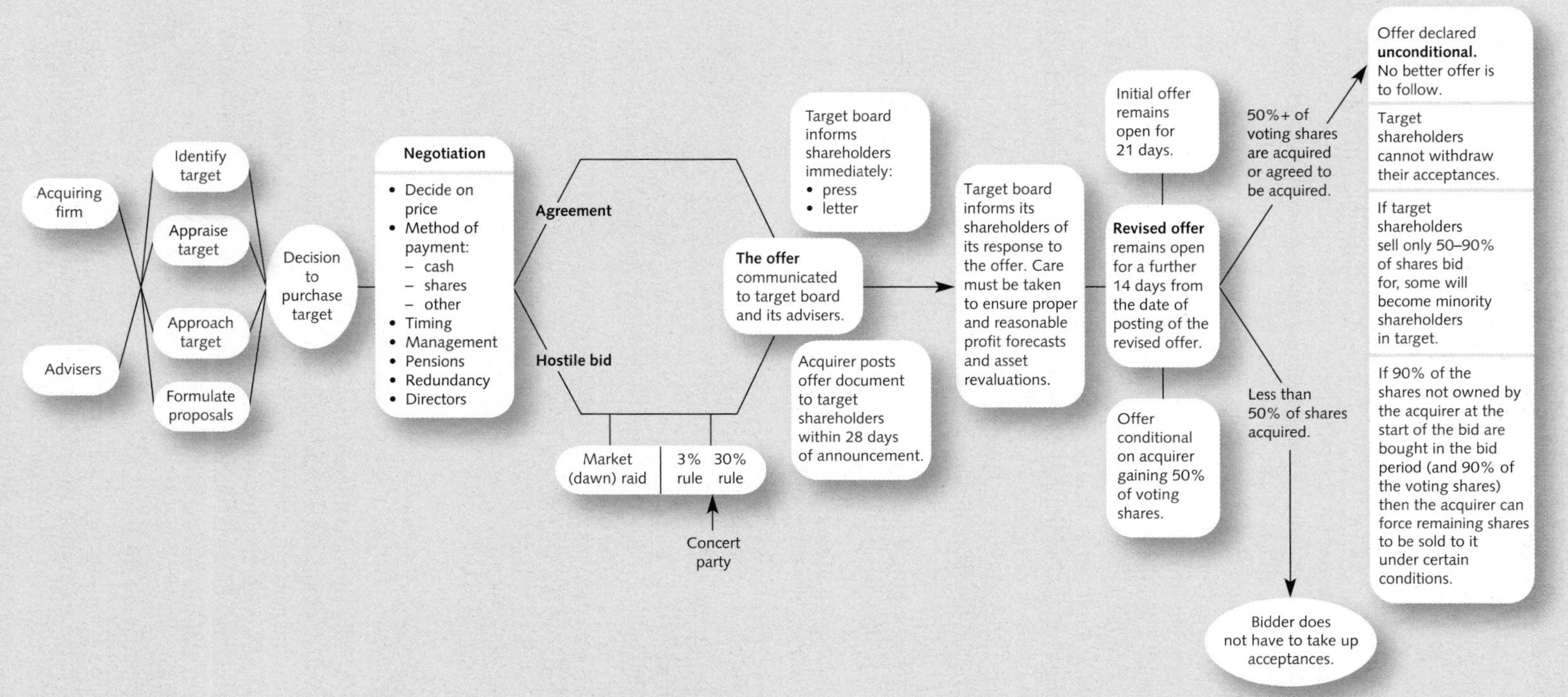

substantial amount of power. It is very difficult for anyone else to bid successfully for the firm when someone already has 30 per cent. It is surprising how often one reads in the financial press that a company or individual has bought a 29.9 per cent holding so that they have as large a stake as possible without triggering a **mandatory bid.**

Sometimes, in the past, if a company wanted to take over another it would, to avoid declaring at the 3 per cent level (or 5 per cent as it was then), or to avoid bidding at the 30 per cent level, sneak up on the target firm's management and shareholders. It would form a '**concert party**' by persuading its friends, other firms and individuals to buy stakes in the target. Each of these holdings would be below the threshold levels. When the acquirer was ready to pounce it would already have under its control a significant, if not a majority, controlling interest. Today all concert party holdings are lumped together for the purposes of disclosure and trigger points.

Once a company becomes a bid target any dealings in the target's shares by the bidder (or an associate) must be publicly disclosed no later than 12 noon on the business day following the transaction. Furthermore, once an offer is under way, any holder of 1 per cent or more of either the bidder or the target must publicly disclose dealings by midday of the next business day. An investor holding 1 per cent must disclose any dealings in the bidder's or target's shares, warrants, convertibles, contracts for difference, options, other derivatives and all other securities in the company.

A tactic that has become common recently is for a potential bidder to announce that it is thinking of making a bid rather than actually doing it – it makes an '**indicative offer**' (dubbed a '**virtual bid**'), saying it might bid but not committing itself to the expense and strict timetable of a formal offer. Shareholders in targets may gain from having potential bidders announce an interest in buying their shares and are in favour of allowing time for the bid to be put together. On the other hand, it is not in the shareholders' interest for the management continually to feel under siege. The Takeover Panel permits indicative offers, but after a few weeks (generally six to eight) without a genuine offer emerging it declares that the potential bidder has to 'put up or shut up' before a deadline date. Once that period has expired the virtual bidder must walk away for at least six months.

Traps for bidders to avoid

If the bidder purchases shares carrying 10 per cent or more of the voting rights in the offer period or in the previous 12 months before a bid, the offer must include a cash alternative at the highest price paid by the bidder. A potential bidder, therefore, should be careful not to buy any shares at a price higher than a fair value.

If the bidder buys shares in the target at a price above the offer price during a bid the offer must be increased to that level. So, the bidder should be careful of topping up acceptances by offering a high price to a few shareholders.

The bid

In both a friendly and a hostile bid the acquirer is required to give notice to the target's board and its advisers that a bid is to be made. The press and the Stock Exchange are usually also informed. The target management must immediately inform their shareholders (and the Takeover Panel). This is done through an announcement to the Stock Exchange and a press notice (disseminated on numerous free financial websites), which must be quickly followed by a letter explaining the situation. In a hostile bid the target management tend to use phrases like 'derisory offer' or 'wholly unacceptable'.

Within 28 days of the initial notice of an intention to make an offer the offer document has to be posted to each of the target's shareholders. Details of the offer, the acquirer and its plans will be explained. If the acquisition would increase the total value of the acquirer's assets by more than 15 per cent the acquirer's shareholders need to be informed about the bid. If the asset increase is more than 25 per cent then shareholders must vote in favour of the bid proceeding. They are also entitled to vote on any increase in authorised share capital.

The target management have 14 days in which to respond to the offer document by writing to all its shareholders. Assuming that they recommend rejection, they will attack the rationale of the merger and the price being offered. They may also highlight the virtues of the present management and reinforce this with revised profit forecasts and asset revaluations. There follows a period of attack and counter-attack through press releases and other means of communication. Public relations consultants may be brought in to provide advice and to plan tactics.

The offer remains open for target shareholders to accept for 21 days from the date of posting the offer document. If the offer is revised it must be kept open for a further 14 days from the posting date of the revision.[15] However, to prevent bids from dragging on endlessly the Panel insists that the maximum period for a bid is 60 days from the **offer document date** (posting day). The final offer day is day 46, which allows 14 days for acceptances. There are exceptions: if another bidder emerges, then it has 60 days, and its sixtieth day becomes the final date for both bidders; or if the board of the target agrees to an extension; if the bid is referrred to the CC the Panel can 'stop the clock'. If the acquirer fails to gain control within 60 days then it is forbidden to make another offer for a year, to prevent continual harassment.

Post-bid

Usually an offer becomes unconditional when the acquirer has bought, or has agreed to buy, 50 per cent of the target's shares. Prior to the declaration of the **offer as unconditional** the bidding firm would have said in the offer documents that the offer is conditional on the acquirer gaining (usually) 50 per cent of the voting shares. This allows the bidding firm to receive acceptances from the target shareholders without the obligation to buy.[16] Once the bid is declared unconditional the acquirer is making a firm offer for the shares which it does not already have, and indicating that no better offer is to follow. Before the announcement of unconditionality those target shareholders who accepted the offer are entitled to withdraw their acceptance. After it, they are forbidden to do so.

Usually in the days following unconditionality the target shareholders who have not already accepted quickly do so. The alternative is to remain a minority shareholder – still receiving dividends (if management and majority shareholders decide to pay dividends) but with power concentrated in the hands of a majority shareholder. There is a rule to avoid the frustration of having a small group of shareholders stubbornly refusing to sell. If the acquirer has bought nine-tenths of the shares (and 90 per cent of voting shares) it bid for, it can, within three to six months of the last date on which the offer can be accepted, insist that the remaining shareholders sell at the final offer price.

If the bid has lapsed or not been declared unconditional the bidder cannot bid again for a 12-month period. However, the bidder is allowed to bid again if a bid is made by another company or the bidder's renewed offered is recommended by the target management.

A scheme of arrangement is an alternative way of taking over another company – *see* **Exhibit 23.16**.

The impact of mergers

There has been a significant amount of empirical research into mergers and their impact. Some of the questions asked and answered will be considered in this section.

Are target firms poor performers?

One of the proclaimed benefits of mergers is that they can be a spur to increased efficiency. Surely, it is argued, the most inefficient managers will be removed through a takeover by more efficient managers, won't they? Some evidence suggests that those firms which become targets are no less

---

[15] If an offer is revised all shareholders who accepted an earlier offer are entitled to the increased payment.

[16] If 90 per cent of the target shares are offered, the bidder must proceed (unless there has been a material adverse change of circumstances). At lower levels of acceptance, it has a choice of whether to declare unconditionality.

Exhibit 23.15 Defence tactics

Roughly one-half of UK hostile bids are unsuccessful. Here are a few of the tactics employed by target managers to prevent a successful bid or to reduce the chances of a bid occurring.

Before bidding starts

- ***Eternal vigilance*** Be the most effective management team and educate shareholders about your abilities and the firm's potential. Cultivate good relationships with unions, work force and politicians. Polish social image.
- ***Defensive investments*** Your firm buys a substantial proportion of the shares in a friendly firm, and it has a substantial holding of your shares.
- ***Forewarned is forearmed*** Keep a watch on the share register for the accumulation of shares by a potential bidder.

After bidding has started

- ***Attack the logic of the bid*** Also attack the quality of the bidder's management.
- ***Improve the image of the firm*** Use revaluation, profit projections, dividend promises, public relations consultants.
- ***Attack the value creating (destroying) record of the bidder.***
- ***Try to get an OFT block or Competition Commission inquiry.***
- ***Encourage unions, the local community, politicians, customers and suppliers to lobby on your behalf.***
- ***White Knight*** Invite a second bid from a friendly company.
- ***Lobby your major shareholders.***
- ***Buy another business to make the firm too big or incompatible with the bidder.***
- ***Arrange a management buyout of your company.***
- ***Begin litigation against the bidder*** Bidders sometimes step over the legal boundary in their enthusiasm – e.g. making false statements, gaining private information by going through dustbins – a court case could be embarrassing.
- ***Employee share ownership plans (ESOPs)*** These can be used to buy a substantial stake in the firm and may make it more difficult for a bidder to take it over.
- ***Share repurchase*** Reduces the number of shares available in the market for bidders.

The following tactics are likely to be frowned upon or banned by the Takeover Panel in the UK, but are used in the USA and in a number of continental European countries.

- ***Poison pills*** Make yourself unpalatable to the bidder by ensuring additional costs should it win – for example, target shareholders are allowed to buy shares in target or acquirer at a large discount should a bid be successful.
- ***Crown jewels defence*** Sell off the most attractive parts of the business.
- ***Pac-Man defence*** Make a counter-bid for the bidder.
- ***Asset lock-up*** A friendly buyer purchases those parts of the business most attractive to the bidder.
- ***Stock lock-up*** (***White squire***) Target shares are issued to a friendly company or individual(s).
- ***Golden parachutes*** Managers get massive pay-offs if the firm is taken over.
- ***Give in to greenmail*** Key shareholders try to obtain a reward (for example, the repurchase of their shares at premium) from the company for not selling to a hostile bidder or for not becoming a bidder themselves. (Green refers to the colour of a US dollar.)
- ***Limit voting rights*** In some European states the management have the ability to limit voting rights to say a maximum of 15 per cent regardless of the actual shareholding.

profitable than those which do not. Singh (1971) has provided some evidence on the best way to avoid becoming a takeover victim. It has little to do with performance and more to do with size. Singh concluded that once firms reach an average profitability there is no incentive to increase profits further in order to avoid being taken over. His rules to avoid being taken over are:

- For *small firms with low profitability* – increase profitability to just above average, (note: satisficing not maximising).
- *For medium and large firms* – increase size rather than the rate of profit.

Other researchers who have identified larger size as a factor that decreases the likelihood of being taken over include Hasbrouck (1985), Palepu (1986), Ambrose and Megginson (1992), Levine and Aaronovitch (1981), Powell and Thomas (1994) and Louis (2004b). This evidence suggests that the threat of takeovers, rather than inducing profit maximisation, encourages firms to grow bigger and faster.

Exhibit 23.16

Bid tactics

by Martin Dickson

FT

Are conventional takeover bids an endangered species? You might think so, judging by recent trends. Yesterday New Look, the fashion chain, received a buy-out bid, to be carried out via a scheme of arrangement – the same mechanism Wm Morrison is using for its takeover of Safeway, approved by shareholders on Wednesday.

A scheme is an increasingly popular bid mechanism that involves a target company convening an extraordinary meeting where the takeover is voted on. Approval requires 75 per cent of the shares voted and the courts then sanction the deal. It is an alternative to the more traditional route, whereby a bidder offers to buy a target's shares and wins once it has got acceptances for more than 50 per cent.

A scheme has three big advantages over a traditional bid. It often can be completed much faster; it can be cheaper, since it is not subject to stamp duty; and private equity bidders – which account for a large proportion of takeovers – like it.

This is because they automatically end up with 100 per cent of the company. Under a conventional bid, they can only force out minority shareholders if 90 per cent of investors have accepted the offer – and there have been several recent cases of large fund managers blocking this.

However, schemes are not as flexible as conventional bids and put control of the process in the hands of the target company, which calls the EGM. So it is not appropriate for a hostile offer, where the target is fighting to the death . . .

Source: Financial Times, 14 February 2004, p. M2. Reprinted with permission.

Franks and Mayer (1996) found that hostile bids in the UK do not appear to be directed at poorly performing firms. Bhide's (1993) research, on the other hand, showed that US target firms generally had poor, or at best mediocre, performance records. Targets of friendly mergers were more likely to be well managed.

Does society benefit from mergers?

One way in which society could benefit from a merger is if the resulting combination could produce goods at a lower cost as a result of economies of scale or improved management. However set alongside this is the fact that mergers may also result in social costs in the form of monopoly power. Investigators have attempted to weigh up these two offsetting outcomes of mergers in general.

The conclusions of researchers in this area generally are that at best mergers are neutral for society.[17] In some studies the cost is seen as greater than the benefit.[18] These analyses are based on the average outcome. They do not exclude the possibility that many mergers do produce social gains greater than the social cost.

The balance of social gains and losses was considered in the case of the bid by GEC (now Marconi) for the submarine maker VSEL. Two of the Monopolies and Merger (now the Competition) Commission commissioners said that the cost reductions resulting from the rationalisation of the shipyard industry would benefit the customer (the government) more than the disbenefit resulting from the loss of competition. The other four commissioners believed that the loss of competition was too great a price to pay. The President of the Board of Trade overruled the majority verdict of the MMC – *see* **Exhibit 23.17**.

[17] For example, *see* Singh (1971), Firth (1980) and Lev (1992).

[18] For example, Cowling *et al.* (1980) concluded that in many cases efficiency was not improved but monopoly profits were made available to the acquirer.

Exhibit 23.17

GEC given go-ahead to bid for VSEL

FT

Heseltine overrules monopolies commission report after assurances on competition

Mr Michael Heseltine, trade and industry secretary, yesterday cleared General Electric Company to bid for VSEL, the submarine maker, overruling a recommendation by the Monopolies and Mergers Commission that GEC's pursuit should be blocked.

GEC, however, has had to agree – if successful in its bid – to maintain separate teams at VSEL's Barrow yard and its own Yarrow site on the Clyde to bid for future contracts in competition with each other.

British Aerospace, the other company pursuing VSEL, was cleared by the commission, and is also able to bid. A bidding war is now likely to resume in the stock market with BAe renewing its share offer for VSEL and GEC offering cash.

The commission was split over whether to block GEC, with two of the six members recommending that GEC should proceed if it could provide adequate safeguards. Mr Heseltine said that as GEC had offered assurances on competition and having taken into account the views of the Ministry of Defence, he would allow GEC's bid to proceed.

The commission's majority report said the proposed takeover of VSEL by GEC would reduce competition. As a result, the MoD would pay a higher price for ships and there would be a loss of potential design and production improvements. Assurances from GEC could not wholly replace the pressure of competition, they said.

In a minority report, however, two of the six members said they thought assurances from GEC would be enough to ensure the procurement system was not abused. They added that the reduction in costs that would flow from GEC's rationalisation of the shipyard industry would also benefit taxpayers.

Source: Bernard Gray, *Financial Times*, 24 May 1995. Reprinted with permission.

Do the shareholders of acquirers gain from mergers?

Some of the evidence on the effects of acquisitions on the shareholders of the bidding firm is that in slightly over half of the cases shareholders benefit. However, most studies show that acquiring firms give their shareholders poorer returns on average than firms that are not acquirers. Even studies which show a gain to acquiring shareholders tend to produce very small average gains – *see* **Exhibit 23.18**.

Exhibit 23.18 Summary of some of the evidence on merger performance from the acquiring shareholders' perspective

Study	Country of evidence	Comment
Meeks (1977)	UK	At least half of the mergers studied showed a considerable decline in profitability compared with industry averages.
Firth (1980)	UK	Relative share price losses are maintained for three years post merger.
Ravenscraft and Scherer (1987)	USA	Small but significant decline in profitability on average.
Limmack (1991)	UK	Long-run underperformance by acquirers.
Franks and Harris (1989)	UK and USA	Share returns are poor for acquirers on average for the two years under one measurement technique, but better than the market as a whole when the CAPM is used as a benchmark.

Sudarsanam, Holl and Salami (1996)	UK	Poor return performance relative to the market for highly-rated (judged by price to earnings ratio) acquirers taking over low-rated targets. However some firms do well when there is a complementary fit in terms of liquidity, slack and investment opportunities.
Manson, Stark and Thomas (1994)	UK	Cash flow improves after merger, suggesting operating performance is given a boost.
Gregory (1997)	UK	Share return performance is poor relative to the market for up to two years post merger, particularly for equity-financed bids and single (as opposed to regular) bidders.
Loughran and Vijh (1997)	US	In the five post-merger years firms that offer shares as payment show negative returns relative to the market. Those that offer cash show positive market-adjusted returns.
Rau and Vermaelen (1998)	US	Acquirers underperform post merger. This is due to overoptimism by investors leading to overpricing of some acquirers regarded as glamour stocks at the time of the merger.
Sudarsanam and Mahate (2003)	UK	Generally acquirers underperform. Cash acquirers generate higher returns than equity payment acquirers. High price to earnings ratio (and low book to market ratio) acquirers do not perform as well as low PER acquirers (and low book to market ratio acquirers).
Goergen and Renneboog (2004)	Europe-wide study	On average bidder performance is roughly the same as the market during the four months around the merger announcement date. Bids financed by equity produce better announcement period returns than those financed by cash.
Conn, Cosh, Guest, and Hughes (2005)	UK	Quoted companies acquiring UK companies results in poor returns around the announcement date and over the subsequent three years on average (–22 per cent). UK acquirers in cross-border mergers of quoted companies also poor performers. However, private UK (not on stock market) acquirers tend to produce zero post-acquisition returns on average.
Gregory (2005)	UK	Acquirers underperform the market by 19.9 per cent over 60 months. Acquirers with a high level of free cash flow perform better than acquirers with low free cash flow in the five years following merger as measured by total return.
Moeller, Schingemann and Stulz (2005)	US	On average acquirer shareholders experience a poor return in the few days around acquisition announcement – particularly in 1998–2001 (hi-tech boom period).
Cosh, Guest, and Hughes (2006)	UK	The larger the holding of shares in the company by the chief executive the better the post-merger long-term share returns.
Powell and Stark (2005)	UK	Takeovers result in modest improvements in operating performance of acquirers.

KPMG sent a report to the press showing the poor performance of cross-border mergers in terms of shareholder value. They then, embarrassed, tried to retrieve the report before it received publicity. Many commentators said that the evidence, that only 17 per cent of cross-border mergers increased shareholder value, would not help KPMG win business assisting firms conducting such mergers – *see* **Exhibit 23.19**.

Exhibit 23.19

KPMG withdraws merger study

FT

Report casts doubt on effectiveness of cross-border deals

by Norma Cohen, Property Correspondent

KPMG, the accountancy and consultancy firm increasingly involved in advising on mergers, this weekend sought to withdraw a study which concluded that 83 per cent of cross-border mergers have not delivered shareholder value.

The high proportion of mergers that fail to add value raises questions about the effectiveness of many cross-border deals – an area in which 'Big Five' firms such as KMPG are increasingly seeking to expand their advisory role.

KMPG sent the report to journalists last week, noting that it was embargoed for publication today. However, late on Friday it asked that the report be withdrawn, saying it was postponing publication . . .

The study, commissioned by KPMG but carried out via confidential interviews by a third-party consultant, looked at a sample taken from the top 700 cross-border deals by value between 1996 and 1998.

In all, 107 companies world-wide participated. Of these, the study found 53 per cent destroyed shareholder value, while another 30 per cent produced no discernible difference. The conclusions came after an analysis of share price movements relative to those of similar competitors in the first year following the merger.

Source: Financial Times, 29 November 1999, p. 23. Reprinted with permission.

Much of the recent research has drawn attention to differences in post-acquisition performance of acquirers that are highly rated by investors at the time of the bid ('glamour shares') and the post-acquisition performance of low rated acquirers ('value shares'), e.g. with low price–earnings ratios or low share price relative to balance sheet net asset value. This overvaluation of glamorous shares seems to be at least a partial explanation for subsequent underperformance. Over time investors reassess the price premium placed on the glamour shares, bringing their prices down – whether they are acquirers or not.

Do target shareholders gain from mergers?

Acquirers usually have to pay a substantial premium over the pre-bid share price to persuade target shareholders to sell. The empirical evidence in this area is overwhelming – target shareholders gain from mergers.

Do the employees gain?

In the aftermath of a merger it sometimes happens that large areas of the target firm's operations are closed down with a consequent loss of jobs. Often operating units of the two firms are fused and overlapping functions are eliminated, resulting in the shedding of staff. However, sometimes the increased competitive strength of the combined entity saves jobs and creates many more.

Do the directors of the acquirer gain?

The directors of the acquirers often gain increased status and power. They also generally receive increased remuneration packages – *see* **Exhibit 23.20**.

Exhibit 23.20

Funds furious over RBS bonuses

FT

by Simon Targett, Investment Correspondent

The National Association of Pension Funds is to recommend that its members vote against the re-election of two Royal Bank of Scotland directors in protest against the pay-out to executives of 'takeover' bonuses worth £2.5m . . .

But last night Sir George Mathewson, RBS executive deputy chairman, told the FT the size of the bonuses paid to him and three other executives – £2.5m in total – 'wouldn't have given you bragging power in a Soho wine bar'.

Sir George, who received a takeover bonus of £759,000 for his part in the acquisition of NatWest, said the special bonuses were not discussed with shareholders prior to their award in March 2000. 'Frankly, [the award of the bonuses] was not worthwhile talking to shareholders about,' he said . . .

The NAPF's opposition to RBS's takeover bonuses follows its protest against telecoms group Vodafone for last year paying a £10m bonus to Chris Gent, its chief executive, for winning the race to buy Mannesmann of Germany.

Institutional shareholders dislike takeover bonuses because they reward executives for completing acquisitions rather than building shareholder value.

Source: Financial Times, 27 March 2001, p. 1. Reprinted with permission.

Do the directors of the target gain?

We do not have a definitive answer as to whether the directors of the target gain. In the press they are often unfairly described as the failed managers and therefore out of a job. They are the losers in the '**market for managerial control**'. In reality they often receive large pay-offs on their lengthy employment contracts and then take on another highly paid directorship.

Do the financial institutions gain?

The financial institutions benefit greatly from merger activity. They usually receive large fees, regardless of whether they are on the winning side in a bid battle.

Warren Buffett sums up the evidence on the winners from mergers:

> They are a bonanza for the shareholders of the acquiree; they increase the income and status of the acquirer's management; and they are a honey pot for the investment bankers and other professionals on both sides. But, alas, they usually reduce the wealth of the acquirer's shareholders, often to a substantial extent.[19]

Managing mergers

Many mergers fail to produce shareholder wealth and yet there are companies that pursue a highly successful strategy of expansion through mergers. This section highlights some of the reasons for failure and some of the requirements for success.

The three stages of mergers

There are three phases in merger management. It is surprising how often the first and third are neglected while the second is given great amounts of managerial attention. The three stages are:

- preparation;
- negotiation and transaction;
- integration.

---

[19] Letter to shareholders in the *Berkshire Hathaway Annual Report 1995*.

In the preparation stage strategic planning predominates. A sub-set of the strategic thrust of the business might be mergers. Targets need to be searched for and selected with a clear purpose – shareholder wealth maximisation in the long term. There must be a thorough analysis of the potential value to flow from the combination and tremendous effort devoted to the plan of action which will lead to the successful integration of the target.

The negotiation and transaction stage has two crucial aspects to it.

1 ***Financial analysis and target evaluation*** This evaluation needs to go beyond mere quantitative analysis into fields such as human resources and competitive positioning.

2 ***Negotiating strategy and tactics*** It is in the area of negotiating strategy and tactics that the specialist advisers are particularly useful. However, the acquiring firm's management must keep a tight rein and remain in charge.

The integration stage is where so many mergers come apart. It is in this stage that the management need to consider the organisational and cultural similarities and differences between the firms. They also need to create a plan of action to obtain the best post-merger integration.

The key elements of these stages are shown in **Exhibit 23.21**.

Exhibit 23.21 The progression of a merger

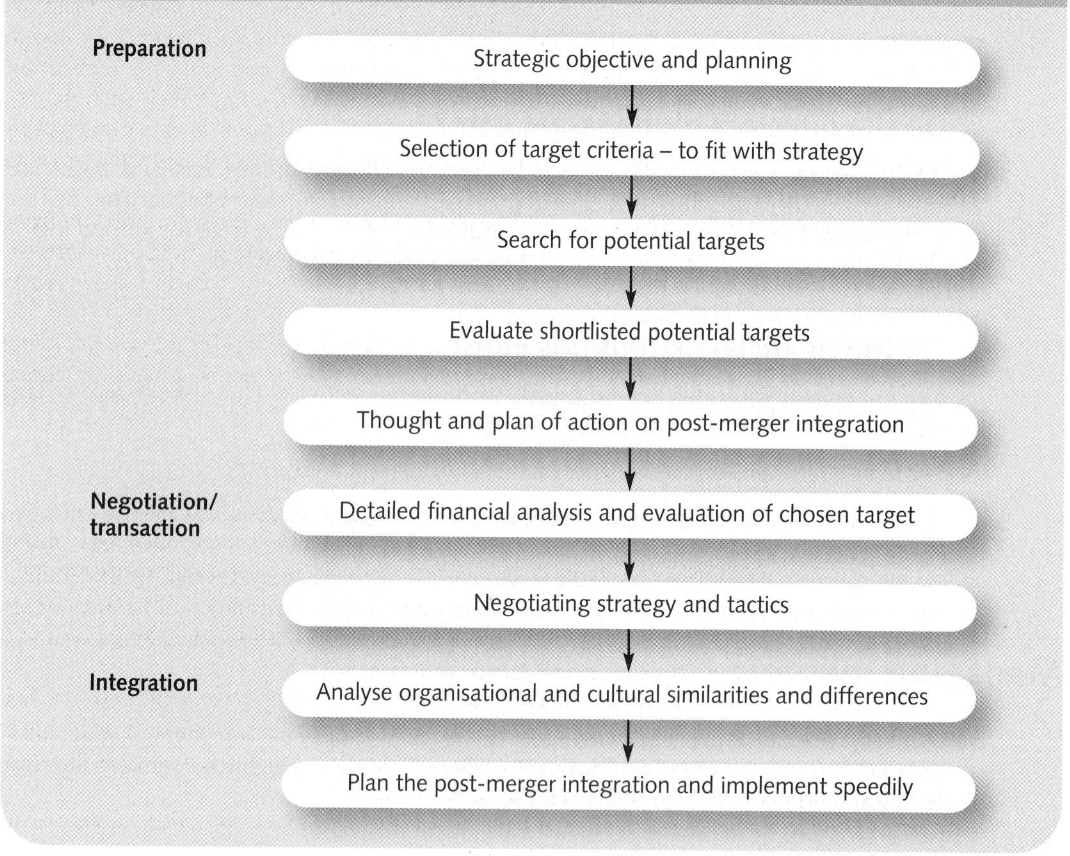

Too often the emphasis in managing mergers is firmly on the 'hard' world of identifiable and quantifiable data. Here economics, finance and accounting come to the fore. There is a worrying tendency to see the merger process as a series of logical and mechanical steps, each with an obvious rationale and a clear and describable set of costs and benefits. This approach all but ignores the potential for problems caused by non-quantifiable elements, for instance, human reactions and interrelationships. Matters such as potential conflict, discord, alienation and disloyalty are given little attention.[20] There is also a failure to make clear that the nature of decision making in this area relies as much on informed guesses, best estimates and hunches as on cold facts and figures.

[20] For a more thorough consideration of the human side of mergers consult Haspeslagh and Jemison (1991), Cartwright and Cooper (1992) and Buono and Bowditch (2003).

The organisational process approach

The organisational process approach takes into account the 'soft' aspects of merger implementation and integration. Here the acquisition process, from initial strategic formulations to final complete integration, is perceived as a complex, multifaceted programme with the potential for a range of problems arising from the interplay of many different hard and soft factors. Each merger stage requires imaginative and skilled management for the corporate objective to be maximised. (Sudarsanam (2003) is an excellent guide.)

Problem areas in merger management

We now examine some of the areas where complications may arise.

The strategy, search and screening stage

The main complicating element at the stage of strategy, search and screening is generated by the multitude of perspectives regarding a particular target candidate. Each discipline within a management team may have a narrow competence and focus, and thus there is potential for a fragmented approach to the evaluation of targets. For example, the marketing team may focus exclusively on the potential for marketing economies and other benefits, the research and development team on the technological aspects and so on. Communication between disparate teams of managers can become complicated and the tendency will be to concentrate the communication effort on those elements which can be translated into the main communicating channel of business, that is, quantifiable features with 'bottom lines' attached. This kind of one-dimensional communication can, however, all too easily fail to convey the full nature of both the opportunities and the problems. The more subtle aspects of the merger are likely to be given inadequate attention.

Another problem arises when senior managers conduct merger analysis in isolation from managers at the operating level. Not only may these 'coal-face' managers be the best informed about the target, its industry and the potential for post-merger integration problems; their commitment is often vital to the integration programme.

There is an obvious need to maximise the information flow effort both to obtain a balanced, more complete view of the target, and to inform, involve and empower key players in the successful implementation of a merger strategy.

The bidding stage

Once a merger bid is under way a strange psychology often takes over. Managers seem to feel compelled to complete a deal. To walk away would seem like an anticlimax, with vast amounts of money spent on advisers and nothing to show for it. Also they may feel that the investment community will perceive this management as being one unable to implement its avowed strategic plans. It may be seen as 'unexciting' and 'going nowhere' if it has to retreat to concentrate on its original business after all the excitement and promises surrounding a takeover bid.

Managers also often enjoy the thrill of the chase and develop a determination to 'win'. Pay, status and career prospects may hinge on rapid growth. Additionally, acquirers may be impelled to close the deal quickly by the fear of a counter-bid by a competitor, which, if successful, would have an adverse impact on the competitive position of the firm.

Thus mergers can take on a momentum which is difficult to stop. This is often nurtured by financial advisers keen on completing a transaction.

These phenomena may help to explain the heavy emphasis given to the merger transaction to the detriment of the preparation and integration stages. They may also go some way to explaining merger failure – in particular, failure to enhance shareholder value as a result of the winner's curse.

Expectations of the acquiring firm's operational managers regarding the post-merger integration stage

Clarity and planning are needed to avoid conflict and disappointment amongst managers. For example, the integration strategy may outline a number of different tasks to be undertaken in the 12–24 months following an acquisition. These may range from disposal of assets and combining operating facilities to new product development and financial reconstruction. Each of these actions may be led by a different manager. Their expectations regarding the speed of implementation and the order in which each of these actions will be taken may be different. A clear and rational resource-planning and allocation mechanism will reduce ambiguity and improve the co-ordination of decision making.

Aiming for the wrong type of integration

There are different degrees of integration when two firms come together under one leadership. At the one extreme is the complete **absorption** of the target firm and the concomitant fusing of two cultures, two operational procedures and two corporate organisations. At the other extreme is the **holding company, preservation or portfolio approach** where the degree of change of the acquired subsidiary may amount merely to a change in some financial control procedures, but otherwise the target firm's management may continue with their own systems, unintegrated operations and culture.

The complete integration approach is usually appropriate in situations where production and other operational costs can be reduced through economies of scale and other synergies, or revenues can be enhanced through, say, combined marketing and distribution. The preservation approach is most suitable when it is recognised that the disbenefits of forcing organisations together outweigh the advantages, for example when the products and markets are completely different and the cultures are such that a fusion would cause an explosive clash. These arm's-length mergers are typical of the acquisitive conglomerates. In such mergers general management skills are transferred along with strict financial performance yardsticks and demanding incentive schemes, but little else is changed.

With **symbiosis-based** mergers there is a need to keep a large degree of difference, at least initially, in culture, organisation and operating style, but at the same time to permit communication and cross-fertilisation of ideas. There may also be a need to transfer skills from one part of the combined organisation to another, whether through training and teaching or by personnel reassignment. An example might be where a book publisher acquires an Internet publisher; each is engaged in a separate market but there is potential for profitable co-operation in some areas. As well as being aware of the need for mutual assistance each organisation may be jealous of its own way of doing things and does not want its *esprit de corps* disrupted by excessive integration.

Exhibit 23.22 expresses the failure of some acquirers to plan a merger properly or to allow adequately for the complicating human factor.

Exhibit 23.22

How to make a corporate marriage work

FT

The tendency to relax after the deal has been done must be resisted – this is the make or break period for a takeover

says Stefan Stern

The deal has been signed, the analysts have been charmed and the press conference is over. But before placing an extra order for tomorrow's newspapers, the wise chief executive will remember that the hardest part of a merger or acquisition is just about to start.

Bringing two companies together is an enormous task, as executives at Proctor & Gamble and Gillette, the consumer goods giants that announced a deal last month, will now be discovering. There are grand, big-picture questions that need to be resolved, such as the new group's strategy and direction. There are also administrative, logistical and technical challenges. Will new contracts of employment be required? Where should the headquarters of the combined operations be located? How can the companies' information technology systems be integrated?

'It takes a certain humility to make a merger work,' says Charles Hampden-Turner, co-author of *Building Cross-cultural Competence*. 'It doesn't follow that your company is a better one simply because it has

Exhibit 23.22 continued

taken another company over. It just means that you've got more money and have been prepared to pay,' he says. 'You should be ready to sit down and learn from the acquired business. There may be expertise there that needs to be respected.'

Work on bringing the partners together should start well before the deal becomes public knowledge. Ravi Chanmugam, a partner at Accenture, the management consultancy, says: 'In essence, there should not be separate M&A and postmerger integration processes, but a holistic approach to the deal, from strategy to target identification and valuation to integration.'

But how can executives start planning integration without the news leaking out? Some use a so-called 'clean room', where trusted counterparties to a deal can meet and discuss future plans confidentially. Computer manufacturers Hewlett-Packard and Compaq, for example, adopted this approach in their $25bn (£13.3bn) merger in 2002.

Speed is of the essence. Roger Pudney of the UK's Ashridge business school says: 'There is often a tendency for companies to relax once the deal is signed, but this is precisely the point at which speed of implementation becomes crucial. Successful M&A companies stress the importance of quick wins as a way of demonstrating that the new combination is already producing added value.'

HP and Compaq ran a series of 'Fast Start' seminars for their staff as soon as their deal was announced to provide reassurance and a sense of direction – seminars that have been planned in advance in the clean room. Offering employees detailed information is essential at the early stage.

An internal human resources website set up for HP and Compaq staff received 2m hits on the day the merger was unveiled.

Managers will inevitably be occupied with practical, administrative changes, such as establishing new terms and conditions and pushing through any redundancies. Yet dealing with the cultural issues in a merger is more subtle and challenging. And when things go wrong in this context they can go wrong very quickly. Witnesses to board meetings of the newly-merged Carnaud Metal Box in 1989, for instance, recalled that French and British directors at times refused even to speak to each other.

Michelle Bligh, a professor at Claremont Graduate University, California, has suggested measures leaders should take to avoid the worst consequences of mergers.

After studying a merger of health organisations in the US, Prof Bligh advised leaders to avoid taking a dictatorial, top-down approach or micro-managing the transition. They need to respond as the new situation demands, she says, and must 'help followers negotiate, modify and even manipulate cultural similarities and differences in the post-merger environment.'

Prof Bligh identifies a few simple ground rules. Managers should recognise cultural differences between the companies, for example, by learning about the history of the new partner. They should give employees reasons why change is necessary, and find practical ways of communicating. As one manager told her: 'When you sit down and start showing employees the nitty-gritty, you get buy-in a lot quicker.'

Symbolism matters too. 'Instead of making great speeches,' Dr Hampden-Turner suggests, 'why not start acting differently and providing a lead that way? Words are too easy, but actions will be noticed.'

Even apparently mundane gestures can count. Discussing employees' new working conditions and being visible on the 'shop floor', for example, may reassure staff that management has an interest in their well-being. One manager in Prof Bligh's study said: 'We have to start with the little things: they really matter to people.'

Nevertheless, the post-merger period can be a draining, emotionally charged time for staff. Reflecting on her experience of the healthcare merger, a nurse said: 'The emotions were so strong, I would rather have my skin peeled off than go through that again.' Counselling services or an employee assistance programme can provide a useful outlet for tensions among staff.

How do the most successful acquirers handle the process of merger integration? General Electric, the US engineering conglomerate, has made more than 400 acquisitions in the past 20 years. But it is still learning how to make these deals work better. When GE bought Amersham, the UK bioscience company, in 2003 for $9bn, it made a big effort to reassure the acquired business that it would not be steam-rollered.

Steve Bolze, now president and chief executive of GE Healthcare Technologies International, led the integration team on the deal. 'This is the first major GE business to be headquartered outside the US,' he says. 'That sends a strong signal to the employees.'

The deal was also based on robust business principles. 'We have very clear revenue and cost-saving targets in year one,' he adds, 'and we carried out six months' planning between the announcement and the close of the deal, with people from both companies on the steering committee. We beat our specific integration targets, managing over $100m of synergies in 2004.'

Talk of a revival in merger and acquisitions activity is on the rise. Investment bankers and management consultants are once again seeking out potential deals and making flattering noises as they lead candidates to the altar. But marriages succeed or fail in the years following the wedding. Even before the hangover has worn off, the hard work has to begin.

Source: Financial Times, 7 February 2005, p. 10. Reprinted with permission.

Next steps in making that merger work

- Should you be starting from here? Are there compelling strategic reasons for this deal? Or is the company under pressure from investors and the media? Is the chief executive looking for a last hurrah before moving on?
- Get your integration plan right. Set target dates for major decisions on structure
- Define key functions in the new entity – including finance, HR, IT, legal – as soon as you can
- Plan to resolve cultural differences; this will largely happen through good communication
- Be careful to give customers priority during the transition; employees will not be the only stakeholder feeling unsettled

Why do mergers fail to generate value for acquiring shareholders?

A definitive answer as to why mergers fail to generate value for acquiring shareholders cannot be provided, because mergers fail for a host of reasons. However, there do appear to be some recurring themes.

The strategy is misguided

History is littered with strategic plans which turned out to be value destroying rather than value creating. Daimler-Benz in combining Mercedes with Fokker and Dasa tried to gain synergies from an integrated transport company then it tried to become a global car producer by merging with Chrysler. Marconi sold off its defence businesses to concentrate on telecommunication equipment. It spent a fortune buying companies at the forefront of technology only to slam into the high-tech recession in 2001 – its shares lost 98 per cent of their value. At the turn of the millennium TimeWarner thought it needed to pay a very high price to merge with AOL so that it could take a leading part in the convergence of media and information/communication technology. Fashion also seems to play its part, as with the conglomerate mergers of the 1960s, the cross-border European mergers of the early 1990s prompted by the development of the single market and the dot.com merger frenzy around the turn of the millennium.

Overoptimism

Acquiring managers have to cope with uncertainty about the future potential of their acquisition. It is possible for them to be over-optimistic about the market economics, the competitive position and the operating synergies available. They may underestimate the costs associated with the resistance to change they may encounter, or the reaction of competitors. Merger fever, the excitement of the battle, may lead to an openness to persuasion that the target is worth more than it really is (*see* **Exhibit 23.23**). A common mistake is the underestimation of the investment required to make a merger work, particularly in terms of managerial time.

Exhibit 23.23

On masquerading skimmed milk, lame horses and sexy deals

We believe most deals do damage to the shareholders of the acquiring company. Too often, the words from HMS Pinafore apply: 'Things are seldom what they seem, skim milk masquerades as cream.' Specifically, sellers and their representatives invariably present financial projections having more entertainment value than educational value. In the production of rosy scenarios, Wall Street can hold its own against Washington.

In any case, why potential buyers even look at projections prepared by sellers baffles me. Charlie and I never give them a glance, but instead keep in mind the story of the man with an ailing horse. Visiting the vet, he said: 'Can you help me? Sometimes my horse walks just fine and sometimes he limps.' The Vet's reply was pointed: 'No problem – when he's walking fine, sell him.' . . .

Talking to *Time Magazine* a few years back, Peter Drucker got to the heart of things: 'I will tell you a secret: Dealmaking beats working. Dealmaking is exciting and fun, and working is grubby. Running anything is primarily an enormous amount of grubby detail work . . . dealmaking is romantic, sexy. That's why you have deals that make no sense.'

. . . I can't resist repeating a tale told me last year by a corporate executive. The business he grew up in was a fine one, with a long-time record of leadership in its industry. Its main product, however, was distressingly glamorless. So several decades ago, the company hired a management consultant who – naturally – advised diversification, the then-current fad. ('Focus' was not yet in style.) Before long, the company acquired a number of businesses, each after the consulting firm had gone through a long – and expensive – acquisition study. And the outcome? Said the executive sadly: 'When we started we were getting 100% of our earnings from the original business. After ten years, we were getting 150%.'

Source: Warren Buffett. Letter to shareholders, *Berkshire Hathaway Annual Report 1995*. Reprinted with permission © Warren E. Buffett and Berkshire Hathaway Inc.

Failure of integration management

One problem is the over-rigid adherence to prepared integration plans. Usually plans require dynamic modification in the light of experience and altered circumstances. The integration programme may have been based on incomplete information and may need post-merger adaptation to the new perception of reality.

Common management goals and the engendering of commitment to those goals is essential. The morale of the workforce can be badly damaged at the time of a merger. The natural uncertainty and anxiety has to be handled with understanding, tact, integrity and sympathy. Communication and clarity of purpose are essential as well as rapid implementation of change. Cultural differences need to be tackled with sensitivity and trust established. According to a former Safeway executive, Morrison's were very insensitive when they took over: 'When they marched into Safeway, there were lots of capable, competent people. I know Martin Ackroyd's [finance director of Morrison] opening words when he arrived were "don't think this is a merger, this is a takeover" . . . Overnight everyone was disaffected and wanted to leave as quickly as they could'.[21] As a result of the mass of resignations Morrison struggled to understand and use Safeway's accounting system and failed in many other managerial areas. Morrison's share price plummeted.

Lord Browne, formerly of BP, advises quick integration: 'It's very important to mix the cultures early on. If the entities that existed previously still exist, then there is great reluctance to change anything.' He also suggests using a third party to help select the best managers. Following the merger with Amoco BP sent 400 top executives to an independent recruitment agency for assessment. 'When you merge with a company, you basically play with half a deck [of cards] because you know all your people, and they know all theirs. So how do you find a way of actually knowing everything about everyone – the answer is get a third party in.'[22]

The absence of senior management commitment to the task of successful integration severely dents the confidence of target and acquired managers.

Coopers & Lybrand, the international business advisers, conducted 'in-depth interviews with senior executives of the UK's top 100 companies covering 50 deals'. There emerged some factors which seem to contribute to failure, and others which are critical for raising the chances of success. These are shown in **Exhibit 23.24**.

The ten rules listed in **Exhibit 23.25** are NOT recommended for shareholder-wealth-orientated managers.

Exhibit 23.24 Survey on the reasons for merger failure and success – Coopers & Lybrand

The most commonly cited causes of failure include:		The most commonly cited reasons for success include:	
Target management attitudes and cultural differences	85%	Detailed post-acquisition plans and speed of implementation	76%
Little or no post-acquisition planning	80%	A clear purpose for making acquisitions	76%
Lack of knowledge of industry or target	45%	Good cultural fit	59%
Poor management and poor management practices in the acquired company	45%	High degree of management co-operation	47%
Little or no experience of acquisitions	30%	In-depth knowledge of the acquiree and his industry	41%

[21] *Financial Times*, 24 March 2005, p. 23

[22] Lord Browne quoted in David Buchan and Tobias Buck, 'Refining BP's management', *Financial Times*, 1 August 2002, p. 21. Reprinted with permission

Exhibit 23.25 Arnold's ten golden rules for alienating 'acquired' employees

1 Sack people in an apparently arbitrary fashion.

2 Insist (as crudely as possible) that your culture is superior. Attack long-held beliefs, attitudes, systems, norms, etc.

3 Don't bother to find out the strengths and weaknesses of the new employees.

4 Lie to people – some of the old favourites are:
- 'there will not be any redundancies';
- 'this is a true merger of equals'.

5 Fail to communicate your integration strategy:
- don't say why the pain and sacrifice is necessary, just impose it;
- don't provide a sense of purpose.

6 Encourage the best employees to leave by generating as much uncertainty as possible.

7 Create stress, loss of morale and commitment, and a general sense of hopelessness by being indifferent and insensitive to employees' needs for information.

8 Make sure you let everyone know that you are superior – after all, you won the merger battle.

9 Sack all the senior executives immediately – their knowledge and experience and the loyalty of their subordinates are cheap.

10 Insist that your senior management appear uninterested in the boring job of nuts-and-bolts integration management. After all knighthoods and peerages depend upon the next high-public-profile acquisition.

Exhibit 23.26 highlights some aspects not yet covered, including:

- a management and personnel audit;
- an alternative to merger is a strategic alliance;
- acquirers that fail to deliver value often become targets themselves.

Exhibit 23.27 summarises Cadbury Schweppes' lessons from its great experience of mergers.

Exhibit 23.26

A sometimes fatal attraction

FT

The problems with takeovers go beyond faulty strategic logic or paying too high a price. Even good deals founder if they are poorly managed after the merger . . .

The task of successfully implementing an acquisition or merger is formidable. If the acquiring company's shareholders are to make money from the deal, sales must be increased and costs reduced to a level that compensates for the premium over the share price paid for the company. This is rarely less than 20 per cent.

Unless there is a large overlap between the companies there are few easy savings. The targets of hostile bids are not necessarily poor performers, according to a study of takeovers in the mid-1980s by the London Business School . . .

[Most] companies delude themselves about the scale and nature of the task. They focus on revenue-enhancement opportunities rather than cost reduction, according to David Wightman, global head of strategy practice at PA Consulting Group. 'In fact revenue synergies are not often achieved in any great quantity, and frequently not at all.'

Companies also often delude themselves about the speed at which they should act. The desire to respect the culture of the acquired company and prevent the defection of important staff often slows the pace of integration . . .

The disadvantage with a slow approach to integration is that it tends to dissipate momentum and enthusiasm. Moreover, delays can dilute the financial benefits of a deal . . .

Nonetheless, the practical difficulty of integrating companies with different cultures cannot be underestimated. Recent research by London's Imperial College into European cross-border deals found that differences in management style – the formality of procedures, the adherence to job descriptions, the structure of communications – bore a strong correlation to deals' chances of failure . . .

[Consultants] urge managers to adopt different styles of management for different types of deal. Bill

Exhibit 23.26 continued

Pursche of McKinsey argues that different styles are appropriate depending on the degree of business overlap, the relative size of companies, the companies' skills, the urgency and source of the expected returns and the style of leadership.

For example, if cost savings are the main rationale of the merger, targets should be set at the top and passed through the organisation. If the goal is to achieve revenue synergies or longer-term skill transfers, then a more participatory approach, drawing recommendations from the 'grass roots', is appropriate. Pursche calls this 'empowering the troops' and says it can result in strong morale. But it is more common in merging companies to find poor morale, rising staff turnover and falling productivity.

There is probably no easy solution to poor morale. Reassuring staff about job security may not be possible – and may be counterproductive if proved false. Even so, companies are invariably advised to try to reduce uncertainty and explain the merger's rationale, through newsletters and meetings between senior executives and employees.

Unsurprisingly, pay is one of the most marked influences on morale. A London Business School study in 1987 found that in two-thirds of successful takeovers, the acquired management reported either improved performance incentives, better pension entitlements, better career prospects, or the introduction of share options.

The same study highlighted another important influence on the ultimate success of the acquisition: a thorough audit of the target company before the takeover.

Whereas all the buyers in the LBS study conducted financial audits of the acquired companies before they bought them, only 37 per cent carried out a management or personnel audit. Moreover, although buyers stressed the importance of the purchased company's middle management, 70 per cent did not meet these managers before the takeover.

The paucity of pre-merger planning causes frustration, particularly among managers concerned with human resources. A seminar of directors and financiers involved in takeovers sponsored by People in Business, a consultancy, uncovered a strongly held view that deals were too focused on financial measures . . .

However, institutional investors are imposing a tougher discipline on bidders than 10–15 years ago, according to Julian Franks of London Business School. 'People who acquire badly, frequently become targets themselves,' he says.

Another feature of the 1990s is the growth in strategic alliances as a cheaper, less risky route to a strategic goal than takeovers.

Source: Vanessa Houlder, *Financial Times*, 11 September 1995. Reprinted with permission.

Exhibit 23.27

Hearts and minds: Cadbury's recipe for merger success

The acquisition of Adams, the US gum manufacturer, in late 2002 was the culmination of nearly 20 years of smaller acquisitions by Cadbury Schweppes costing nearly £10bn, says Todd Stitzer. The cumulative lessons were:

1. Pick the right partner. Adams was founded in the late 1800s, but it was owned for much of the last century by pharmaceutical companies, most recently Pfizer. 'Many of the Adams people felt as if they were coming home,' Mr Stitzer says. The two companies were also complementary in geographical terms: 70 per cent of Adams' business was in the Americas, while Cadbury Schweppes' confectionery operations there were confined to Canada and Argentina.

2. Plan the integration well in advance. 'We started two years before we did the deal. We retained on a part-time basis six or seven old Adams executives who gave us insights into the operations and the culture of the company.'

3. Address the fear and anxiety of people in the target company. 'You have to demonstrate you're being utterly fair and objective in evaluating how they fit together in the new world. A long time ago, we adopted a principle we call "best person, right job"'. External evaluators work with the human resources team or job appointments. In several cases, Cadbury Schweppes executives lost out to Adams people.

4. Communicate. Mr Stitzer, John Sunderland, chairman, and Bob Stack, head of human resources, went to Adams' headquarters in New Jersey to address 11,000 employees by video link before the deal was closed. 'Acquisitions are big investments of shareowners' money. The single best challenge is winning the hearts and minds of the people you're coming together with.'

Source: *Financial Times*, 27 April 2005, p. 11. Reprinted with permission.

Concluding comments

At a minimum this chapter should have made it clear that following a successful merger strategy is much more than simply 'doing the deal'. Preparation and integration are usually of greater significance to the creation of value than the negotiation and transaction stage. And yet, too often, it is towards this middle stage that most attention is directed.

Doubts have been raised about the purity of the motives for mergers but we should restrain ourselves from being too cynical as many mergers do create wealth for shareholders and society. Industries with a shifting technological or market base may need fewer larger firms to supply goods at a lower cost. The savings from superior managerial talent are genuine and to be praised in many cases. Restructuring, the sharing of facilities, talent and ideas, and the savings from the internalisation of transactions are all positive outcomes and often outweigh the negative effects.

Like many tools in the armoury of management, growth through mergers can be used to create or destroy.

Key points and concepts

- **Mergers are a form of investment** and should, theoretically at least, be evaluated on essentially the same criteria as other investment decisions, for example using NPV. However there are complicating factors:
  - the benefits from mergers are difficult to quantify;
  - acquiring companies often do not know what they are buying.
- **A merger is the combining of two business entities under common ownership**. It is difficult for many practical purposes to draw a distinction between merger, acquisition and takeover.
- A **horizontal** merger is when the two firms are engaged in similar lines of activity.
- A **vertical** merger is when the two firms are at different stages of the production chain.
- A **conglomerate** merger is when the two firms operate in unrelated business areas.
- **Merger** activity has occurred in waves. **Cash** is the most common method of payment except at the peaks of the cycle when **shares** are a more popular form of consideration.
- **Synergistic merger motives**:
  - market power;
  - economies of scale;
  - internalisation of transactions;
  - entry to new markets and industries;
  - tax advantages;
  - risk diversification.
- **Bargain-buying merger motives**:
  - elimination of inefficient and misguided management;
  - undervalued shares.
- **Managerial merger motives**:
  - empire building;
  - status;
  - power;
  - remuneration;
  - hubris;
  - survival;
  - free cash flow.
- **Third-party merger motives**:
  - advisers;
  - at the insistence of customers or suppliers.

- **Value is created from a merger** when the gain is greater than the transaction cost.

  $$PV_{AB} = PV_A + PV_B + \text{gain}$$

  The gain may go to A's shareholders, or B's, or be shared between the two.
- The **winner's curse** is when the acquirer pays a price higher than the combined present value of the target and the potential gain.
- **Cash as a means of payment**

  For the acquirer

  Advantages
  - Acquirers' shareholders retain control of their firm.
  - Greater chance of early success.

  Disadvantages
  - Cash flow strain.

  For the target shareholders

  Advantages
  - Certain value.
  - Able to spread investments.

  Disadvantages
  - May produce capital gain tax liability.
- **Shares as a means of payment**

  For the acquirer

  Advantages
  - No cash outflow.
  - The PER game can be played.

  Disadvantages
  - Dilution of existing shareholders' control.
  - Greater risk of overpaying.
  - Unquoted acquirers may not be able to do this.

  For the target shareholders

  Advantages
  - Postponement of capital gains tax liability.
  - Target shareholders maintain an interest in the combined entity.

  Disadvantages
  - Uncertain value.
  - Not able to spread in the investment without higher transaction costs.
- The **City Code on Takeovers and Mergers** provides the main governing rules. It applies to quoted and unlisted public companies. It is self-regulatory with some statutory back-up. Its objective is to ensure fair and equal treatment for all shareholders.
- The **Office of Fair Trading (OFT)** and the **Competition Commission** investigate potential cases of competition constraints.
- **Pre-bid**
  - advisers appointed;
  - targets identified;
  - appraisal;
  - approach target;
  - negotiate.
- A **'dawn raid'** is where a substantial stake is acquired with great rapidity.
- Shareholdings of **3 per cent** or more must be notified to the company.
- A stake of **30 per cent** usually triggers a bid.
- **Concert parties**, where a group of shareholders act as one, but each remains below the 3 per cent or 30 per cent trigger levels, are now treated as one large holding for the key trigger levels.

- **The bid**
  - notice to target's board;
  - offer document sent within 28 days;
  - target management respond to offer document;
  - offer open for 21 days, but can be frequently revised and thereby kept open for up to 60 days (or longer if another bidder enters the fray).
- **Post-bid**
  - When a bid becomes unconditional (usually at 50 per cent acceptances), the acquirer is making a firm offer and no better offer is to follow.
- **Target firms are not on average poor performers** relative to others in their industry.
- **Society sometimes benefits** from mergers **but some studies suggest a loss**, often through the exploitation of monopoly power.
- The **shareholders of acquirers tend to receive returns lower than the market** as a whole after the merger. However many acquirers do create value for shareholders.
- Target **shareholders, directors of acquirers and advisers gain significantly** from mergers. For the **directors of targets and other employees** the evidence is mixed.
- **There are three stages of mergers**. Most attention should be directed at the first and third, but this does not seem to happen. These stages are:
  - preparation;
  - negotiation and transaction;
  - integration.
- **Non-quantifiable**, 'soft', human elements often determine the success or otherwise of mergers.
- **Mergers fail for three principal reasons**:
  - the strategy is misguided;
  - overoptimism;
  - failure of integration management.

References and further reading

Ambrose, B.W. and Megginson, W.L. (1992) 'The role of asset structure, ownership structure, and takeover defences in determining acquisition likelihood', *Journal of Financial and Quantitative Analysis*, 27(4), pp. 575–89.

Bhide, A. (1993) 'The causes and consequences of hostile takeovers', in Chew, Jr, D.H. (ed.), *The New Finance: Where Theory Meets Practice*. New York: McGraw-Hill.
Target firms are poor performers.

Buffett, W. (1982) Letter to Shareholders accompanying the Berkshire Hathaway Annual Report. Omaha, NE. www.berkshirehathaway.com.
Words of wit and wisdom forged by business experience.

Buffett, W. (1995) Letter to Shareholders accompanying the Berkshire Hathaway Annual Report. Omaha, NE. www.berkshirehathaway.com.
Words of wit and wisdom forged by business experience.

Buono, A. and Bowditch, J. (2003) *The Human Side of Mergers and Acquisitions*. Beard Books, US.
Explains the importance of the management of people during and after merger.

Cartwright, S. and Cooper, C. (1992) *Mergers and Acquisitions: The Human Factor*. Oxford: Butterworth Heinemann.
Cultural and other 'soft' issues of mergers are discussed.

Conyon, M.J. and Clegg, P. (1994) 'Pay at the top: a study of the sensitivity of top director remuneration to specific shocks', *National Institute of Economic and Social Research Review*, August.
Growth of the firm (sales) is positively related to directors' pay.

Coopers & Lybrand and OC & C (1993) *A review of the acquisition experience of major UK companies*. London: Coopers & Lybrand.
An interesting survey of the top 100 firms' reasons for difficulties and triumphs in post-merger management.

Conn, R.L., Cosh, A., Guest, P.M. and Hughes, A. (2005) 'The impact on UK acquirers of domestic, cross-border, public and private acquisitions', *Journal of Business Finance & Accounting*, 32(5) and (6), June/July.

UK quoted companies acquiring UK companies results in relatively poor returns around the announcement date and over the subsequent three years on average (–22 per cent). UK acquirers in cross-border mergers of quoted companies are also poor performers. However, private UK (not on stock market) acquirers tend to produce zero post-acquisition returns on average.

Cosh, A., Guest, P.M. and Hughes, A. (2006) 'Board share-ownership and takeover performance', *Journal of Business Finance &Accounting*, 33(3/4), Apr/May pp. 459–510.

UK study. The larger the holding of shares in the company by the chief executive the better the post-merger long-term share returns.

Cowling, K., Stoneman, P. and Cubbin, J. *et al.* (1980) *Mergers and Economic Performance*. Cambridge: Cambridge University Press.

Discusses the societal costs and benefits of mergers.

Devine, M. (2004) *Successful Mergers: Getting the people issues right*. London: The Economist/Profile Books.

An accessible introduction to the 'soft' managerial issues.

The Economist (2000) 'Merger Briefs' (two-page post-merger analysis of successes and failures) in the following editions: DaimlerChrysler, 29 July 2000; HypoVereinsbank, 5 August 2000; Boeing, 12 August 2000; Compaq, 22 July 2000; AOL Time Warner, 19 August 2000; Citicorp, 26 August 2000.

Epstein, M.J. (2005) 'The determinants and evaluation of merger success', *Business Horizons*, 48, pp. 37–46.

Offers six key factors needed for merger success; US case study incorporated.

Fee, C.E. and Thomas, S. (2004) 'Sources of gains in horizontal mergers: evidence from customer, supplier, and rival firms', *Journal of Financial Economics*, 74(3), Dec., pp. 423–60.

Improved productivity and buying power as a result of merger.

Firth, M. (1980) 'Takeovers, shareholders' returns and the theory of the firm', *Quarterly Journal of Economics*, 94, March, pp. 235–60.

UK study. Results: **a** The target shareholders benefit; **b** the acquiring shareholders lose; **c** the acquiring firm's management increases utility; **d** the economic gains to society are, at best, zero.

Firth, M. (1991) 'Corporate takeovers, stockholder returns and executive rewards', *Managerial and Decision Economics*, 12, pp. 421–8.

Mergers leading to increased size of firm result in higher managerial remuneration.

Franks, J. and Harris, R. (1989) 'Shareholder wealth effects of corporate takeovers: the UK experience 1955–85', *Journal of Financial Economics*, 23, pp. 225–49.

Study of 1,800 UK takeovers. Gains of 25–30 per cent for targets. Zero or modest gains for acquirers. Overall there is value created for shareholders.

Franks, J. and Mayer, C. (1996) 'Hostile takeovers and correction of managerial failure', *Journal of Financial Economics*, 40, pp. 163–81.

Ghosh, A. (2004) 'Increasing market share as a rationale for corporate acquisitions', *Journal of Business Finance & Accounting*, 31(1) & (2), January/March, pp. 209–47.

US study of 2,000 acquisitions. Increasing market share following merger is correlated with positive acquirer abnormal returns and operating performance.

Goergen, M. and Renneboog, L. (2004) 'Shareholder wealth effects of European domestic and cross-border takeover bids', *European Financial Management*, 10(1), pp. 9–45.

Europe-wide study. On average bidder performance is roughly the same as the market during the four months around the merger announcement date. Bids financed by equity produce better announcement period returns than those financed by cash.

Gregory, A. (1997) 'An examination of the long-run performance of UK acquiring firms', *Journal of Business Finance and Accounting*, 24(7–8), Sept., pp. 971–1002.

More evidence on the poor performance of acquirers.

Gregory, A. (2005) 'The long run abnormal performance of UK acquirers and the free cash flow hypothesis', *Journal of Business Finance & Accounting*, 32(5) & (6), June/July, pp. 777–814.

UK acquirers underperform the market by 19.9 per cent over 60 months 1984–92. Acquirers with a high level of free cash flow perform better than acquirers with low free cash flow in the five years following merger as measured by total return.

Harding, D., Rovit, S. and Corbett, A. (2005) 'Three steps to avoiding merger meltdown', *Harvard Management Update*, March, pp. 1–5.

A short article offering post-merger integration advice.

Hasbrouck, J. (1985) 'The characteristics of takeover targets: q and other measures', *Journal of Banking and Finance*, 9, pp. 351–62.

Haspeslagh, P. and Jemison, D. (1991) *Managing Acquisitions*. New York: Free Press.

A thorough and well-written guide to the management of firms that engage in mergers.

Higson, C. and Elliot, J. (1993) 'The returns to takeovers – the UK evidence', *IFA Working Paper*. London: London Business School.

More evidence on the poor performance of the shares of acquiring firms.

Hunt, J.W., Lees, S., Grumber, J. and Vivian, P. (1987) *Acquisitions: The Human Factor*. London: London Business School and Egan Zehnder International.

Forty UK companies investigated. Merger motives, success or failure rates and success factors (particularly people factors) are explored.

Jensen, M.C. (1986) 'Agency costs of free cashflow, corporate finance and takeovers', *American Economic Review*, May, p. 323.
Dividend payouts reduce managers' resources and lead to greater monitoring if they go to the capital markets for funds. Internal funding is thus preferred and surplus cash flow leads to value-destroying mergers. Easy to read.

Jensen, M.C. and Meckling, W.H. (1976) 'Theory of the firm: managerial behavior, agency cost and ownership structure', *Journal of Financial Economics*, October, pp. 305–60.
An important paper on agency theory.

Kuehn, D. (1975) *Takeovers and the theory of the firm: An empirical analysis for the United Kingdom 1957–1969.* Basingstoke: Macmillan.
Acquiring firms that engage in multiple acquisitions display profitability, growth rates, etc., that are no different from those of firms which engage in few takeovers.

Lev, B. (1992) 'Observations on the merger phenomenon and a review of the evidence'. Reprinted in J.M. Stern and D. Chew (eds), *The revolution in corporate finance.* 2nd edn. Oxford: Blackwell.
Merger motives, and who wins from mergers, are discussed in an introductory style.

Levine, P. and Aaronovitch, S. (1981) 'The financial characteristics of firms and theories of merger activity', *Journal of Industrial Economics*, 30, pp. 149–72.
An early paper on mergers.

Limmack, R. (1991) 'Corporate mergers and shareholder wealth effect, 1977–86', *Accounting and Business Research*, 21(83), pp. 239–51.
'Although there is no net wealth decrease to shareholders in total as a result of takeover activity, shareholders of bidder firms do suffer wealth decreases.'

Loughran, J. and Vijh, A.M. (1997) 'Do long term shareholders benefit from corporate acquisitions?', *Journal of Finance*, 52(5), pp. 1765–90.
Empirical evidence on post-merger performance.

Louis, H. (2004a) 'Earnings management and the market performance of acquiring firms' *Journal of Financial Economics*, 74(1), Oct., pp. 121–48.
Evidence suggesting that acquiring firms overstate earnings in quarter before acquiring – linked to poor post-merger performance.

Louis, H. (2004b) 'The cost of using bank mergers as defensive mechanisms against takeover threats' *Journal of Business*, 77(2) pt.1, pp. 295–310.
Evidence to show that by acquiring other banks managers can avoid being taken over.

Lynch, P. (1990) *One Up on Wall Street.* New York: Penguin.
One of the greatest investors comments on companies and managers in a witty fashion.

Manson, S., Stark, A. and Thomas, H.M. (1994) 'A cash flow analysis of the operational gains from takeovers', *Research Report 35.* London: Chartered Association of Certified Accountants.
Post-merger and pre-merger consolidated operating performance measures are compared. Operational gains are produced on average. A study of 38 companies.

McKinsey and company (Koller, T., Goedhart, and Wessels, D.) (2005) *Valuation.* 4th edn. New York: John Wiley and Sons Ltd.
Provides some useful and easy-to-follow guidance on merger management.

Meeks, G. (1977) *Disappointing Marriage: A Study of the Gains from Mergers.* Cambridge: Cambridge University Press.
Evidence on merger failure from the acquiring shareholders' point of view.

Meeks, G. and Whittington, G. (1975) 'Director's pay, growth and profitability', *Journal of Industrial Economics*, 24(1), pp. 1–14.
Empirical evidence that directors' pay and firm sales (size of firm) are positively correlated.

Mitchell, M.L. and Lehn, K. (1990) 'Do bad bidders become good targets?', *Journal of Political Economy*, 98(2), pp. 372–98.
'Hostile bust-up takeovers often promote economic efficiency by reallocating the targets' assets to higher valued uses . . . In aggregate, we find that the returns to acquiring firms are approximately zero; the aggregate data obscure the fact that the market discriminates between "bad" bidders which are more likely to become takeover targets, and "good" bidders, which are less likely to become targets.'

Moeller, S.B., Schlingemann, F.P. and Stulz, R.M. (2004) 'Firm size and the gains from acquisitions', *Journal of Financial Economics*, 73, pp. 201–228.
US study. Acquiring firm announcement period abnormal return is on average slightly positive for small firms but negative for large firms. Given that larger firms offer larger acquisition premiums and enter acquisitions with negative dollar synergy gains 'the evidence is consistent with managerial hubris playing more of a role in the decisions of large firms'.

Moeller, S.B., Schlingemann, F.P. and Stulz, R.M. (2005) 'Wealth destruction on a massive scale? A study of acquiring-firm returns in the recent merger wave', *The Journal of Finance*, LX(2), April, pp. 757–82.
US study. On average acquirer shareholders experience a poor return in the few days around acquisition announcement – particularly so in the period 1998–2001 (hi-tech boom period).

Morosini, P. and Steger, U. (eds) (2004) *Managing Complex Mergers: Real world lessons in implementing successful cross-cultural M&As.* Harlow: Financial Times Prentice Hall.
Provides an accessible overview of thinking on the issue of merger failure and merger management.

Palepu, K.G. (1986) 'Predicting takeover targets: a methodological and empirical analysis', *Journal of Accounting and Finance*, 8, pp. 3–35.

The Panel on Takeovers and Mergers, The City Code www.thetakeoverpanel.org.uk

The complex set of rules are laid out in reasonably easy-to-follow fashion. Updated regularly.

Powell, R.G. and Stark, A.W. (2005) 'Does operating performance increase post-takeover for UK takeovers? A comparison of performance measures and benchmarks', *Journal of Corporate Finance*, 11(1 & 2), March, p. 293–317.

Powell, R.G. and Thomas, H.M. (1994) 'Corporate control and takeover prediction', Working paper 94/07 (Department of Accounting and Financial Management, University of Essex).

Rappaport, A. (1998) *Creating Shareholder Value*. New York: Free Press.

Revised and updated. Chapter 8 provides a shareholder value perspective on mergers.

Rau, P.R. and Vermaelen, T. (1998) 'Glamour, value and the post-acquisition performance of acquiring firms', *Journal of Financial Economics*, 49(2), pp. 223–53.

Ravenscraft, D. and Scherer, F. (1987) *Mergers, Sell-Offs and Economic Efficiency*. Washington, DC: Brookings Institution.

An overview of mergers: rationale, activity, profitability, economics. US based.

Roll, R. (1986) 'The hubris hypothesis of corporate takeovers', *Journal of Business*, 59(2), pt. 1, April, pp. 197–216. Also reproduced in R. Thaler (ed.) (1993) *Advances in Behavioral Finance*. New York: Russell Sage Foundation.

'Bidding firms infected by hubris simply pay too much for their targets.'

Schweiger, D. (2002) *M&A integration: A framework for executives and managers*, Oxford: McGraw-Hill Education.

Deals with post-merger management.

Singh, A. (1971) *Takeovers*. Cambridge: Cambridge University Press.

Provides evidence on the type of firms which become targets.

Sirower, M.L. (1997) *The Synergy Trap: How Companies Lose the Acquisition Game*. New York: Free Press.

A practical, easy-to-read guide to mergers and the reasons for the failure to create value.

Stahl, G. and Mendenhall, M. (2005) *Mergers and Acquisitions: Managing Culture and Human Resources*. Stanford, CA: Stanford University Press.

The human aspect of mergers.

Sudarsanam, S. (2003) *Creating value from mergers and acquisitions: The challenge*. Harlow: Financial Times Prentice Hall.

An easy-to-read comprehensive guide to all aspects of mergers – well worth reading.

Sudarsanam, S. and Mahate, A. (2003) 'Glamour acquirers, methods of payment and post-acquisition performance: The UK evidence', *Journal of Business Finance and Accounting*, 30(1 & 2), pp. 299–341.

Sudarsanam, S., Holl, P. and Salami, A. (1996) 'Shareholder wealth gains in mergers: Effect of synergy and ownership structure', *Journal of Business Finance and Accounting*, July, pp. 673–98.

A study of 429 UK mergers, 1980–90. Financial synergy dominates operational synergy. A marriage between companies with a complementary fit in terms of liquidity slack and surplus investment opportunities is value creating for both groups of shareholders. But high-rated acquirers taking over low-rated firms lose value.

Van de Vliet, A. (1997) 'When mergers misfire', *Management Today*, June.

An excellent, easy-to-read overview of merger problems with plenty of examples.

Websites

www.berkshirehathaway.com
www.ft.com
www.kpmg.co.uk
www.londonstockexchange.com
www.thetakeoverpanel.org.uk
www.competition-commission.org.uk
www.oft.gov.uk

Video presentations

Chief executives and finance directors discuss their recent mergers (e.g. motives, people problems, and financial success) on Cantos.com (wwwcantos/com/cantos) – this is free to view.

Case study recommendations

Please see www.pearsoned.co.uk/arnold for case study synopses

- The Royal Bank of Scotland: Masters of Integration. Authors: Nitin Nohria and James B. Weber (2005) Harvard Business School.
- BP and the Consolidation of the Oil Industry – 1988–2002. Authors: Forest Reinhardt, Ramon Casadesus-Mansanell and David J Hanson (2003). Harvard Business School.
- Making the Deal Real: How GE Capital Integrate Acquisitions. Authors: Ronald N. Ashkenar, Lawrence J. DeMonaco and Suzanne C. Francis (1998) Harvard Business Review Article. (January–February pp. 5–15.)
- Vodafone AirTouch's Bid for Mannesmann. Author: Simi Kedia (2003) Harvard Business School.

Self-review questions

1 List as many motives for mergers as you can.

2 Briefly describe the alternative methods of payment for target firms and comment on their advantages and disadvantages.

3 Explain the significance of the following for the merger process:

- a concert party;
- the 3% rule;
- the 30% rule;
- the Takeover Panel;
- the OFT;
- the Competition Commission;
- a dawn raid.

4 List the potential beneficiaries from mergers and briefly explain whether, on average, they do gain from mergers.

5 What are the three stages of a merger?

6 List some actions which might assist a successful post-merger integration.

7 Explain the following in the context of mergers:

- synergy;
- the internalisation of transactions;
- bargain buying;
- hubris;
- the survival motive;
- the free cash flow merger motive.

8 How do mergers differ from other investment decisions?

9 Explain the terms horizontal mergers, vertical mergers and conglomerate mergers.

10 What is the winner's curse?

11 What does it mean when an offer goes 'unconditional'?

Questions and problems

myfinancelab **Questions with an icon are also available for practice in MyFinanceLab with additional supporting resources.**

For those questions marked with an asterisk* the answers are given in the Lecturer's guide.

1* Large plc is considering the takeover of Small plc. Large is currently valued at £60m on the stock market while Small is valued at £30m. The economies of scale and other benefits of the merger are expected to produce a market value for the combined firm of £110m. A bid premium of £20m is expected to be needed to secure Small. Transaction costs (advisers' fees, etc.) are estimated at £3m. Large has 30 million shares in issue and Small has 45 million. Assume the managers are shareholder-wealth maximisers.

Required

a Does this merger create value for Large plc?
b If the purchase is made with cash what will be the price offered for each of Small's shares?
c What would be the value of each of Large's shares after this merger? ?

2 Which of the following mergers is horizontal, vertical or conglomerate?

a Marks & Spencer and Next.
b Northern Foods and Sainsbury's.
c Philips and HMV.
d Rolls Royce and Electrolux.
e Ford and Microsoft.

3* Box plc is considering the acquisition of Circle plc. The former is valued at £100m and the latter at £50m by the market. Economies of scale will result in savings of £2.5m annually in perpetuity. The required rate of return on both firms and the combination is 11 per cent. The transaction costs will amount to £1m.

Required

a What is the present value of the gain from the merger?
b If a cash offer of £70m is accepted by Circle's shareholders what is the value created for Box's shareholders?
c If shares are offered in such a way that Circle's shareholders would possess one-third of the merged entity, what is the value created for Box's shareholders? ?

4* High plc has an historic PER of 22 and Low plc has an historic PER of 12. Both companies have 100 million shares in issue and produced earnings of £20m in the last financial year. High has offered three of its shares for every five held by Low's shareholders.

Required

a If you held 1,000 shares in Low and accepted the offer from High, by how much would your wealth increase assuming High's shares remain at the pre-bid price?
b What is the bid premium being offered?
c If High was able to increase the rate of growth of Low's earnings to the same as High's and therefore place them on the same PER as High, what would High's share price move to?
d If High makes no changes to Low's operations and so earnings growth continues at its present rate what will the intrinsic value of a share in High be, assuming the current PERs reflect accurately future growth in earnings?
e Explain the PER game and how High could continue to acquire firms, make no changes to underlying earnings and yet show a rising earnings per share trend. ?

5* Consider the following companies:

	A	B
Earnings per share (recent)	50p	10p
Dividends per share (recent)	25p	5p
Number of shares	5m	3m
Share price	£9.00	75p

The cost of equity capital for both firms is 12 per cent. B is expected to produce a growth in dividends of 5 per cent per annum to infinity with its current strategy and management. However if A acquired B and applied superior management and gained benefits from economies of scale the growth rate would rise to 8 per cent on the same capital base. The transaction costs of the merger would amount to £400,000.

Required

a What value could be created from a merger?
b If A paid £1.20 cash for each of B's shares what value created by the merger would be available for each group of shareholders?
c If A gave one of its shares for seven of B's what value created by the merger would be available for each group of shareholders?
d If none of the merger benefits is realised, because of problems of integration, what is the loss or gain in value to A and B shareholders under both the cash offer and the shares offer? ?

6 White plc and Black plc have made seperate all-share bids for Blue plc.

	White	Black	Blue	White + Blue	Black + Blue
Pre-merger share price	£4	£3	£1		
Number of shares issued	1m	2m	1.5m		
Market capitalisation	£4m	£6m	£1.5m	£6.8m	£8.0m

Assume no transaction costs.

Required

a If you were the managing director of White what is the maximum number of White shares you would offer for every 10 Blue shares? (Fractions of shares may be used.)
b If you were the managing director of Black, what is the maximum number of Black shares you would offer for every 10 Blue shares? (Fractions of shares may be used.)
c Some mergers produce increased returns for the acquirer's shareholders, whereas others do not. Discuss the reasons for merger failure from the acquirer's shareholders' perspective. ?

7 (*Examination level*) Some of the motives for mergers lead to benefits for society, some to shareholders, some to the management of the acquirer and others result in benefits to more than one group. Describe these in the form of an essay.

8 (*Examination level*) The directors of Trajectory plc have decided to expand rapidly through mergers. You have been asked to explain the process itself, from appointing an adviser to the offer going unconditional. Do this in the form of an essay.

9 (*Examination level*) Mergers fail to produce value for the shareholders of acquirers in many cases. Describe and explain some reasons for merger failure.

myfinancelab *Now retake your diagnostic test for Chapter 23 to check your progress and update your study plan.*

Assignment

Obtain as much information as you can on a recent merger. Relate the elements discussed in this chapter (merger motives, process, planning and integration) to the merger under examination. Write a report and make recommendations for improvement should any future mergers be contemplated.

PART 6

Managing risk

CHAPTER 24

Derivatives

LEARNING OUTCOMES

This chapter describes the main types of derivatives. Continued innovation means that the range of instruments broadens every year but the new developments are generally variations or combinations of the characteristics of derivatives discussed here. At the end of this chapter the reader should be able to:

- explain the nature of options and the distinction between different kinds of options, and demonstrate their application in a wide variety of areas;
- show the value of forwards, futures, FRAs, swaps, caps and floors markets by demonstrating transactions which manage and transfer risk.

Introduction

A **derivative instrument** is an asset whose performance is based on (derived from) the behaviour of the value of an underlying asset (usually referred to simply as the 'underlying'). The most common **underlyings** include commodities (for example, tea or pork bellies), shares, bonds, share indices, currencies and interest rates. Derivatives are contracts which give the right, and sometimes the obligation, to buy or sell a quantity of the underlying, or benefit in another way from a rise or fall in the value of the underlying. It is the legal *right* that becomes an asset, with its own value, and it is the right that is purchased or sold. Derivative instruments include the following: futures, options, swaps, forward rate agreements (FRAs), forwards.

The derivatives markets have received an enormous amount of attention from the press in recent years. This is hardly surprising as spectacular losses have been made and a number of companies brought to the point of collapse through the employment of derivative instruments. Some examples of the unfortunate use of derivatives are:

- Procter & Gamble, which lost $102m speculating on the movements of future interest rates in 1994;
- Barings, Britain's oldest merchant bank, which lost over £800m on Nikkei Index (the Japanese share index) contracts on the Singapore and Osaka derivatives exchanges, leading to the bank's demise in 1995;
- Sumitomo, which lost £1.17bn on copper and copper derivatives over the ten years to 1996;
- Long-Term Capital Management, which attempted to exploit the 'mispricing' of financial instruments, by making use of option pricing theory. In 1998 the firm collapsed and the Federal Reserve Bank of New York cajoled 14 banks and brokerage houses to put up $3.6bn to save LTCM and thereby prevent a financial system breakdown;
- China Aviation Oil, the State-owned monopoly importer of jet fuel, lost £288m in 2004 – more than its market capitalisation. It lost this money by betting that the price of oil would fall by dealing in options on the Singapore Exchange.
- Numerous financial institutions were destroyed in 2007 by buying derivatives whose value depended on US mortgage borrowers continuing to be able to pay their mortgages. When a proportion (10–20 per cent) could not pay their debts, the derivatives (of asset-backed securitised bonds) became either valueless or very difficult/impossible to value. The uncertainty surrounding the value of these derivatives led to a freezing of the short-term debt markets for months, which in turn led to financial distress for financial institutions that had no connection with the US mortgage market or the related derivatives, e.g. Northern Rock.

In many of the financial scandals derivatives have been used (or misused) to speculate rather than to reduce risk. This chapter examines both of these applications of derivatives but places particular emphasis on the hedging (risk-mitigating) facility they provide. These are powerful tools and managers can abuse that power either through ignorance or through deliberate acceptance of greater risk in the anticipation of greater reward. However, there is nothing inherently wrong with the tools themselves. If employed properly they can be remarkably effective at limiting risk.

A long history

Derivative instruments have been employed for more than two thousand years. Olive growers in ancient Greece unwilling to accept the risk of a low price for their crop when harvested months later would enter into **forward agreements** whereby a price was agreed for delivery at a specific time. This reduced uncertainty for both the grower and the purchaser of the olives. In the Middle Ages forward contracts were traded in a kind of secondary market, particularly for wheat in Europe. A futures market was established in Osaka's rice market in Japan in the seventeenth century. Tulip bulb options were traded in seventeenth-century Amsterdam.

Commodity futures trading really began to take off in the nineteenth century with the Chicago Board of Trade regulating the trading of grains and other futures and options, and the London Metal Exchange dominating metal trading.

So derivatives are not new. What is different today is the size and importance of the derivatives markets. The last quarter of the twentieth century witnessed an explosive growth of volumes of trade, variety of derivatives products, and the number and range of users and uses. In the twenty years to 2007 the face value of outstanding derivatives contracts rose dramatically to stand at about US$415 trillion (US$415,000,000,000,000). Compare that with a UK annual GDP of £1.2 trillion.

Options

An **option** is a contract giving one party the right, but not the obligation, to buy or sell a financial instrument, commodity or some other underlying asset at a given price, at or before a specified date. The purchaser of the option can either exercise the right or let it lapse – the choice is theirs.

A very simple option would be where a firm pays the owner of land a non-returnable ***premium*** (say £10,000) for an option to buy the land at an agreed price because the firm is considering the development of a retail park within the next five years. The property developer may pay a number of option premiums to owners of land in different parts of the country. If planning permission is eventually granted on a particular plot the option to purchase may be ***exercised***. In other words the developer pays the price agreed with the farmer at the time that the option contract was arranged, say £1,000,000, to purchase the land. Options on other plots may be ***allowed to lapse*** and will have no value. By using an option the property developer has 'kept the options open' with regard to which site to buy and develop and, indeed, whether to enter the retail park business at all.

Options can also be *traded*. Perhaps the option to buy could be sold to another company keener to develop a particular site than the original option purchaser. It may be sold for much more than the original £10,000 option premium, even before planning permission has been granted.

Once planning permission has been granted the greenfield site may be worth £1,500,000. If there is an option to buy at £1,000,000 the option right has an ***intrinsic value*** of £500,000, representing a 4,900 per cent return on £10,000.

From this comparison we can see the gearing effect of options: very large sums can be gained in a short period of time for a small initial cash outlay.

Share options

Share options have been traded for centuries but their use expanded dramatically with the creation of traded option markets in Chicago, Amsterdam and, in 1978, the London Traded Options Market. In 1992 this became part of the London International Financial Futures and Options Exchange, LIFFE (pronounced 'life'). Euronext bought LIFFE in 2002 and it is now called Euronext.liffe.

A **share call option** gives the purchaser a right, but not the obligation, to *buy* a fixed number of shares at a specified price at some time in the future. In the case of traded options on Euronext.liffe, one option contract relates to a quantity of 1,000 shares. The seller of the option, who receives the premium, is referred to as the ***writer***. The writer of a call option is obligated to sell the agreed quantity of shares at the agreed price some time in the future. **American-style options** can be exercised by the buyer at any time up to the expiry date, whereas **European-style options** can only be exercised on a predetermined future date. Just to confuse everybody, the distinction has nothing to do with geography: most options traded in Europe are American-style options.

Call option holder (call option buyers)

Now let us examine the call options available on an underlying share – BSkyB on 30 October 2007. There are a number of different options available for this share, many of which are not reported in the table presented in the *Financial Times*. A section of this table is reproduced as **Exhibit 24.1**.

Exhibit 24.1 Call options on BSkyB shares, 30 October 2007

	Call option prices (premiums) pence		
Exercise price	November	December	January
660p	25	36.5	42
680p	13.5	25	31
Share price on 30 October 2007 = 675.5p			

Source: Financial Times. Reprinted with permission.

So, what do the figures mean? If you wished to obtain the right to buy 1,000 shares on or before late December 2007, at an **exercise price** of 680p, you would pay a premium of £250 (1,000 × 25p). If you wished to keep your option to purchase open for another month you could select the January call. But this right to insist that the writer sells the shares at the fixed price of 680p on or before a date in late January[1] will cost another £60 (the total premium payable on one option contract = £310). This extra £60 represents additional ***time value***. Time value arises because of the potential for the market price of the underlying to change in a way that creates intrinsic value.

The intrinsic value of an option is the pay-off that would be received if the underlying were at its current level when the option expires. In this case, there is currently (30 October 2007) no intrinsic value because the right to buy is at 680p whereas the share price is 675.5p. However, if you look at a call option with an exercise price of 660p then the right to buy at 660p has intrinsic value because if you purchased at 660p by exercising the option, thereby obtaining 1,000 shares, you could immediately sell at 675.5p in the share market: intrinsic value = 15.5p per share, or £155 for 1,000 shares. The longer the time over which the option is exercisable the greater the chance that the price will move to give intrinsic value – this explains the higher premiums on more distant expiry options. Time value is the amount by which the option premium exceeds the intrinsic value.

The two exercise price (also called **strike price**) levels presented in Exhibit 24.1 illustrate an ***in-the-money option*** (the 660 call option) and an ***out-of-the-money option*** (the 680 call option). The underlying share price is above the strike price of 660 and so this call option has an intrinsic value of 15.5p and is therefore in-the-money. The right to buy at 680p is out-of-the-money because the share price is below the option exercise price and therefore has no intrinsic value. The holder of a 680p option would not exercise this right to buy at 680p because the shares can be bought on the stock exchange for 675.5p. (It is sometimes possible to buy an ***at-the-money option***, which is one where the market share price is equal to the option exercise price.)

To emphasise the key points: the option premiums vary in proportion to the length of time over which the option is exercisable (e.g. they are higher for a January option than for a December option). Also, call options with lower exercise prices will have higher premiums.

An illustration

Suppose that you are confident that BSkyB shares are going to rise significantly over the next three months to 750p and you purchase a January 660 call at 42 pence.[2] The cost of this right to purchase 1,000 shares is £420 (42p × 1,000 shares). If the share rises as expected then you could exercise the right to purchase the shares for a total of £6,600 and then sell these in the market for £7,500. A profit of £900 less £420 = £480 is made before transaction costs (the brokers' fees, etc. would be in the region of £20–£50). This represents a massive 114 per cent rise before costs (£480/£420).

[1] The expiry date is the third Wednesday of the expiry month.

[2] For this exercise we will assume that the option is held to expiry and not traded before then. However in many cases this option will be sold on to another trader long before the expiry date approaches (probably at a profit or loss).

However, the future is uncertain and the share price may not rise as expected. Let us consider two other possibilities. First, the share price may remain at 675.5p throughout the life of the option. Secondly, the stock market may have a severe downturn and BSkyB shares may fall to 500p. These possibilities are shown in **Exhibit 24.2**.

Exhibit 24.2 Profits and losses on the January 660 call option following purchase on 30 October 2007

	Assumptions on share price in January at expiry		
	750p	**675.5p**	**500p**
Cost of purchasing shares by exercising the option	£6,600	£6,600	£6,600
Value of shares bought	£7,500	£6,755	£5,000
Profit from exercise of option and sale of shares in the market	£900	£155	Not exercised
Less option premium paid	£420	£420	£420
Profit (loss) before transaction costs	£480	–£265	–£420
Percentage return over 3 months	114%	–63%	–100%

In the case of a standstill in the share price the option gradually loses its time value over the three months until, at expiry, only the intrinsic value of 15.5p per share remains. The fall in the share price to 500p illustrates one of the advantages of purchasing options over some other derivatives: the holder has a right to abandon the option and is not forced to buy the underlying share at the option exercise price – this saves £1,600. It would have added insult to injury to have to buy at £6,600 and sell at £5,000 after having already lost £420 on the premium for the purchase of the option.

A comparison of **Exhibits 24.3** and **24.4** shows the extent to which the purchase of an option gears up the return from share price movements: a wider dispersion of returns is experienced. On 30 October 2007, 1,000 shares could be bought for £6,755. If the price rose to £7,500, an 11 per cent return would be made, compared with a 114 per cent return if options are bought. We would all like

Exhibit 24.3 Profit if 1,000 shares are bought in BSkyB on 30 October 2007 at 675.5p

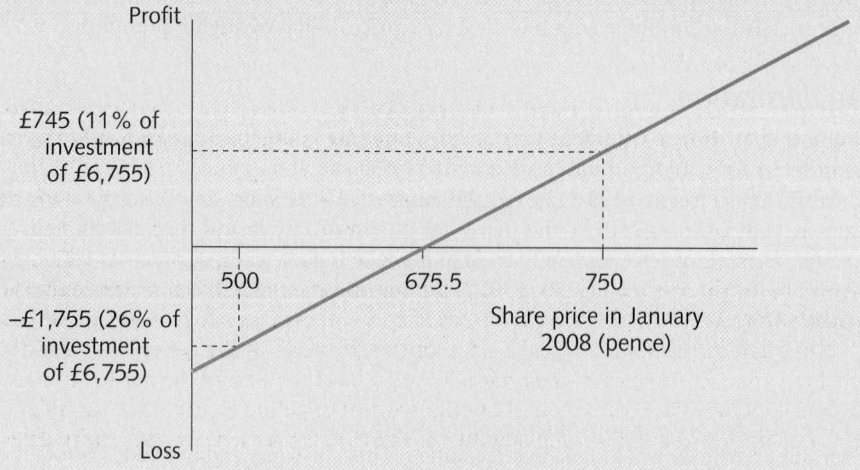

Exhibit 24.4 Profit if one 660 January call option contract (for 1,000 shares) in BSkyB is purchased on 30 October 2007 and held to maturity

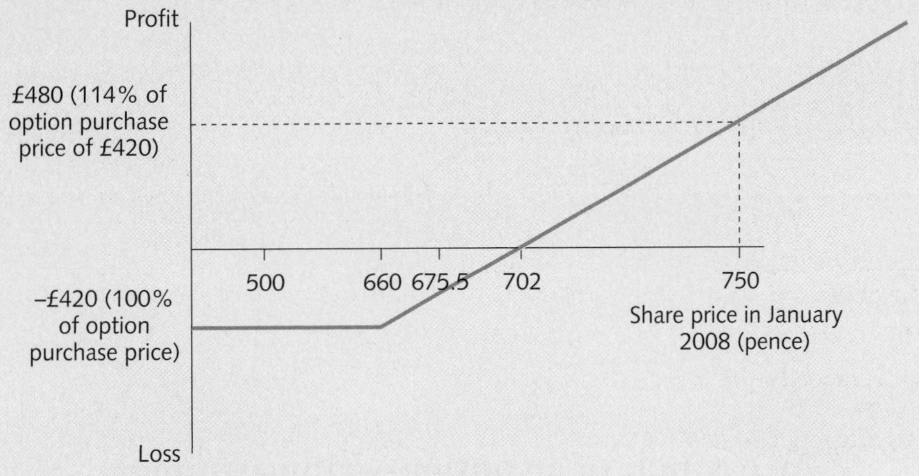

the higher positive return on the option than the lower one available on the underlying – but would we all accept the downside risk associated with this option? Consider the following possibilities:

- If share price remains at 675.5p:
  - Return if shares are bought: 0%
  - Return if one 660 January call option is bought: –63% (paid £420 for the option which declines to its intrinsic value of only £155[3])
- If share price falls to 500p:
  - Return if shares are bought: –26%
  - Return if one 660 January call option is bought: –100% (the option is worth nothing)

The holder of the call option will not exercise unless the share price is at least 660p: at a lower price it will be cheaper to buy the 1,000 shares on the stock market. Break-even does not occur until a price of 702p because of the need to cover the cost of the premium (660p + 42p). However, at higher prices the option value increases, penny for penny, with the share price. Also the downside risk is limited to the size of the option premium.

Call option writers

The returns position for the writer of a call option in BSkyB can also be presented in a diagram (*see* **Exhibit 24.5**). With all these examples note that there is an assumption that the position is held to expiry.

If the market price is less than the exercise price (660p) in January the option will not be exercised and the call writer profits to the extent of the option premium (42p per share). A market price greater than the exercise price will result in the option being exercised and the writer will be forced to deliver 1,000 shares for a price of 660p. This may mean buying shares on the stock market to supply to the option holder. As the share price rises this becomes increasingly onerous and losses mount.

Note that in the sophisticated traded option markets of today very few option positions are held to expiry. In most cases the option holder sells the option in the market to make a cash profit or loss. Option writers often cancel out their exposure before expiry – for example they could purchase an option to buy the same quantity of shares at the same price and expiry date.

[3] £155 is the intrinsic value at expiry (675.5p – 660p) × 1,000 = £155.

Exhibit 24.5 **The profit to a call option writer on one 660 January call contract written on 30 October 2007**

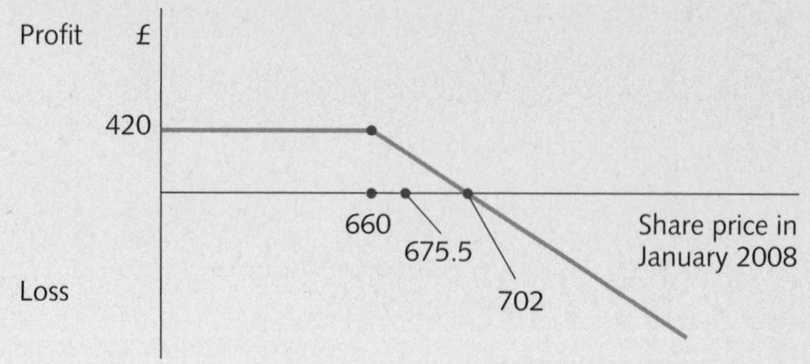

An example of an option-writing strategy

Joe has a portfolio of shares worth £100,000 and is confident that while the market will go up steadily over time it will not rise over the next few months. He has a strategy of writing out-of-the-money (i.e. no intrinsic value) call options and pocketing premiums on a regular basis. Today (30 October 2007) Joe has written one option on January calls in BSkyB for an exercise price of 680p (current share price 675.5p). In other words, Joe is committed to delivering (selling) 1,000 shares at any time between 30 October 2007 and near the end of January 2008 for a price of 680p at the insistence of the person who bought the call. This could be very unpleasant for Joe if the market price rises to, say, 780p. Then the option holder will require Joe to sell shares worth £7,800 to him/her for only £6,800. However, Joe is prepared to take this risk for two reasons. First he receives the premium of 31p per share up front – this is 4.6 per cent of each share's value, equivalent to double the annual dividend. This £310 will cushion any feeling of future regret at his actions. Secondly, Joe holds 1,000 BSkyB shares in his portfolio and so would not need to go into the market to buy the shares to then sell them to the option holder if the price did rise significantly. Joe has written a **covered call option** – so called because he has backing in the form of the underlying shares. Joe only loses out if the share price on the day the option is exercised is greater than the strike price (£6.80) plus the premium (31p). He is prepared to risk losing some of the potential upside (above 680p + 31p = 711p) to gain the premium. He also reduces his loss on the downside: if the shares in his portfolio fall he has the premium as a cushion.

Some speculators engage in **uncovered (naked) option writing**. It is possible to lose a multiple of your current resources if you write many option contracts and the price moves against you. Imagine that Joe had only £10,000 in savings and entered the options market by writing 40 BSkyB January 2008 680 calls receiving a premium of $0.31 \times 40 \times 1{,}000$ = £12,400.[4] If the price moves to £7.80 Joe has to buy shares for £7.80 and then sell them to the option holders for £6.80, a loss of £1 per share: £1 $\times 40 \times 1{,}000$ = £40,000. Despite receiving the premiums Joe has wiped out his savings.

LIFFE share options

The *Financial Times* lists over seventy companies' shares in which options are traded (*see* **Exhibit 24.6**).

[4] This is simplified. In reality Joe would have to provide margin of cash or shares to reassure the clearing house that he could pay up if the market moved against him. So it could be that all of the premium received would be tied up in margin held by the clearing house (the role of a clearing house is explained later in the chapter).

Exhibit 24.6 Equity options shown in the *Financial Times*

FT

Share price at the end of the trading day

Option		Calls Nov	Calls Dec	Calls Jan	Puts Nov	Puts Dec	Puts Jan
AstraZenenca	2300	97.5	140	157	34	62.5	70.5
(*2356)	2400	41	81	100.5	78	104.5	114.5
Aviva	720	33	48	56.5	10	21	26.5
(*740.5)	740	20.5	37	45	18	30	35
Barclays	580	30	44	50.75	13.25	23.75	28.25
(*595)	600	18.5	32.75	39.5	21.5	32.5	36.5
BHP Billiton	1800	79.5	128.5	155	56	94.5	113.5
(*1818)	1850	54	103	158	80.5	118.5	136.5
BP	620	12	22.25	28.25	12.25	19.5	23
(*622.5)	640	4	13	18.5	25	30.5	33.5
BSkyB	660	25	36.5	42	7.5	15	18
(*675.5)	680	13.5	25	31	15.5	23.5	26.5
BT Group	320	11.75	17.75	19.25	7.25	11.5	16
(*323.5)	330	7	12.5	14.25	12.5	16	21.25
Diageo	1050	54.5	70	78.5	4	13	17
(*1097)	1100	18	36	44.5	18	29	33
GlaxoSmKl	1200	39.5	60	71	12	26	32
(*1236)	1250	12.5	32.5	43	35.5	49	54.5

Option		Calls Dec	Calls Mar	Calls Jun	Puts Dec	Puts Mar	Puts Jun
3i Group	1050	62.5	100.5	–	39	62	–
(*1070)	1102	37.5	72	–	66	86.5	–
Allce & Leics	760	76	113.5	116	61	88	113.5
(*768)	780	64.5	–	–	69.5	–	–
ARM	145	9.25	–	–	6.75	–	–
(*146.25)	150	6.5	12.25	16.25	9	12.75	15.75
BAE Systems	490	27	–	–	18.75	–	–
(*494)	500	22	–	–	23.5	–	–
BG Group	860	63.25	–	–	35.5	–	–
(*880)	880	53.75	82.25	101.25	45.75	62.25	73.25
Br Airways	430	28	–	–	23	–	–
(*434.5)	440	23	39	48	28	38	46
BAT	1800	68.5	110.5	136	51.5	94	114.5
(*1801)	1850	45	–	–	78.5	–	–
Cable & Wire	190	12	18.75	22.25	8.75	12.75	16.25
(*193.600)	195	9.5	–	–	11.25	–	–
Cadbury Sch	620	37.5	–	–	16.5	–	–
(*635)	640	26	47	56	25.5	37.5	47

Strike or exercise price for this line of options

Premium payable per share (pence) for put options with a December 2007 expiry date

Source: *Financial Times*, 31 October 2007, p. 41. Reprinted with permission

Put options

A **put option** gives the holder the right, but not the obligation, to sell a specific quantity of shares on or before a specified date at a fixed exercise price.

Imagine you are pessimistic about the prospects for BSkyB on 30 October 2007. You could purchase, for a premium of 26.5p per share (£265 in total), the right to sell 1,000 shares in or before late January 2008 at 680p (*see* Exhibit 24.6). If a fall in price subsequently takes place, to, say, 550p, you can insist on exercising the right to sell at 680p. The writer of the put option is obliged to purchase shares at 680p while being aware that the put holder is able to buy shares at 550p on the stock exchange. The option holder makes a profit of 680 – 550 – 26.5 = 103.5p per share, a 391 per cent return (before costs).

For the put option holder, if the market price exceeds the exercise price, it will not be wise to exercise as shares can be sold for a higher price on the stock exchange. Therefore the maximum loss, equal to the premium paid, is incurred. The option writer gains the premium if the share price remains above the exercise price, but may incur a large loss if the market price falls significantly (*see* Exhibits 24.7 and 24.8).

As with calls, in most cases the option holder would take profits by selling the option on to another investor via Euronext.liffe rather than waiting to exercise at expiry.

Using share options to reduce risk: hedging

Hedging with options is especially attractive because they can give protection against unfavourable movements in the underlying while permitting the possibility of benefiting from favourable movements. Suppose you hold 1,000 shares in BSkyB on 30 October 2007. Your shareholding is worth £6,755. There are rumours flying around the market that the company may become the target of a takeover bid. If this materialises the share price will rocket; if it does not the market will be disappointed and the price will fall dramatically. What are you to do? One way to avoid the

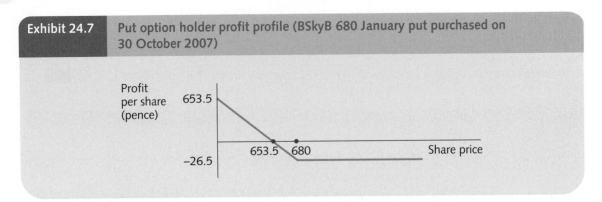

Exhibit 24.7 Put option holder profit profile (BSkyB 680 January put purchased on 30 October 2007)

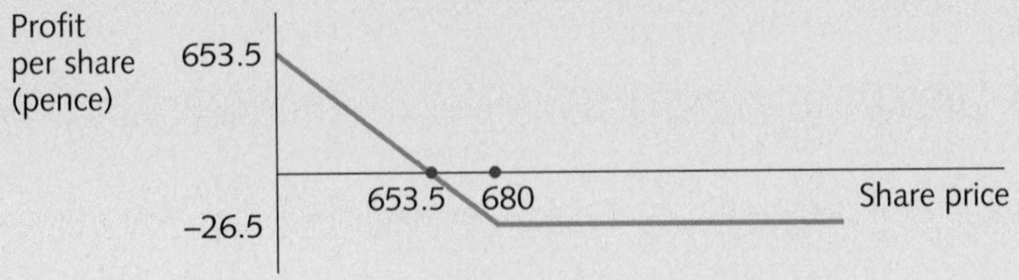

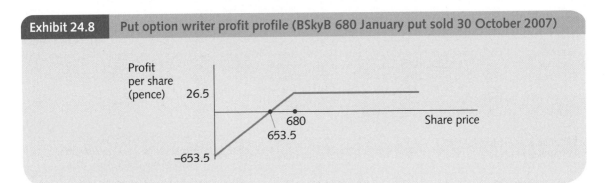

Exhibit 24.8 Put option writer profit profile (BSkyB 680 January put sold 30 October 2007)

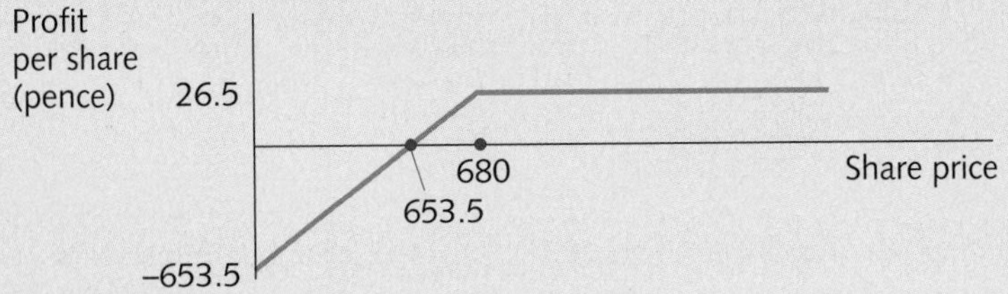

downside risk is to sell the shares. The problem is that you may regret this action if the bid does subsequently occur and you have forgone the opportunity of a large profit. An alternative approach is to retain the shares and buy a put option. This will rise in value as the share price falls. If the share price rises you gain from your underlying share holding.

Assume a 660 January put is purchased for a premium of £180 (*see* Exhibit 24.6). If the share price falls to 450p in late January you lose on your underlying shares by £2,255 ((675.5p – 450p) × 1,000). However, the put option will have an intrinsic value of £2,100 ((660p – 450p) × 1,000), thus reducing the loss and limiting the downside risk. Below 660p, for every 1p lost in a share price, 1p is gained on the put option, so the maximum loss is £335 (£155 intrinsic value + £180 option premium). The size of the gain should the share price rise is limitless, as is shown in **Exhibit 24.9**.

This hedging reduces the dispersion of possible outcomes. There is a floor below which losses cannot be increased, while on the upside the benefit from any rise in share price is reduced. If the share price stands still at 675.5p, however, you may feel that the premium you paid to insure against an adverse movement at 18p or 2.7 per cent of the share price was excessive. If you keep buying this type of 'insurance' through the year it can reduce your portfolio returns substantially.

A simpler example of risk reduction occurs when an investor is fairly sure that a share will rise in price but is not so confident as to discount the possibility of a fall. Suppose that the investor wished to buy 10,000 shares in Diageo, currently priced at 1097p (on 30 October 2007) – *see* Exhibit 24.6. This can be achieved either by a direct purchase of shares in the market or through the purchase of an option. If the share price does fall significantly, the size of the loss is greater with the share purchase – the option loss is limited to the premium paid.

Suppose that ten January 1100 call options are purchased at a cost of £4,450 (44.5p × 1,000 × 10). **Exhibit 24.10** shows that the option is less risky because of the ability to abandon the right to buy at 1100p.

Writing a put option can be a very risky thing to do, as General Motors found out to its cost – see **Exhibit 24.11**.

Exhibit 24.9 Profit profile for a put option and shares

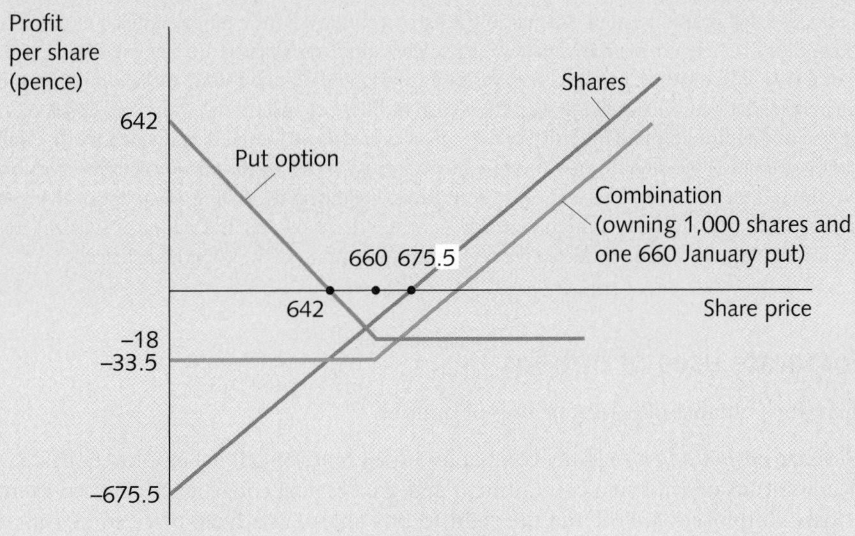

Exhibit 24.10 Losses on alternative buying strategies

Diageo share price falls to:	Loss on 10,000 shares	Loss on 10 call options
1050	£4,700	£4,450
1000	£9,700	£4,450
950	£14,700	£4,450
900	£19,700	£4,450
850	£24,700	£4,450

Exhibit 24.11

GM pays Fiat €1.55bn to end joint ventures

by Adrian Michaels in Milan and Bernard Simon in Toronto

General Motors and Fiat ended threats of legal action yesterday when the US industrial group agreed to pay €1.55bn (£1.07bn) to terminate the companies' joint venture agreements and forestall attempts to force it to take over the Italian company's lossmaking car division.

GM is paying a heavy price to cancel an agreement it signed with Fiat in headier days for both companies five years ago. In 2000 GM took a 20 per cent stake in Fiat Auto, subsequently reduced to 10 per cent, and agreed to a 'put' arrangement that gave Fiat the option to sell the rest of its car unit to GM.

Neither company dreamed the put would become an issue but both have stumbled badly. GM was keen to avoid taking over Fiat Auto and argued that the Italian company invalidated the put by restructuring.

About two-thirds of GM's €1.55bn payment will go towards settling the put option. The remaining third will pay for GM's stake in the Polish diesel engine plant and for technology currently held by Fiat on two diesel engines installed in GM vehicles.

Source: Financial Times, 14 February 2005, p. 1. Reprinted with permission.

Exhibit 24.12 Aunt Agathas and derivatives

Millions of ordinary small investors (Aunt Agathas in the City jargon) have their money applied to the derivatives markets even though they may remain blissfully unaware that such 'exotic' transactions are being conducted on their behalf. Take the case of equity-linked bonds. Investors nervous of investing in the stock market for fear of downward swings are promised a guarantee that they will receive at least the return of their original capital, even if the stock market falls. If it rises they will receive a return linked to the rise (say the capital gain element – excluding dividends). The bulk of the capital invested in these equity-linked bonds may be placed in safe fixed-interest investments, with the stock-market-linked return created through the use of options and other derivatives. Following the Barings Bank fiasco there was some discussion over the wisdom of using such highly geared instruments. However the financial services industry easily defended itself by pointing out the risk-reducing possibilities of these products if properly managed.

Corporate uses of options

There are a number of corporate uses of options.

1 ***Share option schemes*** Many companies now grant (or sell to) employees share options (calls) as a means of achieving commitment and greater goal congruence between agents and principals. Employees are offered the right to buy shares at a fixed price some time in the future. They then have the incentive over the intervening years to perform well and push up the share price so as to realise a large gain when the options may be exercised.

2 ***Warrants*** A share warrant is an option issued by a company which gives the owner the right, but not the obligation, to purchase a specified number of shares at a specified price over a given period of time. Note that it is the company that writes the option rather than speculators or hedgers.

3 ***Convertible bonds*** A convertible bond can be viewed as a bundle of two sets of rights. First, there are the usual rights associated with a bond, for example interest and principal payments, and secondly, there is the right, but not the obligation, to exercise a call option and purchase shares using the bond itself as the payment for those shares.

4 ***Rights issues*** In a rights issue shareholders are granted the right, but not the obligation, to purchase additional shares in the company. This right has value and can be sold to other investors.

5 ***Share underwriting*** Effectively when an underwriter agrees to purchase securities, if investors do not purchase the whole issue, a put option has been bought with the underwriting fee, and the company has the right to insist that the underwriter buys at the price agreed.

6 ***Commodities*** Many firms are exposed to commodity risk. Firms selling commodities, or buying for production purposes, may be interested in hedging against price fluctuations in these markets. Examples of such firms are airlines, food processors, car manufacturers, chocolate manufacturers, which may hedge oil, metals, cocoa, sugar, etc.

7 ***Taking control of a company*** A novel use of options occurred in 2003 when the family that founded the retail chain Monsoon sold put options to shareholders owning 19.5 per cent of Monsoon's shares. The holders of the put bought a right to sell their shares at 140p. If the share price on the stock market remains below 140p many holders will exercise the option. The founding family controlled 72.5 per cent of the company and saw the use of put options as a cheap way of raising their stake to over 90 per cent (cheaper than a full takeover bid).

8 ***Protecting the company from foreign exchange rate losses*** This topic is covered in Chapter 25.

9 ***Real options*** These are options that arise from business operations. *See* Chapter 6.

Forwards

Imagine you are responsible for purchasing potatoes to make crisps for your firm, a snack food producer. In the free market for potatoes the price rises or falls depending on the balance between buyers and sellers. These movements can be dramatic. Obviously you would like to acquire potatoes at a price which was as low as possible, while the potato producer wishes to sell for a price that is as high as possible. However, both parties may have a similar interest in reducing the uncertainty of price. This will assist both to plan production and budget effectively. One way in which this could be done is to reach an agreement with the producer(s) to purchase a quantity of potatoes at a price agreed today to be delivered at a specified time in the future. Bensons, the UK crisp producer, buys 80 per cent of its potatoes up to 19 months forward. Once the forward agreements have been signed and sealed Bensons may later be somewhat regretful if the spot price (price for immediate delivery) subsequently falls below the price agreed months earlier. Unlike option contracts, forwards commit both parties to complete the deal. However, Bensons is obviously content to live with this potential for regret in order to remove the risk associated with such an important raw material.

*A **forward contract** is an agreement between two parties to undertake an exchange at an agreed future date at a price agreed now.*

The party buying at the future date is said to be taking a ***long position***. The counterparty which will deliver at the future date is said to be taking a ***short position***.

There are forward markets in a wide range of commodities but the most important forward markets today are for foreign exchange, in which hundreds of billions of dollars worth of currency are traded every working day – this will be considered in Chapter 25.

Forward contracts are tailor-made to meet the requirements of the parties. This gives flexibility on the amounts and delivery dates. Forwards are not traded on an exchange but are '**over-the-counter instruments**' – private agreements outside the regulation of an exchange. This makes them different from futures, which are standardised contracts traded on exchanges. A forward agreement exposes the counterparties to the risk of default – the failure by the other to deliver on the agreement. The risk grows in proportion to the extent to which the spot price diverges from the forward price as the incentive to renege increases.

Forward contracts are difficult to cancel, as agreement from each counterparty is needed. Also to close the contract early may result in a penalty being charged. Despite these drawbacks forward markets continue to flourish – an example of which you can see in **Exhibit 24.13**.

Exhibit 24.13

Northern Foods passes price rises to customers

FT

by Lucy Warwick-Ching and Ed Crooks

Customers will be hit by higher food prices as Northern Foods, maker of Fox's biscuits and Goodfellas's pizza, prepares to pass on £40m of rising commodity costs to customers, including the big supermarkets.

Stefan Barden, chief executive, said that in the last three months short supplies and high demand had pushed up the prices of cereals, diary products, cocoa and fats. Poor harvests have also hit vegetables prices.

These cost increases are expected to add £32m–£40m to Northern Foods' £400m raw material bill, an increase of 8–10 per cent. However, Mr Barden said that, thanks to long-term contracts, forward buying and hedging, the increase this year would only be between 4–5 per cent, resulting in an extra £16m–£20m.

Source: Financial Times, 10 October 2007, p. 25. Reprinted with permission.

Futures

Futures contracts are in many ways similar to forward contracts. They are agreements between two parties to undertake a transaction at an agreed price on a specified future date. However, they differ from forwards in some important respects.

Futures contracts are exchange-based instruments traded on a regulated exchange. The buyer and the seller of a contract do not transact with each other directly. The **clearing house** becomes the formal **counterparty** to every transaction. This reduces the risk of non-compliance with the contract significantly for the buyer or seller of a future, as it is highly unlikely that the clearing house will be unable to fulfil its obligation.

In contrast to buying options, which give you the choice to walk away from the deal, with futures you are committed and are unable to back away. This is a very important difference. In purchasing an option the maximum you can lose is the premium paid whereas you can lose multiples of the amount you employ in taking a futures position.

A simple example will demonstrate this. Imagine a farmer wishes to lock in a price for his wheat, which will be harvested in six months. You agree to purchase the wheat from the farmer six months hence at a price of £60 per tonne. You are hoping that by the time the wheat is delivered the price has risen and you can sell at a profit. The farmer is worried that all he has from you is the promise to pay £60 per tonne in six months, and if the market price falls you will walk away from the deal. To reassure him you are asked to put money into what the farmer calls a ***margin account***. He asks and you agree to deposit £6 for each tonne you have agreed to buy. If you fail to complete the bargain the farmer will be able to draw on the money from the margin account and then sell the wheat as it is harvested at the going rate for immediate ('spot') delivery. So, as far as the farmer is concerned, the price of wheat for delivery at harvest time could fall to £54 and he is still going to get £60 for each tonne: £6 from what you paid into the margin account and £54 from selling at the spot price.

But what if the price falls below £54? The farmer is exposed to risk – something he had tried to avoid by entering a futures deal. It is for this reason that the farmer asks you to top up your margin account on a daily basis so that there is always a buffer. He sets a ***maintenance margin*** level of £6 per tonne. This means you have to maintain at least £6 per tonne in the margin account. So, if the day after you buy the future, the harvest time price in the futures market falls to £57 you have only £3 per tonne left in the margin account as a buffer for the farmer. You agreed to buy at £60 but the going rate is only £57. To bring the margin account up to a £6 buffer you will be required to put in another £3 per tonne. If the price the next day falls to £50 you will be required to put up another £7 per tonne. You agreed to buy at £60, with the market price at £50 you have put a total of £6 + £3 + £7 = £16 into the margin account. By putting in top-ups as the price moves against you, you will always ensure there is at least £6 per tonne, providing security for the farmer. Even if you go bankrupt or simply renege on the deal he will receive at least £60 per tonne, either from the spot market or from a combination of a lower market price plus money from the margin account. As the price fell to £50 you have a £10 per tonne incentive to walk away from the deal except for the fact that you have put £16 into an account that the farmer can draw on should you be so stupid or unfortunate. If the price is £50 per tonne at expiry of the contract and you have put £16 in the margin account you are entitled to the spare £6 per tonne of margin.

It is in the margin account that we have the source of multiple losses in the futures markets. Say your life savings amount to £10 and you are convinced there will be a drought and shortage of wheat following the next harvest. In your view the price will rise to £95 per tonne. So, to cash in on your forecast you agree to buy a future for one tonne of wheat. You have agreed with the farmer that in six months you will pay £60 for the wheat, which you expect to then sell for £95. (The farmer is obviously less convinced than you that prices are destined to rise.)

To gain this right to buy at £60 you need only have £6 for the ***initial margin***. The other £4 might be useful to meet day-to-day ***margin calls*** should the wheat price fall from £60 (temporarily, in your view). If the price does rise to £95 you will make a £35 profit, having laid out only £6 (plus some other cash temporarily). This is a very high return of 583 per cent over six months. But what if the price at harvest time is £40? You have agreed to pay £60, therefore the loss of £20 wipes out your savings and you are made bankrupt. You lose over three times your initial margin. That is the downside to the gearing effect of futures.

The above example demonstrates the essential features of futures market trading, but in reality participants in the market do not transact directly with each other, but go through a regulated exchange. Your opposite number, called a *counterparty*, is not a farmer but an organisation that acts as counterparty to all futures traders, buyers or sellers, called the *clearing house*. This reduces the risk of non-compliance with the contract significantly for the buyer or seller of a future, as it is highly unlikely that the clearing house will be unable to fulfil its obligation.

In the example we have asumed that the maintenance margin level is set at the same level as the initial margin. In reality it is often set at 70 to 80 per cent of the initial margin level.

The exchange provides standardised legal agreements traded in highly liquid markets. The contracts cannot be tailor-made. The fact that the agreements are standardised allows a wide market appeal because buyers and sellers know what is being traded: the contracts are for a specific quality of the underlying, in specific amounts with specific delivery dates. For example, for sugar traded on Euronext.liffe (*see* **Exhibit 24.14**) one contract is for a specified grade of sugar and each contract is for a standard 50 tonnes with fixed delivery days in late August, October, December, March and May.

Exhibit 24.14 Commodity prices

FT

Energy		Price*	Change
WTI Crude Oil†	Dec	95.53	+2.04
Brent Crude Oil‡	Dec	91.92	+2.20
RBOB Gasoline†	Dec	2.4302	+0.0870
Heating Oil†	Dec	2.5681	+0.0558
Natural Gas†	Dec	8.388	–0.249
Ethanol ◆	Nov	1.830	+0.035
Uranium		85.00	nc
Carbon Emissions‡	Dec	€21.68	–1.14
Diesel (French)		859.75	+47.00
Unleaded (95R)		805.00	+5.50
globalCOAL RB Index		82.35	+0.2
Base metals (♠ LME 3 Month)			
Aluminium		2581.00	+29.00
Aluminium Alloy		2275.00	+17.50
Copper		7525.75	–151.75
Lead		3695.00	+84.75
Nickel		32175.00	+225.00
Tin		16547.50	–40.00
Zinc		2746.25	+1.00
Precious Metals (PM London Fix)			
Gold		796.50	+6.25
Silver		1432.00	–4.00
Platinum		1439.00	–4.00
Palladium		369.00	–1.00
Agricultural & Cattle Futures			
Corn ◆	Dec	377.25	+8.50
Wheat ◆	Dec	777.50	–0.75
Soyabeans ◆	Nov	1001.00	+10.25
Soyabeans Meal ◆	Dec	274.4.	+2.30
Cocoa ✠	Dec	954	–7
Coffee (Robusta) ✠	Nov	2334	–37
Coffee (Arabica) ♥	Dec	118.90	–3.70
White Sugar ✠	Dec	282.5	+0.2
Cotton ♥	Dec	64.37	+0.63
Orange Juice ♥	Nov	142.70	–1.00
Palm Oil	Nov	940.00	–10.00
Live Cattle ♣	Dec	94.775	+0.450
Feeder Cattle ♣	Nov	108.300	–0.250
Lean Hogs ♣	Dec	52.550	nc
Frozen Pork Bellies ♣	Feb	84.700	+3.000
Baltic Dry Index		10548	–33

Source: † NYMEX, ‡ ECX/ICE, ◆ CBOT, ✠ Euronext.liffe, ♥ NYBOT, ♣ CME, ♠ LME/London Metal Exchange.
*$ unless otherwise stated. London Closing prices

Source: *Financial Times*, 1 November 2007. Reprinted with permission.

In examining the table in Exhibit 24.14, it is important to remember that it is the contracts themselves that are a form of security bought and sold in the market. Thus the December future priced at $282.5 per tonne is a derivative of sugar and is not the same thing as sugar. To buy this future is to enter into an agreement with rights. The rights are being bought and sold and not the commodity. When exercise takes place then sugar is bought. However, as with most derivatives, usually futures positions are cancelled by an offsetting transaction before exercise.

Exhibit 24.15 describes the importance of commodity hedging to a number of companies.

Exhibit 24.15

Groups share shelter from the elements

FT

The expanding market in hedging against commodity exposure

Gillian Tett and Kevin Morrison

Industrial companies around the world have reeled as commodity prices surged. But at BPB the blow has been less painful than it might have been.

The British plasterboard group used to be vulnerable to every shift in raw material and energy costs but in the past couple of years its corporate treasury department has taken control of commodity price risk and started hedging some of this for the first time.

'It's a big change. Now we hedge all our energy costs in the UK and want to roll this out across the world and move into [hedging on] other products,' says Jon Drown, treasurer at BPB,

BPB's move into commodity hedging points to a much bigger trend. Many UK companies have become highly adept at protecting their businesses from unexpected interest rate or currency swings, and banks have developed an extensive financial toolkit to help them do this, based on the existence of mature and liquid markets, and instruments such as swaps and derivatives.

But until recently commodities had been oddly under-represented in this process. For while swings in raw material prices can affect profits as badly as currencies or interest rates, far fewer companies have attempted to control their exposure to raw material costs. And with the expectation of items such as oil, liquid markets in commodity derivatives have been less developed than in other financial areas.

'It is quite strange but it seems that corporate treasuries have usually not been that involved in commodity risks at all,' says Martin O'Donovan of the Association of Corporate Treasurers.

An ACT survey two years ago suggested that commodity price risk received by far the lowest level of attention of any financial issue among corporate treasurers.

However, this year's survey by the ACT and Ernst & Young, the accountants, shows that three-quarters of UK companies with commodity exposure now hedge these risks, compared with slightly more than half last year.

As commodity prices rise, shareholders increasingly are demanding evidence that senior managers have – at the minimum – quantified their raw material price risks via internal reviews. 'The days when you could go to investors and say, "Sorry, we didn't expect this" have gone,' admits one senior manager. 'You are supposed to have a precise calculation for the impact of every act of God.'

In some cases, these internal reviews have led companies to conclude that it is not worth hedging a risk. 'It is a big decision for companies, because executives are concerned about signing their name to a hedging programme that runs the risk of losing the company money if prices go against them,' says Wayne Harburn, head of commodity derivatives at ABN Amro.

However, at other groups, corporate treasuries are creating a unified policy for the first time.

'More companies are taking a risk management approach to commodities rather than leaving it to the procurement department to buy metals and energy,' says Tim Owen, global head of commodities and currencies at JPMorgan.

Switching policies is not an easy step. Procurement departments often bitterly resent losing any power to treasurers, and the word 'derivatives' often makes senior managers – or boards of directors – nervous.

Moreover, companies wanting to hedge face a practical problem: the markets are so under-developed that it is not always possible to hedge the right product over the right timescale. There is often a structural mismatch between buyers and sellers.

Rexam, the European global packaging group, has hedged its energy exposure for several years and recently started hedging aluminium, But as Chris Bowmer, its corporate treasurer, explains: 'We try to make sure that we are not involved in the short end of the [aluminium] market – it tends to be driven by fund managers and speculators and is a lot more volatile than the long end, which is mostly driven by long-term producers and consumers. Our objective is to manage risks for the long term, not speculate.'

But though this logic means that Rexam focuses on the long end of the market, the rub is that this area is less

▶

Exhibit 24.15 continued

liquid because far fewer investors want to play here.

'That means we probably do end up paying the banks [to structure products]', Mr Bowmer concludes.

Worse still, some of the other markets that Rexam wants to use simply do not exist. The company would like, for example, to hedge resin prices and has worked with the London Metal Exchange to develop a suitable contract. But the product remains so untested that Rexam's board has not yet approved the step.

Meanwhile, BPB would like to hedge steel costs and polystyrene but similarly cannot do that. 'With some esoteric products, the market isn't there yet . . . even in electricity it can be hard to hedge more than two years out in the UK, and in some countries the markets barely exist,' explains Mr Drown.

Obstacles such as these are unlikely to vanish soon, particularly given the fragmented nature of commodities.

But that is unlikely to dent the enthusiasm of investment banks. 'The more we have events such as hurricanes Rita and Katrina, the more opportunity there will be,' says one banker.

Or as Mr Drown echoes: 'Just look at how energy prices have risen in the past couple of years. This is not going away as an issue any time soon.'

Additional reporting by Jeremy Grant

Source: *Financial Times*, 18 October 2005, p. 25. Reprinted with permission.

Marking to market and margins

With the clearing house being the formal counterparty for every buyer or seller of a futures contract, an enormous potential for credit risk is imposed on the organisation – given the volume of futures traded and the size of the underlying they represent. (Euronext.liffe has an average daily volume of around 3 million contracts worth hundreds of billions of pounds.) If only a small fraction of market participants fail to deliver this could run into hundreds of millions of pounds. To protect itself the clearing house operates a margining system. The futures buyer or seller has to provide, usually in cash, an initial margin. The amount required depends on the futures market, the level of volatility of the underlying and the potential for default; however it is likely to be in the region of 0.1 per cent to 15 per cent of the value of the underlying. The initial margin is not a 'down payment' for the underlying: the funds do not flow to a buyer or seller of the underlying but stay with the clearing house. It is merely a way of guaranteeing that the buyer or seller will pay up should the price of the underlying move against them. It is refunded when the futures position is closed (if the market has not moved adversely).

The clearing house also operates a system of daily ***marking to market***. At the end of every trading day the counterparty's profits or losses created as a result of that day's price change are calculated. The counterparty that made a loss has his/her ***member's margin account*** debited. The following morning the losing counterparty must inject more cash to cover the loss if the amount in the account has fallen below a threshold level, called the maintenance margin. An inability to pay a daily loss causes default and the contract is closed, thus protecting the clearing house from the possibility that the counterparty might accumulate further daily losses without providing cash to cover them. The margin account of the counterparty that makes a daily gain is credited. This may be withdrawn the next day. The daily credits and debits to members' margin accounts are known as the ***variation margin***.

Worked example 24.1 illustrates the effect of leverage in futures contracts. The initial margin payments are small relative to the value of the underlying. When the underlying changes by a small percentage the effect is magnified for the future, and large percentage gains and losses are made on the amount committed to the transaction:

$$\text{Underlying change (Monday–Friday)} \ \frac{55{,}000 - 50{,}000}{50{,}000} \times 100 = 10\%$$

$$\text{Percentage return to buyer of future} \ \frac{5{,}000}{5{,}000} \times 100 = 100\%$$

$$\text{Percentage return to seller of future} \ \frac{-5{,}000}{5{,}000} \times 100 = -100\%$$

Worked example 24.1 Margins

Imagine a buyer and seller of a future on Monday with an underlying value of £50,000 are each required to provide an initial margin of 10 per cent, or £5,000. The buyer will make profits if the price rises while the seller will make profits if the price falls. In the following table (*see* **Exhibit 24.16**) it is assumed that counterparties have to keep all of the initial margin permanently as a buffer.[5] (In reality this may be relaxed by an exchange.)

Exhibit 24.16 Example of initial margin and marking to market

£	Monday	Tuesday	Wednesday	Thursday	Friday
	Day				
Value of future (based on daily closing price)	50,000	49,000	44,000	50,000	55,000
Buyers' position					
Initial margin	5,000				
Variation margin (+ credited) (– debited)	0	–1,000	–5,000	+6,000	+5,000
Accumulated profit (loss)	0	–1,000	–6,000	0	+5,000
Sellers' position					
Initial margin	5,000				
Variation margin (+ credited) (– debited)	0	+1,000	+5,000	–6,000	–5,000
Accumulated profit (loss)	0	+1,000	+6,000	0	–5,000

At the end of Tuesday the buyer of the contract has £1,000 debited from his/her member's account. This will have to be paid over the following day or the exchange will automatically close the member's position and crystallise the loss. If the buyer does provide the variation margin and the position is kept open until Friday the account will have an accumulated credit of £5,000. The buyer has the right to buy at £50,000 but can sell at £55,000. If the buyer and the seller closed their positions on Friday the buyer would be entitled to receive the initial margin plus the accumulated profit, £5,000 + £5,000 = £10,000, whereas the seller would receive nothing (£5,000 initial margin minus losses of £5,000).

To lose all the money committed to a financial transaction may seem disappointing but it is nothing compared with the losses that can be made on futures. It is possible to lose a multiple of the amount set down as an initial margin. For example, if the future rose to £70,000 the seller would have to provide a £20,000 variation margin – four times the amount committed in the first place. Clearly playing the futures market can seriously damage your wealth. This was proved with a vengeance by Nick Leeson of Barings Bank. He bought futures in the Nikkei 225 Index – the main Japanese share index – in both the Osaka and the Singapore derivative exchanges. He was betting that the market would rise as he committed the bank to buying the index at a particular price. When the index fell margin payments had to be made. Leeson took a double or quits attitude, 'I mean a lot of futures traders when the market is against them will double up'.[6] He continued to buy futures. To generate some cash, to make variation margin payments, he wrote

[5] Initial margin is the same as maintenance margin in this case.
[6] Nick Leeson in an interview with David Frost reported in *Financial Times*, 11 September 1995.

combinations of call and put options ('**straddles**'). This compounded the problem when the Nikkei 225 Index continued to fall in 1994. The put options became an increasingly expensive commitment to bear – counterparties had the right to sell the index to Barings at a price much higher than the prevailing price. Over £800m was lost (*see* **Exhibit 24.17**).

Exhibit 24.17

Leeson hid trading from the outset

FT

Mr Nick Leeson opened 88888, the account in which he hid his unauthorised trading, just two days after Barings began trading on Simex at the start of July 1992.

The Singapore inspectors, who have had access to Simex data not made available to the Bank of England, show that Mr Leeson's secret futures and options positions grew slowly at first.

After losing S$10.7m (£4.8m) between July and October 1992, Mr Leeson brought the balance on the hidden 88888 account back close to zero in July 1993. This tallies with his own account, given in a television interview, of the relief he felt when he made back his losses in mid-1993.

But it appears that the main method by which Mr Leeson recovered his losses, initially made on futures positions, was by selling options in a way which stored up trouble. When the market moved against him and his futures lost money, he tended to write 'straddles', a combination of options.

These produced an immediate premium which reduced the deficit in the 88888 account. But the options, on the Nikkei index of Japanese stocks, exposed Mr Leeson to a movement in the market in either direction.

They produced an initial profit, with a counterbalancing risk of loss on expiry of the options contracts. It was a highly risky form of borrowing.

From the timing of Mr Leeson's trading, it appears that the sale of these 'straddles' was an attempt to plug the hole left by punts on the market which had gone awry.

For example, in November 1993, Mr Leeson's futures losses had mounted to S$4.2bn from S$788m the previous month. This coincided with Mr Leeson's most intense bout of options trading, which lifted the value of the options portfolio to a surplus of S$478m the following month.

Losses on account 88888

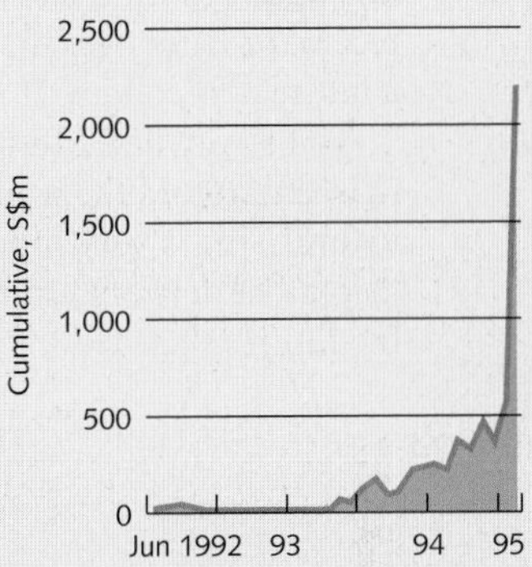

Source: Inspectors re port

But their value collapsed after the Kobe earthquake, which triggered a sharp increase in the volatility of the Japanese stock market. In any case, Mr Leeson's profits on options in 1994 were not sufficient to offset his other losses.

Source: Nicholas Denton., *Financial Times*, 18 October 1995, p. 8. Reprinted with permission.

Settlement

Historically the futures markets developed on the basis of the ***physical delivery*** of the underlying. So if you had contracted to buy 40,000 lb. of lean hogs you would receive the meat as settlement. However in most futures markets today (including that for lean hogs) only a small proportion of contracts result in physical delivery. The majority are **closed out** before the expiry of the contract and all that changes hands is cash, either as a profit or as a loss. Speculators certainly do not want to end up with five tonnes of coffee or 15,000 lb. of orange juice and so will ***reverse their trade*** before the contract expires; for example, if they originally bought 50 tonnes of white sugar they later sell 50 tonnes of white sugar.

Hedgers, say confectionery manufacturers, may sometimes take delivery from the exchange but in most cases will have established purchasing channels for sugar, cocoa, etc. In these cases they may use the futures markets not as a way of obtaining goods but as a way of offsetting the risk of the prices of goods moving adversely. So a confectionery manufacturer may still plan to buy, say, sugar, at the spot price from its longstanding supplier in six months and simultaneously, to hedge the risk of the price rising, will buy six-month futures in sugar. This position will then be closed before expiry. If the price of the underlying has risen the manufacturer pays more to the supplier but has a compensating gain on the future. If the price falls the supplier is paid less and so a gain is made here, but, under a perfect hedge, the future has lost an equal value.

As the futures markets developed it became clear that most participants did not want the complications of physical delivery and this led to the development of futures contracts where **cash settlement** takes place. This permitted a wider range of futures contracts to be created. Futures contracts based on intangible commodities such as a share index or a rate of interest are now extremely important financial instruments. With these, even if the contract is held to the maturity date one party will hand over cash to the other (via the clearing house system).

Equity index futures

Equity index futures are an example of a cash settlement market. The underlyings here are collections of shares, for example 225 Japanese shares for the Nikkei 225. Hedgers and speculators do not want 225 different shares to be delivered say one month from now. They are quite content to receive or hand over the profit or loss made by buying and then selling (or the other way around) a future of the index.

The equity index futures table (**Exhibit 24.18**) from FT.com shows futures in indices from stock markets around the world for 1 November 2007. We will focus on the line for the FTSE 100 index future. This is very much a cut-down version of the futures available to traders. As well as the December delivery future shown Euronext.liffe also offers traders the possibility of buying or selling futures that 'deliver' in March, June and September.

Exhibit 24.18

Equity Index Futures FT

Nov 1		Open	Sett	Change	High	Low	Est. vol.	Open int.
DJIA	Dec	13940.0	13608.0	−328.0	13949.0	13575.0	319	34,247
Mini Dow	Dec	13940.0	13608.0	−328.0	13949.0	13571.0	221,170	108,041
e-Mini Russell 2000	Dec	828.30	796.0	−35.40	828.60	795.50	27	33,080
DJ Euro Stoxx‡	Dec	4514.0	4429.0	−75.0	4515.0	4402.0	53	59,759
S&P 500	Dec	1552.50	1515.80	−39.10	1554.80	1514.50	5,544	583,398
Mini S&P 500	Dec	1552.50	1515.75	−39.25	15550.00	1513.50	1957,311	2048,010
Nasdaq 100	Dec	2251.50	2215.50	−37.00	2256.25	2209.75	416	58,770
Mini Nasdaq	Dec	2250.50	2215.50	−37.00	2256.25	2208.00	433,914	442,465
CAC 40	Nov	5852.0	5728.5	−114.5	5855.0	5697.0	172,518	404,394
DAX	Dec	8067.0	7910.5	−149.0	8078.5	7896.0	187,503	289,033
AEX	Nov	549.85	541.65	−6.35	550.45	538.35	48,190	67,083
MIB 30	Dec	40685.0	40329.0	−511.0	40745.0	39670.0	16,813	20,617
IBEX 35	Nov	15827.0	15743.5	−16.5	15896.0	15689.0	20,418	72,642
SMI	Dec	9051.0	8934	−114.0	9069.0	8876.0	51,213	193,075
FTSE 100	Dec	6741.0	6628.5	−120.0	6759.0	6582.0	148,815	483,067
Hang Seng	Dec	31691.0	31285.0	−85.0	31840.0	31261.0	59,208	112,463
Nikkei 225†	Dec	16900.00	16850	+140.0	16910.0	16840.0	2,344	306,240
Topix	Dec	1631.0	1638.5	≠+22.0	1640.5	1629.0	43,299	410,041
KOPSI 200	Dec	264.95	263.40	+1.60	264.95	260.40	166,565	88,024

North American Latest. Contracts shown are among the 25 most traded based on estimates of average volumes in 2004. CBOT volume, high & low for pit & electronic trading at settlement. Previous day's Open Interest. † Osaka contract. ‡ Eurex contract.

Source: FT.com, 2 November 2007. Reproduced with permission.

The table shows the first price traded at the beginning of the day (Open), the **settlement price** used to mark to market (usually the last traded price), the change from the previous day's settlement price, the highest and lowest prices during the day's settlement price, the number of contracts traded that day (Est. vol.) and the total number of open contracts (these are trading contracts opened over the last few months that have not yet been closed by an equal and opposite futures transaction).

Each point on the UK's FTSE 100 share index future is worth £10, by convention. So if the future rises from 6500 to 6550 and you bought a future at 6500 you have made 50 × £10 = £500 if you were to now sell at 6550.

Worked example 24.2 **Hedging with a share index future**

It is 1 November 2007 and the FT 100 is at 6586. A fund manager wishes to hedge a £13,000,000 fund against a decline in the market. A December FTSE 100 future is available at 6628.5 – *see* Exhibit 24.18. The investor retains the shares in the portfolio and *sells* 196 index futures contracts. Each futures contract is worth £66,285 (6628.5 points × £10). So 196 contracts are needed to cover £13,000,000 (£13,000,000/(£10 × 6628.5) = 196).

Outcome in December

For the sake of argument assume that the index falls by 10 per cent to 5,927, leaving the portfolio value at £11,700,000 (assuming the portfolio moves exactly in line with the FT 100 index). The closing of the futures position offsets this £1,300,000 loss by buying 196 futures at 5927 to close the position producing a profit[7] of:

Able to sell at	6628.5 × 196 × £10	= £12,991,860
Able to buy at	5927 × 196 × £10	= –£11,616,920
		£1,374,940

These contracts are cash settled so £1,374,940 will be paid. Furthermore, the investor receives back the margin laid down, less broker's fees.

Buying and selling futures

A trader in futures must deal through a registered broker. Euronext.liffe provides a list of designated brokers (these follow rules and codes of conduct imposed by the regulators and the exchange). Gone are the days of open pit trading and those brightly coloured jackets in the UK. Trades are now conducted over a computer system on Euronext.liffe. Prices are set by competing market makers on **LIFFE CONNECT™**. Traders can place a price limit for their trade – a maximum they are willing to pay if buying or a minimum if they are selling. Alternatively traders can make an **'at-the-market order'**, that is, one to be executed immediately at the price determined by current supply and demand conditions. The buyer of a contract is said to be in a long position – he/she agrees to receive the underlying. The seller who agrees to deliver the underlying is said to be in a short position.

Traders may be asked to inject money into their margin accounts every day the position is open so they cannot buy/sell a future and then ignore the markets (unless they leave plenty of cash with the broker to meet margin calls). Real-time market prices are available on the Internet, as well as historical prices (*see*, for example, www.nyxdata.com).

Short-term interest rate futures

Trillions of pounds worth of trading takes place every year in the **short-term interest rate futures** markets. These are notional fixed-term deposits, usually for three-month periods starting at a specific time in the future. The buyer of one contract is buying the (theoretical) right to deposit money at a particular rate of interest for three months.

So if the current time is November you could arrange a futures contract for you to 'deposit' and 'receive interest' on, say £1,000,000, with the deposit starting next June and ending in September. The rate of interest you will 'receive' over the three summer months is agreed in November. (This is a notional receipt of interest, as these contracts are cash settled rather than actual deposits being made and interest received – *see* below for an example.) So you now own the right to deposit £1m and receive *x* per cent interest for three months (at least in notional terms).

[7] Assuming that the futures price is equal to the spot price of the FTSE 100. This would occur close to the expiry date of the future.

Short-term interest rate futures will be illustrated using the three-month sterling market, that is, deposits of pounds receiving notional interest for three months starting at some point in the future. Note, however, that there are many other three-month deposits you could make. For example, you could 'deposit' euros for three months, the interest rate on which is calculated with reference to 'Euribor 3m', which is the interest rate highly rated banks pay to other banks for three-month deposits of the currency of the Eurozone countries, the euro. Other three-month deposits are often for money held outside the jurisdiction of the currency's country of origin (i.e. 'Euro' currencies, in the sense of being international money and *not* the new currency in the Eurozone) include Swiss francs deposited in London (Euroswiss), Eurodollars and Euroyens – *see* **Exhibit 24.19**. (Eurocurrency is discussed in Chapter 11.)

The unit of trading for a three-month sterling time deposit is £500,000. Cash delivery by closing out the futures position is the means of settlement, so the buyer would not actually require the seller of the future to accept the £500,000 on deposit for three months at the interest rate indicated by the futures price. Although the term 'delivery' no longer has significance for the underlying it does define the date and time of the expiry of the contract. This occurs in late September, December, March and June and the nearest three consecutive months. (*See* www.euronext.com for precise definitions and delivery dates.)

Exhibit 24.19

INTEREST RATE FUTURES

FT

Nov 1		Open	Sett	Change	High	Low	Est. vol.	Open int.
Euribor 3m*	Dec	95.46	95.48	+0.02	95.50	95.46	152,949	792,707
Euribor 3m*	Mar	95.55	95.61	+0.03	95.63	95.55	225,254	619,247
Euribor 3m*	Jun	95.57	95.66	+0.04	95.68	95.57	224,676	473,666
Euribor 3m*	Sep	95.60	95.70	+0.04	95.71	95.59	186,091	420,697
Euroswiss 3m*	Dec	97.11	97.13	+0.01	97.18	97.09	9,431	65,437
Euroswiss 3m*	Mar	97.07	97.11	+0.02	97.15	97.15	12,766	58,583
Sterling 3m*	Dec	93.79	93.83	–0.02	93.86	93.78	72,187	482,395
Sterling 3m*	Mar	94.05	94.11	–0.01	94.14	94.01	145,340	592,187
Sterling 3m*	Jun	94.25	94.35	+0.02	94.36	94.22	194,913	529,366
Sterling 3m*	Sep	94.38	94.49	+0.03	94.50	94.35	124,801	384,230
Eurodollar 3m†	Dec	95.23	95.26	+0.01	95.29	95.20	386,099	1520,738
Eurodollar 3m†	Mar	95.49	95.59	+0.08	95.65	95.46	427,479	1466,719
Eurodollar 3m†	Jun	95.60	95.75	+0.13	95.79	95.56	494,724	1493,435
Eurodollar 3m†	Sep	95.68	95.83	+0.14	95.86	95.63	502,691	1295,204
Fed Fnds 30d ‡	Oct	95.250	95.250	+0.005	95.250	95.245	1,923	72,330
Fed Fnds 30d‡	Nov	95.510	95.515	+0.010	95.520	95.505	43,948	141,474
Fed Fnds 30d‡	Dec	95.575	95.610	+0.035	95.635	95.565	21,490	76,659
Euroyen 3m‡‡	Dec	99.190	99.185	–	99.190	99.175	24,128	894,130
Euroyen 3m‡‡	Mar	99.175	99.185	–0.005	99.175	99.160	31,683	779,159
Euroyen 3m‡‡	Jun	99.150	99.145	–	99.150	99.135	22,875	454,459

Contracts are base on volumes traded in 2004.

Sources: * LIFFE, † CME, ‡ CBOT, ‡‡ TIFFE

Notes: Euribor 3m: A benchmark interest rate in euros for three-month deposits.
Euroswiss 3m: Three-month interest rate in Euro-Swiss francs.
Sterling 3m: Sterling three-month interest rate.
Eurodollar 3m: Three-month notional deposit rate for Eurodollars.
Fed Fnds 30d: Federal funds 30-day interest – a US benchmark rate.
Euroyen 3m: Three-month interest rate for euroyen deposits.

Source: Financial Times, 2 November 2007, p. 45. Reprinted with permission.

Short-term interest contracts are quoted on an index basis rather than on the basis of the interest rate itself. The price is defined as:

$P = 100 - i$
where:
P = price index;
i = the future interest rate in percentage terms.

Thus, on 1 November 2007 the settlement price for a June three-month sterling future was 94.35, which implies an interest rate of 100 – 94.35 = 5.65 per cent for the period June to September – *see* Exhibit 24.19. Similarly the September quote would imply an interest rate of 100 – 94.49 = 5.51 per cent for the three months September to December 2008.

In both cases the implied interest rate refers to a rate applicable for a notional deposit of £500,000 for three months on expiry of the contract – the June futures contract expires in June (i.e. the right to 'deposit' in June through to September expires in June) and the September future expires in September. The 5.65 per cent rate for three-month money starting from June 2008 is the *annual* rate of interest even though the deal is for a deposit of only one-quarter of a year.

The price of 94.35 is not a price in the usual sense – it does not mean £94.35. It is used to maintain the standard inverse relationship between prices and interest rates. For example, if traders in this market one week later, on 8 November 2007, adjusted supply and demand conditions because they expect generally raised inflation and raised interest rates by the middle of 2008, they would push up the interest rates for three-month deposits starting in June 2008 to, say, 6.0 per cent. Then the price of the future would fall to 94.00. Thus, a rise in interest rates for a three-month deposit of money results in a fall in the price of the contract – analogous to the inverse relationship between interest rates offered on long-term bonds and the price of those bonds.

In relation to short-term interest rate futures it is this inverse change in capital value when interest rates change that it is of crucial importance to grasp. Understanding this is more important than trying to envisage deposits of £500,000 being placed some time in the future.

Worked example 24.3 Hedging three-month deposits

An example of these derivatives in use may help with gaining an understanding of their hedging qualities. Imagine the treasurer of a large company anticipates the receipt of £100m in late September 2008, almost 11 months hence. She expects that the money will be needed for production purposes in January 2009 but for the three months following late September it can be placed on deposit. There is a risk that interest rates will fall between now (November 2007) and September 2008 from their present level of 5.51 per cent per annum for three-month deposits starting in late September. (The Sterling 3m September future in Exhibit 24.19 shows a price of 94.49, indicating an interest rate of 5.51.)

The treasurer does not want to take a passive approach and simply wait for the inflow of money and deposit it at whatever rate is then prevailing without taking some steps to ensure a good return.

To achieve certainty in September 2008 the treasurer buys, in November 2007, September 2008 expiry three-month sterling interest rate futures at a price of 94.49. Each future has a notional value of £500,000 and therefore she has to buy 200 to hedge the £100m inflow.

Suppose in September 2008 that three-month interest rates have fallen to 4 per cent. Following the actual receipt of the £100m the treasurer can place it on deposit and receive a return over the next three months of £100m × 0.04 × $^3/_{12}$ = £1m. This is significantly less than if September 2008 three-month deposit interest rates had remained at 5.51 per cent throughout the 11-month waiting period.

Return at 5.51 per cent (£100m × 0.0551 × $^3/_{12}$)	= £1,377,500
Return at 4.00 per cent (£100m × 0.040 × $^3/_{12}$)	= £1,000,000
Loss	£377,500

However, the caution of the treasurer pays off because the futures have risen in value as the interest rates have fallen.

The 200 futures contracts were bought at 94.49. With interest rates at 4 per cent for three-month deposits starting in September the futures in September have a value of 100 – 4 = 96.00. The treasurer in September can close the futures position by selling the futures for 96.00. Thus, a purchase was made in November 2007 at 94.49 and a sale in September 2008 at 96, therefore the gain that is made amounts to 96.00 – 94.49 = 1.51.

This is where a ***tick*** needs to be introduced. A tick is the minimum price movement on a future. On a three-month sterling interest rate contract a tick is a movement of 0.01 per cent on a trading unit of £500,000.

One-hundredth of 1 per cent of £500,000 is equal to £50, but this is not the value of one tick. A further complication is that the price of a future is based on annual interest rates whereas the contract is for three months. Therefore £50/4 = £12.50 is the value of a tick movement in a three-month sterling interest rate futures contract. In this case we have a gain of 151 ticks with an overall value of 151 × £12.50 = £1,887.5 per contract, or £377,500 for 200 contracts. The profit on the futures exactly offsets the loss of anticipated interest when the £100m is put on deposit for three months in September.

Note that the deal struck in November was not to enter into a contract to actually deposit £100m with the counterparty on the Euronext.liffe market. The £100m is deposited in September with any one of hundreds of banks with no connection to the futures contract that the treasurer entered into. The actual deposit and the notional deposit (on Euronext.liffe) are two separate transactions. However, the transactions are cleverly arranged so that the value movements on these two exactly offset each other. All that is received from Euronext.liffe is the tick difference, based on the price change between buying and selling prices of the futures contracts – no interest is received.

Worked example 24.4 Hedging a loan

In November 2007 Holwell plc plans to borrow £5m for three months at a later date. This will begin in June 2008. Worried that short-term interest rates will rise Holwell hedges by *selling* ten three-month sterling interest rate futures contracts with June expiry. The price of each futures contract is 94.35, so Holwell has locked into an annual interest rate of 5.65 per cent or 1.4125 per cent for three months. The cost of borrowing is therefore:

£5m × 0.01412.5 = £70,625

Suppose that interest rates rise to annual rates of 6 per cent, or 1.5 per cent per quarter. The cost of borrowing for Holwell will be:

£5m × 0.015 = £75,000

However, Holwell is able to *buy* ten futures contracts to close the position on the exchange. Each contract has fallen in value from 94.35 to 94.00 (100 – 6); this is 35 ticks. The profit credited to Holwell's margin account on Euronext.liffe will now stand at:

Bought at 94.00, sold at 94.35:
35 ticks × £12.50 × 10 contracts = £4,375

Holwell pays interest to its lender for the three months June to September at 6 per cent annual rate. The extra interest is an additional £4,375 (£75,000 – £70,625) compared with the rate in the market for June to September deposits when Holwell was looking at the issue back in November. However, the derivative profit offsets the extra interest cost on the loan Holwell takes out in June.

Note that if interest rates fall Holwell will gain by being charged lower interest on the actual loan, but this will be offset by the loss of the futures. Holwell sacrifices the benefits of potential favourable movements in rates to reduce risk.

As Exhibit 24.20 shows, the prices of short-term interest rate futures are followed closely as they give an indication of the market view on the level of short-term interest rates a few months hence.

Exhibit 24.20

Betting on interest rates

FT

The short sterling market has its own advice to offer

As the chancellor and the governor of the Bank of England sit down to ponder interest rate policy at their monthly monetary meeting today, a £40bn-a-day industry will be pronouncing its own judgment on where rates are going next.

The betting in the so-called 'short sterling' futures market is that policy-makers will leave rates unchanged until well into next year. Banks and companies use this market to protect themselves against adverse changes in rates, while speculators use it to gamble on how rates might move.

Short sterling futures are traded on the London International Financial Futures and Options Exchange. Their current price implies a prediction that base rates will still be at $6^3/_4$ per cent by the end of this year, rising to 7 per cent by the end of next year. With more than £10,000bn each year backing these bets, this is a forecast that policy-makers ignore at their peril.

'Short sterling takes in all the latest economic and political news to give an indication of where the money market thinks short-term interest rates will be going in the future,' said Mr Nigel Richardson, an economist at Yamaichi International, a Japanese bank.

The companies and banks buying short sterling futures are making a simple bet. The price of the short sterling contract is equal to 100 minus whatever interest rate is expected when the three month contract expires, so the price of the contract rises when interest rates fall.

If a company thought interest rates would be $6^3/_4$ per cent by December it would expect the price of the December contract to be 93.25. If the current price of the December contract was below 93.25 – in other words the market expected interest rates to be higher than $6^3/_4$ per cent at the end of the year – then the company could buy the contract and expect to profit when it expired in December.

This allows a short sterling trader to protect itself against a possible interest rate movement, effectively fixing the interest rate at which it borrows or lends. A more aggressive investor can use short sterling to gamble on an interest rate change.

Imagine a company has a sum of money to invest in a bank, but fears interest rates will fall. The company could buy a short sterling contract expiring in three months. If, by then, interest rates had not fallen, the company would have lost nothing. If rates did fall the company would get a lower return on its investment, but this would have been offset by a rise in the price of the futures contract.

Another company might want to borrow money, but fear that interest rates are set to rise. It could hedge against this risk by selling short sterling futures. If rates did rise the company's borrowing costs would be higher, but it would be able to buy the contract back at a lower price and use the profit to offset the cost.

This is useful for banks providing fixed-rate mortgages. They use the short sterling market to fix the interest rates at which they borrow, which they can then pass on to customers.

Economists in the City use the forecast provided by the short sterling market as a basis for their own projections. 'It is very useful. It tells you what the market is predicting and you then take the market into account when making your own forecast,' said Mr Stuart Thomson, economist at Nikko, a Japanese bank.

But there have been times when the forecasts have been very different – and short sterling has not always been right. This year the short sterling market was expecting interest rates to be close to 9 per cent by December. Economists were expecting a more modest increase, and in the event they were proved more accurate.

Similarly, after the pound's exit from the European exchange rate mechanism in 1992, short sterling predicted that interest rates would have to remain high. In the event they were cut aggressively.

'If you just want an average of the views of everybody acting in the market, then short sterling is fine,' said Mr Ian Shepherdson, an economist at HSBC Markets. 'But if you want an opinion, you need an economist. Short sterling gives the consensus, but the consensus is not always right.'

Policymakers will no doubt draw solace from the fact that markets can be wrong sometimes too.

Source: Graham Bowley, *Financial Times*, 1 November 1995. Reprinted with permission.

Forward rate agreements (FRAs)

FRAs are useful devices for hedging future interest rate risk. They are agreements about the future level of interest rates. The rate of interest at some point in the future is compared with the level agreed when the FRA was established and compensation is paid by one party to the other based on the difference.

For example, a company needs to borrow £6m in six months' time for a period of a year. It arranges this with bank X at a variable rate of interest. The current rate of interest is 7 per cent. (For the sake of argument assume that this is the Libor rate for borrowing starting in six months and lasting one year, and that this company can borrow at Libor.) The company is concerned that by the time the loan is drawn down interest rates will be higher than 7 per cent, increasing the cost of borrowing.

The company enters into a separate agreement with another bank (Y) – an FRA. It 'purchases' an FRA at an interest rate of 7 per cent. This is to take effect six months from now and relates to a 12-month loan. Bank Y will never lend any money to the company but it has committed itself to paying compensation should interest rates (Libor) rise above 7 per cent.

Suppose that in six months spot one-year interest rates are 8.5 per cent. The company will be obliged to pay Bank X this rate: £6m × 0.085 = £510,000; this is £90,000 more than if the interest rates were 7 per cent. However, the FRA with Bank Y entitles the company to claim compensation equal to the difference between the rate agreed in the FRA and the spot rate. This is (0.085 – 0.07) × £6m = £90,000. So any increase in interest cost above 7 per cent is exactly matched by a compensating payment provided by the counterparty to the FRA.[8] However, if rates fall below 7 per cent the company makes payments to Bank Y. For example, if the spot rate in six months is 5 per cent the company benefits because of the lower rate charged by Bank X, but suffers an equal offsetting compensation payment to Bank Y of (0.07 – 0.05) × £6m = £120,000. The company has generated certainty over the effective interest cost of borrowing in the future. Whichever way the interest rates move it will pay £420,000.

This example is a gross simplification. In reality FRAs are generally agreed for three-month periods. So this company could have four separate FRAs for the year. It would agree different rates for each three-month period. If three-month Libor turns out to be higher than the agreed rate, Bank Y will pay the difference to the company. If it is lower the company pays Bank Y the difference.

The 'sale' of an FRA by a company protects it against a fall in interest rates. For example, if £10m is expected to be available for putting into a one-year bank deposit in three months from now the company could lock into a rate now by selling an FRA to a bank. Suppose the agreed rate is 6.5 per cent and the spot rate in three months is 6 per cent, then the depositor will receive 6 per cent from the bank into which the money is placed plus $^1/_2$ per cent from the FRA counterparty bank.

The examples above are described as 6 against 18 (or 6 × 18) and 3 against 15 (or 3 × 15). The first is a 12-month contract starting in six months, the second is a 12-month contract starting in three months. Typically sums of £5m–£100m are hedged in single deals in this market. Companies do not need to have an underlying lending or borrowing transaction – they could enter into an FRA in isolation and make or receive compensating payments only.

There is more on FRAs in Appendix 24.2.

A comparison of options, futures, forwards and FRAs

We have covered a great deal of ground in the field of derivatives. It is time to summarise the main advantages and disadvantages of the derivatives covered so far – *see* **Exhibit 24.21**.

---

[8] All figures are slightly simplified because we are ignoring the fact that the compensation is received in six months whereas interest to Bank X is payable in 18 months.

Exhibit 24.21 A comparison of options, futures, forwards and forward rate agreements

Options	Futures	Forwards and FRAs
Advantages		
Downside risk is limited but the buyer is able to participate in favourable movements in the underlying.	Can create certainty: specific rates are locked in.	Can create certainty: specific rates are locked in.
Available on or off exchanges. Exchange regulation and clearing house reduce counterparty default risk for those options traded on exchanges.	Exchange trading only. Exchange regulation and clearing house reduce counterparty default risk.	Tailor-made, off-exchange. Not standardised as to size, duration and terms. Good for companies with non-standard risk exposures.
	No premium is payable. (However margin payments are required.)	No margins or premiums payable. (Occasionally a good faith performance margin is required by one or more parties in a forward. Also credit limits may be imposed.)
For many options there are highly liquid markets resulting in keen option premium pricing and ability to reverse a position quickly at low cost. For others trading is thin and so premiums payable may become distorted and offsetting transactions costly and difficult.	Very liquid markets. Able to reverse transactions quickly and cheaply.	
Disadvantages		
Premium payable reduces returns when market movements are advantageous.	No right to let the contract lapse. Benefits from favourable movements in underlying are forgone.	No right to let the contract lapse. Benefits from favourable movements in underlying are forgone.
	In a hedge position if the underlying transaction does not materialise the future position owner can experience a switch from a covered to an uncovered position, the potential loss is unlimited.	In a hedge position if the underlying transaction does not materialise the forward/FRA position owner can experience a switch from a covered to an uncovered position, the potential loss is unlimited.
Margin required when writing options.	Many exchange restrictions – on size of contract, duration (e.g. only certain months of the year), trading times (e.g. when euronext.liffe is open).	Greater risk of counterparty default – not exchange traded therefore counterparty is not the clearing house.
		Generally the minimum contract size is for millions rather than a few thousand (as on the futures or options markets).
	Margin calls require daily work for 'back office'.	More difficult to liquidate position (than with exchange-traded instruments) by creating an offsetting transaction that cancels position.

Caps

An **interest rate cap** is a contract that gives the purchaser the right effectively to set a maximum level for interest rates payable. Compensation is paid to the purchaser of a cap if interest rates rise above an agreed level. This is a hedging technique used to cover interest rate risk on longer-term borrowing (usually two to five years). Under these arrangements a company borrowing money can benefit from interest rate falls but can place a limit to the amount paid in interest should interest rates rise.

Worked example 24.5 Interest rate cap

Oakham plc wishes to borrow £20m for five years. It arranges this with bank A at a variable rate based on Libor plus 1.5 per cent. The interest rate is reset every quarter based on three-month Libor. Currently this stands at an annual rate of 7 per cent. The firm is concerned that over a five-year period the interest rate could rise to a dangerous extent.

Oakham buys an interest rate cap set at Libor of 8.5 per cent. For the sake of argument we will assume that this costs 2.3 per cent of the principal amount, or £20m × 0.023 = £460,000 payable immediately to the cap seller. If over the subsequent five years Libor rises above 8.5 per cent in any three-month period Oakham will receive sufficient compensation from the cap seller to offset exactly any extra interest above 8.5 per cent. So if for the whole of the third year Libor rose to 9.5 per cent Oakham would pay interest at 9.5 per cent plus 1.5 per cent to bank A but would also receive 1 per cent compensation from the cap seller (a quarter every three months), thus capping the interest payable. If interest rates fall Oakham benefits by paying bank A less.

The premium (£460,000) payable up front covers the buyer for the entire five years, with no further payment due.

The size of the cap premium depends on the difference between current interest rates and the level at which the cap becomes effective; the length of time covered; and the expected volatility of interest rates. The cap seller does not need to assess the creditworthiness of the purchaser because it receives payment of the premium in advance. Thus a cap is particularly suitable for highly geared firms, such as leveraged buyouts.

Floors and collars

Buyers of interest rate caps are sometimes keen to reduce the large cash payment at the outset. They can do this by simultaneously selling a **floor**, which results in a counterparty paying a premium. With a floor, if the interest rate falls below an agreed level, the seller (the **floor writer**) makes compensatory payments to the floor buyer. These payments are determined by the difference between the prevailing rates and the floor rate.

Returning to Oakham, the treasurer could buy a cap set at 8.5 per cent Libor for a premium of £460,000 and sell a floor at 6 per cent Libor receiving, say, £200,000. In any three-month period over the five-year life of the loan, if Libor rose above 8.5 per cent the cap seller would pay compensation to Oakham; if Libor fell below 6 per cent Oakham would save on the amount paid to bank A but will have to make payments to the floor buyer, thus restricting the benefits from falls in Libor. Oakham, for a net premium of £260,000, has ensured that its effective interest payments will not diverge from the range 6 per cent + 1.5 per cent = 7.5 per cent at the lower end, to 8.5 per cent + 1.5 per cent = 10 per cent at the upper end.

The combination of selling a floor at a low strike rate and buying a cap at a higher strike rate is called a **collar**.

Swaps

A **swap** is an exchange of cash payment obligations. An **interest-rate swap** is where one company arranges with a counterparty to exchange interest-rate payments. For example, the first company may be paying fixed-rate interest but prefers to pay floating rates. The second company may be paying floating rates of interest, which go up and down with Libor, but would benefit from a switch to a fixed obligation. For example, imagine that firm S has a £200m ten-year loan paying a fixed rate of interest of 8 per cent, and firm T has a £200m ten-year loan on which interest is reset every six months with reference to Libor, at Libor plus 2 per cent. Under a swap arrangement S would agree to pay T's floating-rate interest on each due date over the next ten years, and T would be obligated to pay S's 8 per cent interest.

One motive for entering into a swap arrangement is to reduce or eliminate exposure to rises in interest rates. Over the short run, futures, options and FRAs could be used to hedge interest-rate exposure. However, for longer-term loans (more than two years) swaps are usually more suitable because they can run for the entire lifetime of the loan. So if a treasurer of a company with a large floating-rate loan forecasts that interest rates will rise over the next four years, he/she could arrange to swap interest payments with a fixed-rate interest payer for those four years.

Another reason for using swaps is to take advantage of market imperfections. Sometimes the interest-rate risk premium charged in the fixed-rate borrowing market differs from that in the floating-rate market for a particular borrower. See **Worked example 24.6**.

Worked example 24.6 Swaps

Take the two companies, Cat plc and Dog plc, both of which want to borrow £150m for eight years. Cat would like to borrow on a fixed-rate basis because this would better match its asset position. Dog prefers to borrow at floating rates because of optimism about future interest-rate falls. The treasurers of each firm have obtained quotations from banks operating in the markets for both fixed- and floating-rate eight-year debt. Cat could obtain fixed-rate borrowing at 10 per cent and floating rate at Libor +2 per cent. Dog is able to borrow at 8 per cent fixed and Libor +1 per cent floating:

	Fixed	**Floating**
Cat can borrow at	10%	Libor +2%
Dog can borrow at	8%	Libor +1%

In the absence of a swap market Cat would probably borrow at 10 per cent and Dog would pay Libor +1 per cent. However, with a swap arrangement both firms can achieve lower interest rates.

Notice that because of Dog's higher credit rating it can borrow at a lower rate than Cat in both the fixed- and the floating-rate market – it has an absolute advantage in both. However the risk premium charged in the two markets is not consistent. Cat has to pay an extra 1 per cent in the floating-rate market, but an extra 2 per cent in the fixed-rate market. Cat has an absolute disadvantage for both, but has a comparative advantage in the floating-rate market.

To achieve lower interest rates each firm should borrow in the market where it has comparative advantage and then swap interest obligations. So Cat borrows floating-rate funds, paying Libor +2 per cent, and Dog borrows fixed-rate debt, paying 8 per cent.

Then they agree to swap interest payments at rates which lead to benefits for both firms in terms of: **a** achieving the most appropriate interest pattern (fixed or floating), and **b** the interest rate that is payable, which is lower than if Cat had borrowed at fixed and Dog had borrowed at floating rates. *One* way of achieving this is to arrange the swap on the following basis:

- Cat pays to Dog fixed interest of 9.5 per cent;
- Dog pays to Cat Libor +2 per cent.

This is illustrated in Exhibit 24.22.

Exhibit 24.22 An interest rate swap

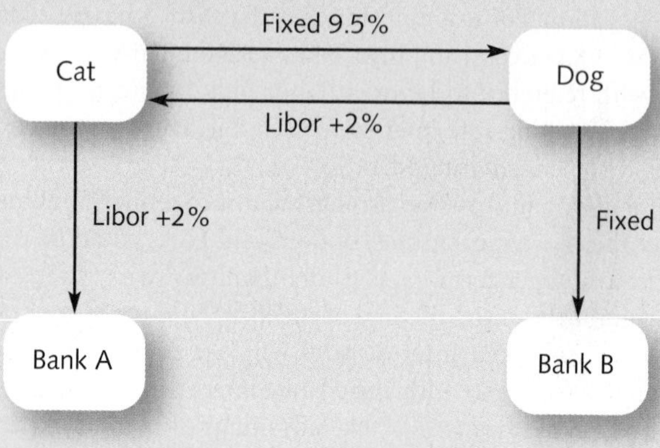

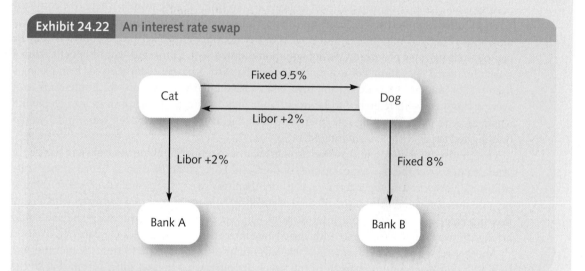

Now let us examine the position for each firm.

Cat pays Libor +2 per cent to a bank but also receives Libor +2 per cent from Dog and so these two cancel out. Cat also pays 9.5 per cent fixed to Dog. This is 50 basis points (0.5 per cent) lower than if Cat had borrowed at fixed rate directly from the bank. On £150m this is worth £750,000 per year.

Cat:

Pays	Libor +2%
Receives	Libor +2%
Pays	Fixed 9.5%
Net payment	Fixed 9.5%

Dog takes on the obligation of paying a bank fixed interest at 8 per cent while receiving 9.5 per cent fixed from Cat on the regular payment days. The net effect is 1.5 per cent receivable less the Libor +2 per cent payment to Cat – a floating-rate liability of Libor +0.5 per cent.

Dog:

Pays	Fixed 8%
Receives	Fixed 9.5%
Pays	Libor +2%
Net payment	Libor +0.5%

Again there is a saving of 50 basis points or £750,000 per year.[9] The net annual £1.5m saving is before transaction costs.

Prior to the widespread development of a highly liquid swap market each counterparty incurred considerable expense in making the contracts watertight. Even then, the risk of one of the counterparties failing to fulfil its obligations was a potential problem. Today intermediaries (for example banks) take counterparty positions in swaps and this reduces risk and avoids the

[9] Under a swap arrangement the principal amount (in this case £150m) may never be swapped and Cat retains the obligation to pay the principal to bank A. Neither of the banks is involved in the swap and may not be aware that it has taken place. The swap focuses entirely in the three-monthly or six-monthly interest payments.

necessity for one corporation to search for another with a corresponding swap preference. The intermediary generally finds an opposite counterparty for the swap at a later date. Furthermore, standardised contracts reduce the time and effort to arrange a swap and have permitted the development of a thriving secondary market, and this has assisted liquidity.

A practical use of a swap arrangement by an individual is shown in **Exhibit 24.23**. The mortgage holder starts by paying base rate plus 1 per cent to the mortgage company (5.5% + 1%) but agrees a swap whereby he pays 6.2 fixed rate and receives base rate.

Exhibit 24.23

Rate rise is music to the ears of 'swappers'

FT

Unlike many home owners, those who have taken out interest rate swaps will be hoping that the Bank of England raises interest rates sooner rather than later.

One client of Stonehenge, which advises wealthy families, recently arranged an interest rate swap on his £5m mortgage for three years. Due to the size of the loan he had to take out a variable mortgage at a rate of 6.5 per cent. Convinced that interest rates will increase significantly over the next three years he was concerned that his variable rate left him vulnerable to the possibility of large and changeable repayments.

He decided to take out a swap, which effectively takes the cost of his mortgage to 7.2 per cent. This meant taking out a 3 year swap priced at 6.2 per cent, 0.7 of a percentage point above base rates of current base rates of 5.5 per cent.

If base rates go above his swap rate of 6.2 per cent, the bank will pay him the difference between his fixed rate and the interest rate, effectively insuring him against further interest rate hikes. If base rates stay below this level he pays out the difference.

The benefits come if the Bank of England raises rates higher. If rates rise to 6.5 per cent, say, his variable mortgage would jump to 7.5 per cent and each year he would need to pay £375,000. While rising interest rates will push up his variable rate, they will also push up the amount he receives back from his bank on his swap.

In this case he would get back the difference between his swap rate of 6.2 per cent and the interest rate of 6.5 per cent. He can then use this 0.3 per cent payment of 7.5 per cent, keeping his payments at a fixed rate of 7.2 per cent.

But by using an interest rate swap, he has ensured that his payments never exceed 7.2 per cent – or £360,000 per year.

Source: Elaine Moore, *Financial Times*, 30 June 2007, Money, p. 2. Reprinted with permission.

There are many variations on the swaps theme. For example, a '**swaption**' is an option to have a swap at a later date. In a **currency swap** the two parties exchange interest obligations (or receipts) and the principal amount for an agreed period, between two different currencies. On reaching the maturity date of the swap the principal amounts will be re-exchanged at a pre-agreed exchange rate. An example of such an arrangement is shown in **Exhibit 24.24**.

There is more on swaps in Appendix 24.2.

Exhibit 24.24

TVA, EIB find winning formula

FT

The back-to-back swap deal priced yesterday for the Tennessee Valley Authority and the European Investment Bank will give both cheaper funding than they could obtain through conventional bond issuance.

TVA, the US government-owned power utility, is issuing a 10-year DM1.5bn eurobond with a Frankfurt listing, while EIB is raising $1bn with a 10-year issue in the US market. The issuers will swap the proceeds.

Speaking in London yesterday, the treasurers of both organisations said the arrangement – now relatively unusual in the swaps market – had allowed them to reduce borrowing costs, although they did not specify by what amount.

Two elements of the deal were important in this respect. First, the EIB has a much stronger comparative advantage over TVA in funding in dollars than it does in D-Marks. Lehman Brothers, co-bookrunner on both deals, said the EIB priced its 10-year dollar paper at 17 basis points over Treasuries, about 6 to 7 points lower than TVA could have done.

Exhibit 24.24 continued

In the German market EIB enjoys a smaller advantage; it could raise funds at about 4 basis points less than the 17 points over bonds achieved by TVA.

Second, by swapping the proceeds on a back-to-back basis rather than through counterparties, bid/offer spreads were eliminated and transaction costs reduced.

Resulting savings were pooled, providing benefits for both borrowers.

Both also diversified their funding sources. Lehman said some 65 per cent of the TVA bonds were placed in Europe, 20 per cent in Asia, and 15 per cent in the US. About half the EIB issue was placed in the US, 35 per cent in Europe, and 15 per cent in Asia.

Source: Richard Lapper, Capital Markets Editor, *Financial Times*, 12 September 1996. Reprinted with permission.

Derivatives users

There are three types of user of the derivatives markets: hedgers, speculators and arbitrageurs.

Hedgers

To **hedge** is to enter into transactions which protect a business or assets against changes in some underlying. The instruments bought as a hedge tend to have the opposite-value movements to the underlying. Financial and commodity markets are used to transfer risk from an individual or corporation to another more willing and/or able to bear that risk.

Consider a firm which discovers a rich deposit of platinum in Kenya. The management are afraid to develop the site because they are uncertain about the revenues that will actually be realised. Some of the sources of uncertainty are that: **a** the price of platinum could fall, **b** the floating-rate loan taken out to develop the site could become expensive if interest rates rise and **c** the value of the currencies could move adversely. The senior managers have more or less decided that they will apply the firm's funds to a less risky venture. A recent graduate steps forward and suggests that this would be a pity, saying: 'The company is passing up a great opportunity, and Kenya and the world economy will be poorer as a result. Besides, the company does not have to bear all of these risks given the sophistication of modern financial markets. The risks can be hedged, to limit the downside. For example, the platinum could be sold on the futures market, which will provide a firm price. The interest-rate liability can be capped or swapped into a fixed-rate loan. Other possibilities include using the FRA and the interest futures markets. The currency risk can be controlled by using currency forwards or options.' The board decide to press ahead with development of the mine and thus show that derivatives can be used to promote economic well-being by transferring risk.

Speculators

Speculators take a position in financial instruments and other assets with a view to obtaining a profit on changes in price. Speculators accept high risk in anticipation of high reward. The gearing effect of derivatives makes speculations in these instruments particularly profitable, or particularly ruinous. Speculators are also attracted to derivatives markets because they are often more liquid than the underlying markets. In addition the speculator is able to sell before buying (to 'short' the market) in order to profit from a fall. More complex trading strategies are also possible.

The term speculator in popular parlance is often used in a somewhat critical fashion. This is generally unwarranted. Speculators are needed by financial markets to help create trading liquidity. Prices, it is argued, are more, not less, likely to be stable as a result of speculative activity. Usually speculators have dissimilar views regarding future market movements and this provides two-way liquidity which allows other market participants, such as hedgers, to carry out a transaction quickly without moving the price. Imagine if only hedgers with an underlying were permitted to buy or sell derivatives. Very few trades would take place each day. If a firm wished to make a large hedge this would be noticed in the market and the price of the derivative would be greatly affected. Speculators also provide a kind of insurance for hedgers – they accept risk in return for a premium.

Arbitrageurs

The act of **arbitrage** is to exploit price differences on the same instrument or similar assets. The arbitrageur buys at the lower price and immediately resells at the higher price. So, for example, Nick Leeson claimed that he was arbitraging Nikkei 225 Index futures. The same future is traded in both Osaka and Singapore. Theoretically the price should be identical on both markets, but in reality this is not always the case, and it is possible simultaneously to buy the future in one market and sell the future in the other and thereby make a risk-free profit. An arbitrageur waits for these opportunities to exploit a market inefficiency. The problem for Barings Bank was that Nick Leeson obtained funds to put down as margin payments on arbitrage trades but then bought futures in both markets – surreptitiously switching from an arbitrage activity to a highly risky, speculative activity. True arbitrageurs help to ensure pricing efficiency – their acts of buying or selling tend to reduce pricing anomalies.

Over-the-counter (OTC) and exchange-traded derivatives

An OTC derivative is a tailor-made, individual arrangement between counterparties, usually a company and its bank. Standardised contracts (exchange-traded derivatives) are available on dozens of derivatives around the world, for example the Chicago Board of Trade (CBOT), the Chicago Board Options Exchange (CBOE), the Chicago Mercantile Exchange (CME), Euronext.liffe, the MATIF in France and the Eurex in Germany and Switzerland. Roughly one-half of outstanding derivatives contracts are traded on exchanges.

Many derivatives markets are predominantly, if not exclusively, OTC: interest-rate FRAs, swaps, caps, collars, floors, currency forwards and currency swaps. Exhibit 24.25 compares OTC and exchange-traded derivatives.

Exhibit 24.25 OTC and exchange-traded derivatives

OTC derivative

Advantages

- Contracts can be tailor-made, which allows perfect hedging and permits hedges of more unusual underlyings.

Disadvantages

- There is a risk (credit risk) that the counterparty will fail to honour the transaction.
- Low level of market regulation with resultant loss of transparency and price dissemination.
- Often difficult to reverse a hedge once the agreement has been made.
- Higher transaction costs.

Exchange-traded derivative

Advantages

- Credit risk is reduced because the clearing house is counterparty.
- High regulation encourages transparency and openness on the price of recent trades.
- Liquidity is usually much higher than for OTC – large orders can be cleared quickly due to high daily volume of trade.
- Positions can be reversed by closing quickly – an equal and opposite transaction is completed in minutes.

Disadvantages

- Standardisation may be restrictive, e.g. standardised terms for quality of underlying, quantity, delivery dates.
- The limited trading hours and margin requirements may be inconvenient.

Concluding comments

From a small base in the 1970s derivatives have grown to be of enormous importance. Almost all medium and large industrial and commercial firms use derivatives, usually to manage risk, but occasionally to speculate and arbitrage. Banks are usually at the centre of derivatives trading, dealing on behalf of clients, as market makers or trading on their own account. Other financial institutions are increasingly employing these instruments to lay off risk or to speculate. They can be used across the globe, and traded night and day.

The trend suggests that derivatives will continue their relentless rise in significance. They can no longer be dismissed as peripheral to the workings of the financial and economic systems. The implications for investors, corporate institutions, financial institutions, regulators and governments are going to be profound. These are incredibly powerful tools, and, like all powerful tools, they can be used for good or ill. Ignorance of the nature of the risks being transferred, combined with greed, has already led to some very unfortunate consequences. However, on a day-to-day basis, and away from the newspaper headlines, the ability of firms to quietly tap the markets and hedge risk encourages wealth creation and promotes general economic well-being.

Key points and concepts

- **A derivative instrument** is an asset whose performance is based on the behaviour of an underlying asset (the underlying).
- **An option** is a contract giving one party the right, but not the obligation, to buy (call option) or sell (put option) a financial instrument, commodity or some other underlying asset, at a given price, at or before a specified date.
- The **writer of a call option** is obligated to sell the agreed quantity of the underlying at some time in the future at the insistence of the option purchaser (holder). A **writer of a put** is obligated to sell.
- **American-style options** can be exercised at any time up to the expiry date whereas **European-style options** can only be exercised on a predetermined future date.
- An **out-of-the-money option** is one that has no intrinsic value.
- An **in-the-money option** has intrinsic value.
- **Time value** arises because of the potential for the market price of the underlying, over the time to expiry of the option, to change in a way that creates intrinsic value.
- **Share options** can be used for hedging or speculating on shares.
- **Corporate uses of options include**:
  - share options schemes;
  - warrants;
  - convertible bonds;
  - rights issues;
  - share underwriting;
  - commodity options;
  - taking control of a company;
  - protecting the company from foreign exchange losses;
  - real options.
- A **forward contract** is an agreement between two parties to undertake an exchange at an agreed future date at a price agreed now. Forwards are tailor-made, allowing flexibility.
- **Futures** are agreements between two parties to undertake a transaction at an agreed price on a specified future date. They are exchange-traded instruments with a clearing house acting as counterparty to every transaction standardised as to:
  - quality of underlying;
  - quantity of underlying;
  - legal agreement details;
  - delivery dates;

- trading times;
- margins.

- For futures, **initial margin** (0.1 per cent to 15 per cent) is required from each buyer or seller. Each day profit or losses are established through **marking to market**, and **variation margin** is payable by the holder of the future who loses.
- The majority of futures contracts are **closed** (by undertaking an equal and opposite transaction) **before expiry** and so **cash losses or profits** are made rather than settlement by delivery of the underlying. Some futures are settled by cash only – there is no physical delivery.
- **Short-term interest-rate futures** can be used to hedge against rises and falls in interest rates at some point in the future. The price for a £500,000 notional three-month contract is expressed as an index:

  $P = 100 - i$

  As interest rates rise the value of the index falls.
- **Forward rate agreements** (FRAs) are arrangements whereby one party pays the other should interest rates at some point in the future differ from an agreed rate.
- An interest rate **cap** is a contract that gives the purchaser the right effectively to set a maximum interest rate payable through the entitlement to receive compensation from the cap seller should market interest rates rise above an agreed level. The cap seller and the lender are not necessarily the same.
- A **floor** entitles the purchaser to payments from the floor seller should interest rates fall below an agreed level. A **collar** is a combination of a cap and a floor.
- A **swap** is an exchange of cash payment obligations. An interest-rate swap is where interest obligations are exchanged. In a currency swap the two sets of interest payments are in different currencies.
- Some **motives for swaps**:
  - to reduce or eliminate exposure to rising interest rates;
  - to match interest-rate liabilities with assets;
  - to exploit market imperfections and achieve lower interest rates.
- **Hedgers** enter into transactions to protect a business or assets against changes in some underlying.
- **Speculators** accept high risk by taking a position in financial instruments and other assets with a view to obtaining a profit on changes in value.
- **Arbitrageurs** exploit price differences on the same or similar assets.
- **Over-the-counter (OTC)** derivatives are tailor-made and available on a wide range of underlyings. They allow perfect hedging. However, they suffer from counterparty risk, low regulation and frequent inability to reverse a hedge.
- **Exchange-traded** derivatives have lower credit (counterparty) risk, greater regulation, higher liquidity and greater ability to reverse positions than OTC derivatives. However, standardisation can be restrictive.

Appendix 24.1 Option pricing

This appendix describes the factors that influence the market value of a call option on a share. The principles apply to the pricing of other options. The complex mathematics associated with option pricing will be avoided because of their unsuitability for an introductory text. Interested readers are referred to the References and further reading list later in this chapter.

Notation to be used:

C = value of call option
S = current market price of share
X = future exercise price
r_f = risk-free interest rate (per annum)
t = time to expiry (in years)
σ = standard deviation of the share price
e = mathematical fixed constant: 2.718 . . .

The factors affecting option value

1 ***Options have a minimum value of zero***

$$C \geq 0$$

Even if the share price falls significantly below the exercise price of the option the worst that can happen to the option holder is that the option becomes worth nothing – no further loss is created.

2 ***The market value of an option will be greater than the intrinsic value at any time prior to expiry*** This is because there is a chance that if the option is not exercised immediately it will become more valuable due to the movement of the underlying – it will become (or will move deeper) in-the-money. *An option has time value* that increases, the longer the time to expiry.

$$\text{Market value} = \text{Intrinsic value} + \text{Time value}$$

3 ***Intrinsic value (S – X) rises as share price increases or exercise price falls*** However this simple relationship needs to be made a little more sophisticated because S – X is based on the assumption of immediate exercise when the option is about to expire. However if the option is not about to expire there is some value in not having to pay the exercise price until the future exercise date. (Instead of buying the share a call option could be purchased and the remainder invested in a risk-free asset until the exercise date.) So intrinsic value is given a boost by discounting the exercise price by the risk-free rate of return:

$$\text{Intrinsic value} = S - \frac{X}{(1 + r_f)^t}$$

4 ***The higher the risk-free rate of return the higher will be intrinsic value,*** because the money saved by buying an option rather than the underlying security can be invested in a riskless rate of return until the option expires.

5 ***The maximum value of an option is the price of the share***

$$C \leq S$$

6 ***A major influence boosting the time value is the volatility of the underlying share price*** A share which has a stable, placid history is less likely to have a significant upward shift in value during the option's lifetime than one which has been highly variable. In option pricing models this factor is measured by the variance (σ^2) or standard deviation (σ) of the share price.

Black and Scholes' option pricing model

Black and Scholes' option pricing model (BSOPM) was published in 1973 and is still widely employed today despite the more recent modifications to the original model and the development of different option-pricing models. The BSOPM is as follows:

$$C = SN(d_1) - Xe^{-r_f t}N(d_2)$$

where:

N (.) = cumulative normal distribution function of d_1 and d_2

$$d_1 = \frac{\ln(S/X) + (r_f + \sigma^2/2)t}{\sigma\sqrt{t}}$$

ln = natural log

$$d_2 = d_1 - \sigma\sqrt{t}$$

NatWest Markets was seriously damaged by the revelation of a long-standing failure of senior managers to recognise the mispricing of options – £77m was lost but the damage in terms of reputation was far greater than that (*see* **Exhibit 24.26**).

Exhibit 24.26

Options mispricing caused loss

FT

The role of Mr Kyriacos Papouis, the 30-year-old former trader at NatWest Markets, in apparently building up over-valuations of £90m in its option books, has not been examined directly during the initial stage of NatWest's inquiry.

However, an outline of what Mr Papouis appears to have done is emerging. Although it involved mis-valuations of options for two years, the bulk of the losses are accounted for by a relatively small number of large trades.

Mr Papouis appears to have amassed small losses as part of routine swaps and options market-making in 1995. However, the fact that option prices are derived from estimates of likely volatility in markets provided a loophole.

Mr Papouis could adjust his estimates of volatility in less liquid swaps and options so as to boost their values. He then managed to persuade risk managers in NatWest Markets to agree to his volatility estimates and valuations.

It is not clear why he was able to persuade other managers that he was right. NatWest says that there was no gap between computer models available to risk managers and to traders, so the mispricing came from volatility estimates.

As the potential losses that would emerge in future rose in size, Mr Papouis appears to have made a few large and complex trades in which volatility estimates were so awry that they offset a high proportion of potential losses.

Source: John Gapper, *Financial Times*, 14 March 1997, p. 6. Reprinted with permission.

Appendix 24.2 The relationship between FRAs and swaps

If a corporation buys (or sells) a sequence of Libor-based FRAs stretching over, say, two years, in which each of the three-month periods making up that two years is covered by an FRA then we have an arrangement very similar to a two-year swap. The company has made a series of commitments to pay or receive differences between the FRA agreed rate and the prevailing spot rate at three-month intervals.

For example, Colston plc has a loan for £100m. This is a floating-rate liability. Interest is set at three-month Libor every three months over its two-year life. So, every three months, whatever the rate that London banks are charging for three-month loans to each other is to be charged to Colston. (This rate can be observed in the *Financial Times*. It changes daily, even by the minute – once agreed it is fixed for the three months.)

Thus the company is vulnerable to interest rate rises. The current time is June and spot Libor rate is set at 5.09 per cent. This is the annualised rate that Colston will pay for the next three months (it will pay one-quarter of this for three-month borrowing). To lock in a rate for the next rollover date, i.e. in September, the company could buy (in June) an FRA set at Libor for the three months starting in September and ending in December (a 3 × 6 forward rate agreement). This FRA is priced at 5.71 per cent. The amount covered can be exactly £100m because FRA arrangements are flexible to suit the client, being an over-the-counter market. The £100m is known as the notional amount.

The FRA buyer (Colston) has technically agreed to deliver to the FRA seller 5.71 per cent. In return the FRA seller will pay Colston whatever is the spot rate for Libor in September. Of course, it would be inefficient to have these two payments made when only one payment set as the difference between these rates is needed. So, if Libor is 5.71 per cent in September no payment is made by either side. However, if Libor in September resets at 6.2 per cent Colston will receive a settlement cash flow of 0.49 per cent, or 49 basis points, on £100m for the three-month period. Thus a payment of £122,500 is received (£100m × 0.0049 × 3/12) from the FRA seller.[10]

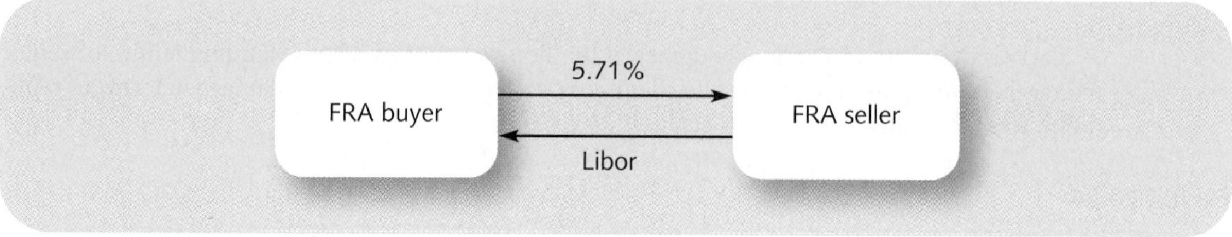

If, however, the spot Libor in September is 5.5 per cent, Colston will pay a settlement cash flow of 21 basis points: £100m × 0.0021 × 3/12 = £52,500.

FRAs are priced at-the-money, i.e. the current rate in the market for future Libor. In the case of Colston in June this is 5.71 per cent for September three-month FRA. The participants in this market consider that the market rate has zero initial value to both parties. However, as rates change the contract gains value for one or other of the contractors.

Colston has locked in the interest rate it will pay for the three months September to December, but what about the other months of the two-year loan commitment? It could enter a series of FRAs for each of the remaining rollover dates. The rates that would be set are shown in **Exhibit 24.27**.

Exhibit 24.27 FRA prices for the next two years

Time	Libor rate quoted in June for three-month periods starting at various dates over next two years
June 2008 (Spot)	5.09
Sept. 2008	5.71
Dec. 2008	6.05
Mar. 2009	6.42
June 2009	6.70
Sept. 2009	6.98
Dec. 2009	7.06
Mar. 2010	7.18

By executing seven FRAs at these rates Colston would pay its lender 5.09 per cent (annualised rate) for the first three months. Thereafter, regardless of how Libor moves the effective cost of the loan is 5.71 per cent for the second three months, 6.05 per cent for the third, and so on. Each one of these FRA deals is like a mini swap, with Colston committed to delivering the rate shown in the exhibit and the FRA seller committed to delivering Libor to Colston. Or, rather, net payments on the difference between the FRA rate and Libor are made. So, to illustrate for the first four payments:

[10] This is the amount payable in December for the September FRA. If the agreement is for payment to be made in September the amount will be reduced (discounted) at the annualised rate of 6.2 per cent.

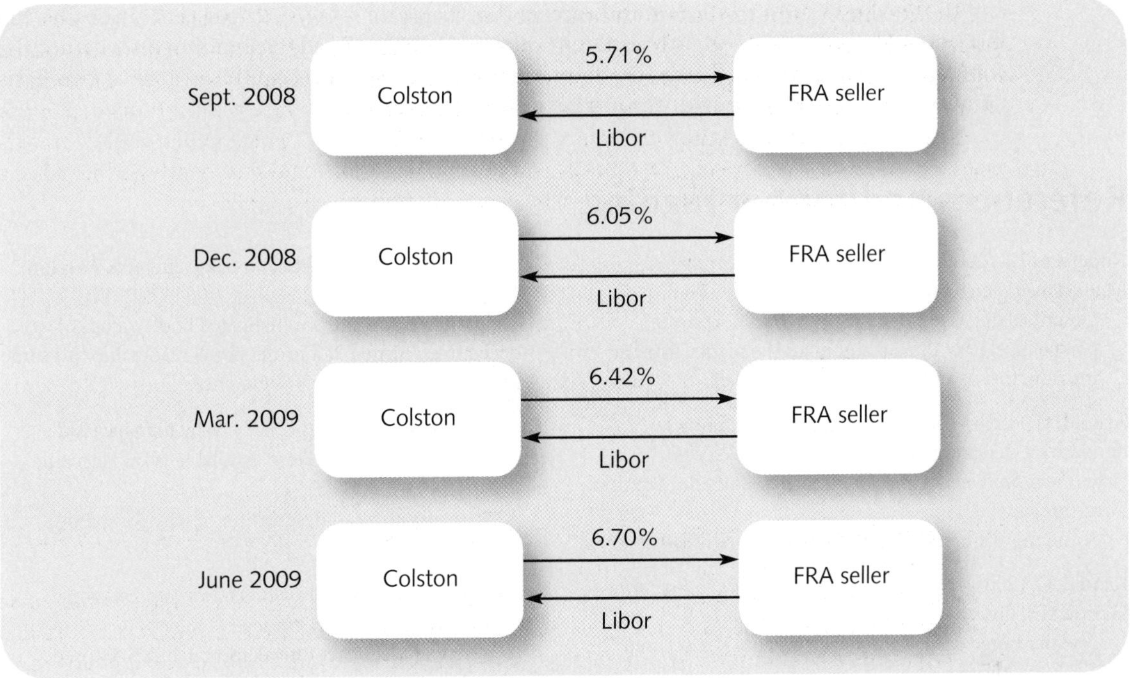

Using FRAs in this way Colston knows how much it has to pay out over the next two years and so is not vulnerable to unexpected changes in Libor. But note that the interest rates are different from one three-month period to another. An alternative open to Colston is to buy a contract with the same rate payable in each of the eight quarters. This rate would be an approximate average of the FRA rates stretching over the two years. This is called a swap. A rough average of the eight Libor rates payable in Exhibit 24.27 is 6.39 per cent. The interest rate swap arrangement is shown in **Exhibit 24.28**. For each three-month period Colston pays the counterparty the swap rate (6.39 per cent) and receives Libor. If interest rates rise above 6.39 per cent Colston would benefit from the swap arrangement because it receives payments from the swap counterparty, which amount to the difference between 6.39 per cent and Libor. This enables Colston to accept any increase in Libor with equanimity, as the effective cost of the loan is constant at 6.39 per cent regardless of how much is paid to the lender.

The swap rates quoted by banks in the financial markets are largely determined by the average of the forward rates to create one fixed rate for all quarterly settlements. The banks act as market makers quoting prices both for those who want to make fixed payments (as in the case of Colston)

Exhibit 24.28 Colston's payouts and receipts under a swap

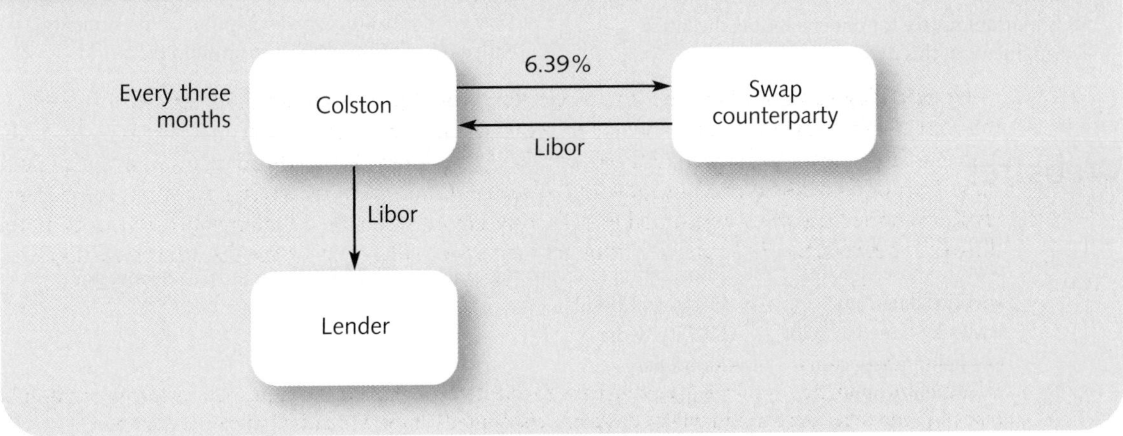

and those who wish to pay Libor and receive the swap rate – say, 6.39 per cent. In reality the market maker will charge slightly different rates (a bid/ask spread) depending on whether the company wants to receive the fixed rate or pay the fixed rate. This can be as little as two basis points but is sufficient to provide the market maker with a profit.

References and further reading

Andersen, T.J. (2006) *Global Derivatives: A Strategic Management Perspective.* Harlow: FT Prentice Hall.
Describes the use of derivatives from a corporate perspective. Easy to read and takes the reader from an introductory level to an intermediate level.

Arnold, G. (1996) 'Risk management using financial derivatives', in Gardener, E. and Molyneux. P. (eds), *Investment Banking: Theory and Practice.* 2nd edn. London: Euromoney.
Some more applications of derivatives are illustrated.

Arnold, G. (2004) *The Financial Times Guide to Investing.* Harlow: FT Prentice Hall.
A wider range of derivative instruments is discussed.

Bank of England Quarterly Bulletins.
An important and easily digestible source of up-to-date information.

Black, F. and Scholes, M. (1973) 'The pricing of options and corporate liabilities', *Journal of Political Economy*, May/June, pp. 637–59.
The first useful option pricing model – complex mathematics.

Blake, D. (2000) *Financial Market Analysis.* 2nd edn. Chichester: Wiley.
Some very useful material – but your maths has to be up to scratch!

Buckley, A. (2003) *Multinational Finance.* 5th edn. London: FT Prentice Hall.
Contains some easy-to-follow chapters on derivatives.

The Economist.
Valuable reading for anyone interested in finance (and world affairs, politics, economics, science etc. etc.)

Financial Times.
An important source for understanding the latest developments in this dynamic market.

Galitz, L. (1998) *Financial Engineering.* 2nd edn. London: FT Prentice Hall.
A clearly written and sophisticated book on use of derivatives. Aimed at a professional readership but some sections are excellent for the novice.

Headley, J.S. and Tufano, P. (2001) 'Why manage risk?' Harvard Business School Note. Available from Harvard Business Online.
A short easy-to-read description of why companies hedge risk.

McDonald, R.L. (2006) *Derivatives Markets.* 2nd edn. Harlow: Pearson/Addison Wesley.
A more technical/theoretical approach. US focused.

Miller, M.H. (1997) *Merton Miller on Derivatives.* New York: Wiley.
An accessible (no maths) account of the advantages and disadvantages of derivatives to companies, society and the financial system.

Pilbeam, K. (2005) *Finance and Financial Markets.* 2nd edn. Palgrave Macmillan.
Contains a few introductory chapter on derivatives.

Taylor, F. (2007) *Mastering Derivatives Markets.* 3rd edn. London: FT Prentice Hall.
A good introduction to derivative instruments and markets.

Vaitilingam, R. (2005) *The Financial Times Guide to Using the Financial Pages.* 5th edn. London: FT Prentice Hall.
Explains the tables displayed by the *Financial Times* and provides some background about the instruments – for the beginner.

Valdez, S. (2007) *An Introduction to Global Financial Markets.* 5th edn. Basingstoke: Macmillan.
Very good introductory description of instruments, with a description of markets around the world.

Websites

www.money.cnn.com	CNN Financial News
www.liffeinvestor.com	Information and learning tools from LIFFE to help the private investor
www.nyxdata.com	Prices on LIFFE
www.ukcitymedia.co.uk	UKCityMedia
www.bloomberg.com	Bloomberg
www.reuters.com	Reuters

www.wsj.com	*Wall Street Journal*
www.ft.com	*Financial Times*
www.fow.com	*Futures and Options World*
www.cbot.com	Chicago Board of Trade
www.euronext.com	London International Financial Futures and Options Exchange (Euronext.liffe)
www.cboe.com	Chicago Board Options Exchange
www.amex.com	American Stock Exchange
www.nyse.com	New York Stock Exchange
www.eurexchange.com	Eurex, the European Derivative Exchange
www.isda.org	International Swaps and Derivatives Association

Self-review questions

1 What are derivatives and why do they have value?

2 Why can vast sums be made or lost in a short space of time speculating with derivatives?

3 Describe the following:

- traded option
- call option
- put option
- in-the-money option
- out-of-the-money option
- intrinsic value
- time value
- index option
- option writer

4 Compare the hedging characteristics of options and futures.

5 Distinguish between delivery of the underlying and cash settlement.

6 List and briefly describe the application of options to industrial and commercial organisations.

7 Explain the advantages of entering into a forward contract.

8 How do futures differ from forwards?

9 Describe the following:

- clearing house
- initial margin
- marking to market
- variation margin

10 Explain forward rate agreements, caps, floors and collars.

11 Describe what is meant by a swap agreement and explain why some of the arrangements are entered into.

12 Distinguish between a hedger, a speculator and an arbitrageur.

13 Why do the over-the-counter markets in derivatives and the exchange-based derivatives markets coexist?

Questions and problems

myfinancelab **Questions with an icon are also available for practice in MyFinanceLab with additional supporting resources.**

For those questions marked with an asterisk* the answers are given in the Lecturer's guide.

1 You hold 20,000 shares in ABC plc which are currently priced at 500p. ABC has developed a revolutionary flying machine. If trials prove successful the share price will rise significantly. If the government bans the use of the machine, following a trial failure, the share price will collapse.

Required

a Explain and illustrate how you could use the traded options market to hedge your position.
Further information
Current time: 30 January.
Traded option quotes on ABC plc on 30 January:

		Calls			Puts		
	Option	March	June	Sept.	March	June	Sept.
ABC plc	450	62	88	99	11	19	27
	500	30	50	70	30	42	57
	550	9	20	33	70	85	93

b What is meant by intrinsic value, time value, in-the-money, at-the-money and out-of-the-money? Use the above table to illustrate.

?

2 Palm's share price stands at £4.80. You purchase one March 500p put on Palm's shares for 52p. What is your profit or loss on the option if you hold the option to maturity under each of the following share prices?

a 550p
b 448p
c 420p

?

3 What is the intrinsic and time value on each of the following options given a share price of 732p?

Exercise price	Calls Feb.	Puts Feb.
700	$55^1/_2$	$17^1/_2$
750	28	40

Which options are in-the-money and which are out-of-the-money?

?

4 Adam, a speculator, is convinced that the stock market will fall significantly in the forthcoming months. The current market index (14 August) level is 4997 (FTSE 100). He is investigating a strategy to exploit this market fall:

Sell five FTSE 100 Index futures on Euronext.liffe with a December expiry, current price 5086.
Extracts from the Financial Times

FTSE 100 Index Futures (LIFFE) £10 per full index point

	Open	Sett. price
Sept.	5069	5020
Dec.	5128	5086

Assume: No transaction costs.

Required

i What would the profit (loss) be if the index rose to 5500 in December under the strategy?
ii What would the profit (loss) be if the index fell to 4500 in December under the strategy?
iii Discuss the relative merits of using traded options rather than futures for speculation. ?

5 On 14 August British Biotech traded options were quoted on LIFFE as follows:

		Calls			Puts		
	Option	Sept.	Dec.	March	Sept.	Dec.	March
British Biotech	160	$30^1/_2$	40	53	$7^1/_2$	$16^1/_2$	$23^1/_2$
($177^1/_2$)	180	$20^1/_2$	31	$45^1/_2$	$16^1/_2$	27	$34^1/_2$

Assume: No transaction costs.

Required

a Imagine you write a December 180 put on 14 August. Draw a graph showing your profit and loss at share prices ranging from 100p to 250p.
b Add to the graph the profit or loss on the purchase of 1,000 shares in British Biotech held until late December at share prices between 100p and 250p.
c Show the profit or loss of the combination of a and b on the graph. ?

6* A manager controlling a broadly based portfolio of UK large shares wishes to hedge against a possible fall in the market. It is October and the portfolio stands at £30m with the FTSE 100 Index at 5020. The March futures price is 5035 (£10 per Index point).

Required

a Describe a way in which the manager could hedge against a falling market. Show the number of derivatives.
b What are the profits/losses if the FTSE 100 Index moves to 4000 or 6000 in March?
c Draw a profit/loss diagram for the strategy. Show the value of the underlying portfolio at different index levels, the value of the derivative and the combined value of the underlying and the derivative. ?

7 (*Examination level*) A buyer of a futures contract in Imaginationum with an underlying value of £400,000 on 1 August is required to deliver an initial margin of 5 per cent to the clearing house. This margin must be maintained as each day the counterparties in the futures are marked to market.

Required

a Display a table showing the variation margin required to be paid by this buyer and the accumulated profit/loss balance on her margin account in the eight days following the purchase of the future. (Assume that the maintenance margin is the same as the initial margin.)

Day	1	2	3	4	5	6	7	8
Value of Imaginationum (£000s)	390	410	370	450	420	400	360	410

b Explain what is meant by 'gearing returns' with reference to this example.
c Compare forwards and futures markets and explain the mutual coexistence of these two. ?

8* A corporate treasurer expects to receive £20m in late September, six months hence. The money will be needed for expansion purposes the following December. However in the intervening three months it can be deposited to earn interest. The treasurer is concerned that interest rates will fall from the present level of 8 per cent over the next six months, resulting in a poorer return on the deposited money.

A forward rate agreement (FRA) is available at 8 per cent.
Three-month sterling interest futures starting in late September are available, priced at 92.00.
Assume: No transaction costs and that a perfect hedge is possible.

Required

a Describe two hedging transactions that the treasurer could employ.
b Show the profit/loss on the underlying and the derivative under each strategy if market interest rates fall to 7 per cent, and if they rise to 9 per cent. ?

9*a Black plc has a £50m ten-year floating-rate loan from Bank A at Libor + 150 basis points. The treasurer is worried that interest rates will rise to a level that will put the firm in a dangerous position. White plc is willing to swap its fixed-interest commitment for the next ten years. White currently pays 9 per cent to Bank B. Libor is currently 8 per cent. Show the interest-rate payment flows in a diagram under a swap arrangement in which each firm pays the other's interest payments.
b What are the drawbacks of this swap arrangement for Black?
c Black can buy a ten-year interest-rate cap set at a Libor of 8.5 per cent. This will cost 4 per cent of the amount covered. Show the annual payment flows if in the fourth year Libor rises to 10 per cent.
d Describe a 'floor' and show how it can be used to alleviate the cost of a cap. ?

10 Three-month sterling interest-rate futures are quoted as follows on 30 August:

	£500,000 points of 100% Settlement price
Sept.	91.50
Dec.	91.70
Mar.	91.90

Red Wheel plc expects to need to borrow £15m at floating rate in late December for three months and is concerned that interest rates will rise between August and December.

Assume: No transaction costs.

Required

a Show a hedging strategy that Red Wheel could employ to reduce uncertainty.

b What is the effective rate of interest payable by Red Wheel after taking account of the derivative transaction if three-month spot rates are 10 per cent in December? Show the gain on the derivative.

c What is the effective rate of interest after taking account of the derivative transaction if three-month spot rates are 7 per cent in December? Show the loss on the derivative.

d Compare short-term interest-rate futures and FRAs as alternative hedging techniques for a situation such as Red Wheel's. ?

11 'The derivatives markets destroy wealth rather than help create it; they should be made illegal.' Explain your reasons for agreeing or disagreeing with this speaker.

12 Invent examples to demonstrate the different hedging qualities of options, futures and forwards.

13 Speculators, hedgers and arbitrageurs are all desirable participants in the derivatives markets. Explain the role of each.

myfinancelab *Now retake your diagnostic test for Chapter 24 to check your progress and update your study plan.*

Assignments

1 Describe as many uses of options by a firm you know well as you can. These can include exchange-traded options, currency options, other OTC options, corporate uses of options (for example underwriting) and operational and strategic decision options.

2 Investigate the extent of derivatives use by the treasury department of a firm you know well. Explain the purpose of derivatives use and consider alternative instruments to those used in the past.

CHAPTER 25

Managing exchange-rate risk

LEARNING OUTCOMES

By the end of this chapter the reader should be able to:

- explain the role and importance of the foreign exchange markets;
- describe hedging techniques to reduce the risk associated with transactions entered into in another currency;
- consider methods of dealing with the risk that assets, income and liabilities denominated in another currency, when translated into home-currency terms, are distorted;
- describe techniques for reducing the impact of foreign exchange changes on the competitive position of the firm;
- outline the theories designed to explain the reasons for currency changes.

Introduction

This chapter discusses how changes in exchange rates can lead to an increase in uncertainty about income from operations in foreign countries or from trading with foreign firms. Shifts in foreign exchange rates have the potential to undermine the competitive position of the firm and destroy profits. This chapter describes some of the techniques used to reduce the risk associated with business dealings outside the home base.

Case study 25.1

What a difference a few percentage point moves on the exchange rate make

Until autumn 1992 sterling was a member of the European exchange rate mechanism (ERM), which meant the extent it could move in value *vis-à-vis* the other currencies in the ERM was severely limited. Then came 'Black Wednesday' when in order to prop up the value of sterling the UK government increased bank base rates to 15 per cent and instructed the Bank of England to buy billions of pounds to offset the selling pressure in the markets. It was all to no avail. The pound fell out of the ERM, the government gave up the fight, and by the end of the year £1 could only buy you about Deutschmarks 2.35 compared with DM2.90 in the summer (a 19 per cent decline).

George Soros was one of the speculators who recognised economic gravity when he saw it, and bet the equivalent of $10bn against sterling by buying other currencies. After the fall the money held in other currencies could be converted back to make $1bn profit in just a few days. He was dubbed the man who 'broke the Bank of England'. While this was not exactly true, he and others did cause severe embarrassment. When sterling was highly valued against other currencies exporters found life very difficult because, to the foreign buyer, British goods appeared expensive – every DM, franc or guilder bought few pounds. However, in the four years following 'Black Wednesday' UK exporters had a terrific boost and helped pull the economy out of recession as overseas customers bought more goods. Other European companies, on the other hand, complained bitterly. The French government was prompted by its hard-pressed importers to ask for compensation from the European Commission for the 'competitive devaluations by their neighbours'. Then things turned around. Between 1996 and 2001 the pound rose against most currencies. For example, whereas you could buy only DM2.2 at the beginning of 1996 by 2001 you could buy DM3.09 for every pound. Looked at from the German importers' viewpoint UK goods relative to domestic goods rose in price by something of the order of 30–40 per cent.

UK firms lined up to speak of the enormous impact the high pound was having on profits. British Steel (Corus) cut thousands of jobs in response to sterling's rise and started losing money at an alarming rate. It also passed on the pain by telling 700 of its UK suppliers to cut prices. In addition, it suffered because its UK customers which exported ordered less steel.

James Dyson, the vacuum cleaner entrepreneur, announced in 2000 that he was planning to build a factory in East Asia rather than Britain because of the strength of the pound. The Japanese car makers, Toyota, Honda and Nissan, which had established plants in Britain, complained bitterly about the high level of the pound. Their factories were set up to export cars. They were hurt by having to reduce prices and also by their commitment to buy 70 per cent of components from UK suppliers (continental European suppliers benefited from a 30–40 per cent price advantage because of the high pound). Then things turned around again. The euro shot up against the pound and against the dollar. European companies had a very hard time trying to export, particularly into the US market because between 2002 and 2007 the dollar declined against the euro by around 50 per cent making European goods 50 per cent more expensive in the eyes of US consumers. Worse, US exporters could compete against their European rivals more effectively when selling to countries in Asia and elsewhere because of the rise in the euro. Heineken, exporting beer to the USA and elsewhere, to maintain profits should have raised its export prices by 50 per cent between 2002 and 2007 , but found competition meant it could only raise them 2–3 per cent per year. Operating profit from its US unit alone fell by an estimated two-thirds. Similar difficulties were experienced by a whole range of European exporters, from German car makers to Scotch whisky distillers.

The message from the ups and downs of sterling and other currencies over the last fifteen years is that foreign exchange shifts and the management of the associated risk are not issues to be separated and put into a box marked 'for the attention of the finance specialists only'. The profound implications for jobs, competitiveness, national economic growth and firms' survival mean that all managers need to be aware of the consequences of foreign exchange rate movements and of how to prepare the firm to cope with them.

The effects of exchange-rate changes

Shifts in the value of foreign exchange, from now on to be referred to as simply '**forex**' (FOReign EXchange),[1] can impact on various aspects of a firm's activities:

- ***Income to be received from abroad*** For example, if a UK firm has exported goods to Canada on six months' credit terms, payable in Canadian dollars (C$), it is uncertain as to the number of pounds it will actually receive because the dollar could move against the pound in the intervening period.
- ***The amount actually paid for imports at some future date*** For example, a Japanese firm importing wood from the USA may have a liability to pay dollars a few months later. The quantity of yen (¥) it will have to use to exchange for the dollars at that point in the future is uncertain at the time the deal is struck.
- ***The valuation of foreign assets and liabilities*** In today's globalised marketplace many firms own assets abroad and incur liabilities in foreign currencies. The value of these in home-currency terms can change simply because of forex movements.
- ***The long-term viability of foreign operations*** The long-term future returns of subsidiaries located in some countries can be enhanced by a favourable forex change. On the other hand firms can be destroyed if they are operating in the wrong currency at the wrong time.
- ***The acceptability, or otherwise, of an overseas investment project*** When evaluating the value-creating potential of major new investments a firm must be aware that the likely future currency changes can have a significant effect on estimated NPV.

In summary, fluctuating exchange rates create risk, and badly managed risk can lead to a loss of shareholder wealth.

Volatility in foreign exchange

Exhibits 25.1 to 25.3 show the extent to which forex rates can move even over a period as short as a few weeks – 5 or 10 per cent point shifts are fairly common.

In the mid-1970s a regime of (generally) floating exchange rates replaced the fixed exchange-rate system which had been in place since the 1940s. Today most currencies fluctuate against each other, at least to some extent.

If a UK firm holds dollars or assets denominated in dollars and the value of the dollar rises against the pound a forex profit is made. Conversely, should the pound rise relative to the dollar, a forex loss will be incurred. These potential gains or losses can be very large. For example, between November 2005 and November 2007 the dollar depreciated by 20 per cent against the pound so you could have made a large gain by exchanging dollars and then holding sterling even before the money was put to use, say, earning interest. In other periods fluctuating forex rates may wipe out profits from a project, an export deal or a portfolio investment (for example a pension fund buying foreign shares).

[1] It is also shortened to FX.

Exhibit 25.1 Exchange-rate movements, US$ to £, November 1982 to November 2007 (monthly)

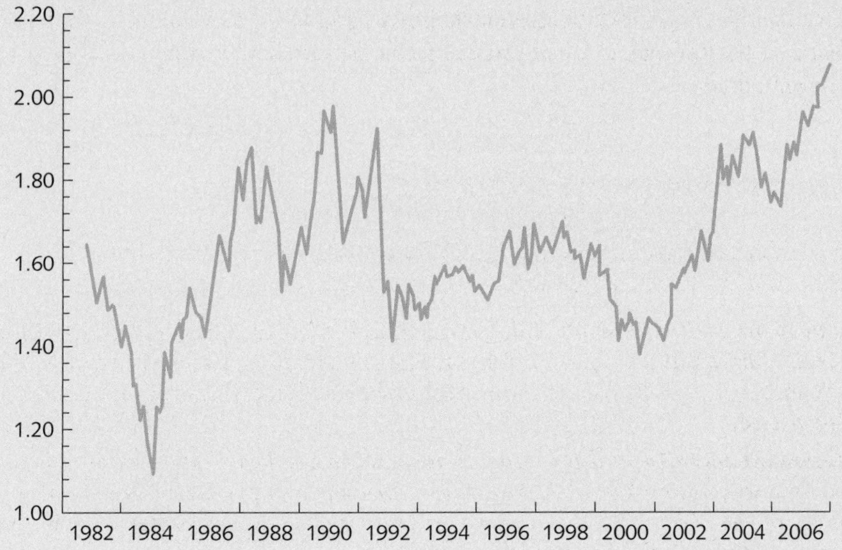

Source: DATASTREAM. Reproduced with permission of Thomson Financial Datastream.

Exhibit 25.2 Exchange rate movements £ to euro, January 1999 to November 2007 (weekly)

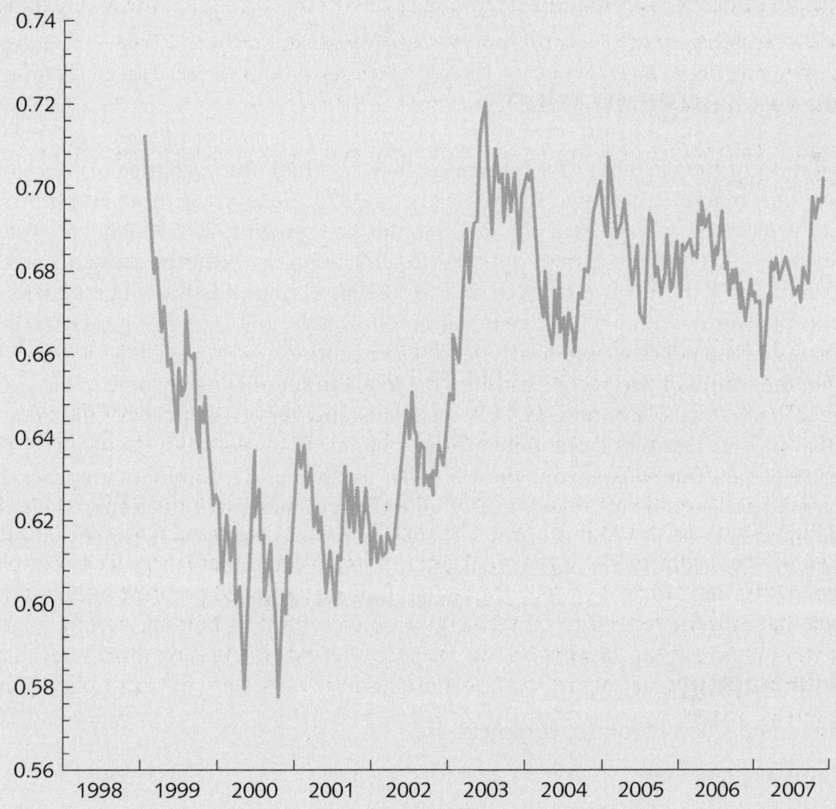

Source: DATASTREAM. Reproduced with permission of Thomson Financial Datastream.

Exhibit 25.3 Exchange rate movements US$ to euro, January 1999 to November 2007 (weekly)

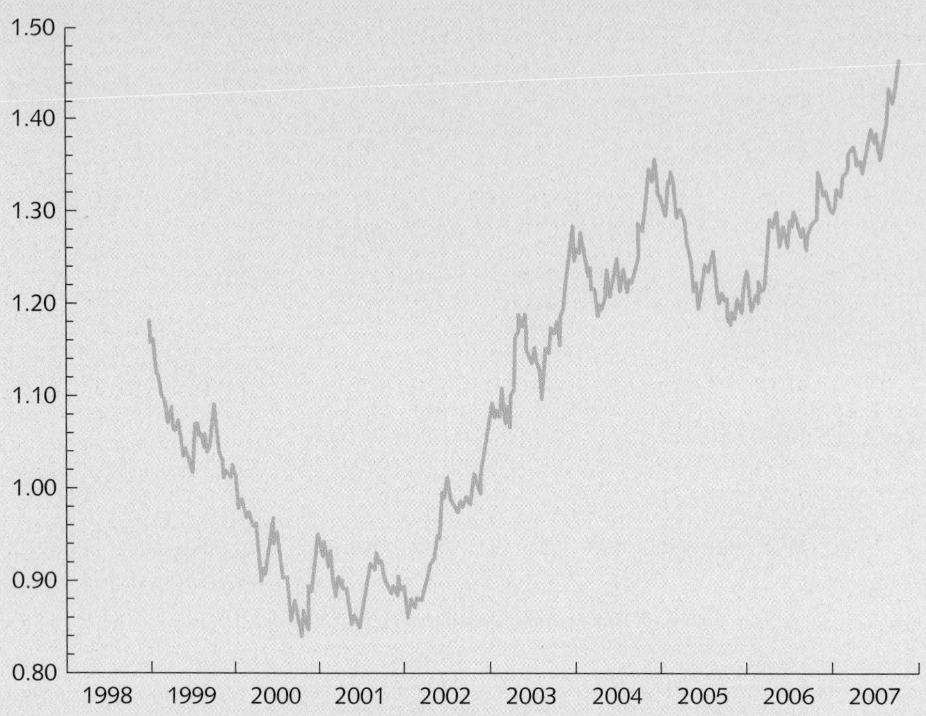

Source: DATASTREAM. Reproduced with permission of Thomson Financial Datastream.

The foreign exchange markets

The function of the currency (forex) market is to facilitate the exchange of one currency into another. This market has grown dramatically. In 1973 the equivalent of US$10bn was traded around the globe on average each day. By 1986 this had grown to US$300bn, and just three years later, by 1989, this had more than doubled to US$590bn. In 1998 the daily turnover was over US$1,490bn. In 2007 it was estimated at US$3,210bn. London is the biggest currency trading centre in the world, with a 34 per cent share, followed by the USA (17 per cent), Japan (6 per cent), Singapore (6 per cent) and Switzerland (6 per cent).

To put the figures in perspective consider the total output of all the people in the UK in one day (GDP): this amounts to around US$7bn – less than a quarter of 1 per cent of the value of the currency that changes hands in London in one day.

The euro is starting to challenge the US dollar as the world's dominant currency. In 2007 the euro entered on one side of 37 per cent of all foreign exchange transactions, whereas the dollar was on one side in 86 per cent of cases. (The yen was on one side of 16.5 per cent of trades and sterling was involved in 15 per cent of trades.)

Exhibit 25.4 explains why London dominates the forex market.

Who is trading?

The buyers and sellers of foreign currencies are:

- exporters/importers;
- tourists;

Exhibit 25.4

London's dominance of global forex grows

FT

By Peter Garnham

London's dominance of the global foreign exchange market has grown sharply while New York's share has slipped, a survey revealed yesterday.

The UK's share of foreign exchange trading volumes jumped from 31.3 per cent in 2004 to 34.1 per cent in April 2007, the latest triennial survey from the Bank for International Settlements shows.

This was more than double that of the US, its nearest rival, which saw its share of the market fall from 19.2 per cent to 16.6 per cent. London's rise in the world's largest financial market will be a fresh blow to New York, which has seen its position as a financial centre come under competitive pressure.

Analysts said London's preeminent global position allowed currency investors to benefit from economies of scale. 'The biggest investors like to trade where there is liquidity,' said David Woo at Barclay's Capital. 'Once you obtain critical mass, it has a tendency to feed off itself.'

The city has benefited as the preferred trading centre for Asian central banks, which have built up huge foreign exchange reserves in recent years. Analysts said London's time zone made it a much more convenient place for them to trade.

'London has always been seen as more international than the US; it's clear that it is staying ahead of the market,' said Rob Close, chief executive of CLS Bank, which settles more than half of global currency trades.

The survey showed that global average daily volumes on the foreign exchange markets rose 71 per cent from $1,880bn in April 2004 to $3,210bn in April 2007.

The BIS said that the jump had been fuelled by growing hedge fund activity, particularly by funds using quantitative trading models, and increased interest from retail investors. The increasing use of foreign exchange as an asset class by institutions, such as pension funds, had boosted volumes.

Source: *Financial Times*, 26 September 2007, p. 1. Reprinted with permission.

- fund managers (pensions, insurance companies, etc.);
- governments (for example, to pay for activities abroad);
- central banks (smoothing out fluctuations);
- speculators;
- banks.

The first five groups account for only a small fraction of the transactions. The big players are the large commercial banks and speculators, such as hedge funds. In addition to dealing on behalf of customers, or acting as market makers, the banks carry out **'proprietary' transactions** of their own in an attempt to make a profit by taking a position in the market – that is, speculating on future movements. Companies and individuals usually obtain their foreign currencies from the banks.

Foreign exchange interbank brokers often act as intermediaries between large buyers and sellers. They allow banks to trade anonymously, thus avoiding having the price move simply because of the revelation of the name of a bank in a transaction.

Roughly one half of deals are still made over the telephone and later confirmed in writing. The new electronic trading systems in which computers match deals automatically have taken a rapidly increasing share of deals. The market has changed significantly from 10 years ago. Then banks would deal for clients and for themselves over the telephone. Today the larger clients increasingly deal alongside banks on a number of electronic platforms. The new platforms also allow smaller banks to access the best prices and provide them with the opportunity to deal alongside the large banks on an even basis because of the transparency of the systems. Rapid price dissemination has, to a great extent, 'levelled the playing field', whereas in the old days only the large banks could 'see' the market prices through their telephone contacts – *see* **Exhibit 25.5**.

Exhibit 25.5

The mouse takes over the floor

FT

Jennifer Hughes charts the decline of the human factor and the rise of the click

Reuters' first screen-based trading system was launched in 1982 for the interbank market, where the majority of foreign exchange dealing takes place. The company launched a conversational dealing product in 1989 and an anonymous 'matching' platform in 1992, but faced its first stiff competition only in 1993 with the launch of Electronic Broking Services (EBS), a platform owned by a number of the big banks and designed with the express purpose of preventing Reuters gaining a monopoly position. Now, both platforms still dominate the interbank market but face competition from the internet, where a number of web-based portals are encouraging new participants to trade directly.

In simple volume terms the online platforms look like minnows. EBS reports average daily volumes worth about $100bn whereas the larger internet platforms have average volumes between $15bn and $20bn. But Justyn Trenner of ClientKnowledge calculates the combined value of all online trading is now worth $100bn a day and highlights the rapid growth in the sector.

Platforms such as FXA11, Hotspot FXi and e-Speed are quick to dismiss suggestions of direct competition with the giants. Instead, they say they offer different parties, such as corporate treasurers or fund managers, the opportunity to participate directly and trade outside their usual banking relationships.

If electronic technology in the interbank market helped smaller banks access price transparency in the interbank market, the latest generation of internet platforms is doing the same for those banks' clients.

'We're not going for the interbank market; we live in the space where banks face out to clients,' says John Eley, chief executive of Hotspot foreign exchange, who says bank clients, who would previously call three or four dealers for quotes, can get the same range in seconds off a web-based platform, and then deal themselves.

'Multibank portals lower the barriers for third-party foreign exchange trades by cutting costs and reducing risk,' adds Mark Warms, chief marketing officer at FXA11, who says the volumes traded by hedge funds have tripled on the platform.

Rick Sears, head of foreign exchange at the Chicago Mercantile Exchange, says volumes in its foreign exchange products had risen sharply since its electronic Globex platform allowed investors to trade its futures contracts 24 hours a day . . .

Source: Financial Times, 27 May 2004, p. 2. Reprinted with permission.

Twenty-four hour trading

Dealing takes place on a 24-hour basis, with trading concentration moving from one major financial centre to another. Most trading occurs when both the European and New York markets are open – this is when it is afternoon in Frankfurt, Zurich and London and morning on the east coast of the Americas. Later the bulk of the trade passes to San Francisco and Los Angeles, followed by Sydney, Tokyo, Hong Kong and Singapore. There are at least 40 other trading centres around the world in addition to these main ones.

Most banks are in the process of concentrating their dealers in three or four regional hubs. These typically include London as well as New York and two sites in Asia, where Tokyo, Hong Kong and Singapore are keen to establish their dominance.

The vast sums of money traded every working day across the world means that banks are exposed to the risk that they may irrevocably pay over currency to a counterparty before they receive another currency in return because settlement systems are operating in different time zones. A bank could fail after receiving one leg of its foreign exchange trades but before paying the other leg – this is called **Herstatt risk** after a German bank that failed in 1974 leaving the dollars that it owed on its foreign exchange deals unpaid. Its failure caused panic and gridlock in the forex market, which took weeks to unravel. A new organisation, the **CLS Bank**, allows both legs of the trade to be paid simultaneously, eliminating the risk that one bank might fail in midstream. Under CLS (Continuous Linked Settlement) payments are made by banks to an orderly schedule in a five-hour slot the day after the deal. A second major advantage of this system is that the net values of the trades are settled rather than the gross amount of trades. So if a bank sold $1 billion, but also bought $900 million the settlement is for only $100 million.

Exchange rates

We now look more closely at exchange rates. We start with some terms used in forex markets. First, we provide a definition of an **exchange rate**:

An exchange rate is the price of one currency expressed in terms of another.

Therefore if the exchange rate between the US dollar and the pound is US$2.05 = £1.00 this means that £1.00 will cost US$2.05. Taking the reciprocal, US$1.00 will cost 48.78 pence. The standardised forms of expression are:

US$/£ : 2.05
or
US$2.05/£

Exchange rates are expressed in terms of the number of units of the first currency per single unit of the second currency. Also forex rates are normally given to five or six significant figures. So for the US$/£ exchange rate on 15 November 2007 the more accurate rate is:

US$2.0455/£

However, this is still not accurate enough because currency exchange rates are not generally expressed in terms of a single 'middle rate' as above, but are given as a rate at which you can buy the first currency (bid rate) and a rate at which you can sell the first currency (offer rate). In the case of the US$/£ exchange rate the market rates on 15 November 2007 were:

US$2.0455/£ 'middle rate'

	bid rate	*offer rate*
	↓	↓
US$/£	2.0454	2.0456
	↑	↑
	You can buy dollars from a bank or broker at this rate.	You can sell dollars to a bank or a broker at this rate.

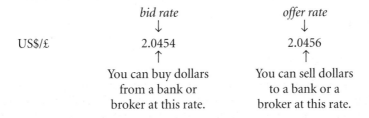

So if you wished to purchase US$1m the cost would be:

$$\frac{\$1,000,000}{2.0454} = £488,902$$

However, if you wished to sell US$1m you would receive:

$$\frac{\$1,000,000}{2.0456} = £488,854$$

The foreign exchange dealers make profit in two ways. First, they *may* charge commission on a deal. Depending on the size of the transaction this can vary, but it is generally well below 1 per cent. Secondly, these institutions are dealing with numerous buyers and sellers every day and they make a profit on the difference between the bid price and offer price (the bid/offer spread). In the above example if a dealer sold US$1m and bought US$1m with a bid/offer spread of 0.02 of a cent a profit of £488,902 – £488,854 = £48 is made.

Worked example 25.1 **Forex**

The basic elements of forex are so important for the rest of the chapter that it is worthwhile to pause and consolidate understanding of the quoted rates through some exercises.

Answer the following questions on the basis that the euro/US$ exchange rate is 1.1168–1.1173, that is, €1.1168/US$ or €1.1173/US$ depending on whether you are buying or selling euros.

1 What is the cost of buying €200,000?
2 How much would it cost to purchase US$4m?
3 How many dollars would be received from selling €800,000?
4 How many euros would be received from selling US$240,000?

Answers

1 $\frac{200,000}{1.1168}$ = US$179,083

2 4,000,000 × 1.1173 = €4,469,200

3 $\frac{800,000}{1.1173}$ = US$716,012

4 240,000 × 1.1168 = €268,032

The spot and forward exchange markets

There are two main forex markets.

1 ***The 'spot' market*** In the **spot market** transactions take place which are to be settled quickly. Officially this is described as immediate delivery, but this usually takes place two business days after the deal is struck. However, this is reduced to the next morning (central European time) for trades going through CLS.

2 ***The 'forward' market*** In the **forward market** a deal is arranged to exchange currencies at some future date at a price agreed now. The periods of time are generally one, three or six months, but it is possible to arrange an exchange of currencies at a predetermined rate many years from now.

Forward transactions represent about one-third to one-half of all forex deals. There are many currencies, however, for which forward quotes are difficult to obtain. The so-called **exotic currencies** generally do not have forward rates quoted by dealers. These are currencies for which there is little trading demand to support international business, etc. On the other hand, spot markets exist for most of the world's currencies.

The *Financial Times* reports the previous day's trading in the forex market. The figures shown in **Exhibit 25.6** relate to dealing on 15 November 2007. Of course by the time a newspaper reader receives the information in this table the rates have changed as the 24-hour markets follow the sun around the world. However, FT.com and other websites provide much more up-to-the-minute and detailed information.

The prices shown under the pound columns in Exhibit 25.6 are the middle price of the foreign currency in terms of £1 in London the previous afternoon.[2] So, for instance, the mid-price of £1 for immediate delivery is 2.2948 Australian dollars. For the US dollar columns the prices for the pound and euro are the number of dollars per currency unit, either per pound or per euro. However, for other currencies the rate shown is the number of units of the other currency per US$1 – for example, 0.9782 Canadian dollars per US dollar. For the euro columns the rate shown is the number of units of the other currency per euro – for example the spot mid-rate against the pound is 71.52 pence per euro.

[2] The *Financial Times* takes a representative sample of rates from major dealers in London at 4 p.m.

Exhibit 25.6

Currency rates

www.ft.com/currencydata

FT

Nov 15	Currency	DOLLAR Closing mid	DOLLAR Day's change	EURO Closing mid	EURO Day's change	POUND Closing mid	POUND Day's change
Argentina	(Peso)	3.1275	–0.0040	4.5748	–0.0256	6.3972	–0.0708
Australia	(A$)	1.1219	+0.0117	1.6411	+0.0101	2.2948	+0.0018
Bahrain	(Dinar)	0.3759	–	0.5498	–0.0025	0.7688	–0.0076
Bolivia	(Boliviano)	7.6400	–	11.1755	–0.0481	15.6273	–0.1528
Brazil	(R$)	1.7463	+0.0100	2.5544	+0.0037	3.5720	–0.0141
Canada	(C$)	0.9782	+0.0219	1.4309	+0.0260	2.0009	+0.0258
Chile	(Peso)	506.940	+2.0400	741.527	–0.1968	1036.92	–5.9253
China	(Yuan)	7.4228	–0.0025	10.8577	–0.0504	15.1830	–0.1536
Colombia	(Peso)	2042.80	+11.8500	2988.11	+4.5386	4178.45	–16.380
Costa Rica	(Colon)	518.910	–	759.036	–3.2692	1061.41	–10.378
Czech Rep.	(Koruna)	18.1566	+0.0206	26.5585	–0.0840	37.1384	–0.3204
Denmark	(DKr)	5.0952	+0.0226	7.4530	+0.0011	10.4219	–0.0552
Egypt	(Egypt £)	5.5245	+0.0030	8.0810	_0.0304	11.3001	–0.1043
Estonia	(Kroon)	10.6967	+0.0459	15.6465	–	21.8794	–0.1192
Hong Kong	(HK$)	7.7857	–0.0034	11.3885	–0.0541	15.9252	–0.1629
Hungary	(Forint)	173.519	+0.7408	253.815	–0.0050	354.925	–1.9405
India	(Rs)	39.3050	–0.0150	57.4934	–0.2696	80.3965	–0.8170
Indonesia	(Rupiah)	9312.00	+92.0000	13621.10	+76.4870	19047.20	+3.7814
Iran	(Rial)	9329.00	–1.0000	13646.00	–60.242	19082.00	–188.65
Israel	(Shk)	3.9405	+0.0155	5.7640	–0.0020	8.0601	–0.0468
Japan	(Y)	110.905	–0.4800	162.226	–1.4038	226.851	–3.2096
One Month		110.515	+0.0012	161.739	+0.0012	225.849	+0.0291
Three Month		109.740	–0.0020	160.703	+0.0114	223.791	+0.0568
One Year		107.093	+0.0290	156.700	+0.0132	216.349	+0.1419
Kenya	(Shilling)	66.3000	–0.2500	96.9804	–0.7849	135.613	–1.8424
Kuwait	(Dinar)	0.2762	–	0.4040	–0.0017	0.5650	–0.0056
Malaysia	(M$)	3.3715	+0.0265	4.9317	+0.0178	6.8962	–0.0127
Mexico	(New Peso)	10.9109	+0.0412	15.9599	–0.0082	22.3177	–0.1330
New Zealand	(NZ$)	1.3195	+0.0119	1.9302	+0.0092	2.6990	–0.0018
Nigeria	(Naira)	119.325	+0.0750	174.543	±0.6416	244.073	–2.2316
Norway	(NKr)	5.4654	+0.0736	7.9945	+0.0737	11.1791	+0.0427
Pakistan	(Rupee)	61.2000	+0.0600	89.5203	±0.2974	125.182	–1.1001
Peru	(New Sol)	2.9948	–0.0028	4.3806	–0.0230	6.1256	–0.0657
Philippines	(Peso)	43.2000	+0.02850	63.1908	+0.1465	88.3635	–0.2754

Nov 15	Currency	DOLLAR Closing mid	DOLLAR Day's change	EURO Closing mid	EURO Day's change	POUND Closing mid	POUND Day's change
Poland	(Zloty)	2.4995	+0.0176	3.6561	+0.0100	5.1126	–0.0137
Romania	(New Leu)	2.3643	+0.0178	3.4583	+0.0111	4.8360	–0.0106
Russia	(Rouble)	24.5135	+0.0605	35.8572	–0.0655	50.1412	–0.3653
Saudi Arabia	(SR)	3.7325	–0.0085	5.4597	–0.0360	7.6347	–0.0922
Singapore	(S$)	1.4515	+0.0052	2.1232	–0.0015	2.9690	–0.0182
Slovakia	(Koruna)	22.5910	+0.1187	33.0450	+0.0320	46.2088	–0.2068
South Africa	(R)	6.6853	+0.0685	9.7789	+0.0586	13.6744	+0.0077
South Korea	(Won)	915.550	+1.9500	1339.22	–2.9034	1872.71	–14.283
Sweden	(SKr)	6.3229	+0.0459	9.2488	+0.0276	12.9331	–0.0317
Switzerland	(SFr)	1.1244	+0.0034	1.6446	–0.0020	2.2997	–0.0155
Taiwan	(T$)	32.2900	+0.0060	47.2322	–0.1947	66.0476	–0.6334
Thailand	(Bt)	33.8550	–0.0050	49.5214	–0.2206	69.2487	–0.6874
Tunisia	(Dinar)	1.2237	+0.0033	1.7900	–0.0028	2.5030	–0.0176
Turkey	(Lira)	1.1788	+0.0069	1.7243	+0.0028	2.4111	–0.0093
U A E	(Dirham)	3.6710	–0.0004	5.3698	–0.0236	7.5089	–0.0742
UK (0.4889)*	(£)	2.0455	–0.0200	0.7152	+0.0039	–	–
One Month		2.0436	+0.0001	0.7162	–	–	–
Three Month		2.0393	+0.0003	0.7181	–0.0001	–	–
One Year		2.0202	–0.0001	0.7243	–0.0001	–	–
Uruguay	(Peso)	21.9750	–	32.1440	–0.1385	44.9488	–0.4395
USA	($)	–	–	1.4628	–0.0063	2.0455	–0.0200
One Month		–	–	1.4635	–	2.0436	+0.0001
Three Month		–	–	1.4644	+0.0001	2.0393	+0.0003
One Year		–	–	1.4632	–0.0005	2.0202	–0.0001
Venezuela †	(Bolivar)	2147.30	–	3140.96	–13.528	4392.20	–42.946
Vietnam	(Dong)	16062.00	–2.5000	23494.70	–104.86	32854.00	–326.40
Euro (0.6836)*	(Euro)	1.4628	–0.0063	–	–	1.3984	–0.0076
One Month		1.4635	–	–	–	1.3964	+0.0002
Three Month		1.4644	+0.0001	–	–	1.3926	+0.0002
One year		1.4632	–0.0005	–	–	1.3807	+0.0004
SDR	–	0.6320	+0.0014	0.9245	–0.0018	1.2927	–0.0095

Rates are derived fromWM/Reuters at 4pm (London time). *The closing mid-point rates for the Euro and £ against the $ are shown in brackets. The other figures in the dollar column of both the Euro and Sterling rows are in the reciprocal form in line with market convention.
†Official rate set by Venezuelan government is 2150 mid per USD; the WM/Reuters rate is for the valuation of capital assets. Some values are rounded by the F.T. The exchange rates printed in this table are also available on the internet at **http://www.FT.com/marketsdata**
Source: Financial Times, 16 November 2007. Reprinted ith permission.

The first forward price (middle price) is given as the 'One month' rate. So you could commit yourself to the sale of a quantity of dollars for delivery in one month at a rate that is fixed at about US$2.0436 per pound. In this case you will need fewer US dollars to buy £1 in one month's time compared with the spot rate of exchange, therefore the dollar is at a ***premium*** on the one-month forward rate.

The forward rate for one month shows a different relationship with the spot rate for the euro against the US dollar. Here more dollars are required ($1.4635) to purchase a euro in one month's time compared with an 'immediate' spot purchase ($1.4628), therefore the dollar on one-month forward delivery is at a ***discount*** to the euro.

The *Financial Times* table lists quotations up to one year, but, as this is an over-the-counter market (*see* Chapter 24), you are able to go as far forward in time as you wish – provided you can find a counterparty. For many currencies trading in three-month and one-year forwards is so thin as to not warrant a quotation in the table. However for the major currencies such as the US dollar, sterling, the euro, and the Japanese yen, forward markets can stretch up to ten years. Airline companies expecting to purchase planes many years hence may use this distant forward market to purchase the foreign currency they need to pay the manufacturer so that they know with certainty the quantity of their home currency they are required to find when the planes are delivered.

The table in Exhibit 25.6 displays standard periods of time for forward rates. These are instantly available and are frequently traded. However, forward rates are not confined to these particular days in the future. It is possible to obtain rates for any day in the future, say, 74 or 36 days hence. But this would require a specific quotation from a bank.

(The Special Drawing Rights (SDRs) of the International Monetary Fund (IMF) shown at the bottom of the table are artificial currencies made up from baskets of other currencies.)

Covering in the forward market

Suppose that on 15 November 2007 a UK exporter sells goods to a customer in France invoiced at €5,000,000. Payment is due three months later. With the spot rate of exchange at €1.3984/£ (*see* Exhibit 25.6) the exporter, in deciding to sell the goods, has in mind a sales price of:

$$\frac{5{,}000{,}000}{1.3984} = £3{,}575{,}515$$

The UK firm bases its decision on the profitability of the deal on this amount expressed in pounds.

However, the rate of exchange may vary between November and February: the size and direction of the move is uncertain. If sterling strengthens against the euro, the UK exporter makes a currency loss by waiting three months and exchanging the euro received into sterling at spot rates in February. If, say, one pound is worth €1.6 the exporter will receive only £3,125,000:

$$\frac{5{,}000{,}000}{1.6} = £3{,}125{,}000$$

The loss due to currency movement is:

$$\begin{array}{r} £3{,}575{,}515 \\ -\ £3{,}125{,}000 \\ \hline £450{,}515 \\ \hline \end{array}$$

If sterling weakens to, say, €1.3/£ a currency gain is made. The pounds received in February if euro are exchanged at the spot rate are:

$$\frac{5{,}000{,}000}{1.3} = £3{,}846{,}154$$

The currency gain is:

$$\begin{array}{r} £3,846,154 \\ -\ £3,575,515 \\ \hline £270,639 \\ \hline \end{array}$$

Rather than run the risk of a possible loss on the currency side of the deal the exporter may decide to cover in the forward market. Under this arrangement the exporter promises to sell €5,000,000 against sterling in three months (the agreement is made on 15 November for delivery of currency in February). The forward rate available[3] on 15 November is €1.3926/£ (*see* Exhibit 25.6). This forward contract means that the exporter will receive £3,590,406 in February regardless of the way in which spot exchange rates move over the three months.

$$\frac{5,000,000}{1.3926} = £3,590,406$$

In February the transactions shown in **Exhibit 25.7** take place.

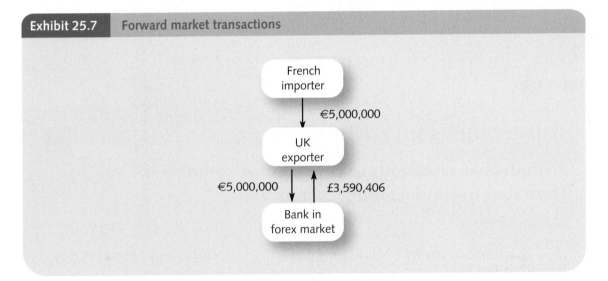

Exhibit 25.7 Forward market transactions

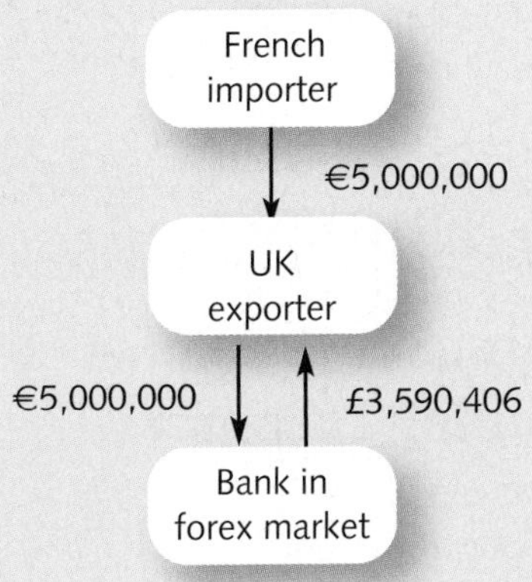

From the outset (in November) the exporter knew the amount to be received in February (assuming away credit risk). It might, with hindsight, have been better not to use the forward market but to exchange the euro at a spot rate of, say, €1.3/£. This would have resulted in a larger income for the firm. But there was uncertainty about the spot rate in February when the export took place in November. If the spot rate in February had turned out to be €1.6/£ the exporter would have made much less. Covering in the forward market is a form of insurance which leads to greater certainty – and certainty has a value.

Types of foreign-exchange risk

There are three types of risk for firms which operate in an international marketplace:

- transaction risk;
- translation risk;
- economic risk.

[3] If we ignore the market makers' bid/offer spread and transaction costs.

Transaction risk

Transaction risk is the risk that transactions already entered into, or for which the firm is likely to have a commitment in a foreign currency, will have a variable value in the home currency because of exchange-rate movements.

This type of risk is primarily associated with imports or exports. If a company exports goods on credit then it carries a figure for debtors in its accounts. The amount it will receive in home-currency terms is subject to uncertainty if the customer pays in a foreign currency.

Likewise a company that imports on credit will have a creditor figure in its accounts. The amount that is finally paid in terms of the home currency depends on forex movements, if the invoice is in a foreign currency. Transaction risk also arises when firms invest abroad, say, opening a new office or manufacturing plant. If the costs of construction are paid for over a period the firm may be exchanging the home currency for the foreign currency to make the payments. The amounts of the home currency required are uncertain if the exchange rate is subject to rate shifts. Also the cash inflows back to the parent are subject to exchange-rate risk.

In addition, when companies borrow in a foreign currency, committing themselves to regular interest and principal payments in that currency, they are exposed to forex risk. This is a problem that beset a number of Brazilian companies in 2002. They had committed themselves to paying off borrowings in a hard currency (e.g. US dollars, sterling). This became a serious problem when the debt rose by 40 per cent simply because of the decline in their currency against the hard currency – *see* **Exhibit 25.8**.

Exhibit 25.8

Balance sheets left reeling by Real

FT

Hedging has saved only a few Brazilian companies from the effects of a falling currency

writes Jonathan Wheatley

It has been a bizarre year for Brazilian companies. Whether or not they supported the campaign of president-elect Luiz Inácio Lula da Silva – and many of them did – senior executives have felt the impact of his election even though he does not take office until January 1.

Concern among investors that a left-wing government under Lula – as he is universally known – might presage a default on Brazil's debts has caused the currency to shed more than 40 per cent of its value to the end of September, wreaking havoc on companies' balance sheets . . .

For most big companies, many of which borrow in dollars but make their income in Reals, the devaluation has been little short of calamitous . . .

'They are extremely vulnerable,' he says. 'Even if only a small part of a

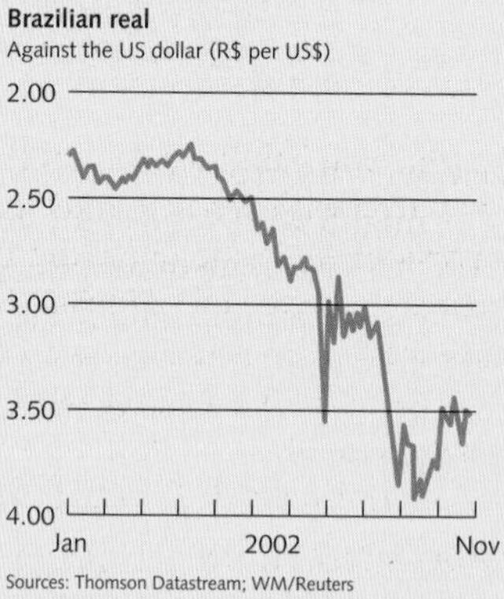

company's debt is unhedged, a devaluation on this scale causes an enormous disaster.'

Many Brazilian companies began hedging their dollar debts when the Real began to slide during the second quarter, as opinion polls showed Lula leading the presidential campaign. But few imagined that the Real would fall so far.

As the situation worsened and international banks began reducing their exposure to Brazil, the cost of hedging became increasingly prohibitive. Many concluded – incorrectly, as it turned out – that hedging was not worth the expense . . .

Usiminas, one of Brazil's biggest steel producers, saw the value of its sales rise by 37 per cent in the third quarter over last year, to R$1.68bn. Nevertheless, it recorded a net loss of R$684m, because both the operating company and, especially, Cosipa, a subsidiary, were not fully hedged.

'Cosipa is one of the most leveraged companies in the industry. Hedging just became too expensive,' says Katia Brullo of Corretora Unibanco, a São Paulo brokerage . . .

Source: Financial Times, 26 November 2002, p. 30. Reprinted with permission.

Translation risk

Translation risk arises because financial data denominated in one currency are then expressed in terms of another currency. Between two accounting dates the figures can be affected by exchange-rate movements, greatly distorting comparability. The financial statements of overseas business units are usually translated into the home currency in order that they might be consolidated with the group's financial statements. Income, expenses, assets and liabilities have to be re-expressed in terms of the home currency. Note that this is purely a paper-based exercise; it is translation and not the conversion of real money from one currency to another. If exchange rates were stable, comparing subsidiary performance and asset position would be straightforward. However, if exchange rates move significantly the results can be severely distorted. For example, GlaxoSmithKline, the UK-based pharmaceutical company found that even though overseas earnings rose in local currency terms, when the figures were translated into sterling a fall in profits was reported. This was mainly because sterling rose against the dollar. *See* **Exhibit 25.9**

Exhibit 25.9

Exchange rate woes hit GSK

FT

by Andrew Jack

The strengthening pound pegged back first-quarter earnings per share at GlaxoSmithKline, the UK-based pharmaceutical group to 27p – a modest 2 per cent. Pre-tax profit in cash terms fell 1 per cent to £2.1bn for the quarter.

At constant exchange rates, earnings per share rose 14 per cent and the company said its guidance for the year on the same terms remained unchanged at 8–10 per cent.

The weakening dollar reduced sales in cash terms to £5.6bn (£5.8bn), though adjusted pharmaceutical sales in the key US market rose 3 per cent to £2.4bn and 3 per cent to £4.8bn worldwide, in spite of challenges from generic drugs.

Jean-Pierre Garnier, chief executive, dismissed the short-term headline exchange rate effect, arguing that the market had seen through the figures to the underlying performance.

'There is nothing we can do about [the weakening dollar]. What comes up must come down,' he said. 'It's a hit like the weather: you have to live with it.'

Source: Financial Times, 26 April 2007, p. 22. Reprinted with permission.

There are two elements to translation risk.

1 ***The balance sheet effect*** Assets and liabilities denominated in a foreign currency can fluctuate in value in home-currency terms with forex-market changes. For example, if a UK company acquires A\$1,000,000 of assets in Australia when the rate of exchange is A\$2.2/£ this can go into the UK group's accounts at a value of £454,545. If, over the course of the next year, the Australian dollar falls against sterling to A\$2.7/£, when the consolidated accounts are drawn up and the asset is translated at the current exchange rate at the end of the year it is valued at only £370,370 (1,000,000/2.7), a 'loss' of £84,175. And yet the asset has not changed in value in A\$ terms one jot. These 'losses' are normally dealt with through balance sheet reserves.

2 ***The profit and loss account effect*** Currency changes can have an adverse impact on the group's profits because of the translation of foreign subsidiaries' profits. This often occurs even though the subsidiaries' managers are performing well and increasing profit in terms of the currency in which they operate, as the case of GSK (*see* Exhibit 25.9) indicates.

Economic risk

A company's economic value may decline as a result of forex movements causing a loss in competitive strength. The worth of a company is the discounted cash flows payable to the owners. It is possible that a shift in exchange rates can reduce the cash flows of foreign subsidiaries and home-based production far into the future (and not just affect the near future cash flows as in transaction exposure). There are two ways in which competitive position can be undermined by forex changes:

- ***Directly*** If your firm's home currency strengthens then foreign competitors are able to gain sales and profits at your expense because your products are more expensive (or you have reduced margins) in the eyes of customers both abroad and at home.
- ***Indirectly*** Even if your home currency does not move adversely *vis-à-vis* your customer's currency you can lose competitive position. For example suppose a South African firm is selling into Hong Kong and its main competitor is a New Zealand firm. If the New Zealand dollar weakens against the Hong Kong dollar the South African firm has lost some competitive position.

  Another indirect effect occurs even for firms which are entirely domestically oriented. For example, the cafés and shops surrounding a large export-oriented manufacturing plant may be severely affected by the closure of the factory due to an adverse forex movement.

Economic risk can badly damage a business – see **Exhibit 25.10**.

Exhibit 25.10

Small fry flounder in the wake of surge

FT

Raphael Minder

Hank Morrison, whose Philippine company makes model aircraft, says he could be out of business within six months if the Filipino peso continues to rally against the US dollar.

'With the way the peso is going, it's become almost impossible,' he says. 'I'm not only operating at a loss but in effect the more I make the more I lose.'

As an emergency step, Mr Morrison has decided to halve his production of model aircraft, 95 per cent of which end up in America on the shelves of collectors or industry buyers such as Boeing. That is bad news both for Mr Morrison's 60 Filipino employees and for Philippine exports.

Source: Financial Times, 10 October 2007, p. 15. Reprinted with permission.

Transaction risk strategies

This section illustrates a number of strategies available to deal with transaction risk by focusing on the alternatives open to an exporter selling goods on credit.

Suppose a UK company exports £1m of goods to a Canadian firm when the spot rate of exchange is C$2.20/£. The Canadian firm is given three months to pay, and naturally the spot rate in three months is unknown at the time of the shipment of goods. What can the firm do?

Invoice the customer in the home currency

One easy way to bypass exchange-rate risk is to insist that all foreign customers pay in your currency and your firm pays for all imports in your home currency. In the case of this example the Canadian importer will be required to send £1m in three months.

However, the exchange-rate risk has not gone away, it has just been passed on to the customer. This policy has an obvious drawback: your customer may dislike it, the marketability of your products is reduced and your customers look elsewhere for supplies. If you are a monopoly supplier you might get away with the policy but for most firms this is a non-starter.

Do nothing

Under this policy the UK firm invoices the Canadian firm for C$2.2m, waits three months and then exchanges into sterling at whatever spot rate is available then. Perhaps an exchange-rate gain will be made, perhaps a loss will be made. Many firms adopt this policy and take a 'win some, lose some' attitude. Given the fees and other transaction costs of some hedging strategies this can make sense.

There are two considerations for managers here. The first is their degree of risk aversion to higher cash flow variability, coupled with the sensitivity of shareholders to reported fluctuations of earnings due to foreign exchange gains and losses. The second, which is related to the first point, is the size of the transaction. If £1m is a large proportion of annual turnover, and greater than profit, then the managers may be more worried about forex risk. If, however, £1m is a small fraction of turnover and profit, and the firm has numerous forex transactions, it may choose to save on hedging costs. There is an argument that it would be acceptable to do nothing if it was anticipated that the Canadian dollar will appreciate over the three months. Be careful. Predicting exchange rates is a dangerous game and more than one 'expert' has made serious errors of judgement.

Netting

Multinational companies often have subsidiaries in different countries selling to other members of the group. **Netting** is where the subsidiaries settle intra-organisational currency debts for the *net* amount owed in a currency rather than the *gross* amount. For example, if a UK parent owned a subsidiary in Canada and sold C$2.2m of goods to the subsidiary on credit while the Canadian subsidiary is owed C$1.5m by the UK company, instead of transferring a total of C$3.7m the intra-group transfer is the net amount of C$700,000 (*see* **Exhibit 25.11**).

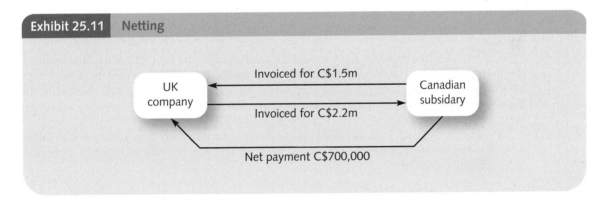

Exhibit 25.11 Netting

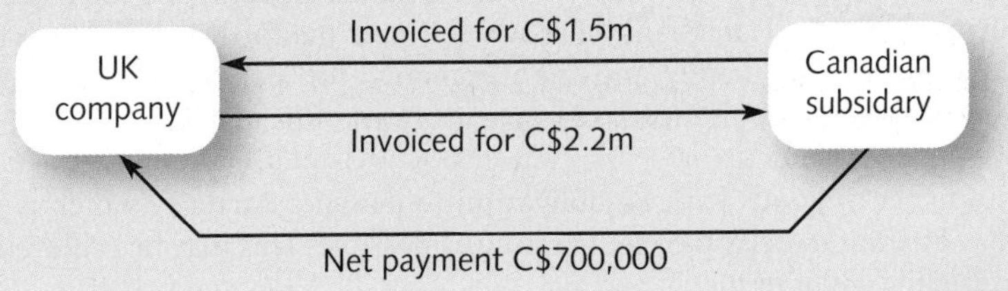

The reduction in the size of the currency flows by offsetting inflows and outflows in the same currency diminishes the net exposure which may have to be hedged. It also reduces the transaction costs of currency transfers in terms of fees and commissions.

This type of netting, involving two companies within a group, is referred to as **bilateral netting**, and is simple to operate without the intervention of a central treasury. However, for organisations with a matrix of currency liabilities between numerous subsidiaries in different parts of the world, **multilateral netting** is required. A central treasury is usually needed so that there is knowledge at any particular time of the overall exposure of the firm and its component parts. Subsidiaries will be required to inform the group treasury about their overseas dealings which can then co-ordinate payments after netting out intra-company debts. The savings on transfer costs levied by banks can be considerable.

Matching

Netting only applies to transfers within a group of companies. **Matching** can be used for both intra-group transactions and those involving third parties. The company matches the inflows and outflows in different currencies caused by trade, etc., so that it is only necessary to deal on the forex markets for the unmatched portion of the total transactions.

So if, say, the Canadian importer is not a group company and the UK firm also imported a raw material from another Canadian company to the value of C$2m it is necessary only to hedge the balance of C$200,000 (*see* **Exhibit 25.12**).

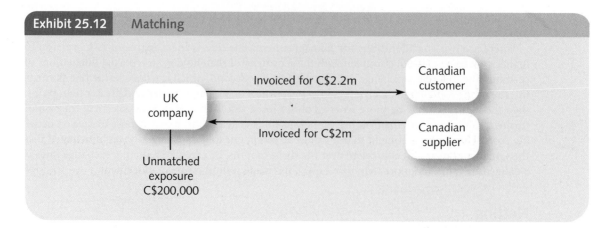

Exhibit 25.12 Matching

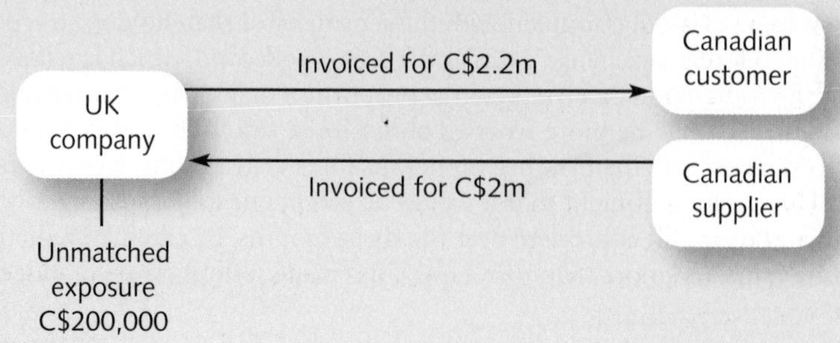

Naturally, to net and match properly, the timing of the expected receipts and payments would have to be the same.

Leading and lagging

Leading is the bringing forward from the original due date of the payment of a debt. **Lagging** is the postponement of a payment beyond the due date. This speeding up or delaying of payments is particularly useful if you are convinced exchange rates will shift significantly between now and the due date.

So, if the UK exporter which has invoiced a Canadian company for C$2.2m on three months' credit expects that the Canadian dollar will fall over the forthcoming three months it may try to obtain payment immediately and then exchange for sterling at the spot rate. Naturally the Canadian firm will need an incentive to pay early and this may be achieved by offering a discount for immediate settlement.

An importer of goods with an obligation to pay in a currency which is anticipated to fall in value may attempt to delay payment as long as possible. This may be achieved either by agreement or by exceeding credit terms.

Forward market hedge

Although other forms of exchange-risk management are available, forward cover represents the most frequently employed method of hedging. A contract is agreed to exchange two currencies at a fixed time in the future at a predetermined rate. The risk of forex variation is removed.

So if the three-month forward rate is C$2.25/£ the UK exporter could lock in the receipt of £977,778 in three months by selling forward C$2.2m.

$$\frac{\text{C\$2.2m}}{2.25} = \text{£}977{,}778$$

No foreign exchange-rate risk now exists because the dollars to be received from the importer are matched by the funds to be exchanged for sterling. (There does remain the risk of the importer not paying, at all or on time, and the risk of the counterparty in the forex market not fulfilling its obligations. However, these risks can be reduced considerably – *see* Buckley (2003) for some of these techniques, such as the use of documentary letters of trading.)

Money market hedge

Money market hedging involves borrowing in the money markets. For example, the exporter could, at the time of the export, borrow in Canadian dollars on the money markets for a three-month period. The amount borrowed, plus three months' interest, will be equal to the amount to be received from the importer (C$2.2m).

If the interest rate charged over three months is 2 per cent then the appropriate size of the loan is:

$$C\$2.2m = C\$?\ (1 + 0.02)$$

$$C\$? = \frac{C\$2.2m}{1.02} = C\$2,156,863$$

Thus the exporter has created a liability (borrowed funds) which matches the asset (debt owed by Canadian firm).

The borrowed dollars are then converted to sterling on the spot market for the exporter to receive £980,392 immediately:

$$\frac{C\$2,156,863}{2.2} = £980,392$$

The exporter has removed forex risk because it now holds cash in sterling.

Three months later C$2.2m is received from the importer and this exactly matches the outstanding debt:

Amount borrowed + Interest = Debt owed at end of period

$$C\$2,156,863 + C\$2,156,863 \times 0.02 = C\$2.2m$$

The receipt of £980,392 is £19,608 less than the £1m originally anticipated. However, it is received three months earlier and can earn interest.

The steps in the money market hedge are as follows:

1 Invoice customer for C$2.2m.
2 Borrow C$2,156,863.
3 Sell C$2,156,863 at spot to receive pounds now.
4 In three months receive C$2.2m from customer.
5 Pay lender C$2.2m.

An importer could also use a money market hedge. So a Swiss company importing Japanese cars for payment in yen in three months could borrow in Swiss francs now and convert the funds at the spot rate into yen. This money is deposited to earn interest, with the result that after three months the principal plus interest equals the invoice amount.

Futures hedge

A **foreign currency futures** contract is an agreement to exchange a specific amount of a currency for another at a fixed future date for a predetermined price. Futures are similar to forwards in many ways. They are, however, standardised contracts traded on regulated exchanges. Forwards can be tailor-made in a wide range of currencies as to quantity of currency and delivery date, whereas futures are only available in a limited range of currencies and for a few specific forward time periods.

The Chicago Mercantile Exchange (CME) and the New York Board of Trade (NYBOT) operate futures markets in currencies.[4] The CME includes the following currency pairs: US$/£, US$/¥, US$/SFr (Swiss franc), US$/€, US$/Mex. Peso, US$/C$ and US$/A$. A single futures contract is for a fixed amount of currency. For example, a sterling contract is for £62,500. It is not possible to buy or sell a smaller amount than this, nor to transact in quantities other than whole-number multiples of this. To buy a sterling futures contract is to make a commitment to deliver a quantity of US dollars and receive in return £62,500. One contract for a euro is for €125,000.

[4] Euronext.liffe also trades US dollar/euro futures.

On 15 November 2007 the CME and NYBOT quoted contracts (shown at www.ft.com) for delivery in late December and March (and for no months in between)[5] – *see* **Exhibit 25.13**. For example, the March contract for euros and US$ was priced at 1.4678 at the end of the trading day (the 'Open' column indicates the rate at the start of trading on 15 November, the 'Sett' column indicates closing prices.) This means that if you *buy* one contract you are committed to deliver US$1.4678 for every euro of the €125,000 you will receive in late March, that is US$183,475. If you *sold* one contract at 1.4678 you would deliver €125,000 and receive US$183,475.

Exhibit 25.13

CURRENCY FUTURES

FT

Nov 16		Open	Sett	Change	High	Low	Est. vol.	Open int.
€-Sterling*	Dec	0.7160	0.7159	–0.0007	0.7173	0.7163	176	9,185
€-Yen*	Dec	160.55	161.75	+0.86	161.60	160.39	996	11,451
$-Can $ †	Dec	1.0130	1.0262	+0.0114	1.0304	1.0111	48,299	108,519
$-Euro € †	Dec	1.4625	1.4665	+0.0044	1.4681	1.4589	167,961	216,215
$-Euro € †	Mar	1.4629	1.4678	+0.0043	1.4693	1.4604	981	4,339
$-Sw Franc †	Dec	0.8925	0.8962	+0.0039	0.8980	0.8909	42,643	79,802
$-Yen †	Dec	0.9089	0.9055	–0.0030	0.9141	0.9012	133,010	165,580
$-Yen †	Mar	0.9196	0.9148	–0.0028	0.9232	0.9105	305	10,991
$-Sterling †	Mar	2.0414	2.0495	+0.0081	2.0515	2.0334	65,231	121,530
$-Aust $ †	Dec	0.8837	0.8885	+0.0043	0.8927	0.8804	49,872	74,665
$-Mex Peso †	Dec	91225	91265	–	01450	91150	9,644	83,568

Sources: * NYBOT: Sterling €100,000 and Yen: €100,000. † CME: Australian $: A$100,000, Canadian $: C$100,000, Euro: €125,000: Mexican Peso: 500,000, Swiss Franc: SFr125,000: Yen ¥12.5m ($ per ¥100): Sterling: £62,500. CME volume, high & low for pit & electronic trading at settlement. Contracts shown are based on the volume traded in 2004.
Source: www.ft.com

A firm hedging with currency futures will usually attempt to have a futures position that has an equal and opposite profit profile to the underlying transaction. Frequently the futures position will be closed before delivery is due, to give a cash profit or loss to offset the spot market profit or loss (for more details on futures *see* Chapter 24) – although physical delivery of the currency is possible. For example, if a US firm exports €125,000 worth of goods to a German firm on 15 November 2007 on four months' credit for payment in late March and the current spot exchange rate is US$1.4628/€ there is a foreign exchange risk. If the March future is trading at a price of US$1.4629 per euro the exporter's position could be hedged by selling one euro futures contract on CME.

If in March the euro falls against the dollar to US$1.10/€ the calculation is:

Value of €125,000 received from customer when converted to dollars at spot in March (€125,000 × 1.10)	US$137,500
Amount if exchange rate was constant at US$1.4628/€	US$182,850
Forex loss	US$45,350

However, an offsetting gain is made on the futures contract:

Sold at US$1.4629/€ (€125,000 × 1.4629)	US$182,863
Bought in March to close position at US$1.10/€ (€125,000 × 1.10)	US$137,500
Futures gain	US$45,363

[5] The CME and NYBOT trade other months than those shown by the *Financial Times*, but these, are usually at three-month intervals.

Alternatively the exporter could simply deliver the €125,000 received from the importer to CME in return for US$182,863.

(Note that the futures contract rate of exchange in March converges with the spot rate at the date of expiry, in late March, i.e. US$1.10/€.)

In the above example a perfect hedge was not achieved because the gain on the futures contract did not exactly offset the loss on the underlying position (i.e. the euros to be received from the German customer). Perfect hedging is frequently unobtainable with futures because of their standardised nature. Perhaps the amount needed to be hedged is not equal to a whole number of contracts, for example €125,000, or the underlying transaction takes place in February (when no future is available).

Currency option hedge

The final possible course of action to reduce forex transaction risk to be discussed in this chapter is to make use of the currency option market.

A **currency option** is a contract giving the buyer (that is, the holder) the right, but not the obligation, to buy or sell a specific amount of currency at a specific exchange rate (the strike price), on or before a specified future date.[6]

A call option gives the right to buy a particular currency.

A put option gives the right to sell a particular currency.

The option writer (usually a bank) guarantees, if the option buyer chooses to exercise the right, to exchange the currency at the predetermined rate. Because the writer is accepting risk the buyer must pay a premium to the writer – normally within two business days of the option purchase. (For more details on options *see* Chapter 24.)

Currency options premiums are shown for the currency rates between the US$ and the euro, and the US$ and the UK pound in **Exhibit 25.14**. This data is taken from the website of the Chicago Mercantile Exchange (CME). For the US$/UK£ call options the purchaser has the right but not the obligation to purchase pounds for dollars. The potential call option buyer has a number of possible rates of exchange open to him/herself. The ones shown in the exhibit ($2040/£ to $2070/£) represent just a few of the possibilities. The premiums payable, shown in the body of

Exhibit 25.14 Currency options displayed on Chicago Marcantile Exchange website. (19 November 2007)

CURRENCY OPTIONS FT

US $/€ OPTIONS (CME)

Strike price	.... CALLS			.... PUTS		
Nov 19	Dec	Mar	Jun	Dec	Mar	Jun
1450	3.18	3.57	4.26	0.54	1.72	2.46
1460	2.38	2.96	3.71	0.86	1.90	2.89
1470	1.72	2.45	3.23	1.33	2.58	–
1480	1.15	2.00	2.78	1.94	3.12	3.92

US $/UK£ OPTIONS (CME)

Strike price	.... CALLS			.... PUTS		
Nov 19	Dec	Mar	Jun	Dec	Mar	Jun
2040	2.38	4.18	4.72	1.60	4.05	5.25
2050	1.82	3.69	–	2.04	4.55	–
2060	1.37	3.25	–	2.59	5.10	–
2070	1.00	2.85	3.47	3.21	5.67	6.93

Source: www.cme.com

[6] With some currency options the exercise can take place at any time up to the expiry date, rather than only on the expiry date.

the table, are quoted as US cents per pound. One contract is for £62,500, and you are only able to purchase whole numbers of contracts on the exchange. If you purchased a 2050 call option for expiry in March you would pay a premium of 3.69 US cents per UK pound (the total premium payable would be $\$0.0369 \times 62,500 = \$2,306$) giving you the right to buy pounds with dollars in March at a rate of $2.05/£. Note that a less favourable exchange rate, e.g. 2070($2.07), commands a lower premium, only 2.85 cents per pound under the contract.

The purchase of a put option gives you the right but not the obligation to *sell* pounds and receive dollars. Again the quantity of a contract is for £62,500.

The $/€ call and put premiums are quoted at US cents per euro under the contract. One contract is for €125,000.

The CME quotes option prices for many more exchange rates than those shown – *see* www.cme.com.

The crucial advantage an option has over a forward is the absence of an obligation to buy or sell. It is the option buyer's decision whether to insist on exchange at the strike rate or to let the option lapse.

With a forward there is a hedge against both a favourable and an unfavourable movement in forex rates. This means that if the exchange rate happens to move in your favour after you are committed to a forward contract you cannot take any advantage of that movement. We saw above that if the forward rate was C$2.25/£ the exporter will receive £977,778 in three months. If the spot exchange rate had moved to, say, C$1.9/£ over the three months the exporter would have liked to abandon the agreement to sell the dollars at C$2.25/£, but is unable to do so because of the legal commitment. By abandoning the deal and exchanging at spot when the Canadian firm pays the exporter will receive an income of:

$$\frac{\text{C\$2.2m}}{1.9} = £1,157,895$$

This is an extra £180,117.

An option permits both:

- hedging against unfavourable currency movement; and
- profit from favourable currency movement.

Worked example 25.2 **Currency option contract**

Now, imagine that the treasurer of the UK firm hedges by buying a three-month sterling call option giving the right but not the obligation to deliver Canadian dollars in exchange for pounds with a strike price of C$2.25/£ when the goods are delivered to the Canadian firm. To induce a bank to make the commitment to exchange at the option holder's behest a premium will need to be paid up front. Assume this is 2 per cent of the amount covered, that is, a non-refundable $0.02 \times$ C$2,200,000 = C$44,000 is payable two business days after the option deal is struck.[7]

Three months later

The dollars are delivered by the importer on the due date. The treasurer now has to decide whether or not to exercise the right to exchange those dollars for sterling at C$2.25/£. Let us consider two scenarios.

Scenario 1

The dollar has strengthened against the pound to C$1.9/£. If the treasurer exercises the right to exchange at C$2.25/£ the UK firm will receive:

$$\frac{\text{C\$2,200,000}}{2.25} = £977,778$$

[7] We are assuming in this example that over-the-counter options are written by a bank rather than exchange-based options on, say, the CME.

If the treasurer takes the alternative and lets the option lapse – 'abandons it' – and exchanges the dollars in the spot market, the amount received will be:

$$\frac{C\$2{,}200{,}000}{1.9} = £1{,}157{,}895$$

Clearly in this case the best course of action would be not to exercise the option, but to exchange at the spot rate. Note that the benefit of this action is somewhat reduced by the earlier payment of C$44,000 for the premium.

Scenario 2

Now assume that the dollar has weakened against sterling to C$2.5/£. If the treasurer contacts the bank (the option writer) to confirm that the exporter wishes to exercise the option the treasurer will arrange delivery of C$2,200,000 to the bank and will receive £977,778 in return:

$$\frac{C\$2{,}200{,}000}{2.25} = £977{,}778$$

The alternative, to abandon the option and sell the C$2.2m in the spot forex market, is unattractive:

$$\frac{C\$2{,}200{,}000}{2.5} = £880{,}000$$

Again, the option premium needs to be deducted to give a more complete picture.

With the option, the worst that could happen is that the exporter receives £977,778, less the premium. However the upside potential is unconstrained.

(*Note*: It is possible to elect for cash settlement (i.e. profit if the market value is greater than exercise value) on the option rather than the physical exchange of the currencies.)

Option contracts are generally for sums greater than US$1,000,000 on the OTC (over-the-counter) market (direct deals with banks) whereas one contract on the CME is, for example, for £62,500. The drawback with exchange-based derivatives is the smaller range of currencies available and the inability to tailor-make a hedging position.

It can be very difficult to determine the correct hedging strategy – as the case of Air Products illustrates in **Exhibit 25.15**.

Exhibit 25.15

Choose the correct path for a viable deal

FT

James Politi evaluates the options available to those implementing currency hedging strategies

In May 2002, Air Products & Chemicals came out with a sobering announcement. Because of opposition from regulators at the US Federal Trade Commission, the Pennsylvania-based industrials group would drop an $11.2bn deal to buy British rival BOC that it had sealed with France's Air Liquide a year earlier.

In addition to being forced to abandon a crucial strategic move, there was another reason for Air Products and its investors to be gloomy. A strong fluctuation in the dollar/pound exchange rate in previous months meant Air Products would have to take a charge of nearly $300m, mostly from losses on the currency hedge that the company had put in place for the BOC deal in January 2000.

The Air Products case illustrates the challenges facing corporate chiefs and investment banks as they study ways to manage foreign exchange risk during M&A deals. A tricky balance has to be struck between properly managing currency exposure, and not hedging so much that it underlines the economics of a deal.

Paul Huck, chief financial officer of Air Products, grappled with these issues. Speaking to the FT today, he believes his company had little choice ▶

Exhibit 25.15 continued

FX OPTION

A foreign exchange option gives the buyer of the option the right to purchase the currency at a specific price. The client would buy a call option to protect itself against a rising currency and would pay a premium for the option – typically in the range of 50–200 basis points (depending on the maturity and price of the strike). The most money one can lose on an option is the premium that one pays for it, which makes it a particularly good strategy for cross-border M&A. With an option you will always know how much you will spend on your hedge, which makes budgeting for the hedge relatively easy. An option is also a marketable asset and could be sold in the free market in the event the hedge needs to be liquidated. The only disadvantage of an option is its upfront cost.

DO NOTHING

'Clients may adopt this strategy, particularly early in the M&A process, as the uncertainty surrounding deal completion can be significant,' says Leo Civitillo and Steve Zannetos at Morgan Stanley.

'When the deal progresses and the probability of completion increases, execution of a currency hedge is typically warranted. However, there may also be other considerations that drive a decision not to hedge, including a view on the market, the implied costs of hedging, and accounting considerations.

'The risk of remaining unhedged is that the currency could significantly move against the company and adversely affect the economics of the acquisition.'

NATURAL HEDGE

'A natural hedge would essentially be issuing the debt for the acquisition in the target's local currency, which would negate the need for foreign exchange hedge', says Courtney McLaughlin, head of the foreign exchange capital markets group in the investment banking division at Credit Suisse, the Swiss bank.

'If the deal is signed and the currency appreciates, the acquirer will pay more for the business in dollar terms, but because they are issuing debt in the local currency market they are getting more (in dollar terms) for the debt they are issuing, thereby creating the natural hedge.'

FX FORWARD

'FX forwards are simply an obligation to exchange one currency or another at a specified rate on a future date,' say Mr Civitillo and Mr Zannetos at Morgan Stanley.

'We typically do not recommend that clients employ vanilla FX forwards to hedge the currency risk embedded in a cross-border transaction until we are absolutely certain that the deal will close. The reason is that the potential breakage or unwind cost of an FX forward can be significant, if the underlying transaction does not close as expected. However, assuming that all of the deal risks have passed, forward contracts can be a very efficient and cost effective way to lock-in the price of a foreign asset.'

DEAL-CONTINGENT FWD

A deal-contingent forward is similar to a vanilla forward with two key differences: the ability of the client to walk away from the contract if the deal is not consummated, and its price. A deal-contingent forward allows a client to exchange one currency for another at a specified rate on a future date. The client would define contingencies that, if met, would allow the client to walk away from the forward with no cost or obligation. Typical contingencies are: material adverse change clauses, shareholder approvals and regulatory approvals. A deal-contingent forward has an implicit cost that is paid for by striking the forward rate slightly off market. It allows the client to enjoy the efficiency of a forward without the out-of-pocket cost of an option.

but to put a hedge in place once it expected the BOC takeover to be approved. Air Products was paying for a collection of assets outside the UK in sterling – Air Liquide was slated to take over the British BOC business – and as such was heavily exposed to any movements in the UK currency between announcement and closing.

'We still feel we did the right thing in hedging the transaction,' says Mr Huck. 'When you do M&A you worry about having the economics of a deal change because of currency movements, and we're not in the business of making currency bets.'

The trouble with the hedge put in place buy Air Products – a mix of options and forward contracts – is that its structure may have been too optimistic. While forwards are less expensive than options because they carry no fee, they leave the company heavily exposed to a currency shift in the wrong direction if the deal does not close. Options, on the other hand, can be expensive, carrying hefty up-front fees.

However, if the currency moves in the wrong direction and the deal does not close, the company can simply let the options expire.

'If I had been willing to do this [use more options and less forwards] and pay higher premiums, it would have been very expensive, and might have hurt the deal [if the FTC had approved it],' says Mr Huck.

Hedging currency risk in M&A deals has become an increasingly popular product in the universe of risk management.

As global M&A volumes have grown, the markets for derivatives – the primary hedging instruments – have become increasingly liquid, banks have been able to match supply and demand on foreign exchange risk with a series of customised hedging packages (see above).

Source: *Financial Times*, 25 January 2007, Special Report: Corporate Finance, p. 2. Reprinted with permission.

Managing translation risk

The effect of translation risk on the balance sheet can be lessened by matching the currency of assets and liabilities. For example, Graft plc has decided to go ahead with a US$190m project in the USA. One way of financing this is to borrow £100m and exchange this for dollars at the current exchange rate of US$1.9/£. Thus at the beginning of the year the additional entries into the consolidated accounts are as shown in Worked example 25.3.

Worked example 25.3 Translation risk

Opening balance sheet

Liabilities		*Assets*	
Loan	£100m	US assets	£100m

The US$190m of US assets are translated at US$1.9/£ so all figures are expressed in the parent company's currency.

Now imagine that over the course of the next year the dollar depreciates against sterling to US$2.30/£. In the consolidated group accounts there is still a £100m loan but the asset bought with that loan, while still worth US$190m,[8] is valued at only £82.61m when translated into sterling. In the parent company's currency terms, £17.39m needs to be written off:

Year-end balance sheet

Liabilities		*Assets*	
Loan	£100m	US assets	£82.61m
	£100m		£82.61m
Forex loss	–£17.39m		

Alternatively Graft plc could finance its dollar assets by obtaining a dollar loan. Thus, when the dollar depreciates, both the asset value and the liability value in translated sterling terms becomes less.

Opening balance sheet

Liabilities		*Assets*	
Loan	£100m	US assets	£100m

If forex rates move to US$2.30/£:

Year-end balance sheet

Liabilities		*Assets*	
Loan	£82.61m	US assets	£82.61m

There is no currency loss to deal with.

One constraint on the solution set out in Worked example 25.3 is that some governments insist that a proportion of assets acquired within their countries is financed by the parent firm. Another constraint is that the financial markets in some countries are insufficiently developed to permit large-scale borrowing.

[8] Assuming, for the sake of simplicity, no diminution of asset value in dollar terms.

Many economists and corporate managers believe that translation hedging is unnecessary because, on average over a period of time, gains and losses from forex movements will even out to be zero. **Exhibit 25.16** considers the reasons for most companies taking no steps to hedge against profit translation risk.

Exhibit 25.16

When a hedge is not a gardener's problem

FT

As the half-yearly company reporting season has got under way, so too have the protests from UK companies that the strength of sterling is cutting profits.

BOC, the gas producer, estimated that sterling's rapid rise in the last 12 months would cut £46m off its annual profits because of the cost of translating foreign currency earnings into sterling.

But, as one letter writer to the Financial Times recently asked, surely UK companies could avoid these problems by hedging their currency exposure, using financial instruments to protect against exchange rate fluctuations?

In fact, exporters use a number of techniques to lower currency risks. An engineering firm exporting machinery to Germany, for example, could price its contracts in sterling and shift the exchange rate risk on to its customers. Exporters can also buy forward contracts for an exchange rate fixed at a future date.

An unpublished survey of corporate treasurers by Record Treasury Management, a London consultancy, found that 77 per cent of respondents used forward contracts and other currency derivatives.

But Les Halpin, chief executive of RTM, said while many companies were happy to use derivatives to hedge their cash positions, almost none was prepared to use similar instruments to protect profits earned overseas.

The result is companies with substantial overseas operations, such as BOC, Imperial Chemical Industries and Reuters, have reported translation losses in converting foreign profits. ICI said interim pre-tax profits were down £90m because of the rapid rise in sterling. It attributed £30m to the translation into sterling.

So why not use derivatives to hedge translation costs? UK companies rarely do, according to Mr Halpin, because they often don't understand them.

The RTM survey found that 30 per cent said 'complexity' was the main risk in using derivatives. 'Most company executives think a hedge is something they get their gardener to trim,' grumbled one City equities analyst.

Another 35 per cent of treasurers said 'lack of control' was a significant risk – the fear that the spirit of Nick Leeson may live in a graduate trainee within the finance department. Since future profit levels are unknown, deciding how much to hedge is one barrier.

Sandvik, the Swedish industrial group, was recently caught out by currency hedging, as it reported an 18 per cent fall in first-half profits. In its case, the weakening of the krona meant its hedged positions made a loss.

UK finance directors are reluctant to hedge for several reasons. Profits lost in translation can often be 'paper losses' – it is only when the profits are converted into sterling that a loss is made. And there are complex accounting problems for representing derivatives on balance sheets, especially for instruments spanning several years.

But the most important reservation may be psychological.

If a corporate treasurer gets permission to hedge overseas earnings, and a currency shift makes the hedge unnecessary, then the cost and blame for the decision can be easily identified. But if the treasurer decides not to hedge, then the company is at the whim of the currency markets, an act of God for which no one is responsible.

Ironically, many corporate treasurers are happy to let their organisations dabble in currency speculation – even though treasurers are no better than anyone else in predicting rate movements . . .

Hedging cannot protect a company from extended currency movements. John Rennocks, finance director of British Steel, said: 'Hedging is an important part of any exporter's business activity, but can only defer the impact of violent currency swings.'

But, Mr Halpin replied, well judged hedging can give a company 'breathing space', enabling it to take decisions on moving production or resources before the full impact of a currency swing is felt.

Source: Richard Adams, *Financial Times*, 18 August 1997. Reprinted with permission.

Managing economic risk

Economic exposure is concerned with the long-term effects of forex movements on the firm's ability to compete, and add value. These effects are very difficult to estimate in advance, given their long-term nature, and therefore the hedging techniques described for transaction risk are of limited use. The forwards markets may be used to a certain extent, but these only extend for a short period for most currencies. Also the matching principle could be employed, whereby overseas assets are matched as far as possible by overseas liabilities.

The main method of insulating the firm from economic risk is to position the company in such a way as to maintain maximum flexibility – to be able to react to changes in forex rates which may be causing damage to the firm. Firms which are internationally diversified may have a greater degree of flexibility than those based in one or two markets. For example, a company with production facilities in numerous countries can shift output to those plants where the exchange rate change has been favourable. The international car assemblers have an advantage here over the purely domestic producer.

Forex changes can impact on the costs of raw materials and other inputs. By maintaining flexibility in sourcing supplies a firm could achieve a competitive advantage by deliberately planning its affairs so that it can switch suppliers quickly and cheaply.

An aware multinational could allow for forex changes when deciding in which countries to launch an advertising campaign. For example, it may be pointless increasing marketing spend in a country whose currency has depreciated rapidly recently, making the domestically produced competing product relatively cheap. It might be sensible to plan in advance the company's response to a forex movement with regard to the pricing of goods so that action can be rapid. For example, a UK company exporting to Norway at a time when sterling is on a rising trend can either keep the product at the same price in sterling terms to maintain profits and face the consequential potential loss of market share, or reduce the sterling price to maintain a constant price in kroner and thereby keep its market share. Being prepared may avert an erroneous knee-jerk decision.

The principle of contingency planning to permit quick reaction to forex changes applies to many areas of marketing and production strategies. This idea links with the notion of the real option described in Chapter 6. The option to switch sources of supply and output, or to change marketing focus, may have a high value. Despite the cost of creating an adaptable organisation, rather than a dedicated fixed one, the option to switch may be worth far more in an uncertain world.

Exhibit 25.17 describes the moves made by a number of UK companies to reduce their economic risk exposure by setting up manufacturing operations in a range of countries.

Exhibit 25.17

A test of company strategy

FT

Peter Marsh

The US employees of Industrial Acoustics Company, a Winchester-based business that is a world leader in making noise-proof enclosures for installations such as jet testing centres and power stations, could soon be among the beneficiaries of the dollar's weakening.

Brian Quarendon, the company's chief executive, says he is considering switching the manufacture of anti-noise products to IAC's New York plant to meet strong demand from the Middle East. They will be made more cheaply in the US than in the company's factories in the UK and continental Europe. 'We are hoping for another $25m worth of business in the Middle East in the next two years. The way the dollar has been moving, I envisage most of this being produced from the US,' says Mr Quarendon.

IAC's reaction to the dollar's fragility illustrates the way company managers are thinking about altering their strategies now that several years of relative currency stability appear to be ending. If the dollar's weakness continues and the euro maintains its new-found robustness, how much opportunity does this give UK-based businesses to change the way they operate?

In the short term, the winners are UK-based companies exporting to the rest of Europe. The losers are those selling to dollar-denominated regions, including China and other nations in south-east Asia.

But according to Sir David Lees, chairman of the GKN engineering group, many UK companies are now so internationally spread that they are highly unlikely to make big changes in strategy on the back of short-term currency shifts.

'In GKN's case, we would never decide to switch production from our plants in Germany to the US on the grounds that the dollar has become weak,' says Sir David. 'In six months' time, the situation could reverse and we'd have to switch back again.'

The case of Imperial Chemical Industries shows how globalisation strategies provide inbuilt protection against currency swings. Two decades ago, any sudden weakening of sterling against continental European currencies would have boosted ICI, which was then a large maker of commodity chemicals sold globally but produced mainly in the UK. Today ICI mainly makes smaller-volume, high-value materials that are produced in plants around the world and used in markets close by. Therefore, the company says, the dollar's weakness makes little difference to how it seeks to run its business.

▶

Exhibit 25.17 continued

JCB, the UK's biggest maker of construction machinery, is another case in point. Until four years ago, all the company's plants were in Britain, giving the business much more exposure to changes in exchange rates. JCB now has several factories outside the UK, including a US plant employing 200.

'To some degree we anticipated the kind of change [the dollar weakening] that we have seen in the past few months,' says John Patterson, JCB's chief executive. 'Having our own US factory puts us in a much better position to respond if currencies move in an unexpected manner.'

In the past few years, many UK-based manufacturers have also sourced more parts from companies based in continental Europe, capitalising on the euro's relative weakness at the time.

Because UK industry has spread its risk to currency swings in this way, Harry Rawlinson, managing director of Aqualisa, a Kent-based shower manufacturer, says that today 'it is a moot point' whether it is in the best interests of UK industry for the pound to be strong or weak against the euro.

If most of UK industry has less reason to worry about currency swings than in the past, most industrial managers would argue that this is how it should be: rather than spend time fretting about the ups and downs of currencies, they can get on with making and selling better products.

Source: Financial Times, 10 January 2004. Reprinted with permission.

Exchange-rate determination

A number of factors influence the rate of exchange between currencies. This section briefly considers some of them.

Purchasing power parity

The theory of **purchasing power parity (PPP)** is based on the idea that a basket of goods should cost the same regardless of the currency in which it is sold. For example, if a basket of goods sold for £10,000 in the UK and an identical "basket" sold for US$15,000 in the USA then the rate of exchange should be US$1.50/£. Imagine what would happen if this were not the case; say, for example, the rate of exchange was US$3.00/£. Now British consumers can buy a basket of goods in the US market for half the price they would pay in the UK market (£5,000 can be exchanged for US$15,000). Naturally the demand for dollars would rise as UK consumers rushed out of sterling to buy dollars. This would cause the forex rates to change – the dollar would rise in value until the purchasing power of each currency was brought to an equilibrium, that is, where there is no incentive to exchange currencies to take advantage of lower prices abroad because of a misaligned exchange rate.

The definition of PPP is:

Exchange rates will be in equilibrium when their domestic purchasing powers at that rate of exchange are equivalent.

So, for example:

Price of a basket of goods in UK in sterling	×	US$/£ exchange rate	=	Price of a basket of goods in USA in dollars
£10,000	×	1.50	=	US$15,000

The PPP theory becomes more interesting if relationships over a period of time are examined. Inflation in each country will affect the price of a basket of goods in domestic currency terms. This in turn will influence the exchange rate between currencies with different domestic inflation rates.

Let us suppose that sterling and the US dollar are at PPP equilibrium at the start of the year with rates at US$1.50/£. Then over the year the inflation rate in the UK is 15 per cent so the same basket costs £11,500 at the end of the year. If during the same period US prices rose by 3 per cent the US domestic cost of a basket will be US$15,450. If the exchange rate remains at US$1.50/£ there will be a disequilibrium and PPP is not achieved. A UK consumer is faced with a choice of either buying £11,500 of UK-produced goods or exchanging £11,500 into dollars and buying US goods. The consumer's £11,500 will buy US$17,250 at US$1.50/£. This is more than one basket; therefore the best option is to buy goods in America. The buying pressure on the dollar will shift exchange rates to a new equilibrium in which a basket costs the same price in both countries. To find this new equilibrium we could use the following formula:

$$\frac{1 + I_{US}}{1 + I_{UK}} = \frac{\text{US\$/£}_1}{\text{US\$/£}_0}$$

where:

I_{US} = US inflation rate;
I_{UK} = UK inflation rate;
$\text{US\$/£}_1$ = the spot rate of exchange at the end of the period;
$\text{US\$/£}_0$ = the spot rate of exchange at the beginning of the period.

$$\frac{1 + 0.03}{1 + 0.15} = \frac{\text{US\$/£}_1}{1.50}$$

$$\text{US\$/£}_1 = \frac{1 + 0.03}{1 + 0.15} \times 1.50 = 1.3435$$

The US dollar appreciates against sterling by 10.43 per cent because inflation is lower in the USA over the period.

At this new exchange rate a basket of goods costing US$15,450 in the USA has a sterling cost of 15,450/1.3435 = £11,500 and thus PPP is maintained.

The pure PPP concludes that the country with the higher inflation rate will be subject to a depreciation of its currency, and the extent of that depreciation is proportional to the relative difference in the two countries' inflation rates. The PPP theory has some serious problems when applied in practice:

- ***It only applies to goods freely traded internationally at no cost of trade***
Many goods and services do not enter international trade and so their relative prices are not taken into account in the determination of currency rates. Medical services, haircuts, building and live entertainment, to name but a few, are rarely imported; therefore they are not subject to PPP. The theory also has limited applicability to goods with a high transportation cost relative to their value, for example, road stone or cement. The PPP disequilibrium would have to be very large to make it worthwhile importing products of this kind. There may also be barriers inhibiting trade, for example regulations, tariffs, quotas, cultural resistance.

- ***It works in the long run, but that may be years away***
Customers may be slow to recognise the incentive to purchase from another country when there is a PPP disequilibrium. There is usually some inertia due to buying habits that have become routine. Furthermore, governments may manage exchange rates for a considerable period, thus defying the forces pressing toward PPP. In addition, in the short term there are other elements at play such as balance of payments disequilibria, capital transactions (purchase of assets such as factories, businesses or shares by foreigners) and speculation.

The evidence is that relative inflation is one influence on exchange rates, but it is not the only factor. There have been large deviations from PPP for substantial periods.

Exhibit 25.18 applies the PPP idea in a light-hearted way.

Exhibit 25.18

The Big Mac Index

Sizzling

Food for thought about exchange-rate controversies

American politicians bash China for its policy of keeping the yuan weak. France blames a strong euro for its sluggish economy. The Swiss are worried about a falling franc. New Zealanders fret that their currency has risen too far.

All these anxieties rest on a belief that exchange rates are out of whack. Is this justified? *The Economist's* Big Mac Index, a light-hearted guide to how far currencies are from fair value, provides some answers. It is based on the theory of purchasing-power parity (PPP), which says that exchange rates should equalise the price of a basket of goods in any two countries. Our basket contains just a single representative purchase, but one that is available in 120 countries: a Big Mac hamburger. The implied PPP, our hamburger standard, is the exchange rate that makes the dollar price of a burger the same in each country.

Most currencies are trading a long way from that yardstick. China's currency is the cheapest. A Big Mac in China costs 11 yuan, equivalent to just $1.45 at today's exchange rate, which means China's currency is undervalued by 58%. But before China's critics start warming up for a fight, they should bear in mind that PPP points to where currencies ought to go in the long run. The price of a burger depends heavily on local inputs such as rent and wages, which are not easily arbitraged across borders and tends to be lower in poorer countries. For this reason PPP is a better guide to currency misalignments between countries at a similar stage of development.

Cash and carry
The hamburger standard

	Big Mac prices in dollars*	Implied PPP† of the dollar	Under (–)/ over (+) valuation against the dollar, %
United States‡	3.41	–	–
Britain	4.01	1.71§	+18
Canada	3.68	1.14	+8
China	1.45	3.23	–58
Denmark	5.08	8.14	+49
Euro area**	4.17	1.12††	+22
Japan	2.29	82.1	–33
New Zealand	5.89	1.35	+73
Russia	2.03	15.2	–41
Singapore	2.59	1.16	–24
South Africa	2.22	4.55	–35
Sweden	4.86	9.68	+42
Switzerland	5.20	1.85	+53

*At current exchange rates †Purchasing-power parity; local price dividend by price in United States. ‡Average of New York, Chicago, Atlanta and San Francisco. §Dollars per pound **Weighted average of prices in euro area ††Dollars per euro

Sources: McDonald's; *The Economist*

The most overvalued currencies are found on the rich fringes of the European Union: in Iceland, Norway and Switzerland. Indeed, nearly all rich-world currencies are expensive compared with the dollar. The exception is the yen, undervalued by 33%. This anomaly seems to justify fears that speculative carry trades, where funds from low-interest countries such as Japan are used to buy high-yield currencies, have pushed the yen too low. But broader measurers of PPP suggest the yen is close to fair value. A New Yorker visiting Tokyo would find that although Big Macs were cheap, other goods and services seemed pricey. A trip to Europe would certainly pinch the pocket of an American tourist: the euro is 22% above its fair value.

The Swiss franc, like the yen a source of low-yielding funds for foreign-exchange punters, is 53% overvalued. The franc's recent fall is a rare example of carry traders moving a currency towards its burger standards. That is because it is borrowed and sold to buy high-yieding investments in rich countries such as New Zealand and Britain, whose currencies look dear against their burger benchmarks. Brazil and Turkey, two emerging economies favoured by speculators, have also been pushed around. Burgernomics hints that their currencies are a little overcooked.

Sources: The Economist, 7 July 2007, p. 82. Reprinted with permission.

Interest rate parity

PPP is concerned with differences in spot rates at different points in time and relating these to inflation rates. However, **interest rate parity (IRP)** concerns the relationship between spot rates and forward rates, and links differences between these to the nominal interest rates available in each of the two currencies.

The interest rate parity theory holds true when the difference between spot and forward exchange rates is equal to the differential between interest rates available in the two currencies.

The outcome of the IRP theory is that if you place your money in a currency with a high interest rate you will be no better off when you convert the sum back into your home currency via a prearranged forward transaction than you would have been if you had simply invested in an interest-bearing investment carrying a similar risk, at home. What you gain on the extra interest you lose on the difference between spot and forward exchange rates.

For example, suppose a UK investor is attracted by the 8 per cent interest rate being offered on one-year US government bonds. This compares well with the similarly very low risk one-year UK government bond offering 6 per cent interest. The IRP theory says that this investor will not achieve an extra return by investing abroad rather than at home because the one-year forward rate of exchange will cause the US$ to be at a discount relative to the present spot rate. Thus, when the investment matures and the dollars are converted to sterling the investor will have achieved the same as if the money had been invested in UK government bonds.

Consider these steps:

1 *Beginning of year*
   - **a** Exchange £1m for US$1.5m at the spot rate of US$1.5/£.
   - **b** Buy US$1.5m government bonds yielding 8 per cent.
   - **c** Arrange a one-year forward transaction at US$1.5283/£ to sell dollars.

2 *End of year*
   Exchange US$1.62m (US$1.5m × 1.08) with the bank which agreed the forward exchange at the beginning of the year at the rate 1.5283 to produce 1.62 ÷ 1.5283 = £1.06m. This is equal to the amount that would have been received by investing in UK government bonds, 6 per cent over the year. The differential between the spot and forward rates exactly offsets the difference in interest rates.

The formula which links together the spot, forward and interest rate differences is:

$$\frac{1 + r_{\text{US}}}{1 + r_{\text{UK}}} = \frac{\text{US\$/£}_F}{\text{US\$/£}_S}$$

where: r_{US} = interest rate available in the USA;
r_{UK} = interest rate available in the UK (for the same risk);
$\text{US\$/£}_F$ = the forward exchange rate;
$\text{US\$/£}_S$ = the spot exchange rate.

To test this relationship consider the case where both the spot rate and the forward rate are at US$1.50/£. Here the investor can prearrange to convert the dollar investment back into sterling through a forward agreement and obtain an extra 2 per cent by investing in the USA. However, the investor will not be alone in recognising this remarkable opportunity. Companies, forex dealers and fund managers will turn to this type of trading. They would sell UK bonds, buy dollars spot, buy US bonds and sell dollars forward. However, this would quickly lead us away from disequilibrium as the pressure of these transactions would lower UK bond prices and therefore raise interest rates, cause a rise in the value of the spot dollar against sterling, a rise in the price of US bonds and therefore a fall in interest rates being offered and a fall in the dollar forward rate. These adjustments will eliminate the investment return differences and re-establish IRP equilibrium.

The IRP insists that the relationship between exchange and interest rates is:

- ***High nominal interest rate currency*** Currency trades at a discount on the forward rate compared with spot rate.
- ***Low nominal interest rate currency*** Currency trades at a premium on the forward rate compared with spot rate.

The IRP theory *generally* holds true in practice. However, there are deviations caused by factors such as taxation (which alters the rate of return earned on investments), or government controls on capital flows, controls on currency trading and intervention in foreign exchange markets interfering with the attainment of equilibrium through arbitrage.

The article in **Exhibit 25.19** describes a serious challenge to those who believe the IRP holds in practice.

Exhibit 25.19

Carry on speculating

How traders have been triumphing over economic theory

No comment on the financial markets these days is complete without mention of the 'carry trade', the borrowing or selling of currencies with low interest rates and the purchase of currencies with high rates. The trade is often blamed for the weakness of the Japanese yen and the unexpected enthusiasm of investors for the New Zealand and Australian dollars.

But why does the carry trade work? In theory, it shouldn't – or not for as long as it has. Foreign-exchange markets operate under a state of 'covered interest parity'. In other words, the difference between two countries' interest rates is exactly reflected in the gap between the spot, or current, exchange rate and the forward market. High-interest-rate currencies are at a discount in the forward market; low-rate currencies at a premium.

If that were not so, it would be possible for a Japanese investor to sell yen, buy dollars, invest those dollars at high American interest rates for 12 months and simultaneously sell the dollars forward for yen to lock in a profit in a year's time. The potential for arbitrage means such profits cannot be earned.

However, economic theory also suggests that 'uncovered interest parity' should operate. Countries that offer high interest rates should be compensating investors for the risk that their currency will depreciate. In other words, the forward rate should be a good guess of the likely future spot rate.

In the real world, uncovered interest parity has not applied over the past 25 years or so. A recent academic study* has shown that high-rate currencies have tended to appreciate and low-rate currencies to depreciate, the reverse of theory. Carry-trade strategies would have brought substantial profits, not far short of stockmarket returns, although dealing costs would have limited the size of the bets traded could make.

Academics have struggled for some time to explain this discrepancy. One possibility is that investors demand a risk premium, separate from the better interest rate, to compensate them for investing in a foreign currency. As this risk premium varies, it might overwhelm the effects of interest-rate changes. For example, American investors might worry about the credibility of the Bank of Japan, but Japanese investors may regard the dollar as a 'safe haven'. This would drive the dollar up and the yen down.

However, according to Andrew Scott, of the London Business School, it has been a struggle to find risk premiums that are large enough to explain exchange-rate volatility. So academics have been looking at the structure of foreign-exchange markets, to see if behavioural factors might be at work.

One obvious possibility is that the actions of carry traders are self-fulfiling; when they borrow the yen and buy the dollar, they drive the former down and the latter up. If other investors follow 'momentum' strategies – jumping on the bandwagon of existing trends – this would tend to push up currencies with high interest rates.

Financial jaywalking

Such a strategy has its dangers. It has been likened to 'picking up nickels in front of steamrollers': you have a long run of small gains but eventually get squashed. In the currency markets, this would mean a steady series of profits from the interest-rate premium that are all wiped out of a large, sudden shift in exchange rates: think of the pound's exit from the European exchange-rate mechanism in 1992. The foreign-exchange markets have been remarkably calm since the Asian crisis of 1998 (when the yen rose sharply, hitting many carry traders). So a whole generation of investors may have grown up in a state of blissful innocence, unaware that their carry strategy has severe dangers.

Inflation may provide an alternative explanation. The theory of purchasing-power parity (PPP) implies that high-inflation currencies should depreciate, relative to harder monies. In other words, while nominal exchange rates might vary, real rates should be pretty constant. And over the very long term, this seems to happen. A study by the London Business School†, with ABN Amro, a Dutch bank, found that real exchange rates in 17 countries moved by less than an average of 0.2% a year over the period 1900–2006.

Other things being equal (such as roughly similar real interest rates across countries) nominal interest rates should be higher in countries with higher inflation rates. So this should give support to uncovered-interest parity and deter the carry trade. Clearly, though, PPP has not been a useful guide over the past ten years, as the deflation-prone yen has declined against the dollar.

Perhaps the success of the carry trade reflects biases built up in an earlier era, during the inflationary 1970s and 1980s. Currencies prone to inflation back then, such as sterling and the dollar, have had to pay higher interest rates to compensate investors for their reputation. In fact, because inflation has declined, investors in Britain and America have been overcompensated for the risks – a windfall gain that has been exploited by followers of the carry trade.

▶

However, it is hard to believe that this effect could have lasted for as long as it has. So the reasons for the success of the carry trade remain a bit of a mystery.

What does seem plain, however, is that the carry trade tends to break down when markets become more turbulent. In such conditions, those who borrowed yen to borrow to buy other assets (such as emerging-market shares) might face a double blow as the yen rose while asset prices fell. If the turbulence were sufficiently large, many years' worth of profits from the carry trade might be wiped out. A steamroller could yet restore the reputation of economic theory.

* 'The Returns to Currency Speculation', by Craig Burnside, Martin Eichenbaum, Isaac Kleschelski and Sergio Rebelo, www.nber.org/papers/w12489
† Global Investment Returns Yearbook 2007

Source: The Economist, 24 February 2007, p. 88. Reprinted with permission. © The Economist Newspaper Limited 2007.

Expectations theory

*The **expectations theory** states that the current forward exchange rate is an unbiased predictor of the spot rate at that point in the future.*

Note that the theory does not say that the forward rate predicts precisely what spot rates will be in the future; it is merely an unbiased predictor or provides the statistical expectation. The forward rate will frequently underestimate the actual future spot rate. However, it will also frequently overestimate the actual future spot rate. On (a statistical) average, however, it predicts the future spot rate because it neither consistently under- nor consistently over-estimates.

Traders in foreign currency nudge the market towards the fulfilment of the expectations theory. If a trader takes a view that the forward rate is lower than the expected future spot price there is an incentive to buy forward. Then when the forward matures and the trader's view on the spot rate turns out to be correct the trader is able to buy at a low price and immediately sell at spot to make a profit. The buying pressure on the forward raises the price until equilibrium occurs, in which the forward price equals the market consensus view on the future spot price, which is an unbiased predictor.

The general conclusions from the empirical studies investigating the truthfulness of the expectations theory is that for the more widely traded currencies it generally works well. However, there may be numerous periods when relative interest rates (under IRP theory) are the dominant influence. For the corporate manager and treasurer the forward rate can be taken to be unbiased as a predictor of the future spot rate. That is, it has an equal chance of being below, or of being above, the actual spot rate. However, it is a poor predictor – sometimes it is wide of the mark in one direction and sometimes wide of the mark in the other.

This knowledge may be useful to a corporate manager or treasurer when contemplating whether to hedge through using forward rates, with the attendant transaction costs, on a regular basis or whether to adopt a 'do nothing' policy, accepting that sometimes one loses on forex and sometimes one wins. For a firm with numerous transactions, the future spot rate will average the same as the forward rate, and so the 'do nothing' policy may be the cheaper and more attractive option.

The influence of a current-account deficit and capital flows

Another influence on exchange rate movements is the presence or otherwise of an unsustainable balance of payments. If an economy is importing more goods and services than it is exporting it is said to have a **current-account deficit**. The exchange rate will move (in theory) so as to achieve current-account balance. So, an overvalued exchange rate makes exporting difficult and encourages consumers to buy goods produced in other countries. If the exchange rate then declines exporters can sell more abroad and consumers are more likely to purchase the domestically produced version of a product as it becomes cheaper relative to imported goods. The trade deficit is eventually eliminated through this mechanism. The **Fundamental Equilibrium Exchange Rate (FEER)** is the exchange rate that results in a sustainable current-account balance. Any movement away from the FEER is a disequilibrium that sets in train forces that tend to bring the exchange rate back to equilibrium. That is the theory. In reality, there are many factors other than the trade balance causing forex rates to move.

Less than 1 per cent of all forex transactions are related to imports and exports of goods and services. Exchange rates can diverge from FEER for many years if foreign investors are willing to continue to finance a current-account deficit. They do this by buying assets (bonds, shares, companies, property, etc.) in the country with the negative balance of payments. The main influence on these capital transfers of money (and therefore demand for the deficit country's currency) is investors' expectations regarding the returns available on financial assets. If investors believe that the economy with a current-account deficit nevertheless offers good future returns on the bond market or the equity market, say, they will still bid up the value of its currency as they buy it to invest.

In the period 2000–4 the USA ran a very large current-account deficit and yet the currency did not fall in value. Foreign investors thought that the returns offered on US financial assets, particularly shares, were attractive and so continued to support the dollar as they pumped money into the economy. While the American people went on a spending spree (with expenditure higher than take-home pay), in the process buying mountains of foreign-produced goods, money flowed in as financial assets were bought, thus allowing the dollar to remain high. In the later stages of this unsustainable deficit the major buyers of US assets were Asian central banks as countries such as China and Japan bought US Treasury bills and bonds to inject demand for dollars so that their exporters did not suffer from a rising currency against the dollar. Of course, it was widely recognised that the dollar could plummet should overseas investors ever start to believe that the US economic miracle is over (or that it was not really a productivity miracle after all) as they sell US financial assets, sell the dollar and move funds to somewhere else in the world offering more exciting (or safer) returns. This is what happened in 2004–7.

The efficiency of the currency markets

Whether the forex markets are efficient at pricing spot and forward currency rates is hotly debated. If they are efficient then speculators on average should not be able to make abnormal returns by using information to take positions. In an efficient market the best prediction of tomorrow's price is the price today, because prices move in a random walk fashion, depending on the arrival of new information. Prices adjust quickly to new information, but it is impossible to state in advance the direction of future movements because, by its nature, news is unpredictable (it might be 'bad' or it might be 'good').

If the market is efficient, forecasting by corporate treasurers is a pointless exercise because any information the treasurer might use to predict the future will have already been processed by the market participants and be reflected in the price.

There are three levels of market efficiency:

- ***Weak form*** Historic prices and volume information is fully reflected in current prices, and therefore a trader cannot make abnormal profits by observing past price changes and trying to predict the future.
- ***Semi-strong form*** All publicly available information is fully reflected in prices, and therefore abnormal profits are not available by acting on information once it is made public.
- ***Strong form*** Public and private (that is, available to insiders, for example those working for a central bank) information is reflected in prices.

Much empirical research has been conducted into currency market efficiency and the overall conclusion is that the question remains open. Some strategies, on some occasions, have produced handsome profits. On the other hand, many studies show a high degree of efficiency with little opportunity for abnormal reward. Most of the studies examine the major trading currencies of the world – perhaps there is more potential for the discovery of inefficiency in the more exotic currencies. Central bank intervention in foreign exchange markets also seems to be a cause of inefficiency.

As far as ordinary humble corporate treasurers are concerned, trying to outwit the market can be exciting, but it can also be dangerous. Alan Greenspan, former chairman of the US Federal Reserve, said, 'To my knowledge no model projecting movements in exchange rates is superior to tossing a coin.'[9]

---

[9] Quoted in Samuel Brittan, 'The dollar needs benign neglect', *Financial Times*, 30 January 2004, p. 21.

Concluding comments

Managers need to be aware of, and to assess, the risk to which their firms are exposed. The risk that arises because exchange rates move over time is one of the most important for managers to consider. Once the extent of the exposure is known managers then need to judge what, if anything, is to be done about it. Sometimes the threat to the firm and the returns to shareholders are so great as to call for robust risk-reducing action. In other circumstances the cost of hedging outweighs the benefit. Analysing and appraising the extent of the problem and weighing up alternative responses are where managerial judgement comes to the fore. Knowledge of derivatives markets and money markets, and of the need for flexible manufacturing, marketing and financing structures, is useful background, but the key managerial skill required is discernment in positioning the company to cope with forex risk. The ability sometimes to stand back from the fray, objectively assess the cost of each risk-reducing option and say, 'No, this risk is to be taken on the chin because in my judgement the costs of managing the risk reduce shareholder wealth with little to show for it,' is sometimes required.

Key points and concepts

- An **exchange rate** is the price of one currency expressed in terms of another.
- **Exchange rates are quoted** with a bid rate (the rate at which you can buy) and an offer rate (the rate at which you can sell).
- **Forex shifts can affect:**
  - income received from abroad;
  - amounts paid for imports;
  - the valuation of foreign assets and liabilities;
  - the long-term viability of foreign operations;
  - the acceptability of an overseas project.
- The **foreign exchange market** grew dramatically over the last quarter of the twentieth century. Over US$2,310bn is now traded each day. Most of this trading is between banks rather than for underlying (for example, import/export) reasons.
- **Spot market** transactions take place which are to be settled quickly (usually one or two days later). In the **forward market** a deal is arranged to exchange currencies at some future date at a price agreed now.
- **Transaction risk** is the risk that transactions already entered into, or for which the firm is likely to have a commitment in a foreign currency, will have a variable value.
- **Translation risk** arises because financial data denominated in one currency then expressed in terms of another are affected by exchange-rate movements.
- **Economic risk** Forex movements cause a decline in economic value because of a loss of competitive strength.
- **Transaction risk strategies:**
  - invoice customer in home currency;
  - do nothing;
  - netting;
  - matching;
  - leading and lagging;
  - forward market hedge;
  - money market hedge;
  - futures hedge;
  - currency option hedge.

- One way of **managing translation risk** is to try to match foreign assets and liabilities.
- The **management of economic exposure** requires the maintenance of flexibility with regard to manufacturing (for example, location of sources of supply), marketing (for example, advertising campaign, pricing) and finance (currency).
- The **purchasing power parity (PPP) theory** states that exchange rates will be in equilibrium when their domestic purchasing powers at that rate are equivalent. In an inflationary environment the relationship between two countries' inflation rates and the spot exchange rates between two points in time is (with the USA and the UK as examples):

$$\frac{1 + I_{US}}{1 + I_{UK}} = \frac{US\$/£_1}{US\$/£_0}$$

- The **interest rate parity (IRP) theory** holds true when the difference between spot and forward exchange rates is equal to the differential between the interest rates available in the two currencies. Using the USA and the UK currencies as examples:

$$\frac{1 + r_{US}}{1 + r_{UK}} = \frac{US\$/£_F}{US\$/£_S}$$

- The **expectations theory** states that the current forward exchange rate is an unbiased predictor of the spot rate at that point in the future.
- The **Fundamental Equilibrium Exchange Rate** (FEER) is the exchange rate that results in a sustainable current account balance.
- **Flows of money for investment** in financial assets across national borders can be an important influence on forex rates.
- The currency markets are generally **efficient**, but there is evidence suggesting pockets of inefficiency.

References and further reading

Buckley, A. (2003) *Multinational Finance.* 5th edn. London: FT Prentice Hall.

There is much more in this book than in this chapter on FX risk and other aspects of companies dealing overseas.

Desai, M.A. (2004) 'Foreign exchange markets and transactions'. Harvard Business School note. (Available at Harvard Business School website.)

A very easy-to-follow introduction to the basics of forex markets.

Eiteman, D.K, Stonehill, A.I and Moffett, M.H. (2007) *Multinational Business Finance.* 11th edn. Reading, MA: Pearson/Addison Wesley.

A good introduction to many financial aspects of running a multinational business. Easy to read. Useful case studies.

Hallwood, C.P. and MacDonald, R. (2000) *International Money and Finance.* 3rd edn. Massachusetts and Oxford: Blackwell.

Detailed discussion of economic aspects of forex.

Levi, M.D. (2005) *International Finance.* 4th edn. New York: Routledge.

Covers the international markets and the international aspects of finance decisions for corporations in an accessible style. US based.

Madura, J. and Fox, R. (2007) *International Financial Management.* London: Thomson.

A good introductory book that goes into much more depth than this chapter.

Taylor, F. (2003) *Mastering Foreign Exchange and Currency Options.* 2nd edn. London: FT Prentice Hall.

A good introduction to the technicalities of the forex markets and their derivatives. Plenty of practical examples.

Taylor, F. (2007) *Mastering Derivatives Markets.* 3rd edn. London: FT Prentice Hall.

Contains some easy-to-read sections on currency derivatives.

Vaitilingam, R. (2005) *The Financial Times Guide to Using the Financial Pages.* 5th edn. London: FT Prentice Hall.

A helpful guide to the way in which the *Financial Times* reports on the forex markets, among others.

Valdez, S. (2007) *An Introduction to Global Financial Markets.* 5th edn. Basingstoke: Palgrave Macmillan.

A clear and concise introduction to the international financial scene.

Websites

www.bis.org	Bank for International Settlements
www.bloomberg.co.uk	Bloomberg
www.reuters.co.uk	Reuters
www.ft.com	*Financial Times*
www.bankofengland.co.uk	Bank of England
www.ecb.int	European Central Bank
www.nybotlive.com	New York Board of Trade
www.cme.com	Chicago Mercantile Exchange
www.euronext.com	Euronext-liffe

Case study recommendations

- Jaguar plc. – 1984. Authors: Timothy A. Luehrman and William T. Schiano (1990). Harvard Business School.
- Dozier Industries. Author: Bruce McKern (2002) Stanford Graduate School of Business (available on Harvard website).
- Hedging Currency risks at AIFS. Authors: Mihir A. Desai, Vincent Dessain and Anders Sjôman (2005) Harvard Business School.
- Foreign exchange hedging strategies at General Motors: Transactional and translational exposures. Authors: Mihir A Desai and Mark F. Veblen (2005) Harvard Business School.

Please see www.pearsoned.co.uk/arnold for case study synopses

Self-review questions

1 Describe the difference between the spot and forward currency markets.

2 Explain through a simple example how the forward market can be used to hedge against a currency risk.

3 Define the following in relation to foreign exchange:

a transaction risk;
b translation risk;
c economic risk.

4 What are the advantages and disadvantages of responding to foreign exchange risk by: **a** invoicing in your currency; **b** doing nothing?

5 Draw out the difference between netting and matching by describing both.

6 What is a money market hedge, and what are leading and lagging?

7 How does a currency future differ from a currency forward?

8 Compare hedging using forwards with hedging using options.

9 Describe how you would manage translation and economic risk.

10 Explain the purchasing power parity (PPP) theory of exchange-rate determination.

11 Describe the relationship between spot rates and forward rates under the interest rate parity (IRP) theory.

12 What is the expectations theory?

Questions and problems

myfinancelab **Questions with an icon are also available for practice in MyFinanceLab with additional supporting resources.**

For those questions marked with an asterisk* the answers are given in the Lecturer's guide.

1 Answer the following given that the rate of exchange between the Japanese yen and sterling is quoted at ¥/£188.869 – 189.131:

- a How many pounds will a company obtain if it sold ¥1m?
- b What is the cost of £500,000?
- c How many yen would be received from selling £1m?
- d What is the cost of buying ¥100,000?

2 On 1 April an Australian exporter sells A$10m of coal to a New Zealand company. The importer is sent an invoice for NZ$11m payable in six months. The spot rate of exchange between the Australian and New Zealand dollars is NZ$1.1/A$.

Required

- a If the spot rate of exchange six months later is NZ$1.2/A$ what exchange rate gain or loss will be made by the Australian exporter?
- b If the spot rate of exchange six months later is NZ$1.05/A$ what exchange rate gain or loss will be made by the Australian exporter?
- c A six-month forward is available at NZ$1.09/A$. Show how risk can be reduced using the forward.
- d Discuss the relative merits of using forwards and options to hedge forex risk.

3 Describe the main types of risk facing an organisation which has dealings in a foreign currency. Can all these risks be hedged, and should all these risks be hedged at all times?

4* (*Examination level*)

a A UK company exports machine parts to South Africa on three months' credit. The invoice totals R150m and the current spot rate is R7.46/£. Exchange rates have been volatile in recent months and the directors are concerned that forex rates might move so as to make the export deal unprofitable. They are considering three hedge strategies:

- i forward market hedge;
- ii money market hedge;
- iii option hedge.

Other information:

- three-month forward rate: R7.5/£;
- interest payable for three months' borrowing in rand: 2.5 per cent for the three months (not an annual rate);
- a three-month American-style rand put, sterling call option is available for R150m with a strike price of R7.5/£ for a premium payable now of £400,000 on the over-the-counter market.

Required

Show how the hedging strategies might work. Use the following assumed spot rates at the end of three months in order to illustrate the nature of each of the hedges:

R7.00/£.
R8.00/£.

b Explain why it may not always make sense for a company to hedge forex risk. ?

5 British Steel (Corus) suffered greatly as a result of the high value of sterling because it is a major exporter (as are many of its customers). Consider the range of approaches British Steel could have taken to reduce both its transaction and economic exposure.

6 Describe how foreign exchange changes can undermine the competitive position of the firm. Suggest some measures to reduce this risk.

7 a A basket of goods sells for SFr2,000 in Switzerland when the same basket of goods sells for £1,000 in the UK. The current exchange rate is SFr2.0/£. Over the forthcoming year inflation in Switzerland is estimated to be 2 per cent and in the UK, 4 per cent. If the purchasing power parity theory holds true what will the exchange rate be at the end of the year?

b What factors prevent the PPP always holding true in the short run? ?

8 a The rate of interest available on a one-year government bond in Canada is 5 per cent. A similar-risk bond in Australia yields 7 per cent. The current spot rate of exchange is C$1.02/A$. What will be the one-year forward rate if the market obeys the interest rate parity theory?

b Describe the expectation theory of foreign exchange. ?

9* (*Examination level*) Lozenge plc has taken delivery of 50,000 electronic devices from a Malaysian company. The seller is in a strong bargaining position and has priced the devices in Malaysian dollars at M$12 each. It has granted Lozenge three months' credit.

The Malaysian interest rate is 3 per cent per quarter.

Lozenge has all its money tied up in its operations but could borrow in sterling at 3 per cent per quarter (three months) if necessary.

Forex rates	Malaysian dollar/£
Spot	5.4165
Three-month forward	5.425

A three-month sterling put, Malaysian dollar call currency option with a strike price of M$5.425/£ for M$600,000 is available for a premium of M$15,000.

Required

Discuss and illustrate three hedging strategies available to Lozenge. Weigh up the advantages and disadvantages of each strategy. Show all calculations. ?

10 The spot rate between the euro and the US dollar is €1.77/US$ and the expected annual rates of inflation are expected to be 2 per cent and 5 per cent respectively.

a If the purchasing power parity theory holds, what will the spot rate of exchange be in one year?

b If the interest rates available on government bonds are 6 per cent in the Eurozone and 9 per cent in the USA, and the interest rate parity theory holds, what is the current one-year forward rate?

11 The spot rate of exchange is Won1,507/£ between Korea and the UK. The one-month forward rate is Won1,450/£. A UK company has exported goods to Korea invoiced in Won to the value of Won1,507m on one month's credit.

To borrow in Won for one month will cost 0.5 per cent, whereas to borrow in sterling for one month will cost 0.6 per cent of the amount borrowed.

Required

a Show how the forward market can be used to hedge.
b Show how the money market can be used to hedge.

?

myfinancelab ***Now retake your diagnostic test for Chapter 25 to check your progress and update your study plan.***

Assignments

1 Examine a recent import or export deal at a company you know well. Write a report detailing the extent of exposure to transaction risk prior to any hedge activity. Describe the risk-reducing steps taken, if any, and critically compare alternative strategies.

2 Write a report for a company you know well, describing the extent to which it is exposed to transaction, translation and economic risk. Consider ways of coping with these risks and recommend a plan of action.

Appendices

Appendix I
Future value of £1 at compound interest

Interest rate

Periods	1	2	3	4	5	6	7	8	9	10	11	12	13	14	15	
1	1.0100	1.0200	1.0300	1.0400	1.0500	1.0600	1.0700	1.0800	1.0900	1.1000	1.1100	1.1200	1.1300	1.1400	1.1500	1
2	1.0201	1.0404	1.0609	1.0816	1.1025	1.1236	1.1449	1.1664	1.1881	1.2100	1.2321	1.2544	1.2769	1.2996	1.3225	2
3	1.0303	1.0612	1.0927	1.1249	1.1576	1.1910	1.2250	1.2597	1.2950	1.3310	1.3676	1.4049	1.4429	1.4815	1.5209	3
4	1.0406	1.0824	1.1255	1.1699	1.2155	1.2625	1.3108	1.3605	1.4116	1.4641	1.5181	1.5735	1.6305	1.6890	1.7490	4
5	1.0510	1.1041	1.1593	1.2167	1.2763	1.3382	1.4026	1.4693	1.5386	1.6105	1.6851	1.7623	1.8424	1.9254	2.0114	5
6	1.0615	1.1262	1.1941	1.2653	1.3401	1.4185	1.5007	1.5869	1.6771	1.7716	1.8704	1.9738	2.0820	2.1950	2.3131	6
7	1.0721	1.1487	1.2299	1.3159	1.4071	1.5036	1.6058	1.7138	1.8280	1.9487	2.0762	2.2107	2.3526	2.5023	2.6600	7
8	1.0829	1.1717	1.2668	1.3686	1.4775	1.5938	1.7182	1.8509	1.9926	2.1436	2.3045	2.4760	2.6584	2.8526	3.0590	8
9	1.0937	1.1951	1.3048	1.4233	1.5513	1.6895	1.8385	1.9990	2.1719	2.3579	2.5580	2.7731	3.0040	3.2519	3.5179	9
10	1.1046	1.2190	1.3439	1.4802	1.6289	1.7908	1.9672	2.1589	2.3674	2.5937	2.8394	3.1058	3.3946	3.7072	4.0456	10
11	1.1157	1.2434	1.3842	1.5395	1.7103	1.8983	2.1049	2.3316	2.5804	2.8531	3.1518	3.4785	3.8359	4.2262	4.6524	11
12	1.1268	1.2682	1.4258	1.6010	1.7959	2.0122	2.2522	2.5182	2.8127	3.1384	3.4985	3.8960	4.3345	4.8179	5.3503	12
13	1.1381	1.2936	1.4685	1.6651	1.8856	2.1329	2.4098	2.7196	3.0658	3.4523	3.8833	4.3635	4.8980	5.4924	6.1528	13
14	1.1495	1.3195	1.5126	1.7317	1.9799	2.2609	2.5785	2.9372	3.3417	3.7975	4.3104	4.8871	5.5348	6.2613	7.0757	14
15	1.1610	1.3459	1.5580	1.8009	2.0789	2.3966	2.7590	3.1722	3.6425	4.1772	4.7846	5.4736	6.2543	7.1379	8.1371	15
16	1.1726	1.3728	1.6047	1.8730	2.1829	2.5404	2.9522	3.4259	3.9703	4.5950	5.3109	6.1304	7.0673	8.1372	9.3576	16
17	1.1843	1.4002	1.6528	1.9479	2.2920	2.6928	3.1588	3.7000	4.3276	5.0545	5.8951	6.8660	7.9861	9.2765	10.7613	17
18	1.1961	1.4282	1.7024	2.0258	2.4066	2.8543	3.3799	3.9960	4.7171	5.5599	6.5436	7.6900	9.0243	10.5752	12.3755	18
19	1.2081	1.4568	1.7535	2.1068	2.5270	3.0256	3.6165	4.3157	5.1417	6.1159	7.2633	8.6128	10.1974	12.0557	14.2318	19
20	1.2202	1.4859	1.8061	2.1911	2.6533	3.2071	3.8697	4.6610	5.6044	6.7275	8.0623	9.6463	11.5231	13.7435	16.3665	20
25	1.2824	1.6406	2.0938	2.6658	3.3864	4.2919	5.4274	6.8485	8.6231	10.8347	13.5855	17.0001	21.2305	26.4619	32.9190	25

Periods	16	17	18	19	20	21	22	23	24	25	26	27	28	29	30	
1	1.1600	1.1700	1.1800	1.1900	1.2000	1.2100	1.2200	1.2300	1.2400	1.2500	1.2600	1.2700	1.2800	1.2900	1.3000	1
2	1.3456	1.3689	1.3924	1.4161	1.4400	1.4641	1.4884	1.5129	1.5376	1.5625	1.5876	1.6129	1.6384	1.6641	1.6900	2
3	1.5609	1.6016	1.6430	1.6852	1.7280	1.7716	1.8158	1.8609	1.9066	1.9531	2.0004	2.0484	2.0972	2.1467	2.1970	3
4	1.8106	1.8739	1.9388	2.0053	2.0736	2.1436	2.2153	2.2889	2.3642	2.4414	2.5205	2.6014	2.6844	2.7692	2.8561	4
5	2.1003	2.1924	2.2878	2.3864	2.4883	2.5937	2.7027	2.8153	2.9316	3.0518	3.1758	3.3038	3.4360	3.5723	3.7129	5
6	2.4364	2.5652	2.6996	2.8398	2.9860	3.1384	3.2973	3.4628	3.6352	3.8147	4.0015	4.1959	4.3980	4.6083	4.8268	6
7	2.8262	3.0012	3.1855	3.3793	3.5832	3.7975	4.0227	4.2593	4.5077	4.7684	5.0419	5.3288	5.6295	5.9447	6.2749	7
8	3.2784	3.5115	3.7589	4.0214	4.2998	4.5950	4.9077	5.2389	5.5895	5.9605	6.3528	6.7675	7.2058	7.6686	8.1573	8
9	3.8030	4.1084	4.4355	4.7854	5.1598	5.5599	5.9874	6.4439	6.9310	7.4506	8.0045	8.5948	9.2234	9.8925	10.6045	9
10	4.4114	4.8068	5.2338	5.6947	6.1917	6.7275	7.3046	7.9259	8.5944	9.3132	10.0857	10.9153	11.8059	12.7614	13.7858	10
11	5.1173	5.6240	6.1759	6.7767	7.4301	8.1403	8.9117	9.7489	10.6571	11.6415	12.7080	13.8625	15.1116	16.4622	17.9216	11
12	5.9360	6.5801	7.2876	8.0642	8.9161	9.8497	10.8722	11.9912	13.2148	14.5519	16.0120	17.6053	19.3428	21.2362	23.2981	12
13	6.8858	7.6987	8.5994	9.5964	10.6993	11.9182	13.2641	14.7491	16.3863	18.1899	20.1752	22.3588	24.7588	27.3947	30.2875	13
14	7.9875	9.0075	10.1472	11.4198	12.8392	14.4210	16.1822	18.1414	20.3191	22.7374	25.4207	28.3957	31.6913	35.3391	39.3738	14
15	9.2655	10.5387	11.9737	13.5895	15.4070	17.4494	19.7423	22.3140	25.1956	28.4217	32.0301	36.0625	40.5648	45.5875	51.1859	15
16	10.7480	12.3303	14.1290	16.1715	18.4884	21.1138	24.0856	27.4462	31.2426	35.5271	40.3579	45.7994	51.9230	58.8079	66.5417	16
17	12.4677	14.4265	16.6722	19.2441	22.1861	25.5477	29.3844	33.7588	38.7408	44.4089	50.8510	58.1652	66.4614	75.8621	86.5042	17
18	14.4625	16.8790	19.6733	22.9005	26.6233	30.9127	35.8490	41.5233	48.0386	55.5112	64.0722	73.8698	85.0706	97.8622	112.4554	18
19	16.7765	19.7484	23.2144	27.2516	31.9480	37.4043	43.7358	51.0737	59.5679	69.3889	80.7310	93.8147	108.8904	126.2422	146.1920	19
20	19.4608	23.1056	27.3930	32.4294	38.3376	45.2593	53.3576	62.8206	73.8641	86.7362	101.7211	119.1446	139.3797	162.8524	190.0496	20
25	40.8742	50.6578	62.6686	77.3881	95.3962	117.3909	144.2101	176.8593	216.5420	264.6978	323.0454	393.6344	478.9049	581.7585	705.6410	25

Appendix II

Present value of £1 at compound interest

Interest rate

Periods	1	2	3	4	5	6	7	8	9	10	11	12	13	14	15	
1	0.9901	0.9804	0.9709	0.9615	0.9524	0.9434	0.9346	0.9259	0.9174	0.9091	0.9009	0.8929	0.8850	0.8772	0.8696	1
2	0.9803	0.9612	0.9426	0.9246	0.9070	0.8900	0.8734	0.8573	0.8417	0.8264	0.8116	0.7972	0.7831	0.7695	0.7561	2
3	0.9706	0.9423	0.9151	0.8890	0.8638	0.8396	0.8163	0.7938	0.7722	0.7513	0.7312	0.7118	0.6931	0.6750	0.6575	3
4	0.9610	0.9238	0.8885	0.8548	0.8227	0.7921	0.7629	0.7350	0.7084	0.6830	0.6587	0.6355	0.6133	0.5921	0.5718	4
5	0.9515	0.9057	0.8626	0.8219	0.7835	0.7473	0.7130	0.6806	0.6499	0.6209	0.5935	0.5674	0.5428	0.5194	0.4972	5
6	0.9420	0.8880	0.8375	0.7903	0.7462	0.7050	0.6663	0.6302	0.5963	0.5645	0.5346	0.5066	0.4803	0.4556	0.4323	6
7	0.9327	0.8706	0.8131	0.7599	0.7107	0.6651	0.6227	0.5835	0.5470	0.5132	0.4817	0.4523	0.4251	0.3996	0.3759	7
8	0.9235	0.8535	0.7894	0.7307	0.6768	0.6274	0.5820	0.5403	0.5019	0.4665	0.4339	0.4039	0.3762	0.3506	0.3269	8
9	0.9143	0.8368	0.7664	0.7026	0.6446	0.5919	0.5439	0.5002	0 4604	0.4241	0.3909	0.3606	0.3329	0.3075	0.2843	9
10	0.9053	0.8203	0.7441	0.6756	0.6139	0.5584	0.5083	0.4632	0.4224	0.3855	0.3522	0.3220	0.2946	0.2697	0.2472	10
11	0.8963	0.8043	0.7224	0.6496	0.5847	0.5268	0.4751	0.4289	0.3875	0.3505	0.3173	0.2875	0 2607	0.2366	0.2149	11
12	0.8874	0.7885	0.7014	0.6246	0.5568	0.4970	0.4440	0.3971	0.3555	0.3186	0.2858	0.2567	0.2307	0.2076	0.1869	12
13	0.8787	0.7730	0.6810	0.6006	0.5303	0.4688	0.4150	0.3677	0.3262	0.2897	0.2575	0.2292	0.2042	0.1821	0.1625	13
14	0.8700	0.7579	0.6611	0.5775	0.5051	0.4423	0.3878	0.3405	0.2992	0.2633	0.2320	0.2046	0.1807	0.1597	0.1413	14
15	0.8613	0.7430	0.6419	0.5553	0.4810	0.4173	0.3624	0.3152	0.2745	0.2394	0.2090	0.1827	0.1599	0.1401	0.1229	15
16	0.8528	0.7284	0.6232	0.5339	0.4581	0.3936	0.3387	0.2919	0.2519	0.2176	0.1883	0.1631	0.1415	0.1229	0.1069	16
17	0.8444	0.7142	0.6050	0.5134	0.4363	0.3714	0.3166	0.2703	0.2311	0.1978	0.1696	0.1456	0.1252	0.1078	0.0929	17
18	0.8360	0.7002	0.5874	0.4936	0.4155	0.3503	0.2959	0.2502	0.2120	0.1799	0.1528	0.1300	0.1108	0.0946	0.0808	18
19	0.8277	0.6864	0.5703	0.4746	0.3957	0.3305	0.2765	0.2317	0.1945	0.1635	0.1377	0.1161	0.0981	0.0829	0.0703	19
20	0.8195	0.6730	0.5537	0.4564	0.3769	0.3118	0.2584	0.2145	0.1784	0.1486	0.1240	0.1037	0.0868	0.0728	0.0611	20
25	0.7795	0.6095	0.4776	0.3751	0.2953	0.2330	0.1842	0.1460	0.1160	0.0923	0.0736	0.0588	0.0471	0.0378	0.0304	25
30	0.7419	0.5521	0.4120	0.3083	0.2314	0.1741	0.1314	0.0994	0.0754	0.0573	0.0437	0.0334	0.0256	0.0196	0.0151	30
35	0.7059	0.5000	0.3554	0.2534	0.1813	0.1301	0.0937	0.0676	0.0490	0.0356	0.0259	0.0189	0.0139	0.0102	0.0075	35
40	0.6717	0.4529	0.3066	0.2083	0.1420	0.0972	0.0668	0.0460	0.0318	0.0221	0.0154	0.0107	0.0075	0.0053	0.0037	40
45	0.6391	0.4102	0.2644	0.1712	0.1113	0.0727	0.0476	0.0313	0.0207	0.0137	0.0091	0.0061	0.0041	0.0027	0.0019	45
50	0.6080	0.3715	0.2281	0.1407	0.0872	0.0543	0.0339	0.0213	0.0134	0.0085	0.0054	0.0035	0.0022	0.0014	0.0009	50

Periods	16	17	18	19	20	21	22	23	24	25	26	27	28	29	30	
1	0.8621	0.8547	0.8475	0.8403	0.8333	0.8264	0.8197	0.8130	0.8065	0.8000	0.7937	0.7874	0.7812	0.7752	0.7692	1
2	0.7432	0.7305	0.7182	0.7062	0.6944	0.6830	0.6719	0.6610	0.6504	0.6400	0.6299	0.6200	0.6104	0.6009	0.5917	2
3	0.6407	0.6244	0.6086	0.5934	0.5787	0.5645	0.5507	0.5374	0.5245	0.5120	0.4999	0.4882	0.4768	0.4658	0.4552	3
4	0.5523	0.5337	0.5158	0.4987	0.4823	0.4665	0.4514	0.4369	0.4230	0.4096	0.3968	0 3844	0.3725	0.3611	0.3501	4
5	0.4761	0.4561	0.4371	0.4190	0.4019	0.3855	0.3700	0.3552	0.3411	0.3277	0.3149	0.3027	0.2910	0.2799	0.2693	5
6	0.4104	0.3898	0.3704	0.3521	0.3349	0.3186	0.3033	0.2888	0.2751	0.2621	0.2499	0.2383	0.2274	0.2170	0.2072	6
7	0.3538	0.3332	0.3139	0.2959	0.2791	0.2633	0.2486	0.2348	0.2218	0.2097	0.1983	0.1877	0.1776	0.1682	0.1594	7
8	0.3050	0.2848	0.2660	0.2487	0.2326	0.2176	0.2038	0.1909	0.1789	0.1678	0.1574	0.1478	0.1388	0 1304	0.1226	8
9	0.2630	0.2434	0.2255	0.2090	0.1938	0.1799	0.1670	0.1552	0.1443	0.1342	0.1249	0.1164	0.1084	0.1011	0.0943	9
10	0.2267	0.2080	0.1911	0.1756	0.1615	0.1486	0.1369	0.1262	0.1164	0.1074	0.0992	0.0916	0.0847	0.0784	0.0725	10
11	0.1954	0.1778	0.1619	0.1476	0.1346	0.1228	0.1122	0.1026	0.0938	0.0859	0.0787	0.0721	0.0662	0.0607	0.0558	11
12	0.1685	0.1520	0.1372	0.1240	0.1122	0.1015	0.0920	0.0834	0.0757	0.0687	0.0625	0.0568	0.0517	0.0471	0.0429	12
13	0.1452	0.1299	0.1163	0.1042	0.0935	0.0839	0.0754	0.0678	0.0610	0.0550	0.0496	0.0447	0.0404	0.0365	0.0330	13
14	0.1252	0.1110	0.0985	0.0876	0.0779	0.0693	0.0618	0.0551	0.0492	0.0440	0.0393	0.0352	0.0316	0.0283	0.0254	14
15	0.1079	0.0949	0.0835	0.0736	0.0649	0.0573	0.0507	0.0448	0.0397	0.0352	0.0312	0.0277	0.0247	0.0219	0.0195	15
16	0.0930	0.0811	0.0708	0.0618	0.0541	0.0474	0.0415	0.0364	0.0320	0.0281	0.0248	0.0218	0.0193	0.0170	0.0150	16
17	0.0802	0.0693	0.0600	0.0520	0.0451	0.0391	0.0340	0.0296	0.0258	0.0225	0.0197	0.0172	0.0150	0.0132	0.0116	17
18	0.0691	0.0592	0.0508	0.0437	0.0376	0.0323	0.0279	0.0241	0.0208	0.0180	0.0156	0.0135	0.0118	0.0102	0.0089	18
19	0.0596	0.0506	0.0431	0.0367	0.0313	0.0267	0.0229	0.0196	0.0168	0.0144	0.0124	0.0107	0.0092	0.0079	0.0068	19
20	0.0514	0.0433	0.0365	0.0308	0.0261	0.0221	0.0187	0.0159	0.0135	0.0115	0.0098	0.0084	0.0072	0.0061	0.0053	20
25	0.0245	0.0197	0.0160	0.0129	0.0105	0.0085	0.0069	0.0057	0.0046	0.0038	0.0031	0.0025	0.0021	0.0017	0.0014	25
30	0.0116	0.0090	0.0070	0.0054	0.0042	0.0033	0.0026	0.0020	0.0016	0.0012	0.0010	0.0008	0.0006	0.0005	0.0004	30
35	0.0055	0.0041	0.0030	0.0023	0.0017	0.0013	0.0009	0.0007	0.0005	0.0004	0.0003	0.0002	0.0002	0.0001	0.0000	35
40	0.0026	0.0019	0.0013	0.0010	0.0007	0.0005	0.0004	0.0003	0.0002	0.0001	0.0001	0.0001	0.0001	0.0000	0.0000	40
45	0.0013	0.0009	0.0006	0.0004	0.0003	0.0002	0.0001	0.0001	0.0001	0.0000	0.0000	0.0000	0.0000	0.0000	0.0000	45
50	0.0006	0.0004	0.0003	0.0002	0.0001	0.0001	0.0000	0.0000	0.0000	0.0000	0.0000	0.0000	0.0000	0.0000	0.0000	50

Appendix III

Present value of an annuity of £1 at compound interest

$$\frac{1 - 1/(1 + i)^n}{i} \times A$$

Interest rate

Periods	1	2	3	4	5	6	7	8	9	10	11	12	13	14	15	
1	0.9901	0.9804	0.9709	0.9615	0.9524	0.9434	0.9346	0.9259	0.9174	0.9091	0.9009	0.8929	0.8850	0.8772	0.8696	1
2	1.9704	1.9416	1.9135	1.8861	1.8594	1.8334	1.8080	1.7833	1.7591	1.7355	1.7125	1.6901	1.6681	1.6467	1.6257	2
3	2.9410	2.8839	2.8286	2.7751	2.7232	2.6730	2.6243	2.5771	2.5313	2.4869	2.4437	2.4018	2.3612	2.3216	2.2832	3
4	3.9020	3.8077	3.7171	3.6299	3.5460	3.4651	3.3872	3.3121	3.2397	3.1699	3.1024	3.0373	2.9745	2.9137	2.8550	4
5	4.8534	4.7135	4.5797	4.4518	4.3295	4.2124	4.1002	3.9927	3.8897	3.7908	3.6959	3.6048	3.5172	3.4331	3.3522	5
6	5.7955	5.6014	5.4172	5.2421	5.0757	4.9173	4.7665	4.6229	4.4859	4.3553	4.2305	4.1114	3.9975	3.8887	3.7845	6
7	6.7282	6.4720	6.2303	6.0021	5.7864	5.5824	5.3893	5.2064	5.0330	4.8684	4.7122	4.5638	4.4226	4.2883	4.1604	7
8	7.6517	7.3255	7.0197	6.7327	6.4632	6 2098	5.9713	5.7466	5.5348	5.3349	5.1461	4.9676	4.7988	4.6389	4.4873	8
9	8.5660	8.1622	7.7861	7.4353	7.1078	6.8017	6.5152	6.2469	5.9952	5.7590	5.5370	5.3282	5.1317	4.9464	4.7716	9
10	9.4713	8.9826	8.5302	8.1109	7.7217	7.3601	7.0236	6.7101	6.4177	6.1446	5.8892	5.6502	5.4262	5.2161	5.0188	10
11	10.3676	9.7868	9.2526	8.7605	8.3064	7.8869	7.4987	7.1390	6.8052	6.4951	6.2065	5.9377	5.6869	5.4527	5.2337	11
12	11.2551	10.5753	9.9540	9.3851	8.8633	8.3838	7.9427	7.5361	7.1607	6.8137	6.4924	6.1944	5.9176	5.6603	5.4206	12
13	12.1337	11.3484	10.6350	9.9856	9.3936	8.8527	8.3577	7.9038	7.4869	7.1034	6.7499	6.4235	6.1218	5.8424	5.5831	13
14	13.0037	12.1062	11.2961	10.5631	9.8986	9.2950	8.7455	8.2442	7.7862	7.3667	6.9819	6.6282	6.3025	6.0021	5.7245	14
15	13.8651	12.8493	11.9379	11.1184	10.3797	9.7122	9.1079	8.5595	8.0607	7.6061	7.1909	6.8109	6.4624	6.1422	5.8474	15
16	14.7179	13.5777	12.5611	11.6523	10.8378	10.1059	9.4466	8.8514	8.3126	7.8237	7.3792	6.9740	6.6039	6.2651	5.9542	16
17	15.5623	14.2919	13.1661	12.1657	11.2741	10.4773	9.7632	9.1216	8.5436	8.0216	7.5488	7.1196	6.7291	6.3729	6.0472	17
18	16.3983	14.9920	13.7535	12.6593	11.6896	10.8276	10.0591	9.3719	8.7556	8.2014	7.7016	7.2497	6.8399	6.4674	6.1280	18
19	17.2260	15.6785	14.3238	13.1339	12.0853	11.1581	10.3356	9.6036	8.9501	8.3649	7.8393	7.3658	6.9380	6.5504	6.1982	19
20	18.0456	16.3514	14.8775	13.5903	12.4622	11.4699	10.5940	9.8181	9.1285	8.5136	7.9633	7.4694	7.0248	6.6231	6.2593	20
25	22.0232	19.5235	17.4131	15.6221	14.0939	12.7834	11.6536	10.6748	9.8226	9.0770	8.4217	7.8431	7.3300	6.8729	6.4641	25
30	25.8077	22.3965	19.6004	17.2920	15.3725	13.7648	12.4090	11.2578	10.2737	9.4269	8.6938	8.0552	7.4957	7.0027	6.5660	30
35	29.4086	24.9986	21.4872	18.6646	16.3742	14.4982	12.9477	11.6546	10.5668	9.6442	8.8552	8.1755	7.5856	7.0700	6.6166	35
40	32.8347	27.3555	23.1148	19.7928	17.1591	15.0463	13.3317	11.9246	10.7574	9.7791	8.9511	8.2438	7.6344	7.1050	6.6418	40
45	36.0945	29.4902	24.5187	20.7200	17.7741	15.4558	13.6055	12.1084	10.8812	9.8628	9.0079	8.2825	7.6609	7.1232	6.6543	45
50	39.1961	31.4236	25.7298	21.4822	18.2559	15.7619	13.8007	12.2335	10.9617	9.9148	9.0417	8.3045	7.6752	7.1327	6.6605	50

Periods	16	17	18	19	20	21	22	23	24	25	26	27	28	29	30	
1	0.8621	0.8547	0.8475	0.8403	0.8333	0.8264	0.8197	0.8130	0.8065	0.8000	0.7937	0.7874	0.7812	0.7752	0.7692	1
2	1.6052	1.5852	1.5656	1.5465	1.5278	1.5095	1.4915	1.4740	1.4568	1.4400	1.4235	1.4074	1.3916	1.3761	1.3609	2
3	2.2459	2.2096	2.1743	2.1399	2.1065	2.0739	2.0422	2.0114	1.9813	1.9520	1.9234	1.8956	1.8684	1.8420	1.8161	3
4	2.7982	2.7432	2.6901	2.6386	2.5887	2.5404	2.4936	2.4483	2.4043	2.3616	2.3202	2.2800	2.2410	2.2031	2.1662	4
5	3.2743	3.1993	3.1272	3.0576	2.9906	2.9260	2.8636	2.8035	2.7454	2.6893	2.6351	2.5827	2.5320	2.4830	2.4356	5
6	3.6847	3.5892	3.4976	3.4098	3.3255	3.2446	3.1669	3.0923	3.0205	2.9514	2.8850	2.8210	2.7594	2.7000	2.6427	6
7	4.0386	3.9224	3.8115	3.7057	3.6046	3.5079	3.4155	3.3270	3.2423	3.1611	3.0833	3.0087	2.9370	2.8682	2.8021	7
8	4.3436	4.2072	4.0776	3.9544	3.8372	3.7256	3.6193	3.5179	3.4212	3.3289	3.2407	3.1564	3.0758	2.9986	2.9247	8
9	4.6065	4.4506	4.3030	4.1633	4.0310	3.9054	3.7863	3.6731	3.5655	3.4631	3.3657	3.2728	3.1842	3.0997	3.0190	9
10	4.8332	4.6586	4.4941	4.3389	4.1925	4.0541	3.9232	3.7993	3.6819	3.5705	3.4648	3.3644	3.2689	3.1781	3.0915	10
11	5.0286	4.8364	4.6560	4.4865	4.3271	4.1769	4.0354	3.9018	3.7757	3.6564	3.5435	3.4365	3.3351	3.2388	3.1473	11
12	5.1971	4.9884	4.7932	4.6105	4.4392	4.2784	4.1274	3.9852	3.8514	3.7251	3.6059	3.4933	3.3868	3.2859	3.1903	12
13	5.3423	5.1183	4.9095	4.7147	4.5327	4.3624	4.2028	4.0530	3.9124	3.7801	3.6555	3.5381	3.4272	3.3224	3.2233	13
14	5.4675	5.2293	5.0081	4.8023	4.6106	4.4317	4.2646	4.1082	3.9616	3.8241	3.6949	3.5733	3.4587	3.3507	3.2487	14
15	5.5755	5.3242	5.0916	4.8759	4.6755	4.4890	4.3152	4.1530	4.0013	3.8593	3.7261	3.6010	3.4834	3.3726	3.2682	15
16	5.6685	5.4053	5.1624	4.9377	4.7296	4.5364	4.3567	4.1894	4.0333	3.8874	3.7509	3.6228	3.5026	3.3896	3.2832	16
17	5.7487	5.4746	5.2223	4.9897	4.7746	4.5755	4.3908	4.2190	4.0591	3.9099	3.7705	3.6400	3.5177	3.4028	3.2948	17
18	5.8178	5.5339	5.2732	5.0333	4.8122	4.6079	4.4187	4.2431	4.0799	3.9279	3.7861	3.6536	3.5294	3.4130	3.3037	18
19	5.8775	5.5845	5.3162	5.0700	4.8435	4.6346	4.4415	4.2627	4.0967	3.9424	3.7985	3.6642	3.5386	3.4210	3.3105	19
20	5.9288	5.6278	5.3527	5.1009	4.8696	4.6567	4.4603	4.2786	4.1103	3.9539	3.8083	3.6726	3.5458	3.4271	3.3158	20
25	6.0971	5.7662	5.4669	5.1951	4.9476	4.7213	4.5139	4.3232	4.1474	3.9849	3.8342	3.6943	3.5640	3.4423	3.3286	25
30	6.1772	5.8294	5.5168	5.2347	4.9789	4.7463	4.5338	4.3391	4.1601	3.9950	3.8424	3.7009	3.5693	3.4466	3.3321	30
35	6.2153	5.8582	5.5386	5.2512	4.9915	4.7559	4.5411	4.3447	4.1644	3.9984	3.8450	3.7028	3.5708	3.4478	3.3330	35
40	6.2335	5.8713	5.5482	5.2582	4.9966	4.7596	4.5439	4.3467	4.1659	3.9995	3.8458	3.7034	3.5712	3.4481	3.3332	40
45	6.2421	5.8773	5.5523	5.2611	4.9986	4.7610	4.5449	4.3474	4.1664	3.9998	3.8460	3.7036	3.5714	3.4482	3.3333	45
50	6.2463	5.8801	5.5541	5.2623	4.9995	4.7616	4.5452	4.3477	4.1666	3.9999	3.8461	3.7037	3.5714	3.4483	3.3333	50

Appendix IV
Future value of an annuity of £1 at compound interest

$$A\left[\frac{(1+i)^n - 1}{i}\right]$$

Interest rate

Periods	1	2	3	4	5	6	7	8	9	10	12	14	16	18	20	25	30	35	40	45	50
1	1.0000	1.0000	1.0000	1.0000	1.0000	1.0000	1.0000	1.0000	1.0000	1.0000	1.0000	1.0000	1.0000	1.0000	1.0000	1.0000	1.0000	1.0000	1.0000	1.0000	1.0000
2	2.0100	2.0200	2.0300	2.0400	2.0500	2.0600	2.0700	2.0800	2.0900	2.1000	2.1200	2.1400	2.1600	2.1800	2.2000	2.2500	2.3000	2.3500	2.400	2.4500	2.5000
3	3.0301	3.0604	3.0909	3.1216	3.1525	3.1836	3.2149	3.2464	3.2781	3.3100	3.3744	3.4396	3.5056	3.5724	3.6400	3.8125	3.9900	4.1725	4.3600	4.5525	4.7500
4	4.0604	4.1216	4.1836	4.2465	4.3101	4.3746	4.4399	4.5061	4.5731	4.6410	4.7793	4.9211	5.0665	5.2154	5.3680	5.7656	6.1870	6.6329	7.1040	7.6011	8.1250
5	5.1010	5.2040	5.3091	5.4163	5.5256	5.6371	5.7507	5.8666	5.9847	6.1051	6.3528	6.6101	6.8771	7.1542	7.4416	8.2070	9.0431	9.9544	10.9456	12.0216	13.1875
6	6.1520	6.3081	6.4684	6.6330	6.8019	6.9753	7.1533	7.3359	7.5233	7.7156	8.1152	8.5355	8.9775	9.4420	9.9299	11.2588	12.7560	14.4834	16.3238	18.4314	20.7813
7	7.2135	7.4343	7.6625	7.8983	8.1420	8.3938	8.6540	8.9228	9.2004	9.4872	10.0890	10.7305	11.4139	12.1415	12.9159	15.0735	17.5828	20.4919	23.8534	27.7255	32.1719
8	8.2857	8.5830	8.8923	9.2142	9.5491	9.8975	10.2598	10.6366	11.0285	11.4359	12.2997	13.2328	14.2401	15.3270	16.4991	19.8419	23.8577	28.6640	34.3947	41.2019	49.2578
9	9.3685	9.7546	10.1591	10.5828	11.0266	11.4913	11.9780	12.4876	13.0210	13.5795	14.7757	16.0853	17.5185	19.0859	20.7989	25.8023	32.0150	39.6964	49.1526	60.7428	74.8867
10	10.4622	10.9497	11.4639	12.0061	12.5779	13.1808	13.8164	14.4866	15.1929	15.9374	17.5487	19.3373	21.3215	23.5213	25.9587	33.2529	42.6195	54.5902	69.8137	89.0771	113.330
11	11.5668	12.1687	12.8078	13.4864	14.2068	14.9716	15.7836	16.6455	17.5603	18.5312	20.6546	23.0445	25.7329	28.7551	32.1504	42.5661	56.4053	74.6967	98.7391	130.162	170.995
12	12.6825	13.4121	14.1920	15.0258	15.9171	16.8699	17.8885	18.9771	20.1407	21.3843	24.1331	27.2707	30.8502	34.9311	39.5805	54.2077	74.3270	101.841	139.235	189.735	257.493
13	13.8093	14.6803	15.6178	16.6268	17.7130	18.8821	20.1406	21.4953	22.9534	24.5227	28.0291	32.0887	36.7862	42.2187	48.4966	68.7596	97.6250	138.485	195.929	276.115	387.239
14	14.9474	15.9739	17.0863	18.2919	19.5986	21.0151	22.5505	24.2149	26.0192	27.9750	32.3926	37.5811	43.6720	50.8180	59.1959	86.9495	127.913	187.954	275.300	401.367	581.859
15	16.0969	17.2934	18.5989	20.0236	21.5786	23.2760	25.1290	27.1521	29.3609	31.7725	37.2797	43.8424	51.6595	60.9653	72.0351	109.687	167.286	254.738	386.420	582.982	873.788
16	17.2579	18.6393	20.1569	21.8245	23.6575	25.6725	27.8881	30.3243	33.0034	35.9497	42.7533	50.9804	60.9250	72.9390	87.4421	138.109	218.472	344.897	541.988	846.324	1311.68
17	18.4304	20.0121	21.7616	23.6975	25.8404	28.2129	30.8402	33.7502	36.9737	40.5447	48.8837	59.1176	71.6730	87.0680	105.931	173.636	285.014	466.611	759.784	1228.17	1968.52
18	19.6147	21.4123	23.4144	25.6454	28.1324	30.9057	33.9990	37.4502	41.3013	45.5992	55.7497	68.3941	84.1407	103.740	128.117	218.045	371.518	630.925	1064.70	1781.85	2953.78
19	20.8109	22.8406	25.1169	27.6712	30.5390	33.7600	37.3790	41.4463	46.0185	51.1591	63.4397	78.9692	98.6032	123.414	154.740	273.556	483.973	852.748	1491.58	2584.68	4431.68
20	22.0190	24.2974	26.8704	29.7781	33.0660	36.7856	40.9955	45.7620	51.1601	57.2750	72.0524	91.0249	115.380	146.628	186.688	342.945	630.165	1152.21	2089.21	3748.78	6648.51
25	28.2432	32.0303	36.4593	41.6459	47.7271	54.8645	63.2490	73.1059	84.7009	98.3471	133.334	181.871	249.214	342.603	471.981	1054.79	2348.80	5176.50	11247.1990	24040.7	50500.3
30	34.7849	40.5681	47.5754	56.0849	66.4388	79.0582	94.4608	113.283	136.308	164.494	241.333	356.787	530.312	790.948	1181.88	3227.17	8729.99	23221.6	60501.1	154107	383500
35	41.6603	49.9945	60.4621	73.6522	90.3203	111.435	138.237	172.317	215.711	271.024	431.663	693.573	1120.71	1816.65	2948.34	9856.76	32422.9	104136	325400	987794	2912217
40	48.8864	60.4020	75.4013	95.0255	120.800	154.762	199.635	259.057	337.882	442.593	767.091	1342.03	2360.76	4163.21	7343.86	30088.7	120393	466960	1750092	6331512	22114663
45	56.4811	71.8927	92.7199	121.029	159.700	212.744	285.749	386.506	525.859	718.905	1358.23	2590.56	4965.27	9531.58	18281.3	91831.5	447019	2093876	9412424	40583319	167933233
50	64.4632	84.5794	112.797	152.667	209.348	290.336	406.529	573.770	815.084	1163.91	2400.02	4994.52	10435.6	21813.1	45497.2	280256	1659761	9389020	50622288	260128295	1275242998

Appendix V
Areas under the standardised normal distribution

z	0.00	0.01	0.02	0.03	0.04	0.05	0.06	0.07	0.08	0.09
0.0	0.0000	0.0040	0.0080	0.0120	0.0160	0.0199	0.0239	0.0279	0.0319	0.0359
0.1	0.0398	0.0438	0.0478	0.0517	0.0557	0.0596	0.0636	0.0675	0.0714	0.0753
0.2	0.0793	0.0832	0.0871	0.0910	0.0948	0.0987	0.1026	0.1064	0.1103	0.1141
0.3	0.1179	0.1217	0.1255	0.1293	0.1331	0.1368	0.1406	0.1443	0.1480	0.1517
0.4	0.1554	0.1591	0.1628	0.1664	0.1700	0.1736	0.1772	0.1808	0.1844	0.1879
0.5	0.1915	0.1950	0.1985	0.2019	0.2054	0.2088	0.2123	0.2157	0.2190	0.2224
0.6	0.2257	0.2291	0.2324	0.2357	0.2389	0.2422	0.2454	0.2486	0.2517	0.2549
0.7	0.2580	0.2611	0.2642	0.2673	0.2704	0.2734	0.2764	0.2794	0.2823	0.2852
0.8	0.2881	0.2910	0.2939	0.2967	0.2995	0.3023	0.3051	0.3078	0.3106	0.3133
0.9	0.3159	0.3186	0.3212	0.3238	0.3264	0.3289	0.3315	0.3340	0.3365	0.3389
1.0	0.3413	0.3438	0.3461	0.3485	0.3508	0.3531	0.3554	0.3577	0.3599	0.3621
1.1	0.3643	0.3665	0.3686	0.3708	0.3729	0.3749	0.3770	0.3790	0.3810	0.3830
1.2	0.3849	0.3869	0.3888	0.3907	0.3925	0.3944	0.3962	0.3980	0.3997	0.4015
1.3	0.4032	0.4049	0.4066	0.4082	0.4099	0.4115	0.4131	0.4147	0.4162	0.4177
1.4	0.4192	0.4207	0.4222	0.4236	0.4251	0.4265	0.4279	0.4292	0.4306	0.4319
1.5	0.4332	0.4345	0.4357	0.4370	0.4382	0.4394	0.4406	0.4418	0.4429	0.4441
1.6	0.4452	0.4463	0.4474	0.4484	0.4495	0.4505	0.4515	0.4525	0.4535	0.4545
1.7	0.4554	0.4564	0.4573	0.4582	0.4591	0.4599	0.4608	0.4616	0.4625	0.4633
1.8	0.4641	0.4649	0.4656	0.4664	0.4671	0.4678	0.4686	0.4693	0.4699	0.4706
1.9	0.4713	0.4719	0.4726	0.4732	0.4738	0.4744	0.4750	0.4756	0.4761	0.4767
2.0	0.4772	0.4778	0.4783	0.4788	0.4793	0.4798	0.4803	0.4808	0.4812	0.4817
2.1	0.4821	0.4826	0.4830	0.4834	0.4838	0.4842	0.4846	0.4850	0.4854	0.4857
2.2	0.4861	0.4864	0.4868	0.4871	0.4875	0.4878	0.4881	0.4884	0.4887	0.4890
2.3	0.4893	0.4896	0.4898	0.4901	0.4904	0.4906	0.4909	0.4911	0.4913	0.4916
2.4	0.4918	0.4920	0.4922	0.4925	0.4927	0.4929	0.4931	0.4932	0.4934	0.4936
2.5	0.4938	0.4940	0.4941	0.4943	0.4945	0.4946	0.4948	0.4949	0.4951	0.4952
2.6	0.4953	0.4955	0.4956	0.4957	0.4959	0.4960	0.4961	0.4962	0.4963	0.4964
2.7	0.4965	0.4966	0.4967	0.4968	0.4969	0.4970	0.4971	0.4972	0.4973	0.4974
2.8	0.4974	0.4975	0.4976	0.4977	0.4977	0.4978	0.4979	0.4979	0.4980	0.4981
2.9	0.4981	0.4982	0.4982	0.4983	0.4984	0.4984	0.4985	0.4985	0.4986	0.4986
3.0	0.4987	0.4987	0.4987	0.4988	0.4988	0.4989	0.4989	0.4989	0.4990	0.4990

Appendix VI

Answers to the mathematical tools exercises in Chapter 2, Appendix 2.1

1 a £124 b £125.97

2 a £26,533 b £163,665

3 a 14.2 years b 4.96 years

4 Present values of the four options:

a £1,000,000
b £1,104,883
c £1,500,000
d £1,283,540

Given the time value of money of 9 per cent per annum and certainty about the future (e.g. that you will live to enjoy the perpetuity) then the official answer is c. You may like to question whether this is what you would really go for. If you prefer another option, try to explain what that option says about your time value of money.

5 6%

6 £675

7 14.93%

8 a £32.20 b £31.18

9 £4,731

10 £6,217, 8.24%

11 Present value of a ten-year £800 annuity = £4,711. Therefore you could invest £4,711 @ 11% and receive £800 per year for ten years. Reject Supersalesman's offer.

12 £6,468

Appendix VII
Solutions to selected questions and problems

This Appendix provides suggested solutions to those end-of-chapter numerical questions and problems not marked with an asterisk*. Answers to questions and problems marked * are given in the *Lecturer's Guide*. Answers to discussion questions, essays and reports questions can be found by reading the text.

Chapter 1

No numerical questions; answers to all questions may be found by reading the text.

Chapter 2

1 Proast plc

a

	Project A			*Project B*		
Point in time (yearly intervals)	*Cash flow*	*Discount factor*	*Discounted cash flow*	*Cash flow*	*Discount factor*	*Discounted cash flow*
0	–120	1.0	–120.00	–120	1.0	–120.00
1	60	0.8696	52.176	15	0.8696	13.044
2	45	0.7561	34.025	45	0.7561	34.025
3	42	0.6575	27.615	55	0.6575	36.163
4	18	0.5718	10.292	60	0.5718	34.308
		NPV	4.108		NPV	–2.460
			£4,108			–£2,460

Advice: Accept project A and reject project B, because A generates a return greater than that required by the firm on projects of this risk class, but B does not.

b The figure of £4,108 for the NPV of project A can be interpreted as the surplus (in present value terms) above and beyond the required 15 per cent return. Therefore, Proast would be prepared to put up to £120,000 + £4,108 into this project at time zero, because it could thereby obtain the required rate of return of 15 per cent. If Proast put in any more than this, it would generate less than the opportunity cost of the finance providers.

Likewise, the maximum cash outflow at time zero (0) for project B which permits the generation of a 15 per cent return is £120,000 – £2,460 = £117,540.

2 Highflyer plc

a First, recognise that annuities are present (to save a lot of time).

Project A: Try 15% –420,000 + 150,000 × 2.855 = +£8,250.
Try 16% –420,000 + 150,000 × 2.7982 = –£270.

$$\text{IRR} = 15 + \frac{8{,}250}{8{,}250 + 270} \times (16 - 15) = 15.97\%$$

Project B: Try 31% and 32%.

Point in time (yearly intervals)	*Cash flow*	*Discounted cash flow @ 31%*	*Discounted cash flow @ 32%*
0	–100,000	–100,000	–100,000
1	75,000	57,252	56,818
2	75,000	43,704	43,044
		+956	–138

$$\text{IRR} = 31 + \frac{956}{956 + 138} \times (32 - 31) = 31.87\%$$

b NPV: *Project A*
–420,000 + 150,000 × 3.0373 = +£35,595

Project B
–100,000 + 75,000 × 1.6901 = +£26,758

c Comparison:

	IRR	*NPV*
Project A	15.97%	+£35,595
Project B	31.87%	+£26,758

If the projects were not mutually exclusive, Highflyer would be advised to accept both. If the firm has to choose between them, on the basis of the IRR calculation it would select B, but, if NPV is used, project A is the preferred choice. In mutually exclusive situations with projects generating more than the required rate of return, NPV is the superior decision-making tool. It measures in absolute amounts of money rather than in percentages and does not have the theoretical doubts about the reinvestment rate of return on intra-project cash inflows.

4

Point in time (yearly intervals)	*0*	*1*	*2*	*3*
Cash flow	−300	+260	−200	+600
Discount factor	1.0	0.885	0.7831	0.6931
Discounted cash flow	−300	+230.1	−156.62	+415.86

NPV = +£189.31

This project presents unconventional cash flows (more than one change in sign). Therefore there is more than one IRR, making a nonsense result.

5 a

Point in time (yearly intervals)	t_1	t_2	t_3	t_4	Total
Cash flow (£)	+200	+300	+250	+400	
Terminal (t_4) value (£)	+304.2	+396.8	+287.5	+400	1,388.5

b

$$\sqrt[4]{\frac{1,388.5}{900}} - 1 = 0.1145 \text{ or } 11.45\%$$

c Try 10%.

$$-900 + \frac{200}{1.10} + \frac{300}{(1.10)^2} + \frac{250}{(1.10)^3} + \frac{400}{(1.10)^4} = -9.2$$

Try 9%.

$$-900 + \frac{200}{1.09} + \frac{300}{(1.09)^2} + \frac{250}{(1.09)^3} + \frac{400}{(1.09)^4} = +12.4$$

$$\text{IRR} = 9 + \frac{12.4}{12.4 + 9.2}(10 - 9) = 9.57\%$$

6 a Modified internal rate of return

Point in time (yearly intervals)	t_1	t_2	t_3	t_4	Total
Cash flow (£)	5,400	3,100	2,800	600	
Terminal value	8,000.3	4,028.8	3,192	600	15,821.1

$$\sqrt[4]{\frac{15,821.1}{9,300}} - 1 = 0.142 \text{ or } 14.2\%$$

This project is accepted under the MIRR decision rule.

b Internal rate of return

Try 14%.

$$-9{,}300 + \frac{5{,}400}{1.14} + \frac{3{,}100}{(1.14)^2} + \frac{2{,}800}{(1.14)^3} + \frac{600}{(1.14)^4} = +67.4$$

Try 15%.

$$-9{,}300 + \frac{5{,}400}{1.15} + \frac{3{,}100}{(1.15)^2} + \frac{2{,}800}{(1.15)^3} + \frac{600}{(1.15)^4} = -76.2$$

$$14 + \frac{67.4}{67.4 + 76.2}(15 - 14) = 14.47\%$$

This project is accepted under the IRR decision rule.

Chapter 3

1 Tenby-Saundersfoot Dock Company

a London head office cost allocation is irrelevant as this is non-incremental.

Point in time (yearly intervals)	*0 £000*	*1→∞ £000*
Fees		255
Repairs	–250	
Employees		–70
Administration, etc.		–85
Electricity		–40
Other docks		–20
Cash flow	–250	+40

Additional overhead costs are included, but those which would have occurred, whether or not the dock project proceeded, are excluded. The loss of trade to other profit centres (docks) is included in the assessment of this project because this is an incidental effect which only occurs because of this new project.

b $\text{NPV} = -250 + \frac{40}{0.17} = -14.706$ or £14,706.

2 Railcam

Point in time (yearly intervals)	*20X2 £m*	*20X3 £m*	*20X4 £m*
Sales	+22	+24	+21
Debtor adjustments			
Opening debtors	5.00	5.50	6.00
Closing debtors	5.50	6.00	5.25
	–0.50	–0.50	+0.75
Wages	–6.00	–6.00	–6.00
Materials	–11.00	–12.00	–10.50
Creditor adjustments			
Opening creditors	2.50	2.75	3.00
Closing creditors	2.75	3.00	2.625
	+0.25	+0.25	–0.375
Overhead	–5.00	–5.00	–5.00
	–0.25	+0.75	–0.125

3 Pine Ltd

a Recognition of sunk cost: £20,000 research.
Recognition of irrelevant data: depreciation.

£000s	*20X1 start*	*20X1 end*	*20X2*	*20X3*	*20X4*	*20X5*	*20X6*
Sales		+400	+400	+400	+320	+200	
Equipment	–240					+40	
Stock	–30					+30	
Working capital	–20					+20	
Overheads		–8	–8	–9.6	–9.6	–9.6	
Materials		–240	–240	–240	–192	–120	
Variable costs		–40	–40	–40	–32	–20	
Debtors adjustment							
Opening debtors		0	400	400	400	320	200
Closing debtors		400	400	400	320	200	0
		–400	0	0	+80	+120	+200
Cash flow	–290	–288	+112	+110.4	+166.4	+260.4	+200
Discount factor	1.0	0.8929	0.7972	0.7118	0.6355	0.5674	0.5066
Discounted cash flow	–290	–257.2	+89.3	+78.6	+105.7	+147.8	+101.3

NPV = –£24,500

A negative NPV indicates that the project produces less than the opportunity cost of capital of the finance providers. This firm would serve its shareholders best by not proceeding with this project.

b The answer should explain, with a minimal use of technical language, the following:

- The time value of money.
- Discounting cash flows to a common point in time.
- Opportunity cost of investors' funds.
- Minimum rate of return required on a project.
- NPV = shareholder wealth increase.
- NPV decision rule
- The significance of being cash flow based rather than profit based.
- Only incremental cash flows are considered.

6 NPV = –5,000 + 2,000 × 0.885 + 2,200 × 0.7831 + 3,500 × 0.6931 = £919

$$\text{AEA} = \frac{\text{NPV}}{\text{annuity factor}} = \frac{919}{2.3612} = £389$$

9 Quite plc

Incremental cash flows for replacement:

Point in time (yearly intervals)	*0*	*1 → 15*	*15*
	+2,000	+500	+500
	–7,000		
	–5,000		

Incremental NPV = –5,000 + 500 × 8.0607 + 500 × 0.2745 = –£832.40

Incremental cash flows for overhaul:

Point in time (yearly intervals)	*0*	*1 → 15*
	–2,500	+300

–2,500 + 300 × 8.0607 = –£81.79

Recommendation: The best course of action is to continue with the old, unoverhauled machine.

11 The Borough Company

Machine X

–20,000 – 5,000 × 2.3612 = –31,806

$$\text{AEA} = \frac{-31{,}806}{2.3612} = -£13{,}470$$

Machine Y

$$-25{,}000 - 4{,}000 \times 2.9745 = -36{,}898$$

$$\text{AEA} = \frac{-36{,}898}{2.9745} = -12{,}405$$

Borough should buy Machine Y because this has the lower annual equivalent annuity cost.

13 Clipper plc

Point in time (yearly intervals)	*NPV*		
0	10,000	=	10,000
1	12,000 × 0.9091	=	10,909
2	14,000 × 0.8264	=	11,570
3	15,500 × 0.7513	=	11,645
4	16,500 × 0.6830	=	11,270

The best time to cut the trees is in three years' time.

15 Hazel plc

a NPV of A: $-200 + \frac{220}{1.15} + \frac{242}{(1.15)^2} = +174$

b NPV of B: $-240 + \frac{220}{1.15} + \frac{242}{(1.15)^2} + \frac{266}{(1.15)^3} = +309$

c AEA of A: $\frac{174}{1.6257} = +107$

AEA of B: $\frac{309}{2.2832} = +135$

Preferred machine: Machine B.

d If C is used for a further five years:

£000s

$$(160 \times 3.3522) + (20 \times 0.497) + \frac{135/0.15}{(1.15)^5} = £993{,}751$$

If C is scrapped now:

£000s

$$87 + \frac{135}{0.15} = £987{,}000$$

Recommended option: do not scrap at time 0.

e Explanations in plain English are required, not passages of technical jargon.

Chapter 4

1 Payback

A: 6 years   B: 3 years   C: 4 years   D: 4 years   E: 5 years

Discounted payback

A	£	*Cumulative*
500× 0.893	446.5	446
500 × 0.797	398.5	845
500 × 0.712	356	1,201
500 × 0.636	318	1,519
500 × 0.567	283.5	1,802
500 × 0.507	253.5	2,056
500 × 0.452	226	2,282

Discounted payback is not achieved (shareholder wealth-destroying project).

B	£	*Cumulative*
2,000 × 0.893	1,786	1,786
5,000 × 0.797	3,985	5,771
3,000 × 0.712	2,136	7,907
2,000 × 0.636	1,272	9,179

Discounted payback is not achieved (shareholder wealth-destroying project).

C	£	*Cumulative*
5,000 × 0.893	4,465	4,465
4,000 × 0.797	3,188	7,653
4,000 × 0.712	2,848	10,501
5,000 × 0.636	3,180	13,681
10,000 × 0.567	5,670	19,351

Discounted payback at year 5.

D	£	*Cumulative*
1,000 × 3.0373	3,037	3,037
7,000 × 0.5674	3,972	7,008

Discounted payback at year 5.

E	£	*Cumulative*
500 × 2.4018	1,201	1,201
2,000 × 0.6355	1,271	2,472
5,000 × 0.5674	2,837	5,309
10,000 × 0.5066	5,066	10,375

Discounted payback at year 6.

2 Payback: 3 years in both cases. Yet the first project is clearly superior to the second.

4 **a** Payback: 4 years

b

Point in time (yearly intervals)	*Cash flow*	*Discount factor*	*Discounted cash flow*	*Cumulative discounted cash flow*
0	(6,250)	1	(6,250)	(6,250)
1	1,000	0.9091	909.1	(5,340.9)
2	1,500	0.8264	1,239.6	(4,101.3)
3	2,000	0.7513	1,502.6	(2,598.7)
4	1,750	0.6830	1,195.3	(1,403.4)
5	1,500	0.6209	931.3	(472.1)
6	1,000	0.5645	564.5	92.4
7	500	0.5132	256.6	349.0
8	500	0.4665	233.3	582.3

Discounted payback = 6 years.

c NPV = £582.30.

5 **Maple plc**

A possible solution.

a ***Project A*** *£000s*

Year	*1*	*2*	*3*	*4*	*5*
Profit before depreciation	800	800	800	800	800
Depreciation $\frac{2,300 - 300}{5}$	400	400	400	400	400
Profit after depreciation	400	400	400	400	400
Asset value at start of year	2,300	1,900	1,500	1,100	700
ARR	$\frac{400}{2,300}$ = 17.4%	$\frac{400}{1,900}$ 21.1%	$\frac{400}{1,500}$ 26.7%	$\frac{400}{1,100}$ 36.4%	$\frac{400}{700}$ 57.1%

Average ARR 31.7%

Project B

Year	*1*	*2*	*3*	*4*	*5*
Profit before depreciation	250	250	250	250	250
Depreciation					
$\frac{660 - 60}{5}$	120	120	120	120	120
Profit after depreciation	130	130	130	130	130
Asset value at start of year	660	540	420	300	180
ARR	$\frac{130}{660}$	$\frac{130}{540}$	$\frac{130}{420}$	$\frac{130}{300}$	$\frac{130}{180}$
	= 19.7%	24.1%	31%	43.3%	72.2%

Average ARR = 38.1%

b NPV:

Project A

NPV = –2,300,000 + 800,000 × 3.3522 + 300,000 × 0.4972 = +£530,920

Project B

–660,000 + 250,000 × 3.3522 + 60,000 × 0.4972 = +£207,882

Project A has the higher NPV and therefore generates most shareholders value.

Chapter 5

Self-review questions

2 $(1 + m) = (1 + h)(1 + i)$

$(1 + 0.09) = (1 + h)(1 + 0.05)$

$$(1 + h) = \frac{1.09}{1.05} - 1$$

$h = 3.81\%$

Questions and problems

1 Plumber plc

a *Project A*:

NPV = –1.5 + 0.5 × 0.8929 + 0.5 × 0.7972 + 1 × 0.7118 + 1 × 0.6355 = +0.69235

Accept.

Project B:

NPV = –2.0 + 4 × 0.6355 = +0.542.

Accept.

Project C:
NPV = −1.8 + 1.2 × 0.7118 + 1.2 × 0.6355 = −0.1832
Reject.

Project D:
NPV = −3.0 + 1.2 × 3.0373 = +0.64476
Accept.

Project E:
NPV = −0.5 + 0.3 × 3.0373 = +0.41119
Accept.

Project	*Investment £m*	*NPV £m*	*NPV/investment*	*Ranking*
A	1.5	0.69235	0.4616	2
B	2.0	0.542	0.271	3
D	3.0	0.64476	0.215	4
E	0.5	0.41119	0.822	1

Allocation of £5m:

Project	*Investment £m*	*NPV*
E	0.5	0.41119
A	1.5	0.69235
B	2.0	0.54200
D × $^1/_3$	1.0	0.21492
	5.0	1.86046

Maximum NPV available given the capital constraint = £1.86046m.

b £2,290,300.

c

Project	*NPV*
A	0.69235
D	0.64476
E	0.41119
	1.74830

2 The Telescope Company

Project	*Investment*	*NPV*
C	10,000	6,000
E	7,000	2,100
A × 0.5	3,000	600
	20,000	8,700

3 Premiums: £25,194.

$PV = 25{,}194/(1.17)^3 = £15{,}730$

5 Hose plc

Point in time (yearly intervals)		*Money cash flow £000*		*Discounted money cash flow £000*
0		–800		–800
1	150 × 1.06	159	159 × 0.885	141
2	150 × 1.1236	169	169 × 0.7831	132
3	150 × 1.1910	179	179 × 0.6931	124
4	150 × 1.2625	189	189 × 0.6133	116
5	150 × 1.3382	201	201 × 0.5428	109
6	150 × 1.4185	213	213 × 0.4803	102
7	150 × 1.5036	226	226 × 0.4251	96
				20

This project produces a positive NPV and should therefore be accepted, all other things being equal.

6

Point in time (yearly intervals)	*Annual writing down allowance*	*Written down value £*
0	0	10,000
1	2,500	7,500
2	1,875	5,625
3	1,406	4,219
4	1,055	3,164
5	791	2,373

Taxable profit can be reduced by £1,406 in the third year.
Present value of WDA in year 4 = £1,055 × 0.30 × 0.6830 = £216.17.

Balancing adjustment if the machine has a scrap value of £1,000 after 5 years:

Amount written off	10,000 – 2,373 =	7,627
Depreciation		9,000
		1,373

9 a Oppton

NPV and profitability index

Project 1

NPV = –35 + 60 × 0.8264 = 14.6
PI = 49.6 ÷ 35 = 1.42

Project 2

NPV = –50 + 30 × 2.4869 = 24.6
PI = 74.6 ÷ 50 = 1.49

Project 3

NPV = –20 + 10 × 3.1699 = 11.7
PI = 31.699 ÷ 20 = 1.58

Project 4

NPV = –30 + 15 × 3.1699 = 17.5
PI = 47.55 ÷ 30 = 1.58

Project 5

NPV = –60 + 70 × 0.9091 = 3.6
PI = 63.6 ÷ 60 = 1.06

Optimal allocation

	Capital (£000s)		*NPV (£000s)*
All of 3	20		11.7
All of 4	30		17.5
All of 2	50		24.6
10/35 of 1	10		4.2
	110	Total NPV	58.0

10 Cartma

Maximum NPV if there are no limits on investment = £16.53m.

Project	*Benefit–cost ratio*
A	5/10 = 0.5
B	3.95/15 = 0.26
C	2.83/8 = 0.35
D	2.58/5 = 0.52
E	2.17/4 = 0.54

Allocation

	Capital (£m)		*NPV (£m)*
All of E	4		2.17
All of D	5		2.58
All of A	10		5.00
All of C	8		2.83
11/15 of B	11		2.90
	38	Total NPV	15.48

Chapter 6

1 +£348.7K **a** +£269.7K **b** +£198.8K

4 a *Annual cash flows:*

		£
Sales	22,000 × 21	462,000
Variable direct costs	22,000 × 16	–352,000
		110,000

$$-400{,}000 + 110{,}000 \times \text{af} = 0$$

$$\text{af} = \frac{400{,}000}{110{,}000} = 3.6364$$

From annuity tables: $24 + \dfrac{3.6819 - 3.6364}{3.6819 - 3.5705}(25 - 24) = 24.4\%$

IRR = 24.4%

b *Sales volume:*

		£
Sales	20,900 × 21	438,900
VDC	20,900 × 16	–334,400
		104,500

$$\text{af} = \frac{400{,}000}{104{,}500} = 3.8278$$

$$22 + \frac{3.9232 - 3.8278}{3.9232 - 3.7993}(23 - 22) = 22.8$$

IRR = 22.8%

Sales price:		£
Sales	22,000 × 19.95	438,900
Variable direct costs		−352,000
		86,900

$$\text{af} = \frac{400{,}000}{86{,}900} = 4.6030$$

$$17 + \frac{4.6586 - 4.6030}{4.6586 - 4.4941}(18 - 17) = 17.3$$

IRR = 17.3%

Variable direct costs:		£
Sales	22,000 × 21	462,000
Variable direct costs	22,000 × 16.8	−369,600
		92,400

$$\text{af} = \frac{400{,}000}{92{,}400} = 4.3290$$

$$19 + \frac{4.3389 - 4.3290}{4.3389 - 4.1925}(19 - 18) = 19.1\%$$

IRR = 19.1%

c Consult the chapter for details.

5 Project W

Return	p_i	$R \times p_i$	*Expected return*	$(R_i - \bar{R})^2 p_i$
2	0.3	0.6	3.4	0.588
4	0.7	2.8	3.4	0.252
		3.4		0.840

Standard deviation £0.917m.

Project X

Return	p_i	$R \times p_i$	*Expected return*	$(R_i - \bar{R})^2 p_i$
−2	0.3	−0.6	5.0	14.7
8	0.7	5.6	5.0	6.3
		5.0		21.0

Standard deviation £4.58m.

Observations: W has a lower return and a much lower standard deviation than X.
X has a higher return than Y, but also a higher risk.

6 $\dfrac{-80{,}000 - 220{,}000}{160{,}000} = 1.875$

Probability of insolvency = 50% – 46.96% = 3.04%

7 Toughnut plc

a

Year 1		*Year 2*	
8,000 × 0.1 =	800	4,000 × 0.3 =	1,200
10,000 × 0.6 =	6,000	8,000 × 0.7 =	5,600
12,000 × 0.3 =	3,600		6,800
	10,400		

$$\text{Expected NPV} = -15{,}000 + \frac{10{,}400}{1.11} + \frac{6{,}800}{(1.11)^2} = -112$$

b *Cash flow (£000s)*

Year 1	*Year 2*	*Prob.*	p_i	*NPV*	$NPV \times p_i$	$(NPV_i - \overline{NPV})^2 p_i$
8	4	0.1 × 0.3 =	0.03	–4.55	–0.136	0.591
8	8	0.1 × 0.7 =	0.07	–1.30	–0.091	0.099
10	4	0.6 × 0.3 =	0.18	–2.74	–0.493	1.243
10	8	0.6 × 0.7 =	0.42	0.50	0.2100	0.157
12	4	0.3 × 0.3 =	0.09	–0.94	–0.085	0.062
12	8	0.3 × 0.7 =	0.21	2.30	0.4830	1.222
			1.00		–0.112	3.374

Standard deviation $\sqrt{3.374} = 1.837$

c $Z = \dfrac{0 - (-0.112)}{1.837} = 0.061$

Probability of the NPV being between zero and –0.112 = 2.39%. Therefore the probability of the NPV being less than zero is 50% + 2.39% = 52.39%.

8

	Outcome	*Probability*	$R_i \times p_i$	$(R_i - \bar{R})p_i$
a	272,321	0.10	27,232	12,125,368,620
b	–46,556	0.10	–4,656	86,071,824
c	–75,255	0.56	–42,143	228,660
d	–234,694	0.24	–56,327	6,052,185,600
		Expected return	–75,894	18,263,854,710

Standard deviation £135,144.

9	*NPV (£000s)*	*Prob.*	$NPV \times p_i$	$(NPV_i - \overline{NPV})p_i$
Recession	–178.8	0.3	–53.6	30,912
Growth	177.8	0.5	88.9	634
Boom	534.5	0.2	106.9	30,780
		Expected NPV	142.2	62,326

Standard deviation $= \sqrt{62{,}326} = 250$

10 a NPVs
RJW's projections, +£138m
More optimistic scenario, +£1,077m
More pessimistic scenario, –£578m

NPV	*pi*	$NPV \times p_i$	$(NPV - \overline{NPV})^2 p_i$
138	0.5	69	9,591
1,077	0.3	323.1	192,240
–578	0.2	–115.6	146,034
Expected return		276.5	347,865

Standard deviation 590.

b $$\frac{-550 - 276.5}{590} = -1.4$$

Probability of avoiding liquidation = 50% + 41.92% = 91.92%.

c $$\frac{100 - 276.5}{590} = 0.3$$

Probability of a rapidly moving share price = 50% + 11.79% = 61.79%.

11 Alder plc

a A: £45,455 B: £105,785 C: £126,446 D: £40,194

Ranking C, B, A, D

b Possibilities: Ranking problem, multiple solutions, no solutions, additivity, reinvestment assumption. Explain each of these.

c	*Profitability index*	*Ranking*
A	1.09	4
B	1.53	1
C	1.18	3
D	1.27	2

Allocation	Outlay (£000s)	NPV (£000s)
All of B	200	105.785
All of D	150	40.194
Half of C	350	63.223
	700	209.202

d

Outcome	Prob.	NPV	$NPV \times p_i$	$(NPV - \overline{NPV})p_i$
A	0.3 × 0.5 = 0.15	19,621	2,943	75,890,257
B	0.5 × 0.7 = 0.35	–105,752	–37,013	3,704,503,040
C	0.5 × 0.6 = 0.30	79,112	23,734	2,016,412,877
D	0.5 × 0.4 = 0.20	37,320	7,464	323,079,373
	1.00		–2,872	6,119,885,547
			Standard deviation = 78,230	

$$Z = \frac{0 - (-2872)}{78{,}230} = 0.037 \text{ standard deviations}$$

Probability of a loss = 50% + 1.4 = 51.4% (approximately).

Chapter 7

1 32%

2 4.17%; 17.7% annualised return

3 22.74%; 84.9%

7 a 30%; 7.16%
b 32%, 16.7%

8 a and b

Expected returns (%) S		Expected returns (%) T		Standard deviations (%) S	Standard deviations (%) T
0.15 × 45 =	6.75	0.15 × 18 =	2.7	99.5	0.15
0.70 × 20 =	14.0	0.70 × 17 =	11.9	0.4	0.00
0.15 × –10 =	–1.5	0.15 × 16 =	2.4	128.3	0.15
	19.25		17.0	σ^2 228.2	σ^2 0.30
		Standard deviations		15.11	0.548

c *Covariances*

	Returns		*Expected returns*		*Deviations*		
Prob.	*S*	*T*	*S*	*T*	*S*	*T*	
0.15	45	18	19.25	17	25.75	1	25.75 × 1 × 0.15 = 3.86
0.70	20	17	19.25	17	0.75	0	0.75 × 0 × 0.7 = 0.00
0.15	–10	16	19.25	17	–29.25	–1	–29.25 × –1 × 0.15 = 4.39
							Covariance = 8.25

$$\text{Correlation coefficient} = \frac{8.25}{15.11 \times 0.548} = +1$$

d Expected return = 18.5%
Standard deviation = 10.25%

9 Any proportion of S and T may be selected. If, say, 50:50 allocation is made the results are:

Expected return = 18.125
Standard deviation = 7.83

The results should plot along a straight line, given the perfect positive correlation.

10 a

Portfolio	*Expected return (%)*	*Standard deviation (%)*
A	10.0	5
B	12.5	4.3
C	15.0	6.0
D	17.5	8.8
E	20.0	12

b Covariance = –0.2 × 5 × 12 = –12

$$\frac{144 - (-12)}{25 + 144 - (2 \times -12)} = 0.81 \text{ or } 81\%$$

Minimum standard deviation is when 81% of fund is devoted to Trent. Then:

Expected return = 11.9%
Standard deviation = 4.2%
} Plot point F in diagram below.

c and d

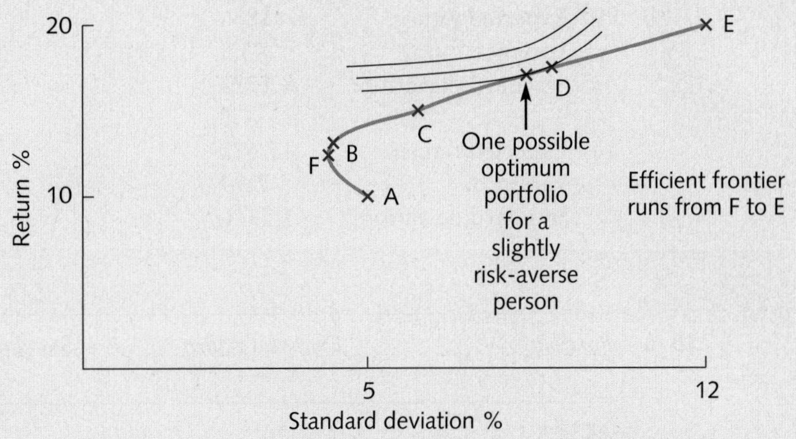

11 Big Trucks plc

a	*Expected returns*	*Standard deviation*
Midlands	18	1.55
Far East	27	19.52

b Expected return = 22.5%; Standard deviation = 10.5%; Covariance = 30.

12 a Expected return = 21%; Standard deviation = 2%.

b Covariance = –1 × 6 × 10 = –60

$$\frac{100 - (-60)}{36 + 100 - 2 \times -60} = 0.625 \text{ or } 62.5\%$$

Allocate 62.5% of the fund to F, 37.5% to G.

13 a Ihser: 21%; 429; 20.7%
Resque: 15%; 15; 3.87%

Covariance

$R_I - \bar{R}_I$	$R_R - \bar{R}_R$	p_i	$(R_I - \bar{R}_I)(R_R - \bar{R}_R)p_i$
19	–5	0.3	–28.5
9	0	0.4	0.0
–31	+5	0.3	–46.5
			–75.0

b (i) Expected return: 18%
Variance: 73.5
Standard deviation: 8.57%

(ii) Expected return 15.6%
Variance: 2.94
Standard deviation: 1.71%

15 a

Portfolio	*Expected return* %	*Standard deviation* %
All in A	20	7.1
1	26.6	20.3
2	22.2	7.3
3	20.9	6.1
All in B	28.75	27.7

Covariance

$R_A - \bar{R}_A$	$R_B - \bar{R}_B$	p_i	$(R_A - \bar{R}_A)(R_B - \bar{R}_B)p_i$
–10	–13.75	0.25	34.38
0	26.25	0.50	0.00
10	–38.75	0.25	–96.88
			–62.50

b

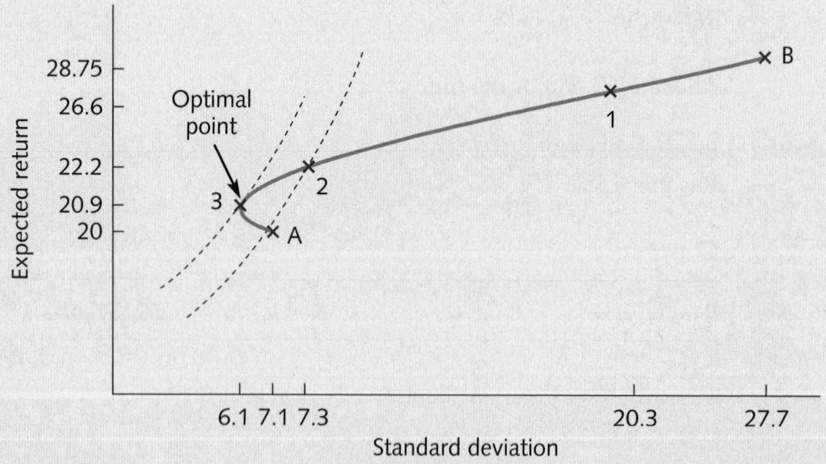

c The efficient region for the risk-return line drawn is between portfolio 3 and B.

The inefficient region is between 3 and A.

d Indifference curves for a highly risk-averse individual are displayed, which result in portfolio 3 being optimal. Indifference curves with other slopes are acceptable, provided the optimal portfolio is shown to be where an indifference curve is tangential to the risk-return line – the highest achievable in the NW direction.

e *See* Chapter 7 for a description of the market portfolio; also *consult* Chapter 8.

Chapter 8

1 14.5%

3 A: 17% B: 9.5% C: 12%

4 7.33

5 a r_f = 10%; risk premium = 8%.

b P is above SML, offering a high return for risk level. The price will rise until the return offered is 23.6%.

c Q is below SML, offering a low return for its risk level. The price will fall until the return offered is 16.4%.

7 Threshold rate for discussion is 10 + 1.4(5) = 17%.

8 a Projects 1, 3 and 4.

9 a False **b** False **c** True **d** False **e** True **f** False

10 a (24,000/80,000) × 0.8 + (20,000/80,000) × 1.2 + (36,000/80,000) × 1.1 = 1.035

b 6.5 + 1.035(5) = 11.68

Chapter 9

No numerical questions.

Chapter 10

12 £1.82; 8p.

Chapter 11

1 a £95.20 **b** 8.06%

2 a £100 **b** 10.15% **c** £103.62

3 **a** $9 \times 6.278 + 100/(1.095)^{10} =$ £96.86

b $9 \times 6.561 + 100/(1.085)^{10} =$ £103.28

c 8.25%

d 8.57%

4 **a** £105.30 **b** £63.79

5 **a** $\frac{100}{(1.05)^5} =$ £78.35

b $\frac{100}{(1.10)^5} =$ £62.09

6 Bond 1: £96.36 Bond 2: £101.82

10 16.08%

11 7.5%

13 **a** £78.71m

b

Year	*1*	*2*	*3*	*4*	*5*
Payments (£m)	4.75	4.75	4.75	4.75	54.75

c

Year	*1*	*2*	*3*	*4*	*5*
Payments (£m)	14.75	13.80	12.85	11.90	10.95
Outstanding at the beginning of the year		40.00	30.00	20.00	10.00

16 **a** 100/40 = £2.50

b (2.50 – 1.90)/1.90 = 31.6%

c £1.90 × 40 = £76

Chapter 12

1

Interest on overdraft	£
$180,000 \times {}^3/_{12} \times 0.1$	4,500
$150,000 \times {}^3/_{12} \times 0.1$	3,750
$200,000 \times {}^3/_{12} \times 0.1$	5,000
	13,250
Arrangement fee	3,000
	16,250

Interest on loan

200,000 × 0.1	20,000
Less Interest receivable	
200,000 × $^3/_{12}$ × 0.04	2,000
20,000 × $^3/_{12}$ × 0.04	200
50,000 × $^3/_{12}$ × 0.04	500
	£17,300

The loan is significantly more expensive. If cost is the only consideration, then the overdraft should be selected.

2 Snowhite

a Payment on the 10th day: saving = £500,000 × 0.01 = £500
Saving on overdraft interest if payment is on 30th day:

$$d = \sqrt[365]{1 + 0.12} - 1 = 0.0003105$$

Twenty days' interest: $(1 + 0.0003105)^{20} - 1 = 0.006229$
49,500 × 0.006229 = £308.34
Conclusion: pay on the 10th day

b Pay on the 10th day, saving £500
Pay on the 60th day: $49{,}500\ (1 + 0.0003105)^{50} - 1 = £774$
Conclusion: pay on the 60th day

4 Overdraft interest over a 40-day period:

$$(1 + d)^{365} = (1 + i)$$

$$\sqrt[365]{1 + 0.11} - 1 = 0.000285959$$

$$(1 + 0.000285959)^{40} - 1 = 0.011502 \text{ or } 1.15\%$$

$$9{,}800 \times 0.011502 = £112.72$$

The value of the discount, £200, is greater than the cost of the additional overdraft and therefore Biscuit should pay on the 10th day.

9 Glub Ltd.

Benefits:
Daily credit granted = £6,000,000/365 = £16,438
Immediate cash boost: £16,438 × 80 × 0.8 = £1,052,055

Annual interest saving £1,052,055 × 0.11 =	£115,726
Plus interest saving on earlier settlement:	
£16,438 × 20 × 0.2 × 0.11 =	£7,233
plus administration saving =	£80,000
	£202,959

Costs:

$0.017 \times 6{,}000{,}000$	£102,000.0
$1{,}052{,}055 \times 0.1$	£105,205.5
$6{,}000{,}000 \times 0.8 \times 0.01$	£48,000.0
	£255,205.0

On a strict interpretation of the data, Glub should favour continuing without the help of the factoring company because the charges are higher than the savings (even with the assumption of immediate reduction if the credit period is taken from 80 days to 60 days). However, there are at least three other considerations that may affect the decision. First, real businesses often feel the pressure of cash flow shortages (the capital markets are not perfect). Therefore the managers may value the cash flow boost more highly than allowed for. Second, senior management time devoted to the problem of debtors may not have been included in 'adminstration costs'. Third, customer relationships may be damaged by the actions of a factor keen in reducing the average debtor period.

10 $\sqrt[365]{1.09} - 1 = 0.000236131$

$(1.000236131)^{46} - 1 = 0.01092$ or 1.09%

It is more attractive to accept a discount of 1.5%.

11 a $\sqrt[365]{1.15} - 1 = 0.000382983$

Interest over 63 days:
$(1 + 0.000382983)^{63} - 1 = 0.02441$ or 2.441%

This is more than the discount and therefore Penguin should continue to pay on the 70th day.

Chapter 13

1 Cash flows: £10m/52 = £192,308 per week

Monday	*Tuesday*	*Wednesday*	*Thursday*	*Friday*
£82,418	£27,473	£27,473	£27,473	£27,473

$$Q = \sqrt{\frac{2 \times 35 \times 10{,}000{,}000}{0.11}} = £79{,}772$$

It is worthwhile for Tollhouse to pay in when cash exceeds £79,772; therefore it makes sense to pay in on Monday, but not to pay in every day of the week. It also makes sense to pay in on Thursday rather than Friday.

4 $EOQ = \sqrt{\frac{2 \times 300{,}000 \times 200}{10}} = 3{,}464$ units

$$\text{Orders per year} = \frac{300{,}000}{3{,}464} = 86.6$$

$$\text{Total inventory cost} = \frac{AC}{Q} + \frac{HQ}{2}$$

(300,000 × 200)/3,464 + (10 × 3,464)/2 = £34,641

5 a $EOQ = \sqrt{\frac{2 \times 10{,}000 \times 50}{7}} = 378$ units.

b Inventory cost: (10,000 × 50)/378 + (7 × 378)/2 = £2,646
Number of orders per year: 10,000/378 = 26.46

c Stock reorder level = 10,000/52 = 192 units

d Maximum inventory holding = 378 + 192 = 570 units

7 a

£000	*October*	*November*	*December*
Previous month's sales	165	180	45
Previous month's sales	55	315	385
This month's sales	90	110	140
Inflows	310	605	570
Materials	–270	–330	–420
Labour and other costs	–45	–55	–70
Total outflows	–315	–385	–490
Balances			
Opening balance	–70	–75	145
Net cash surplus (deficit)	–5	220	80
Closing balance	–75	145	225

Whitborrow will have sufficient cash to purchase the new equipment in December.

9 $\sqrt{\frac{2 \times 20 \times 520{,}000}{0.10}} = £14{,}422$

Davy should pay in every day or every other day. Certainly it should pay in on Mondays if income is received at the weekend.

10 a $EOQ = \sqrt{\frac{2 \times 100{,}000 \times 250}{1.20}} = 6{,}455$ units

$$\frac{AC}{Q} + \frac{HQ}{2} = \frac{100{,}000 \times 250}{6{,}455} + \frac{1.2 \times 6{,}455}{2} = £7{,}746$$

b One week's usage = $\frac{100,000}{52}$ = 1,923

Maximum buffer stock = 3 × 1,923 = 5,769

Chapter 14

2 Theory: 275p.
Practice: the scrip issue may be interpreted by the market as an optimistic signal from management that earnings and dividends will continue to grow in a satisfactory or better manner, and therefore the share price could settle above 275p. Fama *et al.* (1969) showed this phenomenon for US companies.

Chapter 15

8 a Value: $10m + \frac{10m}{0.13} = £86.92m$

b Value: $\frac{12m}{0.13} = £92.31m$

Earnings rise to £12m each year.
This is good investment, as the present value of the additional cash inflows (2/0.13 = £15.4m) is greater than the sacrifice (£10m). Here a rise in earnings coincides with a rise in value.

c Value: $5m + \frac{10.5m}{0.13} = £85.77m$

Earnings rise to £10.5m each year.
This is bad investment, as the present value of the additional cash inflows (0.5/0.13 = £3.8m) is less than the sacrifice at time 0 (£5m). Here a rise in earnings is achieved but value is lost.

9 Annual value creation: £300,000 × (0.19 – 0.13) = +£18,000
Performance spread = 0.19 – 0.13 = 0.06 or 6%
Value of the firm: 300,000 + 18,000 × 5.9176 = £406,517

Chapter 16

No numerical exercises.

Chapter 17

1 Blue plc

a Consumer: £1m × (0.18 –0.15) = +£30,000
Cooker: £2m × (0.14 – 0.16) = –£40,000
Export: £1.5m × 0.02 = +£30,000

b Consumer: £30,000 × 3.3522 = +£100,566
Cooker: –£40,000 × 4.0386 = –£161,544
Export: £30,000 × 3.5892 = +£107,676

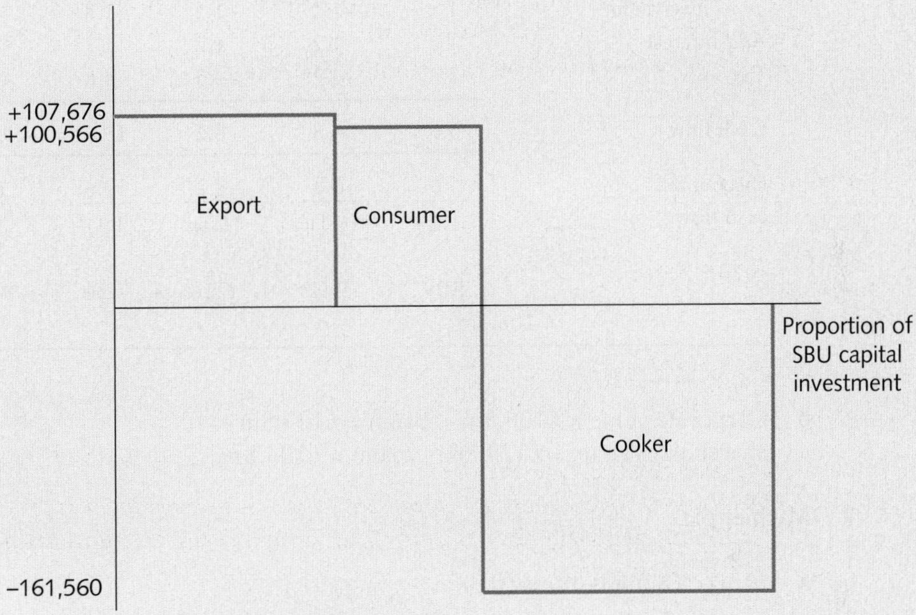

5 Tops plc

EP = operating profit after tax – invested capital × WACC
= £5m – £50 × 0.14 = –£2m

6 Buit plc

Point in time	*1* *£m*	*2* *£m*	*3* *£m*	*4* *£m*	*5 → infinity* *£m*
Forecast profits	12	14	15	16	16
Add depreciation	2	2	3	3	3
Less Fixed capital investment	–5	–5	–5	–3	–3
Less Working capital investment	–1	–1.2	–1.5	–1.8	0
Add Interest	1.2	1.2	1.2	1.2	1.2
Tax	–3.6	–4.2	–4.5	–4.8	–4.8
Cash flow	5.6	6.8	8.2	10.6	12.4

Discounted cash flow

$$\frac{5.6}{1.1} + \frac{6.8}{(1.1)^2} + \frac{8.2}{(1.1)^3} + \frac{10.6}{(1.1)^4} + \frac{12.4}{0.1} \times \frac{1}{(1.1)^4}$$

$$5.09 + 5.62 + 6.16 + 7.24 + 84.69$$

$$= 108.8\text{m}$$

b Corporate value = £108.8m + £16m = £124.8m
Shareholder value = £124.8m – £20m = £104.8m

7 Mythier plc

a £1m – (£8m × 0.08) = £0.36m

b (£1m – £0.24) – (£4m × 0.1) = £0.36m

Chapter 18

1 a $\frac{580 - 600}{600} \times 100 = -3.3\%$

$\frac{580 - 450}{450} \times 100 = 28.9\%$

$\frac{580 - 125}{125} \times 100 = 364\%$

b To put additional meaning to TSR calculations, it is often useful to compare them with a benchmark:

Share index returns	3 years	24%
	5 years	68%
	10 years	210%

On the basis of these calculations, we observe that Tear has performed relatively well over a ten-year period but relatively poorly over three-year and five-year periods. This leads to a problem with TSR: it is highly dependent on the time period chosen.

Additional issues:
- It is important to relate relative returns to risk class.
- It measures in percentage terms rather than absolute terms.

c *Ten years*

$45.5\text{m} - ((12.5\text{m} \times (1.09)^{10}) - 12.5\text{m}) = £28.4\text{m}$

Five years

$13\text{m} - ((45\text{m} \times (1.09)^{5}) - 45\text{m}) = £11.25\text{m}$

2 Sity and Pity

a 90 – 15 = £75m

b 90/15 = 6

c *See* Chapter 18.

d *Sity*

	£m
$2\ (1.08)^5 =$	2.939
$3\ (1.08)^3 =$	3.779
Market value of shares	90.000
Actual wealth	96.718

Expected wealth = $15(1.08)^{25}$ = £102.727m
Excess return = actual wealth – expected wealth

–£6.01m = £96.718m – £102.727m

Pity

	£m
Dividends 5 years (future value table)	
6.1051 × 2 =	12.21
Market value of shares =	90.00
Actual wealth	102.21

Expected wealth = $15(1.1)^5$ = 24.16
Excess return = £102.21m – £24.16m = £78.05m

Chapter 19

2 **a** $$-80 + \frac{5}{1 + K_{DBT}} + \frac{5}{(1 + K_{DBT})^2} + \frac{5}{(1 + K_{DBT})^3} + \frac{5}{(1 + K_{DBT})^4} + \frac{105}{(1 + K_{DBT})^5} = 0$$

Try 10%: +1.05

Try 11%: –2.178

$K_{DBT} = 10.32\%$

$K_{DAT} = 10.32(1 - 0.31) = 7.12\%$

b $K_E = r_f + \beta\,(r_m - r_f)$

$= 6 + 1.3(5) = 12.5\%$

c $K_{BANK} = (9 + 2)(1 - 0.31) = 7.59\%$

$$\begin{aligned} \text{WACC} &= K_E W_E + K_{DAT} W_D + K_{BANK} W_{BANK} \\ &= 12.5 \times 0.526 + 7.12 \times 0.211 + 7.59 \times 0.263 \\ &= 10.07\% \end{aligned}$$

Market values	*£*	*Weight*
Equity	2m	0.526
Loan	1m	0.263
Bond	0.8m	0.211
	3.8m	1.000

d *Corporate value*

£m	*1*	*2*	*3*	*4*	*5*	*6 → ∞*
Sales	1.1	1.21	1.331	1.464	1.6105	1.6105
Profit	0.11	0.121	0.1331	0.1464	0.16105	0.16105
Tax	–0.0341	–0.0375	–0.04126	–0.0454	–0.0499	–0.0499
IFCI	–0.017	–0.0187	–0.02057	–0.0226	–0.0249	0
IWCI	–0.006	–0.0066	–0.00726	–0.008	–0.0088	0
Operating free cash flow	0.0529	0.0582	0.06401	0.0704	0.07745	0.11115

Discounted cash flows (@10.07%)
= 0.0481 + 0.048 + 0.048 + 0.048 + 0.048 + 0.6832
= £0.9233m

Shareholder value = £0.9233m – £1.8m
= –£0.8767m

Pre-interest cash flows are insufficient to cover the return to finance providers and therefore shareholder value is negative.

e A possible element to the answer:
Operating profit margin = 15%
Planning horizon = 8 years

£m	1	2	3	4	5	6	7	8	9
Sales	1.1	1.21	1.331	1.464	1.6105	1.7716	1.949	2.1436	2.1436
Profit	0.165	0.1815	0.1997	0.2196	0.2416	0.2657	0.2924	0.3215	0.3215
Tax	−0.0512	−0.0563	−0.0619	−0.0681	−0.0749	−0.0824	−0.0906	−0.0997	−0.0997
IFCI	−0.017	−0.0187	−0.02057	−0.0226	−0.0249	−0.0274	−0.0302	−0.0331	0
IWCI	−0.006	−0.0066	−0.00726	−0.008	−0.0088	−0.0097	−0.0106	−0.0117	0
OFC	0.0908	0.0999	0.10997	0.1209	0.133	0.1462	0.161	0.1770	0.2218

$$\frac{0.0908}{1.1007}+\frac{0.0999}{(1.1007)^2}+\frac{0.10997}{(1.1007)^3}+\frac{0.1209}{(1.1007)^4}+\frac{0.133}{(1.1007)^5}+\frac{0.1462}{(1.1007)^6}+\frac{0.161}{(1.1007)^7}+\frac{0.177}{(1.1007)^8}+\frac{0.2218/0.1007}{(1.1007)^8}$$

Discounted cash flows:

0.0825 + 0.0825 + 0.0825 + 0.0824 + 0.0823 + 0.0822 + 0.0823 + 0.0822 + 1.0223 = £1.6812m

Shareholder value = £1.6812m − £1.8m
= −£0.1188m

3 Diversified

a $K_E = r_f + \beta\,(r_m - r_f)$
$= 7 + 1.5(5) = 14.5\%$

$K_{DAT} = K_{DBT}\,(1 - T) = 12\,(1 - 0.3) = 8.4$

$WACC = K_E W_E + K_{DAT} W_D$
$= 14.5 \times 0.6667 + 8.4 \times 0.333 = 12.47$

b *See* Chapter 19.

c *See* Chapter 19.

4 a WACC = 11 × (7/9) + 6% (1 − 0.3) × (2/9) = 9.49%
Enterprise value = £1m/0.0949 = £10.54m

b WACC = 16% × (4/9) + 7% (1 − 0.3) × (5/9) = 9.83%
Enterprise value = £1m/0.0983 = £10.17m
WACC rises and firm value falls.

5 $k_E = 4.5\% + 0.9\,(5\%) = 9\%$
WAAC = 9% × (20/40) + 7.5% × (5/40) + 6.5% (1 − 0.3) (15/40) = 7.14%

Chapter 20

3 $$g = \sqrt[5]{\frac{21}{12}} - 1 = 11.8$$

$$P_0 = \frac{21(1 + 0.059)}{0.13 - 0.059} = 313\text{p}$$

4 240p

5 **Tented**

$k_E = 7 + 1.5(5) = 14.5$

Year	Pence per share	Discounted dividends		
1	13.75	13.75/1.145	=	12.01
2	17.19	$17.19/(1.145)^2$	=	13.11
3	21.48	$21.48/(1.145)^3$	=	14.31
4	26.86	$26.86/(1.145)^4$	=	15.63
5	33.57	$33.57/(1.145)^5$	=	17.06

Price at year 5 = $P_5 = \frac{P_6}{k_E - g} = \frac{33.57(1.05)}{0.145 - 0.05} \div (1.145)^5 =$ 188.54

Value of one share 260.66p

6 **Blueberry plc**

a $$\frac{P_0}{E_0} = \frac{205}{14} = 14.6$$

b $$\sqrt[5]{\frac{14}{9}} - 1 = 0.0923 \textit{ or } 9.23\%$$

c 6.5 + 1.2(5) = 12.5%

d $$\frac{P_0}{E_1} = \frac{d_1/E_1}{k_E - g}$$

$$\frac{P_0}{14(1.0923)} = \frac{0.5}{0.125 - 0.0923} = 15.3$$

$P_0 = 15.3 \times 14(1.0923) = 234\text{p}$

Shares are underpriced.

7 Tes plc

a

NAV in BS	3,588
Building	–100
Debtors	–16
Stock	–30
Investments	151
	£3,593 m

d $\sqrt[16]{\frac{9.60}{0.82}} - 1 = 16.62\%$ $\quad 16.62 \times 0.5 = 8.31$

$k_E = 6.25 + 0.77(5) = 10.1\%$

$$P_0 = \frac{d_1}{k_E - g} = \frac{9.6(1 + 10.0831)}{0.101 - 0.0831} = 580.90p$$

c Some ideas:
The assumed *g* could be inaccurate.
The market might be undervaluing.
The constant growth assumption could be wrong.
k_E could be wrong, especially given the doubts about the CAPM.

f $\frac{P_0}{E_1} = \frac{580.90}{21.9(1 + 0.0831)} = 24.5$

g 21.9, 10.96

h $k_{DBT} = 6.91\%$, $k_{DAT} = 6.91(1–0.30) = 4.84\%$

Market value of equity: £8,000m, of debt: 598(105.50/100) = £631m
Total capital £8,631m
Weights: Equity = 0.93, Debt = 0.07

WACC = $k_{DAT}W_D + k_E W_E = 4.84 \times 0.07 + 10.1 \times 0.93 = 9.73\%$

9 Green plc

a

	£m	
Balance sheet NAV	210	
Tangible assets	50	
Debtors	–60	
Stock	–30	
	170	£170m/300m = 56.7 pence

b *See* Chapter 20.

c $$g = \sqrt[8]{\frac{9.2}{5}} - 1 = 0.079$$

$$k_E = 0.065 + 1.3(0.05) = 0.13$$

$$P_0 = \frac{d_0(1+g)}{k_E - g} = \frac{9.2(1.079)}{0.13 - 0.079} = 194.6\text{p}$$

d Debenture rate of return

$$103 = \frac{8}{1 + k_{DBT}} + \frac{8}{(1 + k_{DBT})^2} + \frac{108}{(1 + k_{DBT})^3}$$

Try 7%

Right hand side = 102.62

Try 6%

Right hand side = 105.35

$$6 + \frac{105.35 - 103}{105.35 - 102.62}(7 - 6) = 6.86\%$$

$$k_{DAT} = 6.86(1 - 0.3) = 4.8\%$$

Weights

Equity = 300m × £1.946 = £584m   584/687 = 85%

$$\text{Debt} = \frac{103}{100} \times 100 = 103 \quad \frac{103}{687} = 15\%$$

$$\text{WACC} = k_E W_E + k_{DAT} W_D$$

$$= 13 \times 0.85 + 4.8 \times 0.15 = 11.77\%$$

Chapter 21

2 Eastwell plc

a	£	£	£
Cash flow	60,000	160,000	300,000
All-equity structure			
Return on equity	$\frac{60,000}{1,000,000} = 6\%$	$\frac{160,000}{1,000,000} = 16\%$	$\frac{300,000}{1,000,000} = 30\%$
40% gearing			
Debt interest @ 12%	48,000	48,000	48,000
Earnings avaliable for shareholders	12,000	112,000	252,000
Return on equity	$\frac{12,000}{600,000} = 2\%$	$\frac{112,000}{600,000} = 18.67\%$	$\frac{252,000}{600,000} = 42\%$
80% gearing			
Debt interest @ 13%	104,000	104,000	104,000
Earnings available for shareholders	–44,000	56,000	196,000
Return on equity	$\frac{-44,000}{200,000} = -22\%$	$\frac{56,000}{200,000} = 28\%$	$\frac{196,000}{200,000} = 98\%$

a and b Expected returns and standard deviations

Return R_i%	*Probability*	*Return × probability*		$(R_i - \bar{R})^2p$
All equity				
6	0.25	1.50		30.25
16	0.50	8.00		0.50
30	0.25	7.50		42.25
Expected return, $\bar{R}$		17.00%	σ^2	73.00
Standard deviation, σ				8.54%
40% gearing				
2	0.25	0.5		84.04
18.67	0.50	9.335		1.39
42	0.25	10.50		117.34
Expected return, $\bar{R}$		20.335%	σ^2	202.77
Standard deviation, σ				14.24%
80% gearing				
–22	0.25	–5.5		756.25
28	0.50	14.0		12.50
98	0.25	24.5		1,056.25
Expected return, $\bar{R}$		33.0	σ^2	1,825.00
Standard deviation, σ				42.72%

c

Gearing	*Expected return* %	*Standard deviation* %	*Business risk* %	*Remaining risk due to financial risk* %
All equity	17	8.54	8.54	
40%	20.34	14.24	8.54	5.7
80%	33	42.72	8.54	34.18

Business risk: The variability of the firm's operating income.
Financial risk: The additional variability in returns to shareholders due to debt in the financial structure.

d Consult main text, Chapter 21.

3 a $\text{WACC} = k_E W_E + k_{DAT} W_D$

$\text{WACC} = 15 \times 0.7 + 9(1 - 0.30) \times 0.3 = 12.39\%$

Value of the firm:

$$\frac{750{,}000}{0.1239} = £6{,}053{,}268$$

b *Director A*

$\text{WACC} = 15 \times 0.4 + 9(1 - 0.30) \times 0.6 = 9.78\%$

$$\text{Value of the firm} = \frac{750{,}000}{0.0978} = £7{,}668{,}712$$

Director B

$\text{WACC} = 23.7 \times 0.4 + 9(1 - 0.30) \times 0.6 = 13.26\%$

$$\text{Value of the firm} = \frac{750{,}000}{0.1326} = £5{,}656{,}109$$

Director C

$\text{WACC} = 17 \times 0.4 + 9(1 - 0.30) \times 0.6 = 10.58\%$

$$\text{Value of the firm} = \frac{750{,}000}{0.1058} = £7{,}088{,}847$$

Director D

$\text{WACC} = 28 \times 0.4 + 9(1 - 0.30) \times 0.6 = 14.98\%$

$$\text{Value of the firm} = \frac{750{,}000}{0.1498} = £5{,}006{,}676$$

6 a $6.1 \times 0.4 + 14.5 \times 0.6 = 11.14$
40% debt, 60% equity

9 $\text{WACC} = 30 \times 0.4 + 9 \times 0.6$
$= 17.4\%$

Chapter 22

4 Vale plc

a

	No of shares (million)	*Profit per share*
This year	100.000	10.8p
t – 1	100.000	8.9p
t – 2	76.923	8.19p
t – 3	76.923	7.15p
t – 4	38.4615	9.10p
t – 5	38.4615	6.76p

b

$$g = \sqrt[5]{\frac{5.4}{3.38}} - 1 \quad = 9.82\%$$

$$k_E = 6.5 + 0.9(5) = 11\%$$

$$P = \frac{5.4\ (1.0982)}{0.11 - 0.0982} = 502.6\text{p}$$

The current market price is below the value given by the dividend valuation model and therefore the shares are a good buy.

5 Tesford plc

a

Year	*Net cash flows*	*Investment*	*Cash flows after investment (for dividends)*	*Dividend per share*
	£m	*£m*	*£m*	*(p)*
1	3	2	1	4.17
2	12	2	10	41.67
3	5	3	2	8.33
4	6	3	3	12.50
5	5	3	2	8.33

b

Year	*Cash flows paid out as regular dividends*	*Maintainable regular dividends per share*	*Cash flows available for special dividends or share repurchase*	*Special dividends or share repurchase per share*
	£m	*(p)*	*£m*	*(p)*
1	1.000	4.17	0	0
2	1.189	4.95	8.811	36.71
3	1.414	5.89	0.586	2.44
4	1.682	7.01	1.318	5.49
5	2.000	8.33	0	0

In practice a special dividend or share repurchase in consecutive years is unlikely. Perhaps Tesford directors will choose to have one or two special payouts which distribute the surplus cash over the five-year period.

7 a $g = 7.46$

$P_0 = 155\text{p}$

	Discounted
b $d_1 = 4\text{p}$	3.54
$d_2 = 4\text{p}$	3.13
$d_3 = 10\text{p}$	6.93
$P_3 = \frac{d_4}{k-g} = \frac{10(1.09)}{0.13-0.09} = 272.5$	188.86
	202.46

Answer 202p.

Therefore the sacrifice of short-term dividends is worthwhile.

c Issues to be discussed: signalling, information asymmetry, clientele effects and residual theory.

Chapter 23

6 a 4.667 shares

b 4.444 shares

Chapter 24

1 A possible hedging strategy:

Purchase 20 June 450 put options and hold to expiry.

If share price falls to 400p:

Loss on shares	£1 × 20,000	20,000
Gain on options	50p × 20,000	10,000
Less Option premium		3,800
		£6,200

Overall loss £13,800

If share price rises to 600p:

Gain on shares	£1 × 20,000	20,000
Less Option premium		3,800
Overall gain		£16,200

2 **a** £520 loss

b £520 – £520 = 0

c £800 – £520 = £280 profit

3

Option	*Intrinsic value*	*Time value*
700 call	32p	23.5p
750 call	0	28p
700 put	0	17.5p
750 put	18p	22p

In-the-money options: 700 call, 750 put.
Out-of-the-money options: 750 call, 700 put.

4 **i**

Sold @ 5,086 × £10 × 5	=	254,300
Bought @ 5,500 × £10 × 5	=	275,000
Loss		£20,700

ii	Sold @ 5,086 × £10 × 5	254,300
	Bought @ 4,500 × £10 × 5	225,000
	Gain	£29,300

5

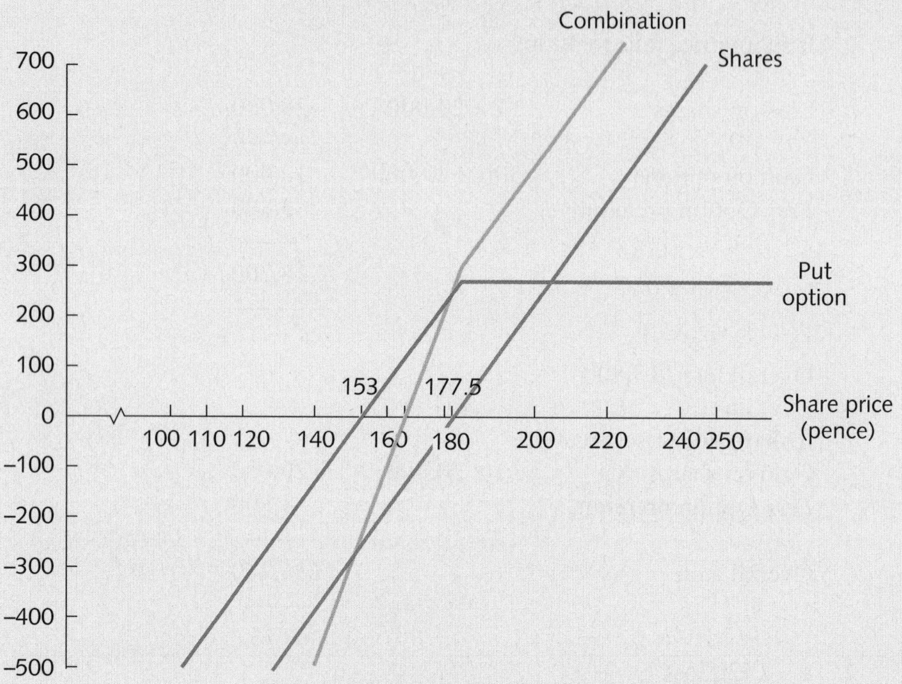

7 a

£000s

Day	*1*	*2*	*3*	*4*	*5*	*6*	*7*	*8*
Value of future	390	410	370	450	420	400	360	410
Initial margin	20	–	–	–	–	–	–	–
Variation margin	−10	20	−40	+80	−30	−20	−40	50
Accumulated profit (loss)	−10	+10	−30	+50	+20	0	−40	+10

10 a Red Wheel could sell 30 three-month sterling interest rate futures dated for December at 91.70.

b Rate of interest = 8.30%.
Gain on derivative: 91.70 – 90.00 = 170 ticks.
This exactly offsets the additional interest paid to the lender:
Gain on derivative: 170 × 12.50 × 30 = £63,750.
Loan interest above 8.3%:
£15m × 0.017 × $^{3}/_{12}$ = £63,750.

c Rate of interest = 8.30%.

Loss on derivative: 91.70 – 93.00 = 130 ticks.

130 × 12.50 × 30 = –£48,750.

Gain from interest rate being lower than 8.3%:

£15m × 0.013 × $^{3}/_{12}$ = £48,750.

Chapter 25

1 a £5,287.34

b ¥94,565,500

c ¥188,869,000

d £529.47

2 a

Expected income	A$10m
Actual income $^{11}/_{1.2}$	A$9.167m
Exchange rate loss	A$0.8333m

b

	A$10.0000m
A$10m $^{11}/_{1.05}$ =	A$10.4762m
Exchange rate gain	A$0.4762m

c Exporter agrees to deliver NZ$11m in six months to forward market counterparty. It will receive 11m/1.09 = A$10.09174m regardless of spot exchange rates in six months' time.

d *See* Chapter 25.

7 a $\frac{1 + 0.02}{1 + 0.04} \times 2 =$ SFr1.9615/£

8 a $\frac{1 + 0.05}{1 + 0.07} \times 1.02 =$ C$1.0009/A$

10 a $\frac{1.02}{1.05} \times 1.77 =$ €1.7194/US$

b $\frac{1.06}{1.09} \times 1.77 =$ €1.7213/US$

11 a Forward purchase of sterling

$$\frac{\text{Won } 1{,}507\text{m}}{1{,}450} = £1.03931\text{m.}$$

b Borrow in Won and exchange for sterling immediately.

Amount borrowed: $\frac{1{,}507\text{m}}{1.005} = \text{Won } 1{,}499.5\text{m}$

Exchange: $\frac{1{,}499.5\text{m}}{1{,}507} = £995{,}023$

In one month the lender is paid with the Won received from the customer.

Glossary

'A' shares Sometimes the 'A' shares are the ordinary shares that carry fewer or no votes. However, in many companies 'A' shares carry more votes than the 'B' shares. The shares may also differ with regard to the size of dividend.

Abandon The choice made by a holder of a warrant or option to allow it to expire without exercise.

Abnormal return (residual return) A return greater than the market return after adjusting for differences in risk.

Absolute advantage A firm, person, organisation or country has an absolute advantage if it can obtain a benefit at a lower cost than other firms, people, organisations or countries. For example Costa Rica has an absolute advantage in growing bananas *vis-à-vis* Europe.

Acceptance credit (bank bill) An institution (e.g. bank) commits itself to the payment of a sum of money in the future as stated in the acceptance credit document. The borrower is given this document (which can be passed on to a supplier) in return for a promise to pay a sum on the maturity date to the institution. The acceptance credit can be sold in the discount market to obtain funds for the borrower (or to pass on to a supplier).

Accounting rate of return (ARR) A measure of profitability based on accounting numbers. Profit divided by assets devoted to the activity (e.g. project, entire business) as a percentage.

Accounting standards A set of formal rules and conventions set by the accounting profession to calculate accounting numbers.

Accounts payable Short-term debts owed by a firm to its creditors for goods and services received. A term used more in the USA – in the UK '**creditors**' is usually used.

Accounts receivable Customer debts to this company. A term used more in the USA – in the UK '**debtors**' is usually used.

Acid test *See* Quick ratio.

Additivity Ability to add up.

Administration An administrator ('administrative receiver') takes over the running of a distressed company following the failure to abide by loan agreements to recover debt due to the creditor(s). Administrators often keep the business running as a going concern, but may have no alternative to liquidation to release money for the creditor(s).

Adverse selection problem When there is an opportunity or incentive for some firms/individuals to act to take advantage of their informational edge over others then the firm/individual doing that activity will be disproportionately those taking advantage rather than being truly representative of the population as a whole, e.g. the tendency for poorer-than-average risks to continue with insurance. This will raise the cost of insurance for the whole group, including those of less-than-average risk. This is caused by asymmetric information in which the poorer-than-average risk policy holder knows more about their risk level than the insurer does.

Affirmative covenants Loan agreement conditions that require positive action on the part of the borrower, e.g. a statement that a bond will pay regular dividends, or that the borrower will distribute information regularly.

Ageing schedule The total debtor figure is broken down to show how long invoices have been outstanding (i.e. have remained unpaid).

Agency Acting for or in the place of another with his/her/their authority.

Agency costs Costs of preventing agents (e.g. managers) pursuing their own interests at the expense of their principals (e.g. shareholders). Examples include contracting costs and costs of monitoring. In addition there is the agency cost of the loss of wealth caused by the extent to which prevention measures have not worked and managers continue to pursue non-shareholder wealth goals.

Agent A person who acts for or in the place of another with that other person's authority (the '**principal**').

Aggressive shares Shares having a beta value greater than 1.

AGM *See* Annual general meeting.

AIM admission document The document needed for a company to be quoted on the Alternative Investment Market in the first instance. It is similar to a prospectus.

Allocation of capital The mechanism for selecting competing investment projects leading to the production of a mixture of goods and services by a society. This can be influenced by the forces of supply and demand; and by central authority direction. The term may also be used for selection of securities (e.g. shares) by investors or business units and activities by managers.

Allocational efficiency of markets Efficiency in the process of allocating society's scarce resources between competing real investments.

Allotment In a new issue of shares, if more shares are demanded at the price than are available, they may be apportioned (allotted) between the applicants.

All-paper deal When a bidder offers to buy shares in a target the payment is entirely in the form of shares in the bidder.

Alpha (Alpha coefficient, α) A measure of performance greater than or less than the market as a whole after allowing for beta in the capital asset pricing model (q.v.). That portion of a share's return that cannot be explained by its responsiveness to moves in the market as a whole. Sometimes called stock-specific return.

Alternative Investment Market (AIM) The lightly regulated share market operated by the London Stock Exchange, focused particularly on smaller, less well-established companies.

Alternative investments Outside the mainstream, e.g. art, stamps, coins, wine.

American Depositary Receipts (ADRs) Depositary receipts issued in the USA.

American-style option (American option) An option which can be exercised by the purchaser at any time up to the expiry date.

AMEX The American Stock Exchange. Trades equities, options and exchange-traded funds.

Amortisation The repayment of a debt by a series of instalments.

Amortisation of assets The reduction in book value of an intangible asset such as goodwill.

Analyst A researcher of companies' prospects and predictor of their share price performance. Also analyses other securities.

Angel – *See* Business angels.

Annual equivalent annuity (AEA) A regular annual amount which is equivalent, in present value terms, to another set of cash flows.

Annual equivalent rate (AER) – *See* Annual percentage rate.

Annual general meeting (AGM) A limited company must hold in each calendar year an annual general meeting. It is an opportunity for shareholders to meet and talk with each other and with those who run the company on their behalf. The managers give an account of their stewardship. All shareholders are entitled to attend and vote. Election of directors may take place.

Annual percentage rate (APR) The true annual interest rate charged by a lender. It takes full account of the timing of payments of interest and principal.

Annual results Annual company accounts. This term is often used for the preliminary results.

Annuity An even stream of payments (the same amount each time) over a given period of time with a fixed frequency of payments.

Annuity due An annuity where the cash flows occur at the start of each period rather than at the end – the first payment is due now, not in one year's time.

Arbitrage The act of exploiting price differences on the same instrument or similar securities by simultaneously selling the overpriced security and buying the underpriced security.

Arbitrage pricing theory (APT) A type of multi-factor model which relates return on securities to various non-diversifiable risk factors. The expected return on any risky security is a linear combination of these factors.

Arithmetic mean or average The average of a set of numbers equals the sum of the observations divided by the number of observations.

Arrangement fee A fee for agreeing and setting up a financial transaction such as a bank loan.

Articles of association Internal rules governing a company. Can be unique to a company.

Asset In the financial markets an asset is anything that can be traded as a security, e.g. share, option, commodity, bond.

Asset allocation An investment methodology, which specifies the proportion of funds to be invested in different asset classes, e.g. property, shares, bonds.

Asset-backed (SPE) (SPV) or entity securities (ABS) *See* Securitisation.

Asset backing The value of the assets held in the business – often measured on a per share basis.

Asset class Asset types, e.g. bonds, shares.

Asset liquidity The extent to which assets can be converted to cash quickly and at a low transaction cost.

Asset lock-up In a hostile takeover situation, the target sells to a friendly firm those parts of the business most attractive to the bidder.

Asset securitisation *See* Securitisation.

Asset transformers Intermediaries who, by creating a completely new security – the intermediate security – mobilise savings and encourage investment. The primary security is issued by the ultimate borrower to the intermediary, who offers intermediate securities to the primary investors.

Associated company A company in which an investor (usually a holding company) holds a participating interest and exercises significant influence over the entity. 'Interest' includes shares, options and convertible securities. 'Participating' means the interest is held on a long-term basis and there is significant influence. Usually a 20 per cent or more holding of the shares is presumed to be participating.

Asymmetric information One party in a negotiation or relationship is not in the same position as other parties, being ignorant of, or unable to observe, some information which is essential to the contracting and decision-making process.

At-the-money option The current underlying price is equal to the option exercise price.

Audit committee A group of independent non-executive directors responsible for validating financial figures.

Auditor Auditors determine whether the company's financial statements are misleading and whether the accounts show a true and fair view.

Authorised but unissued ordinary share capital Shares that have not yet been sold by the company to investors. However, they have been created (authorised by shareholders) and may be sold or given to existing shareholders or sold to new shareholders.

Authorised share capital The maximum amount of share capital that a company can issue. The limit can be changed by a shareholder vote.

Average collection period (ACP) The average number of days it takes to collect debts from customers. The total debtors outstanding divided by the average daily sales.

Back office That part of a financial institution which deals with the settlement of contracts, accounting, regulatory matters and management information processes.

Back-to-back loan Company A and Company B lend to each other the same amount with the same maturity but in different currencies. The purpose is to hedge against currency fluctuations.

Bad debts Debts that are unlikely to be paid.

Bad growth When a company increases investment in an area of business that generates returns less than the opportunity cost of capital.

Balance of payments A record of the payment for goods and services obtained by a country and other transfers of currency from abroad and the receipts for goods and services sold and other transfers of currency abroad. The balance on the current account (visible trade and invisible trade) is the difference between national income and national expenditure in the period. The capital account is made up of such items as the inward and outward flow of money for investment and international grants and loans.

Balance sheet Provides a picture of what a company owned, what it owes and is owed on a particular day in the past. It summarises assets, liabilities and net worth (capital).

Balance sheet hedge To counter the risk of forex (q.v.) translation or economic exposure a company may hedge (q.v.) by borrowing in the same currency as the denomination of the assets.

Balloon repayment on a loan The majority of the repayment of a loan is made at or near the maturity date, with the final payment substantially larger than the earlier payments.

Ballot In a new issue of shares when a company floats on a stock exchange if the demand is greater than the supply, the shares are allocated to some applicants but not others, selected at random.

Bancassurance Companies offering both banking and insurance.

Bank bill *See* Acceptance credit.

Bank covenants *See* Covenant.

Bank for International Settlements (BIS) Controlled by central banks, the BIS was established to assist international financial co-ordination. It promotes international monetary co-ordination, provides research and statistical data, co-ordination and trusteeship for intergovernmental loans and acts as a central bank for national central banks, accepting deposits and making loans.

Bank of England The central bank of the United Kingdom, responsible for monetary policy. It oversees the affairs of other financial institutions, issues banknotes and coins, manages the national debt and exchange rate, and is lender of last resort.

Banker's draft A payment drawn upon the bank itself rather than the customer. It is therefore very reassuring to the supplier, because of the higher probability of being paid compared with a standard cheque.

Bankruptcy Commonly used to describe an individual or company that cannot meet its fixed commitments on borrowing which leads to legal action. However, technically, in the UK individuals become bankrupt whereas firms become insolvent.

Barriers to entry The obstacles that a company entering a market for the first time has to overcome to do well in that market.

Base-case strategy A continuation of current strategy.

Base rate The reference rate of interest that forms the basis for interest rates on bank loans, overdrafts and deposit rates.

Basic (FRS 3) earnings per share Includes deductions from profit of one-off exceptional items and goodwill amortisation.

Basis point (bp) One-hundredth of 1 per cent, usually applied to interest rates.

Bear An investor who takes the view that prices are likely to fall.

Bear fund Designed to do well when shares are falling in price.

Bearer bond The ownership of a bond is not recorded on a register. Possession of the bond is sufficient to receive interest, etc.

Bells and Whistles Additional features placed on derivatives or securities, such as bonds, that are designed to attract investors or reduce issue costs.

Benchmark index An index of shares or other securities that sets a standard for fund manager performance, e.g. a fund manager controlling a portfolio of pharmaceutical shares would measure performance against a pharmaceutical index. This is calculated by an independent person to be representative of the sector.

Benefit–cost ratio A measure of present value per £ invested. Benefit–cost ratio = Net present value (NPV) (q.v.) divided by Initial outlay.

Beta A measure of the systematic risk of a financial security. In the capital asset pricing model (q.v.) it is a measure of the sensitivity to market movements of a financial security's return, as measured by the covariance between returns on the asset and returns on the market portfolio divided by the variance of the market portfolio. In practice a proxy (e.g. FTSE 100 index) is used for the market portfolio.

Bid premium The additional amount an acquirer has to offer above the pre-bid share price in order to succeed in a takeover offer.

Bid price The price at which a market maker will buy shares or a dealer in other markets will buy a security or commodity.

Bid–offer spread ('Bid–ask spread' in USA) The difference between the market maker's buy and sell prices.

Bid yield The yield to maturity on a bond given the market price at which the market makers will buy from investors.

Bill A legal document with a promise to pay or a demand for payment.

Bill of exchange A document setting out a commitment to pay a sum of money at a specified point in time, e.g. an importer commits itself to paying a supplier. Bills of exchange may be discounted – sold before maturity for less than face value.

BIMBO A buy-in management buyout. A combination of a management buyout and a buy-in. Outside managers join forces with existing managers to take over a company, subsidiary or unit.

Bird-in-the-hand fallacy The belief that dividends received earlier are discounted at a lower annual rate than those received in more distant years.

Black Monday 19 October 1987, the date of a large fall in stock market prices (also Monday 28 October 1929 in USA).

Black Wednesday 16 September 1992, a day of severe currency turbulence when sterling and the Italian lira devalued significantly and were forced to leave the Exchange Rate Mechanism.

Blue chip A company regarded as of the highest quality – little risk of a sharp decline in profits or market value.

Board of Directors People elected by shareholders to run a company.

Bond A debt obligation with a long-term maturity (more than one year), usually issued by firms and governments.

Bond covenant *See* Covenant.

Bonus issue *See* Scrip issue.

Bookrunner *See* Book-building

Book value Balance sheet value. Can be expressed on a per share basis.

Book-building A book runner (lead manager) invites major institutional investors to suggest how many shares (or other financial securities) they would be interested in purchasing and at what price in a new issue or secondary issue of shares (or other financial securities). This helps to establish the price and allocate shares.

Book-to-market equity ratio The ratio of a firm's balance sheet net asset value to the total market value of its shares.

Bootstrapping game *See* Price-earnings ratio game.

Borrowing capacity Limits to total borrowing levels imposed by lenders, often determined by available collateral.

Bottom line Profit attributable to the shareholders.

Bought deal An investment bank (the 'lead manager', perhaps together with co-managers of the issue), buys an entire security issue (e.g. shares) from a client corporation raising finance. The investment bank usually intends to then sell it out to institutional clients within hours.

Bourse Alternative name for a stock exchange. A French word, but used in other countries, particularly in Continental Europe.

Break-even analysis Analysing the level of sales at which a project, division or business produces a zero profit (accounting emphasis).

Break-even NPV The point at which when a single variable is changed, the net present value (NPV) (q.v.) of a proposed project switches from positive to negative (or vice versa).

Break-up value The total value of separate parts of the company if the parts are sold off to the highest bidder.

British Bankers Association (BBA) Trade association of British banks. Sets model contracts, publishes interest rates, e.g. interbank rates, advocates on behalf of banks.

Broker Assists in the buying and selling of financial securities by acting as a 'go-between', helping to reduce search and information costs.

Broker-dealer An individual acting as agent for buyers and sellers, but who, at the same time, trades for his own account and may also be a market maker.

Bubble An explosive upward movement in financial security or other asset prices not based on fundamentally rational factors, followed by a crash.

Budget (national) Sets out government expenditure and revenue for the financial year. In the UK it is presented by the Chancellor of the Exchequer to the British Parliament.

Buffer stock Stock (raw material, work-in-progress or finished goods) held to reduce the negative effects (stock-out costs) of an unusually large usage of stock.

Building society A UK financial institution, the primary role of which is the provision of mortgages. Building societies are non-profit-making mutual organisations. Funding is mostly through small deposits by individuals.

Bulge bracket A leading investment bank.

Bull An investor taking the view that prices will rise.

Bulldog A foreign bond issued in the UK.

Bullet bond A bond where all the principal on a loan is repaid at maturity.

Bulletin board A computer-based site for infrequently traded shares on which investors (via brokers) can display their unfilled orders in the hope of finding a match.

Business angels Wealthy individuals prepared to invest between £10,000 and £250,000 in a start-up, early-stage or developing firm. They often have managerial and/or technical experience to offer the management team as well as equity and debt finance. Medium- to long-term investment in high-risk situation.

Business risk The risk associated with the underlying operations of a business. The variability of the firm's operating income, before interest income: this dispersion is caused purely by business-related factors and not by the debt burden.

Buy-back *See* Share repurchase.

BVCA British Venture Capital Association.

CAC 40 (Compagnie des Agents de Change 40 Index) A stock market index of French shares quoted in Paris.

Cadbury report The Committee on the Financial Aspects of Corporate Governance chaired by Sir Adrian Cadbury made recommendations on the role of directors and auditors, published in 1992.

Call-back features *See* Call option.

Call option This gives the purchaser the right, but not the obligation, to buy a fixed quantity of a commodity, financial instrument or some other underlying asset at a given price, at or before a specified date.

Called-up (issued) share capital The total value of shares sold by a company when expressed at par or nominal value.

Cap (1) An interest rate cap is a contract that effectively gives the purchaser the right to set a maximum level for interest rates payable. Compensation is paid to the purchaser of a cap if interest rates rise above an agreed level. (2) (Derivatives) Any feature that sets a maximum return, payout or cost.

Capex *See* Capital expenditure

Capital (1) Funding for a business – can be equity only or equity plus debt. (2) Another term for net worth – total assets minus total liabilities.

Capital Asset Pricing Model (CAPM) An asset (e.g. share) pricing theory which assumes that financial assets, in equilibrium, will be priced to produce rates of return which compensate investors for systematic risk as measured by the covariance of the assets' return with the market portfolio return (i.e. beta).

Capital budgeting The process of analysing and selecting long-term capital investments.

Capital expenditure (Capex) The purchase of long-lived (more than one year) assets (that is, fixed assets).

Capital gearing The extent to which the firm's total capital is in the form of debt.

Capital lease *See* Finance lease and Leasing.

Capital market Where those raising finance can do so by selling financial investments to investors, e.g. bonds, shares.

Capital rationing When funds are not available to finance all wealth-enhancing (positive NPV) projects.

Capital reconstruction (restructuring) Altering the shape of the firm's liabilities. E.g. increases/ decreases in the amount of equity; increases/ decreases in debt; lengthening/ shortening debt maturities.

Capital structure The proportion of the firm's capital which is equity or debt.

Capitalisation (1) An item of expenditure is taken on to the balance sheet and capitalised as an asset rather than written off against profits. (2) Short for market capitalisation (q.v.).

Capitalisation factor A discount rate.

Capitalisation issue *See* Scrip issue.

Capitalisation rate Required rate of return for the class of risk.

Capped bonds The floating interest rate charged cannot rise above a specified level.

Captives A venture capital organisation that raises its capital from one institution (or a small group of institutions).

Cartel A group of otherwise competing firms entering into an agreement to set mutually acceptable prices, output levels and market shares for their products.

Cash-conversion cycle The stock-conversion period plus the debtor-conversion period minus the credit period granted by suppliers. It focuses on the length of time between the company's outlay on inputs and the receipt of money from the sale of goods.

Cash cow A company with low growth and stable market conditions with low investment needs. The company's competitive strength enables it to produce surplus cash.

Cash dividend A normal dividend by a company, paid in cash rather than a scrip dividend.

Cash settled In the derivatives market some contracts are physically settled at expiry date (e.g. pork bellies are delivered in return for cash under the derivative contract). However, many derivatives are not physically delivered; rather, a cash difference representing a gain or loss on the closed derivative position changes hands.

Causal ambiguity A potential imitator is unable to see clearly which resource is giving the sustainable competitive advantage to a firm or it is difficult to identify the way in which the extraordinary resource was created in the first place.

CBOT *See* Chicago Board of Trade.

CEO (Chief Executive Officer) The director with the highest power over the actions of the firm.

Central bank A bankers' bank and lender of last resort, which controls the credit system of an economy, e.g. controls note issue, acts as the government's bank, controls interest rates and regulates the country's banking system.

Central Counter-party (CCP) clearing house *See* Clearing house.

Certainty equivalent The value of a risk-free cash flow that would make the investor indifferent as to the choice between this safe cash flow or an alternative risky cash flow.

Certificate of deposit (CD) A deposit is made at a bank. A certificate confirming that a deposit has been made is given by the bank to the lender. This is normally a bearer security. Most CDs can then be sold in the secondary market whenever the depositor (firm or investor) needs cash.

CHAPS (Clearing House Automated Payment System) The UK same-day interbank clearing system for sterling payments (computer based).

Characteristic line The line that best relates the return on a share to the return on a broad market index.

Chartism Security analysis that relies on historic price charts (and/or trading volumes) to predict future movements.

Chicago Board of Trade (CBOT) The futures and options exchange in Chicago, USA – the world's oldest (established 1848).

Chicago Board Options Exchange (CBOE) The largest options exchange in the world, trading options on shares, indices and interest rates.

Chicago Mercantile Exchange (CME) An exchange which trades a wide range of currency futures and options, interest rate futures and options, commodity futures and options and share index futures and options.

Chief executive officer (CEO) The manager/director in overall charge of the running of the business.

Chief executive's review (operational review) A comment, contained in a company's annual report and accounts, on performance, strategy and managerial intentions.

Chinese walls Barriers within a financial service company designed to prevent sensitive information being passed on to another branch of the organisation.

CHIPS (Clearing House Interbank Payment System) The US system for settling US dollar payment the same day between banks.

Circle of competence The business areas that an individual thoroughly understands and is equipped to analyse.

City Code on Takeovers and Mergers Provides the main governing rules for UK-based companies engaged in merger activity. Self-regulated and administered by the Takeover Panel.

City of London A collective term for the financial institutions located in the financial district to the east of St Paul's Cathedral in London (also called the Square Mile). However, the term is also used to refer to all UK-based financial institutions, wherever they are located.

Clawback Existing shareholders often have the right to reclaim shares sold under a placing as though they were entitled to them under a rights issue.

Clean price On a bond the prices are generally quoted 'clean', that is without taking account of the accrued interest since the last coupon payment.

Clearing a trade The stock exchange ensures that (1) all reports of a trade are reconciled to make sure all parties are in agreement as to the number of shares traded and the price; and (2) the buyer and seller have the cash and securities to do the deal.

Clearing bank Member of the London Bankers' Clearing House, which clears cheques, settling indebtedness between two parties.

Clearing house An institution which registers, monitors, matches and settles mutual indebtedness between a number of individuals or organisations. The clearing house may also act as a counterparty.

Clientele effect In dividend theory the level of dividend may be influenced by shareholders preferring a dividend pattern which matches their consumption pattern and/or tax position.

Closed-end funds Collective investment vehicles (e.g. investment trusts) that do not create or redeem shares on a daily basis in response to increases and decreases in demand. They have a fixed number of shares for lengthy periods.

Closing out a futures position The act of taking a second action in the futures market (say, selling the future) which is exactly opposite to the first action (say, buying the future). Also called reversing the trade.

CLS bank *See* Continuous linked settlement.

Coefficient of determination, R-squared For single linear regression this is the proportion of variation in the dependant variable that is related to the variation in the independent variable. A measure of the 'goodness of fit' in a regression equation.

Co-lead manager The title given to an underwriter (e.g. for a bond sale) who has joint lead manager status and may sometimes be engaged in structuring the transaction. Usually part of the selling group. Usually does not act as a bookrunner.

Collar A ceiling and floor interest rate placed on the variability of interest payable on a debt, often achieved by the simultaneous purchase of an interest rate cap and sale of an interest rate floor.

Collateral Property pledged by a borrower to protect the interests of the lender.

Collective funds *See* Pooled funds.

Combined Code A set of guidelines for best practice corporate governance. The latest alterations were made by the Higgs committee (*see* Hampel report). The United Kingdom Listing Authority (q.v.) requires compliance or an explanation.

Commercial banking A range of banking services undertaken, including taking deposits and making loans, chequing facilities, trustee services, securities advisory services.

Commercial bill (bank bill or trade bill) A document expressing the commitment of a borrowing firm to repay a short-term debt at a fixed date in the future.

Commercial paper (CP) An unsecured note promising the holder (lender) a sum of money to be paid in a few days – average maturity of 40 days. If they are denominated in a foreign currency and placed outside the jurisdiction of the authorities of that currency then the notes are Eurocommercial paper.

Commitment fee A fee payable in return for a commitment by a bank to lend money at some future date. In some cases the fee is only payable on the undrawn portion of the loan, in others the fee also applies to funds already drawn down under the arrangement.

Commodity product (1) Undifferentiated compared with competitor offerings in any customer-important way by factors such as performance, appearance, service support, etc. For example, many personal computers are said to be commodity products. (2) Raw materials and foodstuffs.

Common stock The term used in the USA to describe ordinary shares in a company.

Companies Acts The series of laws enacted by Parliament governing the establishment and conduct of incorporated business enterprises. The Companies Act 2006 consolidated the Acts that preceded it.

Companies House The place where records are kept of every UK company. These accounts, etc. are then made available to the general public.

Company registrar *See* Registrar.

Comparative advantage A firm or a country has a comparative advantage in the production of good X if the opportunity cost of producing a unit of X, in terms of other goods forgone, is lower, in that country compared with another country, or in that firm compared with another firm.

Competition Commission The Commission may obtain any information needed to investigate possible monopoly anti-competitive situations referred to it. It may then block anti-competitive action.

Competitive advantage (edge) The possession of extraordinary resources that allow a firm to rise above the others in its industry to generate exceptional long-run rates of return on capital employed.

Competitive floor Where shareholders receive a rate of return that only just induces them to put money into the firm and hold it there. This minimal rate of return occurs because of the high level of competition in the market for the firm's product.

Competitive position The competitive strength of the firm *vis-à-vis* rivals, suppliers, customer and substitutes in a product market.

Complementary product One that is generally bought alongside the product in question.

Compliance Methods of ensuring that financial market operators meet any legal and supervisory requirements.

Compound interest Interest is paid on the sum which accumulates, whether or not that sum comes from principal or from interest received at intermediate dates.

Compound return The income received on an investment is reinvested in the investment and future returns are gained on both the original capital and the ploughed-back income.

Concert party A group of investors, acting together or under the control of one person, which buys shares in a company.

Conflict of preferences There is a conflict of preferences between the primary investors wanting low-cost liquidity and low risk on invested funds, and the ultimate borrowers wanting long-term risk-bearing capital.

Conglomerate A holding company with subsidiaries with operations in different business areas.

Conglomerate bank A bank with a wide range of activities, products and markets.

Conglomerate merger The combining of two firms which operate in unrelated business areas.

Consideration The price paid for something.

Consolidated accounts All the income, costs, assets and all the liabilities of all group companies, whether wholly or partially owned, are brought together in the consolidated accounts. Consolidation must take place if 50 per cent or more of a subsidiary's shares are held by the parent. If less than 50 per cent of the shares are held consolidation may still be required.

Consolidation of shares The number of shares is reduced and the nominal value of each remaining share rises.

Consumer price index (CPI) A measure of general inflation.

Continuing obligations Standards of behaviour and actions required of firms listed on the London Stock Exchange, enforced by the United Kingdom Listing Authority (q.v.).

Continuous Linked Settlement (CLS) A system designed to reduce the risk of failure of one counterparty to a foreign exchange transaction to fulfil an obligation. Payment of the two sides of the currency deal is made the day after the deal, organised by the CLS Bank.

Continuous order book Throughout the trading day orders are automatically matched and executed against one another.

Contract for differences (CFD) The buyer and seller agree to pay, in cash, at the closing of the contract, the difference between the opening and closing price of the underlying shares, multiplied by the number of shares in the contract. *See* Arnold, G.C. (2004) *The Financial Times Guide to Investing* (Harlow: FT Prentice Hall) for more detail.

Contractual theory Views the firm as a network of contracts, actual and implicit, which specify the roles to be played by various participants. Most participants bargain for low risk and a satisfactory return. Shareholders accept high risk in anticipation of any surplus returns after all other parties have been satisfied.

Contrarian Taking the opposite position to the generality of investors.

Controlling shareholder Any shareholder able to control the composition of the board of directors and therefore the direction of the company. Strictly speaking this is 50 per cent, but even a 30 per cent shareholder can exercise this degree of power, and therefore 30 per cent is used as the cut-off point for some purposes.

Conventional cash flows Where an outflow is followed by a series of inflows, or a cash inflow is followed by a series of cash outflows.

Convergence The coming together of the futures price and the underlying share price as the final trading day of a futures contract approaches.

Conversion premium The difference between the current share price and the conversion price, expressed as a percentage of the current share price for convertible bonds.

Conversion price The share price at which convertible bonds may be converted.

Conversion ratio The nominal (par) value of a convertible bond divided by the conversion price. The number of shares available per bond.

Conversion value The value of a convertible bond if it were converted into ordinary shares at the current share price.

Convertible bonds Bonds which carry a rate of interest and give the owner the right to exchange the bonds at some stage in the future into ordinary shares according to a prearranged formula.

Convertible currency A currency that may be exchanged into another with no or few restrictions on individuals, companies or institutions, such as government prohibitions.

Convertible loan stock Same definition as Convertible bond.

Convertible preferred stock A preferred share that can be changed into another type of security, e.g. an ordinary share, at the holder's option.

Coredeal An international exchange for international debt-related securities, owned by the International Securities Markets Association (ISMA).

Corporate bond A bond issued by a company.

Corporate acquisition *See* Takeover (acquisition).

Corporate broker Stockbrokers that act on behalf of companies quoted on an exchange. For example, they may provide advice on market conditions or may represent the company to the market. Corporate brokers are knowledgeable about the share and other financial markets. They advise companies on fund raising (e.g. new issues). They try to generate interest amongst investors for the company's securities. They stand prepared to buy and sell companies' shares.

Corporate finance department of investment banks The department assisting firms in raising funds (e.g. rights issues, bond issues) and managing their finances.

Corporate governance The system of management and control of the corporation.

Corporate raider An organisation that makes hostile takeover approaches for quoted companies.

Corporate value The present value of cash flows for the entire corporation within the planning horizon plus the present value of cash flows after the planning horizon plus the saleable value of assets not required for cash flow generation. Includes cash flows attributable to equity and debt holders.

Corporate venturing Large companies fostering the development of smaller enterprises through, say, joint capital development or equity capital provision.

Corporation tax A tax levied on the profits of companies.

Correlation coefficient A measure of the extent to which two variables show a relationship, expressed on a scale of –1 to +1.

Correlation scale A scale between –1 and +1 showing the degree of co-movement of two variables, e.g. the return on two shares. A value of –1 indicates exact opposite movement, a value of +1 indicates perfect movement in the same direction.

Cost leadership strategy Standard no-frills product. Emphasis on scale economies and other cost advantages.

Cost of capital The rate of return that a company has to offer finance providers to induce them to buy and hold a financial security.

Counterparty The buyer for a seller or the seller for a buyer.

Counterparty risk The risk that a counterparty to a contract defaults and does not fulfil its obligations.

Country risk Risk to transactions overseas or assets held abroad due to political, legal, regulatory or settlement changes or difficulties, e.g. nationalisation or law forbidding repatriation of profits.

Coupons An attachment to bond or loan note documents which may be separated and serve as evidence of entitlement to interest. Nowadays it refers to the interest itself: the nominal annual rate of interest expressed as a percentage of the principal value.

Covariance The extent to which two variables move together.

Covenant A solemn agreement.

Cover Offsetting one position in a financial security with an equal and opposite transaction in the same or linked (e.g. derivative) security.

Covered call option writing Writing a call option on an underlying when the writer owns at least the number of underlying securities included in the option.

Covered warrants The same as warrants except that financial institutions issue them, selling the right to buy or sell shares in industrial and commercial companies.

Creative accounting The drawing up of accounts which obey the letter of the law and accounting body rules but which involve the manipulation of accounts to show the most favourable profit and balance sheet.

Credit derivative An instrument for which the payoff is linked to changes in the underlying's credit standing, e.g. if the credit rating changes on a bond issued by a company from BBB– to D the holder will receive a payout on a credit derivative (sold by a financial institution) which takes as its underlying that particular company's bond.

Credit facility or Credit line A short-term borrowing arrangement with a bank or other lender under which borrowing may fluctuate at the behest of the borrower up to a fixed total amount, e.g. overdraft, revolving facility.

Credit insurance An insurance policy that pays out on trade debts held by the firm when customers fail to meet their obligations.

Credit period The average length of time between the purchase of inputs and the payment for them. Equal to the average level of creditors divided by the purchases on credit per day.

Credit rating An estimate of the quality of a debt from the lender's viewpoint in terms of the likelihood of interest and capital not being paid and of the extent to which the lender is protected in the event of default. Credit-rating agencies are paid fees by companies, governments, etc. wishing to attract lenders.

Credit risk The risk that a counterparty to a financial transaction will fail to fulfil its obligation.

Credit risk premium or credit spread The additional yield (over, say, reputable government bonds) on a debt instrument due to the borrower's additional perceived probablity of default.

Credit union A non-profit organisation accepting deposits and making loans, operated as a co-operative.

Creditor One to whom a debt is owed.

Crest or CREST An electronic means of settlement and registration of shares and other securities following a sale on the London Stock Exchange, operated by CRESTCo.

Crown jewels defence In a hostile merger situation, the target sells off the most attractive parts of the business.

Cum-dividend (1) When an investor buys a government bond (q.v.) when it is still designated cum-dividend or cum-coupon he/she is entitled to the accrued interest since the last coupon was paid. (2) A share (q.v.) designated cum-dividend indicates that the buyer will be entitled to a dividend recently announced by the company.

Cum-rights Shares bought on the stock market prior to the ex-rights day are designated cum-rights and carry to the new owner the right to subscribe for the new shares in the rights issue.

Cumulative If a payment (interest or dividend) on a bond (q.v.) or share (q.v.) is missed in one period those securities are given priority when the next payment is made. These arrears must be cleared up before shareholders received dividends.

Currency swap *See* Swap.

Current account deficit *See* Balance of payment.

Current asset value (net) Current assets (cash, accounts receivable, inventory) minus current liabilities (also called working capital).

Current assets Cash and other assets that can be rapidly turned into cash. Includes stocks of raw materials, partially finished goods and finished goods, debtors and investments expected to be sold within one year.

Current liabilities Amounts owed that the company expects to have to pay within the next year.

Current ratio The ratio of current liabilities to the current assets of a business.

Current yield (flat yield, income yield or running yield) The ratio of the coupon (q.v.) on a bond (q.v.) to its current market price.

Cyclical companies (industries, shares) Those companies in which profits are particularly sensitive to the growth level in the economy, which may be cyclical.

Daily Official List (DOL) The daily record setting out the prices of all trades in securities conducted on the London Stock Exchange.

Darling A stock market darling is one which receives a lot of attention and is regarded as very attractive.

Dawn raid An acquirer acts with such speed in buying the shares of the target company that the raider achieves the objective of a substantial stake in the target before its management has time to react.

DAX 30 (Deutsche Aktienindex) A stock market index of German shares quoted on Deutsche Börse (q.v.).

Debentures Bonds issued with redemption dates a number of years into the future or irredeemable. Usually secured against specific assets (mortgage debentures) or through a floating charge on the firm's assets (floating debentures). In the USA debenture means an unsecured debt with a fixed coupon.

Debt An obligation to pay

Debt capital Capital raised with (usually) a fixed obligation in terms of interest and principal payments.

Debt maturity The length of time left until the repayment on a debt becomes due.

Debt-to-equity ratio The ratio of a company's long-term debt to shareholders' funds.

Debtor conversion period The average number of days to convert customer debts into cash. Equal to the average value of debtors divided by the average value of sales per day.

Debtors Those who owe a debt.

Declining (reducing) balance method of depreciation The amount by which an asset is depreciated declines from one year to the next as it is determined by a constant percentage of the asset's depreciated value at the start of each year.

Deep discounted bonds Bonds sold well below par value, usually because they have little or no coupon.

Deep discounted rights issue A rights issue price is much less than the present market price of the old shares.

Default A failure to make agreed payments of interest or principal, or failure to comply with some other provision.

Defensive industries Those industries where profits are not particularly sensitive to the growth level in the economy.

Defensive shares Having a beta value of less than 1.

Deferred ordinary shares (1) Rank below preferred ordinary shares for dividends. So, if profits are low deferred ordinary holders may not receive a dividend. However, if the company achieves a predetermined level of profit or other performance target the deferred ordinary shares often entitle the owner to a higher than normal dividend. (2) The right to the dividend is deferred for a set period, after which the holders rank equal with ordinary shareholders.

Deferred tax With a fixed asset the writing down allowance, which can be used to reduce current tax payable, is often greater than the depreciation charge as determined by the company's accounting policy. The differences is called a timing difference. A Deferred tax provision is the difference between (i) the corporation tax actually payable on the taxable trading profit and (ii) the tax that would have been payable if the taxable trading profit is the same as the accounting profit (using normal depreciation not writing down allowance).

Dematerialisation Traditionally the evidence of financial security ownership is by written statements on paper (e.g. share certificates). Increasingly such information is being placed on electronic records and paper evidence is being abandoned.

Demerger The separation of companies or business units that are currently under one corporate umbrella. It applies particularly to the unravelling of a merger.

Depletion A reduction in the value of a natural resource, e.g. oil in the ground, owned by a company.

Depositary receipts Certificates, representing evidence of ownership of a company's shares (or other securities) held by a depository. Depositary Receipts (DRs) are negotiable (can be traded) certificates which represent ownership of a given number of a company's shares which can be listed and traded independently from the underlying shares. There are a number of forms of DRs including American Depositary Receipts (ADRs), Global Depositary Receipts (GDRs), Euro Depositary Receipts (EDRs) and Retail Depositary Receipts (RDRs).

Derivative A financial asset (instrument), the performance of which is based on (derived from) the behaviour of the value of an underlying asset.

Deutsche Börse AG The German Stock Exchange based in Frankfurt.

Development capital Second-stage finance (following seed finance – *see* Seedcorn capital or money *and* Early-stage capital) to permit business expansion.

Differentiated product One that is slightly different in significant ways from those supplied by other companies. The unique nature of the product/service offered allows for a premium price to be charged.

Diluted earnings per share Takes into account any additional shares that may be issued in the future under executive share option schemes and other commitments.

Dilution The effect on the earnings and voting power per ordinary share from an increase in the number of shares issued without a corresponding increase in the firm's earnings.

Diminishing marginal utility Successive equal increments in quantity of a good (money) yield smaller and smaller increases in utility.

Direct foreign investment The cross-border purchase of commercial assets such as factories and industrial plant for productive purposes.

Directors' dealings The purchase or sale of shares in their own company. This is legal (except at certain times of the company's year). Some investors examine directors' dealings to decide whether to buy or sell.

Directors' report Information and commentary on company performance and other matters contained in a company's annual report and accounts.

Dirty price On a bond a buyer pays a total of the clean price and the accrued interest since the last coupon payment.

Disclosure of shareholdings If a stake of 3 per cent or more is held by one shareholder in a UK public company, then this has to be declared to the company.

Discount (1) The amount below face value at which a financial claim sells, e.g. bill of exchange or zero coupon bond. (2) The extent to which an investment trust's shares sell below the net asset value. (3) The amount by which a future value of a currency is less than its spot value. (4) The action of purchasing financial instruments, e.g. bills, at a discount. (5) The degree to which a security sells below its issue price in the secondary market. (6) The process of equating a cash flow at some future date with today's value using the time value of money.

Discount house An institution that purchases promissory notes and resells them or holds them until maturity.

Discount market deposit Originally it was money deposited with a London discount house. However, there is now a collection of UK institutions and dealers in money market instruments such as trade bills. These are normally repayable at call or very short term. Clearing banks are the usual depositors.

Discount rate (1) The rate of return used to discount cash flows received in future years. It is the opportunity cost of capital given the risk class of the future cash flows. (2) The rate of interest at which some central banks lend money to the banking system.

Discounted cash flow Future cash flows are converted into the common denominator of time zero money by adjusting for the time value of money.

Discounted payback The period of time required to recover initial cash outflow when the cash inflows are discounted at the opportunity cost of capital.

Discounting The process of reducing future cash flows to a present value using an appropriate discount rate.

Disintermediation Borrowing firms bypassing financial institutions and obtaining debt finance directly from the market.

Disinvest To sell an investment.

Diversifiable risk *See* Unsystematic risk.

Diversification To invest in varied projects, enterprises, financial securities, products, markets, etc.

Divestiture (Divestment) The selling off of assets or subsidiary businesses by a company or individual.

Dividend That part of profit paid to ordinary shareholders, usually on a regular basis.

Dividend cover The number of times net profits available for distribution exceed the dividend actually paid or declared. Earnings per share divided by gross dividend per share *or* Total post-tax profits divided by total dividend payout.

Dividend discount model – *See* Dividend valuation models.

Dividend payout ratio The percentage of a company's earnings paid out as dividends.

Dividend per share The total amount paid or due to be paid in dividends for the year (interim and final) divided by the number of shares in issue.

Dividend policy The determination of the proportion of profits paid out to shareholders over the longer term.

Dividend reinvestment plan (DRIP) A shareholder receives shares in lieu of a cash dividend. This avoids the cost and trouble of receiving cash and then reinvesting.

Dividend valuation models (DVM) These methods of share valuation are based on the premise that the market value of ordinary shares represents the sum of the expected future dividend flows, to infinity, discounted to present value.

Dividend yield The amount of dividend paid on each share as a percentage of the share price.

Divisible projects It is possible to undertake a fraction of a project.

Divorce of ownership and control In large corporations shareholders own the firm but may not be able to exercise control. Managers often have control because of a diffuse and divided shareholder body, proxy votes and apathy.

Dominance When one (investment) possibility is clearly preferable to a risk-averse investor because it possesses a better expected return than another possibility for the same level of risk.

Dow or Dow Jones Industrial Average The best known index of movements in the price of US stocks and shares. There are 30 shares in the index.

Drawdown arrangement A loan facility is established and the borrower uses it (takes the money available) in stages as the funds are required.

Due diligence When a transaction is contemplated, such as a merger or a loan, a detailed investigation of the company is carried out, usually by specialists, to ensure that its condition is suitable for the transaction.

Early-settlement discount The reduction of a debt owed if it is paid at an early date.

Early-stage capital Funds for initial manufacturing and sales for a newly formed company. High-risk capital available from entrepreneurs, business angels and venture capital funds.

Earn-out The purchase price of a company is linked to the future profits performance. Future instalments of the purchase price may be adjusted if the company performs better or worse than expected.

Earning power The earning (profit) capacity of a business in a normal year. What the company might be expected to earn year after year if the business conditions continue unchanged.

Earnings Profits, usually after deduction of tax.

Earnings guidance A company guiding analysts to estimates of profits for the current period.

Earnings multiple Price–earnings ratio.

Earnings per share (EPS) Profit after tax and interest divided by number of shares in issue.

Earnings yield Earnings per share divided by current market price of share.

EBIT A company's earnings (profits) before interest and taxes are deducted

EBITDA Earnings before interest, taxation, depreciation and amortisation. Or as cynics have it: Earnings Before I Tricked The Dumb Auditor.

Economic book value A term used by Stern Stewart & Co. It is based on the balance sheet capital employed figure subject to a number of adjustments.

Economic exposure *See* Economic risk.

Economic franchise Pricing power combined with strong barriers to entry. The strength and durability of an economic franchise are determined by (1) the structure of the industry; and (2) the ability of the firm to rise above its rivals in its industry and generate exceptional long-run rates of return on capital employed.

Economic order quantity (EOQ) The quantity of inventory items (e.g. raw materials) to order on each occasion which minimises the combined costs of ordering and holding stock.

Economic profit (EP) For a period the economic profit is the amount earned by a business after deducting all operating expenses and a charge for the opportunity cost of the capital employed.

Economic risk The risk that a company's economic value may decline as a result of currency movements causing a loss in competitive strength.

Economic value added (EVA) Developed by Stern Stewart & Co. A value-based metric of corporate performance which multiplies the invested capital (after adjustments) by the spread between the (adjusted) actual return on capital and the weighted average cost of capital (q.v.). The adjustments are to the profit figures to obtain the actual return and to the balance sheet to obtain the invested capital figure.

Economies of scale Larger size of output often leads to lower cost per unit of output.

Economies of scope The ability to reduce the unit costs of an item by sharing some costs between a number of product lines, e.g. using the same truck to deliver both ketchup and beans to a store.

EDX London An equity derivative exchange based in London owned by the London Stock Exchange and OM AM of Sweden.

Effective annual rate *See* Annual percentage rate.

Efficient market hypothesis (EMH) The EMH implies that new information is incorporated into a share price (1) rapidly and (2) rationally. *See also* Efficient stock market.

Efficient portfolio A portfolio that offers the highest expected return for a given level of risk (standard deviation) and the lowest risk for its expected return.

Efficient stock market Share prices rationally reflect available information. In an efficient market no trader will be presented with an opportunity for making an abnormal return, except by chance. *See also* Efficient market hypothesis.

EGM *See* Extraordinary general meeting.

Electronic funds transfer at a point of sale (EFTPOS) A computerised system allowing the automatic transfer of money from a buyer to a seller of goods or services at the time of sale.

Electronic settlement Transferring shares from sellers to buyers without certificates – it is a computer entry only.

Emerging markets Security markets in newly industrialising countries and/or capital markets at an early stage of development.

Employee share ownership plans (ESOP) Schemes designed to encourage employees to build up a shareholding in their company.

Endowment policies (savings schemes) Insurance policies in which a lump sum is payable, either at the end of the term of the policy or on death during the term of the policy.

Enfranchisement Granting voting rights to holders of non-voting shares.

Enterprise investment scheme (EIS) Tax relief is available to investors in qualifying company shares (unquoted firms not involved in financial investment and property).

Enterprise value The sum of a company's total equity market capitalisation and borrowings.

Entrepreneur Defined by economists as the owner-manager of a firm. Usually supplies capital, organises production, decides on strategic direction and bears risk.

Equilibrium in markets When the forces of supply and demand are evenly balanced.

Equities An ownership share of a business, each equity share representing an equal stake in the business. The risk capital of a business.

Equitisation An increasing emphasis placed on share (equity) finance and stock exchanges in economies around the world. A growing equity culture.

Equity approach An economic profit approach to value measurement that deducts interest from operating profit as well as tax. From this is deducted the required return on equity funds devoted to the activity only (i.e. does not include required return for debt capital).

Equity indices Baskets of shares indicating the movement of the equity market as a whole or sub-sets of the markets.

Equity kicker (sweetener) The attachment to a bond or other debt finance of some rights to participate in and benefit from a good performance (e.g. to exercise an option to purchase shares). Often used with mezzanine finance (q.v.) and high-yield bonds.

Equity-linked bonds *See* Convertible bonds.

Equity shareholders' funds *See* Shareholders' funds.

Equity warrants A security issued by a company that gives to the owners the right but not the obligation to purchase shares in the company from the company at a fixed price during or at the end of a specified time period.

Euribor Short-term interest rates in the interbank market (highly stable banks lending to each other) in the currency of euros.

Euro The name of the single European currency in use since 1999 in the eurozone.

Euro medium-term notes (EMTN) *See* Medium-term note.

Eurobond Bond sold outside the jurisdiction of the country in whose currency the bond is denominated. For example, a bond issued in yen outside Japan.

Eurocommercial paper *See* Commercial paper.

Eurocredit A market in credit outside the jurisdiction of the country in whose currency the loan is denominated. (Borrowers can gain access to medium-term bank lending, for 1–15 years.)

Eurocurrency Currency held outside its country of origin, for example, Australian dollars held outside Australia. Note: this market existed long before the creation of the currency in the eurozone. It has no connection with the euro.

Eurocurrency banking Transactions in a currency other than the host country's currency. For example, transactions in Canadian dollars in London. No connection with the currency in the eurozone.

Eurocurrency deposits Short-term wholesale money market deposits made in the eurocurrency market.

Eurodeposit account Short-term wholesale money market deposits are made into an account set up for that purpose made in the eurocurrency market.

Eurodollar A deposit or credit of dollars held outside the regulation of the US authorities, say in Tokyo, London or Paris. No connection with the currency in the eurozone.

Euromarkets Informal (unregulated) markets in money held outside the jurisdiction of the country of origin, e.g. Swiss francs lending outside the control of the Swiss authorities – perhaps the francs are in London. No connection with the euro, the currency in use in the eurozone. Euromarkets began in the late 1950s and now encompass the eurocurrency, eurocredit and eurobond markets as well as over-the-counter derivatives and commodity markets.

Euronext The combined financial stock market comprising the French, Dutch, Belgian and Portuguese bourses.

Euronext.liffe Euronext, the organisation combining the French, Dutch, Belgian and Portuguese stock markets, bought LIFFE (q.v.) and renamed it Euronext. liffe.

Euronotes A short-term debt security. These are normally issued at a discount to face value for periods of one, three and six months' maturity. They are tradable once issued and are bearer securities. They are issued outside the jurisdiction of the currency stated on the note. They are backed up by a revolving underwriting facility which ensures that the issuer will be able to raise funds.

European Monetary Union (EMU) A single currency with a single central bank having control over interest rates being created for those EU member states which join. The process of moving towards a monetary union began in 1999.

European-style options Options which can only be exercised by the purchaser on a predetermined future date.

Eurosecurities Financial securities such as bonds, commercial paper, ordinary shares, convertibles, floating rate notes, medium-term notes, and promissory notes offered on or traded in the euromarkets.

Eurosterling Sterling traded in the eurocurrency market.

Euro Swiss francs Swiss francs traded in the eurocurrency market.

Euroyen Japanese yen traded in the eurocurrency market.

Eurozone Those countries that joined together in adopting the euro as their currency in 1999.

Event risk The risk that some future event may increase the risk on a financial investment, e.g. an earthquake event affects returns on Japanese bonds.

Ex-ante Intended, desired or expected before the event.

Ex-coupon A bond sold without the right to the next interest payment.

Ex-dividend When a share or bond is designated ex-dividend a purchaser will not be entitled to a recently announced dividend or the accrued interest on the bond since the last coupon – the old owner will receive the dividend (coupon).

Ex-post The value of some variable after the event.

Ex-rights When a share goes 'ex-rights' any purchaser of a share after that date will not have a right to subscribe for new shares in the rights issue.

Ex-rights price of a share The theoretical market price following a rights issue.

Exceptional items Gains or costs which are part of the company's ordinary activities but either are unusual in themselves or have an exceptionally large impact on profits that year.

Excess return (ER) (1) The return above the level expected given the level of risk taken. (2) A value metric that examines the amount of capital invested in previous years and then charges the company for its use over the years. It also credits companies for the returns shareholders can make from the money paid to them (e.g. as dividends) when reinvested in the market. Excess return expressed in present value terms equals actual wealth expressed in present value terms minus expected wealth expressed in present value terms.

Exchange controls The state controls the purchase and sale of currencies by its residents.

Exchange rate The price of one currency expressed in terms of another.

Exchangeable bond A bond that entitles the owner to choose at a later date whether to exchange the bond for shares in a company. The shares are in a company other than the one that issued the bond.

Exclusive franchise *See* Economic franchise.

Execution-only brokers A stockbroker who will buy or sell shares cheaply but will not give advice or other services.

Executive directors Manages day-to-day activities of the firms as well as contributing to boardroom discussion of company-wide policy and strategic direction.

Exercise price (strike price) The price at which an underlying will be bought (call) or sold (put) under an option contract.

Exit (1) The term used to describe the point at which a venture capitalist can recoup some or all of the investment made. (2) The closing of a position created by a transaction.

Exit barrier A factor preventing firms from stopping production in a particular industry.

Exotic A term used to describe an unusual financial transaction, e.g. exotic option, exotic currency (i.e. one with few trades).

Expansion capital Capital needed by companies at a fast-development phase to increase production capacity or to increase working capital and capital for the further development of the product or market. Venture capital is often used.

Expectations hypothesis of the term structure of interest rates (yield curve) Long-term interest rates reflect the market consensus on the changes in short-term interest rates.

Expectations theory of foreign exchange The current forward exchange rate is an unbiased predictor of the spot rate at that point in the future.

Expected return The mean or average outcome calculated by weighting each of the possible outcomes by the probability of occurrence and then summing the result.

Experience curve The cost of performing a task reduces as experience is gained through repetition.

Expiry date of an option The time when the rights to buy or sell the option cease.

External finance Outside finance raised by a firm, i.e. finance that it did not generate internally, for example through profits retention.

External metrics Measures of corporate performance which are accessible to individuals outside the firm and concern the performance of the firm as a whole.

extraMARK A grouping or sub-set of investment companies and products on the Official List (q.v.) of the London Stock Exchange.

Extraordinary general meeting (EGM) A meeting of the company (shareholders and directors) other than the annual general meeting (q.v.). It may be convened when the directors think fit. However, shareholders holding more than 10 per cent of the paid-up share capital carrying voting rights can requisition a meeting.

Extraordinary resources Those that give the firm a competitive edge. A resource which when combined with other (ordinary) resources enables the firm to outperform competitors and create new value-generating opportunities. Critical extraordinary resources determine what a firm can do successfully.

Face value *See* Par value.

Factor model A model which relates the returns on a security to that security's sensitivity to the movements of various factors (e.g. GDP growth, inflation) common to all shares.

Factor risk/Non-factor risk A factor risk is a systematic risk in multi-factor models describing the relationship between risk and return for fully diversified investors. Non-factor risk is unsystematic risk in multi-factor models.

Factoring To borrow against the security of trade debtors. Factoring companies also provide additional services such as sales ledger administration and credit insurance.

Fair game In the context of a stock market this is where some investors and fund raisers are not able to benefit at the expense of other participants. The market is regulated to avoid abuse, negligence and fraud. It is cheap to carry out transactions and the market provides high liquidity.

Fair value (Fair-market value) The amount an asset could be exchanged for in an arm's-length transaction between informed and willing parties.

Fallen angel Debt which used to rate as investment grade but which is now regarded as junk, mezzanine finance (q.v.) or high-yield finance.

FEER The Fundamental Equilibrium Exchange Rate (FEER) is the exchange rate between two currencies that results in a sustainable current-account balance. The exchange rate is expected to move (in theory) so as to achieve current-account balance.

Filter approach to investment A technique for examining shares using historic price trends. The trader focuses on the long-term trends by filtering out short-term movements.

Final dividend The dividend announced with the annual accounts. The final dividend plus the interim dividend make the total dividend for the year for a company that reports results every six months.

Finance house A financial institution offering to supply finance in the form of hire purchase, leasing and other forms of instalment credit.

Finance lease (also called **capital lease, financial lease** or **full payout lease**) The lessor expects to recover the full cost (or almost the full cost) of the asset plus interest, over the period of the lease.

Financial assets (securities, instruments) or Financial claim Contracts that state agreement about the exchange of money in the future, e.g. shares, bonds, bank loans, derivatives.

Financial distress Obligations to creditors are not met or are met with difficulty.

Financial gearing (leverage) *See* Gearing.

Financial Reporting Council (FRC) The UK's independent regulator responsible for ensuring high quality corporate reporting, accounts and governance.

Financial risk The additional variability in a firm's returns to shareholders and the additional risk of insolvency which arises because the financial structure contains debt.

Financial Services and Markets Act The 2000 Act (and orders made under it) form the bedrock of financial regulations in the UK.

Financial Services Authority (FSA) The chief financial services regulator in the UK.

Financial slack Having cash (or near-cash) and/or spare debt capacity available to take up opportunities as they appear.

Financing gap The gap in the provision of finance for medium-sized, fast-growing firms. Often these firms are too large or fast growing to ask the individual shareholders for more funds or to obtain sufficient bank finance. Also they are not ready to launch on the stock market.

Financing-type decision In an investment project the initial cash flow is positive.

Finished goods inventory period The number of days for which finished goods await delivery to customers. Equal to the average value of finished goods in stock divided by the average goods sold per day.

Fisher's equation The money rate of return m is related to the real rate of return h and the expected inflation rate i through the following equation: $(1 + m) = (1 + h)(1 + i)$.

Fixed assets Those not held for resale, but for use in the business.

Fixed charge (e.g. **fixed charged debenture or loan**) A specific asset(s) assigned as collateral security for a debt.

Fixed cost A cost that does not vary according to the amount of goods or services that are produced. Those business costs that have to be paid regardless of the firm's turnover and activity.

Fixed exchange rate The national authorities act to ensure that the rate of exchange between two currencies is constant.

Fixed interest (Fixed rate) Interest on a debt security is constant over its life.

Fixed-interest securities Strictly, the term applies to securities, such as bonds, on which the holder receives a predetermined interest pattern on the par value (e.g. gilts, corporate bonds, eurobonds). However, the term is also used for debt securities even when there is no regular interest, e.g. zero-coupon bonds (q.v.), and when the interest varies, as with floating rate notes (q.v.), for example.

Flat rate The rate of interest quoted by a hire purchase company (or other lender) to a hiree which fails to reflect properly the true interest rate being charged as measured by the annual percentage rate (APR) (q.v.).

Flat yield *See* Yield.

Float (1) The difference between the cash balance shown on a firm's chequebook and the bank account. Caused by delays in the transfer of funds between bank accounts. (2) An exchange rate that is permitted to vary against other currencies. (3) An issuance of shares to the public by a company joining a stock market. (4) For insurance companies it is the pool of money held in the firm in readiness to pay claims.

Floating charge The total assets of the company or an individual are used as collateral security for a debt. There is no specific asset assigned as collateral.

Floating exchange rate A rate of exchange which is not fixed by national authorities but fluctuates depending on demand and supply for the currency.

Floating-rate notes (FRNs) Notes issued in which the coupon fluctuates according to a benchmark interest rate charge (e.g. LIBOR – q.v.). Issued in the euromarkets generally with maturities of 7 to 15 years. **Reverse floaters** Those on which the interest rate declines as LIBOR rises.

Floating-rate borrowing (floating interest) The rate of interest on a loan varies with a standard reference rate, e.g. LIBOR.

Floor An agreement whereby, if interest rates fall below an agreed level, the seller (floor writer) makes compensatory payments to the floor buyer.

Flotation The issue of shares in a company for the first time on a stock exchange.

Focus strategy The selection of a segment in the industry to serve to the exclusion of others.

'Footsie' Nickname for FTSE 100 index. Trademarked.

Foreign banking Transactions in the home currency with non-residents.

Foreign bond A bond denominated in the currency of the country where it is issued when the issuer is a non-resident.

Foreign exchange control Limits are placed by a government on the purchase and sale of foreign currency.

Foreign exchange markets (Forex or FX) Markets that facilitate the exchange of one currency into another.

Forex A contraction of 'foreign exchange'.

Forfaiting A bank (or other lender) purchases a number of sales invoices or promissory notes from an exporting company; usually the importer's bank guarantees the invoices.

Forward A contract between two parties to undertake an exchange at an agreed future date at a price agreed now.

Forward agreement *See* Forward.

Forward-rate agreement (FRA) An agreement about the future level of interest rates. Compensation is paid by one party to the other to the extent that market interest rates deviate from the 'agreed' rate.

Founders' shares Dividends are paid only after all other categories of equity shares have received fixed rates of dividend. They usually carry a number of special voting rights over certain company matters.

Free cash flow Cash generated by a business not required for operations or for reinvestment. Profit before depreciation, amortisation and provisions, but after interest, tax, capital expenditure on long-lived items and increases in working capital necessary to maintain the company's competitive position and accept all value-generating investments.

Free float (Free capital) The proportion of a quoted company's shares not held by those closest (e.g. directors, founding families) to the company who may be unlikely to sell their shares.

Frequency function (probability or frequency distribution) The organisation of data to show the probabilities of certain values occurring.

Friendly mergers The two companies agree to a merger.

Friendly Society A mutual (co-operative) organisation involved in saving and lending.

FRS 3 *See* Basic (FRS 3) earnings per share.

FTSE 100 share index An index representing the UK's 100 largest listed shares. An average weighted by market capitalisation.

FTSE Actuaries All-Share Index (the 'All-Share') The most representative index of UK shares, reflecting about 700 companies' shares.

FTSE Eurofirst300 An index of European shares.

FTSE Global All Cap An index of share price movements around the world.

FTSE International (*Financial Times* and the London Stock Exchange) This organisation calculates a range of share indices published on a regular (usually daily) basis.

Full-payout lease *See* Leasing.

Fund management Investment of and administering a quantity of money, e.g. pension fund, insurance fund, on behalf of the fund's owners.

Fund raising Companies can raise money through rights issues, etc.

Fundamental analysts Individuals that try to estimate a share's true value, based on future returns to the company. Data from many sources are used, e.g. company accounts, economic trends, social trends, technological changes, etc.

Fundamental beta An adjustment to the risk premium on the average share, developed by Barr Rosenburg and others, which amalgamates a number of operating and financial characteristics of the specific company being examined.

Fungible Interchangeable securities; can be exchanged for each other on identical terms.

Future A contract between two parties to undertake a transaction at an agreed price on a specified future date.

GAAP Generally accepted accounting principles. United States accounting rules for reporting results. However, the term has come to mean any widely accepted set of accounting conventions.

GDP (nominal, real) Gross domestic product, the sum of all output of goods and services produced by a nation. Nominal means including inflation, and real means with inflation removed.

Gearing (financial gearing) The proportion of debt capital in the overall capital structure. Also called leverage. High gearing can lead to exaggeratedly high returns if things go well or exaggerated losses if things do not go well.

Gearing (operating) The extent to which the firm's total costs are fixed. This influences the break-even point and the sensitivity of profits to changes in sales level.

General inflation The process of steadily rising prices resulting in the diminishing purchasing power of a given nominal sum of money. Measured by an overall price index which follows the price changes of a 'basket' of goods and services through time.

General insurance Insurance against specific contingencies, e.g. fire, theft and accident.

Geometric mean The geometric mean of a set of n positive numbers is the nth root of their product, e.g. the geometric mean of 2 and 5 is $\sqrt{2 \times 5} = \sqrt{10} = 3.16$. The compound rate of return.

Gilts (gilt-edged securities) Fixed-interest UK government securities (bonds) traded on the London Stock Exchange. A means for the UK government to raise finance from savers. They usually offer regular interest and a redemption amount paid years in the future.

Globalisation The increasing internationalisation of trade, particularly financial product transactions. The integration of economic and capital markets throughout the world.

Goal congruence The aligning of the actions of senior management with the interests of shareholders.

Going concern A judgement as to whether a company has sufficient financial strength to continue for at least one year. Accounts are usually drawn up on the assumption that the business is a going concern.

Going long Buying a financial security (e.g. a share) in the hope that its price will rise.

Going public Market jargon used when a company becomes quoted on a stock exchange (the company may have been a public limited company, plc, for years before this).

Going short *See* Short selling.

Golden handcuffs Financial inducements to remain working for a firm.

Golden parachutes In a hostile merger situation, managers will receive large pay-offs if the firm is acquired.

Golden shares Shares with extraordinary special powers over the company, e.g. power of veto over a merger.

Good growth When a firm grows by investment in positive-performance-spread activities.

Goodwill An accounting term for the difference between the amount that a company pays for another company and the sum of the market value of that company's individual assets (after deducting all liabilities). Goodwill is thus an intangible asset representing things like the value of the company's brand names and the skills of its employees.

Grace period A lender grants the borrower a delay in the repayment of interest and/or principal at the outset of a lending agreement.

Greenbury Committee report Recommendations on corporate governance (1995).

Greenmail Key shareholders try to obtain a reward (e.g. the repurchase of their shares at a premium) from the company for not selling to a hostile bidder or becoming a bidder themselves.

Greenshoe An option that permits an issuing house, when assisting a corporation in a new issue, to sell more shares than originally planned. They may do this if demand is particularly strong.

Grey market A market in shares where the shares have not yet come into existence, e.g. in the period between investors being told they will receive shares in a new issue and the actual receipt they may sell on the expectation of obtaining them later.

Gross dividend yield

$$\frac{\text{Gross (before tax) dividend per share}}{\text{Share price}} \times 100$$

Gross domestic product *See* GDP.

Gross margin *See* Gross profit margin.

Gross present value The total present value of all the cash flows, excluding the initial investment.

Gross profit Turnover less cost of sales.

Gross profit margin (gross margin) Profit defined as sales minus cost of sales expressed as a percentage of sales.

Gross redemption yield (Gross yield to redemption) A calculation of the redemption yield (*see* Yield) before tax.

Growth industries Those industries which grow almost regardless of the state of the economy.

Guaranteed loan stock (bond) An organisation other than the borrower guarantees to the lender the repayment of the principal plus the interest payment.

Hampel report A follow-up to the Cadbury (1992) and Greenbury (1995) reports on corporate governance. Chaired by Sir Ronald Hampel and published in 1998.

Hang Seng Index Main index for Hong Kong shares.

Hard capital rationing Agencies external to the firm will not supply unlimited amounts of investment capital, even though positive NPV projects are identified.

Hard currency A currency traded in a foreign exchange market for which demand is persistently high. It is unlikely to depreciate by large percentages. The major currencies (e.g. US dollar, euro and sterling) are considered hard currencies.

Headline (underlying, adjusted or normalised) earnings per share Directors produce these profit per share numbers by excluding one-off costs, exceptional items and goodwill amortisation to show underlying profit per share trend (or just to make the managerial performance look better).

Hedge or Hedging Reducing or eliminating risk by undertaking a countervailing transaction.

Hedge fund A collective investment vehicle that operates relatively free from regulation allowing it to take steps in managing a portfolio that other fund managers are unable to take, e.g. borrowing to invest, shorting the market.

Her Majesty's Revenue and Customs (HMRC) The prinicipal tax collecting authority in the UK.

Herstatt risk In 1974 the German bank Herstatt was closed by the Bundesbank. It had entered into forex transactions and received deutschmarks from counterparties in European time, but had not made the corresponding transfer of US dollars to its counterparties in New York time. It is the risk that arises when forex transactions are settled in different time zones.

Higgs Committee report Recommendations on corporate governance published in 2003.

High-yield debt *See* Mezzanine finance or Junk bonds.

High-yield shares (yield stocks, high yielder) Shares offering a high current dividend yield because the share price is low due to the expectation of low growth in profits and dividends or because of perceived high risk. Sometimes labelled value shares.

Hire-purchase (HP) The user (hiree) of goods pays regular instalments of interest and principal to the hire-purchase company over a period of months. Full ownership passes to the hiree at the end of the period (the hiree is able to use the goods from the outset).

Historical PER (P_0/E_0) Current share price divided by the most recent annual earnings per share.

Holding company *See* Parent company.

Holding period returns Total holding period returns on a financial asset consist of (1) income, e.g. dividend paid; and (2) capital gain – a rise in the value of the asset.

Homemade dividends Shareholders creating an income from shareholdings by selling a portion of their shareholding.

Horizontal merger The two companies merging are engaged in similar lines of activity.

Hostile merger The target (acquired) firm's management is opposed to the merger.

Hubris Overweaning self-confidence.

Hurdle rate The required rate of return. The opportunity cost of the finance provider's money. The minimum return required from a position, making an investment or undertaking a project.

Hybrid finance A debt issue or security that combines the features of two or more instruments, e.g. a convertible bond is a package of a bond with an option to convert. Also used to indicate that a form of finance has both debt risk/return features (e.g. regular interest and a right to receive principal at a fixed date) and equity risk/return features (e.g. the returns depend to a large extent on the profitability of the firm).

Idiosyncratic risk An alternative name for unsystematic risk.

Impact day The day during the launch of a new issue of shares when the price is announced, the prospectus published and offers to purchase solicited.

Imperfect hedge The hedge position will partly, but not exactly, mirror the change in price of the underlying.

In-the-money option An option with intrinsic value. For a call option (q.v.) the current underlying price is more than the option exercise price. For a put option (q.v.) the current price of the underlying is below the exercise price.

Income gearing The proportion of the annual income streams (i.e. pre-interest profits or cash flow) devoted to the prior claims of debt holders. The reciprocal of income gearing is the interest cover.

Income reinvested The performance of shares, other securities or portfolios is usually expressed as 'total return' including both capital gains or losses and the accumulated benefit of periodic reinvestment of income distributions in further shares or securities of the same kind as the original investment.

Income statement Alternative title for profit and loss account.

Income yield *See* Yield.

Incorporation The forming of a company (usually offering limited liability to the shareholders), including the necessary legal formalities.

Incremental cash flow The new cash flows that occur as a result of going ahead with a project.

Incremental effects Those cash flows indirectly associated with a project, e.g. the cash flows on an existing project are boosted if the new project under consideration goes ahead.

Incremental fixed capital investment Investment in fixed assets which adds to the stock of assets and does not merely replace worn-out assets.

Incubators Organisations established to assist fast-growing young firms. They may provide finance, accounting services, legal services, offices, etc.

Independent director One that is not beholden to the dominant executive directors. Customers, suppliers or friends of the founding family are not usually regarded as independent.

Independents A venture capital organisation that raises its capital from the financial markets – it is not owned by one institution.

Independent variables The two variables are completely unrelated; there is no co-movement.

Index *See* Market index.

Index option An option on a share index, e.g. FTSE 100 or Standard & Poor's 500.

Index funds (trackers) Collective investment funds (e.g. unit trusts) which try to replicate a stock market index rather than to pick winners in an actively managed fund.

Index-linked gilts (stocks) The redemption value and the coupons rise with inflation over the life of the UK government bond.

Indices *See* Market index.

Industry attractiveness The economics of the market for the product(s), part of which is determined by the industry structure.

Industry structure The combination of the degree of rivalry within the industry among existing firms; the bargaining strength of industry firms with suppliers and customers; and the potential for new firms to enter and for substitute products to take customers. The industry structure determines the long-run rate of return on capital employed within the industry.

Inevitables Companies that are likely to be dominating their field for many decades due to their competitive strength.

Inflation The process of prices rising resulting in the fall of the purchasing power of one currency unit.

Inflation risk The risk that the nominal returns on an investment will be insufficient to offset the decline in the value of money due to inflation.

Informal venture capitalist An alternative name for business angel (q.v.).

Information asymmetry One party to a transaction (e.g. loan agreement) has more information on risk and return relating to the transaction than the other party.

Information costs The cost of gathering and analysing information, e.g. in the context of deciding whether to lend money to a firm.

Informed investors Those that are highly knowledgeable about financial securities and the fundamental evaluation of their worth.

Initial margin An amount that a derivative contractor has to provide to the clearing house when first entering upon a derivative contract.

Initial public offering (IPO) (New Issue) The offering of shares in the equity of a company to the public for the first time.

Insider trading (dealing) Trading shares, etc. on the basis of information not in the public domain.

Insolvent A company unable to pay debts as they become due.

Instalment credit A form of finance to pay for goods or services over a period through the payment of principal and interest in regular instalments.

Institutional neglect Share analysts, particularly at the major institutions, may fail to spend enough time studying small firms, preferring to concentrate on the larger 100 or so.

Institutionalisation The increasing tendency for organisational investing, as opposed to individuals investing money in securities (e.g. pension funds and investment trusts collect the savings of individuals to invest in shares).

Insurable risk Risk that can be transferred through the payment of premiums to insurance companies.

Intangible assets Those that you cannot touch – they are non-physical, e.g. goodwill.

Interbank brokers Brokers in the forex markets who act as intermediaries between buyers and sellers. They provide anonymity to each side.

Interbank market The wholesale market in short-term money and foreign exchange in which banks borrow and lend among themselves. It is now extended to include large companies and other organisations.

Interest-withholding tax *See* Withholding tax.

Interest rate cap *See* Cap.

Interest cover The number of times the income (profit or cash flow) of a business exceeds the interest payments made to service its loan capital.

Interest rate parity (IRP) of exchange rate determination The interest rate parity theory holds true when the difference between spot and forward exchange rates is equal to the differential between interest rates available in the two currencies.

Interest rate risk The risk that changes in interest rates will have an adverse impact.

Interest rate swap *See* Swap.

Interest yield *See* Yield.

Interim dividend A dividend related to the first half-year's (or quarter's) trading.

Interim profit reports A statement giving unaudited profit figures for the first half of the financial year, shortly after the end of the first half-year.

Intermediaries offer A method of selling shares in the new issue market. Shares are offered to financial institutions such as stockbrokers. Clients of these intermediaries can then apply to buy shares from them.

Intermediate debt See Mezzanine finance or Junk bonds.

Intermediate security To help solve the conflict of preferences between savers (investors) in society and the ultimate borrowers' intermediaries (e.g. banks) create intermediate securities (e.g. bank account) offering the characteristics attractive to investors, i.e. high liquidity, low risk and the ability to deal in small amounts.

Internal finance Funds generated by the firm's activities, and available for investment within the firm after meeting contractual obligations.

Internal metrics Measures of corporate performance available to those inside the company. They can be used at the corporate, SBU (q.v.) or product-line level.

Internal rate of return (IRR) The discount rate that makes the present value of a future stream of cash flows equal to the initial investment(s).

Internalisation of transactions By bringing together two firms at different stages of the production chain in a vertical merger, an acquirer may achieve more efficient co-ordination of the different levels.

International banking Banking transactions outside the jurisdiction of the authorities of the currency in which the transaction takes place.

International bonds Some people use the term to mean the same as eurobonds, others extend the definition to encompass foreign bonds as well.

International Capital Market Association (ICMA) A self-regulatory organisation designed to promote orderly trading and the general development of the euromarkets.

International Petroleum Exchange (IPE) The energy futures and options exchange in London.

Interpolation Estimating intermediate data points on a set of data where observed points are at intervals.

Intrinsic value (company) The discounted value of the cash that can be taken out of a business during its remaining life.

Intrinsic value (options) The payoff that would be received if the underlying is at its current level when the option expires.

Introduction A company with shares already quoted on another stock exchange, or where there is already a wide spread of shareholders, may be introduced to the market. This allows a secondary market in the shares even though no new shares are issued.

Inventory *See* Stock.

Investing-type decision In an investment project the initial cash flow is negative.

Investment bank or Merchant bank Banks that carry out a variety of financial services, usually excluding high street banking. Their services are usually fee based, e.g. fees for merger advice to companies.

Investment grade debt Debt with a sufficiently high credit rating (BBB– or Baa and above) to be regarded as safe enough for institutional investors that are restricted to holding only safe debt.

Investment trusts (investment companies) Collective investment vehicles set up as companies selling shares. The money raised is invested in assets such as shares, gilts, corporate bonds and property.

Invoice An itemised list of goods shipped, usually specifying the terms of sale and price.

Invoice discounting Invoices sent to trade debtors are pledged to a finance house in return for an immediate payment of up to 80 per cent of the face value.

Invoice finance A method of receiving finance secured by receivables (trade debtors). A finance house advances funds to a firm. When a customer pays on the invoice the company pays the finance house with interest.

IOU A colloquialism intended to mean 'I owe you'. The acknowledgement of a debt.

Irredeemable Financial securities with no fixed maturity date at which the principal is repaid.

Irrelevancy of the dividend proposition (by Modigliani and Miller) If a few assumptions can be made, dividend policy is irrelevant to share value.

Issued share capital That part of a company's share capital that has been subscribed by shareholders, either paid up or partially paid up.

Issuing house *See* Sponsor.

Joint stock enterprise The ownership (share) capital is divided into small units, permitting a number of investors to contribute varying amounts to the total. Profits are divided between stockholders in proportion to the number of shares they own.

Joint venture A business operation (usually a separate company) is jointly owned by two or more parent firms. It also applies to strategic alliances between companies where they collaborate on, for example, research.

Junior debt (junior security) *See* Subordinated debt.

Junk bonds Low-quality, low credit-rated company bonds. Rated below investment grade (less than BBB– or Baa). Risky and with a high yield.

Just-in-time stock holding Materials and work-in-progress are delivered just before they are needed and finished goods are produced just before being sent to customers.

Kicker *See* Equity kicker.

Lagging The postponement of a payment beyond the due date. A tactic used in international trade when the debtor expects the relative value of the currency in which the debt is expressed to fall.

Laissez-faire The principle of the non-intervention of government in economic affairs.

landMARK Groups of London Stock Exchanges Official List companies from particular UK regions.

LCH Clearnet (LCH) Settles mutual indebtedness between a number of organisations. It settles ('clears') trades for equity traders, derivative traders, bond traders and energy traders, and guarantees all contracts. It often acts as counterparty to all trades on an exchange.

Lead manager In a new issue of securities (e.g. shares, bonds, syndicated loans) the lead manager controls and organises the issue. There may be joint lead managers, co-managers and regional lead managers.

Lead steer A term used to describe a dominant person with the power to induce others to follow.

Lead time The delay between placing an order with a supplier and the order being delivered.

Leading The bringing forward from the original due date of the payment of a debt.

Leasing The owner of an asset (lessor) grants the use of the asset to another party (lessee) for a specified period in return for regular rental payments. The asset does not become the property of the lessee at the end of the specified period. *See also* Finance lease and Operating lease.

Lender of last resort This is usually the central bank, which provides a group of financial institutions with funds if they cannot otherwise obtain them.

Lessee The user of an asset under a lease.

Lessor The provider of an asset under a lease.

Leverage *See* Gearing.

Leveraged buyout (LBO) The acquisition of a company, subsidiary or unit by another, financed mainly by borrowings.

Leveraged recapitalisation The financial structure of the firm is altered in such a way that it becomes highly geared.

LIBOR (London Interbank Offered Rate) The rate of interest offered on loans to highly rated (low-risk) banks in the London interbank market for a specific period (e.g. three months). Used as a reference rate for other loans.

Lien A right is given to a lender to seize possession of the assets belonging to a borrower under the lien.

Life cycle stage of value creation The longevity of competitive advantage and favourable industry economics can be represented in terms of a life cycle with four stages: development, growth, maturity and decline. In the early stages superior long-term value performance is expected because of a sustainable competitive advantage and favourable long-term industry economics.

Life insurance or life assurance Insurance under which the beneficiaries receive payment upon death of the policyholder or other person named in the policy. Endowment policies offer a savings vehicle as well as cover against death.

LIFFE (London International Financial Futures and Options Exchange) The main derivatives exchange in London – now owned by NYSE-Euronext (q.v.).

LIFFE CONNECT™ The computer system used by Euronext.liffe (q.v.) for trading derivatives (q.v.).

Limit bid In a book-building exercise a potential institutional investor states that it will buy a given number of shares at a particular price.

Limit prices An order to a broker to buy a specified quantity of a security at or below a specified price, or to sell it at or above a specified price.

Limited companies (Ltd) 'Private' companies with no minimum amount of share capital, but with restrictions on the range of investors who can be offered shares. Limited liability for the debts of the firm is granted to the shareholders. They cannot be quoted on the London Stock Exchange.

Limited liability The owners of shares in a business have a limit on their loss, set as the amount they have committed to invest in shares.

Line of credit *See* Credit facility.

Line of least resistance Taking the path with the least hassle.

Liquidation value *See* Liquidation of a company.

Liquidation of a company The winding-up of the affairs of a company when it ceases business. This could be forced by an inability to make payment when due or it could be voluntary when shareholders choose to end the company. Assets are sold, liabilities paid (if sufficient funds) and the surplus (if any) is distributed to shareholders.

Liquidity The degree to which an asset can be sold quickly and easily without loss in value.

Liquidity-preference hypothesis of the term structure of interest rates The yield curve is predominately upward sloping because investors require an extra return for lending on a long-term basis.

Liquidity risk The risk that an organisation may not have, or may not be able to raise, cash funds when needed.

Listed companies Those on the Official List (q.v.) of the London Stock Exchange.

Listing agreement The UK Listing Authority (q.v.) insists that a company signs a listing agreement committing the directors to certain standards of behaviour and levels of reporting to shareholders.

Listing particulars *See* Prospectus.

Listing Rules The regulations concerning the initial flotation of a company on the London Stock Exchange and the continuing requirements the company must meet.

Lloyds Insurance Market A medium-sized insurance business in London founded over two centuries ago. 'Names' supply the capital to back insurance policies. Names can now be limited liability companies rather than individuals with unlimited liability to pay up on an insurance policy.

LME London Metal Exchange.

Loan stock A fixed-interest debt financial security. May be unsecured.

Local authority bills/deposits Lending money to a UK local government authority.

London Metal Exchange (LME) Trades metals (e.g. lead, zinc, tin, aluminium and nickel) in spot, forward and option markets.

London Stock Exchange (LSE) The London market in which securities are bought and sold.

London Traded Option Market (LTOM) Options exchange which merged with LIFFE in 1992.

Long bond Often defined as bonds with a time to maturity greater than 15 years, but there is some flexibility in this, so a 10-year bond is often described as being long.

Long-form report A report by accountants for the sponsor of a company being prepared for flotation. The report is detailed and confidential. It helps to reassure the sponsors when putting their name to the issue and provides the basis for the short-form report included in the prospectus.

Long position A positive exposure to a quantity – if the market rises the position improves. Owning a security or commodity; the opposite of a short position (selling).

Long-range structural analysis A process used to forecast the long-term rates of return of an industry.

Long-term incentive plan (LTIP) A scheme designed to motivate senior managers and directors of a company by paying bonuses if certain targets are surpassed (e.g. share price has risen relative to the market index).

Low-grade debt *See* Mezzanine finance or Junk bonds.

Low-yield shares (stocks) Shares offering a relatively low dividend yield expected to grow rapidly. Often labelled growth stocks.

Ltd Private limited company.

M & A Merger and acquisition.

Macroeconomics The study of the relationships between broad economic aggregates: national income, saving, investment, balance of payments, inflation, etc.

Main Market The Official List of the London Stock Exchange, as opposed to the Alternative Investment Market (qq.v.).

Maintenance margin (futures) The level of margin that must be maintained on a futures account (usually at a clearing house). Daily marking to market of the position may reveal the need to put more money into the account to top up to the maintenance margin.

Making a book Market makers offering two prices: the price at which they are willing to buy (bid price) and the price they are willing to sell (offer price).

Management buy-in (MBI) A new team of managers makes an offer to a company to buy the whole company, a subsidiary or a section of the company, with the intention of taking over the running of it themselves. Venture capital often provides the major part of the finance.

Management buyout (MBO) A team of managers makes an offer to its employers to buy a whole business, a subsidiary or a section so that the managers own and run it themselves. Venture capital is often used to finance the majority of the purchase price.

Managementism/Managerialism Management not acting in shareholders' best interests by pursuing objectives attractive to the management team. There are three levels: (1) dishonest managers; (2) honest but incompetent managers; (3) honest and competent but as humans, subject to the influence of conflicts of interest.

Mandatory bid If 30 per cent or more of the shares of a company are acquired the holder is required under the Takeover Panel rules to bid for all the company's shares.

Marché à Terme d'Instruments Financiers (MATIF) The French futures and options exchange.

Margin (futures) Money placed aside to back a futures purchase or sale. This is used to reassure the counterparty to the future that money will be available should the purchaser/seller renege on the deal.

Market capitalisation The total value at market prices of the shares in issue for a company (or a stock market, or a sector of the stock market).

Market entry Firms that previously did not supply goods or services to this industry now do so.

Market in managerial control Teams of managers compete for control of corporate assets, e.g. through merger activity.

Market index A sample of shares is used to represent a share (or other) market's level and movements.

Market makers Organisations that stand ready to buy and sell shares from investors on their own behalf (at the centre of the London Stock Exchange's quote-driven system of share trading).

Market portfolio A portfolio which contains all assets. Each asset is held in proportion to the asset's share of the total market value of all the assets. A proxy for this is often employed, e.g. the FTSE 100 index.

Market power The ability to exercise some control over the price of the product.

Market risk *See* Systematic risk.

Market segmentation hypothesis of the term structure of interest rates The yield curve is created (or at least influenced) by the supply and demand conditions in a number of sub-markets defined by maturity range.

Market-to-book ratio (MBR) The market value of a firm divided by capital invested. ('Capital invested' is usually taken to be balance sheet net assets)

Market value added The difference between the total amount of capital put into a business by finance providers (debt and equity) and the current market value of the company's shares and debts.

Marking to market The losses or gains on a derivative contract are assessed daily in reference to the value of the underlying price.

Matador A foreign bond issued in the Spanish domestic market.

Matched-bargain systems *See* Order-driven trading system.

Matching The company matches the inflows and outflows in different currencies covered by trade, etc., so that it is only necessary to deal on the currency markets for the unmatched portion of the total transactions.

Matching principle The maturity structure of debt matches the maturity of projects or assets held by the firm. Short-term assets are financed by short-term debt and long-term assets are financed by long-term debt.

Maturity, Maturity date or Final maturity (Redemption date) The time when a financial security (e.g. a bond) is due to be redeemed and the par value is paid to the lender.

Maturity structure The profile of the length of time to the redemption and repayment of a company's various debts.

Maturity transformation Intermediaries offer securities with liquid characteristics to induce primary investors to purchase or deposit funds. The money raised is made available to the ultimate borrowers on a long-term, illiquid basis.

Maximisation of long-term shareholder wealth The assumed objective of the firm in finance. It takes into account the time value of money and risk.

Mean (1) arithmetic mean: a set of numbers are summed, and the answer is divided by the number of numbers; (2) geometric mean: calculated as the *n*th root of the product of *n* number, e.g. the geometric mean of 2 and 5 is $\sqrt{2} \times 5 = \sqrt{10} = 3.16$.

Mean reversion *See* Reversion to the mean.

Mean-variance rule If the expected return on two projects is the same but the second has a higher variance (or standard deviation) (qq.v.), then the first will be preferred. Also, if the variance on the two projects is the same but the second has a higher expected return, the second will be preferred.

Medium-term note (MTN) A document setting out a promise from a borrower to pay the holders a specified sum on the maturity date and, in many cases, a coupon interest in the meantime. Maturity can range from nine months to 30 years (usually one to five years). If denominated in a foreign currency they are called euro medium-term notes.

Memorandum of Association Lays down the rules which govern a company and its relations with the outside world, e.g. states the objective of the company.

Merchant bank *See* Investment bank.

Merger The combining of two business entities under common ownership.

Metric Method of measurement.

Mezzanine finance Unsecured debt or preference shares offering a high return with a high risk. Ranked behind secured debt but ahead of equity. It may carry an equity kicker (q.v.).

Minority shareholder A shareholder who owns less than 50 per cent of a company's ordinary shares.

Mobilisation of savings The flow of savings primarily from the household sector to the ultimate borrowers to invest in real assets. This process is encouraged by financial intermediaries.

Model Code for Directors' Dealings London Stock Exchange rules for directors dealing in shares of their own company.

Modified internal rate of return (MIRR) The rate of return which equates the initial investment with a project's terminal value, where the terminal value is the future value of the cash inflows compounded at the required rate of return (the opportunity cost of capital).

Momentum investing Buying shares that have recently risen and selling shares that have recently fallen.

Monetary policy The deliberate control of the money supply and/or rates of interest by the central bank.

Money cash flow All future cash flows are expressed in the prices expected to rule when the cash flow occurs.

Money markets Wholesale financial markets (i.e. those dealing with large amounts) in which lending and borrowing on a short-term basis takes place (< 1 year). Examples of instruments: banker's acceptances, certificates of deposit, commercial paper, treasury bills.

Money rate of return The rate of return which includes a return to compensate for inflation.

Monopoly One producer in an industry. However for Competition Commission purposes a monopoly is defined as a market share of 25 per cent.

Moral hazard The presence of a safety net (e.g. an insurance policy) encourages adverse behaviour (e.g. carelessness). An incentive to take extraordinary risks (risks that tend to fall on others) aimed at rectifying a desperate position. The risk that a party to a transaction is not acting in good faith by providing misleading or inadequate information.

Mortgage debentures Bonds secured using property as collateral.

Mortgage-style repayment schedule A regular monthly amount is paid to a lender which covers both interest and some capital repayment. At first most of the monthly payment goes towards interest. As the outstanding debt is reduced, the monthly payment pays off a larger and larger amount of the capital.

Mutual funds A collective investment vehicle the shares or units of which are sold to investors – a very important method of investing in shares in the USA.

Mutually owned organisations Organisations run for the benefit of the members (usually the same as the consumers of the organisation's output) and not for shareholders. Examples include some insurance organisations, building societies and the co-operative societies.

Naked (or uncovered) Long or short positioning a derivative without an offsetting position in the underlying. *See also* Uncovered call option writing.

NASDAQ (National Association of Securities Dealers Automated Quotation system) A series of computer-based information services and an order execution system for the US over-the-counter securities (e.g. share) market.

National Savings Lending to the UK government through the purchase of bonds, and placing money into savings accounts.

Near-cash (near-money, quasi-money) Highly liquid financial assets but which are generally not usable for transactions and therefore cannot be fully regarded as cash, e.g. treasury bills.

Negative covenants Loan agreements conditions that restrict the actions and rights of the borrower until the debt has been repaid in full.

Negotiability (1) Transferable to another – free to be traded in financial markets. (2) Capable of being settled by agreement between the parties involved in a transaction.

Net assets (Net worth), Net asset value (NAV) Total assets minus all the liabilities. Fixed assets, plus stocks, debtors, cash and other liquid assets, minus long-and short-term creditors.

Net current assets The difference between current assets and current liabilities (qq.v.).

Net present value (NPV) The present value of the expected cash flows associated with a project after discounting at a rate which reflects the value of the alternative use of the funds.

Net profit (Net income) Profit after interest, tax and extraordinary charges and receipts.

Net realisable value What someone might reasonably be expected to pay less the costs of the sale.

Net worth Total assets minus total liabilities.

Netting When subsidiaries in different countries settle intra-organisational currency debts for the net amount owed in a currency rather than the gross amount.

Neuer Markt German stock exchange for smaller young companies. Now closed due to financial scandals and loss of confidence among investors.

New entrant A company entering a market area to compete with existing players.

New issue The sale of securities, e.g. debentures or shares, to raise additional finance or to float existing securities of a company on a stock exchange for the first time.

Newstrack A small company news service and a place where share prices for companies trading on PLUS market (q.v.) are posted.

Niche company A fast-growing small to medium-sized firm operating in a specialist business with high potential.

Nikkei index or Nikkei 225 Stock Average A share index based on the prices of 225 shares quoted on the Tokyo Stock Exchange.

Nil paid rights Shareholders may sell the rights to purchase shares in a rights issue without having paid anything for these rights.

Noise trading Uninformed investors buying and selling financial securities at irrational prices, thus creating noise (strange movements) in the price of securities.

Nominal return (or interest rate) The return on an investment including inflation. If the return necessary to compensate for the decline in the purchasing power of money (inflation) is deducted from the nominal return we have the real rate of return.

Nominal value *See* Par value.

Nominated adviser (Nomad) Each company on the AIM (q.v.) has to retain a nomad. They act as quality controllers, confirming to the London Stock Exchange that the company has complied with the rules. They also act as consultants to the company.

Nominated brokers Each company on the AIM (q.v.) has to retain a nominated broker, who helps to bring buyers and sellers together and comments on the firm's prospects.

Nominee accounts An official holder of an asset is not the beneficial owner but merely holds the asset in a nominee account for the beneficiary. In the stock market, the most common use of nominee accounts is where execution-only brokers act as cominees for their clients. The shares are registered in the name of the broker, but the client has beneficial ownership of them.

Non-executive director (Outside director) A director without day-to-day operational responsibility for the firm.

Non-recourse A lending arrangement, say in project finance, where the lenders have no right to insist that the parent company(s) pay the due interest and capital should the project company be unable to do so.

Non-voting shares A company may issue two or more classes of ordinary shares, one of which may be of shares that do not carry any votes.

Normal rate of return A rate of return that is just sufficient to induce shareholders to put money into the firm and hold it there.

Normalised earnings per share *See* Headline earnings per share.

Note (promissory note) A financial security with the promise to pay a specific sum of money by a given date, e.g. commercial paper, floating rate notes. Usually unsecured.

Note issuance facility (Note purchase facility) A medium-term arrangement allowing borrowers to issue a series of short-term promissory notes (usually 3–6 month maturity). A group of banks guarantees the availability of funds by agreeing to purchase any unsold notes at each issue date while the facility is in place.

NYSE The New York Stock Exchange.

NYSE-Euronext The organisation that controls and integrates the stock exchanges in New York, Paris, Brussels, Amsterdam and Lisbon as well as owning Liffe.

Objective probability A probability that can be established theoretically or from historical data.

Off-balance-sheet finance Assets are acquired in such a way that liabilities do not appear on the balance sheet, e.g. some lease agreements permit the exclusion of the liability in the accounts.

Offer as unconditional *See* Unconditionality.

Offer document (1) A formal document sent by a company attempting to buy all the shares in a target firm to all the shareholders of the target setting out the offer. (2) The legal document for an offer for sale in a new issue.

Offer for sale A method of selling shares in a new issue. The company sponsor offers shares to the public by inviting subscriptions from investors. (1) Offer for sale by fixed price – the sponsor fixes the price prior to the offer. (2) Offer for sale by tender – investors state the price they are willing to pay. A strike price is established by the sponsors after receiving all the bids. All investors pay the strike price.

Offer for subscription A method of selling shares in a new issue. The issue is aborted if the offer does not raise sufficient interest from investors.

Offer price (1) The price at which a market maker in shares will sell a share, or a dealer in other markets will sell a security or asset. (2) The price of a new issue of securities, e.g. a new issue of shares.

Office of Fair Trading (OFT) The Director-General of Fair Trading has wide powers to monitor and investigate trading activities, and take action against anti-competitive behaviour. He can also refer monopoly situations to the Competition Commission (q.v.).

Official List (OL) The daily list of securities admitted for trading on highly regulated UK markets such as the London Stock Exchange. It does not include securities traded on the Alternative Investment Market (AIM) (q.v.).

Offshore investment Outside investors' home country jurisdiction and financial regulation, usually in tax havens.

Oligopoly A small number of producers in an industry.

Onshore fund A fund authorised and regulated by the regulator in the investor's home country.

Open-ended funds The size of the fund and the number of units depends on the amount investors wish to put into the fund e.g. a unit trust. The manager adds to or liquidates part of the assets of the fund depending on the level of purchases or sales of the units in the fund.

Open-ended investment companies (OEIC) Collective investment vehicles with one price for investors. OEICs are able to issue more shares if demand increases from investors, unlike investment trusts. OEICs invest the finance raised in securities, primarily shares.

Open interest The sum of outstanding long and short positions in a given futures or option contract. Transactions have not been offset or closed out, thus there is still exposure to movements in the underlying (q.v.).

Open offer New shares are sold to a wide range of external investors (not existing shareholders). However, under clawback provisions, existing shareholders can buy the shares at the offer price if they wish.

Open outcry Where trading is through oral calling of buy and sell offers and hand signals by market members.

Operating gearing *See* Gearing.

Operating lease The lease period is significantly less than the expected useful life of the asset and the agreed lease payments do not amount to a present value of more than 90 per cent of the value of the asset.

Operating margin *See* Operating profit margin.

Operating profit (operating income) The accounting income remaining after paying all costs other than interest.

Operating profit margin (operating margin, trading margin) Operating profit as a percentage of sales.

Operational efficiency of a market Relates to how the market minimises the cost to buyers and sellers of transactions in securities on the exchange.

Operational risks The risks that come from the business activity itself rather than from, say, financial risks such as interest rates changing.

Opportunity cost The value forgone by opting for one course of action; the next best use of, say, financial resources.

Opportunity cost of capital The return that is sacrificed by investing finance in one way rather than investing in an alternative of the same risk class, e.g. a financial security.

Option A contract giving one party the right, but not the obligation, to buy or sell a financial instrument, commodity or some other underlying asset at a given price, at or before a specified date.

Option premium The amount paid by an option purchaser (holder) to obtain the rights under an option contract.

Order book system *See* Order-driven trading system.

Order-driven trading system Buy and sell orders for securities are entered on a central computer system, and investors are automatically matched according to the price and volume they entered (also called matched bargain systems) – SETS is an example (q.v.).

Ordinary resources Those that give the firm competitive parity. They provide a threshold competence.

Ordinary shares The equity capital of the firm. The holders of ordinary shares are the owners and are therefore entitled to all distributed profits after the holders of preference shares, debentures and other debt have had their claims met. They are also entitled to control the direction of the company through the power of their votes – usually one vote per share.

Organic growth Growth from within the firm rather than through mergers.

Out-of-the-money option An option with no intrinsic value. For a call option (q.v.) the current price of the underlying is less than the exercise price. For a put option (q.v.) the current price of the underlying (q.v.) is more than the exercise price.

Over-allotment issue Same as Greenshoe (q.v.).

Over-capacity An industry or company has significantly more capacity to supply a product than is being demanded.

Over-subscription In a new issue of securities investors offer to buy more securities (e.g. shares) than are made available.

Over-the-counter trade (OTC) Securities trading carried on outside regulated exchanges. These bilateral deals allow tailor-made transactions.

Overdraft A permit to overdraw on an account (e.g. a bank account) up to a stated limit; to take more out of a bank account than it contains. This arrangement is usually offered for a period, say six months or one year, but most banks retain the right to call in the loan (demand repayment) at any time.

Overhang Blocks of securities or commodities that are known to be available for sale. This can lead to share (or commodity) price depression due to the anticipated sale of the large block of shares (or the commodity).

Overhead The business expenses not chargeable to a particular part of the work or product: a cost that is not directly associated with producing the merchandise.

Overtrading When a business has insufficient finance to sustain its level of trading (turnover). Too much cash is tied up in stocks and debtors, and too little is available to pay creditors and meet day-to-day expenses. A business is said to be overtrading when it tries to engage in more business than the investment in working capital will allow. This can happen even in profitable circumstances.

Owner earnings Earnings plus depreciation, depletion, amortisation and certain other non-cash charges less the amount of expenditure for plant and machinery and working capital, etc. that a business requires to fully maintain its long-term competitive position, its unit volume and to invest in value-generating opportunities.

PacMan defence or strategy In a hostile merger situation the target makes a counterbid for the bidder.

Paid-up capital The amount of the authorised share capital that has been paid for or subscribed for by shareholders.

Panel on Takeovers & Mergers *See* Takeover panel.

Paper A term for some securities, e.g. certificates of deposit, commercial paper.

Paper bid In a merger the acquirer offers shares in itself to buy shares in the target.

Par value (nominal, principal or **face value)** A stated nominal value of a share or bond. Not related to market value.

Parent company (Holding company) The one that partially or wholly owns other companies.

Partnership An unincorporated business formed by the association of two or more persons who share the risk and profits.

Pathfinder prospectus In a new issue of shares a detailed report on the company is prepared and made available to potential investors a few days before the issue price is announced.

Payables Trade credit received from suppliers.

Payback The period of time it takes to recover the initial cash put into a project.

Payment-in-kind (PIKs) notes and loans High risk debt offering a very high rate of return (900 basis points over LIBOR or more). They do not pay out a coupon; they pay out in the form of more bonds or loans.

Payout ratio The percentage of after-tax profit paid to shareholders in dividends.

Pecking order theory of financial gearing Firms exhibit preferences in terms of sources of finance. The most acceptable source of finance is retained earnings, followed by borrowing and then by new equity issues.

Pension funds These manage money on behalf of members to provide a pension upon the member's retirement. Most funds invest heavily in shares.

Pension holiday When a pension fund does not need additional contributions for a time, it may grant the contributors, e.g. companies and/or members, a break from making payments.

PER *See* Price-earnings ratio.

Perfect competition (perfect market) Entry to the industry is free and the existing firms have no bargaining power over suppliers or customers. Rivalry between existing firms is fierce because products are identical. The following assumptions hold: (1) There is a large number of buyers. (2) There is a large number of sellers. (3) The quantity of goods bought by any individual transaction is so small relative to the total quantity traded that individual trades leave the market price unaffected. (4) The units of goods sold by different sellers are the same – the product is homogeneous. (5) There is perfect information – all buyers and all sellers have complete information on the prices being asked and offered in other parts of the market. (6) There is perfect freedom of exit from the market.

Perfect hedge Eliminates risk because the movements in the value of the hedge (q.v.) instrument are exactly contrary to the change in the value of the underlying (q.v.).

Perfect market *See* Perfect competition.

Perfect negative correlation When two variables (e.g. returns on two shares) always move in exactly opposite directions by the same proportional amount.

Perfect positive correlation When two variables (e.g. returns on two shares) always move in the same direction by the same proportional amount.

Performance spread The percentage difference between the actual rate of return on an investment and the required rate given its risk class.

Perpetuity A regular sum of money received at intervals forever.

Personal guarantee An individual associated with a company, e.g. director, personally guarantees that a debt will be repaid.

Personal pension A pension scheme set up for an individual by that individual. Contributions to the fund are subject to tax relief.

Physical delivery Settlement of a futures contract by delivery of the underlying (q.v.) rather than cash settlement based on price movement during the holding of the open position.

Placing, place or placement A method of selling shares and other financial securities in the primary market. Securities are offered to the sponsors' or brokers' private clients and/or a narrow group of institutions.

Plain vanilla A bond that lacks any special features such as a call or put provision.

Planning horizon The point in the future after which an investment will earn only the minimum acceptable rate of return.

Plc Public limited company.

PLUS-Markets Group plc This is a provider of primary and secondary equity market services independent of the London Stock Exchange. It operates and regulates the PLUS service.

Poison pills Actions taken, or which will be taken, which make a firm unpalatable to a hostile acquirer.

Political risk Changes in government or government policies impacting on returns and volatility of returns.

Pooled funds Organisations (e.g. unit trusts) that gather together numerous small quantities of money from investors and then invest in a wide range of financial securities.

Portfolio A collection of investments.

Portfolio approach to merger integration *See* Preservation approach to merger integration.

Portfolio investment (1) Investment in a variety of instruments; (2) (in national accounting) investment made by firms and individuals in bonds and shares issued in another country. An alternative form of foreign investment is direct investment, buying commercial assets such as factory premises and industrial plant.

Portfolio optimiser A computer program designed to select an optimal portfolio in terms of risk and return.

Portfolio planning Allocating resources within the company to those Strategic business units (q.v.) and product/customer areas offering the greatest value creation, while withdrawing capital from those destroying value.

Portfolio theory Formal mathematical model for calculating risk-return trade-offs as securities are combined in a portfolio.

Post-completion audit The monitoring and evaluation of the progress of a capital investment project through a comparison of the actual cash flows and other benefits with those forecast at the time of authorisation.

Precautionary motive for holding cash This arises out of the possibility of unforeseen needs for cash for expenditure in an unpredictable environment.

Pre-emption rights The strong right of shareholders of UK companies to have first refusal to subscribe for further issues of shares. *See* Rights issue.

Preference share These normally entitle the holder to a fixed rate of dividend but this is not guaranteed. Holders of preference shares precede the holders of ordinary shares, but follow bond holders and other lenders, in payment of dividends and return of principal. *Participating preference share*: share in residual profits. *Cumulative preference share*: share carries forward the right to preferential dividends. *Redeemable preference share*: a preference share with a finite life. *Convertible preference share*: may be converted into ordinary shares.

Preferred ordinary shares Rank higher than deferred ordinary shares for an agreed rate of dividend or share of profits. They carry notes. Not the same as preference shares.

Preliminary annual results (Preliminary profit announcements, prelims) After the year-end and before the full reports and accounts are published, a statement on the profit for the year and other information is provided by companies quoted on the London Stock Exchange.

Premium (1) (On an option) The amount paid to an option writer to obtain the right to buy or sell the underlying. (2) (Foreign exchange) The forward rate of exchange stands at a higher level than the current spot rate. (3) (Investment trusts) By how much the share price exceeds the net asset value per share.

Present value The current worth of future cash flows when discounted.

Preservation approach to merger integration Little is changed in the acquired firm in terms of culture, systems or personnel. General management skills might be transferred from the parent along with strict financial performance yardsticks and demanding incentive schemes.

Press Collective name for newspapers and periodicals.

Pre-tax margin *See* Pre-tax profit margin.

Pre-tax profit Profit on ordinary activities before deducting taxation.

Pre-tax profit margin (pre-tax margin) Profit after all expenses including interest expressed as a percentage of sales.

Price discovery The process of forming prices through the interaction of numerous buy and sell orders in an exchange.

Price-earnings ratio (PER, Price-earnings multiple, PE multiple, PE ratio, P/E ratio) Share price divided by earnings per share over the latest twelve months. *Historic*: Share price divided by most recently reported annual earnings per share. *Forward* (prospective): share price divided by anticipated annual earnings per share.

Price-earnings ratio game (bootstrapping) Companies increase earnings per share by acquiring other companies with lower price-earnings ratios than themselves. The share price can rise despite the absence of an economic value gain.

Price formation The mechanisms leading to a price for an asset, e.g. many buyers and sellers in a company's shares through their buy or sell actions (e.g. via market makers or on a computerised system) arrive at a price to carry out transactions.

Price-sensitive information That which may influence the share price or trading in the shares.

Price-to-book ratio (market to book) The price of a share as a multiple of per share book (balance sheet) value.

Pricing power An ability to raise prices even when product demand is flat without the danger of losing significant volume or market share.

Primary investors The household sector contains the savers in society who are the main providers of funds used for investment in the business sector.

Primary market A market in which securities are initially issued to investors rather than a secondary market in which investors buy and sell to each other.

Principal (1) The capital amount of a debt, excluding any interest. (2) A person acting for their own purposes accepting risk in financial transactions, rather than someone acting as an agent for another. (3) The amount invested.

Principal–agent problem In which an agent, e.g. a manager, does not act in the best interests of the principal, e.g. the shareholder.

Private equity Share capital invested in companies not quoted on an exchange.

Private Equity Investment Trusts (PEIT) These are investment vehicles allowing investors to buy in to an established private equity fund run by an experienced management team. The PEIT shares are bought and sold on the stock market.

Private limited company (Ltd) A company which is unable to offer its shares to the wider public.

Privatisation The sale to private investors of government-owned equity (shares) in state-owned industries or other commercial enterprises.

Pro forma earnings Projected or forecast earnings. These are not audited and may be unreliable.

Profit and loss account Records whether a company's sales revenue was greater than its costs.

Profit margin Profits as a percentage of sales.

Profitability index A measure of present value per pound invested.

Project An investment within the business requiring medium- to long-term commitment of resources.

Project appraisal The assessment of the viability of proposed long-term investments in real assets within the firm.

Project finance Finance assembled for a specific project. The loan and equity returns are tied to the cash flows and fortunes of the project rather than being dependent on the parent company/companies.

Promissory note A debtor promises to pay on demand or at a fixed date or a date to be determined by circumstances. A note is created stated this obligation.

Proprietary transactions (Proprietary trading) A financial institution, as well as acting as an agent for a client, may trade on the financial markets with a view to generating profits for itself, e.g. speculation on forex (q.v.).

Prospectus A document containing information about a company (or unit trust/OEIC – q.v.), to assist with a new issue (initial public offering) by supplying detail about the company and how it operates.

Provision (1) Sum set aside in accounts for anticipated loss or expenditure. (2) A clause or stipulation in a legal agreement giving one party a right.

Proxy votes Shareholders unable to attend a shareholders' meeting may authorise another person, e.g. a director or the chairman, to vote on their behalf, either as instructed or as that person sees fit.

Public limited company (Plc) A company which may have an unlimited number of shareholders and offer its shares to the wider public (unlike a limited company – q.v.). Must have a minimum share value of £50,000. Some Plcs are listed on the London Stock Exchange.

Purchasing power parity (PPP) theory of exchange rate determination Exchange rates will be in equilibrium when their domestic purchasing powers at that rate of exchange are equivalent. Movements in exchange rates will be a function of the differential in the two currencies' inflation rates.

Put features *See* Put options.

Put option This gives the purchaser the right, but not the obligation, to sell a financial instrument, commodity or some other underlying asset at a given price, at or before a specified date.

Qualitative analysis Relying on subjective elements to take a view, e.g. valuing shares by judging quality of management and strategic position.

Quant (Quantum) analysis Quantitative analysis using complex mathematical models.

Quick asset value (net) Current assets minus stock minus current liabilities (qq.v.).

Quick ratio (acid test) The ratio of current assets, less stock, to total current liabilities (qq.v).

Quota Quantitative limits placed on the importation of specified goods.

Quote-driven trading system Market makers post bid and offer prices on a computerised system.

Quoted Those shares with a price quoted on a recognised investment exchange (RIE) or AIM (e.g. the Official List of the London Stock Exchange (qq.v.)).

Random walk theory The movements in (share) prices are independent of one another; one day's price change cannot be predicted by looking at the previous day's price change.

Ranking (debt) Order of precedence for payment of obligations. Senior debt receives annual interest and redemption payments ahead of junior (or subordinated) debt. So, if the company has insufficient resources to pay its obligations the junior debt holders may receive little or nothing.

Rappaport's value drivers The seven key factors which determine value are: (1) Sales growth rate. (2) Operating profit margin. (3) Tax rate. (4) Incremental fixed capital investment. (5) Incremental working capital investment. (6) The planning horizon. (7) The required rate of return.

Rating *See* Credit rating.

Raw materials stock period The average number of days raw materials remain unchanged and in stock. Equal to the average value of raw materials stock divided by the average purchase of raw materials per day.

Real assets Assets used to carry on a business. These assets can be tangible (e.g. buildings) or intangible (e.g. a brand) as opposed to financial assets.

Real cash flows Future cash flows are expressed in terms of constant purchasing power.

Real option An option to undertake different courses of action in the real asset market (strategic and operational options), as opposed to a tradable option on financial securities or commodities.

Real rate of return The rate that would be required (obtained) in the absence of inflation. The nominal return minus inflation.

Recapitalisation A change in the financial structure, e.g. in debt to equity ratio.

Receivable (Accounts receivable) A sum due from a customer for goods delivered: trade credit.

Receiver A receiver takes control of a business if a creditor successfully files a bankruptcy petition. The receiver may then sell the company's assets and distribute the proceeds among the creditors.

Recognised investment exchange (RIE) A body authorised to regulate securities trading in the UK, e.g. the London Stock Exchange.

Recourse If a financial asset is sold (such as a trade debt), the purchaser could return to the vendor for payment in the event of non-payment by the borrower.

Redemption The repayment of the principal amount, or the par value, of a security (e.g. bond) at the maturity date resulting in the retirement and cancellation on the bond.

Redemption yield *See* Yield.

Registrar An organisation that maintains a record of share (and other securities) ownership for a company. It also communicates with shareholders on behalf of the company.

Regulated exchange market A market where there is a degree of supervision concerning market behaviour or other controls on the freedom of participants.

Regulatory News Service (RNS) A system for distributing important company announcements and other price-sensitive financial news run by the London Stock Exchange.

Reinvestment rate The rate of return on the periodic cash flows generated by a project when invested.

Relationship banking A long-term, intimate and relatively open relationship is established between a corporation and its banks. Banks often supply a range of tailor-made services rather than one-off services.

Rembrandt A foreign bond issued in The Netherlands.

Remuneration committee A group of directors of a company, all of which are independent of management, decide the remuneration of executive directors.

Repayment holiday *See* Grace period.

Reporting accountant A company planning to float on the London Stock Exchange employs a reporting accountant to prepare a detailed report on the firm's financial controls, track record, financing and forecasts.

Required return The minimum rate of return given the opportunity cost of capital.

Rescheduling Rearranging the payments made by a borrower to a lender – usually over a long period.

Rescue rights issue A company in dire trouble, in danger of failure, carries out a rights issue to raise capital.

Residual income An alternative term for economic profit.

Residual theory of dividends Dividends should only be paid when the firm has financed all its positive NPV projects.

Resistance line A line drawn on a price (e.g. share) chart showing the market participants' reluctance to push the price below (or above) the line over a period of time.

Resolution A proposal put to the vote at a shareholders' meeting.

Resolution of uncertainty theory of dividends The market places a greater value on shares offering higher near-term dividends because these are more certain than more distant dividends.

Restructuring costs The costs associated with a reorganisation of the business, e.g. closing factories, redundancies.

Retail banking Banking for individual customers or small firms, normally for small amounts. High-volume, low-value banking.

Retail Service Providers (RSPs) Some market makers also offer automated computer dealing service to investors as RSPs.

Retained earnings That part of a company's profits not paid as dividends.

Retention ratio Retained profits for the year as a proportion of profits after tax attributable to ordinary shareholders for the year.

Return on capital employed (ROCE); return on investment (ROI) Traditional measures of profitability. Profit return divided by the volume of resources devoted to the activity. Resources usually includes shareholders' funds, net debt and provisions. Cumulative goodwill, previously written off, may be added back to the resources total. *See also* Accounting rate of return.

Return on equity (ROE) Profit attributable to shareholders as a percentage of equity shareholders' funds.

Revaluation reserve A balance sheet entry that records accumulated revaluations of fixed assets.

Reverse floater *See* Reverse floating-rate notes.

Reverse floating-rate notes *See* Floating-rate notes.

Reverse takeover The acquiring company is smaller than the target in terms of market capitalisation and offers newly created shares in itself as consideration for the purchase of the shares in the acquirer. So many new shares are created that the former shareholders in the target become the dominant shareholders in the combined entity.

Reversing the trade *See* Closing out a futures position.

Reversion to the mean The behaviour of financial markets is often characterised as reverting to the mean, in which an otherwise random process of price changes or returns tends over the medium to long term to move towards the average.

Revolving credit An arrangement whereby a borrower can draw down short-term loans as the need arises, to a maximum over a period of years.

Revolving underwriting facility (RUF) A bank(s) underwrites the borrower's access to funds at a specified rate in the short-term financial markets (e.g. by issuing euronotes) throughout an agreed period. If the notes are not bought in the market the underwriter(s) is obliged to purchase them.

Reward-to-variability ratio Alternative name for Sharpe ratio (q.v.).

Reward-to-volatility ratio An alternative name for Treynor's ratio (q.v.).

Rights issue An invitation to existing shareholders to purchase additional shares in the company in proportion to their existing holdings.

Risk A future return has a variety of possible values. Sometimes measured by standard deviation (q.v.).

Risk arbitrage Taking a position (purchase or sale) in a security, commodity, etc., because it is judged to be mispriced relative to other securities with similar characteristics. The comparator securities are not identical (e.g. shares in Unilever and in Procter & Gamble) and therefore there is an element of risk that the valuation gap will widen rather than contract. An extreme form of risk arbitrage is to take a position hoping to make a profit if an event occurs (e.g. a takeover). If the event does not occur there may be a loss. The word 'arbitrage' has been stretched beyond breaking point, as true arbitrage should be risk free.

Risk averter Someone who prefers a more certain return to an alternative with an equal expected return but which is more risky.

Risk lover (seeker) Someone who prefers a more uncertain alternative to an alternative with an equal but less risky outcome.

Risk management The selection of those risks a business should take and those which should be avoided or mitigated, followed by action to avoid or reduce risk.

Risk premium The extra return, above the risk-free rate for accepting risk.

Risk transformation Intermediaries offer low-risk securities to primary investors to attract funds, which are then used to purchase higher-risk securities issued by the ultimate borrowers.

Risk-free rate of return (RFR) The rate earned on riskless investment, denoted r_f. A reasonable proxy is short-term lending to a reputable government.

Risk-return line A line on a two-dimensional graph showing all the possible expected returns and standard deviation combinations, available from the construction of portfolios from two assets. This can also be called the two-asset opportunity set or feasibility set.

Roadshow Companies and their advisers make a series of presentations to potential investors, usually to entice them into buying a new issue of securities.

Rolled-over overdraft Short-term loan facilities are perpetuated into the medium and long term by the renewal of the overdraft facility.

Rolling settlement Shares and cash are exchanged after a deal has been struck a fixed number of days later – usually after three days – rather than on a specific account day.

RPI (retail price index) The main UK measure of general inflation.

R-squared, R^2 *See* Coefficient of determination.

Running yield *See* Yield.

Safe haven Investing in a safe investment in time of trouble, such as major financial turmoil. UK or US government bonds and treasury bills, for example, are usually regarded as safe havens.

Sale and leaseback Assets (e.g. land and buildings) are sold to another firm (e.g. bank, insurance company) with a simultaneous agreement for the vendor to lease the asset back for a stated period under specific terms.

Sales ledger administration The management of trade debtors: recording credit sales, checking customer creditworthiness, sending invoices and chasing late payers.

Samurai A foreign bond, yen-denominated, issued by a non-Japanese entity in the domestic Japanese market.

S&P 500 Standard & Poor's index of 500 leading US shares.

Satisficed When a contributor to an organisation is given just enough of a return to make their contribution, e.g. banks are given contracted interest and principal, and no more.

Scaledown In a new issue, when a company floats on a stock exchange, if demand is greater than supply at the offer price the applicants receive less than they applied for, according to a prearranged formula.

Scenario analysis An analysis of the change in NPV (q.v.) brought about by the simultaneous change in a number of key inputs to an NPV analysis. Typically a 'worst case scenario', when all the changes in variables are worsening, and a 'best case scenario', when all variable changes are positive, are calculated.

Scrip dividends Shareholders are offered the alternative of additional shares rather than a cash dividend.

Scrip issue The issue of more shares to existing shareholders according to their current holdings. Shareholders do not pay for these new shares. Company reserves are converted into issued capital.

SEAQ (Stock Exchange Automated Quotation System) A real-time computer screen-based quotation system for securities where market makers on the London Stock Exchange report bid-offer prices and trading volumes, and brokers can observe prices and trades.

SEAQI (Stock Exchange Automated Quotation International) A real-time computer screen-based quotation system for securities that allows market makers in international shares based on the London Stock Exchange to report prices, quotes and trading volumes.

Search costs The cost of finding another person or organisation with which to transact business/investment.

Seasoned Equity Offerings (SEOs) Companies that have been on a stock exchange for some time selling new shares, e.g. via a rights issue.

Second lien loans Low ranking loans paying high rates of return. The owners of the loans are in line behind senior secured creditors in a liquidation.

Secondary buy-out A company that has been backed by private equity finance is then sold to another private equity firm(s).

Secondary market Securities already issued are traded between investors.

Secondary market trading facility A system to allow current holders of shares or other securities to trade between themselves.

Second-tier markets Not those trading markets provided for the leading (biggest company) shares and other securities.

Securities and Exchange Commission (SEC) The US federal body responsible for the regulation of securities markets (exchanges, brokers, investment advisers, etc.).

Securities house This may mean simply an issuing house. However, the term is sometimes used more broadly for an institution concerned with buying and selling securities or acting as agent in the buying and selling of securities.

Securitisation Financial payments (e.g. a claim to a number of mortgage payments) which are not tradable can be repackaged into other securities (e.g. bonds) and then sold. These are called asset-backed securities.

Security (1) A financial asset, e.g. a share or bond. (2) Asset pledged to be surrendered in the event of a loan default.

Security market line (SML) A linear (straight) line showing the relationship between systematic risk and expected rates of return for individual assets (securities). According to the capital asset pricing model (q.v.) the return above the risk-free rate of return (q.v.) for a risky asset is equal to the risk premium for the market portfolio multiplied by the beta coefficient.

SEDOL Stock Exchange Daily Official List. A journal published daily giving prices and deals for shares on London's Official List. Companies are given SEDOL numbers to identify them.

Seedcorn capital or money (Seed capital or money) The financing of the development of a business concept. High risk; usually provided by venture capitalists, entrepreneurs or business angels.

Self-amortising A reduction in the amount outstanding on a loan by regular payments to the lender.

Self-regulation Much of the regulation of financial services in the UK is carried out by self-regulatory organisations (SROs), i.e. industry participants regulate themselves within a light-touch legislated framework.

Selling the rights nil paid In a rights issue those entitled to new shares (existing shareholders) are entitled to sell the rights to the new shares without the need to purchase the new shares.

Semi-annual Twice a year at regular intervals.

Semi-captives A venture capital organisation that raises its capital from the financial markets, but is dominated by the participation of an organising institution.

Semi-strong efficiency Share prices fully reflect all the relevant, publicly available information.

Senior debt *See* Subordinated debt.

Sensitivity analysis An analysis of the effect on project NPV of changes in the assumed values of key variables, e.g. sales level, labour costs. Variables are changed one at a time. It is a 'what-if' analysis, e.g. what if raw material costs rise by 20 per cent?

Separate legal person A company is a legal entity under the law. It is entitled to make contracts and be sued, for example, separately from the owners of the company.

Separation principle The decision on asset allocation can split into (1) selecting the optimum market portfolio on the efficiency frontier, and (2) allocating wealth between the optimum portfolio and the risk-free asset.

Serious Fraud Office (SFO) Investigates and prosecutes crimes of serious fraud in the UK.

SETS (Stock Exchange Electronic Trading System) An electronic order book-based trading system for the London Stock Exchange. Brokers input buy and sell orders directly into the system. Buyers and sellers are matched and the trade executed automatically. The system is used for the largest UK shares.

SETSsq A share trading system run by the London Stock Exchange with a focus on lightly traded shares (few trades per day).

Settlement The completion of a transaction, e.g. upon the sale of a share in the secondary market cash is transferred as payment, in return ownership is transferred.

Settlement price The price calculated by a derivatives exchange at the end of each trading session as the closing price that will be used in determining profits and losses for the marking-to-market process for margin accounts.

Share Companies divide the ownership of the company into ordinary shares. An owner of a share usually has the same rights to vote and receive dividends as another owner of a share. Also called equity (q.v.).

Share buy-back The company buys back a proportion of its shares from shareholders.

Share certificate A document showing ownership of part of the share capital of a company.

Share markets Institutions which facilitate the regulated sale and purchase of shares; includes the primary and secondary markets.

Share option scheme Employees are offered the right to buy shares in their company at a modest price some time in the future.

Share premium account A balance sheet entry represented by the difference between the price received by a company when it sells shares and the par value of those shares.

Share repurchase The company buys back its own shares.

Share split (stock split) Shareholders receive additional shares from the company without payment. The nominal (par) value of each share is reduced in proportion to the increase in the number of shares, so the total book value of shares remains the same.

Shareholder value analysis A technique developed by Rappaport (q.v.) for establishing value creation. It equals the present value of operating cash flows within the planning horizon *plus* the present value of operating cash flows after the planning horizon *plus* the current value of marketable securities and other non-operating investments *less* corporate debt.

Shareholder wealth maximisation The maximising of shareholders' purchasing power. In a pricing efficient market, it is the maximisation of the current share price.

Shareholders' funds (Equity) The net assets of the business (after deduction of all short- and long-term liabilities and minority interests) shown in the balance sheet.

Sharpe ratio A measure relating risk and return. The extent to which a portfolio's (or share's) return has been greater than a risk-free asset divided by its standard deviation (q.v.).

Shell company A company with a stockmarket quotation but with very little in the way of real economic activity. It may have cash but no production.

Short position In a derivative contract the counterparty in a short position is the one that has agreed to deliver the underlying (q.v.).

Short selling The selling of financial securities (e.g. shares) not yet owned, in the anticipation of being able to buy at a later date at a lower price.

Short-term sterling interest rate future (colloquially known as **short sterling**) The three-month sterling interest rate future contract traded on LIFFE (q.v.). Notional fixed-term deposits for three-month periods starting at a specified time in the future.

Short-termism A charge levelled at the financial institutions in their expectations of the companies to which they provide finance. It is argued that long-term benefits are lost because of pressure for short-term performance.

Shorting Same as Short selling.

Shorts UK government bonds (gilts) with less than five years to maturity.

Sight bank account (current account) One where deposits can be withdrawn without notice.

Sigma A measure of dispersion of returns, standard deviation (q.v.).

Signalling Some financial decisions are taken to be signals from the managers to the financial markets, e.g. an increase in gearing, or a change in dividend policy.

Simple interest Interest is paid on the original principal; no interest is paid on the accumulated interest payments.

Sinking fund Money is accumulated in a fund through regular payments in order eventually to repay a debt.

SIS x-clear SIS x-clear AG is part of the corporate group Swiss Financial Market Services AG, the integrated Swiss financial market infrastructure provider. As Central Counterparty (CCP) Swiss x-clear offers clearing and risk management services for SWX Europe and SWX Swiss Exchange.

Small firm effect (Size effect) The tendency of small firms to give abnormally high returns on the stock market.

Soft capital rationing Internal management-imposed limits on investment expenditure.

Solvency The ability to pay legal debts.

South Sea Bubble A financial bubble (*see* Bubble) in which the price of shares in the South Sea Company were pushed to ridiculously high levels on a surge of over-optimism in the early eighteenth century.

Special dividend An exceptionally large dividend paid on a one-off basis.

Special purpose vehicle or entity Companies set these up as separate organisations (companies) for a particular purpose. They are designed so that their accounts are not consolidated with those of the rest of the group.

Special resolution A company's shareholders vote at an AGM or EGM with a majority of 75 per cent of those voting. Normally special resolutions are reserved for important changes in the constitution of the company. Other matters are dealt with by way of an ordinary resolution (50 per cent or more of the votes required).

Special drawing rights (SDRs) A composite currency designed by the International Monetary Fund (IMF). Each IMF member country is allocated SDRs in proportion to its quota.

Specific inflation The price changes in an individual good or service.

Specific risk *See* Unsystematic risk.

Speculative grade Bonds with a credit rating below investment grade.

Speculative motive for holding cash This means that unexpected opportunities can be taken immediately.

Speculators Those that take a position in financial instruments and other assets with a view to obtaining a profit on changes in their value.

Sponsor Lends its reputation to a new issue of securities, advises the client company (along with the issuing broker) and co-ordinates the new issue process. Sponsors are usually merchant banks or stockbrokers. Also called an issuing house.

Spot market A market for immediate transactions (e.g. spot forex market, spot interest market), as opposed to an agreement to make a transaction some time in the future (e.g. forward, option, future).

Spot rate of interest *See* Spot market.

Spread The difference between the price to buy and the price to sell a financial security. Market makers quote a bid–offer spread for shares. The lower price (bid) is the price an investor receives if selling to the market maker. The higher (offer) price is the price if the investor wishes to buy from the market maker.

Stakeholder A party with an interest (financial or otherwise) in an organisation, e.g. employees, customers, suppliers, the local community.

Standard and Poor's 500 An index of leading (largest) 500 US shares listed in the New York Stock Exchange. Companies are weighted by market capitalisation of the NYSE.

Standard deviation A statistical measure of the dispersion around an average. A measure of volatility. The standard deviation is the square root of the variance. A fund or a share return can be expected to fall within one standard deviation of its average two-thirds of the time if the future is like the past.

Start-up capital Finance for young companies which have not yet sold their product commercially. High risk; usually provided by venture capitalists, entrepreneurs or business angels.

Statistically independent shares The movement of two variables is completely unrelated (e.g. the returns on two shares are unrelated).

Statutory Established, regulated or imposed by or in conformity with laws passed by a legislative body, e.g. Parliament.

Sterling bonds Corporate bonds which pay interest and principal in sterling.

Stock Another term for inventory of raw materials, work-in-progress and finished items.

Stock exchange A market in which securities are bought and sold. In continental Europe the term bourse may be used.

Stock Exchange Automated Quotations *See* SEAQ.

Stock market *See* Stock exchange.

Stock-out costs The cost associated with being unable to draw on a stock of raw material, work-in-progress or finished goods inventory (loss of sales, profits and goodwill, and also production dislocation).

Stocks and shares There is some lack of clarity in the distinction between stocks and shares. Shares are equities in companies. Stocks are financial instruments that pay interest, e.g. bonds. However, in the USA shares are also called 'common stocks' and the shareholders are sometimes referred to as the stockholders. So when some people use the term stocks they could be referring to either bonds or shares.

Straight bond One with a regular fixed rate of interest and without the right of conversion (to, say, shares) or any other unusual rights.

Strategic analysis The analysis of industries served by the firm and the company's competitive position within the industry.

Strategic business unit (SBU) A business unit within the overall corporate entity which is distinguishable from other business units because it serves a defined external market where management can conduct strategic planning in relation to products and markets.

Strategic objectives These goals are used as the criteria to guide the firm, e.g. market share targets. However, they may not always be good indicators of whether shareholder wealth is being maximised.

Strategic position A firm's competitive position within an industry and the atractiveness of the industry.

Strategy Selecting which product or market areas to enter/exit and how to ensure a good competitive position in those markets/ products.

Strategy planes chart Maps a firm's, SBU's or product line's position in terms of industry attractiveness, competitive advantage and life cycle stage of value potential.

Strike bid In a book-building exercise a potential institutional investor states that it will buy a given number of shares within the initial price range.

Strike price (1) In the offer for sale by a tender it is the price selected that will sell the required quantity of shares given the offers made. (2) The price paid by the holder of an option when/if the option is exercised – *See* Exercise price.

Strong form efficiency All relevant information, including that which is privately held, is reflected in the share price.

Subjective probability Probabilities are devised based on personal judgement of the range of outcomes along with the likelihood of their occurrence.

Subordinated debt A debt which ranks below another liability in order of priority for payment of interest or principal. Senior debt ranks above junior (subordinated) debt for payment.

Subscription rights A right to subscribe for some shares.

Subsidiary A company is a subsidiary of another company if the parent company holds the majority of the voting rights (more than 50%), or has a minority of the shares but has the right to appoint or remove directors holding a majority of the voting rights at meetings of the board on all, or substantially all, matters or it has the right to exercise a dominant influence.

Summary financial statement Companies often send small

investors a summary of the financial statements rather than the full report and accounts. This suits many investors and saves the company some money. However, an investor is entitled to receive a full annual report and accounts. It may be necessary to make a request for this.

Sunk cost A cost the firm has incurred or to which it is committed that cannot be altered. This cost does not influence subsequent decisions and can be ignored in, for example, project appraisal.

Super normal returns A rate of return above the normal rate.

Survivorship bias In empirical studies of share price performance the results may be distorted by focusing only on companies which survived through to the end of the period of study. Particularly poor performers (i.e. liquidated firms) are removed from the sample, thus biasing the results in a positive direction.

Swap An exchange of cash payment obligations. An interest rate swap is where one company arranges with a counterparty to exchange interest-rate payments. In a currency swap the two parties exchange interest obligations (receipts) for an agreed period between two different currencies.

Swaption or swap-option An option to have a swap at a later date.

Symbiosis type of post-merger integration Large differences between acquired and parent firms in culture, systems, etc., are maintained. However, collaboration in communications and the cross-fertilisation of ideas are encouraged.

Syndicated loan A loan made by one or more banks to one borrower.

Synergy A combined entity (e.g. two companies merging) will have a value greater than the sum of the parts.

Systematic (Undiversifiable or market or residual) risk That element of return variability from an asset which cannot be eliminated through diversification (q.v.). Measured by beta (q.v.). It comprises the risk factors common to all firms.

Systemic risk The risk of failure within the financial system causing a domino-type effect bringing down large parts of the system.

Take-out Market expression of bid made to a seller to 'takeout' his position – e.g. venture capital backed companies are bought allowing the venture capitalist to exit from the investment.

Takeover (acquisition) Many people use these terms interchangeably with merger. However, some differentiate takeover as meaning a purchase of one firm by another with the concomitant implication of financial and managerial domination. Usually applied to hostile (without target management approval) mergers.

Takeover Panel The committee responsible for supervising compliance with the (UK) City Code on Takeovers and Mergers (q.v.).

Tangible assets Those that have a physical presence.

Tariff Taxes imposed on imports.

Tax allowance An amount of income or capital gain that is not taxed.

Tax avoidance Steps taken to reduce tax that are permitted under the law.

Tax evasion Deliberately giving a false statement or omitting a relevant fact.

Tax haven A country or place with low rates of tax.

Tax shield The benefit for a company that comes from having some of its capital in debt form, the interest on which is tax deductible, resulting in a lower outflow from the company to the tax authorities.

Taxable profit That element of profit subject to taxation. This frequently differs from reported profit.

techMARK The London Stock Exchange launched techMARK in 1999. It is a subsection of the shares within the LSE's Official List (q.v.). It is a grouping of technology companies. It imposes different rules on companies seeking a flotation from those that apply to the other companies on the Official List (e.g. only one year's accounts are required).

Technical analysis Analysis of share price movements and trading volume to forecast future movements from past movements.

Tender offer A public offer to purchase securities.

Term assurance Life assurance taken out for less than the whole life – the insured sum is paid only in the event of the insured person dying within the term.

Term loan A loan of a fixed amount for an agreed time and on specified terms, usually with regular periodic payments. Most frequently provided by banks.

Term structure of interest rates The patterns of interest rates on bonds with differing lengths of time to maturity but with the same risk. Strictly it is the zero coupon implied interest rate for different lengths of time. *See also* Yield curve.

Terminal value The forecast future value of sums of money compounded to the end of a common time horizon.

Three-day rolling settlement (T+3) After a share transaction in the stock exchange investors pay for shares three working days later.

Tick The minimum price movement of a security or derivative contract.

Tier one ratio of core capital That part of a bank's capital defined as shareholders' equity plus irredeemable and non-cumulative preference shares.

Tiger economies (or countries) The first four industrialised economies in Asia excluding Japan: Taiwan, South Korea, Singapore and Hong Kong (also referred to as dragon economies).

'Time adjusted' measures of profitability The time value of money is taken into account.

Time value That part of an option's value that represents the value of the option expiring in the future rather than now. The longer the period to expiry, the greater the chance that the option will become in-the-money before the expiry date. The amount by which the option premium exceeds the intrinsic value.

Time value of money A pound received in the future is worth less than a pound received today – the present value of a sum of money depends on the date of its receipt.

Total (or market) capitalisation *See* Market capitalisation

Total shareholder return (TSR) or Total return The total return earned on a share over a period of time: dividends per share plus capital gain divided by initial share price.

Touch prices *See* Yellow strip.

Tracker An investment fund which is intended to replicate the return of a market index. Also called an index fund or passive fund.

Trade acceptance *See* Acceptance credit.

Trade credit Where goods and services are delivered to a firm for use in its production and are not paid for immediately.

Trade debtor A customer of a firm who has not yet paid for goods and services delivered.

Trade sale A company buys another company in the same line of business.

Traded option An option tradable on a market separate from the underlying (q.v.).

Trading floor A place where traders in a market (or their representatives) can meet to agree transactions face to face. However investment banks often have 'trading floors' where they 'meet' counterparties on other trading floors to conduct transactions via the telephone or computer.

Trading margin *See* Operating profit margin.

Traditional option An option available on any security but with an exercise price fixed as the market price on the day the option is bought. Bilateral contracts between the option buyer and the option writer rather than exchange-traded instruments. All such options expire after three months and cannot be sold to a secondary investor.

Transaction risk The risk that transactions already entered into, or for which the firm is likely to have a commitment in a foreign currency, will have a variable value in the home currency because of exchange-rate movements.

Transactional banking Banks compete with each other to offer services at the lowest cost to corporations, on a service-by- service basis.

Transactional motive for holding cash Money is used as a means of exchange; receipts and payments are rarely perfectly synchronised and therefore an individual or business generally needs to hold a stock of money to meet expenditure.

Translation risk This risk arises because financial data denominated in one currency are then expressed in terms of another currency.

Treasury UK government department responsible for financial and economic policy

Treasury bill A short-term money market instrument issued (sold) by the central bank, mainly in the UK and the USA, usually to supply the government's short-term financing needs.

Treasury management To plan, organise and control cash and borrowings so as to optimise interest and currency flows, and minimise the cost of funds. Also to plan and execute communications programmes to enhance investors' confidence in the firm.

Treynor's ratio or index A measure relating return to risk. It is the return on a portfolio (or share) minus the risk-free rate of rate of return divided by beta.

TRRACK system A system to assist the analysis of a company's extraordinary resources under the headings: tangible; relationships; reputation; attitude; capabilities; and knowledge.

Trust deed A document specifying the regulation of the management of assets on behalf of beneficiaries of the trust.

Trustees Those that are charged with the responsibility for ensuring compliance with the trust deed.

Tulipmania A seventeenth-century Dutch bubble. *See* Bubble.

Turnover (revenue or sales) (1) Money received or to be received by the company from goods and services sold during the year. (2) In portfolio management, the amount of trading relative to the value of the portfolio.

Ultimate borrowers Firms investing in real assets need finance which ultimately comes from the primary investors.

Uncertainty Strictly (in economists' terms), uncertainty is when there is more than one possible outcome to a course of action; the form of each possible outcome is known, but the probability of getting any one outcome is not known. However, the distinction between risk (the ability to assign probabilities) and uncertainty has largely been ignored for the purposes of this text.

Unconditionality In a merger (q.v.), once unconditionality is declared, the acquirer becomes obliged to buy. Target shareholders who accepted the offer are no longer able to withdraw their acceptance.

Unconventional cash flows A series of cash flows in which there is more than one change in sign.

Uncovered (naked) call option writing Writing a call option (q.v.) on an underlying (q.v.) when the writer does not own the underlying securities included in the option.

Underlying The asset (e.g. share, commodity) that is the subject of a derivative contract.

Underlying earnings per share *See* Headline earnings per share.

Underwriters These (usually large financial institutions) guarantee to buy the proportion of a new issue of securities (e.g. shares) not taken up by the market, in return for a fee.

Undifferentiated product One that is much the same as that supplied by other companies.

Undiversifiable risk *See* Systematic risk.

Uninformed investors Those that have no/little knowledge about financial securities and the fundamental evaluation of their worth.

Unique risk *See* Unsystematic risk.

Unit trust An investment organisation that attracts funds from individual investors by issuing units to invest in a range of securities, e.g. shares or bonds. It is open ended, the number of units expanding to meet demand.

United Kingdom Listing Authority (UKLA) This organisation is part of the Financial Services Authority (q.v.) and rigorously enforces a set of demanding rules on companies at the time when they join the stock market and in subsequent years.

Universal banks Financial institutions involved in many different aspects of finance including retail banking and wholesale banking.

Unlisted Shares and other securities not on the Main Market of the London Stock Exchange (qq.v.) are described as unlisted.

Unquoted firms Those shares with a price not quoted on a recognised investment exchange, RIE (e.g. the Official List or AIM of the London Stock Exchange – qq.v.).

Unsecured A financial claim with no collateral or any charge over the assets of the borrower.

Unsystematic (unique or diversifiable or specific) risk That element of an asset's variability in returns which can be eliminated by holding a well-diversified portfolio.

Utility (1) The satisfaction, pleasure or fulfilment of needs derived from consuming some quantity of a good or service. (2) A business involved in basic goods and services, e.g. water, electricity.

Valuation risk (price risk) The possibility that, when a financial instrument matures or is sold in the market, the amount received is less than anticipated by the lender.

Value action pentagon This displays the five actions for creating value: (1) Increase the return on existing capital. (2) Raise investment in positive spread units. (3) Divest assets from negative spread units to release capital for more productive use. (4) Extend the planning horizon. (5) Lower the required rate of return.

Value chain The interlinking activities that take place within an organisation or between organisations in the process of converting inputs into outputs. Identifying these activities and finding ways to perform them more efficiently is a way for companies to gain competitive advantage over their rivals.

Value creation The four key elements are: (1) Amount of capital invested. (2) Actual rate of return on capital. (3) Required rate of return. (4) Planning horizon (for performance-spread persistence).

Value creation profile An analysis of the sources of value creation within the firm from its products and market segments, which maps value creation against the proportion of capital invested.

Value drivers Crucial organisational capabilities, giving the firm competitive advantage. Different from Rappaport's value drivers (q.v.).

Value investing The identification and holding of shares which are fundamentally undervalued by the market, given the prospects of the firm.

Value-based management A managerial approach in which the primary purpose is long-term shareholder wealth maximisation. The objective of the firm, its systems, strategy, processes, analytical techniques, performance measurements and culture have as their guiding objective long-term shareholder wealth maximisation.

Vanilla bond *See* Straight bond.

Variable costs Costs that rise or fall with product output and sales.

Variable rate bond (loan) The interest rate payable varies with short-term rates (e.g. LIBOR six months).

Variance A measure of volatility around an average value. It is the square of the standard deviation.

Variation margin The amount of money paid after the payment of the initial margin required to secure an option or futures position, after it has been revalued by the exchange or clearing house. Variation margin payments may be required daily to top the account up to the maintenance margin level.

Vendor placing Shares issued to a company to pay for assets, or issued to shareholders to pay for an entire company in a takeover are placed with investors keen on holding the shares in return for cash. The vendors can then receive the cash.

Venture and development capital investment trusts (VDCIT) Standard investment trusts (without tax breaks) with a focus on more risky developing companies.

Venture capital (VC) Finance provided to unquoted firms by specialised financial institutions. This may be backing for an entrepreneur, financing a start-up or developing business, or assisting a management buyout or buy-in. Usually it is provided by a mixture of equity, loans and mezzanine finance. It is used for medium-term to long-term investment in high-risk situations.

Venture capital trusts (VCTs) An investment vehicle introduced to the UK in 1995 to encourage investment in small and fast-growing companies. The VCT invests in a range of small businesses. The providers of finance to the VCT are given important tax breaks.

Vertical merger Where the two merging firms are from different stages of the production chain.

Virtual bid When a proper merger offer of one company for another has not been made, but the potential acquirer has raised the possibility of making a bid for the target firm.

Virt-x A share market operating electronically across borders. It mostly trades large Swiss company shares (it is part owned by SWX Swiss Exchange). It is a recognised investment exchange supervised by the FSA in the UK.

Volatility The speed and magnitude of price movements over time, measured by standard deviation or variance (qq.v.).

Volume transformation Intermediaries gather small quantities of money from numerous savers and repackage these sums into larger bundles for investment in the business sector or elsewhere.

Warrant A financial instrument which gives the holder the right to subscribe for a specified number of shares or bonds at a fixed price at some time in the future.

Weak-form efficiency Share prices fully reflect all information contained in past price movements.

Wealth added index (WAI) A value metric devised and trademarked by Stern Stewart & Co. It measures the increase in shareholder's wealth through dividend and capital gains over a number of years after deducting the cost of equity capital, defined as the return required for shares of that risk class.

Weighted average cost of capital (WACC) The weighted average cost of capital (the discount rate) is calculated by weighting the cost of debt and equity in proportion to their contributions to the total capital of the firm.

White knight A friendly company which makes a bid for a company that is the subject of a hostile takeover bid. The white knight's bid is welcomed by the directors of the target company.

Whole-of-life policies Life assurance that pays out to beneficiaries when the insured dies (not limited to, say, the next 10 years).

Wholesale bank One that lends, arranges lending or supplies services on a large scale to corporations and within the interbank market. As opposed to retail banks dealing in relatively small sums for depositors and borrowers.

Wholesale financial markets Markets available only to those dealing in large quantities. Dominated by interbank transactions.

Winding-up The process of ending a company, selling its assets, paying its creditors and distributing the remaining cash among shareholders.

Winner's curse In winning a merger battle, the acquirer suffers a loss in value because it overpays.

Witholding tax Taxation deducted from income by the payer of that income (e.g. company paying interest or dividends) and then sent to tax authorities.

Work-in-progress period The number of days to convert raw materials into finished goods. Equal to the average value of work-in-progress divided by the average cost of goods sold per day.

Working capital The difference between current assets and current liabilities – net current assets or net current liabilities (qq.v.).

Working capital cycle Typically, investment in raw materials, work-in-progress and finished goods is followed by sales for cash or on credit. Credit sales funds are usually collected at a later date. Investment is needed at each stage to finance current assets. The cycle may be expressed in terms of the length of time between the acquisition of raw materials and other inputs and the flow of cash from the sale of goods.

Write down (Write off) Companies change the recorded value of assets when they are no longer worth the previously stated value.

Writer of an option The seller of an option contract, granting the right but not the obligation to the purchaser.

Writing-down allowance (WDA) (Capital allowance) Reductions in taxable profit related to a firm's capital expenditure (e.g. plant, machinery, vehicles).

Yankees A foreign bond, US dollar-denominated, issued by a non-US entity in the domestic US market.

Yellow strip The yellow band on a SEAQ or SETS screen which displays the highest bid and the lowest offered prices that competing market makers are offering in a security. They are known colloquially as the 'touch' or 'yellow strip' prices.

Yield The income from a security as a proportion of its market price. The flat yield (interest yield, running yield and income yield) on a fixed interest security is the gross interest amount, divided by the current market price, expressed as a percentage. The redemption yield or yield to maturity of a bond is the discount rate such that the present value of all cash inflows from the bond (interest plus principal) is equal to the bond's current market price.

Yield curve A graph showing the relationship between the length of time to the maturity of a bond and the interest rate.

Yield stock *See* High yield shares.

Yield to maturity *See* Yield.

Z statistic A measure of the number of standard deviations away from the mean (average) value a point (say an NPV outcome) is.

Zero-cost option A combination of option purchase and option writing. The price of the written option (premium) is the same as the price (premium) paid for the option that is purchased, so the net cost is zero.

Zero coupon bond (or zero coupon preference share) A bond that does not pay regular interest (dividend) but instead is issued at a discount (i.e. below par value) and is redeemable at par, thus offering a capital gain.

For a much wider range of definitions and descriptions consult: Moles, P. and Terry, N. (1997) *The Handbook of International Financial Terms* (Oxford: Oxford University Press).

The following websites provide definitions of financial terms:
www/financial-dictionary.thefreedictionary.com
www.financial-terms.co.uk
www.global-investor.com
www.investopedia.com
www.investorwords.com
www.moneyterms.co.uk

Bibliography

3i (1993) 'Dividend Policy'. Reported in *Bank of England Quarterly Review* (1993), August, p. 367.

Abraham, A. and Ikenberry, D. (1994) 'The individual investor and the weekend effect', *Journal of Financial and Quantitative Analysis*, June.

Accounting Standards Committee (1984) *Accounting for leases and hire purchase contracts*, SSAP 21. Also see International Accounting Standard IAS 17. London: Accounting Standards Committee.

Adedeji, A. (1997) 'A test of the CAPM and the Three Factor Model on the London Stock Exchange', paper presented to the British Accounting Association Northern Accounting Group 1997 Annual Conference, 10 Sept. 1997, Loughborough University.

Aggarwal, R. (2001) 'Using economic profit to assess performance: A metric for modern firms', *Business Horizons*, Jan/Feb, pp. 55–60.

Al-Ali, J. and Arkwright, T. (2000) 'An investigation of UK companies' practices in the determination, interpretation and usage of the cost of capital', *Journal of Interdisciplinary Economics*, 11, pp. 303–19.

Alkaraan, F. and Northcott, D. (2006) 'Strategic capital investment decision-making: a role for emergent analysis tools? A study of practice in large UK manufacturing companies', *British Accounting Review*, 38, pp. 149–73.

Alti, A. (2006) 'How persistent is the impact of market timing on capital structure?', *Journal of Finance*, 61(4), August, pp. 1681–710.

Ambrose, B.W. and Megginson, W.L. (1992) 'The role of asset structure, ownership structure, and takeover defences in determining acquisition likelihood', *Journal of Financial and Quantitative Analysis*, 27(4), pp. 575–89.

Amran, M. and Kulatilaka, N. (1999) *Real Options: Managing Strategic Investment in an Uncertain World*. Boston, MA: Harvard Business School Press.

Anderson, A.M., Bey, R.P. and Weaver, S.C. (2005) 'Economic value Added®® Adjustments: Much ado about nothing'. Working paper. Bethlehem, PA: Lehigh University.

Anderson, K. and Brooks, C. (2006) 'The long-term price-earnings ratio', *Journal of Business Finance and Accounting*, 33 (7&8), pp. 1063–86.

Anderson, R.C., Mansi, S.A. and Reeb, D.M. (2003) 'Founding family ownership and the agency cost of debt', *Journal of Financial Economics*, 68, pp. 263–85.

Anderson, T.J. (2006) *Global Derivatives: A Strategic Management Perspective*. Harlow: Financial Times Prentice Hall.

Anthony, R.N. (1960) 'The trouble with profit maximisation', *Harvard Business Review*, Nov.–Dec., pp. 126–34.

Arnold, G.C. (1996a) 'Risk management using financial derivatives', in E. Gardener and P. Molyneux (eds), *Investment Banking: Theory and Practice*. 2nd edn. London: Euromoney.

Arnold, G.C. (1996b) 'Equity and corporate valuation', in E. Gardener and P. Molyneux (eds), *Investment Banking: Theory and Practice*. 2nd edn. London: Euromoney.

Arnold, G.C. (2000) 'Tracing the development of value-based management'. In Glen Arnold and Matt Davies (eds), *Value-based Management: Context and Application*. London: Wiley.

Arnold, G.C. (2002) *Valuegrowth Investing*. London: Financial Times Prentice Hall.

Arnold, G.C. (2004) *The Financial Times Guide to Investing*. Harlow: Financial Times Prentice Hall.

Arnold, G.C. and Baker, R.D. (2007) 'Return reversal in UK shares'. Salford Business School Working Paper 107/07. Available at: www.mams.salford.ac.uk/mams/resources/uploads/File/working-papers.

Arnold, G.C. and Baker, R.D. (2005) 'Return reversal in UK shares', University of Salford Working Paper.

Arnold, G.C. and Davies, M. (eds) (2000) *Value-Based Management*. London: Wiley.

Arnold, G.C. and Davis, P. (1995) Profitability trends in West Midlands industries. A study for Lloyds Bowmaker. Edinburgh: Lloyds Bowmaker.

Arnold, G.C. and Davis, P. (1996) Profitability trends in East Midlands industries. A study for Lloyds Bowmaker. Edinburgh: Lloyds Bowmaker.

Arnold, G.C. and Hatzopoulos, P.D. (2000) 'The theory practice gap in capital budgeting: evidence from the United Kingdom', *Journal of Business Finance and Accounting*, 27(5) and (6), June/July, pp. 603–26.

Arnold, G.C. and Shi, J. (2005) 'Profitability of momentum strategies in UK bull and bear market conditions'.

Arnold, G. and Smith, M. (1999) *The European High Yield Bond Market: Drivers and Impediments*. London: Financial Times Finance Management Report.

Arnold, G.C. and Xiao, Y. (2007) 'Financial statement analysis and the return reversal effect'. Salford Business School Working Paper 108/07. Available at: www.mams.salford.ac.uk/mams/resources/uploads/File/working-papers.

Arnott, R. and Bernstein, P. (2002) 'What risk premium is normal?', *Financial Analysts Journal*, March/April.

Arya, A., Fellingham, J.C. and Glover, J.C. (1998) 'Capital budgeting: some exceptions to the net present value rule', *Issues in Accounting Education*, 13(3), August, pp. 499–508.

Atkins, A.B. and Dyl, E.A. (1993) 'Reports of the death of the efficient markets hypothesis are greatly exaggerated', *Applied Financial Economics*, 3, pp. 95–100.

Baba, N. and Kozaki, M. (1992) 'An intelligent forecasting system of stock prices using neural networks', *Proceedings of International Joint Conference on Neural Networks*, Baltimore, MD, vol. 1, pp. 371–7.

Baker, A. and Wurgler, J. (2002) 'Market timing and capital structure', *Journal of Finance*, 62(1), February, pp. 1–32.

Baker, M. and Wurgler, J. (2004) 'A catering theory of dividends', *Journal of Finance*, 59(3), June, pp. 1125–65.

Baker, M.K., Powell, G.E. and Veit, E.T. (2002) 'Revisiting management perspectives on dividend policy', *Journal of Economics and Finance*, 26(3), pp. 267–83.

Ball, M., Brady, S. and Olivier, C. (1995) 'Getting the best from your banks', *Corporate Finance*, July, pp. 26–47.

Ball, R. (1995) 'The theory of stock market efficiency: Accomplishments and limitations', *Journal of Applied Corporate Finance*, Winter and Spring, pp. 4–17.

Ball, R. (2001) 'The theory of stock market efficiency: accomplishments and limitations', in D.H. Chew (ed.) *The New Corporate Finance*, 3rd edn. New York: McGraw-Hill Irwin.

Ball, R. and Brown, P. (1968) 'An empirical evaluation of accounting income numbers', *Journal of Accounting Research*, Autumn, pp. 159–78.

Ball, R. and Kothari, S.P. (1989) 'Nonstationary expected returns: Implications for tests of market efficiency and serial correlation in returns', *Journal of Financial Economics*, 25, pp. 51–94.

Ball, R., Kothari, S.P. and Shanken, J. (1995) 'Problems in measuring portfolio performance: An application to contrarian investment strategies', *Journal of Financial Economics*, May, vol. 38, pp. 79–107.

Bank of England Quarterly Bulletins.

Bank of England, www.bankofengland.co.uk.

Banz, R. (1981) 'The relationship between return and market value of common stock', *Journal of Financial Economics*, 9, pp. 3–18.

Banz, R.W. and Breen, W.J. (1986) 'Sample-dependent results using accounting and market data: Some evidence', *Journal of Finance*, 41, pp. 779–93.

Barber, B.M. and Odeon, T. (1999) 'The courage of misguided convictions', *Financial Analysts Journal*, 55, November–December, pp. 41–55.

Barber, B. and Odeon, T. (2000) 'Trading is hazardous to your wealth: the common stock investment performance and individual investors', *Journal of Finance*, 55(2), April, pp. 773–806.

Barberis, B., Schleifer, A. and Vishny, R.W. (1998) 'A model of investor sentiment', *Journal of Financial Economics*, 49, 307–43.

Barclays Capital (annual) *Equity Gilt Study*. London: Barclays Capital.

Barker, R. (2001) *Determining Value: Valuation models and financial statements*. Harlow: Financial Times Prentice Hall.

Barry, C.B., Peavy J.W. III and Rodriguez, M. (1998) 'Performance characteristics of emerging capital markets', *Financial Analysts Journal*, January/February, pp. 72–80.

Basu, S. (1975) 'The information content of price-earnings ratios', *Financial Management*, 4, Summer, pp. 53–64. Evidence of a market inefficiency for low PER shares.

Basu, S. (1977) 'Investment performance of common stocks in relation to their price/earnings ratios: A test of the efficient market hypothesis', *Journal of Finance*, 32(3), June, pp. 663–82.

Basu, S. (1983) 'The relationship between earnings' yield, market value and return for NYSE stocks – Further evidence', *Journal of Financial Economics*, June, pp. 129–56.

Baumol, W.J. (1952) 'The transactions demand for cash: An inventory theoretic approach', *Quarterly Journal of Economics*, November, pp. 545–56.

Benartzi, S. and Thaler, R. (1995) 'Myopic loss aversion and the equity premium puzzle', *Quarterly Journal of Economics*, 110(1), pp. 73–92.

Bernard, V. (1993) 'Stock price reaction to earnings announcements', in R. Thaler (ed.) *Advances in Behavioural Finance*. New York: Russell Sage Foundation.

Berle, A.A. and Means, G.C. (1932) *The Modern Corporation and Private Property*. New York: Macmillan.

Bernard, V.L. and Thomas, J.K. (1989) 'Post-earnings-announcement drift: Delayed price response or risk premium?', *Journal of Accounting Research*, 27 (Supplement 1989), pp. 1–36.

Berry, A. *et al.* (1990) 'Leasing and the smaller firm', The Chartered Association of Certified Accountants, Occasional Research Paper No. 3.

Better Payment Practice Group (1998) 'Better payment practice' (www.payontime.co.uk).

Bevan, A.A. and Danbelt, J. (2004) 'Testing for inconsistencies in the estimation of UK capital structure determinants', *Applied Financial Economics*, 14, pp. 55–66.

Bhasker, K. (1979) 'A multiple objective approach to capital budgeting', *Accounting and Business Research*, Winter.

Bhide, A. (1993) 'The causes and consequences of hostile takeovers', in D.H. Chew, Jr (ed.), *The New Finance: Where Theory Meets Practice*. New York: McGraw-Hill.

Bierman, H. (1988) *Implementing Capital Budgeting Techniques*, revised edn. Cambridge, MA: Ballinger Publishing.

Bierman, H. and Smidt, S. (1992) *The Capital Budgeting Decision*, 8th edn. New York: Macmillan.

Bierman, H. and Smidt, S. (2006) *Advanced Capital Budgeting*. London: Routledge.

Black, F. (1972) 'Capital market equilibrium with restricted borrowing', *Journal of Business* (July), pp. 444–55.

Black, F. (1976) 'The dividend puzzle', *Journal of Portfolio Management*, 2, pp. 5–8.

Black, F. (1986) 'Noise', *Journal of Finance*, 41(3), July, pp. 529–34.

Black, F. (1993) 'Beta and return', *Journal of Portfolio Management*, 20, Fall, pp. 8–18.

Black, F., Jensen, M.C. and Scholes, M. (1972) 'The Capital Asset Pricing Model: some empirical tests', in M. Jensen (ed.), *Studies in the Theory of Capital Markets*. New York: Praeger.

Black, F. and Scholes, M. (1973) 'The pricing of options and corporate liabilities', *Journal of Political Economy*, May/June, pp. 637–59.

Blake, D. (2000) *Financial Market Analysis*. 2nd edn. London: Wiley.

Blume, M.E. (1971) 'On the assessment of risk', *Journal of Finance*, 26(1), March, pp. 1–10.

Blume, M.E. (1975) 'Betas and their regression tendencies', *Journal of Finance*, 30(3), June, pp. 785–95.

Blume, M. and Friend, I. (1973) 'A new look at the Capital Asset Pricing Model', *Journal of Finance*, March, pp. 19–33.

Boardman, C.M., Reinhard, W.J. and Celec, S.G. (1982) 'The role of the payback period in the theory and application of duration to capital budgeting', *Journal of Business Finance and Accounting*, 9(4), Winter, pp. 511–22.

Bodie, Z., Kane, A. and Marcus, A.J. (2005) *Investments*. 6th edn. New York: McGraw-Hill.

Booth, L., Aivazian, V., Demirgue-Kunt, A. and Maksimovic, V. (2001) 'Capital Structures in Developing Countries', *Journal of Finance*, 61(1) February, pp. 87–130.

Bower, D.H., Bower, R.S. and Logue, D.E (1986) 'A primer on arbitrage pricing theory', in J.M. Stern and D.H. Chen (eds), *The Revolution in Corporate Finance*. Oxford: Basil Blackwell.

Bower, J.L. (1972) *Managing the Resource Allocation Process*. Homewood, IL: Irwin.

Brav, A., Graham, J.A., Harvey, C.R., and Michaely, R. (2005) 'Payment policy in the 21st century', *Journal of Financial Economics*, 77, pp. 483–527.

Brealey, R.A., Cooper, I.A. and Habib, M.A. (2001) 'Using Project Finance to Fund Infrastructure Investments', in D.H. Chew (ed.), *The New Corporate Finance*. 3rd edn. New York: McGraw Hill Irwin.

Brealey, R.H. (1986) 'Does dividend policy matter?', in J.M. Stern and D.H. Chew (eds), *The Revolution in Corporate Finance*. Oxford: Basil Blackwell.

Brealey, R.M. and Myers, S.C. (2003) *Principles of Corporate Finance*. 7th edn. New York: McGraw-Hill.

Breedon, F. and Twinn, I. (1996) 'The valuation of sub-underwriting agreements for UK rights issues', *Bank of England Quarterly Bulletin*, May, pp. 193–6.

Brennan, M. (1971) 'A note on dividend irrelevance and the Gordon valuation model', *Journal of Finance*, December, pp. 1115–21.

Brennan, M.J. and Schwartz, E.S. (1985) 'Evaluating Natural Resource Investments', *Journal of Business*, Vol. 58, pp. 135–57.

Brennan, M.J. and Trigeorgis, L. (eds) (2000) *Project Flexibility, Agency, and Competition: New Developments in the Theory and Application of Real Options*. Oxford, New York: Oxford University Press. 5th edn. London: Random House.

Brett, M. (2003) *How to Read the Financial Pages*. 5th edn. London: Random House Business Books.

Brierley, P. and Bunn, P. (2005) 'The determination of UK capital gearing', *Bank of England Quarterly Bulletin*, Autumn, pp. 356–66.

Brigham, E.F. (1966) 'An analysis of convertible debentures: Theory and some empirical evidence', *Journal of Finance*, March, pp. 35–54.

Brigham, E.F., Gapenski, L.C. and Ehrhardt, M.C. (2001) *Financial Management: Theory and Practice*. 10th edn. Fort Worth, TX: Dryden Press.

Bris, A. (2005) 'Do insider trading laws work?' *European Financial Management*, 11(3), pp. 267–312.

British Private Equity and Venture Capital Association, London (www.bvca.co.uk).

Brock, W., Lakonishok, J. and LeBaron, B. (1992) 'Simple technical trading rules and the stochastic properties of stock returns', *Journal of Finance*, 47, December, pp. 1731–64.

Bromwich, M. and Bhimani, A. (1991) 'Strategic investment appraisal', *Management Accounting*, March.

Brown, S.J., Goetzmann, W.N. and Kumar, A. (1998) 'The Dow theory: William Peter Hamilton's track record reconsidered', *Journal of Finance*, 53(4), pp. 1311–13.

Brunnermeier, M.K. and Nagel, S. (2004) 'Hedge funds and the technology bubble', *Journal of Finance*, LIX(5), October, pp. 2013–40.

Brusa, J., Liu, P. and Schulman, C. (2003) 'The weekend and "Reverse" weekend effects: An analysis by month of the year, week of month, and industry', *Journal of Business Finance and Accounting*, 30(5) and (6), June/July, pp. 863–90.

Buckle, M. and Thompson, J. (2004) *The UK Financial System*. 4th edn. Manchester: Manchester University Press.

Buckley, A. (2000) *Multinational Finance*. 4th edn. Harlow: Financial Times Prentice Hall.

Buckley, A. (2004) *Multinational Finance*. 5th edn. Harlow: FT Prentice Hall.

Buffett, W. (1982) Letter to Shareholders accompanying the Berkshire Hathaway Annual Report. Omaha, NE. www.berkshirehathaway.com.

Buffett, W. (1984a) *Berkshire Hathaway Annual Report*. Omaha, NE: Berkshire Hathaway.

Buffett, W.E. (1984b) 'The superinvestors of Graham-and-Doddsville', an edited transcript of a talk given at Columbia University in 1984.

Buffett, W. (1995) Letter to Shareholders accompanying the Berkshire Hathaway Annual Report. Omaha, NE. www.berkshirehathaway.com.

Buffett, W.E. (2000) Letter to shareholders included with the 2000 Annual Report of Berkshire Hathaway Inc: www.berkshirehathaway.com.

Bunn, R. and Young, G. (2004) Corporate capital structure in the United Kingdom: determinants and adjustment. Bank of England Working paper 226 (www.bankofengland.co.uk/index.html).

Buono, A. and Bowditch, J. (1989) *The Human Side of Mergers and Acquisitions*. San Francisco: Jossey-Bass.

Buono, A. and Bowditch, J. (2003) *The Human Side of Mergers and Acquisitions*. Washington, DC: Beard Books.

'The Cadbury Report' (1992) Report of the Committee on the Financial Aspects of Corporate Governance. London: Gee.

Campbell, K. (2003) *Smarter ventures: A survivor's guide to venture capital through the new cycle*. Harlow: Financial Times Prentice Hall.

Capaul, C., Rowley, I. and Sharpe, W.F. (1993) 'International value and growth stock returns', *Financial Analysts Journal*, 49, January–February, pp. 27–36.

Carsberg, B.V. (1975) *Economics of Business Decisions*. Harmondsworth: Penguin.

Carsberg, B.V. and Hope, A. (1976) *Business Investment Decisions Under Inflation: Theory and Practice*. London: Institute of Chartered Accountants in England and Wales.

Cartwright, S. and Cooper, C. (1992) *Mergers and Acquisitions: The Human Factor*. Oxford: Butterworth Heinemann.

Chan, A. and Chui, A.P.L. (1996) 'An empirical re-examination of the cross-section of expected returns: UK evidence', *Journal of Business Finance and Accounting*, 23, pp. 1435–52.

Chan, L.K.C., Hamao, Y. and Lakonishok, J. (1991) 'Fundamentals and stock returns in Japan', *Journal of Finance*, 46, pp. 1739–64.

Chan, L.K.C., Jegadeesh, N. and Lakonishok, J. (1996) 'Momentum strategies', *Journal of Finance*, 51, Dec., pp. 1681–713.

Chan, L.K.C. and Lakonishok, J. (1993) 'Are the reports of beta's death premature?', *Journal of Portfolio Management*, 19, Summer, pp. 51–62. Reproduced in S. Lofthouse (ed.), *Readings in Investment*. Chichester: Wiley (1994).

Chan, L.K.C. and Lakonishok, J. (2004) 'Value and growth investing: review and update', *Financial Analysts Journal*, January/February, pp. 71–86.

Chartered Institute of Public Finance and Accountancy (1983) 'Management of capital programmes', *Financial System Review*, 8.

Chew, D.H. (ed.) (1993) *The New Corporate Finance*. New York: McGraw-Hill.

Chew, D.H. (ed.) (2001) *The New Corporate Finance*. 3rd edn. New York: McGraw Hill Irwin.

Chi-Hsiou, D., Shackleton, M. and Xu, X. (2004) 'CAPM, higher co-moment and factor models of UK stock returns', *Journal of Business Finance and Accounting*, 31(1–2), January/March, pp. 87–112.

Childs, P.D., Ott, S.M. and Triantis, A.J. (1998) 'Capital Budgeting for Interrelated Projects: A Real Options Approach', *Journal of Financial and Quantitative Analysis*, 33(3), pp. 305–34.

Chittenden, F. and Darregia, M. (2004) 'Capital investment decision-making: some results from studying entrepreneurial businesses', www.icaew.co.uk.

Chopra, N., Lakonishok, J. and Ritter, J.R. (1992) 'Measuring abnormal performance: Do stocks overact?', *Journal of Financial Economics*, 31, pp. 235–68.

Christy, G.A. (1966) *Capital Budgeting – Current Practices and their Efficiency*. Bureau of Business and Economic Research, University of Oregon.

Churchill, N.C. and Mullins, J.W. (2001) 'How fast can your company afford to grow?', *Harvard Business Review*, May.

City of London/London Stock Exchange/Oxera (2006) 'The cost of capital: an international comparison' (available for download: www.londonstockexchange.com).

Clare, A. and Thomas, S. (1995) 'The overreaction hypothesis and the UK stock market', *Journal of Business Finance and Accounting*, 22(7), October, pp. 961–73.

Clark, T.M. (1978) *Leasing*. Maidenhead: McGraw-Hill.

Cochrane, J.H. (2001) *Asset Pricing*. Princeton, NJ, and Oxford: Princeton University Press.

Collier, P., Cooke, T. and Glynn, J. (1988) *Financial and Treasury Management*. Oxford: Heinemann CIMA series.

Collis, D.J. and Montgomery, C.A. (2005) *Corporate Strategy: A Resource-based Approach*. New York: McGraw Hill.

Competition Commission (2007) BAA Ltd. A report on the economic regulation of the London airport companies (download from website).

Conn, R.L., Cosh, A., Guest, P.M. and Hughes, A. (2005) 'The impact on UK acquirers of domestic, cross-border, public and private acquisitions', *Journal of Business Finance & Accounting*, 32 (5 & 6), June/July.

Conyon, M.J. and Clegg, P. (1994) 'Pay at the top: a study of the sensitivity of top director remuneration to specific shocks', *National Institute of Economic and Social Research Review*, August.

Cooper, D.J. (1975) 'Rationality and investment appraisal', *Accounting and Business Research*, Summer, pp. 198–202.

Cooper, I. and Kaplanis, E. (1994) 'Home bias in equity portfolios, inflation hedging and international capital market equilibrium', *Review of Financial Studies*, 7(1), pp. 45–60.

Coopers & Lybrand and OC & C (1993) *A review of the acquisition experience of major UK companies*. London: Coopers & Lybrand.

Copeland, T. and Antikarov, V. (2001) *Real Options: A Practitioner's Guide*. New York: Texere.

Copeland, T. and Tufano, P. (2004) 'A real-world way to manage real options', *Harvard Business Review*, March, pp. 1–11.

Corhay, A., Hawawini, G. and Michel, P. (1987) 'Seasonality in the risk-return relationship: some international evidence', *Journal of Finance*, 42, pp. 49–68.

Corporate Finance Magazine. London: Euromoney.

Cornelius, I. and Davies, M. (1997) *Shareholder Value*. London: Financial Times: Financial Publishing.

Cosh, A., Guest, P.M. and Hughes, A. (2006) 'Board share-ownership and takeover performance', *Journal of Business Finance & Accounting*, 33(3/4), Apr/May, pp. 459–510.

Coulthurst, N.J. (1986a) 'Accounting for inflation in capital investment: state of the art and science', *Accounting and Business Research*, Winter, pp. 33–42.

Coulthurst, N.J. (1986b) 'The application of the incremental principle in capital investment project evaluation', *Accounting and Business Research*, Autumn.

Cowling, K., Stoneman, P. and Cubbin, J. *et al.* (1980) *Mergers and Economic Performance*. Cambridge: Cambridge University Press.

Credit Management Research Centre, Leeds University Business School (2005) 'Credit policy in the UK economy'. Prepared for the Small Business Service (www. payontime.co.uk).

Crossland, M., Dempsey, M. and Moizer, P. (1991) 'The effect of cum- to ex-dividend changes on UK share prices', *Accounting and Business Research*, 22(85), pp. 47–50.

Cuthbertson, K. (1996) *Quantitative Financial Economics*. Chichester: Wiley.

Damodaran, A. (1999) *Applied Corporate Finance: A User's Manual*. 2nd edn. New York: Wiley.

Damodaran, A. (2002) *Investment Valuation*. 2nd edn. New York: Wiley.

Damodaran, A. (2005) *Applied Corporate Finance: A User's Manual*. New York: Wiley.

Daniel, K., Hirshleifer, D. and Subrahmanyam, A. (1998) 'Investor psychology and security market under- and overreactions', *Journal of Finance*, 53(6), pp. 1839–85.

Daniel, K. and Titman, S. (1997) 'Evidence on the characteristics of cross-sectional variation in common stock returns', *Journal of Finance*, 52, pp. 1–33.

Daniel, K. and Titman, S. (2006) 'Market reactions to tangible and intangible information', *Journal of Finance*, 61, pp. 1605–43.

Davies, M. (2000) 'Lessons from Practice: VBM at Lloyds TSB', in G.C. Arnold and M. Davies (eds) *Value-Based Management*. London: Wiley.

Davies, M., Arnold, G.C., Cornelius, I. and Walmsley, S. (2001) *Managing For Shareholder Value*. London: Informa Publishing Group.

Dawson, E.R. and Steeley, J.M. (2003) 'On the existence of visual technical patterns in the UK stock market', *Journal of Business Finance and Accounting*, 30(1) and (2), January–March, pp. 263–97.

Dean, J. (1951) *Capital Budgeting*. New York: Columbia University Press.

De Bondt, W.F.M. and Thaler, R.H. (1985) 'Does the stock market overreact?', *Journal of Finance*, 40(3), July, pp. 793–805.

De Bondt, W.F.M. and Thaler, R.H. (1987) 'Further evidence on investor overreaction and stock market seasonality', *Journal of Finance*, 42(3), pp. 557–81.

De Long, J.B., Shleifer, A., Summers, L.H. and Waldmann, R.J. (1989) 'The size and incidence of the losses from noise trading', *Journal of Finance*, 44(3), July, pp. 681–96.

De Long, J.B., Shleifer, A., Summers, L.H. and Waldmann, R.J. (1990) 'Noise trader risk in financial markets', *Journal of Political Economy*, 98, pp. 703–38.

Demirag, I. and Goddard, S. (1994) *Financial Management for International Business*. Maidenhead: McGraw-Hill.

Demski, J.S. (1994) *Managerial Uses of Accounting Information*. Boston, MA: Kluwer.

Desai, M.A. (2004) 'Foreign exchange markets and transactions', Harvard Business School Note. Available from Harvard Business Online.

Devine, M. (2004) *Successful Mergers: Getting the people issues right*. London: The Economist/Profile Books.

De Wit, B. and Meyer, R. (2004) *Strategy: Process, Content, Context*. 3rd edn. Cincinnati, OH: South-Western College Publishers.

Dhamani, A. (2005) 'Corporate dividend policy: the views of British financial managers', *Journal of Business Finance and Accounting*, 32(7 & 8), Sept/Oct, pp. 1625–72.

Dhrymes, P.J., Friend, I. and Gultekim, N.B. (1984) 'A critical reexamination of the empirical evidence on the arbitrage pricing theory', *Journal of Finance*, 39, June, pp. 323–46.

Dimson, E. (ed.) (1988) *Stock Market Anomalies*. Cambridge: Cambridge University Press.

Dimson, E. and Marsh, P.R. (1986) 'Event study methodologies and the size effect: The case of UK press recommendations', *Journal of Financial Economics*, 17, pp. 113–42.

Dimson, E. and Marsh, P.R. (1999) 'Murphy's law and market anomalies', *Journal of Portfolio Management*, 25(2), pp. 53–69.

Dimson, E. and Marsh, P.R. (2007) *The Hoare Govett smaller companies (HGSC) index report 2007*. London: ABN AMRO and London Business School.

Dimson, E., Marsh, P.R. and Staunton, M. (2001) *The Millennium Book II: 101 Years of Investment Returns*. London: London Business School and ABN Amro.

Dimson, E., Marsh, P.R. and Staunton, M. (2002) *The Triumph of the Optimists: 101 years of global investment returns*. Princeton, NJ: Princeton University Press.

Dimson, E., Marsh, P.R. and Staunton, M. (2006) The Worldwide Equity Premium: A Smaller Puzzle. EFA 2006 Zurich, 7 April. Meeting papers available at SSRN: http://ssrn.com/abstract=891620.

Dimson, E., Marsh, P.R., Staunton, M. and Elgeti, R. (2007) *Global Investment Returns Yearbook 2007*. ABN AMRO.

Dissanaike, G. (1997) 'Do stock market investors overreact?', *Journal of Business Finance and Accounting*, 24(1), January, pp. 27–49.

Divecha, A.B., Drach, J. and Stefek, D. (1992) 'Emerging markets: a quantitative perspective', *Journal of Portfolio Management*, Fall, pp. 41–50.

Dixit, A. and Pindyck, R. (1994) *Investment Under Uncertainty*. Princeton, NJ: Princeton University Press.

Dixit, A.K. and Pindyck, R.S. (1995) 'The Options Approach to Capital Investment', *Harvard Business Review*, May–June. (Also reproduced in J. Rutterford (ed.) *Financial Strategy*. New York: John Wiley, 1998.)

Donaldson, G. (1961) *Corporate debt policy and the determination of corporate debt capacity*. Boston, MA: Harvard Graduate School of Business Administration.

Donaldson, G. (1963) 'Financial goals: management vs. stockholders', *Harvard Business Review*, May–June, pp. 116–29.

Doyle, P. (1994) 'Setting business objectives and measuring performance', *Journal of General Management*, Winter, pp. 1–19.

Dreman, D. (1998) *Contrarian Investment Strategies: The Next Generation*. New York: Wiley.

Dreman, D. and Berry, M. (1995) 'Overreaction, underreaction, and the low P/E effect', *Financial Analysts Journal*, 51, July/August, pp. 21–30.

Drury, J.C. and Braund, S. (1990) 'The leasing decision: A comparison of theory and practice', *Accounting and Business Research*, Summer, pp. 179–91.

Eaker, M., Fabozzi, F. and Grant, D. (1996) *International Corporate Finance*. Orlando, FL: Dryden.

Eales, B.A. (1995) *Financial Risk Management*. Maidenhead: McGraw-Hill.

Easterbrook, F.H. (1984) 'Two agency-cost explanations of dividends', *American Economic Review*, 74(4), September, pp. 650–60.

Economist, The (1991) 'School brief: risk and return', 2 February.

Economist, The (1992) 'Beating the market: Yes – it can be done', 5 December.

Economist, The (1996) 'Economic focus: stay-at-home shareholders', 17 February.

Economist, The (1996) 'A survey of corporate risk management', 10 February.

Economist, The (2000) 'Merger Briefs' 22 July, 29 July, 5 August, 12 August, 19 August, 26 August.

Economist, The (2005) 'A survey of corporate social responsibility', 22 January.

Eiteman, D.K., Stonehill, A.I. and Moffett, M.H. (2003) *Multinational Business Finance*. 10th edn. Reading, MA: Addison-Wesley.

Eiteman, D.K., Stonehill, A.I. and Moffett, M.H. (2007) *Multinational Business Finance*. 11th edn. Reading, MA: Pearson Addison Wesley.

Ekanem, I. (2005) 'Bootstrapping the investment decision-making process in small firms', *British Accounting Review*, 37, pp. 299–318.

Elton, E.J. and Gruber, M.J. (1970) 'Marginal stockholder tax rates and the clientele effect', *Review of Economics and Statistics*, February, pp. 68–74.

Elton, E.J., Gruber, M.J., Brown, S.J. and Goetzmann, W.N. (2003) *Modern Portfolio Theory and Investment Analysis*, 6th edn. Chichester: Wiley.

Elton, E.J., Gruber, M.J. and Mei, J. (1994) 'Cost of capital using arbitrage pricing theory: a case study of nine New York utilities', *Financial Markets, Institutions and Instruments*, 3, August, pp. 46–73.

Elton, E.J., Gruber, M.J. and Rentzler, J. (1983) 'A simple examination of the empirical relationship between dividend yields and deviations from the CAPM', *Journal of Banking and Finance*, 7, pp. 135–46.

Emmanuel, C., Otley, D. and Merchant, K. (1990) *Accounting for Management Control*, 2nd edn. London: Chapman and Hall.

Epstein, M.J. (2005) 'The determinants and evaluation of merger success', *Business Horizons*, 48, pp. 37–46.

Fabozzi, F.J. (2003) *Bond Markets, Analysis and Strategies*. 5th edn. Harlow: Financial Times Prentice Hall.

Fama, E.F. (1965) 'The behaviour of stock market prices', *Journal of Business*, January, pp. 34–106.

Fama, E.F. (1970) 'Efficient capital markets: A review of theory and empirical work', *Journal of Finance*, May, pp. 383–417.

Fama, E.F. (1980) 'Agency problems and the theory of the firm', *Journal of Political Economy*, Spring, pp. 288–307.

Fama, E.F. (1981) 'Stock returns, real activity, inflation and money', *American Economic Review*, 71 (Sept.), pp. 545–64.

Fama, E.F. (1991) 'Efficient capital markets II', *Journal of Finance*, 46(5), December, pp. 1575–617.

Fama, E.F. (1998) 'Market efficiency, long-term returns, and behavioural finance', *Journal of Financial Economics*, 49, September, pp. 283–306.

Fama, E.F., Fisher, L., Jensen, M.C. and Roll, R. (1969) 'The adjustment of stock prices to new information', *International Economic Review*, 10(1), February, pp. 1–21.

Fama, E.F. and French, K.R. (1988) 'Permanent and temporary components of stock prices', *Journal of Political Economy*, 96, pp. 246–73.

Fama, E.F. and French, K.R. (1992) 'The cross-section of expected stock returns', *Journal of Finance*, 47, pp. 427–65.

Fama, E.F. and French, K.R. (1993) 'Common risk factors in the returns on stocks and bonds', *Journal of Financial Economics*, 33, pp. 3–56.

Fama, E.F. and French, K.R. (1995) 'Size and book-to-market factors in earnings and returns', *Journal of Finance*, 50(1), March, pp. 131–55.

Fama, E.F. and French, K.R. (1996) 'Multifactor explanations of asset pricing anomalies', *Journal of Finance*, 50(1), March, pp. 55–84.

Fama, E.F. and French, K.R. (1998) 'Value versus growth: The international evidence', *Journal of Finance*, 53(6), December, pp. 1975–99.

Fama, E.F. and French, K.R. (2001) 'Disappearing dividends: changing firm characteristics or lower propensity to pay?', *Journal of Financial Economics*, 60(1), April, pp. 3–43.

Fama, E.F. and French, K.R. (2002) 'The Equity Premium', *Journal of Finance*, 57(2), April, pp. 637–59.

Fama, E.F. and French, K.R. (2005) 'Financing decisions: who issues stocks?', *Journal of Financial Economics*, 76, pp. 549–82.

Fama, E.F. and French, K.R. (2006) 'The value premium and the CAPM', *Journal of Finance*, LXI(5), October, pp. 2163–85.

Fama, E.F. and MacBeth, J. (1973) 'Risk, return and equilibrium: empirical test', *Journal of Political Economy*, May/June, pp. 607–36.

Fama, E.F. and Miller, M.H. (1972) *The Theory of Finance*. Orlando, FL: Holt, Rinehart & Winston.

Fama, E.F. (1978) 'The effects of a firm's investment and financing decisions', *American Economic Review*, 68(3), June, pp. 272–84.

Fee, C.E. and Thomas, S. (2004) 'Sources of gains in horizontal mergers: evidence from customer, supplier, and rival firms', *Journal of Financial Economics*, 74 (3), Dec., pp. 423–60.

Fifield, S.G.M., Power, D.M. and Sinclair, C.D. (2005) 'An analysis of trading strategies in eleven European stock markets', *European Journal of Finance*, 11, pp. 531–48.

Finance and Leasing Association (FLA) Annual Report. London: FLA.

Financial Reporting Council. Various publications on corporate governance displayed on the FRC website (www.frc.org.uk) including the updated Combined Code.

Financial Services Authority (2003) The Combined Code on corporate governance. London. www.fsa.gov.uk/pubs/ukl

Financial Times. Students of finance, or any managerial discipline should get into the habit of reading the *Financial Times* and the *Economist* to (a) reinforce knowledge gained from a course, and (b) appreciate the wider business environment.

Finnie, J. (1988) 'The role of financial appraisal in decisions to acquire advanced manufacturing technology', *Accounting and Business Research*, 18(70), pp. 133–9.

Firth, M. (1980) 'Takeovers, shareholders' returns and the theory of the firm', *Quarterly Journal of Economics*, 94, March, pp. 235–60.

Firth, M. (1991) 'Corporate takeovers, stockholder returns and executive rewards', *Managerial and Decision Economics*, 12, pp. 421–8.

Firth, M.A. (1977a) 'An empirical investigation of the impact of the announcement of capitalisation issues on share prices', *Journal of Business Finance and Accounting*, Spring, p. 47.

Firth, M.A. (1977b) *The Valuation of Shares and the Efficient Markets Theory*. Basingstoke: Macmillan.

Fisher, F.M. and McGowan, J.I. (1983) 'On the misuse of accounting rates of return to infer monopoly profits', *American Economic Review*, 73, March, pp. 82–97.

Fisher, I. (1930) *The Theory of Interest*. Reprinted in 1977 by Porcupine Press.

Flannery, M.J. and Rangan, K.P. (2006) 'Partial adjustment toward target capital structures', *Journal of Financial Economics*, 79, pp. 469–506.

Foster, G. (1979) 'Briloff and the capital markets', *Journal of Accounting Research*, 17, pp. 262–74.

Foster, G., Olsen, C. and Shevlin, T. (1984) 'Earnings releases, anomalies, and the behaviour of security returns', *Accounting Review*, 59(4), October, pp. 574–603.

Francis, G. and Minchington, C. (2000) 'Value-based Metrics as Divisional Performance Measures', in G.C. Arnold and M. Davies (eds) *Value-Based Management*. London: Wiley.

Frank, M.Z. and Goyal, V.K. (2003) 'Testing the pecking order theory of capital structure', *Journal of Financial Economics*, 67, pp. 217–48.

Franks, J. and Harris, R. (1989) 'Shareholder wealth effects of corporate takeovers: the UK experience 1955–85', *Journal of Financial Economics*, 23, pp. 225–49.

Franks, J. and Mayer, C. (1996) 'Hostile takeovers and correction of managerial failure', *Journal of Financial Economics*, 40, pp. 163–81.

Frazzini, A. (2006) 'The disposition effect and underreaction to news', *Journal of Finance*, LXI(4), August, pp. 2017–46.

Friedman, M. (1970) 'The social responsibility of business is to increase its profits', *New York Times Magazine*, 30 Sept.

Friend, I. and Blume, M. (1970) 'Measurement of portfolio performance under uncertainty', *American Economic Review*, September, pp. 561–75.

Friend, I., Westerfield, R. and Granito, M. (1978) 'New evidence on the Capital Asset Pricing model', *Journal of Finance*, 33, June, pp. 903–20.

Froot, K.A. and Dabora, E. (1999) 'How are stock prices affected by the location of trade?', *Journal of Financial Economics*, 53, pp. 189–216.

Frost, P.A. and Savarino, J.E. (1986) 'Portfolio size and estimation risk', *Journal of Portfolio Management*, 12, Summer, pp. 60–4.

Fuller, R.J., Huberts, L.C. and Levinson, M.J. (1993) 'Returns to E/P Strategies, Higgledy-Piggledy Growth,

Analysts' Forecast Errors, and Omitted Risk Factors', *Journal of Portfolio Management*, Winter, pp. 13–24.
Fuller, R.J. and Wong, G.W. (1988) 'Traditional versus theoretical risk measures', *Financial Analysts Journal*, 44, March–April, pp. 52–7. Reproduced in S. Lofthouse (ed.), *Readings in Investment*. Chichester: Wiley (1994).
Gadella, J.W. (1992), 'Post-project appraisal', *Management Accounting*, March, pp. 52 and 58.
Galbraith, J. (1967) 'The goals of an industrial system' (excerpt from *The New Industrial State*). Reproduced in H.I. Ansoff, *Business Strategy*. London: Penguin, 1969.
Galitz, L. (1998) *Financial Engineering*. 2nd edn. London: FT Prentice Hall.
Ghosal, S. (2005) 'Bad management theories are destroying good management practices', *Academy of Management's Learning and Education*, 4(1), pp. 75–9.
Ghosh, A (2004) 'Increasing market share as a rationale for corporate acquisitions', *Journal of Business Finance & Accounting*, 31(1 & 2), January/March, pp. 209–47.
Gitman, L.J. and Forrester, J.R. (1977) 'A survey of capital budgeting techniques used by major US firms', *Financial Management*, Fall, pp. 66–76.
Gitman, L.J. and Maxwell, C.E. (1987) 'A longitudinal comparison of capital budgeting techniques used by major US firms: 1986 versus 1976', *The Journal of Applied Business Research*, Fall, pp. 41–50.
Gitman, L.J. and Mercurio, V.A. (1982) 'Cost of capital techniques used in major US firms', *Financial Management*, Winter, pp. 21–9.
Goergen, M. and Renneboog, L. (2004) 'Shareholder wealth effects of European domestic and cross-border takeover bids', *European Financial Management*, 10(1), pp. 9–45.
Goetzman, W.N., Lingfeng, L. and Kouwenhorst, K.G. (2005) 'Long-term global market correlations', *Journal of Business*, 78, pp. 1–38.
Goffin, K and Mitchell, R. (2006) 'Learning to avoid the net present value trap', *Financial Tines*, Mastering Financial Management (part 1), 26 May, p. 2.
Gordon, L.A. and Myers, M.D. (1991) 'Postauditing capital projects', *Management Accounting* (US), January, pp. 39–42.
Gordon, L.A. and Stark, A.W. (1989) 'Accounting and economic rates of return: a note on depreciation and other accruals', *Journal of Business Finance and Accounting*, 16(3), pp. 425–32.
Gordon, M.J. (1959) 'Dividends, earnings and stock prices', *Review of Economics and Statistics*, 41, May, pp. 99–105.
Gordon, M.J. (1962) *The Investment, Financing and Valuation of the Corporation*. Homewood, IL: Irwin.
Gordon, M.J. (1963) 'Optimal investment and financing policy', *Journal of Finance*, May.
Gordon, M.J. and Shapiro, E. (1956) 'Capital equipment analysis: the required rate of profit', *Management Science*, III, pp. 102–10.
Graham, B. (1973) *The Intelligent Investor*, revised 4th edn. New York: Harper Business (reprinted 1997).
Graham, B. (2003) *The Intelligent Investor*, revised edition, updated by Jason Zweig. New York: Harper Business Essentials.
Graham, B. and Dodd, D. (1934) *Security Analysis*. New York: McGraw-Hill.
Graham, J.R. and Harvey, C.R. (2001) 'The theory and practice of corporate finance: evidence from the field', *Journal of Financial Economics*, 60(2–3), May, pp. 187–243.
Graham, J.R. and Kumar, A. (2006) 'Do dividend clienteles exist? Evidence on dividend preferences and rational investors', *Journal of Finance*, 61(3), June, pp. 1305–36.
Grayson, C.J. (1966) 'The use of statistical techniques in capital budgeting', in A.A. Robichek (ed.), *Financial Research and Management Decisions*. New York: Wiley, pp. 90–132.
'The Greenbury Report' (1995) Directors' remuneration: report of a Study Group chaired by Sir Richard Greenbury. London: Gee.
Gregory, A. (1997) 'An examination of the long-run performance of UK acquiring firms', *Journal of Business Finance and Accounting*, 24(7–8), Sept., pp. 971–1002.
Gregory, A. (2005) 'The long run abnormal performance of UK acquirers and the free cash flow hypothesis', *Journal of Business Finance & Accounting*, 32(5 & 6), June/July, pp. 777–814.
Gregory, A., Harris, R.D.F. and Michou, M. (2001) 'An Analysis of Contrarian Investment Strategies in the UK', *Journal of Business Finance and Accounting*, 28(9) and (10), November–December, pp. 1193–228.
Gregory, A. Harris, R.D.F. and Michou, M. (2003) 'Contrarian investment and macroeconomic risk', *Journal of Business Finance and Accounting*, 30(1) and (2), January–March, pp. 213–55.
Gregory, A. and Rutterford, J. (1999) 'The cost of capital in the UK: a comparison of industry and the city'. CIMA monograph, May. Evidence on UK practice.
Grinblatt, M. and Han, B. (2005) 'Prospect theory, mental accounting and momentum', *Journal of Financial Economics*, 78, pp. 311–39.
Grinyer, J.R. (1986) 'An alternative to maximisation of shareholder wealth in capital budgeting decisions', *Accounting and Business Research*, Autumn, pp. 319–26.
Grullon, G. and Michaely, R. (2002) 'Dividends, share repurchases, and the substitution hypothesis', *Journal of Finance*, 57(4), pp. 1649–84.
Gurnani, C. (1984) 'Capital budgeting: theory and practice', *Engineering Economist*, Fall, pp. 19–46.
Gustavo, G. and Roni, M. (2004) 'The information content of share repurchase programs', *Journal of Finance*, 59(2), April, pp. 651–80.
Hajdasinski, M.M. (1993) 'The payback period as a measure of profitability and liquidity', *Engineering Economist*, 38(3), Spring, pp. 177–91.
Haka, S.F., Gordon, L.A. and Pinches, G.E. (1985) 'Sophisticated capital budgeting selection techniques and firm performance', *Accounting Review*, October, pp. 651–69.
Hallwood, C.P. and MacDonald, R. (2000) *International Money and Finance*. 3rd edn. Massachusetts and Oxford: Blackwell.
'The Hampel Report' (1998) The Committee on Corporate Governance, Final report. London: Gee.
Harding, D., Rovit, S. and Corbett, A. (2005) 'Three steps to avoiding merger meltdown', *Harvard Management Update*, March, pp. 1–5.
Harris, A. (1996) 'Wanted: Insiders', *Management Today*, July, pp. 40–1.
Harris, M., Kriebel, C.H. and Raviv, A. (1982) 'Asymmetric information, incentives and intrafirm resource allocation', *Management Science*, 28(6), June, pp. 604–20.
Harris, M. and Raviv, A. (1991) 'The theory of capital structure', *Journal of Finance*, 46, pp. 297–355.

Hart, O.D. (1995a) *Firms, Contracts and Finanical Structure*, Oxford: Oxford University Press.

Hart, O.D. (1995b) 'Corporate governance: some theory and implications', *Economic Journal*, 105, pp. 678–9.

Harvey, C.R., Lins, K.V. and Roper, H. (2004) 'The effect of capital structure when expected agency costs are extreme', *Journal of Financial Economics*, 74, pp. 3–30.

Hasbrouck, J. (1985) 'The characteristics of takeover targets: q and other measures', *Journal of Banking and Finance*, 9, pp. 351–62.

Haspeslagh, P. and Jemison, D. (1991) *Managing Acquisitions*. New York: Free Press.

Haugen, R.A. (2001) *Modern Investment Theory*, 5th edn. Upper Saddle River, NJ: Prentice-Hall.

Hawawini, G. and Klein, D.B. (1994) 'On the predictability of common stock returns: Worldwide evidence', in R.A. Jarrow, V. Maksinovic and W.T. Ziembas (eds) *Finance*. Amsterdam: North-Holland.

Hawawini, G.A. and Michel, P.A. (eds) (1984) *European Equity Markets, Risk, Return and Efficiency*. New York: Garland Publishing.

Hayek, F.A. (1969) 'The corporation in a democratic society: in whose interests ought it and will it be run?' Reprinted in H.I. Ansoff, *Business Strategy*. London: Penguin, 1969.

Headley, J.S. and Tufano, P. (2001) 'Why manage risk?', Harvard Business School Note. Available from Harvard Business Online.

Hertz, D.B. (1964) 'Risk analysis in capital investment', *Harvard Business Review*, January/ February, pp. 95–106.

Hertz, D.B. and Thomas, H. (1984) *Practical Risk Analysis: An Approach through Case Histories*. Chichester: Wiley.

Hickman, B.G. (1958) 'Corporate bond quality and investor experience', *National Bureau of Economic Research*, 14, Princeton.

Hicks, J.R. (1946) *Value and Capital: An Inquiry into some Fundamental Principles of Economic Theory*. 2nd edn. Oxford: Oxford University Press.

'The Higgs Report' (2003) Review of the role and effectiveness of non-executive directors. London: The Department of Trade and Industry. www.dti. pdf file available.

Higson, C. and Elliot, J. (1993) 'The returns to takeovers – the UK evidence', *IFA Working Paper*. London: London Business School.

Hillier, F.S. (1963) 'The derivation of probabilistic information for the evaluation of risky investments', *Management Science*, April, pp. 443–57.

Hirshleifer, J. (1958) 'On the theory of optimal investment decision', *Journal of Political Economy*, 66 (August), pp. 329–52.

Hirshleifer, J. (1961) 'Risk, the discount rate and investment decisions', *American Economic Review*, May, pp. 112–20.

Ho, S.M. and Pike, R.H. (1991) 'Risk analysis techniques in capital budgeting contexts', *Accounting and Business Research*, 21(83), pp. 227–38.

Hodgkinson, L. (1987) 'The capital budgeting decision of corporate groups', Plymouth Business School Paper.

Hon, M.T. and Tonks, I. (2003) Momentum in the UK stock market', *Journal of Multinational Financial Management*, 13, pp. 43–70.

Hong, H. and Stein, J.C. (1999) 'A unified theory of underreaction, momentum trading and overreaction in asset markets', *Journal of Finance*, 54(6), pp. 2143–84.

Howell, S., Stark, A., Newton, D., Paxson, D., Cavus, M. and Pereira, J. (2001) *Real Options: Evaluating Corporate Investment Opportunities in a Dynamic World*. Harlow: Financial Times Prentice Hall.

Howells, P. and Bain, K. (2004) *Financial Markets and Institutions*, 4th edn. Harlow: Financial Times Prentice Hall.

Hunt, J.W., Lees, S., Grumber, J. and Vivian, P. (1987) *Acquisitions: The Human Factor*. London: London Business School and Egan Zehnder International.

Ikenberry, D., Lakonishok, J. and Vermaelen, T. (1995) 'Market underreaction to open market share repurchases', *Journal of Financial Economics*, October–November, pp. 181–208.

Ikenberry, D., Rankine, G. and Stice, E. (1996) 'What do stock splits really signal?', *Journal of Financial and Quantitative Analysis*, 31, pp. 357–75.

International Accounting Standards Board (2007) *IAS 17 Leases*. London: IASB.

Investors Chronicle (1997) 'A week in the markets', 18 April, p. 10.

Jaffe, J., Keim, D.B. and Westerfield, R. (1989) 'Earnings yields, market values and stock returns', *Journal of Finance*, 44, pp. 135–48.

Jagannathan, M., Stephens, C.P. and Weisbach, M.S. (2000) 'Financial flexibility and the choice between dividends and stock repurchases', *Journal of Financial Economics*, 57(3), September, pp. 355–84.

James, A.N.G. and Peterson, P.P. (1984) 'The leasing puzzle', *Journal of Finance*, September.

Jegadeesh, N. and Titman, S. (1993) 'Returns to buying winners and selling losers: Implications for stock market efficiency', *Journal of Finance*, 48, March, pp. 65–91.

Jenkinson, T. and Ljungquist, A. (2001) *Going Public: The Theory and Evidence on How Companies Raise Equity Finance*. 2nd edn. Oxford: Clarendon.

Jensen, M.C. (1968) 'The performance of mutual funds in the period 1945–64', *Journal of Finance*, 23, May, pp. 389–416.

Jensen, M.C. (1986) 'Agency costs of free cash flow, corporate finance and takeovers', *American Economic Review*, 76, pp. 323–9.

Jensen, M.C. (1989) 'Eclipse of the public corporation', *Harvard Business Review*, September–October, pp. 61–74.

Jensen, M.C. (2001) 'Value Maximisation, Stakeholder Theory, and the Corporate Objective Function', *Journal of Applied Corporate Finance*, 14(3), Fall.

Jensen, M.C. and Meckling, W.H. (1976) 'Theory of the firm: managerial behavior, agency costs and ownership structure', *Journal of Financial Economics*, Oct., 3, pp. 305–60.

Johnson, G. and Scholes, K. (2001) *Exploring Corporate Strategy*. 6th edn. Harlow: Pearson Education.

Jones, G. and Gallagher-Kernstine (2004) '"Walking on a tightrope": maintaining London as a financial centre?' *Harvard Business Review*, 27 May.

Jones, T.C. and Dugdale, D. (1994) 'Academic and practitioner rationality: the case of investment appraisal', *British Accounting Review*, 26, pp. 3–25.

Jorion, P. (1992) 'Portfolio optimisation in practice', *Financial Analysts Journal*, 48, January/February, pp. 68–74.

Journal of Economic Perspectives (1988) Vol. 2, Issue 4, Fall. (See article by Miller, M.H., 'The Modigliani – Miller propositions after thirty years', pp. 99–120).

Julio, B. and Ikenberry, D.L. (2004) 'Reappearing dividends', *Journal of Applied Corporate Finance*, 16(4), Fall, pp. 89–100.

Kahneman, D., Slovic, P. and Tversky, A. (1982) *Judgment under uncertainty heuristics and biases*. London: Cambridge University Press.

Kahnemann, D. and Tversky, A. (2000) *Choices, Values and Frames*. Cambridge: Cambridge University Press.

Kamijo, K.-I. and Tanigawa, T. (1990) 'Stock price recognition – approach', *Proceedings of International Joint Conference on Neural Networks*, San Diego, CA, vol. 1, pp. 215–21.

Kaplan, R. and Norton, D.P. (1996) *The Balanced Scorecard*. Boston, MA: Harvard Business School Press.

Kaplan, R. and Roll, R. (1972) 'Investor evaluation of accounting information: Some empirical evidence', *Journal of Business*, 45, pp. 225–57.

Kaplan, R.S. (1986) 'Must CIM be justified by faith alone?', *Harvard Business Review*, March/April, pp. 87–95.

Kaplan, R.S. and Atkinson, A.A. (1998) *Advanced Management Accounting*, International Edition. Englewood Cliffs, NJ: Prentice-Hall.

Kaplanis, E. (1996) 'Benefits and costs of international portfolio investments', *Financial Times Mastering Management*, January.

Kaplanis, E. and Schaefer, S. (1991) 'Exchange risk and international diversification in bond and equity portfolios', *Journal of Economics and Business*, 43, pp. 287–307.

Kay, J. (1993) *Foundations of Corporate Success*. New York: Oxford University Press.

Kay, J. (2004) 'Forget how the crow flies', *Financial Times Magazine*, 17–18 January, pp. 17–21.

Kay, J.A. (1976) 'Accountants, too, could be happy in a golden age: the accountant's rate of profit and the internal rate of return', *Oxford Economic Papers*, 28, pp. 447–60.

Keane, S. (1974) 'Dividends and the resolution of uncertainty', *Journal of Business Finance and Accountancy*, Autumn.

Keasey, K., Thompson, S. and Wright, M. (1997) *Corporate Governance*. Oxford: Oxford University Press.

Kee, R. and Bublitz, B. (1988), 'The role of payback in the investment process', *Accounting and Business Research*, 18(70), pp. 149–55.

Keim, D.B. (1983) 'Size-related anomalies and stock return seasonality: Further empirical evidence', *Journal of Financial Economics*, 12, pp. 13–32.

Keim, D.B. (1988) 'Stock market regularities: A synthesis of the evidence and explanations', in E. Dimson (ed.) *Stock Market Anomalies*, Cambridge: Cambridge University Press, and in S. Lofthouse (ed.) (1994) *Readings in Investment*, Chichester: Wiley.

Keim, D.B. and Ziemba, W.T. (eds) (2000) *Security Market Imperfections in World Wide Equity Markets*. Cambridge: Cambridge University Press.

Kendall, M. (1953) 'The analysis of economic time-series prices', *Journal of the Royal Statistical Society*, 96, pp. 11–25.

Kennedy, A. and Mills, R. (1993a) 'Post completion auditing in practice', *Management Accounting*, October, pp. 22–5.

Kennedy, A. and Mills, R. (1993b) 'Experiences in operating a post-audit system', *Management Accounting*, November.

Kennedy, J.A. and Mills, R. (1990), *Post Completion Audit of Capital Expenditure Projects*. London: CIMA. Management Accounting Guide 9.

Keynes, J.M. (1936) *The General Theory of Employment, Interest and Money*. London: Harcourt, Brace and World.

Kim, S.H. (1982) 'An empirical study of the relationship between capital budgeting practices and earning performance', *Engineering Economics*, 27(3), Spring, pp. 185–96.

Kim, S.H., Crick, T. and Kim, S.H. (1986) 'Do executives practice what academics preach?', *Management Accounting* (US), November, pp. 49–52.

Kim, S.H. and Farragher, E.J. (1981) 'Current capital budgeting practices', *Management Accounting* (US), June, pp. 26–33.

Kindleberger, C.P. (1996) *Manias, Panics and Crashes: A History of Financial Crises*, 3rd edn. New York: Macmillan.

King, P. (1975), 'Is the emphasis of capital budgeting theory misplaced?', *Journal of Business Finance and Accounting*, 2(1), p. 69.

Kisgen, D.J. (2006) 'Credit ratings and capital structure', *Journal of Finance*, 61(3), June, pp. 1035–72.

Klammer, T., Koch, B. and Wilner, N. (1991) 'Capital budgeting practices – a survey of corporate use', *Journal of Management Accounting Research*, Fall, pp. 447–64.

Koch, A.S and Sun, A.X. (2004) 'Dividend changes and the persistence of past earnings changes', *Journal of Finance*, 59(5), October, pp. 2093–116.

Korajeczyk, R.A. and Levy, A. (2003) 'Capital structure choice: macroeconomic conditions and financial constraints', *Journal of Financial Economics*, 68, pp. 75–109.

Kothari, S.P., Shanken, J. and Sloan, R.G. (1995) 'Another look at the cross-section of expected stock returns', *Journal of Finance*, 50(1), March, pp. 185–224.

Kuehn, D. (1975) *Takeovers and the theory of the firm: An empirical analysis for the United Kingdom 1957–1969*. Basingstoke: Macmillan.

Lakonishok, J. and Shapiro, A.C. (1984) 'Stock returns, beta, variance and size: an empirical analysis', *Financial Analysts Journal*, 40, July–August, pp. 36–41.

Lakonishok, J. and Shapiro, A.C. (1986) 'Systematic risk, total risk and size as determinants of stock market returns', *Journal of Banking and Finance*, 10, pp. 115–32.

Lakonishok, J., Shleifer, A. and Vishny, R. (1994) 'Contrarian investment extrapolation and risk', *Journal of Finance*, 49, pp. 1541–78.

Lakonishok, J., Vishny, R.W. and Shleifer, A. (1993) 'Contrarian investment, extrapolation and risk', *National Bureau of Economic Research Working Paper*, No. 4360, May.

Lamont, O.A. and Thaler, R.H. (2003) 'Can the market add and subtract? Mispricing in tech price equity carve-outs', *Journal of Political Economy*, 111(2 April), pp. 227–68.

La Porta, R. (1996) 'Expectations and the cross-section of stock returns', *Journal of Finance*, 51(5), December, pp. 1715–42.

La Porta, R., Lakonishok, J., Shleifer, A. and Vishny, R. (1997) 'Good news for value stocks: Further evidence on market efficiency', *Journal of Finance*, 52(2), pp. 859–74.

Lawrence, A.G. and Myers, M.D. (1991) 'Post-auditing capital projects', *Management Accounting*, January, pp. 39–42.

Leary, M.T. and Roberts, M.R. (2005) 'Do firms rebalance their capital structures?', *Journal of Finance*, 60(6), December, pp. 25–75.

Lee, D.R. and Verbrugge, J.A. (1996) 'The efficient market theory thrives on criticism', *Journal of Applied Corporate Finance*, 9(1), pp. 3–11.

Lefley, F. (1996) 'Strategic methodologies of investment appraisal of AMT projects: a review and synthesis', *Engineering Economist*, 41(4), Summer, pp. 345–61.

Lefley, F. (1997) 'The sometimes overlooked discounted payback method', *Management Accounting* (UK), November, p. 36.

Lev, B. (1992) 'Observations on the merger phenomenon and a review of the evidence'. Reprinted in J.M. Stern and D. Chew (eds), *The revolution in corporate finance*. 2nd edn. Oxford: Blackwell.

Levi, M.D. (2005). *International Finance*. 4th edn. New York: Routledge.

Levine, P. and Aaronovitch, S. (1981) 'The financial characteristics of firms and theories of merger activity', *Journal of Industrial Economics*, 30, pp. 149–72.

Levine, R. and Zervos, S. (1996a) 'Capital control liberalisation and stock market development', *World Bank Policy Research Working Paper* No. 1622. Washington, DC: World Bank.

Levine, R. and Zervos, S. (1996b) 'Stock markets, banks and economic growth', *World Bank Policy Research Working Paper*. Washington, DC: World Bank.

Levinson, M. (2002) *Guide to Financial Markets*. 3rd edn. London: The Economist Books.

Levis, M. (1989) 'Stock market anomalies: A reassessment based on UK evidence', *Journal of Banking and Finance*, 13, pp. 675–96.

Levis, M. (1990) 'The winner's curse problem, interest costs and the underpricing of initial public offerings', *Economic Journal*, 100, March, pp. 76–89.

Levy, H. (1978) 'Equilibrium in an imperfect market: a constraint on the number of securities in the portfolio', *American Economic Review*, September, pp. 643–58.

Levy, R.A. (1971) 'On the short-term stationarity of beta coefficients', *Financial Analysts Journal*, Nov.–Dec., pp. 55–62.

Lewellen, J. (2004) 'Predicting returns with financial ratios', *Journal of Financial Economics*, 74, pp. 209–35.

Lewellen, W.G., Stanley, K.L., Lease, R.C. and Schlarbaum, G.G. (1978) 'Some direct evidence of the dividend clientele phenomenon', *Journal of Finance*, December, pp. 1385–99.

Lewis, K. (1996) 'Consumption, stock returns, and the gains from international risk-sharing', *NBER Working Paper*, No. 5410, January.

Limmack, R. (1991) 'Corporate mergers and shareholder wealth effect, 1977–86', *Accounting and Business Research*, 21(83), pp. 239–51.

Lintner, J. (1956) 'Distribution of income of corporations among dividends, retained earnings and taxes', *American Economic Review*, 46, May, pp. 97–113.

Lintner, J. (1965) 'The valuation of risky assets and the selection of risky investments in stock portfolios and capital budgets', *Review of Economics and Statistics*, 47, February, pp. 13–37.

Lister, R. (2005) 'Cost of capital: the case for the prosecution', *Investment Management and Financial Innovations*, 2, pp. 142–57.

Lister, R. (2006) 'Cost of capital is beyond our reach', *Accountancy*, December, pp. 42–3.

Little, I.M.D. (1962) 'Higgledy Piggledy Growth', *Institute of Statistics Bulletin* 24(4), pp. 387–412.

Litzenberger, R.H. and Ramaswamy, K. (1979) 'The effect of personal taxes and dividends on capital asset prices: Theory and empirical evidence', *Journal of Financial Economics*, 7, pp. 163–95.

Litzenberger, R. and Ramaswamy, K. (1982) 'The effects of dividends on common stock prices: tax effects or information effects?', *Journal of Finance*, May, pp. 429–43.

Litzenberger, R.M. and Joy, O.M. (1975) 'Decentralized capital budgeting decisions and shareholder wealth maximisation', *Journal of Finance*, 30(4), pp. 993–1002.

Liu, W., Strong, N. and Xu, X. (1999) 'The profitability of momentum investing', *Journal of Business Finance and Accounting* 26(9) and (10), November–December, pp. 1043–91.

Ljungquist, A. (2004) 'IPO underpricing', in Eckbo, E. (ed.) *Handbook of Corporate Finance*. Vol. 1. New York: Elsevier.

Lockett, M. (2001) 'Calculating the Cost of Capital for the Regulated Electricity Distribution Companies', Aston University MBA Project.

Lockett, M. (2002) 'Calculating the cost of capital for the regulated electricity distribution companies', *Power Engineering Journal*, October, pp. 251–63.

Lofthouse, S. (ed.) (1994) *Readings in Investment*. Chichester: Wiley.

Lofthouse, S. (2001) *Investment Management*, 2nd edn. Chichester: Wiley.

London, S. (2003) 'The Long View: Lunch with the FT, Milton Friedman', *Financial Times Magazine*, 7–8 June, pp. 12–13.

London Stock Exchange (2004) *A Practical Guide to Listing on the London Stock Exchange*.

London Stock Exchange Website. An excellent overview of the role and activities of the LSE.

Longmore, D.R. (1989) 'The persistence of the payback method: a time-adjusted decision rule perspective', *Engineering Economist*, 43(3), Spring, pp. 185–94.

Loughran, J. and Vijh, A.M. (1997) 'Do long term shareholders benefit from corporate acquisitions?', *Journal of Finance*, 52 (5), pp. 1765–90.

Louis, H. (2004a) 'Earnings management and the market performance of acquiring firms', *Journal of Financial Economics*, 74 (1), Oct., pp. 121–48.

Louis, H. (2004b) 'The cost of using bank mergers as defensive mechanisms against takeover threats', *Journal of Business*, 44(2), pt. 1, pp. 295–310.

Lowe, J. (1997) *Warren Buffett Speaks*. New York: Wiley.

Lowe, J. (1999) *The Rediscovered Benjamin Graham*. New York: Wiley.

Lowenstein, L. (1991) *Sense and Nonsense in Corporate Finance*. Reading, MA: Addison Wesley.

Luehrman, T.A. (1997) 'Using APV: A better tool for valuing operations', *Harvard Business Review*, 75 (May–June), pp. 145–54.

Lumijäärvi, O.P. (1991) 'Selling of capital investments to top management', *Management Accounting Research*, 2, pp. 171–88.

Lutz, F.A. and Lutz, V.C. (1951) *The Theory of Investment in the Firm*. Princeton, NJ: Princeton University Press.

Lynch, P. (1990) *One Up on Wall Street* (with John Rothchild). New York: Penguin Books. (Originally published by Simon & Schuster, 1989.)

Lynch, P. (1994) *Beating the Street* (with John Rothchild). New York: Simon & Schuster.

Macqueen, J. (1986) 'Beta is dead! Long live Beta!', in J.M. Stern and D.H. Chen (eds), *The Revolution in Corporate Finance*. Oxford: Basil Blackwell.

Madura, J. and Fox, R. (2007) *International Financial Management*. London: Thomson.

Magee, J.F. (1964a) 'Decision trees for decision making', *Harvard Business Review*, July/August, pp. 126–38.

Magee, J.F. (1964b) 'How to use decision trees in capital investment', *Harvard Business Review*, September/October, pp. 79–96.

Malkiel, B.G. (1999) *A Random Walk Down Wall Street*. New York: W.W. Norton & Co.

Maness, T.S. and Zietlow, J.T. (1993) *Short-term financial management*. St Paul, MN: West Publishing Company.

Manson, S., Stark, A. and Thomas, H.M. (1994) 'A cash flow analysis of the operational gains from takeovers', *Research Report 35*. London: Chartered Association of Certified Accountants.

Markowitz, H.M. (1952) 'Portfolio selection', *Journal of Finance*, 7, pp. 77–91.

Markowitz, H.M. (1959) *Portfolio Selection: Efficient Diversification of Investments*. New York: Wiley (1991); 2nd edn: Cambridge, MA: Basil Blackwell.

Markowitz, H.M. (1991) 'Foundations of portfolio theory', *Journal of Finance*, June.

Markowitz, H.M. (2005) 'Market efficiency: a theoretical distinction and so what?', *Financial Analysts Journal*, September/October, pp. 17–30.

Marsh, P. (1982) 'The choice between equity and debt: An empirical study', *Journal of Finance*, 37, March, pp. 121–44.

Marsh, P. (1994) 'Underwriting of rights issues: a study of the returns earned by sub-underwriters from UK rights issues', *Office of Fair Trading Research Paper No. 6*.

Martikainen, T. and Puttonen, V. (1996) 'Finnish days-of-the-week effects', *Journal of Business Finance and Accounting*, 23(7), September, pp. 1019–32.

Martin, J.D. and Petty, J.W. (2000) *Value Based Management: Corporate response to the shareholder revolution*. Boston, MA: Harvard Business School Press.

Mason, C. and Harrison, R. (1997) 'Business angels – heaven-sent or the devil to deal with?' in S. Birley and D.F. Muzyka, (eds) *Mastering Enterprise*, London: Pitman Publishing/Financial Times.

McDaniel, W.R., McCarty, D.E. and Jessell, K.A. (1988) 'Discounted cash flow with explicit reinvestment rates: Tutorial and extension', *The Financial Review*, August.

McDonald, R.L. (2006) *Derivative Markets*. 2nd edn. Harlow: Pearson Addison Wesley.

McIntyre, A.D. and Coulthurst, N.J. (1986) *Capital Budgeting Practices in Medium-Sized Businesses – A Survey*. London: Institute of Cost and Management Accountants.

McIntyre, A.D. and Coulthurst, N.J. (1987) 'Planning and control of capital investment in medium-sized UK companies', *Management Accounting*, March, pp. 39–40.

McKinsey and Co. (Koller, T., Goedhart, M. and Wessels, D.) (2005) *Valuation*. 4th edn. New York: McKinsey & Co. and Wiley.

McLaney, E., Pointon, J., Thomas, M. and Tucker, J. (2004) 'Practitioners' perspectives on the UK cost of capital', *European Journal of Finance*, 10, April, pp. 123–38.

McTaggart, J.M., Kontes, P.W. and Mankins, M.C. (1994) *The Value Imperative*. New York: Free Press.

Meeks, G. (1977) *Disappointing Marriage: A Study of the Gains from Mergers*. Cambridge: Cambridge University Press.

Meeks, G. and Whittington, G. (1975) 'Director's pay, growth and profitability', *Journal of Industrial Economics*, 24(1), pp. 1–14.

Mehra, R. (2003) 'The equity premium puzzle. Why is it a puzzle?' *Financial Analysts Journal*, 59, pp. 54–69.

Mehra, R. and Prescott, E.C. (1985) 'The Equity Premium: A Puzzle', *Journal of Monetary Economics*, 15, pp. 145–61.

Mehra, R. and Prescott, E.C. (2006) 'The equity premium: what have we learned in 20 years?' in R. Mehra (ed.) *Handbook of Investments: Equity Risk Premium* in the Handbook of Economics and Finance series. Amsterdam: Elsevier.

'Mergers and acquisitions' (1995) *Bank of England Quarterly Bulletin*, August, pp. 278–9.

Merton, R.C. (1998) 'Application of Option-Pricing Theory: Twenty-Five Years Later', *American Economic Review*, June, No. 3, pp. 323–49.

Merton, R.C. (2005) 'You have more capital than you think', *Harvard Business Review*, November, pp. 1–10.

Michaely, R., Thaler, R. and Womack, K. (1995) 'Price reaction to dividend initiations and omissions: Overreaction or drift?', *Journal of Finance*, 50, pp. 573–608.

Michaud, R.O. (1989) 'The Markowitz optimization enigma: Is "optimized" optimal?', *Financial Analysts Journal*, 45, January–February, pp. 31–42.

Michaud, R.O., Bergstorm, G.L., Frashure, R.D. and Wolahan, B.K. (1996) 'Twenty years of international equity investment', *Journal of Portfolio Management*, Fall, pp. 9–22.

Miles, D. and Timmermann, A. (1996) 'Variations in expected stock returns: evidence on the pricing of equities from a cross-section of UK companies', *Economica*, 63, pp. 369–82.

Miller, M.H. (1977) 'Debt and taxes', *Journal of Finance*, 32, May, pp. 261–75.

Miller, M.H. (1988) 'The Modigliani–Miller propositions after thirty years', *Journal of Economic Perspectives*, (Fall). Also reproduced in D.H. Chew (ed.) (2001) *The New Corporate Finance*. New York: McGraw-Hill. 3rd edn.

Miller, M.H. (1991) 'Leverage', *Journal of Finance*, 46, pp. 479–88.

Miller, M.H. (1997) *Merton Miller on Derivatives*. New York: Wiley.

Miller, M.H. and Modigliani, F. (1961) 'Dividend policy, growth and the valuation of shares', *Journal of Business*, 34, October, pp. 411–33.

Miller, M.N. and Orr, D. (1966) 'A model of the demand for money by firms', *Quarterly Journal of Economics*, August, pp. 413–35.

Mills, R.W. (1988) 'Capital budgeting techniques used in the UK and the USA', *Management Accounting*, January, pp. 26–7.

Mills, R.W. and Herbert, P.J.A. (1987) 'Corporate and divisional influence in capital budgeting', *Chartered Institute of Management Accountants*, Occasional Paper Series.

Mills, R., Robertson, J. and Ward, T. (1992) 'Why financial economics is vital in measuring business value', *Management Accounting* (UK), January, pp. 39–42.

Mitchell, M.L. and Lehn, K. (1990) 'Do bad bidders become good targets?', *Journal of Political Economy*, 98(2), pp. 372–98.

Modigliani, F. and Miller, M.H. (1958) 'The cost of capital, corporation finance and the theory of investment', *American Economic Review*, 48, June, pp. 261–97.

Modigliani, F. and Miller, M.H. (1963) 'Corporate income taxes and the cost of capital: A correction', *American Economic Review*, 53, June, pp. 433–43.

Modigliani, F. and Miller, M.H. (1969) 'Reply to Heins and Sprenkle', *American Economic Review*, 59, September, pp. 592–5.

Moel, A. and Tufano, P. (2002) 'When Are Real Options Exercised? An Empirical Study of Mine Closings', *The Review of Financial Studies*, Spring, 15(1), pp. 35–64.

Moeller, S.B., Schingemann, F.P. and Stulz, R.M. (2004) 'Firm size and the gains from acquisitions', *Journal of Financial Economics*, 73, pp. 201–28.

Moeller, S.B., Schingemann, F.P. and Stulz, R.M. (2005) 'Wealth destruction on a massive scale: A study of acquiring-firm returns in the recent merger wave', *The Journal of Finance*, LX(2), April, pp. 757–82.

Montier, J. (2002) *Behavioural Finance: Insights into irrational minds and markets.* London: J. Wiley.

Morgan, G. and Thomas, S. (1998) 'Taxes, divided yields and returns in the UK equity market', *Journal of Banking and Finance*, 22, pp. 405–23.

Morosini, P. and Steger, U. (eds) (2004) *Managing Complex Mergers: Real world lessons in implementing successful cross-cultural M&As.* Harlow: Financial Times Prentice Hall.

Mossin, J. (1966) 'Equilibrium in a capital asset market', *Econometrica*, 34, October, pp. 768–83.

Mougoué, M. and Rao, R.P. (2003) 'The information signalling hypothesis of dividends: Evidence from cointegration and causality tests', *Journal of Business Finance and Accounting*, 30(3) and (4), April/May, pp. 441–78.

Myers, S.C. (1974) 'Interaction of corporate financing and investment decisions – implications for capital budgeting', *Journal of Finance*, 29 (March), pp. 1–25.

Myers, S.C. (1984) 'The capital structure puzzle', *Journal of Finance*, 39, July, pp. 575–82.

Myers, S.C. (1996) 'Fischer Black's contributions to corporate finance', *Financial Management*, 25(4), Winter, pp. 95–103.

Myers, S. and Majluf, N. (1984). 'Corporate financing and investment decisions when firms have information investors do not have', *Journal of Financial Economics*, June, pp. 187–221.

Neale, C.W. and Holmes, D.E.A. (1988) 'Post-completion audits: the costs and benefits', *Management Accounting*, 66(3), pp. 27–30.

Neff, J. (1999) *John Neff on Investing* (with S.L. Mintz). New York: Wiley.

Nichols, N.A. (1993) 'Efficient? Chaotic? What's the New Finance?', *Harvard Business Review*, March–April, pp. 50–8.

Nissim, D. and Ziv, A. (2001) 'Dividend changes and future profitability', *Journal of Finance*, 56(6), pp. 2111–33.

Northcott, D. (1991) 'Rationality and decision making in capital budgeting', *British Accounting Review*, Sept., pp. 219–34.

Ofcom (2005) Ofcom's approach to risk in the assessment of the cost of capital (www.ofcom.org.uk).

Ofgen (2004) Electricity Distributed Price Control reviews: Background information on the cost of capital (www.ofgen.gov.uk).

Office for National Statistics (2006) *Share Ownership: A report on ownership of shares as at 31st December 2006.* Norwich: HMSO.

Ogier, T., Rugman, J. and Spicer, L. (2004) *The real cost of capital.* London: FT Prentice Hall.

Outram, R. (1997) 'For what it's worth', *Management Today*, May, pp. 70–1.

Palepu, K.G. (1986) 'Predicting takeover targets: a methodological and empirical analysis', *Journal of Accounting and Finance*, 8, pp. 3–35.

Panel on Takeovers and Mergers, The City Code (www.thetakeoverpanel.org.uk).

Park, C-H. and Irwin, S.H. (2007) 'What do we know about the profitability of technical analysis?' *Journal of Economic Surveys*, 21(4), pp. 786–826.

Passov, R. (2006) 'How much cash does your company need?', *Harvard Business Review*, November, pp. 1–8.

Patterson, C.S. (1989) 'Investment decision criteria used by listed New Zealand companies', *Accounting and Finance*, 29(2), November, pp. 73–89.

Peters, E.E. (1991) *Chaos and Order in the Capital Markets.* New York: Wiley.

Pettit, R.R. (1977) 'Taxes, transaction costs and clientele effects of dividends', *Journal of Financial Economics*, December.

Pike, R.H. (1982) *Capital Budgeting in the 1980s.* London: Chartered Institute of Management Accountants.

Pike, R.H. (1983a) 'A review of recent trends in formal capital budgeting processes', *Accounting and Business Research*, Summer, pp. 201–8.

Pike, R.H. (1983b) 'The capital budgeting behaviour and corporate characteristics of capital-constrained firms', *Journal of Business Finance and Accounting*, 10(4), Winter, pp. 663–71.

Pike, R.H. (1985) 'Owner-manager conflict and the role of payback', *Accounting and Business Research*, Winter, pp. 47–51.

Pike, R.H. (1988) 'An empirical study of the adoption of sophisticated capital budgeting practices and decision-making effectiveness', *Accounting and Business Research*, 18(72), Autumn, pp. 341–51.

Pike, R.H. (1996) 'A longitudinal survey of capital budgeting practices', *Journal of Business Finance and Accounting*, 23(1), January.

Pike, R.H. and Wolfe, M. (1988) *Capital Budgeting in the 1990s.* London: Chartered Institute of Management Accountants.

Pilbeam, K. (2005a) *Finance and Financial Markets.* 2nd edn. Basingstoke: Palgrave Macmillan.

Pilbeam, K. (2005b) *International Finance.* 3rd edn. London: Macmillan Business.

Pinches, G.E. (1982) 'Myopia, capital budgeting and decision-making', *Financial Management*, Autumn, pp. 6–19.

Piotroski, J.D. (2000) 'Value investing: the use of historical financial statement information to separate winners from losers', *Journal of Accounting Research*, 38, Supplement, pp. 1–51.

Pitman, B. (2003) 'Leading for value', *Harvard Business Review*, April, pp. 41–6.

Pohlman, R.A., Santiago, E.S. and Markel, F.L. (1988) 'Cash flow estimation practices of larger firms', *Financial Management*, Summer.

Pontiff, J. and Schall, L.D. (1998) 'Book-to-market ratios as predictors of market returns', *Journal of Financial Economics*, 49, pp. 141–60.

Porter, M.E. (1980) *Competitive Strategy.* New York: Free Press.

Porter, M.E. (1985) *Competitive Advantage.* New York: Free Press.

Porterfield, J.T.S. (1965) *Investment Decisions and Capital Costs.* Upper Saddle River, NJ: Prentice-Hall.

Poterba, J.M. and Summers, L.H. (1988) 'Mean reversion in stock prices: Evidence and implications', *Journal of Financial Economics*, 22, pp. 27–59.

Powell, R.G. and Stark, A.W. (2004) 'Does operating performance increase post-takeover for UK takeovers? A comparison of performance measures and benchmarks', *Journal of Corporate Finance.*

Powell, R.G. and Thomas, H.M. (1994) 'Corporate control and takeover prediction', Working paper 94/07 (Department of Accounting and Financial Management, University of Essex).

Prahalad, C.K. and Hamel, G. (1990) 'The core competence of the corporation', *Harvard Business Review*, 68(3), May–June, pp. 79–91.

Quigg, L. (1993) 'Empirical testing of Real Option Pricing Models', *Journal of Finance*, 48 (2), pp. 621–40.

Rappaport, A. (1998a) *Creating Shareholder Value.* New York: Free Press.

Rappaport, A. (1998b) *Creating Shareholder Value.* (Revised and updated version.) New York: Free Press.

Rappaport, A. (1999) *Creating Shareholder Value.* New York: Free Press. Revised and updated.

Rau, P.R. and Vermaelen, T. (1998) 'Glamour, value and the post-acquisition performance of acquiring firms', *Journal of Financial Economics*, 49(2), pp. 223–53.

Ravenscraft, D. and Scherer, F. (1987) *Mergers, Sell-Offs and Economic Efficiency.* Washington, DC: Brookings Institution.

Reimann, B.C. (1989) *Managing for Value.* Oxford: Basil Blackwell.

Reinganum, M.R. (1981) 'Misspecification of capital asset pricing: Empirical anomalies based on earnings' yields and market values', *Journal of Financial Economics*, 9, pp. 19–46.

Reinganum, M.R. (1982) 'A direct test of Roll's conjecture on the firm size effect', *Journal of Finance*, 37, pp. 27–35.

Reinganum, M.R. (1988) 'The anatomy of a stock market winner', *Financial Analysts Journal*, March–April, pp. 272–84.

Reinhardt, U.E. (1973) 'Break-even analysis for Lockheed's Tristar: an application of financial theory', *Journal of Finance*, 28, pp. 821–38, September.

Rendleman, R.J., Jones, C.P. and Latané, H.E. (1982) 'Empirical anomalies based on unexpected earnings and the importance of risk adjustments', *Journal of Financial Economics*, November, pp. 269–87.

Ridley, M. (1993) 'Survey of the frontiers in finance', *The Economist*, 9 October.

Ritter, J.R. (2003) 'Differences in European and American IPO markets', *European Financial Management*, 9, pp. 421–34.

Ritter, J.R. and Chopra, N. (1989) 'Portfolio rebalancing and the turn-of-the-year effect', *Journal of Finance*, 44, pp. 149–66.

Roberts, H.V. (1959) 'Stock market "patterns" and financial analysis: Methodological suggestions', *Journal of Finance*, March, pp. 1–10.

Roberts, R. (2007) *The City: A guide to London's global Financial Centre.* 2nd edn. London: The Economist Newspaper/Profile books.

Roll, R. (1977) 'A critique of the Asset Pricing Theory's tests: Part 1: On past and potential testability of the theory', *Journal of Financial Economics*, 4 March, pp. 129–76.

Roll, R. (1981) 'A possible explanation for the small firm effect', *Journal of Finance*, September.

Roll, R. (1986) 'The hubris hypothesis of corporate takeovers', *Journal of Business*, 59(2), pt. 1, April, pp. 197–216. Also reproduced in R. Thaler (ed.) (1993) *Advances in Behavioral Finance.* New York: Russell Sage Foundation.

Roll, R. (1994) 'What every CFO should know about scientific progress in financial economics: What is known and what remains to be resolved', *Financial Management*, 23(2) (Summer), pp. 69–75.

Roll, R. and Ross, S.A. (1980) 'An empirical investigation of the Arbitrage Pricing Theory', *Journal of Finance*, 35, December, pp. 1073–103.

Roll, R.W. and Ross, S.A. (1983) 'Regulation, the Capital Asset Pricing Model and the Arbitrage Pricing Theory', *Public Utilities Fortnightly*, 111, 26 May, pp. 22–8. Reproduced in S. Lofthouse (ed.), *Readings in Investment.* Chichester: Wiley (1994).

Ross, S. (1977) 'The determination of financial structure: The incentive-signalling approach', *Bell Journal of Economics*, 8, pp. 23–40.

Ross, S.A., Westerfield, R.W. and Jaffe, J. (2004) *Corporate Finance.* 6th international edn. New York: McGraw-Hill.

Rosenberg, B., Reid, K. and Lanstein, R. (1985) 'Persuasive evidence of market inefficiency', *Journal of Portfolio Management*, 11, Spring, pp. 9–16.

Rosenberg, B. and Rudd, A. (1986) 'The corporate uses of Beta', in J.M. Stern and D.H. Chew (eds) *The Revolution in Corporate Finance.* Oxford: Basil Blackwell.

Ross, S.A. (1974) 'Return, risk and arbitrage', in I. Friend and J.L. Bicksler (eds) *Risk and Return in Finance.* New York: Heath Lexington.

Ross, S.A. (1976) 'The arbitrage theory of capital asset pricing', *Journal of Economic Theory*, 13, December, pp. 341–60.

Ross, S.A. (1995) 'Uses, abuses, and alternatives to the net-present-value rule', *Financial Management*, 24(3), Autumn, pp. 96–102

Ross, S.A., Westerfield, R.W. and Jaffe, J. (2002) *Corporate Finance.* 6th edn. New York: McGraw-Hill.

Roth, P. (1996) *Mastering Foreign Exchange and Money Markets.* London: Pitman Publishing.

Rouwenhorst, K.G. (1998) 'International Momentum Strategies', *Journal of Finance*, 53(1), February, pp. 267–84.

Rouwenhorst, K.G. (1999) 'Local return factors and turnover in emerging stock markets', *Journal of Finance*, 54, August, pp. 1439–64.

Rouwenhorst, K.G., Heston, S. and Wessels, R.E. (1999) 'The role of beta and size in the cross-section of European stock returns', *European Financial Management*, 4.

Rozeff, M. (1986) 'How companies set their dividend payout ratios'. Reprinted in J.M. Stern and D.H. Chew (eds) *The Revolution in Corporate Finance.* Oxford: Basil Blackwell.

Rutterford, J. (2000) 'The cost of capital and shareholder value', in G.C. Arnold and M. Davies (eds) *Value-Based Management.* London: Wiley.

Samuels, J.M., Wilkes, F.M. and Brayshaw, R.E. (1996) *Management of Company Finance*, 6th edn. London: Chapman and Hall.

Sangster, A. (1993) 'Capital investment appraisal techniques: a survey of current usage', *Journal of Business Finance and Accounting*, 20(3), April, pp. 307–33.

Scapens, R.W. and Sale, J.T. (1981) 'Performance measurement and formal capital expenditure controls in divisionalised companies', *Journal of Business Finance and Accounting*, 8, pp. 389–420.

Scapens, R.W., Sale, J.T. and Tikkas, P.A. (1982) 'Financial Control of Divisional Capital Investment.' London: Institute of Cost and Management Accountants, Occasional Papers Series.

Schoenburg, E. (1990) 'Stock price prediction using neural networks', *Neurocomputing*, 2, pp. 17–27.

Scholes, M. (1972) 'The market for securities: Substitution versus price pressure effects of information on share prices', *Journal of Business*, April, pp. 179–211.

Schwartz, E.S. and Trigeorgis, L. (eds) (2001) *Real Options and Investment Under Uncertainty: Classical Readings and Recent Contributions*. Cambridge, MA and London: MIT Press.

Schweiger, D. (2002) *M&A Integration: A Framework for Executives and Managers*. Oxford: McGraw-Hill Education.

Sharpe, W.F. (1963) 'A simplified model for portfolio analysis', *Management Science*, 9, pp. 277–93.

Sharpe, W.F. (1964) 'Capital asset prices: a theory of market equilibrium under conditions of risk', *Journal of Finance*, 19, Sept., pp. 425–42.

Sharpe, W.F., Alexander, G.J. and Bailey, J.V. (1999) *Investments*, 6th edn. Upper Saddle River, NJ: Prentice-Hall.

Shefrin, H. (2000) *Beyond Greed and Fear*. Boston, MA: Harvard Business School Press.

Shefrin, H.M. and Statman, M. (1984) 'Explaining investor preference for cash dividends', *Journal of Financial Economics*, 13, pp. 253–82.

Shiller, R.J. (1981) 'Do Stock Prices Move Too Much to Be Justified by Subsequent Changes in Dividends?', *American Economic Review*, 71, pp. 421–36.

Shiller, R.J. (2000) *Irrational Exuberance*. Princeton, NJ: Princeton University Press.

Shivakumar, L. (2006) 'Accruals, cash flows and the post-earnings-announcement drift', *Journal of Business Finance and Accounting*, Jan.–Mar., 33(1), pp. 1–25.

Shleifer, A. (2000) *Inefficient Markets: An Introduction to Behavioural Finance*. Oxford: Oxford University Press.

Shyam-Sunder, L. and Myers, S.C. (1999) 'Testing static trade off against pecking order models of capital structure', *Journal of Financial Economics*, 51, pp. 219–44.

Siegel, J.J. (2005) 'Perspectives on the equity risk premium', *Financial Analysts Journal*, Nov./Dec., pp. 61–73.

Simon, H.A. (1959) 'Theories of decision making in economics and behavioural science', *American Economic Review*, June.

Simon, H.A. (1964) 'On the concept of organisational goals', *Administrative Science Quarterly*, 9(1), June, pp. 1–22.

Singh, A. (1971) *Takeovers*. Cambridge: Cambridge University Press.

Sirower, M.L. (1997) *The Synergy Trap: How Companies Lose the Acquisition Game*. New York: Free Press.

Smith, A. (1776) *The Wealth of Nations*. Reproduced in 1910 in two volumes by J.M. Dent, London.

Smith, C. (1986) 'Investment banking and the capital acquisition process', *Journal of Financial Economics*, 15, pp. 3–29.

Smith, R. (Chair) (2003) Audit committees combined code guidance. Published by the Financial Reporting Council. www.frc.org.uk.

Solnik, B.H. (1974) 'Why not diversify internationally rather than domestically?', *Financial Analysts Journal*, July–August, pp. 48–54.

Solnik, B.H. and McLeavey, D. (2003) *International Investments*, 5th edn. Boston, MA: Pearson Education.

Solomon, E. (1963) *The Theory of Financial Management*. New York: Columbia University Press.

Solomons, D. (1965) *Divisional Performance: Measurement and Control*. Reproduced (1983) Connecticut: M. Weiner Publishing.

Solomons, D. (1985) *Divisional Performance, Measurement and Control*. 2nd edn. (1st edn, 1965). Princeton, NJ: Markus Wiener Publishing.

Soros, G. (1987) *The Alchemy of Finance*. New York: Wiley.

Soros, G. (1995) *Soros on Soros*. New York: Wiley.

Soros, G. (1998) *The Crisis of Global Capitalism*. New York: Public Affairs.

Spiedell, L.S. and Sappenfield, R. (1992) 'Global diversification in a shrinking world', *Journal of Portfolio Management*, Fall, pp. 57–67.

Stahl, G. and Mendenhall, M. (2005) *Mergers and Acquisitions: Managing Culture and Human Resources*. Stanford, CA: Stanford University Press.

Standard & Poor's (1999) Ratings Performance 1998: Stability and Transition, January.

Statman, M. (1982) 'The persistence of the payback method: a principal–agent perspective', *Engineering Economist*, Summer, pp. 95–100.

Statman, M. and Sepe, J.F. (1984) 'Managerial incentive plans and the use of the payback method', *Journal of Business Finance and Accounting*, 11(1), Spring, pp. 61–5.

Steele, R. and Albright, C. (2004) 'Games managers play at budget time', *MIT Sloan Management Review*, Spring, pp. 81–4.

Stein, J.C. (1996) 'Rational capital budgeting in an irrational world', *Journal of Business*, 69, pp. 429–55.

Stephens, G. and Funnell, J. (1995) 'Take your partners . . .', *Corporate Finance*, London: Euromoney monthly journal, July.

Stern, J. (1998) 'The capital structure puzzle', *Journal of Applied Corporate Finance*, II(I), Spring, pp. 8–23.

Stern, J.M., Stewart, G.B. and Chew, D.H. (2001) 'The EVA®® Financial Management System', in D.H. Chew, (ed.) *The New Corporate Finance*. New York: McGraw-Hill/Irwin. Stern Stewart's website provides some additional literature: www/sternstewart.com

Stewart, G.B. (1990) *The Quest for Value*. New York: Harper Business.

Stewart, G.B. (1991) *The Quest for Value*. New York: Harper Business.

Stewart, G.B. (2001) 'Market Myths'. in Chew, D.H., *The New Corporate Finance* (ed.) New York: McGraw-Hill/Irwin.

Strong, N. and Xu, X.G. (1997) 'Explaining the cross-section of UK expected stock returns', *British Accounting Review*, 29(1), pp. 1–23.

Sudarsanam, S. (2003) *Creating value from mergers and acquisitions: The challenge*. Harlow: Financial Times Prentice Hall.

Sudarsanam, S., Holl, P. and Salami, A. (1996) 'Shareholder wealth gains in mergers: Effect of synergy and ownership structure', *Journal of Business Finance and Accounting*, July, pp. 673–98. A study of 429 UK mergers, 1980–90.

Sudarsanam, S. and Mahate, A. (2003) 'Glamour acquirers, methods of payment and post-acquisition performance: The UK evidence', *Journal of Business Finance and Accounting*, 30(1 & 2), pp. 299–341.

Sullivan, R., Timmermann, A. and White, H. (1999) 'Data-snooping, technical trading rule performance, and the bootstrap', *Journal of Finance*, 54(5), pp. 1647ff.

Swalm, R.O. (1966) 'Utility theory – insights into risk taking', *Harvard Business Review*, November/December, pp. 123–36.

'Symposium on some anomalous evidence on capital market efficiency' (1977). A special issue of the *Journal of Financial Economics*, 6, June.

Taylor, F. (2000) *Mastering Derivatives Markets*. 2nd edn. London: FT Prentice Hall.

Taylor, F. (2004) *Mastering Foreign Exchange and Currency Options*. 2nd edn. London: FT Prentice Hall.

Thaler, R.H. (ed.) (1993) *Advances in Behavioural Finance*. Vol. II. Princeton, NJ: Russell Sage Foundation.

Tirole, J. (2005) *The Theory of Corporate Finance*. Princeton, NJ: Princeton University Press.

Tobin, J. (1958) 'Liquidity preference as behaviour toward risk', *Review of Economic Studies*, February, 26, pp. 65–86.

Torstila, S. (2003) 'The clustering of IPO gross spreads: international evidence', *Journal of Financial and Quantitative Analysis*, 38, pp. 673–94.

Train, J. (1980) *The Money Masters*. New York: Harper Business (reprinted 1994).

Train, J. (1987) *The Midas Touch*. New York: Harper & Row.

The Treasurer (a monthly journal). London: Euromoney.

The Treasurers Handbook. London: Association of Corporate Treasurers.

Treynor, J. (1965) 'How to rate management of investment funds', *Harvard Business Review*, Jan–Feb.

Triantis, A.J. and Barisan, A. (2001) 'Real Options: State of the Practice', *Journal of Applied Corporate Finance*, 14, Summer, pp. 8–24.

Triantis, A.J. and Hodder, J.E. (1990) 'Valuing Flexibility as a Complex Option', *Journal of Finance*, 45 pp. 545–66.

Trigeorgis, L. (1996) *Real Options: Managerial Flexibility and Strategy in Resource Allocation*. Cambridge, MA: MIT Press.

Tse, C-B. (2005) 'Use dividends to signal or not: an examination of the UK dividend payout patterns', *Managerial Finance*, 31(4), pp. 12–33.

Tully, S. (1993) 'The real key to creating wealth', *Fortune*, 20 September, pp. 38–50.

Tyrrall, D.E. (1998) 'Discounted cash flow: rational calculation or psychological crutch?', *Management Accounting* (UK), February, pp 46–8.

Urry, M. (1996) 'The $45bn man makes his pitch', *Financial Times, Weekend Money*, 11/12 May, p. 1.

US Office of Business Economics (1966) *The National Income and Product Accounts of the United States 1929–1965*. Washington: Government Printing Office.

Vaitilingam, R. (2000) *The Financial Times Guide to Using the Financial Pages*. 4th edn. London: FT Prentice Hall.

Vaitilingam, R. (2006) *The Financial Times Guide to Using the Financial Pages*. 5th edn. London: FT Prentice Hall.

Valdez, S. (2007) *An Introduction to Global Financial Markets*. 5th edn. London: Palgrave Macmillan.

Valdez, S. and Wood, J. (2003) *An Introduction to Global Financial Markets*. 4th edn. Basingstoke: Palgrave Macmillan.

Van de Vliet, A. (1997) 'When mergers misfire', *Management Today*, June.

van Putten, A.B. and MacMillan, I.C. (2004) 'Making real options really work', *Harvard Business Review*, December, pp. 1–8.

Wagner, W.H. and Lau, S. (1971) 'The effects of diversification on risk', *Financial Analysts Journal*, November–December.

Wallace, J.S. (1997) 'Adapting residual income-based compensation plans: do you get what you pay for?', *Journal of Accounting and Economics*, 24, pp. 275–300.

Wardlow, A. (1994) 'Investment appraisal criteria and the impact of low inflation', *Bank of England Quarterly Bulletin*, 34(3), August, pp. 250–4.

Watson, R. and Wilson, N. (2002) 'Small and medium size enterprise financing: A note of some empirical implications of a pecking order', *Journal of Business Finance and Accounting*, 29(3) and (4) April/May, pp. 557–78.

Weaver, S.C. (2001) 'Measuring Economic Value Added®®: a survey of the practices of EVA®® proponents', *Journal of Applied Finance*, Fall/Winter, pp. 7–17.

Weingartner, H.M. (1969) 'Some new views on the payback period and capital budgeting', *Management Science*, 15, pp. 594–607.

Weingartner, H.M. (1977) 'Capital rationing: *n* authors in search of a plot', *Journal of Finance*, December, pp. 1403–31.

Welch, J. (2004) 'Capital structure and stock options', *Journal of Political Economy*, 112(1), pp. 106–31.

West, K.D. (1988) 'Bubbles, fads and stock price volatility tests: A partial evaluation', *Journal of Finance*, 43(3), pp. 639–56.

Westerman, W. and van Eije, H. (2005) 'Multinational cash management in Europe towards centralisation and disintermediation: the Philips case', *Management Finance*, 31(10), pp. 65–74.

Westwick, C.A. and Shohet, P.S.D. (1976) 'Investment Appraisal and Inflation', ICAEW Research Committee, Occasional Paper, No. 7.

Wilkes, F.M. (1980) 'On multiple rates of return', *Journal of Business, Finance and Accounting*, 7(4).

Wilkes, F.M. (1983) *Capital Budgeting Techniques*, 2nd edn. Chichester: Wiley.

Williamson, O. (1963) 'Managerial discretion and business behaviour', *American Economic Review*, 53, pp. 1033–57.

Wilson, N. and Summers, B. (2002) 'Trade Credit terms offered by small firms: survey evidence and empirical analysis', *Journal of Business Finance and Accounting*, 29 (3) and (4), April/May, pp. 317–51.

Winstone, D. (1995) *Financial Derivatives*. London: Chapman & Hall.

Winstone, D. (2000) *Financial Derivatives*. London: Thompson Learning.

Wright, S, Mason, R., Satchell, S., Hari, M. and Baskaya, M. (2006) Smither's and Co.'s report on the cost of capital provided to Ofgen (www.ofgen.gov.uk).

Xiao, Y. and Arnold, G.C. (2007) 'Testing Benjamin Graham's Net Current Asset Value Strategy in London'. Salford Business School Working Paper 109/07. Available at: www.mams.salford.ac.uk/mams/resources/uploads/File/working-papers.

Young, D.S. and O'Byrne, S.F. (2001) *EVA and Value-based Management: A practical guide to implementation.* New York: McGraw-Hill.

Zider, B. (1998) 'How venture capital works', *Harvard Business Review*, November–December, pp. 131–9.

Zimmerman, J.L. (1997) *Accounting for Decision Making and Control*, 2nd edn. Boston, MA: Irwin/McGraw-Hill.

Index